THE FATE OF THE
Romanovs

THE FATE OF THE
Romanovs

Greg King
and
Penny Wilson

WILEY

JOHN WILEY & SONS, INC.

Published by John Wiley & Sons, Inc., Hoboken, New Jersey
Published simultaneously in Canada

Photo credits: pages 32, 47, 52, 61, 81, 100, 107, 108, 109, 111, 113, 114, 122, 130, 139, 162, 173, 193, 201, 239, 248, 266, 304, 306, 404, 492, 519: *Atlantis Magazine*; pages 64, 65, 148, 252, 412, 427, 522: Dimitri Volkogonov; pages 121, 224, 269, 273, 323, 354, 361, 439: Ian Lilburn.

Design and production by Navta Associates, Inc.

For general information about our other products and services, please contact our Customer Care Department within the United States at (800) 762-2974, outside the United States at (317) 572-3993 or fax (317) 572-4002.

Wiley also publishes its books in a variety of electronic formats. Some content that appears in print may not be available in electronic books. For more information about Wiley products, visit our web site at www.wiley.com.

ISBN 0-471-20768-3

Printed in the United States of America

10 9 8 7 6 5 4 3 2 1

To Peter Kurth

Loyalty to petrified opinions never yet broke a chain
or freed a human soul in this world—and never will.
—MARK TWAIN

Contents

Foreword		ix
Cast of Characters		1
Introduction		10
Authors' Note		26

1	The Ruin of an Empire	28
2	A Traitor to the Revolution	71
3	The House of Special Purpose	103
4	"It Was Dreadful, What They Did . . ."	129
5	The Seventy-eight Days	154
6	Russia in Chaos	183
7	The First to Die	201
8	The June Conspiracies	212
9	"A Happy Hour with the Grandest People in the World"	233
10	The Coming Storm: Enter Yurovsky	263
11	Murderous Intentions	282
12	Götterdämmerung	296
13	The Four Brothers	316
14	Aftermath	332
15	The Investigations	346
16	"Holy Relics of Our Saints"	368
17	Unearthing the Past	381

18   "An Unknown Grave from the Soviet Period"   400

19   Bones of Contention   417

20   "It's All Secret, All Political"   435

21   The Secret of Koptyaki Forest   458

22   "Drowned in This Mist of Holiness"   472

Epilogue   504

Appendix 1   Ekaterinburg Guards   529

Appendix 2   Inventory of Romanov Possessions
              in Ekaterinburg   533

Appendix 3   The Romanovs' Jewels   541

Acknowledgments   546

Notes   556

Bibliography   619

Index   634

Foreword

When Greg King and Penny Wilson asked me to write a short fore-word for this book, I said that I'd be honored. This statement conceals more than it looks. After thirty years' involvement in what I happily call the Romanov Wars, I find myself still entrenched among the rebels—if anything, somewhat farther to the left. In 1983, my first book, *Anastasia: The Riddle of Anna Anderson*, argued for a complete revision of thinking about the most famous "Anastasia" claimant, who died the following year. I pled her case again, briefly, in *Tsar: The Lost World of Nicholas and Alexandra* (1995), even though, by that time, DNA testing on Mrs. Anderson's remains had seemed to prove conclusively that she was a fraud. I still think otherwise, and am known in the trenches either as Anna Anderson's "tireless champion" or—more often—as some kind of nut on this story.

In saying this, I salute Greg and Penny's courage in asking me aboard, but imply nothing about the independence of their work. They know that they've entered both a quagmire and a minefield, and that their account of the last days and murder of the Russian imperial family will find objection in many quarters. It has never been otherwise. When I began researching the story seriously in 1970, the accepted version of the death of the Romanovs had hardened into stone. This is the tale that everyone knows—of the tsar, his wife, their five children, and four remaining servants held prisoner by the Bolsheviks at the Ipatiev House in Ekaterinburg, who were woken in the early hours of July 17, 1918, ordered to dress, and taken downstairs to a "cellar," where all eleven were shot, stabbed, and bludgeoned to death. The bodies were taken into the forest, "hacked to pieces," "soaked in petrol," and burned; the larger bones were then "dissolved in sulfuric acid," and what remained was tossed down an abandoned mineshaft, leaving noth-ing behind but a suspicious trail of immediately identifiable objects: icons, jewelry, belt buckles, the burned remains of six women's corsets—accounting exactly for the number of female victims—and "Jemmy," "Anastasia's dog," who was supposedly yapping like mad during the execution and callously "killed with his mistress." Looking back, I can scarcely believe how naive we were.

It wasn't until the Soviet Union collapsed in 1991 that anything like a clear picture of the Ekaterinburg murders emerged. In the West, this process had started sometime before, first at the marathon "Anastasia" trials in Germany, and later in a series of books that knocked holes in the "Sokolov Report," the official record of the White Russian army's investigation of the Romanovs' disappearance. Murders without corpses are difficult to prove, and when these murders are royal they explode exponentially, touching every chord of history, passion, symbolism, patriotism—and intrigue. In 1992, Edvard Radzinsky's *The Last Tsar*, edited by the late Jacqueline Kennedy Onassis, was an international best-seller, reproducing for the first time documents, testimony, and interviews about the Ekaterinburg murders from Russian archives. These proved, if nothing else, the incompetence, bewilderment, and almost comical bad timing of the tsar's assassins. But they also proved, to any open mind, that the Bolsheviks were liars lying to liars, and that this was especially the case if they were asked to sign their names to official reports. In 1989, the remains of the imperial family had been found in the woods outside Ekaterinburg—all but two of them, that is, Alexei and one of his sisters—though whether it's Anastasia or Marie remains a source of predictable discord and controversy.

I went to Ekaterinburg myself in 1992, after the first forensic examination of the Romanov bones by American scientists. The city's nose was still out of joint. Many were convinced that the skeletons couldn't possibly be authentic; others resented the decision of "the Center"—Moscow—to invite American scientists to Ekaterinburg over the heads of the local authorities, all of whom, in any case, were at war with each other: the coroner, the district governor, the archivists, the scientists, the Church, the men who found the bodies, and the sudden profusion of monarchists, who urged me not to trust this one or that one "because he is *out* with the members of the emperor's family!" In the meantime, as my translator said, "It is forbidden to take pictures of the skeletons, and above all to sell them to foreigners." The only person I met in Ekaterinburg whose passions weren't inflamed was Dr. Ludmilla Koryakova, an archaeologist at Ural State University, who was ordered "practically at gunpoint" in 1991 to excavate the bones. Her words bear emphasis:

> There was nothing like the proper atmosphere or precaution, no preparation, no tools and no instruments. . . . We had one bulldozer, some military trucks, and several spades. Everything was done too quickly. . . . Everybody got digging, not just the experts. The evidence had already

been considerably destroyed by earlier excavations. The skeletons were no longer lying in the way they had been dumped. . . . Many were destroyed. I thought at first that the corpses had been dismembered, because they were so brutally treated. The skulls were smashed beyond recognition—there were just holes where the faces had been. I've seen a lot of skulls and bones but never so many that were so badly damaged.

This is the subject of the book you're about to read, the first comprehensive account of the Romanov murders to appear since their bones were walled up in 1998 at the Cathedral of Peter and Paul in St. Petersburg. There they will remain, I imagine, in perpetuity. All but two of them, that is. I am indeed a "nut" on this story, and am confident in predicting that many of you will be, too, when you discover what follows.

—Peter Kurth

Cast of Characters

THE IMPERIAL FAMILY

Nicholas II (1868–1918), the last emperor of Russia.

Alexandra Feodorovna (1872–1918), the last empress of Russia, consort of Nicholas II. Born Princess Alix of Hesse und bei Rhine.

Alexei Nikolaievich (born 1904), tsesarevich, heir to the Russian throne, and only son of Nicholas and Alexandra. His body, missing from the mass grave in the Koptyaki Forest, has never been found.

Olga Nikolaievna (1895–1918), grand duchess, eldest daughter of Nicholas and Alexandra.

Tatiana Nikolaievna (1897–1918), grand duchess, second daughter of Nicholas and Alexandra.

Marie Nikolaievna (1899–1918), grand duchess, third daughter of Nicholas and Alexandra.

Anastasia Nikolaievna (born 1901), grand duchess, youngest daughter of Nicholas and Alexandra. Her body, missing from the mass grave in the Koptyaki Forest, has never been found.

THE HOUSE OF ROMANOV

Alexander II (1818–1881), emperor of Russia, grandfather of Nicholas II, assassinated by the revolutionary group Narodnaya Volya (People's Will).

Alexander III (1845–1894), emperor of Russia, father of Nicholas II.

Alexander Mikhailovich (1866–1933), grand duke, grandson of Nicholas I, husband of Grand Duchess Xenia Alexandrovna.

Dimitri Konstantinovich (1860–1919), grand duke, cousin of Nicholas II. Executed by the Bolsheviks.

Elizabeth Feodorovna (1864–1918), grand duchess, wife of Grand Duke Serge Alexandrovich. Known in the family as Ella, she was born Princess Elizabeth of Hesse und bei Rhine, elder sister of Empress Alexandra. Executed by the Bolsheviks.

George Alexandrovich (1871–1899), grand duke, second brother of Nicholas II.

George Mikhailovich (1863–1919), grand duke, cousin of Nicholas II. Executed by the Bolsheviks.

Helen Petrovna (1884–1962), princess of Russia, only daughter of King Peter of Serbia; married Prince Ioann Konstantinovich in 1911.

Igor Konstantinovich (1894–1918), prince. Executed by the Bolsheviks.

Ioann Konstantinovich (1886–1918), prince, husband of Helen Petrovna. Executed by the Bolsheviks.

Konstantin Konstantinovich (1890–1918), prince. Executed by the Bolsheviks.

Marie Feodorovna (1847–1928), empress of Russia, consort of Alexander III (1881–1894), dowager empress (1894–1917), mother of Nicholas II. Born Princess Dagmar, daughter of King Christian IX of Denmark.

Michael Alexandrovich (1878–1918), grand duke, youngest brother of Nicholas II. Known in the family as Misha, contracted morganatic marriage. Refused throne after Nicholas's abdication. Executed by Bolsheviks in Perm, his body has never been found.

Nicholas Mikhailovich (1859–1919), grand duke, cousin of Nicholas II. Executed by the Bolsheviks.

Nicholas Nikolaievich (1856–1929), grand duke, Nicholas II's uncle, known in the family as Nikolasha. From 1914 to 1915, was supreme commander of the Russian armies.

Olga Alexandrovna (1883–1960), grand duchess, youngest sister of Nicholas II.

Paul Alexandrovich (1860–1919), grand duke, Nicholas II's uncle. Executed by Bolsheviks in 1919.

Serge Alexandrovich (1857–1905), grand duke, uncle and brother-in-law of Nicholas II. Assassinated in 1905.

Serge Mikhailovich (1869–1918), grand duke, cousin of Nicholas II. Executed by the Bolsheviks.

Xenia Alexandrovna (1875–1960), grand duchess, eldest sister of Nicholas II, wife of Grand Duke Alexander Mikhailovich.

THE IMPERIAL COURT, SUITE,
AND HOUSEHOLD

Benckendorff, Paul (1833–1921), count, grand marshal of the imperial court.

Botkin, Eugene (1865–1918), personal physician to the empress. With his two children Gleb and Tatiana, went voluntarily into exile with the Romanovs, and was murdered with them in Ekaterinburg.

Buxhoeveden, Sophie (1884–1956), baroness, freilina (lady-in-waiting) to Empress Alexandra. Betrayed the Romanovs in exile.

Chemodurov, Terenty (1849–1919), valet to Nicholas II, imprisoned briefly with the Romanovs in the Ipatiev House.

Demidova, Anna (1878–1918), maid to Empress Alexandra, imprisoned and shot with the Romanovs in Ekaterinburg.

Derevenko, Nicholas (1906–1999), son of court physician Vladimir Derevenko. Known as Kolya, was one of the tsesarevich's few friends.

Derevenko, Vladimir (1879–1936), court physician and surgeon to the tsesarevich, accompanied the Romanovs into exile.

Dolgoruky, Vassili (1868–1918), prince, adjutant-general in imperial suite, accompanied the Romanovs into Siberian exile. Executed by the Bolsheviks.

Ersberg, Elizabeth (1882–1942), third lady's maid to the empress.

de Freedericksz, Vladimir (1838–1927), minister of the imperial court.

Gibbes, Charles Sidney (1876–1963), tutor of English to the imperial children.

Gilliard, Pierre (1879–1962), of Swiss origin, tutor of French to the imperial children. In exile, married the former nursery maid Alexandra Tegleva.

Hendrikova, Anastasia, lady-in-waiting to the empress. Executed by the Bolsheviks in 1918.

Kharitonov, Ivan (1870–1918), chef. Executed with the Romanovs in the Ipatiev House.

Nagorny, Klementy (1889–1918), former sailor on the imperial yacht *Standart*, diadka (sailor-nanny) to the tsesarevich. Executed by the Bolsheviks in Ekaterinburg.

Schneider, Catherine (1886–1918), lectrice to Empress Alexandra. Executed by the Bolsheviks.

Sednev, Ivan (1886–1918), former crewman on the imperial yacht *Standart*, footman to the grand duchesses. Executed by the Bolsheviks.

Sednev, Leonid (1904–1927), nephew of Ivan Sednev, assistant cook, friend of the tsesarevich. Removed from the Ipatiev House only hours before the execution and sent back to Kaluga District.

Tatishchev, Ilya (1859–1918), count, adjutant-general in imperial suite, accompanied Romanovs into Siberian exile. Executed by the Bolsheviks.

Tegleva, Alexandra, nursery maid, married Pierre Gilliard in 1922.

Trupp, Alexei (1856–1918), footman, executed with the Romanovs in Ekaterinburg.

Tutelberg, Maria, second lady's maid to the empress.

Volkov, Alexei, kammer-diner (valet de chambre) to the empress.

Zanotti, Madeleine, first lady's maid to the empress.

ROYAL RELATIVES

Alexandra (1844–1925), queen of Great Britain and Ireland. Born Princess Alexandra of Denmark, she was the elder sister of Nicholas's mother Maria Feodorovna.

Ernst Ludwig (1868–1937), grand duke of Hesse und bei Rhine, only brother of Empress Alexandra.

George V (1865–1936), king of Great Britain and Ireland, first cousin to both Nicholas and Alexandra, forced his government to withdraw an offer of asylum to the imperial family.

Wilhelm II (1859–1941), emperor of Germany, first cousin to Empress Alexandra, repeatedly attempted to intercede on behalf of the Romanovs.

THE REVOLUTIONARIES

Avdayev, Alexander (1887–1947), first commandant of the Ipatiev House.

Beloborodov, Alexander (1891–1938), chairman of the Ural Regional Soviet.

Berzin, Reinhold (1888–1939), commander of the Northern Siberian Ural Front.

Bykov, Paul, member of the Ekaterinburg Soviet, produced the only authorized Soviet account of the Ekaterinburg murders.

Chicherin, G. V. (1872–1936), people's commissar for foreign affairs.

Dzerzhinsky, Felix (1877–1926), founder of the Cheka.

Ermakov, Peter (1884–1952), military commissar for Verkh-Isetsk.

Goloshchokin, Philip [Isaac] (1876–1941), military commissar of the Ural Regional Soviet.

Ioffe, Adolf (1883–1927), Soviet ambassador to Germany.

Kerensky, Alexander (1881–1970), president of the Provisional Government.

Khokhryakov, Paul (1893–1918), Bolshevik charged with transferring the imperial children to Ekaterinburg.

Kosarev, Vladimir (1881–1945), chairman of the Western Siberian Soviet in Omsk.

Kudrin, Michael (1890–1963), member of the Ural Regional Cheka. Born Michael Medvedev.

Lenin, Vladimir (1870–1924), chairman of the Council of People's Commissars. Born Vladimir Ilyich Ulyanov.

Lukoyanov, Feodor (1894–1947), chairman of the Ural Regional Cheka.

Lyukhanov, Serge (1875–1954), official chauffeur to the House of Special Purpose in Ekaterinburg.

Nikulin, Gregory (1892–1964), member of the Ural Regional Cheka, deputy commandant of the Ipatiev House under Yurovsky.

Rodzinsky, Isai (1891–1964), member of the Ural Regional Cheka.

Safarov, Gregory (1891–1941), member of the Presidium of the Ural Regional Soviet.

Stalin, Josef (1879–1953), secretary-general of the Communist Party from 1922.

Sverdlov, Yakov (1885–1919), chairman of the Central Executive Committee.

Trotsky, Leon (1879–1940), people's commissar for military affairs.

Voikov, Peter (1888–1927), Ural Regional Soviet commissar of supplies; later Soviet ambassador to Poland.

Yakovlev, Vassili (1886–1938), Soviet extraordinary commissar charged with removing the Romanovs from Moscow; born Konstantin Myachin.

Yurovsky, Yakov (1878–1938), last commandant of the House of Special Purpose.

Zinoviev, Gregory (1883–1936), chairman of the Petrograd Soviet.

INTERESTED PARTIES

Bittner, Klaudia (1878–1935), tutor to the imperial children in Tobolsk; later married Colonel Eugene Kobylinsky.

Bulygin, Paul, bodyguard to Nicholas Sokolov, assisted in White Russian army investigation into the Ekaterinburg murders.

Dehn, Julia (1880–1963), known as Lili, friend of Empress Alexandra.

Deterikhs, Michael (1874–1937), General in the White Russian army; supervised the White Russian investigation into the Ekaterinburg murders.

Hermogen (1858–1918), bishop of Tobolsk Province. Born George Dolganyov, he was involved in plots to rescue the prisoners from Tobolsk.

Ipatiev, Nicholas (1867–1938), retired engineer, owner of the Ekaterinburg house where the Romanovs were imprisoned and killed.

Kobylinsky, Eugene (1879–1927), captain, commander of the Special Detachment that guarded the Romanovs in Tobolsk. Later married Klaudia Bittner.

Kolchak, Alexander (1873–1920), supreme commander of the White Russian army in Siberia; authorized the Sokolov investigation into the Ekaterinburg murders.

Lvov, George (1861–1925), prince, first prime minister of the Provisional Government, later incarcerated in Ekaterinburg. Made numerous unreliable assertions regarding the imprisonment and death of the Romanovs.

Markov, Serge, former cornet in the Crimean Horse Guards Regiment. Worked with Boris Soloviev to free the prisoners in Tobolsk.

Mirbach, Wilhelm (1871–1918), count, German ambassador in Moscow.

Nametkin, Alexander, first White Russian investigator into the imperial family's fate.

Sergeyev, Ivan, second White Russian army investigator into the fate of the Romanovs.

Sokolov, Nicholas (1882–1924), last White Russian army investigator of the murder of the Romanovs.

Soloviev, Boris (1893–1926), husband of Marie Rasputin. Acted as courier for Anna Vyrubova, Lili Dehn, and others in passing correspondence and money to the prisoners in Tobolsk. Attempted to organize a rescue attempt. Wrongly implicated in theft of rescue funds.

Vassiliev, Alexander, priest at the Annunciation Church in Tobolsk. Involved with Hermogen in rescue attempts and implicated in theft of money intended for the Romanovs.

Vyrubova, Anna, friend of Empress Alexandra.

Wilton, Robert, correspondent for the *Times* of London; assisted in the White Russian army investigation into the Ekaterinburg murders.

THE MODERN INVESTIGATORS

Abramov, Sergei, doctor, director of the Department of New Technology in the Russian Federation's Central Forensics Medicine Division in the Ministry of Health. Worked extensively on identification of remains.

Avdonin, Alexander, retired geologist who, together with Geli Ryabov, located the Koptyaki grave in 1979.

Baden, Michael, director of New York State Police Forensic Services Division; member of 1992 American forensic team.

Blokhin, Alexander, Sverdlovsk regional deputy.

Falsetti, Anthony, professor at the C. A. Pound Human Identification Laboratory at the University of Florida; examined remains in 1998.

France, Diane, professor, forensic expert, and member of NecroSearch International; examined remains in 1998.

Gill, Peter, genetics expert at the British Home Office's Forensic Science Services Laboratory; conducted genetic testing of Romanov remains.

Gritsaenko, Peter, deputy head of the Sverdlovsk Regional Forensic Medicine Bureau.

Gurtovaya, Svetlana, doctor; serological and fiber expert from the Ministry of Health.

Ivanov, Pavel, doctor; genetics expert in the Russian Ministry of Health who worked with Peter Gill on genetic testing of the Romanov remains.

Koryakova, Ludmilla, doctor of archaeology at the Laboratory of the History and Archaeology Institute of the Urals Science Center of the USSR Academy of Sciences. Participated in first 1991 exhumation.

Levine, Lowell, forensic odontologist with New York State Police Forensic Services Division; member of the 1992 American forensic team.

Maples, William, professor; director of the C. A. Pound Human Identification Laboratory at the University of Florida. He assembled and led the 1992 American forensic team. Died in 1998.

Nevolin, Nikolai, director of the Sverdlovsk Regional Forensic Bureau.

Nikitin, Sergei, specialist in facial reconstruction.

Plaskin, Vladislav, doctor; chief medical examiner in Russia's Ministry of Health.

Popov, Vyacheslav, professor; forensic odontologist from the St. Petersburg Academy of Military Medicine.

Rossel, Edvard, head of the Sverdlovsk Regional Executive Committee in 1991.

Ryabov, Geli, former official in the Soviet Ministry of the Interior, mystery writer, and part-time filmmaker who, with Alexander Avdonin, discovered the Koptyaki grave.

Sykes, Brian, professor of human genetics in the Institute of Molecular Medicine at Oxford University in Great Britain.

Viner, Vadim, chairman of the International Independent Commission to Investigate the Murder of the Romanov Family.

Volkov, V., assistant prosecutor in the Sverdlovsk Region.

Yeltsin, Boris, former president of the Russian Federation.

Zaitzev, N., Sverdlovsk regional prosecutor.

Zvyagin, Victor, chief of the Physical and Technical Department of the Russian Ministry of Health.

INSTITUTIONS

Central Executive Committee, ruling Soviet body, ruled by a Presidium (VTsIK).

Cheka, the All-Russian Extraordinary Commission for the Struggle with Counter-revolution and Sabotage, founded by Felix Dzerzhinsky in 1918. Successor to the Imperial Okhrana, it was followed by the GPU, NKVD, and KGB.

Constituent Assembly, parliamentary institution closed by order of the Central Executive Committee, January 1918.

Sovnarkom, Council of Peoples' Commissars. Headed by Lenin, it was the executive branch of the Soviet government.

Ural Regional Soviet, headed by a Presidium, body that controlled the western Siberian provinces from Ekaterinburg.

Introduction

If it was your relations who have wrought my death, then no
one of your family, none of your children or relations, will
remain alive for more than two years. They will be killed by
the Russian people

—FINAL LETTER OF GREGORY RASPUTIN
TO NICHOLAS II, DECEMBER 1916[1]

IN JANUARY 1613, in the midst of Russia's "Time of Troubles," a
specially elected assembly of nobles, the Zemskii Sobor, met in
Moscow and decided to offer the vacant throne to sixteen-year-old
Michael Romanov, a grandnephew of Ivan the Terrible's wife, Anastasia.
A delegation left Moscow for the Volga River town of Kostroma, where
young Michael had taken refuge with his mother. It was here, in the
Ipatiev Monastery, that they informed the terrified boy of their decision. At first Michael refused, fearing that the throne was too unstable,
and worried that he would fall victim to either the endless intrigues of
the Moscow court, or to the plots of foreign invaders. But the representatives prevailed, and that summer Michael was duly crowned as the
first Romanov tsar in Moscow. Three centuries later, Nicholas II, the
eighteenth sovereign of the Romanov Dynasty, died in a hail of bullets
in the basement of the Ipatiev House in Ekaterinburg.

In its most basic form, it is the stuff of legend: a great royal love
affair, within the opulent palaces of a vanished empire, played out
against a background of war and revolution; a family tragedy, a mad
monk, faded photographs evoking a lost world; an ornate little villa in

an isolated Siberian town, a brutal massacre of women and children; an enduring mystery, missing corpses, and claims of survival. The story of Nicholas II and his family, less than a century old yet rooted in history, continues to this day amid ever-increasing affection for, and religious devotion to, Russia's last imperial family. Eighty-five years after the Ekaterinburg murders, these seven victims evoke both enormous interest and surprisingly strong feelings among devotees. Few transformations, from historical personages to objects of veneration, are as precise as that of the Romanovs. In the early morning hours of July 17, 1918, when they stepped across the threshold of a small basement room in the Ural Mountains, they passed from discredited former sovereigns into adoring myth.

Nicholas II was not the first Romanov sovereign to fall at the hand of an assassin. Peter III had been overthrown and strangled by those who placed his wife, Catherine the Great, on the Russian throne; her son, Paul I, was strangled and bludgeoned by a group of aristocratic conspirators acting with the knowledge of his own son and successor, Alexander I. Nicholas II's grandfather Alexander II was the victim of a terrorist bomb, and bled to death before the horrified eyes of his family in 1881. In 1905 Nicholas II's uncle and brother-in-law, Grand Duke Serge Alexandrovich, was literally blown to pieces by a revolutionary group.

Revolutions beget violence. In 1649, Charles I was beheaded with the approval of Oliver Cromwell following his trial before Parliament. Louis XVI and Marie Antoinette fell victim to the vengeance of the French Revolution, and tried before the Convention, which declared them guilty of innumerable crimes. In 1867 Emperor Maximilian was arrested and shot when Benito Juárez seized control of the Habsburg-ruled Mexican Empire. And the beginning of the twentieth century was marked with another act of brutality: in 1903, King Alexander and Queen Draga of Serbia were massacred in a conspiracy carried out with the knowledge of Russian officials, their bodies defiled and dumped naked into the square in front of their palace.[2]

With the exception of the Serbian king and queen, however, there is a substantial difference between the execution of Nicholas II and those of his fellow monarchs. Charles I, Louis XVI, and Maximilian of Mexico were all publicly executed, following trials at which evidence was laid before a commission charged with assessing guilt. Nicholas II was shot without trial. And while the French Revolution took vengeance on Marie Antoinette, the Russian Revolution deemed it necessary to eliminate not only the monarch but also members of both his immediate and extended family. The execution of Nicholas II was not unexpected; the massacre of his wife and innocent children, merely because they were inconvenient reminders of the fallen dynasty, shocked the world. Arguably more words have been spilled over the seven Romanovs who died in the Ekaterinburg massacre than any other similar group of twentieth-century victims. Some of that allure stems from the sheer scale of their sorrowful story. Yet the intensity that still surrounds Nicholas, Alexandra, and their family transcends ordinary interest, and has evolved into a phenomenon unique to the century in which they died; they have become the crowned equivalents of pop idols, complete with worshipful fans.

This has led many historians to view the Ekaterinburg massacre as a pivotal event in twentieth-century history, a position best described by historian Richard Pipes, who termed it "a prelude to twentieth-century mass murder," and spoke of the symbolic nature of the crime:

> When a government arrogates to itself the power to kill people, not because of what they had done or even might do, but because their death is "needed," we are entering an entirely new moral realm. Here lies the symbolic significance of the events that occurred in Ekaterinburg in the night of July 16–17. The massacre, by secret order of the government, of a family that for all its Imperial background was remarkably commonplace, guilty of nothing, desiring only to be allowed to live in peace, carried mankind for the first time across the threshold of deliberate genocide. The same reasoning that had led the Bolsheviks to condemn them to death would later be applied in Russia and elsewhere to millions of nameless beings who happened to stand in the way of one or another design for a new world order.[3]

The late Russian historian Dimitri Volkogonov expressed a slightly more adamant view:

> The extermination of the Imperial Family symbolized the vast tragedy of a great nation which had yielded to class hatred and fratricide. The tragedy which took place in the Ipatiev House, ostensibly an episode in the deadly Civil War, synthesized the hypocrisy of Bolshevik propaganda, the cruelty of the regime, and the duplicity of its leaders. The murders in Ekaterinburg highlighted the inability of the Bolsheviks to handle problems without unrestrained violence or state terror. The authorities in Moscow could not admit to themselves that, even in defeat, they feared Nicholas as long as he was alive. They did not believe that their revolution was irreversible, and Nicholas inspired in them a mystical fear as the symbol of the nation which might, when it had become disillusioned with the Bolsheviks, turn back to their monarch.[4]

These historians—one American, one Russian—aptly summarized the two most common modern assessments of the Ekaterinburg murders.

It was an execution that transcended its basic form to assume greater symbolic importance than any of those involved in the actual event could ever have imagined. At the same time, this single act represented all the brutality of the Bolshevik regime, and the suffering of Russia. Add to this another element, that of the Russian Orthodox Church, which canonized the imperial family precisely because of their murder, and the massacre has become endowed with a deep spiritual significance as well.

Yet these assessments, rendered after decades of worldwide carnage and the collapse of the totalitarian Soviet regime, reflect a modern imputation of motivations at the expense of 1918 realities. A political execution, originally driven by a people's vengeance, has thus been shrouded with influences and wrapped in meanings not intended nor even considered by its participants, all in an effort to explain its extraordinary pull. Such opinions, which seek to place the murders within clearly defined contemporary moral parameters, in reference to unforeseen events that followed, appeal to popular sentiment. Yet they also often fail to reflect the larger historical truths behind the Ekaterinburg murders.

Even today, the murder of Nicholas II and his family remains one of the most divisive chapters of Russian history. The few known historical facts surrounding the last months of captivity and ultimate murder of the last Russian imperial family have been subsumed in an eighty-five-year-old propaganda war waged by Reds and Whites, Bolsheviks and monarchists, historians and Romanov devotees. Political and religious agendas, introduced even before the murder itself, continue to plague the case. Official Soviet history paid little attention to the fate of the Romanovs; the murders were justified as necessary for the survival of the Revolution, ignoring the slaughter of four young women and a young boy who, by any standard, were guilty of nothing but a misfortune of birth. The Ekaterinburg massacre was wrapped in tales of monarchist plots, Civil War exigencies, a clear answer to a world throwing off the shackles of oppressive monarchies as its young men fought and died in the trenches of World War I.

These Bolshevik characterizations never took hold beyond the Soviet Union, leaving monarchists, Russian émigrés, and historians to depict Lenin and his regime as bloodthirsty butchers after the Ekaterinburg murders. Few questioned this interpretation of events; it was, after all, useful propaganda. At the time of his death, Nicholas II was all but forgotten except for a few intermittent queries from his royal relatives in Europe, and a handful of monarchists haphazardly pursuing any number of ultimately futile rescue plots. Those who might reasonably have been expected to look on the sovereign with sympathy—generals and officers from the Imperial Army—had no use for him. His extended Romanov family had openly plotted against him while

Nicholas was still on the throne, and saw no role for him in the Russia of the future. Allied governments alongside whose soldiers Russia had so valiantly fought, welcomed the news of his abdication. The autocracy was dead, and the former sovereign was a political nonentity. His death, and that of his family, eliminated potential worries from all sides over his future role. At the same time, the massacre solidified the growing distrust of Bolshevism and the Soviet Union, a culmination of revolutionary hatred and an ominous portent of the evils of totalitarianism, its bloody details laid bare for the world's condemnation. In death Nicholas II became a potent banner on which the flags of nationalism, Orthodoxy, anti-Semitism, counterrevolution, and democracy have all been proudly hung.

With the passage of time, such sentiments have formed the overwhelming Western view of the end of the Romanovs. The passion of Nicholas and Alexandra, the suffering of their hemophiliac son, the scandal of Rasputin, the murders, and the rumored survival of Anastasia have spread across the pages of countless books, been portrayed in films, and filled the lyrics of songs, a lingering specter to one of the twentieth century's most haunting tragedies. In the process, Russia's last imperial family has been enveloped in a protective cocoon of myth, where they no longer belong to history but to the new Russia, struggling to come to terms with its past by rejecting the Soviet state in favor of wishful sentiment for the brutal regime it replaced; to monarchist groups; to the church; and to those who look on the last Russian imperial family as representatives of some unreal, imaginary, vanished world of golden nostalgia.

This is not putting too fine a point on it. The collapse of the Soviet Union and the release of previously unsuspected archives have rejuvenated the story of the Romanovs. Letters and diaries, filtered through the romantic pens of sympathetic writers, and nostalgic photographs, flickering across television screens to the faint strain of haunting music, have become the predominant images of the fallen dynasty. Rather than view Nicholas II's disastrous reign as political drama, history has largely focused on the Romanovs as individuals, praising their virtues and seeking to examine their personalities. The swell of discontent enveloping the Russian Empire, with its ponderous bureaucracy, corrupt church, impoverished peasants, starving workers, official anti-Semitism, student strikes, bloodshed, and wars, has fallen victim to the Romanov cult of personality.

Most figures of the past grow shadowy and less distinct as they recede into the reaches of history; they fail to resonate in a complex and increasingly dangerous modern world. Yet Nicholas, Alexandra, and their children defy that trend. Through retrospective adulation, they have been transformed into powerful symbols endowed with every grace and pure intent, utterly devoid of anything that hints at the ordinary course of life for lesser mortals: disagreements, strife, and resentments are swept away in favor of faded photographs of the white-gowned empress and her beautiful daughters in their Edwardian picture hats, the sick tsesarevich in his sailor suits. They have become the objects of prayer and devotion, undiluted sympathy, and a curious insistence on viewing them, as one author wrote, as "the most pure, holy family."[5] Such quasi-religious exaltation often borders on, and in many cases transcends, the line between historical interest and literal idolization, a trend particularly encouraged by the universal growth of the Internet. Today there are hundreds of sites and groups devoted to Nicholas and Alexandra, where contributors post gushing poetic tributes to the grand duchesses; animated candles of remembrance flicker eternally; players enact re-creations of the last years of empire; and Orthodox priests post prayers to their "tsar-martyr," listing litanies of miraculous cures from drug and alcohol abuse, unemployment, and illness, all attributed to the intervention of the Romanovs. These spiritual yearnings and sentimental fantasies attempt to imbue the Romanovs with modern sensibilities and contemporary relevance, to wish illusion into reality.

The final chapter in the Romanov story began on April 22, 1918, when Vassili Yakovlev, an extraordinary commissar sent from Moscow, arrived in the town of Tobolsk, charged with the task of safely transporting the imperial prisoners out of Siberia. Eight days later, Nicholas, Alexandra, and their third daughter, Marie, were in the hands of the mutinous Ural Regional Soviet, imprisoned in the Siberian mining town of Ekaterinburg. Joined three weeks later by the rest of their family and a handful of retainers, the prisoners were confined to a large mansion, carefully hidden from curious eyes by a tall wooden palisade.

The seventy-eight days of their Ekaterinburg captivity are shrouded in mystery, speculation, allegation, and controversy. Countless works, by monarchists, White Russian émigrés, Western historians, and, more recently, Russian analysts, have painted this period as a vivid orgy of drunken barbarity by their first jailer, Alexander Avdayev; labeled the men who guarded them as brutes who delighted in inflicting ingenious new humiliations on the unfortunate captives; condemned those who carried out the executions as unredeemed, cold-blooded liars; and at the same time elevated the imperial family to the status of martyrs. Beginning in 1920, with the publication of journalist Robert Wilton's grossly prejudiced and inaccurate work on the Romanovs, an endless torrent of vulgar depravities has been ascribed to these seventy-eight days. "The Ekaterinburg period," Wilton contended, "was one long martyrdom for the Romanovs, growing worse, with one short interval, as the hour of their death approached." He termed their first guards "brutal," the last "alien," all possessing a "fiendish ingenuity in tormenting their helpless captives," "coarse, drunken criminals" with "evil-smelling bodies" who watched over the Romanovs with "drunken, leering eyes."[6] To Wilton this added up to "ill-treatment, amounting to horrible torture, mental if not physical."[7]

Such hellish interpretations have cast the imperial family's murder into curious perambulations, echoing the Russian idea of *sudba*, an inescapable, inexorable fate that brought predetermined tragedy and suffering to all. It was an idea Nicholas II himself willingly embraced in life; in death, such sentiments were echoed by others. The murders, asserted tutor Pierre Gilliard, were the "inevitable fulfillment, the climax, of one of the most moving tragedies that humanity has ever known," the "last stage in their long martyrdom," when mercifully "death refused to separate those whom life had so closely banded together," and swept away "all seven, united in one faith and one love."[8] Another author declared, "It was a mercy of God that they all died together," thus saving the "innocents" from "a fate worse than death."[9] This insistence that "all seven, united in one faith and one love" perished at the hands of their Bolshevik executioners, has become a major tenet in the Romanov story. It speaks less to the possibility of potential survival than to the necessity of those who have romanticized the end of the Romanovs to view them, up to the last minute, as moral symbols, at the same time damning not only those who shot them but also the entire Soviet system as culpable for the distant events of 1918.

The grotesque picture has passed into accepted history. It served the propaganda needs of loyal monarchists, White Russians, and the Orthodox faithful in presenting a sympathetic portrait of the last days of the Romanovs, while at the same time resorting to descriptions of imagined abuses and exaggerated tales of squalid insults in an effort to heighten their suffering. It is difficult to establish why such provocative tales have been endlessly repeated by serious historians; few have questioned their validity, and of these, only three—Richard Pipes, Mark Steinberg, and Vladimir Krustalev—have boldly declared that they range from distortion to outright fabrication.[10] Steinberg and Krustalev note that many of the stories

were told to White investigators by survivors from the Tsar's Suite, or by former guards who had been arrested by the Whites and were on trial during the Civil War for their role in persecuting and killing the Tsar. The White investigators themselves posed questions and wrote reports that clearly sought to adduce every possible instance of the moral suffering of the Tsar and his family at the hands of the Bolsheviks. Tales were solicited and readily believed, for they confirmed the perception of adherents to the old order that the Revolution had brought rough and resentful plebeians to power.[11]

Given the importance of the Ekaterinburg murders, it is somewhat surprising that, for most of the twentieth century, historians have relied on only a handful of sources to illuminate the event. Foremost among these was a book by Nicholas Sokolov, *Enquete judiciare sur l'Assassinat de la Famille Imperiale Russe*, published in Paris in 1924. Sokolov's position as the last officially appointed investigator lent his book the air of authority lacking in previous works. Sokolov's book, however, was in no way a complete examination of the murders and the investigations that followed, but rather more along the lines of a carefully prepared judicial brief, a case for the monarchist prosecution. As a result, he ignored much testimony and evidence that contradicted the official view, these depositions and statements left to molder in the eleven volumes of Sokolov's dossier.[12]

Three other books, written by those who worked closely with Sokolov during the investigation in Russia, also became pivotal in Western interpretation of the Romanov executions. The first of these—and the first book devoted solely to the Ekaterinburg murders—was Robert Wilton's *The Last Days of the Romanovs*, published in 1920. It drew heavily on his own personal copy of Sokolov's dossier, as he himself admitted.[13] Wilton included four depositions he had been given by George Telberg, the last minister of justice in Admiral Kolchak's Omsk regime, including those of Paul Medvedev and Anatoly Yakimov. These previously unpublished accounts—coupled with Wilton's close proximity to the case and those involved in the official investigation—lent his account a presumed air of authority.

A two-volume work by White Army general Michael Deterikhs followed in 1922. Deterikhs' book, *Ubiistvo tsarskoi sem'i i chlenov doma Romanovykh na Urale* (The murder of the imperial family and members of the House of Romanov in the Urals), was published by the Vladivostok Military Academy. Although both Wilton and Deterikhs had access to copies of Sokolov's dossier, the general also was in the unique position of having read and reviewed every deposition or testimony, and examined all the evidence as a member of the White government that had commissioned the judicial inquiry into the Ekaterinburg murders. In many ways, Deterikhs' book was more complete and insightful than Sokolov's official report of 1924, if more blatant in its overt political and racial assertions. Deterikhs discussed the various investigations into first the imperial family's disappearance, then presumed murder, detailing the inquiries that eventually led to Sokolov's appointment. Deterikhs provided a far more extensive inventory of items discovered at the Ipatiev House and at the Four Brothers Mine, indicating precisely where each had been found, in contrast to Sokolov, who gave only a general listing. Deterikhs also made the unique claim that Goloshchokin had personally severed the heads of the victims, placed them in steel drums filled with alcohol, and taken them to Moscow as trophies. He offered no evidence to support this bizarre assertion, other than his own personal speculation that this accounted for the complete absence of any teeth at the Four Brothers mine.[14] Deterikhs' book, however, languished in obscurity. When he tried to have it produced in Great Britain, he found it condemned as too anti-Semitic; no publisher was willing to stand behind his incendiary rhetoric. Today it holds the questionable distinction of being the only major work by an important participant in the murder investigation never to have been translated or republished in any other form or language.

Eleven years after Sokolov's death, his compatriot Paul Bulygin published his own account of both the Ekaterinburg murders and the investigation into the crime. Bulygin's essay, "The Sorrowful Quest," was grouped with "The Road to Tragedy," an account written by Alexander Kerensky that dealt with both the fall of the Russian monarchy and the imperial family's Siberian exile and eventual murder, and a book, *The Murder of the Romanovs*, was the result. It was published in 1935 in an English-language edition, with a somewhat larger French version appearing at the same time.[15] Bulygin dedicated his book to Sokolov, "for the memory of his warm friendship and noble character."[16] He explained that he wished to "popularize the conclusions at which he, as an experienced investigator, was able to arrive."[17]

In these years, official Soviet silence was broken only twice. Portions of Sokolov's conclusions were seemingly confirmed when Paul Bykov wrote an article "The Last Days of the Last Emperor," which appeared in a small book by him, *Rabochaya revolyutsiya na Urale* (The workers' revolution in the Urals), published in Ekaterinburg in 1921. As the former chairman of the Ekaterinburg City Soviet, Bykov was in a unique position to offer an authoritative commentary on the Romanov murders. But his article often seemed merely to repeat—albeit from a Soviet point of view—many of the details previously suggested by Wilton, who in turn drew on his copy of Sokolov's dossier. Bykov's article was extracted and published in *Arkhiv Russkoy Revolyutsii* in Berlin and Prague and thus became known to Sokolov and others then living in Europe. But the book in which it had appeared, of which only ten thousand copies were printed, was ordered seized and destroyed by Moscow. Only a few copies, which had made their way to the West, survived.[18] In 1926 Bykov was allowed to expand his article into book form. *Posledniye dni Romanovykh* (The last days of the Romanovs) was published in Ekaterinburg—newly rechristened Sverdlovsk—by a local state publishing house, Uralkniga; in 1934, English-language translations appeared in both Great Britain and America, titled, respectively, *The Last Days of Tsardom* and *The Last Days of Tsar Nicholas.* Bykov, however, did add one new detail, which stood in direct contradiction to the works of Wilton, Deterikhs, and Sokolov. According to Bykov's account, the bodies of the victims had not been chopped apart, burned, and the remains then dissolved in acid, but rather had been buried "in a swamp."[19] Until the publication of the Yurovsky note in 1989, this single sentence was the only Russian hint that the fate of the remains might have been different from that asserted by the official investigation.

In the 1930s, a highly questionable account of the Ekaterinburg murders appeared. Written by author Richard Halliburton, it was said to be the firsthand story of Peter Ermakov, and contained a lurid account of both the shooting and the disposal of the corpses. Halliburton, an American journalist who specialized in travel adventures, was staying in Moscow in the fall of 1934 when he ran into William Stoneman of the *Chicago Daily News* at the Hotel Metropole. Stoneman told him that it might be possible to travel to the Urals and interview one of the actual participants in the Romanov execution. Halliburton quickly arranged to hire Stoneman's interpreter, a man identified only as Walter, and set off to Sverdlovsk.[20] There Halliburton was taken first to the Ipatiev House, then to Ermakov's apartment. He found Ermakov lying on his self-proclaimed deathbed; the former assassin dramatically told his American visitor that he suffered from throat cancer and that this interview would undoubtedly be his last. Halliburton listened intently as Ermakov spilled out his story; some of the details he gave regarding general events, and the life of the imperial family in the Ipatiev House, did correspond largely with the facts as we now know them. But while Ermakov also was known to have been among the members of the execution squad, his account of that night differs greatly in detail from the memoirs of other participants. In fact, he simply repeated the assertion made by Sokolov and others that the bodies had been chopped apart; burned; and, as a final dramatic flourish, their ashes cast to the wind.[21] Halliburton's interview was published twice, first in an American magazine, and then in his book *Seven League Boots.* Like much of what he wrote, it drew a mixed reaction. "Nobody," wrote Halliburton's biographer, "believed the Ermakov yarn—except most of Richard's readers."[22] In fact, Soviet authorities had carefully managed the entire Ermakov "confession." His translator, the mysterious Walter, was later discovered to have been an agent of the GPU, successor to the Cheka.[23] Many years later, Stoneman speculated that the entire affair had been designed to "feed" Halliburton, as an unsuspecting dupe, "with Moscow's pre-packaged 'facts.'"[24]

The collapse of the former Soviet Union, and a hidden wealth of archival documents, brought forth stunning and often controversial materials on the fate of the Romanovs, making it possible to present a new, comprehensive examination of the Ekaterinburg period and their eventual murders. From the Romanovs, there are the diaries of Nicholas and Alexandra—his kept regularly until the middle of June, then much more sporadically; hers, daily. There also are a few letters from this period which survive—several from Alexandra, but most from the grand duchesses; however, the authenticity of some of these last letters is open to doubt. Only one letter from Alexei, written at Ekaterinburg, is known to exist. From those imprisoned with the family, we have accounts from three sources: two letters written by their physician Dr. Eugene Botkin; statements made by the emperor's valet Terenty Chemodurov after Ekaterinburg fell to the advancing Czech and White forces; and a number of secondhand, hearsay accounts, said to derive from Chemodurov, Alexei's sailor-nanny Klementy Nagorny, and the footman Ivan Sednev, and related by Alexandra's valet Alexei Volkov, the tutors Pierre Gilliard and Sydney Gibbes, lady-in-waiting Baroness Sophie Buxhoeveden, and former prime minister Prince George Lvov.

From those in charge of the Romanovs and their retainers, the memoirs are more abundant. First and foremost we have the guard duty book from the Ipatiev House, which noted daily events: the time of their walks, and their duration; visitors; any changes in guard; and special requests or extraordinary occurrences surrounding their captivity. Alexander Avdayev left a set of memoirs, while Yakov Yurovsky, the last commandant of the House of Special Purpose, left five varied accounts of his life, his time in the Ipatiev House, and the eventual murders, the most important and detailed of which, written in 1922, has never before been published. Of the 105 guards, 17 gave statements or wrote memoirs, and 5 secondhand statements were given by their parents, sisters, or wives. The memoirs of seven of those involved in the execution also drew on eyewitness experiences to touch briefly on life within the Ipatiev House: Peter Ermakov (who left three accounts), Peter Voikov, Isai Rodzinsky, Michael Kudrin, Alexei and Michael Kabanov, and Victor Netrebin. Nine secondary witnesses also gave firsthand accounts of scenes they witnessed at the Ipatiev House: Victor Vorobyev, editor of the local newspaper *Uralskii rabochii;* three women who washed the floors in the Ipatiev House on several occasions; two nuns, Sisters Antonina and Maria, from the Novotikhvinsky Monastery, as well as their mistress of novices, Sister Agnes; Father Storozhev, who conducted religious services for the prisoners; and Catherine Tomilova, a worker at the local Bolshevik canteen who brought food to the Ipatiev House.

These diverse sources, taken with Western materials and the information collected by the White Army investigators, make it possible to accurately reconstruct the daily life of the prisoners in the Ipatiev House over those eleven weeks. At the same time, previously unknown archival documents help shatter the decades-old portrait of hardened, brutal revolutionary guards who delighted in the deliberate torment of their prisoners. Between April 30 and July 8, 105 men served guard duty at the Ipatiev House: 97 had been raised in the Orthodox faith, and 72 still considered themselves members of the church at the time of their duty; and more than half were married, with children of their own. Twenty-six were members of the Bolshevik Party, while a mere 13 had previously been involved in any criminal or revolutionary activity. Only 14 of these men were over age twenty-five; most were younger than twenty-three-year-old Grand Duchess Olga, the eldest of the imperial children.[25] Such facts provide a powerful correction to the usual depiction of these men as toughened Bolshevik criminals. Finally, in examining the murders, these newly uncovered memoirs, coupled with forensic evidence drawn from the remains themselves, allow for a more complete, disturbing, and ultimately realistic account of what took place in the basement of the Ipatiev House on the night of July 16–17, 1918.

In 1989, Geli Ryabov, author and former adviser to the Soviet Ministry of the Interior, startled the world by announcing that he and a small team of amateur sleuths had discovered the bodies of the Romanov family, buried—not burned and dissolved in acid, as Sokolov and others had declared—just outside of Ekaterinburg. The news coincided with the burgeoning of Mikhail Gorbachev's glasnost. The secrets of history were slowly being revealed, even as the Soviet Union itself collapsed under the immensity of its own tedious weight. Official and amateur investigations followed; forensic, anthropological, and genetic tests conducted on the nine sets of exhumed remains; unknown accounts of the murder revealed; and new claims asserting that some or all of the imperial family survived the execution in 1918 cast on the public. The Romanovs have twice been canonized, by two rival branches of the Russian Orthodox Church—once, in 1981, as martyrs, the second time, in 2000, as passion bearers. Their exhumed remains have been buried in St. Petersburg, in the same cathedral that, for two hundred years, served as the traditional resting place for members of the imperial dynasty.

And yet, despite the apparent finality that the 1998 funeral promised, the case of the murders of the Romanovs remains surprisingly enigmatic, awash with inaccuracies; contradictions; and enduring, unanswered questions. The Russian Orthodox Church within Russia has consistently refused to recognize the remains exhumed as those of the Romanovs; it is one of the few commonalities shared with the virulently monarchist Russian Orthodox Church Outside Russia, which holds that the genuine remains of the imperial family are in a mysterious box encased in a cathedral in Brussels. In 1992, Russian forensic and anthropological experts identified one set of remains as those of the famous Anastasia; since then, they have been repeatedly challenged by teams of American experts who contend that Anastasia is still missing. The genetic testing in 1993 on the remains seemed conclusive at the time; yet this verdict, too, has been challenged, not only by changes in technique but also, most recently, by Japanese geneticists. Two bodies remain missing, leaving the ultimate fate of two of the imperial children unknown. Despite the best efforts of scientists and historians, mystery cloaks the Romanov case. These questions lead back to events preceding the massacre itself, setting off an inexorable, cataclysmic tide that ended for the Romanovs in a hail of bullets.

This present book had its genesis in a series of articles, originally published in *Atlantis Magazine: In the Courts of Memory*, which sought to reexamine some of these outstanding questions.[26] Ironically, years earlier, we had each embarked on separate manuscripts concerning the murder of the Romanovs; the investigation into their deaths; and the stories of survival. As our individual work progressed, it only made sense to join as we explored these outstanding questions. After extensive research, the sheer amount of new material necessitated a much narrower focus than at first planned: in the end, we have elected to examine only the Ekaterinburg period; the murders themselves; and the 1991 exhumation and subsequent controversies over the identification of the Romanov remains.

We have approached the end of the Romanovs from an investigative position. This has been dictated first and foremost by an effort to combine here all available source material, old and new, published and unpublished, Russian and Western, to form a comprehensive portrait from which we attempt to extract, through analysis, something of the truth in the Romanov case. Any new examination of the last days and murder of the Romanovs must be undertaken with cautious, open minds, aware of the historic significance of the events. What we have attempted to do in these pages is look closely and critically at both old theories and new, known and previously unpublished evidence, in an effort to re-create the crucial months of April to July 1918, and the issues of identification, testing, burial, and canonization that followed from them.

It is a complex subject, and one that demanded an examination of everything related to these events—whether rumor, allegation, or historically accepted fact, as filtered by monarchists, Bolsheviks, Whites, recent historians, or the Romanovs themselves. In analyzing and re-creating these crucial months, we have utilized, wherever possible, primary source material. All too often, the end of the Romanovs has been characterized by books in which authors repeat the same assertions that have come to be accepted as truth; one of the authors of this present work, in his biography of Alexandra, was himself guilty of falling into this historical trap.[27] If the present work thus appears as a sharp break with what has come before, it does so in unapologetic terms, in the firm belief that this necessity drives any worthwhile history.

Examining the last seventy-eight days of captivity for the Romanovs in Ekaterinburg, evidence has now emerged that clearly challenges long-held beliefs—brutal abuse; insolent Bolshevik guards; and even the tranquil, rose-colored portrait of the imperial family itself, willingly, almost eagerly, going to their martyrdom—that can now be exposed largely as exercises in propaganda. The true portrait of those weeks and days; of the family and their retainers who endured them; the story of the men who guarded them; the reasons for the murders themselves; the question of who precisely ordered them; the actual executions; the disposal of the bodies; the investigation into the crimes; the motivations of those involved; the discovery of the Romanov remains; their identification; and the conflicting claims made about these bones—these issues have remained largely unresolved. We offer here new interpretations, fresh evidence, and careful analysis of the Romanov case, based on years of extensive research. Our conclusions, while controversial, follow only from this evidence; unlike many who have approached the story, our only goal has been to tear away some of the layers obscuring the few remaining fragments of discernible truth.

Such a task involves challenges, particularly given the romantic and religious sentiments still surrounding this case. As historians, we have had to divorce ourselves from such considerations and, indeed, from the strong feelings that initially brought each of us to this subject when we were much younger. This will cause considerable consternation among some readers, expecting to read the usual portrait of the loving, devoted imperial family and their "evil" Bolshevik jailers. But such tales are well known, and will be challenged here. Of necessity, the story focuses on deconstruction of what is most widely known and accepted as historical fact—what might be termed the émigré-monarchist myths surrounding the last days of the Romanovs—in an effort to reveal the individual personalities and characters who lived through these events. Nevertheless, we have attempted to maintain a narrative structure that conveys the drama of the story. The necessary though sometimes ponderous arguments and evidence have been largely confined to notes, where critical readers may examine for themselves the bases for our analyses and interpretations.

Many accounts reproduced here for the first time emanate from former Soviet archives, written by those directly involved in the fate of the Romanovs. Some were Bolsheviks, but, surprisingly, the vast majority were not. Nevertheless, historical accuracy forces us to read these accounts with extreme care; when they contain assertions of a dramatic nature, we have pursued, as far as is possible, corroborative evidence. The same standard also has been applied to evidence drawn from the opposite end of the political spectrum—the testimonies, accounts, and memoirs of those attached to the Romanovs. Few would question the judicious use and analysis of these former Soviet accounts, yet there remains a strident insistence among certain members of the émigré community that all such evidence is, of necessity, tainted and unreliable. This carries personal prejudice across the boundary of opinion, seeking to impose it on history itself, a danger that has, from the very first days following the 1918 murders, threatened to overwhelm the Romanov case.

Such dismissals, on the basis of proven or even presumed loyalties, ignore the fact that the only accounts of the murder of the imperial family—whether those utilized by Sokolov or the more recent revelations—derive from these sources. Aware of this widespread prejudice, we have considered the roles, sympathies, and positions of those men controlling the destinies of the imperial family. It has become all too common to color those involved in the Ekaterinburg drama in either black or white, yet all—from the Romanovs to the men who murdered them—possessed shades of gray. Membership in the Bolshevik Party of 1918 does not automatically equate to an alliance with the worst excesses of the regime. The Russia of this period was a morass of political motivations, not all easily delineated, and while in this story there may appear to be only monarchists and Bolsheviks, Whites and Reds, the lines of demarcation were never quite as solidly entrenched as might be assumed. Just as the former imperial generals fighting for the Whites spanned the political spectrum, ranging from rabidly anti-Semitic promonarchists to those who had actively plotted against Nicholas II before the February Revolution, so, too, did the Bolshevik Party encompass nuance and divergent points of view; in the first half of 1918, Lenin's rule was maintained only by embracing such diversity in what was formed as a coalition government. Even within the ruling body of the Central Executive Committee, independent men such as Trotsky and Zinoviev clashed with Lenin over policy issues, often in a very public manner. Given such circumstances among the ruling authorities, it is scarcely surprising that Soviets scattered across the enormous nation contained and tolerated the fearsome radical and the political novice, the hardened revolutionary and the shrewd opportunist, the cold pragmatist and the eager young idealist dreaming only of a better world.

A few of those who have left accounts do indeed fit the émigré portrait of the drunken, barbaric Bolshevik, most notably Peter Ermakov. Many of these memoirs contain factual errors and contradictions, which we have been careful to acknowledge. At the same time, because we know that these men were indeed present during these momentous events, it would be irresponsible to simply dismiss their accounts. Therefore we have opted to analyze these varied testimonies contextually, pointing out where and why we believe the evidence supports portions of one while at the same time stating when they conflict with known fact. We believe that this is the only responsible method of reconciling the allegations and often contradictory assertions within this case. This book, however, also calls for the critical eye of the reader; in several places we have presented our own hypotheses, which we offer only as logical, if plausible, theories on what may have taken place. Readers should gauge for themselves the evidentiary value of what is related, weigh and assess it as we ourselves have done.

We have tried to examine all participants equally, be they members of the imperial family or the Bolshevik Party, devoted courtiers or wide-eyed revolutionaries. The young men guarding the former imperial family, sure that they were contributing to the creation of a new Russian utopia, were largely unwilling witnesses to the brutal and sordid murder of their charges. Sympathy for the murder of innocent imperial children has thus been shared with those young men unwittingly caught up in the terrible drama—who stood aghast in the courtyard after the execution vomiting, hurled abuse at the assassins, and who were later murdered themselves by the vengeful White Army, or who, suffering from depression over the slaughter, committed suicide.

Despite any number of recently published books that have claimed for themselves the last word or the final chapter in the Romanov case, history continues to unfold: documents appear, scientists argue and challenge, and new versions come to the surface. What we offer here is in no way intended as the end of the story. It is, however, what we believe to be the most comprehensive contemporary examination of the outstanding issues in the case. Further accounts of these events do exist, and undoubtedly future works will appear that will both add to our own research and challenge our interpretations. If our own contribution spurs debate and incites interest in the subject, it will not have been in vain.

Authors' Note

THE USE OF THE TITLES "tsar," "tsarina," "tsaritsa," "emperor," and "empress" can be confusing. Until 1721, all Romanov rulers were called tsar, a title that derived from the Latin word Caesar. Peter the Great, enamored of all things modern and Western, officially adopted the title *gosudar imperator*, meaning sovereign emperor. From 1721 until the end of the Romanov Dynasty in 1917, this title was the correct form of address. Even so, the emperor was commonly referred to as tsar, with his wife, the empress, being known as the tsarina or, properly in Russian, tsaritsa. Nicholas II, being himself a Slavophile, preferred the ancient tsarist title, while Alexandra used empress. We have elected to use the correct form, and to refer to the imperial pair as the emperor and empress wherever possible. When quoting another who has used "tsar" or its female derivations, we have not tampered with the original.

Nicholas and Alexandra's son, Alexei, is most often referred to as the tsarevich. This is the ancient form of his title, meaning "the son of the tsar." Since 1721, the correct title of the empire's heir has been "tsesarevich," literally meaning "the son of Caesar" or of the emperor. Again, wherever possible without altering original sources and quotations, we have opted to call the boy "Tsesarevich Alexei."

In the transliteration of Russian names we have followed the Library of Congress method with certain exceptions. Unless attached to a living person, all proper names have been rendered in English for the ease of readers; thus we have "Paul" for "Pavel," "Marie" in place of "Mariya," and "Nicholas" instead of "Nikolai." The sole important exception is the name of the tsesarevich, who remains the traditional "Alexei."

A few words about dates, times, and measurements. In Russia, until the October Revolution, the Julian calendar was in official use. As a result, dates in the nineteenth century were twelve days behind those in Western Europe, where the Gregorian calendar was—and still is—in use. In the twentieth century, the Julian calendar lagged thirteen days behind, and in the twenty-first century it trails the Gregorian by fourteen days. So when Nicholas II abdicated his throne on March 2, 1917, according to the Russian Julian calendar, in the West it was already March 15. The difference in calendar usage officially ended when the Bolsheviks instituted use of the Gregorian calendar in February 1918, although many people dated their letters and diaries according to whichever calendar they preferred, without regard to officialdom. With a few exceptions noted in the text, nearly all incidents discussed in this book took place after the Bolsheviks changed the calendar, and we have therefore rendered them according to this system. Also on May 31, 1918, Lenin ordered the use of daylight saving time throughout Russia, which generally altered clocks by two hours. Further explanations of date and time are provided in the text when and where needed. Finally, and particularly in some quoted documents, original Russian measurements are used; we have provided equivalents for these as encountered, with one exception, noted here: the Russian measurement of one *verst*, used to calculate distance, is roughly equal to 1.06 kilometers, or 0.66 mile.

I

The Ruin of an Empire

A SHRILL WHISTLE SHATTERED the silence of the snowy afternoon as the Red Cross train slowly steamed into the siding at Tarnopol. Weary soldiers, bundled against the freezing rain, shuffled noiselessly along the crowded platform, heads bent low, eyes hollow and resigned. Amid the sea of disconsolate faces, J. P. Demidov, muffled in a thick astrakhan coat and hat, made his way across the siding, jumped into a waiting motorcar, and left the despair of the station in his wake.

It was the first winter of the Great War. In the devastation of Russian-occupied Galicia, a rising tide of miseries threatened to overtake the Imperial Army. Four months earlier, poorly trained, uneducated peasants proudly wore their new uniforms as they marched west, toward the advancing German and Austro-Hungarian armies under the late summer sun; for many, the clean leather boots had been the first pair of decent shoes they owned. But the four months could have been four years for the changes they wrought. Uniforms were ragged, muddied, stained with food, sweat, urine, and their comrades' blood, and the new boots—so impressive in the bright August sunshine—revealed their shabby manufacture as the Imperial Army waded through the marshes of Poland and the Danube. Disease and dejection hung like specters over these men, slowly replacing the patriotic ideals and short conflict promised in the far-off days of summer.

Demidov's motorcar snaked through the streets of Tarnopol, clogged with refugees shuffling through the slush among the ruins of bombed buildings as they dodged piles of fallen brick and burned timbers. The pale, expansive sky, dotted with leafless fingers of gnarled trees, disappeared into a shadowy stretch of swirling snow, broken only by ribbons of black crows that scattered and spread at the distant thud of enemy artillery fire. Misery was everywhere.

The Red Cross train on which Demidov arrived sat at the platform, angrily belching smoke into the winter sky. Dispatched by the Duma, the Russian parliament, it carried new bandages, linens, uniforms, supplies, and fresh medical personnel to replace the depleted Russian stores. Russia's presence in Galicia was hard-won, a much-needed boost to the nation following disastrous defeats in eastern Prussia. But the Galician campaign, waged by hungry and demoralized men slowly overwhelmed by growing discontent of war, marked the beginning of a weary bond shared by soldiers across the Continent.

As a deputy in the Duma, Demidov had supervised the legislature's Red Cross train on its journey across the vast sweep of the Russian Empire; having safely delivered it, he remained in Tarnopol, directing the distribution of supplies. One night he met a middle-aged woman, said to be a mystic. Without warning, she fell into a trance and began to murmur a string of prophecies. When Demidov asked about the war, she replied that the Russian army would suffer defeat in Galicia, soldiers giving themselves over to the enemy. The Allies would be victorious, but Russia would not last out the war.

"What about the emperor?" Demidov asked.

"I can see him in a room, on the floor, killed," she slowly answered.

"And the empress?" Demidov pressed.

"Dead, by his side," she replied.

"Where are the children, then?"

"I cannot see them," she announced. "But beyond the corpses of the emperor and the empress, I can see many more bodies."[1]

Demidov left, shaken. The following day he boarded a train and returned across the frozen winter landscape to Petrograd. The capital provided a stark contrast to the wretched scenes in Galicia: here, the wide boulevards were jammed with French motorcars and fashionable carriages, conveying privileged passengers to the pastel palaces lining the icy Neva River. Here, life carried on largely as before; in Galicia, it had ground to a tragic halt. But the tranquillity would not last. In twenty-six months the mighty Russian Empire collapsed, victim of a revolution that enveloped the glittering world of the imperial court. And the seer's vision of regicide became horrific fact only eighteen months later, when the 304-year-old Romanov Dynasty came to its bloody, inexorable end in a small cellar room in the Ural Mountains mining town of Ekaterinburg.

+   +   +

THE ROMANOV DYNASTY had ruled Russia for nearly three hundred years when, in 1894, Nicholas II acceded to the imperial throne. As the empire entered the twentieth century, the decades of fear and respect enveloping the imperial house had eroded, replaced with antipathy and alienation. The dynasty languished on an ethereal plane, subsumed in its own Byzantine opulence and a sense of impending doom. Shortly after the last emperor came to the throne, the young writer Dimitri Merezhovskii ominously recorded: "In the House of the Romanovs . . . a mysterious curse descends from generation to generation. Murders and adultery, blood and mud. . . . Peter I kills his son; Alexander I kills his father; Catherine II kills her husband. And besides these great and famous victims there are the mean, unknown and unhappy abortions of the autocracy . . . suffocated like mice in dark corners, in the cells of the Schlusselburg Fortress. The block, the rope and poison—these are the true emblems of Russian autocracy. God's unction on the brows of the Tsars has become the brand of Cain."[2]

In their centuries of rule, the Romanovs had wavered between failed reforms and brutal repression, bourgeois domesticity interrupted by murderous family plots. Though rich in artistic and cultural wealth, their empire bore little resemblance to a modern industrial state. The vast majority of Russia's 140 million subjects were uneducated peasants, their lives governed by a centuries-old struggle for survival; the handful of privileged aristocrats lived in splendid isolation in their baroque and neoclassical palaces in St. Petersburg and Moscow, spoke French and English instead of Russian, and spent holidays gambling away fortunes in Baden-Baden, Nice, and Monte Carlo. Yet between these two extremes stretched a growing class of urbanized peasants seeking a better life as factory workers, only to discover poverty and despair; and the small intelligentsia of merchants, lawyers, and students who devoured philosophical works and questioned the autocracy.

Russia entered the twentieth century poised on the edge of a volcano, demanding a steady hand and firm character to guide it through the uncertain waters of the modern era. It was the empire's misfortune, and Nicholas II's personal tragedy, that he took the throne at this crucial moment. Hopelessly ill equipped to deal with the burdens of his exalted position, and incapable of decisive action in the face of impending catastrophe, he presided over the dynasty's last years as an impotent spectator, unwilling and unable to avoid the wave of horrors that swept over Russia and drowned his country and his family. Even his birth on May 6, 1868, seemed to hint at the tragedy to come. In the liturgical calendar of the Russian Orthodox Church, it was the Feast of St. Job, an ill omen to the impressionable Nicholas. With tragic fatalism, Nicholas passively ascribed every catastrophe that befell his empire, every terrible drama suffered in his private life, to "God's will."

He was the eldest of the six children born to the future emperor Alexander III and his wife, Marie Feodorovna, a daughter of King Christian IX of Denmark. A second son, Alexander, was born in 1869, but lived for less than a year.[3] In Nicholas's first fourteen years, the family grew rapidly. He was joined in the nursery by two brothers, Grand Duke George Alexandrovich, who was born in 1871, and Grand Duke Michael Alexandrovich, in 1878; and two sisters, Grand Duchess Xenia Alexandrovna, in 1875, and Grand Duchess Olga Alexandrovna, in 1882. Raised in an atmosphere of familial love that stressed subservience as a cardinal virtue, Nicholas was unfailingly deferential, yet suffered under his father's heavy hand. Alexander made no attempt to disguise his disappointment in the shy, sensitive young boy who would one day follow him to the imperial throne. He "loathed everything that savored of weakness," recalled one official, and his eldest son bore the brunt of his wrath.[4] In an attempt to shape Nicholas in his own image, Alexander bullied him, crushing his instincts and even insulting him in front of his friends by yelling, "You are a little girlie!"[5]

Never one to argue, Nicholas simply accepted this treatment; with each passing year he became increasingly quiet and withdrawn, hampered by indecision and a lack of self-confidence, a situation his mother encouraged. Not particularly well educated, Marie Feodorovna was a clinging, possessive woman who spoiled Nicholas as much as her husband bullied him. She kept her son in an oppressive cocoon where he remained emotionally dependent. Friends and influences beyond this artificial world were regarded with suspicion, and allowed only with great reluctance. Happy though they may have been with this bourgeois family life, Alexander and Marie fatally crippled their eldest son. He passed into adulthood immature and incapable of reasoned judgment; instead, he was subject only to emotion, relying on instinct and on passion—whether familial love or religious fervor—when making important decisions.

This claustrophobic existence was heightened by the terrible uncertainty surrounding the imperial throne. At age twelve, Nicholas watched helplessly as his grandfather Alexander II bled to death before his eyes, victim of a revolutionary bomb. Six years later, on the anniversary of the tragedy, Nicholas and his family barely escaped assassination themselves when six men, carrying the workings of crude bombs, were discovered in the streets of St. Petersburg. An investigation found that they were part of a larger plot, driven by revolutionary students at St. Petersburg University; after a brief trial, the conspirators were found guilty and hung, the last public executions in imperial Russia.[6] Among those who went to the gallows was a young man named Alexander Ulyanov, elder brother of the boy who would become Vladimir Lenin.

Such incidents seared Nicholas's own conception of his future, a situation exacerbated by Konstantin Pobedonostsev, the political tutor who warned that violence was the natural outcome of any move toward democracy in Russia. The tutor made no intellectual distinction between the violent revolutionaries who engaged in acts of terror, and the majority of students and the intelligentsia who peacefully campaigned for reform, a dangerous and inaccurate foundation on which the young Nicholas built his few political views. Pobedonostsev emphasized the mystical nature of the Russian autocracy as a unique bond between sovereign and people. According to him, "real" Russians, loyal Russians, stood unquestionably behind the imperial throne, accepted the autocracy as divinely mandated, and prayed fervently for their sovereign. In turn, the emperor was endowed with divine grace, answerable to no one but his own conscience. Democratic concessions, Pobedonostsev declared, only disguised encroachment of the emperor's divine rights, a severing of this mystical relationship with the Russian people.

Nothing in Nicholas's education prepared him for what was to come. He had a passion for history; spoke Russian, French, German, Danish, and English; liked dancing; and impressed those whom he met with his quiet, thoughtful demeanor. Nor did his five-year career as an officer in the Preobrajensky Guards Regiment provide any intellectual or moral development. Rather than assume leadership, Nicholas reacted passively to military life, happy to take orders and follow a regimented routine with a rigidly defined hierarchy where his entire path was laid out for him by senior officers, leaving no unwelcome questions of choice. Even when he came to the imperial throne, at age twenty-six, Nicholas remained distinctly naive and immature, lacking the vision and force of will necessary to guide his country through the tumultuous decades that followed.

Nicholas and Alexandra, 1914.

Nicholas had a string of diverting youthful romances, but his true passion lay elsewhere. He first met Princess Alix of Hesse and by Rhine when she attended the wedding of her sister Elizabeth, known as Ella, to his uncle Grand Duke Serge Alexandrovich, in 1884. Within a week the sixteen-year-old tsesarevich was convinced of his love for the shy, twelve-year-old German princess, and this conviction deepened in the winter of 1889, when she stayed with her sister and brother-in-law in St. Petersburg. That winter, Nicholas was a handsome young officer with light brown hair and deep blue eyes, a dashing figure in his Imperial Guards uniform if, at five feet, seven inches tall, just slightly shorter than the princess herself. Alix, too, had blossomed into a quietly beautiful young woman, with golden hair and blue-gray eyes. The skating parties, balls, and dinners gave way to an extensive correspondence after she returned to her home in Darmstadt, and the young lovers found eager conspirators in Serge and Ella, who used their position at court to influence Alexander III and Marie Feodorovna.

In the case of Alix of Hesse, there was much to overcome. Beautiful though she was, she failed to win over the imperial couple during her visits to Russia. Confirmed into the Lutheran Church at age sixteen, Alix was preternaturally serious, and consumed with religious passion; coupled with a prim Victorian morality and distaste for frivolity, she left unfavorable impressions on those she encountered. Her emotions were guarded, her social skills undeveloped, creating a veneer of boredom, of disinterest, and of distinct unease. Her cousin Queen Marie of Romania later declared that Alix was "not of 'those who win'; she was too distrustful, too much on the defensive. . . . She had no warm feeling for any of us and this was of course strongly felt in her attitude, which was never welcoming. Some of this was no doubt owing to shyness, but the way she closed her narrow lips after the first rather forced greeting gave you the feeling that this was all she was ready to concede and that she was finished with you then and there. . . . She made you, in fact, feel an intruding outsider, which is of all sensations the most chilling and uncomfortable. The pinched, unwilling, patronizing smile with which she received all you said as if it were not worth while answering, was one of the most disheartening impressions I ever received. When she talked, it was almost in a whisper, and hardly moving her lips as though it were too much trouble to pronounce a word aloud. Although there was little difference in age between us, she had a way of making me feel as though I were not even grown up."[7]

After her mother's premature death in 1878, Alix found herself in a world dominated by forceful women. Grand Duke Ludwig IV, loving and devoted father though he was, had always been a submissive figure, and easily gave way to his mother-in-law, Queen Victoria, as she selected tutors and outlined lessons for her Hessian grandchildren.

Under her direction, as well as that of the tutor Margaret Jackson, Alix quickly developed into a shy, serious young woman, willful and stubborn, with an innate belief in the superiority of her own limited intellect. Her models were of feminine power and domination of weak men, a pattern that characterized her childhood, youth, and later married life.

A flurry of letters, as well as the tsesarevich's diaries, chronicled Nicholas's battle to win Alix's hand. Not only did his parents object, but also Alix herself refused to abandon the Lutheran faith for Orthodoxy, a necessity for the wife of the future emperor of Russia. Only in 1894, at the wedding of her brother, did she finally relent and agree to Nicholas's proposal. The marriage of Nicholas and Alexandra—the name Alix took on her conversion to the Russian Orthodox faith—rested on a peculiar foundation. Nicholas awakened in Alexandra a convergence of feelings. The longing in her heart was filled with a man who adored her, and needed her at his side. Like the other men in Alexandra's life, Nicholas was weak, accustomed to following the dictates of his father and especially his mother; in seeking Alexandra out, he supplied himself with a lover, substitute mother, stern nanny, and stronger will than he himself possessed. In turn, his shy, gentle character greatly appealed to her; she recognized his weakness, and came to believe that it was her role not only to support him, but also to prod—and provoke—him to greatness. As a man who would one day rule his great empire as an autocrat, regarded as God's anointed on earth, Nicholas engaged the deeply religious Alexandra. By marrying him, she assumed her proper place in the divinely inspired plan she was certain lay in store for them both.

On October 20, 1894, at 2:30 P.M., Alexander III died of nephritis at Livadia, in the Crimea. The emperor was only forty-nine; although he had been unwell for months, his premature death came as a shock to his empire, and no one was more overwhelmed than the new emperor himself. Nicholas II panicked at the thought of his crushing responsibilities. Isolated from affairs of state by his father, Nicholas himself had shown absolutely no interest in his future role until it was thrust on him. "To the end of his life," wrote Count Paul von Benckendorff, who knew Nicholas well, "he lacked balance, nor could he grasp the principles that are necessary for the conduct of so great an Empire. Hence his indecision, his limitations, and the fluctuations which lasted throughout his reign. He was very intelligent, understood things at once, and was very quick, but he did not know how to reconcile decisions with fundamental political principles, which he entirely lacked."[8]

Nicholas II left an enduring legacy as a faithful, loving husband; a devoted father; a modest, charming man marked with a deep religious faith equal to his undoubted patriotism. Colonel Eugene Kobylinsky, who came to know him under less than ideal circumstances when he assumed command of the Special Detachment guarding the Romanovs after the Revolution, said that Nicholas "was a very clever man, well informed, and very interesting to talk with; he had a remarkable memory." He noted the emperor's passion for "physical labor" and recalled that he "was very modest in his needs."[9] At the same time, remembered Charles Sydney Gibbes, the English tutor at the imperial court, the emperor's "extremely honest character" and "compassionate heart" were balanced by a firm imperial reserve, a "hatred of any sort of familiarity."[10]

The emperor's private virtues, however, played little part in his disastrous reign. Though dedicated to his role as sovereign, and sincere in his attempts to rule as he thought best for Russia, Nicholas unwittingly acted as the chief architect of his empire's doom. Distrusting ministers and other officials, and resentful at the merest whisper of any infringement on what he considered his divine rights, Nicholas ruled his empire as a man might jealously guard his mistress, keeping secrets from his own government and neglecting to inform one ministry what the other was doing, in an attempt to maintain the illusion that only he truly remained in control. So complete was this jealousy that he would not even have a private secretary, for fear that another might come between him and his prerogatives.[11]

Nicholas did not understand the need for urgent reform if his empire was to survive the dramatic changes enveloping Russia at the turn of the century. The rapid industrialization of the nineteenth century created Russia's first working class, an unknown in a country where fewer than 5 percent of the population owned nearly everything, and where serfdom had existed only forty years earlier. Factory owners grew rich while their workers labored for up to eighteen hours a day under unsafe and frequently deadly conditions, paid a miserable wage from which their meager food and abysmal housing in disease-filled company barracks were deducted. Children as young as eight years worked alongside their parents, with conditions in the country's iron mines and oil fields much worse. Peasants in the countryside starved, or wallowed in cheap vodka, while officials of the Russian Orthodox Church, a body renowned for its corruption, happily accepted bribes and looked the other way.

The autocratic system was rotting away, yet Nicholas never sensed the inexorable explosion. Instead, he submerged himself in fantasy, basking in his own bucolic myth: happy peasants working in the fields, loyal to authority; an unseen population devoted to the throne; and a devout church dedicated to the principles of their Orthodox sovereign. It was as unreal as the portrait of Nicholas as a bloodthirsty tyrant painted by the growing number of revolutionaries, yet one that Nicholas eagerly embraced.

Nicholas reigned by resignation, submersing himself in such myths and in the comforting delusion that his fate—and therefore that of his empire—was predestined by God. He believed fully in the Russian idea of *sudba*, an overwhelming, inexorable force controlling the destinies of an impotent humanity. *Sudba* decreed that misfortune was inescapable, to be passively accepted, and it became a signature of Nicholas's reign. When, in 1905, he learned that the Russian navy had mutinied at Kronstadt, he remarked to one official: "If you find me so little troubled, it is because I have the firm and absolute faith that the destiny of Russia, my own fate, and that of my family are in the hands of Almighty God, who has placed me where I am. Whatever may happen, I shall bow to his will."[12] By embracing disaster as his inexorable fate, Nicholas abdicated his responsibilities in favor of a philosophical delusion of convenience that absolved him of personal obligation for the misfortunes plaguing Russia. It was a view he shared with Alexandra as they willingly—almost enthusiastically—gave themselves and their children over to the fate of the Revolution. Even in exile, they questioned not the emperor's own lack of leadership, which had helped bring them to this point, but the will of an unfathomable God who saw fit to punish Russia for the sins of its citizens against the throne.

For the first time, under Nicholas II, the Russian autocracy became a spiritual, and not just a political, ideology, enshrined in an elaborate myth that it was an institution ordained by God, an earthly priesthood where the emperor acted as benevolent pastor to his secular flock. Thus Nicholas once declared: "I shall never, under any circumstances, agree to a representative form of government because I consider it harmful to the people whom God has entrusted to my care."[13] He never understood that the autocratic system had long passed into oblivion, and as Russia tumbled from catastrophe to catastrophe, his blind devotion to its principles drove the country headlong to revolution.

From his father's premature death, Nicholas's reign unfolded with tragedy at every turn. His hasty marriage to Princess Alix, just a week after Alexander III's funeral, earned her the epithet of "the funeral bride" as people whispered, "She has come to us behind a coffin. She brings misfortune with her."[14] Just three months after his accession, Nicholas dismissed the pleas of a provincial delegation asking for a larger role in self-governance as "senseless dreams," a devastating remark that resounded throughout the empire.

At Nicholas and Alexandra's coronation in May 1896, more than a thousand people were killed, crushed to death in a crowd awaiting the appearance of the imperial couple at an open-air feast. That same night, they attended a previously scheduled ball given by the French ambassador, leaving an unfortunate image of a heartless imperial couple, dancing as their subjects died in Moscow's hospitals. Both Nicholas and Alexandra regarded such incidents as personal tragedies, yet as the reign progressed, the emperor sunk deeply into reaction, cementing unfavorable impressions and creating the turmoil threatening to overwhelm his empire. Gentle and modest though he may have been in his private life, Nicholas often urged repression and even bloodshed in an effort not only to maintain law and order but also to uphold the phantom principles of the autocracy itself.

Very quickly he alienated the country's growing base of industrial workers. In April 1895, employees at a textile factory in Yaroslavl went on strike over unsafe conditions; in response, a division of soldiers broke up their meeting, killing thirteen men. "I am very satisfied with the way the troops behaved at Yaroslavl during these factory uprisings," Nicholas commented on the official report.[15] While such comments contrast with the usual picture of Nicholas, they are not unique. In the first ten years of his reign, he responded to student disturbances with orders for exile and hard labor, ordering blood to flow after a wave of violent political assassinations struck the country between 1900 and 1904. The Russo-Japanese War of 1904–1905, an unhappy conflict largely brought about by the emperor's reckless Far Eastern policy, ended with nearly half a million dead, and Russia suffering a humiliating defeat.

Animosity against the imperial regime led to the Revolution of 1905, the culmination of a year filled with violence. On January 9 a group of striking factory workers had trudged over the frozen canals and down the windswept streets of St. Petersburg, intent on assembling in front of the Winter Palace and presenting Nicholas with a petition for better living conditions, an end to child labor, and a minor increase in pay. Thousands of men, women, and children—carrying icons and portraits of the emperor and singing hymns—crossed the snowy capital, to be met not by the emperor, who had retreated to his suburban palace at Tsarskoye Selo, but by his soldiers, who leveled their guns at the unarmed crowds and opened fire, leaving the early morning rent with the screams and the snow littered with bodies and spreading pools of blood. The massacre, called "Bloody Sunday," left several hundred dead, an unknown number injured, and helped demolish the traditional view of the emperor as paternalistic sovereign. Revolutionaries evoked the massacre as further evidence that Nicholas despised his people, treating them not as human beings but as cogs in the enormous wheel of empire, to be disposed of according to his own capricious moods. Those who fell on "Bloody Sunday" were not shot on the emperor's orders, but many of the thousands who perished over the sixteen months that followed certainly were.

Within two weeks the emperor's uncle and brother-in-law, Grand Duke Serge Alexandrovich, was killed by an anarchist's bomb in Moscow. Factory strikes, student protests, and mutinies in the army and navy launched a wave of violence that tore across Russia as peasants killed aristocratic landowners and burned their estates, and as officials were gunned down by terrorists. Such activities were brutally suppressed, often on Nicholas's direct orders. Reading a report that Cossacks in Saratov had "unfortunately" beaten a group of doctors suspected of assisting local peasants, Nicholas underlined the word "unfortunately," added a question mark, and wrote, "Very well done!"[16] Hearing that a revolt in the Caucasus had passed without bloodshed, Nicholas replied, "That is no good! In such cases one must always shoot!"[17] In the Baltic provinces, a certain Lieutenant Captain Richter began, on his own authority, to execute suspects without benefit of trials or even official arrests; learning this, Nicholas commented, "What a fine fellow!"[18] When a group of anarchists who had seized a small enclave surrendered their arms, Nicholas was beside himself with anger: "The town should have been destroyed!" he declared.[19] He expressed similar sentiments on learning that a group of demonstrators in Vladivostok had been dispersed without violence: "You should have shot them!" he told the official in charge.[20]

By the fall of 1905, Russia was in chaos. Railways had stopped running, and students and factory workers in all major cities were on strike. With the country collapsing around him, Nicholas finally took decisive action to save his throne. He favored declaring martial law, suspending all court trials, and appointing his uncle Grand Duke Nicholas Nikolaievich as dictator; on learning of this, the grand duke stormed into his nephew's study, brandishing a pistol and threatening to shoot himself on the spot unless the emperor granted a constitution. Faced with this, Nicholas reluctantly signed the Manifesto of October 17, 1905, which created Russia's first elected legislature, the Duma.

The sweep of a pen had transformed Russia from an autocracy to a constitutional monarchy, but Nicholas refused to accept the change. He stubbornly clung to the mistaken belief that he remained an autocrat, responsible to no one but God for his rule. He had nothing but contempt for the parliament he created; both the first and the second Dumas were illegally closed on Nicholas's orders when they insisted on launching investigations into government-sponsored pogroms.[21] In 1907, in anticipation of the third Duma, the emperor illegally altered the voting laws to prevent those he considered too liberal from winning seats.[22]

Another outcome of these troubled years was the rise of Russian anti-Semitism. The vast majority of Russia's Jews were restricted to the infamous Pale of Settlement, created by Catherine the Great in 1791 to house her most undesirable subjects.[23] Following Alexander II's assassination, his successor enacted the infamous "May Laws" of 1882, exacting punitive revenge on the Jews whom Alexander III despised. Thousands were killed in pogroms while officials looked on in approval; shops and houses were seized, and families were turned out into the street; education was restricted; and Jewish professionals were dismissed from their posts.

Nicholas II inherited both his father's personal anti-Semitism and his public anti-Semitic policies. He firmly believed in a worldwide Jewish conspiracy against the Russian empire in general and himself in particular.[24] He once denied an orchestra permission to perform in Yalta on the excuse that it contained Jewish musicians; on another occasion, learning that the widow of a Jewish doctor in Yalta had been evicted from her home and applied for permission to return, Nicholas dismissed her request by writing, "There are too many Yids already."[25]

The systematic pogroms of Nicholas II's reign were far more vicious than anything witnessed under Alexander III. The notorious Easter Massacre at Kishinev in 1903 was organized by Vyacheslav Plehve, the minister of the interior, with the emperor's knowledge and support. Alexei Lopukhin, director of the Imperial Police Department, recalled that leaflets inciting the violence were printed under Plehve's direction on Ministry of the Interior presses; the text had been personally approved by General Trepov on the emperor's behalf, and the costs borne by Nicholas himself.[26] Some fifty Jews were dragged from their houses and murdered in the streets, with another six hundred beaten and tortured with the assistance of the local police.[27] The world was stunned, and the slaughter at Kishinev was roundly condemned, though Nicholas himself was satisfied at the outcome. He fully approved, he told his minister of war, adding that the Jews "ought to be taught a lesson, that they have got above themselves and are taking the lead of the revolutionary movement."[28]

Kishinev set an ominous pattern for the wave of anti-Semitic violence that erupted during the Revolution of 1905. In eleven days alone—October 18–29—a total of 690 separate pogroms took place, leaving hundreds of Jews dead and tens of thousands homeless.[29] The single worst episode occurred in Odessa, where nearly 1,000 Jews were murdered, hacked to pieces with sabers and axes as their horrified families looked on, held back by police who did nothing to halt the slaughter.[30] Nicholas rarely raised a protest against such indiscriminate violence. He was never able to separate the minority of revolutionaries who happened to be Jews from the vast majority of his Jewish citizens, even when the victims included women and children.[31]

Such violence played on the deep anti-Semitism of most Russians, codified into repressive law by Alexander III. In the fall of 1906 the Council of Ministers unanimously recommended that the most restrictive measures against the Jews be lifted. Nicholas, however, refused to give ground, explaining "an inner voice ever more insistently repeats to me that I should not take this decision upon myself. So far my conscience has never deceived me. Therefore, in this case also, I intend to follow its dictates. . . . I bear a terrible responsibility before God for all authorities set up by me and at any time I am ready to answer for them to Him."[32] Thus he justified the continued discrimination that marked the Jews out for violence on the whims of conscience.

The emperor's own anti-Semitic views were bolstered by the infamous *Protocols of the Elders of Zion*, a piece of literary fiction promoted by Alexandra's sister Grand Duchess Elizabeth Feodorovna. In 1900 Nicholas and Alexandra fell under the influence of Philippe Nazier-Vachot, a French mystic of dubious history and talent. Finding themselves increasingly shut out, Grand Duke Serge Alexandrovich and his wife—loathe to lose their hold on the imperial couple—embarked on a scheme that played directly on the emperor's prejudices.

Versions of the *Protocols* had been in circulation for nearly a hundred years, but they first appeared in Russia shortly after 1901, greatly altered by the Okhrana, the Secret Police. On Serge and Ella's instructions, they were again rewritten, this time to include not only allegations against the Jews but also the Freemasons, a group with which Nazier-Vachot was known to be involved.[33] The grand duchess worked closely with Serge Nilus, a reactionary, ultra-Orthodox writer known for his controversial publications and, conveniently, married to one of her ladies-in-waiting. Together, Serge and Ella introduced him to influential members of the court and helped raise the necessary funds for his work.[34]

Nilus's book was published in 1903. Nicholas eagerly devoured it, though its intended mission failed. Philippe fell from favor at court, but only after he wrongly predicted several pregnancies for the empress. The seed, however, had been planted. Nicholas viewed the *Protocols* not as a clumsy forgery but as a statement of political and religious truth. "What depth of thought!" he wrote of Nilus's book. "Everywhere one sees the directing and destroying hand of Jewry!"[35] Two years later, the book was republished. Nilus called the new version *The Great in the Small and the Coming of the Antichrist as a Future Probability: The Protocols of the Zionist Elders*, declaring that the six-pointed Star of David was the biblical "mark of the Beast," foretold in the Book of Revelation. The

Protocols, he asserted, exposed the Jewish plan for world domination, a scheme whose principal aim was the introduction of Satan on earth and the destruction of Holy Orthodox Russia. With Nicholas's permission, Nilus dedicated the book to the emperor, who himself paid for its publication and distribution by the Court Chancellery at Tsarskoye Selo.[36]

An investigation ordered by Prime Minister Peter Stolypin eventually revealed the sordid plot, and with some reluctance Nicholas ordered his Chancellery to halt distribution, commenting, "A just cause cannot be defended through dirty means."[37] Yet he continued to believe that exposure of this alleged Jewish conspiracy was "a just cause." As a prisoner in Tobolsk he complained bitterly to one of his children's tutors that the "Yids" had incited the Russian people to revolution, and repeatedly turned to the pages of Nilus's fabrication, noting that it made for "very timely reading."[38]

In the aftermath of the Revolution of 1905 and the publication of the *Protocols*, Russian anti-Semitism became firmly entrenched, supported as it was by the emperor himself. Several odious groups, including the Black Hundreds and the Union of the Russian People, rose to the forefront of the movement, determined to uphold the vanished autocracy and promote devastating pogroms. To both groups, Jews were purely and simply evil, condemned in the speeches of their leaders, their bulletins, and in their propaganda, as collectively guilty of Russia's misfortunes and the rise in revolutionary activity. Jews, they warned, hoped to exploit peasants and workers, smash the Russian Orthodox Church, and overthrow the Romanov Dynasty; if these same bodies did not support their anti-Semitic policies, they would be engulfed when the tide of Jewish revolution swept across the empire.[39]

Both the Union and the Black Hundreds found an enthusiastic and ardent supporter in Nicholas II. Although at times he questioned their methods, he stood wholeheartedly behind their aims and believed fiercely in their views. On December 23, 1905, he happily received a deputation from the Union, accepting honorary membership for both himself and his infant son with these words: "Unite the Russian people—I am counting on you!"[40] He was likewise steadfast in his support for the Black Hundreds, once telling Count Konovnizin, their leader, "I know that Russian courts are too severe toward the participants in the pogroms. I give you my Imperial word that I shall always lighten their sentences, on the application of the Union of the Russian People, so dear to me."[41] The Union also received official support from the imperial government—in one year some 2.5 million rubles alone for their propaganda—while the emperor and empress sponsored its activities with private contributions that helped fund new pogroms.[42]

With pogroms favorably discussed in government-owned newspapers and local authorities inciting the masses to riot, a crisis was inevitable. It came in March 1911, when a thirteen-year-old boy from Kiev was found murdered, stabbed forty-seven times. The local press eagerly described it as established Jewish ritual slaughter, and crowds clamored for blood. Although an investigation found that the boy had been killed by a band of local Russian thieves, senior police officials told their men to "find a Yid" on whom to pin the crime.[43] Chaplinsky, the Kiev District prosecutor, candidly admitted that finding the real culprit was unimportant, urging that the crime be used to prove to the world that Jews practiced ritual murder.[44] It took some time, but the prosecutor, "with the personal blessing of the emperor," was finally able to uncover a "witness" of questionable honesty, who claimed to have seen a young Jew, Mendel Beilis, kidnap and murder the boy.[45] Beilis was arrested in August, but it took Chaplinsky two years to fabricate a case against him.[46] Nicholas II himself read the official reports of perjury and manufactured evidence, but refused to intervene as the case moved forward.[47] Worse still, even though he knew Beilis to be innocent, the emperor actively conspired with his government to frame him for the crime.[48] He sent the assistant public prosecutor of the St. Petersburg District to work with Chaplinsky in Kiev, where the pair bribed witnesses and forced the coroner to alter his official report.[49]

Shortly before the trial began, Nicholas summoned the presiding judge, handed him a gold watch, and promised a future promotion if the government won the case he knew to be fabricated.[50] When it came to trial, the case—as Duma official Paul Miliukov declared—embodied "all the falsehood of the regime, all its personal violence."[51] On October 28, 1913, as the prosecutor warned that "the Jews would destroy Russia!" the jury found Beilis not guilty. It was stunning news, received with disbelief within the imperial regime; the official government newspaper *Novyoe Vremya* even declared that "all Russia has suffered a defeat."[52]

The verdict came in the midst of celebrations marking the three-hundredth anniversary of Romanov rule, falling like a stone in a sea churning with discontent. Strikes and riots threatened to overwhelm the country: just six months before the festivities, hundreds of workers were massacred near Baku during a demonstration. The number of political arrests and forced exiles to Siberia increased dramatically, providing an ominous mise-en-scène for the celebrations.

Nicholas looked to the ceremonies—which included services and balls in both St. Petersburg and Moscow and a visit to the Ipatiev Monastery in Kostroma, where young Michael Romanov had been offered the vacant Russian throne in 1613—as a chance to evoke public support for his faltering regime. The Revolution of 1905 and its aftermath left the empire uncertain, and the imperial family left their cloistered life in the Alexander Palace at Tsarskoye Selo rarely, exchanging its protections for their estate at Peterhof, on the Gulf of Finland; cruises aboard their favorite yacht, *Standart*, in the Finnish skerries; journeys west to their Polish hunting lodges; and holidays at the imperial compound of Livadia, in the Crimea. This pattern guaranteed that they remained hidden from the outside world.

It was all as Alexandra and, to a lesser extent, Nicholas himself, wished. They valued the sanctity of their family with a jealous passion, resenting public duties as an encroachment on their private lives. As historian Edward Crankshaw noted, the empress spent these years "trying to confine her children and Nicholas himself to a sort of everlasting cosy tea-party at Tsarskoye Selo."[53] They never realized, added Russian diplomat Dimitri Abrikossow, "that as Emperor and Empress, they were no longer private individuals with personal sympathies, that duty toward the country rather than absorption in family life should have been their prime consideration."[54] The former glories of the imperial court were abandoned, the enormous rooms of the magnificent Winter Palace cloaked in silence.

The empress forced herself through rare public appearances, though by 1913 she was increasingly unwell. Alexandra had never been particularly strong, inheriting her mother's fragile health, and even in her first years in Russia she suffered from innumerable complaints: sciatica, fatigue, shortness of breath, and incessant headaches. The sheer number of medical consultations was staggering: in 1898, when she was only twenty-six, Alexandra saw court doctors on more than two hundred separate occasions, and in 1900 there were more than a hundred examinations. In addition to her other complaints, by the beginning of the twentieth century Alexandra had been diagnosed with acute otitis.[55]

The symptoms were genuine, though the empress's ill health was rooted in her increasingly nervous condition, a diagnosis confirmed by Dr. Eugene Botkin, the court physician-in-ordinary who treated the family and shared their eventual assassination. In a letter to his brother Peter, Botkin reported: "I am very pained about the malady of the Empress; it is a nervousness of the heart related to the cardiac muscles. This is confirmed by physicians here who I have consulted. I spoke without restriction because I believed it to be in the best interests of the Empress. I like to let my imagination free to search for different names for the Empress's condition."[56]

Alexandra used her declining health to absolve herself of her ceremonial duties as empress, in much the same way that Nicholas eagerly looked on his self-declared fate as releasing him from responsibility as the empire crumbled away. During World War I, however, the empress unwittingly revealed the true nature of her troubles. "I want to help others in life," she once explained, "to help them fight their battles and bear their crosses."[57] Cast into this role of caregiver, Alexandra completely forgot her own struggles and focused her energies on others. Thus, she attempted, often successfully, to impose her will on her husband—to help him bear "his cross" of ruling—and spent hours engaged in ordinary hospital work as a nursing sister, roles that freed her and at the same time allowed Alexandra to cloak herself in the mantle of champion of the sick; the downtrodden; and, in her husband's case, the weak.

In the empress's isolated world, where she saw few people, she purposely surrounded herself with a pair of trustworthy and uncritical women. Lili Dehn, wife of Karl Akimovich von Dehn, a Russian naval officer who commanded the cruiser *Varyag*, was the first and most astute; the second, Anna Vyrubova, offered the empress, as Pierre Gilliard wrote, a "fiery and sincere devotion." It was, he declared, just as Alexandra wished: "Imperious as she was, she wanted her friends to be hers, and hers alone. She only entertained friendships in which she was quite sure of being the dominating partner. Her confidence had to be rewarded by complete self-abandonment."[58]

Having gone voluntarily—or been subsumed by his wife's more forceful character—into this narrow world, Nicholas attempted to use the 1913 celebrations to promote the historical link between the Romanov Dynasty and the Russian people, and to assert his own vision of his role as emperor. As shortsighted as Nicholas could be, in one respect he was far ahead of his contemporary monarchs: with an uncanny sense of the value of his own family, he eagerly offered them up as paragons of modern morality, launching a propaganda war that continues to this day.

Nicholas took the unprecedented step of commissioning an authorized biography, published in Russian, English, and French, that portrayed him in glowing terms as the most pious, patriotic, and paternalistic Russian ever to occupy the imperial throne. To a large extent, the book focused on his private life, a previously forbidden subject now laid bare in an attempt to win back the affection of his subjects. He had lost control of Russia, been forced to grant the hated Duma, and bow repeatedly to his wife's wishes, yet there was one area over which he still remained master: the presentation of his family to the nation and the world, and Nicholas was not shy in using them, especially his beautiful daughters and handsome young son, to evoke patriotism and loyalty to the throne. Descriptions of their simple family life—complete with declarations that all enjoyed only Russian food, found comfort in the Russian Orthodox Church, and read only Russian literature—crafted an image to accompany the hundreds of official photographs and postcards, creating a cult of personality that lingered far beyond the end of the Romanov Dynasty.

Despite the proliferation of photographs, postcards, and newsreels depicting them, the five children of Nicholas and Alexandra remained enigmas to Russia, unknown by all but a handful of court officials and infrequently seen relatives. After the murders in Ekaterinburg, their sad, sheltered lives were often portrayed in the most unrealistic terms: a closely knit, loving imperial family, doting parents and adoring children who did not resent their imposed isolation but, as Baroness Sophie Buxhoeveden, one of Alexandra's ladies-in-waiting, wrote, looked on their parents "as delightful companions."[59] Like any family, however, they endured struggles, fights, and insecurities, realities made all the more clear in their letters and diaries.

In her first six years of marriage, Alexandra gave birth to four daughters: the Grand Duchesses Olga, Tatiana, Marie, and Anastasia Nikolaievna. Enveloped though they were in privilege and surrounded by a bevy of fawning courtiers, they endured sad, shadowy lives made all the more tragic by the murders in Ekaterinburg. Weighed down by the burdens of office, Nicholas spent little more than an hour with them each evening, and often this, too, was sacrificed to the demands of the throne. Alexandra acted as their principal influence, a loving if obsessive mother who had difficulty allowing her children their foibles, mistakes, and pleasures. She retained a Victorian distaste for anything that hinted at idleness; from their earliest days her daughters were taught not to be frivolous, but to occupy themselves at all times with something useful, be it reading, writing letters, piano lessons, needlework, or painting. In such a narrow environment there was little opportunity for youthful high spirits, and as the girls grew older they frequently clashed with their forceful mother. "The children," Alexandra once complained to Nicholas, "with all their love still have quite other ideas and rarely understand my way of looking at things, the smallest, even, they are always right and when I say how I was brought up and how one must be, they can't understand, find it dull."[60]

In this repressive atmosphere, the children learned quickly that the empress ruled the palace. All except Tatiana favored their father, with whom they shared confidences and could act according to their vibrant characters; with their mother, they were often guarded, aware that any infraction might bring disapproval. Queen Marie of Romania remembered that the four grand duchesses "were natural, gay and pleasant and quite confidential with me when their mother was not present; when she was there, they always seemed to be watching her every expression so as to be sure to act according to her desires."[61]

With the empress often unwell, the girls, as Pierre Gilliard noted, "arranged matters in such a way that they could take turns of 'duty' with their mother, keeping her company for the day."[62] Increasingly, though, Alexandra interacted with her daughters only in brief letters, exchanged beneath the same roof. For such healthy girls, coping with both their mother's fragile mental and physical state and her passive acceptance of suffering as "God's will" took its toll. In 1908, thirteen-year-old Olga wrote, "So sorry that I never see you alone Mama dear, can not talk so should try to write to you what could of course better say, but what is to be done if there is no time, and neither can I hear the dear words which sweet Mama could tell me."[63] A year later, twelve-year-old Tatiana wrote to her mother: "I hope you won't be today very tired and that you can get up to dinner. I am always so awfully sorry when you are tired and when you can't get up."[64] This deliberate isolation began to take an emotional toll on the relationships. "Mother came over and lay down nearby," Olga candidly reported to her grandmother the dowager empress in 1913. "As usual, her heart isn't well. It's all so unpleasant."[65] And even Tatiana, the most subservient and dutiful of the four girls, once complained, "Mama, sweet, I am so awfully sad. I see so little of you. I hate going away for so long. Really, we never see you now."[66]

To these heartfelt letters, Alexandra usually replied with typical fatalism. To eleven-year-old Marie she once explained: "It is my great sorrow not to be able to be more with you all and to read and shout and play together—but we must bear all. He has sent His cross which must be borne. I know it's dull having an invalid mother but it teaches you all to be loving and gentle."[67] Such exhortations brought little comfort to the grand duchesses, who idolized their remote mother yet, as the years passed, grew increasingly distant from her.

Olga, the eldest daughter, was born in November 1895, one week before her parents' first wedding anniversary. She most resembled her father, with his light chestnut hair and deep blue eyes. Gleb Botkin, son of the imperial physician, recalled that she was "probably the least pretty of the four, but because of her personality, the most attractive."[68] It was this personality—"open, somewhat brisk," as Queen Marie recalled—that singled Olga out among the girls.[69] The quietest of all the children, she also was the most thoughtful. Well-read, she liked to retire by herself for hours with a book, or sit and ponder life. "She was by nature a thinker," Gleb Botkin remembered, "and as it later seemed to me, understood the general situation better than any member of her family, including even her parents. At least I had the impression that she had little illusions in regard to what the future held in store for them, and in consequence was often sad and worried."[70]

The four grand duchesses, 1914. From left: Marie, Anastasia, Tatiana, and Olga.

Olga struck many as intensely serious, an undoubted echo of her mother; Alexandra imbued all of her children with a sense of purpose, but Olga, as the first, seems to have borne the most criticism. The empress often lectured her "to be an example of what a good little obedient girlie ought to be. You are the eldest and must show the others how to behave. Learn to make others happy, think of yourself last of all. Be gentle and kind, never rough or rude. In manners, as well as in speech, be a real lady."[71]

As she grew older, Olga resented this oppression, and frequently clashed with her mother. Charles Sidney Gibbes, her English tutor, noted that Olga was "easily irritated" and that "her manners were a little harsh."[72] And Anna Vyrubova, who knew the grand duchesses well, wrote that Olga possessed "a hot temper" and "a strong will and singularly straightforward habit of thought and action. Admirable qualities in a woman, these same characteristics are often trying in childhood, and Olga as a little girl sometimes showed herself willful and even disobedient."[73] In her letters to Nicholas when he was at army headquarters during World War I, Alexandra often complained of her eldest daughter's behavior: "Olga is the whole time grumpy, sleepy, angry to put on a tidy dress and not nurse's [uniform] for the hospital and to go there officially—she makes everything more difficult by her humor," she once wrote.[74] She termed her "always most unamiable about every proposition" the empress made, writing that she "sulks with me" when corrected.[75] In turn, those who knew her agreed that Olga's relationship with her mother was strained. "She loved her father more than anybody else," Gibbes remembered, a sentiment echoed by Colonel Eugene Kobylinsky.[76]

Tatiana was born in 1897. With her long, lean figure and fine features, she most resembled her mother. "You could hardly find anyone so thin," recalled Gibbes.[77] Alexander Mossolov, head of the Imperial Chancellery, wrote that she was "the best looking of all the sisters."[78] Proud and exceptionally refined, Tatiana impressed everyone with her grace and soft character. "She was a poetical creature," recalled Lili Dehn, "always yearning for the ideal and dreaming of great friendships."[79]

In manner, Tatiana was "gentle and reserved," according to Anna Vyrubova, so protective of her siblings that they called her "the Governess."[80] Gilliard thought her "essentially well balanced," with "a will of her own, though she was less frank and spontaneous than her elder sister."[81] Gibbes, however, dissented, saying that Tatiana was "reserved, haughty, and not open hearted," though he also noted that she was "the most positive" of the imperial children. "She was always preoccupied and pensive and it was impossible to guess her thoughts."[82] And Colonel Kobylinsky, who got to know her well during the family's Siberian exile, perceptively added: "She was quite different from her sisters. You recognized in her the same features that were in her mother— the same nature and the same character. You felt that she was the daughter of an emperor. She had no liking for art. Maybe it would have been better for her had she been a man."[83]

Tatiana shared her mother's streak of melancholy, which only increased as she grew older. "It was impossible to guess her thoughts," recalled Gibbes.[84] Even so, Tatiana was, like her mother, the most decided in her opinions: she drew lines between those whom she liked and those whom she did not. It was Tatiana who inherited her mother's sense of purposeful authority and unquestioning acceptance of their privileged lives. In turn, Alexandra indulged her second daughter, treating her as an intimate in a way she found impossible with the headstrong Olga.

Above all, Tatiana was, as her mother wished, subservient to her wishes, dutiful and loyal. To please the empress, she tried to copy her religious piety, diligently recording conversations with Rasputin and his letters to the family.[85] But she was unable to exhibit the same depth of feeling. To Tatiana, said Gibbes, religion was a "duty" imposed on her, in contrast to her elder sister Olga, who felt it "in her heart."[86]

Unable to match Alexandra's religious fervor, Tatiana assumed the role of caretaker. "She was closest in sympathy to her mother and was the definite favorite of both her parents," recalled Baroness Buxhoeveden. "She was completely unselfish, always ready to give up her own plans to go for a walk with her father, to read to her mother, to do anything that was wanted."[87] And Gilliard noted that Tatiana "knew how to surround" the empress "with unwearying attentions and never gave way to her own capricious impulses."[88] With Tatiana, the empress mirrored the behavior of her own aunt, Queen Alexandra, and had treated her daughter Princess Victoria like "a glorified maid," according to Grand Duchess Olga Alexandrovna.[89]

The two youngest daughters had only just begun to reveal their individual personalities and talents when the Revolution erupted. Marie, born in 1899, was the most beautiful of the sisters, "a typical Russian beauty," said Gleb Botkin, "rather plump and with cheeks red as apples."[90] With her thick, golden hair and deep blue eyes, she attracted many admirers, among them her cousin Prince Louis of Battenberg, later Lord Mountbatten, who kept her photograph beside his bed until his assassination in 1979.[91]

Broadly built, Marie inherited her grandfather Alexander III's strength, and liked to amuse herself by grabbing her male tutors and lifting them up in the air.[92] Modest and simple, she was generous and gregarious, the most unassuming of the children and who continually flirted with the young officers surrounding the family. She often would sneak away from the palace and slip into the guards' dining room, chatting with the soldiers who told her of their lives, their wives, and their children. "All the intimate affairs in such cases were always known to her," recalled Kobylinsky.[93] Her greatest desire, she often declared, was to one day marry and raise a large family.[94]

Marie passionately adored her father, and as a young girl constantly followed him about the palace; she felt less affection for her mother. As the third daughter, Marie believed she had been unwanted and was unloved, a situation unwittingly exacerbated by the empress. When Marie once confided her insecurities to her mother, Alexandra responded in typical though far from reassuring fashion. Rather than speak to her troubled daughter, she composed a letter to the eleven-year-old girl in which she urged her daughter to "try to be good," promising that "then all will love you."[95] The mere fact that, in the midst of this emotional crisis, the empress felt compelled, through habit or discomfort, to confine her assurances to paper speaks volumes of the emotional distance between Alexandra and her children. Nor did her response, promising that her daughter would be loved provided she behaved, prove any more comforting to the sensitive young girl. Marie, in turn, replied with a pleading, childish letter of her own, which resulted not in personal assurances but a second letter from the empress, who lacked the necessary parental skills to successfully navigate this common dilemma: "Your letter made me quite sad. Sweet child, you must promise me never again to think that nobody loves you. How did such an extraordinary idea get into your little head? Get it quickly out again. We all love you very tenderly, only when too wild and naughty and won't listen then must be scolded; but to scold does not mean that one does not love, on the contrary, one does it so as that you may cure your faults and improve. You generally keep away from the others, think that you are in the way and remain alone . . . instead of being with them; now you are getting a big girl it is good that you should be more with them. Now do not think any more about it, and remember that you are just as precious and dear as the other four and that we love you with all our heart."[96]

The fourth and youngest daughter, Anastasia, was born in 1901. The idea that she, too, had been unwanted undoubtedly led to Anastasia's famously roguish behavior. She was the rebel of the family, her small, boyish frame well suited to her wild pursuits. She climbed trees, then refused to come down; terrorized her tutors with practical jokes; and made frequent, often barbed comments at the expense of those around her. Once, when discussing portraits of her children with a visiting artist, the empress declared, "It is Anastasia who will give you trouble."[97] Gleb Botkin thought Anastasia "witty, vivacious, hopelessly stubborn, delightfully impertinent, and in general a perfect enfant terrible," noting that "she undoubtedly held the record for punishable deeds in her family, for in naughtiness she was a true genius."[98] Although generally good-natured, Tatiana Botkin recalled that Anastasia also was "full of a good dose of mischief."[99] This "mischief" often took the form of purposefully mean-spirited and obnoxious behavior, particularly with her young cousins. One, Princess Nina Georgievna, later declared that Anastasia was "considered nasty to the point of being evil," and recalled long afternoons of play where she cheated, kicked, and scratched to get her own way, a "frightfully temperamental" girl, "wild and rough" who resented any challenge.[100]

Short and somewhat overweight, Anastasia was described by one tutor as the only ungraceful member of the imperial family.[101] Her auburn, shoulder-length hair, as Gibbes remembered, "was not wavy and soft, but lay flat on her forehead."[102] Of all the children, it was Anastasia, as Tatiana Botkin recalled, who had "the most extraordinary blue eyes of the Romanovs, of great luminescence."[103]

Deprived of true confidantes, the grand duchesses befriended the young women who comprised the household within the palace— the maids, dressers, and nurses. "They took the greatest interest in the Household from the highest to the lowest," recalled Baroness Buxhoeveden, "and were considerate in little ways, often doing things for themselves so as to enable their maids to go out."[104] Although they occasionally played with their Romanov cousins, none of the girls had any real friendships.[105] Olga, remembered Tatiana Botkin, "longed pathetically" for real friends, yet none were ever allowed.[106] Their closest companions were two of their mother's young ladies-in-waiting, Anastasia Hendrikova, who acted as a sort of unofficial governess, and Baroness Sophie Buxhoeveden, who, at age twenty-eight, was appointed one of their mother's ladies-in-waiting in 1913. The latter noted sadly that "no young girls were ever asked to the Palace."[107]

For the girls, these friendships became their only contact with the outside world. "The Empress thought that the four sisters should be able to entertain one another," commented Buxhoeveden.[108] Such unfortunate circumstances soon became widely known. In 1912, the author of an American magazine article titled "Royal Mothers and Their Children" referred to the children as "inmates of the imperial nursery," watched over by their "nerve-wracked mother" who suffered from "abnormal fears" for their futures.[109]

Their upbringing, coupled with the isolation imposed by their mother, meant that none of the girls was prepared to face the harsher realities of the world that lay beyond their palace gates, a world into which they were plunged after the Revolution. As Alexandra wished, the girls were certainly unaffected by their positions, yet this innocence came at a price: not only did the empress deny her daughters any semblance of a normal youth, but also, in so doing, she deprived them of the healthy interaction that led to maturation. "I never heard the slightest word suggestive of the modern flirtation," recalled Alexander Mossolov. "Even when the two eldest had grown into real young women, one might hear them talking like little girls of ten or twelve."[110] And while they could behave properly when the occasion demanded, Elizabeth Naryshkina-Kuryakina, the empress's mistress of the robes, wrote that "they generally behaved like young savages."[111]

As loved as the girls were, Romanov succession laws demanded a male heir. Both Nicholas and Alexandra grew frantic, seeking the intervention of a number of dubious holy men such as Nazier-Vachot, and reputed saints. When their only son, Tsesarevich Alexei, was born in 1904, their joy was replaced with despair on learning that he had inherited hemophilia from his mother, who, in turn, had received the defective gene through Queen Victoria. The discovery shattered the couple's lives. Nicholas submissively accepted his son's illness as another manifestation of "God's will," but Alexandra, her physical and mental health devastated by the knowledge that she had passed the disease to her only son, turned to mystics for comfort.

When, in 1905, Gregory Rasputin first appeared, the imperial couple were so emotionally overwrought that they readily accepted him and his mysterious ability to relieve their son's illness. Born in the small Siberian village of Pokrovskoye, Rasputin, contrary to popular legend, was never a monk, but rather a starets, a pilgrim who wandered the empire in search of God. On arriving in St. Petersburg, he impressed the Orthodox hierarchy with his piety and growing reputation as a powerful healer. Rasputin never shed his peasant roots, and he moved through this world of gilded palaces and aristocratic admirers with undisguised pride, openly boasting of his influence over the imperial couple, who increasingly relied on his apparent power to relieve their son's suffering. Surrounded by those seeking power, often drunk, and finding no shortage of women willing to share his bed, the peasant fell victim to intrigues and to his own inability to resist the temptations of his privileged position. Alexei's illness remained a carefully guarded secret. The public knew only that the heir to the throne was frequently ill; no one understood the true nature of the disease, and rumor replaced fact. The reasons for the imperial couple's reliance on Rasputin were never revealed, and his scandals and sexual indiscretions attached themselves to Nicholas and Alexandra, doing much to undermine the last remaining vestiges of public affection for the Romanovs.

"Alexei was the center of this united family, the focus of all its hopes and affections," wrote tutor Pierre Gilliard. "His sisters worshipped him. He was his parents' pride and joy. When he was well, the palace was transformed. Everyone and everything in it seemed bathed in sunshine."[112] A handsome baby when he was born, Alexei grew into a

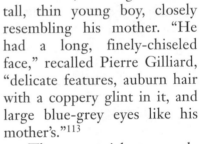

tall, thin young boy, closely resembling his mother. "He had a long, finely-chiseled face," recalled Pierre Gilliard, "delicate features, auburn hair with a coppery glint in it, and large blue-grey eyes like his mother's."[113]

The tsesarevich constantly struggled against the barriers his hemophilia placed on his life, begging his parents for a bicycle or to row or play tennis; but such activities were dangerous, and Alexei was almost always refused.[114] He grew up sheltered and isolated, denied even the most common of childhood pleasures. His parents surrounded him with two sailors, Derevenko and Nagorny, referred to as diadkas,

The heir Tsesarevich Alexei Nikolaievich, 1914.

who followed the boy everywhere, watched while he played, warned him when he overexerted himself, and spent long hours carrying him about when he was unable to walk owing to his illness. Derevenko, the older of the pair, was a large man, and the young boy seemed to take particular delight in ridiculing the sailor's efforts to keep up with him. He habitually called Derevenko "The Fat One," and often would humiliatingly yell loudly, "Look at Fatty run!" as the sailor struggled to keep up in public processions.[115]

Alexei was undoubtedly affected by his illness. He had great empathy for those who also suffered, and could be unusually thoughtful for a boy of his young age. He rarely complained about his own health, just the restrictions his illness placed on how he could live. "Disagreeable things he bore silently and without grumbling," recalled Gibbes. "He was kind hearted and during the last period of his life he was the only one who liked to give things away."[116]

Although usually polite, Alexei also possessed more than a hint of autocratic temperament and could behave imperiously. "Influenced only through his emotions," wrote Gibbes, "he rarely did what he was told, but he obeyed his father; his mother, loving him passionately, could not be firm with him, and through her, he got most of his wishes granted."[117] Wild and uncorrected, he could embarrass family members with his undisciplined behavior. Grand Duke Konstantin Konstantinovich, after his wife lunched with the imperial family, recorded in his diary, "He wouldn't sit up, ate badly, licked his plate and teased the others. The Emperor often turned away, perhaps to avoid having to say anything, while the Empress rebuked her elder daughter Olga, who sat next to her brother, for not restraining him. But Olga cannot deal with him."[118]

Indulgence, in Alexei's case, often led to bad manners and temper tantrums that left his young Romanov cousins startled. One day, at Livadia, he sent a message to the youngest sons of Grand Duchess Xenia to come have tea with him; at the appointed hour they arrived, but Prince Rostislav, Alexei's favorite cousin, was being punished and remained behind. When he saw that Rostislav was not present, Alexei rudely told his other cousins, "You can all go home!" and walked back inside the palace.[119]

Catherine Mikhailovna Frolova-Bagreeva, whose family had a small dacha just down the hill from Livadia, recalled that "it was not always pleasant to see the Heir coming, because he was a 'mischievous' child as our parents taught us to say. He liked to greet people who bowed to him with a bloody nose by hitting them in the face as they bowed. I remember one day his sailor-nanny taking him by the hand so that he couldn't greet people with a bloody nose, and so the Heir greeted us, in public, with very bad language."[120] Eventually Alexei began to grow out of such behavior, but neither of his parents did much to correct the problem. Nicholas saw his children far less than he wished, and the empress indulged her son and could not bring herself to scold him, even when he behaved in the most appalling fashion. "While I fully shared the general devotion to him," wrote Gleb Botkin, "his manners seemed to me considerably worse than those of his sisters, and his restlessness rather depressing."[121]

Heartbreakingly, the five children remained hopeful and naive, their early years behind palace walls having drained them of the ability to judge character and recognize the darker forces gathering in their father's empire. Once, in the midst of an English history lesson on Llewellyn, Olga optimistically declared, "I really think people are much better now than they used to be. I'm very glad I live now when people are so kind."[122] Only in the last year of her life, having watched her father abdicate and herself and her family imprisoned first by the Provisional Government then by the Bolsheviks, did Olga come to understand just how ugly people could be.

AT 7:10 P.M. ON AUGUST 1, 1914, Germany declared war on Russia. There was great optimism for a swift victory in the first days, when both the British and French presses dubbed their ally "the Russian steamroller."[123] But all the Imperial Army had in its favor was sheer manpower: in 1914 it stood at 3.1 million men.[124] To every yard of railway track in Russia, Germany had ten, and the kaiser's factories outnumbered the emperor's by the hundreds. Ammunition was in short supply: after soldiers fired their stock, they had to wait for resupply, under bombardment of German artillery. Each Russian soldier traveled an average of eight hundred miles to the front, compared to two hundred for the Germans.[125]

Initial enthusiasm temporarily dispelled the growing discontent with the imperial regime and, for the first time in his reign, Nicholas found himself enveloped in popular adulation. It was not to last. In September two hundred thousand Russian troops surged through the bogs and marshes of Poland and eastern Prussia. Led by cavalry swinging their sabers, General Paul Rennenkampf's First Imperial Army and General Alexander Samsonov's Second Imperial Army marched into the forests at Tannenberg, to be mowed down by enemy artillery.[126] Samsonov was so humiliated that he rode off into the woods and shot himself.[127] Within a few months the Germans managed to rout the Second Imperial Army; by the time they retreated, the Russians had lost nearly half of their men.[128] Most Russian soldiers had never seen the weapons they now used, and knew nothing of the modern world; on seeing airplanes for the first time, some peasants took it as a sign that God was fighting on the side of the enemy and fled their positions.[129] By the end of 1914 the Russians had lost some 1 million men.[130]

In March 1915 the Russians captured Austria-Hungary's strongest fortress, Przemsyl, and a month later held most of the Carpathian Mountains. But Germany came to Austria's aid with heavy artillery, and the Russians lost—killed and wounded—more than fifteen thousand men in just four hours.[131] "The retreat from Galicia was one vast tragedy for the Russian Army," recalled General Anton Denikin. "The German heavy artillery swept away whole lines of trenches, and their defenders with them. We hardly replied—there was nothing with which we could reply. Our regiments, although completely exhausted, were beating off one attack after another by bayonet. . . . Blood flowed unendingly, the ranks became thinner and thinner; the number of graves constantly multiplied."[132]

More disaster followed near the end of the summer, when Warsaw fell. Much of Russian Poland had to be evacuated in advance of the German offensive, and, as the kaiser's armies marched toward the Baltic provinces, there was even talk to possible occupation of the imperial capital itself. As summer turned to fall, nearly half of the Russian army of the previous year was gone: 1.4 million killed or wounded, and 976,000 prisoners.[133]

The fall of Warsaw was a major strategic and moral blow to the Russians, and prompted Nicholas II to take over as supreme commander of the Imperial Army himself. He was prompted and supported by the empress, who believed that the former supreme commander, Grand Duke Nicholas Nikolaievich, deliberately undermined her husband's prestige and power to win laurels for himself.[134] The emperor took up residence at Stavka, the military headquarters that had been established at Mogilev, hundreds of miles from the actual front. In truth, the move was largely symbolic: important decisions were made by General Michael Alexeiev, the emperor's chief of staff, and Nicholas did little more than review troops, inspect field hospitals, and preside over military luncheons.

Nicholas's assumption of the post as supreme commander made little difference in the conduct of the war, but the damage proved fatal— if not in fact, then certainly in perception. He abandoned the capital, leaving Alexandra responsible for reviewing reports and receiving ministers on his behalf. Had Nicholas remained at Tsarskoye Selo, it is unlikely he would have followed a different course in the unfolding political drama of those years, subject as he would still have been to his wife's exhortations and advice. Members of the government, however, together with a majority of his subjects, saw it as evidence of the imperial couple's gross incompetence, and believed that this single decision hastened the end of the monarchy. In this case, perception—however inaccurate—became accepted reality. All the misfortunes that followed, both political and military, were laid at the feet of the emperor, the empress, and Rasputin, who, it was assumed, controlled them both and dictated Russian policy.

It all came to its unbelievable, incredible end in the early morning hours of December 17, 1916, when Rasputin was murdered by a group of conspirators led by Felix Yusupov, the wealthy, flamboyant homosexual prince married to Nicholas II's niece Princess Irina Alexandrovna. Rasputin's death, like his life, became legend, the conspirators convinced that in their cold-blooded act of poisoning, stabbing, beating, shooting, and finally drowning the peasant, they would be hailed as Russia's saviors, that his elimination would somehow cause a sudden and radical shift in Nicholas II's policies. Such reasoning was as ill-conceived as the murder itself, and nothing changed. Nicholas remained obdurate, bowing to the wishes of his stronger wife, who failed to suffer the complete physical and moral collapse the assassins had predicted.

Rasputin's murder was the provocation that many had anticipated in an autumn of discontent. The war staggered from disaster to disaster, soldiers were demoralized, and arms shortages increased daily. Unwisely, the government poured all effort and energy into the struggle, neglecting the swelling tide of misery in the cities. The situation was particularly bad in Petrograd, as Nicholas had patriotically renamed St. Petersburg at the beginning of the war. Inflation rose to incredible heights, making daily life a struggle; the hungry factory workers, exhausted from their grueling shifts, trudged through banks of snow to wait in long lines for the meager food a few kopecks could purchase, only to discover the shelves empty. "In a country teeming with food," reported Robert Wilton of the *Times* of London, "we are bereft of the most elementary necessities of life."[135]

Trains carried not food to Petrograd, but arms away from its factories to the distant front, blocking regular supplies to the capital. As winter set in, fuel was scarce, and food growing more so. The wealthy still managed to give splendid parties in their palaces along the frozen Neva River: lavish ballrooms scented with the aroma of fresh flowers, diamonds and gold braid flashing through the haze of blue cigarette smoke as guests plucked glasses of champagne from silver trays held aloft by liveried footmen. Beyond their windows, however, the suffering multiplied, the misery grew, the hunger rose among the silent masses.

The inevitable crisis finally erupted in late February, when starving factory workers and social unrest converged in the frozen streets. Daily demonstrations led to general strikes, followed by looting, open calls for the emperor's abdication, and imperial guards abandoning their regiments to join the revolutionaries. Events moved quickly, and within a week the imperial regime had collapsed, replaced by a Provisional Government. Nicholas, trying to return to Petrograd from Mogilev, found his train blocked by rebel garrisons; he eventually ordered it to Pskov, to learn that the new Provisional Government and his generals insisted on his immediate abdication.

The succession laws in 1917 dictated that the throne should go to Alexei. In the early afternoon of March 2, 1917, this is exactly what Nicholas did, abdicating for his twelve-year-old son, with Nicholas's brother Grand Duke Michael Alexandrovich as regent. The decision was inevitable; he had learned that two representatives from the Provisional Government, Alexander Guchkov and Vassili Shulgin, were already on their way to Pskov, to demand that he do so; rather than appear to bow to the pressure of the Revolution, Nicholas acted himself. Having signed the manifesto, the former emperor could do nothing but wait, a long winter afternoon and evening interrupted by a conversation with one of Alexei's doctors. Contrary to Nicholas's expectations, he was told that he would almost certainly be separated from his son and forced, with his family, into some form of external exile.[136]

Hearing this, Nicholas—indecisive to the last—changed his mind, abdicating a second time, for himself and for Alexei, in favor of his brother Michael. This was illegal; Nicholas did not possess the power to alter the succession law in such a way, though no one challenged him. The abdication manifesto, for whose patriotism and dignity Nicholas II was personally praised, was, in fact, written not by the emperor but by Prince Nicholas Basily.[137] Although the final version was signed at 11:40 P.M. on March 2, it was given a time of 3:00 P.M., to preserve the illusion that Nicholas had not acted under pressure from the government.[138] The following day, Michael refused to accept the throne unless called on to do so by a representative body, ending the 304-year-old rule of the Romanov Dynasty.

On March 8, General Lavr Kornilov arrived at the Alexander Palace with orders from the Provisional Government to arrest the empress. He told her that the emperor would return on the following day and that both would be placed under the protection of the Provisional Government.[139] In her diary, Alexandra wrote: "From now on, we are to be considered prisoners: shut up—may see nobody from outside."[140] Nicholas's arrival at Tsarskoye Selo on March 9 marked the first of 481 days of imprisonment for the Romanovs, ending only on July 17, 1918, with their assassination.[141]

The former imperial family passed their first five months as prisoners in the Alexander Palace. The circumstances of their confinement were marked with minor annoyances rather than real fear. All doors were locked and sealed, and only the new palace commandant had a set of keys. Telephone lines were severed, and all correspondence was subject to censorship. Though restricted to a small portion of the imperial park, the Romanovs had ample provisions; enjoyed wine from the imperial cellars; and continued to be attended by nearly a hundred members of their suite and household.[142]

As the weeks wore on, no one knew what to expect. "Our captivity in Tsarskoye Selo did not seem likely to last long," Pierre Gilliard wrote, "and there was talk about our imminent transfer to England. Yet the days passed and our departure was always being postponed."[143] Nicholas had hoped for exile to England; the day after his abdication, he sent a formal request to Prince George Lvov, prime minister in the new Provisional Government, asking for safe passage for his family from Murmansk, and he made frequent mention in his diary of packing his belongings in anticipation of leaving Russia.[144]

King George V of Great Britain was a first cousin to both Nicholas and Alexandra, and the imperial couple expected to find sanctuary in his country. The king, however, wanted nothing to do with his Russian cousins, and forced his government to withdraw its offer of asylum. The question of what to do with the former sovereign and his family fell to Alexander Kerensky, who became prime minister of the Provisional Government after an abortive Bolshevik coup d'état in July 1917. In Petrograd's long, pale "white nights," he wrestled with the difficulties posed by their continued presence near the capital. There was some talk of the Crimea as a possible destination, but, like England, this, too, vanished.

In the end, Kerensky selected the small Siberian town of Tobolsk as a place of exile. Being isolated, it promised a brief respite from the chaos of the Revolution until he could arrange for their safe transport out of Russia. In addition, as Kerensky himself noted, it boasted a large residence, the Governor's House, which would be suitable for the Romanovs and their servants. After placing Colonel Eugene Kobylinsky, a former officer in the Petrograd Imperial Life Guards Regiment, in charge of the three hundred soldiers of the Special Detachment who would guard the Romanovs, Kerensky broke the news to the prisoners, who quickly began packing their belongings.

The afternoon of July 31, 1917, hung heavily over the Alexander Palace, its lemon-yellow facade and white Corinthian colonnade washed by the soft northern sunlight. Within, the imperial family wandered through the deserted rooms; shafts of light sliced across the marble and wooden floors, bathing the dust-covered furniture and draped crystal chandeliers in the pale evening glow. "After supper we waited for our constantly postponed hour of departure to be set," Nicholas wrote in his diary.[145] With their rooms locked, they gathered in the semicircular hall, with tall French doors opening onto the park beyond, the marble floor covered with luggage and steamer trunks.[146]

Kerensky arrived shortly after eleven that night.[147] He found the empress, dressed in a traveling suit, sitting in a corner weeping "like any ordinary woman and mother."[148] "We have not suffered enough for all the faults we have committed," she commented bitterly.[149] Trucks finally arrived 1:30 A.M. to convey the luggage to the train on which the Romanovs would travel. As the night wore on, and the family waited, the anxiety only increased. "The Tsesarevich," wrote Kerensky, "was full of excitement and exceedingly frolicsome. He kept on trying to escape from the inner rooms into our room, to find out what was going on in the Emperor's Study."[150] Midway through the night, however, the pressure overwhelmed him, and he burst into tears, crying, "Why don't they kill us at once, and be done with it? It would be better than murdering us slowly in this way!"[151] Nicholas stood quietly in a corner, incessantly smoking cigarette after cigarette, while the four grand duchesses, clad in white summer dresses, "wept copiously."[152]

Two o'clock passed, then three, yet no train had arrived. After making several telephone calls, Kerensky learned that rail workers in Petrograd had prevented its departure. Throughout the long night, Kerensky hovered over the telephone, trying to negotiate an uneasy truce. All through the pale, half light of the northern night, figures moved in and out of the Alexander Palace, silhouetted against the glow from the tall windows. At 5:15 A.M., Kerensky finally learned that the train had arrived at the Alexandrovsky Station at Tsarskoye Selo.[153]

A string of motorcars pulled into the driveway and up to the ramp, and Nicholas and Alexandra, followed by their children, walked through the doors and climbed into the open vehicles. Alexandra's face, recalled one witness, "was ashy white as she went out of the door of her home for the last time."[154] Above, the sky had turned a fiery pink, and shafts of early-morning sun slanted through the tops of the tall trees. As the cars drove away, the family turned and watched as the Alexander Palace shrunk away in the distance; thirty minutes later, their train steamed off in the pale morning light, toward Siberia.[155]

"History," commented one Bolshevik historian, "probably can record no criminal furnished by his jailers with such a vast staff of servants as Nicholas enjoyed with the personal consent of Kerensky."[156] In all, forty-two persons accompanied the Romanovs into exile, including Adjutant General Count Ilya Tatischev; Prince Vassili Dolgoruky, who served as grand marshal of the imperial court in exile; Countess Anastasia Hendrikova, lady-in-waiting to the empress; Mademoiselle Catherine

Schneider, the court lectrice; two physicians, Dr. Eugene Botkin and Dr. Vladimir Derevenko; Pierre Gilliard, tutor of French to the imperial children; ladies' maids Marie Tutelberg, Anna Demidova, and Elizabeth Ersberg; Alexandra Tegleva, nursery assistant; Terenty Chemodurov, the emperor's valet; Alexei Volkov, valet de chambre to the empress; Ivan Sednev, footman to the grand duchesses; Klementy Nagorny, the tsesarevich's attendant; seven additional footmen, including Alexei Trupp; a kitchen superintendent; four cooks, including Ivan Kharitonov; Leonid Sednev, kitchen assistant; Alexander Kirpichnikov, a secretary; a hairdresser; and a sommelier. In the fall and winter of 1917, six others arrived in Tobolsk to share the imperial family's captivity: Charles Sydney Gibbes, tutor of English to the children; Klaudia Bittner, brought in to instruct the children in music; Madeleine Zanotti, the empress's dresser; the maids Anna Romanova and Anna Utkin; and Baroness Sophie Buxhoeveden, who arrived in December 1917. These last three were not admitted to the house where the Romanovs were confined.[157]

Prince Vassili Dolgoruky, who acted as adjutant during the imprisonment at Tsarskoye Selo, was the stepson of Count Paul von Benckendorff, grand marshal of the imperial court; in Siberia he assumed his stepfather's place as grand marshal of the nonexistent court. Tatischev, like Dolgoruky, was an aristocrat, a member of the suite who remained dedicated to the Romanovs. "A better and more loyal man than he it would be hard to find," wrote Grand Duke Kirill Vladimirovich.[158]

Of the women who formed the imprisoned suite, the eldest was Mademoiselle Catherine Schneider. A niece of the former imperial physician Dr. Hirsch, as a young lady she was charged with helping Alexandra's sister Grand Duchess Elizabeth Feodorovna learn Russian, a task she repeated for the empress in her position as lectrice. "She adored the Empress and her children," recalled one official. "She was infinitely sweet tempered and good hearted."[159] She shared the empress's strict morality, once forbidding the grand duchesses from staging a play that contained the word "stockings."[160] Countess Anastasia Hendrikova, who served at court with the rank of freilina, or lady-in-waiting, was of aristocratic stock, daughter of a master of ceremonies under Alexander II and Alexander III. Like Mademoiselle Schneider, she remained faithful to the Romanovs to the end, paying for her loyalty with her life at the hands of the Bolsheviks.

The third of the court ladies who remained was Baroness Sophie Buxhoeveden, who became a freilina in 1913 at age twenty-nine.[161] As one of the youngest women at court, she often accompanied the grand duchesses on their official engagements, taking the place of their frequently ill mother. The girls, especially Olga and Tatiana, looked on her as a confidante, calling her "Isa" and treating her with the friendship their mother prevented them from extending to any girls their own age. Illness prevented her from accompanying the Romanovs on their journey to Tobolsk; when she eventually arrived, in December, she was denied permission to join them in the Governor's House.

Eugene Sergeievich Botkin, court doctor.

Of the two doctors who shared the imperial family's confinement, the most important and devoted was Eugene Sergeievich Botkin. Born in 1865, Botkin came from a family whose great passion was medicine. His father, Serge Botkin, had served as court physician to both Alexander II and Alexander III, and his brother Serge also became a doctor. They took advantage of early marketing, and "Botkin's Powder's" and various other cures were widely manufactured and distributed across Russia.

Botkin's brother Peter memorialized him as a living saint, a man who embodied all known virtues: "From a very tender age, his beautiful and noble nature was complete," he wrote. "He was never like other children. Always sensitive, of a delicate, inner sweetness of extraordinary soul, he had a horror of any kind of struggle or fight. We other boys would fight with fury. He would not take part in our combats, but when our pugilism took on a dangerous character he would stop the combatants at the risk of injuring himself. He was very studious and conscientious in his studies. For a profession he chose medicine: to help, to succor, to soothe, to heal without end."[162]

Eugene Botkin studied medicine at the University of St. Petersburg before taking courses at the Universities of Berlin and Heidelberg. When he returned to Russia he was appointed chief physician at St. Georgievsky Hospital in St. Petersburg, and frequently lectured on medical matters at the Academy of Medical Sciences.[163] During the Russo-Japanese War he served with distinction as a volunteer aboard the St. Georgievsky Hospital Red Cross train.[164]

In 1908 Botkin received an appointment as personal physician-in-ordinary to the imperial family. "My responsibility is great but this is not only vis-à-vis the family," he wrote to his brother Peter. "I find myself with a great burden, a responsibility toward not only the family but the whole country."[165] Botkin was one of the few members of the imperial suite conversant in languages, often speaking to the empress in her native German, and occasionally acting as her translator when she had to receive Russian delegations.[166] The imperial family relied heavily on Botkin, and he was a favorite among the children. "Your brother is a true friend to me," Nicholas once said to Peter Botkin, "we take everything to heart, and we feel comfortable describing our maladies to him."[167]

Botkin married "a poor young woman," in the words of his brother Peter.[168] The couple had four children who survived: three boys— Dimitri, Yuri, and Gleb; and one daughter, Tatiana. In time the Botkin marriage became strained: with the empress's increasingly bad health, Dr. Botkin sacrificed his own family life to look after his imperial patients, and his wife, feeling neglected, began a scandalous affair with a German tutor, eventually demanding a divorce, which her husband granted with some reluctance.[169]

At the beginning of World War I, both of the eldest Botkin sons, Dimitry and Yuri, joined the army. Dimitry, recently graduated from the elite Corps des Pages in St. Petersburg, became a lieutenant in a Cossack regiment assigned to the Eastern Front, where he was killed in December 1914.[170] Botkin was devastated by his son's death, and Gleb noticed an increasing fatalism: "He grew more and more orthodox in his religious conceptions," he wrote, "and developed a veritable abhorrence of the 'flesh.'"[171]

By the time of the Revolution, Botkin was a saddened, prematurely aged man, tall and stout. Habitually attired in an immaculate waistcoat, jacket, trousers, stiff shirt, and tie, he wore a gold-rimmed pince-nez perched midway down his nose. His one indulgence was his love of scent: the grand duchesses used to tease him by chasing him around the palace, sniffing the air to follow his trail.[172]

Botkin's colleague Dr. Vladimir Derevenko owed his position at court to his fellow physician, who had hired him as an assistant to help care for the tsesarevich. Before this Derevenko had served as physician to the emperor's Cossack *Konvoi* regiment.[173] "A capable surgeon he was," Gleb Botkin recalled, "however, of peasant stock and showed it only too clearly in his manners and speech."[174] Derevenko remained with the Romanovs after the Revolution and followed them into exile, but he was intensely bitter. "Some job you've found for me, I'm telling you!" he often shouted at Botkin.[175] His loyalty to the Romanovs was always pliable; he owed his devotion first and foremost to his own family, who followed him into Siberian exile. His son Nicholas Vladimirovich was one of the few playmates allowed to the tsesarevich. Known as Kolya, he was born in 1906, two years after Alexei Nikolaievich, and attended the Emperor Nicholas Gymnasium in Tsarskoye Selo. Alexei adored him, and in Siberia he and Kolya became close friends.

At the time of the imperial family's departure for Siberia, only one of the children's tutors, Pierre Gilliard, lived with them, and he was the only tutor allowed to accompany them to Tobolsk. Gilliard, of Swiss nationality, had joined the imperial court in 1905, having previously worked for Duke George of Leuchtenberg.[176] Although undoubtedly devoted to the imperial family, Gilliard was, Gleb Botkin recalled, "a very ordinary type of French teacher," and whatever abilities he brought to his position were largely constrained by both the empress's attitudes and the children's own educational disinterest.[177] Gilliard later married Alexandra Tegleva, nursery maid to the tsesarevich, described by Gleb Botkin as "a very nice woman but a complete nonentity."[178]

Gilliard's English colleague, Charles Sydney Gibbes, who lived in a wing of the Catherine Palace, tried unsuccessfully to gain admission to the Alexander Palace after the Revolution.[179] Born in Yorkshire, he came to the imperial court a few years after Gilliard, attempting, not altogether successfully, to teach the children English. Having received Kerensky's permission to join the Romanovs, he arrived in Tobolsk shortly before the Bolshevik Revolution in October. The third tutor, Klaudia Bittner, had not held any court position, but obtained her place in the household through the influence of Colonel Kobylinsky, whom she later married.

The female members of the empress's household who followed their mistress into exile were led by Madeleine Zanotti, who held the rank of Ober-Kamer-Jungferi, a post roughly equivalent to first lady's maid and imperial dresser. At the beginning of the Revolution, when offered the chance by General Kornilov to leave the Alexander Palace, Zanotti declared proudly, "In good times we served the family. Never will we forsake them now!"[180] Arriving in Tobolsk in December, she was not allowed to share their captivity in the Governor's House. Her two assistants, Maria Tutelberg and Elizabeth Ersberg, who held the ranks of second and third Kamer-Jungferi (ladies' maids), respectively, traveled with the Romanovs to Tobolsk, but were denied permission to follow them into the Ipatiev House in Ekaterinburg; later they assisted White Army investigators in identifying the imperial family's belongings.

The only female member of the household who did follow the Romanovs to both Tobolsk and into the Ipatiev House was Anna Stepanovna Demidova. Born in 1878, Demidova was a tall, statuesque woman, with light blond hair and blue eyes, and came to court after the intercession of her friend Elizabeth Ersberg, who secured her a position as komnatnoye devyushki, or parlor maid. The pair became inseparable, and Demidova soon fell in love with Ersberg's brother Nicholas Nikolaievich, who was an official for the State Railway Inspection Board; at one point they were engaged, but for unknown reasons, the

Anna Stepanovna Demidova,
Alexandra's last maid.

proposed marriage fell through.[181] During her service at court, Demidova became enamored of Charles Sydney Gibbes, the young English tutor to the imperial children. The homosexual Gibbes, however, took no notice; he once described her as "of a singularly timid and shrinking disposition."[182]

Of the emperor's household, only one man remained with the Romanovs and accompanied them into the Ipatiev House, Terenty Chemodurov. Born in 1849, Chemodurov came to the imperial court by way of the army, as did so many members of the household. In 1908 the emperor appointed the fifty-nine-year-old man as his valet. During their Siberian exile Chemodurov became increasingly senile, and was finally removed from the Ipatiev House to a local hospital just three weeks after the Romanovs arrived in Ekaterinburg.[183]

Alexei Volkov was born to a peasant family in Tambov Province in 1859; at sixteen he joined the Imperial Army, and eventually he came to the Pavlovsky Guards Regiment. In this capacity he became valet to the emperor's uncle Grand Duke Paul Alexandrovich. After Paul's morganatic marriage and European exile in 1902, Volkov was given a position in the emperor's household, though he eventually switched and became the empress's Kammer-diner, or valet de chambre.[184]

The tsesarevich's diadka, his male sailor-nanny who remained with him after the Revolution, was Klementy Nagorny. Nagorny was twenty-nine, a tall, muscular man with jet-black hair and, as one man recalled, "guileless honesty and clarity in his gray eyes."[185] Tall and thin, with light, closely cropped red hair, Nagorny was a striking figure, with "skin as clear and delicate as that of a woman," as one guard later declared.[186] Throughout the imperial family's exile in Tobolsk, it was Nagorny who patiently attended to Alexei, and carried him when he was unable to walk. One guard recalled that Nagorny had "huge shoulders. His face bore the slavish expression of a peasant in uniform, though this particular peasant also had an infinite patience and tenderness in his face."[187]

An uncle and a nephew also accompanied the Romanovs into exile and finally into the Ipatiev House. Ivan Dimitrievich Sednev was born in 1886 in Yaroslavl; at age eighteen he joined the crew of the imperial yacht *Standart*, acting as an orderly. At twenty-five he left the yacht to join the imperial household as kammer-diner (valet de chambre) to the grand duchesses. Sednev had cut a striking figure in his court livery: he was exceptionally tall, with red hair and a neatly trimmed Vandyke beard and mustache. Like so many others who followed the Romanovs into exile, he paid the ultimate price, being shot by the Bolsheviks in Ekaterinburg, leaving behind a wife and three children.

Sednev's brother died when he himself began service at the imperial court, leaving a young son, Leonid Ivanovich, called Lenka by his family. Ivan arranged for the young boy to live with him. Though two years younger than the tsesarevich, Leonid Sednev was, in many ways, infinitely more mature, and, in exile, displayed remarkable patience with, and concern for, Alexei, whom he befriended. The young boy was described by one guard as "tall for his age, thin," with a pale face and jet black hair.[188]

Two other male servants followed the imperial family to both Tobolsk and into the Ipatiev House, where they were murdered with the Romanovs. Alexei Trupp, fifty-nine at the time of the Revolution, had been a colonel in the military before joining the imperial household, where he served as a footman. Trupp was distinguished by his great height and sturdy build.[189] Ivan Kharitonov, forty-five at the time of the Revolution, served in the imperial kitchen as a cook. His wife and small daughter accompanied him into Siberian exile, but remained behind in Tobolsk when he went to Ekaterinburg.[190] He was somewhat small, though powerfully built, with, as Proskuryakov recalled, "black hair and a small black mustache."[191] On his left cheek, a mole sprouted thick hairs if he neglected to shave it.[192]

In Tobolsk, the Romanovs lived in the former Governor's House, with members of their extensive suite and household scattered between this residence and the Kornilov House, a large, ornate villa across the street. Tobolsk was a quiet town, protected from the tide of revolutionary ardor by its isolation. The closest railway connection was in the town of Tyumen, itself

Alexei Igorovich Trupp, footman.

Ivan Mikhailovich Kharitonov, chef.

separated by a hundred miles of desolate taiga, and linked by the Irtysh and Tobol Rivers, frozen from late October until early May. Here the former imperial family passed the long, uneventful autumn and winter, events unfolding in distant Petrograd as Lenin and the Bolsheviks overthrew Kerensky's Provisional Government and came to power. Their incarceration was not as comfortable as it had been in Tsarskoye Selo. The harsh Siberian winter kept the house cold, and unpleasant incidents increased as the months passed: the imperial family was forbidden to attend religious services; the members of the Special Detachment demanded that the emperor remove the epaulettes from his coats; and the prisoners were subjected to unwelcome searches and growing hostility from their guards.

Isolated, the Romanovs fell victim to a number of shadowy conspiracies, led by monarchists and double agents. Within two months of their captivity in Tobolsk, the money provided by the Provisional Government for the upkeep of both the prisoners and the members of the Special Detachment ran out. Kobylinsky, together with Tatischev and Dolgoruky, was forced to sign a bill of personal responsibility to local merchants to ensure continued provisions.[193]

In Petrograd, Count Paul von Benckendorff, the former grand marshal of the imperial court, gradually raised funds to support the prisoners. The largest amount came from Karol Yaroshinsky, a wealthy industrialist who had been one of the principal benefactors of the military hospital under the patronage of Grand Duchesses Marie and Anastasia Nikolaievna. Between November 1917 and April 1918, Yaroshinsky donated some 175,000 rubles toward the imperial family's upkeep in Siberia.[194] The majority of this money was sent to Siberia through Benckendorff, as the latter indicated in his memoirs.[195] But other money also was being gathered in the fall of 1917, both to help maintain the Romanovs in Tobolsk and to finance a rescue attempt. The two prime figures behind this secondary collection of funds were the empress's two closest friends, Lili Dehn and Anna Vyrubova.

In the autumn of 1917, Lili Dehn, in her attempts to assist the Romanovs in their Siberian exile, fell in with a thoroughly disreputable man, Nicholas Markov, known as Markov II, an extreme reactionary and former member of the Imperial State Duma. His beliefs were simple: the Jews, Masons, and Bolsheviks were all working together to destroy Russia. He collected funds necessary to enact the rescue operation he freely described to all he met, including a young officer, Serge Markov, formerly cornet of the Crimean Horse Guards Regiment under the patronage of the empress herself. Markov II warned that the chief task was "to raise larger sums, for there was no lack of faithful and reliable men; they were all well organized and ready to start for Tobolsk at a moment's notice." He claimed that an agent, Nicholas Sedov, was already in Tobolsk, gathering men.[196]

Serge Markov realized that Markov II's chief concern was money. Before they parted, he asked the young officer to introduce him to Anna Vyrubova; when they met, Markov II insisted that "he was the only person who had made any attempt to try to organize a rescue." He repeated his assertion that trusted men awaited his orders, and warned that Vyrubova "must trust in him and help him out."[197]

A third man tied to the Romanovs' tenure in Tobolsk was Boris Soloviev, the twenty-seven-year-old son of a former treasurer of the Holy Synod and trusted friend of both Rasputin and Anna Vyrubova.[198] After the transfer of the Romanovs to Tobolsk, Soloviev married the peasant's younger daughter Maria Rasputin, and the pair set off for her home village of Pokrovskoye in Siberia.[199] In November 1917 Soloviev traveled to Tobolsk to investigate the Romanovs' position.[200] He met with the highest ecclesiastical authorities, including Bishop Hermogen and Father Alexei Vassiliev, priest at the Church of the Annunciation, where the imperial family had attended irregular services, handing over a number of letters and a large sum of money; Vassiliev promised to deliver them to the Romanovs.[201]

Soloviev told both men that a rescue effort was being prepared, adding that Rasputin's "family and his friends are active."[202] Hermogen himself volunteered the services a certain Staff Captain Lepilin, head of the Local Assembly of Soldiers of the Front, in any rescue.[203] All of this talk was built on a precarious foundation. Soloviev himself related that some three hundred faithful former officers were gathering to enact the attempt; when this news reached the empress, she asked that the organization be named the Brotherhood of St. John of Tobolsk.[204]

When Soloviev returned to Tobolsk on February 2, 1918, his story took a dramatic turn. For eighty-five years, Soloviev has been condemned as an adventurer, the Brotherhood of St. John of Tobolsk labeled a deliberate fabrication on his part, designed to win the confidence of the Romanovs and those acting on their behalf to further his own financial ends. In fact, Soloviev, while inept, was himself nothing more than Markov II's scapegoat in the latter's own nefarious schemes involving the Romanovs.

Soloviev had brought with him another installment of money and letters for the prisoners. When he met with Hermogen and Vassiliev and asked how the rescue plans were progressing, the clerics were confused. Neither had ever heard of Markov II or his assistant Nicholas Sedov, whom Markov II had claimed was organizing the three hundred men in Tobolsk. Nor had they received any of the money Markov II had collected in Petrograd.[205] Soloviev was stunned to learn that nothing had been done.[206] Markov II's Brotherhood of St. John of Tobolsk, declared to be under Sedov's organization, had been nothing more than a financial shield used to drain the accounts of those gullible enough to hand over their funds. Soloviev had known nothing of this when he first informed Hermogen and Vassiliev of the plans Markov II had related. Now Soloviev realized the extent of the swindle.[207]

Shaken, Soloviev handed over 50,000 rubles he had brought from the capital. Some of this money reached the Romanovs through the valet Volkov, who was in close contact with Vassiliev, for on February 4 the empress wrote in a letter to Vyrubova: "Tenderly we thank through you K. Yarochinsky. Really it is touching that even now we are not forgotten."[208] Vassiliev, however, apparently kept most of it for himself.

When Alexandra learned that Soloviev was in Tobolsk, she hastily wrote him: "Let us know what you think of our situation. Our common wish is to achieve the possibility of living tranquilly, like an ordinary family, outside politics, struggle and intrigue. Write frankly, for I will accept your letter with faith in your sincerity."[209] Realizing the full extent of Markov's betrayal, Soloviev responded: "Deeply grateful for the feelings and trust expressed. The situation is on the whole very serious and could become critical, and I am certain that it will take the help of devoted friends, or a miracle, for everything to turn out all right, and for you to get your wish for a tranquil life. Your sincerely devoted Boris."[210]

Soloviev returned to Petrograd, where he met with Anna Vyrubova and Lili Dehn, telling them what he had learned from Hermogen and Vassiliev. Both women were horrified to discover that Markov II had apparently kept, for his own use, money intended to help the prisoners.[211] Before he left Petrograd, Soloviev apparently was given 200,000 rubles, collected by Count Paul von Benckendorff for the prisoners.[212] In his book, Benckendorff did not reveal the name of the courier, simply writing that "the money reached its destination, thanks to the devotion and energy of X."[213] Maria Rasputin later recalled: "Just before the Bolsheviks moved the capital, Boris was in Petrograd to collect a rather substantial sum for Their Majesties. This he did and conveyed it into trusted hands."[214]

Soloviev was back in Tobolsk on February 21, when he turned over the 200,000 rubles to a certain "Mademoiselle X, a lady of the court," as Serge Markov called her. This mysterious woman was, Markov said, ill at the time the Romanovs were originally sent to Tobolsk, arrived at a later date, but "the guards refused her entry to the Governor's House." She lived in her own apartment in town.[215] Markov clearly meant Baroness Sophie Buxhoeveden, the only "lady of the court" who had not joined the imperial family due to illness; who later came to

Tobolsk; who was refused admission to the Governor's House; and who had her own apartment in the town. "I left the money and letters with her," Soloviev later said, "which she promised to give to Volkov next day. We made arrangements for a meeting the following evening and I went home full of bright hopes." When he returned the following day, Buxhoeveden told him that everything had already been smuggled in to the prisoners, with the exception of a few books and some cologne. Believing the issue closed, Soloviev returned to Pokrovskoye.[216]

That Soloviev turned this money over to Buxhoeveden on February 21 is confirmed by four separate sources: Soloviev himself; Serge Markov; Maria Rasputin; and by Staff Captain Lepilin, Hermogen's envoy.[217] Yet Buxhoeveden did not hand over the money to Volkov, as she had claimed. On February 27, just six days after Soloviev gave Buxhoeveden the packages, the prisoners learned that as of March 1 they would all be put on ordinary soldiers' rations. According to Kobylinsky, who had assumed responsibility for the Romanovs' finances, the move came just in time as, "by the beginning of March, all of the money previously sent had vanished, and no more arrived for us."[218]

No further sums were ever turned over to the Romanovs or those imprisoned with them. In April, as Prince Vassili Dolgoruky told his stepfather Count von Benckendorff, the Bolsheviks learned that a member of the former suite living in Tobolsk had a large sum of the money intended for the imperial family. This led to an increase in surveillance on the prisoners and ultimately, he believed, to their transfer to the Urals.[219] In fact, early on the morning of April 25, Buxhoeveden and her companion Miss Annie Mather were awakened by a contingent of Bolshevik soldiers, who spent two hours searching their small apartment. An hour after the first group left, a second squad arrived, carrying "all kinds of murderous weapons." They, too, insisted on searching the entire apartment.[220]

Buxhoeveden herself offered no explanation for this nocturnal raid, though it is likely the men knew of Soloviev's funds. Buxhoeveden's behavior in swindling the Romanovs was starkly at odds with the devoted young woman who acted as confidante to the grand duchesses and who, in exile, wrote three lovingly detailed books on the imperial family and the Russian Empire. Yet this would not be her only act of treachery during the imperial family's Siberian captivity.

A tide of uncertainty was gathering around the Romanovs. Members of the Special Detachment, initially friendly to the prisoners, were dismissed, replaced by men who, having suffered the horrors of World War I and the brutalities of prison and political exile, held no affection for their former sovereign. By the spring of 1918 the Romanovs began to attract the unwelcome attention of revolutionaries in Siberia's larger cities, who complained about the relative comfort of their life in the provincial town. Amid the swirling Siberian snows, the Romanovs looked from their windows to see mounted patrols of Bolshevik soldiers arriving daily, faces unknown and rifles at their side as they scrutinized the prison compound.

As these events played themselves out, the Romanovs grew increasingly nervous. When they left Tsarskoye Selo, they had brought an immense cache of jewelry with them. Charles Sydney Gibbes later estimated that the empress and her daughters had not less than 1 million rubles' worth of jewelry in Tobolsk (£3,000,000, or $4,890,000 in 2003 currency).[221] In fact, a portion of this collection of tiaras, diadems, brooches, bracelets, necklaces, and other jeweled objets d'art held by the prisoners in the Governor's House was later valued at some 2,662,528 rubles (£7,987,584, or $13,0197,619 in 2003 currency). Another 216,402 rubles (£649,206, or $1,058,206 in 2003 currency) of jewelry was found in Ekaterinburg after the imperial family's murder, representing a total of 2,878,930 rubles' (£8,636,790, or $14,077,968 in 2003 currency) worth of jewels in the Romanovs' possession in Tobolsk.[222]

The imperial family could easily have used this vast fortune in jewels to purchase their safe release. Colonel Kobylinsky was kindly disposed toward a rescue attempt, and for the first five months of captivity the members of the Special Detachment were chiefly concerned with money, not punishment of their former sovereign. Instead, however, the Romanovs began to disperse the larger pieces of jewelry to trusted servants. Brooches, diadems, and jeweled sabers were carefully wrapped in paper and cloth, concealed in packages or beneath the clothing of those who had access to the Governor's House, and smuggled out to Vassiliev at the Abalatsky Monastery; to Hermogen in the Bishop's Palace; to the nuns of the nearby Ivanovsky Convent; and to members of the suite.[223]

An uneasy tension settled over the Governor's House as the days passed, heightened by the sea of strange faces parading through the streets of Tobolsk. No one knew what to expect, though everyone sensed the growing menace. Unknown to the Romanovs, as they shivered through the last days of the harsh Siberian winter, two rival groups of Bolsheviks were engaged in a struggle whose outcome would seal the fate of the prisoners.

2

A Traitor to the Revolution

O N THE COLD, WINDY AFTERNOON of Monday, April 22, 1918, a mounted detachment of 150 soldiers rode into Tobolsk, snow flying as their horses raced along Freedom Street.[1] At their head was Vassili Yakovlev, a thirty-three-year-old extraordinary commissar sent by the Central Executive Committee in Moscow. Watching their arrival from the windows of the Governor's House, Alexandra grew increasingly worried, noting in her diary: "More soldiers on foot and on horseback daily arrive from almost all over the place." But there was something ominous in this latest group, which led the empress and her daughters to begin burning their personal letters and papers.[2]

The Romanovs, isolated and nearly abandoned, had no idea that the arrival of this new squadron would effectively seal their fate. For nine months they had been largely ignored in the chaotic struggles enveloping Russia, culminating in the October Revolution, which swept Kerensky and his Provisional Government from power and installed the Bolshevik regime. As the Siberian winter melted into spring, however, the fate of the Romanovs began to attract a diverse collection of powerful Bolshevik factions, each intent on seizing the prisoners and exacting their own revolutionary vengeance.

After the October Revolution, their future lay in the hands of Vladimir Lenin, an enigmatic man of nearly unfathomable personality, and his band of Bolshevik comrades. Lenin himself came from privileged stock, a sore point often ignored in Soviet history. His mother, Maria Alexandrovna Blank, was the fourth of five daughters of a wealthy St. Petersburg doctor who owned a substantial country estate complete with a number of serfs, near the Volga River. Blank himself had been a state counselor and a proud member of the Kazan District Nobility Association.[3] Lenin's own father, Ilya Ulyanov, served as school inspector of the Volga District, and held the rank of actual councilor of state; as such, he and his children were entitled to sign themselves "Hereditary Nobles" in official documents.[4]

Events moved quickly for the Ulyanov family in 1886 and 1887. Ilya died early in 1886, and Alexander, the eldest son who had been studying biology at the University of St. Petersburg since 1883, fell in with the terrorist group Narodnaya Voliya (The People's Will). In 1887 he was arrested, tried, and convicted of a terrorist plot to assassinate Emperor Alexander III. These years forged the Lenin of history, yet for all the trauma, Vladimir Ulyanov continued his daily life much as before. As a student in the imperial capital for five years, Alexander had been only an occasional visitor to his parents' home in Simbirsk, and had ceased to have much influence over his younger brother.

The assertion that Lenin was somehow set upon a revolutionary path of vengeance on learning of his brother's execution is easily exposed. As their sister Anna recalled, the two brothers had not been close.[5] The more considerate and thoughtful of the pair, Alexander disliked his brother's cold and pompous manner. "Volodya," Anna said of Vladimir, "had reached that transitional age when a youngster is especially sharp and quarrelsome. He was very brash and self-confident, and even more so after the death of father."[6] Young Vladimir was especially rude to his mother following his father's death. So dismissive was he of her requests that once a visiting Alexander told him, "You either go and do what Mama asks, or I shall not play with you again."[7] "He's obviously very gifted," Alexander complained to his sister, "but we don't really get on."[8]

Alexander's execution in 1887 was his own personal sacrifice after he refused to enter into any agreement that might potentially spare his life. He went to the gallows unrepentant, but in so doing, he single-handedly destroyed the comfortable way of life his family had previously enjoyed. After this, young Vladimir nursed a growing resentment against the imperial system that had condemned his brother as well as against Alexander himself, whose actions cast the family into the role of social outcasts.

Lenin got a taste of this when he participated in his first student demonstration at the University of Kazan. It was a minor disturbance, yet he was expelled from both the institution and the city, principally because his brother was regarded by the state as a criminal, and his family was therefore suspect.[9] At every turn, Lenin found himself shunned by educational institutions and watched by suspicious police officials. Yet Vladimir Ulyanov was determined to find for himself a place within the imperial system, and he did not strike out at official authority but instead tried to become part of it. He thus continued to sign himself as "Hereditary Nobleman Vladimir Ulyanov" in plea after plea to educational officials, and in 1891 officially registered as gentry of Simbirsk Province.[10]

The imperial regime, however, had no use for the younger brother of a condemned terrorist. Lenin's growing anger in these years stemmed from this deliberate exclusion as a result of his brother's activities, not any perceived resentment he bore against the system that had condemned him. Only when his attempts to assume what he considered his rightful place within this society were opposed did Vladimir Ulyanov begin his political transformation into the man who would become Lenin.

In this, he was overwhelmingly influenced by the writings of Serge Nechayev. Throughout his life, Lenin expressed nothing but admiration for Nechayev, regarding him as a visionary thinker who had clearly delineated not only the necessity for revolution but also dictated the personal qualities necessary in those who would lead it. His *Revolutionary Catechism* became Lenin's bible. Nechayev wrote that a revolutionary should have "no personal interests, no business affairs, no emotions, no attachments, no property, and no name." A true revolutionary, he explained, "excludes all sentimentality, romanticism, infatuation, and exaltation. All private hatred and revenge must also be excluded. Revolutionary passion, practiced at every moment of the day until it becomes a habit, is to be employed with cold calculation. At all times and in all places the revolutionary must obey not his personal impulses but only those which serve the cause of the revolution." Nechayev also warned against personal vengeance: "When a list of whose who are condemned is made and the order of execution is prepared, no private sense of outrage should be considered, nor is it necessary to pay attention to the hatred provoked by these people among the comrades or the people. Hatred and the sense of outrage may even be useful in so far as they incite the masses to revolt."[11]

Those words drove—indeed, formed—Lenin; they shaped his character, his thinking, his manner, and his relations with others. There is, uniquely, no indication that Lenin ever disagreed with these tenets; instead, he put them into practice in a ruthlessly dispassionate manner. Vladimir Voitinsky, who knew Lenin well, described him as "the most unemotional man I have ever met in politics. No hate, no compassion, not even irritation against his opponents. His ruthlessness in polemics never stemmed from a personal grudge—each word, even each slanderous innuendo in his writings was coldly calculated."[12]

This abrupt manner, this reason before passion, ruled every aspect of Lenin's life. Even his few known pronouncements on the Romanovs themselves echoed and even quoted Nechayev. Once, in discussing this, Lenin quoted Nechayev's answer to the question "Which member of the ruling dynasty should be destroyed?" The answer, Nechayev asserted, was "The entire ruling house." "This," Lenin commented in admiration, "is simplicity to the point of genius." These words reflected not a desire for personal vengeance against the Romanovs, but a clear political philosophy, as Lenin explained: "This is so simply and clearly formulated that it can be understood by everyone living in Russia at a time when the Orthodox Church is a powerful force, and the majority of the people, in one way or another, attend church. Every one of these people would know that 'the entire ruling house' meant all members of the Romanov Dynasty."[13] Thus this oft-cited passage reflected not Lenin's personal view on the Romanov Dynasty but rather his admiration for the simplicity of Nechayev's message.

Lenin was far from well disposed toward Nicholas II; indeed, in exile before the Revolution, he spoke of the necessity of his death.[14] Yet nothing suggests that such political considerations ever extended to the imperial family. On one occasion Lenin declared, "It is necessary to behead at least one hundred Romanovs." Like the quotation from Nechayev, however, this was not meant to convey his personal animosity and future murderous intent. It came in a 1911 essay in which Lenin wrote: "If, in such a cultured country as England, which had never known the Mongol yoke, serfdom, bureaucratic oppression, or the tyranny of a military caste, it was necessary to behead one crowned criminal in order to teach their kings to be constitutional monarchs, then in Russia, it is necessary to behead at least one hundred Romanovs to achieve the same results."[15] Lenin spoke not of a specific plan of vengeance, but of a political philosophy, an example of the dramatic change necessary in the Russian Empire. No evidence suggests that Lenin ever altered these views. Nicholas II was a man for whom he had no use; his death was necessary, but it was death that would follow his public trial and predetermined guilt.

In the first months following the October Revolution, Lenin gave little thought to the fate of the Romanovs. Other, more pressing concerns demanded his full attention. He faced a crisis over the Constituent Assembly, a relic from Kerensky's Provisional Government. Lenin had no use for an elected, representative body, especially one that threatened his own government. "It's an obvious mistake," he declared. "We have already won power, and yet we have to take military measures to win it all over again."[16] These "military measures" were not long in coming. Lenin ordered the regular Electoral Commission in Petrograd disbanded and its members arrested. He placed Michael

Uritsky in charge, supposedly to supervise the election of deputies, but in actuality to ensure a Bolshevik victory. A contingent of Latvian Guards, loyal to the Bolsheviks, engaged in menacing tactics to discourage potential counterrevolutionary parties from receiving a majority of votes.[17]

Despite these measures, the initial round of elections resulted in solid victories for the Mensheviks, Constitutional Democrats, Socialist Revolutionaries, and Left SRs. In Siberia alone, the Constitutional Democrats and the SRs won one-third to three-fourths of all votes.[18] A total of 703 deputies were elected, nearly half of whom belonged to the Socialist Revolutionary Party, while the Bolsheviks received only 168 seats.[19] In response, the Soviet Central Executive Committee issued a decree that invalidated the election of those deputies they deemed "did not hold the confidence of the people," a flimsy excuse by which they eliminated those who opposed them.[20]

But the Bolsheviks could not throw out 535 deputies, and reluctantly allowed the Assembly to move forward. On January 5, 1918, those deputies who had not been illegally deprived of their seats assembled in Petrograd to begin their formal sitting. The Constituent Assembly lasted a day; when the deputies returned on January 6, they found the doors locked and a heavily armed detachment of Latvian Guards surrounding the building. Thus ended the Constituent Assembly.

Lenin's hold on power was fragile. On February 21 the Council of People's Commissars issued a directive, "The Socialist Fatherland in Danger!," warning that the Revolution itself was threatened. This led to a general decree, authored by Lenin, that launched the Revolution on wide-scale, state terror, authorizing executions "on the spot," without any charges or trial, for those believed to be counterrevolutionaries, and labeled as "enemy agents speculators, thieves, hooligans, anti-Bolshevik agitators, German spies," and a whole host of other suspects.[21] This caused considerable consternation among the members of the Soviet hierarchy, precisely because it was the antithesis of Lenin's public policy. Yet behind this public mask was a brain willing to embrace the idea of state terror as a means to an end if it saved the Revolution.

Lenin's terror was deeply ideological, designed only to save what his comrades had won; nevertheless, it was just as brutal and widespread, with or without his personal participation. "He took care," wrote Robert Payne, "to speak of the terror only in the abstract, disassociating himself from individual acts of terrorism, the murders in the basement of the Lubyanka and in all the other basements."[22] Lenin's definition of Red terror was that enacted by the state for the greater good of the Revolution; he once explained this in an essay in which he wrote that the former dynasty and the bourgeoisie had "practiced terror against the workers, soldiers, and peasants in the interests of a small group of landowners and bankers, whereas the Soviet regime applies decisive measures against landowners, plunderers, and their accomplices in the interests of the workers, soldiers, and peasants."[23]

When Isaac Steinberg, the Left SR commissar of justice in the Soviet government, once complained about state terror, Lenin replied simply, "You certainly don't think we'll survive this as the winners if we don't use the most brutal revolutionary terror?" Steinberg seemed less than convinced, and Lenin added, as if to reassure him: "We don't use terror as a weapon, the same way that the French Revolution did—a sharp guillotine against the necks of all the people. It's my sincere hope that we'll never resort to such measures in the future, nor need we as long as we're in power."[24] But Steinberg was not won over. He regarded Lenin's proposal as "a system of violence, dispensed from above . . . a planned and quasi-legal program to intimidate and terrify a people into submission."[25] Exasperated, one day he finally confronted Lenin, screaming, "Why do we bother to have a Commissariat of Justice? Let's be honest and call it the Commissariat for Social Extermination and be done with it!" According to Steinberg, "Lenin's face brightened suddenly." Slowly, deliberately, he replied, "Well put. That's exactly what it should be called. But we can't say that."[26]

On the heels of the "Socialist Fatherland in Danger!" announcement came an ominous hint of what was to come. The February 23, 1918, edition of *Pravda* reported: "The Cheka hitherto has always been tolerant in its struggle against the enemies of the people. But now, when the hydra of counterrevolution, encouraged by the treacherous attack of the Germans, grows bolder every day, and the world bourgeoisie is trying to crush the vanguard of international revolution, i.e., the Russian proletariat, the Cheka sees no means of combating counterrevolutionaries, spies, speculators, thugs, roughs, saboteurs, and other parasites, except by mercilessly destroying them on the spot."[27]

It fell to Felix Dzerzhinsky, head of the Cheka, to carry out these threats. "Terror," he once said, "is an absolute necessity during times of revolution. We terrorize the enemies of the Soviet government in order to stop crime at its inception."[28] His Cheka, the Extraordinary Commission for Combating Counterrevolution and Sabotage, was a true successor to Ivan the Terrible's infamous Oprichniki, far more brutal than the tsarist Okhrana, as they openly engaged in torture and murder.[29]

These concerns diverted Lenin's attention from the question of the Romanovs, but he also faced the dilemma of the continuing war. On December 3 the Bolsheviks had proposed a separate peace with Germany and, within three weeks, negotiations were under way. On

February 12 the Soviets announced that as far as they were concerned, the war was over for Russia, and that their troops would no longer fight. By giving the game away so early, they undoubtedly played into the hands of the German negotiators.

Bolshevik support for a treaty was never widespread, even within the party. Throughout the winter of 1918, while negotiations were under way, the Bolshevik Party was divided into two factions: the first, led by Lenin, which supported the idea of a treaty, and the second, composed largely of left-Communists who vehemently opposed any negotiations with the Germans that would result in loss of territory for Russia. This was a contest of ideological and political wills: Lenin needed to preserve his fragile hold on power by any means necessary, while Bukharin's contingent believed firmly that the Revolution must be exported to other countries in order for that in Russia to survive.[30]

Russia was at the mercy of the kaiser's representatives, who extracted demand after demand from the Soviet delegation led by Leon Trotsky. By the time the Treaty of Brest-Litovsk was signed on March 3, 1918, Russia had agreed to cede to Germany 34 percent of her population, 32 percent of her arable land, 54 percent of her heavy industries, and fully 89 percent of her coal mines.[31] This was a devastating loss—the whole of the Ukraine and the Crimea were gone, along with most of Russia's former western provinces and interests. Lenin was keenly aware of the desperate situation that forced him to sign the treaty. He recognized, from the very beginning, the impossibility of its conditions. "I don't mean to read it," he declared, "and I don't mean to fulfill it, except in so far as I am forced."[32] When the terms of the treaty were released, the Socialist Revolutionaries who had formed Lenin's fragile coalition government resigned en masse. So great were fears of a German invasion that the Soviet government officially moved from Petrograd to Moscow on March 10, 1918, "a signal," as Dimitri Volkogonov noted, "to Germany that Russia would not defend her frontier."[33]

The signing of the Treaty of Brest-Litovsk signaled a new chapter in the fate of the Romanovs. Suspicion that the German government—and specifically Kaiser Wilhelm II—was engaged in some conspiracy to rescue the imperial family from Siberia and bring them to the relative safety of Europe haunted the imagination of the Soviet regime. On February 10, 1918, just two weeks before the Treaty of Brest-Litovsk was signed, *Pravda* carried an article titled "The German Emperor and the Russian Emperor," in which they called for the removal of the Romanovs from Tobolsk to "a secure place. It is urgent that he be deprived of all freedom of contact with any persons, and to confine him in prison while he awaits an immediate trial."[34]

While the Romanovs were at Tobolsk, the empress's brother Grand

Duke Ernst Ludwig of Hesse and by Rhine apparently called on Adolf Ioffe, the Bolshevik representative in Berlin, offering to mediate between Germany and Russia during the Brest negotiations. One of his promises was a suspension or reduction of the 300 million rubles Russia was to hand over to Germany as her war indemnity.[35] The Kaiser himself allowed Ernst Ludwig to write his sister, offering help in rescuing the imperial family. The grand duke gave the letter to Serge Markov, who apparently delivered the letter through secret channels to the prisoners. On receiving it, Nicholas refused German assistance. Alexandra, however, felt compelled to answer and explained to Ernst why the offer could not be accepted. Markov took the letter back to Germany. According to General Deterikhs, "the letter which Markov brought actually existed. It was seen by others. It was seen by people who could know the Empress's handwriting."[36]

Markov himself made no mention of any such letter in his book, though at the time it was written he was living in exile, relying heavily on money from Ernst Ludwig to support himself. But the emperor's cousin Grand Duke Andrei Vladimirovich reported that Markov had contacted Ernst Ludwig through the German embassy in Moscow, offering his services, "received a personal letter from the Grand Duke of Hesse to be given to the Emperor, and the instruction to apply for assistance to two German agents in Russia who served German intelligence during the War. With their help he reached Tobolsk."[37] Apparently this letter contained some possible mention of German support for a restoration of the throne, with the grand duke offering himself as regent for his nephew Tsesarevich Alexei. Grand Duke Andrei noted: "The mention of his name as Regent prompts the assumption that he knew everything. That the conduct of the Germans was not disinterested requires no proofs."[38]

These developments were followed with ominous concern in the major Bolshevik strongholds in Siberia, particularly Ekaterinburg, the largest, most important city in the Ural Mountains. Its ruling Ural Regional Soviet had proudly declared Ekaterinburg "the citadel of the Revolution," and this was not an idle boast.[39] The Urals in general, and Ekaterinburg in particular, had always been politically independent and prone to such militancy. Siberia was too vast a land, too remote, too sparsely populated, to demand attention from authorities in St. Petersburg, and consequently the region was largely left to develop on its own. The Trans-Siberian Railway changed this, but the network of tracks that crossed the mountains and plains only served to emphasize the enormous gulfs—both geographical and political—between European Russia and the land beyond the Ural Mountains.

The ruling Ural Regional Soviet was a constant thorn in Moscow's side, troublesome, hostile, and openly contemptuous of the Central Executive Committee's authority. In the first few months of the new Bolshevik regime, the Ural Soviet, composed largely of terrorists, factory workers, and former political prisoners, humored Lenin, but by the beginning of 1918 relations had degenerated to the point that the Ural Soviet had one of Lenin's cousins shot for participating in a strike; Lenin himself had to intervene to save his uncle from the same fate.[40] This tenuous relationship between Ekaterinburg and Moscow— between the rigid ideologies practiced by Lenin and the practicalities endured by the Ural Bolsheviks struggling for survival on the front lines of the Civil War—heavily influenced the events of that momentous spring and summer.

Beginning at the end of February, the Ural Regional Soviet, headed by Chairman Alexander Beloborodov, bombarded Yakov Sverdlov and the Central Executive Committee with cables, first asking for resolution to the issue of security in Tobolsk, then demanding the transfer of the prisoners to Ekaterinburg.[41] "We worried," recalled Alexander Avdayev, one of their members, "that the spring thaw would allow for possible rescue."[42] To this end, as Ural Bolshevik Paul Bykov later admitted, the Ekaterinburg contingent cynically elected Philip [Isaac] Goloshchokin, the Ural Regional military commissar, to go to Moscow at the end of March and speak with Sverdlov—a personal friend—about the possible transfer. "This," Bykov wrote, "allowed us to make a statement regarding our ability to securely guard the family, once in our custody, while, at the same time, displaying a subtle show of our military strength to the central authorities."[43]

Bykov's admission indicates that authorities in Ekaterinburg were unimpressed with Moscow's power, and willing to make their own moves on the Romanovs. They sought permission and counsel, but in the end willingly assumed responsibility themselves. On March 14 the Ural Regional Soviet dispatched two undercover agents to Tobolsk: Tatiana Teumina, whose mother lived in the district, allowing her to move without notice; and Paul Khokhryakov, a former sailor who later married Teumina.[44] A few days later, Alexander Avdayev arrived in Tobolsk under false identity papers; with him were sixteen Bolsheviks, who quickly infiltrated the town. Avdayev had been given "extraordinary powers by the Ural Regional Soviet, with a view to taking all steps necessary to prevent the liberation of the Romanovs."[45] A few days later, a second armed detachment of Bolsheviks, led by former factory worker Semyon Zaslavsky, arrived from Ekaterinburg and insisted that the Romanovs be incarcerated in the local prison.[46]

For seven days, members of the Special Detachment guarding the Romanovs and the Ekaterinburg men maintained an uneasy standoff.

On the night of April 3 Zaslavsky attempted to storm the Governor's House and seize the prisoners by force, aided by his few dozen soldiers.[47] Members of the Special Detachment managed to repulse the attack, but the situation was desperate. Colonel Kobylinsky was impotent to act, but a third group took matters into its own hands. This was a contingent of Bolshevik forces from Omsk, bitter enemies of Ekaterinburg who, on April 4, drove Zaslavsky and his brigade, including Avdayev, out of town. Kobylinsky was forced to turn to the Omsk detachments for assistance, and together they instituted a new system of armed patrols and watches around the Governor's House, ready to repel any new attack.[48] Only Khokhryakov remained, quietly hidden in his fiancée's house.[49]

News of these events sent a wave of panic through the Ural Regional Soviet. On April 6 they demanded "the transfer of the prisoners to the Urals."[50] Without waiting for an answer, they took matters into their own hands, ordering Zaslavsky back to Tobolsk, this time accompanied by two hundred heavily armed soldiers charged with bringing the Romanovs to Ekaterinburg.[51]

When his efforts to gain admittance to the Governor's House were rebuffed, Zaslavsky had Colonel Kobylinsky summoned to a general meeting of the Tobolsk Soviet, where Zaslavsky angrily denounced him and again insisted that the Romanovs immediately be taken to the local prison. He made a fatal mistake, however, in insisting that members of the Special Detachment could no longer be trusted, and should likewise be incarcerated.[52] This suggestion created an uproar. The members of the Special Detachment, unhappy in their situation, were initially friendly to the overtures of the Bolsheviks but, when they learned of this proposal, quickly threw in their lot with Kobylinsky, as did the rival Bolsheviks from Omsk, who were willing to do anything to keep the Romanovs out of reach of their hated Ekaterinburg comrades.[53]

Zaslavsky reported these events to Ekaterinburg. On April 13 Boris Didkovsky, the deputy chairman of the Ural Regional Soviet, dispatched an urgent cable to Lenin and Sverdlov in Moscow: "We ask you to solve the Tobolsk question by calling an emergency session. In four–five days roads will be clear. It is necessary to know how Nicholas II and the others are being guarded against the outside world. The route to the sea will be open, and so will the way to China. The way things are in the East, it might already be too late." Once again, to the authorities in Moscow, they "insisted" on "the immediate transfer" of the Romanovs from Tobolsk, adding, "we suggest the Urals."[54]

Moscow, however, had already discussed the situation. On April 1, 1918, the Presidium of the Central Executive Committee voted to send a new commissar to Tobolsk, who, "should the possibility arise, immediately transfer all of the prisoners to Moscow." This decision, the transcript noted, was to remain secret.[55] Five days later, however, on April 6, the Presidium, "as a supplement to the previously adopted Resolution," announced that Sverdlov was to "communicate with Ekaterinburg and Omsk over the direct line about the appointment of reinforcements for the detachment guarding Nicholas Romanov and about the transfer of all the arrested to the Urals."[56]

Did this reflect a sudden change in policy by Moscow? Almost certainly not. All evidence indicates that Vassili Yakovlev, the new extraordinary commissar, was charged with bringing the Romanovs to Moscow. Rather, the first resolution, that the Romanovs would be brought to Moscow, remained a secret, while the second, for public consumption, announced that they would be transferred to the Urals. This second decision, then, seems to have been adopted only to deceive Ekaterinburg as to Yakovlev's intent. On April 9 Sverdlov informed the Ural Regional Soviet that Yakovlev's mission was to "deliver Nicholas to Ekaterinburg alive, and hand him over to Chairman Beloborodov or to Goloshchokin," noting that he had received "precise, detailed instructions."[57]

The new extraordinary commissar left Moscow on April 9. For most of the past eighty-five years, Vassili Vassilievich Yakovlev has remained an enigma, subject of theories that veer wildly across the spectrum of possibility to form an impenetrable web of conflicting assertions built on rumor and innuendo. In fact, he was born near Ufa in 1885 as Konstantin Myachin.[58] After a period of revolutionary activity in Russia, Myachin fled to Europe, where he first used the alias of Yakovlev.[59] Yakovlev joined the Bolshevik Party in 1905 but apparently felt constrained by their principles. His political development took him steadily to the left, and he eventually joined the Socialist Revolutionary Party, where he found an extreme ideology more fitting to his own beliefs.[60]

Following the February Revolution, Myachin joined the stream of political exiles hurrying back to Russia. Curiously enough, his first assignment brought him face to face with Nicholas II. On March 9, 1917, the day on which the abdicated emperor returned to the Alexander Palace as a prisoner, the Soviet Executive Committee passed a resolution

Vassili Vassilievich Yakovlev, Moscow's man assigned to transfer the Romanovs back to the Red capital.

that the former imperial family must be imprisoned in the Trubetskoy Bastion of the Fortress of St. Peter and St. Paul in Petrograd.[61] They charged a certain Serge Maslavsky with arresting the emperor and his family at Tsarskoye Selo and bringing them back to the capital; at his side was a man identified as Staff Captain Tarasov-Rodionov, a new alias adopted by Yakovlev.[62] The men, accompanied by three armored cars, reached the palace and, after a series of frustrated negotiations, finally agreed that they would leave if they could simply view the emperor, to reassure the Soviet that he was incarcerated. Nicholas duly appeared before them, walking through a corridor, and Yakovlev had his first encounter with Nicholas II.[63]

At the beginning of 1918 the Central Executive Committee considered appointing Yakovlev as military commissar of the Urals, with a seat on the Ural Regional Soviet. Authorities in Ekaterinburg, however, protested, and raised one of their own men, Philip Goloshchokin, to the position.[64] It was a sign of Lenin's relative weakness that a provincial Soviet, however fierce and strong, would reject a proposal from the central authorities, and do so without reprisal.

Yakovlev's journey to Tobolsk took fourteen days. On April 13 he arrived in Ufa, where he met Goloshchokin, the Ural Regional military commissar. According to fellow Ural Soviet member Paul Bykov, Goloshchokin was in Ufa on official business, though the meeting seems to have been arranged by Moscow to secure the cooperation of the Ekaterinburg Bolsheviks. During this meeting, Yakovlev showed Goloshchokin his papers, which included two mandates to transfer the Romanovs from Tobolsk. These stated that Yakovlev was a member of the VTsIK charged with a "mission of special importance," and carried Moscow's authority to shoot anyone who disobeyed his orders. According to Colonel Kobylinsky, who himself saw the two mandates, neither disclosed where the prisoners were to be taken.[65] One mandate was signed by Sverdlov, while the second was signed by Lenin himself.[66]

After showing Goloshchokin his orders, Yakovlev insisted that secrecy was imperative, presumably to prevent any attempts to interfere with the transfer. Only a few days earlier, Goloshchokin had received Sverdlov's assurance that Ekaterinburg would be allowed to take possession of the Romanovs; with some reluctance, Goloshchokin agreed to instruct all members of the Ekaterinburg and Ural Regional Soviets to obey the extraordinary commissar on penalty of death.[67]

From Ufa, Yakovlev and his men traveled through Chelyabinsk to Ekaterinburg, from where they turned north, to Tyumen. Here he met Alexander Avdayev, sent by the Ural Regional Soviet to spy on Moscow's man.[68] As Yakovlev turned north, riding across the frozen taiga and through the snow-clad forests toward Tobolsk, he learned that a contingent of heavily armed Bolshevik guards, led by a Commissar Brusyatsky, had been dispatched by Ekaterinburg. They lay in wait in the forest, instructed, as Bykov himself admitted, to bring Nicholas to Ekaterinburg "alive or dead," and to defend the interests of the Ural Regional Soviet against any "outside forces."[69]

Ekaterinburg was clearly suspicious of both Moscow and its extraordinary commissar, despite having received guarantees that the Romanovs were to be transferred into its hands. The Ural Regional Soviet trusted no one, and was willing, in open defiance of Moscow, to take the Romanovs by force, either "alive or dead." If Yakovlev was charged with bringing the Romanovs to Moscow, the attitude of the Ural Bolsheviks itself explains the government's secrecy, and their two decisions that gave contradictory destinations, all in an effort to deceive the Ural Regional Soviet while at the same time ensuring their actual objective.

On arriving at Tobolsk, Yakovlev showed Kobylinsky his credentials. Yakovlev bore three different mandates. The first was signed by Sverdlov and countersigned by both Ovanessov, the vice chairman of the VTsIK, and Isaac Steinberg, the Soviet commissar of justice. This named Yakovlev as "a member of the VTsIK entrusted with a mission of special importance, empowered to shoot anyone who disobeyed his orders."[70] The second order, addressed to the members of the Special Detachment, placed them directly under Yakovlev's authority. The third mandate formed Yakovlev's traveling papers, an official pass from the VTsIK instructing all officials to cooperate with his demands, on orders of the Soviet government.[71]

Kobylinsky led Yakovlev on an inspection of the Governor's House, joined by the new commissar's secretary, Serge Galkin; Paul Matveyev, chairman of the Special Detachment; and Alexander Avdayev, representing the Ekaterinburg District Soviet. Near the end of the upper corridor, Kobylinsky directed Yakovlev to an open door, out of which stepped Nicholas II, followed by three of the grand duchesses.[72] Yakovlev, Nicholas wrote, appeared "clean-shaven, smiling, and embarrassed."[73]

"Are you satisfied with the guard?" Yakovlev asked Nicholas. "Do you have any complaints to make?"

"No, no, very pleased," the emperor replied.[74]

Yakovlev then asked to see the tsesarevich. "Alexei Nikolaievich is quite ill," Nicholas told him.

"It is extremely important that I see him," Yakovlev replied.

"Well," Nicholas answered, "all right, but only you alone." He led him through the doorway, and into the tsesarevich's bedroom. Yakovlev later described Alexei as "very ill," with a "yellow complexion" and an "appearance which gave the impression he was not long for this world."[75] Only a week earlier, Alexei had injured himself while tobogganing down the main staircase.[76] Within a day of the accident, Alexei took to his bed with pain in his leg: it was the beginning of his worse attack of hemophilia since 1912, when the tsesarevich had nearly died at the Polish hunting lodge of Spala.

On hearing that the empress still was not dressed, Yakovlev agreed to return later. He finished his inspection of the Governor's House "without stopping," as Nicholas noted, rushing from room to room, poking his head through doorways, and all the while apologizing for the interruption.[77]

Shortly before eleven that morning, Yakovlev returned to take tea with the emperor and empress. He addressed the emperor as "Your Majesty," and spoke to Pierre Gilliard, who was present, in fluent French.[78] He was, Alexandra later told Alexei Volkov, "somewhat lecturing in the tone of his voice," but added that he "was well behaved and very polite."[79] The empress noted in her diary that he reminded her of "an intelligent, highly nervous workman or engineer."[80] Before he left, Yakovlev asked if the prisoners had much luggage, which Gilliard took as a hint that they might soon be moved.[81]

Yakovlev left the Governor's House and went straight to the telegraph office, where he informed Sverdlov of the tsesarevich's condition, and asked for further instructions: "Probable that only principal part of baggage can be transferred. Both you and Comrade Sverdlov suspected this." The reply was quick in arriving: "Your intention to remove only principal part is approved."[82]

On the morning of April 25 Yakovlev finally told Kobylinsky that he was to move the imperial family from Tobolsk. "How?" Kobylinsky asked. "And Alexei—he's sick! He cannot travel!"

"This has been the difficulty," Yakovlev said. "I had to contact the Central Committee by direct line. I have received the order to take the emperor and leave the family if necessary. How ironic is that?"[83]

From his talks with Yakovlev, Kobylinsky assumed that the destination was to be Moscow.[84] Although Yakovlev asked to meet with the emperor privately, Alexandra was immediately suspicious, and refused to leave her husband's side. As soon as Yakovlev entered, she asked, "Why should you want to speak to the emperor alone? I never leave him alone to speak with anyone." Yakovlev was forced to relent; rather than cause a scene, he allowed the empress to remain.[85]

Yakovlev began to explain his mission, but Nicholas cut him off, asking, "Where are you taking me?" When the commissar indicated that he could not reveal the destination, Nicholas announced flatly, "In that case, I will not leave."[86]

"I beg you not to refuse," Yakovlev told him. "I am compelled to execute the order. In case of your refusal I must take you by force or resign. In the latter case they would probably decide to send a less scrupulous sort of man to take my position. Be calm, I am responsible with my life for your security. If you do not want to go alone you could take with you the people you desire. Be ready, we are leaving tomorrow at four o'clock."[87]

Alexandra, as Yakovlev recalled, became hysterical. "What are you going to do with him?" she screamed. "You want to tear him away from his family! How can you? How? His son is sick! He can't go, he must stay with us! This is too cruel! I can't believe you would do this!" She paced up and down the room, "like an animal, muttering loudly to herself."[88] Both Yakovlev and Colonel Kobylinsky, standing nearby, overheard her words to Tatischev as she passed: "If he is taken alone, he'll do something stupid, like he did before. Without me, they can force him to do whatever they want."[89] Having witnessed this scene, Yakovlev concluded: "Apparently, Alexandra Feodorovna did not have a very high opinion of her husband's intelligence and judgment."[90]

As soon as Yakovlev departed, the prisoners discussed the situation. Kobylinsky suggested that Yakovlev was most likely taking the emperor to Moscow, based on the travel time the extraordinary commissar had estimated for the journey. "I imagine," Nicholas declared angrily, "that they want to force me to sign the Treaty of Brest-Litovsk. But I won't! I'd rather cut off my right hand than sign that treaty!"[91]

Pierre Gilliard later recalled that "Kobylinsky told us that Yakovlev at first informed him that the final destination was to be Moscow, but that he later said he did not know where the emperor was going to be taken."[92] Yet Kobylinsky contradicted this. "I felt sure," Kobylinsky later said, "that Yakovlev, representing Moscow, worked in accordance with its desires, fulfilled the instructions he got from them in Moscow, and that that was the place where the imperial family was to be taken."[93]

All of those with whom Yakovlev spoke confirmed later that Moscow was indeed the intended destination. Nicholas Nemtsov, chairman of the Presidium of the Perm Regional Soviet, met Yakovlev as he passed through Tyumen on his way to Tobolsk. Yakovlev, Nemtsov recalled, "showed me his mandate, which called for the removal of Nicholas Romanov from Tobolsk and his transfer to Moscow."[94] Yakovlev also had shown Avdayev the same mandate, which indicated Moscow.[95] Before the group left Tobolsk, Yakovlev spoke to Matveyev, chairman of the Special Detachment, and asked if he had ever had to carry out secret military instructions. "I gave him an affirmative reply, and Yakovlev announced that he had been given the task of transferring the former Emperor to Moscow."[96] Dr. Vladimir Derevenko also spoke to Yakovlev before he left Tobolsk. He later told Princess Helen, wife of Prince Ioann Konstantinovich, that Yakovlev's mission had been the transfer of the imperial family to Moscow, where, he theorized, Nicholas was to discuss the idea of reestablishing the throne under German protection.[97] Prince Vassili Dolgoruky later said that he understood, from Yakovlev himself, that the mission had been to bring the Romanovs to Moscow, and, from there, take them out of the country, through Riga."[98]

Yakovlev himself told Tatiana Botkin that they were to go to Moscow, where the emperor would stand trial. But when Tatiana asked Colonel Kobylinsky about this, he seemed surprised. "Trial!" he exclaimed. "Nonsense! There won't be any trial. From Moscow, they are to be taken to Petrograd, Finland, and Sweden, to Norway."[99] Tatiana and her brother Gleb had the same story from their father. Dr. Botkin himself spoke with Yakovlev, and that afternoon related his conversation to his children: "Yakovlev has finally announced that he has come to take us all to Moscow. He had a long talk with Kobylinsky who said that as long as he lived he would not permit the imperial family to be taken away, unless he were convinced that no harm would be done to them. But Yakovlev has shown him all his papers, mandates and secret instructions. It is actually true that the Soviets have promised Germany to release the imperial family. But the Germans have had the decency not to demand that the imperial family go to Germany. Accordingly it was decided that we shall be sent to England. To satisfy the masses, however, we are to pass through Moscow, where a short trial of the emperor will be held. He will be found guilty of whatever the revolutionists care to accuse him, and be condemned to deportation to England."[100]

That night witnessed a long, agonized struggle in the Governor's House. "I can't let the Emperor go alone!" Alexandra cried to Pierre Gilliard. "They want to separate him from his family, as they did before. . . . I ought to be at his side in the time of trial. But the boy is still so ill. . . . Oh, God! What ghastly torture! For the first time in my life, I don't know what to do. I've always felt inspired whenever I had to take a decision and now I can't think."[101]

Alexandra was uncertain what to do. The empress, Gilliard declared, "was so agitated from this frightful trouble that I had never seen her in such condition, not even in Spala, when Alexei was so sick, nor at the time of the abdication of the Emperor. She could not stay still, nor find a moment of peace. She paced up and down with her fists clenched, talking to herself. The Emperor stayed away from her. He spent that night alone."[102]

With each passing minute, the empress became more hysterical. Marie Tutelberg, one of her maids, later remembered how "violently upset" Alexandra had been. "She suffered much more than she had even at the beginning of the Revolution. She was terribly agitated." But when Tutelberg attempted to speak to her, the empress angrily told her, "Please don't add to my grief!"[103]

Tatiana, Gilliard remembered, "had to take a hand and calm her mother down."[104] "But Mother, if Father has to go, whatever we say, something must be decided," Tatiana said.[105] "You cannot go on tormenting yourself like this."[106] Alexandra continued to pace up and down the room, talking to herself. Suddenly she said, "Yes, that will be best; I'll go with the Emperor."[107]

Her decision made, she went to her husband, who replied quietly, "I can see your mind is made up." Gilliard watched as they disappeared into their bedroom. A short time later, when they emerged, Prince Dolgoruky asked Nicholas, "Which of us will accompany you, me or Tatischev?" Nicholas looked at his wife and asked, "Which would you like?" Alexandra told him Dolgoruky, and the decision was made.[108]

She then went to Alexei's room and told him that she and Nicholas would be leaving in the morning. "She was crying," remembered Volkov, "but she managed to keep her face calm for the boy; tears were running down her cheeks."[109]

Throughout the long night, Tatiana Botkin noted, the windows of the Governor's House blazed with light.[110] At ten-thirty, the emperor and empress asked the members of the suite and household to take tea with them in the second-floor drawing room. Alexandra half reclined on a sofa, her eyes red and swollen from crying, with two of her daughters sitting beside her.[111] "It was the most mournful and depressing party I ever attended," recalled Gibbes. "There was not much talking and no pretense at gaiety. It was solemn, tragic, a fit prelude to inescapable tragedy." As they said their farewells, the emperor shook hands with everyone and thanked them for their faithful service, while they filed past the empress and kissed her hand. As the group departed, Anna Demidova, who was to accompany the emperor and empress, turned to Gibbes and said, "I am so frightened of the Bolsheviks, Mr. Gibbes. I don't know what they will do to us."[112]

Although they expected the worst, Alexandra continued to pray that they would not be forced to leave. "I know, I am convinced, that the river will overflow tonight, and then our departure must be postponed. This will give us time to get out of this terrible position. If a miracle is necessary, I am sure a miracle will take place."[113]

But there was no miracle for Alexandra that night. Just after two that morning, Tatiana Botkin watched as a group of carriages flew down Freedom Street, bells jingling and snow flying from the runners.[114] Snow continued to flurry in the long hours leading up to the departure. "The Governor's House and barracks were brilliantly lighted," Tatiana Botkin later wrote. "Outside the fences of the enclosure, the sleighs and vozaks stood in line, waiting for the gates to open. . . . From time to time, some unknown, mounted soldiers would appear—evidently of Yakovlev's detachment. At last the gates opened and the sleighs drove up to the front door, one after the other. The yard became animated, the figures of servants and soldiers, dragging luggage, appeared. . . . My father came out of the house repeatedly, wearing Dolgoruky's fur-lined coat, because his big, deerskin coat was used to wrap up Her Majesty and Marie Nikolaievna, who had nothing heavier than their light winter coats."[115]

Alexandra had asked her daughter Marie to accompany them on their journey. Tatiana would be left in charge of Alexei, while Anastasia was too young. Only the eldest daughter, Olga, seemed, according to Klaudia Bittner, to understand "the tragic situation in which they found themselves. She sobbed very hard throughout as her parents were leaving."[116]

Just before five that morning, the emperor and empress left their rooms and descended to the first floor of the Governor's House. Both Alexandra and her daughter Marie wore long coats of Persian lamb to guard against the cold.[117] At the bottom of the staircase, Nicholas walked up to Volkov, embraced and kissed him, and said quietly, "All will be well—I hope." The empress, following behind him, extended her hand to the valet and said, "Guard Alexei."[118]

The vehicles selected for the trip were a mixture of peasant carts, koveshas, and tarantasses. The first, drawn by two horses and similar to an open sleigh, was intended for Yakovlev and the emperor; the second, drawn by three horses, was fitted with a cloth hood to provide some protection from the elements but had neither springs nor seats. One man, who had the misfortune to travel in a Siberian tarantass, later described the experience: "As there are no roads and only the roughest of tracks with fearful ruts and soft places where water lingers, with sometimes a sloping bank down to a stream, and, as the wild driver keeps his horses at their full speed, one is hurled violently and roughly about the whole time, sleep, for me at least, is beyond my wildest hopes from start to finish."[119] In an effort to make the tarantass more comfortable, a few of the servants swept up some straw from the pigsty and covered the floor with it; on top of this, Pierre Gilliard placed an old mattress, to help cushion the bumps.[120] In these vehicles, the journey of some two hundred miles to Tyumen would be made.[121]

As the Romanovs emerged from the Governor's House, Yakovlev met them on the steps. "It was about 5:00 A.M.," recalled Tatiana Botkin, "and in the dawn of a pale spring day, they could all be clearly seen. Commissar Yakovlev was walking beside the emperor and saying something to him respectfully, constantly touching his tall fur cap."[122]

Although both ladies were wrapped in heavy furs, Yakovlev insisted that the empress take Dr. Botkin's overcoat as well. The emperor came out, wearing his usual military officer's greatcoat.

"What!" Yakovlev exclaimed. "You're only wearing an overcoat!"

"That's all I ever wear," Nicholas replied. But Yakovlev insisted that he take a second greatcoat as well.[123]

Alexandra climbed into her cart slowly, assisted by Nicholas and her daughter. The emperor attempted to follow her, but Yakovlev stopped him, saying that he must ride with the extraordinary commissar in the first cart. As Nicholas duly climbed in, Yakovlev stood at attention and saluted.[124]

Marie then climbed in beside her mother. Dr. Botkin and Prince Vassili Dolgoruky rode by themselves in a third cart; even in these desperate circumstances, the servants—valet Terenty Chemodurov, maid Anna Demidova, and footman Ivan Sednev—were meticulously separated by rank and forced to follow in a fourth sled. The gates of the compound swung open, and escorted by a cavalry regiment, the group of carts sped down the street and out into the Siberian night. "My father," remembered Tatiana Botkin, "saw me, and turning around, signed me repeatedly with the Cross, giving me his blessing." She watched as "all this dashed past me with incredible rapidity and vanished around the corner. I looked in the direction of the Governor's House. There on the doorsteps stood three figures in grey suits and gazed for a long time into the distance, then turned and slowly one after the other entered the house."[125]

The prisoners knew only that Yakovlev was taking them to Tyumen, the nearest town on the railroad line, and, from there, presumably to Moscow. Just after 8:00 A.M. on Friday, April 26, the party had to cross the Irtysh River, awash with swiftly churning water and ice floes. The horses waded out into the torrent, struggling to pull the carts as they sank into the mud. In a letter to Zenaide Tolstoy, Marie described the ride as difficult, noting, "we were all terribly shaken."[126] The constant sleet, coupled with the howling wind, melting snow, and deeply rutted roadway, left the empress "fearfully shaken." At eight that night they stopped at the village of Yevlevo, where Yakovlev had arranged for the group to stay in an old post house and shop. Nicholas and Alexandra had camp beds, while Marie slept on a mattress on the floor. "Got to bed at 10, dead tired and ached all over," Alexandra wrote in her diary. "One does not tell us where we are going from Tyumen—some imagine Moscow, the little ones are to follow as soon as river free and Baby well. By turn each carriage lost a wheel or something else smashed. Luggage always late—heart aches, enlarged, wrote to the children through our first coachman."[127]

On Saturday, April 27, the prisoners were woken at four in the morning to begin their journey, but they were delayed while Yakovlev, who had overslept, explained that he had misplaced a piece of luggage.[128] Alexandra noted that Yakovlev seemed "fidgety, running about, telegraphing."[129] In fact, the extraordinary commissar had good reason to be worried. When he awoke that morning, he discovered that, on orders of the Ural Regional Soviet, Zaslavsky had arrived at Yevlevo, accompanied by an armed detachment bearing machine guns, ready to attack the group and take the prisoners.[130]

Alexander Nevolin, a member of the Fourth Ural Regiment of the Red Army, recalled that he and his comrades received an order on April 16 from the chief of staff to "bring a certain person, dead or alive, back to Ekaterinburg." The regiment was dispatched to Tyumen, and from there, on horse to meet Zaslavsky. On learning of Yakovlev's departure from Tobolsk they were told to attack the convoy, and "seize all of their weapons and Romanov." Nevolin thought this was too dangerous, and so a second plan, which called for an ambush on the road outside Tyumen, was adopted. "You must cut off Yakovlev completely, and shred his detachment with machine guns," the group was told. "Don't say a word to anyone." Nevolin, worried that the entire episode would end in disaster, crept away from the group in the middle of the night and found Yakovlev at Yevlevo that morning, quickly informing him of the plot.[131]

There is no question that the Presidium of the Ural Regional Soviet was behind the plan. In August 1918 Nicholas Sakovich, Ekaterinburg's commissar of public health, recalled an ominous meeting he attended shortly after Yakovlev had arrived in Tobolsk: "Someone, I do not remember who, suggested staging a train wreck during the former Emperor's transfer. This was even put to a vote and the decision was made to remove the sovereign from Tobolsk to Ekaterinburg."[132] This meeting was later confirmed by Paul Bykov, who recalled that "all present expressed their definite distrust of Yakovlev, and it was decided if necessary to attack his detachment on the road and carry off the Romanovs."[133] He added that they took another vote, which called for "the immediate execution of Nicholas, to prevent his flight and possible restoration to the Throne."[134]

When Yakovlev learned of these plans, he simply told the emperor and empress that he had misplaced some luggage and must search for it. Instead, however, he went straight to the telegraph office and dispatched an urgent cable to Goloshchokin in Ekaterinburg: "I have just received information that your people, commanded by Zaslavsky, Khokhryakov, the leader of the guards, or others—want to disarm us and take the baggage by force. If you do not act at once, bloodshed will be inevitable. Inform Tyumen in detail at once. Zaslavsky left Tobolsk secretly before I could arrest him. I am leaving Yevlevo." He sent a second cable, to Tyumen, requesting a detachment of "thirty armed men, prepared for military action," to meet him along the route.[135]

Nevolin knew only that Zaslavsky's Ural Bolsheviks lay in wait at some point along the route. After he left, however, Zaslavsky's contingent was joined by another, led by Brusyatsky, also heavily armed.[136] Given these circumstances, Yakovlev proceeded cautiously. When they reached the Tobol River, they found it awash with ice floes. Yakovlev directed that planks be laid across the shifting ice, and the Romanovs had to cross the river on foot. It was, as both Nicholas and Alexandra noted in their diaries, a beautiful spring day, "excellent and very warm," the emperor declared.[137]

Yakovlev had arranged a number of halts along the route, to change horses. At noon they stopped at one staging post in Pokrovskoye, where the carts pulled up directly beneath Rasputin's house. His widow, Praskovie, stood in one of the windows, looking down, her daughter Maria at her side. Staring at Alexandra, she carefully made the sign of the cross, then disappeared behind the curtain.[138]

From Pokrovskoye, the convoy continued, Yakovlev uneasily watching the edges of the thick forest for any sign of activity. Along the journey, Yakovlev sent several cables from the empress to the remaining children in Tobolsk; for security, he signed them himself. That afternoon he cabled to Kobylinsky: "Proceeding safely. God bless you. How is the little one?"[139] While he was momentarily away, a peasant approached and asked where the contingent was taking the former emperor. One of the soldiers told him Moscow, to which the man replied, "Glory be to the Lord! To Moscow! That means we will now have order again in Russia."[140]

According to Yakovlev, Nicholas seemed happy enough on the journey, relieved to finally be freed from eight months of captivity behind the wooden stockade surrounding the Governor's House in Tobolsk. He was able to walk while the horses were changed, and Yakovlev ordered his men to leave the emperor alone during these excursions. The empress, Yakovlev noted, was different, "silent, talked to no one, and acted proud and unapproachable." Neither she nor her husband, however, "complained of anything." Yakovlev was "struck by their inherent humbleness."[141]

Late in the afternoon they reached the village of Borki, where the last change of horses took place. As he stepped from his cart, however, Dr. Botkin suddenly collapsed with sharp kidney pains. Yakovlev had to wait while they took him to a nearby house and let him rest in bed for ninety minutes.[142] By twilight, Botkin had recovered sufficiently for them to continue their journey. It was, as Nicholas noted, a lovely, pleasant night, "with a beautiful moon in the sky."[143] Some of the soldiers had tied bells onto the conveyances, and, as they "tore along at wild rate," the empress recorded, the sound of the bells jingled as they flew across the snow-covered landscape.[144]

A few miles outside Tyumen, the contingent of armed soldiers Yakovlev had requested met the group and escorted them into the town. It was dark, past nine at night, when the group finally arrived in Tyumen on April 27. At the Tyumen railroad station, a train, composed of a locomotive, a first-class passenger coach, and three second-class cars, stood waiting along the deserted, heavily guarded siding. Over the next two hours, Yakovlev supervised the transfer of the Romanovs, along with Botkin, Dolgoruky, Chemodurov, Demidova, and Sednev, to the railroad cars, along with the few pieces of luggage they had been allowed to carry with them. He explained that they would wait for morning to leave. Saying he must go off to the telegraph office, he bid the prisoners good night.[145]

What happened over the two days that followed makes sense only if Yakovlev believed his mission was to bring the Romanovs to Moscow. There were two railroad lines to Moscow. One passed directly from Tyumen through Ekaterinburg, and then on to Moscow. The second, southern route, ran from Omsk to the Soviet capital, but it bypassed Ekaterinburg completely. The distance from Tyumen to Ekaterinburg was some two hundred miles; a journey by way of Omsk, followed by a switch to the lower railroad line, involved a delay of several extra days. At the railroad station Yakovlev sent a series of urgent cables. One went to Goloshchokin in Ekaterinburg:

> Your detachments have only the single goal of destroying the baggage. They attempted a number of measures along the route, but my detachment was stronger and they failed. I have a prisoner from the detachment who told me everything. I can't explain all now, but most important is that Zaslavsky concealed himself before I left to avoid arrest, saying that you had summoned him to return to Ekaterinburg. But he set out to attack us, presumably on our train as we approach Ekaterinburg. Did you know about this? I cannot but think you are being deceived, since they mock you in their conversations and belittle you. They have decided that if I don't give them the baggage, they will finish them off, along with me and the entire detachment. I will do all in my power to break these hooligans, but as you know there is a strong feeling in Ekaterinburg which supports destroying the baggage. Do you guarantee preservation of the baggage? Remember, the Sovnarkom stands behind us to keep us safe. I await your reply.[146]

To Sverdlov in Moscow, Yakovlev cabled:

I have only brought part of the baggage here. I want to change the route, due to extremely desperate circumstances. Certain people came to Tobolsk from Ekaterinburg before myself, intent on destroying the baggage. When I first arrived, we barely repulsed an attack and avoided bloodshed. Still, they hinted strongly that the baggage need not be delivered to its destination. I managed to put them off, but they warned me not to sit next to the baggage on the journey. Thus, it was clear they would attempt to destroy it on the route. I naturally sat next to the baggage to ensure its safety. I know that the Ekaterinburg detachments have but one goal—destruction of the baggage. Therefore I had my Chief Guzakov and others guard the entire route from Tobolsk to Tyumen, but the Ekaterinburg detachments have decided to attack us outside Ekaterinburg and massacre us if I do not hand over the baggage. I and Guzakov know this because we heard it directly from a member of the Ekaterinburg detachment who came over to us. With the exception of Goloshchokin, Ekaterinburg has but one goal: to eliminate the baggage no matter what.[147]

To this, Sverdlov replied: "Perhaps you are too nervous? Are the fears exaggerated? Can the old route be taken?" Yakovlev cabled back: "Is it possible to go to Omsk and obtain further instructions there?" Sverdlov replied: "Proceed to Omsk. Telegraph when you arrive. Report to [Vladimir] Kosarev [chairman of the soviet]. Proceed conspiratorially. Further instructions in Omsk."[148]

The word "route" in Yakovlev's cable is given in Russian as *mashrut*, one of two Russian words denoting the English equivalent. *Mashrut* signifies an informal route, with the destination being by implication more important than the way in which it is reached. The word *trassa* describes an actual planned and plotted travel itinerary. When he cabled the sentence "I want to change the route, due to extremely desperate circumstances," Yakovlev was not saying that he meant to change the intended destination, but rather the manner in which he was to reach it. This is an extremely important point, for it clearly indicates that the original destination remained intact. Yakovlev had no confusion about how to proceed until he encountered the Ural Bolsheviks, who presumably informed him that they had been promised possession of the Romanovs in a letter from Sverdlov on April 9. This agreed with the resolution adopted by the VTsIK for publication on April 6, but not with their private resolution of April 1. Yakovlev would have had no reason to question which "route" to take had he not learned of the plans to ambush the convoy and seize and kill the Romanovs. If Moscow had told their extraordinary commissar to simply deliver the Romanovs to Ekaterinburg, there should have been no misunderstandings.

Throughout the enfolding drama, Yakovlev never once acted on his own authority, or made any decision, without consulting with Moscow.

Developments in Ekaterinburg, however, forced Yakovlev to alter his plans. Despite having received assurances from Sverdlov in the public VTsIK decision of April 6, apparently no one in the Ural Regional Soviet believed that Moscow was about to hand over the prisoners as promised. Moscow had little control over the actions of the Ural Regional Soviet; indeed, with only a handful of armed men to assist Yakovlev in the transfer, Moscow was at Ekaterinburg's mercy until the prisoners were safely out of Siberia. Neither Lenin nor Sverdlov dared provoke a conflict with Ekaterinburg on their home territory—a battle the government's forces would almost certainly lose. Deliberate deception became the only alternative if Moscow hoped to bring the Romanovs to the capital without harm.

The change of plan authorized by Moscow meant that Yakovlev and his prisoners would have to travel in a roughly circular manner, doubling back on a lower railroad line to avoid passing through Ekaterinburg. If Ekaterinburg was the intended destination all along, such a measure made no sense. Yakovlev still retained Moscow's full confidence, as evidenced in a cable dispatched by Sverdlov to Vladimir Kosarev, chairman of the Omsk Soviet: "Yakovlev, about whom you have been informed, will arrive in Omsk with baggage. Trust completely. Follow only our orders, no one else's. I place full responsibility on you; proceed with necessary secrecy. Yakovlev acts on our direct orders. Immediately send order up Omsk–Tyumen line to render assistance in every possible way to Yakovlev."[149]

This cable alone demonstrates that Yakovlev's mission continued under Sverdlov's authority, a mission that now involved bringing the Romanovs to Omsk and, presumably from there, to Moscow via the southern railroad line. Sverdlov's cable is important for another reason: his demand that Kosarev "follow only our orders, no one else's" indicates that Moscow was attempting to outmaneuver Ekaterinburg and undermine their authority in Siberia.

After these telegraphic conversations, Yakovlev returned to the train, where he made the mistake of telling Avdayev, who had accompanied him on the journey from Tobolsk, of the change of plan. According to the accounts of both Avdayev and Bykov, Yakovlev was definite in his statement that the destination was to be Moscow.[150] This was reinforced by a certain Count Kapnist, a member of the French military mission in Siberia. He happened, by chance, to travel with the same conductor who had served on Yakovlev's train, and the railroad employee told him that he had overheard conversations between the extraordinary commissar and the emperor that confirmed Moscow as the destination.[151]

Yakovlev's train had left Omsk at five on the morning of Sunday, April 28—Palm Sunday in the Russian Orthodox Church. It slowly steamed out of the railroad station at Tyumen, heading west, toward the Urals. Within two hours, under cover of the creeping dawn, a new engine quietly pulled the railroad cars bearing the Romanovs back through Tyumen, its lights extinguished as it headed east, toward Omsk. When the Romanovs rose, Nicholas looked out his compartment window and noted by the name of the stations they passed that they were heading east. "Where will they take us after Omsk—to Moscow or Vladivostok?" he wrote in his diary. "The commissars said nothing, of course."[152]

The journey was without incident. In an effort to try to learn what was taking place, Nicholas and Alexandra sent Marie, alone, to speak with the Bolshevik soldiers several times, but to no avail.[153] Yakovlev himself spent several hours with the emperor. Two weeks later, in an interview with *Izvestia*, Yakovlev described Nicholas as "noticeably healthier" in the year since his abdication, since he had first encountered him in the Alexander Palace at Tsarskoye Selo. "He has spent a lot of time outside, chopping wood and clearing snow; as a result, his hands are tough, but he is in good spirits, and feels marvelous. I think he's made peace with his present situation." After these lengthy conversations, however, Yakovlev was "surprised at his colossal narrow-mindedness." Alexandra inevitably came across as less sympathetic. "She seems exhausted," he noted, "but tried to conceal it. In general, she remained aloof and proud. She has an enormous influence on her husband. During the entire trip, she remained completely by herself, and did not leave her compartment all day. She did not want to even accept the slightest kindness from us. The corridors in the railway carriage were very narrow, and when two people met, one would have to stand back to allow the other to pass. Alexandra Feodorovna refused to allow us to even do this for her, so she would get up every morning at four or five, to wash and use the lavatory so that she would not encounter a sentry. If she happened to spot one in the corridor, she quickly retreated either back into her compartment, or into the lavatory, locking herself in until the passage was again empty."[154]

Unknown to Yakovlev, before the train left Tyumen, Avdayev had run to the telegraph office, reporting this new development to the Ural Regional Soviet.[155] Ekaterinburg received the news with undisguised horror, and issued orders to all railroad officials between Tyumen and Omsk to stop Yakovlev's train and turn it back toward the Urals. Alexander Beloborodov, the chairman of the Ural Regional Soviet, immediately wired Sverdlov:

> Your Commissar Yakovlev brought Romanov to Tyumen, put him on the train, and headed for Ekaterinburg. Halfway to the next station, he

changed directions and went back. The train with Nicholas is now headed to Omsk. We cannot understand this, and consider it an act of treason. According to your letter of April 9, Nicholas is supposed to come to Ekaterinburg. What is meant by this? The Ural Regional Soviet and the Regional Party Committee have adopted resolutions calling for the train to be diverted at all costs, and to arrest and deliver both Yakovlev and Nicholas to Ekaterinburg. We have no intention of paying attention to the documents Yakovlev might present or cite in his defense, since his actions have shown him to be a criminal, under instructions of some outside force.[156]

Without waiting for a reply, the Presidium of the Ural Regional Soviet openly branded Yakovlev "a traitor to the Revolution," and dispatched further cables to the Omsk Soviet demanding that it stop the train and send the prisoners to Ekaterinburg. Beloborodov also wired a request to Kosarev, the chairman of the Western Siberian Regional Soviet, asking that he send armed troops to the rail junction at Kulominzo outside of Omsk, to arrest Yakovlev and seize the prisoners.[157]

Within a few hours, Ekaterinburg had its answer from Sverdlov, who cabled to Beloborodov: "All that Yakovlev does is according to our direct orders, received from me at 4:00 A.M. Do not issue any orders regarding Yakovlev. Give him your full trust. Do not interfere."[158] The intent of Yakovlev's mission thus remained the same: the delivery of the Romanovs to Moscow.

Ekaterinburg, however, was intent on forcing the issue. Despite having received direct instructions from Sverdlov not to interfere with Yakovlev, and to obey his orders, they simply ignored the Soviet government and proceeded according to their own agenda. On April 28 the Ural Regional Soviet dispatched cables to the railroad stations in Kurgan, Petropavlovsk, Omsk, Chelyabinsk, and half a dozen other cities, demanding that they arrest Yakovlev and his prisoners and transport them all to Ekaterinburg.

As the journey was nearing its end, Yakovlev somehow learned of Ekaterinburg's moves against him, and had his train stopped at Lyubinskaya. It now became a race against time. The Omsk Soviet hastily dispatched a detachment of soldiers to Kulominzo, where the railroad line connected to the southern spur to Chelyabinsk. Yakovlev unhitched the train's engine and, leaving the prisoners in their railroad cars, himself completed the journey to Omsk to speak directly with Sverdlov.[159]

In Omsk, Yakovlev found himself surrounded by "a thick crowd of people" as he made his way to the telegraph office, where he began an intense round of negotiations with Sverdlov.[160] When he cabled Moscow for instructions, Yakovlev received a startling reply: "Return immediately to Tyumen. Have reached understanding with Ural Soviet. They agree to guarantee personal responsibility for the safety of the baggage. Hand over all baggage in Tyumen to the chairman of the Ural Regional Soviet. Your mission remains the same. Ekaterinburg will brief you with details."[161]

This news must have come as a shock to Yakovlev, for he replied: "As always, I will obey your instructions. I will deliver the baggage wherever you say. But it is my duty to warn you again that the danger to the baggage, as both Tyumen and Omsk can confirm, is real. If the baggage is taken by the first route, you won't ever be able to retrieve it safely. There, the baggage will be in danger.[162]

Sverdlov, however, refused to reconsider his decision, and Yakovlev was forced to take the prisoners to Ekaterinburg. What brought about this sudden change? Yakovlev himself was remarkably consistent during his mission. On his way to Tobolsk, in the town itself, to the members of the Special Detachment, to Avdayev, to the railroad conductor, to his own soldiers, to members of the imperial suite and household, and to the prisoners, he was direct, saying that the Romanovs were being taken to Moscow. He may have said more, given the statements about exile from Russia. The frantic exchange of telegrams, and Yakovlev's own efforts to outrun the Ural Bolsheviks, both preclude the possibility that he was simply telling these people what he thought they wanted to hear, when his intention all along was to remove them to Ekaterinburg. This is supported in the two resolutions adopted by the VTsIK: one private, noted in the minutes of the session as "secret" and "not for publication"; and the second, authorizing transfer of the Romanovs to Ekaterinburg, for public dissemination. The truth of Yakovlev's mission was to be concealed until he successfully spirited the prisoners out of reach of the Ural Bolsheviks.

It has been argued that Sverdlov lied to Yakovlev, forcing the extraordinary commissar into an inevitable showdown by pitting his mandate against the more powerful Ekaterinburg forces. In this way Moscow relieved itself of the undoubted problems the presence of the Romanovs would create in the capital, while at the same time either securely stashing them away in a hostile city where they would be diligently guarded against any possible rescue, or deliberately placing them in an environment where their deaths would be inevitable.[163]

Such a hypothesis, however, fails to accord with the evidence. Under such a scenario, Moscow had no need for such elaborate subterfuge, with Yakovlev warned to "proceed conspiratorially" and the Ural Regional Soviet repeatedly warned to follow his orders. Why did Moscow dispatch an extraordinary commissar on a journey that took him and his men across thousands of miles, when the Ural Regional Soviet could have supplied local agents to fulfill the mission?

After handing over the Romanovs, Yakovlev attempted to leave Ekaterinburg, but was prevented from doing so by an armed guard of Ural Bolsheviks who surrounded his train. In response, the extraordinary commissar wired an appeal to Moscow, saying, "I have resigned my mandate, since it cannot be fulfilled. I cannot answer for the consequences."[164] Yakovlev's words are pregnant with importance, indicating that with the Romanovs imprisoned in Ekaterinburg, he could not fulfill his mission. Had that mission been their removal from Tobolsk to the Urals, such an excuse would be inexplicable.

Authorities in Ekaterinburg kept Yakovlev a prisoner for nearly a week, forcing him to explain his actions over and over again. Under such conditions did they present him with a typed statement that, in part, declared that Yakovlev's intent had been the transfer of "the family of the former emperor Nicholas Romanov from Tobolsk to Ekaterinburg," and that the confusion had resulted from the extraordinary commissar's "hasty departure from Moscow," which had left him "unacquainted with all the necessary facts."[165] Yakovlev had little choice but to sign the document, but its contents stand in stark contrast to every statement he had made about his mission. At the mercy of the Ural Regional Soviet, under pressure, and in circumstances that found him a virtual prisoner in Ekaterinburg, Yakovlev's signature cannot be read as a statement of historical fact.

When Yakovlev eventually returned to Moscow, he was received by both Sverdlov and Lenin, and even rewarded, first with a temporary post as an aide to Dzerzhinsky in the offices of the Cheka, and then with a position leading a Red Army battalion on the Ural Front of the Civil War. Clearly, Moscow had no worries as to Yakovlev's reliability, or any quarrel with his actions concerning the Romanovs. Moscow itself was remarkably silent on the entire issue, though this is not surprising, given that revelation of the truth would be tantamount to an admission that Moscow had lost control of the Romanovs to a provincial soviet.

After his telegraphic exchange with Sverdlov, Yakovlev reluctantly returned to the prisoners, informing them of what had transpired. "Omsk Soviet would not let us pass Omsk, and feared one wished to take us to Japan," Alexandra noted in her diary.[166] As the train turned around and steamed back toward Ekaterinburg, the emperor walked into the compartment occupied by Paul Matveyev. He saw a piece of black bread from the table, grabbed it, then quickly apologized. Matveyev told him that it was stale, but Nicholas, as he recalled, continued to chew the dry crust, "more out of frustration than anything else." After a few moments he broke his silence, and asked Matveyev, "Is it definitely settled that we will remain in Ekaterinburg?" When Matveyev replied that it seemed to have been decided, Nicholas said quietly, "I would have gone anywhere but to the Urals. Judging from the papers, the workers there are bitterly hostile to me."[167]

Yakovlev's train arrived in the capital of the Urals at 8:40 A.M. on Tuesday, April 30, 1918, and slowly pulled to a stop at the main Ekaterinburg Station. It was a brilliant, cloudless day, warm and full of the promise of the approaching summer.[168] Yakovlev lowered the windows of his compartment to see "an immense crowd, hundreds of faces, all agitated," swept up in "threats and shouts, repeated over and over again." A cordon of local Bolshevik sentries had been hastily arranged, but "they made no effort to keep the crowd away, and gradually it advanced toward us." As they surged forward, there were angry screams: "We ought to hang them here!" and "We finally have them in our hands!" Even the stationmaster himself cried, "Yakovlev! Come out! Show us the Romanovs and let me spit in their filthy faces!"[169]

Confronted with this scene, all of Yakovlev's worst fears were suddenly confirmed. He quickly ordered his soldiers to ring the train with an armed guard, all the while shouting, "Grab the machine guns!" Hearing this, the mob began to retreat in fear.[170]

At that moment an open motorcar rumbled up the station, bearing three men: Alexander Beloborodov, chairman of the Ural Regional Soviet; Isaac Goloshchokin, the Ural Regional military commissar; and Boris Didkovsky, Beloborodov's assistant. They quickly made their way through the crowd and entered the rattling train.[171]

Over the next three hours, the simmering conflict between Yakovlev and the Ekaterinburg authorities finally erupted. Yakovlev insisted that he be allowed to proceed to Moscow, saying that the mob scene he had just witnessed proved that the Ural Regional Soviet could not control the situation.[172] The Romanovs, forbidden to open their shades, or look out of their compartment windows, listened as the confrontation escalated into a "violent quarrel" amid threats and angry shouts.[173]

While this continued, the mob reassembled, their threats once again drowning out the shouts between Yakovlev and the Ural Bolsheviks. Sensing that they were indeed about to lose control of the situation, Beloborodov ordered Yakovlev's train to pull out of the main station and proceed to Ekaterinburg II, the goods depot two miles west of the city, which could be more easily guarded.[174]

At Ekaterinburg II, the entire area had been surrounded, as Avdayev recalled, by "a heavily armed detachment of Red Army soldiers." Here, another fight ensued, as Yakovlev made one last attempt to proceed to Moscow.[175] The train, and its precious cargo, sat in the middle of the siding for another three hours, as Alexandra noted in her diary.[176] Finally a detachment of armed Ural Bolsheviks arrived and, on Beloborodov's orders, surrounded the train. Yakovlev was told to hand

Yakovlev delivering the Romanovs to the Ural Bolsheviks on April 30, 1918. From a painting by
Chelyin. The original hung in Demidova's former room in the Museum of the People's Vengeance.

over his prisoners, or face an ambush at the hands of the superior
Ekaterinburg forces.[177] "Yakovlev had to give us over to the Ural
Regional Soviet," the empress wrote bitterly in her diary.[178]

Beloborodov forced Yakovlev to formally sign over custody of the
prisoners, in a receipt that itemized the prisoners:

> On April 30, 1918, I, the undersigned Chairman of the Ural Regional
> Soviet of Workmen's, Peasants' and Soldiers' Deputies, Alexander
> Beloborodov, received from the Extraordinary Commissar of the All-
> Russian Central Executive Committee, Vassili Vassilievich Yakovlev,
> the following persons, transferred from the town of Tobolsk: (1) The
> former Ruler Nicholas Alexandrovich Romanov; (2) the former tsaritsa,
> Alexandra Feodorovna Romanova; (3) the former Grand Duchess
> Marie Nikolaievna Romanova—all of them to be kept under guard in
> the town of Ekaterinburg.[179]

At four that afternoon, Beloborodov entered the coach where
Nicholas, Alexandra, and Marie had remained hidden throughout the
long fracas. He introduced himself, and told the prisoners that Moscow
had ordered the Romanovs detained in Ekaterinburg until a trial for the
former emperor could be arranged. He told them to gather their luggage and follow him outside, explaining that those who had accompanied them from Tobolsk, as well as the remainder of the baggage, would
follow later that same day.[180]

Nicholas came out of the carriage first, wearing an officer's greatcoat from which the epaulettes had been removed. Alexandra and Marie
Nikolaievna followed, in dark Persian lamb coats and hats and carrying
small valises. Beloborodov directed them to the side of the clearing,

where two open cars waited. Nicholas climbed into the rear of the first, followed by Alexandra and her daughter. Beloborodov himself sat in the front seat next to Parfen Samokhavlov, the driver dispatched from the Ural Regional Soviet's military garage. Avdayev, Goloshchokin, and Didkovsky followed in the second motorcar.[181]

The convoy set off down the roadway, followed by an open truck whose bed was filled with Bolshevik soldiers "armed to their teeth," as Alexandra noted.[182] They drove through the deserted back streets of the city until they arrived at their destination, a large house belonging to a retired engineer, Nicholas Ipatiev, which had been commandeered only two days earlier.[183] The Ural Regional Soviet surrounded the property with a ten-foot-high wooden stockade, and whitewashed the windows; ominously, they renamed the mansion "The House of Special Purpose."[184] Walking ahead of the trio as they climbed from the motorcar, a triumphant Goloshchokin opened the front door and, turning to the Romanovs, gestured with his hand, saying, "Citizen Romanov, you may enter."[185]

Within half an hour, a second convoy pulled up before the Ipatiev House and delivered the remainder of those who were to be allowed to share the Romanovs' captivity. This included Dr. Botkin, Anna Demidova, Terenty Chemodurov, and Ivan Sednev. Prince Vassili Dolgoruky was not among them; he had been arrested at the station, accused of plotting to free the Romanovs, and was incarcerated in Ekaterinburg City Prison.[186]

With the arrival of Botkin, Demidova, Chemodurov, and Sednev came a truck loaded with baggage—valises, cases, and steamer trunks—belonging to the Romanovs. "As the Emperor's family had gone from an eighteen-room house in Tobolsk to a five-room flat in Ekaterinburg," recalled Avdayev, "Comrade Didkovsky and I had to examine their luggage to see what would be allowed into the house, and what could be stored in exterior sheds, as space was limited." As the two men examined the contents of each case, Avdayev noted "fur coats; knives, swords, and ceremonial daggers; and several sets of binoculars." All of the weaponry, as well as the binoculars, were confiscated under the watchful eyes of the prisoners. Alexandra immediately protested, whispering to Botkin, who kept repeating, "But Kerensky allowed that in!"[187]

Alexandra continued to fight, and Nicholas, seeing her agitation, himself became increasingly irate, walking up and down the room and muttering, "This is damnable! Thus far, we have had polite treatment, and men who behaved like gentlemen, but now—"[188] He was interrupted by Didkovsky: "I ask you to remember that you are all under investigation and arrest."[189]

There were other altercations. When told that they would no

longer be addressed by their former titles, neither Nicholas nor Marie, Avdayev recalled, "seemed to care about the change, but Alexandra Feodorovna exploded, demanding to know why this was now so. I explained to her that the Revolution had swept away the use of such false vanities." When she attempted to protest in English to Botkin, Avdayev informed her that no foreign languages were to be spoken inside their new prison.[190]

Before she left Tobolsk, Alexandra wrote to her friend Anna Vyrubova of what the future held. "The atmosphere around us is fairly electrified. We feel that a storm is approaching, but we know that God is merciful and will care for us. . . . Though we know that the storm is coming nearer and nearer, our souls are at peace. Whatever happens will be through God's will."[191]

3

The House of Special Purpose

STRETCHED ON THE EASTERN SLOPE of the Ural Mountains, the city of Ekaterinburg rose and fell across a series of low hills, mirrored in low-lying lakes fringed by dark forests of pine and birch. Just under fifty miles east of the continental border separating European Russia from Asia, it was a city of great contrasts: wealth and poverty; mansions and squalid hovels; joyous abandon and discontent—a mirror of the former empire itself. Capped by a flat, pale sky hung with thick clouds of black, industrial smoke, Ekaterinburg hovered precariously between hope and despair on that early spring day in 1918 when the train carrying the Romanovs arrived at the goods depot on the outskirts of the city.

Ekaterinburg was the most important city in the Ural Mountains. Founded in 1721, it took its name from Catherine, second wife of Peter the Great, and the first woman to rule Russia as empress in her own right after the death of her husband. In the eighteenth century, intrepid miners first discovered rich deposits of gold, platinum, and silver; marble, porphyry, malachite, jasper, and lapis lazuli; and immense supplies of iron ore and coal, all in the surrounding hills. This mineral wealth transformed the burgeoning city into a vast industrial center. By the beginning of the twentieth century the Ekaterinburg region boasted forty gold and platinum mines, five ironworks plants, and nearly a hundred mining operations devoted to precious and semiprecious stones.[1] Before the Revolution, these mines produced fully 90 percent of the world's platinum.[2]

Unlike most Siberian cities, Ekaterinburg possessed a large industrial base, drawn from local peasants who toiled in the city's factories and mines. The most important of these were the Zlokazov and Verkh-Isetsk factories, in the suburbs of Ekaterinburg, and the Syssert Mining Works, some ten miles beyond the city, which produced cast iron, marble, and gold.[3] The headquarters of the Ural Mining Institute was situated here, along with a mining chemical laboratory; the Imperial School of Mining; the State Mint; and the Imperial Lapidary.[4]

The discovery of these resources quickly distinguished Ekaterinburg from other early settlements in Siberia, and the town flourished. By the beginning of the twentieth century, Ekaterinburg was the fastest-growing town in Siberia, with some eighty thousand residents. Wealthy merchants sponsored improvements to their town: elegant avenues, shaded with lime and linden trees, were laid out, and a large municipal garden skirted the Lower Iset Pond, lying in the foothills. In the 1880s, electricity arrived, with noisy tramways and telephone exchanges.[5] The city was sufficiently important to possess consulates for the United States, Switzerland, Germany, Sweden, Denmark, France, and Great Britain, the latter two housed in elaborate little buildings on Voznesensky Prospekt, near the center of town.[6]

Pierre Pascal, a French lieutenant who passed several days in Ekaterinburg in May 1918, was not impressed. "This city," he wrote, "is, in reality, a village. A few factories. A lot of Chinese, soldiers and workers. It is something less than luxurious."[7] There was undoubtedly something exotic about the city: "Ekaterinburg," wrote New York journalist Carl Ackerman, "does not resemble any American city I know, because the streets are at least twice as wide as any of our broadest thoroughfares. The buildings differ in architecture from ours and none of them is more than two or three stories high. Often, in riding about the city, one finds beautiful modern buildings and residences next door to frame huts."[8]

The main railroad station, at the northern edge of the town, had been built in 1878. "I do not know any railway station in Russia proper that can compare with that of Ekaterinburg," wrote one foreign visitor, "just where Siberia really begins, in all its arrangements for the traveling public and especially in the equipment of its restaurants and dining rooms, where every comfort in the way of good food and good service is provided for the traveler, and French and German are freely spoken."[9] From the station square flowed Voznesensky Prospekt, a broad, three-mile-long roadway that ran in a straight line through the town. "On arrival at the station one saw wooden one-storey houses," recalled British consul Thomas Preston, "but as you approached the center of the town you were pleasantly surprised to see big and spacious mansions, the homes of gold and platinum miners and rich merchants, situated in picturesque garden settings." In contrast to Pascal, he concluded, "Ekaterinburg could compare favorably with any towns of similar size in Western Europe."[10]

For all its rough edges, Ekaterinburg was careful to present a refined public face: in summer, the broad avenues and city parks were shaded with birch, aspen, alder, and poplar trees, and brass bands played in rose-covered pergolas stretched along the edges of wide expanses of mown lawns, or the stone quays of Lower Iset Pond. Resources from the surrounding mines took visible form in the richly decorated, Empire- and neo-Baroque-style villas and mansions of the city's merchants and mineral kings, their rough-brick walls hidden beneath plaster veneers pierced with arched double windows of expensive plate glass and topped with curved, cast-iron roofs topped with decorative finials.[11]

A mile down Voznesensky Prospekt from the main rail station was Voznesensky Square, named after the blue-and-white Baroque Cathedral of the Ascension that stood in its center, its five-storied spire dominating the city's skyline. This was the most fashionable neighborhood for the city's wealthy merchants and industrialists.[12] The immense Kharitonov Palace, with its string of neoclassical columned porticos, filled the northern side of the square, facing the equally magnificent Demidov Mansion, built by an industrial family who rose to great prominence in the first years of the city's life.[13]

On the outskirts of the city, shielded from its bustling streets and noisy electric trams, was the Novotikhvinsky Monastery and Convent, one of the largest religious complexes in all of Siberia. In addition to the cathedral and a separate chapel, there was the monastery itself; a convent; almshouse; hospital; convent school; the ecclesiastical school; the orphanage; the art studio; and an extensive agricultural works. According to William Bury, who visited the complex in 1912, it was "a most imposing group of buildings, stretching along an extended front, with cupolas, spires, and pinnacles, and is much frequented by pilgrims from far and near who come to pray in its chapel before a famous icon."[14]

Bury visited Novotikhvinsky during rehearsal for the "Te Deum" celebrating the emperor's birthday. He was drawn to the cathedral, through the open doors of which floated the melodies of the choir inside, "the most beautiful thing I had ever heard from women's voices."[15] At the conclusion of the service, Bury was introduced to the young deacon, Vassili Afanasievich Buimirov, "a remarkably good-looking man, with a wonderfully rich voice," who, six years later, would help conduct services for the Romanovs in the Ipatiev House. Bury learned that Buimirov had given up a burgeoning career in the opera to join the church; asked if he ever regretted his decision, the deacon answered, "Oh, well, of course I missed things at first, but I'm gradually getting used to it." Later, with a smile, Abbess Magdelena confided to

Bury that, "sometimes, from the way he offered the incense," she wondered if he still fancied himself on the stage.[16]

On the eve of World War I, Empress Alexandra's sister Princess Victoria of Battenberg passed through Ekaterinburg and left an ominous account of her visit: "I did not think the town attractive and the population did not seem particularly pleased at the official visit. I noticed it especially at an evening entertainment of fireworks, where the crowd was quite unenthusiastic."[17] As she drove past Voznesensky Square, the princess noticed a jumble of wooden huts, mingled with a scattering of gnarled birches and pleached linden trees, spread along the western side of the broad avenue. And, in their midst, poised at the edge of the hillside, a large villa: it belonged, the princess was told, to a local merchant.[18]

This was the home of Nicholas Nikolaievich Ipatiev, a forty-eight-year-old former captain in the Army Corps of Engineers, and his wife, Marie. Born in St. Petersburg, Ipatiev attended the Nikolaievsky Engineering School before graduating from the Military Engineering Academy. At the turn of the century he moved to Ekaterinburg, where he served as engineering director at the Ural Mining Institute. Ipatiev rose to great prominence in the city, where he served as a member of the Ekaterinburg Duma and chaired a number of important committees. After his retirement he invested the bulk of his fortune in two local mining enterprises, which proved successful and provided him with a steady income.[19]

In 1908 Ipatiev purchased the large house that stood at the corner of Voznesensky Prospekt and Voznesensky Lane from a local merchant named Charaviev, the same man who in 1897 had built it.[20] In 1918 it was one of the finest private residences in Ekaterinburg. Ipatiev ordered the main floor of the house completely redecorated and the latest technologies installed, including new plumbing and a system of call bells for his servants, who occupied a few rooms on the lower, ground floor. He planned to use a three-room suite at the southern end of the ground floor—a hallway with a separate entrance door to the lane, a small room with a vaulted ceiling, and a storeroom—as his offices, but he never got around to furnishing them.

The Ipatiev House stood at 49 Voznesensky Prospekt, along the crest of a gently sloping hillside directly across from the Cathedral of the Ascension. The property covered this slope, which fell away from the square toward the Lower Iset Pond, a quarter mile down the hill. Viewed from Voznesensky Square, the eastern facade of the Ipatiev House appeared to be only a single story, built atop a raised basement. But at the sides and rear, where the hillside fell away from the prospekt, this basement gradually exposed itself as a full two stories. Voznesensky Prospekt, some five feet higher than the Ipatiev House, was separated by a steep bank and a narrow, secondary roadway marked by a small, ornate shrine dedicated to St. Nicholas, its onion dome crowned with a burnished Orthodox cross.[21] Ominously, in view of what was to transpire within its walls, the house not only bore the name of Ipatiev, an echo of the beginnings of the Romanov Dynasty in 1613 at the Ipatiev Monastery, but also had been built atop the ruins of the first Voznesensky Church and its seventeenth-century cemetery.[22]

One man, who visited the Ipatiev House in the early 1920s, wrote that it "was distinguished from buildings of more provincial design, and would not have disgraced itself, but rather would have fit in well, with the houses in the aristocratic quarters of Moscow or St. Petersburg."[23] Constructed of brick and stone and covered in plaster whitewash, the Ipatiev House was a mixture of elaborate, late Empire style with stucco ornaments, pilasters, carved cornices and lintels, decorative iron railings, and curved attic dormer windows sunk deep into the green iron roof, modeled on medieval Russian architecture. A wide flight of six granite steps led to the double doors facing Voznesensky Square. Heavy batten gates, set between stone piers in an archway topped with iron railing, opened to a courtyard at the northern end of the property, edged by a two-story carriage house; a bathhouse; a storage shed; a pergola overlooking the gardens; and a small cottage for the servants which, during the Romanovs' imprisonment, became a guardhouse. A second entrance, on the southern side of the house, opened to Voznesensky Lane.[24] At the rear of the property, a double balcony, its floors linked by an exterior staircase, overlooked the garden, a steep

Voznesensky Prospekt in the 1890s. The Hotel Amerika stands in the left foreground of this photograph. In the distance is the spire of Voznesensky Cathedral. Directly across the street from the cathedral is the rounded roof of the old Voznesensky Church, which stands on the future location of the Ipatiev House.

plot of land shaded by linden, birch, poplar, and fir trees. From the pergola, arbors covered with roses, lilac, and acacia provided relief from the summer sun and views to the Lower Iset Pond.[25]

The front doors of the Ipatiev House led to the floral-papered foyer, where a wide flight of stone stairs rose from the level of the street to the main floor between balusters and railings of carved oak.[26] From the landing, a set of white, paneled double doors

The main entrance of the Ipatiev House, showing the inner palisade where it attached to the wall.

opened to an anteroom, while a jib door, nearly concealed in the thick pattern of the wallpaper, opened to a secondary hallway. The floor here was covered in wide pine boards, the walls hung with a subtly striped paper; the secondary staircase, between two windows and enclosed by a balustrade of turned wooden spindles and oak posts, descended to the floor below. At the rear of the hall was the lavatory, its linoleum floor cracked from the constant drip of the exposed pipes; and the bathroom, with a large enamel tub, and stove and copper steam boiler to heat the water.[27]

Ipatiev's former study had become the commandant's room. Above the carved oak wainscot, the walls were hung with a wine-colored paper

A view of the back and side of the Ipatiev House, looking along Voznesensky Lane. The arched window of the murder room is visible next to the side entrance with an awning.

stamped with golden palm fronds; from the center of the ceiling hung a silver Art Nouveau–style chandelier. The furniture was sparse: below a mounted stag's head, a low sofa, with tapestry-covered bolsters, was used by Moshkin, the commandant's assistant, as a bed; a mahogany bookshelf with glass-fronted doors; a few chairs; and a table, covered in green oilcloth and piled with two small lamps, a gramophone, ashtrays, and a stack of writing paper headed "Commandant of the House of Special Purpose of the Ural Soviet Committee."[28]

Beyond the anteroom and study, double doors opened to the drawing room, and an adjoining sitting room separated by a wide, open arch with carved and gilded coffers. This was the most elaborate room in the house, the white wainscot carved with beading picked out in gilt; the walls covered in light gray, brown, and white oak leaf cluster patterned paper; and heavily carved and gilded cornices stretching to the deep coves of the ceiling. In one corner, a stove of decorative faience tiles stood next to a mahogany piano; above the parquet floor hung an electrified crystal and ormolu chandelier, purchased in Italy by Nicholas Ipatiev. The room reflected the Ipatievs' wealth and bourgeois values, filled with expensive furniture of carved oak upholstered in velvet brocades. In the adjoining sitting room there was a large writing desk, several bookshelves, an étagère filled with porcelain, and an ornate suite of rococo-revival chairs and sofa, gilded and covered in gold damask.[29]

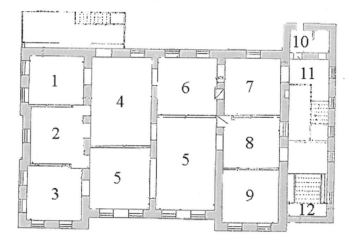

A floor plan of the upper level of the Ipatiev House: 1. The room used by maid Anna Demidova. 2. The bedroom of the four grand duchesses. 3. The bedroom of the emperor and empress, shared with their son, Alexei. 4. The dining room. 5. The two halves of the drawing room, separated by an archway, as seen in Figure 21. 6. The main stair hall. 7. The kitchen. 8. The general anteroom. 9. The commandant's study or office, used by both Avdayev and Yurovsky. 10. The bathroom and lavatory. 11. The secondary stair hall. 12. The vestibule and front outer doors.

The study, drawing room, and sitting room all overlooked Voznesensky Square; on the western side, facing the garden and distant Lower Iset Pond, were three further rooms, including the kitchen, with a large wood-burning stove and enamel sink; and the stair hall, its staircase closed off by doors in a wood and plaster partition. During the Romanovs' imprisonment, the doors on both the ground floor and in the stair hall above were locked, to prevent the prisoners from using them and to preclude access by the guards.[30]

The large dining room was lit by two tall windows, one of which opened onto the covered balcony and connected to the terrace below by the narrow, exterior staircase; before the Romanovs arrived, this door was locked and covered with a rug. As an important businessman, Ipatiev frequently entertained, and the room's dark, carved oak wainscot; crimson-and-gold-patterned wallpaper; and expensive, four-light brass and crystal chandelier reflected his prosperity. The furniture was oppressive and ornate—a pier glass decorated with black marble panels; an elaborately carved buffet; and the oak table and matching chairs upholstered in leather—and the room's grandeur was reflected in the variegated marble mantel carved with scrolls, bunches of grapes, oak leaf clusters, and cherubs.[31]

The last three rooms on the main floor were ranged along the southern end of the house. At the southwestern corner was a bedroom, with wine-colored floral carpet and white plaster walls. Although its western wall formed one side of the balcony, there was no entrance or exit from this room other than the double doors from the dining room. Opposite these, two tall, double-glazed windows, set within a single frame, overlooked Voznesensky Lane.

The middle room, lit by a single, tall arched window, had originally served as a dressing room; when the prisoners arrived, it became the grand duchesses' bedroom. If the heavy, masculine atmosphere of the study, drawing room, and dining room reflected the taste of Nicholas Ipatiev, this and the adjoining corner bedroom mirrored that of his wife. Two corner stoves warmed the room, with its parquet floor and walls covered in pink, red, and green floral paper. The furnishings, too, were simpler: in one corner stood a tall pier glass, with a table, bookcase, and several Biedermeier and Bentwood chairs scattered across the Oriental carpet. A fire screen, painted with flowers, stood in front of one of the stoves. From the ceiling hung another of Ipatiev's Italian purchases: an electric chandelier, decorated with clusters of green bronze leafs and three handblown, tulip-shaped shades of red and white Venetian glass.[32]

The main bedroom occupied the southeastern corner; its four tall windows, draped with tulle curtains sewn with lace roses, made it the brightest room in the house. It also was the most isolated room on the main floor, and could be reached only through the dining room and the adjacent dressing room. Walls covered in pale yellow and white striped paper and topped with a painted frieze of pansies and irises reflected the feminine influence. From the center of the ceiling hung an Art Nouveau–style bronze chandelier, with hanging frosted glass globes; below, the parquet floor was covered with a red, green, and yellow floral carpet. A baize-topped writing table; étagère filled with porcelain, books, and plants; mahogany dressing table with an oval mirror; overstuffed armchair upholstered in velvet brocade; bookcase; and a few Biedermeier chairs with embroidered cushions comprised the majority of the room's furnishings. Against the northern wall stood a marble-topped vanity with a washbasin; a tall mahogany wardrobe; and two bedsteads, pushed back into the corner.[33]

The ground floor of the Ipatiev House contained another fourteen rooms, including a second kitchen; a bathroom; lavatory with toilet; several rooms for servants; and the suite of three rooms ranged along the southern end of the house that Ipatiev had originally intended to use as his new offices, reached from Voznesensky Lane through a doorway set beneath an ornate wrought iron canopy. Most of the rooms, however, were bare, used only for storage.[34]

When the emperor, empress, and grand duchess Marie arrived at the Ipatiev House on April 30, 1918, they were given five rooms for

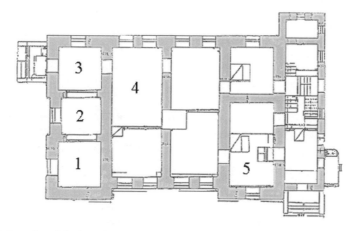

A floor plan of the lower level of the Ipatiev House: 1. The storeroom behind the murder room. 2. The murder room. 3. The corridor/entryway with the side door leading to Voznesensky Lane and a back window overlooking the garden. From here, Ivan Kleshchev watched the murders. 4. The guards' dayroom. On the night of the murders, Alexander Strekotin was on guard duty here. 5. The room occupied by Rudolf Lacher, from which he later claimed to have witnessed the dead Romanovs carried out of the house—a real impossibility.

their daily use. Nicholas, Alexandra, and their daughter took the large corner bedroom, with Demidova on a cot in the dining room, and Botkin and the two male servants lodged on cots and mattresses in the drawing room and its adjoining sitting room.[35] Nicholas described the new prison as "nice and clean," though he noted the tall wooden palisade and string of sentries that surrounded the walls of the house.[36]

If the Ipatiev House was not particularly large, its ornate wallpapers, Oriental carpets, parquet floors, and elaborate furnishings at least offered the illusion of comfort. In a letter written to Zenaide Tolstoy on May 17, and smuggled from the Ipatiev House by a friendly member of the guard, Marie described it as "small, but nice."[37] On that first afternoon in the Ipatiev House, on the window frame of what was to become her last bedroom, Alexandra scrawled a swastika, her favorite good-luck symbol, and penciled the date: 17/30 April, 1918.[38]

With the former emperor, his wife, and one of their daughters safely installed in the Ipatiev House, the Ural Regional Soviet celebrated their victory. That night, the windows of the Hotel Amerika on Voznesensky Prospekt blazed with light. Beneath the elaborate wrought iron and glass canopy shielding the lobby doors of the three-story brick building, Bolshevik sailors, armed with grenades and pistols, menacingly halted those who tried to enter, arresting anyone who aroused their displeasure.[39] The marble halls and gilded reception rooms, decorated with columns of malachite and jasper from the Urals and hung with crystal chandeliers, witnessed a motley parade of soldiers, Chekists, and members of the Red Guard who climbed the staircase and disappeared into room 3 on the hotel's main floor. Through the blue haze of cigarette smoke, a dozen men sprawled in gilded armchairs around a large, Empire-style table, discussing the imperial family.[40]

The men gathered in room 3 were tired, faces unshaven and eyes red from lack of sleep and too much alcohol. At their head sat Alexander Beloborodov, chairman of the Presidium of the Ural Regional Soviet, a tall, thin man with pale features and a receding hairline. Born in 1891, the son of a factory worker, Beloborodov quit school at age twelve to apprentice as a electrician, but soon found the conditions deplorable. At sixteen he joined the Ural Consortium of Electricians, taking odd jobs in area factories before landing a steady position at the Nazedzhdinsky factory; that same year, he joined the Bolshevik Party and became involved in their underground network. A year later, at seventeen, he was arrested for distributing seditious propaganda and sentenced to forty years in prison. After four years, however, he was set free, moved to the Urals, married, and settled in Perm to raise his family. White General Michael Deterikhs described him as "a typical Bolshevik, of middle Russian proletarian stock, not especially clever, not especially grammatical in speech, not original in ideas, but strong in belief."[41]

Despite Beloborodov's position as chairman, the most powerful member of the Ural Regional Soviet, and the only man with substantial ties to the authorities in Moscow, was Philip Goloshchokin. Born in 1876 in Vitebsk, Goloshchokin eventually moved to St. Petersburg, where he studied at the Imperial School of Dentistry; ironically, one of his lecturers served as the court dentist to Nicholas and Alexandra.[42] In 1903 Goloshchokin left the

The commissars of the Ural Regional Soviet. From left: Alexander Beloborodov, Georgy Safarov, Philip Goloshchokin.

school and spent a year wandering aimlessly in the imperial capital. During the Russo-Japanese War of 1904–1905, he joined the Bolshevik Party, and quickly gained a reputation for fierce revolutionary activity. In 1906, following a revolt of sailors at the naval base of Kronstadt, he was arrested by Okhrana agents and sentenced to two years in the grim Schlusselburg Fortress.[43]

Released in 1907, Goloshchokin remained free for less than a year before being arrested again for revolutionary activities. This time he managed to elude authorities and fled to Europe but, like so many émigrés, longed for his homeland and returned to Russia in 1909, where he was quickly arrested and sentenced to hard labor in a Siberian prison camp. His tenure there was brief: after less than a year he escaped, was caught, and managed to escape again, eventually taking up residence in Switzerland, where he met Lenin and other Bolshevik leaders. In 1912, while still in exile, Goloshchokin attended a Party conference in Prague and was elected a member of the Bolshevik Central Executive Committee.[44] Sent back to Russia by the Central Committee, he helped organize a Bolshevik cell in Moscow that the authorities soon discovered. On this, the occasion of his fifth arrest, Goloshchokin's luck did not hold: he was sent to a heavily guarded prison camp in the grim Turukhansk Region.[45]

It was here that he met Yakov Sverdlov, and the two men formed a close bond, "linked not only by common views but also by personal friendship," as Sverdlov's wife later wrote.[46] Both men were freed from Turukhansk in February 1917 and quickly became leading members of the Bolshevik Party. In November, while serving as a Ural delegate at the Bolshevik Party Congress of Soviets in Petrograd, Goloshchokin renewed his acquaintance with Lenin who, on the strength of Sverdlov's recommendation, appointed him as Ural Regional Soviet Military Commissar.[47] The Central Executive Committee had good cause to keep vigilant watch on their Ekaterinburg comrades even at this early stage, fearing provincial rebellion at a time when Lenin's power was not yet consolidated. Once installed in Ekaterinburg, Goloshchokin was derisively called "the eyes of the Kremlin" by his fellow Ural Bolsheviks.[48]

Goloshchokin's character was tempered by his experiences. The virulently anti-Bolshevik journalist Robert Wilton, correspondent for the *Times* of London, described Goloshchokin as "a homicidal sadist. He never attended executions, but insisted upon hearing a detailed account of them. He huddled in bed shivering and quaking till the executioner came with his report, and would listen to his description of tortures with a frenzy of joy, begging for further details, gloating over the expressions, gestures and death throes of the victims as they passed before his diseased vision."[49] Such a literary flight of fancy, however, is without foundation. In fact, Goloshchokin seems to have been a rather thoughtful man, a firm believer in the Revolution and the necessity for state terror, but one who, like Lenin, valued reason over passion. This cautious approach, in fact, helped Goloshchokin win his position in Ekaterinburg; with his cold, calculating political mind, Lenin would scarcely have sent a sadistic, bloodthirsty tyrant who reveled in the personal sufferings of others to manage the crucial task of directing the Bolshevik war effort in the Urals.

If Beloborodov and Goloshchokin were somewhat circumspect in their behavior, with reasoned ideological pursuits, the same could not be said for a third man at the table, Peter Ermakov. Born in 1884 in the Ekaterinburg suburb of Verkh-Isetsk, he launched his career as a terrorist during the 1905 Revolution, when he joined the Bolshevik Party and began a series of robberies intended to help fund the movement. He stole horses, robbed trains and banks, and acted as a sort of latter-day highwayman; in 1911, following his raid on the treasury of the Verkh-Isetsk factory, he was arrested for the murder of the night watchman, whose head he had brutally sawed off.[50] For this Ermakov was sentenced to hard labor in a Siberian

Peter Ermakov.

prison camp. In 1917, following the February Revolution and the Provisional Government's general amnesty, he was released from prison and returned to his home in Verkh-Isetsk, where he received a hero's welcome. In October 1917 he became military commissar of Verkh-Isetsk and presided over the large Bolshevik contingent attached to the factory there.[51]

Ermakov was a dedicated revolutionary, a man dedicated to his role as an agent of the local Extraordinary Commission for Combating Counterrevolution and Sabotage, the dreaded Cheka. Founded by Lenin's comrade Felix Dzerzhinsky, the Cheka never pretended that their work was confined to arrests; it extended to terror and even murder, but it was murder justified in the name of the state. Led by Feodor Lukoyanov, the Ekaterinburg Cheka included Ermakov; Yakov Yurovsky; Gregory Nikulin; and Michael Medvedev, who went by his Party name of Kudrin. These men were intimidating, with hardened faces, menacing eyes, and belts of ammunition thrown over the shoulders of their leather coats. Yet they also attracted a good deal of loyal devotion and even worship. In speaking of Yurovsky, Nikulin, and Ermakov—all men who participated in the murder of the Romanovs—one Ekaterinburg woman later said quite happily: "I have made love to all three of them! It is not in the fashion of professors and bourgeois now—we proletarian girls make love with whomever we admire! The Chekists are the best, always elegant, always generous. They entertain you, give you presents, take you to the theater, they are without equal. It is especially enjoyable for your body to be caressed with the strong clean hands that fired the shots. They are most knowledgeable in the arts of love, and often give pointers to the young graduates of the Red Army School."[52]

If Beloborodov and Goloshchokin provided Ekaterinburg's brains, it was Ermakov who happily drenched the Urals in blood. "His hands itched to kill," one man recalled. This blood lust earned him the nickname of "Comrade Mauser."[53] In appearance, Ermakov was striking. Tall and broadly built, with a unkempt mane of black hair and dark eyes, he glowered when he spoke. He took pride in his position as military commissar, and in his work for the Cheka, though his menacing and wild appearance owed much to his perpetual drunken stupor.

Wherever Ermakov went, he was inevitably accompanied by his close friends and confidants the brothers Victor and Stephan Vaganov, the latter described by one acquaintance as "a hooligan and very much a tramp."[54] Ermakov also had a special Verkh-Isetsk detachment, composed of Red Army soldiers and members of the Cheka, with which he terrorized the city: after the Romanov executions, these men would be called on to help transport the corpses.[55]

One member of the Ural Regional Soviet, Peter Voikov, stood apart from his comrades. Born in 1888 into a solidly middle-class family of schoolteachers, Voikov was raised in a house where education was prized above all other virtues. In Voikov's case, this quest for knowledge led him at an early age to revolutionary pamphlets: when he was just eleven, Voikov was expelled from grammar school when he attempted to incite his fellow students to riot. After joining the Bolshevik Party in 1903 at age fifteen, Voikov moved to St. Petersburg to attend the Imperial Mining Institute. During the 1905 Revolution, his activities forced him to flee into European exile to avoid a lengthy prison sentence. Voikov lived first in Paris, where he completed his secondary education, then in Geneva, where he graduated with honors from the university. In exile, his life was far different from that of the usual revolutionary: Voikov married the daughter of a wealthy Polish factory owner, and the two lived in considerable comfort from her family's money. After the February Revolution he returned to Russia, moving to Ekaterinburg, where he intended to put his training as a mining engineer to use; instead, he quickly became involved in local politics, first as a member of the Ekaterinburg City Soviet and, in January 1918, as the Ural Regional Soviet's commissar of supplies.[56]

Voikov was tall and thin, with dark blond hair, pale blue eyes, and a dashing little mustache that—even amid the revolutionary turmoil of the Civil War—he carefully kept waxed and curled at the ends. One Ekaterinburg resident later called him "very pleasant," noting that he "from time to time would throw out a bon mot in Latin or English," and that he liked to wear "heavy eye powders like the girls. He was trained as an actor, and could alter his manner and voice in several ways."[57]

A fifth man destined to play a part in the final drama of the Romanovs was Serge Lyukhanov, born in 1875 in a small peasant village in Chelyabinsk Province. Having quit school after the fourth grade to work in a local factory, Lyukhanov held a number of industrial positions in the Urals before moving to Chelyabinsk, where he worked as a telephone station technician for the Pokrovsky Brothers Company; in off-hours he acted as private chauffeur to the owner, accompanying him to St. Petersburg on business trips.[58] In 1899 Lyukhanov married Augusta Avdayeva, a teacher four years his senior, and a year later their son Valentin—who served in the guard at the Ipatiev House—was born, followed by Vladimir, Alexei, and Antonina. In 1907 he joined the Bolshevik Party, though his revolutionary ardor grew weaker with the passing years. In the summer of 1916 his brother-in-law Alexander Avdayev—first commandant of the Ipatiev House—got him a job at the Zlokazov Brothers factory on the outskirts of Ekaterinburg as a machinist.[59] When the Romanovs arrived in Ekaterinburg, Lyukhanov was appointed the official driver to the House of Special Purpose.[60]

A number of others from the Ural Regional Soviet crowded around the table, including thirty-five-year-old Boris Didkovsky, son of a former imperial officer, who acted as Beloborodov's vice chairman. Educated at the St. Petersburg Military Academy, Didkovsky later attended the University of Geneva, where he met fellow mining student Peter Voikov. Didkovsky returned to Russia and took an official position with the Ural Regional Soviet at the beginning of 1918.[61] Gregory Safarov, another member of the Presidium, had returned from exile in Switzerland with Lenin aboard the infamous "sealed" train.[62] Serge Chukazev, a member of both the Ural Regional Soviet and the Ekaterinburg Cheka, would act as liaison between the local authorities and the foreign consuls in the city who expressed repeated worries over the safety of the Romanovs.[63] A final member of the Ural Regional Soviet drawn into the fate of the Romanovs was Paul Bykov, the twenty-year-old chairman of the Ekaterinburg City Soviet.

On April 27, 1918, three days before the Romanovs arrived in Ekaterinburg, these men had met in room 3 to discuss their expected prisoners. Having decided, at the urging of Peter Voikov, to appropriate the Ipatiev House as the imperial family's place of imprisonment, they turned to the question of who would be charged with their supervision. They offered the post of commandant of the House of Special Purpose to Alexander Dimitrievich Avdayev, a member of the Ural Regional Soviet and of the Bolshevik Party. On this night they gave him his final instructions. From April 30 until July 4, 1918, when he was replaced, Avdayev presided over the Ipatiev House and the prisoners confined within.

History, forged by nearly a century of monarchist and White émigré memoirs, has inevitably painted Avdayev as a bloodcurdling figure, an "inveterate drunkard" who "showed great ingenuity in daily inflicting fresh humiliations on those in his charge," as Pierre Gilliard, tutor to the imperial children, later alleged.[64] Yet this grotesque picture, shaped by the propaganda needs of those who sought to portray all Ekaterinburg Bolsheviks connected with the incarceration and eventual murder of the Romanovs as inhuman sadists, is little more than myth.

Avdayev was born in 1887 in a small village on the outskirts of Ekaterinburg. Together with his sister Augusta, he attended the local grammar and secondary schools, and seems to have been an educated man. At the end of his education he became an apprentice locksmith in Perm. During World War I he joined the Bolshevik Party, and following the October Revolution, became a member of the Ural Regional Soviet.[65] In November 1917 Avdayev got a position at the Zlokazov

Brothers factory. "He bothered his fellow workers with his Bolshevik blather," recalled Abbess Magdalena of the Novotikhvinsky Convent in Ekaterinburg, who knew him well.[66] In December the Ural Bolsheviks arrested factory owner Nicholas Zlokazov; in his place, they appointed a Revolutionary Commissariat chaired by Avdayev.[67]

Avdayev impressed those at the Zlokazov factory as "a true Bolshevik."[68] He openly campaigned for the position of commandant of the House of Special Purpose, as his fellow Zlokazov comrade and future Ipatiev House guard Anatoly Yakimov recalled. "I will promise you all access to the house," Avdayev said, "and you will be able to be in the same room as the Emperor and his family." Yakimov remembered: "It was at this time that I first heard the name 'Nicholas the Bloody.' Avdayev said it, and kept saying it, and soon everyone was saying it."[69] This animosity, as Yakimov admitted, "wasn't personal but because of the War. He said that the Emperor wanted a War, and for three years spilled the blood of the workers, with a great number of workers shot during that period for daring to strike."[70]

At the time he became commandant, Avdayev was thirty years old, tall, with light brown hair and a small, neatly trimmed mustache. Although Colonel Kobylinsky thought him "uncultivated" when they first met in Tobolsk, he also noted that his face "bore no signs of drunkenness."[71] A surprisingly favorable analysis of his character was given by Sister Agnes, mistress of novices at the Novotikhvinsky Convent in Ekaterinburg, who had known him since his youth. According to Sister Agnes, Avdayev "could absolutely play the role of the leader, happy to exercise his passion for his cause, but he was only capable of cruelty through terrible comments, not actions. It is somewhat true that he drank, but he never inclined to entertain himself by making the prisoners suffer. His personal demons ate at him night and day and never stopped pursuing him. When one hears of Avdayev these days, we see him always through a haze of alcohol, but I think it is important not to exaggerate its influence on him. . . . In his first impression, he would seem like an inflexible tyrant, and would appear to be unrestrained and in a terrible mood, but soon his true self would emerge and he would become accommodating." Avdayev, as Sister Agnes recalled, "played at being an inflexible Commandant, but this was only lip service. His world was one of bluster and wine. He used a lot of virulent words, and made a big show of Bolshevik fire, but he didn't have it in him to hurt anyone."[72]

Nikita Tchernikin, another man who knew him well, declared that Avdayev "contained all colors of personality. He encouraged his subordinates to think of him as a bandit so that they would be afraid of him. He was irascible and audacious, but he had a good heart."[73] This lack of revolutionary ardor, as Ekaterinburg Cheka member Isai Rodzinsky wrote, marked Avdayev from his first days as commandant. He was, Rodzinsky said, "an able comrade" but "not very good at his job."[74]

Such views contrast strongly with the usual depiction of Avdayev as a cruel tyrant, particularly in the works of those connected to the later White Army investigation into the murder of the Romanovs. Their goal was to present all Bolsheviks in the most disreputable and repugnant light imaginable, and those who had some part in the final drama of the Romanovs as veritable embodiments of evil. Yet, just as every official in the imperial regime was not a reactionary, virulent anti-Semite, not every Bolshevik was a bloodthirsty tyrant who delighted in carnage and humiliation, despite the efforts of those who, for political reasons, needed them to appear so to history.

Avdayev's true feelings about the Romanovs remain enigmatic, but his words and his actions in the Ipatiev House underscore a man torn between political expectation and personal inclination. He seems to have tried to act as he thought was expected, as a Bolshevik commissar should with his men, filling the air with loud boasts designed to show his mastery over the former sovereign, a man who, as Sister Agnes recalled, "played" at his role but who did not feel it. He presented himself as the loud, swaggering drunkard of history, angrily refusing every request made by the Romanovs to cause them torment, while at the same time quietly and eventually relenting, a pattern repeated throughout his tenure as commandant.

While Avdayev was nothing of the monster often described, the same cannot be said of his assistant, Alexander Mikhailovich Moshkin. Moshkin, twenty-eight years old in 1918, had, like Avdayev, been trained as a locksmith, and worked at the Zlokazov factory. If Avdayev's reputation was that of a drunken brute, Moshkin lived up to the description in practice. Many of the humiliating incidents suffered by the imperial family in the Ipatiev House can be traced not to Avdayev but to Moshkin, who did indeed take great delight in his authority over his former emperor.

The Ural Regional Soviet met late into the night as these men argued the final details of the prisoners' incarceration. Of prime concern was the question of a reliable guard. Ekaterinburg's successful seizure of the Romanovs from Yakovlev was an unanticipated event, despite the Ural Regional Soviet's repeated efforts, and no adequate preparations had been made to look after the prisoners. The first Ipatiev House guards were, as official White Army investigator Nicholas Sokolov later confirmed, "hastily pulled from factories and prisons."[75] Composed largely of workers from the local Makarov factory, they "were appointed haphazardly," as one member recalled. "They did not have the frame for unity or the ability to complement each others' strengths and weaknesses. These guards came from different detachments and they were never a unit."[76]

Between April 30 and July 8, a total of 105 men served guard duty at the Ipatiev House; this number does not include Magyar prisoners of war, for whom no reliable records of service exist. The vast majority were drawn from four local factories: the Makarov, Syssert, Verkh-Isetsk, and Zlokazov Works near Ekaterinburg. Somewhat surprisingly, only 26 were members of the Bolshevik Party, and of these, one—Paul Medvedev—had let his Party membership lapse.[77] Only 14 of the 105 men were over age twenty-five: 53 were younger than Grand Duchess Olga Nikolaievna (twenty-three years old); 29 younger than Tatiana (twenty-one); 19 younger than Grand Duchess Marie (nineteen); and 2, Sadurov and Letemin, were just seventeen, the same age as Grand Duchess Anastasia. Ninety-seven of these men had been raised in the Orthodox faith, and 72 still regarded themselves as members of the church at the time of their duty. Just over half were married, and of these, 41 had children of their own. Thirteen of the men had previously been arrested for various crimes, but the vast majority had never before been in any trouble with the law. A total of 102 of the men were ethnic Russians: the only exceptions were the 2 Mishkevich brothers, of Polish extraction; and Mohammed Abdul Latypov, a Muslim from neighboring Georgia.

The vast majority of these men had no professional training as guards, a strong contrast to the usual historical portrait of hardened revolutionaries who delighted in brutal humiliation of the prisoners. Only a handful of the guards—principally those from the Verkh-Isetsk and Zlokazov factories—held to fanatical political views, and few took the job because they relished the idea of using their positions of power to lash out against their former emperor.[78] Many men were drawn to the job for financial reasons. The recruits were promised a salary of 400 rubles per month, along with free housing and board in Ekaterinburg; provision also was made for those who wished to keep their factory positions and work part-time when off-duty, to further supplement their income.[79]

There was, however, a second, more immediate reason that led the majority of these men to volunteer for duty in the Special Detachment. On April 22 the Soviet government had announced that all men between ages eighteen and forty were to undergo an eight-week training course, in advance of conscription. This meant certain action—and possible death—for those unluckily dispatched to the front lines of the bloody Civil War. Exceptions were to be made, however, for members of the Special Detachment—a fact that led many of these young men to join the safe ranks of the new guard.[80]

The Special Detachment, drawn as it was from local factories that tended to employ generations of the same families, contained a number of relatives. There were eleven sets of brothers in the guard: Alexei and Michael Kabanov; Stephan and Philip Khokhryakov; Ivan and Alexander Kotlov; Kuzma and Michael Letemin; Ivan and Vassili Loginov; Nicholas and Stanislaus Mishkevich; Avksenti and Vassili Petrov; Nicholas and Boris Sadchikov; Michael and Alexander Smorodyakov; Alexander and Andrei Strekotin; and Paul and Stephan Vyatkin. Two sets of cousins also were in the guard: Alexander and Ivan Kotegov; and Alexander and Konstantin Ukraintsev. There was even a father and son, Andrei and Ivan Starkov.

Beyond brief work histories, ages, and religious and party affiliations, the vast majority of these guards remain frustratingly enigmatic. Among the oldest members of the Special Detachment was Ivan Cherepanov. A worker from the Syssert factory, he joined the Special Detachment in May as a means of providing additional support to his large family. "Steadfast and solid," recalled Alexander Strekotin, "he repeatedly refused to join the Bolshevik Party."[81] Another older Syssert worker, Nicholas Zaitsev, signed with the guard when his job as a stonecutter became too physically demanding; in the Special Detachment, he often worked as a cook. Like Cherepanov, he refused to join the Bolshevik Party.[82]

Ivan Kleshchev was a stout, twenty-one-year-old member of the guard with romantic notions and a weak character. Born in 1897 in Shadrinsk, a suburb of Ekaterinburg, until the February Revolution Kleshchev lived with his parents, Nicholas and Tatiana, while he worked at the Holy Exaltation of the Cross Cloth Factory in Ushakov, close to Ekaterinburg, where his father also was employed, as a mechanic.[83] Nicholas Kleshchev was, according to White Army general Michael Deterikhs, "not always sober," though he "worked well, accurately, and of his own volition."[84] Just before the February Revolution, Ivan quit his job and left for Tyumen, accompanied by a gang of friends.[85] His mother chased after him, stormed into the house where he lived, and, after telling him off in front of his friends, dragged her son back home, having arranged for him to return to his former job. In February 1918 Kleshchev joined a group of workers who stormed into the house of the Zlokazov factory manager, stole his belongings, and forced him to hand over his factory to a new, revolutionary commissariat.[86] Nicholas Kleshchev refused to have

Guard Ivan Kleshchev.

anything to do with the Bolshevik Party, but his wife, eager to see her son rise, attended meetings and organized groups of workers herself.[87] On learning that men were needed to form the Ipatiev House guard, Tatiana Kleshchev herself signed up her son. During his tenure as a guard, Kleshchev frequently showed his parents small photographs, souvenirs, and books that he had pilfered from the imperial family's belongings. Throughout, Kleshchev himself never joined the Bolshevik Party, though he mingled with its members and counted them as his friends.[88]

Michael Ivanovich Letemin was seventeen when he was signed from his job at the Syssert factory to join the Ipatiev House detachment. Like most of the men, he was not a member of the Bolshevik Party; according to fellow guard Alexander Strekotin, Letemin was completely uninterested in politics.[89] He joined the guard detachment for the same reason he had joined the Red Army earlier that year: money.[90] According to Sokolov, he had, in the past, been tried on an unspecified morals charge, an enigmatic incident that led Deterikhs to term him a "heinous convict" and "a beast."[91]

Paul Spiridonovich Medvedev, the senior guard commander at Ipatiev House, had formerly been a worker at the Syssert factory. Born in 1890, Medvedev—like most members of the guard—was raised as a practicing Russian Orthodox in the Syssert district of suburban Ekaterinburg.[92] Medvedev attended school for several years, but left without any secondary education to work in the Syssert factory at age fourteen as a welder. In 1910 he married Maria Danilovna, and the couple had one daughter, Zoya, born in 1911, and two sons, Andrei, born in 1913, and Ivan, born in late 1917. Medvedev was an industrious man, a hard worker who made extra money as a shoemaker in his spare time. This brought him a measure of financial stability: he owned a small but neatly kept house in Syssert, where neighbors recalled him as quiet but pleasant, a handsome young man devoted to his wife and who doted on his children. He was, said his comrade Alexander Strekotin, a man of "good will," with a generous character.[93] Before the executions of the Romanovs, Medvedev had never participated in or been charged with any criminal activity: in many ways, he exemplified Nicholas II's own vision of the Russian working class, diligent and dedicated to his family, his community, his

Paul Medvedev.

church, and his country. In 1914 he volunteered for service as a fighter in the First Class Irregular Army, and was eventually sent to Militia Detachment 33 in Verkhoturye in Siberia. After two months of military service, however, Medvedev was honorably discharged as a factory munitions worker needed for national defense and security, and he returned to his job at the Syssert factory.[94]

In April 1917 Medvedev joined the Bolshevik Party because, he said, "the majority of the factory workers did so."[95] In the spring of 1918, however, he stopped paying his Party dues and let his membership lapse. He later explained that he did not wish to engage in or encourage any Party work or activity.[96] In January 1918 Medvedev was drafted into the Red Army and sent to the Dutov Front under command of Serge Mrachkovsky. When Medvedev returned to Syssert in April on three weeks' leave, Mrachkovsky visited his factory and asked for volunteers to form a detachment for the Ipatiev House. Not wishing to return to the front, and, as he said, "missing my family," Medvedev signed on for guard duty.[97] During his service in the Ipatiev House, Medvedev also worked as a courier for the Ekaterinburg Cheka.[98]

Eighteen-year-old Philip Proskuryakov, one of Medvedev's comrades at the Syssert factory, joined the Ipatiev House detachment on May 11, 1918. The son of the Syssert factory foreman, he attended the Syssert Five Class School for three years but, as with so many members of the guard, his education came to an abrupt halt when, at age ten, he began his apprenticeship as a factory electrician. Proskuryakov hated the factory, and attempted to start his own business; when this failed, he got a job working in the Central Electrical plant in Ekaterinburg in March 1918. On May 9 his friend Ivan Talapov told him that Mrachkovsky was recruiting guards for the Ipatiev House.[99] "I was anxious to see the Emperor," he recalled, "so I ignored my father's advice and on the next day enlisted."[100] Deterikhs characterized him as a "hooligan," though—like most members of the detachment—Proskuryakov had never engaged in any criminal activity, nor was he a Bolshevik.[101]

The youngest member of the guard, Alexander Feodorovich Sadurov, had just turned seventeen when he was signed from the Syssert factory on May 11. Too young to have any interest in political issues, he resolutely refused to join the Bolshevik Party, opposing their stern ideology. He was, according to Alexander Strekotin, the "most handsome" of all the guards, "the darling of the whole company," which called him "Kerensky" after his Christian name and patronymic.[102]

One of the few guards to join the Special Detachment from political conviction was twenty-seven-year-old Andrei Strekotin, from the Syssert factory. "Why," he asked, "would we give the Emperor such boundless power? Why did he drown in riches and excess? And now his

Court is here, and all he has from all the people who came with him from Petrograd to Tobolsk to Ekaterinburg are three or four people. And we here have had long lives of hard work with our backs and our hands, we are half-starved and half-angry at having been put in his battalions to fight his wars. We should already have pulled him off the throne a long time ago. And naturally, he should have been shot."[103]

Andrei's brother, twenty-one-year-old fellow Syssert worker Alexander Strekotin, did not share his feelings. He recalled: "We were offered the opportunity to sign up and serve in the Red Guard unit that was to be in charge of guarding the family of Nicholas II. This offer was restricted to those Red Guards who already lived in Ekaterinburg and the first places were to be filled by those who had served on the Dutov Front. In this number were my brother Andrei Andreievich and I. The money was good, so I agreed."[104]

Anatoly Alexandrovich Yakimov joined the Ipatiev House detachment from his job at the Zlokazov factory on June 11, 1918. Born in 1887, the son of a peasant, Yakimov was raised in Perm. His father died when Yakimov was twelve; at the time, young Yakimov was in his third year of study at the Ekaterinburg Ecclesiastical Seminary School and, as a result, he grew up devoutly Orthodox. Even as a guard at the Ipatiev House, he continued to attend daily services.[105]

His father's death forced Yakimov to quit school and take a job as an errand boy at the Motovilikhia Works in Perm, to help supplement his family's income.[106] At age sixteen, Yakimov got a job working in the plant itself, and in 1906 he married the daughter of a fellow worker. In 1916 he volunteered for the Imperial Army and was recruited to the 494th Vereisky Regiment of the 124th Division, fighting on the Romanian Front. After the Revolution he returned to Motovilikhia, where he worked as a lathe operator, and was elected as a worker representative to the regimental committee in charge of the factory. In November 1917 he moved to Ekaterinburg, where he got a job working under Avdayev at the Zlokazov factory.[107]

Yakimov refused to join the Bolshevik Party, though in sentiment he agreed with many of their early Utopian principles.[108] He provides perhaps the best example of how the common Russian saw the Revolution: a road to a better life, paved not with the blood of the Civil War, or the still unsuspected purges of the future, but with opportunity. "I still think," Yakimov explained after being captured by the Whites, "that there will be a good and just life only when there aren't any rich and poor, as there are now, and this will happen only when all of the people understand through education that such a life does not yet exist. I viewed the Emperor as the number one capitalist, who always will be holding hands with the capitalists and not with the workers. For that reason, I did not want an Emperor, and thought it was necessary to keep him under guard, imprisoned for the safety of the Revolution."[109]

If some of these men were disillusioned with the former imperial regime, the key to this unhappiness is revealed in the story of their lives. The vast majority of the men were poorly educated; schools had been available to most, but circumstances prevented them—even had they wished—from pursuing any higher education. Yakimov is a typical example, a boy of twelve forced to quit school on his father's death and join the labor force to help support his family. The same holds true for others who were forced to quit school at an early age and become child laborers. The lack of any adequate governmental system to protect these children and their families provided a dangerous breeding ground for rural discontent, their misery—if not quite equal to that of their comrades who worked in the country's squalid urban factories—driving an ultimately fatal sense of abandonment. Most were certainly pragmatic and cynical, but they were hardened not by the Revolution or incendiary Bolshevik talk but by the experiences of their lives.

Even as they met late into the night of April 30, 1918, the Ural Regional Soviet discussed the prison regime at the Ipatiev House. "At any given time," recalled Avdayev, "we needed a force of about thirty soldiers, to do sentry duty in the house itself, in the garden, and around the palisade." On May 8 the first guards from the Makarov factory were supplemented with prisoners of war, mainly Magyars, hastily pulled from Ekaterinburg City Prison.[110] A second contingent, of twenty-four men, drawn from the Verkh-Isetsk factory, also were brought into the Ipatiev House that week and given interior posts; the Makarov workers and Magyars were reassigned to exterior duty.[111]

The Ural Regional Soviet had ordered Serge Mrachkovsky, a military commissar in the Red Army, to recruit men from the factories in the surrounding suburbs to form a new guard.[112] On May 9 Mrachkovsky visited the Syssert factory where, assisted by Paul Medvedev, he conducted interviews. Of the thirty Syssert workers signed that day, only eleven were members of the Bolshevik Party.[113]

The Syssert detachment arrived in Ekaterinburg on Sunday, May 12; for the first twelve days, they were housed near the New Gostiny Dvor.[114] On May 13 they elected Paul Medvedev and Alexei Nikiforov as their senior guard representatives and, on the following day, began their duties at the Ipatiev House.[115] With their arrival, the Makarov factory workers who had formed the first guard were finally dismissed.[116] Two weeks later, on Friday, May 24, the Syssert detachment finally moved into the Ipatiev House, taking rooms on the lower floor, where camp beds were set up in the storerooms and in the corridors.[117] With them, they brought their own cook, Ivan Kotegov, later replaced by Andrei Starkov.[118]

A week later, on May 30, the Workers' Committee at the Zlokazov factory on the outskirts of Ekaterinburg received a request from the Ural Regional Soviet to provide an additional ten guards for the Ipatiev House.[119] Fourteen men were chosen for this detail, joining the Syssert guards; on this same day, an additional fifteen workers from the Verkh-Isetsk factory joined the men who formed the "Special Detachment for the House of Special Purpose."[120] On Saturday, June 1, the Magyar detachment was relieved of its duty, disbanded, and the men sent back to their prison cells.[121] On that same day, the original twenty-four guards from Verkh-Isetsk also were relieved of their duties and ordered back to their factory; they were replaced the following day with the new Zlokazov guards, who moved into the Ipatiev House.[122]

As the number of guards grew, living conditions on the lower floor of the Ipatiev House became increasingly cramped, and the men from the Syssert factory complained that they had no place in which to be alone with their visiting wives and girlfriends.[123] To solve this problem, the Ural Regional Soviet commandeered the upper floor of the Popov House, a two-storied brick building directly opposite the Ipatiev House at the corner of Voznesensky Prospekt and Voznesensky Lane. The lower floor contained several small apartments, rented by Ekaterinburg workers and merchants, who remained throughout the occupation.[124]

On June 4 six more Zlokazov workers were selected as Ipatiev House guards; one declined his position, and an alternate was named in his place.[125] A week later, on June 11, Alexander Avdayev was dismissed from his position at the Zlokazov factory. According to Anatoly Yakimov, "a feeling of discontent toward Avdayev grew very strong at that time among the Zlokazov workers, who felt he spent too much time at the Ipatiev House," and had him fired.[126] When he left, he took fifteen men, giving them positions as guards at the Ipatiev House.[127]

With these new men, the guard was completely reorganized. Paul Medvedev was elected senior guard commander, in charge of both Syssert and Zlokazov workers, and three assistants, called "guard seniors," were selected by their men: Anatoly Yakimov for the Zlakozov men, and Benjamin Safonov and Konstantin Dobrynin for the Syssert detachment.[128] Day-to-day supervision of the detachment was left to the guard seniors, themselves responsible to Medvedev, who reported directly to the commandant of the Ipatiev House. As senior guard commander, Medvedev was charged with the overall management of the Ipatiev House; neither the commandant of the House of Special Purpose nor his assistant had much to do with the daily operation of the prison or the care of its inmates. Medvedev ordered household goods; ensured the delivery of meals and, later, foodstuffs for the family; served as liaison between the Romanovs and the commandant; and supervised the daily guard shifts. He worked from the commandant's study, next to the drawing room on the main floor of the house, where he was expected to remain for his daily twelve-hour shift. Only after Dobrynin became the third senior was Medvedev allowed to work eight-hour shifts.[129] Medvedev and the three guard seniors worked in rotation, with shifts from 6:00 A.M. to 2:00 P.M.; 2:00 P.M. to 10:00 P.M.; and 10:00 P.M. to 6:00 A.M. The guards themselves worked four six-hour shifts: 8:00 A.M. to 2:00 P.M.; 2:00 P.M. to 8:00 P.M.; 8:00 P.M. to 2:00 A.M.; and 2:00 A.M. to 8:00 A.M.[130]

In addition to regular telephone lines between the Ipatiev and Popov Houses, commanders and sentries communicated through a system of bells within the House of Special Purpose itself. This call system, an addition made by the Ipatievs, included bells at the front door; the secondary hallway; a third, in the study; a fourth, in the kitchen; and four on the lower floor, as well as call bells installed in the Popov House. But the system functioned erratically throughout the imperial family's imprisonment, making such communications infrequent.[131]

When the Romanovs arrived in Ekaterinburg on April 30, the Ipatiev House was surrounded by a ten-foot-high stockade fence, hastily and clumsily erected from rough planks. This fence enclosed the garden along Voznesensky Lane, stretching to the top of the hillside, where it extended north along the main facade of the house to end just before the front door, where it was anchored into the wall with iron ties. "In this way," recalled Anatoly Yakimov, "the fence made a little courtyard, which could be entered only from the main entrance of the house which was facing Voznesensky Prospekt."[132] On June 5 a second palisade was erected, higher and longer than the first, which completely enclosed the property.[133] At the corner of Voznesensky Prospekt and Voznesensky Lane, near the edge of the second palisade, a small sentry box was built, connected to the commandant's office by a telephone line strung along the facade of the house.[134]

From April 30 to July 5 there were ten guard posts at the Ipatiev House. Post 1, in the foyer on the main floor, was manned around the clock. Post 2 was in the secondary hall that led to the bathroom and lavatory, at the head of the staircase that connected the lower floor. Post 3 was just inside the courtyard gates. Post 4 stood on the exterior side of the gates, on Voznesensky Prospekt. Post 5 was a sentry box near the northern end of the outer palisade, surveying the length of the avenue. Post 6 stood in the sentry box at the intersection of Voznesensky Prospekt and Voznesensky Lane, at the crest of the hillside. Post 7 was between the house and the first palisade, in a sentry box on the southern side of the house along Voznesensky Lane. Post 8 was in the Ipatiev House garden. Post 9 was on the balcony, situated off the western side of the main floor, and connected to the terrace below by a narrow staircase. The last post, 10, was directly beneath the dining room, in a large storeroom near the southern end of the lower floor.[135]

Until the arrival of the Zlokazov workers on June 11, Syssert and Verkh-Isetsk workers had performed guard duty on all ten sentry posts, but Avdayev replaced them with his friends and former coworkers. Only men from the Zlokazov factory did guard duty on Posts 1 and 2, situated on the main floor, and enjoyed access to the main floor, where the Romanovs lived. These guards slept in the commandant's room, the foyer, or in the anteroom, on mattresses laid on the floors.[136] This privileged treatment eventually erupted, as one guard recalled, into jealousies between the interior and exterior detachments.[137]

These sentries were armed with rifles fixed with triangular-shaped bayonets; in addition, the exterior guard had their own Russian Nagant revolvers, and carried hand grenades.[138] There were four machine guns: one on the balcony of the house, overlooking the garden; a second below that, at Post 10; a third in the dormer window overlooking the intersection of Voznesensky Prospekt and Voznesensky Lane, directly above the room occupied by Nicholas and Alexandra; and a fourth in the bell tower of Voznesensky Cathedral, in the middle of the square just opposite the house.[139] With these defenses, the Ipatiev House assumed the appearance of an impregnable fortress from which the imperial family could not escape.

4

"It Was Dreadful,
What They Did . . ."

WEDNESDAY, MAY 1, 1918, dawned bright and clear over Ekaterinburg. Behind the rough wooden palisade ringing the property, the Ipatiev House gradually stirred to life, guards sloshing through the brown sludge of melting snow as they took up their sentry positions. That morning, the prisoners woke to brilliant spring sunshine. Through the open window of the corner bedroom she shared with her parents, Grand Duchess Marie listened as the singing of birds was gradually drowned out by the clanging bells of electric streetcars noisily making their way along Voznesensky Prospekt. Peering out from the upper pane, she saw nothing but the blue and white spire of the Cathedral of the Annunciation, its gilded Orthodox cross shimmering in the golden light.[1] Thus began the first of the seventy-eight days the former emperor and his family were to pass as prisoners of the Ural Regional Soviet.

May Day was a public holiday. By midday, Ekaterinburg was thronged with noisy workers parading through the streets, red flags and proletariat banners waving in the bracing air, accompanied by the discordant sounds of brass bands and voices singing the "Internationale." Hearing this cacophony, Nicholas raised himself to the single open windowpane; he could see nothing of what was taking place in the square just beyond the palisade.[2] The crowd eventually dispersed, replaced by the first curious groups who gathered daily around the ornate little villa, "craning their necks" in an attempt to catch a glimpse of the prisoners. The guards, under strict orders to prevent such displays, would shout, "Walk on, citizens, walk on! There's nothing to see here!"

"If there's nothing to see here," they asked, "then why can't we just stand here if we want? Is this the house where the Emperor is staying?" In the end, the flash of a sentry's rifle was usually enough to send the crowds scurrying away.[3]

The Romanovs spent an uneasy first day as captives of the Ural Regional Soviet. The previous evening, exhausted from their perilous journey across Siberia and surrounded by hostile jailers, Nicholas, Alexandra, and Marie had retreated to the quiet of their corner bedroom, enveloped in the silence of their new prison. "It's not clear how things will be here," the empress wrote in a letter to Tobolsk, her cautious words barely concealing the nervous uncertainty of their situation.[4] The four retainers imprisoned with them—Dr. Eugene Botkin, maid Anna Demidova, valet Terenty Chemodurov, and footman Ivan Sednev—carefully unpacked the few valises allowed the group when they left Tobolsk. With crowds still gathered on the square beyond the palisade, Alexander Avdayev decreed it too dangerous for the prisoners to walk in the garden; the empress spent the afternoon arranging treasured icons, photographs, and books she had brought from the Governor's House.

As night fell over Ekaterinburg, the prisoners settled into the drawing room, lit by the soft glow from the Italian chandelier. As they took tea, the Romanovs were surprised to see a friendly face: unbelievably, they knew one of the men guarding them. Konstantin Ukraintsev, Avdayev's first deputy commandant, was a former imperial soldier from the Crimean town of Gagra. During the imperial family's annual holidays at Livadia, Ukraintsev had served as a beater for Grand Duke

The drawing room in the Ipatiev House.

Michael Alexandrovich on hunts, and also played with the emperor's sister Grand Duchess Olga Alexandrovna. Alexandra spoke with him at length, asking about Ukraintsev's family, his job in the Ipatiev House, and questioning him about the other guards and how the security system had been arranged.[5] "In short," Grand Duchess Marie wrote to her sisters in Tobolsk, "he told us many interesting things about his life."[6]

After a volatile first day, the prisoners gradually settled into an uncertain, monotonous routine the following morning. It was a "beautiful, warm, sunny day," as Alexandra noted, though the chill Siberian spring wind howled through the single open window in the corner bedroom.[7] Assembling for prayers, they found the dining room in shadow, the bright sunshine blocked by a carpet Avdayev had hung across the window to the balcony. As they prepared to take tea, they found the samovar on the oak sideboard empty; the guards stationed on the main floor had used all the hot water earlier that morning. When Avdayev learned of this, he ordered his men to boil water so the prisoners could have their tea.[8]

Alexandra spent much of the day in bed, utterly exhausted. Ever dutiful, Marie remained with her mother while the others walked in the garden for an hour that afternoon, reading aloud to her.[9] The prisoners still had no word of Prince Dolgoruky, who had accompanied them from Tobolsk, only to be arrested on arriving in Ekaterinburg. While these discussions were taking place, the Romanovs worried over the continued absence of Prince Dolgoruky. "From vague hints from those around us," Nicholas wrote in his diary, "we understand that poor Valia is no longer at liberty, and that an inquiry is ordered against him before he will be freed: there is no possibility of contacting him, despite Botkin's best efforts."[10] Before allowing any further retainers into the Ipatiev House, Avdayev warned, the Romanovs must draw up a list of those people incarcerated with them as well as those who remained in Tobolsk, explaining their functions. "How difficult it is once again," Marie wrote to her sisters. "For eight months, we had peaceful lives, and now it begins anew."[11]

A brief snowstorm, followed by bright afternoon sunshine, greeted Good Friday on May 3. The prisoners asked for a priest, but this was denied; instead, Nicholas read the Gospels before a makeshift altar, covered by the empress with an embroidered cloth and the family's icons.[12] The following evening, however, Avdayev relented, and at eight-thirty two men arrived at the Ipatiev House, Father Anatoly Meledin and his deacon, Vassili Buimirov.[13] "They conducted the service quickly and well," Nicholas recorded; "it was a great comfort to pray even in such conditions, and to hear 'Christ is risen.'"[14] With some surprise, both Nicholas and Alexandra watched as Ukraintsev led members of the guard in joining the service.[15]

Easter Sunday passed quietly for the prisoners in the Ipatiev House. In previous years, the Romanovs had celebrated this most important of religious holidays amid the splendor of their palaces, an exchange of greetings with hundreds of uniformed members of the imperial court followed by the presentation of a specially commissioned Fabergé Easter egg to the empress. In Ekaterinburg, the day passed quietly, listlessly spent reading or writing letters, interrupted for an afternoon walk in the garden followed by tea.[16]

Although the prisoners had been warned that their correspondence was subject to censorship, Nicholas failed to understand the need for caution. On Easter weekend he wrote a letter to the children at Tobolsk; concealed beneath the lining of the envelope, Nicholas enclosed a rough floor plan of the Ipatiev House.[17] When Avdayev discovered this, he called the emperor into his office, demanding an explanation. Nicholas, Avdayev recalled, "stuttered over his words like a schoolboy, and said he hadn't known it was forbidden to send plans."[18] The commandant, Nicholas noted in his diary, "took it away, saying I could not send it."[19]

Nearly two weeks had passed since the Romanovs had left Tobolsk, or heard anything of the children who remained there. On May 8 Ukraintsev delivered a cable from Grand Duchess Olga: "Thanks letter. All well. Little One already been in garden. We are writing."[20]

It was to be Ukraintsev's last service to the prisoners. Late that morning, a new guard, established by the Ural Regional Soviet, appeared in the Ipatiev House. Composed largely of Magyar prisoners of war culled from Ekaterinburg City Prison, they appeared "dressed in different sorts of jackets," as Nicholas noted, "with all possible types of headgear. The officers stood guard with sabers and rifles. When we went out to walk, all the soldiers who had free time also came to the garden to look at us."[21]

The arrival of these men, according to Nicholas, caused "some sort of big fuss," and the next morning, Avdayev's telephone rang constantly. "We weren't told what happened, of course," the emperor complained to his diary; "perhaps some sort of detachment landed in town and caused confusion among the locals. The mood of the guard, however, was cheerful and very agreeable."[22]

When Ukraintsev failed to appear for his customary shift, Nicholas noted his absence. Only on the following day, however, did they learn from Avdayev that he had been relieved of his position. Marie's indiscreet letter to her sisters in Tobolsk, coupled with the long evenings he had spent amiably chatting with the Romanovs, singled out Ukraintsev as a marked man, and the Ural Regional Soviet ordered him dismissed.[23] In his place, Avdayev appointed Alexander Moshkin, his former assistant at the Zlokazov factory. Nicholas described him as having "a kind face, similar to that of an artist," but the Romanovs quickly learned that Moshkin was a brutal man.[24]

Both Avdayev and his new assistant worked seven days a week. Avdayev generally arrived at nine each morning and left twelve hours later; he never slept at the Ipatiev House, but lived with his sister Augusta and brother-in-law Serge Lyukhanov. Moshkin, however, promptly moved into the Ipatiev House, sleeping on a cot in the commandant's office. In Avdayev's absence, he was in charge. Unlike Avdayev, Moshkin was a vindictive man who delighted in humiliating the prisoners, and his position gave him ample opportunities to indulge his passion. Tales of drunken soldiers, loud revolutionary songs, and other petty but painful incidents usually ascribed to Avdayev in fact took place in the evenings, after he had left.[25] Several of the guards later testified that Moshkin spent his nights drinking, entertaining the girlfriend he slipped into the house after Avdayev departed.[26] Alexandra hinted at this in her diary, writing that Moshkin was "vulgar and unpleasant."[27]

The episode with Ukraintsev clearly worried the Ural Regional Soviet. The Romanovs had been prisoners in Ekaterinburg for just under two weeks, and security at the Ipatiev House was already disintegrating, as guards easily mingled with their captives. The first chief of the guards, a man named Glarner, had—like Ukraintsev—become very friendly with the prisoners, joining Nicholas in the drawing room for evening games of bezique.[28] One morning, Glarner appeared "looking funny," Nicholas wrote, "and was sleepy all day." When questioned, the head of the Special Detachment admitted that he had spent the previous evening dancing at a ball.[29]

In an attempt to regulate security, the Ural Regional Soviet appointed a second assistant commandant, an unknown man Nicholas referred to in his diary as "My enemy" and "the pop-eyed one."[30] There were other changes. At eight-thirty each morning, all of the prisoners, as Alexandra complained, had "to get out of bed for the guards, head of the guards and Commandant, who come to see if we are there."[31] A delegation from the Ural Regional Soviet demanded that the captives hand over all of the money they had with them, "a most unpleasant incident!" as Nicholas wrote.[32] In a letter to her siblings in Tobolsk, Marie warned: "We get nasty surprises here almost daily," adding, "Who would think that after fourteen months imprisonment we would be treated like this?"[33]

More changes came on May 13, when Glarner was relieved of duty and replaced with Alexei Sidorov while the prisoners walked in the garden.[34] The next day they were informed that their daily walk was now restricted to two thirty-minute sessions, one in the morning and one in the afternoon.[35] Nicholas, in particular, grumbled about this, asking why such a move was necessary. "To make it like a prison regime," came the reply.[36] A new detachment of guards drawn from the Syssert factory appeared, led by Paul Medvedev, described by Nicholas as "an imposing young man."[37] The following day, as a final security measure, the windows on the upper floor were whitewashed; "looking through," Nicholas noted, "now all one sees is a fog."[38] A few days later, however, Avdayev himself went outside and scratched the paint from one of the windows, so the prisoners could read the thermometer.[39] As a final measure, new telephone lines were installed, along with additional call bells. The strain proved too much for the Ipatiev House wiring; on several days, the electricity went out, and the prisoners were forced to eat and play cards by candlelight.[40]

Nicholas in particular found these new security measures oppressive. Always fond of physical exercise, he bristled at the regulations limiting his walks, and repeatedly asked to be allowed to clean the garden, or be provided with a hatchet or saw to chop firewood. There was little chance, however, that the Bolsheviks would supply their prisoners with any weaponry, and his requests were denied.[41] Avdayev, however, relented somewhat on the issue of walks, and only rarely enforced the restrictions ordered by the Ural Regional Soviet.[42]

Sunday, May 19, dawned over Ekaterinburg with "glorious, bright sunshine," as Alexandra wrote.[43] On this day, Nicholas turned fifty, recording in his diary, "It even seems strange to me!"[44] At eleven-thirty that morning, Father Meledin and his deacon, Vassili Buimirov, returned to the Ipatiev House to conduct the Easter Service of Intercession. With the weather so improved, Avdayev lengthened the first walk to seventy-five minutes, and allowed a second turn in the garden later that afternoon.[45]

In the three weeks since Nicholas and Alexandra had left Tobolsk, they had received only a few cables and letters from their remaining children, who were to join them in Ekaterinburg as soon as Alexei could travel. Anxious over the separation, they repeatedly asked for news, only to be told that arrangements were being made. On May 21, Avdayev finally told them that the others were expected within a few days, and he opened three new rooms for their use on the main floor: a second bedroom, in the southwestern corner next to the dining room; the main stair hall; and the kitchen, which Sednev had been allowed to use only when warming meals.[46]

A sense of nervous anticipation hung over the Ipatiev House in these days, as the emperor and empress awaited news of their children. On May 22 Nicholas recorded: "We still do not know where the children are or when they shall arrive. Tiresome uncertainty."[47] As he wrote these words, an unexpected snowstorm descended on the Urals; within the Ipatiev House, the prisoners huddled around the warmth of the drawing room stove, unseen gusts of snow thundering against the whitewashed windows and burying Ekaterinburg beneath a white veil. Three hundred miles away, a terrible drama played itself out as the children made their perilous, final journey.

FOLLOWING THE DEPARTURE of Nicholas, Alexandra, and Marie Nikolaievna from Tobolsk, remembered Alexei Volkov, "the sadness of death descended on the Governor's House."[48] On Saturday, April 27, the driver of Alexandra's tarantass returned to Tobolsk, bringing a hastily jotted note from Marie in which she wrote of the extremely bad condition of the roads and discomfort of the carriages.[49] There was further news the following day, when Kobylinsky received a cable saying that the party had safely reached Tyumen at 9:30 P.M. on Saturday. Late that night, a second cable arrived, signed by Yakovlev but dictated by the empress: "Traveling in comfort. How is the boy? God be with you."[50]

Then, after this, there was only silence, and the worry in Tobolsk increased with each passing day. "Where are they?" Gilliard wrote in his diary on Thursday, May 2. "They could have reached Moscow by Tuesday."[51] On May 3 Kobylinsky had a cable from Yakovlev, which Countess Hendrikova noted with a laconic entry in her diary: "News arrived of their arrest in Ekaterinburg. No details."[52] Others, however, were mystified. "What has happened?" Gilliard asked in his diary that evening.[53] "This telegram," recalled Kobylinsky, "caused us all consternation. Why Ekaterinburg? We were stupefied; we always thought that Moscow was their destination."[54]

The Easter of 1918 was the first the children had ever celebrated without their parents, and, as Gilliard noted, everyone was "in low spirits."[55] In anticipation of the midnight liturgy, the grand duchesses and members of the household decorated a portable iconostasis in a corner of the ballroom with flowers and boughs of spruce.[56] A priest came and sang the liturgy for the small congregation, but—as with their parents' day in Ekaterinburg—the contrast to previous years was notably sad. Their Easter "feast" consisted of vegetable broth, cold salami, cold ham, hot slices of turkey, and salad.[57]

The next day, the children finally had a letter from Ekaterinburg. Dictated by Alexandra and written by Anna Demidova, it noted that their belongings had all been searched, even their "medicines," a code word to indicate the family's jewels.[58] Before leaving Tobolsk, the empress informed her daughters that if they received this message, they should conceal their remaining jewelry.[59]

For several days, as Alexandra Tegleva recalled, the three remaining grand duchesses worked at sewing diamonds, rubies, emeralds, sapphires, and pearls into the linings of their clothing. Tegleva said,

> We took several garments of heavy linen. We put the jewels in wadding, covered the wadding with two garments, and then sewed the garments together. In this fashion the jewels were sewn between two garments, which were then covered with wadding on both sides. The jewels of the Empress were sewn in two pairs of garments. In one of such double garments the weight of the jewels together with the garments and wadding was four and a half pounds. The other was of the same weight. Tatiana wore one of them, and Anastasia the other. In these were sewn diamonds, emeralds, and amethysts. The jewels of the Grand Duchesses were sewn into a double garment in the same fashion, and it was worn by Olga. In addition they put many pearls on their bodies, under their blouses. We also sewed jewels into the hats of the Grand Duchesses, between the lining and the velvet. Among the jewels of this type I remember a large pearl necklace and a brooch with a large sapphire and diamonds. The Grand Duchesses had blue outer garments of cheviot. These garments [summer clothes they wore when they left] did not have buttons but sashes, on each of which there were two buttons. We ripped these buttons off and in place of the buttons sewed jewels, diamonds I believe, wrapping them first in wadding and then with black silk. In addition the Grand Duchesses had grey garments of English tricot with black stripes. These were autumn clothing which they also wore during the summer, in bad weather. We also ripped the buttons off these and sewed on jewels, after wrapping them in wadding and black silk.[60]

In her original, Russian-language statement, Tegleva used only the general word *kostyumi* to identify the clothing in which these jewels were sewn; there was no mention of *korset*, the Russian word for "corset." In numerous Russian-language accounts of the executions, however, the word *korslet*, which literally means "armor," was used to describe the solid nature of the garments shielding the upper torsos of the grand duchesses from both bullets and bayonets, and over the years and through improper translation, this has come to be rendered as "corset." Jewelry was concealed in belts, hats, and in buttons on dresses and jackets as well as in undergarments, though precisely what these last were is not known. While both the empress and her daughters had corsets, there is no indication that any jewels were concealed within them. Instead, certain items may have been secreted in camisoles, sewn together to form the double garments of which Tegleva spoke.

Camisoles of the period, with stays and thick bodice panels, would have provided sufficient rigidity and form to allow for concealment.[61]

With each passing day, the Ural Regional Soviet worried that some monarchist force would descend on Tobolsk and rescue the imperial children. By the middle of May they had sent a second Ural Soviet commissar, Nicholas Rodionov, to assist Paul Khokryakov in the transfer of the remaining Romanovs to Ekaterinburg to join their parents.[62] At the same time, the Special Detachment was relieved of its duties, replaced with Rodionov's guard of sixty-three Ural sharpshooters and nine machine gunners from the Second Ural Rifle Regiment.[63] These new guards were Latvians, "very rough and abusive," according to Alexei Volkov.[64]

While Khokhryakov acted humanely, Rodionov was a sinister character. Once installed in the Governor's House, he kept careful watch over the prisoners, passing his days "almost entirely in the guardroom," recalled Volkov, "armed from head to foot."[65] The day after he arrived, Rodionov gave Volkov new instructions for the grand duchesses: "Tell the young ladies that they may not close the door to their bedchamber at night." Volkov immediately protested, but Rodionov said flatly, "Tell them to do it."

"It is absolutely impossible," Volkov objected, "because the guards walk back and forth in front of their door when they're awake, let alone when they're asleep."

"My guards do no such thing!" Rodionov replied. "If you do not do as I have asked you, then I will shoot you where you stand." As he spoke, Rodionov drew his pistol. "I will mount a sentry or two on their door at night," he told Volkov.[66] Thereafter, fearing the worst, the remaining male members of the suite and household organized their own watch over the children.[67]

Rodionov also instituted a daily roll call for the prisoners. Every morning, the grand duchesses and members of the suite and household were required to appear in the ballroom, stepping forth and replying to Rodionov's questions: "Are you Olga Nikolaievna? Tatiana Nikolaievna?"[68] It was humiliating, Tegleva recalled, as he counted them "like so many inanimate objects."[69]

It took the prisoners a week to pack. "The rooms are empty," Alexei wrote in his diary, "little by little everything is packed away. The walls look bare without their pictures."[70] Slowly, the prisoners felt the noose tightening around them. When Tatiana Botkin asked Rodionov for permission to accompany the prisoners to Ekaterinburg, where her and her brother Gleb hoped to rejoin their father, he said flatly, "Why should such a handsome girl as you are want to rot all her life in prison, or even to be shot?"

"The imperial family is not going to rot in prison," Tatiana angrily replied.

"Perhaps not," Rodionov answered. "In all probability they will be shot, instead."

"Indeed?" Tatiana declared with sarcasm. "I doubt it, very strongly. You don't appear to know the facts of the situation. But, in any event, what is it to you if we desire to be killed with them?"

"Nothing," Rodionov replied. "Just the same you're not going to be killed with them. If you don't believe me, you may go with me as far as Ekaterinburg Station. The entry to Ekaterinburg is forbidden to all people without a special permit. So all that will happen to you at Ekaterinburg will be to be arrested at the station and sent back to Tobolsk."[71] In the end, Gleb and Tatiana decided to remain behind in Tobolsk.

Sunday, May 19, was to be the last day spent in Tobolsk. Knowing that the prisoners would be leaving soon, Gleb Botkin walked up and down Freedom Street in front of the Governor's House, hoping to catch a glimpse of his friends. "I saw Anastasia," he remembered, "who beckoned smilingly upon my greeting."[72] He took off his cap, smiled, and waved, dropping her a low bow. Rodionov, who witnessed this scene from the guardroom, immediately ran into the street, shouting, "Nobody is permitted to look at the windows of this house! Pass on, pass on!" Turning to the soldiers of the guard, he yelled, "Comrades, shoot everybody who so much as looks in this direction! Shoot to kill!"[73]

At eight that night, the children took their last meal in Tobolsk: roast veal and macaroni.[74] Gibbes recalled:

> It was only on this last evening that we called for the two remaining bottles of wine. It was impossible to take them away, and it was agreed that the next best thing to do was to drink them. While we were doing so the new Commandant [Rodionov] was heard sneaking down the corridor. We had only just time to hide the bottles and our glasses under the table, concealed by a long trailing cloth, when he walked in. He stood by the door, giving a quizzical look all round, and immediately we felt like little schoolboys caught doing something naughty at school. The situation was so ludicrous that as our eyes met we could contain ourselves no longer, but burst into a wild yell of uncontrollable laughter. The Commandant, more mystified than ever, did not know what to make of it, but as laughter is not generally a concomitant of plotting, he left it at that and went away.[75]

After dinner, the last belongings were packed in anticipation of the following day's move. As she wrapped pictures and bits of porcelain,

Tegleva saw Rodionov eyeing her suspiciously. "Life down there," he ominously told her, referring to Ekaterinburg, "will be very different."[76]

Before dawn on the following morning, May 20, a long line of carts drew up before the Governor's House, stretching along the fenced-in roadway. It took the sixty-three men of the Latvian detachment nearly six hours to load all of the luggage and possessions that were to follow the prisoners to Ekaterinburg.[77] Just after eleven a carriage drew up before the main entrance to the Governor's House, between lines formed from the Lett detachment, who stood armed with rifles, and the prisoners appeared. Nagorny carried the tsesarevich in his arms, gently placing him inside the carriage, while the three grand duchesses, dressed in simple traveling suits, followed with the members of the suite and household who were to accompany them.[78] As he sat in the carriage, Alexei saw crates of dishes, paintings, and furniture from the house, waiting to be moved. "Why are you taking these things?" he asked Rodionov. "They do not belong to us or to you."

"If the master is absent, then everything belongs to us," replied Rodionov.[79]

At the wharf, the steamship *Rus* waited; it was the same vessel that had brought the Romanovs to Tobolsk the previous August. For the first few hours, the girls arranged themselves in the cabins, while the tsesarevich sat on deck in his wheelchair, enjoying the sunshine.[80] Twenty-seven members of the suite and household accompanied them to Ekaterinburg, including Countess Hendrikova; Baroness Buxhoeveden; Mademoiselle Schneider; General Tatishchev; Nagorny; Alexei Volkov; Dr. Derevenko; Elizabeth Ersberg; Pierre Gilliard; Gibbes; Alexandra Tegleva; Kharitonov; Leonid Sednev; Tutelberg; Pauline Mejantz; the maids Katia and Masha; Ivanov; Tutin; Youravsky; Trupp; and Kokichev.[81]

Baroness Buxhoeveden saw the imperial children for the first time since Tsarskoye Selo that morning when she boarded *Rus*. "I was horrified to see how ill the tsesarevich still looked," she wrote. "He was terribly thin and could not walk as his knee had got quite stiff from lying with it bent for so long. He was very pale and his large dark eyes seemed still larger in the small narrow face. Olga Nikolaievna had also greatly changed. The suspense and anxiety of her

Countess Sophie Buxhoeveden in Russian court dress, 1912.

parents' absence, and the responsibility she bore when left as head of the house with her sick brother to look after, had changed the lovely, bright girl of twenty-two into a faded and sad middle-aged woman. She was the only one of the young girls who acutely realized the danger that their parents were in."[82]

While the luggage was loaded, members of the Lett detachment wandered the decks, "singing and playing the accordion," Buxhoeveden recalled.[83] As the hours wore on, the soldiers became more boisterous, drinking and firing their rifles into the air, throwing live grenades over the side of the ship into the river, or letting loose with their machine guns at the distant trees.[84] Occasionally, as Volkov recalled, "they fired at birds, but as often as not they fired at nothing but air."[85] Worried about Alexei, Khokhryakov sought him out and told the tsesarevich not to be frightened.[86] Finally, as the sun stood low on the horizon, a mighty roar of the engines sent a tremble over *Rus*. With a shrill whistle, the boat slowly edged away from the Tobolsk wharf, churning a ribbon of white foam as it steamed across the dark water into the fire of the Siberian sunset. It was the beginning of what Volkov later termed "a savage orgy."[87]

Rodionov and his band of drunken soldiers passed from cabin to cabin, reshuffling passengers, until all of the men were gathered together in a handful of rooms. The doors slammed shut with loud bangs, followed by further, more ominous sounds: padlocks being secured and doors being nailed shut. Within a few minutes, the goal was accomplished: all of the men, as Gibbes recalled, had been locked into their cabins, "so that they could not interfere with the evil intentions of the Red soldiers."[88]

Bands of drunken soldiers roamed the decks, oblivious as Nagorny banged on his cabin door, shouting, "What effrontery! A sick boy! He can't even go out to the washroom!"[89] The women, as Buxhoeveden recalled, had been ordered "to leave our cabin doors open all night. No one undressed."[90] Through the open doors, the soldiers leered at the grand duchesses, refusing, as Volkov later learned, to "leave them in peace."[91]

The abuse reached a crescendo as the night wore on. Gibbes, locked away in his cabin, listened helplessly, as he later told his son George, as the drunken guards harassed the grand duchesses. "It was dreadful, what they did," the former tutor recalled. The "terrified screams" of the girls, Gibbes said, haunted him "to the end of his life."[92]

What happened that night aboard *Rus*, leaving it seared in Gibbes' mind as, according to George Gibbes, his "worst memory," even "more so than learning that the family had been martyred"? The key must lie in Gibbes' account, in the "dreadful" thing done to the girls, an unnamed crime that brought about such "terrified screams" that their tutor was haunted by the memory "to the end of his life." From across the distance of time, a faded photograph, taken the following day aboard *Rus*, whispers of suffering. It is the last photograph of Olga and her brother, the tsesarevich cast in shadow. Olga sits against the dark mahogany paneling of the room, the large mirror, the crystal lantern hanging from the white ceiling; although a warm, late May day, she wears a long, dark skirt; white blouse buttoned to the throat, barely visible beneath a dark jacket; and a dark hat.[93] She clutches her purse, head turned to the window, face pensive and etched with worry.[94] Her look—buttoned, haunted, exhausted—hints heavily at despair and resignation.

Almost certainly, the grand duchesses were subjected to taunts, and perhaps lewd advances at the hands of the drunken Latvian guards; how far this progressed as the evening wore on is impossible to determine. The harassment, as Volkov wrote, continued throughout the night, while Buxhoeveden's comment that the women remained dressed suggests the attention was sexual in nature. Gilliard made no mention of any such incident, yet according to Volkov and Gibbes, the soldiers were persistent in their actions. The near veil of silence surrounding the events of that night, however, is not difficult to understand, given the exalted position of the grand duchesses; the horrific murders in Ekaterinburg; the determination by those intimately connected with the Romanovs to present them as paragons of all moral virtue; and the tenor of the times. Those aboard the ship were unable (being locked up) or unwilling (through fear of reprisal at the hands of the Bolsheviks) to intercede, as Buxhoeveden herself later remarked: "We were prisoners and had to be passive." This may well be key to the events of that night: shame and humiliation at not being able to come to the defense of the helpless grand duchesses might well account for Gibbes' "worst memory."[95]

No matter what took place, it is difficult not to believe that the experience had a profoundly traumatic effect on the young women, particularly Grand Duchess Olga. Once she arrived in Ekaterinburg, Olga was withdrawn, silent, and did not mix with her sisters, perhaps indicating that she had suffered some significant trauma. If the memory of that night haunted Gibbes for the rest of his life, the effect on those who actually suffered at the hands of the Bolsheviks must have been truly horrific, particularly for young women raised in the cloistered world of their father's palaces.

Even as these horrors unfolded, another ominous and, in the end, brutally personal situation played itself out. Unknown to the terrified grand duchesses, a previously trusted member of their father's suite willingly betrayed their secrets. On learning that she had apparently kept Soloviev's money, Baroness Buxhoeveden had come under the penetrating gaze of the Bolsheviks, who suspected her in some unknown plot. Two searches of her apartment early on the morning of April 25 presumably failed to disclose the hidden funds, but the increased pressure left Buxhoeveden in fear for her own welfare.

As the grand duchesses' terrified screams filled the decks of *Rus*, echoing across the placid waters to the darkness beyond, Buxhoeveden acted. Perhaps in an effort to spare herself from the same fate, or to guarantee her later safety, she found Rodionov, telling him not only of the fortune in jewels concealed beneath the clothing of the three young women, but also where the items could be found: "The buttons on her coat aren't buttons," she revealed, "they're diamonds"; "the aigrette of that hat conceals a diamond from the shah of Persia"; and "that belt there—underneath it are ropes of pearls."[96]

Buxhoeveden's revelations were accurate, indicating that while she herself had been forbidden access to the Governor's House and only been reunited with the grand duchesses earlier that morning, someone within the intimate circle had talked. Two further members of the Romanov household also betrayed the imperial family, telling both Buxhoeveden and the Bolsheviks what they knew of the hidden jewels: Countess Hendrikova's maid Alexandrine Nikolaeva, and the maid Anna Romanova. When the prisoners arrived in Ekaterinburg, Rodionov reported this news to the Ural Regional Soviet, and all three women were questioned that same day. Like Buxhoeveden, Nikolaeva crumbled under pressure, according to Ural Regional Soviet member Paul Bykov, "revealing where these things could be found."[97] Anna Romanova, who had arrived with Buxhoeveden in Tobolsk, also readily disclosed the secrets of the family she had served; she later married a Bolshevik commissar and remained in the Soviet Union.[98]

Acting out of fear, Buxhoeveden nevertheless guaranteed her own safety on reaching the Urals. Alone of the former imperial suite, she was not arrested and imprisoned but allowed first to live in a railroad coach at the station in Ekaterinburg, then to leave the Urals unharmed with the members of the household. Both Gilliard and Gibbes later openly questioned how the baroness had managed to escape the fate of Countess Hendrikova and Mademoiselle Schneider, the only other two women of the suite. "My father," said George Gibbes, "rarely spoke of her. When he did, it was in a distasteful way, indicating that she'd been responsible not only for his misery but also that of the imperial family."[99]

Word of this hidden cache of jewels quickly spread among the Ekaterinburg Bolsheviks, weighing heavily on their minds. "It was absurd," recalled Cheka member Isai Rodzinsky. "They didn't have any freedom, but they had such an immense treasure of jewels in their hands. We had decided that these should all go to the Diamond Fund in the Kremlin, but it was laughable—they had their own Diamond Fund in the Ipatiev House. Do you understand how absurd this was? They had incalculable wealth in their hands. One jewel they had hidden was a big diamond, wrapped up in cotton wadding, and sewn to the front of a hat as a button, which we were told had been given to them by the shah of Persia."[100] And in his 1922 memoirs, Yurovsky wrote of "the damn valuables and jewels we knew they had concealed in their clothes when they arrived, which caused troubles to no end."[101] The Romanovs themselves apparently never learned the truth of their former lady-in-waiting's betrayal.

After this long and torturous night, a brilliant sunrise broke over *Rus* as it continued along the banks of the river. That day, by prior arrangement, the children and certain members of the suite and household were given their only meal of the voyage: five portions of veal, two portions of beef Stroganov, and three portions of chicken, along with fruit and four glasses of cocoa, milk, and tea. A request for cigarettes and cigars—perhaps the former for the grand duchesses themselves—appeared on the bill, but was denied.[102] Whatever had taken place, Khokhryakov apparently had no hand in it, though he may have been powerless to oppose either Rodionov or his men. Certainly the grand duchesses bore Khokhryakov no ill will. That afternoon, when he slipped from a ladder, Olga ran to him, explaining that she had worked as a nurse during the war and offering to examine his foot. By this time, members of the Latvian detachment had begun to gather, and Khokhryakov—perhaps fearful of appearing too friendly—"refused gruffly to have it seen to," limping away under the watchful eyes of the soldiers. But all afternoon and into the night, Olga worried, referring to Khokhryakov as her "poor fellow."[103]

At dawn on the morning of May 22, the ship finally docked at Tyumen, where the prisoners were to board a train for Ekaterinburg.[104] By coincidence, Maria Rasputin, daughter of the infamous Siberian peasant, happened to be in Tyumen: "I went to the pier for tickets and saw a ship docked there; but no one was allowed." Approaching the ticket booth, she saw Countess Hendrikova and the tsarevich waving through the dirty windows. "They were like angels," she later said.[105]

Rodionov entered the saloon and read from a list of names. The first group, including Tatishchev, Buxhoeveden, Hendrikova, Schneider, Dr. Derevenko, and Ersberg, followed soldiers of the Latvian detachment up the quayside to a heavily guarded siding, where a string of second-class railroad coaches waited.[106] The grand duchesses followed, escorted along the same muddy path between two rows of soldiers, followed by Nagorny, who carried Alexei in his arms. "News that the Emperor's children were in town had spread," Buxhoeveden recalled, "and a crowd gathered. Some ladies threw flowers at the children, but were rudely pushed aside by the soldiers."[107] Those who remained, including Gilliard, Gibbes, Volkov, Tegleva, Kharitonov, and Leonid Sednev, and the other servants, were placed in a fourth-class goods wagon coupled to the back of the train.[108]

The prisoners had been searched before entering the train. They were not allowed any silver, on the excuse it could be used as a weapon; when it came time to eat, General Tatishchev used his penknife to cut the bread and peel the fruit they had brought with them. "Tatishchev foretold," Buxhoeveden recalled, "that the treatment meted out to us on this journey boded no good for the regime we should find in force at Ekaterinburg." Countess Hendrikova, too, seemed quiet, reflective. According to Buxhoeveden, she had "so fixed her thoughts on approaching death that it had no terror for her. She was very pretty and looked younger than her twenty-eight years, but she welcomed the thought of death, so weary had she become of life and so much detached from earthly interests. I felt her drifting away to higher planes."[109]

In early afternoon, the train pulled away from the siding, heading along the northern spur of the Trans-Siberian Railroad toward the Urals and Ekaterinburg. At midnight it entered the thick forests that ringed the eastern slopes of the Urals; as the train climbed higher, the weather grew steadily more cold, with brief gusts of snow swirling around the darkened cars as they threaded their way along the track. Finally, just before 2:00 A.M., the train eased to a halt at Ekaterinburg II, the goods depot siding, and a heavily armed guard posted around the entire station.[110] Looking out of the door, Volkov saw only the glint of their rifles shimmering in the steady rain.[111]

Thursday, May 23, 1918, dawned cold and clouded over Ekaterinburg; clumps of snow from the previous night still lay on the ground, melting into tiny streams that joined the incessant rain and fed the growing morass of mud surrounding the train.[112] By nine, the entire depot had filled with a curious and hostile public, who had somehow learned of the children's arrival.[113] "I cannot describe the faces I saw," Buxhoeveden recalled. "All the escaped jailbirds and their womenfolk seemed to have forgathered. These were faces that bore the imprint of every vice written in large letters on them: fat faces, lean faces, but all with deadly, intense hatred stamped on them. They mocked and jeered as the luggage was taken out."[114]

Someone in the crowd grabbed a box and pulled it open, revealing some of the emperor's old boots. "He has six pairs, and I have none!" shouted one barefooted man. Hearing him, the crowd chanted, "Death to the tyrant! Death to the bourgeois!" Yet another box was torn open, disclosing the empress's dresses and gowns. "All these boxes contain the gold dresses of these wanton women!" cried another woman, pointing toward the train. "Off with their heads!" A third man climbed onto one of the boxes and exhorted the crowd: "Tovarishi! While these blood suckers were gloating over their ill-gotten gains, we were sweating the sap of our lives in working for them. Now it is their turn; down with them! Hang them! Drown them in the lake!"[115]

The contingent of armed soldiers sent to guard the prisoners laughed as the crowd swelled, the menace growing with every jeer, every round of applause. Finally, Khokhryakov managed to clear the siding and began to remove the luggage. "This and that goes to the Ipatiev House," he would say, "these other things to the Soviet." As Buxhoeveden recalled, "Most of Their Majesties' belongings went to the Soviet or to the lodgings of the Commissars themselves, and were never seen again by their lawful owners."[116]

At ten, Rodionov entered the second-class carriage where the grand duchesses, tsesarevich, and a few members of the suite were gathered. At his side was Alexander Beloborodov, while another group from the Ural Regional Soviet stood impatiently in the rain. Rodionov ordered them to bring their luggage outside, directing them into a string of covered droshkies that had pulled alongside the train.[117] Only Tatiana seemed optimistic as she said her farewells to the members of the suite: "What is the use of all these leave takings? We shall all rejoice in each other's company in half an hour's time!" Hearing this, one of the guards turned to Buxhoeveden, whispering, "Better say 'Good-bye.'"[118]

Alexei left first, carried, as one witness recalled, "with love and care in the strong arms" of Nagorny, who placed him in a waiting droshky.[119] "I'd seen so many pictures of the tsesarevich," recalled one man, "that I recognized him as easily as his father. He looked white as wax, and very sick."[120] Then the young women appeared, "wearing pretty, dark costumes with big buttons. They got down and started to walk unsteadily, for they were each carrying leather suitcases in their hands that looked far too big and heavy for them. Their way was not made easier by the large men's boots they were wearing, or by the fact that it was raining all morning as it sometimes does in the Urals in the springtime. It struck me that for the first time in their lives these girls were carrying their own luggage, and had no control over their situation. They moved slowly and with difficulty. Their movements were refined and delicate, and their faces, when I watched them for the two or three minutes I had while they passed, were young, mobile, and expressive. I will never forget when my eyes met those of one of the girls. They locked for a moment, and I felt pity for her like a dagger in my heart. It was not any one particular expression that I could name, but contained rather all the colors of the rainbow. It was not a sad little tune, but was instead a tragic symphony. Everything was on her face, she was nervous, emotional, excited to see her parents again, she was a young girl trying to suppress her pride, but also trying to suppress her fear in front of hostile strangers, and finally, hauntingly, perhaps a touch of knowledge that her imminent death was now a possibility."[121]

Nagorny ran to assist them, but the sentries roughly pushed him aside.[122] In addition to their luggage, the girls held two of the three dogs they had brought into exile: Jemmy, the King Charles spaniel Anna Vyrubova had given to Tatiana; and Ortino, Tatiana's English bulldog.[123] "I tried to get out," Gilliard later wrote, "but was roughly pushed back into the carriage by the sentry. I came back to the window. Tatiana Nikolaievna came last, carrying her little dog and struggling to drag a heavy brown valise. It was raining and I saw her feet sink into the mud at every step."[124] The grand duchesses filled the remaining droshkies, flanked by armed sentries and a small ring of members of the Ural Regional Soviet. With a shout from Beloborodov, the carts lurched forward into the dark, ominous morning, bouncing down the muddy road and into the veil of mist that enveloped Ekaterinburg.[125]

At the Ipatiev House, Nicholas and Alexandra waited impatiently for their remaining children. Throughout the morning, Avdayev entered the drawing room with the latest news: their train had arrived the previous night; luggage was being removed; the grand duchesses and the tsesarevich were expected soon. Finally, shortly before eleven, the droshkies pulled up before the wooden palisade, and the children hurried through the rain, disappearing into the shelter of the house and their parents' welcoming arms. "What an enormous joy it was to see them again and to embrace them after the four-week separation and uncertainty," Nicholas wrote. The strain of their journey, he noted, was apparent: "The poor things had endured a lot of personal, spiritual suffering both in Tobolsk and during the three-day trip."[126] Darkness descended on the Urals, the fierce wind and renewed snowfall thundering against the ornate villa perched on the edge of Voznesensky Square; beyond the glow of the windows, the Romanovs celebrated the evening with prayers, happy to be reunited in their new prison. They would not leave it alive.

With the children safely removed to the Ipatiev House, members of the suite and household continued to wait in the train near Ekaterinburg II, occasionally staring out the windows onto the rain-drenched crowd, which seemed to grow larger and more hostile with each passing hour. In the early afternoon, a few more cars arrived. Rodionov entered the rail coach and asked, "Is Volkov here?"

"I am Volkov," the valet said.

"Get out," Rodionov told him. "We are leaving."[127] At Rodionov's orders, he was joined by Tatishchev, Hendrikova, Mlle. Schneider, Elizabeth Ersberg, Ivan Kharitonov, and Leonid Sednev.[128] "We climbed into the conveyances," Volkov recalled, "and were driven through the streets, past a house surrounded by a very high enclosure that I imagined the imperial family had been taken to. I had time to think these thoughts, because I was riding by myself in the first carriage. We stopped in front of the house. No one came out of the mansion, and we were not told to get down. Finally, from the last carriage, Kharitonov and the young Sednev were taken. The rest of us were driven on."[129] Later that afternoon, Alexei Trupp joined Kharitonov and Sednev at the Ipatiev House.

The first group from the train eventually arrived at a large building surrounded by a heavily guarded palisade. Beloborodov, who had been riding at the head of the procession, yelled, "Open the doors to receive the prisoners!" "This order clearly explained our predicament," Volkov recalled.[130] Beloborodov took the prisoners through the gates and down a corridor into an office, where he instructed them to register, then conducted them to small cells. The two women, Schneider and Hendrikova, were taken to a hospital ward, while Tatishchev and Volkov shared a cramped cell on an upper floor.[131]

At five that afternoon, Rodionov finally returned to the siding, where the rest of the suite and household had passed an uneasy day. He went first to the fourth-class goods coach, announcing to Gilliard, Gibbes, and the others, "You are free and you can go wherever you like."[132]

In the second-class coach in which the children had traveled, the only member of the suite who remained was Buxhoeveden. When Rodionov had entered the coach earlier that day and taken Tatishchev, Schneider, Hendrikova, Volkov, and others, he apparently made no reference to the baroness. "I was about to follow them," she later wrote, "but the sentries barred the door with their rifles. Rodionov came up and said that as there was no remaining conveyance I should have to wait."[133]

According to Buxhoeveden, when Rodionov returned that evening, he told her that "the local Soviet had examined my case and that I was free." She grabbed her bag and "left the carriage, not knowing where I should wend my steps. Ekaterinburg was under martial law. I knew not a soul in the town and the passport I had was the most incriminating, for it was still the same old diplomatic one. I was at my wits' end when one of the sentries, now off duty, took pity on me and told me he would escort me to the main station, 'where there was a coach full of people of your kind.'" Buxhoeveden was taken to the coach in which Gibbes, Gilliard, and most of the servants remained.[134]

Those who arrived with the children from Tobolsk were divided into categories that ultimately determined their fates. It was segregation based not on foreign-sounding last names or passports, but rather on social positions and whether they held ranks within the suite or the household. Every member of the suite who arrived in Ekaterinburg was imprisoned and killed, while all of the servants of the household were allowed their freedom. Buxhoeveden was conspicuous as the only member of the suite released, something that puzzled the others. "I cannot understand what prompted the Bolsheviks to this decision to save our lives," Gilliard later wrote. "Why, for instance, should Countess Hendrikova be taken to prison while Baroness Buxhoeveden, also a lady-in-waiting to the tsarina, was allowed to go free? Why they and not ourselves? Was there confusion of names or functions?"[135] Gibbes held a similar, though stronger, view: "My father," George Gibbes recalled, "told me he never understood why Baroness Buxhoeveden had gone free, and others detained and killed."[136]

Unknown to both of these men, and ignored by Buxhoeveden in her memoirs, was her interrogation that afternoon. A few members of the Ural Regional Soviet and Ekaterinburg Cheka entered the railroad coach where she waited alone, questioning her at length about her revelations to Rodionov aboard *Rus*. During the session, Buxhoeveden repeated her knowledge of the imperial family's hidden jewelry, a final betrayal that guaranteed her freedom and helped seal the fate of the prisoners.[137]

Another departure was that of Dr. Vladimir Derevenko. That afternoon, a car sent by the Ekaterinburg Cheka arrived for him, and Derevenko was taken to their headquarters at the Hotel Amerika.

Dr. Vladimir Nikolaievich Derevenko on the train on his way into exile, August 1917.

He quickly established a good relationship with the Ural Bolsheviks, and they permitted him to remain at liberty in Ekaterinburg and set up his own practice—the only member of the former suite or household accorded such privileges.[138]

Derevenko's conspicuous freedom made him an inevitable target for monarchist speculation; on this issue, Derevenko's brief memoirs are frustratingly silent.[139] Yet Princess Helen of Serbia offered a possible explanation. The wife of Prince Ioann Konstantinovich, Helen followed her husband into his

Siberian exile, but alone among members of the Romanov family, remained free in Ekaterinburg, where she heard details of Derevenko's favored position from a Madame Atamanov, the woman who ran the rooming house where she lived. According to her, an epidemic of the Spanish flu was raging in Ekaterinburg when Derevenko arrived. One of the victims was Beloborodov's wife, and the commissar apparently asked Derevenko to treat her. When she recovered, Beloborodov, in gratitude, granted Derevenko his freedom.[140] Significantly, Derevenko was not granted his freedom until May 28; had he begun his treatment on May 23—the day he arrived in Ekaterinburg—it is possible that Beloborodov may have believed Derevenko had managed a miraculous cure when, in fact, the influenza had simply run its course.

Derevenko himself offered little in the way of explanation as to why he had remained free, and his own account contradicted the story told by Princess Helen. After the fall of Ekaterinburg to the Whites on July 25, Gleb Botkin had rushed to the city to seek information on his father. "The first man I met was Dr. Derevenko," he recalled. "He welcomed me warmly, but could tell me little. In some miraculous way he had escaped imprisonment. Nor had he been sent back to Tyumen, but permitted to live in Ekaterinburg in perfect freedom, and had managed to establish a good practice." He explained, "rather apologetically," as Botkin wrote, "The Reds must have forgotten me."[141]

Yet he certainly was not forgotten by the Bolsheviks during their hold on the city. In his memoirs, Avdayev noted Derevenko's "astuteness" and wrote, "He was a man of great intelligence and guile, able to see how things were."[142] And Catherine Tomilova, the woman charged with bringing the daily meals to the Ipatiev House from the Soviet soup kitchen, recalled: "Once, in the beginning when I had brought meals, the Doctor passed by a Red Army man into the House, and the Red Army man stood at attention."[143]

Such deference by the Bolsheviks, once it became known, became fodder for monarchists who suspected Derevenko of collaboration. White general Michael Deterikhs was skeptical of the doctor. "Somehow," he wrote, "the ordinary people of the city, with whom Derevenko associated, and who were certainly not partisans of the Bolsheviks, retained very few recollections of stories told by Derevenko about his visits to the Ipatiev prisoners during this extraordinary period in the life of the Imperial Family."[144] And one of the Ipatiev House guards, Anatoly Yakimov, added fuel to the fire when he later recalled that, though he had wanted to speak to Derevenko privately about arranging a possible rescue attempt, he "was doubtful of him. I cannot tell you why I was doubtful. I just thought: I don't know what kind of man he is."[145]

Derevenko seems, as Avdayev put it, to be a man who "was able to see how things were." Unlike Botkin, he was not a courtier, and after the Revolution, he had made no secret of his dissatisfaction with his new situation as a prisoner, complaining loudly about the restrictions and inconveniences of life with the former imperial family. As an ordinary man, he had indeed risen to great heights, and enjoyed an intimate relationship with the Romanovs; his son Kolya even became one of the tsesarevich's few friends. Yet there was never any question, even in Siberian exile, when all were prisoners, of a presumption of equality. Siberian exile, in this case, very often brought to the surface the most unpleasant traits and displays from the empress and her only son, and it is certainly possible that Derevenko resented the charade of power and deference still enacted by the Romanovs. His treatment of Beloborodov's wife gained him both his freedom and the respect of the local Bolshevik authorities, whereas service at court had brought him little but exile and bitterness. He seems never to have abandoned the Romanovs, and was almost certainly instrumental in assisting those who attempted to effect a rescue, but he also had a family of his own to consider.

For those incarcerated in Ekaterinburg, their long ordeal was just beginning. According to Volkov, "around May 25" two guards appeared and escorted Tatishchev from his cell. He was told that the prison warden wished to speak to him and immediately "paled." The guards showed Tatishchev a piece of paper that said he was being released and "expelled from the Ural Region."[146] "We said our good-byes," Volkov later wrote, "and he went out. He left me his beautiful, fur-lined coat, and I asked him to remember me to his aunt, whom I much admired. I thought that it had been difficult for him to part with the coat, but he felt that I would need it more than he would."[147]

The next day, Volkov decided he should return the coat to Tatishchev, and asked to take it to the warden. Later, when he asked a female guard if Tatishchev had received it, she replied that he had been shot in it. She had recognized the general, she told Volkov, because the corpse she had seen wore his distinctive coat.[148] Volkov was not entirely convinced, and asked the prison warden if the corpse could be examined by the prison doctor. The warden agreed, but the doctor was unable to report a definitive conclusion. He had only seen Tatishchev a few times since his incarceration on May 23, and was not familiar with his face.[149] Later, Gilliard wrote, a body was discovered in the prison yard that was thought to be that of Tatishchev, but there never was any identification.[150]

Thomas Preston, the British consul in Ekaterinburg, received "several pencil-written notes" from Prince Dolgoruky, "imploring me to intervene on behalf of the Imperial Family. To avoid compromising him, I never replied to them, but he must have known that I was making daily representations to the Ural Soviet on behalf of the Tsar and his family."[151] At the same time that Tatishchev was taken from his cell and disappeared, according to Preston, Dolgoruky was released from prison and allowed to move into his own rooms. Some time later, officials from the Ekaterinburg Cheka appeared and conducted a search of the premises, finding two maps of the region, with rivers and other means of passage marked and noted, along with a considerable sum of money. He was arrested again and shot a few days later.[152]

Before the prisoners left Tobolsk, a young officer dispatched by Spalaikovich, the Serbian minister in Petrograd, had delivered some 75,000 rubles to be used in event of any emergency. It was divided by Tatishchev and Dolgoruky, each taking half in case they were separated. Volkov believed that each man still carried his half on arrival in Ekaterinburg. It is possible that Dolgoruky, armed with just over 37,000 rubles, might have bribed his way out of prison, believing that once free he could then use the remaining funds to either provide relief for the Romanovs or help effect their escape.[153]

On May 26 the remaining servants, along with the two tutors Gilliard and Gibbes, and Baroness Buxhoeveden—who had been living in the railroad coach in Ekaterinburg—were ordered by the Presidium of the Ural Regional Soviet to leave the province. The railroad line, however, was cut, and the authorities grudgingly allowed them to remain.[154]

Several times, both Gilliard and Gibbes asked Rodionov if they could voluntarily join Alexei in the Ipatiev House, but were refused; in her memoirs, Buxhoeveden writes that she, too, asked for permission, only to be met with a similar response.[155] Buxhoeveden wrote,

My companions and I, though we were officially free, were evidently carefully shadowed. Armed soldiers always prowled about the station and lounged near our car. There were so many of them that it was difficult to guess which was to be our special escort. Whenever we went to dine at the station restaurant soldiers sat on each side of us and listened attentively to every word we uttered. The streets were full of sailors and soldiers, and we generally had the uncomfortable sensation, when we walked abroad, of somebody slinking behind us. I had often had the same feeling at Tobolsk and had got into the way of stopping whenever I noticed this and pretending I was deeply engrossed by something I saw in the street till my "follower" had passed me, when I walked behind him in my turn. I had got so used to this maneuver that I caught myself stopping short in the street when I heard steps behind me for months after my return to Europe. Naturally in these conditions we went about as little as possible, but when we did go into the town we

saw a good deal of movement in the streets. A great many cars rushed
hither and thither, full of commissars. A German Red Cross mission
had just arrived at Ekaterinburg in connection with the repatriation of
the former prisoners-of-war, and the Bolsheviks were doing their best
to be amiable to their guests, as the Germans played a great part after
the Brest-Litovsk Treaty. I saw German generals and nurses being
driven about the town, and their train, a beautiful one, was drawn up on
the main line of the station, not far away from ours. Did this delegation
know of the danger to the Emperor and his family, or were they
deluded into believing in the Bolsheviks' feelings of humanity?
Certainly had they themselves offered to do anything for them the
Emperor and Empress would not have accepted their help, but I always
wondered how it was that through this Red Cross delegation the news
of the desperate plight of the Russian Sovereigns did not filter through
abroad. I personally could not approach the Germans, for I considered
that we were still at war with them, the Emperor never having recognized the peace treaty concluded with them by the Bolsheviks. Even the
civil population of Ekaterinburg that we met in the streets seemed all
akin to the ruffians that we had seen at the station when the luggage was
being dealt with. Ekaterinburg was a large mining center, and it had
become one of the chief strongholds of the Bolsheviks after the
Revolution. Most of the criminal element from the whole of Siberia had
assembled there, which explained the types we saw. I was also struck by
the evidences of class hatred that were shown in the casual conversations we overheard in shops and in the streets. I suppose that all the
more moderate elements in the population were too terrorized to show
themselves. Both the tutors and I were tied hand and foot, for none of
us had valid documents and very little money. We could only stay where
we were and await events. We did not again see the Commissars who
had brought us from Tobolsk, for their mission was now ended.
Everything connected with the state prisoners was so much shrouded in
mystery by the Bolsheviks that many of the townspeople did not even
know of the Emperor's presence in Ekaterinburg. All questions concerning them were regarded with such suspicion that it took us a couple of days even to locate the Ipatiev House.[156]

The remaining members of the household and Baroness
Buxhoeveden spent eleven days living in their railroad coach, unable to
leave Ekaterinburg as ordered but prevented from taking any rooms in
the city. Gilliard and Gibbes both paid several visits to the British and
Swedish consuls in Ekaterinburg, imploring them to help the imperial
family.[157] "The two consuls," Gilliard later wrote, "relieved our minds

by telling us that proceedings had already been taken and that they did not think there was any imminent danger."[158]

On June 2, 1918, the eighteen men and women living in the railroad car at the Ekaterinburg Station had an unexpected visitor: a member of the Presidium of the Ural Regional Soviet, who told them that the rail lines had been repaired and that they had twelve hours to leave the city and the province.[159] "The order was preemptory," Buxhoeveden wrote; "we could do nothing but obey . . . Gilliard, Gibbes and I clubbed together to pay for the fourth-class van in which we were to travel, for the servants had little money. . . . On June 3 we started back along the way we had come, still hoping that we might somehow ultimately manage to get into touch with the unfortunate family who were now completely isolated in the clutches of the Ural Soviet."[160]

The train got only as far as the small town of Kamyshlov, some distance from Tyumen, before it had to be stopped: the advancing Czech forces had taken control of the Trans-Siberian and severed the lines for a second time. Here, in this little village, the train sat for ten days. Finally, Gilliard and Gibbes approached the engineer and asked that their coach be coupled onto the next engine that passed them; he agreed, and within a day, as Gibbes explained in a letter to his aunt, "we arrived at the railway station at Tyumen, where we had to leave the railway to take the boat for Tobolsk."[161]

Tobolsk, however, had fallen to the Whites, ironically at the end of May, just ten days after the Romanov children had left.[162] While the travelers would have been happy to return to Tobolsk and place themselves under the protection of the Whites, members of the Tyumen Soviet would not allow them to do this. Instead, they were told that they could not leave the city, and that they must remain at their own expense.[163] "There was much discussion at Tyumen," Buxhoeveden recalled, "as to whether we were to be arrested or not. Happily it was proved that we were harmless."[164] Gibbes, who disliked Gilliard, took a room by himself, leaving the children's tutor of French to make other arrangements.[165] According to Buxhoeveden, both tutors, being foreigners, "were still treated a shade better than the Russians during the first weeks of our stay."[166] After the Reds fled Tyumen, the remaining members of the household, with the two tutors and Buxhoeveden, finally returned to Tobolsk. Here they remained for several months, uncertain what to do, and not knowing what had become of the imperial family. Only after Ekaterinburg fell to the advancing Czech and Whites forces on July 25, 1918, did they make their way back to the Urals, to learn what had happened to the Romanovs.[167]

5

The Seventy-eight Days

F OR SEVENTY-EIGHT DAYS, the thick, whitewashed walls of the Ipatiev House sheltered the Romanovs and those imprisoned with them under Bolshevik guard. History has shrouded these eleven weeks in speculation and controversy, depicting an orgy of drunken barbarity and cruel humiliations by Avdayev and his men. This thread of alleged abuse runs throughout the vast majority of works on the end of the Romanovs, curiously symptomatic of the necessity to portray them in a sympathetic light while at the same time resorting to squalid, often highly exaggerated tales of insults in an effort to heighten their imagined sufferings.

Robert Wilton, a journalist working with the White Army for the *Times* of London in Siberia, provided a typical example. "The Ekaterinburg period," he contended, "was one long martyrdom for the Romanovs, growing worse, with one short interval, as the hour of their death approached." He termed their first guards "brutal," the last, "alien" guards who possessed a "fiendish ingenuity in tormenting their helpless captives."[1] Avdayev and his men, he declared, "were coarse, drunken, criminal types," who "entered the prisoners' rooms whenever they thought fit, at all hours, prying with drunken, leering eyes into everything that they might be doing. Their mere presence was an offense; but picture the torments of the captives to have to put up with their loathsome familiarities. They would sit down at the table when the prisoners ate, put their dirty hands into the plates, spit, jostle, and reach in front of the prisoners. Their greasy elbows would be thrust, by accident or design, into the ex-Tsar's face. Alexandra was of course a special object of attention. They would crowd round her chair, lolling in such a manner that any movement on her part brought her in contact with their evil smelling bodies."[2] Such snobbish sentiments fell on the eager ears of most monarchists, ready to believe the worst not only of Bolsheviks but also of anyone associated with them, reflecting the class prejudices that helped drive the Revolution. Wilton summarized this as "ill-treatment, amounting to horrible torture, mental if not physical."[3]

The truth of those eleven weeks, however, lies quite some distance from the imaginative pens of Wilton and those loyal monarchists who followed in his footsteps. The imperial family and those imprisoned with them had little comfort or privacy, and endured much that was unpleasant, but the suggestion that these seventy-eight days consisted of humiliation piled on humiliation ignores the available evidence. In large part, the Ekaterinburg period was marked not with abuse but with monotonous uncertainty.

The arrival of the remaining children on May 23 brought relief to their worried parents, reuniting the imperial family under the roof of their last prison. All day, they waited in vain for the nickel-plated camp beds they had brought into exile.[4] On the following day, Gibbes saw them being taken from the train, but it was not until the afternoon of Monday, May 27, that they were finally delivered to the Ipatiev House and taken to the room used by the grand duchesses.[5] The beds were removed after the murders, apparently shipped to Perm with many of the family's other possessions.

The tsesarevich, as the empress noted, was given his sister Marie's bed, while the four grand duchesses slept "on cloaks and cushions on the floor in the adjoining room."[6] Alexei, who still could not walk after his reckless accident sledding down the staircase in the Governor's House, bumped his knee on the edge of the cot as he climbed into bed, "as if on purpose," his father wrote somewhat resentfully in his diary, adding that his son's "terrible suffering all night disturbed our sleep."[7] By the next day, the tsesarevich was in considerable pain, and Avdayev allowed Dr. Derevenko to visit him and put compresses on his leg. The commandant remained throughout, as Alexandra noted in her diary, and she was unable to ask Derevenko for news of the suite and household.[8]

Before the arrival of the children, seven people were incarcerated within the Ipatiev House: Nicholas, Alexandra, and Marie; Dr. Botkin; maid Anna Demidova; valet Terenty Chemodurov; and footman Ivan Sednev. On May 23 that number increased to thirteen, with the arrival of Alexei, Olga, Tatiana, and Anastasia; the cook Ivan Kharitonov; and Leonid Sednev, his assistant. On the following day, the Ural Regional Soviet allowed Klementy Nagorny, Alexei's diadka, and footman Alexei Trupp to join the others in the Ipatiev House. Both men had to sign statements accepting their status as prisoners, agreeing to "submit to and fulfill the orders of the Ural Regional Soviet issued by the Commandant, and consider myself in the same position as the Romanov Family."[9] Nagorny and Trupp brought with them the last of the family's three dogs, Alexei's spaniel Joy.[10] Both men were questioned and searched by Avdayev, and forced to hand over all of their money before joining the other prisoners.[11]

With the arrival of these new prisoners, Nicholas relieved his valet Terenty Chemodurov of his duties. The old man, growing increasingly senile and suffering from nervous exhaustion, was scarcely capable of continuing in service, and the emperor had Avdayev's assurance that he would receive treatment. Chemodurov left the Ipatiev House on May 24, just a few hours after Nagorny and Trupp arrived. Taken to a hospital ward in Ekaterinburg City Prison, Chemodurov remained here until the city fell to the advancing anti-Bolshevik forces on July 25.

In their eleven weeks of captivity in Ekaterinburg, Nicholas and Alexandra shared the southeastern corner bedroom, with the four grand duchesses in the adjacent dressing room. For the first month, Alexei was lodged in the third bedroom, which Avdayev had opened for his parents a few days before the children arrived from Tobolsk; in June he was moved into his parents' room.[12] The remaining servants and Dr. Botkin were disposed in the other rooms allowed to the prisoners. For the first three weeks, Demidova slept on a chaise set up in the dining room; after Alexei moved into his parents' room, Demidova took his old room. Botkin slept on a chaise in the sitting room, off the drawing room, with Trupp, Kharitonov, and Leonid Sednev sleeping on cots set up in the stair hall or kitchen. The three dogs—Jemmy, Joy, and Ortino—were allowed the run of the first floor.

That evening, Alexandra asked Dr. Botkin to write a letter begging that the two tutors Gilliard and Gibbes be allowed to join them in the Ipatiev House. Addressed to Beloborodov, chairman of the Ural Regional Soviet, the letter pointed out that "Alexei Nikolaievich is subject to pains in the joints from bumps that are completely unavoidable in a boy of his age, and that are accompanied by seepage of fluids and resultant excruciating pains. In these events the boy suffers day and night with inexpressible pain, so that none of his closest relatives, not to mention his mother with chronic heart ailments who does not spare herself for him, can stand taking care of him for long. My fading strength is not enough, either." Although Nagorny had just arrived in the Ipatiev House, Botkin described him as "barely able to stand on his feet" after the tumultuous journey to Ekaterinburg. He asked that Gilliard and Gibbes, who "help each other" and "by reading and a change of impressions distract the patient from his suffering during the day," be allowed into the Ipatiev House."[13]

Avdayev, already under suspicion by the Ural authorities over the Ukraintsev affair and his generally indulgent attitude, attempted to learn further details of Alexei's illness before making the request. The emperor and empress refused to discuss the subject, while Botkin dismissed his inquiry, saying, "You wouldn't understand."[14] With no enlightenment forthcoming, Avdayev passed on the letter, but added his own recommendation: "Having examined Dr. Botkin's present request, I believe that even another servant would be one too many, as the children are now present and can look after the patient, and so I suggest that the chairman of the Regional Soviet notify these ladies and gentlemen at once that they have attempted to reach beyond their bounds."[15] In the end, Botkin's plea was ignored, though Avdayev did allow Dr. Derevenko regular access to the Ipatiev House to treat the tsesarevich.

Alexei's recovery was slow. On Saturday, May 25, Alexandra wrote: "Baby spent the day like yesterday, swelling wee bit less but pains off and on very strong."[16] Derevenko examined him that afternoon, and returned the following day, accompanied, as Nicholas noted in his diary, by a "dark-complexioned gentleman who we took for a doctor."[17] The man with Derevenko was not a doctor. It was Yakov Yurovsky, member of the Ural Regional Soviet and the Ekaterinburg Cheka, and the man who, in six weeks, would lead the execution squad against the Romanovs and their retainers.

The following evening, as Nicholas noted in his diary, Avdayev and Moshkin inspected the trunks and other luggage brought from Tobolsk and finally delivered to the Ipatiev House.[18] As these possessions were being searched, Nagorny—hot-tempered and already an enemy of the Ural Bolsheviks—apparently got into an argument with the men. At 6:30 P.M., Nagorny and Ivan Sednev were called to Avdayev's office for questioning and, within a few minutes, were escorted from the Ipatiev House.[19] As Alexandra recorded in her diary, no one appeared to "know the reason."[20]

By coincidence, Gilliard and Gibbes happened to be passing along Voznesensky Prospekt with Dr. Derevenko that evening. "We saw two carriages drawn up and surrounded by a large number of Red Guards," Gilliard recalled. "What was our horror at recognizing in the first Sednev sitting between two guards. Nagorny was going to the second carriage. He was just setting foot on the step with his hand on the side of the carriage when, raising his head, he saw us all there standing motionless a few yards from him. For a few seconds he looked fixedly at us, then, without a single gesture that might have betrayed us, he took his seat. The carriage was driven off and we saw them turn in the direction of the prison."[21]

The removal of Nagorny and Sednev has always remained something of a mystery. It has frequently been claimed that Nagorny was arrested after he protested the theft of a gold cross belonging to the tsesarevich. The story was thirdhand at best, said to have been told by Nagorny himself to former prime minister Prince George Lvov when both men were imprisoned in Ekaterinburg City Prison.[22] Lvov, who was responsible for many of the questionable stories concerning events in the Ipatiev House, was scarcely a credible witness. In an October 1918 letter to U.S. president Woodrow Wilson, Lvov recounted that he had been imprisoned in Ekaterinburg at the end of February 1918; he escaped after three months, and spent five weeks fleeing across Siberia before finally reaching Vladivostok at the beginning of July.[23] Lvov's own timetable virtually eliminates any possibility that he heard firsthand information on what took place in the Ipatiev House from either Nagorny or Sednev, who were both imprisoned only on the evening of May 27. Other statements made by Lvov completely destroy his credibility as a witness. In the fall of 1918, he told both White investigators and Allied representatives looking into the murder of the Romanovs that the entire family, along with their retainers, had been killed in the cell next to his at the City Prison in Ekaterinburg. "They brought them together into the one room," the French foreign minister reported Lvov saying, "and having made them sit down in a row, they spent the entire night inflicting bayonet blows on them before finishing them off next morning, one after the other, with revolver shots: the Emperor, Empress, the Grand Duchesses, the Tsesarevich, the lady-in-waiting [sic], the Empress's female companion, and all the people with the imperial Family."[24] Although a friend of the former prime minister asserted that the foreign minister had "obviously misunderstood" Lvov's meaning, the prince continued to repeat his lurid and patently false account, which was eventually picked up and printed by the U.S. media.[25]

It is possible that such a theft took place, though unlikely. Nagorny was with the other prisoners when called to Avdayev's office that evening; had he witnessed such a scene, it defies common sense that he would not have mentioned this to either the emperor or the empress. Yet their diaries are silent on the issue, expressing only surprise that the men had been removed.[26]

Another variant, also attributed to Lvov, claimed that the soldiers allowed Alexei only one pair of boots from his luggage; when Nagorny violently protested, he was arrested. This is suspiciously similar to a passage from one of Buxhoeveden's books in which she claimed that Anastasia, on asking for a new pair of shoes, was told "that those she had would last for the rest of her life."[27] It is difficult to imagine that any Bolshevik in the Ipatiev House would be foolish enough to suggest that the life of one of their prisoners was about to end, and certainly none of the evidence from the imperial family's letters and diaries; the statements of those interviewed during the White Army investigation into the murders; or the work of Nicholas Sokolov support such a claim. Buxhoeveden was never in the Ipatiev House and, like much of what she wrote about those final weeks of captivity for the Romanovs, it is without proof.

In all likelihood, Nagorny and Sednev were removed from the Ipatiev House precisely because they represented a threat to the power of the Special Detachment. Both were tall, well-built young men capable of protecting the Romanovs if necessary; with their removal, the only men who remained in the Ipatiev House were the middle-aged Nicholas, Botkin, Trupp, and Kharitonov, and the two young boys, Alexei and Leonid Sednev.

Nagorny and Sednev were imprisoned in Ekaterinburg City Prison that same night, and subjected to lengthy interrogations. According to one guard, Nagorny "did not take well to jail life, being a man of complete devotion to his small charge. Never will I forget the guileless honesty and clarity in his gray eyes."[28] On the last day of May, both men were driven a few miles out of town and shot; Peter Ermakov later bragged that his was the bullet that struck down the devoted sailor.[29]

Deprived of Nagorny, Gilliard, and Gibbes—the three men who had attended to his needs and distracted him during his frequent attacks of hemophilia—Alexei was in low spirits, and his recovery was slow. "Baby slept on the whole well, though woke up every hour—pains less strong," Alexandra wrote on May 28.[30] Although Dr. Botkin remained in the Ipatiev House, he had no special proficiency in dealing with the tsesarevich, and it was his colleague Derevenko who faithfully came each afternoon to treat him. Accustomed to the course of the tsesarevich's attacks, Derevenko first brought a narcotic, which relieved the boy's pain and made him sleep. "Baby's night was better," the empress noted the following day.[31] As the blood from the swollen knee began the gradual process of seeping back into the body, the symptoms became more distressing, and Alexei's temperature rose, accompanied by sharp pains that the narcotic did little to relieve. Derevenko did what he could, administering a splint with a plaster of Paris casing to help straighten the knee and hasten reabsorption, but the recovery process was a long and agonizing one for both the tsesarevich and his fatigued mother. Only after twelve long days had passed did Derevenko pronounce him cured.[32]

By the beginning of June, life for the Romanovs and those imprisoned with them had settled into a predictable, if somewhat uneasy, routine. They usually rose between eight and nine in the morning, assembling in the drawing room for prayers and a reading from the Bible; occasionally, as guard Philip Proskuryakov remembered, they sang hymns.[33] The Ural Regional Soviet demanded a daily inspection, usually conducted by Avdayev or, if he was absent, by Moshkin, before the prisoners were dismissed and free to go about their days.[34]

The Romanovs and their retainers ate breakfast together, sharing the same dining room table, as Chemodurov said, "by order of the emperor." The long expanse of the oak table was bare; although the imperial family had brought a trunk filled with table linens, these items apparently were not allowed into the Ipatiev House. Nor, the emperor's elderly valet declared, did the prisoners have "enough knives, forks, or spoons."[35]

Unpleasant and inconvenient as the arrangements were, these few simple facts were quickly distorted after the Ekaterinburg murders by several authors attempting to paint Avdayev and his regime as purposely cruel. British journalist Robert Wilton, who published the first comprehensive examination of the assassination, wrote: "The table cover was a greasy oil cloth. There were not knives or forks or even plates enough to go round. All ate with wooden spoons out of one common dish."[36] And Baroness Buxhoeveden went further, claiming, "There were neither tablecloths nor napkins, and only five forks for seven people."[37] Chemodurov, who lived in the Ipatiev House for twenty-four days, made no mention of a "greasy oil cloth," saying only that the table was uncovered. The shortage of plates, "wooden spoons," and communal dish existed only in Wilton's imagination. Nor, in any of his statements, did the valet ever indicate—contrary to Buxhoeveden's account—how many pieces of silver the prisoners had at their disposal. Given the lack of supporting evidence, the baroness's assertion calls for extraordinary caution if not rejection.

Breakfast for the prisoners, according to Chemodurov, consisted of black bread, "left over from the day before," and tea.[38] Wilton altered this testimony: the bread became "stale," the tea served with "no sugar."[39] Nor did Chemodurov's statement fare any better with Buxhoeveden, who wrote that the prisoners "often had no tea for breakfast as the soldiers used up all the hot water."[40] Chemodurov had said nothing of "stale" bread, a lack of sugar or hot water, or "no tea for breakfast," yet Wilton and Buxhoeveden again distorted fact to paint a more disturbing portrait of captivity. The only reliable mention of a lack of hot water happened on May 2, when the guards on the main floor emptied the samovar to make their own tea; within an hour, Avdayev had it replaced.[41] Twelve days later, Avdayev himself purchased a samovar for the prisoners to avoid any further inconvenience.[42]

Avdayev ordered a small oil stove for the kitchen, later supplemented with supplies and kitchenware so Kharitonov could prepare meals; occasionally, as the commandant recalled, the grand duchesses also assisted.[43] Contrary to Chemodurov's assertion that breakfast consisted of black bread and tea, Avdayev provided the prisoners with a supply of cocoa by the end of their first week of captivity.[44] He followed this with pastries, oatmeal, fruit, and cold meats.[45] Coffee, however, was in short supply; when, on May 16, the prisoners received a package of chocolate and coffee from Grand Duchess Elizabeth Feodorovna, the empress noted this "great treat" in her diary.[46]

Once breakfast ended, the grand duchesses helped Demidova attend to household matters, stripping beds and gathering soiled clothing and linen. For the first six weeks of their incarceration, laundry from the Ipatiev House was sent out to the local Soviet labor committee head-quarters.[47] Soon after the arrival of the remaining children, however, this caused a problem; not only did certain articles—linen, towels with impe-rial crests, and even undergarments with the emperor's monogram—go missing, but also the laundry bill itself became a contentious issue. Avdayev recalled that in the first weeks following May 23, the prisoners accumulated a laundry bill of 87 rubles ($428 or £261 in 2003 currency), because the grand duchesses "insisted on changing their bed linens every day." Presented with this bill, the Ural Regional Soviet deemed it "astro-nomical" and declared that the prisoners would have to wash their own bed linens and towels; clothing still could be sent out. They sent their chairman, Alexander Beloborodov, to speak with the young women per-sonally. As Avdayev recalled, he told the grand duchesses to "busy them-selves with helping Demidova do their own laundry; after all, a little work never hurt anyone." The grand duchesses acquiesced but, with no idea how to proceed, asked Avdayev for instructions. This launched the commandant of the House of Special Purpose on an unlikely quest, as he scoured first the Ekaterinburg Public Library, bookstores, and finally labor unions in search of the elusive instructions. "Despite these efforts," Avdayev recalled, "we could find no written instructions on how to do laundry." In despair, Avdayev finally asked a former worker from the Zlokazov factory named Andreyev to come to the Ipatiev House and instruct the young women. Christened with the absurd title of "Com-rade Laundry Teacher to the House of Special Purpose," Andreyev began his lessons. According to Avdayev, he proved "rather clever at this work, and got on well with the grand duchesses."[48]

Conditions in the Ipatiev House were cramped: with eleven people disposed among eight rooms, privacy was at a minimum. Buxhoeveden, citing a conversation between Chemodurov and Gilliard, insisted that "the doors between the rooms had been taken off their hinges," allow-ing the guards "to look into the rooms whenever they wished," a charge that was patently untrue.[49] As noted during the very thorough inspec-tion of the Ipatiev House by the first White Army investigator, Alexander Nametkin, only one door was missing, that between the imperial couple's corner bedroom and the adjoining dressing room, where the grand duchesses slept. A set of double doors sealed off this suite from the dining room, with two further sets of double doors separating the main stair hall and kitchen, and drawing room and anteroom, thus ensuring some measure of isolation from the northern end of the main floor, where Avdayev and his men worked.

In fact, the guards were deliberately kept away from the prisoners on the main floor. Of the ten posts established during Avdayev's tenure, only two were situated on the upper floor: the post in the foyer, just inside the main door; and the post in the secondary stair hall, adjacent to the doors leading to the bathroom, lavatory, serving kitchen, and corridor.[50] Members of the guard were forbidden access to the prisoners' rooms unless accompanied by the commandant or by the guard commander. The door to the main staircase had even been locked and boarded over, to prevent any access from the lower floor. The door from the drawing room to the anteroom outside Avdayev's office, as guard Anatoly Yakimov himself stated, "was always shut."[51]

To reach the bathroom and lavatory, both situated at the northwestern end of the main floor, the prisoners had to leave their quarters. They could pass through the drawing room and the anteroom outside Avdayev's office, or through the dining room, main stair hall, kitchen, and into the secondary hall. A sentry was always posted here around the clock, men Chemodurov termed "absolutely indecent: they were rude and unrestrained, with cigarettes between their teeth, and impudent in their manners; they inspired disgust and revulsion."[52]

View from Demidova's room through dining room, stair hall, and into the kitchen at the Ipatiev House.

These few indignant sentences from Chemodurov spawned fanciful descriptions from those seeking to heighten the suffering of the prisoners in captivity; the behavior of the men on duty at Post 2 became increasingly distorted in the accounts of others. The unreliable Prince Lvov alleged that these guards routinely harassed the grand duchesses when they went to the lavatory, telling them lewd jokes; for good measure, he claimed that the prisoners could not even use the lavatory "without permission, or without being accompanied by a Red Guard."[53] Robert Wilton had the guards "crowding round the lavatory," adding, "there was only one for the prisoners and the warders."[54] And Buxhoeveden wrote that the sentry on duty made "rude and disgusting" remarks to the women; when Dr. Botkin complained of this, she said, Avdayev ignored him.[55]

The claim that the prisoners could not use the lavatory unless they received permission and were accompanied by a sentry is demonstrably untrue, a piece of anti-Bolshevik gossip from the unreliable Prince Lvov. Wilton's account, too, contained the seeds of its own destruction. Not only were members of the guard forbidden access by Avdayev to the main floor of the Ipatiev House unless on duty at one of the two interior posts, but also the journalist's claim that there was "only one" lavatory shared by the prisoners and their jailers was false. The only members of the guard allowed to use the prisoners' lavatory were those posted in the foyer and in the secondary stair hall, along with Avdayev, Moshkin, Guard Commander Paul Medvedev, and the three guard seniors, a total of eight men. The rest of the guard used a lavatory on the lower floor of the Ipatiev House, directly beneath that above.

It is likely that a few of the soldiers did indeed make "rude and disgusting" remarks, though such incidents were undoubtedly isolated. No reliable evidence indicate that such behavior occurred regularly. In fact, as guard Anatoly Yakimov recalled, when the prisoners used the lavatory, they inevitably went by way of the anteroom, a route that took them directly past Avdayev's office. "They could have gone to the lavatory through the kitchen," he said, "but for reasons I don't know, they never did so."[56] Had the prisoners been subjected to harassment by these men as often alleged, their chosen route—which took them past not only Avdayev's office but also an additional guard post—is inexplicable. That they elected to do so is strong evidence that any unpleasantness by the sentries must have been rare.

A few of the soldiers spent their hours on duty covering the walls of the stair hall and lavatory with graffiti. Alexander Nametkin cataloged that found on the main floor of the Ipatiev House, while his successor, Ivan Sergeyev, compiled a report covering the lower-floor rooms. The men found poems written by members of the guard:

Our Russian Tsar named Nick
Was pulled off the Throne by his prick.

And:

To all the people of Russia,
Nikolasha said,
As for your Republic
Go fuck yourselves instead!

There was also lurid graffiti, describing sexual relations between the empress and Rasputin; the latter clearly captivated the attention of the guards, who scrawled jokes about the size of the peasant's penis, along with pornographic sketches depicting him with Alexandra. A few drawings of this sort, along with juvenile political slogans, decorated the walls of the hallway and lavatory, where they were undoubtedly noticed by the prisoners.[57] The vast majority of the graffiti, however, was found in the lower rooms, used by the guards as a barracks, the work, as guard Philip Proskuryakov recalled, of Andrei Strekotin.[58]

Mornings in the Ipatiev House were filled with the few, simple activities allowed the prisoners: reading, writing letters, and games of cards until it was time for their first walk.[59] As days slipped into weeks, the initial uncertainty of captivity in the Ipatiev House turned to boredom, marked with petty annoyances that, after the murders, were magnified into claims of deliberate mistreatment meted out under Avdayev's drunken approval.

Pierre Gilliard never witnessed what took place in the Ipatiev House, but he testified that, according to Chemodurov, Avdayev was "sometimes drunk" while on duty.[60] Two years later, when he wrote his own book, Gilliard altered the old valet's story. Avdayev had been an "inveterate drunkard" who "gave rein to his coarse instincts" and delighted in "inflicting fresh humiliations upon those in his charge."[61]

Stories of Avdayev's brutal treatment of the prisoners became firmly ensconced as part of the Romanov story. Guard Anatoly Yakimov later said:

Avdayev was a rough and uncouth man, a drunkard. He drank some kind of wheat paste, very strong, which he got at the Zlokazov Factory, at the Ipatiev House. If, during his absence, any member of the Imperial Family asked Moshkin for a favor, he always replied that they must wait for Avdayev. To these pleas, Avdayev would answer, "Let them go to hell!" Sometimes, when he returned from their rooms, Avdayev would say that the Imperial Family had asked him for something or another, and he had refused: apparently, he delighted in refusing their requests, boasting of it with a happy look on his face. I remember that when they asked for permission to open the windows, he told us that he forbade it. I cannot say how he addressed the Imperial Family, but in the Commandant's room he referred to them as "they," and called the Emperor "Nikolasha." He raged when he spoke about him, calling him "The Blood Drinker." This, he said, wasn't personal, but because of the War. He said that the Emperor wanted a War, and for three years spilled the blood of the workers.[62]

Hundreds of witnesses were interviewed by White Army investigators after the murders, yet the only firsthand evidence of Avdayev's misbehavior came from two men, Yakimov and the elderly Chemodurov. Unlike Gilliard, Wilton, Buxhoeveden, or Sokolov, both men lived in the Ipatiev House under Avdayev—Yakimov for twenty-two days, and Chemodurov for twenty-three days. There is little reason to doubt, as they alleged, that Avdayev drank while on duty. Yet this is quite some distance from the "inveterate drunkard" of Gilliard's description. In fact, the prisoners themselves noted only one occasion on which the commandant appeared intoxicated: on June 14, Nicholas deemed him "slightly tipsy" when Avdayev spoke to them in the evening.[63] This single reference does little to support the assertion that Avdayev was often drunk while on duty; rather, its inclusion in the emperor's diary marks it out as an unusual event, supported by the complete silence in the imperial couple's diaries on the subject.

Nor do the letters or diaries of the prisoners record any of the humiliation or brutality they allegedly suffered at Avdayev's hands. The commandant's response to their requests, "Let them go to hell!" has frequently been quoted without reference to the context that Yakimov described. It was, the guard declared, Avdayev's reply to Moshkin, or to his guards, but not to the prisoners themselves. Yakimov himself emphasized this, saying, "I cannot say how he addressed the Imperial Family," an important distinction usually ignored. There is no evidence that Avdayev ever spoke in such a way to the Romanovs or their retainers, nor that he ever referred to the emperor directly as "The Blood Drinker" or "Nikolasha." Such language, as Yakimov said, was used when Avdayev was among the guards, or behind the closed doors of his office; the commandant himself explained that his views were based not on personal antipathy but on the war and the imperial regime's treatment of workers.

A few of the more virulent members of the Special Detachment, as guard Alexander Strekotin recalled, believed that "Avdayev and his adjutant were entirely too friendly and helpful to the Emperor's family."[64] "He encouraged his subordinates to think of him as a bandit so that they would be afraid of him," said another man. "He was irascible and audacious, but he had a good heart."[65]

This last assessment of Avdayev coincides with that of Sister Agnes, mistress of novices at the Novotikhvinsky Convent in Ekaterinburg. Avdayev, she later declared, "played at the role of leader, happy to exercise his passion for his cause, but he was only capable of cruelty through terrible comments, not actions. It is somewhat true that he drank, but he never inclined to entertain himself by making the prisoners suffer. . . . In his first impression, he would seem like an inflexible tyrant, and would appear to be unrestrained and in a terrible mood, but soon his true self would emerge and he would become accommodating."[66]

In some respects, Avdayev was constrained not only by his subordinate position to the fierce Presidium of the Ural Soviet but also by the expectations of his office. His comments about the prisoners almost certainly contained an element of boasting, akin to the way in which Rasputin himself created an image for public consumption and secured a reputation far removed from the realities of his actual influence. As the weeks in the Ipatiev House passed, Avdayev—along with a majority of his guards—came to view the Romanovs not as criminals but as flawed, and scared, human beings; in time, this developed into open sympathy. While Avdayev's true feelings about the prisoners were enigmatic, both his words and his actions grew increasingly conflicted. He presented himself to his men as the loud, swaggering drunkard recorded by history, angrily refusing every request from the Romanovs while at the same time inevitably and quietly relenting. It became the pattern of his tenure as commandant: in the first weeks, he ignored the Ural Regional Soviet's regulations dictating the length of daily walks; purchased food, cocoa, and a samovar for the prisoners; and failed until forced to institute a roll call. He even handed over his own money to the nuns of the Novotikhvinsky Convent, asking that they purchase tobacco for "the Emperor."[67]

The Romanovs themselves bore their first commandant no ill will, perhaps the strongest evidence that the usual portrait of Avdayev rests not on fact but on eighty-five years of propaganda. On learning of his replacement as commandant by the Ural Presidium in July, Nicholas wrote in his diary: "I am sorry for Avdayev, but it was his own fault as he did nothing to keep his men from stealing things out of our trunks in the shed."[68] There is perhaps no more telling sentence related to Avdayev's tenure as commandant of the Ipatiev House. The emperor expressed not joy that Avdayev, the man who, according to history, brutalized his wife and children with insults and repeated denials, was gone; not satisfaction that the man who called him "The Blood Drinker" was cast out of the

Ipatiev House; nor pleasure at being freed from his reign of fear. Instead, he described his personal sorrow for Avdayev, leveling only criticism over the undoubted theft of the imperial family's possessions.

Nor were the soldiers under Avdayev guilty of the most heinous charges laid at their feet for nearly a century. The idea that the imperial family, as Gilliard later claimed, "were very badly treated in the Ipatiev House" runs like a thread throughout the body of Romanov literature.[69] Contrary to the usual portrait of men who, as Buxhoeveden asserted, "had been specially chosen from among the most militant Bolsheviks" and who spared the prisoners "no humiliation they could devise," members of the Special Detachment were, for the most part, quietly curious of their former emperor, then openly sympathetic after they observed the Romanovs firsthand.[70]

"Avdayev was a simple workman," said guard Philip Proskuryakov, "very poorly developed, mentally. Sometimes he was intoxicated. But neither he nor the guards during his time offended or did any wrong to the Imperial Family."[71] Far from the barbaric horde usually described, most of the guards shared Avdayev's complex attitude toward the prisoners. The hardened Bolshevik terrorists of historic myth never existed among the Special Detachment. With less than a fifth even members of the Bolshevik Party, and the overwhelming majority the same age or younger than Grand Duchess Olga Nikolaievna, these soldiers brought nothing of the expected revolutionary fervor or calculated cruelty to the Ipatiev House. Young and immature, with no professional training as guards, they made, as guard Alexander Strekotin recalled, "all kinds of mistakes, like sleeping at their posts, leaving their posts, letting people in for a peek, and talking to people on the street outside. Sometimes, they were even guilty of raising false alarms."[72]

This lack of training resulted in numerous incidents, small in and of themselves, which—like so much of life in the Ipatiev House—became distorted and subject to the whims of propaganda. On the same day when Nagorny and Ivan Sednev were removed, May 27, Nicholas noted in his diary: "The sentry standing under our window shot into our house because he thought something moved by the window."[73] Seven days later, on Monday, June 3, guard Anatoly Dobrynin accidentally shot his rifle into the ceiling of the storeroom directly beneath the bedroom used by the grand duchesses.[74] And on June 24, guard Nicholas Podkorytov accidentally fired his rifle while it was being loaded.[75]

The young men who formed the Special Detachment were frequently careless, as evidenced by these random accidental shots. In time, however, these episodes became muddled. In 1919, when former guard Philip Proskuryakov was interrogated by Sokolov, he testified: "Once I was walking near the house when I saw the youngest daughter of the Emperor, Anastasia, look out the open window. When the sentry on duty noticed it he fired his rifle at her. The bullet missed her and lodged above her in the wood-work of the window frame."[76]

In his book on the murder of the Romanovs, Robert Wilton repeated this statement virtually word for word without attributing it to Proskuryakov.[77] Paul Bykov, author of the only official Soviet account of the Ekaterinburg period, also repeated the claim, but for some inexplicable reason named Tatiana, mistakenly identified as "the eldest daughter of the ex-Emperor."[78] And Alexander Strekotin later wrote: "The Emperor used to stand at the window of their room and stick his head out as high as he could, in an effort to see as much beyond the palisade as possible. Though he was repeatedly warned by the Duty Guard Commander about this, it made no impression on him, and he continued to do this. Then, one day, the Red Guard Benjamin Safonov warned that he would be shot if he repeated his actions. But this apparently left no impression, either, for the Emperor continued to stand at the window and look about; he refused to listen to our warnings. So Safonov waited for the next time he was on duty, and kept a watch on the window. Soon, the Emperor was there, again trying to put his head out. To teach him a lesson, Safonov took aim and shot a bullet into the window frame. Naturally, this caused some alarm, but we noticed that, from that day on, Nicholas stayed away from the window."[79]

These four accounts vary considerably. If Proskuryakov actually observed the incident he described, it could not have been the shooting on May 27, noted by Nicholas in a diary entry that makes no mention of Anastasia. In fact, as Nicholas wrote, he believed that the guard "was just amusing himself with his rifle, as sentries always do."[80] Had a shot been intentionally fired at Anastasia, this passage would be inexplicable. Proskuryakov insisted that his fellow guard Nicholas Podkorytov had deliberately fired at Anastasia. Yet the incident with Podkorytov's gun took place on June 24, when he was on duty at Post 3. This was situated in the main courtyard of the Ipatiev House, separated from the street not only by the gates of the house itself but also by two wooden palisades. Walking on the street as he claimed, Proskuryakov could not have seen the incident. Further, as recorded in the Special Detachment duty book, the incident occurred at 2:30 A.M. Nor, as both Nicholas and Alexandra made clear in their diaries, was there an open window on the northern side of the Ipatiev House's upper floor.

According to Proskuryakov, when the prisoners complained about the shot, Paul Medvedev reported the incident to Yurovsky, who declared, "Well, they must not look out of the window."[81] Yurovsky only took over as commandant of the Ipatiev House on July 4, eliminating not only the possibility that Proskuryakov's incident was the shot described on May 27—the only shot fired at a window—but also that it was that fired by Podkorytov, as recorded in the duty book on June 24. Proskuryakov's story that Anastasia, whom he could not have seen, stuck her head out of a window she could not open, and was fired on by a man he could not possibly have glimpsed, must—along with Wilton's version—be dismissed. Bykov should have been better placed to render a factual account, yet he confused the tale by adding his own details to the testimony left by Proskuryakov. As large portions of Bykov's book were apparently copied from the works of Wilton and Sokolov, his evidence, too, falls under close examination. Only Strekotin's account, in which he named Safonov as the men responsible, contained assertions compatible with the incident on May 27, although even he confused the event by insisting that Nicholas had stuck his head out of the window; in fact, no windows on the upper floor of the Ipatiev House were opened until nearly a month later. Proskuryakov undoubtedly heard a jumbled, secondhand version that, filtered through the boasts of any number of his fellow guards, stretched to include Anastasia and went on to become firmly ensconced in Romanov lore.

Incompetence by their jailers provided the imprisoned Romanovs with much-needed distractions. Nicholas saw nothing malicious in the incident; the imperial family had frequently commented on the absurdities of those charged with guarding them at Tsarskoye Selo and in Tobolsk. Such episodes broke the monotony of days spent reading, writing, playing games of cards, and gathering laundry in the Ipatiev House. One of the few bright spots for the prisoners were their daily walks. Although the instructions from the Ural Regional Soviet called for only one walk, Avdayev ignored this rule; on most days, the prisoners were allowed both a morning and an early-afternoon stroll.[82] Alexandra only occasionally ventured into the garden, preferring to remain inside; to ensure that she was not left alone, one of her daughters stayed at her side, reading aloud while the others walked. Each time the empress did not walk, she thus deprived one of her daughters of exercise as well. To ensure that all could go out at least once every day, the young women arranged a system, with one daughter detailed to her mother in the morning, and a different one in the afternoon.

These daily walks, like many aspects of life in the Ipatiev House, became an issue of contention in the propaganda war waged by those most sympathetic to the Romanovs, propelled by a number of erroneous and fabricated claims. Chemodurov later told investigators that "exercise in the garden was only permitted once a day, for fifteen or twenty minutes; during this period, the garden was entirely surrounded by guards."[83] Yakimov testified: "The girls left the second floor only to walk with their family in the garden for fifteen minutes each day."[84]

Wilton extended this statement to all of those incarcerated: "Only a quarter of an hour was allowed to the prisoners in the open air."[85] Prince Lvov, who claimed to have heard details from Nagorny, told the investigators: "Every day things got worse. At first they were given twenty minutes to go walking but then the time was reduced to five minutes."[86]

With each version, the imagined deprivation was magnified. Yet all four accounts are demonstrably untrue. Of the four giving accounts, only two—Chemodurov and Yakimov—actually lived inside the Ipatiev House. Chemodurov, suffering from exhaustion and encroaching senility, was scarcely an impartial observer, and the diaries of both Nicholas and Alexandra, as well as the Special Detachment duty book for the period of May 1–23, when the elderly valet was in the Ipatiev House, undermine his credibility. The only walk of fewer than thirty minutes during these three weeks took place on May 4, when the prisoners remained in the garden for twenty minutes; as Alexandra noted in her diary, this was due to the heavy snowfall.[87] The remaining walks varied between two (May 3 and May 17), of thirty minutes each, owing to rain; one (May 15) of forty minutes; one (May 9) of forty-five minutes; nine (May 2, 5–8, 12–14, and 16) of one hour; two (May 10 and 20) of seventy-five minutes; and two (May 11 and 19) of ninety minutes.[88] Such facts show the need for extreme caution when examining the testimonies left by Chemodurov. Yakimov's assertions, too, fall under inspection. Of the thirty-six days he served in the Ipatiev House, the prisoners were allowed eighteen walks of one hour; seven walks of ninety minutes; and eleven walks of two hours.[89] His claim, like that of Chemodurov—and by extension, those of Wilton and of Lvov—must be dismissed.

Nor did the authorized Soviet account of the Ekaterinburg period, written by Paul Bykov, convey an accurate impression. "The prisoners," Bykov wrote, "were allowed a daily walk in the little garden belonging to the house, where they could do manual work, the necessary tools being placed at their disposal. They themselves chose the time for their walk."[90] The last two assertions were as patently untrue as those made by Chemodurov, Yakimov, and Wilton. Nicholas, in fact, asked for, and was refused, permission to saw firewood in the garden, much to his consternation.[91]

Despite such unpleasantness, daily walks were one of the few times largely free of stress. If Alexei remained inside, the prisoners left the Ipatiev House by the secondary staircase, descending to the lower floor and out into the garden. With Nagorny removed from the Ipatiev House, it fell to Nicholas to carry Alexei when the tsesarevich felt well enough to venture outside. "He would lift him up very cautiously," recalled Alexander Strekotin, "and hug him to his broad chest, and his son would hold onto his father. The Emperor carried him from the house like that, put him in a special wheelchair, and pushed him down the courtyard to the garden."[92] Usually Leonid Sednev accompanied the tsesarevich, pushing his chair or sitting with him in the sunshine, playing with tin soldiers; occasionally Nicholas would bring his son some small stones or a branch or flower. Alexei, "being a child," said Strekotin, "would look at them then toss them away into the bushes."[93]

The empress, recalled Strekotin, "seldom went out, because she had difficulty in walking which made it hard for her to go down to the garden. She usually sat on the steps of the main entrance."[94] For the others, the daily walk provided a much-needed escape from the confines of the Ipatiev House. "Everyone relaxed more," Strekotin remembered, "and began to talk and laugh with each other." At the beginning of June, when the weather improved, some of the soldiers spent an evening off-duty building and hanging a swing for the grand duchesses from one of the taller trees.[95]

These activities were arranged between breakfast and lunch, which usually took place between one and two in the afternoon. A second, longer walk later in the day preceded tea when, as they had done for twenty years, Nicholas and Alexandra gathered their children around them, Alexei playing with his toy soldiers and the grand duchesses sewing while the emperor read aloud. Alexandra spent much time reading, or writing letters to her friends. While the prisoners could write as many letters as they wished, all of their correspondence was subject to censorship. Usually, as he recalled, Avdayev read through these messages; if a letter was in English, German, or French, he passed them along to Peter Voikov at the Presidium of the Ural Regional Soviet, who spoke all three languages. The few incoming letters they were allowed to receive were subject to these same provisions.[96]

Only a few of these letters reached their intended parties. In her last letter to Anna Vyrubova, found in the Ipatiev House after the murders, the empress wrote: "God won't forsake you. I send you my blessing with the [illegible] and recommend unto her care. Do not wear the image as the ring is not firm, put it on a ribbon with another image on the other side and place it in your Bible. I and N kiss you tenderly."[97] In a last letter from the tsesarevich to his friend Kolya Derevenko, possibly given to the doctor to pass to his son, Alexei wrote of his health: "I feel well myself. How is grandmother's health? What is [illegible] doing? My head was aching all day, but now the pain has gone completely. I embrace you warmly. Greetings to Botkins from all of us. Always yours, Alexei."[98]

Many days, and particularly when in the first few weeks that he was at the Ipatiev House and was still unwell, Alexei was confined to his bed. Here he set out his tin soldiers, read, and played games of chess, checkers, and cards with Leonid Sednev. After he was moved into the southeastern corner bedroom used by his parents in late June, he leaned against the wall and had Sednev mark off his height on the wallpaper with a pencil; to this he added lines for his father and his mother, writing, "Maman" and "Papa" next to them.[99]

In Tobolsk, Alexei often had played with a bow and arrow set; somewhat surprisingly, Avdayev let him bring it into the Ipatiev House. Together with Sednev, the tsesarevich sharpened the arrows and, when he felt better, amused himself in the garden by shooting them at the palisade. After the window in the southeast corner bedroom was opened on June 22, this game took on a more dangerous character: Alexei propped himself against the frame and shot his arrows out over the sill, beyond the palisade, and into Voznesensky Prospekt. This activity, as Avdayev recalled, caused near-disaster on several occasions when the arrows narrowly missed hitting sentries and passersby in the street. The commandant warned Alexei that he could play with the bow and arrow only in the garden; if he continued to shoot arrows into the street, they would be taken from him. With some reluctance, the tsesarevich complied, but the episode reveals something of Avdayev's indulgent attitude toward his prisoners.[100]

There were occasional visitors from beyond the ranks of the Ural Regional Soviet. Derevenko came frequently and, aside from the priests who conducted religious services on several occasions, women from the local labor union washed the floors in the house regularly, the first time on June 21.[101] Avdayev usually was solicitous of the family's requests: when Nicholas asked, the commandant allowed a barber to come to the Ipatiev House to cut his hair and that of the tsesarevich.[102] When the Ural Regional Soviet got wind of this, they forbade Avdayev to allow any further visits. Thereafter, Alexandra herself trimmed her husband's and son's hair.[103]

As with breakfast, all of the prisoners ate dinner together. While Kharitonov was responsible for the first meal of the day, until the middle of June both lunch and dinner were brought in each day from a local Soviet soup kitchen, "the best in town," according to Paul Bykov.[104] One of the workers, Catherine Tomilova, volunteered for the job. She recalled,

> When I brought the meals for the first time, I asked a Bolshevik soldier to let me into the house to get the dishes from the previous day. Soon the Commandant appeared and escorted me through the halls to the Dining Room, where a large table had already been laid for dinner. I placed my boxes on a sideboard and, as I turned, I saw the former Emperor. I recognized him at once. He wore a double-breasted, khaki tunic, with a small order pinned to his chest, and short, patent leather boots. His short hair, parted slightly to the side, seemed quite grey to me, as did his bushy,

The dining room in the Ipatiev House.

square beard. Two other men, also in khaki jackets, stood at his side; they looked like military men. One was of medium height, with a darker beard than the Emperor; the second man was apparently the eldest, though he had less grey in his hair than did the Emperor. I also saw two of the Emperor's daughters that day. When I left with the previous day's dishes, I asked one of the guards if the man I had seen had really been the former Emperor; I also asked which daughters I had encountered. He assured me it had been Nicholas, and told me that the girls were Marie and Anastasia. On another day when I brought meals, I saw the former Heir Alexei Nikolaievich, sitting in a wheelchair. He seemed thin, with an unhealthy look on his face. I only saw the former Empress twice. She was tall, dark, and thin. But I often saw Marie, Anastasia, and their brother Alexei the former Heir. They wheeled him in his chair. I once whispered to him, "Do your legs hurt?" and he replied, "Yes" and nodded his head. A nearby guard had seen this, and said I was not to talk to them. I didn't see the two eldest daughters though I was told they were in the house as well. There was another woman in the house who I saw, dressed nicely; she seemed young to me. A guard told me that she was their maid. When I brought the boxes with the meals, the Commandant or his Assistant always followed me through the halls to the Dining Room and remained until I had gone. No conversation was allowed, and the prisoners were always strangely silent. But they always looked very cheerful and smiled when they saw me.[105]

As with breakfast, lunches and dinners in the Ipatiev House became issues of contention after the Ekaterinburg murders. Although Tomilova later claimed, "I always brought dinner at 1:00 P.M. and supper at 9:00 P.M.," the arrival of these meals varied considerably, and often was quite late, as Alexandra recorded in her diary.[106] Yet Buxhoeveden asserted that not only was the food "scarce and bad," but that "sometimes" it was "forgotten altogether," a claim as false as that of Tomilova.[107] No one who actually lived within the Ipatiev House ever made such a statement, nor do the diaries of the imperial couple or the Special Detachment duty book support the baroness's version.

The food itself, Chemodurov testified, was "very ordinary," consisting of "meat soup and a roast, usually a joint or cutlets of very poor quality."[108] In Wilton's hands, this became "prison fare of the poorest quality," with "thin soup and meat, the latter of doubtful quality."[109] And Buxhoeveden wrote of "coarse food" that the Empress "could scarcely touch."[110] Ordinary the food may have been, but nothing supports Wilton's description of "thin soup" or Buxhoeveden's claim of "coarse food." Certainly meals in the Ipatiev House were very different from those that had regularly appeared on the palace table, but there is no evidence that they were inedible. Alexandra often ate only macaroni, prepared for her over the oil stove by either Kharitonov or Leonid Sednev, but such had been her habit for many years. In fact, as Nicholas noted in his diary after a typical meal from the canteen, "The food was excellent, plentiful, and served on time."[111]

In monarchist works on the Ekaterinburg period, these meals took on a foul character, replete with deliberate humiliation and verbal abuse. Colonel Eugene Kobylinsky, who never set foot in the Ipatiev House, related that Chemodurov told him of soldiers wandering over to the table and reaching for food, saying, "Enough for you, I will take some myself."[112] Wilton repeated the statement word for word, but ascribed it to Avdayev himself, adding the lurid detail that it was said as the commandant "grabbed some food from the Emperor's hand."[113] And Paul Bulygin, who worked closely with Nicholas Sokolov, further embellished the tale, describing how Avdayev had grabbed a piece of meat from Nicholas while commenting, "You've had enough, you idle rich."[114]

Not content with this elaboration, Wilton added further, more menacing assertions: "Avdayev often brought his friends in to watch as the Romanovs ate and purposely humiliated the prisoners to impress his fellow Bolsheviks. Once, Avdayev reached past the Emperor to fetch himself a piece of food, at the same time jabbing Nicholas in the face with his elbow."[115] Buxhoeveden picked up this bit of literary nonsense and repeated it, but she, too, resorted to further distortion, writing of the soldiers "pushing aside the Emperor" to get at the food.[116]

Such stories, endlessly repeated in serious histories of the Ekaterinburg period, bear little relation to fact. Chemodurov himself made no such claims in his testimonies, and it is unlikely he would have neglected to include them in his catalog of shameful behavior had they taken place. Nor do the diaries of Nicholas or Alexandra mention any such humiliation or maltreatment at the dining table. In fact, as one member of the Special Detachment later recalled, the single kernel of truth in these claims could be found in a single occasion, when Avdayev, reaching across the table to set down a bowl of soup for the prisoners, accidentally knocked the emperor in the shoulder with his elbow. "I was there," the former guard explained, "and it certainly wasn't done on purpose, nor was it an act of oafishness. Avdayev himself had restrained manners except when he was drunk, and he apologized profusely for the accident."[117] No evidence exists to support claims of boastful talk, glowering soldiers, grabbing of food from the hands of the prisoners, or members of the guard pushing them roughly aside to get at the table.

After dinner, the imperial family and Dr. Botkin gathered in the drawing room to play bezique, or to listen while Nicholas read aloud; apparently none of the other members of the household were ever invited to join them.[118] In addition to the books they had brought with them, the emperor and empress found numerous titles that had been left behind by the Ipatievs. Incarcerated in the Ipatiev House, Nicholas read *War and Peace* for the first time, along with the works of popular satirist Michael Saltykov-Shchedrin, and, more ominously, a biography of the murdered Emperor Paul I.[119] In addition to religious works, another favorite was *The Great and the Small and the Coming of the Antichrist*, an incendiary, rabidly anti-Semitic work by Serge Nilus; although Nicholas had disavowed the book when confronted with evidence that the Okhrana had helped forge its infamous *Protocols of the Elders of Zion*, he frequently read Nilus's book aloud to his family in both Tobolsk and Ekaterinburg, noting that it made for "very timely reading."[120]

When Avdayev left at nine each evening, the atmosphere in the Ipatiev House disintegrated. Moshkin invited friends from the Zlokazov factory into the prison, drinking far into the night and, as guards Anatoly Yakimov and Philip Proskuryakov recalled, singing a litany of revolutionary songs: "You Fell as a Victim in the Struggle," "Get Cheerfully in Step, Comrades," "Let's Forget the Old World," and "You Do Not Need a Golden Idol."[121] According to Prince Lvov, who named Nagorny and Ivan Sednev as his sources, the grand duchesses "were forced" by the drunken guards "to play the piano" and join in their songs. After the murders, these evenings took on a far more sinister character.[122]

Yakimov, one of the two actual witnesses, qualified his statement by adding that "great noise" took place not in front of the prisoners but "in the Commandant's room."[123] Proskuryakov confirmed this, and, indeed, as Nicholas noted in his diary, the soldiers had moved the piano from the drawing room into Avdayev's office at the end of the first week of May.[124] "Avdayev," Proskuryakov added, "did not know anything about it."[125] Neither Yakimov nor Proskuryakov claimed that the grand duchesses were forced to play the piano, nor do the diaries of the emperor or empress record any incident—an inexplicable omission had they actually taken place. In fact, the single mention of any such activity, recorded in the emperor's diary on May 8, scarcely reflected revulsion as he described "the sound of uneven singing and playing on the piano" coming from Avdayev's office.[126] Coming from the unreliable Prince Lvov, it is an assertion best dismissed.

On these drunken evenings, as the prisoners soon suspected, Moshkin and a few other soldiers began to steal their belongings. When the remaining children arrived in Ekaterinburg on May 23, they were accompanied by a railroad car filled with personal effects, clothing, books, rugs, porcelain, photographs, furniture, and other household objects. A few items were allowed into the Ipatiev House, but the majority was either confiscated off the train at the goods depot, or taken to the prison and locked in a small shed overlooking the garden. When the Romanovs wanted anything, soldiers escorted them across the courtyard to the shed, where the luggage had been stacked. As time went on, the prisoners discovered many objects missing, pilfered by members of the guard. "Often," Yakimov recalled, "they used to go into the storeroom and take out various things in sacks or bags. The bags they took away in a motor car or on horses to their houses or flats."[127] Nicholas made frequent references in his diary to these thefts, which continued unchecked for most of their imprisonment. Discomforts, petty annoyances, uncertainty, and boredom were the prisoners' constant companions in the Ipatiev House, not the deliberate abuse and humiliations later claimed. Unpleasant incidents certainly took place, yet the usual story of these seventy-eight days rests largely on rumor, distortion, and even fabrication, not on fact.

Such was the routine into which the prisoners settled as May eased into June. On Saturday, June 1, Kharitonov pulled Alexei Sidorov, the duty commander, aside, saying he had found something on top of the wardrobe in the main stair hall, previously occupied by Nagorny and Ivan Sednev. Sidorov discovered eight army bombs, all in working condition, pushed to the back of the wardrobe. He quickly summoned Avdayev, who collected the bombs, took them to the guardroom below, and disarmed them.[128] Although the commandant questioned the prisoners, they seemed genuinely surprised at the discovery, and Avdayev was forced to report the matter to Beloborodov. How and why the bombs were in the Ipatiev House is not known, but by turning them over, Kharitonov sealed the fate of his former colleagues: that same night, Nagorny and Sednev were taken from the local prison and shot.

The next day, following a request from Dr. Botkin, Avdayev allowed a priest to come and conduct the liturgy. In place of Meledin, who had previously come, Avdayev sent for Father Ioann Storozhev, priest of the Ekaterinburg Cathedral, who arrived at the Ipatiev House with his deacon, Father Buimirov. On entering the drawing room, where the prisoners had assembled, Storozhev was shocked to see Alexei lying on a cot. Storozhev recalled,

He was pale to such a degree that he seemed transparent. He was gaunt and so tall that I was astounded, though generally he looked extremely sick. Only his eyes were alive and bright, looking at me, a new person, with noticeable interest. He had on a white shirt and was covered to the waist with a blanket. Near his bed was a chair in which Alexandra Feodorovna sat. She had on a loose dress of dark blue color; I did not see any jeweled ornaments on either Alexandra Feodorovna or on her daughters. Alexandra Feodorovna attracted attention with her great height and bearing, which can only be described as stately. She was sitting in a chair but got up with energy and firmness when we entered and left the room and whenever during the service I said, "Peace be to all," when I read the Gospel, and when we sang the most important prayers. [Throughout the service, Avdayev] stood in a corner of the drawing room near the far window, remaining a proper distance from the worshippers. [Nicholas] wore a khaki field shirt, khaki pants, and high boots. On his breast, he wore an officer's Cross of St. George, but had no epaulets. All four daughters, as I recall, wore dark skirts and simple white jackets, and had their hair cut fairly short at the back. They were lively and seemed almost happy. Nicholas Alexandrovich impressed me with his firm bearing, his calm, and particularly his manner of looking straight at one, firmly, in the eyes. I did not see in him any signs of fatigue or spiritual depression. It seemed to me that there were slight traces of grey in his beard. As for Alexandra Feodorovna, she was the only one who appeared tired, or rather ill. The members of the Romanov Family displayed an extraordinary deference to my Holy office, bowing in reply to my silent greeting when I entered the room and also upon completion of the service. Taking our places in front of the table with icons we began the service. The deacon spoke the prayer of petition and I sang. Two female voices accompanied me, I think Tatiana Nikolaievna and one of the others. At times I was also accompanied by the low bass of Nicholas Alexandrovich when he sang, for example, "Our Father" and other hymns. The service went well, they prayed very earnestly. At the end of the service I gave the usual blessing with the Holy Cross and then paused for a moment, not knowing whether I should approach the worshippers with the Cross so they could kiss it, or whether this was forbidden and I, with my false move, might create future difficulties for them when they sought permission for attention to their spiritual needs. I glanced at the Commandant to see what he was doing and how he was reacting to my desire to approach with the Cross, and it seemed that Nicholas Alexandrovich also threw a quick glance in his direction. From his place in the corner, he nodded at me quietly. I took a step forward and at the same time Nicholas Alexandrovich, with firm, direct steps, not turning his direct gaze from me, approached the Cross first and kissed it. Behind him came Alexandra Feodorovna and all four daughters. I went over to Alexei Nikolaievich who was lying on the bed. He looked at me with such lively eyes that I thought: "Now he will surely say something." But Alexei Nikolaievich kissed the Cross in silence. The Deacon gave him the host and also gave it to Alexandra Feodorovna.[129]

The morning left a moving impression on the deeply religious imperial family, who found the lack of regular services the one true hardship of their imprisonment. After the priest and deacon left, the prisoners had lunch, then walked in the garden. "The weather remained marvelous, hot," Nicholas wrote. "We walked after the service and during the day before tea. It's unbearable to sit locked up like this and not be able to go out into the yard when one wants to and to spend a nice evening in the fresh air! The prison regime!"[130]

The following afternoon, guard Anatoly Dobrynin, while setting the bolt on his rifle, accidentally fired a shot into the ceiling of the room directly beneath that used by the grand duchesses. Avdayev rushed in and asked if the bullet had penetrated through the ceiling, and if anyone had been injured, but it had been stopped by the thick plaster of the vaults below.[131]

The lack of ventilation made the rooms "hot and stuffy," as Nicholas wrote in his diary.[132] Although the prisoners repeatedly complained about this to Avdayev, the commandant himself was under orders from the Ural Regional Soviet not to open any windows; instead, he passed along their requests to the Presidium, which, in true Soviet fashion, formed a special Committee for the Examination of the Question of Windows in the House of Special Purpose, which promised to reach a conclusion and settle the issue.[133] The oppressive atmosphere was made worse when, on June 4, the prisoners learned that Lenin had ordered all clocks advanced two hours, an energy-saving measure that began at 10:00 P.M. on May 31, although it took Avdayev four days to inform them of the fact.[134]

By June 5, Alexei was well enough to venture into the garden for the first time; he still could not walk, and Dr. Botkin carried him through the Ipatiev House to the main foyer, where he was placed in the empress's wheelchair. The doors were opened, and, joined by his mother and sister Tatiana, he sat on the front steps for seventy-five minutes, in "glorious" weather, as the empress wrote in her diary.[135] Throughout the afternoon, soldiers erected a second, outer palisade, completely enclosing the Ipatiev House, "so that not even the tops of the trees can be seen," Alexandra noted. Once this was finished, Avdayev told them, the committee would come and open the windows.[136] That night, Dr. Derevenko arrived, accompanied by Avdayev. During this visit, as Alexei Sidorov noted in the duty book, Alexandra spoke to her daughters in German, a language that had been forbidden. Avdayev warned her that if she continued to speak in a language he did not understand in front of Derevenko, the doctor would not be allowed any future visits.[137] The following day, when Derevenko arrived at the Ipatiev House, he was turned away owing to the empress's indiscretion.[138]

On Thursday, June 6, Alexandra turned forty-six. After lunch, Marie—the strongest of the grand duchesses—carried her brother to the main foyer and wheeled him out to the doorstep, where he was joined by Alexandra and Olga. By evening, the rooms had again become "very hot and awfully stuffy," as Alexandra wrote.[139] Nicholas spent much of the day in bed, suffering from hemorrhoids, which caused him "terrible pain."[140] By the following day, the situation was worse, and when Sidorov asked what was wrong, Botkin explained that the emperor was suffering from "enlarged veins." He could not leave his bed and was unable to walk in the garden, though by evening he began to recover.[141]

The following day brought the first of the numerous political developments that almost sealed the fate of the Romanovs. A week earlier, British troops had landed at Archangel in northern Russia; although initially invited by Trotsky on behalf of the Soviet regime to help repel a possible German invasion following the Treaty of Brest-Litovsk, their presence caused general alarm across Russia. Then, on June 8, the armies of the Czech Legion, which had rebelled two weeks earlier and joined forces with the advancing Whites, captured the important town of Samara. Here, anti-Bolshevik forces began to gather, forming a socialist government largely composed of those duly elected members of the Constituent Assembly that Lenin had ordered closed within hours of its first session in January.

That same day, when Derevenko arrived at the Ipatiev House, he was not admitted; nor were the prisoners allowed their regular walk in

the garden.[142] That night, for the first time during his captivity in
Ekaterinburg, Nicholas failed to make his usual diary entry. Although
he had been ill for several days, he had been well enough on the previous day to sit up and make his regular notation. "The omission might
seem trivial," wrote Harrison Salisbury, "but there was no precedent for
this." As Salisbury noted, "He was meticulous in his entries. For him, to
skip a day without even a line on the weather was almost as traumatic as
a heart attack."[143] On the following day, Nicholas returned to his usual
pattern of diary entries, but he skipped June 12, and thereafter he would
record events only periodically.

Various explanations have been offered for this sudden halt to what
had, for thirty-eight years, been the one consistent pattern in Nicholas's
life. Historian Serge Melgunov suggested that the emperor, overwhelmed by the monotony of life in the Ipatiev House, simply abandoned his custom of making regular entries.[144] This seems highly
unlikely; Nicholas was, if anything, a methodical man, accustomed to
regimen, routine, habit. Other diary entries from the period of his captivity spanning August 1917 through July 16, 1918, show that no matter how dull he found life, he regularly recorded the times of his walks,
the weather, when he ate, and what he read. The absence of entries on
certain days remains an enigma. There is, however, one brief hint in
Alexandra's diary. "Great fidgeting going on around us today," she
wrote on June 8, "since three days, don't give us any papers to read, and
made much noise in the night."[145] It is likely that the arrival of the
British expeditionary force in Archangel, coupled with the Czech rebellion and the fall of Samara, set Ekaterinburg on edge.

On Sunday, June 9, another curious incident took place, one that
remained hidden for nearly seventy years. "About midnight, at Machine
Gun Post No. 1," wrote Sidorov in the duty book, "a bomb went off
because of a guard's carelessness. There were no victims or damage."[146]
Alexander Strekotin later recalled: "A member of the Red Guard
Detachment, Ivan Talapov, found himself at his machine gun post on
the upper terrace, and apparently began to devote himself—out of
boredom—to practice at throwing grenades off the gallery. Once, he
accidentally pulled the ring out, and the grenade began to hiss. He
threw it out onto the Lane, and there was a great explosion. This set off
the alarm, not only for the House Commandant, but also for the people of the whole city."[147]

In 1976, British authors Anthony Summers and Tom Mangold,
investigating the murder of the Romanovs and the Sokolov report,
uncovered a reference to an explosion at the Ipatiev House in mid-June.
It was mentioned in an article published on July 12 in the *New York
Times* that suggested that Alexei had died of fright after a bomb was

thrown at his father during his regular afternoon walk.[148] This erroneous report provided the genesis of a Soviet account in *Pravda* that was picked up and reprinted in *Svenska Dagbladt* on July 24, 1918. The *Pravda* article concerned itself with conveying one of the first Soviet accounts of Nicholas II's execution—shot alone following a military court-martial, it alleged. This early bit of official disinformation managed not only to disguise the true circumstances of the murders of the imperial family and those imprisoned with them in the Ipatiev House, but also the basic facts regarding the alleged bomb incident.[149]

Summers and Mangold discovered a further reference to the supposed bomb in a letter written by Danish diplomat Poul Ree: "While I was there, a bomb was thrown over the fences around the Tsar's villa. Lots of noise—little damage. The man got away in the smoke and the dust. Next day there was nothing to see. They say though that the Tsar's heir died of fright and was secretly buried at 6:00 A.M., some say in the prison yard. . . . I think the Government arranged the bomb at Ekaterinburg. I don't believe Alexei died of fright."[150]

It is not surprising that Ree picked up this bit of gossip while in Ekaterinburg. Olga Petrova, an Ekaterinburg resident, later testified to the White investigators: "I do not remember the month last winter when a stranger, Catherine Tomilova, was billeted on Bolshevik orders. She told me she was a waitress at the Soviet canteen and her number was eighteen. A month-and-a-half later, she told me that she carried dinners for the Imperial Family from the Soviet canteen to the house enclosed by a fence made of planks. She told me also that she brought supper to the Imperial Family. That summer there was a rumor going about town that the heir Alexei Nikolaievich was dead. I asked Tomilova about this and she answered that the Heir was alive, but his leg was sore and he was in a wheelchair."[151] And, on June 12, when Derevenko visited the Ipatiev House, he told Alexei Sidorov that "rumors are current in the town that Alexei Romanov had been killed and buried last night."[152]

Even with no "bombing incident," the mood in Ekaterinburg was uneasy, and such that rumors were easily believed. On June 10 Nicholas wrote in his diary: "External attitudes have also changed during recent weeks. The jailers try not to speak to us, though not in their usual mood, as though feeling a kind of fear and sense of danger in our presence. I can't understand it."[153]

That danger erupted on June 12. As Strekotin recalled, a group of anarchists attempted to take over the Verkh-Isetsk factory, and the streets of Ekaterinburg were filled with an angry mob protesting Bolshevik rule. A large counterrevolutionary demonstration, composed of anarchists and Social Democrats, took place in Voznesensky Square, directly opposite the windows of the Ipatiev House.[154] As Avdayev recalled, they demanded "the immediate execution of the former Emperor, insisting that we hand him over so that they might apply their own brand of justice."[155]

This revolt was put down only with great difficulty, and the sound of gunfire echoed across Voznesensky Square. By late afternoon the mob was dispersed, but the demonstration left the Ural Regional Soviet shaken. The day marked the turning point for the Romanovs. That night, three hundred miles to the west, the Bolsheviks made their first strike against a member of the former dynasty.

6

Russia in Chaos

EKATERINBURG'S OMINOUS SEIZURE of the Romanovs was
followed with growing concern by imperial Germany, Russia's
master after the signing of the Treaty of Brest-Litovsk. The
chaotic unrest plaguing the country, coupled with Lenin's loss of control over events in Siberia, made Berlin uneasy. In the oak-paneled
offices along the Wilhelmstrasse, diplomats followed internal events
closely, worried that the terms and conditions of the treaty might push
the Russians into rebellion—the last thing they wanted. On April 26,
Count Wilhelm von Mirbach was appointed German ambassador to
Russia; from the embassy in Moscow, he would follow events over the
ten weeks that followed with increasing alarm.[1]

A distinguished career diplomat, von Mirbach was forty-seven years
old. The scion of a wealthy Prussian aristocrat, von Mirbach rose quickly
through the ranks of the military and entered the diplomatic corps when
he was twenty-four. From 1908 to 1911 he had served as a counselor in
the German embassy in St. Petersburg, where he had met Nicholas II on
several official occasions.[2] Von Mirbach's assistant in Moscow was Kurt
Riezler, a thirty-six-year-old former philosophy student.

The Treaty of Brest-Litovsk freed the German army to launch new
offensives on the Western Front, a move that greatly worried the Allies,
who were stung by Russia's withdrawal from the war and surprised at
her acceptance of such a humiliating peace. The kaiser's army still held
numerical superiority along the French Front. Just three weeks after
signing the treaty with the Bolsheviks, the Germans launched a major
offensive in France. Throughout the spring—from Chemin des Dames
through Flanders and on to Château-Thierry on the Marne—the

Germans advanced, provoking first concern, then panic, among the Allies. At the end of May, with the kaiser's forces rapidly approaching, there was even talk of abandoning Paris.[3]

The situation became so desperate that, in London, Prime Minister Lloyd George actually called a secret meeting of the war cabinet to discuss a worst-case contingency: making immediate peace with the Germans in exchange for a cessation of hostilities, and the grant of all rights to Russia to the kaiser. The ease with which such a proposal was even raised demonstrates how precarious the Allied position was that spring. With the signing of the Treaty of Brest-Litovsk, the Bolsheviks had clearly become anathema, an expendable regime not to be trusted. As much as Allied governments railed against German militarism, clearly "civilized" Germany was preferable to a Bolshevik Russia.[4]

This "growing misapprehension as to the nature of Bolshevism" began to spill into official Allied policies, "which encouraged wishful thinking about its early demise," commented one historian. "As details of Lenin's new social order filtered through to the West, the first signs appeared of the strong anti-Bolshevik sentiment that was soon to become fanatical. It was bad enough for the landed gentry of Britain and France that the Bolsheviks had overthrown their betters in Russia; it was terrifying that they now spoke of spreading this appalling political dogma throughout Europe and perhaps the rest of the world. So when the delegates at the Soviet Congress spoke of 'the coming world revolution of which we are the advance guard,' the *Times* of London responded with an editorial saying, 'The remedy for Bolshevism is bullets.'"[5]

Nothing came of Lloyd George's proposal, but the Allies were deeply worried. If the Germans were not to be given a free hand in Russia, most Western governments were determined to do the next best thing, and force a second front to fracture the kaiser's forces. The first hesitant steps toward this goal were taken in April, when a small expeditionary force composed of British and Japanese troops landed at Vladivostok. This was no more than a test—to provoke a reaction from Moscow—and the forces remained largely confined to Russia's Pacific coast. But as the spring of 1918 wore on, the Allied representatives stepped up efforts for a full-scale landing. On May 2, 1918, David Francis, the American ambassador to Russia, reported to the U.S. State Department: "In my judgment, time for Allied intervention has arrived." Francis went on to say that Russia had completely fallen under the control of the Germans, and warned that the kaiser's forces were daily becoming more deeply entrenched.[6]

Germany, understandably, greeted these rumors with apprehension. It was imperative that Russia remain committed to the Treaty of Brest-Litovsk for the kaiser's armies to prosecute the war on the Western

Front. The last thing they wanted was what the Allies precisely plotted: a renewal of the two-front war. Von Mirbach was instructed to sound out Lenin and members of his government, to ensure that Russia intended to fulfill the terms of the Treaty of Brest-Litovsk. On May 16 the German ambassador held his first meeting with Lenin, and came away with assurances that the Soviets were committed to their publicly stated path.[7]

This suited the German High Command. Both Paul von Hindenburg and Erich Ludendorff recognized the necessity of keeping Russia weak and bound to the terms of the Treaty of Brest-Litovsk. Should Russia waver, any number of possibilities—all unpleasant and most potentially disastrous for the German Empire—opened themselves. Yet, while the German High Command meant to keep Russia under their thumb and thus spare the necessity of expending valuable troops in the East, diplomats along Berlin's Wilhemstrasse had other plans. According to information received by Adolf Ioffe from the German diplomat von Kuhlmann, if the Civil War in Russia proved successful and the Whites managed to advance to the Urals, Germany would do the unthinkable and open a second front—sending troops into the country, march on Moscow, and overthrow the Bolshevik regime.[8]

Throughout the spring of 1918, Germany spent a substantial sum in supporting the Soviet regime, providing funds for use in antiwar propaganda and to help crush resistance to the Bolsheviks. In May the Foreign Ministry in Berlin cabled to von Mirbach in Moscow: "Please make use of greater sums, as it is largely in our interest that the Bolsheviks survive." And, on June 3, 1918, von Mirbach cabled Berlin with a request for 3 million marks a month, to be channeled to the Bolsheviks for anti-Allied propaganda. An official in the German Foreign Ministry estimated that von Mirbach would need upwards of 40 million marks to guarantee this goal.[9]

But Germany also was playing a dangerous double game. While publicly supporting the Bolshevik regime and forcing their adherence to the Treaty of Brest-Litovsk, they behaved in a far different manner in the Ukraine and western Russia, territories that fell under their control when ceded by the treaty. Here the Germans established cordial relations with the Volunteer Army, the most stringent of anti-Bolshevik forces opposing Lenin's government in 1918, and even helped finance their actions. Such was Ludendorff's wish: to keep Germany's future options open. He insisted that the Treaty of Brest-Litovsk be enforced—and by German military units in the streets of Moscow if necessary—to keep Russia weak and unstable, knowing that such conditions would likely result in Lenin's eventual overthrow and the installation of a puppet regime handpicked by Berlin. This was recognized in a secret communiqué from the German embassy in Moscow to the Foreign Ministry in Berlin: "Famine is on the way and is being choked off with terror. People are quietly shot by the hundreds. All this in itself is not so bad, but there can be no doubt that the physical means with which the Bolsheviks are maintaining their power are running out. . . . To facilitate the restoration of a Russia which would again be imperialist is not a pleasant perspective, but the development may perhaps be inevitable."[10]

This bit of realpolitik was played out against the increasingly destructive span of the Russian Civil War. That so much of the conflict took place in Siberia reflected the historical division between European Russia and the vast stretches of land that lay beyond the Ural Mountains. Siberia had never proved particularly receptive to political dogma; the peasants who lived there—owning their land, working for themselves—never suffered the indignities of the serfs in European Russia. Their hostilities were broad, confined mainly to that intangible they described simply as "fate." At the same time, this very difference marked them as independent in thought and action; while the Urals may have been Bolshevik strongholds, this was only in the larger cities, which had factories or industrial works and could boast workers who toiled under deplorable conditions.[11]

Into this fray came the Volunteer Army. Established at the beginning of 1918, the Volunteer Army—or more loosely, the White Army—was composed of former tsarist generals, soldiers from the Imperial Army, monarchists, republicans, Constitutional Democrats, and a number of other polar opposites, all united in their hatred for the Bolsheviks. The White Army never had a unified vision or ultimate goal other than the complete overthrow of Lenin and his regime. Thus some factions supported a restoration of the throne, either with Nicholas II or someone else as sovereign, while the majority fought for a democratic, parliamentary-ruled Russia, with universal suffrage and a truly representative elected body. Certain elements supported Russia's reentry into the war, but most focused only on the country's internal strife. They railed against the Germans as a traditional enemy, and blamed them not only for the introduction of Lenin and the Bolsheviks into Russia but for the continued existence of the Soviet regime as well. They railed against the Jews, another traditional enemy: both the officers and the common ranks of the White Army seethed with anti-Semitic rumor and allegation.

The latter sentiment was particularly strong and widespread. One Jewish writer explained,

> Previously, Russians have never seen a Jew in a position of authority: neither as governor, nor as policeman, nor even as postal employee. Even then, there were, of course, better times and worse times, but the

Russian people had lived, worked and disposed of the fruits of their labor, the Russian nation grew and enriched itself, the Russian name was grand and awe-inspiring. Now the Jew is on every corner and on all rungs of power. The Russian sees him as head of the ancient capital, Moscow, and in charge of the capital on the Neva, and in command of the Red Army, that most perfect mechanism of self-destruction. He sees the Prospekt of St. Vladimir bear the glorious name of Nakhimson, the historic Liteinyi Prospekt renamed the Prospekt of Volodarskii, and Pavlovsk become Slutsk. The Russian now sees the Jew as judge and executioner. He meets Jews at every step—not Communists, but people as hapless as himself, but issuing orders, working for the Soviet regime; and this regime, after all, is everywhere, one cannot escape it. And this regime, had it emerged from the lowest depths of hell, could not be more malevolent or brazen. Is it any wonder, then, that the Russian, comparing the past with the present, concludes that the present regime is Jewish and therefore so diabolical?[12]

Throughout the Civil War that followed, the White Army was divided into three spheres of influence: the first in the Ukraine, where, despite their anti-German rhetoric, they regularly received grants from Berlin to assist in their campaigns and propaganda; the second in the Caucasus and Russian Asia; and the third in Siberia. These forces were led by a handful of former tsarist officers, including Generals Alexeiev, Kornilov, Denikin, and Krasnov.

The Whites and their supporters, particularly émigrés writing after the fact, painted the forces as Russia's last great hope to cast off the shackles of Bolshevism, patriotic men who embodied the noble spirit of their country. Delineation between the "barbaric," atheistic Soviet regime, with its Red Army and brutal Cheka, and Whites took on an especially intransigent attitude, with the latter portrayed as paragons of virtue, opposed to the forces of tyranny. While the White Army never instituted any official organization equivalent to the dreaded Cheka to launch formalized retribution and terror, the hands of the Volunteer Army and their leaders were stained with the blood of thousands of innocent men, women, and children. Largely ignored, these White atrocities certainly took place, and often were as brutal as those instituted by their Bolshevik counterparts.[13]

The two worst offenders on the White side were Dutov, ataman (chief) of the Cossacks; and Semyonov, a rogue Cossack who, supported by the White government established in Siberia, murdered, raped, and pillaged his way from the Pacific to the Urals, leaving behind a wave of human misery unequaled even by the most virulent of Red Army leaders. Dutov was feared for his retribution: on taking a town or village that previously had been in Red hands, he customarily ordered all remaining men tortured, then killed, while his soldiers raped any female unfortunate enough to have remained behind. Tales of child-rape were not uncommon, as were mass executions. Whole families—husbands, wives, and their children—were regularly tortured and killed without any charges or trial.[14]

As terrible as Dutov was, his cruelty was far surpassed by Semyonov; if anything, his campaign of violence was worse, not only in terms of numbers of victims and brutality, but also because it was financed by the White authorities, up to and including Admiral Kolchak, who, aware of Semyonov's bloody work, nonetheless did nothing to stop him and continued to encourage his campaigns. General William Graves, a member of the American expeditionary force in Siberia, witnessed Semyonov's barbarism firsthand. The carnage reached such proportions that, in 1922, the U.S. Senate Committee on Labor and Education conducted hearings into what had taken place in Siberia, and heard evidence from Semyonov himself, who seemed pleased at the attention. Graves and other witnesses supplemented Semyonov's own account, spinning a web of horror. The committee heard how "whole villages were wiped out by the Cossacks and Mongolian Cavalry under Semyonov's command; wholesale executions were practiced, apparently for no other purpose than to keep the Cossacks in training, and to inspire terror." They learned of one incident when ten railroad cars filled with Red Army soldiers captured by Kolchak's forces were seized by Semyonov, who ordered every man—more than a thousand—summarily executed on the spot, "just to show that executions could be held on Sunday as well as on weekdays," as Semyonov explained. Hundreds of towns and villages were burned to the ground, peasant farms destroyed, women and children tortured and raped—all on Semyonov's orders, and without any interference from the White command. In all, more than a hundred thousand men, women, and children were killed by Semyonov and his division, a number without parallel by any other single leader, White or Red, in the Civil War.[15]

The Red Army that faced these men, as Richard Pipes has noted, "existed largely on paper."[16] Where the Whites at least had the benefit of trained soldiers and proven leadership, the Bolshevik forces were largely poorly trained and badly led. The Whites outnumbered the Reds by at least five to one during these first months of the Civil War. In these early days, the Red Army was composed of a few Bolshevik shock troops drawn from front-line soldiers and factory workers, with a scattering of Latvians, and Magyar prisoners of war. Their strongest ally was the Cheka, engaged in barbaric cruelty and systematic torture and murder as they swept from village to village across Russia.

Into this fray, in the spring of 1918, came an unexpected and powerful force. During Russian campaigns in World War I, tens of thousands
of prisoners had been captured in the southeastern thrust into Galicia.
These prisoners were largely Czech and Slovak in nationality, with a few
Magyars; all had been members of the Austro-Hungarian army, but none
of them wished to return and fight for the hated Habsburg Empire. In
1916 the Czechoslovakian National Council, held in Paris, passed a resolution that called for the organization of these prisoners into a special
force that could enter the war and fight for the Allies. This proposal languished until the fall of the imperial regime, when the Provisional
Government—eager for troops to bolster the crumbling army—relented
and allowed the formation of the Czech Corps, which fought for several
months with great success along the Western Front.[17]

As early as spring 1917, Thomas Masaryk, future president of the
Czechoslovak Republic, had attempted to negotiate a return of these
soldiers to the Western Front.[18] By the end of that summer, some
twenty-four thousand Czech and Slovak soldiers, organized into tight,
efficient units, anxiously awaited an end to their Russian tenure.
Kerensky's government relented and agreed that they, as well as any
remaining Czech or Slovak soldiers in prisoner-of-war camps, would be
allowed to return via the Western Front to their homes.

The October Revolution, however, changed this. With the Czech
and Slovak troops restive and increasingly angry, the Allies were quick
to seize the opportunity, recognizing the Czech Corps in Russia as a
distinct and independent army, placed—with the agreement of
Masaryk—under the authority of the Supreme Allied Command. This
sent a wave of panic through Bolshevik circles: the Czechoslovakian soldiers could scarcely be considered friendly to their cause, and it was in
their best interests to rid themselves of these men before a situation
erupted. Negotiations over the Treaty of Brest-Litovsk, which began in
December 1917, further complicated the issue, for by February the
Russians knew that the Germans would occupy vast territories of land
where many of these former Habsburg troops were situated; some
thirty-seven thousand Czech and Slovak troops alone were scattered
across the Ukraine at the end of 1917.[19] Only after the treaty was formalized did Moscow consent to their return.[20]

The original plan had called for evacuation of the soldiers through
Vladivostok, a journey that would take them nearly around the world.[21]
The Germans, when they learned of this, immediately objected: the last
thing they wanted was another fifty thousand soldiers fighting for the
Allies to appear on the Western Front. But Moscow could do little to
control the Czech movement east.[22] The Allies wanted the Czechs
immediately; they suggested that Moscow send them out through the

north, via Murmansk and Archangel; finally Moscow agreed to this, with the proviso that all Czech divisions west of Omsk would leave by the northern route, while those in Siberia would be evacuated as planned through Vladivostok.[23]

The Czechoslovakians were being treated like pawns, and they knew it. These thousands of men—upward of fifty thousand soldiers— were scattered along the Volga, in the Ukraine, and in Siberia. Roughly half made their way east, jumping aboard the Trans-Siberian Railroad when passage could be found, and slowly making their way toward Vladivostok. Conditions were deplorable, and some divisions of the Czech Corps spent two months waiting in overcrowded railroad cars to travel two days.[24] These men traveled, on Masaryk's instructions, in a state of "armed neutrality," forbidden to become embroiled in any domestic Russian affairs, either political or military.[25]

The Czech Corps was subdivided into battalions of a thousand men each for their evacuation; as they would be passing through chaos-ravaged Siberia, they were to be provided with enough arms to defend themselves if the situation arose.[26] Moscow had agreed to these terms, but, as the first divisions were moving east toward Vladivostok, the Bolsheviks panicked. On March 26, Stalin—at Lenin's request—sent a cable to the Czech National Council in Paris that demanded that "the Corps set out immediately for Vladivostok, and that all counterrevolutionary commanders be removed. The Czechs and Slovaks must not travel as fighting Corps, but rather as free citizens, and they must carry only such arms as are necessary to guarantee their safety from counter-revolutionaries."[27]

Stalin's cable demanded that these conditions be met before any city or regional Soviet along the railroad line would let the Czech Corps pass on to Vladivostok. Each train was allowed only 168 rifles, with 300 rounds per rifle, and 1 machine gun with 1,200 rounds; in actual fact, most of the divisions carried two to three times this amount, concealed in the railroad cars that carried them over the long, twisting Trans-Siberian Railroad.[28] The Czech Corps agreed to this in principle, but while turning over some of their arms, they carefully hid others, maintaining a secret cache of rifles, machine guns, and rounds of ammunition.[29]

But Stalin's second demand—that the divisions were to be accompanied to Vladivostok by trusted commissars from the Penza Soviet— caused turmoil.[30] The divisions protested vehemently, but were calmed by their commanders, who assured them that they would be out of the country soon. But days turned into weeks, and, as railroad cars sat idle in depots thronged with desperate refugees, the commissars took advantage of the situation to try to convince the Czech Corps to remain in Russia and fight with the Red Army against the Allies. The men resented this, and their discontent grew steadily to the point where nerves were poised on a knife edge.

Within these divisions, resistance grew. The idea of retribution against the Bolsheviks, first spoken of in whispers, then loud, angry voices, became a consuming passion for some of these men. In this, they were egged on by a twenty-six-year-old Czech officer, Rudolf Gaida, a man who, as one historian wrote, "combined a melodramatic outlook with a predilection for political intrigue."[31] Originally a simple hospital orderly, Gaida quickly made a name for himself in combat situations, demonstrating a fearless recklessness that stunned even his most vehement Bolshevik enemies. Tall and thin, with jet black hair and piercing blue eyes, Gaida was driven by hatred of the two forces he held responsible for untold miseries: the Bolsheviks and the Germans, forces that, to him and to many of the men under his command, became synonymous. He was as ruthless as Dutov or Semyonov, later boasting that he had taken prisoner-of-war camps and executed all of those he found there; with the Bolsheviks he was equally fierce, proudly recalling that during his campaigns, no prisoners were taken, only bodies left behind.[32]

With the Czechs whipped into frenzy, it took only the slightest tremor to set them off. In this case, two disasters followed, one upon the other, compounding reactions and heightening the crisis. The second blow fell almost immediately. The morning of Tuesday, May 14, saw two trains sitting in the crowded, dusty siding at Chelyabinsk: one was filled with a thousand angry, disillusioned Czech troops, the other with Hungarian prisoners of war, both being evacuated. There was no love lost between the Czech and the Hungarian forces, and throughout the hot, sultry morning, insults flew back and forth between the overcrowded cars. As the Hungarian train slowly steamed from the station, one of the soldiers aboard grabbed a piece of cast iron pipe and hurled it at a group of Czechs, striking one of the men in the head. The Czechs poured out of their train, ran across the tracks, seized the locomotive, forced the engineer to halt it, and stormed the cars, pulling out the Hungarian and killing him on the spot.[33]

There the situation might have ended had not the Chelyabinsk Soviet interfered. They arrested the Czechs who had lynched the Hungarian soldier, a move that brought the crisis to a head. Within a day, soldiers poured forth from the crowded train and seized control of the town from the Bolsheviks, freed their imprisoned comrades, and overthrew the soviet.[34]

The second blow came almost immediately, provoked by Leon Trotsky, the new commissar of war and the man charged with hastily establishing a coordinated Red Army. With the Czech Corps making increasingly loud noises, Trotsky ordered their representatives in

Moscow placed under arrest, where they were coerced into agreement with Soviet demands that the Czech Corps be completely disarmed. Trotsky followed this with another demand: all members of the Czech Corps were to be immediately arrested and forced into Red Army units. Those who resisted would be arrested and sent to labor camps.[35]

A few days later came a third demand, this a cable sent to all soviets along the Trans-Siberian Railroad: "Under serious penalty, all soviets on the rail line are ordered to disarm the Czech units. All Czech units discovered on the line possessing arms are to be immediately executed. All military transports conveying a single armed Czech are ordered stopped, Czechs placed in prison camps."[36]

But the Czechs were in control of Chelyabinsk, including the telegraph office, by this time, and they learned of Trotsky's instructions as soon as the cable arrived.[37] As Peter Fleming wrote, Trotsky's cable was, "in effect, a declaration of War against the Czechs," and this is certainly how they perceived it.[38] Within a few days, the Czechs were in open rebellion against the Bolsheviks, determined to march across Siberia, fighting the Red Army as they went.

A later, official Czech account declared: "The Czecho-Slovaks, from their intimate knowledge of political conditions throughout Russia, judged that the feeling against the Bolsheviks was strongest in the very regions where most of their divisions were located, namely in the Urals and western Siberia. The executive committee, therefore, in planning their action, took cognizance of these facts, and planned to take advantage both of the weakness of the Red Army and of the strong popular feeling against the Bolsheviks to force their way through to the east. That their action would be accompanied by or followed by the overthrow of the Soviet Government and the establishment of a new government in western Siberia never entered into their calculations, although later when the fall of the Soviet government was an accomplished fact, the Czecho-Slovaks were the first to welcome the new government and to lend it their moral and armed support."[39]

The Bolsheviks, however, immediately assumed the worst, and not without cause. In general terms, later claims that the Czechs were largely sympathetic to the Bolshevik regime are hard to substantiate, resting principally on a few accounts written after the fact, largely to dispel allegations that the Chelyabinsk incident had been planned by the Allies. In fact, many of the Czechs—and certainly a majority of their leaders—were sympathetic personally not only to the Allied cause but also, more importantly to the events of that summer, to the Romanovs.

During World War I, Czech prisoners of war, captured by the Russians, were allowed to form their own units and fight on the Allied side. Nicholas even received their representatives at Tsarskoye Selo, assuring them that once the war ended, Russia would help free their land of the hated Habsburgs. The Czech Corps thus had very real reasons to oppose the Bolsheviks, side with the Allies, and regard the imprisoned imperial family with some sympathy.[40] Gaida himself later became personally involved in the investigation into the murders in Ekaterinburg, and at least one Czechoslovakian division declared itself monarchist in sentiment.[41]

This view is particularly true when we look at Gaida. During the evacuation east, his train had been stopped at the town of Novo-Nikolayevsk, where Gaida held fairly extensive meetings with a secret anti-Bolshevik organization composed of monarchist officers. During these talks, a course of action was plotted, which called for general rebellion against the Soviet regime. Gaida assured them that his men were ready and willing to act, and he urged the monarchists to organize a similar rising.[42] He ended with a promise: "You just start in, and we'll take care of the Bolsheviks."[43]

Gaida's own version of events has long been ignored, possibly because it appeared only in his memoirs, published by a small press in Prague in the 1920s, and was never widely distributed or translated into any other language. It is evident that there was, before the Czech rebellion at Chelyabinsk, contact, if not exactly coordination, between the evacuated soldiers and anti-Bolshevik organizations, including but not limited to Socialist Revolutionaries and monarchist officers, and that the latter believed they could count on Czech support. This is verified in a second, rather obscure book, published in Prague and authored by a friend of Gaida, Boris Solodovnikov, who writes: "As early as the

Four White Russian generals, Siberia, 1918. From the left: Gaida, Kolchak, Deterikhs, and Domontovich.

beginning of May 1918 I met on one occasion in Moscow, in the apartment of the lawyer Vilenkin and in the presence of the Colonel of the General Staff N. Poradelov, with the well-known Socialist Revolutionary, Colonel V. I. Lebedev, and gained the understanding that in preparing their uprising, the SRs were placing hopes on the Czechoslovaks."[44]

But given these facts, it also must be pointed out that, contrary to later Soviet allegations, there is no evidence to support the idea that the Czech rebellion was either supported or instigated by the Allies or by any other group. What took place in Chelyabinsk was clearly spontaneous, regardless of any meetings or associations by Gaida or others with anti-Bolshevik groups. While these forces agreed in principle that they would work together, there is no reliable evidence that suggests any pattern to the chaotic events of the spring of 1918 in Siberia. As scholar George Kennan wrote: "One is reduced to the conclusion that external instigation or encouragement, either from the Allies or from the central headquarters of the underground Whites, played no significant part in the decision of the Czechs to take arms against the Soviet power."[45]

The Czech Corps advanced rapidly across Siberia. By the end of May they controlled not only Chelyabinsk and Novo-Nikolayevsk but also a ring of important towns around Omsk. The former Bolshevik stronghold of Penza fell on May 29, followed by Petropavlovsk and Tomsk on May 31, and Omsk on June 7.[46] The capture of Omsk was a significant loss to the Bolsheviks, and signaled a far more ominous turn of events. A new Government of Western Siberia was proclaimed there, transferred from Tomsk, and composed largely of Socialist Revolutionaries, monarchists, and Constitutional Democrats, all united in their hatred of the Bolsheviks.[47] As it had in Tomsk, the body remained resolute in its open defiance of Moscow. They raised their own white-and-green flag; rescinded appropriation decrees; abrogated Bolshevik laws; and outlawed all town, city, and regional soviets.[48] Yet, as Pipes notes, they were "content to isolate Siberia from Bolshevism and the Civil War."[49]

On June 8 the Volga town of Samara fell to the Czechs.[50] This was to have a dire consequence for the Bolsheviks. After the Bolsheviks had closed the duly elected Constituent Assembly in January, many of the deputies fled Petrograd, seeking refuge in the South. After the Czechs captured Samara, the town became a magnet for these thwarted politicians, who converged on the Volga and proclaimed themselves the government of the Constituent Assembly. Composed—like their forerunners in Tomsk and Omsk—of a curious mixture of political parties and ideologies, they declared that they were the only legitimate source of authority in all of Russia.[51]

Over the next month, the Czechs continued their advance. In late

June they laid siege to the city of Irkutsk, taking it from the Bolsheviks two weeks later.[52] Vladivostok fell to the Czechs on June 29, and, on July 6, the city of Ufa. Thus, by the end of the first week of July, nearly the entire length of the Trans-Siberian Railroad from Penza to Vladivostok lay in Czech control.[53] Within six weeks, the Bolsheviks had lost nearly every important city between the Volga and the Pacific Ocean; there were two exceptions to this: Perm, and, more ominously for the Romanovs, Ekaterinburg.

In Ekaterinburg itself, concern grew into apprehension, and apprehension into panic, as the city was increasingly encircled by the approaching Czech and White soldiers. Railroad lines were severed, repaired, and cut again; phone and telegraph lines out of the city worked only sporadically, subject to the fortunes of the increasing spiral of the Civil War. And, in the midst of the city, secret agents, spies, counter-revolutionaries, and plots. As Thomas Preston, British consul in Ekaterinburg, later wrote, as early as the end of May an agent had brought him a message informing him that the Allies should support the Czech revolt, and telling him to contact the Czech leaders through secret channels to offer assistance. "My position," Preston recalled, "and that of my Consular colleagues was therefore quite a precarious one, seeing that whilst resident in a town which was the seat of a Bolshevik Government, we were in touch with their enemies, the relieving forces of Czechs and White Russians who were gradually surrounding Ekaterinburg."[54]

These developments cast further, lengthening shadows over Lenin's fragile hold on power. Even two weeks before the Czech rebellion, Lenin chaired a session of VTsIK, during which they agreed to "begin immediately a general evacuation to the Urals."[55] This was a stunning decision, an admission that Lenin was prepared to sacrifice all of European Russia to the Germans, or the Allies, or both, to save his revolution; when word of this plan leaked out, there was panic.[56] In advance of this retreat, some 650 million gold rubles were put on a heavily guarded train and sent to the Urals, where it was to finance Lenin's new government. The train, and its important shipment, however, fell into the hands of the Whites at Kazan, providing them with an unexpected financial gain with which to fund their campaigns.[57]

And there was worse: quietly, Lenin told the VTsIK, he had asked Count von Mirbach to negotiate Russian peace treaties with the Ukraine and Finland, in an attempt to gain time. That he had to admit to his own political impotence was bad enough; coupled with the fact that he was forced to ask the hated occupiers to undertake the task on his behalf was a shameful humiliation. But the worst blow was Lenin's admission that these new treaties would almost certainly "risk new annexations."[58]

While struggling with this growing crisis, Lenin faced another: widespread famine. The two revolutions had been largely concentrated in urbanized, industrial areas, though there were a few incidents of widespread peasant retribution and looting in the summer of 1917. Most peasants, however, were distinctly unconcerned with politics, struggling from day to day to survive. The chaos of revolution—coupled with the complete breakdown in the country's infrastructure—began to starve the larger cities into desperation. To solve this, Lenin ordered bands of Red Army units and armed factory workers into the countryside, to steal grain from the peasants and transport it back to Moscow and Petrograd.[59]

This idea did not originate with Lenin. On December 1, 1917, A. Kosarev, president of the Omsk Regional Military Commissariat, wrote to Yakov Sverdlov: "We have much grain. But it is in the hands of the cooperatives, the defeatists, and other enemies of democracy. Send a train or two, some good competent workers and we will send you millions of pounds of grain, and it's good-bye hunger!"[60]

Peasants revolted, and they were supported by the four largest non-Bolshevik political parties, the Constitutional Democrats, the Mensheviks, the Left Socialist Revolutionaries, and the Socialist Revolutionaries; not surprisingly, the latter three parties enjoyed great support among the masses, setting up a direct conflict to the Bolshevik authorities in Moscow.[61] Throughout the spring of 1918, violent clashes took place. In April a contingent from the Red Army was seized and killed near Perm when they attempted to commandeer the grain of a small village. At the same time, nineteen members of an expeditionary force were killed in a peasant rebellion when they attempted to take local grain supplies; to make matters worse, the rebellion was organized by members of the local Bobrov Soviet—the very men Lenin had counted on to help carry out his program. When the members of the expeditionary force outnumbered the peasants, it was the latter who fell: on June 6, three hundred unarmed peasants were brutally shot and bayoneted when they attempted to halt shipment of a requisitioned load of grain.[62]

Disgust with Lenin's famine policy, coupled with disbelief at the terms of the Treaty of Brest-Litovsk, escalated dramatically. Urged on by these political factors, discontent spread from one village to the next, until only Petrograd, Moscow, and the Urals stood as strongholds of Lenin's regime.[63] Lenin's position was so fragile that he willingly considered sacrificing not just the third of the country that the Germans had won in the Treaty of Brest-Litovsk, but also all Russian territory west of the Urals—half of the former Romanov Empire. If potentially necessary, such considerations also won the Bolsheviks no support. The Treaty of Brest-Litovsk had alienated nearly every other political party in Russia, along with a sizable portion of the country's population; now, faced with the loss of even more territory, members of Lenin's own party began to turn on him as well.

On May 14, faced with imminent crises from all directions, Lenin delivered a report on Russia's foreign policy to a joint session of the VTsIK and Moscow Soviet. "We will do everything," he declared, "in order to prolong this short and unstable breathing space which we gained in March, because we are firmly convinced that we have behind us tens of millions of workers and peasants who know that with every week and with every month that this breathing space lasts they are gaining new strength." He counseled the need for "restraint and calm. There are, as I know well, men who think themselves wise, who insist on their cleverness and even call themselves Socialists, who declare that it was premature for us to seize power before the Revolution had spread to other countries. But such a view is childish nonsense. We all knew what to expect, for revolutions don't come without trials."[64]

Designed to placate the ever-increasing voices of criticism, Lenin's speech, coupled with plans for possible evacuation to the Urals and new territorial demands, instead brought immediate scorn. As Lenin was speaking, Boris Kamkov, a prominent Left SR, stood up and angrily demanded renunciation of the Treaty of Brest-Litovsk, and a wave of attacks on the Germans occupying the Ukraine to drive them from the country. Shouts and applause followed, and an SR deputy named Kogan-Bernstein took advantage of the chaos, leaped to his feet, and called for the dismissal of Lenin and his government, screaming that the Constituent Assembly must be reconvened. Even Lenin's old adversary Menshevik Julius Martov accused Lenin of turning the Revolution into his "personal dictatorship." Yelling "Long live the Russian Republic!" and insisting that the Constituent Assembly be called, he was quickly escorted from the building by members of the Red Army.[65]

Throughout these increasingly chaotic months, as each new crisis seemed to erupt without warning, anti-Bolshevik forces stirred. Those favorable to the Revolution regarded Lenin as a traitor who had sold both their country and their political ideologies for personal power. As defeat followed defeat, rebellion heaped on rebellion, the anti-Bolshevik forces saw their chance to make a grab for control—not only the Whites, Czechs, and monarchists, but also the SRs, Left SRs, Mensheviks, Constitutional Democrats, and Anarchists—all seething with discontent and plotting as spring turned to summer.

In the last two weeks of April, the Left Socialist Revolutionaries met in Moscow to discuss policy issues. A majority called for a final, comprehensive break with Lenin's government, but no action was taken. Violently opposed to the Treaty of Brest-Litovsk, they wanted a renunciation of the peace with Germany, expulsion of von Mirbach and all other Germans from Russian territory, an end to Lenin's famine policy, and a renewal of the war. On June 24 their leaders met secretly and agreed to raise these demands at the forthcoming Fifth Congress of Soviets, to be held in Moscow in the first week of July. If their demands were not met, they would launch an all-out campaign of revolutionary terror intended to bring about the fall of Lenin's regime.[66] Although this decision had been made in secret, word soon leaked out. On June 30, Maria Spiridonovna, leader of the Left SR Party, went so far as to declare that only an armed uprising would now save the Revolution from the Soviets.[67] "This was an alarm signal," wrote Louis Fischer. "The Social Revolutionaries were seizing their old weapon: terror. An explosion seemed imminent."[68]

Discontent from the Treaty of Brest-Litovsk, from the closing of the Constituent Assembly, and from famine coalesced into a swell of strikes and demonstrations. Hunger was a constant companion. As Richard Pipes notes, food shortages, coupled with rations and inflation, resulted in an exodus from Petrograd and Moscow—a loss of more than half of the workforce. By May 1918, only just over 10 percent of Petrograd's industrial workers had jobs.[69]

The spring of 1918 was a litany of unrest. Just after the Constituent Assembly met, a group of workers' representatives met in Petrograd to discuss a course of action.[70] These representatives called for elections to a new Constituent Assembly, disavowal of the Treaty of Brest-Litovsk, and overthrow of the Soviet government.[71] On March 31 the Cheka raided the Petrograd headquarters of the Council of Workers' Representatives, making threats and taking away anti-Bolshevik literature. Throughout April an uneasy truce developed, but this was short-lived. By the beginning of May, talk in Petrograd's factories ran high, and included stunning denunciations of the Bolsheviks. When Bolshevik speakers tried to calm the crowd, they were shouted down, and the group called for immediate dissolution of the Petrograd Soviet, in addition to their previous demands.[72]

On May 28, hungry, depressed, angry at their treatment by the Bolsheviks, the workers at the Putilov factory in Petrograd reiterated their demands. Groups of workers' representatives in Moscow, Orel, Tula, and other large industrial cities adopted nearly identical platforms.[73] The following day, with Moscow's factories erupting in chaos, Lenin declared martial law in the capital. At the same time, most of the Left Communists quit the government, stating publicly that they would support the anti-Bolshevik forces.[74]

Two days later, the Council of Petrograd Workers' Representatives urged their members to strike.[75] Within a few days, they agreed not to strike on condition that a handpicked delegate would be received in Moscow. But when the delegate, on arrival, began to whip up the Moscow workers with anti-Bolshevik rhetoric, the Cheka moved in, arresting him. Within a few days, however, the threats of Moscow workers forced his release.[76]

Next came another crisis: elections to the town, city, and regional soviets. This was a despised but necessary measure, for delegates had to be selected before the Fifth Congress of Soviets, scheduled to take place in Moscow in early July. Like the previous elections to the Constituent Assembly, these proved disastrous to the Bolsheviks, with Mensheviks and Socialist Revolutionaries winning a vast majority of seats.[77] In response, the Bolsheviks took extreme measures to guarantee victory. They postponed the elections for the Moscow and Petrograd Soviets, aware that if they took place as scheduled, they would fail to gain a majority of seats. Stuck with the results already counted, the Bolsheviks resorted to ballet tampering to ensure victory; according to this formula, some Bolshevik candidates were given as many as five individual votes to guarantee their seats.[78] When a second round of elections was ordered, on June 14, the Bolsheviks simply ordered all Mensheviks and Socialist Revolutionaries thrown out of the soviets, declaring that if they were not members, they could not receive votes. The only candidates who remained, therefore, were either Bolshevik or Left SR.[79]

These developments built into a crescendo of chaos. With each passing day there were further strikes, factory walkouts, and calls for the resignation of the Council of People's Commissars, of the Central Executive Committee, and of Lenin himself. More and more, there was talk of armed resistance, met by fierce warnings from the government. On June 9, Dzerzhinsky, in an interview with the Menshevik paper *Novaya Zhizn*, declared that the Cheka intended to fight "the enemies of Soviet authority and of the new way of life. Such enemies are both our political opponents and all bandits, thieves, speculators, and other criminals who undermine the foundations of the socialist order."[80] A week later, the Central Executive Committee allowed publication of a "resolution" that stated that "Revolutionary Tribunals are not bound by any rules in the choice of measures against the counterrevolution except in cases where the law defines the measure in terms of 'no lower than' such punishment."[81]

Four days after this, an SR terrorist named Sergeyev assassinated V. Volodarsky, a member of the Central Committee and the commissar for press and propaganda in the Petrograd Soviet.[82] When the Cheka attempted to arrest suspected agitators and factory leaders, they were met with armed resistance and strikes; the Bolsheviks had to order troops into the industrial areas and to impose martial law in an attempt to suppress the rebellion. Lenin, when he learned of this, was beside himself with anger, both at the assassination, and at the lenient manner with which Zinoviev was dealing with the uprising. He wrote to Zinoviev on June 26: "We are discrediting ourselves; we threaten mass terror . . . yet when it comes to action we obstruct the revolutionary initiative of the masses, a quite correct one. This is impossible; the terrorists will consider us old women. This is wartime above all. We must encourage the energy and mass character of the terror against the counterrevolutionaries, and particularly in Petrograd, the example of which is decisive."[83]

The accumulation of these developments—resentment against Brest-Litovsk, political unrest, rigged elections, increasing strikes, assassinations, the Civil War, and the Czech rebellion—worried the Germans. In Berlin, right-wing military extremists openly called for Russia's immediate obliteration, while even the more cautious voices counseled that the time had come for Germany to sever ties with the Bolsheviks.[84] From Moscow, von Mirbach's assistant Kurt Riezler advised Berlin that, with the rising of the Czech Corps, he did not expect the Soviet regime to last.[85] Such a pessimistic evaluation came from a surprising source: Trotsky, who, on June 13, had commented, "We're already the walking dead."[86] And von Mirbach himself made two ominous reports to Berlin: "After more than two months of cautious watch," he wrote in the last week of June, "I can today report that I no longer have a good impression of the chances of survival of the Bolshevik regime. It is now undoubtedly a sick man; despite brief moments of seeming recovery, in the final analysis he is doomed."[87] A few days later he confidently asserted: "In the event of a change of orientation here, we would not even have to apply a great deal of force, and we could to some extent keep up appearances in our relations with the Bolshevik right up to the last moment. The continual mismanagement here, and the equally violent blows being struck against our interests, could be used as a motive for a military advance at any time we chose."[88]

On July 1, 1918, came the final blow. On this day some four thousand British, French, American, Canadian, and Italian troops landed at Murmansk, in northern Russia. This was the first Allied expeditionary force, and their arrival caused panic. Already soldiers had landed at Vladivostok in the spring, and with that port city firmly in the hands of the Czechs, more soldiers were expected. With the Germans in the South, the Allies coming from the North and the East, and the Whites and Czechs moving in concentric circles ever closer to Moscow, the situation was indeed desperate. Against this tense, traumatic background, the fate of the Romanovs would be played out.

7

The First to Die

WHEN NICHOLAS II abdicated the Russian throne on March 15, 1917, the 304-year-old Romanov Dynasty ended. On that cold winter day, fifty-two members of the imperial house were living in the empire. Over the following two years, seventeen Romanovs were murdered by the Bolsheviks, while thirty-five managed to escape the Revolution.

The first Romanov to die at the hands of the Bolsheviks was Grand Duke Michael Alexandrovich, the emperor's only surviving brother, and the man who, having been named in Nicholas's abdication manifesto as his successor, quickly signed away his own rights, thus ending the rule of the Romanov Dynasty. The grand duke was an uncomplicated, genial man, the favorite of both his parents, and had grown up indulged and spoiled by his entire family. Although he served with distinction in the army during the war, scandal hung heavily over his name. After a series of flaunted romances with ladies at court, he fell hopelessly under the spell of Nathalia Sheremetevskaia Wulfert, the beautiful and headstrong young wife of one of his fellow guards officers. Natasha, as she was known, could be

Grand Duke Michael Alexandrovich, youngest brother of the last emperor. The first Romanov to die in the Urals.

charming and as genial as the weak-willed Michael, but she had a forceful character that quickly subsumed the young man. Although she had
already divorced one husband and was married to a second, she was
determined not to let such an opportunity with the grand duke out of
her reach, and she wove of spell of whispered compliments and sexual
intrigue that bewitched the naive grand duke. When she learned that
she was pregnant, there was no longer any pretense, and the grand
duke openly acknowledged the son as his. Natasha divorced Wulfert,
and set out firmly on her quest to capture for herself the emperor's own
brother as her third husband.

The grand duke was all innocence and naïveté, without guile and
malice. One man who knew him well, Dimitri Abrikossow, later
recalled: "I must say I have never met another man so uncorrupted and
noble in nature; it was enough to look into his clear blue eyes to be
ashamed of any bad thought or insincere feeling. In many ways he was
a grown-up child who had been taught only what was good and moral.
He did not want to admit that there was wickedness and falsehood in
this world and trusted everybody."[1]

It was easy for the dominant Natasha to steer the grand duke to her
plans, despite repeated warnings from both his brother the emperor and
his mother, Dowager Empress Marie Feodorovna. Michael certainly
never gave any sign, in the hundreds of intimate love letters that passed
between him and his mistress, that he was anything but hopelessly in
love with Madame Wulfert, but few others believed there was anything
more to the liaison than sheer lust for power on the part of his para-
mour. In 1912, while on a trip to Europe and under constant surveillance by members of the Okhrana, the pair managed to sneak away and
marry. The union could scarcely be considered legal; not only did the
grand duke marry without the emperor's permission, which invalidated
the marriage according to the Fundamental Laws of the Russian
Empire, but also his bride, with two previous husbands and a solidly
middle-class background, was an untenable choice.

Nicholas II received news of this action at a critical moment—as his
only son lay possibly dying at Spala in Poland; the grand duke com-
pounded his error by writing that the boy's illness—and the possibility
that he might die and thus make his uncle heir apparent—had hastened
his decision. Nicholas responded by forbidding his brother to return to
Russia, a condition that he only relaxed with great reluctance at the
beginning of World War I. But Natasha, who was granted the courtesy
title of Countess Brassova, would never be received by either the
emperor or the empress. During the heady days of autumn 1916 leading
up to the Revolution, Natasha, aware of her position and that of her husband, continually pushed Michael to conspire against his brother with

members of the Duma and liberal elements, seemingly unaware that she could never occupy the imperial throne at his side even if her wishes came true. The grand duke, under her spell and too weak morally and intellectually to resist, actively discussed the need for Alexandra's removal with several officials prior to the events of March 1917.

Following the February Revolution, Michael and Natasha lived quietly in the suburban estate of Gatchina. The exile of the imperial family to Tobolsk in August, however, worried Michael sufficiently that he asked British ambassador Sir George Buchanan to obtain a visa so that he and Natasha could leave Russia and take up residence in England, where the grand duke owned some property. Apparently, however, Michael was unaware of the numerous obstacles that had been thrown in the path of any Romanov being granted asylum; it was not only his own cousin King George V by the end of summer 1917, but the British government as well. To Buchanan's query, the Foreign Office responded: "His Majesty's Government do not wish members of the Imperial Family to come to England during the War."[2]

At the end of 1917, Michael petitioned Lenin to be allowed to change his name to Mr. Michael Brassov. At the same time, he also sought permission to leave Russia. Lenin, however, had no time for this; he declared it was not an issue on which he would act, and he let the matter drop.[3] For several months Michael lived quietly, but the Bolshevik Revolution in October 1917 marked a turning point. Whereas the Provisional Government had not been hostile, the same could not be said of the new regime. Their first full year of power—1918—marked, as authors John Curtis Perry and Constantine Pleshakov remarked, "an orgy of destruction, the deliberate crushing of a culture, the civilization of Imperial Russia."[4] The Romanovs increasingly became targets of this chaotic campaign.

Near the end of March 1918, the Soviet government began a systematic program designed to round up and relocate all remaining members of the dynasty. The Soviet decision was perhaps a natural extension of the Revolution, yet the immediate order seemed predicated on two factors: the signing of the Treaty of Brest-Litovsk on March 3, and the transfer of the capital and all official government offices from Petrograd to Moscow a week later. Lenin had no wish to leave more than two dozen members of the former dynasty in the old capital. He feared that, in what he knew would be a forthcoming German occupation of the immense stretches of European Russia granted to them under the terms of the Treaty of Brest-Litovsk, the kaiser's army would seize the Romanovs and use them to their own political advantage.

After the Treaty of Brest-Litovsk, Michael fell under the watchful eye of the Petrograd Soviet. "The Treaty brought terrible odium to the

Bolshevik regime," notes historian Richard Pipes. "In this atmosphere attempts at restoration could not have been precluded, the more so that the Bolsheviks were aware of pro-monarchist sentiments among German generals. To avoid trouble, precautions were taken to remove the Romanovs from the scene."[5]

This nagging worry led Lenin to his first important action since coming to power involving members of the former dynasty. Six days after the treaty was signed, Lenin ordered Michael arrested; he was imprisoned first at the Smolny Institute in Petrograd, then moved to the headquarters of the city Cheka. Within a few days, however, Lenin ordered him to Perm. According to Paul Bykov,

> The accompanying letter to the Perm Soviet stated that Michael Romanov was being sent to Perm on the responsibility and under the observation of the Soviet but it suggested that no special restrictions be imposed upon him. However the Perm Soviet could not make up its mind to liberate him at once and detained him under domestic arrest in the former Hall of the Nobility. Michael Romanov protested against his arrest and insisted on his release, referring to the Petrograd decision as a justification. However, at the sessions of the town Soviet and at workers' meetings, particularly at the Motovilikhia Works, the workers themselves repeatedly raised the question of shooting Michael Romanov, in order thereby once for all to block the monarchists' inclinations to hunt for a candidate to the Imperial throne.[6]

The Perm Soviet was not at all convinced that Michael should be allowed his freedom; not only did they have a personal desire to imprison him as a member of the former dynasty, but also the Siberia of 1918 seethed with various revolutionary groups, any one of which might be likely to take matters into their own hands and either attempt a rescue of the grand duke or an assassination of him. But Michael went to the Cheka headquarters and complained, and after cabling to both Moscow and Petrograd for instructions, Perm finally received an answer, signed by Vladimir Bonch-Bruyevich, head of the Council of People's Commissars, and Uritsky of the Petrograd Cheka, that they should let Michael have his freedom. He was duly released, but the Perm Cheka warned him that they could not be responsible for his safety.[7]

Given his freedom, Michael, accompanied by his English secretary Nicholas Johnson, his valet Chelyshev, and his chauffeur Borunov, lived first in rooms at the Men's Club in Perm, then at the Hotel Korolev on Siberia Street, the most expensive accommodation in town. He was watched, but free to come and go at will.[8] The only restriction appears to have been a required report to the local Cheka.[9]

According to Bykov, "Michael Romanov was in close contact with his friends and relations, and there was constant communication between Perm and Petrograd."[10] In May, Natasha visited her husband, and the pair attended midnight Easter services in the town's cathedral. "The blatantly monarchist ceremonies of the bourgeoisie and the new Tsar-Savior's almost daily processions to the Cathedral along roads covered with carpets and fresh flowers angered the working class," recalled A. A. Shamarin, a member of the Perm Cheka.[11]

By the beginning of June 1918, officials in Perm seem to have panicked over Michael's continued presence in the city. Following the Czech uprising on May 23, and their rapid advance across Siberia, there were real worries that they might make their way to Perm and rescue the grand duke. In the first few days of the month, newspapers in the city publicly worried that the grand duke might be conspiring to flee and place himself at the head of the anti-Bolshevik Volunteer Army, or set himself up as sovereign.[12]

A great deal of mystery continues to cloud the circumstances of the actual decision to murder Michael, with no clear historical indication of how the decision came about or who was ultimately responsible. The few facts behind the murder are simple enough. On the night of Wednesday, June 12, 1918, a contingent of men arrived at the Korolev Hotel on Siberia Street with the intention of kidnapping and killing Grand Duke Michael. They were led by Gabriel Myasnikov, twenty-nine years old, a member of the Perm Cheka and head of the city garrison. The group included Andrei Markov, commissar for appropriations in the Perm Soviet; Vassili Ivanchenko, head of the Perm military garrison; Nicholas Zhuzhgov, assistant chief of the Motovilikhia factory; and Ivan Kolpashchikov, a member of the Red Army.[13] A sixth man, Igor Novoselov, later wrote an account of the murder, which seems to indicate that he also was present that night in the forest. Another version came from Feodor Lukoyanov, who later claimed to have been involved in the murder. According to his sister Vera, one day he burst into a meeting of the Ekaterinburg Cheka and declared: "If you would give me Nicholas, I would solve this sorry affair, just like I did with Michael!"[14]

Myasnikov worked out the plan. The men would forge an evacuation order, saying that the grand duke had to be removed from the approaching reach of the anti-Bolshevik forces. He would be taken away to a clearing in a forest near the Motovilikhia factory and shot; at the same time, the Perm Cheka would declare that Michael had disappeared—rescued or kidnapped—and arrest the three members of his small household as suspected conspirators. Myasnikov was careful to warn his fellow conspirators that such deception was necessary so that Lenin and Sverdlov would not be compromised.[15]

The events of that night are chronicled in six different accounts.

The grand duke's valet, Vassili Tchelyshev, was later imprisoned with Alexei Volkov, Empress Alexandra's valet de chambre, and told him details of what he had seen; Volkov himself repeated this tale to Nicholas Sokolov, and also to an émigré friend in Europe in the 1920s. Two other men who were present at the Korolev Hotel that night, Kobelev, and Kurumnikov, also gave evidence to the White investigators. Of the actual assassination there are three accounts: that of Mayasnikov, and statements written by Andrei Markov and Igor Novoselov.[16]

The first three witnesses related how, shortly before midnight on June 12, a group of men had arrived at the Korolev Hotel, armed with revolvers, and gone to the grand duke's rooms. He was woken and presented with the evacuation order; apparently Michael suspected it to be a forgery, for he began to protest that he must speak to the local authorities, but the men insisted that they must hurry. One of them, according to Tchelyashev, whispered something to Nicholas Johnson, who in turn passed this along to Michael, explaining that although the men were dressed as Bolsheviks, they were, in fact, monarchists determined to spirit him away from the city. When Johnson insisted that he be allowed to accompany the grand duke, the group relented, and the two prisoners were driven off surrounded by several armed men.[17]

The group drove Michael and Johnson out of the city and into the woods near the Motovilikhia factory. Nearly a mile beyond the kerosene depot, the two carriages came to a halt and Zhuzhgov ordered the prisoners to get out. As Johnson left the carriage, Markov shot him in the head; he "swayed and fell into the dirt." Michael jumped from the carriage and began to run, Kolpashchikov aimed and pulled the trigger on his revolver, but the gun jammed; Zhuzhgov fired, but his shot only wounded the grand duke, and left him standing. Michael ran toward Johnson; as he did so, Markov fired, his shot striking the grand duke in the head and sending him in a spiral into the road, where he died at the side of his secretary. "It was too light to properly bury the bodies," Markov recalled, "and we dragged them into the forest near Motovilikhia, covered them with dirt and branches, and returned to Perm. Later, Zhuzhgov and a trusted member of the Cheka returned that night and properly buried them."[18]

On returning to Perm, the assassins continued their deception. At 2:20 A.M. on June 13, Myasnikov sent a cable to Moscow: "Last night, Michael Romanov and Johnson were kidnapped by unknown persons dressed in military uniform. Search unsuccessful as yet, taking energetic measures."[19] The following day, Permskye Izvestiia, the local Perm newspaper, reported: "During the night of June 12, an organized band of White Guards with forged orders arrived at the Hotel where Michael Romanov and his secretary Johnson resided and kidnapped them, carrying them away to an as yet unknown destination. A search party organized last night has found no trace. The search continues."[20] This rumor was picked up and quickly repeated. On June 17, newspapers in Moscow and Petrograd reported the grand duke's abduction, noting that the search had as yet uncovered no sign of the two men.[21] Within two weeks, it had been picked up by foreign journalists. The July 4 issue of the *New York Times*, quoting an article in the *Times* of London, mentioned rumors of the deaths of both Michael and his brother Nicholas II. It suggested that while there was no confirmation related to the fate of the former emperor, "rumors of the escape of Prince Michael are better founded."[22] Ten days later, the *New York Times* reported that Michael had been seen in Kiev.[23] And just six days after the Ekaterinburg murders, the Press Bureau of the Soviet People's Commissariat released a statement that declared that Michael had last been seen in Omsk and speculated that he had fled to London.[24]

With these various contradictory rumors, no one knew with any certainty just what had become of the grand duke. Rumors appeared from time to time that he was spotted in Vladivostok, the Crimea, or the Ukraine; that he was with Admiral Kolchak, helping to plan a White offensive; and that he had disappeared into European exile.[25] Given this state of affairs, it is not surprising that the German army in Russia believed that the grand duke had escaped; throughout that summer of 1918, as authors Rosemary and Donald Crawford have written, German diplomatic correspondence continually mentions the idea of promoting the grand duke as a figurehead monarch over a Russia controlled by the kaiser's army.[26]

The grand duke's mysterious murder continued to perplex historians for decades. Although Nicholas Sokolov correctly set the date of the execution as the early morning of June 13, his assistant Paul Bulygin, in his book on the murders of the Romanovs, inexplicably gave the date as July 12, while Robert Massie wrote that Michael was killed "on the night of 13 July 1918—three days before the murders in Ekaterinburg."[27] And the authors Maylunas and Mironenko, the latter the curator of the Russian State Archives, which holds most of the relevant documents, placed the date of the murder on the night of June 26, with no apparent justification and based on a seeming lack of understanding over which calendar was in use at the time.[28] Bulygin, along with Sokolov, Wilton, and others, helped contribute to the general confusion, all three men suggesting with great confidence that the bodies had been destroyed in the furnaces of the Motovilikhia factory.[29] The general lack of documentation continues to perplex the case; as recently as 1990, historian Richard Pipes, in his work on the Russian Revolution, claimed that "the remains of Michael and Johnson had been located by the Sokolov Commission" in 1919.[30] Of course, Sokolov never made such a claim, nor have any bodies ever been found, but it is indicative of the veil of fog that continues to surround the grand duke's murder.

Even more of an enigma are questions of ultimate responsibility: Who ordered the execution? Did Moscow know in advance? There are three basic views. The first postulates that Moscow indeed ordered Michael's execution, as a sort of test run for the eventual Ekaterinburg murders, to lay the groundwork for deception and to see what sort of reaction rumors of his death would provoke. A second hypothesis contends that the decision was made by a rogue group of Perm Bolsheviks, without the sanction or knowledge of the Perm Soviet or any higher authorities. And a third view holds that the decision was made jointly by members of the Perm and Ekaterinburg Soviets, either with or without the permission of Moscow.

The issue of Michael's murder and the questions of ultimate responsibility had great bearing on the eventual Ekaterinburg executions. Of the first theory—that the grand duke's murder was ordered by Moscow—there exists absolutely no evidence, though it remains popular among émigré circles. It rests only on the assumption made by the official investigator, Nicholas Sokolov, who concluded in his book on the murder of the Romanovs that Lenin had to have given such an order, based on the view that the authorities in Perm would not have acted on their own without approval, and on his own personal belief that Lenin and Sverdlov were behind the executions of all of the Romanovs. Sokolov wrote,

> It is with the murder of Michael Alexandrovich that the Bolsheviks opened a series of murders on members of the Romanov family. It began with Michael Alexandrovich, who, from the political point of view, was more dangerous than the Emperor, who had renounced the Throne. Moscow had prepared a unique plan, of which the essential element was the lie. The Bolsheviks lied in Ekaterinburg, they lied in Alapayevsk, they lied in Perm, and all in the same way. Before the murder of the Grand Duke, Moscow had decided to start a rumor that the Emperor had been killed. This rumor spread with the desired effect until it made its way in June from Moscow to Ekaterinburg. Once there, attention turned from the Grand Duke to the Emperor. And the version of the kidnapping of Michael Alexandrovich was as gladly accepted as the news of the murder of the Emperor was rapidly being denied by the Bolsheviks themselves.[31]

Unfortunately for Sokolov, this contention contains the seeds of its own destruction. Moscow certainly was not behind the rumors of the emperor's death that circulated in June, as will be shown, nor did these first surface until after the grand duke had already been killed. There is not, with the grand duke's murder, even the slightest hint of a paper trail linking Moscow to the Perm execution, as there is with the Ekaterinburg assassinations. Indeed, both Lenin and Sverdlov seem to have learned of the grand duke's death only after it had occurred. In fact, this is quite definitely shown in the transcripts of a telegraph conversation between Sverdlov in Moscow and Beloborodov in Ekaterinburg. Having received the cable that the grand duke had been abducted, it took Sverdlov only a few days to learn the truth of what took place, but he was still uncertain who was ultimately responsible. He asked Beloborodov: "Whose work was it? Ours, or Motovilikhia's?"[32]

Nor does there appear to be any truth, as the recent Russian author Platonov alleged, that "the Cheka was playing a very deliberate game of subterfuge, designed not only to cover their own tracks, but also to obfuscate where the question of responsibility was concerned."[33] Such an allegation imparts to Myasnikov and the others involved a degree of sophisticated cooperation and coordination with Moscow for which no evidence exists.

Authors Rosemary and Donald Crawford, while admitting that no solid evidence exists to show a collaboration between Moscow and Perm, nevertheless suggest that Moscow's lack of reaction to the murder was "odd" and write: "No vengeful tribunal descended on Perm to exact punishment on those charged with Michael's security. No one demanded an accounting by the local leadership, or the arrest of those whose negligence had permitted the rescue. There was no inquiry, no scapegoat, no consequence."[34] This is true enough, but it misses an obvious argument: Michael's death may have been welcomed by Moscow, and they may well have looked on the actions undertaken by the Perm Cheka with gratitude, having eliminated a man who, at some future point, might very well cause problems for the Bolshevik regime. Further, it is possible that they saw in this independent action an opportunity to gauge likely public reaction—especially from the West—should a similar fate prove necessary for the Romanovs in Ekaterinburg.

But this hypothesis also fails to take into account one last, and perhaps most important, factor. With no evidence to the contrary, Moscow was presented with a fait accompli, an action undertaken by a rogue provincial Party organization without prior approval or even tacit endorsement. The argument that one should have expected Moscow to exact retribution ignores the realities of the very tenuous political situation of the Soviet regime, as well as the well-known independent spirit harbored by the Siberian Bolsheviks, who, by the summer of 1918, were openly regarding Moscow with disdain. Faced with this reality, would Moscow really have admitted that its Perm Cheka and Soviet had acted without approval and needed to be punished, thereby publicly owning up to their own impotence? This is highly unlikely, and any such punitive measures that might have been taken against the authorities in Perm must be viewed in this light.

We do know that Moscow apparently received the news of Michael's death firsthand, in a report delivered by M. P. Turkin, a member of the Perm Soviet, who was sent to Moscow at the end of June to attend the Fifth Congress of Soviets. This must be treated with some caution, however, for it derives not from Turkin himself but from Myasnikov, who was not above distortion in his own statement. According to Turkin's account as relayed by Myasnikov, the deception continued, extending even to Lenin and Sverdlov. Turkin explained the execution of the grand duke as an act of political expediency, saying that Michael had been killed to avert his imminent capture by a band of sympathetic officers in Perm. Turkin apparently spoke to Sverdlov in person, and to Lenin on the telephone, and both men were "pleased" at Perm's action and decided to officially state that the grand duke had escaped.[35]

If the theory that Moscow ordered the grand duke's execution does not stand up to examination, is there any better evidence to suggest that the assassins acted alone, without the approval of any Perm organization? This, too, does not satisfy. "This event was a complete surprise for all the organizations in Perm," Bykov claimed. "A chase was organized immediately which however set out on the false route and could find no traces. At the same time telegrams were sent to Petrograd and in every direction announcing the escape of Michael Romanov. For some time the Perm organizations were in ignorance of the true course of events and only after some time discovered the actual state of affairs from rumors which spread among the rank and file."[36] But this is nonsense. Too many members of the Perm Cheka and the Perm Soviet participated in the conspiracy and the murder to believe that it did not have some official sanction, even if that approval was generally unknown to the members at large.[37]

The third hypothesis—that Perm worked in conjunction with Ekaterinburg—is far stronger. In their own later memoirs, two of the participants in the Ekaterinburg execution—Michael Medvedev, who went by his Bolshevik Party name of Kudrin, and Isai Rodzinsky—both confirmed that all of the Romanov murders that summer in Siberia—in Perm, in Ekaterinburg, and the deaths at Alapayevsk—were the work of the Ural Regional Soviet.[38] It is almost certain that Michael's murder was planned and executed by authorities in Perm in collaboration with the Ural Regional Soviet, who were careful to conceal the true circumstances of their crime from Moscow by setting up an elaborate story of a rescue plot, complete with deceptive cables. This explains Sverdlov's query, asking who was responsible—a clear indication that Moscow had no hand in the murder.

The murder of the grand duke was unknown to the prisoners in the Ipatiev House. There is no indication that they were aware of any of the rumors surrounding his possible fate, widely reported in newspapers across Russia. But this execution was to play a direct and ultimately fatal role in their fate.

8

The June Conspiracies

THE MURDER OF GRAND DUKE Michael Alexandrovich in
Perm signaled a new, ominous chapter in the captivity of the
imperial family at Ekaterinburg. With each passing week,
pressures slowly, inexorably mounted. Lenin struggled to maintain his
precarious hold over the Soviet regime; the Germans occupied Russia;
the Civil War raged ever closer to the few remaining centers of fragile
Bolshevik power; and the rebellious Czechoslovak forces marched
headlong into the Urals, toward Ekaterinburg.

Against this background, concern for the Romanovs took a more
urgent turn. Shortly after the Treaty of Brest-Litovsk was signed, King
Christian X of Denmark—Nicholas II's cousin—wrote to Kaiser
Wilhelm II, imploring him to intervene on behalf of the imprisoned
imperial family. The kaiser replied cautiously, saying that he had to be
careful lest any action on his part be taken for official German endorsement of a Romanov restoration.[1] But he assured the king: "I cannot
deny the Imperial Family my compassion from the human point of
view, and when it lies in my power, I will gladly do my part to ensure
that the Russian Imperial Family has a safe and suitable situation."[2]

This was far from the end of the kaiser's involvement. On May 18,
Harald Scavenius, the Danish minister in Petrograd, reported to
Copenhagen that the dowager empress had fallen under "German con-
trol." Three days earlier, Count von Moltke, the Danish ambassador in
Berlin, had wired Copenhagen that he had consulted with German
diplomatic authorities about possible asylum for the dowager empress
and other members of the Romanov family in the Crimea. The official
German reply stated that Adolf Ioffe, the Russian ambassador in Berlin,

had objected strenuously to the idea of any member of the Romanov Dynasty being granted foreign asylum, ostensibly for their own safety.[3] But the official reply veiled a covert operation then currently taking place. Unbeknownst to the Danish officials, the kaiser himself had ordered intensive diplomatic negotiations undertaken on behalf of his Romanov relations. Throughout the spring and summer of 1918, Wilhelm II repeatedly tried to gain assurances for his cousins' safety.

When Count von Mirbach took up his appointment as German ambassador in Moscow, he did so with Wilhelm II's charge that he work to guarantee the safety of the imperial family. When, in the spring of 1918, a group of monarchists asked for von Mirbach's help, the ambassador said, "Be calm. We Germans have the situation well in hand, and the Imperial Family is under our protection. We know what we are doing and when the time comes, the German Imperial Government will take the necessary measures."[4] To the queries of one monarchist, Prince Dimitri Obolensky, the new ambassador replied: "*Aidez-vous mêmes et Dieu vous aidera.* I would rephrase it thus: Aid yourself and Germany will help you."[5]

By this time, however, the Germans apparently knew of the emperor's refusal to cooperate with any German efforts to rescue his family. When Count Benckendorff wrote a long plea to von Mirbach asking after the imperial family, he received a disturbing reply: "The fate of the Emperor is a matter for the Russian people. We now have to concern ourselves with the safety of the German princesses on Russian territory."[6] Indeed, von Mirbach reported to Berlin that he had presented the Soviet government with "a statement regarding our expectations that the German princesses will be treated with all possible consideration, and specifically that unnecessary petty annoyances, as well as threats against their lives, will not be permitted."[7] The German princesses were likely Alexandra and her sister Ella rather than the empress and her daughters. All this occurred on the kaiser's orders. Cousin Willy, despite his bombastic nature, genuinely worried about his Russian cousins.

On May 10, von Mirbach once again raised the issue of the Romanovs with Lev Karakhan and Karl Radek. Von Mirbach reported: "Without venturing to act as an advocate for the overthrown Regime, I have nevertheless expressed to the commissars the expectation that the German Princesses will be treated with all possible consideration and, in particular, that there will be no minor annoyances, or any threats to their lives. Karakhan and Radek, who represented the indisposed Chicherin, received my remarks in a very forthcoming and understanding manner."[8]

According to Vladimir Burtsev, who knew von Mirbach well, the ambassador also approached Sverdlov, speaking to him at some length.

Later he told Burtsev: "I will do all possible to bring the Emperor to Petrograd, but cannot answer for the results because the local authorities do not make it possible to insist." Burtsev recalled: "I also know that on [von] Mirbach's insistence the Central Committee gave permission for money to be sent to the Emperor. Wilhelm II personally was very anxious about Nicholas II and constantly asked Count [von] Mirbach about the state of affairs."[9]

German concern mounted as spring turned to summer. A number of reports filed by von Mirbach confirm that as late as the end of June, he was making overtures to the Central Executive Committee on behalf of the Romanovs.[10] And the kaiser himself, as late as three weeks before the Ekaterinburg murders, continued to make overtures about his Russian cousins. According to a British Foreign Office report, citing Queen Olga of the Hellenes, Nicholas II's aunt and mother-in-law of the kaiser's sister Sophie, Wilhelm was greatly distressed at the Romanovs' situation, and particularly upset that the emperor had rejected offers of German assistance. Crown Princess Cecilie spoke with the queen at some length, and told her that her father-in-law the kaiser "spends sleepless nights in mourning over the Romanovs' fate."[11]

At the same time, Wilhelm von Kuhlmann, the German state minister, reported a conversation he had had with Ioffe in Berlin: "The Russian representative replied he had been perfectly clear about it and multiple telegraphic messages referred to it, it was important to them to look after the Emperor's family and put them in a suitable place. The decision to let them come to Moscow is also fundamentally ready and prepared when the interruption of the railway line by the Czechoslovakians is cleared. The Soviet Republic is not in a position to do anything in this respect now."[12]

Thus, even without the cooperation of the emperor, the Germans had apparently worked out some diplomatic solution with the Bolsheviks, in which the Germans were guaranteed the safety of the imperial family, and promised that they would be brought to Moscow. It is impossible to say if this was a cynical move by the Bolsheviks, designed to allay German concern, or a genuine offer. In any event, the situation in Russia, coupled with Lenin's increasingly desperate struggle to simply survive, meant that the question of moving the Romanovs fell victim to more pressing matters.

After the Ekaterinburg murders, word of these negotiations inevitably leaked out, and caused considerable consternation among the monarchists and Whites. For many, it was inconceivable that the Romanovs would have fled Russia, and certainly not with the assistance of the Germans. "Apart from the bald assertions of parties interested in spreading false reports," declared Robert Wilton, "there is no evidence of any attempt on the part of the Romanovs to escape from any of their prisons."[13] Yet this is nonsense. We know that the prisoners, while still in Tobolsk, intrigued in several plots that would have resulted in their rescue and safe exile outside of Russia, and while imprisoned in Ekaterinburg they fully cooperated with a proposed rescue attempt.

The prisoners in the Ipatiev House were unaware of these machinations, though Ekaterinburg itself became increasingly swept up in a swirl of plots to rescue the Romanovs. Only a few hours after Grand Duke Michael Alexandrovich was killed, the monotonous routine of life in the Ipatiev House was suddenly shattered. Thursday, June 13, was the Feast of the Ascension, and the prisoners expected a priest to come to conduct a service. By eleven-thirty that morning they had arranged their icons in the drawing room and gathered in anticipation. An hour later, Avdayev appeared and, as Alexandra noted, said that no priest could come, as it "was such a big holiday!"[14]

As the prisoners prepared for their regular walk in the garden, Avdayev returned, saying that they would not be allowed out. He offered no explanation, nor, when Dr. Derevenko came, was he admitted to the Ipatiev House to see Alexei.[15] That evening, Avdayev spoke with Dr. Botkin, explaining that the prisoners must pack their belongings at once. The Ural Regional Soviet, according to Nicholas, "feared an outbreak of Anarchists and that we could therefore, perhaps, anticipate an early departure, probably for Moscow. He asked us to get ready to leave. We began to pack right away but quietly at Avdayev's special request so as not to attract the attention of the rank of the guard."[16]

By eleven that night, the Romanovs and their retainers were ready, their few belongings hastily packed and gathered in their rooms. Then, in the midst of this uncertainty, Avdayev told the prisoners that they would remain in Ekaterinburg for at least a few more days.[17] As Alexandra wrote, he also added that Nagorny and Sednev would most likely be returned to join them on Sunday, June 16; in fact, they had been shot two weeks earlier.[18]

Once again, if only for a moment, the Romanovs hoped for Moscow and eventual exile to the safety of England. The following day, however, these hopes were dashed. The prisoners, as Nicholas wrote, took "walks as usual, in two shifts," uncertain if, when they returned, they would be forced to leave.[19] A veil of unease hung over the Ipatiev House, exacerbated when, during a routine inspection that afternoon, Paul Medvedev discovered that his Nagant revolver had been stolen by someone within the house. It was never discovered, and the guards suspected that one of the prisoners found and kept it for use in a possible escape attempt.[20] Late that evening, after dinner, Avdayev finally returned, telling the prisoners, as Nicholas wrote, "that the Anarchists had been seized, the danger passed, and our departure canceled. After all the preparations it was quite a blow."[21]

The prisoners had no idea what was taking place. But, as both Avdayev and Paul Bykov later wrote, the Ural Regional Soviet apparently feared an attack on the Ipatiev House, either by local anarchists or members of an underground monarchist organization. And, in fact, that evening Paul Khokryakov arrested two anarchists at the Palais Royale Hotel in Ekaterinburg after shots were exchanged.[22] Several men were killed in the exchange of gunfire, including a certain Captain Rostovtsev and a White officer named Mamkin.[23]

The immediate crisis had passed, but the Ural Regional Soviet remained deeply suspicious, once again ordering security tightened at the Ipatiev House. The Presidium of the Ural Regional Soviet asked the Military Commissariat to conduct a house-to-house inspection in the area surrounding the Ipatiev House, to determine who resided in these houses and apartments. When this was established, their names were passed to both Avdayev and Medvedev, who informed members of the Special Detachment that only these people had the right to be wandering up and down the streets outside the House of Special Purpose. There also was a new restriction: For all who entered the Ipatiev House, registration was now required, in exchange for which a pass was received. Altogether, nine passes were issued, including one for Dr. Derevenko.[24]

From this day on, Derevenko's visits to the Ipatiev House became less frequent. Although he usually appeared every afternoon, he was admitted only every few days. When, on June 15, he came, Avdayev turned him away. Before leaving, Derevenko asked if he could send milk and eggs for the prisoners; after some discussion, Avdayev authorized this, partially, as Sidorov noted in the duty book, because "the Guard is also in need of food."[25]

The following day, June 16, was a Sunday. Although Botkin had requested a priest, this was not allowed. The weather, as Alexandra noted in her diary, was splendid, and she joined Alexei, Olga, and Tatiana in sitting outside for an hour before lunch; the other prisoners walked for an hour, between four and five that afternoon.[26] Although Derevenko came, he was not admitted to the Ipatiev House; as promised, however, he did send a basket of eggs and milk, delivered at seven that morning by Sister Antonina Trinkina and Sister Marie Krokhaleva from the Novotikhvinsky Convent.[27]

"At the Ipatiev House," recalled Sister Agnes of the Novotikhvinsky Convent of Avdayev, "my novices found him quite bearable and reasonable, and were always dealt with quickly and efficiently. He would stand for them, and would speak in a polite and honeyed tone, but at flattery, he was feeble. . . . When my novices would first arrive at the house, they would go together with him to see the prisoners, and he would growl like a surly bear being chased from his lair, but then he would calm down and become as sweet and docile as a lamb."[28]

With regular provisions guaranteed, Avdayev told Kharitonov that he would now be responsible for preparing the prisoners' meals, beginning immediately. It was a hot day—"lovely weather," as Alexandra wrote in her diary—and all the prisoners enjoyed sitting in the garden. But the stifling atmosphere of the Ipatiev House, its windows closed and whitewashed against the summer heat of the Urals, became increasingly oppressive. With Kharitonov hard at work preparing dinner, by later afternoon, according to the empress, the entire house was not only "very hot and stuffy" but also smelled "strong of kitchen everywhere." There was brief hope that evening, when members of the Committee for the Examination of the Question of Windows in the House of Special Purpose arrived, going from room to room on an inspection, but after they left, the windows remained closed.[29]

On Tuesday, June 18, Anastasia turned seventeen. The previous evening, Kharitonov had given the grand duchesses lessons in baking bread, the results being produced to accompany lunch. Alexandra thought it "excellent," while Nicholas, somewhat less sure, recorded only that it was "not bad."[30] At 3:15 P.M. all of the prisoners took a walk, Alexei being wheeled out into the garden for the first time. "We all sat there for an hour," Alexandra wrote, "very hot, nice lilac bushes and small honeysuckle, quite pretty foliage, but as untidy as ever."[31] That evening, when Dr. Derevenko arrived, Avdayev brought him into the Ipatiev House and allowed him to examine the tsesarevich's leg; during his visit, however, Alexandra again spoke in German, this time to her daughters. Avdayev warned her for a second time that this was forbidden, though he did not, as he had previously threatened, forbid the doctor any further visits.[32] On the following day, however, Derevenko was refused admittance.[33]

The third week of June 1918 marked a dramatic change for the Romanovs. A number of competing factions established themselves in Ekaterinburg, all conspiring to rescue the imperial family from the Ipatiev House. These scattered groups—often unknown to each other—played an ultimately fatal role in these last weeks; through their efforts to save the prisoners, they instead added to the mounting pressure that brought about their death sentences.

According to Paul Bykov,

> prominent counterrevolutionaries and suspicious characters continued to flock to Ekaterinburg, as they formerly did to Tobolsk, and their aim was still to engineer plots and to liberate Romanov and all his relatives.

With the approach of the Front nearer to Ekaterinburg, the local counterrevolutionary loyalist officers also began to try and get in touch with
the Emperor's family, assiduously corresponding with Nicholas
Romanov and particularly with his wife, who was more active. . . . But
from the very first days of the Romanovs' transfer to Ekaterinburg
there began to flock in monarchists in great numbers, beginning with
half-crazy ladies, countesses and baronesses of every caliber and ending
with nuns, clergy, and representatives of foreign powers. The correspondence addressed by them to Nicholas consisted mainly of greetings
and condolences. Sometimes there were letters of obviously abnormal
persons, describing their dreams, visions and similar nonsense.
Requests for permission to visit either Nicholas or other members of
the Romanov Family were fairly frequent.[34]

These gathering monarchists operated quite openly. Ekaterinburg
Cheka member Michael Medvedev, who went by his Bolshevik Party
name of Kudrin, recalled how "groups of curious people had begun to
gather in Ekaterinburg; they could often be seen wandering round the
stockade of the House of Special Purpose. As a rule, they were questionable characters from Petersburg or Moscow. They constantly tried
to hand over notes or provisions. They sent letters in the post, all of
which we intercepted; every one of these letters promised devotion and
offered services. As members of the Cheka, we had the idea that there
was a White Guard organization in the town, which was trying to contact the Emperor and his wife. . . . Under cover of secrecy, monarchists
came to Ekaterinburg to rescue the prisoners when the chance came."[35]
    Despite his position as one of the city's leading Bolsheviks, Bykov
admitted that, had a rescue operation been enacted, "the success of
such an attempt was not out of the question."[36] Thus, despite precautions by the Ural Regional Soviet, the prisoners remained within the
reach of those who would save them throughout the spring of 1918.
    Those conspiring to free the Romanovs in these weeks moved
freely through Ekaterinburg. The St. Petersburg Military Academy of
the General Staff had been transferred to the Urals from the former
capital, bringing with it hundreds of officials formerly in the service of
the imperial regime. These men were not Bolsheviks; many were right-
wing extremists or monarchists.[37] Why the Bolsheviks permitted such a
body to function openly in the Urals has never been satisfactorily
explained; certainly the academy contained many men sympathetic to
the plight of the Romanovs. Even Bykov acknowledged that these men
"represented a ready-made organized force for anti-Soviet action."[38]
    The situation in Ekaterinburg was exacerbated that spring with the
arrival of a number of important Romanov prisoners. In May the city

was seemingly flooded with members of the former dynasty: the empress's sister Grand Duchess Elizabeth Feodorovna, accompanied by one of her senior nuns, Sister Barbara Yakovleva, who was ultimately to share her fate; Grand Duke Serge Mikhailovich; Princes Ioann, Igor, and Konstantin Konstantinovich; Helen Petrovna, a former princess of Serbia married to Prince Ioann; and Prince Vladimir Paley, morganatic son of Grand Duke Paul Alexandrovich.[39] The prisoners, with the exception of Princess Helen, were taken in heavily guarded motorcars to the Palais Royale Hotel on Voznesensky Prospekt, where they were imprisoned in a suite of rooms ringed with a string of soldiers armed with rifles.[40] Although under arrest, these Romanovs still had a certain degree of freedom. Prince Vladimir Paley reported in letters to his mother how he often walked around Ekaterinburg; on several occasions he strolled past the Ipatiev House but could see nothing.[41] During these days, Princess Helen—who had not been arrested—lived in rooms she had rented from a Cossack couple named Atamanov.[42]

According to Paul Bykov, they lived under "very indifferent observation." They found eager supporters, he declared, "among the bourgeoisie of Ekaterinburg," who "willingly invited these noble guests to their evening parties, at which a secret organization to carry off the Romanovs was formed."[43] A certain Madame Semchevskaya, wife of a monarchist officer attached to the Academy of the General Staff in Ekaterinburg, later recalled that during these dinner parties, plots were indeed openly discussed; according to her account, a group of thirty-seven officers from the Academy of the General Staff were "ready for anything" to save the imperial family.[44]

Within a few weeks, according to Bykov, "the danger of keeping such a large gathering" of Romanovs in Ekaterinburg, "so near the Front, at the height of the struggle against the counterrevolution, was obvious."[45] Accordingly, on May 20 they told the prisoners that they were being transferred to the mining town of Alapayevsk, nearly a hundred miles northeast of Ekaterinburg. Here, they were housed in a red brick building, the School of the Fields, attached to the local factory and mining works. For the first few weeks, although they were still under arrest, they enjoyed relative freedom, being allowed to take walks and attend church services without an escort.[46] Princess Helen, however, worried about her children, who had remained behind at the Palace of Pavlovsk near Petrograd with Prince Ioann's mother. After discussing the situation with Ioann, Helen asked for, and received, permission from the Alapayevsk Soviet to return to Ekaterinburg and discuss her request to be allowed to return to Petrograd. Arriving in Ekaterinburg on June 21, she went to the Hotel Amerika on Voznesensky Prospekt, where she demanded an audience with Beloborodov.[47]

Beloborodov refused her request, saying that travel by train was impossible owing to the military situation in the Urals.[48] She therefore returned to the Atamanovs' and once again rented rooms. In the city she became something of a pest, according to British consul Thomas Preston. According to his memoirs, she made almost daily visits to the consulate, demanding that Preston intervene on behalf of her husband at Alapayevsk; that he speak to the Presidium of the Ural Regional Soviet and guarantee her continued freedom; that he get her a travel visa to Petrograd; and that he obtain for her permission to enter the Ipatiev House to visit the emperor and his family. According to Preston, she insisted that Britain make immediate arrangements to rescue the Romanovs, saying that she was certain the Germans meant to kidnap him and force him to sign the Treaty of Brest-Litovsk. When she was not at the British consulate, she haunted the Hotel Amerika, demanding to see Beloborodov. The Ekaterinburg Cheka finally warned her that if she continued, she would be arrested and put in prison.[49]

Not to be put off by such threats, however, Helen sought out Dr. Derevenko and tried to convince him to go to the authorities on her behalf. After Derevenko warned her that he was under constant surveillance and could do nothing, she declared that she herself would go directly to the Ipatiev House and demand entrance. Despite the doctor's best efforts, she would not be put off. The following day, she went up to the sentry on duty at the main entrance and loudly announced, "I am the wife of a Romanov interned at Alapayevsk, and I am also the daughter of the King of Serbia. As a relative of the Emperor, I have come to get news of him and ask to be allowed to see him." The startled sentry disappeared inside the palisade and into the Ipatiev House; within a few minutes, Avdayev came out to speak to her. He refused her request to be admitted, but promised to let the imperial family know that she had come. "The Commandant," she later wrote, "had a very attractive figure, and lacked nothing of good manners when he came and stood opposite me."[50]

Princess Helen was not the only Serb in Ekaterinburg. One day in late June, a Captain Maximovich, like the princess before him, arrived at the Ipatiev House and demanded to see the emperor. He declared that he wished to discuss questions of a "historic" nature "concerning the War." His request was refused, and he was quickly taken to the Cheka headquarters at the Hotel Amerika. A search revealed a number of letters and some 30,000 rubles hidden among his possessions.[51]

The lack of subtlety displayed by these two Serbs provoked general distrust and paranoia among the Ekaterinburg authorities, who began to suspect plots everywhere. The day after Princess Helen's arrival in Ekaterinburg, Ekaterinburg apparently warned their comrades in Alapayevsk to be vigilant in guarding their imperial prisoners. This followed a cable from Moscow that had advised that the Alapayevsk Soviet could do with the various servants "what they wished," and forbade them, "without permission from either Dzerzhinsky in Moscow or Uritsky in Petrograd or the local Ekaterinburg Soviet," to make any changes in the regime imposed.[52] This cable indicates that, in issues concerning their Romanov prisoners, the Alapayevsk Soviet was under the clear authority of the Ural Regional Soviet in Ekaterinburg.

The Ekaterinburg Cheka knew of—and kept watch over—at least two groups of monarchist officers operating in the city. Isai Rodzinsky named them as the "White Cross Officers' Organization" and the "Red Cross Officers' Organization."[53] Rodzinsky asserted: "There was a Commissar who set up a salon where the Officers would come, thinking they were mixing with the highest echelons of society, and they would discuss their plans. But it was us all the time, listening. This Commissar placed himself as the servant, the personal servant of one such officer. We also planted ladies with them. There were eventually two such organizations engaged in openly plotting a rescue of the prisoners."[54]

The two prime monarchist agents seem to have been Colonel Ivan Sidorov and Captain Dimitri Malinovsky. Sidorov, a monarchist and former adjutant to the emperor, arrived in Ekaterinburg from Odessa in mid-June and promptly made contact with Dr. Derevenko and thus with the imperial family. When he first met Derevenko, Sidorov handed over a number of letters for the Romanovs, which the doctor somehow managed to smuggle in to the Ipatiev House and pass along to the prisoners.[55] The larger group of conspirators, grown by the middle of June to encompass thirty-seven White officers, all living openly in Ekaterinburg, was led by Malinovsky, who arranged meetings with several of the Romanovs who were eventually sent to Alapayevsk. In Ekaterinburg, Malinovsky became one of Dr. Derevenko's few intimates, thus ensuring his contact with the prisoners.[56] As the only civilian authorized to make daily visits to the Ipatiev House, and the only man outside of the local Bolsheviks allowed to see the prisoners, Derevenko moved cautiously. By the third week of June, however, he himself drafted or obtained a plan of the Ipatiev House, which he gave to Malinovsky.[57] Once this plan was in the hands of the conspirators, the group moved quickly, embarking on an ill-conceived adventure that sealed the fate of the imperial family.

These conspirators composed a letter offering to rescue the imperial family that was concealed among the supplies delivered by the nuns from the Novotikhvinsky Convent. At seven on the morning of June 20, the nuns delivered their regular basket of provisions; the conspirators did not know that the baskets were sent not to Kharitonov but rather to Andrei Starkov, who acted as cook for the Special Detachment. As the supplies were unpacked, this letter was discovered, hidden, as Avdayev recalled, in the top of a bottle of cream.[58]

"This secret letter," Avdayev later wrote, "was immediately turned over to Comrade Goloshchokin, who arranged for it to be copied before it was handed to the prisoners."[59] At an urgent meeting of the Ekaterinburg Cheka, a hasty plan of action was accepted.[60] The letter was copied out by Cheka member Isai Rodzinsky, with changes dictated by Peter Voikov, Alexander Beloborodov, and Philip Goloshchokin, composed, as Rodzinsky recalled, "to elicit an answer from them."[61] It was then replaced in the provisions, where Kharitonov presumably discovered it later that day.

Isai Rodzinsky copied out the letter in the original French, a language Peter Voikov spoke fluently. The original message was not preserved, making it impossible to determine its content. The Cheka copy, with deletions and additions, read:

> The friends sleep no longer and hope the hour so long awaited has arrived. The revolt of the Czechoslovaks menaces the Bolsheviks more and more seriously. Samara, Chelyabinsk and the whole of Siberia, eastern and western, are under the control of the provincial national government. The army of the Slavic friends is eighty kilometers from Ekaterinburg. The soldiers of the Red Army do not effectively resist. Be watchful of every movement from without, wait and hope. But at the same time, I beseech you, be prudent, because the Bolshevikii before being defeated are a real and serious danger to you. Be ready all the time, day and night. Make a sketch of your two rooms, the places of the furniture, of the beds. Write exactly when you all go to bed. One of you should not sleep between two and three o'clock all the following nights. Reply in a few words, but give, I beg you, all useful information to your friends outside. It is to the same soldier who gives you this note that you must give your written answer, but do not speak a single word. One who is ready to die for you—An Officer of the Russian Army.[62]

According to Avdayev, the Romanovs waited several days before responding.[63] If the letter was first discovered on June 20 and delivered to them later that same day, the response must have been written and sent no later than June 22. The reply mentioned that the windows of the Ipatiev House were closed and sealed, a fact that changed on June 23, when Avdayev ordered a window in the corner bedroom shared by Nicholas and Alexandra opened.

The answer to this letter was written on the bottom and reverse side of the original, also in French. While it has been suggested that Nicholas himself composed the reply, it did not match his handwriting, nor that of the empress, whose script had a distinctive character. It could, however, have been written by one of the two eldest grand duchesses. The answer read:

> From the corner of the balcony five windows face the street, two the square. All the windows are closed glued and painted shut. The Little One [the tsesarevich] is still sick in bed and cannot walk at all. Every disturbance causes him pain. A week ago, because of the anarchists, we were supposed to leave for Moscow at night. It is important not to risk anything without being absolutely sure of the result. We are almost all the time under watchful observation.[64]

It is not known how the prisoners attempted to send this reply. The most likely explanation is that it was concealed among the empty jugs, crockery, and cans in the baskets from the convent, which the nuns left every morning and exchanged for a basket of fresh provisions each day. The reply, however, never made it beyond the walls of the Ipatiev House: like the first, genuine message, it, too, was confiscated, and taken to the Ekaterinburg Cheka.

Amid this uncertainty, life for the Romanovs carried on. On June 21, six women arrived to wash the floors; while the prisoners waited, Nicholas read aloud from a book of sea stories he had found among the Ipatievs' belongings. At 3:30 P.M., all of the prisoners walked in the garden, exiting the house to find that it was, as the empress wrote, "fearfully hot"; in an attempt to seek relief from the burning sunshine, she sat "under the bushes," watching as her husband and daughters paced back and forth, and Leonid Sednev pushed Alexei up and down the dusty plot of land. As they prepared to return inside, Avdayev appeared, saying that as the weather was so nice, they could remain in the garden for an additional half hour.[65] Early that same evening, Derevenko arrived; Alexei's left arm was slightly swollen, the result of an accidental knock, but the doctor believed it would correct itself. He was more concerned with the tsesarevich's leg, which, though better, still could not fully support him, and used an electrical medical apparatus to stimulate his muscles. Throughout, as the empress noted, Avdayev was present, and she found it "impossible to say even one word" to Derevenko.[66] Undoubtedly she had hoped to question him about the mysterious letter.

Then another surprise. "In the last few days," Nicholas wrote on June 22, "the weather has been marvelous, but very hot. It was terribly stuffy in our rooms, particularly at night."[67] Under such circumstances—and with their requests that a window be opened to provide ventilation denied—Dr. Botkin asked Avdayev to allow the prisoners to remain in the garden beyond the allotted hour. The commandant agreed, and all of the prisoners except for the empress and Olga sat outside for ninety minutes, as they had been allowed to do the previous day.

"The aroma from all of the gardens in the city is quite extraordinary," Nicholas wrote.[68] At about five that afternoon, as the prisoners were taking tea, six men appeared in the Ipatiev House. None of the prisoners recognized them, although they had previously met two: Beloborodov and Goloshchokin. They walked from room to room, examining the house and noting those they encountered; "in our presence they stared at the windows in silence," Nicholas wrote.[69] The empress also recorded the visit, writing of the "people (of the Committee)" who came "(from St. Petersburg?) to see again about the windows."[70] Although Avdayev said nothing, both Nicholas and Alexandra assumed that the group had been sent to determine which, if any, of the windows could be opened to provide ventilation. "The resolution of this question has dragged on for approximately two weeks," Nicholas noted with consternation in his diary.[71]

Unknown to the prisoners, the group was in fact the urgent inspection ordered by Moscow, conducted by Reinhold Berzin, the military commander of the Northern Ural Siberian Front to assure the Soviet government—after the disappearance of Grand Duke Michael Alexandrovich the previous week—that the Romanovs were safe and alive. In the days following Michael's disappearance, rumors spread that the Romanovs in Ekaterinburg had been killed by the Ural Regional Soviet, by a rogue group of Red Army soldiers, or in a botched rescue attempt undertaken by a monarchist group. The first known reference to them came on June 19, in an interview Lenin gave to the liberal newspaper *Nashe Slovo*. While he had received confirmation from the authorities in Perm that Michael had escaped, Lenin declared that he had no information regarding the safety of the Romanovs in Ekaterinburg.[72]

Another view from the Ipatiev House garden, looking toward the house and showing the corridor window, under the balcony, from where Ivan Kleshchev watched the murders.

This was a stunning announcement, prompting a rash of related reports, the first appearing that same afternoon in *Nash Vek*.[73] Over the following days, the rumor that Nicholas II had been killed was picked up and reported in numerous Russian papers. Louis de Robien, a French diplomat then living in Vologda, noted the stories in his diary.[74] Within a week, the story appeared in Western presses as well.[75] The rumors were so widespread that, on June 23, the Soviet Press Bureau took the unprecedented step of confirming that Moscow was unable to determine the fate of the prisoners in Ekaterinburg.[76]

These rumors—and the swell in press coverage devoted to them— caused great concern among the Germans in Moscow. On June 21, von Mirbach had a hasty audience with George Chicherin, the Soviet commissar of foreign affairs, in which von Mirbach urged the Soviet government to provide definite assurances of the Romanovs' safety.[77] In Berlin, Adolf Ioffe, the Soviet ambassador, received similar demands for assurances of the imperial family's safety. To these queries, Ioffe replied that his government had decided to move the Romanovs from Ekaterinburg, owing to its close proximity to the advancing White and Czechoslovak forces, but fighting had cut the railroad lines, and thus Moscow had no way to establish the truth of the rumors then current.[78] This was hardly reassuring, but Berlin could do little but continue to raise the issue through von Mirbach in Moscow daily.

On June 20 the situation was desperate enough that Moscow began to pursue the matter in earnest. On that day, at 2:06 P.M., Vladimir Bonch-Bruyevich, president of the Soviet of Peoples' Commissars and a personal friend of Lenin, dispatched an urgent cable to Beloborodov in Ekaterinburg: "In Moscow rumors spread that former Emperor Nicholas has been killed. Please inform if you have any information. Soviet of Peoples' Commissars Bonch-Bruyevich."[79] The following day, at 7:26 P.M., the government in Moscow sent a second telegram to Beloborodov: "Immediately inform as to reliability of rumors concerning murder of Nicholas Romanov. Signed Stark."[80]

Despite the nonchalant attitude of Lenin's interview on June 19, Moscow was clearly worried. Without waiting for an answer, Lenin himself dispatched Reinhold Berzin, the military commander of the Northern Siberian Ural Front, to investigate the situation at the Ipatiev House.[81] In and of itself, this action demonstrates that Moscow did not trust the word of the Ural Regional Soviet; if nothing else, it was a blunt acknowledgment that the fate of the Romanovs no longer rested entirely with the Soviet government in Moscow.

Berzin received a cable from Bonch-Bruyevich, on Lenin's orders, instructing him to set off for Ekaterinburg at once.[82] This he did, leaving his field headquarters at Perm and traveling the three hundred

miles east to the capital of the Urals. On his arrival he went straight to
the telegraph office at the railroad station, ordered the three operators
on duty from the room, and had his own telegraph operator connect
him with Moscow by the Hughes wireless cable. In a few minutes,
Lenin was on the line. The three duty cable operators later testified that
they listened to the exchange, and heard Lenin order Berzin "to take
under his protective authority the entire Imperial Family, and not to
allow any violence directed against them by any faction. If any violence
did occur, Berzin was responsible for it with his own life."[83]

After this, Berzin went directly to the Hotel Amerika, demanding to
see Beloborodov. Berzin's sudden appearance must have been a profound shock to the authorities in Ekaterinburg, who knew nothing of
his visit. This was not an exercise in nuance; it immediately became
clear that Moscow had sent its own man to check on their reliability.
The Ural Regional Soviet itself was unaware of Moscow's concern; with
the railroad lines cut, the regular cable system functioned only intermittently, and Bonch-Bruyevich's telegram of June 20 had not yet
arrived, nor had the second cable, from Stark.

On Berzin's orders, Beloborodov and Goloshchokin picked up four
other members of the Ural Regional Presidium, who escorted Berzin
down Voznesensky Prospekt to the Ipatiev House, where they passed
through the rooms, eyed by the curious prisoners, who mistook them
for the Committee for the Examination of the Question of Windows in
the House of Special Purpose.[84] Moscow was forced to wait an additional seven days before they received word of this mission. On June 24
they dispatched a third cable, to Vorobyov in Ekaterinburg: "Urgent:
Request confirmation on reliability of rumor of murder of Nicholas
Romanov. Extremely important. Signed Stark."[85] Ironically, on this
same day, Ekaterinburg finally received the first cable sent from
Moscow four days earlier. Although Berzin had been able to get a direct
telegraphic line via the Hughes wireless machine to Moscow to discuss
the situation with Lenin, this method of communication was lost within
a few hours. Only on June 28 did Moscow receive a cable from Berzin:
"I have received Moscow newspapers that carry an item on the murder
of Nicholas Romanov at some railway stop outside Ekaterinburg by
Red Army men. I officially inform you that on 21 June, I, together with
Military Inspectors, and the Military Commissar of the Ural Military
District [Goloshchokin] and members of the All Russian Extraordinary
Committee [Cheka] examined the house to ascertain how Nicholas
Romanov is being confined with his family and to inspect the sentries
and guards. All members of the family and Nicholas himself are alive
and all information about his murder and so forth is a provocation.
Commander of the Northern Siberian Ural Front, Berzin."[86]

Rumors of all sort concerning members of the Romanov Dynasty were rampant that late June 1918, but the safety of the prisoners in Ekaterinburg clearly raised an alarm in Moscow. The episode has often been explained as a deliberate provocation, ordered by Moscow, as historian Richard Pipes believed, "to test the public reaction of the proposed murder of the ex-Tsar."[87] Yet had the rumors been orchestrated by Moscow, it would have been unnecessary for Bonch-Bruyevich to order Berzin to conduct a personal inspection of the Ipatiev House to ensure that the Romanovs were alive. Nor can this easily be explained away as a sort of Bolshevik pantomime; Berzin, as commander of the Northern Siberian Ural Front, was in the midst of a dangerous struggle with the Czech and White forces advancing across Siberia. His very selection suggests the degree of Moscow's concern: clearly, they wanted their own man to give a firsthand report on the situation. Moscow's trust in Ekaterinburg, already fragile when the Ural Regional Soviet forcibly seized the Romanovs from Yakovlev, was, by June, nonexistent. Had Moscow been behind such an adventure, they certainly had no need to dispatch worried cables to Ekaterinburg imploring them for information, especially as there was no expectation that such communiqués would ever be seen by other than trusted Bolshevik eyes. It is, however, entirely possible that the rumors were deliberately spread not by Moscow but by Ekaterinburg itself, to gauge Lenin's response should Nicholas be killed or, like Michael Alexandrovich, be made to disappear.

The day following Berzin's inspection, June 23, was Trinity Sunday in the liturgical calendar of the Russian Orthodox Church. At eleven-thirty that morning, the priest Anatoly Meledin and his deacon, Vassili Buiremov, arrived at the Ipatiev House to conduct, as Nicholas noted in his diary, "a real liturgy with vespers."[88] It was, Nicholas wrote, a "wonderful" day, and even Alexandra recorded the "glorious weather."[89] That morning, after weeks of negotiations, Avdayev finally opened a single window in the corner bedroom shared by the emperor and empress. "Such joy," the empress wrote, "delicious air at last, and one window no longer whitewashed."[90]

Botkin was unwell, suffering from kidney trouble that kept him confined to bed, and Alexandra and Tatiana spent the afternoon looking after him, the latter giving him a shot of the morphine the prisoners were allowed to keep for Alexei to ease his pain.[91] In the afternoon, when the rest of the prisoners took a two-hour walk in the garden, the empress and Tatiana remained inside, with the doctor.[92] That evening, Nicholas learned that the visitors from the previous day had not come from the Ural Regional Soviet; he erroneously reported that they were "commissars from Petrograd."[93]

The prisoners had not yet received a reply from the mysterious monarchist who signed himself "An Officer of the Russian Army." Yet, on this night, as Alexandra wrote in her diary, Tatiana moved her bed to sleep with her brother.[94] Alexei was not particularly unwell, and Derevenko's visit had revealed little out of the ordinary. Almost certainly, this move came in anticipation of a rescue attempt, especially as the tsesarevich would need assistance in any rapid evacuation of the Ipatiev House.

As the Romanovs waited, the Ekaterinburg Bolsheviks planned their next move. Other, genuine letters apparently followed the discovery of the first, concealed, as Ekaterinburg Soviet member Paul Bykov recalled, "in loaves of bread, on parcels, and wrapping paper."[95] Like the first confiscated letter, none of these survived, and only the forgeries composed by the Cheka are known. It is possible that certain elements from these genuine letters were copied, though undoubtedly changed, to maintain some consistency, though the extant correspondence originated with Beloborodov, Goloshchokin, and Voikov.

It was in 1964 that Isai Rodzinsky spoke at length of "the correspondence I carried on with Nicholas." In his account, Rodzinsky clearly recalled the letters he wrote in French. "I remember the red ink with which they were written to the present day," the elderly man said.[96] Rodzinsky, according to his fellow Cheka member Kudrin, had been selected to copy the letters because "he had good handwriting."[97] Rodzinsky also left a telling comment: "We had to be able to show," he said, "evidence that a rescue had been arranged."[98]

This "evidence," as both Rodzinsky and Kudrin later revealed, was never intended for public consumption, but for the eyes of the Central Executive Committee, to prove the existence of a monarchist plot to rescue the Romanovs. The Ural Bolsheviks embarked on this deliberate and dangerous provocation to ensnare the prisoners in a trap that could then be used to justify their eventual execution. Only ten days earlier, the Ural Regional Soviet had almost certainly conspired with their counterparts in Perm to murder Grand Duke Michael Alexandrovich, an execution designed to test both Moscow's reaction, and their own ability to exact the vengeance they deemed necessary for the survival of the Revolution. Avdayev's accidental discovery of the first, genuine "Officer" letter dictated Ekaterinburg's course of action as they pursued their own plot to exterminate the Romanovs.[99]

Monday, June 24, passed quietly for the Romanovs. Alexandra noted that, with the window open all night, they had enjoyed "good air, but so noisy." In the morning, with the weather so warm, the empress and Alexei spent thirty minutes in the garden; in the afternoon, Alexandra, along with Marie and Dr. Botkin, who was still unwell, remained inside while the others walked. At six, Derevenko arrived to look after the tsesarevich. That night, as the empress noted, "Tatiana sleeps with Alexei."[100]

Almost certainly, on this evening, the Romanovs received a second letter, handed to the empress, as both Rodzinsky and Kudrin later recalled, by a member of the interior guard.[101] Like the first, it was written in French, and spoke at length of a rescue attempt:

> With the help of God and your sangfroid, we hope to succeed without any risk. It is absolutely necessary that one of your windows be unglued so that you may be able to open it at the given moment. Please indicate this window accurately. The fact that the little Tsesarevich is not able to walk complicates matters, but we have foreseen this and I do not believe it will be too great an inconvenience. Please write if two persons are necessary to carry him or if one of you may be able to take care of that. Is it possible to make the Little One sleep for one or two hours in case you should know in advance the exact hour? It is the doctor who must give his opinion, but in case it is necessary we may furnish something or other for that purpose. Do not be uneasy. No attempt will be made without being absolutely sure of the result. Before God, before history and our conscience, we give you solemnly this promise. An Officer.[102]

The response, when it came, can only have been written on the following day, June 25:

> The second window from the corner, facing the square, has been open for two days—day and night—the seventh and eighth windows facing the square at the side of the main entrance are always open. The room is occupied by the Commandant and his assistants, who are also the interior guard, about thirteen people at least, all armed with rifles, revolvers and bombs. None of the doors have keys (except ours). The Commandant and his assistants enter our rooms when they please. The one on duty makes the outside round twice each other of the night, and we hear him talk to the sentinel beneath our windows. There is a machine gun on the balcony, another one below for a possible alarm. If there are more, we do not know. Don't forget that we have the doctor, a chambermaid, two men, and a little boy cook with us. It would be ignoble of us, even if they didn't want to burden us, to leave them behind after their following us into exile voluntarily. The doctor has been in bed for two days after an attack in the kidneys but he is recovering. We want all the time the return of our two men [Nagorny and Sednev] who are young and strong, and who have been locked up for a month without our knowing why. In their absence the Little One is being carried around by his father through the rooms and gardens. Our surgeon D[erevenko], who comes almost daily at 5:00 to see the Little

One, lives in the city; do not forget him. We never see him alone. The guards are in a little house across from our five windows on the other side of the street, fifty men. The only things that we still have are in crates in the shed (in the interior courtyard). We are especially worried about AF, No. 9, a small black crate, and a large black crate, No. 13 NA, with his old letters and diaries. Naturally the bedrooms are filled with crates, beds and things, all at the mercy of the thieves who surround us. All the keys and separately, No. 9, are with the Commandant, who has behaved towards us well. In any case, warn us if you can, and answer if you can also bring our people. In front of each sentry post, in the command room, some wires also go to the guard house and elsewhere. If our other people remain, can we be sure that nothing happens to them? Doctor B[otkin] begs you not to think about him and the other men, so your task will not be more difficult. Count on the seven of us and the woman. May God help you; you can count on our sangfroid.[103]

Tuesday, June 25, dawned, as Nicholas noted, "extraordinarily hot." Not even the open window helped cool the rooms in the Ipatiev House.[104] At two-thirty, the prisoners had their usual walk; Alexandra and Tatiana again remained inside with Botkin during the two-hour walk.[105] In the evening, two storms, one after the other, erupted over Ekaterinburg, "freshening the air," as Nicholas wrote with relief.[106] On this night, the prisoners sat up, awaiting a rescue attempt; the following day, Alexandra recorded that she had "scarcely slept, only three hours, as they made so much noise outside."[107]

Nothing happened, but the prisoners remained hopeful. The following morning, the empress "arranged things," almost certainly in anticipation of an expected rescue. It is likely that this was a reference to the jewels the imperial family had brought with them into exile.[108] That evening, Alexei was moved into his parents' corner bedroom— "more air for him and to have him nearer," the empress wrote in her diary.[109] This move almost certainly came in anticipation of a rescue attempt. For a second night, the prisoners sat up, awaiting some signal that a rescue was under way, but none came. The following day, Alexandra wrote that she had "scarcely slept."[110]

On Thursday, June 27, Marie turned nineteen. Alexandra "arranged things all day," as she wrote in her diary, remaining inside with Olga and Dr. Botkin during the afternoon walk in the garden. In the evening, Goloshchokin and Yurovsky arrived at the Ipatiev House, inspecting all of the rooms in the prison.[111] That night, Kharitonov and Sednev were moved into the bedroom next to that of the grand duchesses, which, until the previous day, had been used by Alexei. Alexandra noted that it would be "less hot than their being near the kitchen," but it also concentrated all of the prisoners in the southern rooms of the Ipatiev House, where they could be more easily rescued.[112]

In this tense, uncertain atmosphere, the Cheka plot unfolded as the Ekaterinburg Bolsheviks had hoped. "On watching the Romanovs," recalled Kudrin, "we found that they had indeed spent two or three nights at the suggested time, ready and dressed as if for flight."[113] The peculiar behavior of the prisoners, coupled with their favorable responses, change of rooms, and the lights seen burning in their windows late into the night, gave the Ural Regional Soviet the evidence it needed.

"We passed a night of alarm and sat up in our clothes," Nicholas wrote in his diary that evening. "All of this was due to our recently having received two letters, one after the other, in which we were advised to get ready to be carried off by some loyal people. But the days passed and nothing happened. The waiting and the uncertainty were very upsetting."[114] This entry was to be the last in the emperor's diary for nearly a week. Although he had first skipped his regular diary entries a few weeks earlier, he still maintained some consistency; after his entry of June 27, however, the entries became sporadic. He did not make an entry again until July 4, after six days had passed, and, after this, recorded events in his diary for only five days: July 5, 6, 8, 11, and 13. Such a lapse was completely uncharacteristic.

By Friday, June 28, an air of tension had settled over the Ipatiev House, the uncertainty of the last few days replaced with unease and fear. As Alexandra noted, they heard "the night sentry under our rooms being told quite particularly to watch every movement at our window—they have become again most suspicious since our window is opened and don't allow one to sit on the sill even now."[115] Until this day, as Nicholas's diary entry of June 27 indicated, only two letters had been received; a third almost certainly came on June 28, asking for further details:

> Do not be uneasy about the fifty men who are in the small house opposite your windows; they will not be dangerous when it is necessary to act. Tell us something more precise about your commandant in order to make the beginning easier. One cannot say at this moment whether it will be possible to take all your people. We hope yes, but, in any event, they will not be with you after leaving the house, except the doctor. Are taking steps for Doctor D. We much hope to indicate to you before Sunday the detailed plan of the operation. For the present it is arranged in this way. Upon the expected signal you close and barricade with furniture the door separating you from your guards who will be blockaded and terrorized in the interior of the house. By a rope made specially for this purpose you descend through the window. You are expected below. The rest is not difficult. The means for getting away are not lacking and

the escape (its success) is surer than ever. The main question is taking the Little One down. Is this possible? Answer this question after considering it carefully. In any case it is the father, the mother and the son who must go first. Then the daughters and the doctor follow. Answer if this is possible in your opinion and if you can make a suitable rope, since it is a difficult matter at present to get a rope for you. An Officer.[116]

The Romanovs did not immediately respond. The heightened security, noted by the empress in her diary, coupled with uncertainty, led them to offer a cautious reply, most probably on Saturday, June 29:

We do not want to and cannot flee. We may be rescued only by force as it was by force that we were taken from Tobolsk. Therefore do not count on any active aid on our part. The Commandant has many assistants. They change often and have grown weary. They conscientiously guard our prison as well as our lives and are good to us. We do not want them to suffer for our sakes, nor you for us. Above all, in the name of God, avoid bloodshed. Get information yourselves about them. It is utterly impossible to descend from the window without a ladder. Even if one has descended, one is in great danger on account of the open window in the room of the commandant and from machine guns on the lower floor, which one enters from the inside court. Give up the idea of carrying us off. If you are guarding over us, you may always come and save us in the case of imminent and real danger. We are fully ignorant of what is going on outside, receiving neither papers nor letters. Since it has been permitted to open the windows, the guard has been increased, and one is forbidden to put one's head out of the window, at the risk of receiving a bullet in the face.[117]

Alexandra continued to "arrange things," as she recorded in her diary, perhaps still anticipating a rescue attempt, yet nothing took place. On both Saturday and Sunday she mentioned her exhaustion and lack of sleep, an indication that the prisoners may have again sat up awaiting a rescue that never came. The guards were more watchful, and on Saturday evening Goloshchokin again appeared—"to see if we were all there," Alexandra commented.[118]

As June drew to a close, a violent rainstorm erupted over Ekaterinburg, a bleak portent of what was to come. A genuine plot to rescue the Romanovs and spirit them from the Ipatiev House, foolishly conceived and haphazardly executed, instead become a tool in the hands of the Ural Regional Soviet, used to justify their eventual murders. The fate of the imperial family was fast becoming a thorn in the side of the Ural Bolsheviks. By the beginning of July, time—for both the Romanovs and the Ural Regional Soviet—was quickly running out.

9

"A Happy Hour with the Grandest People in the World"

As the spring of 1918 edged toward summer, the uncertain situation in the Ipatiev House took its toll on the prisoners. After the failed rescue attempt, they became despondent, tired, and weary. The discovery of the plot also put the authorities in Ekaterinburg on edge. Deeply suspicious, and increasingly worried as the White and Czech forces advanced toward the Urals, a conspiracy of circumstance drove the Ural Regional Soviet to the point of no return that June of 1918, sealing the fate of the Romanovs.

Nicholas Sokolov, appointed by the White Army to conduct the official investigation into the Ekaterinburg murders, wrote of the Ipatiev House as "an impregnable fortress," and declared "with such a system of sentries, the Imperial Family was in a trap without an escape."[1] Yet this assertion was far from accurate. The sister of one guard later recalled: "They always had their rifles in their hands like children with toys, and then only for form. I doubt strongly that they would have used them in defense had the enemy attacked the house."[2] This view was echoed by a member of the Special Detachment, who declared that "had a serious, methodical military attack been made on the house, we comrades agreed that we would throw down our rifles. Our machine gunners had never practiced and most of the guards were half-wits who knew nothing."[3]

By the last week of June, security in the Ipatiev House had broken down to such an extent that a majority of the guards no longer could be trusted. Having observed the prisoners under the pressures of confinement, these guards openly sympathized with the imperial family. "After I personally saw them several times," recalled Anatoly Yakimov, "I began to feel entirely different towards them. I began to pity them. I pitied them as human beings. . . . I got into my mind the idea to let them escape, or to do something to help them escape."[4] Together with the discovery of the rescue plot and the willingness of the prisoners to cooperate, the unreliability of the guards provided the Ural Bolsheviks with a convenient excuse to plan the murder of the Romanovs.

This sympathetic tone was set by Avdayev himself and, in the end, led to his downfall. He attempted to act as expected, as a Bolshevik commissar should, filling the air with loud boasts designed to impress his men and show his mastery over their former sovereign. In private, however, he was quite a different man, lax even in enforcing the rules laid down by the Presidium of the Ural Regional Soviet. According to Isai Rodzinsky, Avdayev was "an able comrade, but when he was at the House of Special Purpose, he wasn't very good at his job."[5] It was an opinion shared by many. Alexander Strekotin later commented that Avdayev "was entirely too friendly and helpful to the Emperor's family," while the fierce Peter Ermakov dismissed him as "not so tough after all. He went soft and sentimental toward the Romanovs."[6] And Yakov Yurovsky, who replaced Avdayev as commandant, echoed Ermakov, calling his predecessor "too soft, and not at all the correct choice for such a duty."[7]

Nor were most members of the guard less sympathetic. "After the first days," recalled one sentry, "we quite changed our minds about the Imperial Family. We could not reconcile this face of the family with the one we were prepared to meet."[8] Such attitudes were scarcely surprising, given the composition of the Special Detachment itself, where only fourteen men were older than Grand Duchess Olga Nikolaievna; most described themselves as practicing members of the Russian Orthodox Church; and only a quarter were even Bolsheviks. Having joined the detachment for the pay and to avoid possible conscription into the Red Army, the majority of these guards were young idealists, susceptible to the powerful aura of pathos evoked by their prisoners.

In the Ipatiev House, Avdayev and his men discovered not "Nicholas the Bloody" but a cheerful, slightly pathetic man, overwhelmed by events and apparently without guile. Alexandra, the hated "German bitch," if less genial than her husband, was a sick woman, crippled by illness, who seemingly easily exchanged banter with several members of the guard and even invited them into the privacy of their drawing room to play cards—a privilege not extended to the faithful Demidova, Kharitonov, and Trupp. The popular image of the bloodthirsty Romanovs, accused in revolutionary rhetoric of haughty indifference to Russia and consumed with pomp and power, bore no resemblance to the simple, frightened group before them, the last vestiges of the former dynasty. These men were confronted with a sick thirteen-year-old boy, and four beautiful young women, once accustomed to great luxury but now dressed like impoverished maids. Their few pleasures, cheerful smiles, and devotion to each other were all so ordinary, so unexpected, that few of the soldiers could nurse the revolutionary talk or harbor hatred against the Romanovs.

"Though I did not speak when I first encountered them," recalled Anatoly Yakimov, "I still had an indelible impression that seared itself on my soul." Nicholas, he said later, "was no longer young; his beard was flecked with grey. He always wore the same type of clothes: a khaki soldier's shirt, with an officer's belt and yellow-gold buckle round his waist; khaki trousers; and old, worn-out boots. His eyes were kind, and conveyed a sympathetic impression. He seemed to me friendly, modest, and frank; I often got the impression that he would like to speak to me; he looked as if he wanted to talk to all of us."[9]

Another guard, a former worker from Verkh-Isetsk, remembered:

I had many occasions on which to observe the Sovereign. I knew he was to be considered the same as us, but I also knew that his style, his manners, his behavior were not at all that of a common mortal. When he arrived, he would sit in the sun, his eyelids lowered, as though he was concentrating hard on an inner force. Although Nicholas Alexandrovich was lord of all of us peasants and rustics, he behaved in a quiet, self-effacing manner, he had a pleasant disposition, and would make small jokes and be more than reasonably affable. His voice was sweet and clear, his manners excessively elegant. His eyes were blue and very agreeable. . . . Some of us were open to speaking with him, while others would greet his overtures rudely and crudely. On the whole, he would just talk to us in a friendly and humble manner. I spoke with him twice. The first time, I was on guard in the garden, one day in the spring. I came on duty just as the Emperor and his family were let out for their walk. It seemed to me as I followed them, that they spoke to each other soto voice in English, remarking on the prettiness of the flowers and the freshness of the air and scent of the trees. Then the Emperor turned to me and said "This is an excellent time for working the fields." I answered, "It's true that it is so. It is just time for the peasants to get out and make their fields profitable." I started to take a real interest in our conversation, but just at that moment Avdayev came to the door and yelled out that the time for walking was over. I always called him "Majesty."[10]

Alexei Kabanov remembered him as "very friendly and open, and always willing to speak with us."[11] And Avdayev himself later wrote that Nicholas did not appear to be bothered at all by his captivity, that he had a "natural gaiety" throughout the imprisonment.[12]

Nicholas adapted quickly to the realities of imprisonment, whether at Tsarskoye Selo, Tobolsk, or Ekaterinburg, though he chafed at the restrictions imposed on him. The minor annoyances brought grumbles in the pages of his diary, but he seemed most perplexed by the nature of the captivity itself, which kept him restricted and unable to engage in the strenuous exercise he so enjoyed. Next to nothing, however, is known of his personal feelings; his diary, always a dispassionate rendering of daily events, rarely included any serious reflection on his situation. As with so many other instances in his life, Nicholas seems to have regarded his imprisonment as little more than an extension of his personal, preordained fate; thus he was able to move comfortably through this uncertain world, peopled with his declared enemies, and yet treat them genially, in the belief that they, too, were simply fulfilling their destinies.

"In my opinion," Alexander Strekotin later wrote, "the Emperor didn't resemble anyone's idea of an Emperor. He was always dressed in the same khaki uniform. A small man, of average height, he was solidly built, with a reddish mustache he constantly twirled. But his entire appearance was unremarkable, and he seemed shiftless, without any real thoughts or even concerns."[13] Ural Regional Soviet member Paul Bykov provided a rather more cynical echo of this: "Nicholas Romanov, who was in general, idiotically indifferent to all that went on around him, took the house regulations fairly calmly."[14] In a similar vein, Peter Ermakov later recalled: "The Tsar, kept very quiet, smoked cigarettes all day. Nothing disturbed the Tsar. He didn't seem to realize he wasn't Emperor any more, but just an ordinary Russian, and a prisoner."[15]

After meeting Nicholas, Victor Vorobiev, editor of the Ekaterinburg newspaper *Uralskii Rabochii*, provided him with a subscription so the emperor could follow the progress of the Civil War.[16] After this, as Isai Rodzinsky remembered, "he seldom had no newspapers in his hands. We brought him a lot of magazines, too, and arranged for several subscriptions." Rodzinsky found himself drawn to the emperor, though it was an interest tempered by his strong Bolshevik views: "Nicholas appeared to be such a weak-willed man, generally speaking, and he was interesting, and he wrote a lot on anything he could find. On his night table we later found poems he had written, making fun of us and the Bolsheviks. They were very immature, but they were poetry. He couldn't organize himself to stand up, but he could read in one language or another, and explain in a third, and then again in another, so he wasn't stupid. But he didn't seem to have any common sense, either."[17]

Members of the guard found it more difficult to look favorably on the empress. "She was an honest woman," said one soldier. "It was easy to read her emotions and thoughts on her face. But she was entirely different than her husband. She was haughty, pale as though in the morgue, and would not have anything to do with us. Nicholas and his daughter tried to be friendly. She didn't. She did not seem a truly Russian Empress. She was a completely German type. . . . When she sat alone by herself, she would raise her eyebrows and purse her lips at us."[18]

Anatoly Yakimov, with all of his sympathetic words for the emperor, declared that his wife "was not at all like him. She looked severe, with the appearance and manner of a haughty, serious woman. Sometimes, when we spoke amongst ourselves, we discussed them, and we all thought that Nicholas Alexandrovich was modest, but that she was different, and looked exactly like an Empress should. She even seemed older than he was. Her temples were flecked with grey hair, and her face was no longer young."[19] Isai Rodzinsky condemned her as "very arrogant," noting that "the Family held her in the first place. She had only to give a look for them to obey."[20] Of all the prisoners, Alexandra suffered most from the petty humiliations and lack of previous comforts; as with her years on the imperial throne, she found it impossible to disguise her true feelings. Above all, she found it impossible to reconcile their new position with her absolute conviction that her husband was God's anointed representative on earth, now subject to such unimaginable—if minor—privations and inconveniences and lack of deference.

True to form, she attempted to impose her will on those she encountered, creating endless tension in the Ipatiev House. "She seized every opportunity to protest against the conditions imposed on her by the regulations," claimed Paul Bykov, "and insulted the guard as well as the officials representing the Regional Soviet."[21] While it is difficult to believe that the empress behaved in such a blatant manner, there can be little doubt that she was the least agreeable and cooperative of all the prisoners. Ermakov remembered her, no doubt with a jaundiced eye, as "always angry and quarreling about something. She asked me one day please to have the soldiers stop making so much noise outside her room. I told her the soldiers could make all the noise they liked. They weren't the prisoners, she was."[22]

Despite Ermakov's open hostility, his remarks ring true, and were confirmed by others. "The Empress," wrote Alexei Kabanov, "spoke Russian badly. When we spoke to her in Russian, she did what we asked, but I can't ever remember her answering us in Russian. She used to go out for a walk quite often, but, after a few of the guards asked her questions about Rasputin, she stopped."[23] Victor Vorobiev, who was often at the Ipatiev House, left a telling picture of Alexandra, "spiteful, constantly suffering from migraine and indigestion," writing that despite addressing her she "did not bother to look at me. She spent days on a sofa, her head swathed in a compress."[24]

Of all the prisoners, Alexei aroused the most sympathy. Ermakov remembered him as a "handsome little fellow . . . but a hopeless invalid

... no sort of Emperor for Russia."[25] The emaciated young boy, unable to walk, with wide, saddened eyes staring out from a pale face, evoked unanimous compassion. There was something singularly pathetic about him, as Rodzinsky recalled, that made him "very attractive to us."[26] In the Ipatiev House, one guard from the Verkh-Isetsk factory remembered, the tsesarevich was "pale and transparent, and looked as though a good wind could break him. . . . It was clear to everyone that the boy was not going to be long upon this earth. The tsesarevich was so often ill, and walked outside his room so little, that it was impossible for us to get to know him well enough to guess at his inner thoughts. He came out to the garden very rarely, and to the dinner table even less."[27]

The young men in the Ipatiev House guard were most fascinated by the four grand duchesses. "They were just like all girls," Alexei Kabanov recalled, "stuck up and stupid," though he added that they were "also quite lively, and very friendly to us."[28] Only Olga Nikolaievna seemed remote, perhaps preoccupied with thoughts of her own, uncertain future. "She was thin, pale, and looked very sick," remembered Strekotin. "She took few walks in the garden, and spent most of her time with her brother."[29] When she did venture outside, said another guard, she stood "gazing sadly into the distance, making it easy to read her emotions."[30] Tatiana inevitably struck most of the guards as more refined and prettier than her sisters, yet also more reserved.[31] "She had the same serious and haughty look as her mother," Yakimov recalled.[32] In captivity, she had grown very thin; one guard later commented that she looked "as if she was not far from the morgue."[33]

These men remembered Marie Nikolaievna as the most sympathetic and friendly of the girls. In the first days of captivity in the Ipatiev House, according to one sentry, she suffered "continual reprimands" from her mother, accompanied by "severe and angry whispers" indicating that she was too friendly with members of the guard.[34] Strekotin, too, recalled Marie's "friendly overtures," noting that she "was a girl who loved to have fun."[35] Her simple beauty and efflorescent personality, as another guard later declared, "always provided us with nourishment. She was buxom, and a true Russian beauty with no airs of grandeur about her."[36]

Anastasia, Yakov Yurovsky remembered, was "very attractive. She had rosy cheeks, and a quite lovely face and features. In character, she seemed best adjusted to their position."[37] According to Strekotin, she was "very friendly and full of fun. She was almost always with her sister Marie."[38] And another guard called Anastasia "a very charming devil! She was mischievous, and I think, rarely tired. She was lively, and was fond of performing comic mimes with the dogs, as though they were performing in a circus."[39] Occasionally, though, her pointed barbs gave offense, as had happened even before the Revolution. "She was a child," said one exasperated guard, "offensive, and a terrorist. Under other circumstances, she might have seemed naive and lighthearted, but her remarks sometimes caused tension."[40]

As time passed, animosities and preconceived impressions held by both prisoners and guards rapidly faded. Guards Gregory Suatin and Mohamed Abdul Latypov later testified that members of the Special Detachment were in open sympathy with the captives, and especially the emperor himself. "It is making a man suffer needlessly," they declared among themselves.[41] Another guard added: "Of course we pitied them. But what could we really do?"[42]

Marie and Anastasia, 1914.

Some of the men did risk their positions to help the prisoners. A few smuggled books and provisions into the Ipatiev House, while others—at the empress's request—took her letters and mailed them to friends outside.[43] The captives themselves appreciated these small gestures. In their reply to the third "Officer" letter, they wrote of the members of the Special Detachment: "They conscientiously guard our prison as well as our lives and are good to us. We do not want them to suffer for our sakes."[44]

By the end of June 1918, as even virulently anti-Bolshevik author Paul Bulygin admitted, the Ipatiev House guard was "beginning to simmer down and to regard the prisoners as human beings."[45] Off duty—in their barracks, in their homes, drinking at taverns—these men spoke openly of "the sovereign" and his family, abandoning revolutionary slogans in favor of whispered encounters with members of the former ruling dynasty. A few, like Yakimov's friend Glafira Stepanovna, found the shift distasteful: "In the last weeks before the killing, I noticed that not only Anatoly, but also other guards that I knew became little by little counterrevolutionaries. They began to suffer from troubled consciences, like old women poisoned by religion. In place of the crimes of Nicholas and Alix and her Rasputin, they began to talk like true bourgeois. They completely lost their heads."[46]

The situation deteriorated to the extent that Peter Voikov deemed the Special Detachment "undependable" during a meeting of the Ural Regional Soviet at the end of June.[47] When Yurovsky replaced Avdayev as commandant on July 4, he saw firsthand the degree to which barriers between the prisoners and their jailers had collapsed: "Many of the Emperor's guards," he later wrote, "had assumed an overly sympathetic attitude to them, and did all they could to assist in their secrets. They were so close to the Romanovs and so unreliable that we considered exterminating them to prevent further scandal and possible rescue of the prisoners."[48]

According to the rules laid down by the Presidium of the Ural Regional Soviet, the prisoners were to be kept under constant watch, particularly during their daily walks; conversation between the captives and their guards was expressly forbidden. Yet Avdayev never enforced this, and very quickly, the grand duchesses drew the young men of the Special Detachment into easy exchanges. "Everyone relaxed more," Strekotin recalled, "and began to talk and laugh with each other. We were especially keen to talk to the daughters, except for Olga." There must have been many such conversations, for Strekotin recounted that "they always began" with one of the grand duchesses complaining, "We're so bored! In Tobolsk, there was always something to do. I know! Try to guess the name of this dog!"[49]

Such banter was perfectly natural for the grand duchesses. Having been raised in a military environment at their father's court, they always had felt a natural ease in the company of soldiers, mixing freely with the young officers on the imperial yacht, or the men who formed the Cossack Konvoi Regiment, which guarded the imperial family, playing games of tennis, swimming, or riding while on holiday.[50] Flirtations and frivolous talk with such men had always formed an idle distraction that helped alleviate the boredom of their own ordered, cloistered lives. Marie and Anastasia, in particular—even before the Revolution—held to no false conceit in such relationships, behaving naturally and trustingly toward all. To the men of the Special Detachment, however, such informality with the daughters of the former emperor was an extraordinary, heady experience. In the Ipatiev House, as Alexander Strekotin recalled, the girls "whispered flirtatiously with us, giggling as they went." Some of the sentries eagerly joined in the chatter, while others, "with smiles and winks," answered, "Don't try to distract me with your smooth talk—just keep walking!" The girls, "pretending fright," according to Strekotin, "would hurry away along the path, then burst into giggles, followed by our more subdued laughter."[51]

The girls, as Strekotin related, took advantage of this relaxed atmosphere and receptive, impressionable audience, enticing the young men into lighthearted conversations. "It was especially hard for the men at the posts inside the House," he later wrote. "They tried to remain professional, but the girls would come out of their rooms, smile at them, talk with them for hours, and flirt quite openly. I myself stood at one of these posts when I was not needed on machine gun duty, and saw this firsthand."[52]

While Olga Nikolaievna remained aloof, her three sisters were more open with these guards. Even the usually reserved Tatiana, as one soldier later said, "would be pleasant to the guards if she thought they were behaving in an acceptable and decorous manner."[53] In time, she became more comfortable in their presence; Avdayev remembered how she "would often go up to one of the interior guards, speaking to him about himself, his life, his enjoyments and so on."[54] Yurovsky, too, saw her "frequently open the door to their rooms, outside of which stood a sentry. She took great pains to flirt with him outrageously, apparently in the hope of putting the guards in a good humor with them."[55]

Of all the grand duchesses, it was Marie Nikolaievna who formed the easiest and most intimate bonds with the soldiers of the Ipatiev House guard. Renowned for her lack of pretension, she had always taken great pains to befriend ordinary soldiers serving as members of the imperial guard. The simplest of the four girls, she continued this familiarity with her captors throughout her time at Tsarskoye Selo, and into her imprisonment at both Tobolsk and Ekaterinburg. According to Avdayev, she could often be found with members of the guard, questioning them about their lives and hobbies.[56] In this, Yurovsky later wrote, "she did not behave at all like her elder sisters. Her sincere, modest character was very attractive to the men, and she spent most of her time flirting with them."[57] With her natural gaiety, Marie mixed easily with her jailers, "flirting at every available opportunity," according to Paul Bykov.[58]

Anastasia, too, moved freely among the guards. Like Marie, she cared little for ceremony or pretension, though her mischievous wit and crude humor even put off many of the men. Still, as Yurovsky recalled, she was "most often to be found at the side of her sister Marie, making eyes at the soldiers then laughing at their replies."[59] Even occasional visitors to the Ipatiev House, such as Peter Ermakov, were surprised at the ease between the grand duchesses and members of the Special Detachment, noting, with true Bolshevik indignation, that the soldiers could often be found "talking to the youngest girls and laughing with them."[60]

Inevitably, the men of the Special Detachment fell under the spell of the grand duchesses. "They were brilliantly pretty," recalled one soldier, "and the humane and intelligent among our guard took the necessary steps to raise their morale."[61] As the lines between captives and jailers faded, the young women began to take the men into their confidence. Alexander Strekotin later wrote of "long conversations, in which they spoke of their hopes for the future, and talked about living in England one day." They became so comfortable, he recalled, that the grand duchesses "often came down to our guard room, bringing their photograph albums for us to look at," showing the ghostly images of their former lives. Strekotin was particularly struck by one photograph, showing Rasputin standing with the four girls.[62]

"Their personalities were fascinating to us," Strekotin recalled. "They were the topic of discussion between two or three of us, who passed some sleepless nights together speaking of them. . . . You could look at them in their old and tattered clothes, with bracelets and trinkets just like any poor girls, but yet there was something especially sweet about them. They always looked good to me, and I thought that they would not have looked better even if they had been all covered in gold and diamonds. All in all, we felt that we would not mind so much if they were allowed to escape."[63]

This powerful testimony from a member of the Ipatiev House guard demonstrates something of the infatuation prevalent among the men of the Special Detachment. Further evidence was left by a sentry from the Zlokazov factory who spoke at length of the "scent of their perfumes and luxury soaps, the curiosity of their St. Petersburg dresses, and the tap-tapping sound of their high heels crossing the floors. But this was not what excited us the most. When they would drink tea with us and become talkative, well, we were spending a happy hour with the grandest people in the world."[64]

"It was difficult for us, being we were young and inexperienced," recalled one guard, "to entirely absorb and reconcile our new identities as guards, and to completely abandon our natural instincts, especially when presented with such fodder for our imaginations."[65] Occasionally, sitting drinking tea with the grand duchesses and chatting amiably while examining photographs of their former holidays in the Crimea and aboard the imperial yacht, these young men forgot themselves completely. Once, a guard repeated a risqué joke and Tatiana, "pale as death," ran from the room. Marie, who remained, fixed the offending man with a stare, declaring, "Why are you not disgusted with yourselves when you use such shameful words? Do you imagine that you can woo a well-born woman with such witticisms and have her be well disposed towards you? Be refined and respectable men and then we can get along."[66]

There is something particularly telling in these incidents, with their easy conversation, mutual laughter, and shared confidences. The grand duchesses may have perceived nothing unusual in these friendly relationships with members of the guard, but the young men themselves clearly felt otherwise. One guard later spoke of these "somewhat risky and dangerous amusements" by the grand duchesses, indicating that, with the exception of Olga Nikolaievna, they surprised the men, not only with their friendliness but also "with their lack of modesty." Their "acts and words," he claimed, were made "with coquetry, excitement, and daring," and gave members of the guard "reason to believe" that more than friendly feelings existed.[67]

At least one member of the Special Detachment made no secret of his ambitions. One day twenty-one-year-old Ivan Kleshchev announced that he intended to marry one of the grand duchesses; if her parents objected, he insisted, he would rescue her from the Ipatiev House himself.[68] Kleshchev made this startling declaration in front of his Special Detachment comrades, a clear indication of just how far the barriers separating the prisoners and their jailers had fallen. His boast fell on receptive ears, for Kleshchev was not reprimanded or even reported for engaging in such incendiary talk; he remained a guard at the Ipatiev House until the Romanovs were murdered. Such open sympathies, however, were certainly no secret. Things had become so bad, Peter Ermakov recalled, that the Ural Regional Soviet actually believed that the guards would "be helping the prisoners escape the next thing we knew."[69]

Pressures were inexorably building within the Ipatiev House, as smiles and careless confidences gave way to whispered secrets and outright declarations of mutual sympathy between the prisoners and their jailers. With the barriers separating captive and guard rapidly crumbling, an explosion was inevitable. When, in the third week of June, it finally came, it burst over a tenuous and uncertain situation already poised on the edge of tragedy, a fatal combination of disparate elements that not only fractured the unity of the imperial family but also sealed the fate of the Romanovs.

Thursday, June 27, began quietly in the Ipatiev House. The prisoners wandered through the stifling day in a haze of nervous exhaustion, having sat up most of the previous night awaiting a rescue that never came. At two that afternoon, Grand Duchess Marie, marking her nineteenth birthday, joined her father, brother, Tatiana, and Anastasia as they paced the dusty garden under the relentless Siberian sun.[70]

As the prisoners returned to the house, members of the Special Detachment filled the courtyard and passages as they made their regular afternoon shift change. One of those going off duty was Ivan Skorokhodov, a young man who had formerly worked under Avdayev at the Zlokazov factory. Skorokhodov, who had joined the Special Detachment on June 11, lived in the ground-floor rooms of the Ipatiev House with the other Zlokazov workers.[71] In his first seventeen days of service, he had been assigned to duty on Guard Post 2, in the secondary staircase hall next to the bathroom and lavatory, where he came into daily contact with the prisoners.[72]

Like most of his comrades, including his fellow Zlokazov worker Anatoly Yakimov, Skorokhodov entered the Ipatiev House as a former factory worker, a young man whose knowledge of the prisoners came from half-truths and revolutionary rhetoric. Quickly he found himself exchanging smiles and sipping tea with the former emperor's daughters, an extraordinary experience that seems to have completely over-whelmed him. On this particular day, he had smuggled a cake into the Ipatiev House, to celebrate Marie's birthday. Apparently he pulled her aside, and the pair disappeared.[73]

At five that afternoon, Goloshchokin and Beloborodov arrived at the Ipatiev House and began a thorough inspection of the prison.[74] During their tour they apparently found one of the grand duchesses with a member of the guard, a discovery that provided irrefutable evidence that the soldiers were no longer reliable. Details of this incident remain somewhat uncertain but, from a number of accounts, it is possible to piece together what may have taken place. In 1926, Alois Hochleitner, a former prisoner of war, recalled what he had been told while incarcerated in Ekaterinburg City Prison in July 1918. According to Hochleitner, two of the imperial daughters "apparently often spoke to the guards and held lengthy conversations with them. Flirtations even developed. In the course of an inspection, a sentry was discovered in a situation with one of the Grand Duchesses, whereupon a drastic investigation was ordered and carried out."[75]

Hochleitner had this story secondhand, but others confirmed its basic details. In 1964 Isai Rodzinsky, the member of the Ekaterinburg Cheka who wrote the "Officer" letters, remembered: "The girls often made eyes at the guards at their posts. It once lead to—no, no—I can't say this. . . . No, but it did lead to it."[76] This cryptic account hinted heavily at some incident that developed between a member of the guard and one of the grand duchesses. Ipatiev House guard Victor Netrebin was more direct. On being brought into the Ipatiev House in early July, Yakov Yurovsky warned that he must be cautious with the prisoners. Too much, he declared, had been allowed under Avdayev; things had gone "too far"; and, as Netrebin recalled, one of the soldiers had been caught "consorting with one of the younger Grand Duchesses."[77]

These accounts are problematic, yet their convergence of detail makes it impossible for them to be simply dismissed. Hochleitner was not in a position to observe what took place in the Ipatiev House, and had his details from a prison guard. Members of the Ipatiev House Special Detachment, however, also worked at Ekaterinburg City Prison to supplement their income, making it possible that the story came from a reliable source. Rodzinsky clearly knew intimate details of life in the Ipatiev House, nor, given his place within the prison, is there any reason to question the brief account left by Netrebin.

That some incident occurred involving a member of the guard and one of the grand duchesses seems likely. Further confirmation is found in Yakov Yurovsky's unpublished memoirs. While he himself made no actual reference to the event in question, he recounted a conversation with Father Ioann Storozhev, who on July 14 came to the Ipatiev House to conduct a religious service for the prisoners. The priest, according to Yurovsky, was nervous. Apparently he had somehow learned of the alleged incident, for he commented: "Before this all, we had never met such refined people. Of course, one changes one's opinions, knowing what has happened. It is already a great scandal over the situation. But we at the Church are ready to forgive, and give a pass to an Imperial soul."[78] Storozhev's statement lends circumstantial support to the accounts of Hochleitner, Rodzinsky, and Netrebin, particularly his remark that the Church was "ready to forgive, and give a pass to an Imperial soul." Not "the Imperial souls," but a singular reference, to one specific person involved in some "great scandal over the situation."

What happened in the Ipatiev House? Almost certainly, during their inspection on June 27, Beloborodov and Goloshchokin discovered Grand Duchess Marie and Ivan Skorokhodov, the young member of the Special Detachment who had smuggled in a cake to mark her nineteenth birthday, in circumstances that left little doubt that security had all but irrevocably broken down. This, coupled with the favorable replies of the "Officer" letters, led, in the week that followed, to Avdayev's removal as commandant; new rules that forbade the guards from doing their regular shifts of duty on the main floor posts, replacing them with a specially selected contingent, and expelling them from the Ipatiev House to the Popov House across the street; and, most ominously, to a hasty decision by the Ural Regional Soviet to execute the Romanovs.

Faced with the passage of time and lack of documentary evidence, it is impossible to determine the extent of this incident, yet there are solid reasons to believe that, in some form, it did take place. The one source that should have recorded it, the guard duty book for the Special Detachment kept by Sidorov, provides only silence; indeed, in this methodical record of life in the Ipatiev House, entries for the period between June 24 and July 3 are frustratingly unavailable. This lapse—covering the crucial events following Berzin's inspection; discovery of the genuine rescue plot; the fabricated "Officer" letters; and the incident on June 27—is unique in the duty book. No similar gap exists from May 13, when Sidorov assumed responsibility for its entries, to June 23. Given Sidorov's meticulous habit of recording everything, even to the point, as on May 17, of writing, "No incidents took place or special reports made," it would have been extremely unlikely that nothing had been entered in the duty book during these volatile twelve days.[79] Based on the pattern of Sidorov's entries for May and June, it defies logic that he suddenly would have abandoned his responsibilities, particularly at a time when crucial events were unfolding within the House of Special Purpose. Therefore it is likely that these entries were removed from the record at some later date, after Sidorov was forced to turn over the duty book on July 4 to Yurovsky's assistant Gregory Nikulin.

Nor can the incident be dismissed as clumsy Bolshevik propaganda designed to tarnish the reputation of the imperial family. Rumors of flirtations between the grand duchesses and their guards have always been controversial, given the modern Romanov cult that has ensconced them in a protective cocoon of myth. Yet, if such was the intent of these stories, surely the allegations would have been made in the Soviet press, or in their official account of the murders by Paul Bykov; instead, the memoirs of Rodzinsky, Yurovsky, and Netrebin remained hidden, with the last two never previously published. Nor, if the assertions represented an attempt to discredit the Romanovs, would one expect to find such circumspection and lack of damning detail. None of these three men, dedicated Bolsheviks and all participants in the imperial family's murder, had any great sympathy for the prisoners, yet they displayed a marked reticence in discussing the issue. Hochleitner certainly had no political or national agenda in repeating the story he had heard, though even his account falls far short of the sordid descriptions to be found in numerous fabrications; indeed, representatives of Allied governments were guilty of spreading far more prurient tales of habitual rape and torture of the prisoners than anything contained in these four memoirs.

After this incident, witnesses recalled, a noticeable chill settled over the Ipatiev House. Grand Duchess Olga, as Strekotin later wrote, "refused to associate with her younger sisters."[80] Netrebin, too, remembered that she "stayed mostly alone, away from her younger sisters, behaving like her arrogant mother."[81] And Yurovsky was more specific, linking Olga's behavior to resentment of her younger sister: "Marie did not behave like her elder sisters at all. She spent most time with the sentries. Somehow, she seemed closed off from most of her family. This obviously followed from what happened, because her mother and eldest sister treated her as if she didn't belong, like an outcast."[82]

The grand duchesses, and particularly Marie and Anastasia, had always acted in such a natural way with the guards surrounding them; in Siberian exile, they apparently made no distinction as one contingent of soldiers followed another, judging these men not on their political beliefs but on the strength of their behavior. They bore their jailers, few of whom were actually Bolsheviks, no animosity, and certainly never judged their guards on the basis of their political inclinations. Yet these languid relationships were perceived quite differently by the soldiers, who, unaccustomed to such friendliness and at a loss to understand their actions, mistakenly interpreted the smiles and shared laughter as romantic flirtations.

While it is improbable that Marie's indiscretion extended beyond mere romantic flirtation, her mother and eldest sister clearly felt differently. It is not difficult to understand Alexandra's attitude, given her narrow-minded sensibilities and open contempt for most of the men surrounding them. Held as prisoners by a hostile regime, stripped of power and dignity, the empress could barely tolerate what she perceived as the lack of respect due her husband by virtue of his former position; any dalliance by her third daughter, however innocent, must have seemed a deliberate betrayal, leading Alexandra, as Yurovsky noted, to treat Marie "like an outcast."

Olga, too, was suffering from the strain of captivity. Twenty-three years old, she had tried to act as a dutiful daughter, yet never entirely reconciled her own personal feelings to the expectations of her parents. In Ekaterinburg she grew, as several witnesses recalled, to closely resemble her mother, echoing the empress's stubborn reserve and underlying melancholy. Imprisoned, surrounded by men she alone of the grand duchesses clearly found distasteful, and in a situation no one could have foreseen, the harsh realities of her life undoubtedly brought a sense of helplessness, perhaps tinged with resentment over her family's uncertain predicament. Having lived through the brutal experience aboard *Rus*, Olga almost certainly entered the Ipatiev House an emotionally, if not physically, scarred young woman. Had the incident on *Rus* amounted to harassment and brutal threats, Olga would naturally have been bitter; if the situation deteriorated to physical assaults, her behavior—particularly if she then witnessed her younger sister sharing high-spirited laughs with soldiers she equated with their brutal torment on the vessel—must have reflected profound shock.

After June 27, Nicholas did not write again in his diary for the next six days, the longest such lapse of his recorded life; even when he was ill, he asked his wife to record the fact in the pages of his journal. While the diary assumed a somewhat sporadic nature after the first week of June, the emperor never let more than a few days pass before reverting to habit. The lack of an expected rescue may have led him to abandon temporarily the one constant in his methodical life; it is also possible, however, that his failure to make any entries for six days after June 27 was tied to depression on learning of the incident that evening between his daughter and a member of the guard.

Ivan Skorokhodov himself was removed from the Ipatiev House on the evening of June 27. His comrades in the Special Detachment were told, as Anatoly Yakimov recalled, that he had "suddenly become ill."[83] In fact, he was taken to Ekaterinburg City Prison, after which he simply

Olga and Tatiana, 1914.

vanished from the pages of history.[84]

To members of the Ural Regional Soviet, the episode proved that security at the Ipatiev House had completely collapsed. The extreme ardor and discipline of these hand-picked guards had all but disintegrated, a scenario that itself accounts for the few subdued references to what dedicated Bolsheviks like Yurovsky, Rodzinsky, and Netrebin must have viewed as a blight on the reputation of the revolutionary Urals. Coupled with the discovery of the rescue plot and the prisoners' favorable responses to the fabricated "Officer" letters, it provided the Ural Regional Soviet with final justification to murder the Romanovs.

Authorities in Ekaterinburg were increasingly worried as counter-revolutionary forces drew nearer the Urals. The city hovered uneasily between panic and resignation as the leading Bolsheviks repeatedly met at the Hotel Amerika, attempting to coordinate unified military opposition and plan for an eventual evacuation. There was little doubt, according to Goloshchokin, that the city would fall to the advancing Czech and White Armies; it had been inevitable since June 15, when, as Ural military commissar, Goloshchokin had privately informed Moscow that the Bolsheviks could not keep the Urals.[85] It was now only a question of time: at the end of June, Goloshchokin said, Ekaterinburg might hold out for another week, or two at most. With this uncertain situation, it was imperative to deal with the question of what to do with the imperial prisoners.

The situation with the Romanovs had dragged on since the arrival of the emperor, empress, and Grand Duchess Marie on April 30, with little instruction or even communication on the subject from the authorities in Moscow. Indeed, both Lenin and Sverdlov seemed content to let the prisoners languish, driven, as they were, by the more vital matter of the survival of their own regime. The Ural Regional Presidium welcomed this silence, granting them, as it did, complete authority over prisoners. Yet with authority came responsibility and, by the end of June, the situation in the Ipatiev House had grown far too dangerous to ignore.

Avdayev's discovery of the smuggled letters offering to rescue the prisoners, along with their favorable responses to the Cheka fabrications, unnerved the Ural Regional Soviet. Then, during their inspection of the Ipatiev House on the evening of June 27, Goloshchokin and Beloborodov almost certainly found Grand Duchess Marie with Ivan Skorokhodov; under such conditions, there seem to have been very real fears that the guards at the Ipatiev House might somehow cooperate with, or even institute, a rescue attempt. The fabricated Cheka letters bought the Ural Regional Presidium time, but the breakdown in security, coupled with the advance of the anti-Bolshevik forces, presented Ekaterinburg with an unexpected impetus to finally address the lingering question of the former emperor and his family.

By June 1918 the Bolsheviks held control of both the Ekaterinburg Soviet and the Ekaterinburg Cheka, but only just. The soviet was divided between the Bolsheviks, who had a slim majority, and three other groups: the Socialist Revolutionaries, the Left Socialist Revolutionaries, and the Anarchists. All but the Bolsheviks were vocal in their demands that the Romanovs be executed.[86] "Tempers flared," recalled Kudrin, "particularly in the numerous factories around the city. Long considered hotbeds of Bolshevik activity and support, they should have been our strongest supporters, but instead became our worst critics. Angry workers began to threaten the power of both the Ural Regional Soviet and the Ekaterinburg Cheka, demanding that we put an end to Nicholas." Kudrin admitted that there was "a good deal of indignation among the local workers, which came at an uncertain time for us, just as the enemy was advancing toward Ekaterinburg. There were demonstrations and angry meetings at the Verkh-Isetsk factory, with resolutions calling for the immediate execution of the former Emperor." He spoke of the "difficulty in creating reliable and loyal Red Army units in the city, such was the state of things," and the "constant threat of a massacre of the Romanovs by the workers, who were armed and took themselves very seriously."[87] And Paul Bykov recalled that the Anarchists and Left SRs "were not certain that the Bolsheviks would shoot the ex-Emperor, and decided to take steps to do so with their own forces."[88]

On June 28 the local *Ural'skii rabochii* declared, "The Revolution is in mortal danger!" In an editorial, it urged the city's inhabitants to "take up arms against the counterrevolutionary elements now threatening the Red Urals." Ominously, it warned: "Romanov and his relatives will not escape the hour of the People's Court."[89] Such was the uncertainty of the situation that, on this same day, Beloborodov requested that Moscow grant him direct cable access to the Kremlin, and to Lenin and Sverdlov. Although sent on June 28, the cable was not received in Moscow until July 7.[90]

Saturday, June 29, was another brilliant day in the Urals;

Ekaterinburg sweltered under the heat of a cloudless sky.[91] That afternoon, the marble corridors of the Hotel Amerika on Voznesensky
Prospekt echoed with the angry click of boots as members of the
Presidium of the Ural Regional Soviet and the Ekaterinburg Cheka
made their way past the potted palms and gilded, overstuffed sofas and
chairs. Here, in Room 3, they assembled around the large, Empire-style
table: Beloborodov, Goloshchokin, Didkovsky, Safarov, Chukazev,
Ermakov, Voikov, Yurovsky, Alexei Kabanov, Adolf Lepa, and, from
Perm, Gabriel Myasnikov.

This meeting determined the fate of the Romanovs. After some discussion, Safarov composed and read a resolution:

> The Ural Regional Soviet categorically refuses to take the responsibil-
> ity for transferring Nicholas Romanov in the direction of Moscow as
> has been suggested, and considers it necessary therefore to liquidate
> him. There is grave danger that Citizen Romanov will fall into the
> hands of the Czechoslovaks and other counterrevolutionaries and be
> used to their benefit. We cannot ignore this question. We face a critical
> moment in our revolutionary path: we must move forward, we cannot
> turn away from our duty to the Revolution. Romanov's family and those
> who have elected to remain with him and share his imprisonment must
> also be liquidated at the same time.

The Romanovs imprisoned at Alapayevsk also were condemned to
death. The Presidium decided to send Goloshchokin to Moscow with a
copy of the resolution, to seek the immediate sanction of Lenin and
Sverdlov; these "liquidations" were to take place "no later than July 15,"
the last day on which Goloshchokin believed Ekaterinburg might
remain in Bolshevik hands.[92]

That night, Goloshchokin conducted another inspection of the
Ipatiev House, as Alexandra recorded in her diary.[93] The following day,
June 30, he left for Moscow. With the Urals on the verge of falling to the
Czech and White Armies, Beloborodov was eager to get his wife and
children away from the danger, and asked Gabriel Myasnikov to escort
them from Perm to Moscow. Myasnikov left Perm with Beloborodov's
wife and children on July 8. The group encountered trains crowded with
refugees throughout the Urals. Then, early in the second week of July,
while crossing the Vytchegda River on a crowded ferry, disaster struck.
The vessel capsized, and, though Myasnikov survived, Beloborodov's
wife and three children were swept down the river and drowned.[94]

The adoption of this resolution, along with the dispatch of
Goloshchokin to Moscow, would seal the fate of the prisoners. But it
also indicates that the Ural Regional Soviet—independent of any
instruction or authorization from Lenin—had, of its own volition,

embarked on the final drama of the Romanovs and made the decision to end their lives. Word of this resolution somehow got back to Avdayev, who stormed into the Hotel Amerika and, according to Sister Agnes from the Novotikhvinsky Convent, "raised an outcry, created a scandal, stomped his foot, when he learned about plans to murder them." For several hours the commandant "courageously defended the interests of the poor prisoners to his superiors," but to no avail.[95]

This protest determined the Ural Regional Soviet's second course of action: Avdayev's removal as commandant, and the replacement of his men with a contingent of guards capable of and willing to exact the ultimate vengeance of the Revolution. At a special meeting of the Ural Regional Soviet and Ekaterinburg Cheka on July 3, Isai Rodzinsky spoke of Avdayev's dismissal as necessary "for the special purpose the Ural Presidium had in mind." This "special purpose," he states, were "extreme measures" that remained "at the forefront of our plans for them."[96]

Avdayev apparently had no hint of his pending replacement; on the evening of July 3, he received a telephone call summoning him to the Hotel Amerika. Only when he was seated before the members of the Presidium of the Ural Regional Soviet did they inform him that he had been relieved of his duty as commandant at the Ipatiev House, effective immediately. He was allowed to leave quietly. Alexander Moshkin, his deputy, was not as fortunate: he was arrested and sent to the front.[97]

That same evening, there was a second emergency session of the Presidium of the Ural Regional Soviet at the Hotel Amerika. Earlier that day, the telephone had rung in the small apartment shared by Yakov Yurovsky and his family, summoning him to the ornate, red brick building on Voznesensky Prospekt. Although the evening itself was overcast, a humid pall hung over Ekaterinburg, and the windows of Room 3 were open to the broad avenue beyond, bustling with noise. As Yurovsky took his place in one of the gilded armchairs, Beloborodov informed him that he had been selected to replace Avdayev as commandant of the House of Special Purpose.[98]

Like many cast in the final drama of Ekaterinburg, Yakov Yurovsky has been broadly painted as a villain, a man devoid of humanity, who brutally shot down the helpless women and children in the basement of the Ipatiev House. Thus Baroness Buxhoeveden termed him "the very spirit of evil."[99] Yet the same man who organized the Romanov execution had once been a devout monarchist. His life of grinding poverty and despair led to the gradual development of the revolutionary destined to play the penultimate role in the Romanov tragedy.

Yakov Mikhailovich Yurovsky was born on June 19, 1878, in the Siberian city of Tomsk, the eighth of ten children born to Michael Ilyich Yurovsky and his wife.[100] The Yurovsky family was solidly working class,

Yakov Yurovsky, last commandant
of the House of Special Purpose.

with bourgeois values and traditional dedication to home life; to the church; and, especially, to the Romanov Dynasty. Michael Yurovsky worked as a glazier, while his wife worked as a seamstress from their home. Both were industrious. Yakov Yurovsky would later recall that his parents "worked to the point of exhaustion." With ten children to feed and clothe, money often was tight, and luxuries were nonexistent.[101]

Yet the family was not impoverished. Unlike most families in Tomsk, the Yurovskys had two houses. From June to February the family lived in a wooden dacha along the banks of the wide, flat Ob River, on the outskirts of Tomsk. When the spring thaw brought melting snow and the river overflowed, they retreated to a small, first-floor apartment they kept in the center of town, on Millionaya Street. Situated above a butcher shop, this was less than ideal—small and, as Yurovsky recalled, permeated with the smells of blood and boiling meat from the shop below.[102]

Michael Yurovsky, as his son recalled, was deeply religious. He later wrote of his father's "religious fanaticism. . . . On holidays and regular days the children were forced to pray, and it is not surprising that my first active protest was against religious and nationalistic traditions."[103] As a young boy, Yakov Yurovsky rebelled against this enforced piety. When he was seven or eight years old, he remembered sitting in the courtyard of their wooden dacha, "thinking what a difficult life it was in this world. I thought then that one could go to the Emperor and tell him how hard our life was. But then, of course, we would have been told that such hardships were sent from Heaven." One day he asked his mother why life should be hard for some and easy for others. "Because God wills it," she told him.[104]

This early sense of deprivation and injustice grew steadily in the young boy. After the arrival of a tenth child in 1886, they had outgrown their small apartment. When the spring thaw came that year, catching the family in their dacha beside the Ob, they quickly fled to the Millionaya Street flat. With such cramped conditions, the butcher who owned the building generously asked if the elder children would like to stay in his second-floor apartment. Yet this only brought more discontent from the young Yakov. One day he asked his mother, "Why do we have to live in such a dacha, with water flowing through our rooms, while the children of the building's owner all have a good place to live and sleep upstairs?"

"It is better to be poor, but honest," his mother replied.[105]

Such platitudes did little to assuage the growing social resentment in the fourth Yurovsky son. One Friday he took lunch to his father, and passed a group of Jews on their way to synagogue. When he returned home, he once again peppered his mother with questions indicating the depth of Yurovsky's own anti-Semitism: "How is it that Jews have all the money, and can close their shops to go to synagogue on Friday, when others have to work? Why are they allowed to decide when it is forbidden to work, when the rest of us have to do so?"[106]

To this, his mother gave her usual answer: "Because God wills it."[107]

But, by now, Yakov Yurovsky refused to accept such things. "I used to sit alone," he later wrote, "and think to myself, It would be a great thing if I had money. I would not keep it all to myself and I would give lots of things to others who had nothing."[108] This early deprivation caused a good deal of rebellion and fostered resentment. "Tomsk was a backwater in the far reaches of the Empire," Yurovsky later wrote. "From the time of my birth, my place in life was settled as a worker, just as it had been for my father. There was no escape."[109]

Yurovsky began his education at age six when he was enrolled in the River District Grammar School. In 1890, when he was twelve, his father made him quit to pursue a trade. Yurovsky himself had wanted to continue his education, but, as he later wrote, "Father was very severe, and would not allow any contrary points of view from his children."[110] He was apprenticed to the town's best watchmaker, on Post Office Street, a job he held for the next decade.[111]

On July 5, 1891, thirteen-year-old Yakov Yurovsky unknowingly came face to face with his own destiny. That summer, the future Nicholas II was completing his Far Eastern tour, returning to St. Petersburg across the length of Siberia. Stops were arranged in all major cities and towns along the route, including Tomsk. Beneath a cloudless Siberian sky, church bells rang out in greeting as the procession swept through the city streets, lined with cheering crowds. All schools had been given a holiday, and their students, dressed in crisp, clean uniforms, waved miniature Russian flags.[112] Standing in the doorway of the watch repair shop where he worked, Yakov Yurovsky watched as the tsesarevich sped past him along Post Office Street in a brightly painted troika owned by one of the city's wealthiest Jews. The sight aroused much talk; even Yurovsky remembered thinking: "The Heir should not have been subjected to pernicious Jewish influence."[113]

The governor-general of Tomsk Province greeted the tsesarevich on the steps of the Governor's House with the traditional Russian welcome of bread and salt.[114] "I thought at that time that although I had a special wish to see the heir," Yurovsky recalled, "it didn't really matter. I thought that it would be good to see him, but what would pass between us?" He watched as Nicholas appeared on the balcony of the Governor's House, a few hundred feet down the street. "I remember how handsome the heir was," Yurovsky later wrote, "with his little, neat brown beard." In a few minutes, the boy had joined the cheering crowd below. "It was," he wrote, "a perfect day, with beautiful weather, as the heir nodded and waved to us."[115]

This encounter seemed to have been a highlight for the young Yakov Yurovsky. In his unpublished memoirs, he devoted more space to its telling than to any other incident of his childhood or youth. The Romanovs had always occupied a special place in the Yurovsky household. According to Yurovsky, his father "glorified Nicholas I. I didn't think this was deserved." He remembered one particular family dinner in 1894, when he was sixteen. As usual, his father spoke long about the Romanovs and his favorite emperor, but Yakov interrupted him. "I began to argue that nothing good had happened because of Nicholas I. When something good had happened, it was only because of Alexander II. He had freed the serfs, and was not so coarse, as one heard that Nicholas had been. My father refused to listen; he threw a fork at me, and I ran out, staying away from home for two days."[116]

This particular dinner triggered the cold cynicism for which Yurovsky later became known, severing the last loyalties that bound the young man to the Russian throne. "Father thought that he had merely thrown the fork at me," he later wrote, "but in reality, he was throwing the memory of Nicholas I into the grave. He did not know that times had changed, and this was a different era. And by now, my life had taught me to know this of Nicholas II: he was a fiend, he was a bloodsucker, a killer. Finally, I came to yet another understanding; that everything was made by the hands of workers and peasants and that the Emperor was dependent on us." With an uncanny, chilling presentiment, he concluded: "We controlled their destinies."[117]

In 1897 Russia suffered a wave of violent strikes, student protests, and political demonstrations. By this time, the nineteen-year-old Yakov Yurovsky seethed with anger over his life and over the inequities around him. In a letter to his children, he wrote of his "watchmaker master, who got rich off the sufferings of his adolescent workers." He had no serious political philosophy, only a sense of injustice and the rebellious energy of youth, but this independent spirit led him to join a likeminded group of Tomsk workers. Together they planned the first strikes and demonstrations the isolated city had ever witnessed. Unaccustomed to such action, soldiers of the Tomsk garrison quickly moved in and arrested the strikers, including Yurovsky, whom they quickly identified as the leader. He served only a few months in the town prison but, on his release, he found that he was no longer welcome at his old job in the watchmaker's shop on Post Office Street, nor in any other watch or jewelry shop in Tomsk.[118]

The ill-conceived, badly executed strike made Yakov Yurovsky an outcast in Tomsk and marked him as a revolutionary in the eyes of the tsarist regime. He wandered across Siberia, and eventually settled in Ekaterinburg shortly after the turn of the century. Here, he took a position in a jeweler's shop, and it was through this work that he met his future wife, whom he married in 1904 in a traditional Orthodox ceremony.[119]

Then came the 1905 Revolution, an event that had a profound effect on the burgeoning dissident and that marked a dramatic shift in his political development. Since his youth he had harbored an innate resentment of the rigid financial and social structures that seemingly predetermined the course of his life. His was an ideology of idealism, naive, not yet hardened by war and revolution. The birth of his children, however, heightened his sense of injustice. "My children," he later wrote, "deserved a life different from the one I was forced to live, a life with freedom and hope."[120] Such sentiments led him, in the fall of 1905, to join the Bolshevik Party.[121]

At some point in these difficult years, Yurovsky took his wife and young children and fled to Europe. Information on his time outside of Russia is almost impossible to verify. His own memoirs make only the briefest mention of a few years spent living in Berlin, noting that he became proficient in German. While in Berlin he formally left the Russian Orthodox Church. This does not appear, however, to have been a complete break with organized religion, for he joined the Lutheran Church.[122] This conversion remains a mystery. Usually it has been attributed as a desire to shake off his Jewish roots, yet Yurovsky himself—whatever the ethnic antecedents of his grandparents—was baptized and raised in the Russian Orthodox Church. He had no need, therefore, to cast off one branch of the Christian faith only to embrace a second. His attitude toward religion remained decidedly ambivalent, as, indeed, it did with many revolutionaries who had been born into the Russian Orthodox Church and imbued with its overwhelming presence in their daily lives. Yurovsky himself gave contradictory expression to his own religious feelings. In a letter to his children written shortly before his death in 1938, he railed against religion, echoing the official Soviet line.[123] Yet, just three days before he shot the Romanovs, he watched in silence from a corner of the drawing room as Father Storozhov conducted a last liturgy for the prisoners in the Ipatiev

House. As the priest was leaving, Yurovsky pulled him aside and said, "It is important that one must pray, and one must save one's soul."[124] The episode remains—like the man himself—a historical enigma.

In Berlin, Yurovsky worked first as a watchmaker, then, after becoming interested in photography, took up a position in a Berlin studio, where he quickly absorbed his instructor's lessons. In time he became quite skilled, with a talented eye for composition and keen interest, which led him to abandon his former trade.[125]

Just as little is known of Yurovsky's time in Europe, so the details of his return to Russia remain a mystery. He was back in Russia in 1912, working in the underground Bolshevik movement, when Okhrana agents arrested him. Apparently, however, his involvement was minimal, and the officials lacked enough information to imprison him; instead, he was exiled to Ekaterinburg.[126] There, Yurovsky was allowed to set up his own photographic studio. In these years, his life swelled with contradictions. By day he was a husband and father, a respectable, even prosperous photographer, taking studio portraits of the city's wealthy merchants and industrialists. According to one man who knew him well, "he received business from as far away as Germany and America."[127] Yet, in the evenings, he conducted secret Bolshevik Party meetings in his studio. Having embraced the revolutionary ideals in 1905, he never looked back, convinced, as he later wrote, of "the absolute correctness of our mission."[128]

In 1915 he was drafted into the Russian army; rather than join the ranks of the ordinary soldiers, however, he signed up for medical training, and was assigned to the 198th Perm Infantry Regiment as a field hospital orderly.[129] He took part in the disastrous Carpathian campaign, one of the most bloody and destructive misadventures in the entire war.[130] This carnage hardened Yurovsky. "He lost his decency in the army," recalled one man who knew him. "Like a weather vane, he could change directions and ideas quickly; what was important the day before wasn't anymore. His moral fiber disappeared."[131] When the February Revolution erupted, Yurovsky took advantage of the chaos to desert the army, apparently taking with him a number of like-minded soldiers.[132] He returned to Ekaterinburg where, in the fall of 1917, he became one of the founding members of the Ural Regional Soviet. He was appointed deputy regional commissar of justice, and joined the Regional Cheka.[133]

Yurovsky celebrated his fortieth birthday just two weeks before he was appointed commandant of the Ipatiev House. A tall, sturdy man, with dark hair and eyes, he sported a small, neatly trimmed imperial beard, and almost habitually wore a pair of pince-nez eyeglasses. During these momentous summer days, he shared a small Ekaterinburg apartment with his family. In addition to his widowed mother and his wife there were three children—two sons and a daughter, Rimma.[134]

With his positions in both the Ural Regional Soviet and the Cheka, Yurovsky was an important man in Ekaterinburg, even before his appointment as commandant. He cut a wide swath through the city—he was friendly with many and reviled by others. Opinions varied widely. One Ipatiev House guard, who apparently liked him, later recalled: "He never learned English, or how to dance, or about music, or any other refinement, in his childhood. His school was far more severe—the school of the Revolution! Professionally, he was trained as a military hospital orderly. So Yurovsky did not have the finer things in life, but he was indisputably intelligent and capable. In fact, in his years as an orderly, he picked up quite a bit of medical knowledge, and sometimes used this to surprise doctors by making intelligent recommendations."[135]

Another witness interviewed by the White investigators, Nicholas Sakovich, served as the Ural Regional commissar of public health. He declared: "Yurovsky proved to be an efficient, honest and conscientious worker. . . . He was educated and well read enough to stand out among his colleagues and friends for his knowledge. . . . Yurovsky was kind to me, and often visited me when I fell ill." Yet he added that Yurovsky was also "a cynic to the core."[136]

Sister Agnes, mistress of novices at the Novotikhvinsky Convent, also spoke at length of the Yurovsky known to both her and her nuns:

> They found him very intelligent and very active. He did not drink, not even wine. He did not make unnecessary conversation and he was close to no one. Avdayev played at the role of an inflexible leader, but Yurovsky was one—plus he harbored in his heart an unstoppable hatred for the Imperial Family. He had a great command of language and this, together with his grace of manner, enabled him to crush anyone easily. He was possessed of a dissembling and false character. . . . Despite his good manners and the fact that he didn't drink, my novices disliked him more than Avdayev, and thought he was dangerous. He had an insatiable passion for power and importance. In contrast to Avdayev, he was not content to pay only lip service to the new regime. He loved it. And he seemed to love commanding and organizing. His world was all obedience and command, and he burned with the Red Fire, using passionate words to keep his men in line. My novices became afraid when Yurovsky replaced Avdayev.[137]

Yurovsky assumed his new post charged by the Presidium of the Ural Regional Soviet with two basic instructions. First, he was to strengthen the security surrounding the prisoners. This he did over the course of his first week, embarking, as one guard later recalled, on "a complete reorganization, a complete dis-infection" of the Special Detachment.[138]

His second task was to pave the way for the eventual executions. "At the forefront of the plans," recalled Isai Rodzinsky of Yurovsky's appointment, "was the most extreme measure, execution."[139] And Yurovsky himself later wrote: "I came to my duty knowing that I would have to take a stand on the question of liquidating the Romanovs. The Czechoslovakian forces were coming nearer and nearer the Urals. I was, therefore, to be the source who provided the answer we sought to the outstanding question of their fate."[140] Having reached their decision to assassinate the imperial family and those imprisoned with them, the Ural Regional Soviet never looked back. Goloshchokin's urgent journey to Moscow, to seek approval for their resolution, was nothing more than a charade. Even before Goloshchokin arrived in Moscow and presented the Soviet regime with the Ural Regional Soviet's demands, Ekaterinburg was determined to act.

The Yakov Yurovsky who walked into the Ipatiev House on the afternoon of July 4, 1918, bore only a faint resemblance to the thirteen-year-old boy who had waved so enthusiastically at Tsesarevich Nicholas when he visited Tomsk in 1891, or even to the idealistic young man who in 1905 had joined the Bolshevik Party in an attempt to secure a better future for his newborn son. Now the man who came to control the destinies of the imperial family was hardened—by prison, by exile, by war, by the Revolution. In his memoirs he left but a single sentence to indicate that he fully understood the extraordinary position in which he now found himself: "It was left to me, the son of a worker, to settle the Revolution's score with the Imperial House for centuries of suffering."[141]

In Goloshchokin's absence, Ekaterinburg slipped into the momentous days of July 1918. On July 3, Czech and White forces under the command of General Rudolf Gaida captured the towns of Zlatoust and Kyshtym in the Urals with little resistance; by the end of the first week of July they were fewer than fifty miles from Ekaterinburg itself, pressing closer every day. The long, low Ural horizon was dotted with distant smoke, the faint thud of artillery fire piercing the illusory quiet that hung over the city. As the second week of July began, the distant boom of enemy guns could be heard along Voznesensky Prospekt.

Day and night, a sea of soldiers—tired, hungry, disillusioned—swarmed around the railroad station in Ekaterinburg. Serge Markov, the monarchist officer who had attempted to rescue the Romanovs from Tobolsk, arrived in the city on July 1: "The station was full of traffic, all the rails were occupied by trains, among which I noticed extemporized armored trains, which had been hastily put together from iron coal trucks. Crowds of tattered soldiers were strolling about the platforms and on the lines; only the Letts, who were on guard, had a soldierly appearance."[142]

Soldiers lolled along the length of the railroad siding, the cartridge belts strung across their shoulders and around their waists jingling with every step. Fresh recruits—forced into the Red Army from the city's factories—bade farewell to families amid floods of tears. Here and there, groups of drunken soldiers staggered around, singing lewd songs and ignoring the pleas of old, bent babushkas and the wounded for a few kopecks. At intervals, trains rattled into the station, disgorging hundreds of men from their vermin-infested cars, while the wave of pistols and bayonets crowded their replacements into these goods cars, packed in on floors drenched with urine, feces, vomit, and alcohol. Shrill whistles, drunken shouts, the singsong of alcohol, the occasional crack of a rifle—these were the sounds that sent the men off, toward the thick forests of the Urals and certain death. Behind them, the walls of the station were thick with propaganda: "All to the Front!" read one poster, "To the defense of the Red Urals!" another.[143]

Yet in Ekaterinburg, life continued. Near the Ipatiev House, in the Municipal Gardens, couples still took their afternoon promenades in what passed for fashion in a city caught in the midst of the Civil War. When evening fell on Ekaterinburg, the sun slipping against the gray clouds of waste belched forth from the tall smokestacks of the factories, couples gathered to listen to a motley band, playing in the gardens by the light of strings of electric lights and hanging paper lanterns; up the hill, the faint sound of music could be heard drifting into the ragged Ipatiev House garden. In the city's opera house, with its plush velvet and gilt, performers sang Italian arias before an audience of bourgeoisie dressed in the remnants of their finery, sitting uncomfortably close to workers and factory foremen in peasant blouses and muddy boots, enduring the loud and boisterous singing of "The Marseillaise" and other half-learned revolutionary songs at the beginning and end of the evening.

The city was caught between two worlds, two times, two spheres of influence, two visions of the future. Officers from the General Staff Academy, attired in crisp uniforms, carried bundles of papers and muttered under their breath as they passed crowds of workers, usually drunk by midafternoon, engaged in revelry, boisterous singing of lewd little ditties, and loud guffaws as old babushkas and what was left of the city's merchant class picked their ways along the broad avenues and beneath the lush, green foliage of the pleached linden trees. The Revolution had yet to quite take hold; cafés and restaurants still offered caviar, smoked salmon, sturgeon, and champagne, for exorbitant prices, at tables covered with starched white cloths. The movie theater still managed to captivate occasional audiences with newsreels of the war,

British or French dramas, or American silent comedies. Deprived of their old, private clubs, businessmen warily gathered on park benches and smoked their cigars, discussing the uncertainty of life. Bureaucrats fumbled along the city streets, suspended between the Soviet-controlled government and their formal education and training, which imposed manner, form, and a fair degree of corrupt incompetence on all they did. Every Sunday, the city's churches were still filled with worshipers, as was the Annunciation Cathedral, just across the square from the Ipatiev House, its bells ringing out over the spiky wooden palisade separating the prisoners from the outside world. Across dusty Voznesensky Prospekt, a few monarchists and curiosity seekers still drifted casually along the square, stopping long enough to glance at the ornate house and its green roof, knowing that beneath it languished the former emperor and his family.[144]

Against this background, a surprising number of former officers, monarchists, and foreign agents made their way to Ekaterinburg that first week of July. In addition to Serge Markov, several British agents arrived in Ekaterinburg shortly before the Romanovs were murdered.[145] Czechoslovak spies had already infiltrated the city, visiting Allied consulates and warning them that they should fly their national flags to avoid being fired on when Ekaterinburg fell.[146] A French agent actually hid himself in the British consulate the week before the Romanovs were murdered. At 4:22 P.M. on July 9, he sent a cable that bore the stamp of the French consulate at 27 Voznesensky Prospekt to the French consul in Moscow: "Arrived Ekaterinburg, at present living at British consulate. Rumors about Romanovs false." This cable was signed, rather incautiously, "Boyar," the Russian word for an aristocrat.[147]

Princess Helen of Serbia had been forced to remain in Ekaterinburg, refused permission to continue to Petrograd to join her children. At seven on the evening of July 4, she was joined by four members of her former staff: Serb major Jarko Konstantinovich Michich; Serge Smirnov, who served the princess as master of her household; Sergeant Major Bojitchitch; and Captain Abramovich. The four went directly to the princess, who had remained in her rented rooms at the Atamanov House.[148] The following day, Michich and Smirnov requested an interview with the Presidium of the Ural Regional Soviet. At the Hotel Amerika they presented their credentials as an official delegation dispatched by the Serbian minister Spalaikovich to retrieve the princess and return with her to Petrograd.[149] Authorities in Ekaterinburg, however, decided to clarify the situation, and dispatched a cable to Petrograd asking for information. It is some indication of the difficulty in communications during that period—and particularly the unreliability of the telegraph lines—that it took four days to receive an answer. In this cable they learned that Spalaikovich's request that the princess be allowed to return to the former capital had been refused by officials at the Petrograd Cheka.[150]

Exactly how and why the Serbs thought they would manage to pull off this bit of deception remains a mystery. Presumably their intent was simply to rescue the princess from the Ural Bolsheviks and spirit her to safety, but the clumsy manner in which they attempted to deceive the Ural Regional Soviet—as inept as previous Serbian efforts to contact the Romanovs in the Ipatiev House by marching straight up to the front gate and demanding to see the emperor—doomed their mission. On July 9 a contingent of Red Guards surrounded the Atamanov House, and the Serbs—Princess Helen together with Michich, Smirnov, and the others—were arrested and confined in Ekaterinburg City Prison.[151]

These arrivals made the Ural Bolsheviks nervous. The situation in Ekaterinburg was increasingly grim. On the night of Monday, July 8, Ensign Ardatov, commander of the Ekaterinburg Red Army garrison, gathered his men and fled the city, defecting to the Czechs under the command of General Gaida. Ardatov quickly informed Gaida of Ekaterinburg's lack of proper defenses and mapped out the number of remaining troops, along with their artillery positions.[152] This defection left Ekaterinburg largely unprotected. The only remaining garrison troops belonged to a detachment formed of workers from the Verkh-Isetsk factory, under the questionable direction of Peter Ermakov. Word of Ardatov's flight quickly spread across the city; by the following morning, the widespread discontent among Ekaterinburg's citizens, which had seethed beneath the heavily armed surface, suddenly erupted. At noon an enormous mob gathered in Voznesensky Square, just opposite the Ipatiev House. Composed of Anarchists, SRs, Left SRs, starving peasants, disgruntled soldiers, angry factory workers, and the disenchanted from all walks of life, they shouted their conflicting demands—for wage increases, for food, for a renewal of the war with Germany, for the overthrow of the Bolsheviks, and for the immediate execution of the Romanovs. It took the few factory workers under Ermakov's command several hours to disperse the howling mob.[153]

The demonstration came at the worst possible time for the Bolsheviks. With Ekaterinburg doomed to fall to the approaching Czech and White troops, the Ural Regional Soviet faced the imminent evacuation of the city and the fate of perhaps the seven most important prisoners in all of Russia. Panic set in, and the Ekaterinburg Cheka made one last, dramatic sweep of the city, attempting to round up those suspected of conspiracies to help free the Romanovs. This increased paranoia almost certainly resulted in the executions of General Tatischev and Prince Vassili Dolgoruky. Tatischev, said to have been shot in late May or early June, was never identified, and Prince Dolgoruky, according to British consul Thomas Preston, managed to win his freedom and remain at liberty in Ekaterinburg throughout June. He was only arrested in July, when the Ekaterinburg Cheka searched his rooms and found two maps of the Ural region, annotated with notes on river routes, along with a considerable sum of money.[154] Both men were executed on July 10, shot some distance from the city.[155] Cheka member Gregory Nikulin later recalled how he had picked up Dolgoruky and driven him into the forest. When the prince stepped from the motorcar, Nikulin struck him down with a single revolver shot.[156]

By July 11, when the Czechs captured Irkutsk, the Bolsheviks had lost control of nearly the entire length of the Trans-Siberian Railroad; only isolated segments of a few hundred miles scattered along the three-thousand-mile track remained in Bolshevik hands. With the capture of the Trans-Siberian Railroad, Moscow lost any reliable telegraphic communication with the majority of Siberia. As the last two weeks of imprisonment for the Romanovs began, Ekaterinburg had to rely on the increasingly erratic telegraph lines that ran along the Tyumen–Perm spur of the Kotlas rail line.[157]

Only three days before the Romanov executions, another riot—the second in less than a week—erupted in Voznesensky Square. This was the "Revolt of the Evacuated Invalids," in which disgruntled Red Army soldiers banded together with Socialist Revolutionaries and Anarchists to foment discontent against the Bolsheviks. The few remaining Red Army soldiers of Ermakov's Verkh-Isetsk detachment panicked, and opened fire on the square.[158] This set the ominous tone for the days that followed: Ermakov's men roaming the city streets, shooting dozens of suspected counterrevolutionaries and even, as British vice consul Arthur Thomas recalled, shooting men heard to simply remark on Ekaterinburg's imminent evacuation.[159] The crack of gunfire mingled with the approaching artillery as night closed over the deserted city streets; the Ural Regional Soviet had imposed an early curfew on Ekaterinburg, and citizens kept to their houses, on pain of being shot.[160]

Under such conditions was the final stage of the Romanov drama enacted.

10

The Coming Storm:
Enter Yurovsky

THE FINAL SIXTEEN DAYS of Romanov captivity in the Ipatiev House began on a gray, gloomy Monday morning. The first day of July dawned warm but overcast in Ekaterinburg, an ominous beginning to the two weeks that followed. The day passed—as had so many others—in utter monotony, interrupted only by a walk from three to five that afternoon.[1] An indication of the heightened panic among the Ural Bolsheviks came the following day, as Alexandra noted in her diary: "Now Avdayev has to come morning and evening to see if we are all there. In the daytime came today to ask if I don't go out because of my health, seems committee won't believe it."[2] That evening, Dr. Derevenko paid his last visit to the Ipatiev House.[3]

A cloudless blue sky spread over Ekaterinburg as July 3 broke in the Urals. Alexandra noted the "glorious weather" in her diary that day.[4] That evening, Eugene Botkin began what was to become his last letter, written to a friend:

I am making a last attempt at writing a real letter—a letter from here—although that qualification, I believe, is utterly superfluous. I do not think that I was fated at any time to write anyone from anywhere. My voluntary confinement here is restricted less by time than by my earthly existence. In essence I am dead—dead for my children, for my work. . . . I am dead but not yet buried, or buried alive—whichever: the consequences are nearly identical. . . . My children may hold out hope that we will see each other again in this life . . . but I personally do not indulge in that hope . . . and I look the unadulterated reality right in the eye. . . . I will clarify for you the smallest episodes illustrating my condition. The day before yesterday, as I was calmly reading Saltykov-Shchedrin, whom I was greatly enjoying, I suddenly saw a reduced vision of my son Yuri's face, but dead, in a horizontal position, his eyes closed. Yesterday, at the same reading, I suddenly heard a word that sounded like "Papulya" [Dearest Papa]. I nearly burst into sobs. Again—this is not a hallucination because the word was pronounced, the voice was similar, and I did not doubt for an instant that my daughter, who was supposed to be in Tobolsk, was talking to me. . . . I will probably never hear that voice so dear or feel that touch so dear, with which my little children spoiled me. . . . If "faith is dead without works," then works can live without faith. If any of us does combine faith and works, then it is only out of God's special kindness. One such happy man—through grave suffering, the loss of my firstborn, my half-year-old boy Seryozha—was I. Ever since then my code has significantly expanded and defined itself, and in every case I have also been concerned about the patient's soul. This vindicates my last decision, too, when I unhesitatingly orphaned my own children in order to carry out my physician's duty to the end, as Abraham did not hesitate at God's demand to sacrifice his only son.

This letter was never completed. It was found among a group of papers in the drawing room of the Ipatiev House after the murders.[5]

Thursday, July 4, began like any other day in the Ipatiev House. The prisoners awoke, gathered for prayers, and then had breakfast. Unusually, there was no inspection that morning, and neither Avdayev nor his assistant Moshkin were in the Ipatiev House. The Romanovs and their retainers were just sitting down to lunch when Beloborodov, accompanied by several other men, entered the dining room. He announced that Avdayev had been replaced that morning as commandant; at his side stood Yakov Yurovsky, whom Beloborodov introduced as the new commandant, and Gregory Nikulin, who was to take Alexander Moshkin's place as deputy commandant. Both Nicholas and Alexandra recognized Yurovsky from his two previous visits to the Ipatiev House, each noting that they had believed him to be a doctor as, on the first occasion, he had accompanied Derevenko, and remained at his side examining the tsesarevich.[6]

Both Nicholas and Alexandra assumed they knew the reason for this sudden change. Nicholas, in his first diary entry in a week, wrote: "They explained that an unpleasant incident had occurred in our house, referring to the disappearance of our things."[7] And Alexandra speculated that the Ural Regional Soviet had "found out that they had been stealing our things out of the shed."[8] The change of commandant interrupted the usual routine. The prisoners' regular walk in the Ipatiev House garden was abandoned at Yurovsky's order; instead, the Romanovs were directed to gather in the drawing room at 5:00. At the appointed hour, Yurovsky, together with Nikulin, duly appeared through the double doors leading from the anteroom; in his hands, the new commandant carried a sheaf of papers. He informed the Romanovs that, on orders from the Ural Regional Soviet, they must hand over all of their jewelry. "It was my understanding," he wrote in his unpublished memoirs, "that I should collect all valuables from their hands and keep them out of sight so that none of the guards would take the risk of stealing them."[9]

Over the course of the next hour, the empress and her daughters were forced to divest their jewelry boxes and themselves of the few necklaces, earrings, brooches, and rings they had publicly kept with them. As each piece was handed to Yurovsky, the empress and her daughters provided descriptions, which Nikulin carefully noted in a ledger. "Alexandra Feodorovna," Yurovsky recalled, "made her discontent quite apparent, in a loud, clear voice, when I said I would have to take the gold bracelets from her arm."[10] These bracelets, gifts from her uncle Leopold, Duke of Albany, when she was eleven, proved to be too tight.[11] "We couldn't pull them off," Yurovsky remembered, "and she kept complaining, so we let her keep them."[12] Each of the grand duchesses was allowed to keep a single bracelet, gifts from their parents when they were children, and which were now too tight to be removed. "They were gold," Yurovsky wrote, "but of no great worth."[13]

Nicholas, too, handed over his jewelry, keeping only his engagement ring, which was too tight to remove.[14] "Neither Nicholas nor his children made their dissatisfaction apparent," Yurovsky wrote. "He asked only that Alexei be allowed to keep his watch, otherwise he was bored. I agreed to this."[15] This may have been a last effort on the part of the Ural Regional Soviet to get at the imperial jewels they knew the Romanovs had brought with them into exile. "We knew they had it from what their lady said," Isai Rodzinsky recalled, though short of instituting a search of the prisoners' clothing, the Bolsheviks had no way to get at them.[16] If Yurovsky and the Ural Bolsheviks had hoped that the Romanovs would willingly turn over their hidden jewels, however, they were disappointed. Looking at the minor collection of rings, brooches, necklaces, bracelets, and earrings produced at his request, Yurovsky knew that thousands of rubles worth of jewels remained concealed among the family's clothing. "This question," Yurovsky wrote, "haunted us like a weight around the neck."[17]

Over the twelve full days that followed, the prisoners lived under Yurovsky's increasingly cold, watchful eye, more uncertain of their

Gregory Nikulin.

fate than ever. With him, Yurovsky brought Gregory Petrovich Nikulin, a thirty-year-old member of the Ekaterinburg Cheka. Nikulin, like Yurovsky, came from working-class roots. Nikulin was a native of Ekaterinburg; his father was a bricklayer, his mother a house-wife. Nikulin attended only the first few grades of grammar school, and remained only semiliterate. He worked as a bricklayer at a dynamite factory in 1909, and kept the posi-tion through World War I to avoid compul-sory military service. When the factory closed in spring 1918, Nikulin got a position as treas-urer with the Cheka.[18]

Nikulin was tall and thin, with a lean, ascetic face and brown hair. Paul Medvedev remembered that his voice had a distinct nasal quality.[19] When she was first introduced to him, the empress recorded that he seemed "decent," in contrast to Alexander Moshkin, whom she characterized as "vulgar and unpleasant."[20] Yet behind this seemingly placid exterior lurked the soul of a true revolutionary. Nikulin adopted the revolutionary nom de guerre of "Akulov," the Russian word for "shark." At the Ipatiev House he made concerted efforts to live up to the name in an attempt to impress Yurovsky, whom he worshiped; in turn, Yurovsky doted on him, called him "Sonny," and frequently asked him to his apartment.[21]

Friday, July 5, marked the first full day of Yurovsky's rule in the Ipatiev House. Early that morning, the nuns from Novotikhvinsky Convent had brought their regular food basket to the Ipatiev House. For the first time, these were passed along in their entirety to the pris-oners, the soldiers being forbidden to remove any of the provisions for their own use, as Avdayev had allowed.[22] That afternoon, Yurovsky ordered the Romanovs to assemble in the drawing room, and brought to them all the jewelry he had taken the previous day. As they watched, he checked off each piece, placed it in a small box, and locked and sealed it in their presence. He explained that he would leave the valu-ables in their possession, but that they must keep the box in the draw-ing room, and that he himself would check each day to ensure that the seal had not been broken.[23] Yurovsky recalled that, on entering the drawing room, Nicholas would greet him, announcing, "Your package is complete."[24]

At some point after Yurovsky took over as commandant, the pris-oners received the last of the known communications signed "Officer." This was a Cheka forgery, dictated by Voikov and copied by Isai

Rodzinsky. According to the accounts of both Rodzinsky and Kudrin, a member of the guard must have handed this last letter to the empress; we do not know if the man who passed it to the empress realized that he was being engaged in a Cheka conspiracy. It read:

> The change of guard and the Commandant has prevented our writing to you. Do you know the cause of this? We answer your questions. We are a group of officers in the Russian Army who have not lost consciousness of our duty to Emperor and Country. We are not informing you in detail about ourselves, for reasons you well understand, but your friends D. and T., who are already safe, know us. The hour of deliverance is approaching, and the days of the usurpers are numbered. In any case, the Slavic armies are steadily advancing toward Ekaterinburg. They are a few versts [a verst is 0.6629 mile] from the city. The moment is becoming critical and now one must not fear bloodshed. Remember, the Bolsheviks, in the last moment, will commit any crime. The moment has arrived. We must act. Be certain that the machine gun on the lower floor will not pose any danger. Rest assured that the machine gun downstairs will not be dangerous. As for the Commandant, we will have to take him away. Await the whistle around midnight. That will be the signal. An Officer.[25]

If there was any reply from the prisoners to this letter, it has not been preserved. Perhaps, by this point, the Romanovs suspected a plot. To the Ural Regional Soviet and the Ekaterinburg Cheka, however, any reply—or further communication—was irrelevant. The genuine rescue plot—stumbled on by Avdayev—provided them with the impetus to launch a wider and, in the end, deadly plan to entrap the Romanovs and justify their eventual execution.

The weather that first week of July fluctuated wildly in the Urals. Saturday, July 6, dawned warm and bright, with intense summer sunshine; by midafternoon, Ekaterinburg was deluged with both rain and thunderstorms.[26] The rain cut through the stale, humid air and, as Nicholas noted, "it was not so oppressive in the bedroom."[27] Two women, sent from the local Soviet labor union, arrived to wash the floors in the Ipatiev House; they were forbidden to speak with any of the prisoners.[28] That evening, Yurovsky returned to Nicholas a leather case containing a watch he had found in the guardroom; it had been stolen from their trunks in the courtyard shed.[29]

Although the Romanovs requested a priest to come on Sunday, July 7, Yurovsky did not allow this.[30] The following day marked the last of the dramatic changes in the prisoners' lives. On this day Yurovsky replaced the interior guard at the Ipatiev House.[31] On his first day as commandant in the Ipatiev House, Yurovsky pulled Paul Medvedev aside and asked him to explain how Avdayev had arranged the security system. It was only then that he learned that the old guards—the very men whose behavior and sympathy for the prisoners had caused such trouble and played a direct role in Avdayev's replacement—remained at their posts. "For the present," Yurovsky told him, "you will have to perform duty on the interior posts. Later, I will request men from the Cheka to fill them."[32]

Avdayev's soldiers continued on duty, though they were immediately restricted from access to the main floor, where the prisoners lived. Guard Posts 1 and 2—the first in the entrance hall, the second in the rear hall near the bathroom—were assigned to Medvedev and the three senior guards directly beneath him: Anatoly Yakimov, Konstantin Dobrynin, and—replacing Benjamin Safonov, who was relieved of duty on July 1 due to illness—Ivan Starkov. These were the only members of Avdayev's old detachment allowed, after July 4, on the same floor with the Romanovs.[33]

Yurovsky came into the Ipatiev House charged with a complete reorganization of both the Special Detachment and the security surrounding the prisoners themselves. To this end, he himself drew up a list of rules for both the old soldiers as well as the new guards he brought in on July 8. These rules were not new; in fact, they were nearly identical to the first set of regulations formed by the Provisional Regional Soviet for Avdayev. Members of the Special Detachment were not to engage in any conversation with the prisoners, and were to report all unauthorized communication to Yurovsky personally. They were charged with keeping careful watch on the prisoners, particularly when they were in the garden, and were to ensure that they did not attempt any signaling or communication with people in the street. That such provisions needed to be repeated provides some indication of just how far the lines separating Avdayev's guards from their captives had fallen. A few of the instructions—guards were not permitted to read books or newspapers while on duty at their posts—were absurd, but the majority seem to have been directed toward Yurovsky's desire to maintain a strict hold over the Ipatiev House.[34]

When the seven new guards first appeared in the Ipatiev House, Nicholas referred to them as "Letts."[35] The term "Lett," applied correctly according to Russian usage, indicated someone from the Baltic provinces: Lithuania, Latvia, or Estonia. By 1918, however, it had come to represent nearly anyone of indeterminate European nationality who spoke a foreign language. "I cannot say why," recalled Anatoly Yakimov, "but we used to call all those men Letts. But whether they were Letts none of us knew. It is quite possible that they were not Letts but Magyars."[36] The sister-in-law of another guard later remembered what he had told her: "They spoke Russian fluently, but their religion was not the same as ours, it was the religion that the Italians, Poles and Germans have."[37]

The "Lett" detachment was commanded by Captain Adolf Lepa, of Lithuanian extraction. Under him were two brothers, Michael and Alexei Kabanov, and an enigmatic man named Soames, all from the Baltic provinces; factory worker Victor Netrebin; and two Austro-Hungarian prisoners of war, Andras Verhas and Rudolf Lacher.[38] The group was drawn from the Verkh-Isetsk factory, where they worked, personally selected from the factory battalion, as Netrebin recalled, by Yurovsky himself. He offered them "special duty" at the Ipatiev House, explaining that if they accepted, they would likely be called on "to execute the death penalty on the former Emperor."[39]

Eighteen-year-old Victor Netrebin was the only Russian member of the new detachment. Born in the small village of St. Nikolai-Pavdinsky, he left home at age fifteen and came to Ekaterinburg, where he took a job as a shop assistant. After the Revolution, he volunteered for the Red Army, and served on the notorious Dutov Front, renowned for its terrible casualties and cruelty. "It was then," he recalled, "that I first became acquainted with members of the Bolshevik Party and their ideas."[40] Little is known of Austro-Hungarian prisoner of war Andras Verhas; the life of his comrade Rudolf Lacher is better documented. Born in 1893 in a small village nestled in the Austrian Alps, he had joined the Habsburg Army in 1914 and was sent to the Carpathian Front. In 1915 he was captured by Russian troops in Galicia and sent as a prisoner of war to a labor camp in the Urals, where he spent the next two years working on a state-owned farm. After the Revolution, Lacher remained under nominal imprisonment, though he was allowed, as he recalled, "to do work and get a job provided I had authorization from the local authorities." At the beginning of 1918, the dashing twenty-five-year-old secured a job at the Verkh-Isetsk factory, largely on the strength of his linguistic talents: with so many local workers conscripted into the Red Army, former prisoners of war had been forced into the Ural factories, though unable to speak Russian or understand their new masters. Lacher, who spoke German and Russian,

Rudolf Lacher.

acted as official interpreter, rising quickly through the ranks of his comrades until he came to Yurovsky's notice.[41]

As soon as the new detachment arrived, Yurovsky ordered the members of Avdayev's old guard out of the Ipatiev House and into the Popov
House, across Voznesensky Lane. They continued, however, to man
both the exterior posts, and those posts on the lower floor of the Ipatiev
House. Deeply suspicious of these men, the very soldiers whose frater-
nization with the Romanovs—and particularly the grand duchesses—
had caused such concern, Yurovsky forbade them access to the upper
floor unless accompanied by an escort, and then only to Yurovsky's
office, just off the entrance hall, where they could constantly be
watched.[42] The new guards were installed in the basement rooms formerly occupied by the Syssert, Zlokazov, and Verkh-Isetsk workers.[43]
They ate their meals in the commandant's office on the main floor and,
as Proskuryakov recalled, "did not associate with the old guards."[44]
Guards from the old detachment soon noted this preferential treatment. "Yurovsky," Yakimov later said, "treated the Letts as equals. The
Syssert workers he treated a little better than us, and us [Zlokazov
workers], worst of all."[45]

Yurovsky, as he later wrote, "embarked not only on an organization
of the inner guard, but also a new system of guard posts and communications among the men."[46] In addition to the ten existing guard posts,
Yurovsky added another two: Post 11, at the rear of the garden, and
Post 12, in the dormer window of the attic directly above the corner
bedroom shared by Nicholas, Alexandra, and Alexei. A Russian Maxim
machine gun was placed here, trained down the length of Voznesensky
Prospekt, and the older Colt machine gun mounted in the spire of
Voznesensky Cathedral in the square opposite the Ipatiev House also
was replaced with a new Maxim, aimed directly at the southeastern corner of the prison.[47] On examining the signal system that linked the
Ipatiev and Popov Houses, Yurovsky found "that it did not function
properly, nor had it worked for quite some time. This was just another
example of how Avdayev had been lax in his duties, and completely
wrong for this kind of special assignment."[48]

At first the prisoners' lives continued normally under Yurovsky.
The nuns from the Novotikhvinsky Convent still arrived at seven each
morning, bringing baskets loaded with fresh supplies. Yurovsky soon
discovered that Avdayev had authorized regular delivery of other provisions for the prisoners—pastries, breads, produce, and fruits—which,
he later said, "appeared to me to be too abundant. I ended all of these
deliveries, except those from the Convent. I decided to do all this
because everyone in Ekaterinburg was being rationed, and therefore the
Imperial Family should be rationed like all ordinary citizens. I spoke

with the cook Kharitonov about this, warning that no one must eat more than a quarter pound of meat per day. I explained that the Emperor especially must live just as did everyone else. This made it difficult for Kharitonov to perform his duties, particularly when there was so little with which to cook."[49]

With his previous medical training, Yurovsky was curious about Alexei's condition; apparently, although they knew he was ill, no one in the Ural Regional Soviet had been told that the tsesarevich suffered from hemophilia, despite having made repeated inquiries. "I once asked Dr. Botkin what Alexei's illness was," Yurovsky said, "but he told me it was not possible to speak about it, adding that it was a family illness." Botkin dismissed Yurovsky's queries by saying, "You wouldn't be able to understand anything about it."[50]

To accommodate the prisoners, Yurovsky changed the time of the required daily roll from nine to ten in the morning. Despite this, the empress, as he recalled, "brought her typical bad temper to the situation."

"Why must we get up so early?" she asked him.

"I don't care," the commandant replied, "if you want to spend the whole day in bed. You can do what you like. But everyone must be up by ten for roll, or I'll come into your bedroom and get you up myself."[51]

Tatiana, as Yurovsky recalled, was frequently sent down the hallway by her parents to his office, "to inquire after this or that favor: what time could they walk, could we ask for a priest, could Alexei leave the house and attend church." Yurovsky found her "the most mature of the four girls," and "very much their leader."[52] Despite the new stringent security, the imperial family continued to behave as though nothing had changed. Sitting in his office one afternoon, Yurovsky heard "loud noises and shouts," and ran out into the garden where the prisoners had gathered for their daily walk. Here he found Alexei and Leonid Sednev "lighting and tossing explosive fireworks over the fence and at startled members of the guard." After some questioning he learned that Avdayev had allowed the tsesarevich to keep a box of fireworks to amuse him; Yurovsky quickly confiscated the explosives.[53]

Even Yurovsky's new guards were not immune from encounters with the imperial prisoners. During one walk, Yurovsky spotted Olga deep in conversation with Alexei Kabanov. After a few minutes, she yelled to her father, "Papa! It's our grenadier!" Yurovsky watched as Nicholas hurried over to greet Kabanov. "But I know you!" he exclaimed. "You served in my Grenadier Guards Regiment." Kabanov admitted that they had met during a review several years earlier.[54]

Nicholas, Yurovsky noted, "believed himself to be especially democratic. With his unexceptional face, he appeared to be an ordinary gentleman, simple, and I would say very much like a peasant soldier."

The empress made a less favorable impression. "She held herself especially proud," Yurovsky recalled. "It quickly became apparent that she came from a family where the women dominated the men. Even when he was enjoying a peaceful evening with his family, Nicholas knew that Alexandra Feodorovna's strong hand was over him. He always looked to her for signals when questions were posed, and always bowed to her wishes."[55]

These observations left Yurovsky conflicted. "It was impossible," he wrote, "not to hate what the Imperial Family represented, and have bitterness for all the blood of the people spilled on their behalf. Yet even with these feelings, it was difficult for me to view them in this way. One could not find such simple, unassuming, and generally pleasant people. If I hadn't been given my charge, I would have had no reason to have anything against them after I got to know them. It made my position even more difficult."[56]

Yet, if Yurovsky suffered from any pangs of conscience, he refused to let them interfere with what he clearly saw as his revolutionary duty. Each morning he arrived between eight and nine; reviewed the guard duty book for the previous evening; and received a daily report from Paul Medvedev on the Special Detachment. With each passing day, security was slowly, inexorably tightened. On July 11 Yurovsky ordered a heavy iron grate installed over the single open window in the corner bedroom. "The Empress," he wrote, "frequently stood in front of this window, where she could look out onto the square, waving at people in hopes of being seen. The guards at the post often saw her do this, and I myself went to her and told her she was forbidden to continue such behavior. She, however, refused, and to solve the problem and prevent any communication, I had the iron grate placed over the window."[57]

Despite Yurovsky's warnings, Alexandra speculated that the guards were "always frightful of our climbing out, no doubt, or getting into contact with the sentry."[58] Nicholas noted the addition of the grate in his diary, writing of Yurovsky, "We like this type less and less."[59] His growing distaste for the new commandant was quickly echoed by other prisoners. That same afternoon, Kharitonov got into a heated argument with Nikulin over the issue, while Botkin remarked sarcastically to Yurovsky, "Perhaps you think it might be good if we had bars on all our windows?"[60]

These new security measures came in the face of the chaos enveloping the city beyond the wooden palisade around the Ipatiev House. "Constantly hear artillery passing," Alexandra wrote in her diary on July 12, "infantry and twice cavalry during the course of this week. Also troops marching with music—twice it seems to have been the Austrian prisoners who are marching against the Czechs (also our former prisoners) who are with the troops coming through Siberia and not far from here now. Wounded arrive daily in town."[61] The following day she recorded ominously: "Heard three revolver shots in the night."[62]

On Saturday, July 13, Alexei was well enough to take a bath—his first since leaving Tobolsk. "He managed to get in and out alone," Alexandra wrote, "climb also alone in and out of bed, but can only stand on one foot as yet."[63] The matter of baths had, by this time, become something of an issue, as Yurovsky wrote in his memoirs: "The Romanov family took no small pleasure in having baths several times a day. The Emperor would spend hours soaking, and even had a special foaming liquid he liked to use. The strain on the house's hot water supply was intense, and we often ran short of even enough water to wash dishes. I finally had to forbid them from taking four or five baths a day."[64]

Nicholas, too, recorded the events of that day: "Alexei took his first bath since Tobolsk. His knee gets better, but he cannot yet straighten out his leg completely. The weather was warm and pleasant. We have no news from the outside."[65] This was the last sentence the fifty-year-old emperor wrote in his diary, abruptly ending what had, for him, been a methodical, forty-year habit.

Sunday, July 14, broke over Ekaterinburg with a brilliant sunrise, washing the cloudless blue sky.[66] The previous day, Yurovsky had sent one of the guards to ask Father Anatoly Meledin to return to the Ipatiev

A view of the garden of the Ipatiev House, showing the bathhouse.

House to hold a Sunday service for the Romanovs. Meledin agreed, and made arrangements with Father Ioann Storozhev to take over the liturgy in the cathedral.[67] At the last moment, however, there was a change. "At eight o'clock in the morning," Storozhev recalled, "someone knocked on my apartment door. I immediately got up and unlocked it. It turned out to be the same soldier who previously had summoned me to perform services at the Ipatiev House."

"What can I do for you?" Storozhev asked.

The soldier, according to Storozhev, "replied that the Commandant 'required' me at the Ipatiev House to say Mass. I answered that Father Meledin had already been asked, but the soldier said: 'Meledin has been replaced. They want you.' I did not ask any more questions, and said I would take Father Deacon Buimirov with me—the soldier did not object to this—and that I would be there at ten o'clock. He took his leave and went away, while I dressed, went to the Cathedral, and gathered the necessary articles for the service."[68]

Storozhev and Buimirov arrived at the Ipatiev House at ten that morning. "We had only just passed through the gate," Storozhev recalled, "when I spotted Yurovsky, watching us from the window of the Commandant's office. On entering the Commandant's room, we found the same chaos as before, dirty and desolate. Yurovsky sat behind a table, drinking tea and eating bread with butter. Another man was sleeping, in his clothes, on a bed."[69]

"Someone here asked for the clergy," Storozhev told Yurovsky. "We are here. What do you want us to do?"

According to Storozhev, "Yurovsky did not get up to greet us, but only sat and stared." Finally he said, "Wait here for a while, and then you will say Mass."

"Which liturgy should I celebrate?" Storozhev asked him. "Obednya, or Obednitsia?"

"He wrote Obednitsia," Yurovsky replied, referring to Botkin's written request, which lay on the table before him. He turned back to his tea and bread, watching as Storozhev and Buimirov began to prepare their articles and vestments. Finally he said, as if to reassure himself, "So, your name is . . . S?"

"My name is Storozhev," the priest replied.

"Ah, yes," Yurovsky answered. "Yes, good. You have already performed services here then?"

"Yes, I have," Storozhev responded.

"Yes," Yurovsky said, half muttering, "and so it will be so again for you."

"At this time," Storozhev later recalled, "the Deacon turned to me and began to insist for some reason that we must not celebrate the liturgy of Obednitsia but Obednya. I saw that this disturbed Yurovsky, and he began to examine the Deacon closely. I quickly ended this, telling the Deacon that it was necessary to do as they had requested, and that here, in this house, it was necessary to do as they had said. This apparently placated Yurovsky. On seeing that I was rubbing my hands, as if cold, Yurovsky asked me, with a hint of a smile, what was wrong. I told him that I had been ill recently, and feared that it might return. He began to share his ideas on the best way to cure pleurisy, adding that he himself had undergone an operation on his lungs. We exchanged a few more words. Yurovsky conducted himself above reproach; in general, he seemed pleasant and very correct with us."[70]

Yurovsky called one of the guards and asked him to fill Storozhev's censer with hot coals from one of the stoves; in a few minutes, it was returned to the commandant's room, and Yurovsky told the two priests to go into the drawing room, where the prisoners were waiting. He himself followed them. Storozhev recalled:

At the same time Nicholas Alexandrovich entered through the doors leading into the inner room. Two of his daughters were with him, I did not have a chance to see exactly which ones. I believe Yurovsky asked Nicholas Alexandrovich: "Well, are you all here?" Nicholas Alexandrovich answered firmly: "Yes, all of us." Ahead, beyond the archway, Alexandra Feodorovna was already in place with two daughters and Alexei Nikolaievich. He was sitting in a wheelchair and wore a jacket, as it seemed to me, with a sailor's collar. He was pale, but not so much as at the time of my first service. In general he looked more healthy. Alexandra Feodorovna also had a healthier appearance. She wore the same dress as on June 2. As for Nicholas Alexandrovich, he was wearing the same clothes as the first time. Only I cannot, somehow, picture to myself clearly whether he was on this occasion wearing the St. George cross on his breast. Tatiana Nikolaievna, Olga Nikolaievna, Anastasia Nikolaievna, and Marie Nikolaievna were wearing black skirts with white blouses. Their hair (as I recall they were all the same) had grown and now came to the level of their shoulders at the back. It seemed to me that on this occasion Nicholas Alexandrovich and all of his daughters were—I won't say in depressed spirits—but they gave the impression just the same of being exhausted. On this occasion the members of the Romanov family took exactly the same positions during the service as they had on June 2. Only now Alexandra Feodorovna's chair stood next to that of Alexei Nikolaievich—farther from the archway and a little behind it. Behind Alexei Nikolaievich stood Tatiana Nikolaievna (she pushed his wheelchair when they kissed the Cross after the service), Olga Nikolaievna, and, I think (I don't remember exactly), Marie

Nikolaievna. Anastasia Nikolaievna stood next to Nicholas Alexandrovich, who stood in his usual place by the wall to the right of the archway. Beyond the archway, in the living room, stood Dr. Botkin, a girl and three servants: one tall, another short and stocky, and the third a young boy. Yurovsky stood in the living room at the same far corner window. There was no one else in these rooms during the service. According to the liturgy of the service it was customary at a certain point to read the prayer, "Who Resteth with the Saints." On this occasion for some reason, the Deacon, instead of reading this prayer, began to sing it, and I as well, somewhat embarrassed by this departure from the ritual. But we had scarcely begun to sing when I heard the members of the Romanov family, standing behind me, fall on their knees. After the service everyone kissed the Holy Cross. Father Deacon gave the host to Nicholas Alexandrovich and Alexandra Feodorovna. (Yurovsky's agreement had been obtained beforehand.) As I went out, I passed very close to the former Grand Duchesses and heard the scarcely audible words "Thank you"—I don't think I just imagined this. . . . Father Deacon and I walked in silence to the art school building when he suddenly said to me, "Do you know, Father Archpresbyter, something has happened to them there." Since the Father Deacon's words somewhat confirmed my own impression, I stopped and asked him why he thought so. "Yes, precisely," the Deacon said, "they are all some other people, truly. Why, no one even sang." And it must be said that actually, for the first time, no one of the Romanov family sang with us during the service of July 14.[71]

The morning of July 15 marked a return to the gloomy weather enveloping the Urals that summer. An enormous storm burst over Ekaterinburg, drenching the streets until they turned to mud.[72] At seven that morning, Sisters Antonina and Maria arrived from the Novotikhvinsky Convent with their usual provisions. Yurovsky, who had arrived early, asked them to bring fifty eggs on the following day, along with a container of milk. He also passed along a note from one of the grand duchesses, asking for some thread.[73] At noon, Yurovsky handed an envelope filled with rubles to Paul Medvedev: it was payday for members of the Special Detachment, and Medvedev spent the afternoon handing out salaries as guards came on duty.[74]

At ten-thirty that morning, four women, dispatched from the Union of Professional Housemaids, arrived to wash the floors of the Ipatiev House. Recalled Maria Starodumova,

> From the Ipatiev House they sent us to the Popov House where the Guards were living. There the chief of the guards, Medvedev, ordered us to wash the floor in the command quarters and then took us to the

Ipatiev House which was called the House of Special Purpose. They took us into the yard and up the stairs leading from the lower to the upper floor. They let us into the upper floor where the Emperor was living with his family. I personally washed floors in almost every room set aside for the Imperial Family. We did not wash the floor in the Commandant's room. When we went into the house the Emperor, the Empress, and all the children were in the dining room, with the doctor, another old man, a valet with glasses, a woman, and a young boy. They were playing cards and were gay. The Grand Duchesses were laughing. There was no trace of sadness. Yurovsky was seated in a chair facing the Heir, and he was speaking to him very politely. The Grand Duchesses helped us to move their beds and chatted cheerfully to us. We ourselves did not speak with anyone of the Imperial Family. The Commandant, Yurovsky, was watching us almost the whole time. I saw him sitting in the dining room talking with the Tsesarevich, asking him about his health.[75]

"I also washed floors in the Ipatiev House with Maria Starodumova and the other women," said Varvara Dryagina. "As far as I can remember it was on Monday, July 15 of this year. The chief of the guards, Medvedev, took us into the house. In the house I saw the Emperor, the Empress, the Tsesarevich and the four Grand Duchesses, the doctor, and some old woman. The Tsesarevich was sitting in a wheelchair. The Grand Duchesses were happy and helped us to move the beds in their rooms."[76]

And Eudokia Semyonovna remembered:

Four of us were dispatched to wash the floors in the house where the Emperor and his family were imprisoned. We were happy and excited about this job, for we would be able to see members of the Imperial Family. First of all, we were to go to work in the Popov House, where the guards were living. These filthy guards had turned their quarters into a stable through tramping around in their dirty boots. We had to scrape and scrub. There were thousands of sunflower seed shells. But when we were through with our work at the Popov House, Commandant Medvedev took us across to the Ipatiev House. We entered the first floor and all of a sudden we came upon the Emperor, Empress and all their children who were in the dining room, sitting around the table as though they were having a meeting. We bowed deeply out of politeness, and they responded with friendly smiles. The Grand Duchesses got up and went with we four into their bedroom to move their beds for us. As I remember it, they were neither in the least scared, nor in the least worried. Their eyes shone brightly with fun and high spirits, their short hair was tumbled and in disorder, their cheeks were rosy like apples. They did not dress like Grand Duchesses, but wore short dresses of black with white blouses underneath, and a bit of décolletage showed. The Commandant, Yurovsky, was a snooper. For some time he stood listening at the open door, and would look in to glare at us when we exchanged jokes and pleasantries with the young Grand Duchesses. We were all cautious and spoke in low voices after that. At one time, when Yurovsky withdrew his head from the room, the smallest Grand Duchess, Anastasia, turned to the doorway and made such a face at him that we all laughed, then she put out her tongue and thumbed her nose at his back. I myself burst into laughter, but stopped myself right away. All the girls treated us simply, were friendly and welcoming. Each of their smiles and looks were a gift for us. They had been displaced from their rightful station, poor dears, but they were cheerful and not only moved furniture for us, but got on their knees and helped to wash the floor. . . . All this time we could hear Yurovsky in the dining room asking after the health of the Heir and making a consultation with the doctor. When they began to replace the beds, the Grand Duchesses took this opportunity of helping us to have some fun. I could hear them teasing each other, "Hey! You! You little peasant urchin— move that bed to the left a little—faster!" Joy showed in their eyes that afternoon. . . . The Emperor was always a figure of divinity for me, and so I thought it would be when I was in the Ipatiev House. . . . I had the chance to observe the Emperor and his wife at close quarters for half an hour. Nicholas Alexandrovich was not a giant and was not the image of God Himself, but rather was a small and drab man, somewhat smaller than his wife, and somewhat simpler than she. He did not have the air of a bad or evil man, but he appeared somewhat common. His nose was small, his forehead low, his hair sparse, and one could see a great bald patch on his skull. He was narrow in the shoulders, and his legs were too short for his body. His wife looked tired and sick, but her great pride was still apparent, and in her eyes, you could see how she suffered from this pride. On her face, you could find each of her daughters, but without their smiles and laughter. She also lacked their color, looking pallid. Poor Alexei stayed in his wheelchair or in bed the whole time we were there. His father transported him from room to room and bed to bed. When I saw the poor sick child, it gave me pause for thought: His face was the color of wax, it was transparent, and his eyes were sad with big dark circles under them. He smiled at me and giggled when I bowed profoundly to him. His sisters were spirited and breathed love of life, but he—he was no longer of this world. The Grand Duchesses had well-manicured hands, with highly polished nails, but after helping us, they were dirty and chipped. It took me no more than ten minutes to realize that they were not gods, but were actually ordinary people like us, simple mortals.[77]

Tuesday, July 16, 1918, dawned hot and humid in Ekaterinburg. Low, gray clouds hung scattered across the expansive Siberian sky, threatening the seemingly incessant rain and thunderstorms that had engulfed the Urals that summer. By afternoon, however, the weather had cleared; shafts of sunlight cut through the clouds, temporarily dry-ing the vast, muddy streets encircling the Ipatiev House.[78] Inside the prison, with its closed, whitewashed, and barred windows, the Romanovs and those incarcerated with them baked in the summer heat.

The seventy-eighth day of captivity for the imperial family began like others before it. At seven, Sisters Antonina and Maria arrived, bringing with them the fifty eggs and milk Yurovsky had requested, along with some thread for the grand duchesses.[79] Earlier that morning, guard Philip Proskuryakov had gone on duty at Post 6, at the intersec-tion of Voznesensky Prospekt and Voznesensky Lane. At about nine, a motorcar bearing the insignia of the Ekaterinburg Cheka rattled down the muddy avenue, honked its horn, and turned into the gates of the Ipatiev House; Proskuryakov caught a glimpse of Beloborodov sitting inside. A few minutes later, Yurovsky climbed inside and left toward the center of the city.[80]

When Proskuryakov's shift ended, he met up with fellow guard Igor Stolov, and, armed with their wages from the previous day, both men set off for a local tavern, where they spent the entire afternoon drinking.[81] Proskuryakov missed Yurovsky's return, at eleven that morning, as Nikulin later recalled.[82] The commandant went to conduct his daily inspection of the prisoners and to check the seal on the box of jewels in the drawing room, then bade them to take their morning walk. As usual, Alexandra remained inside, as she would for the afternoon walk, kept company by first Olga, then Tatiana. As the empress later wrote in her diary, during the walk they "arranged our medicines."[83] Thus, on the last full day of their lives, the Romanovs apparently continued to hope for a rescue attempt, organizing their possessions in the event they had to flee. At three that afternoon, a second motorcar arrived at the Ipatiev House. After picking up Yurovsky, it rattled through the muddy streets, pulling up beneath the wrought-iron canopy that sheltered the main door of the Hotel Amerika. Inside, one last, urgent meeting was taking place.[84]

Anatoly Yakimov, on duty in the far corner of the yard, watched as the prisoners paced restlessly up and down beneath the burning sun. Across the muddy stretch of grass, seventeen-year-old Michael Letemin stood smoking, stationed in the courtyard near the door to the Ipatiev House.[85] At four, when the allotted hour had come to an end, the Romanovs and those imprisoned with them reluctantly left the garden, walking across the sloped courtyard and passing Letemin as they entered the house. "I did not notice," he later said, "anything out of the ordinary with them."[86]

Both Proskuryakov and Igor Stolov were to resume guard duty that night on two of the exterior posts. When they arrived back at the Ipatiev House and went to report to Paul Medvedev, however, he saw that both were still drunk. He escorted them across Voznesensky Lane to the Popov House, shoved them into the bathhouse in the yard, and locked the door, telling them he would return and let them out after they were sober.[87]

Yurovsky returned to the Ipatiev House after seven that evening.[88] At eight, just as the prisoners were sitting down to dinner, he came into the room and asked Leonid Sednev to gather his things, explaining that his uncle, Ivan Sednev, wished to take him home.[89] "Sednev was excited, and happy to be going home," Yurovsky recalled.[90] No one in the Ipatiev House knew that Ivan Sednev had been executed nearly six weeks earlier.[91]

The prisoners were deeply suspicious. Yurovsky later wrote of "the turmoil within the Romanov Family that followed this decision. In a short time, they sent Dr. Botkin to my office, and he plied me with questions about the boy: Where had his uncle been? Where was he going? Was he not returning? I gave him the same explanation as I had told Sednev himself. Botkin seemed satisfied with this and left. Then they sent Tatiana to me. She was hysterical, asking more questions. Her brother already missed Sednev, and demanded him back. I had to calm her down before she would listen to the same thing I had already told Botkin. To ease her mind, I told her that he would return shortly. Finally, she seemed calmed, and went back to her family."[92] Despite Yurovsky's continued assurances, the Romanovs remained uneasy. "Wonder whether it's true," Alexandra wrote in her diary that night, "and if we shall see the boy again!"[93]

At ten that night, the regular change of guard shifts took place. Medvedev, the senior guard commander, was otherwise occupied, and asked Anatoly Yakimov, one of the three senior guards in the Ipatiev House, to see to the transfer. He appointed Leonid Brusyanin to Post 3, just inside the courtyard; Gregory Lesnikov to Post 4, at the exterior gates opening onto Voznesensky Prospekt; Nikita Deryabin to Post 7, in the old sentry box between the first and second palisades; and Ivan Kleshchev to Post 8, almost directly beneath the balcony overlooking the garden. Yakimov also was off duty; as senior guard, to work the scheduled four-hour shift from 10:00 P.M. to 2:00 A.M., he appointed Konstantin Dobrynin.[94]

As evening fell over Ekaterinburg, the sound of nearby artillery fire shattered the sky.[95] The White Army and Czechoslovaks stood barely twenty miles from the city, and it was only days before Ekaterinburg fell. When Arthur Thomas, the British vice consul, walked along the street before the Ipatiev House early that evening, the guards at the House of Special Purpose quickly ordered him to the other side of Voznesensky Prospekt.[96] By eight the broad avenues and sloped streets ringing the Ipatiev House were deserted following the curfew imposed by the Ural Regional Soviet.[97] From the windows of the British consulate, Thomas watched as Bolshevik soldiers moved a number of machine guns into Voznesensky Square.[98]

Within the Ipatiev House, the prisoners passed the evening quietly. For an hour after dinner, Nicholas and Alexandra sat in the drawing room, playing bezique. In their corner bedroom, the empress sat for a few minutes, methodically recording the day's events in her diary. She ended the entry with what would become her last notations: "10:30 P.M.: To bed, 15 degrees."[99] By eleven, the southern end of the Ipatiev House was shrouded in the darkness of the brief summer night.

11

Murderous Intentions

D ARK, OMINOUS CLOUDS HUNG over the Urals on the afternoon of Friday, July 12, drenching Ekaterinburg in a torrent
of rain. Streetcars and motorcars struggled along the uneven
avenues, splattered with mud cast from the hoofs of passing horses,
their mounted Red Army soldiers looking grim, guns drawn and cartridge belts jangling as they peered down streets and into doorways,
seeking out those bold enough to venture into the gray downpour.
Nerves were on edge as spies prowled the city, bands of rival revolutionaries threatened the Ural Regional Soviet's precarious hold on
power, and factory workers noisily demanded the immediate execution
of the Romanovs. Above the fringe of forest encircling the capital of the
Urals, the looming thud of enemy artillery fire sent waves of panic over
Ekaterinburg; mile by mile, the White and Czech forces drew nearer,
encircling the once proudly defiant Bolshevik stronghold.

The wind and rain were unrelenting as a stream of motorcars pulled
to a stop beneath the shelter of the Hotel Amerika's wrought-iron
canopy. Inside, past the marble floors caked in mud and up the main
staircase, their passengers filed slowly, wearily to the heavily guarded
doors opening to Room 3. With Ekaterinburg on the verge of falling to
the White and Czech forces, Goloshchokin returned from Moscow,
bringing Lenin's reply to the Ural Regional Soviet's unanimous resolution calling for the execution of the Romanovs. "We all understood,"
recalled Kudrin, "that evacuating the Emperor's family from the city,
not just to Moscow, but even along the Northern route, meant that we
would be giving the monarchists the very opportunity they had wished

for: rescuing their sovereign."[1] As rain continued to pound the city, the Ural Bolsheviks met, determined to settle the fate of the Romanovs.

For eighty-five years, what took place in Room 3 that cold, wet afternoon has formed one of the key questions in the Romanov case: Who ordered the executions? Western historians have followed the pattern as laid out by White Army investigator Nicholas Sokolov in assessing responsibility for the murders. "The fate of the Imperial Family," Sokolov concluded, "was not decided in Ekaterinburg, but in Moscow."[2] It is a view fervently endorsed by émigrés, and resurgent in post-Soviet Russian works on the imperial family, irrevocable evidence of the barbaric nature of Lenin and his Bolshevik regime. Author Robert Massie thus claimed: "From the beginning the annihilation of the Romanovs— their execution and the disappearance of their bodies—had been approved by Moscow."[3] The voices are nearly unanimous. Historian Richard Pipes: "It can be established that the final decision to liquidate the Romanovs was taken personally by Lenin, most likely at the beginning of July."[4] Edvard Radzinsky: "It was all decided in Moscow."[5] And Orlando Figes: "The evidence that has since emerged from the archives shows conclusively that the order came from the party leadership in Moscow."[6] The reality of the situation, however, was far more complex than that suggested by this simplistic reading of history.

The first official Soviet discussion concerning the eventual fate of the Romanovs came in November 1917, shortly after Lenin seized power. No decision was reached, and the question of the former emperor and his family fell victim to more pressing concerns.[7] With the Romanovs safely imprisoned in Tobolsk, Lenin gave them little thought, consumed as he was with the survival of his own regime. In January 1918, Isaac Steinberg, Soviet commissar of justice, declared in the press: "It was originally proposed to try the former sovereign, as is well known, before the Constituent Assembly. Now, however, his fate will apparently be decided by the Sovnarkom."[8] A week later, however, the Sovnarkom called for Nicholas II to be tried before a specially appointed revolutionary tribunal.[9]

The proposed trial was Leon Trotsky's idea, a grand scheme in which he himself would serve as Soviet chief prosecutor; the former lawyer was fascinated at the idea of such a spectacle. It would, he suggested, be "an open court, that would unfold a picture of the entire reign (peasant policy, labor, nationalities, culture, the two wars, etc.). The proceedings would be broadcast to the nation by radio; in the villages accounts of the proceedings would be read and commented upon daily."[10] As such, it offered the fledgling Soviet government several strong incentives. A trial would show that the new regime functioned lawfully, not as a nation adrift in a sea of anarchy, while a recitation of those crimes attributed to Nicholas II against his own people would serve as propaganda, potentially alienating any lingering vestiges of affection for the former dynasty. The verdict also would serve the Soviets; not only would Nicholas II be deemed guilty of crimes against his own people, but also, should the ultimate penalty be imposed, it would have allowed the Bolsheviks an inarguably legal manner of disposing of the troublesome former emperor.

Plans moved swiftly. At the end of January, the Presidium of the Central Executive Committee authorized Nicholas's transfer from Tobolsk to Petrograd, where the trial was to take place, and the Soviet Press Bureau announced that a tentative date had been set for April.[11] On Lenin's orders, Steinberg began to interview witnesses, record depositions, and collect evidence supporting the former emperor's guilt.[12] According to Nicholas Krylenko, chairman of the Supreme Investigatory Commission, Nicholas II would be tried only for those events that took place after signing the 1905 manifesto granting a constitution and parliament; even the Soviet regime acknowledged that the former emperor could not legally be charged with any perceived crimes that had occurred before this date, when he had ruled as an autocrat.[13]

As time wore on, however, doubts about the proposed trial grew. Lenin continued to support it as "a very good thing if it were feasible," but he warned Trotsky that "there might not be time enough" for such a lengthy show trial.[14] Lenin's worries stemmed from the growing German threat; after the signing of the Treaty of Brest-Litovsk, the kaiser's government began a series of overtures, designed both to ensure the imperial family's safety and eventually secure their release. German occupation of a third of the former empire and establishment of their own regime bought the Soviet government time; once entrenched, however, and with the Bolsheviks fast losing their fragile hold on political and military power, German demands concerning the Romanovs grew more insistent. If Berlin pressed the matter, Lenin had no guarantee he would be in any position to refuse the prisoners' release.

Against this background, Goloshchokin arrived in Moscow on the evening of July 3. With him he carried the Ural Regional Soviet's resolution seeking approval for the immediate execution of the Romanovs and those imprisoned with them. "The Ural Soviet," recalled Peter Voikov, "stood categorically for the death of the Emperor, as we told Moscow several times. We said that we had the support of the Ural workers, and the law of revolution on their side."[15] Moscow was less than receptive. Goloshchokin pleaded Ekaterinburg's case to his friend and fellow Ural Bolshevik Yakov Sverdlov, though he ultimately failed in his mission; Lenin was too busy even to meet with him.[16]

It is not surprising that Lenin should have had no time for Goloshchokin during his four days in Moscow. On July 4 the Fifth Congress of Soviets convened at the Bolshoi Theater in Moscow and rapidly disintegrated into open rebellion against the Bolshevik regime. The powerful Left Socialist Revolutionaries (Left SRs), vehemently opposed to the Treaty of Brest-Litovsk and Lenin's internal policies, used the gathering to publicly denounce the Soviet government, accusing them of having sold out the Revolution to foreign interests.[17] Things went badly for the Bolsheviks: when Sverdlov took the stage and delivered a rousing defense of Soviet policy, he was booed from the podium.[18] After calling for a vote of no confidence in the Soviet regime, the Left SRs walked out of the theater, quitting the Bolshevik government, a move that left Lenin's hold on power at its most fragile.[19]

The Left SRs used the occasion to rally support against Brest-Litovsk and Lenin's regime, but they had no intention of waiting. When, on July 6, two Left SRs assassinated German ambassador Wilhelm von Mirbach, they fired the first shots in what became an open war against Lenin's government.[20] The two assassins fled to the safety of the Popov Battalion, composed of several hundred men sympathetic to their cause, and commanded by a member of the Left SR Party.[21] Dzerzhinsky himself went to the Popov barracks, demanding the men immediately be handed over to the Cheka. Despite his threats to shoot the Left SR leaders, however, the men refused, and instead arrested Dzerzhinsky.[22] When he learned of this ominous turn of events, Lenin, according to one witness, "did not turn pale—he turned white."[23] Within a few hours came word that Martin Latsis, Dzerzhinsky's deputy, also had been arrested by Left SRs and was being held hostage in the notorious Lubyanka Prison.[24]

Lenin quickly recognized his precarious position. "Now, at any price," he told Trotsky, "we must influence the character of the German report to Berlin. The motive for military intervention is quite sufficient, particularly when you take into consideration that von Mirbach has continually reported that we are weak and a single blow would suffice"; his presentiment was correct, and within a week Germany would demand the right to station "protective" battalions in Moscow.[25] By five that afternoon, as Lenin drove through to the German embassy to express his regrets, disaster threatened: the Popov Barracks disgorged hundreds of Left SR sympathizers who, joined by disgruntled Red Army soldiers, swelled across the humid city, capturing government offices merely by walking through doors and raising their guns. At the Central Telephone and Telegraph Exchange they dispatched hundreds of cables to Soviets across the country, warning, "Stop all telegrams signed by Lenin, Trotsky, Sverdlov," and announcing that the Bolshevik regime had fallen.[26]

By nightfall the Kremlin was surrounded, the dark sky peppered with artillery flashes as the Popov Battalion and the Red Army opened fire with machine guns. As round after round of ammunition smashed into buildings and shattered windows, Lenin huddled behind its thick brick walls, a steady stream of officials running between his office and the telephone exchange, bringing increasingly desperate news. All that stood between the Left SRs and the fall of the Soviet government were the Kremlin's medieval defenses and a contingent of guards from the Latvian Rifle Division.[27] With gunfire echoing across the citadel, Lenin sent for the Latvian commander, asking a single question indicating just how perilous the situation had become: "Comrade, can we hold out until morning?"[28] Desperate, Trotsky ordered two divisions of Latvian soldiers, loyal to the Bolsheviks, into the streets of Moscow. The early-morning hours of July 7 rang with the sound of gunfire as the Latvians engaged the Left SRs and members of the Popov Battalion and the Red Army in battle. Isolated shootings continued into the morning, but by noon the Bolsheviks had recaptured all government offices and the Central Telephone and Telegraph Exchange.[29]

On the same day that von Mirbach was assassinated, Moscow learned that Czechoslovak forces had captured the important Bolshevik stronghold of Ufa. Over the next forty-eight hours, the news became increasingly worse. A Left SR rebellion erupted in Yaroslavl, with similar coup attempts in several other important cities; General Hermann von Eichhorn, commander of the German occupation army, was assassinated by a Left SR terrorist in Kiev; and General Michael Muravyev, Reinhold Berzin's deputy and commander of the Red Army's Volga Front, defected to the Left SRs, taking his heavily armed battalions and moving from town to town along the great river, inciting open rebellion against the Bolsheviks.[30] The Bolsheviks managed to survive only through sheer luck. While put down, the rebellions served as unwelcome reminders of both the widespread discontent against the Soviet regime and Lenin's fragile hold on power.

Literally fighting for the very survival of his regime, Lenin had no time during that crucial week for Goloshchokin or his demands concerning the prisoners in Ekaterinburg. Even had rebellion not erupted in Moscow and across Russia at this moment, it is unlikely that Lenin would have concerned himself with such matters. The Romanovs had never formed any part of his Revolution or its driving philosophy other than their removal from power, and he continually and pointedly ignored questions over their fate.

It fell to Sverdlov to worry over their future. He himself had gone to Lenin with Ekaterinburg's request, only to learn that he insisted on publicly trying the former emperor. "We must count up the human and material losses to the country the sovereign caused during his reign," Lenin had declared. "We must know how many revolutionaries were hung, how many prisoners died in camps, and how many men fell in a war no one wanted. He himself must answer for all of this, before his former people."[31] To this end, Gleb Boki, deputy chief of the Cheka, had just deposed Vladimir Kokovtsov, telling the former prime minister, "The Soviet Powers have decided to bring the former Emperor's actions before a Court of the People."[32] The trial was scheduled for the end of July, with Trotsky as prosecutor.[33] If Lenin's insistent position was slightly unrealistic, it also was deeply rooted in fear. Having barely survived the Left SR rebellions, the Soviet government now faced increasing pressure from imperial Germany. Just two days after Goloshchokin returned to Ekaterinburg, Berlin delivered the military ultimatum Lenin feared would follow von Mirbach's assassination, demanding that German battalions be stationed in Moscow. With the situation precarious, and in the wake of repeated German overtures on behalf of the Romanovs, Lenin could not afford to antagonize the Germans.

As Peter Voikov recalled, Lenin "still believed that the Romanovs were a great trump card in our hands against Germany." In light of the dramatic developments threatening to overwhelm his government, Lenin considered using the prisoners in negotiations with Berlin. "Several members of the Presidium," Voikov said, "were united with Lenin on one principle: the execution of the children. Lenin pointed out that when the French Revolution took place, the King and Queen were put on trial and lawfully condemned, but that the Dauphin was left untouched. Shooting the Imperial children, he said, would have a terrible impression on the foreign countries threatening us, even in such a radical crisis."[34]

Sverdlov broke this news to Goloshchokin just before he left Moscow on July 8 to return to the Urals. In the midst of this dilemma, and with Lenin completely immersed in the pressing political and foreign policy concerns threatening to overwhelm his country, Sverdlov became the voice of pragmatism. "Luckily," recalled Voikov, "we had an unshakably loyal comrade from the Urals in Sverdlov. He proved to be of the utmost assistance to us in this difficult situation."[35]

In discussions between Goloshchokin and Sverdlov, alternatives were raised. It was a foregone conclusion that Nicholas's trial would result in his death. If events in Siberia brought the Ural Regional Soviet to a dangerously precarious position, with the hasty evacuation of Ekaterinburg and the possibility of a White rescue, Sverdlov apparently suggested that Moscow might well view Nicholas's execution as an act of necessary summary justice.[36] He suggested as much when he told

Goloshchokin, "If you can organize a trial, then do it. If not . . . well then, you know what that means."[37]

Such reluctant provisional permission, predicated on the military situation in the Urals, clearly referred only to Nicholas himself. He was to be the only member of the imperial family put on trial; neither the empress, though popularly believed to have been complicit in the disintegration of the empire, nor her children, were to be implicated or charged with any crime. On this point, as he again told Sverdlov, Lenin was adamant: he vehemently opposed wholesale executions, such as that proposed by Ekaterinburg, which would include the imperial children. This, he repeated, would have a negative effect on public opinion, both in Russia, where it would concentrate discontent against the Bolsheviks, and abroad, where it would be viewed as a moral question.[38]

In Goloshchokin's absence, and on the assumption that Moscow would approve their proposal, the Ural Regional Soviet embarked on its plan. As Ekaterinburg Soviet member Paul Bykov later wrote, the Ural Bolsheviks decided the fate of the Romanovs "in the first days of July."[39] On July 4—the same day Goloshchokin arrived in Moscow—they removed Avdayev as commandant of the Ipatiev House, replacing him with Yakov Yurovsky, who, as he recalled, "came to my duty knowing" he would execute the prisoners; the order, said Cheka member Isai Rodzinsky, called for "extreme measures" against the Romanovs.[40] Four days later, Yurovsky himself brought new, handpicked interior guards into the Ipatiev House, selected, as Victor Netrebin wrote, on the understanding that they would serve as the execution squad.[41] "We in the Ural Regional Soviet," Voikov later explained, "decided this question on our own."[42]

Fewer than twenty-four hours before Goloshchokin returned to Ekaterinburg, a former mining engineer named Ivan Fesenko spotted Yurovsky, Peter Ermakov, and a man described only as a "Lett" riding in Koptyaki Forest outside the city, near an abandoned mine known as the Four Brothers; Fesenko conveniently recorded the precise moment by carving his name and the date on the trunk of a birch tree later discovered by the White Army investigators.[43] The men questioned him at length, asking if he thought a truck carrying at least five hundred pounds of grain could navigate the old roads leading through the forest.[44] As they rode back to the city, they also were seen by a local peasant, who noted the "simple carpenter's ax" in Yurovsky's hands.[45] The men had, in fact, been searching for a suitable place to dispose of the victims.

The Ekaterinburg to which Goloshchokin returned on the early morning of July 12 was poised on the edge of a volcano. With the main

railroad lines cut, and the Trans-Siberian Railroad in the hands of the
White and Czech forces, it was only days before the city itself fell.
Walking into the Hotel Amerika, Goloshchokin called an urgent meeting of the Ural Regional Presidium and leaders of the Ekaterinburg
Cheka.[46] By five that afternoon, the most important Ural Bolsheviks sat
clustered round the baize-topped table at the center of Room 3, listening with tired faces as Goloshchokin delivered a report of his visit to
Moscow.[47] "The Central Executive Committee," he nervously told his
comrades, "is not giving sanction for an execution."[48]

Certain that Moscow would approve their resolution, Ekaterinburg
now learned that Lenin supported the proposed trial. "The Ural Soviet
and the Presidium of the Communist Party," Voikov said, "therefore
stood irreconcilably divided on the issue of the shooting."[49] The men
gathered in Room 3 sat in stunned silence as Goloshchokin unsuccessfully attempted to explain Moscow's position. The crisis had come to a
head: the Ural Bolsheviks must agree to Moscow's demands, and risk
losing the prisoners to their would-be rescuers, or follow the path on
which they had already embarked, to eliminate the entire imperial family, in open defiance of the Soviet government.

It did not take these men long to make their decision. In the first six
months of 1918, Moscow's influence over the Urals had never been
strong, a point uneasily proved when Ekaterinburg forced Yakovlev's
hand and commandeered his imperial prisoners. With the signing of
the Treaty of Brest-Litovsk and German occupation of a third of the
former empire; Lenin's disastrous famine policy; increasing anarchy in
the cities; growing Red Army defeats in the Civil War; and open rebellion against the government itself, Lenin's regime appeared weaker with
each passing day. These larger Soviet struggles were entirely lost on the
Ural Bolsheviks, themselves facing imminent disaster as White and
Czech forces tightened their noose around the uneasy city. Ekaterinburg, the once-proud "capital of the Red Urals," could do nothing but
watch helplessly as the Revolution faltered.

Exhausted, suspicious, resentful, and on the verge of fleeing for
their own lives, these men had no use for the Romanovs. From the very
beginning, as Yakovlev had warned Sverdlov when faced with insistent
Ural demands, Ekaterinburg was determined to exact vengeance on its
former ruling dynasty. Complicit in the murder of Grand Duke
Michael Alexandrovich, the Ural Regional Soviet used his death to test
both Moscow's reaction and public opinion; despite the obvious and
clumsy lies of a kidnapping woven by the Bolsheviks in Perm, Moscow
neither investigated nor sought to punish those responsible. Within a
week of the grand duke's death, officials in Ekaterinburg seized on
Avdayev's accidental discovery of a concealed monarchist letter to enact

their own plot, designed to entrap the Romanovs in a compromising situation and at the same time, as both Rodzinsky and Kudrin readily admitted, provide convincing evidence on which they could justify the execution of the prisoners to Moscow. Having launched themselves on this path, they never looked back: their unanimous resolution of June 29, calling for the wholesale slaughter of the imperial family and their retainers, became their own self-fulfilling prophecy.

Nor did these men have any patience for the niceties demanded by Lenin. It was clear, Bykov later wrote, "that Moscow's vision of a trial was now out of the question."[50] Having propelled themselves into the spotlight when they seized the Romanovs, the Ural Bolsheviks were determined not to fail what they saw as both their historic duty and their revolutionary obligation, particularly to humor a regime in distant Moscow they perceived to be losing the struggle. "At the end of the meeting," Bykov wrote, "the Ural Regional Soviet decided not to obey Moscow's instructions regarding the Romanovs. It was decided not to organize a trial, as Moscow had suggested, but instead to shoot them."[51] It was, Kudrin explained, a political and military necessity: "Either we would lead the workers in the defense of Ekaterinburg and Soviet Russia, or the anarchists or Social Democrats would take matters into their own hands. There was no third option."[52]

It became only a question of how and when. The first matter was left to Yurovsky, while resolution of the second hinged on their military position. Unsure of precisely how much time they had left, the Ural Regional Soviet decided, as Bykov related, to consult "the Army Command, as to the real situation at the Front."[53] To this end they dispatched a cable to Reinhold Berzin, commander of the Northern Ural Front in Perm, seeking his opinion.[54] For ninety hours they nervously awaited Berzin's response. It finally arrived on Tuesday, July 16, and once again the men were summoned to an urgent meeting at the Hotel Amerika. In his report, Berzin predicted the fall of Ekaterinburg within "three days."[55] This news, as Kudrin recalled, was greeted with "a complete, depressed silence. Considering all of these circumstances, it was decided to act that night." During the meeting, Yurovsky suggested that Leonid Sednev should be spared. "What reason is there to kill him?" he asked his comrades. "He was only a playmate for Alexei." After some discussion, the men agreed; the remaining prisoners—Dr. Botkin, Anna Demidova, Ivan Kharitonov, and Alexei Trupp—were condemned to death along with the Romanovs.[56]

When Yurovsky returned to the Ipatiev House, he pulled Nikulin into his office and closed the door. "It's been decided," he told him. "Tonight. The city has just announced a state of siege. We have to carry out the execution tonight, execute everyone." He seemed, Nikulin recalled, "to be in a state of near-panic."[57] Trying, as he later wrote, to organize matters "very quickly, without any proper preparation," Yurovsky phoned the Ekaterinburg Military Garage, asking Serge Lyukhanov to bring a large truck to the Ipatiev House at midnight; he also asked him to find some rolls of canvas, with which they could cover the corpses.[58]

While Yurovsky busied himself at the House of Special Purpose, Beloborodov and Goloshchokin remained at the Hotel Amerika, attempting to sort through the sudden wave of havoc their decision had created. The Ural Bolsheviks had reached the point of no return. Did they now, at the last minute, seek affirmation from Lenin? Just after seven that evening, Goloshchokin dispatched a cable to Gregory Zinoviev in Petrograd: "Inform Moscow that due to military conditions which cannot be delayed, the trial agreed upon with Philip cannot now wait. If your opinion differs, inform immediately."[59]

This cable was transmitted, as Zinoviev noted in an addendum, over the "direct" Hughes telegraph line between Ekaterinburg and Petrograd.[60] Goloshchokin may have attempted to send his advisory to Moscow, but lines in the new Soviet capital were, on that day, functioning only intermittently. At one twenty-seven that afternoon, Lenin had received a cable from the Danish newspaper *National Tidende* asking if rumors that Nicholas II had been shot were true. Lenin had his secretary draft a reply denying the report, and ordered it sent just before 4:00 P.M. The reply, however, was returned to the Kremlin, with the notation "No connection."[61]

As Goloshchokin's cable arrived in Petrograd over the "direct line," no delay was involved in its transmission. Nor, given the urgency involved, did Zinoviev wait before he transmitted the cable to Moscow. In 1918, all official cables used Petrograd time as their standard. Zinoviev forwarded Goloshchokin's message to Lenin at 5:50 P.M. Petrograd time; this was 6:20 P.M. in Moscow and 7:50 P.M. in Ekaterinburg. Swift transmission, however, fell victim to erratic cable lines: it was not received in Moscow until 9:22 P.M. Petrograd time, or 9:52 P.M. Moscow time—three and a half hours after it had been sent on the direct line between the former and new Russian capitals. By the time it reached the Kremlin, it was already 11:22 P.M. in Ekaterinburg.

It has been suggested that "trial" was simply a code word for the murder of the Romanovs, previously agreed on by Moscow while Goloshchokin was staying with Sverdlov. This, author Edvard Radzinsky has speculated, explains the peculiar wording—Ekaterinburg's announcement that the "trial" could not wait.[62] This interpretation, however, rests on the assumption that Moscow had authorized the slaughter of all of the prisoners, something unsupported by the evidence. Yet there is a second possibility: that "trial" was indeed a code word, in this case not for the slaughter of the entire imperial family, but rather the elimination of Nicholas II himself. Refusing to sanction a mass execution, Moscow had allowed, should circumstances force the issue, the shooting of the former emperor. Having reached their decision in open defiance of this directive, the Ural Regional Soviet dispatched a cable so ambiguous that Moscow, anticipating only the fate of Nicholas himself, read its message as a reference to the former emperor. Such obfuscation bought Ekaterinburg time: immediately after the murders, they continued this deception in a cable that informed Moscow that Nicholas had been shot "by a decree of the Presidium of the Ural Regional Soviet" and that his family "has been evacuated to a place of greater safety." This action, they advised, had been necessary owing to both the approach of "counterrevolutionary forces" and "the discovery of a serious White Guard plot designed to rescue the former Emperor and his family," the latter a reference to their own fabricated letters designed to ensnare the prisoners.[63] With this cable, Ekaterinburg informed Moscow not that a previously agreed-upon plot had been enacted, but rather that they themselves had taken the action. The cable also indicates Ekaterinburg's deliberate deception: only Nicholas II had been killed; his family had been evacuated. Only late on the night of July 17 did the Ural Regional Soviet finally inform Moscow that, indeed, the entire family had "suffered the same fate" as Nicholas. Had Moscow ordered the slaughter of the entire family, there was no need to alert them to what they presumably already knew; linked to the cable received in Moscow earlier that morning, however, it followed a pattern of eventual disclosure of the crime by the Ural Regional Soviet, "reflecting," noted historians Steinberg and Krustalev, "perhaps confusion over what had actually occurred, or an attempt to cover up what Moscow had not intended."[64]

Did Moscow answer Ekaterinburg's query through Zinoviev? Author Edvard Radzinsky found the memoirs of Alexei Akimov, a member of the Kremlin guard who claimed that he had personally carried Lenin's message "confirming" the "decision" to execute the imperial family to the telegraph office. To Radzinsky, it "answered the question" of whether Lenin had approved the executions.[65] Though frequently cited as evidence of Lenin's complicity, the assertion is far from convincing. Akimov did not specify a date, or even a time, in his memoirs; he merely referred to "the summer of 1918." Nor did he record the telegram's content, writing only that it "confirmed the decision of the Ural Regional Soviet" to execute the Romanovs.[66] Lacking any reference to July 16, Akimov's story cannot be considered proof of Lenin's prior approval of the executions. Instead, it seems to have been sent after Moscow learned of the murders—as Akimov recalled, a telegram "confirming the decision."

It is another mysterious cable now popularly believed to have provided the Ural Regional Soviet with its answer. In his 1920 account of the murders, the famous Yurovsky note, the man who led the execution wrote: "On July 16, a cable in previously agreed-upon language arrived from Perm, containing the order to execute the Romanovs." This reference to a crucial cable stands alone; it was markedly absent from Yurovsky's 1922 and 1934 accounts. Yurovsky's claim of a cable from Perm presents an evidentiary conundrum. He himself placed its receipt on the afternoon of July 16, before six that evening when, on its strength, "Goloshchokin decreed that the order be carried out."[67] This could not have been, as most historians have suggested, an order from Lenin or Sverdlov; had this been the case, there would have been no need for Goloshchokin to send his cable to Zinoviev at 7:00 P.M. that evening, advising Moscow that Ekaterinburg could not wait. Nor, given this time frame, could it have been Moscow's reply to the Zinoviev cable.

It has been suggested that this mysterious cable came from Berzin, commander of the Northern Ural Front in Perm, who had been asked to convey Moscow's orders.[68] Yet there was no need for Moscow to have sent such an instruction to Perm; Ekaterinburg's cable was in working order.[69] If such a cable existed, clearly it was not an order from Moscow, nor their reply to the Zinoviev cable. There is, however, one possible explanation. On July 12, the Ural Regional Soviet had dispatched a cable to Berzin in Perm, asking his opinion on their situation. His answer, received on July 16, estimated the fall of Ekaterinburg "within three days." Considering this, Berzin may have urged immediate action against the Romanovs. Thus it is likely that the two cables—Berzin's reply to the Ural Regional Soviet, and the enigmatic message from Perm received in Ekaterinburg before six that evening—were one and the same, and not any order from Moscow.

Ultimately, although there is solid evidence that Ekaterinburg informed or attempted to inform Moscow of their murderous intentions, there is absolutely no evidence that Moscow cabled orders requiring that Ekaterinburg carry out the assassinations. All extant evidence points to the conclusion that Moscow may have allowed for the death of Nicholas alone, if circumstances demanded it, but not the massacre of his family.[70]

After the fact, Leon Trotsky left an account that seemingly provided Western historians and Russian émigrés with the evidence of Lenin's complicity they so desperately sought. In his *Diary in Exile*, Trotsky wrote:

The White press at one time hotly debated the question of who it was that ordered the execution of the Tsar's family. The liberals, it seemed, inclined to the opinion that the Ural Regional Committee, being cut off from Moscow, had acted independently. That is not correct. The resolution was adopted in Moscow. The affair took place during a very critical period of the Civil War, when I was spending almost all my time at the Front, and my recollections about the case of the Tsar's family are rather fragmentary. . . . My next visit to Moscow took place after the fall of Ekaterinburg. Talking to Sverdlov, I asked in passing, "Oh yes, and where is the Tsar?" "It's all over," he answered, "he has been shot." "And where is the family?" "And the family along with him." "All of them?" I asked, apparently with a touch of surprise. "All of them" replied Sverdlov, "what about it?" He was waiting to see my reaction. I made no reply. "And who made the decision?" I asked. "We decided it here. Ilyich [Lenin] believed that we shouldn't leave the Whites a live banner to rally round, especially under the present difficult circumstances." I did not ask any further questions, and considered the matter closed.[71]

This was a confident, bold statement from a man who should have known precisely what took place. And yet, on closer examination, there are serious doubts as to Trotsky's credibility on the issue. He claimed not to have been present in Moscow when this decision was supposedly reached; yet, from the official minutes of the meeting of the Council of People's Commissars, it is obvious that Trotsky was indeed in Moscow—and sitting in the same room—with both Lenin and Sverdlov at the precise moment the official announcement of the executions was made.[72] Six years after he wrote the above passage, Trotsky changed his story. It was now Stalin, he claimed, who bore ultimate responsibility for the executions.[73] By 1941 Stalin had replaced Lenin and Sverdlov as Trotsky's primary nemesis. Trotsky believed that Stalin had ordered his son killed, and remained deeply suspicious of the Soviet premier—with good reason, as it turned out.[74] Given Trotsky's habit of assigning blame to whichever Soviet official he most resented, his initial claim regarding Lenin's alleged complicity cannot be considered as the irrefutable evidence so often described by historians.

Lenin had no use for Nicholas II; his death was necessary, but it was death that would follow his public trial and predetermined guilt. Such thoughts were never extended to his immediate family. While Lenin had no difficulty in approving the executions of members of the Romanov Dynasty after the fact, as happened in the case of Grand Duke Michael Alexandrovich, no evidence implicates him in any deliberate effort to exterminate the Romanovs. Indeed, the facts speak against this theory. If Lenin had himself desired the death of all Romanovs, more than eighteen would have been killed in the Russian Revolution. Members of the dynasty in the Crimea, under the control of the Bolsheviks, were not killed but managed to leave Russia. Grand Duke Nicholas Konstantinovich, living in exile in Tashkent, was allowed a considerable degree of freedom, and died in 1918 of natural causes. Other members of the former dynasty were even allowed to leave the country. Had Lenin's desire been simply to kill every member of the Romanov Dynasty, why did he not order their immediate executions once he came to power? Why, once Nicholas II and his family were in the hands of the Ekaterinburg Bolsheviks, were they not simply killed? Why, with Lenin's permission, were Grand Duke Michael Alexandrovich and a number of others allowed great freedom in the first six months of Bolshevik power and not put to death?

The clear answer is that the wholesale slaughter of members of the Romanov Dynasty was not—and indeed had never formed—a part of Lenin's philosophical view of the new Russia. It has been suggested that in eliminating the Romanovs, Lenin was attempting to solidify the position of his own regime by removing all pretenders to the nonexistent throne. Yet, even if Lenin had been able to round up all the grand dukes and princes of the imperial blood then living in Russia, Grand Duke Kirill Vladimirovich and his son were alive in exile, as was Grand Duke Michael Mikhailovich, living in England. The only iconic and monarchist threat to the Soviet regime was represented by Nicholas, who had abdicated amid a sea of discontent and active conspiracy by members of his own family, army, and government.

One inescapable point remains: of the eighteen Romanovs who perished in the Revolution at the height of Soviet power, the greatest number—fourteen—all died at the hands, and under the control, of the Ural Bolsheviks. All evidence indicates that Lenin had nothing to do with these deaths and, indeed, attempted to prevent them. In January 1919, four Romanov Grand Dukes were awaiting execution in Petrograd. According to a well-known story, when writer Maxim Gorky appealed for mercy, Lenin refused. In fact, Gorky himself related that Lenin signed an order for clemency; the writer was on his way to deliver it when he learned that the Petrograd Cheka had presumably acted on their own authority and shot all four Grand Dukes, contrary to the instructions of the Soviet leader.[75]

12

Götterdämmerung

EVENING SLOWLY SETTLED over Ekaterinburg on July 16, the sky washed with a haze of pearl and orange as the sun gradually slipped behind the forested slopes of the Urals. Darkness comes late to the Urals in July; with the clock advanced two hours by the Bolsheviks, that Siberian summer night was particularly short, the first light of dawn piercing the horizon scarcely four hours after twilight. It was still hot; windows left open to catch a passing breeze also brought the ominous sounds of approaching enemy gunfire. Under a Bolshevik-imposed curfew, the broad avenues were empty save for a few isolated soldiers. British vice consul Arthur Thomas later recalled that, on that night, the very air seemed "heavy with a sense of impending tragedy."[1] By midnight, the Ipatiev House stood silent, shrouded in shadow; only the golden light spilling from the two tall windows of the commandant's office burned against the black night. Here, Yurovsky nervously awaited the truck that would carry the corpses of those he intended to shoot.

Earlier that evening, Yurovsky prepared for the impending executions. Although charged with seeing the murder through, Yurovsky had no practical experience in conducting such an operation, nor did anyone he consulted have any idea as how best to enact it. From stabbing or shooting the victims as they lay sleeping to throwing hand grenades in their rooms, various ideas were discussed, then finally abandoned in favor of a mass shooting. It would have been safest to remove the imperial family from the confines of the Ipatiev House, take them to some isolated spot, and there kill them. Such a plan, however, involved danger: with the White and Czech forces so close to the city, there was no guarantee that they might not break through the thin line of Red soldiers defending Ekaterinburg and interrupt the murders. There also was the possibility that if the Ural Regional Soviet attempted to move the imperial family to some isolated spot, something might go wrong, and one or more of the prisoners would escape. The success of the entire operation rested on secrecy.

In the end, Yurovsky had little choice but to kill the Romanovs in the Ipatiev House, in such a way that there was no confrontation and no chance for escape. After examining the ground floor for a suitable spot, he turned to the southern end of the house. From a small hallway, two rooms extended east, toward Voznesensky Prospekt and into the hillside. The first, reached from the hallway by double doors, had been used as a dormitory for the guards. Situated directly beneath the room used by the four grand duchesses, its southern side edged the slope of Voznesensky Lane, overlooked by a high, arched window sunk deep into the thick wall. Above the floor of yellow-painted pine boards, the walls were hung with cream and beige striped paper, topped with a burgundy frieze; being plaster, Yurovsky believed that the walls would absorb any stray bullets.[2] In the corners of the room, lath and plaster piers supported a vaulted ceiling; from its center hung the room's only light, a single electric bulb suspended from the vault. A second set of double doors opened from this room to a storeroom beyond, equipped only with a semicircular window at street level. From here, there was no exit.

For intended murders, the room was small, though not as cramped as usually claimed. Robert Wilton, who personally examined it, gave the measurements as 16 by 18 feet.[3] In time, this has itself been revised by other authors: British researchers Anthony Summers and Tom Mangold claimed that the room was 14 by 17 feet, while Robert Massie reduced this even further, to "only 11 by 13 feet."[4] In fact, as measured by both the first White Army investigators and by Sokolov himself, the room was 7.8 meters by 6.4 meters, or approximately 25 by 21 feet.[5]

Just after eight that night, Yurovsky summoned Paul Medvedev, the senior guard, to his office. "Tonight, Medvedev," he declared, "we will have to shoot them all."[6] He ordered Medvedev to collect the revolvers from all of the guards on exterior duty. When Medvedev returned, he placed the assembled collection on the desk in the commandant's office, leaving Yurovsky to sort through this arsenal with which the crime would be committed. Fourteen guns were used that night. There were six pistols: a .28-caliber (6.43 mm) Browning; a .32-caliber (7.63 mm) Browning; two .45-caliber (11.43 mm) American Colts; and two .32-caliber (7.63 mm) Mausers; and eight revolvers: a .42-caliber (10.66 mm) Smith & Wesson; four .30-caliber (7.62 mm) Nagants; and three .35-caliber (9 mm) Nagants. The most powerful weapons were the two

Mausers, with a velocity of 1,400 feet per second. Of the fourteen guns, nine—all of the Nagants and the Colts—used gunpowder to fire their bullets, causing a discharge of smoke and caustic fumes. Among them, they held a total of 103 shots.[7]

Yurovsky told Medvedev that he would have to warn the men on duty of the executions. This was to be done, however, "only at the last minute, when everything was ready."[8] The necessity of warning the guards was itself unambiguous, but the deliberate confiscation of guns from the members of the old, exterior guard, coupled with Yurovsky's instruction that they not be informed of the shootings until just before they began, indicated his clear unease over both their reliability and their potential reaction. These were, after all, Avdayev's men, the same soldiers whose friendly relationships with the prisoners had caused such anxiety among the Ural Regional Soviet. With the White and Czech Armies advancing toward the city, and Ekaterinburg under curfew, the danger was heightened. It was not the necessity for weaponry that drove Yurovsky's decision, but rather fear of how these men might react to the shootings themselves.

Aside from Yurovsky, only one other man had been selected by the Ural Regional Soviet to participate in the execution: Peter Ermakov, who, with his fearsome reputation and taste for blood, seemed an obvious choice. That evening, Beloborodov summoned Ermakov to the Hotel Amerika, announcing, "You are a lucky man. You have been chosen to execute and bury them in such a way that no one ever finds their bodies, that is your personal responsibility, which we entrust to you as an old revolutionary."[9] Thus did the brutal Ermakov, who only a few days before had assisted Yurovsky in selecting a place to dispose of the corpses, learn that he himself would help carry out the murders of the Romanovs. It was to prove a fateful choice.

It fell to Yurovsky to select the remaining members of the execution squad within a few hours of the shootings themselves. With eleven intended victims, he wanted to have an equal number of shooters, as Kudrin later explained, "so that the family would not suffer and have to witness each other's deaths."[10] Yurovsky added, "executing people is not as easy as some think. This wasn't at the Front, but in what could be called peaceful conditions. Nor were these men bloodthirsty; they were merely fulfilling the onerous duty of the Revolution."[11]

The composition of the execution squad has long remained a mystery. Usually they are identified only as the "Letts" Yurovsky brought into the Ipatiev House shortly after his appointment. Even the memoirs of those directly involved only served to further confuse the issue. In his 1920 note, Yurovsky claimed only that the squad was composed of ten shooters.[12] In neither his 1922 memoirs nor his 1934 statement did he mention a specific number, though both contained references to Ermakov, Gregory Nikulin, and Michael Kudrin.[13] Kudrin named Yurovsky, Nikulin, Ermakov, Paul Medvedev, seven Letts, and himself, while Nikulin contended that he joined Yurovsky, Medvedev, Kudrin, Ermakov, Alexei Kabanov, and two others in carrying out the murders.[14] Paul Medvedev, who consistently denied that he himself had been among the shooters, at first claimed that "ten Letts" were responsible; later he changed his story, indicating that the murders had been carried out by Yurovsky, Nikulin, two members of the Cheka, and seven Letts.[15] Medvedev's wife, Maria, however, contradicted both of his accounts, naming her husband as one of twelve men who killed the Romanovs.[16] Guard Anatoly Yakimov, who had his story secondhand, named Yurovsky, Nikulin, Paul Medvedev, and an unspecified number of Letts.[17] Andrei Strekotin, according to several guards, later claimed that the executions had been conducted by Yurovsky, Medvedev, and members of the Lett detachment, while his brother Alexander—who witnessed the shooting from the corridor—clearly recalled Yurovsky, Nikulin, Medvedev, and "six or seven others," who were unknown to him.[18]

Even with such confusion, one list of alleged shooters, in circulation for many years, is easily dismissed. This seems to have first appeared in print in the 1974 book *Letters of the Tsar's Family from Captivity*, published by the Russian Orthodox Church Outside Russia's Holy Trinity Monastery; subsequently, it often has been reproduced as the only authentic list. It named thirteen shooters: Yurovsky, Ermakov, Kudrin, Medvedev, Nikulin, Serge Vaganov, Lazlo Gorvat, Anzelm Fisher, Isidor Edelshtein, Emil Fekete, Imre Nage, Viktor Grinfeld, and Andras Vergazi.[19] This list originated with a man named Hans Johann Meyer, who forged, then attempted to sell, a number of documents, first to lawyers representing Anna Anderson, then later to the West German magazine *7-Tage*. Although exposed by a West German court in the 1960s, Meyer's forgeries have found recent favor among certain Russian historians. The idea that the murders were carried out by the mysterious "Letts" appealed deeply to many Russians, absolving, as it did, their fellow countrymen of responsibility for the crimes. The string of foreign names played on prevailing contemporary sentiment that Nicholas II and his family were killed by some pernicious alien force, while the inclusion of clearly Jewish names evoked long-standing Russian anti-Semitism and persistent rumors of ritual murder.[20]

In fact, it is now possible to accurately name the ten men who formed the execution squad. Aside from Yurovsky, they included Nikulin, Ermakov, Kudrin, Paul Medvedev, and five members of the Verkh-Isetsk factory battalion brought into the Ipatiev House on July 8: Alexei and Michael Kabanov, Victor Netrebin, a man known only as

Soames, and, almost certainly, Rudolf Lacher.[21] Of the ten, three—the two Kabanovs and Soames—were from Russia's Baltic provinces; Netrebin was Russian. As an Austrian, Lacher would have been the only truly foreign member of the squad.[22]

The Verkh-Isetsk factory battalion had been selected for duty in the Ipatiev House on the understanding that they would execute the prisoners. That night, however, Yurovsky encountered difficulties. "When I called the roll," he wrote, "a few of the Letts said they did not feel able to shoot at the girls, and refused to do it. I felt that it would be for the best to exclude these comrades from the execution so that they would not fail at that important moment in their revolutionary duty."[23] One of those who refused to shoot was, ironically, Adolf Lepa, commander of the factory battalion; the other was Andras Verhas, a Hungarian prisoner of war.[24] Having been dismissed, Lepa and Verhas fled to the Popov House across Voznesensky Lane, where the battalion commander spent the night, as Guard Michael Letemin recalled, complaining about the murders.[25]

Having selected the execution squad, Yurovsky retreated to his office, where he was joined by several members of the Ural Regional Soviet and the Ekaterinburg Cheka, including Kudrin and Goloshchokin. As the hours passed, the men sat in near-silence, nervously chain smoking and glancing at the clock.[26] At ten, the regular change of guards took place. Medvedev, the senior guard commander, was otherwise occupied, and asked Anatoly Yakimov, one of the three senior guards, to supervise the transfer. Yakimov appointed Leonid Brusyanin to Post 3, just inside the courtyard; Gregory Lesnikov to Post 4, at the exterior gates opening onto Voznesensky Prospekt; Nikita Deryabin to Post 7, in the old sentry box between the first and second palisades; and Ivan Kleshchev to Post 8, almost directly beneath the balcony overlooking the garden. Yakimov's own place as senior guard was taken by Konstantin Dobrynin, scheduled to work a four-hour shift from 10:00 P.M. to 2:00 A.M.[27]

Earlier that afternoon, Yurovsky had phoned Serge Lyukhanov, the man appointed as official chauffeur to the House of Special Purpose, and asked him to secure and deliver a truck to the Ipatiev House at midnight. Lyukhanov put in the request at the Ekaterinburg Military Garage, ordering that the truck be brought to the Hotel Amerika just before midnight. As the hour approached, Peter Leonov, chief of the military garage, filled the vehicle with gasoline. It was a one-and-a-half-ton Fiat, with a flat, open bed of wood slats measuring just 6 by 10 feet and enclosed by wooden side rails. A few minutes before midnight, Leonov asked one of his employees, Nikiforov, to deliver the vehicle to the Hotel Amerika. Apparently there was some last-minute confusion as to whether the truck should be dispatched to the Hotel Amerika or to the Ipatiev House itself, resulting in a delay. It was nearly 12:30 A.M. on the morning of July 17 when Nikiforov rumbled through the deserted city streets and pulled up before the ornate wrought-iron and glass canopy shielding the hotel's entrance. Although Nikiforov had expected to drive the vehicle, Lyukhanov ordered him out, grabbing the keys and disappearing inside, leaving Nikiforov to walk back to the garage.[28]

In the Ipatiev House, Kudrin recalled, "it was past midnight." The summer night "became cooler," quieter.[29] Every few minutes, one of the men left the office and crept down the corridor to peer beneath the closed double doors of the drawing room. Finally the lights within were extinguished, and no sound could be heard.[30] Yurovsky was increasingly impatient. "The night was short, and time was passing," he recalled. "As it dragged on, I thought that the truck would never come."[31]

At 12:30 A.M. the nervous silence of his office was shattered by the ringing of the telephone: it was Lyukhanov, saying there had been a delay, but that he would be leaving shortly.[32] Fifteen minutes passed, then thirty, then forty-five; still the truck had not arrived. Finally, just before 1:30 A.M., Lyukhanov telephoned again, apologizing for the delay, but saying that he was now on his way.[33] This was the signal for which Yurovsky had been waiting. He moved quickly, leaving his office and turning left until he stood before the closed double doors of the drawing room.

Eugene Botkin, who used the room as a dormitory, was asleep when Yurovsky knocked on the door at 1:30 A.M. "He came out," Yurovsky recalled, "and asked what was taking place. I told him that everyone had to be woken, and must dress quickly. There was, I said, trouble in the city, and we would have to take them to another, safer place."[34] Leaving Botkin to wake the others, Yurovsky retreated to his office.

Within a few minutes, through the open windows, Yurovsky heard Lyukhanov's truck; with the curfew, it was the only vehicle on Voznesensky Prospekt. The Fiat rumbled past the square and turned through the open gates of the palisade into the sloped courtyard.[35] It now became evident, as Yurovsky later related, what had transpired. Ermakov, having been told earlier that he was to take responsibility for disposing of the bodies, had attempted to circumvent delivery of the truck to Lyukhanov. An argument ensued, carried on by a noticeably inebriated Ermakov, before Lyukhanov could finally get the keys away from him and proceed to the Ipatiev House.[36]

Yurovsky told Lyukhanov to drive to the opposite side of the square, where he was to wait for further instructions. He left the Fiat parked next to the cathedral, while he himself stood in the dusty street, smoking; above him stretched the dark sky, dotted with twinkling stars.[37]

A collection of pistols remained on the desk in Yurovsky's office. Yurovsky was armed with his own Mauser, and a second gun, a Colt; Kudrin, too, had a Colt, as well as a Browning; Nikulin took the other Browning; Paul Medvedev and four of the other men took the Russian Nagants, while the sixth man took the Smith & Wesson. Ermakov had come armed with two Russian Nagants; Yurovsky handed him a Mauser, along with a Nagant. Dangerously weighted down with four revolvers, Ermakov's belt sagged, the sight, as Kudrin recalled, so absurd that "we all had to smile at his armed appearance."[38]

Yurovsky briefed the men on what would take place. Each man was assigned to a particular victim, in the hope, as Yurovsky recalled, that "everything would proceed in an orderly manner."[39] Only Ermakov, "rambling drunkenly and armed to the teeth," according to Yurovsky, would take two victims—the empress and Dr. Botkin.[40] Taking his Nagant revolver, Victor Netrebin momentarily trembled. "My position suddenly became clear," he later wrote, "and, like my comrades, I was extremely nervous at having to carry out the execution."[41]

As the clock neared 2:00 A.M., Medvedev began his rounds, warning the guards of the shootings, and adding that they would be required to work past the end of their shifts. He was assisted by Konstantin Dobrynin, one of the senior guards.[42] On hearing this, Deryabin fled his post in disbelief, running to the southern side of the Ipatiev House, where Medvedev had advised him the executions would soon take place. He took up a position outside the single arched window, through which he could clearly see the cellar room. At the same time, Ivan Starkov and Andrei and Alexander Strekotin arrived to assume their regular shifts. Starkov went directly to his post at the junction of Voznesensky Prospekt and Voznesensky Lane, having missed Medvedev's warning. Andrei Strekotin was due to relieve Ivan Kleshchev at Post 8; walking into the garden, he found Kleshchev standing in the shadows beneath the balcony. Kleshchev offered him a cigarette, and the two men stood in the darkness, smoking.[43]

Alexander Strekotin had gone to get a rifle from the large hall, directly beneath the dining room, when Medvedev appeared, a revolver in his hand. "Why do you have that?" Strekotin asked.

"We're going to start shooting them soon," he answered, then quickly disappeared.[44]

Spotting his brother and Kleshchev through the window, Alexander Strekotin motioned them inside and relayed Medvedev's message. While Andrei stood in silence, smoking his cigarette, Kleshchev "fell apart, seized with panic" at the thought of the impending executions. "This can't be!" he stammered, leaning against the window. "What can be done?"[45]

Within a few minutes, Medvedev again appeared, this time with Nikulin, and a third man Alexander Strekotin did not recognize. They went into the intended murder room, looked around, rattled the doors to the storeroom beyond to ensure that they were locked, then quickly left again, "almost at a run," back through the labyrinth of ground-floor rooms to the northern end of the house. Then, "after two or three minutes had passed," he returned, "looking grim," followed by "six or seven men." They disappeared into a small room, out of view, and closed the single door behind them.[46] "Here," remembered Netrebin, "we waited, guns in our hands, for Yurovsky to come get us."[47]

It took the prisoners some forty-five minutes to wash and dress. "I didn't want to cause them any unnecessary pain," the commandant later wrote, "so I told Botkin that they had plenty of time to get dressed."[48] While Yurovsky sat in his office, Ermakov crept down the corridor, listening through the closed doors. "I heard them walking around in the bedrooms, putting on their clothes and talking," he later recalled.[49] Just after two, they left their rooms.[50] No one seemed alarmed and, as Alexei Kabanov recalled, "no one said anything."[51] Nicholas came first, carrying Alexei in his arms. Both were dressed, according to Paul Medvedev, in field shirts, with military caps on their heads.[52] Alexandra, "skirts rustling," and leaning heavily on her cane, followed.[53] The grand duchesses came next: Olga, Tatiana, Marie, and, as Kudrin recalled, "the chubby Anastasia."[54] All wore white blouses and dark skirts, with no jackets or hats.[55] Anna Demidova held two pillows; sewn deep inside were small metal boxes containing jewelry belonging to the empress and her daughters. Dr. Botkin, Alexei Trupp, and Ivan Kharitonov followed. "Even though I had warned them through Botkin not to take anything with them," Yurovsky later wrote, "they nevertheless had collected all kinds of trifles, pillows, purses, and so on."[56] The Romanovs left their three dogs upstairs; none of the murderers mentioned the presence of the King Charles spaniel Jemmy, the English spaniel Joy, or the French bulldog Ortino during the assassinations.

Yurovsky led the group across the upper floor of the Ipatiev House and down the secondary staircase. "On the landing," Kudrin recalled, "there was a stuffed female bear with two cubs. For some unknown reason, they all crossed themselves as they passed the bears on their way downstairs."[57] As the emperor reached the bottom, he turned to his family, saying, "Well, we're going to get out of this place."[58]

They followed Yurovsky out of the double doors at the bottom of the staircase and into the courtyard at the side of the house. He opened a second set of double doors and gestured the prisoners into the basement, down a short flight of steps, through a series of hallways and guardrooms, toward the opposite end of the house. Peering out from the room where the execution squad waited, Netrebin watched them pass. "Nicholas was calm, silent," he remembered. "His wife, very thin, followed, her grey hair disheveled from being woken so suddenly. Catching sight of us, she gave us a look as if expecting we would bow as she passed." Olga, "arrogant as her mother and all skin and bones," led her three sisters, who "smiled naturally at us in their usual cheerful manner."[59]

At the southern end of the lower floor, Yurovsky opened the double doors to the cellar room selected for the murders, motioning the prisoners inside. "The Romanovs," he recalled, "had no idea what was taking place."[60] Still sleepy from being roused in the middle of the night, they entered in silence. So dim was the single electric light, Kudrin said, "that the two women standing by the closed door looked like ghostly silhouettes; only the two large white pillows held by the maid could clearly be seen."[61] The room was empty. On entering, Alexandra asked, "Why is there no chair here? Is it forbidden to sit down?"[62] Yurovsky ordered two chairs brought in, "the final thrones of the condemned Dynasty," as Kudrin noted.[63] Alexandra sat in the first, next to the arched window, while Nicholas "gently set his son in the second in the middle of the room," remembered Yurovsky, then stood "directly in front, so that he shielded him."[64] Trupp and Kharitonov leaned against the northern wall, while Botkin stood just behind Alexei. Demidova had gone to the far southeastern corner, standing against the locked storeroom doors. The four grand duchesses waited behind their mother: Tatiana, directly behind the empress; Anastasia behind her; and Olga and Marie leaning against the wall of the storeroom.[65] With all of the

The courtyard of the Ipatiev House, showing the two doors that the imperial family passed through on their way to the basement room.

intended victims before him, the room, Yurovsky noted, "suddenly seemed very small."[66]

The prisoners, Yurovsky announced, would have to wait until the arrival of a truck; he then disappeared.[67] Before the commandant closed the doors and exited the room, Kudrin took a quick glimpse back over his shoulder: "The Romanovs were completely calm, no suspicions."[68] As if on cue, Alexei Kabanov remembered, "they all faced the door."[69]

Yurovsky found Ermakov, and sent him across Voznesensky Prospekt to summon the truck.[70] Goloshchokin had disappeared; Ermakov found him standing with Lyukhanov, pacing back and forth as Goloshchokin smoked.[71] On Ermakov's instructions, Lyukhanov hopped into the cab, driving the Fiat across the prospekt and through the open courtyard gates. Because of the steep slope of the courtyard, he decided to back the truck through the gate, leaving it at the top of the incline beneath the archway; once loaded, he worried that the weight of the corpses would prevent the truck from making its way back up the incline and out the gate. This meant that the bodies would have to be taken from the murder room, at the opposite, southern end of the ground floor, through the labyrinth of basement rooms, up a short flight of stairs, out into the courtyard, then carried some forty feet up the incline to the waiting truck. Once in position, Lyukhanov gunned his engine, as Yurovsky had ordered, in an attempt to muffle the shots within the basement.[72]

In a few minutes, Yurovsky, having checked on the truck, returned to the lower floor, where he collected the members of the execution squad and led them into the corridor, before the closed double doors shielding the Romanovs.[73] There was "complete silence," followed by "the roar of Lyukhanov's engine in the courtyard." The Fiat was so loud, Yurovsky remembered, that the glass in the windows "rattled in its frame." It was 2:15 A.M.[74]

Yurovsky opened the double doors and quickly stepped into the room. The executioners followed, crowding around and peering over his shoulder at the scene. "Nicholas II, the empress, and Botkin," Kudrin recalled, "stared at us, watching us closely. We were new faces, unfamiliar to them." Nikulin moved in to Yurovsky's left, standing directly in front of the tsesarevich; on the other side of Yurovsky stood Kudrin, then Ermakov, opposite the empress.[75] These four men formed the first rank of the execution squad; the rest of the group, remembered Alexei Kabanov, "stood in the doorway, and had to fire over the shoulders of the men in front of us."[76] Peering over his comrades' shoulders, Netrebin spotted Alexei, "sickly looking and waxy," staring out "with wide, curious eyes" at the men. "I suddenly thought, how very short his sad life had been," Netrebin wrote, "and I silently prayed we would all be good shots."[77]

The basement murder room in the Ipatiev House, showing sections of plaster removed by White Russian investigators.

"I ordered the prisoners to all stand," Yurovsky wrote.[78] The empress, "with a flash of anger in her eyes," as Kudrin recalled, pulled herself erect.[79] With everything ready, Yurovsky faced Nicholas, who viewed him curiously. "In view of the fact that your relatives continue their offensive against Soviet Russia," he declared loudly, "the Presidium of the Ural Regional Soviet has decided to sentence you to death."[80]

"Lord, oh, my God!" Nicholas stuttered. "Oh, my God! What is this?" As he turned to face his family, a cry arose from the back of the room: "Oh, my God! No!" No one seemed to understand what was taking place. "So we're not going to be taken anywhere?" Botkin asked.[81]

Nicholas, as Nikulin recalled, "could not even grasp what was happening."[82] Instead, he turned around and said to Yurovsky, "I can't understand you. Read it again, please."[83]

Irritated, Yurovsky again read from the crumpled paper he clutched in his hand. The others now understood, and the empress and Olga began to cross themselves.[84] Nicholas, however, seemed frozen. He looked at Yurovsky and repeated again, "What? What?"[85]

"This!" Yurovsky answered, pulling out his pistol. His finger caught the trigger, and, with a flash of smoke and a deafening noise, the first bullet smashed into Nicholas's chest. "He reeled suddenly," remembered Andrei Strekotin.[86] In an instant his khaki tunic exploded in blood, as "all ten people firing" took direct aim at their former emperor.[87] "I shot Nicholas," Yurovsky later wrote, "and everyone else also shot him."[88] Kudrin, who opened fire the same instant as Yurovsky, squeezed off five rounds in rapid succession, each ripping into Nicholas, who, Strekotin remembered, "stood quivering as shot after shot pierced his body."[89] Three of these wounds, to the left side of his chest, were, in and of themselves, fatal, tearing through Nicholas's rib cage, into the pericardial cavity, into his heart, and exiting out his back.[90] With "wide, vacant eyes," Alexei Kabanov recalled, "Nicholas lurched forward and toppled to the floor."[91]

Everyone had aimed directly at Nicholas, contrary to Yurovsky's instructions that the men should shoot at specific individual victims. "No one seemed to understand my meaning," the commandant recalled, "and I couldn't stop them once it began."[92] Without doubt, each man standing in the cellar that night had come to kill Nicholas, to fulfill the vengeance of the Russian people. Shooting down the helpless women, sick tsesarevich, and faithful retainers offered no personal satisfaction or revolutionary glory. This instinctual firing had another effect: all of the first shots were directed to the center and left, northern side of the room, where all of the men stood.

"Women's screams and moans" rose over the sound of the gunfire. The executioners were so closely crowded into the double doors that they themselves were injured in the shooting. "One of the soldiers," Kudrin recalled, "was wounded in the finger and the neck, either from a ricochet, or from a bullet fired by the men behind, who could not see through the thick smoke from the guns."[93] As Yurovsky continued to fire, "bullets from the men behind flew past my head," the noise reverberating in his ears.[94] "There were so many arms with revolvers pointing ahead," Alexei Kabanov recalled, "that those standing at the front suffered burns from the shots of their comrades behind."[95] Above the deafening echo of gunfire, Yurovsky "tried to shout my intent, but the shooters took too long to understand my words."[96]

As the men continued to fire, the shooting, as Yurovsky recalled, became "increasingly disorderly," with "bullets flying about the room" and the air growing thick with smoke.[97] "My hope that the wooden wall at the back would hold the bullets," he remembered, "was immediately proved wrong, causing disaster."[98] Unable to take proper aim, confused by the victims' cries and barely discernible shouts from their leader, those standing in the open doors to the corridor held their guns high, shooting not victims but into the walls; ripping through the striped wallpaper, they hit plaster, sending "dust flying in the air," and "ricocheting around the room like hailstones."[99]

Within seconds of Yurovsky's first shot, the cloud of smoke was so thick that only legs could be seen, stumbling back and forth beneath the haze. The shouts, horrified screams, and incessant firing mingled into a cacophony of death. "No one could hear anything," Yurovsky remembered.[100] With bullets flying, panic set in, and the execution squad fired randomly, shooting through clouds of smoke and dust at vague shadows, barely visible in the dim light cast by the single electric bulb.[101] "It was complete chaos," Netrebin remembered.[102]

Bullets that missed Nicholas hit Botkin, Kharitonov, and Trupp. Botkin, standing closest to the emperor, took two shots to the abdomen: one bullet lodged against his lower lumbar vertebrae, the other in the soft tissue of his pelvis. Though injured, the devoted doctor turned toward the body of the emperor, only to be hit by a third bullet, fired at his legs. It shattered both his kneecaps, breaking his legs, and Botkin, unable to stand, crashed forward onto the floor.[103]

With the first shot, Trupp turned from the execution squad toward the northeastern corner of the room; two bullets, fired in rapid succession, struck his left thigh, shattering his femur and breaking his leg. Unable to stand, Trupp crumpled to his knees; seeing him beneath the thick layer of smoke, one of the executioners in the first row took aim, firing a bullet into the right side of his head. Smashing through his skull, it killed him instantly. Kharitonov, standing against the northern wall, was hit with several bullets at once, the force so powerful, Yurovsky recalled, that he "sat down and died."[104]

"Only a few shots," Strekotin recalled, "had been aimed at the far corner of the room."[105] The women first stood in place, frozen with fear; then, as bullet after bullet tore across the room, huddled together in the southeastern corner, screaming for help that never came. Drunk and consumed with his own lust for blood, Ermakov turned from Nicholas to Alexandra, who, he recalled, stood "only six feet away."[106] He raised his Mauser as she turned her head away and began to cross herself; before she could finish, as Andrei Strekotin recalled, he pulled the trigger.[107] A bullet slammed into the left side of her skull, a spray of blood and brain tissue exploding from her right ear as the force drove her violently back, knocking her onto the floor.[108] Above, peering through the heavy grating covering the window, Konstantin Deryabin watched in horrified silence.

At the rear of the room, Marie broke away from the group of girls and "began to hurl herself against the closed door of the storeroom," pounding against it and rattling the knobs. Hearing her frenzy, Ermakov stepped away from the center of the room. His Mauser now empty, he grabbed a second gun from his belt and aimed beneath the veil of smoke. His bullet struck her in the thigh and, as Kudrin recalled, "she fell suddenly" to the floor.[109] In the farthest corner, Anna Demidova turned her back as the shots began to fly wildly around the room. "Through the haze of smoke," Kudrin remembered, "a white pillow moved in the far corner." Seeing this, one of the assassins aimed low, under the cloud of smoke: the bullet caught Demidova in the upper left thigh, breaking her bone and sending her sprawling to the floor.

"The smoke was so thick that it blocked out the single light," Strekotin recalled.[110] Overwhelmed with the combination of plaster dust and thick, noxious smoke from the guns, Yurovsky, as he recalled, "was forced to stop the shooting, which had become haphazard."[111] The assassins stumbled from the room, eyes stinging and lungs full of toxic fumes from the gunpowder, leaving behind a room filled with writhing, screaming victims.

The doors to the corridor were thrown open, to clear the murder room of its toxic fumes. A few of the assassins, overwhelmed by the gases and the carnage, fell against the corridor walls, coughing and crying; Kudrin saw Paul Medvedev, doubled over and trembling, "deathly pale and vomiting."[112] Seconds ticked away as they waited for the smoke to dissipate; standing in the hall, the men heard "moans, screams, and low sobs" from within the still-foggy cellar room.[113]

"We had," Yurovsky wrote, "to go back in to finish the operation."[114] Pushing through the men, he led Kudrin, Nikulin, Ermakov, and Alexei Kabanov back across the threshold. "Everything was confused," Kabanov recalled, "chairs turned over, blood, people moving about."[115] Only Nicholas, Alexandra, Trupp, and Kharitonov had perished in the first volley.[116] When Yurovsky entered the room, he saw Botkin, covered in blood, leaning on his right arm as he tried to raise himself from the floor. He stepped across the pool of blood spreading from the emperor's body, held his Mauser close to Botkin's head, and pulled the trigger. The bullet ripped through the doctor's head, exiting out the lower right side of his skull, its force slamming his body against the floor in a shower of gore.[117]

At the center of the room, Alexei sat rigid in his chair, "terrified," as Yurovsky recalled.[118] His "ashen face," Netrebin remembered, was spattered with "his father's blood."[119] Nikulin, Yurovsky vividly wrote, held his Browning pistol "in quivering hands" as he stood before the thirteen-year-old, firing off five bullets in quick succession until there was nothing left: he had spent his "entire cartridge clip."[120] Yurovsky fired the last bullets from his Mauser directly into the tsesarevich, who slowly slipped from his chair and crumpled to the floor.[121] Paul Medvedev, who had staggered back into the room, saw Alexei on the floor, "moaning and alive."[122] Out of bullets, Yurovsky yelled to Ermakov, who turned back to the center of the room, pulling an eight-inch, triangular bayonet from his belt as he stumbled over the growing pile of arms and legs.[123] Crouched on the floor, he raised the knife; over and over, the glint of steel flashed in the dim electric light as he stabbed the supine boy, blood flying from the blade with each arc and seeping across the once-yellow floorboards. Yurovsky watched in horror as Alexei struggled against the powerful, wild Ermakov: "nothing seemed to work," Yurovsky wrote. "Though injured, he continued to live."[124] None of the assassins knew that, beneath his tunic, the tsesarevich wore a shirt wrapped with jewels, which shielded his torso from both bullets and Ermakov's bayonet. Finally, "unable to stand by," Yurovsky pulled his second gun, a Colt, from his belt, pushed Ermakov aside, and fired two shots into the boy.[125]

The room was again filled with thick smoke, the light barely cut through the haze, illuminating the horrific scene. Bodies lay crumpled on the floor, half concealed by the fallen chairs, pillows and purses surrounded by a lake of brain tissue and urine.[126] Blood was everywhere: spattered across the pale, striped wallpaper, spotting the faces of the assassins, and seeping across the floor in "a mass as thick as liver," as Paul Medvedev remembered.[127]

Huddled in the corner, Olga, Tatiana, and Anastasia all remained alive and unhurt, having escaped the hail of gunfire; following Yurovsky's last shot, their agonized screams filled the deafening silence.[128] The men fired at them through the smoke but, as Yurovsky recalled, "they wouldn't die."[129] With bullets flying around the room, Olga and Tatiana "wrapped their arms around each other," the commandant later wrote.[130] Yurovsky and Ermakov stepped over bodies at the front of the room, slipping in "the miasma of death" spread across the floor; seeing them coming, the two young women "crouched on the floor" next to the storeroom door, "covering their heads with their arms" and "screaming and crying."[131]

With the two men nearly upon them, the two grand duchesses struggled to get to their feet. Yurovsky, standing behind Tatiana, aimed his Colt and fired.[132] The bullet tore into the rear of her head; it ripped through her skull instantly, blowing out the right front of her face in "a shower of blood and brains" that covered her screaming sister.[133]

In an instant, Ermakov, "wild-eyed and face spattered with blood," moved forward.[134] As Olga tried to rise, he violently kicked her back, sending her spinning toward the floor; at the same time, he squeezed the trigger of his Nagant revolver. With a flash of smoke, the bullet caught her as she fell, just beneath her chin, breaking her jaw as it seared through her skull, lacerating her brain before smashing through the top of her forehead. In a second, she toppled across her sister, dead.[135]

Kudrin and Kabanov, both standing in the open door to the corridor, looked across this scene of carnage and saw "flashes of white, barely visible through the smoke," from the far corner of the room.[136] "It was the Emperor's two youngest daughters," Kabanov wrote, "suddenly alive and crying out for help."[137] Marie, only wounded in the leg, had fallen to the floor in front of the storeroom door, hidden with Anastasia when Demidova and her pillows collapsed against them.[138] Hearing their terrified screams, Ermakov turned from the lifeless body of their eldest sister, rounding on them with his blood-stained bayonet. Kabanov watched as he grabbed Marie, "stabbing her in the chest over and over again."[139] Yurovsky looked on in horror as Ermakov attacked her, but "the bayonet would not pierce her bodice."[140] She was, Yurovsky wrote, "finished off" with a shot to the head.[141]

Anastasia had backed into the corner next to the storeroom door. Ermakov turned on her, slashing frenziedly "through the air" as he approached.[142] Drunk and crazed, he struck the pier, his bayonet slicing deeply into the plaster, before drawing back the blade and plunging it into Anastasia's chest as she struggled to fend him off. In an increasing spiral of savagery, he swung his knife repeatedly, unable to penetrate her bodice. "Screaming and fighting," Yurovsky wrote, she fell only after Ermakov put his gun to her head and pulled the trigger.[143]

Yurovsky and Ermakov had reached the open door to the corridor when, as Kudrin recalled, "something white moved in the corner." It was Anna Demidova, who had fallen in a faint after being shot in the leg. "Thank God!" she screamed. "God has saved me!"[144] She tried to get to her feet, but Ermakov, bayonet held high, reached her, swinging out in delirium. "She grabbed it with her hands," Kabanov remembered, "screaming and crying."[145] With her hands sliced to ribbons and unable to defend herself, finally she, too, fell still.

The room was quiet, the screams and cries and echoes of gunfire silenced by death. In a mad frenzy, Ermakov, bayonet glistening, stumbled drunkenly around the room, stabbing viciously both at any perceived movement and out against those he hated most. Reaching the lifeless body of the emperor, he brought the bayonet down with such vengeance and force that he drove the blade through the sternum, cracking the bone and pinning Nicholas to the floor.[146] Turning to the empress, he stabbed her in the stomach and chest; one blow was so powerful that it cracked her ribs and chipped her spine.[147]

Yurovsky and Kudrin moved about the room, taking pulses. Yurovsky, in 1922, wrote, "after checking again to see that all were dead, I ordered the men to start moving them."[148] The entire executions had taken fewer than ten minutes.[149]

Across Voznesensky Lane, a peasant named Victor Buivid had left his apartment in the basement of the Popov House just after two in the morning; feeling ill, he stood in the garden, vomiting. In a few minutes, he heard "muffled volleys, about fifteen. These shots were not from rifles. They came from the Ipatiev House, and they had a muffled sound, as though they were from the basement." In a few minutes, this was followed by "three or four individual shots." Fearing the worst, Buivid quickly fled back inside.[150]

Others, too, had heard the shooting. Paul Medvedev, sent by Yurovsky to the Popov House to collect men to carry the bodies to the waiting truck, was in the middle of Voznesensky Lane when another "two or three shots" were heard from within the basement. A number of guards, including Dobrynin and Ivan Starkov, ran up to him, questioning him as to what had happened, and then disappearing to tell their comrades.[151] Very quickly, these men filled the basement of the Ipatiev House. As they encountered members of the assassination squad, they erupted in anger, shouting accusations of "Murderers!" and "Butchers!" Three members of the exterior guard then on duty—Lesnikov, Kleshchev, and Deryabin—were so upset, as they later told Anatoly Yakimov, that they fled their posts; a forth, Brusyanin, on seeing the murder room, was so overcome by the sight of the bloodstained bodies that he ran screaming from the Ipatiev House.[152] Ermakov passed a few of these men along the corridor, which, as he recalled, was "full of soldiers. Some of them got sick at the sight of so much blood and had to go out again."[153]

Yurovsky ordered the men to carry the bodies out to the truck. "We noticed," he later said, "that there was blood everywhere. I immediately ordered them to get some khaki cloth, and spread it over the rear of the truck."[154] Onto this, the bodies would be laid.[155] By this time, Peter Voikov had arrived from the Hotel Amerika. He stepped into the basement room and immediately recoiled: "Bodies lay in an appalling jumble," he recalled, "eyes staring in horror, clothing covered in blood. The floor was slick and slippery as a skating rink, with blood, brains, and gore."[156]

In the courtyard, Kudrin saw Goloshchokin, who warned him that he had been walking in Voznesensky Square and clearly heard the shots and screams from the basement. As they passed the secondary staircase, the two men saw Ortino, Tatiana's bulldog, whimpering at the top. The dog rushed down the staircase in search of his mistress. A nearby soldier grabbed a bayonet, impaled the quivering body, then heaved it into the rear of the Fiat. "A dog's death to dogs!" Goloshchokin commented.[157]

No one had given any thought as to the best way to remove the victims. Before he left, Yurovsky had told Kudrin to simply wrap them in some blankets and carry them through the basement to the Fiat in the courtyard. They began at the front of the murder room, working their way back, starting with Nicholas himself.[158] Alexander Strekotin watched as the men struggled with the heavy bundle, Kudrin following closely behind.[159] After the first few bodies, the blankets were drenched in blood. When the corpse of Dr. Botkin was placed within the blanket, it simply slipped from their hands with a thud back onto the floor.[160] Someone, Yurovsky recalled, "suggested stretchers. We removed the poles from a sleigh in the courtyard, and stretched a sheet between them."[161] The sheets, as Kudrin later wrote, were affixed to the poles using ropes.[162]

With the operation under way, Yurovsky told Kudrin to supervise the removal of the bodies.[163] He himself disappeared upstairs, into his office, closing the doors behind him.[164] The events of the night had clearly proved too much for him to bear; a few minutes later, he was found lying on his sofa, a cold compress across his forehead.[165]

Both Yurovsky and Kudrin stated unequivocally that they checked the bodies for signs of life and found none.[166] If so, this must have been a very quick—and ultimately flawed—procedure: after this had been done, several of the intended victims were still alive. Ten minutes after the shooting had finally ended, as the bodies were being carried out of the Ipatiev House, one of the daughters, Strekotin recalled, "was picked up. She cried out and covered her face with her hands. Another daughter also was alive. They couldn't shoot anymore, because a guard had come running in from the street saying that the shots could be heard from all over the neighborhood."[167] Voikov, standing in the corridor, saw one of the grand duchesses "spit blood from her mouth; strange, guttural noises came from her." Seeing this, he immediately got sick and ran from the room.[168]

The men were terrified. The nerves of several of the soldiers gave way completely, and they ran from the scene, vomiting or seeking refuge from the shattering wails coming from the bloody bodies. "Ermakov," Strekotin recalled, "took a rifle with a bayonet, and started stabbing frenziedly at all those who were still living." Once again, the bayonets failed to penetrate the bodies, but Ermakov continued to thrust repeatedly, finally turning the rifle around and using the butt to smash at the quivering bodies until the screams stopped.[169] "It was our dishonor," Voikov later said, "that they did not all fall quickly, but had to suffer through such terrible deaths."[170]

In Kudrin's absence, a few of the soldiers began to pilfer from the bodies. Andrei Strekotin later confessed to Philip Proskuryakov that he had joined in the looting, stealing a watch from Botkin.[171] Lacher, searching the pockets of the emperor's tunic, found his distinctive cigarette holder.[172] Kudrin walked in on this scene: "Red Guards taking rings and bracelets and watches from the corpses and putting them into their own pockets."[173]

Kudrin ran up the secondary staircase, shouting Yurovsky's name; he found the commandant standing in his office. Quickly, he informed Yurovsky of what was taking place below. "I realized," Yurovsky later said, "that apparently they had brought many of their valuable things with them."[174] For a moment, Yurovsky was uncertain what to do. Then, with determination, he ran back to the murder room and demanded that anyone who had taken personal articles from the corpses immediately hand them over. "After refusing," he recalled, "two of the men returned the valuables they had taken. I threatened to shoot anyone else caught looting, and expelled the two men from the house."[175]

Kudrin, however, warned that more men had been involved. "Alone myself," Yurovsky later wrote, "I decided on the spot to gather everyone that was there. Nikulin and I called everybody to my office and demanded that they turn over everything they had taken."[176] This included the shooters, Kudrin, and, as Strekotin recalled, those members of the guard who were on duty, including himself, and who had run to the room as soon as they heard the shooting.[177] Beneath them, temporarily abandoned, were the corpses, some lying wrapped in sheets in the rear of the Fiat truck, some curled in bloodsoaked blankets in the corridor, and still others lying in crumpled heaps where they had fallen. According to Kudrin, only Serge Lyukhanov and Goloshchokin remained by the truck; inside the basement, old exterior guards wandered among the bodies, overcome with shock.[178]

Once they were gathered in his office, Yurovsky addressed the men: "All of you who took valuables from the Romanovs must put them on my desk. You have thirty seconds to consider it. Then I will search you all. If anyone has kept anything, I will have them immediately shot." Soon, Kudrin recalled, "a pile of gold appeared on the desk: diamond brooches, pearl necklaces, wedding rings, diamond stickpins, and gold pocket watches."[179]

"We just wanted something," a few of the men offered, "a reminder of the event."[180]

In the darkened courtyard of the Ipatiev House, the Fiat truck waited with its grisly cargo. "I went down to the truck and counted the bodies again," Kudrin noted; "all eleven were in place—and I covered them with the free end of the cloth."[181]

Finally, Yurovsky appeared in the courtyard. "Though I had hoped," he later wrote, "that I would be able to turn over the further work of the night to Comrade Ermakov, it had become clear to me that he would not be able to carry this out in an orderly fashion. So I decided to go with them. Nikulin I left behind, to explain what had happened to the guards who had not been on duty and did not know what had taken place."[182] He climbed into the cab alongside Ermakov and Lyukhanov.[183] In the rear of the truck, as Yurovsky recalled, were "three people from the interior guard."[184] In addition to Soames and Lacher, significantly this included Verhas, one of those who, only an hour before, had refused to open fire on the women and children.

Lyukhanov started the Fiat's engine, and slowly the truck eased its way up the sloping drive and out of the Ipatiev House courtyard onto Voznesensky Prospekt. It passed down the broad, deserted avenue, bereft of all traffic. Night watchman Peter Tsetsegov, stationed half a mile down Voznesensky Prospekt from the Ipatiev House, heard the approach of the truck as it rumbled through the city; before it reached him, it turned off, in the direction of Verkh-Isetsk and Koptyaki Forest. Tsetsegov glanced at his watch: it was exactly 3:00 A.M.[185]

13

The Four Brothers

T HE FIAT TRUCK SWUNG out of the Ipatiev House gates and turned right, "through the sleeping city with the remains of the Romanovs," as Kudrin recalled. Yurovsky, Ermakov, and Lyukhanov were squeezed together in the cab; in the rear, armed with rifles and crouched in pools of blood, uncomfortably close to the mound of protruding arms and legs, were Soames, Lacher, and Verhas.[1] Flimsy wooden side rails along the bed of the truck shielded the heap of bodies, preventing them from rolling off as the Fiat twisted and turned through the city.

From the Ipatiev House, the Fiat rolled onto Voznesensky Prospekt, turned right on Voznesensky Lane, and followed the steep hillside as it descended to Lower Iset Pond, its placid surface reflecting the dark sweep of sky above. A left turn brought the truck onto Yakova Street; it followed the embankment to Moskovskaya Prospekt, turning right along the broad avenue and across the earthen dam spanning the pond. A mile west, where the road divided, the Fiat turned onto Isetsky Road, rumbling past the racetrack toward Verkh-Isetsk. It took Lyukhanov some fifteen minutes to maneuver through the dark city and into the suburbs of Ekaterinburg.

The one-and-a-half-ton Fiat contained a sixty-horsepower engine, adequate enough for ordinary purposes, but now under heavy pressure from the enormous weight the vehicle carried. Three men sat in the cab, eleven victims lay in the rear of the truck, along with the three guards. The total combined weight of these seventeen people—living and dead—must have been at least twenty-two hundred pounds. This weight caused the truck to struggle, and the engine began to overheat.

It was running hot and loud, and as the Fiat passed through Verkh-Isetsk, the roar of the engine awakened a young boy just before 3:30 A.M.[2] As they passed the darkened factory, Yurovsky turned to Ermakov and asked if he had brought all of the necessary equipment to dig a proper grave. Still drunk, Ermakov could only mumble apologetically that he had a shovel; perhaps someone else, he suggested, could bring something with them. "It was thus obvious," Yurovsky later wrote, "that the entire operation had been placed in the hands of the wrong man. I was determined to see the operation successfully completed myself."[3]

A mile and a half beyond Verkh-Isetsk, the road skirted the shore of Upper Iset Pond, passing the Zlokazov factory before turning northwest and heading out of the industrial suburb and into Koptyaki Forest, where it stretched the twelve miles to the small village of Koptyaki, at the edge of Lake Iset. Just before entering Koptyaki Road, Lyukhanov maneuvered the Fiat over the Perm railroad line, at Grade Crossing 803, without any difficulties. A quarter mile beyond, however, the truck reached Grade Crossing 187, with its sharper incline over the Kungursk line. The Fiat struggled as Lyukhanov coerced it up the slope, but on reaching the top the wheels sank between tracks, refusing to move. Overheated and weighed down, the truck struggled as Lyukhanov gunned the engine; gears began to grind, and a wisp of steam rose from beneath the hood as the truck finally lurched over the line and down onto Koptyaki Road, its engine growing increasingly hot.[4]

Here, Koptyaki Road abruptly changed from a paved, well-traveled artery to a narrow, rutted road of unevenly compacted earth; the rainstorm of July 15 had left the road pocked with enormous stretches of mud and pools of black, stagnant water concealing perilous holes. In the gray shadows of the early dawn, they passed fields hung with low mist, haystacks standing like sentinels against the growing light. The Fiat bounced roughly over the uneven surface, jolting the three men squeezed inside the cramped cab. A few times, the wheels sank into deep ruts, and the men had to get out and push the vehicle back onto the roadway; the engine itself became so hot that Lyukhanov twice had to turn it off and let the truck rest before they could continue.[5]

When the journey resumed, Lyukhanov dared not push the truck's fragile engine; they traveled through the forest, Yurovsky later recalled, at five to seven miles an hour.[6] "Somehow," Ermakov wrote, "it took us nearly two hours to travel the ten short miles."[7] As the truck reached Grade Crossing 185, where an overgrown road led north to a series of abandoned copper mines and industrial works, it came upon a group of mounted guards, armed with rifles, with half a dozen open carts. "What is this?" Yurovsky asked Ermakov.

"Oh, these are the men who have come to help us out," he explained, saying that these were his comrades from Verkh-Isetsk.

"But why so many people?" continued Yurovsky. "And why all of these carts?"

"I thought the Romanovs would be brought here alive," Ermakov confessed. "They were to finish them off." In anger, he added: "I didn't know we'd be bringing them in their hearse."[8]

The men quickly galloped toward the Fiat, surrounding it and peering inside. "We thought you would deliver them to us alive!" the men howled. "And now look at them, they're dead!"[9] The discovery that they were not to have the honor of killing the Romanovs, Yurovsky recalled, "quickly settled in disappointment on their faces, then anger."[10]

Followed by this mounted detachment, the Fiat continued down the muddy road for just over a mile, until it reached Grade Crossing 184, in a large, open clearing fringed by the dense forest. Here the road was crossed by the Gorno–Uralsk Railroad line, extending north into Koptyaki Forest to the abandoned mines and works. As Lyukhanov attempted to cross the old railroad line, the Fiat again stalled. He barely managed to drive the vehicle over the slight rise and back down onto the roadway.[11]

Nearly a mile beyond, the Fiat sank into a muddy patch of roadway in a clearing known as Pig's Meadow; Lyukhanov gunned the engine, but a burst of steam from the radiator brought his efforts to an abrupt halt. The truck was not only stuck, but its engine dangerously over-heated. At Yurovsky's order, Ermakov's men unloaded the corpses from the rear of the truck, tossing them in the long, dew-covered grass. Even freed of its cargo, the truck's engine was still too hot; with each attempt to extricate the vehicle, it sunk deeper into the mud.[12]

Vassili Lobukhin, the guard at Grade Crossing 184, was roused from his sleep by an insistent banging on his door. It was Lyukhanov, asking for water for his radiator; he also asked if Lobukhin had anything the men could use to extricate the truck. The guard directed him to a pile of railroad ties stacked against the side of the hut. Ermakov's men took these and laid them across the road, forming a bridge over the mud, then pushed as Lyukhanov gunned the engine. With a roar, the truck eased out of the depression and up onto the platform of ties, and the corpses were loaded into the bed.[13]

It was now nearly four-thirty in the morning; it had taken ninety minutes for the truck to travel the seven miles to Grade Crossing 184. Nearly two miles past Lobukhin's hut lay Grade Crossing 183, where Koptyaki Road was crossed by deeply rutted forest tracks leading west to Lake Melkoye and northeast to an old copper works. Just beyond this crossing, Ermakov directed Lyukhanov off the road across a small clearing; here the trees parted, disclosing a narrow, overgrown road disappearing into the forest beyond.

The sky above was already suffused with daylight as the truck turned into the sleeping forest. Within half a mile, however, the road narrowed as it passed between the trunks of two tall pine trees; as Lyukhanov tried to maneuver the Fiat, it slipped sideways and spun itself off the uneven, muddy road. He tried to gun the engine and pull the truck back onto the road, but suddenly the air was filled with grinding and the splintering of wood as the Fiat again slipped, lodging itself firmly between the trunks of the two trees.[14]

Uncertain what to do, Yurovsky asked how much farther it was to the abandoned mine. Ermakov thought it was perhaps another mile west, although he himself appeared confused; several disused tracks disappeared into the forest ahead. Together with Ermakov, Yurovsky borrowed horses from the members of the Verkh-Isetsk detachment and set off down one of the trails, hoping to find the intended destination, but to no avail. In a few minutes they returned to the clearing, where the Fiat lay at an angle. With the truck lost to them, Yurovsky ordered Ermakov's men to unload the bodies and place them in the open carts they had brought. As the men began to transfer the corpses, a few began to prod at them, ripping at the blouses of the grand duchesses and touching imperial flesh. First one, then another, saw, concealed beneath the women's clothing, flashes of diamonds and other jewels, visible through the rips and tears in bodices. Quickly, as Yurovsky recalled, "they began stealing these things." Seeing this, Yurovsky pulled out his revolver, waving it in the air and threatening to shoot anyone caught stealing from the victims.[15]

This brought the operation to a temporary halt. There was, Yurovsky recalled, "much grumbling, and the men complained they had been deprived of executing the Romanovs." Now Yurovsky had to worry not only over the disposal of the corpses, but also the behavior—and, as he later confessed, the "potential revolt"—of Ermakov's men. To solve this dilemma, he ordered another search for the intended burial place. He and Ermakov would again go off in one direction, but he also ordered the Verkh-Isetsk detachment to conduct searches, in an effort "to separate them from the troublesome corpses." The remaining soldiers from Verkh-Isetsk were ordered back through the forest and out onto Koptyaki Road, to stand guard and turn back anyone they might encounter. Before he himself rode away from the clearing, Yurovsky pulled Lyukhanov and the three soldiers from the Ipatiev House aside, warning that they were to stand guard over the bodies. They were not to allow the men from Verkh-Isetsk near them; if anyone attempted to approach, these men were to open fire on them.[16]

Four miles away, dawn broke over Koptyaki, on the edge of Lake Iset. The village was no more than a collection of wooden dachas scattered between the placid edge of the lake and the encircling forest of pine and birch, home to the twenty families who lived here, "engulfed in the primeval remoteness of the Ural backwoods," as Nicholas Sokolov would later say. They were farmers, supplementing their incomes with fresh fish from the lake and game from the surrounding forests, gathered and taken to market in Ekaterinburg.[17]

This Wednesday morning of July 17, Natasha Zukova left Koptyaki Village with her son Nicholas and his wife, Maria, their cart loaded with freshly caught fish from the lake. Hoping to get the best price at the Ekaterinburg market by arriving early, they departed just after 5:30 A.M. Some three miles along the road, they were surprised to see a group of Bolshevik soldiers, some standing, some with wagons, and some on horseback. Spying their approach, two of the mounted guards quickly turned their horses and galloped down the road to meet them.[18]

Natasha Zukova recognized one of the men as Stephan Vaganov, a former sailor, and a worker from the Verkh-Isetsk factory. With his pistol raised in the air, he shouted, "Turn back! Turn back!" He pointed the gun at the terrified group of peasants, waving them back toward Koptyaki. Natasha Zukova asked no questions; turning her cart, she raced back along the muddy road, Vaganov and the other mounted guard following closely for half a mile, guns in the air. Just once did she turn her head again, only to be met with Vaganov's shout of "Don't turn around, or I'll shoot you!"[19]

As they approached the tiny hamlet, the Zukovs encountered Feodor Zvyorgin, a neighbor who had just set out for Ekaterinburg. They warned him of the guards on the road ahead, and he, too, turned around. When they reached Koptyaki, Nicholas Zukov ran through the streets, screaming, "Get out! Run! They are bringing weapons out here! The troops are coming!"[20]

A few of the villagers decided to investigate, and silently crept back along the road. They encountered no soldiers but, in the clearing where the old road disappeared into Koptyaki Forest, they noticed tree limbs bent back, the long meadow grass crushed by the obvious weight of some conveyance that had passed into the woods.[21] Suddenly they heard hoofbeats approaching from Koptyaki Forest, and a mounted detachment of soldiers appeared, armed with revolvers, rifles, hand grenades, and even a sword. In answer to their questions, one of the soldiers explained, "The front has been entered. We're merely scouting and practicing. But don't be afraid if you hear shots." As the group turned back toward Koptyaki, they thought they heard the sounds of several explosions in the distance.[22]

While Vaganov and his comrades from the Verkh-Isetsk detachment were thus engaged, Yurovsky and Ermakov continued their futile search. Drunk and confused, Ermakov "could not find the spot," and Yurovsky, "weary and angry," returned to the clearing just as one of the Verkh-Isetsk parties thundered down a distant tract. "We've found a shaft!" one of them cried. Yurovsky ordered that they finish loading the corpses; they lay scattered among the bed of the Fiat, the carts, and on the wet floor of the forest meadow, eyes open and staring, features twisted in death and covered in dried blood, the entire macabre scene bathed in the brilliant early-morning light.[23]

The carts set off, Yurovsky promising Lyukhanov they would return and help him remove the Fiat "within a few hours."[24] Threading their way through the forest, the Verkh-Isetsk men led the cortege along a narrow, twisting trail, overgrown with weeds, deeper and deeper into Koptyaki Forest, until the trees finally parted to reveal an expansive meadow surrounded by a shield of tall trees. As Yurovsky looked closer, he spotted a group of peasants crouched around a bonfire near one of the open shafts. "Evidently," he later recalled, "they had been mowing hay in a nearby meadow, and spent the night here."[25]

"I ordered the group to get up and leave the area immediately," Yurovsky later wrote, "telling them that the Czech troops were in the forest, and that shooting was likely to erupt without warning." According to Yurovsky, they quickly grabbed their few belongings and fled the scene, "a look of terror in their eyes."[26]

The men had arrived at the Ganina Works, some eleven miles northwest of Ekaterinburg and just under two miles from the village of Koptyaki. Yurovsky and Ermakov, in fact, had previously scouted the mine only a week earlier, when they had been spotted by several men. The area took its more evocative name of the Four Brothers from four ancient pine trees that had once grown near the shafts; by July 1918, only two stumps remained. The clearing had previously been mined for iron ore; mounds of clay and earth lay abandoned near the mouths of the pits and shafts. The two open pits had caved in; Yurovsky found them filled with accumulated rain and runoff from the surrounding, marshy ground. There were, however, two shafts. The first, a small, narrow channel some thirty-six feet deep, was lined with wooden planking and divided by a wooden wall. During the mining operation, one side of the shaft had been used for descent, the other for pumping the constant flow of water. The second shaft was larger, a shallow opening extending into a pool of black water nine feet below the ground. The entire area, neglected and covered with weeds, was isolated, hidden from view by the surrounding forest.[27]

It was nearly seven in the morning by the time the cortege reached the Four Brothers. The pearl-colored sunrise had long since faded into a sky washed with the deep blue of the Siberian summer. The arrival of these men shattered the silence of the abandoned clearing. Suddenly there were shouts, the sloshing of boots across the muddy grass, horses neighing and snorting in the early morning as the men began to move the corpses from the carts to the clay surface surrounding the two shafts. The peasants who had fled the scene had left their fire from the previous night; cold and tired from their searches, the men crowded around in an effort to warm themselves.[28] No one had thought to bring any wood to burn, and the few branches collected from the surrounding forest were soaked from the recent storm.

A few of the men from the Verkh-Isetsk detachment began to circle the corpses, crouching down and pulling at the bloodstained clothing to get a better look, as Yurovsky recalled, at "the damn valuables the Romanovs had hidden beneath their clothes." This invasive curiosity gave Yurovsky the excuse he had been seeking since encountering the group. "Ermakov's men," he later said, "were all wrong for this kind of operation, and there were too many of them. I decided to send them all away, because it would be impossible to continue our mission with them there. If they remained, everything could have been ruined."[29]

Turning to the group, he shouted, "Young men! This isn't going to be a big job. You must leave now."

There followed "further grumbling, but I told them that they must return to the city, where undoubtedly they had many important tasks to attend to. It was most important that they leave at once. I knew only a few of them, and didn't know if they could be trusted." Yurovsky kept, as he later recalled, only five men at the mine to assist him.[30] In addition to Ermakov and the three members of the Ipatiev House interior guard this included Kudrin, who had arrived from Ekaterinburg.[31]

Alone with these five men, Yurovsky ordered the corpses stripped. He recalled that valuables were found on the bodies of Olga, Tatiana, and Anastasia, but not on the body of Grand Duchess Marie. "I was not surprised by this," he later wrote, "because once again, it reflected her disgraced position in the Romanov Family at the end."[32] Kudrin, too, later remembered finding valuables on only three of the grand duchesses.[33]

From around Alexandra's waist, Yurovsky pulled several long strands of pearls wrapped in silk; there also was a large, thin strand of gold, wrapped in a coil, hidden beneath her clothes.[34] Around the necks of the empress and her daughters they discovered amulets containing miniature portraits of Gregory Rasputin and the text of a prayer.[35] The jewels—diamonds, sapphires, emeralds, rubies, necklaces, brooches, and bracelets—concealed beneath clothing and hidden in the pillows carried by Demidova—weighed approximately seventeen pounds.

Yurovsky collected them, to be handed over later to the authorities in Moscow.[36]

Once the corpses were stripped—"completely naked," as both Yurovsky and Kudrin recalled—the bloody clothes were burned in the nearby fire.[37] As Yurovsky explained in 1934, he supervised the destruction of all of the bloody clothing "so that there would be no clues if for some reason the corpses were ever found."[38] Morning painted a grisly portrait: the pile of naked corpses, stiff from rigor mortis, lay on the muddy ground, torsos, arms, legs, and hands pierced with bayonet wounds, faces smashed and hair smeared with dried blood, eyes staring and mouths open in the twisted cries of death. One by one, the men dragged them to the edge of the larger shaft, casting them into the black water at the bottom.[39] Yurovsky had assumed that this shaft was as deep as its neighbor; now, as body after body piled one atop the other, he realized it was "very shallow," stretching no more than ten feet below the surface.[40] The water, which he had hoped would swallow the corpses, instead stood in a stagnant pool only three feet deep.[41] It "scarcely covered" the first few bodies, while those above were completely untouched.[42]

In despair, Yurovsky attempted to blow up the shaft, hoping to cover the bodies with debris. A few grenades were tossed down the hole, but did no more than rip into the corpses at the top, sending a shower of dirt from the upper walls of the shaft into the murky water below.[43] "In the process, a few pieces were torn off," Yurovsky recalled.[44] "Nothing," according to the luckless commandant, "was working. It was obvious that we had to find another place for them, but where?"[45]

Ganin's Pit at the Four Brothers, as collapsed by the Bolshevik grenades.

Uncertain what to do, Yurovsky ordered the top of the shaft covered with brush and dirt, in a feeble effort to conceal the twisted arms and legs protruding above the surface.[46] Leaving the three men from the Ipatiev House to stand guard, he decided to return to Ekaterinburg and seek advice on how to proceed. It was just after 9:30 A.M. when the group left the Four Brothers and made their way back through the forest toward Koptyaki Road.[47]

Yurovsky was back in Ekaterinburg by noon; apparently some of Ermakov's Verkh-Isetsk men had already reported on events in the forest, and Yurovsky was himself summoned to an emergency meeting of the Presidium of the Ural Regional Soviet.[48] He stood before his comrades and, as he later recalled, admitted that "things were not good."[49] The meeting proved to be an unpleasant experience; Isai Rodzinsky cryptically recalled, "I can't imagine that they didn't demand a full explanation of things from him."[50] A few minutes into the session, Yurovsky later wrote, "it became obvious how things were going to be settled," Yurovsky recalled. "I explained that I needed to find another place where we could completely dispose of the bodies. Beloborodov and Safarov gave me no answer. After a while, Goloshchokin himself took me aside and warned that I had to dispose of the corpses in a different way."[51]

As Yurovsky prepared to leave, he saw Ermakov standing in the corridor, "red-eyed" and looking "more disheveled than usual; apparently the previous night had finally caught up with him."[52] With some reluctance, Ermakov entered Room 3 in the Hotel Amerika; Yurovsky could hear the ensuing argument, during which Ermakov was "soundly berated" for his failure to conduct the operation as agreed.[53] "What a comrade he was!" recalled Isai Rodzinsky. "He was very provincial, and boasted that he knew everything, knew how to hide things, but no one bothered to ask him where he intended to conceal the bodies. He did not work for us, but instead among the suburban authorities, who apparently decided that he would know more about the countryside and how to go about things there. That was why he was used, but the results, as we quickly learned, were terrible!"[54]

Yurovsky himself faced further, unpleasant questions about the events of that night: Beloborodov had warned him that he was to report immediately to the Executive Committee of the Cheka.[55] Off he went, to find himself faced with "questions over what had gone wrong, but no answers."[56] At the end of the interrogation, Yurovsky sought out his friend Serge Chukazev, chairman of the Ekaterinburg Soviet, asking if he knew of any deep mines in the surrounding forests. Chukazev recommended one shaft, on the opposite side of Koptyaki Road from the Four Brothers area near the abandoned copper mines, and gave Yurovsky directions on how to find it.[57]

These meetings had taken most of the afternoon. In the early evening, Yurovsky asked his friend Pavlushin to help him inspect the new location. As they rode through the forest, however, Yurovsky's horse slipped on the muddy roads, sending him sprawling onto the ground; his horse landed on top of his leg, injuring it. "For several minutes," Yurovsky recalled, "I lay there in a daze, unable to move. Finally, I looked around, and saw that Pavlushin, too, had fallen from his horse on crossing the uneven surface." Both men struggled to their feet, limping heavily, and climbed back on their mounts to ride off into the woods.[58]

In the growing evening, the men proceeded to the old copper mine. This, as Yurovsky recalled, "was deep, surrounding a swampy area, and a clay surface which would make covering our trail easy." He decided to bring the corpses here and dispose of them that same night. During the ride back to town, Pavlushin suggested that Yurovsky attempt to burn several of the bodies, in an attempt to confuse any White investigators who might search the forest for the imperial remains. Yurovsky agreed in principle, though he himself had no experience in cremating bodies.[59]

As they rode down the Koptyaki Road, the two men encountered a group of young Red Army soldiers loitering at the edge of the woods. Worried that they were Ermakov's men and would interfere with what, of necessity, needed to be a secret operation, he asked Pavlushin to report them to the Cheka, requesting that a car of armed agents be sent to arrest them. Pavlushin agreed and went off, while Yurovsky himself returned to the Hotel Amerika to report to the Ural Regional Soviet. Here he found Peter Voikov, the regional commissar of supplies, and asked him to gather a large quantity of gasoline and sulfuric acid to be used in disposing of some of the corpses. He agreed, but warned, "These things aren't so easy to obtain."[60]

It was after eight that night when Voikov finally sent his assistant Zimin to the Russian Company's Chemist's Shop in Ekaterinburg, the city's largest industrial supplier, with a written request: "I instruct you, without delay or excuses, to deliver to the bearer of this five pouds [about 180 pounds] of sulfuric acid from your supply." A few hours later, Zimin was back with a second note: "I instruct you to deliver to the bearer of this note three additional containers of Japanese sulfuric acid."[61] This amounted to roughly fifteen gallons of acid. Yurovsky had ordered a truck sent to the Hotel Amerika to pick up the destructive agent. With the White and Czech forces approaching the city, Ekaterinburg was enveloped in a frenzy of activity, and Peter Leonov, manager of the Ekaterinburg Military Garage, had to wait until nearly one the next morning before he had a vehicle he could dispatch.[62] After the mishaps of the previous morning, Yurovsky had ordered that the truck stay clear of the mine; instead, it stopped at Grade Crossing 184, where it remained for the next twenty-four hours, waiting for the arrival of horse-drawn carts to transport the materials to the mine.[63]

Pavlushin had agreed to join Yurovsky that night in retrieving the corpses from the Four Brothers. Yurovsky waited impatiently at the Hotel Amerika for his return, the night growing longer and the Siberian sky darker. At eleven, he went off to find him. At the offices of the Cheka, he learned that Pavlushin had gone home; angry, Yurovsky immediately set off to find him. When he arrived at his apartment, however, he found Pavlushin in bed, his ankle swathed in a bandage. "I can't walk," Pavlushin explained weakly. "Thus," Yurovsky wrote, "the business of burning the bodies fell upon me, and on my men, who had absolutely no experience with such an operation."[64]

At the same time, Yurovsky phoned the military garage and ordered a car immediately delivered to the Hotel Amerika. "Oh, I know what for!" said Paul Gorbunov, deputy director of the garage. "I'll send it at once."[65] It was nearly four in the morning when Yurovsky finally arrived at the Four Brothers mine. He was surprised to find not only the men from the Ipatiev House guard but also "some twenty men, of whom I knew only two or three. Once again, the entire operation threatened to be ruined by the intrusion of other people."[66]

These men had been gathered from the nearby Kusvinsky factory. One, Gregory Sukhorukov, recalled how a few Bolshevik officials had appeared that evening, saying, "Comrades! A state secret is now entrusted to you. You must die with it." Their task, they learned, was to exhume the bodies from the mine and then bury them. "We arrived very early in the morning," Sukhorukov recalled. Immediately, the men were drawn to the piles of ash scattered in the clearing, sorting through the cold embers where they found several diamonds and other neglected bits of jewelry that had remained in the clothes when they were burned.[67] According to Kudrin, who was not present but heard details from his Cheka comrade Isai Rodzinsky, the water in the shaft had been so deep and so cold that the bodies "looked as if they were alive—the faces of the sovereign, the girls, and the women even had rosy cheeks."[68] Rodzinsky himself recalled the moment the emperor's body was pulled from the mine. "They laid him out on the grass," he said, "and we all paused to admire his wonderful physique. He was very powerfully built, with very developed muscles in his arms, back, and legs"; peculiarly, Rodzinsky and his Bolshevik friends poked and prodded him, as he later recalled, "wondering at his body; he had a particularly nice, firm rear."[69]

Yurovsky was beside himself with anger when he caught sight of this absurd spectacle, and quickly ordered the entire area cleared. "I sent these men to Koptyaki village," he wrote, "to instruct the people there not to leave because a search was under way, and it was possible that they might be caught in an exchange of gunfire. We then resumed work when the riders left us. By morning, we had recovered the bodies."[70]

It was already hot, and Yurovsky had not slept for two days. He listened as the few remaining men grumbled: "Why can't we just bury them here? What difference does it make?" With some reluctance, Yurovsky agreed that to make the transportation of the bodies to the new shaft easier, they would bury a few of the corpses at the Four Brothers. The men quickly dug a grave into the clay surface; after a foot, they hit the swampy earth, and the hole flooded with water. "We were all so tired," Yurovsky later wrote, "that we decided to just throw Nicholas and Alexei in, and cover the grave back over." As they finished their preparations, however, Yurovsky spotted an unknown face peering at this activity through the distant trees. "Hey!" he yelled. "Who is that? Come here at once!"

With reluctance, the man appeared, "head moving from side to side in an attempt to see the corpses behind us." As he came forward, Ermakov, sitting forlornly on the muddy ground, jumped up. "Oh, no!" he shouted. "He's a friend of mine. He hasn't seen anything, and in any case, he can be trusted."[71]

Yurovsky would have none of this. Though uncertain what the man had actually seen, he sent him away on the threat of being shot. Once again, the entire operation, Yurovsky later wrote, had "been ruined because of Ermakov and his damn friends. Now we had to abandon the grave, and move all of the corpses to the other shaft across the highway." Frustrated, Yurovsky berated Ermakov. "Next time I see one of your men here," he screamed, "or some friend of yours spying from the forest, I'll shoot him on the spot myself!"[72]

The men dragged the corpses to the edge of the clearing, covering them with brush and dirt, before Yurovsky returned to Ekaterinburg, leaving the men from the Ipatiev House standing guard over the macabre scene. On arriving in the city, however, he discovered another problem: Ermakov and his men had spent the previous day drinking together at the Verkh-Isetsk Factory Club, freely discussing the executions and burials so loudly that many people heard them. "Everyone in Upper Isetsk was talking about the execution of Nicholas II," remembered Kudrin, "and that the bodies had been thrown into an abandoned mine near Koptyaki. It was unbelievable—some secret!"[73]

At the Hotel Amerika, Yurovsky again reported on "the disastrous situation at the mine." It was early afternoon when he returned to Koptyaki Forest. Although Lyukhanov's Fiat had been extricated and now sat at Grade Crossing 184, Yurovsky approached the mine using a different tract farther down Koptyaki Road; the tract cut through the forest and doubled back. He had brought with him changes of clothes for the men, as well as food and drink; as they ate, he asked whether they had seen anyone since he had left. On hearing that no one had been spotted, Yurovsky, for the first time in days, "felt relieved." Climbing back into his car, he set off for the city, to make final preparations for the burial of the corpses. His optimism was misplaced. As the car lurched through the forest and neared Koptyaki Road, it first stalled, then simply quit altogether. "I spent more than an hour," he later wrote, "trying to repair it, but without luck. I had to leave on foot, which wasn't easy as my leg still hurt me a good deal."[74]

As he limped along the road on his eleven-mile walk back to Ekaterinburg in the hot afternoon sunshine, Yurovsky saw two riders approaching. At first, because the road itself had been blocked to traffic by the guard established the previous morning, Yurovsky assumed that these must be Ermakov's men. As they grew closer, however, he saw that they were strangers, teenage boys.

"Young men!" he called. "Tell me, friends, where are you going?"

"Hey, look!" one of them said. "It's Comrade Yurovsky!"

"Yes, I'm Yurovsky. Now listen to me, lads. I must return to the city, but my car has had an accident. You must help me to bring it back to Ekaterinburg." The two young men agreed, doubling up on one horse so that Yurovsky could have the other. He led them back through the forest to the abandoned car, and managed to secure it to the horses using some rope. It was, Yurovsky remembered, "slow going, with the horses straining to pull the car across the forest and uneven road, but eventually we returned to the city."[75]

It was nearly six in the evening when Yurovsky walked into the military garage, demanding another car, as well as a truck. "I have a car," said the young man in charge of the garage, "but only one lightweight truck."

"What difference does it make to me?" Yurovsky declared. "Give it to me." He loaded the truck with a few supplies—shovels, ropes, and several large concrete blocks with which he intended to weight the bodies before throwing them into the new shaft—and returned to the Hotel Amerika, where he managed to locate a second, heavier truck, ordering both out to the Four Brothers mine, along with a contingent of soldiers from the Cheka to help transport the corpses across Koptyaki Road for disposal at the abandoned copper works.[76]

Inspired by the urgency of the situation, Goloshchokin himself drove out to the Four Brothers that evening to oversee the disposal of the imperial corpses. As Yurovsky was returning to Ekaterinburg, Goloshchokin was spotted by Catherine Privalova, a guard at Grade Crossing 803, sitting in a car with several men that passed along the road and toward Koptyaki.[77]

It was ten o'clock that night before Yurovsky left the city, riding the ten miles to the forest by horse. At the edge of the wood, just opposite Grade Crossing 184, he found Serge Lyukhanov, waiting with his ill-fated Fiat. Yurovsky asked him to drive off the road and across the clearing, stopping in a dense grove of trees, which shielded the truck from view; rather than risk further disaster, the corpses would be brought to Lyukhanov. Just after midnight, Yurovsky rode into the clearing at the Four Brothers. Half a dozen carts were ranged around the side of the meadow, surrounded by a string of men enlisted to help transfer the remains. A few of the bodies had already been loaded onto the open carts, their bloated, naked limbs a pale, ghostly white in the light of the flaming torches. As Yurovsky looked on, the remaining corpses were dragged across the muddy clearing and swung into the waiting carts; finally, just before two that morning, the cortege set off into the depths of Koptyaki Forest, led by a weary Yurovsky who, as he recalled, "was barely able to keep my seat from lack of sleep."[78]

Even without the encumbrance of the Fiat, the journey through the forest, Yurovsky recalled, was "slow going, and seemed to take hours" as the carts jostled over the uneven, muddy ground. Near the edge of the forest, the procession reached the nervous Lyukhanov, and the corpses were quickly transferred to the rear of the truck. Cautiously, Lyukhanov started the engine and steered the Fiat out of the black forest, toward Koptyaki Road.[79]

Just after 4:00 A.M., the truck—followed by Yurovsky and a number of men on horseback—entered the clearing known as Pig's Meadow, ringed by a fringe of birch trees, their white trunks shimmering in the early-dawn light. There was no road here, only the same, uneven muddy ground Lyukhanov had first crossed forty-eight hours earlier, and the Fiat bounced and jostled as it rose and fell over the undulating glade. Then, disaster. The truck slipped in a worn spot, a miasma of mud and stagnant water from which it could not escape. Once again the quiet forest echoed with the sound of grinding gears as Lyukhanov gunned the engine.[80] "All our efforts to move the truck," Sukhorukov later wrote, "were unsuccessful."[81]

For Yurovsky, it was the breaking point, "the final straw" in a mis-adventure that had, from the executions themselves, plagued his mind and body. He had been up for seventy hours; spent an uneasy two days appearing before urgent meetings of the Ural Regional Soviet and Ekaterinburg Cheka; been kept on a continual run between the city and the Four Brothers; contended with the continual, unwelcome presence of Ermakov and his dubious friends attempting to inject themselves into the Romanovs drama; eaten little; fractured his leg; and, despite his best efforts, been unable to rid himself of troublesome remains. "Nothing could be done," Yurovsky recalled. "It was already light, my men were exhausted, expecting that any minute we would encounter White or Czech forces. I had to find another way to dispose of the corpses."[82]

Pig's Meadow lay just a mile north of Grade Crossing 184, fewer than five hundred feet from Koptyaki Road, itself just visible in the early-morning light through the thin shield of trees. In a last effort to free the Fiat, the men unloaded the corpses, tossing them from the dirty bed into the long, wet grass. With the truck lightened, they struggled to remove it, their boots sinking deeply into the swampy grass as they heaved and pushed the vehicle up and out of the mud. Standing in the meadow, Yurovsky's attention was drawn to the hole left in the meadow. It was only a few feet from the spot where the Fiat had become stuck on the morning of July 17, the forest road marked with their bridge of railroad ties. "I decided then," he recalled, "to bury them right there, in the middle of the clearing."[83] He set the men to widening the hole, digging down deep enough to conceal the corpses. "I must say," he declared in 1934, "that everyone was so damned tired that they didn't even want to dig the grave. But, as soon as two or three of the men got to work, the others joined in, and soon we all took up shovels and finished the pit."[84]

As this work continued, Yurovsky later wrote, he decided to burn two of the corpses.[85] "The horses were unhitched, the bodies unloaded, and the barrels of gasoline were opened," he recalled. "I ordered that we begin with Alexei. We laid his body down, and soaked it with gasoline, just to see if it would work, since no one knew how to go about this."[86] According to Kudrin, the bodies, "which were frozen, smoked and hissed";[87] the smell, Isai Rodzinsky later said, "was terrible."[88]

"We wanted to burn Alexei and Alexandra," he said in 1920, "but by mistake, instead of her we burned the lady-in-waiting [sic] and Alexei."[89] According to Yurovsky, this cremation began at 4:30 A.M. and was finished within an hour. The men took what remained, dug a hole on the spot where the bodies had been burned, threw the remains into it, covered it with earth, built another fire atop the soil, and then compacted the entire area.[90] Just before 5:30 A.M. the mass grave was ready. The faces of the other bodies were smashed with rifle butts and doused with sulfuric acid, "both so that they wouldn't be recognized if they were ever found," said Yurovsky, "and also to prevent any stench as they rotted."[91] Into the grave they went: Nicholas, Alexandra, three of their daughters, and the four retainers whose faithful loyalty had brought them only death, the last remnants of the ruling dynasty flung haphazardly into a muddy pit flooded with murky water. More acid was poured over the naked corpses, dripping from body to body as it burned away fat and flesh before being concealed with earth, brush, and stones. Atop this they placed the railroad ties, shoveling earth on them to disguise what lay beneath. Lyukhanov drove the Fiat back and forth over the grave, compacting the ties deeply into the soil and sealing them into the earth.[92]

Yurovsky gathered the men around him. They must, he warned, "forget all that they had seen," and "never speak of what had taken place" in Koptyaki Forest "to anyone."[93] By six on the morning of July 19, it was all over.[94] Within a few minutes, as Sokolov's investigation later revealed, the cordon of Bolshevik soldiers that had blocked Koptyaki Road for the past forty-eight hours was lifted, and the inhabitants of the tiny village on the shores of Lake Iset could again pass freely along its length.[95] Exhausted, Yurovsky climbed into the cab and, for the last time, Lyukhanov drove the Fiat down Koptyaki Road, rumbling along beneath a pale, glorious Siberian sunrise.

14

Aftermath

As soon as the fiat carrying the bodies swung out of the Ipatiev House gates at 3:00 A.M. on the morning of July 17, 1918, several guards were brought in to clean the scene of the slaughter. When a sleepy Philip Proskuryakov entered the murder room, he found the walls splattered with blood and pocked with bullet holes; even an hour after the execution, the thick smoke from the assassins' guns lingered in the room, "like a fog."[1] The two chairs in which the empress and the tsesarevich had sat lay toppled on the floor, its yellow wooden boards awash, as Ermakov later recalled, in "a red lake." A trail of blood led from the murder room through the corridor, the guardrooms, up the flight of stairs, and out into the courtyard, indicating the path by which the corpses had been removed. On Paul Medvedev's orders, the soldiers washed down the walls, scrubbing away the lifeblood of their former sovereign and his family. Carefully picking their ways across the room, they collected the "slippers and pillows and handbags and odds and ends" that "swam round" in the congealing pools of blood, brain tissue, and bodily fluids.[2] Once the room had been cleared, they rinsed the floor with water, sprinkling it with sand to absorb the pools of gore; only after this gruesome mixture dried and was swept up did Medvedev release the men.

At seven that morning, the two nuns from the Novotikhvinsky Monastery returned to the Ipatiev House with the supplies Yurovsky had requested the day before the murders. They waited to see the commandant himself, but one of the guards told them that he was out. Confused, the two nuns stood outside the palisade gate with their provisions until one of the sentries yelled, "Go away! Don't bring things anymore!"[3]

Across Voznesensky Lane, the early morning had passed uneasily in the Popov House as news of the executions quickly spread among the exterior guards. Leonid Sednev, having been sent from the Ipatiev House only hours before the shooting, heard these horrifying details from sympathetic sentries, and collapsed in tears.[4] Although Yurovsky had promised that he was to be reunited with his uncle, the young boy now feared for his own life. Every few hours, Medvedev checked on him: before leaving for Koptyaki Forest, Yurovsky had ordered that Sednev was not to leave the Popov House. To discourage him from attempting to sneak away, the commandant had confiscated most of Sednev's clothes, giving him in exchange only a "large pair of old black trousers, and an old school shirt, also black, which buttoned up the back."[5]

The guards themselves, having grown close to the prisoners, and openly sympathetic to their plight, were largely devastated by the murders. Several simply fled their positions in the Special Detachment, while others, like Yakimov, made a great show of emotion, breaking down repeatedly and crying as he recalled their fate. At eight that morning, unable to sleep, Yakimov suddenly appeared at the apartment of his sister, "looking horribly upset," as she later recalled, "exhausted and nervous," his face "convulsed in terror and his body trembling all over." Finally he collapsed in sobs, muttering, "It's all over!" and tearfully relating what he had heard of the murders.[6] "After the assassinations," recalled the sister-in-law of one of these men, "they were all filled with remorse, troubled by their participation in those events. In those few days before the Whites arrived, many of the guards took to drinking, in an effort to erase the memory of what had happened."[7] Twenty-one-year-old Nicholas Sadchikov, who had openly declared that he "would like to take all the Romanovs and deliver them into the hands of the White Army," was so overwhelmed that three days after the executions, he collapsed in tears in the market, mourning the fate of the grand duchesses;[8] unable to overcome this depression, he later committed suicide.[9]

At two that afternoon, a reluctant and weary Anatoly Yakimov walked through the courtyard gates and into the Ipatiev House. He later recalled:

> On the table in the Commandant's Office lay many different kinds of valuables. They were stones, earrings, pins with stones, and beads. Many were ornamented. Some were in cases. The cases were all open. The door leading from the anteroom into the rooms which had been occupied by the Imperial Family was closed as before, but there was no one in the rooms. This was obvious. No sound came from there.

Before, when the Imperial Family lived there, there were always sounds of life in their rooms: voices, steps. At this time there was no life there. Only their little dog [Alexei's spaniel Joy] stood in the anteroom, at the door to the rooms where the Imperial Family had lived, waiting to be let in. I well remember thinking at the time: you are waiting in vain.[10]

In Yurovsky's office, he saw Paul Medvedev and two members of the Verkh-Isetsk factory battalion sitting quietly, "depressed," he recalled, "and nervous. They would not talk at all or answer any of my questions."[11] Before returning to Koptyaki Forest, Yurovsky ordered Paul Medvedev to relieve these men of their posts; only Netrebin and the two Kabanov brothers—significantly, three men who had participated in the executions—were allowed to remain, to pack the prisoners' belongings. The rest were to be immediately sent to the Ural Front of the Civil War.[12]

It was an anxious day in Ekaterinburg. At 4:00 A.M. Beloborodov had sent a cable to Moscow, addressed to both Lenin and Sverdlov:

> In view of the rapid advance of enemy troops on Ekaterinburg, and the discovery [by] the Cheka of a significant White Guard plot to abduct the former emperor Nicholas Romanov and his family, for which we possess the relevant documents, we have passed and acted upon the following resolution: Nicholas Romanov was shot on the night of July 16. His family has been evacuated to a place of greater safety.

The cable also included the text of an announcement written by the Ural Regional Soviet:

> In view of the advance of counterrevolutionary bands on the Red capital of the Urals, and the possibility of the crowned hangman escaping the people's justice (a plot has been uncovered involving White Guards whose express purpose was to abduct Nicholas Romanov and his family, along with the relevant supporting documents), the Ural Regional Soviet, moved by the iron will of the Revolution, resolved to execute the former emperor. This sentence was carried out on July 16, 1918. Romanov's family, detained with him under guard, has been evacuated from Ekaterinburg for safety.

Signed by Beloborodov, the cable informed the Presidium of the Central Executive Committee that the documents that provided evidence of the alleged White Guard plot were being dispatched to Moscow.[13]

This cable informed Moscow of the Ural Regional Soviet's apparent fait accompli. Nevertheless, it indicated distinct unease on Ekaterinburg's part. In this, their first communication with Moscow after the executions, they deliberately lied, not only in saying that Nicholas alone had been killed, but also in asserting that a serious

White Guard plot had existed, bent on rescuing the Romanovs, which had forced this extreme measure.

Such a message would be inexplicable had Moscow ordered the wholesale execution of the prisoners. Instead, the cable revealed Ekaterinburg's deception; having received unequivocal instructions on Goloshchokin's return that Lenin insisted on the proposed trial, the Ural Regional Soviet had simply proceeded with their previous resolution of June 29, which called for the execution of all the Romanovs in Siberia. Only at the last minute, late on the evening of July 16, did they inform Moscow, in their cable to Zinoviev, that they had rejected the trial. They did not ask for permission or authority to act, only to be informed if Moscow objected.

Goloshchokin had possibly obtained discreet approval from Sverdlov authorizing the Ural Regional Soviet to dispose of Nicholas II if circumstances became critical. Lenin, however, remained adamant where the rest of the imperial family was concerned. In executing all of the Romanovs, the Ural Bolsheviks had acted on their own initiative, without any order or authorization from Lenin or Sverdlov. Such action by the Ural Bolsheviks would inevitably be discovered; while the murder of Grand Duke Michael Alexandrovich in Perm could be safely disguised behind a veil of lies evoking a White kidnap plot, the Ural Regional Soviet faced an entirely different position with the Romanovs in Ekaterinburg. Beloborodov's first cable of July 17 bought the Ural Bolsheviks time with Moscow—a few hours in which to determine how best to reveal that they had acted on their own authority and against Lenin's orders. Within eighteen hours, they themselves voluntarily relinquished the first lie: that only Nicholas himself had been killed, and his family transferred. It was obvious that they could not maintain the pretense that the Romanovs had all been moved to a new, safe location: Moscow would quickly demand to know where this was. Yet their second lie—that they possessed documentary evidence of a White Army plot to rescue the prisoners, which had necessitated the former emperor's immediate execution—was never abandoned. It became, for the Ural Bolsheviks, the only justification they could offer, their one hope that no retribution would follow.

Beloborodov's cable represented Ekaterinburg's first hesitant steps in presenting the news of the murders to Moscow, an opportunity to gauge official reaction. Throughout that day, the Presidium of the Ural Regional Soviet met in urgent session at the Hotel Amerika, attempting to control the swelling crisis that had erupted in Koptyaki Forest with the bodies, and to organize an approach to Moscow that would reveal their deed. That same evening, Beloborodov followed his first cable with a second, in which the Ural Bolsheviks finally admitted the extent of their action:

"Tell Sverdlov entire family suffered same fate as head. Officially family will perish in evacuation."[14]

Received at eleven that night in Moscow, this cable thus alerted Lenin and Sverdlov that all the prisoners had perished. Had Moscow known of the executions in advance, such peculiar wording would be inexplicable; instead, taken together with Zinoviev's forwarded cable of July 16, which made no such statement regarding the imperial family, and Beloborodov's earlier telegram, the pattern of Ekaterinburg's duplicitous behavior was laid bare for the eyes of the Soviet government. They had first warned Moscow only that they could not wait for the proposed trial—which was to have been conducted for Nicholas II alone; taken with Ekaterinburg's first cable of July 17, the clear inference was that only the former emperor had been executed. From this first cable, Moscow already knew what "fate" Nicholas himself had suffered, but they did not know what had become of his family, except for the reference to the family being sent to "a place of greater safety." These cables only confirm the hypothesis that Moscow issued no orders regarding the execution of the entire imperial family.

Further evidence that the Ural Regional Soviet alone dictated the fate of the Romanovs in Siberia came within twenty-four hours of the Ekaterinburg murders. On the night of July 17, Grand Duchess Elizabeth Feodorovna, Grand Duke Serge Mikhailovich, Princes Ioann, Igor, and Konstantin Konstantinovich, and Prince Vladimir Paley—together with the grand duke's secretary, Feodor Ramez, and Barbara Yakovleva, a nun from the grand duchess's convent—were all murdered, flung down an abandoned mine in the village of Alapayevsk, where they had been held prisoner. With the exception of Grand Duke Serge Mikhailovich, who was shot, all were struck on the head before being thrown into the shaft. Contrary to numerous monarchist legends that later sprung up regarding their eventual deaths, they perished not from starvation and exposure but from hemorrhages sustained from their head injuries.[15]

The Ural Regional Soviet had confirmation of these murders in a cable received in Ekaterinburg from the Alapayevsk Soviet at 3:15 A.M. on July 18. However, that same morning, Beloborodov dispatched a cable to Lenin and Sverdlov informing them that, following an attack by White Guards, the Alapayevsk Romanovs "have been abducted. There are victims on both sides. Searches are under way for the prisoners."[16] As in the murder of Grand Duke Michael Alexandrovich, and the murders in Ekaterinburg, the Ural Regional Soviet thus deliberately lied to Moscow, concealing the true circumstances of the crimes. This itself was later confirmed by both Kudrin and Nikulin, who wrote in their memoirs that the victims in Alapayevsk were all killed only on the direct orders of the Ural Regional Soviet.[17]

Nicholas Sokolov himself, while he attributed the Ekaterinburg murders to Lenin and Sverdlov, had no doubt that the Ural Regional Soviet itself was solely responsible for those in Alapayevsk. "It is incontestable," he wrote, "that the murders were carried out on the orders of Ekaterinburg. There is no sign that these men carried out a plan devised by Moscow."[18]

Before any announcements concerning the executions in Ekaterinburg were made public, the members of the government were informed. On the evening of July 18, as the commissar of health was reading a draft of a new proposal to the Council of People's Commissars in Moscow, Sverdlov entered the room and whispered a few words to Lenin.

"Comrade Sverdlov wants to make a statement," Lenin said.

"I have to say," Sverdlov announced, "that we have had a communication that in Ekaterinburg, by a decision of the Regional Soviet, Nicholas has been shot. The Presidium has resolved to approve." Silence fell over the room. Then Lenin said slowly and deliberately, "Let us now go on to read the draft clause by clause."[19]

The minutes of the meeting of the Central Executive Committee for July 18, 1918, confirm that they indeed learned of Ekaterinburg's decision the day after the sentence had been carried out:

> Report on the First Sessions of the Presidium of the Central Executive Committee on the execution of Nicholas II:

> July 18, 1918.

> Received the report of the execution of Nicholas Romanov (cable from Ekaterinburg). The Presidium passed the following resolution in relation to this discussion:

> The Presidium of the Central Executive Committee recognizes the decision of the Ural Regional Soviet as correct and proper. Comrades Sverdlov, Sosnovsky, and Avanesov are charged with the composition of appropriate news releases for the press. Information related to the former Emperor Nicholas Romanov (diaries, letters, etc.) will be transferred to the Central Executive Committee in Moscow, which will publish any relevant information. Comrade Sverdlov is charged with the creation of a special committee to collate these documents and arrange for publication.

> V. Avanesov, Chairman of the Presiding Committee.[20]

That same evening, Robert Bruce Lockhart sent the first known cable in which Nicholas's execution was revealed: "Ex-Emperor of Russia was shot on the night of July 16 by order of Ekaterinburg local

Soviet in view of approaching danger of his capture by Czechs. The Central Executive at Moscow has approved action."[21]

On July 19, 1918, both *Pravda* and *Izvestia* published the following text: "The Presidium of the Ural Regional Soviet passed a resolution to execute Nicholas Romanov and carried it out on July 16. Romanov's wife and son have been sent to a safe place."[22] This announcement maintained Ekaterinburg's original lie that only Nicholas had been killed. Lenin himself, as he had told Sverdlov, opposed the wholesale slaughter of the empress and her children for fear of public reaction, both in Russia and in the West. With his own regime in a precarious position, threatened not only by powerful political opponents within Russia but also by the unabated flow of Allied expeditionary forces in general and the more immediate danger of a hostile Germany in the wake of von Mirbach's assassination, news of the Romanov murders—received the night of July 17, 1918—came at the worst possible moment. Now that the Ural Regional Soviet had acted of their volition and done the very thing he feared, Lenin was forced to participate in their charade of deception, in an effort to keep news of the true fate of the rest of the imperial family from providing his enemies with further ammunition against the faltering Soviet state.

The executions had not yet been announced in Ekaterinburg, although, by July 19, almost everyone knew they had taken place. On the morning of July 19, a group of Bolsheviks sitting in the garden of the Communist Club at Verkh-Isetsk, just outside of Ekaterinburg, spoke loudly of the executions of the entire family, describing the victims in detail; the shootings themselves; and the fact that the bodies had still been "warm" when they touched them.[23] A second group of soldiers, "under the strong influence of alcohol," gleefully announced to a group of peasants, "We burned your Nicholas and all of them."[24]

The Ural Regional Soviet was uncertain what to do, and spent a tense day awaiting Moscow's reply to news of their actions. Only on the evening of July 18 did they have a reply from Moscow: "The Central Executive Committee of the Councils of Deputies of Workers, Peasants, Red Guards and the Cossacks, in the Person of their President, approve the action of the Presidium of the Council of the Urals. The President of the Central Executive Committee. Sverdlov."[25]

This cable, as Kudrin later recalled, came as an immense relief. He saw Beloborodov, who was so ecstatic that the two men "embraced and congratulated" each other on their successful deception. "This," Kudrin recalled, "meant that Moscow had understood the complex situation we faced, and that, as a result, Lenin had approved our actions." Until this time, said Kudrin, Beloborodov had been "afraid that Lenin would hold him personally responsible for executing the Romanovs without the approval of the VTsIK."[26]

On July 20, Sverdlov held a telegraphic conversation with Beloborodov during which the latter asked when they should announce the executions, and what form it should take.[27] Sverdlov replied by simply resending to Ekaterinburg the essence of their initial cable of July 17, stating that Nicholas had been executed following the discovery of a White Guard plot, and that his family had been evacuated:

> In view of the fact that Czechoslovakian bands are threatening the Red Capital of the Urals, Ekaterinburg; that the crowned executioner may escape from the tribunal of the people (a White Guard plot to carry off the whole Imperial Family has just been discovered); the Presidium of the Divisional Committee in pursuance of the will of the people, has decided that the ex-Emperor, Nicholas Romanov, guilty before the people of innumerable crimes, shall be shot. The decision of the Presidium of the Divisional Council was carried out on the night of July 16–17. Romanov's family has been transferred from Ekaterinburg to a place of greater safety.[28]

That same afternoon, Goloshchokin addressed a hastily called open meeting at the Ekaterinburg Municipal Theater. "The Czechs," he said, "those hirelings of French and British capitalists, are close at hand. The old Imperial generals are with them. The Cossacks also are coming; and they all think that they will get their Emperor back. But they never shall. We shot him last night."[29]

Information as to the reception of this news is extremely contradictory. Bykov wrote that it was met with "a storm of enthusiasm."[30] And Kudrin declared that "the ovations from the audience seemed to go on forever. The news uplifted the spirits of all the workers."[31] According to General Michael Deterikhs, however, there were cries of "Show us the body!"[32] Surprisingly, this was confirmed by Isai Rodzinsky, who was present: "The audience was a curious group: average people, women in their evening hats. There were no workers there due to the hour of the meeting. I don't know exactly why the meeting was organized in such a way. The audience gave the impression that all the Philistines had come. Some of the ladies in their hats were crying. We watched closely. Someone said he didn't believe the execution. He said that the Bolsheviks were lying. We heard more of this after the meeting. People didn't believe the Emperor had been killed."[33]

Within a day, the Ekaterinburg newspaper *Uralskii rabochii* reported: "White Guards attempted to kidnap the ex-Emperor and his family. Their plot has been discovered. The Ural Regional Soviet, thinking quickly, foresaw this criminal action, and executed the Murderer of All Russians. This should be a first warning! The enemies of the people will not achieve a restoration of the Autocracy any more than they succeeded in sparing the Crowned executioner."[34]

Yurovsky himself left Ekaterinburg on July 19, within six hours after he had finally disposed of the corpses. A coachman, Yelkin, later recalled arriving at the Ipatiev House early that afternoon: "Some young people came out of the house and with the help of an old Red Army man brought out seven pieces of luggage and put them in my carriage. There was a wax seal on one of them, a black leather suitcase of medium size."[35] Nikulin traveled with Yurovsky, carrying luggage loaded with the Romanovs' belongings. In addition to jewelry, the two men took with them most of the correspondence of the imperial family: letters from the emperor to the empress; cables and notes exchanged between the children and their parents during their separation in Tobolsk and Ekaterinburg; and many of the private photograph albums they had brought with them from Tsarskoye Selo.

They also carried two of the letters written in French to the imperial family by the Cheka. As Kudrin recalled: "Beloborodov thought that these two documents would show the Executive Committee that there was an officers' organization that had set itself the goal of kidnapping the Imperial Family." Kudrin also made it clear that the intent was deception of the authorities in Moscow: "These letters would be used to show the circumstances which had forced us to act on our own and execute the Romanovs." He added, somewhat cynically: "Yurovsky and Nikulin were to personally show these to Sverdlov, and tell him about the situation in Ekaterinburg, to get their reaction."[36] Yurovsky and Nikulin acted as the Ural Regional Soviet's sacrificial lambs, dispatched to the capital to convey not only a lie, but also fabricated evidence that supported that lie.

Two days earlier, Yurovsky had ordered the remaining members of the Verkh-Isetsk factory battalion to begin packing up the imperial family's belongings. These, he explained, were to be sent by rail to Moscow. He warned that the work would have to be completed by July 19, when he planned to leave the city.[37]

"I collected together and stacked the diaries and journals of the executed," recalled Victor Netrebin. "But time was so short that there could not be a detailed reading of them. Someone did read parts aloud to us as we worked. I don't know that anything was especially interesting. I, of course, did not want to hand over everything that had been written by their hands, I am ashamed to say."[38]

As the men flipped through the diaries, they found postcards, photographs, letters, and little notes, jammed haphazardly between pages. One such note, discovered in the emperor's diary, was a list of offensive words, written in Nicholas's hand; a second note, which fell from his diary, recounted how, suffering from hemorrhoids, he had one day sat on the toilet in the Ipatiev House for hours, watching a spider slowly build its web across the ceiling.[39]

It took these men an entire day to sort through the imperial family's clothing, both within the Ipatiev House itself, and that stored in a number of steamer trunks and suitcases in the shed off the courtyard. In one of Alexandra's trunks they found a long red silk shirt, blue silk pants, and a tasseled silk belt that had belonged to Rasputin and that she had brought with her family into their unknown exile.[40] A few of the men, Netrebin recalled, began to sort through a pile of undergarments on the floor of the grand duchesses' room that, having been worn, were ready to be sent to the laundry. These were passed around, the men sniffing them loudly and laughing. In examining a black velvet belt, one of the men tossed it across the room, only to hear it crack as it fell to the wooden floor. As they gathered around, they saw that it had concealed a number of diamonds, which spilled out from beneath the velvet. "We all stood there," recalled Netrebin, "like we were rooted to the ground, impressed with the cunning of our former prisoners. We rechecked all their clothes, even the hatpins of the former Grand Duchesses, where we found even more jewels and diamonds."[41]

They also discovered, hidden in a bureau drawer in the corner bedroom shared by Nicholas and Alexandra, "a diverse selection of condoms," as Netrebin recalled, "of different shapes and types." Exploring further in their quest for "unusual things," they found a number of merkins, pubic wigs that had belonged to the empress.[42] These items were all packed and shipped out of Ekaterinburg by train, via Perm, to Moscow.

The Bolsheviks began to evacuate Ekaterinburg on July 19, within a few hours of Yurovsky's departure. By the morning of July 21, most of the important members of the Ural Regional Soviet and Ekaterinburg Cheka had fled northwest, toward Perm. Over the three days that followed, there were gun battles in the city streets, and skirmishes in Koptyaki Forest as the net slowly closed around the capital of the Urals. On the evening of July 24 the entire city was encircled by White and Czech troops; within hours, by dawn on July 25, they finally entered Ekaterinburg.

That first morning, the Whites went straight to the Ipatiev House. The Special Detachment had been disbanded several days earlier, and the ornate little villa now sat ominously silent, its rooms empty of life. Here, everything was in disorder: books and papers lay piled on the floors, next to ashes that spilled from the porcelain stoves; drawers had been pulled from chests; and dressers and their contents dumped on the floors, pilfered by the Bolsheviks. From the icons, letters, books, and bottles of medicine it was apparent that, whatever had happened to the Romanovs and those imprisoned with them, it had happened quickly, without warning, and without opportunity to pack their belongings.

On the afternoon of July 25, 1918, Major General Golitsyn, head of the new White Army Ekaterinburg garrison, established a military guard around the abandoned villa, to prevent any potential intrusion into what was believed to be a crime scene, and to forestall any possible pilfering of imperial belongings. Seven days later, following his appointment as the official judicial investigator, Alexander Nametkin began an extensive inspection and inventory of the Ipatiev House. In all, he spent nineteen hours, spread over five days, carefully examining the former prison and its contents, leaving a final glimpse of the last days of life for the Romanovs and their retainers in the Ipatiev House.[43]

Nametkin examined only the upper floor, beginning in the foyer. He noted a pile of greasy flannel rags left on the floor at the side of the staircase. Above these he found an inscription scrawled on the side of the staircase in black ink: "Commissar of the House of Special Purpose Alexander Avdayev." The hallway beyond, with its secondary staircase descending to the basement below, was free of any graffiti or imperial possessions. In the bathroom, Nametkin noted a pile of discarded French newspapers, with the name of guard Alexei Sidorov written across them. A discarded hand mirror, identified as having belonged to the empress, lay atop a tin ventilator. Next to the bathtub were several linen sheets embroidered with imperial crowns and sewn with the initials of Grand Duchess Tatiana Nikolaievna and of the empress. Pushed beneath the edge of the raised tub was a small wooden box containing three distinct colors of hair, which Chemodurov identified as having come from three of the grand duchesses; more hair, from all four girls, was discovered on a corner shelf.

The toilet was in a small room just outside of the bathroom. Here Nametkin found a few lewd jokes penciled on the walls; these, and a few similar obscenities in the bathroom, were the only graffiti noted in any of the upper rooms occupied by the Romanovs. Shoved behind the toilet, hidden next to a pipe, Nametkin found a small book, its pages filled with a curious—and indecipherable—code used by the emperor and empress in their personal correspondence; on the flyleaf the empress had written, "To My Own Darling Nicky, to remind him of his Spitzbub when he is far away from her. From his loving Alix, Osborne, July, 1894."

In the corridor outside the commandant's office Nametkin cataloged a number of items: six pages from the *Graphic* newspaper of

London, dated November 21, 1914; a collection of back issues of *Izvestia*, along with copies of Ekaterinburg's *Uralski rabochii*, and a copy of the *Petrograd Evening Post* from January 1918; a few magazines; and a collection of odd volumes of the collected works of Saltykov. A large oak bookcase held an extensive collection of medicine bottles, later identified as having been used by the empress and the tsesarevich, and six vials of oil for an icon lamp. There also was a box of hair—four colors—identified as those of the grand duchesses.

In Yurovsky's office, Nametkin found a small electroshock machine that Derevenko had recommended for the tsesarevich, as well as a second electroshock machine prescribed by the Ekaterinburg physician Dr. Anatoly Belogradsky. In a small cabinet, Nametkin discovered bottles of medicine belonging to the empress, as well as small containers of holy oil, and a black steel Fabergé engraved pencil case. Several of the tsesarevich's board and card games were piled on a small side table, next to an Ekaterinburg telephone directory and more medicine bottles, these prescribed for the empress by Rasputin's friend Dr. Badmayev. Yurovsky's desk was piled with books and papers, including a small notebook with "House of Special Purpose" written on the cover; gray-and-white stationery marked "Commandant of the House of Special Purpose"; several ashtrays; a few gramophone records; and a stack of women's sanitary belts and napkins. Beneath the sofa, Nametkin found a cypress rosary, which Chemodurov identified as having belonged to the empress. A small table and bookshelf were crammed with papers, including letters written by members of the imperial family more than a decade earlier and brought into exile by them; prayer books; novels; and another box of hair cut from the heads of the grand duchesses.

The drawing room and adjoining sitting room through the open arch held a number of objects. The potted palm near the double doors to the dining room tilted to the side, dying from lack of water. A few coats, marked with imperial monograms, hung on a wooden coat rack near the double doors to the corridor, including a velvet cloak embroidered with the initials "A. F." A corner desk in the sitting room contained a number of letters written in French by the tsesarevich; atop this was a box labeled "Jewels Belonging to Anastasia Nikolaievna." A number of newspapers, books, bottles of perfume and cologne, and photographs of the Romanovs lay scattered in the drawing room.

The dining room contained a number of objects. Between the two windows overlooking the garden, on the black marble shelves of a two-tiered floor-length mirror, were dozens of bottles of wine marked "Imperial Court Cellars." The large gilt clock above the buffet had stopped at 9:57. The buffet itself was crowded with yet more bottles of wine, as well as bottles of ointment labeled "Imperial Court Pharmacist

Rozmarin," which Chemodurov identified as belonging to the tsesarevich. A number of dishes—fifteen faience soup plates and other china marked with the monogram "N. II" and bearing the dates 1909, 1913, and 1914—lay piled next to a large white samovar with a gold spout, which Avdayev had purchased for the prisoners in May. Inside the buffet, Nametkin found a number of icons: St. Antonina, St. Ioann, St. Mustafiya, St. Seraphim Sarov, and a number of icons representing the Mother of God. Finally, he noted a large bottle of foaming bubble bath, which Chemodurov explained had been the emperor's—apparently Nicholas enjoyed taking bubble baths. Beyond the left window, on the terrace, was a plate with a number of bones—the last remains of the three dogs' dinner on July 16.

Piles of clothes were stacked on the floral carpet in Demidova's corner bedroom, all later identified by Chemodurov as having belonged to Alexei. There also was a small bag of coins that had belonged to the tsesarevich, as well as a third electroshock machine. In the bedroom used by the four grand duchesses, a plaid lap rug bearing the monogram of the emperor had been spread across the parquet floor; atop this were stacks of books, a number of letters, postcards, and icons. A velvet-lined box contained several icons, their frames studded with diamonds. A corner bookshelf held a number of titles, including *War and Peace* and Serge Nilus's *The Great in the Small*, which contained the infamous *Protocols of the Elders of Zion*. Nametkin found a few postcards and half-written letters, along with notes in English on a play the children had performed at Tobolsk in February. The doors of both corner stoves stood open, spilling ashes onto the floor.

In the adjoining bedroom, used by the emperor, empress, and tsesarevich, Nametkin found a number of items that had been used by Alexei, including a large, flat board on which he had played with his tin soldiers; his bedpan, tucked beneath his bed; a chess set; and a number of books. The wall calendar had last been torn off on July 6 (June 23 O.S.). On the empress's corner dressing table were a number of bottles of Brocard's English eau de cologne; two small bottles of other English scents; a box of lavender bath salts; a dish of cold cream labeled "Imperial Pharmacy"; feminine hygiene belts and pads; bottles of medicine; and a carafe, still filled with water. Nametkin also found a number of books here, including the empress's Bible and an exercise book from 1883, in which Nicholas had written a number of prayers. Nametkin inventoried a total of 251 books and 57 icons, the most important of which was the Feodorovsky Mother of God, the empress's favorite. The halo had been stripped of its diamond-encrusted crown.[44]

On searching the lower floor of the Ipatiev House, the Whites found the cellar room where the murders had taken place. Here there was clear evidence of violence. The walls bore bullet holes, the wallpaper was torn in places from bayonet marks, and both the walls and the yellow floorboards were still stained with blood. Standing in the gloomy light that filtered in through the single window, they came to an inescapable conclusion: it was obvious that some murderous activity had occurred here, the mute evidence of death and destruction all around them.

15

The Investigations

W HEN THE WHITE and Czech Armies took Ekaterinburg on July 25, 1918, they found the Ipatiev House deserted, the imperial family's rooms full of debris. The sinister basement room, its walls pocked by bullets and stained with blood, bore mute witness to some terrible, though as yet unknown, tragedy. Although both Moscow and Ekaterinburg had announced the execution of the emperor, there remained the very real possibility that the rest of the family might still be alive. During the following year, no fewer than five separate investigations into their fate were undertaken. Three of these were judicial; the other two—the Officers' Commission inquiry and the Military-Criminal Investigating Division report—were sponsored by the White Army.

Two days after the fall of Ekaterinburg, Lieutenant Andrei Sheremetievsky, a White Army officer who had been hiding in Koptyaki for several weeks, visited the commander of the 8th Municipal District. He described the mysterious events in Koptyaki Forest before the Bolsheviks had fled the city: the comings and goings of trucks; the roadblocks; patrols of armed Bolsheviks; and explosions at the abandoned Four Brothers mine. When the Whites took Ekaterinburg, Sheremetievsky led a small group of peasants out to the mine, where they discovered a number of important items: burned and scorched bits of clothing; buttons from coats and jackets; belt buckles, including one with the Romanov double-headed eagle; and jewelry, including a large emerald cross. Sheremetievsky handed these over to the White officials, explaining that they had been found in the shaft itself; ground into the surrounding earth; and in the ashes of several bonfires at the edges of the clearing.[1]

These discoveries seemed ominous. Two days later, a man named Feodor Gorshkov appeared before Alexander Kutuzov, assistant public prosecutor in Ekaterinburg, declaring he had information about the imperial family. Gorshkov explained that his story was fifthhand, told to him by the city coroner, Tomashevsky, who had heard it from Gregory Agafonov; Agafonov was married to Capitolina Yakimova, sister of Anatoly Yakimov, former guard at the Ipatiev House, who himself heard of the murders from several members of the guard. In the process, the tale had become garbled: "The whole Imperial Family were gathered in the dining room, where they were told that they were to be shot. Immediately after this, the Letts fired at the Imperial Family, and all fell to the floor. After this, as the Letts checked pulses to ensure that all were dead, they found that Grand Duchess Anastasia Nikolaievna still lived. She screamed when they touched her. They beat her over the head with their rifles, and stabbed her thirty-two times."[2]

Inaccurate though it was, Gorshkov's statement indicated the worst. It was duly entered into a file marked "The Case of Emperor Nicholas II"—the first document in what would eventually form some eleven volumes of evidence and testimony regarding the end of the imperial family. Men dug up the entire garden of the Ipatiev House; soldiers combed the surrounding forests; and yet another contingent dragged Upper Iset Pond near the Verkh-Isetsk factory, all searching in vain for the corpses of the Romanovs.[3]

By the end of July, three official investigations, under nominal charge of White Army general Michael Deterikhs, were under way. The Officers' Commission, led by Prince Riza-Kuli-Mirza, the ruling military governor of the captured city, examined Koptyaki Forest and tracked down witnesses but never produced any report of their inquiries.[4] The second body, the Military-Criminal Investigating Division, operated under the authority of the White Army but proved more contentious. Headed by Alexander Kirsta, assistant to the chief of military intelligence in Siberia, it pursued hundreds of rumors and allegations, a tendency that brought it into direct conflict with both Deterikhs and the White Army. Deterikhs complained, "Again and again, the Military-Criminal Investigating Division embarked on the quest for ideas discovered in various reports, which reflected not the truth but the wishes of those who had committed the crime—rumors spread by secret agents of the Bolsheviks themselves. Without identifying these sources, questioning their motivations, verifying their veracity, or investigating the background of those involved, they eagerly used this information to begin their work. Any search for the truth was thus lost."[5]

It was obvious from the beginning that, to Deterikhs, there was only one avenue of possible exploration in the case—that the entire imperial family had been killed; any evidence that suggested otherwise he simply dismissed as "nonsense."[6] But the Military-Criminal Investigating Division refused to bow to pressure, and pursued the theory that while Nicholas II had himself apparently been killed—probably with the four retainers left in the Ipatiev House—the empress and her children had been evacuated northwest by the Bolsheviks. Among the cables discovered in Ekaterinburg were a number sent by Beloborodov in late June and early July, referring to the dispatch of a train of valuables to Perm. Without any evidence to the contrary, the Military-Criminal Investigating Division believed that these valuables had, in fact, been the Romanovs. The emperor, it was said, had been "dragged away in chains," and the entire imperial family put on a train northwest. Half a dozen witnesses testified that they had personally seen all of this.[7] The fall of Perm brought further accounts, depositions from those who claimed to have seen one or more of the imperial women there, held prisoner by the local Bolsheviks. The evidence was somewhat less than compelling: most of those who encountered these "imperial women" had never before seen any of the Romanovs, and often failed to accurately select their photographs from the MCID selections. Nonetheless, Kirsta seemed convinced that Alexandra and her daughters had survived, a suggestion that, for political reasons, the White Army authorities considered dangerous. In the end, the Military-Criminal Investigating Division's inquiry into the fate of the Romanovs—like that of the Officers' Commission—was officially closed on General Deterikhs's orders.

The most important investigations into the fate of the Romanovs were the three judicial inquiries. The first began on July 30, when Kutuzov appointed Alexei Nametkin, Criminal Investigator for the Most Important Cases in Ekaterinburg, to conduct the inquiry. Little is known of Nametkin or his background, though he had apparently served in his position for a number of years. He held his post for just eight days before being unceremoniously fired, but accomplished a considerable amount of work, including a methodical inventory of the Ipatiev House. His results formed the basis of all investigations to follow.

To assist Nametkin, Kutuzov appointed Captain Dimitri Malinovsky, the White Army officer who had previously been involved with Dr. Derevenko in attempting to organize a rescue attempt.[8] On July 30, the day of his appointment, Nametkin traveled to Koptyaki Forest to investigate the abandoned mines. He discovered a number of small items: burned parts of shoes; buttons; and more jewelry and jewel fragments, most significantly, a large diamond found in the grass near the mouth of the deepest shaft. Before he left, Nametkin asked Malinovsky to arrange to have the water in the shafts pumped out, so they could be further investigated.[9] While waiting for a suitable pump, Nametkin concentrated his energies on the Ipatiev House itself. He spent six days measuring each room on the upper floor, describing and meticulously cataloging their contents down to each individual medicine bottle, book, and icon the Romanovs had left behind.[10]

On August 7, however, Nametkin was removed from the investigation during a closed-door session of the Ekaterinburg Regional Court. A number of reasons for this abrupt dismissal have been offered. According to Nicholas Sokolov, Nametkin's "conduct" was responsible for his termination.[11] Sokolov gave no details, but those with whom he worked did. Robert Wilton alleged, erroneously, that Nametkin "did not even go near the woods," and thus failed to investigate Koptyaki Forest.[12] Sokolov's faithful aide Paul Bulygin declared, on no evidence, that Nametkin had to be forced "almost at the point of a revolver" to investigate the Four Brothers mine because he did not want "to compromise himself in the murderers' eyes."[13] And Deterikhs charged: "From the first days of Nametkin's work, Kutuzov realized that he was completely unfit to conduct such an important matter. During his term, Nametkin distinguished himself not only by his laziness and the careless manner of his work, but in his clear ignorance of even the most basic duties of an investigator."[14]

In Nametkin's place, the Ekaterinburg Regional Court appointed Ivan Sergeyev, Examining Magistrate for Cases of Special Importance. Ironically, Sergeyev was from Simbirsk, the same Volga River town in which both Lenin and Kerensky had been born. The son of a career military officer, Sergeyev received a law degree from Moscow University in 1894 and, three years later, moved to Ekaterinburg, where he established his own practice. By the beginning of World War I, he had distinguished himself to such an extent that he was raised to his judicial position by an imperial decree from Nicholas II himself.[15]

Sergeyev carefully examined the basement room where the suspected crimes had taken place. He found a number of bullet holes and bloodstains; upon testing, the blood proved to be human. Sergeyev also supervised the pumping of the Ganina pit on August 19, collecting more than sixty items of charred clothing and jewelry, all identified as having belonged to the imperial family. Sergeyev cast his net widely, collecting as much evidence and testimony as possible, whether bearing directly on the search for the Romanovs or not. General Deterikhs, however, alleged, "Sergeyev, in the work accomplished, demonstrated a complete absence of the most modest investigative talents, and an absolute lack of understanding of the investigator's profession. His interrogation of witnesses consisted in the mere notation of what the witness, or the criminal himself, wanted to tell. He made no effort to direct the questioning in accordance with a definite thought, a definite plan, or ask resultant questions; only when the witness himself, accidentally, provided such insights were they recorded in the dossier. He ignored the possibility of establishing facts through investigation and thorough examination of items of material evidence."[16]

In fairness to Sergeyev, he faced overwhelming odds from the beginning. "The military authorities," according to Deterikhs, "were in general very much prejudiced against Sergeyev personally."[17] The military governor of the Urals, according to Wilton, refused to provide him with "the monthly stipend for a typist," and he even had trouble in obtaining the necessary funds to travel and conduct interviews.[18] Despite these conditions, Deterikhs readily complained of Sergeyev's work. He hinted heavily that Sergeyev's lack of speed, and his refusal to implicate the central Soviet authorities without proof, were influenced by his supposed background, declaring, "The investigation was in the hands of a member of the murderers' race—a Jew."[19]

Such was the state of confusion in the fall of 1918 that high-level Allied expeditions eagerly swallowed the latest turgid versions of the end of the family, which spilled forth in shocking abundance. American journalist Carl Ackerman, of the *New York Times*, supposedly interviewed a man named "Parfen Alekseivich Domnin," described as the emperor's "personal attendant," who recalled Nicholas II's execution and his family's removal in an absurdly melodramatic and error-ridden tale that was believed by members of the American expeditionary force in Siberia.[20] The Domnin account, and the ease with which it was believed, clearly pointed out the weakness of all foreign military intelligence operations in Siberia in 1918, when officers eagerly seized on the latest reports without bothering to verify their validity.

By the end of 1918, Sergeyev had collected depositions from a number of former guards at the Ipatiev House, who testified that they had heard second- and thirdhand stories of the basement shootings. These were not the only tales in circulation. At the same time, a series of increasingly barbaric and gruesome versions filtered through both intelligence services and the investigation itself. On December 5, a French Secret Service report declared that "the prisoners were tied to their chairs, after which the soldiers abused them, especially the Grand Duchesses. . . . The young girls were abused and raped, and the Tsar, in chains, was obliged to watch this scene. After the young girls had been killed, the Tsar begged that the Tsarina should at least be killed without further outrage."[21] This story cut a wide swath through European ministries, and apparently reached Buckingham Palace, where it was believed to be true. "About six months after the Tsar's death," recalled Lord Mountbatten, "King George V showed me

Secret Service reports that they had all been raped. The King advised me not to tell my mother."[22]

Three weeks later, on December 29, 1918, M. Pichon, the French foreign minister, reported that he had received information about the end of the Romanovs from Prince George Lvov: "Prince Lvov was in a cell next to the one the members of the Imperial Family were in. . . . They brought them together into the one room and having made them sit down in a row, they spent the entire night inflicting bayonet blows on them before finishing them off next morning, one after the other, with revolver shots: the Emperor, the Empress, the Grand Duchesses, the Tsesarevich, the lady-in-waiting, the Empress's female companion, and all the people with the Imperial Family, so that according to what Prince Lvov has told me, the room was literally a pool of blood."[23]

Despite being one of the most unreliable sources in the entire case, Lvov's version was widely reported and, for a time, believed. As the weeks passed, further tales also filtered out of Siberia, equally horrific in their claims. A secondhand account, said to have derived from one of the assassins, alleged that the executioners "jeered at the Sovereign, the Empress, and the Grand Duchesses. They beat them, spat on them, hit them in the face, and raped the girls. The Sovereign asked the men to take him, and to spare the family. Nobody responded to that. Then the sailor-convict said, 'I was in prison because of you, and suffered. Now it's your turn.' That is what he said, and exactly what he meant, and did, raping the Sovereign. Then he shot, and everyone began firing, and the Red Army men bayoneted them."[24]

Another equally lurid version reached the White investigators in January 1919, said to derive from a certain George Biron as related to a traveling companion during a train journey. According to this tale, "the servants were taken to the City Prison, and that evening a group of eight men arrived at the Ipatiev House. Lots were drawn to determine whom they would kill, although not the Emperor, since Pashka Berzin, a sailor from Latvia, had already demanded that he be allowed the honor. When the murderers reached the Ipatiev House they found Nicholas sitting alone at a table, drinking tea. He said, 'It's hot and stuffy. I could do with a drink.' Then he saw their revolvers and began to tremble and Berzin laughed, saying that his time was up. Nicholas fell to his knees and begged for mercy, while Berzin laughed at him and kicked and taunted him, finally shooting him in the head. Alexandra was then brought into the room naked—Biron said 'she was naked, but her body was very beautiful.' She was killed with two shots and fell across her dead husband. One by one the girls were brought into the room and shot, and Alexei last of all. Nicholas's body was weighted and sunk into a nearby marsh while the bodies of his family were buried in a forest outside of town."[25]

The truth of what had taken place in the Ipatiev House was rapidly subsumed in such tales, each more lurid than the previous. Sergeyev came under increasing pressure from officials in the White Army. On November 17, the lawful White government in Omsk was overthrown in a military coup, which installed Admiral Alexander Kolchak as the new supreme ruler.[26] From this moment on, the White Army controlled every aspect of the Romanov investigation, an inquiry that now fell under the authority of General Deterikhs, Kolchak's chief of staff in Omsk.

Kolchak was ready and eager to believe the worst about the fate of the Romanovs, conveniently pointing the finger of blame at the Jews, Bolsheviks, and Germans. In his mind, the first two were often lumped together as one entity, financed and promoted by the third, to create a sort of nefarious triptych of evil. His favorite book, it was said, was the infamous *Protocols of the Elders of Zion*.[27] Deterikhs clearly absorbed these ideas, and took to passing out copies of the *Protocols* to members of his own staff. As Russians, these men had been inculcated in such beliefs by both the state and the Russian Orthodox Church, but their paranoia spread to others. The British general Sir Alfred Knox, head of the British military mission in Siberia who worked closely with both Kolchak and Deterikhs, summed up this attitude in a 1919 cable he dispatched to the Foreign Office, in which he referred to the "blood-stained, Jew-led Bolsheviks."[28]

Knox, in fact, also was responsible for the spread of a fair amount of anti-Semitic rhetoric involving the murder of the Romanovs. On February 5, 1919, Knox reported that the murders in Ekaterinburg had been conceived and enacted by a group of five Jews.[29] Knox himself apparently commanded little confidence among British officials. Robert Bruce Lockhart complained to Arthur Balfour that Knox's "complete misunderstanding of the situation has been one of the chief reasons for our failure in this country."[30] The story, however, was apocryphal, having emanated from a group of virulently anti-Semitic Russians including the OSVAG, General Denikin's anti-Bolshevik propaganda office. This did not stop it from being endlessly repeated across Europe.[31] Among certain monarchist elements, however, it found a welcome home, adding further "evidence" to their belief that Jewish elements had been behind the Ekaterinburg murders.[32]

Deterikhs himself was quite conscious of the historical nature of the murders. "From the point of view of the ideology of the Russian people," he wrote, "there is still another aspect of this question—the spiritual symbol personified by the figure of the Emperor as anointed of God. The investigation considered itself obliged to exert every effort to display the murdered Emperor and Empress in as far as possible in this aspect, proceeding from the following considerations: the overthrow of an Emperor who is regarded by the people as merely a ruler is a crime of 'form,' a civil-political crime; but the overthrow of an Emperor who is regarded by the people as being also the anointed of God is a crime of the 'spirit,' which strikes at the roots of the whole historic, national, and religious outlook of the people, knocking out from under its feet the moral props of its life and existence."[33]

Such sentiments explain, to some extent, both the nationalistic attitudes so prevalent in the Romanov case and the intense religious feelings attached to the imperial family, twin threads that have largely remained hallmarks of not only the Ekaterinburg murders but also of discussions of the family of Nicholas and Alexandra. Such beliefs drove not only Deterikhs but also Wilton, Gilliard, Sokolov, and dozens of other authors who were to follow over the next eighty-five years. Objectivity was supplanted by larger considerations that built on the foundations of a fragile myth.

Such beliefs galvanized Deterikhs. He despised the Bolsheviks; he hated the Germans. Most of all, Deterikhs reviled Jews. Like his superior Admiral Kolchak, he passionately believed in *The Protocols of the Elders of Zion*, and even had special pamphlets printed for his troops titled *The Jews Have Killed the Emperor*.[34] In his own book on the Ekaterinburg murders, Deterikhs launched on the most vitriolic anti-Semitic attacks in any work dealing with the Romanovs. A single page gave ample evidence of his racial prejudices: he referred to "the Jew Zinoviev," "the Jew Zaslavsky," "the base, criminal Jews Dutzmann and Zaslavsky," "the Jews Safarov, Yankel [sic] Yurovsky, Pinkus [sic] Voikov, and Krasnov," and wrote, "Of the twelve members of the Ural Regional Soviet, seven were stinking Jews."[35] Such references peppered nearly every page of his book, with individuals frequently identified not only by ethnicity but also by a host of appellations ranging from "rotten Jew" to "filthy Jew."[36]

The White Army—and Deterikhs in particular—had no wish to draw out the investigation as it pursued various rumors, and stories that one or more of the imperial family had been rescued. With such attitudes in place, Sergeyev was a marked man. Although both Deterikhs and Sokolov accused Sergeyev of mishandling the Romanov investigation, there is no evidence to suggest this. Almost certainly, he lost his post for political reasons. His willingness to consider alternatives to the official White position ran counter to the wishes of those in Omsk, who, for propaganda and political purposes, seem to have determined that the murder of all the Romanovs was the only acceptable answer to the question of their fate.

On February 7, 1919, Deterikhs appointed Nicholas Sokolov, special investigator for the Omsk Provincial Court, to head all further investigations into the murders of the imperial family. Sokolov was a dedicated monarchist, a man who, for all of his judicial training, could be counted on to produce an acceptable version of the murders. Thus, with little more than the testimony of two guards, a room stained with blood, and a collection of burned items that had belonged to the imperial family, the Romanovs were formally declared to be dead. Thereafter, the investigation focused only on proving this assertion, at the same time ignoring evidence to the contrary.

Nicholas Sokolov was born in 1882 in Mokshan, Penza District, into a simple, provincial background. He graduated from the gymnasium in Penza and went on to study law at Kharkov University. Until the Revolution, he was a minor official in the Department of Justice in Penza. Learning of the rise of the Bolsheviks, Sokolov quit his job and, disguised as a peasant, made his way on foot across Siberia, eventually offering his services to the Omsk Regional Court. His wife, who served as his typist, accompanied him on this perilous journey.[37] Prior to his appointment, Sokolov was vested with the title of Official Investigator for Cases of Exceptional Importance. This, however, bore little relation to his own experiences. In reality, Sokolov was nothing more than a provincial public prosecutor of no great prominence or even promise. He was, however, capable and, more important to the White officials in Omsk, pliable. He was recommended to Deterikhs and Kolchak by an old friend, General Rozanov, a former shooting partner, who assured the military leaders that Sokolov could be trusted.[38] Sokolov understood that his mission was not to pursue any evidence that pointed to any conclusion other than what Deterikhs had instructed him to find, and his inquiry became less a search for truth than simply a prosecutorial legal brief with which the Whites hoped to indict the entire Soviet system. From the beginning, the White Army regulated Sokolov's mission; in a letter, General Deterikhs referred to the Sokolov investigation as a "military command."[39]

Sokolov was a curious man, of medium height, "lean, even emaciated," as Deterikhs recalled, with thinning hair and a glass eye that was cracked.[40] He struck those whom he encountered as overtly nervous, "pulling and biting"

Nicholas Sokolov posing in peasant disguise in Siberia, 1918.

his mustache, "swaying from side to side and slowly rubbing his hands" when speaking, and constantly "twitching."[41] He was passionate in his hatreds, not only for the Bolsheviks but also for the former Provisional Government and Kerensky, who, as Deterikhs recalled, he despised "to the depths of his soul."[42]

Sokolov may have genuinely believed that the Romanovs were all dead and that Moscow had ordered their assassination. There certainly was circumstantial evidence that the family had been killed, and although there was no proof of Moscow's involvement in their fate, it was not an unreasonable assumption. But Sokolov conducted his investigation—and produced his final report of that investigation—at the expense of impartiality. Evidence supporting his beliefs was included in his book; that which did not, offered alternative solutions, or even raised troublesome questions, was simply ignored, and buried in his dossiers. His final, published results were heavily edited to the extent that he removed contradictory passages in many of the statements made by the four captured Ipatiev House guards—Medvedev, Yakimov, Letemin, and Proskuryakov—simply to conceal what he himself made no effort to explain.

During the course of his investigation, Sokolov was to be shadowed and assisted by two men, Paul Bulygin and Robert Wilton, both of whom produced their own accounts of the end of the Romanovs. Bulygin, a former officer in the Life Guards, had gone to Siberia in a failed attempt to rescue the imperial family at the request of Dowager Empress Marie Feodorovna. In January 1919 she asked him to investigate what had become of her son and his family. He presented himself at Kolchak's headquarters in Omsk and was quickly appointed Sokolov's assistant; later he also would serve as his personal bodyguard.[43] Bulygin vividly recounts his first night in Omsk, when he dined with Deterikhs: "I first learnt the exact position: all the Emperor's family were dead, beyond a shadow of a doubt; the Imperial captives of Alapayevsk and Perm were also dead; the investigation was being conducted by a gifted and energetic judicial official, Sokolov, who was the third man to tackle the task, the first two having proved useless."[44]

The second man, Robert Wilton, was a former correspondent for the *Times* of London. Wilton was later fired from the *Times* as unreliable—a condemnation more than borne out by the number of wild inaccuracies in his eventual book. Wilton was formally in Russia to follow Kolchak, but he attached himself to General Deterikhs and actually became a member of his staff, thus compromising, as Philip Knightly noted, "any claim to objective reporting."[45] Wilton was scarcely a neutral observer, nor a credible recorder of fact. During his time in Siberia he repeatedly clashed with not only Russian officials but also members

of the British high commission and military mission. This led to a startling cable in June 1919 from General Knox, in which he implored that
Wilton be recalled immediately.[46] A Foreign Office communication,
not surprisingly, referred to Wilton as "inaccurate as to the facts."[47]

Wilton's own book *The Last Days of the Romanovs*, was published in
1920, and seemed equally devoted to a personal vendetta against both
the Germans and the Jews, the latter inevitably lumped together with
the Bolsheviks. His book, like that of Deterikhs, was littered with incendiary references. He claimed, for example, that Lenin's government had
ordered a statue of Judas Iscariot erected in a Moscow square, as "one of
its three main heroes."[48] His book was filled with anti-Semitic references
of the most blatant and offensive kind. Thus he wrote of "Yankel [sic]
Sverdlov, the Red Jewish Autocrat of All the Russias,"[49] "the Red-Jew
Government,"[50] "Jew-ruled Moscow,"[51] "the Jew murderers,"[52] "the
hellish design of the Jew fiend, Yankel [sic] Sverdlov,"[53] and "the hand of
the Red-Jew murderer."[54] He summed up this pathological hatred thus:
"The murder of the Tsar, deliberately planned by the Jew Sverdlov (who
came to Russia as a paid agent of Germany) and carried out by the Jews
Goloshchekin, Syromolotov, Safarov, Voikov and Yurovsky, is the act not
of the Russian people but of this hostile invader."[55]

Wilton was a man of definite ideas, particularly where the Romanovs
were concerned. Joseph Lasies, a French officer then in Ekaterinburg,
later recounted a curious conversation he had with Wilton at the train
station in Ekaterinburg in May 1919. During their talk, Lasies openly
expressed doubts as to the idea that the entire imperial family had been
killed. Wilton responded fiercely, growing more agitated by the minute,
until finally he declared, "Commandant Lasies, even if the Imperial
Family are alive, it is necessary to say that they are dead!"[56]

In the five months Sokolov worked on the Romanov case in Siberia,
he himself did far less than most have assumed. The work undertaken
during his tenure amounted to little more than a reexamination of the
murder room; a new search of the Four Brothers, which brought forth
sixty previously undiscovered objects; and the questioning of several
dozen witnesses, most of whom were members of the former imperial
suite and household. Sokolov's great benefit, however, was that he took
all of his investigative materials—the dossiers begun by Nametkin and
more than tripled in length by Sergeyev—into European exile, where
he continued to interview witnesses and compose his final brief. Even
so, Sokolov's eventual conclusions left much to be desired. His evidence that the entire imperial family had been killed, and their bodies
completely destroyed by being burned then subjected to acid, was itself
problematic and rested on a number of false assumptions and unsup-
portable science.

He built his case on four key pieces of evidence, the first of which was the testimony of four former Ipatiev House guards—Medvedev, Yakimov, Letemin, and Proskuryakov—all of whom testified that the entire imperial family had been murdered. Of this number, Yakimov's tale became known, in garbled form, through Sergeyev's interrogations of his sister and brother-in-law, while Letemin was questioned at Sergeyev's instruction by Kirsta. Only Medvedev claimed to have actually seen the corpses himself, and strenuously denied—in contradiction to the testimony of both his wife and the other captured guards—that he himself had been involved in the execution. Anatoly Yakimov had his tale secondhand, told to him by Kleshchev, Brusyanin, and Deryabin, and later added to by Medvedev himself. As such, Yakimov's evidence had only inferential value. Nevertheless, Sokolov openly questioned his veracity, and asked in his book, "Did Yakimov witness the murder with his own eyes, or did he know about it only through the words of others?"[57] Letemin's evidence was of even less value, having heard—like Yakimov—the story of the murder second- and even thirdhand. The same held true for Proskuryakov, who could offer nothing except a tale that, filled though it was with multiple contradictions to the other testimonies, seemed to clearly indicate that the Romanovs had been murdered in the basement of the Ipatiev House.

Of these guards, the most important was Paul Medvedev. He was arrested after the fall of Perm, and first questioned by a White general, Alexeiev, on February 11, 1919. Sokolov himself was in Omsk at the time; rather than returning to the Urals to interview this most important of all witnesses in his case himself, he asked Ivan Sergeyev—the man he had replaced—to undertake this examination on his behalf. It speaks volumes of Sergeyev's character that he agreed to do so. Medvedev was brought to Ekaterinburg, where Sergeyev interviewed him on February 21 and 22. Shortly thereafter, on March 25, Medvedev died while still incarcerated, the cause officially listed as typhus.[58]

Sokolov's second key piece of evidence was the murder room itself. The first examination of the murder room was conducted by Sergeyev in August 1918. Nametkin himself had concentrated on the upper floor, compiling an extensive inventory of the hundreds of items left by the imperial family. He had sealed the presumed murder room, and Sergeyev had to break the seal to begin his investigation. The one warranted criticism Sokolov was to level at Sergeyev was that the latter had not bothered to photograph the room in the condition in which it was found; the only photographs of it were taken after holes had been cut into the walls, spilling plaster onto the floor, leaving an impression of far more damage than had actually been present.[59]

Sergeyev noticed that the floor of the corridor outside the room had recently been washed, and bore traces of blood. Sand was still affixed to the surface when it was wet with blood, and the combination of these two elements had left clear signs on the yellow-painted wooden boards. On opening the double doors to the presumed murder room, Sergeyev noticed the same patterns of sand mixed with crimson stains spread across the entire surface of the floor. "In the corners," Sergeyev noted, "there are thicker layers of the same dried mixture of sand and whitening; stains of a reddish hue are visible on the surface of the floor." As he looked further, he saw "running stains, having the appearance of blood." These stained sections of flooring were cut away and removed for testing.[60]

In the walls, doors, and floor, Sergeyev found a total of twenty-seven bullet holes. There were two bullet holes in the set of double doors leading into the hallway to Voznesensky Lane; one bullet hole in the doorframe; two bullet holes on the southern wall just below the window; six bullet holes in the floor to the left of the doors to the hallway; and sixteen bullet holes clustered to the left of the double doors to the storeroom on the eastern wall.[61]

The majority of the bullet holes were in the lower parts of the walls, indicating to the first investigators that the victims had been shot while kneeling or seated on the floor itself. In fact, the bullet holes provided mute evidence of the chaotic nature of the executions, clear indications that the smoke mentioned in most of the accounts was so thick that the only parts of the victims visible to the shooters were their legs. A number of bullets were recovered from the walls, including those that had been fired from an 11.43 mm Colt revolver; from a 10.66 mm Smith & Wesson revolver; from a 6.43 mm Browning and from a 7.63 mm Browning; and from Russian 7.62 and 9 mm Nagant revolvers.[62]

Sergeyev removed substantial portions of wallpaper stained with blood; Sokolov apparently discovered several other, small splashes, which were submitted for testing and proved to be human. Of the blood, however, Sokolov also made some startling claims. "This wall," he wrote in one report, "was spattered with the blood of one of the Grand Duchesses," and again he declared, "Near the damaged wall the blood of the Empress is to be seen."[63] Blood grouping as a science had not yet been developed, nor did Sokolov possess any blood samples from members of the imperial family with which the bloodstains could be compared and tested. In his determination to prove what had, in fact, taken place, Sokolov engaged in deliberate distortion of evidence to suit his own ends.

Sergeyev also noted several inscriptions on the walls. There were crude pornographic drawings of the empress with Rasputin and, below the window, an inscription that read:

Belsatzar ward in selbiger Nacht
Von seinen Knechten umgebracht.

It was a quotation from the twenty-first stanza of the poem "Balshazzar" by the German poet Heinrich Heine. In translation it read:

Belsatzar was that very night
Seized by his slaves and killed outright.

Whoever had written the inscription was certainly educated, and had more than a passing acquaintance with German poetry. The inscriber also had changed the spelling from the original "Belshazzar" to read "Belsatzar," as if to indicate that the emperor, the "tzar" indicated, had been seized and killed by his former slaves.[64] In the hands of Wilton, this inscription became a clear indication that the execution had been enacted by Jews—in his book he even reproduced a photograph of it captioned, "The hand of the Red-Jew murderer."[65]

Below the window, on the same wall on which the inscription had been made, were four small marks, written in thick, black ink.[66] Sokolov himself reproduced them in his book without comment. In 1923 a Russian émigré, Michael Skariatin, wrote a small booklet called *Sacrifice* under the pseudonym "Enel," in which he contended that three of the symbols were the letter *l* in Hebrew, Samaritan, and Greek—languages, he asserted, that had been used by the Jews throughout history. Skariatin concluded, without attempting to consider precisely who among the assassins spoke Hebrew, Greek, and Samaritan, that the writer was a Jew, and the marks somehow connected to the murder of the Romanovs.[67] From this highly speculative analysis, any number of anti-Semitic accusations have flowed, usually insistent that the execution was a "ritual Jewish murder" of a Christian sovereign, enacted on the orders of a worldwide Jewish conspiracy.[68]

The convincing, although circumstantial, evidence, coupled with both the sworn testimony gathered by Sergeyev and by Sokolov himself from several former guards at the Ipatiev House, led Sokolov to the following conclusion:

It is demonstrated that between July 17 and 22, 1918, when Ipatiev renewed the interrupted possession of his house, a murder occurred in it. This did not occur on the upper floor, where the Imperial Family lived: there is not even a hint of violence being employed there, against anyone. The bloody carnage took place in one of the rooms of the lower, basement, floor. The selection alone of this room speaks for itself: the murder was strictly premeditated. From it there is no escape: behind it there is a deep storeroom without exit; its only window, with two sashes, is covered on the outside with a thick iron grating. It is deeply sunk in the ground and completely concealed from the outside by a high fence. This room is, in full degree, a torture chamber. The murder was perpetrated with revolvers and bayonets. More than thirty shots were fired, because it cannot be assumed that all of the blows were trans-piercing and that no bullets remained in the bodies of the victims. Several people were murdered, because it cannot be supposed that one person could change his position in the same room to such an extent and submit to so many blows. Some of the victims were, before death, in positions along the east and south walls, others were nearer to the center of the room. Several were hit while they were already lying on the floor. If the Imperial Family and those living with them were murdered here, there is no doubt that they were lured here from their living quarters by some false pretext.[69]

The evidence collected at the Four Brothers mine shaft by Sheremetievsky, Nametkin, the members of the Officers Commission, Sergeyev, and Sokolov was almost entirely circumstantial, in no way pointing directly to Sokolov's conclusion that the entire imperial family and their retainers had been killed. As such, it was the weakest aspect of Sokolov's case—his inability to prove precisely what had happened to the corpses. In addition to the collection of items discovered by Sheremetievsky and Nametkin, Sergeyev located a number of important finds. These included more jewels, including pearls concealed in buttons, earrings, topaz beads, and fragments from emeralds, diamonds, and sapphires; pieces of a hand grenade; shattered glass vials; buttons; portions of burned clothing and footwear; personal accessories such as tie clasps, stickpins, parts of cufflinks, and watch chains; a number of animal bones; the upper plate from a pair of false teeth, identified as having belonged to Dr. Botkin; two pieces of skin; and a severed finger—the last three items the only indisputably human remains ever discovered during the various White investigations.[70]

After the fall of Ekaterinburg, both Gilliard and Gibbes had hastily returned to the city, hoping to discover what had become of the Romanovs. Now, joined by Dr. Derevenko and Terenty Chemodurov, the emperor's old valet who had been incarcerated in a hospital ward of Ekaterinburg City Prison since late May, these four men began the lengthy process of attempting to identify these items.[71] Much of the clothing recovered was too badly destroyed to be accurately identified, although enough remained intact that these men were able to determine that a great many pieces represented either items similar to those

that belonged to the imperial family, or were, in fact, Romanov possessions. A few of the jewels, too, were too fragmented to be satisfactorily
identified, but the vast majority were determined to represent items
that had belonged either to the empress or to her daughters.[72]

Sokolov was forced to wait until the arrival of spring 1919 before he
could fully examine the Four Brothers area. In late May he first investigated the area, walking from Ekaterinburg out along Koptyaki Road
and past Grade Crossing 184, to the place where several witnesses had
indicated clear evidence that, the previous summer, a truck had passed
through the trees. During his examination, he found and photographed
the road that cleaved through Pig's Meadow, including the railroad ties
sunk into the swampy ground that, in fact, concealed the Romanov
graves. Although he had collected the testimonies of those who recalled
the truck breaking down and the collection of railroad ties from the hut
at Grade Crossing 184, Sokolov simply assumed that they had been
placed across the muddy lane to provide the vehicle with better traction.
Suspicious though they were, he made no effort to extricate them, or
more fully examine what they possibly concealed.[73]

The only human remains discovered were two small pieces of skin,
and the severed finger, the latter highly contentious. Dr. Derevenko
examined it and declared confi-
dently that it had belonged to his
colleague Dr. Botkin.[74] Sokolov,
however, declared that an unnamed
"commission of experts" believed it
to be the finger of a middle-aged
woman, with long, thin fingers,
"accustomed to manicuring, as it
presented a well-groomed appearance."[75] Sokolov's compatriots
Bulygin and Wilton both confidently asserted in their respective
books that it had, indeed, belonged
to the empress.[76] Both identifications—those of Derevenko and that
of Sokolov's unnamed "commission
of experts"—were, quite simply,
ridiculous. The photograph of the
finger that Sokolov reproduced
in his book did not show a long,
thin finger that was "accustomed
to manicuring" and had a "well-
groomed appearance." Rather, it

Investigator Sokolov on the road through the
Koptyaki Forest. Unknowingly, he is standing
in the vicinity of the Romanov graves.

was large, ungainly, and the fingernail was broken off. Nor, in 1919, was it possible to determine either the gender of the finger's original owner, nor even who that person might have been. Derevenko was reaching, but his identification did not, as did Sokolov's, form part of the official historical record. Clearly, it was necessary, given the complete absence of corpses, for Sokolov to attempt to prove his case, as his exaggerated claims regarding the severed finger and its presumed owner show. With the upper plate of false teeth known to have come from Botkin, he needed something to represent the physical remains of the empress. One can only conclude that Sokolov either engaged in extremely naive, wishful thinking, or was himself guilty of manipulating his own evidence.

The various investigations failed to locate any identifiable human remains. Deterikhs later claimed that on the visit to the Four Brothers, members of the Officers' Commission had discovered a "completely burnt rib" that, when touched, "crumbled into a fine ash."[77] Sokolov built on this by asserting that "splinters of shattered and burned bones" also were discovered at the mine but that Nametkin had thrown them away.[78] It may be that Sokolov believed this, but any such bones allegedly found at the Four Brothers could not have come from any of the victims in the Romanov case. Accepting the story that two of the corpses were burned, the Ural Bolsheviks were quite clear that this was done not at the Four Brothers but rather in Pig's Meadow, several miles away. This same argument also applies to the forty-two bone fragments, which Sokolov identified only as those of a "mammal." Apparently these were found at the Four Brothers, and bore signs of having been subjected to blows from a sharp-bladed object as well as being burned. Sokolov quoted a doctor in his book as saying, "I do not exclude the possibility that these bones are all human."[79] This is inexplicable. Had Sokolov submitted the bones to any qualified examiner, it could easily have been determined whether the bones were human. Sokolov, perhaps unwilling to pursue the matter, let the doctor's statement stand, apparently confirming, as it did, that these bone fragments could very well be the only actual remains of the imperial family and their retainers. It is more likely, as several forensic experts have asserted after having studied the photographs of the bones, that they came from an animal, not from a human body.[80]

Sokolov was perplexed by the lack of human remains. He wandered around the Four Brothers, asking aloud, "Where are the cinders? That is the question; we have found too few."[81] Even given Sokolov's assumption that the bodies of all eleven victims had been fully destroyed by being burned, then dissolved in acid, one important item remained missing: teeth, which are nearly indestructible. Had his conclusions been correct, Sokolov should have found teeth—or even a single tooth—to show that corpses had in fact been destroyed at the mine. He ignored this major flaw in his theory, but both Wilton and Deterikhs attempted to explain it by asserting that the heads had all been severed and taken back to Moscow by Yurovsky, on Sverdlov's orders.[82] It is a tale still vehemently believed by some members of the Russian Orthodox Church Outside Russia to this day.

According to Sokolov, "the open shaft" provided "the solution to the entire mystery. It was not difficult to resolve. All that was required was to lower oneself to the bottom of the shaft."[83] Here, according to Sokolov, on June 25, 1919, investigators discovered the corpse of Jemmy, one of three dogs the Romanovs had taken with them into their Siberian exile. Sokolov described this as "the corpse of a female dog," which, "thanks to the low temperature at the bottom of the shaft, had been well preserved."[84] It did not take long for the animal to be identified by the tutor Gibbes as Jemmy; he erroneously described it as Anastasia's pet, an error repeated by Gilliard that quickly became embodied in Romanov literature, despite the fact that Anna Vyrubova, in her own memoirs, indicates that the dog had been a gift from herself to Tatiana Nikolaievna.[85]

How did this important piece of evidence remain undiscovered for eleven months, and how did it manage to survive in nearly pristine condition? Wilton claimed that the Bolsheviks had hidden it beneath a false floor that they affixed to the bottom of the shaft.[86] Yet Sokolov himself made no such claim, stating that it was "noticeable to the eye" and found lying at the "bottom of the open shaft."[87] Yet the shaft had been pumped out twice—once by Sergeyev, and once by Sokolov himself—and nothing had been discovered at the bottom except sludge. Nor did Sokolov ever claim that the corpse had been concealed beneath a false floor. He did, however, repeat Wilton's assertion that the low temperature in the shaft, coupled with the Siberian winter, had left the dog in its remarkable state.[88]

Like Wilton's story of a false floor, however, this assertion was wrong, and it is here, with the issue of Jemmy's corpse, that Sokolov's most strident critics, Summers and Mangold, discovered the one piece of certain false evidence planted in the Romanov case. They conducted an extensive investigation into the weather and temperature conditions for the shaft and thus were able to disprove Sokolov's and Wilton's claims regarding the permanent ice at the bottom of the shaft.[89] Nor, as they discovered, did the condition of the dog in any way resemble that of an animal that had been dead for eleven months and been immersed in water. Given the autopsy report, which included details on the lungs, and the general condition of the corpse itself, forensic pathologists believed that the dog had been dead for perhaps no more than a week when discovered on June 25, 1919.[90]

This indicated that the dog had not—as Sokolov asserted—died with its mistress on the night of July 17, but had only recently been killed. This itself was not out of the question; when Michael Letemin was arrested the previous summer, he was found to have Alexei's spaniel Joy with him. Joy was subsequently taken by a member of the British military mission to England, where he lived on a farm in Berkshire.[91] As Kudrin recalled, one dog was killed on the night of the murders, as it came down the staircase of the Ipatiev House. This must, then, have been Ortino, whose corpse was never found. It is entirely possible, given the few bones discovered at the Four Brothers, that Ortino's corpse was, in fact, burned at the mine—a process that would have been relatively easy to accomplish given the two days on which guards were on duty in Koptyaki Forest. If, as seems likely, this is the case, then the forty-two bone fragments discovered by Sokolov represented not the imperial family or their retainers, but rather one of their pets.

Sokolov's final explanation of what happened in Koptyaki Forest included a large dose of unproved assertion, as time would show:

> On the clay area, at the open shaft, the corpses were stripped. The clothing was crudely removed, torn away and cut with knives. Several of the buttons were destroyed in the process, hooks and eyes stretched. The concealed jewels were of course exposed. Several of them which fell with many others on the clay area of the shaft remained unnoticed, and were trampled in the upper layers of this area. The main purpose was to destroy the bodies. For this, it was necessary, first of all, to dissect the corpses, to cut them up. This was done on the clay area. The blows of the sharp, cutting instruments, cutting the corpses apart, cut some of the jewels that were trampled into the earth. A commission of experts established that several of the jewels were destroyed by strong blows of some hard objects; not sharp, cutting instruments. These were jewels that had been sewn into the brassieres of the Grand Duchesses and destroyed by the bullets entering their bodies at the time of the murders. The dissected bodies were burned in the bonfires with the aid of gasoline and destroyed with sulfuric acid. The bullets, which remained in the bodies, fell into the fires. The lead was melted, ran into the ground and then, cooling, acquired the shape of hardened drops. The empty bullet casings remained. The corpses, burned on the bare ground, gave up fat. Running out it impregnated the soil. The torn and cut pieces of clothing were burned in the same fires. In several there were hooks, eyes and buttons. They were preserved in burned form. Several hooks and eyes, having been burned, remained fastened

together. Noticing some of the objects remaining, the criminals threw them into the shaft, after having first broken the ice in it. Then they covered them with earth.[92]

In July 1919 Ekaterinburg fell to the advancing Bolsheviks, marking the beginning of the end of White rule in Siberia. White and Czech forces fled east from the Urals, preceded by overcrowded railroad cars jammed with refugees, including Sokolov, who carried a number of cases; most contained depositions and transcripts of interviews with those involved in the Romanov case, but two held items recovered from the Four Brothers mine in Koptyaki Forest—the presumed last remnants of the Russian imperial family. Sokolov spent some time in Chita, where he was almost executed by none other than the maniacal Cossack Semyonov, who apparently wished to silence the official White version of the end of the Romanovs.[93] This episode did little to calm Sokolov's notoriously fragile nerves. When General Deterikhs offered him safe transport out of Russia, the investigator refused, warning his colleague Captain Paul Bulygin that it was all part of a plot to separate him from his precious boxes.[94]

The murder of Admiral Kolchak at the beginning of 1920—coupled with suspicions that the French had conspired in handing him over to the Bolsheviks—signaled a general panic among the remaining White and monarchist elements in Siberia. Sokolov soon fled to Vladivostok, where—ironically—he placed himself under the protection of General Janin, head of the French mission and commander of the Allied expeditionary forces in Siberia.[95] In spring 1920 Sokolov left Russia, sailing aboard the French ship *André le Bon*. The vessel was crammed with refugees, among them Colonel Kirill Naryshkin and his wife, who dutifully did as Sokolov asked and slept with one of his cases beneath her bunk. Presumably this contained the items—a few charred bones, the severed finger, bits of clothing, smashed jewelry, and other relics—found at the Four Brothers mine in Koptyaki Forest.[96] Throughout the voyage, Sokolov remained deeply suspicious, convinced that all around him plots were developing to rob him of his investigative materials.[97]

In Europe, Sokolov took rooms in the Hôtel du Bon Lafontaine, on the Rue des St. Peres, in Paris. This hotel became something of a magnet for like-minded émigrés: in addition to Sokolov, his wife, and their child, Bulygin also shared the apartment, with Pierre Gilliard and his new wife, the former imperial nurse Alexandra Tegleva, just one flight up.[98] A frequent visitor was journalist Robert Wilton, another companion from the days of the Romanov investigations in Siberia.[99] Sokolov spent the next three years working on a book that would encompass the results of his investigation and present the nearest thing to an official account of the murders of the Romanovs to history.[100] On several occasions he attempted to meet with members of the exiled dynasty, but no one among them seemed to want anything to do with him. He planned to take his records to Copenhagen, where Dowager Empress Marie Feodorovna was living, and present her with the evidence he had accumulated. When the dowager empress got wind of this, she hastily sent a cable, through her daughter Grand Duchess Olga Alexandrovna, to Paris: "Entreat Sokolov and Bulygin not to come." Nor was the investigator any more successful in his attempts to meet Grand Duke Nicholas Nikolaievich, then living in exile in southern France. The dowager empress did, however, send Sokolov £1,000 to help finance his work. Thus, recalled Bulygin, "the investigation was saved."[101]

The money sent by the dowager empress, however, only went so far, and soon Sokolov found himself without funds. At this desperate moment he met Prince Nicholas Orlov. The son of Prince Vladimir Orlov, who had served as the last head of the Imperial Chancellery, Prince Nicholas was, like Sokolov, a dedicated monarchist émigré, and agreed to supply him with both a stipend and an apartment on his estate near Fontainebleau.[102] Despite this brief respite in his fortunes, Sokolov, as Orlov recalled, was plagued with "disappointments and difficult experiences." The prince wrote:

> Alone, supported by no one, deeply convinced of the extraordinary importance of the truth of the murder of the Emperor and his family, believing that this truth properly belonged to the future National Russia, that it must be preserved for the Russian people—Sokolov had to wage a long and painful struggle for its defense against those who tried to use it in their personal interests. Some insisted upon silence at all costs because the truth—death—was not to their liking. Others, on the contrary, wanted to use this truth for the benefit of their own personal interests. Nicholas Alexeievich did not falter. . . . He guarded this truth for future generations, guarding it from every encroachment of personal intrigue. He determined to proclaim the truth himself—on his own, and not under the banner of any political party whatsoever.[103]

In his last months, Sokolov became embroiled with automotive magnate Henry Ford, a virulently anti-Semitic proponent of the idea that a worldwide Jewish conspiracy did indeed exist. Ford published a company newspaper in which he gave full vent to his views, and over the course of the 1920s he was sued several times for libel for his assertions. In late 1923 Boris Brasol, chairman of the Russian National Society, told Ford that it would be worth his time to invite Nicholas Sokolov to America, as his investigation "showed conclusively that the murder of the Imperial Family was instigated by Jews and the actual killing was done by a group of men composed, with the exception of three, entirely of Jews."[104]

After some negotiations, Sokolov, accompanied by Prince Nicholas Orlov and his wife, Princess Nadejda Orlov, left Europe for America, arriving in Boston at the end of January 1924. An article in the *New York Times* reported their arrival, saying that the group had come to interview a woman claiming to be a rescued grand duchess.[105] Eight days later, Sokolov issued an official denial, saying that the visit to the United States was concerned only with the future publication of his work.[106] The trio journeyed to Dearborn, Michigan, and Ford's headquarters. After meeting with the automotive baron, Sokolov agreed that, in exchange for funding from Ford, his official report would declare that "the assassination had been planned and carried out by the Jews." This rather shameful episode, wrote researchers Anthony Summers and Tom Mangold, reduced the "the work begun in Ekaterinburg, fan-fared as an unbiased judicial investigation into the fate of the most powerful monarch on earth," to "a tawdry racist transaction in a Michigan office block."[107]

Sokolov returned to Paris completely exhausted. His health was poor, his nerves shattered, his funds gone, and the promise of money from Ford lay in the future. Sokolov complained that "everything is completely disintegrating here and I cannot get any funds."[108] To Bulygin he wrote: "The old engine is worn out. . . . Must finish up the work and that will be the end. . . . Why are you so far away, dear? I am lonely. The end is near. I feel we shall not see each other again. . . . I send you from afar my parting embrace."[109]

Sokolov barely finished his work on the murder of the Romanovs. On November 23, 1924, he suffered a massive heart attack and died. He was only forty-two. He was buried in a small churchyard in the village of Salbris, beneath a tombstone erected by his friends. Its inscription declared simply: "Your Truth is Truth Eternal."[110]

16

"Holy Relics of Our Saints"

WHEN SOKOLOV FLED RUSSIA in 1920, he carried with him three suitcases, and a small wooden chest, covered in mauve cloth, that had belonged to the empress. Carefully wrapped and locked inside were 311 objects, discovered in the Ipatiev House and at the Four Brothers mine: "about thirty fragments of bone, a little human fat which had dripped off the logs, some hair, an amputated finger which expert knowledge identified as one of the Empress's ring fingers, charred remains of jewelry, small icons, scraps of clothing, and of shoes, such metal accessories as buttons, shoe buckles, the buckles of the Tsesarevich's belt, bits of bloodstained carpet, revolver bullets," and other items.[1] Bulygin also detailed "thirteen drops of blood," preserved "in arsenic capsules."[2]

These four cases followed Sokolov from Ekaterinburg to Omsk, Omsk to Chita, and Chita to Harbin. On January 7, 1920, General Deterikhs wrote to Miles Lampson, the British high commissioner in Siberia:

> To the last possible moment I wished to retain in my own hands and in Russia, in the revival of which I still continue to trust, the affair of the Imperial Family, i.e., the substantial evidence in the matter and the Remains of Their Imperial Majesties, which it has been possible to find on the place where Their Corpses were burnt. The turn which events are taking, however, shows that in order to ensure the safety of these Sacred Relics, it is essential that They should not be connected with my fate. I cannot leave Russia; the German orientation in Chita may compel me temporarily to seek refuge in the forest. Under such conditions

I am of course unable to carry with me the Great National Sacred Relics. I have decided to entrust you, as the Representative of Great Britain, with the safe-keeping of these Sacred Objects. I think you will understand without my having to explain, why I wish it to be Great Britain; you and we have one common historical foe, and the tortuous murder of the Members of the Imperial Family, a deed unprecedented in history, is the deed of this foe, aided by their assistants, the Bolsheviks. I should like to add that if circumstances compel you to take the Imperial Remains and the documents out of Russia, and if England cannot return Them to me, I consider that they can be only handed over to the Grand Duke Nicholas Nikolaievich or General Denikin.[3]

According to an official report, written by Lampson and lodged in the files of the Public Record Office at Kew, the boxes in question were definitely turned over to the high commissioner on January 8, 1920.[4] Lampson turned the box or boxes over to U.S. vice consul Ernest Harris, to be carried out of Siberia aboard his train to Harbin.[5] It seems that both Lampson and Harris each traveled with a part of Sokolov's cargo, for both men speak in their respective accounts of the case or cases they brought with them.

In 1925, a curious story by Arthur Elliot Sproul appeared in the *New York Times*, which confirmed British and American involvement in the affair. Sproul wrote:

I was in Russia in 1917 and 1918. . . . While in Moscow I became intimately acquainted with an American gentleman who had formerly held important posts in our consular service but who was then connected with a large New York bank in its Russian department. . . . Owing to the strenuous conditions then prevailing it proved impossible for this official to retain a permanent headquarters. At first his office was in Omsk; but he was compelled to move gradually eastward, until he found himself in Ekaterinburg. . . . My friend kept on his slow way until he finally reached Vladivostok—thence taking ships to this country, which he reached in the summer of 1920, where he told me this story: "I personally brought the bones of all members of the former Royal Family of Russia out of Siberia in a trunk, together with the icons and minor articles of jewelry that were worn by the victims at the time of their assassination. The bones and personal belongings were delivered to me in Ekaterinburg, after being removed from the disused mine shaft where the bodies were flung after the event. Those who requested me to care for and remove the bones and the articles indicated told me that they did so because I was an American and they felt differently toward me for that reason than they would toward any European. . . . I accepted the trust; and when I left Ekaterinburg, not long thereafter, the trunk and its contents naturally formed part of my consular baggage. As I was bound for Vladivostok, however, and not to China, I turned over the trunk and contents to British officials at Harbin on the Mongolian frontier—taking their receipt—who were then to forward them to Peking and deliver them to the Russian Legation in that city.[6]

The American official was Ernest Harris. He was said to have carried the box containing the remains across Siberia.

Sokolov was in Harbin, awaiting safe passage to Vladivostok and then to Europe, when he was overcome with one of his frequent bouts of nervous paranoia. "I found myself in Harbin," Sokolov later wrote, "in a most difficult position." In February 1920 he wrote to Lampson, "asking him if he could arrange to send the documents to Europe for me. I told him that these were the victims' remains and I emphasized the Germans' role in the affair. On 23 February the Ambassador's secretary . . . told me that the Ambassador had telegraphed to London for instructions. On 19 March the English Government's reply was communicated to me by Mr. Sly, the British Consul at Harbin. It was negative."[7]

The answer Lampson received from Whitehall was adamant: neither Sokolov nor his cases would be welcome in England. In the official notification, Lampson was warned that "it would be a source of great embarrassment to have that dispatch box in England; the King spoke to me about this the other day. If it can be handed over to a suitable Russian we shall be well rid of it."[8] Even after the Ekaterinburg murders, King George V pointedly refused to grant asylum even to the presumed bones of his dead relatives.

The number of reports left by Lampson, as well as the letter from Deterikhs, make it quite clear that the high commissioner indeed had the boxes in Siberia and, in turn, handed them over to Harris. This seems to have taken place in January 1920, while Sokolov himself was awaiting official word on whether he would be allowed to come to Great Britain with the documents and cases. Lampson reported to London: "Sokolov is getting restive at the absence of any reply and states that he is in danger from German agents. . . . Sokolov's letter seems to me somewhat hysterical. . . . I am tempted to think he has German machinations on the brain."[9]

Harris later recounted how he had traveled across Siberia with the small wooden box said to contain the chopped bones, finger, fat mixed with earth, drops of blood, and other relics found at the Four Brothers mine. He recalled the "small wooden box, tied up hastily with rope like an immigrant's luggage," which he kept beneath the table in his compartment.[10] Both Lampson and Harris headed for Harbin, aboard separate trains. According to tutor Charles Sydney Gibbes, Lampson reached the city first, followed some days later by Harris. But Gibbes thought that the box carried by Harris contained not the actual remains from the Four Brothers mine but rather a number of documents that implicated the Germans in the Ekaterinburg murders.[11]

In Harbin, Sokolov attempted to find safe passage for the cases. "On the same day," he wrote, "I found the French General Janin who was in Harbin. Janin told General Deterikhs, who accompanied me, and myself, that he considered the mission we entrusted to him to be a debt of honor to a faithful ally. Thanks to him, the dossiers were saved and taken to a safe place."[12]

Pierre Gilliard, who happened to be in Harbin with Sokolov, Deterikhs, and Bulygin, himself later wrote: "They were in a state of great agitation, for the situation in Manchuria was growing daily more precarious, and it was expected that at any moment the Chinese Eastern Railway might fall into the hands of the Reds. Bolshevik spies were already beginning to swarm over the station and its surroundings. What was to be done with the documents of the inquiry? Where could they be put in safety? General Deterikhs and N. Sokolov had appealed to the British High Commissioner before his departure for Peking, asking him to take to Europe the relics of the Imperial Family and the evidence of the inquiry. He had asked for instructions from his Government. The reply was a long time coming. It came at last. It was in the negative! I then appealed personally to General Janin, informing him of the situation." According to Gilliard, Janin replied: "I am quite ready to help you. I can do it on my own responsibility, as there is not time to refer the matter to my government. But it shall not be said that a French General refused the relics of one who was the faithful ally of France. Ask General Deterikhs to furnish me with a written request expressing his certainty of my consent; I should consider doubt as a reflection on me." The requested document was, Gilliard recorded, duly sent. "Two days later," Gilliard wrote, "General Deterikhs, his two orderly officers, N. Sokolov, and myself took on our shoulders the heavy valises prepared beforehand and carried them to General Janin's train, which was standing a short distance from the station."[13]

Sokolov and Gilliard were at odds as to precisely who approached General Janin and requested passage for the cases. As Sokolov was the official White investigator, and the man who so zealously guarded the cases, it would be reasonable to assume that his was the correct account, a fact later confirmed by General Janin.[14] Why Gilliard felt the need to inject himself into the episode when he clearly played no role remains a mystery.

Janin presumably took possession of the three suitcases and the wooden box covered in mauve cloth in Harbin. Janin had the box and cases sealed, and selected a special guard of officers to stand watch over them "for the duration of the voyage."[15] According to Gilliard, the luggage was loaded aboard Janin's train on March 19, 1920, in Harbin. The following day, the train—carrying not only Janin but also Sokolov, Deterikhs, Bulygin, Gilliard, and Gibbes—left the city en route to Vladivostok, where the French vessel *André le Bon* waited to take them to Marseilles.[16]

Madame Naryshkina later recalled sleeping with a small box tucked beneath her bunk, and believed this to have contained the presumed imperial remains.[17] Janin, in a later letter to the French periodical *Petit Journal* recalled that another four cases traveled aboard a different French ship, locked in a strong room belowdecks and watched over by his specially selected guards.[18] Janin, it seems, stood guard over the imperial family's possessions but not their presumed remains.

Eventually the cases arrived in Marseilles. Janin refused to hand them over to French authorities, but instead kept them in the basement of his country house near Grenoble. He intended to hand them over personally to the dowager empress in Copenhagen or, failing this, to Grand Duke Nicholas Nikolaievich at his residence in the south of France. The dowager empress, however, refused to receive the cases, and Janin had no better luck with the grand duke. Nor would the exiled White general Denikin accept the relics. On the grand duke's advice, Janin apparently turned the cases over to the former Russian ambassador in Rome, Nicholas de Giers.[19]

The twenty-nine cases that contained the items removed from the Ipatiev House—clothing, photograph albums, porcelain, the tsesarevich's toys, and the imperial family's linens—seem to have been taken from Marseilles to London, and then to Buckingham Palace. Apparently the boxes were taken down The Mall to Marlborough House, residence of Queen Alexandra, sister of the dowager empress, where King George V and Queen Mary joined Grand Duchess Xenia Alexandrovna for their unpacking. The contents were investigated, checked, and found to contain little of material interest. Only later did the grand duchess, after receiving information from Baroness Sophie Buxhoeveden, discover some of Empress Alexandra's jewels, hidden in a rolled-up cloth packed between some clothing that had belonged to Countess Hendrikova.[20]

A persistent rumor also contends that the small box presumed to contain the remains of the Romanovs made its way into British royal hands. Lampson was said to have delivered it to Queen Alexandra at Marlborough House, as Lady Violet Kirkpatrik, who worked with the former high commissioner in the Foreign Office, later recalled. She wrote that one day in 1920 "Mr. Lampson came into my room and left a leather bag with me. He returned later and told me he had a very painful thing to do. He was going straight to Marlborough House to give the box which was in the bag to Queen Alexandra as it contained all the remains of the Imperial Family which were not destroyed by being burnt."[21] This story was confirmed by Sir Thomas Preston, who himself apparently heard it from the king in February 1921. At that time, George V had complained: "The relics were in such a state that they had to be fumigated before they could be touched."[22] Two other accounts held that the remains were also delivered to the British royal family; ironically, both came from exiled Russians. Prince Felix Yusupov, according to an interview given by Prince Serge Obolensky in 1971, said that he himself had seen the box with the remains at Buckingham Palace.[23] And Prince Dimitri Alexandrovich, son of Grand Duchess Xenia, publicly declared that the box, with its grisly contents, was in Windsor Castle as late as the 1950s.[24]

The box may, in fact, have temporarily been in the possession of the British royal family in the first years after the Revolution. But there is something unconvincing about the stories that the presumed remains continued to be held in their possession for nearly four decades. First, King George V was adamant that he was unwilling to receive them; he may, as Lady Kirkpatrik's evidence suggests, later have relented somewhat, but this seems to have been only temporary. Even then, the box was not kept by the king at either Buckingham Palace or Windsor Castle, but sent to his mother, Queen Alexandra, at Marlborough House, to be passed along to her sister the dowager empress. According to Grand Duchess Olga Alexandrovna, the dowager empress and her two daughters were duly given the box. Grand Duchesses Xenia and Olga Alexandrovna "wept over the little box before it went to France."[25]

Janin apparently had possession of the relics only until he could pass them on to Lampson. But Janin's own account contradicted this. According to his version, as published in the December 1930 issue of *Petit Journal*, the box still rested in the vaults beneath his house near Grenoble.[26] And yet, according to Janin's book, published three years later, he had indeed handed over the box to de Giers at the request of Grand Duke Nicholas Nikolaievich some years earlier.[27]

The mystery, if not entirely resolved, is perhaps at least partially explained by the fact that multiple boxes and cases connected with the Romanovs, and to Sokolov's investigation, were brought out of Russia, and seem to have, at various times, been in France, Great Britain, Denmark, and Italy. Undoubtedly, with the cases sealed and rumors rampant, some of those involved may have confused not only what they saw but also their speculation on what was contained within.

The most important box—which contained the presumed remains

of the imperial family—almost certainly ended up in the possession of de Giers in Rome. In November 1923 Grand Duke Kirill Vladimirovich, head of the imperial house, wrote a letter to de Giers, asking him to confirm that he had the remains; de Giers, however, equivocated, replying only that "these objects are kept in a reliable place, and under my personal responsibility."[28] The grand duke made further inquiries and learned that Nicholas Nikolaievich had refused to take possession of the box, asking that it be left with de Giers. In 1924 Kirill Vladimirovich again wrote to de Giers, asking that the remains be turned over to him. He would assume responsibility for them, and place them in an appropriate consecrated vault. The former diplomat apparently took this letter to Grand Duke Nicholas Nikolaievich, who harbored personal animosity toward Kirill Vladimirovich and refused to discuss the issue. After "determining that all attempts were futile," Grand Duke Kirill Vladimirovich, in a letter of August 8, 1924, expressed "my most heartfelt outrage that these Holy Imperial Relics" remained in the hands of a "private citizen, without proper burial."[29]

According to Prince Sidamon-Eristov, de Giers held this box at least through 1931.[30] On April 15 of that same year, Grand Duke Kirill Vladimirovich privately established the Committee for the Investigation and Preservation of the Holy Imperial Relics, and appointed A. Bashmakov as its chairman; the membership included V. Khrustaev, Nicholas Markov, former senator N. Korevo, and Prince Chachavadze. After discussing the issue, the committee approached de Giers and formally requested on behalf of the grand duke that the remains be turned over to them for their safekeeping.[31]

Was the box in fact turned over at this point? It is possible. Sometime before the outbreak of World War II, however, the box was once again transferred, this time to Paris, where it was stored in the vault of the Sécurité Générale Insurance Company. During the occupation of Paris, the building was seized by German troops, who raided the vault.[32]

Thereafter, the fate of the box is, officially, an enigma. Such inquiries were not helped—and this was perhaps the point—by obvious though ambiguous leaks over the years from various Russian émigrés. Professor Pierre Kovalevsky, for example, related, rather improbably, that the box was in the possession of a group of trusted aristocrats, passed from member to member, and that "whoever has them at that time simply keeps them on top of a cupboard."[33] Author Victor Alexandrov, writing in 1966, reported "an unconfirmed rumor, circulating among the old Russian émigré taxi drivers in Paris," that the box was "securely stored in the safe of a Manhattan bank."[34]

But two other versions of the fate of the box with the presumed imperial remains have become, over time, the most popular and frequently repeated. One holds that the remains were buried in the Cemetery of St. Genevieve de Bois in Paris, final resting place of many notable Russian émigrés. Seeming confirmation of this story came when Ian Vorres's authorized biography of Grand Duchess Olga Alexandrovna was published in the 1960s. In this book, Vorres repeated the grand duchess's assertion that the box "went back to France, there to find its last resting place together with a few other relics in the Russian cemetery outside Paris."[35] Yet, throughout the years, as the rumor spread, authorities at the cemetery issued repeated—if somewhat cryptic—denials that they knew the whereabouts of the box.[36]

The second tangent to this story—and the most widely accepted version—holds that the box and its pathetic contents is carefully protected in the Russian Orthodox Church of St. Job the Sufferer in Brussels. Thus, author Robert Massie asserted, "everyone knows that it is kept in the Russian Orthodox Church of St. Job," adding that "the contents of the box have been described by witnesses but the Church will not endorse their reports."[37] During the intensive investigation into the identification of the Ekaterinburg remains in the 1990s, officials, headed by Yuri Yarov, then vice premier of the Russian Federation, made repeated requests that they be allowed to examine the box and its contents. These requests were inevitably met with firm refusals by church officials in Belgium, not surprising given the general and widespread belief among Russian émigrés, and most particularly the Russian Orthodox Church Outside Russia, that the grave eventually exhumed in Koptyaki Forest was nothing more than a KGB fabrication.

The Church of St. Job the Sufferer was erected and dedicated to the memory of Nicholas II, named after the saint who, in the Orthodox liturgical calendar, shared his name day. Begun in the 1930s, it was believed to have received the mysterious box in 1936, in time for it to be walled up in a portion of the altar. A number of former imperial belongings are, in fact, kept in the church, including icons the Romanovs took with them into exile and an inscribed Bible from the empress to the tsesarevich.[38]

Authorities in Brussels had always refused to confirm or deny these rumors, though, as author William Clarke has pointed out, the Church of St. Job the Sufferer seems a logical resting place for the presumed remains.[39] On these rumors, any number of allegations have been constructed, including accounts whose authors have claimed to have been told of the contents of the box by the authorities there. In 1994, for example, Prince Alexis Scherbatow, the elderly president of the Russian Nobility Association, told author Robert Massie that he had been assured that the box "absolutely" contained the human remains "from two bodies."[40]

Such a claim, of course, would rather neatly wrap up the enigma of the two bodies known to be missing from the grave exhumed in 1991, yet it cannot be taken seriously. We know precisely what Sokolov placed in this box in the way of presumed human remains. The list included some forty-two small pieces of bone, never even identified as human; a severed finger; Dr. Botkin's false teeth; two small pieces of skin; thirteen drops of blood preserved in capsules; and several small vials containing a mixture of greasy earth, which Sokolov believed to have been human fat, burned off of the bodies when they were subjected to fire. Such meager remains can scarcely be held to account, as Scherbatow claimed, for two bodies, much less even part of one; nor is it known if the small bone fragments, which Sokolov and his experts could only identify as "mammal bones," were human. The thirteen drops of blood came from the Ipatiev House. Discounting Dr. Botkin's dentures, we are left with only one severed finger, two small pieces of skin, the questionable bones, and the earth mixed with fat. Even the latter must be called into question as having any bearing on the Romanov case, particularly as Sokolov's earth came from the Four Brothers mine, while, as Yurovsky's accounts convey, the bodies supposedly burned were subjected to cremation several miles away, at the eventual common grave. Claims that the box itself contains the remains of "two people," as Scherbatow asserted, cannot be maintained.

In 1998, as the final work on identification of the Ekaterinburg remains ended, and plans for a funeral were finally under way, the issue of the Sokolov box once again took center stage. Metropolitan Vitaly of the Russian Orthodox Church Outside Russia broke decades of official silence to declare in an interview that the remains were, in fact, in the Church of St. Job the Sufferer in Brussels. He refused to even consider exhuming the box and submitting the alleged contents to testing, saying, "How could we ever dare turn them over to some Soviet Commission? These are Holy Relics of our Saints." At the same time, Vitaly declared that the remains unearthed in Koptyaki "were not genuine relics of the Imperial Family."[41]

These, then, are the conflicting accounts. There is, however, a larger problem where the box is concerned. Author William Clarke boldly and correctly asserted that the presumed human remains were not in the Brussels church at all.[42] The final solution to this mystery centers on the late Grand Duke Vladimir Kirillovich, son of Grand Duke Kirill Vladimirovich and the head of the imperial house until his death in 1992. Speaking in 1971, the grand duke confirmed that the box had been safely locked away in the Paris vault until the German occupation during World War II. Agents of the Gestapo, he related, broke into the vault and opened the box, clearly in the belief that it contained imperial jewelry. The grand duke did not elaborate on its fate after the war, though he added enigmatically, "There seems to be a mystery about what Sokolov brought back and I don't know why."[43]

As the grand duke hinted, there was no mystery—at least not to him. His father, Grand Duke Kirill Vladimirovich, was involved in negotiations over the fate of the mysterious box in the early 1930s; it temporarily ended up in a bank vault in Paris, as his son Vladimir later confirmed. The actual papers and documents detailing the movement of the box and its precise locations in these years, however, have been lost. But the actual human remains were removed after 1931, when the box came into Kirill Vladimirovich's possession. What remained were pieces of charred clothing, jewelry, and other artifacts retrieved from the Four Brothers mine. These items—along with the actual earth retrieved by Sokolov— were handed over to the archbishop in Brussels.[44]

And what of the other items in the box? German film producer Maurice Philip Remy, while making a documentary on the Anastasia–Anna Anderson case, achieved the impossible: the authorities at the Church of St. Job the Sufferer in Brussels not only told Remy that they did not have any actual human remains, but also pulled out a file that detailed, along with photographs, very precisely, and item by item, exactly what materials they did possess that had belonged to the imperial family. These included a number of icons, dozens of buttons, hooks and eyes, pieces of charred cloth, and pieces of glass vials—in short, nearly all of the material evidence Sokolov and the other investigators had collected from the Four Brothers mine, but not the human remains from his fabled mauve-colored box. These items were placed within a larger box, sealed within one of the church walls during construction, and the site marked with a small plaque.[45]

Members of the Russian Orthodox Church Abroad continue to venerate the presumed contents of the box walled in the Church of St. Job the Sufferer as remnants of the imperial family, relics of those they believe to be holy martyrs. Authorities at the church are largely silent on the issue, and over the past decade there has been widespread criticism of the church's refusal to hand over the box or allow its contents to be examined in an attempt to provide a scientific link—as Scherbatow suggested—to the missing Romanov bodies. If the human remains are no longer in the box, however, there would be no reason to break apart the wall or conduct any tests. Yet the mythology of the Sokolov box has long served a valuable propaganda role, not only a testament and presumed validation that Sokolov's conclusions were all correct—and thus, no one could possibly have survived—but also as an unseen, if widely believed, reminder that the Bolsheviks had so ruthlessly slaughtered Nicholas II, a phantom of the evils of the now phantom Soviet Union.

And what of the actual presumed human remains, which passed to

Grand Duke Kirill Vladimirovich? Unfortunately, at this point a veil of secrecy once again covers the trail. It is likely, however, that, having taken possession of these remains, the grand duke had them quietly laid to rest—perhaps even in the Paris cemetery of St. Genevieve de Bois, as so many have suggested. Despite the church's recent claims, the best evidence thus indicates that the bone fragments, finger, blood, pieces of skin, and dentures do not remain in Brussels.

The battle over the presumed Brussels remains underlined not only the violent schism between the church in Russia and the Russian Orthodox Church Outside Russia, but also the increasing religious exaltation surrounding Nicholas II and his family. Beginning with the publication of Robert Wilton's work on the Romanov case in 1920, a flood of magazine and newspaper articles, books, and even motion pictures kept the story of the imperial family very much alive in twentieth-century popular imagination; the fate of Grand Duchess Anastasia—and the claim made by Anna Anderson to be the rescued imperial daughter—generated even more interest in the doomed Romanovs and their ultimate fate. This trend reached its climax in 1981, when Nicholas II and his family were canonized as martyred saints.

Among members of the émigré community, such a proposition had often been discussed. Many Russians were divided; some encouraged such talk, undoubtedly not only because they regarded the imperial family as martyrs, but also because such a decision served a larger purpose of marking out the Bolsheviks not just as murderers but also as symbolic destroyers of the old, Orthodox order. Others were more skeptical, including members of the Romanov family in exile, who regarded the idea of canonization as "ridiculous."[46]

Even in the first years of the Soviet Union, monarchist nostalgia led many to quietly express such sentiments. In the 1920s, author Valentin Speranski visited a church near Novgorod and was surprised to find the ceiling covered with a new fresco over the apse, depicting the imperial family surrounded by a sea of angels.[47] In 1936, two events confirmed this growing mood. In Belgrade, a monument was dedicated to Nicholas II; during the ceremony, Orthodox metropolitan Dosifei declared that "Serbia honors the Sovereign Emperor Nicholas II as a saint of the Church."[48] That same year, the cornerstone was laid for the Church of St. Job the Sufferer in Brussels, which subsequently became a place of veneration for the faithful who believed that the physical remains discovered at the Four Brothers mine in 1918 were enshrined within its walls.

The issue of honoring the Romanovs as saints became politicized early on, strongly promoted, as it was, by the Russian Orthodox Church Outside Russia, a fiercely anti-Communist organization that broke away from the main body of the church in the 1920s. The Russian Orthodox

Church Outside Russia, in its early years, was largely composed of émigrés who, not surprisingly given their experiences, cherished what had been lost, and virulently denounced the Soviet Union, which had taken its place. In the process, and through vehement condemnations of the Moscow patriarch, they managed not only to isolate themselves from the Church within Russia but also from the Orthodox Church Abroad, a completely separate and autocephalous institution that remained in communion with Moscow. These two exile branches of the Russian Orthodox Church held strongly contrasting views on the Romanovs, with the Orthodox Church Abroad, the larger and more established of the two, remaining circumspect in its pronouncements. It was a breach further widened when the Russian Orthodox Church Outside Russia made the controversial decision to canonize the imperial family.

The 1981 canonization was, in fact, the fulfillment of decades of church policy. Historian Robert Warth tellingly referred to it as "an extreme example" of Nicholas II's "apotheosis."[49] The church had long been active in promoting the idea of Nicholas II's personal sanctity and in presenting a carefully crafted image of the Romanovs as martyred saints. These manifestations often took form as books, produced by their Holy Trinity Monastery, extolling the virtues of the Romanovs while at the same time promoting a virulently anti-Communist political position.

The decision to canonize Nicholas II and his family, declared Metropolitan Philaret, head of the church, was based solely on the manner of his death, though the explanation seemed as bent on making the event into a political statement. He said,

> Never in recorded history has evil manifested itself so insolently, so blatantly, as it does now. Never before have we heard such revolting abuse, such insane blasphemy of God and all that is sacred, shouted to the high heavens, as we now hear in Soviet Russia. . . . One must not forget that in slaying the Imperial Family the Communist malefactors intended to wipe out the very memory of how Russia had lived for the many centuries of its existence. They tried to tear away, to destroy, to extirpate from the souls of the much suffering Russian people that radiant spirit which prevailed in Holy Orthodox Russia, the spirit of an Orthodox statehood, and implant in its stead the abominable spirit of theomachy and fratricidal communism. The criminal murder of the imperial family was not merely an act of hatred and vengeance; it was not only an act of political retaliation—but it was principally a spiritual act aimed at destroying the Orthodoxy of the Russian people and replacing it with an unnatural and evil communist spirit. That was the purpose of the criminal liquidation of the Tsar and his family. The last of the Tsars was murdered with his

family precisely because he was the crowned representative and bearer of the lofty ideals of Orthodox statehood. He was killed precisely because he was an Orthodox Tsar, because of his Orthodoxy.[50]

Such sentiments undoubtedly found favor with many in the church but had little to do with reality. That the Romanovs were deliberately executed because they were Orthodox is an idea that the Russian Orthodox Church Outside Russia was almost alone in promoting, and bore no resemblance to the facts of the case. It was, however, a convenient way in which to link the murders to a larger political and religious issue, and to turn the canonization into a political—and therefore, anti-Communist—rather than a religious, issue.

The imperial family were not the only martyrs canonized by the church. Some thirty thousand other victims of the Revolution, the Civil War, and even Soviet purges were included in the decision, further underlining the political nature of the ceremony. This number included the four retainers who had been killed with the imperial family— Botkin, Trupp, Demidova, and Kharitonov—as well as the Romanovs killed in Perm, Alapayevsk, and Petrograd, with the notable exception of Grand Duke Nicholas Mikhailovich, who was excluded on the grounds that he was a Freemason and therefore somehow suspect.

The ceremony took place in New York City, at the Cathedral of Our Lady of the Sign in Manhattan, on October 31, 1981. More than a thousand Orthodox faithful packed the church to witness the service, including the rightful claimant to the throne, Grand Duke Vladimir Kirillovich. During the five-hour service, dozens of new icons, commissioned especially for the canonization, were solemnly carried in procession by black-robed priests to the iconostasis, one depicting the Romanovs, their familiar features flattened and distorted in a quasi-Byzantine reinterpretation ordered by the church. At the end of the service the choir burst into a new hymn, "We Glorify You, O Martyred Tsar!," which only served to reinforce the emphasis on the Romanovs, despite the church's attempts to include other victims of communism.[51]

The canonization of 1981 gave the Russian Orthodox Church Outside Russia a new canon of saints, but the decision was roundly criticized by the Orthodox Church Abroad, which refused to acknowledge it, perhaps recognizing it as an act whose roots were political, not religious. Throughout the 1980s, the Russian Orthodox Church Outside Russia continued to fight over the right to claim the deaths of the Romanovs for its own ends; at the same time, events in Russia were unfolding that would bring both a dramatic conclusion to the Romanov story and inadvertently open more questions in one of the twentieth century's most enigmatic mysteries.

17

Unearthing the Past

I N THE LATE 1970S, unknown to the rest of the world, two men had taken it upon themselves to track down and uncover the grave of the Romanovs. This work, carried out in the dark forests of the Urals, closed one chapter of the Romanov mystery and inadvertently opened another. One of those involved was Alexander Nikolaievich Avdonin, a native of Ekaterinburg. Born twelve years after the murders, Avdonin recalled: "While still a teenager, I took a great interest in natural sciences, including geography, biology, geology, and in the study of local lore. This inevitably led to the investigation of historical and folklore documents. Toward the end of the 1940s I inspected all our museums and read books in history, particularly about the Romanovs. Later, our scanty, insipid history compelled me to think seriously of collecting information, documents, material evidence and other historical facts for restoring unknown spots in the history of our Region for use not then, but in the future."[1]

Avdonin's interest in the Romanovs came at a time when such matters could easily have marked him as a danger to society in the eyes of Soviet authorities. "I was interested in the burial place of their remains," he said. "I read related literature and talked to various people who knew about it. In the 1960s I had a conversation with Gennady Lisin. He was about eighty years old at the time. He gave me the rough location of the site where the remains of Nicholas II's family had been burned. He knew about this because in 1919 he assisted Investigator Sokolov in the search for the burial place of the Romanovs." Avdonin also read a copy of Bykov's book, which claimed that the remains had been "dumped into a swamp." Using an association with a local official, Avdonin managed to see copies of local files "that contained information about the Romanovs' execution in the Ipatiev House. I kept them. Finally I decided that when I had the time I would try to find the Romanovs' burial place."[2]

Avdonin's research was confined to the Urals, but this changed in 1976, when he met Geli Ryabov. Somewhat older than Avdonin, Ryabov came from an important family. His father was an official in the Red Army, while his mother was active in Bolshevik circles. He later described himself as "brainwashed by decades of Soviet propaganda—Stalin, Beria—they totally destroyed my life."[3] Ryabov himself was a well-known mystery writer; a part-time filmmaker; and, most importantly, an official who worked for Nicholas Schelekov, the Soviet minister of the interior. "I first became interested in this subject in 1952," Ryabov later said. "I wanted to understand not really why, but how the Romanov family disappeared and I began my investigation. Actually, my initial approach into this issue occurred when I looked at some old photographs from the time when Yurovsky murdered the Tsarist family. In 1967 I read in the newspaper *Komsomolskaya Pravda* how it happened."[4]

In 1976, Ryabov arrived in Sverdlovsk, as Ekaterinburg had been renamed by the Soviets in the 1920s, to attend a screening of his new film, *Born to the Revolution*. As he later recalled, he had personally been asked by Schelekov to make the journey.[5] Met by local officials on his arrival, Ryabov "asked them to take me to the Ipatiev House. They seemed curious at this request and I myself am not sure why I asked them to do it." That night, Ryabov remembered, "I couldn't sleep. I went over to the window and saw the silhouette of Voznesensky Church on the horizon. I can't explain why, but I felt that the house of Ipatiev must be there, so at four in the morning I left the hotel and started out to find this place. It was no surprise that Ipatiev's House was right there where I thought it to be. It was a gloomy structure, about one and a half storeys. Behind it was an overgrown garden surrounded by a fence. I walked around that house the entire night. Strange, astonishing thoughts assaulted me: I cannot even say what they actually were."[6]

On the following day, Red Army colonel Ivan Korlykhanov, head of the Internal Affairs Office in the Sverdlovsk Regional Police Department, arrived at Ryabov's hotel and asked if he wanted to tour the Ipatiev House.[7] According to Ryabov, they "showed me everything inside—the room of Commandant Yurovsky, the rooms where the family of Nicholas II had lived, Dr. Botkin and all the others. Then we went down to the basement and there was the area where the Romanov family had been shot and killed. This place interested me more than anything else." Wandering through these rooms, Ryabov later said he "felt that I, too, was responsible for all the cruelty that cannot be erased in my country's history, for everything that came with the great cataclysms that shook Russia. I decided it was my duty to discover the truth about the execution and burial of the Romanovs, and to tell people. There must be no blank spots and no black spots in our history. Throwing light on them is our own repentance before history itself."[8]

Ryabov recalled that Korlykhanov "told me that he knew a person who was interested in that period, and who knew a lot about it, and he promised to introduce me to him. After a while we went to the man's apartment."[9] Thus did the two men who would find the grave of the Romanovs meet, in an encounter arranged by one of the highest-ranking Communist officials in the city, and the man who served as head of the Internal Affairs Office in the Sverdlovsk Regional Police Department, on a trip ordered by Soviet minister of the interior Schelekov, for whom Ryabov worked.[10] Avdonin, Ryabov recalled, was immediately suspicious, particularly on seeing Ryabov's official badge.[11] Nor, when Ryabov proposed a search for the Romanov grave, was Avdonin convinced. "Who cares now?" he asked Ryabov. "It ended long ago. Why dig up the past?"[12]

Ryabov persisted, and, as he later recalled, Avdonin "looked at me like I was crazy."

"Have you lost your mind?" Avdonin asked him. "Not only have sixty years passed, but sulfuric acid was poured over their bodies to destroy any remains. We will never find anything there. Also, some roads have been built and the site has been covered forever."[13]

Suddenly confronted by these two Soviet officials, asking pointed questions about a forbidden topic, Avdonin remained skeptical throughout the meeting. "He said," Ryabov recalled, "that any attempt to do this now would fail because now there were railways and houses where it all could have happened. I insisted that my idea had merit. Why I thought so I cannot explain, because I had no special documents on the matter. I said that we should look at the documents and then decide if it would be worthwhile. Avdonin asked if I could obtain such documents and study them. I said that I could. He said if I found any-thing that would help start a search for the grave, I should come to him; he would be ready to help me in the work."[14] Even so, according to Ryabov, Avdonin was less than enthusiastic. At the end of their meeting he merely "shrugged his shoulders, and reluctantly agreed to work together."[15]

Avdonin took Ryabov to meet a retired employee of the newspaper *Uralskii Rabochii* who, Ryabov recalled, "told me that the daughter of one of the participants in the murder of the emperor, Rimma Yurovsky, lived in Leningrad. He recommended that I contact her and learn details of the period from her."[16] Before leaving the city, Ryabov warned Avdonin to "be careful, and there will be no problem."[17] Ryabov gave no indication of what this problem might be, but the entire visit left Avdonin uneasy. Ryabov was an official in the Ministry of Internal Affairs, working directly for the minister of the interior himself. Schelekov had sent him to Sverdlovsk, where not only a tour of the Ipatiev House but also a fortuitous meeting with Avdonin had been arranged by a Red Army colonel, the man who headed the Internal Affairs Office in the Sverdlovsk Regional Police Department, to discuss the Romanovs. As such, the suggested adventure bore every indication of an officially endorsed Soviet action. Ryabov himself admitted that his ties with the Soviet Ministry of the Interior were strong and deep: "I had many connections and friends there," he said. In speaking of the search for the Romanov story, he later acknowledged the "wonderful support" he had received from Schelekov, who "helped me find out about the truth of this story."[18] According to Avdonin, Ryabov told him that they "would work on behalf of Schelekov."[19] Later, Avdonin added that Ryabov had continually assured him "that he would guarantee our safety" owing to his important government connections.[20]

Such circumstances raised troubling questions. At a time when the Romanovs were a dangerous topic, and members of the Politburo in Moscow were secretly debating a proposal by Yuri Andropov to raze the Ipatiev House to eliminate it as a reminder of the past, the search for the Romanov grave was firmly rooted and, indeed, approvingly launched by Soviet officialdom, approved by the minister of the interior, and coordinated by one of the highest-ranking Communist officials in the Urals. Under these conditions, the extent of the Soviet government's involvement in the affair cannot easily be dismissed. This itself was later hinted at by Peter Gritsaenko, one of the Russian scientists involved in the Romanov case. "Geli Ryabov's position in society," he declared, "is very different; he was more free to speak. He belonged to a part of society where you can express yourself more openly, and not worry that you might be somehow punished for it. The approval he got made things easier for them."[21]

Ryabov himself apparently returned to Moscow. He gave two contradictory stories as to his next step. Speaking in 1989, he claimed that he had spent several years conducting research on the Romanov case, then gone to Leningrad to meet with Yurovsky's surviving children, when he obtained a copy of Yurovsky's 1920 note.[22] Two years later, in an official deposition, he asserted: "I want to emphasize that I read the books by Sokolov, Deterikhs and others in the special book depositories after my talk with Yurovsky."[23] Ryabov, by his own account, told the minister of the interior that he wanted access to documents on the murder of the

Romanovs. It is some measure of the sensitivity of the subject that, aside from the documents on the case, the State Central Archives of the October Revolution also held three books—those by Bykov, Deterikhs, and Sokolov—carefully locked away from inquisitive eyes in a "special depository."[24] He pored over these accounts, he related, examining maps and illustrations, for two years, from 1976 to 1978.[25] His contacts, however, were not limited to Schelekov. In fact, as Ryabov himself later admitted in a candid moment, "I had many connections, many friends. I received maps and materials from the KGB to help in my search."[26] Thus not only the Soviet minister of the interior but also the KGB were privy to this "secret" quest for the Romanov grave.

These same connections, Ryabov recalled, assisted in the next step: the search for Rimma Yurovsky in Leningrad. "I got the militia to look for her," he later confessed. "These friends finally managed to locate her." In the winter of 1977 he traveled to Leningrad to meet her. "She was a fat old woman," he later said, "with a deep voice." Ryabov began to question her about the executions, but she quickly cut him off. "What do you want me to say?" she asked. "Nicholas II was a bloodthirsty man, a tyrant. The Ural Soviet gave an order, and my father executed it." She refused to say anything further; after Ryabov continued pleading with her, however, she finally told him, "Look, I have a younger brother named Alexander. He's a bit crazy, like you, about these things. Go and see him."[27]

Supplied with an address, Ryabov quickly located Alexander Yurovsky, then an elderly man living in poverty in the suburban sprawl of modern Leningrad. The two men spent the entire day discussing the murder. Yurovsky, as Alexander recalled, "had only answered questions about his role in the Emperor's execution with great reluctance. I understood that his father was sorry for what had happened."[28] At the end of the afternoon, Alexander Yurovsky called Ryabov into a small room and said, "Look, I'm going to give you something that no one else has seen—my father's note that he wrote at the time. It's his personal account of the murders held in the Soviet Archives."[29] "This note," Ryabov later acknowledged, "doesn't contain any coordinates, nothing."[30] Only on the typed original, with Yurovsky's written corrections, did historian Michael Pokrovsky append this information at the bottom. While useful in describing the secret burial, the copy of the Yurovsky note handed to Ryabov did not contain any directions on how to find it.

Ryabov continued to pore over the resources at his disposal. It was while reading Sokolov that he learned of the statement of Vassili Lobukhin, the watchman at Grade Crossing 184 along Koptyaki Road, who had testified about being woken by the movement of trucks, and the taking of railroad ties from his yard early on the morning of July 19. This, as Ryabov knew from reading Yurovsky's note, had been done at the place where the truck carrying the corpses had broken down, and marked the burial site.[31] A photograph of the site had appeared in Sokolov's book, and Ryabov shared this with Avdonin. "We needed to locate this place and examine it," Avdonin said, "as it was the only spot connected to the transportation of the remains."[32]

Unaware of the political machinations taking place within the Soviet government as it eagerly cooperated with Ryabov, Avdonin led the actual search. To assist him, he asked a friend and fellow geologist, Michael Kochurov.[33] They used the photograph from Sokolov's book as their guide. "Our first goal," Avdonin said, "was to find that spot, and ensure it was the only one linked to the removal of the bodies. After a thorough search of all the roads and possible routes on and around Koptyaki Road, however, we could find no planking. We began to suspect that it must be hidden under the earth."[34]

Avdonin and Kuchurov made a topographical survey of Koptyaki Road between Grade Crossing 184 and the Four Brothers mine, the area in which they knew the truck must have broken down.[35] Kuchurov, "being a real pathfinder," as Avdonin later said, "immediately defined the whereabouts of the old road; two places where burials could have been made." According to Ryabov, Kuchurov discovered these sites when, unable to locate anything by examining the ground, he climbed a pine tree next to the old road; from this point he spotted the two depressions in the earth.[36]

Avdonin and Kuchurov used "a very simple instrument, resembling a large iron corkscrew, about 1.5 meters in length, which we turned into the ground in the area around Pig's Meadow. In this general area, while conducting our test, the instrument hit something wooden, at a depth of about 40 centimeters. We probed this area and found that the wooden planking covered an area of about seven by ten feet. Beneath this, we suspected we would find the remains concealed."[37]

This took place in September 1978. Feeling certain that they had located the burial site, Avdonin wrote to Ryabov: "We know that we have now found the site for which we are looking. I am amazed by one thing, however: in sixty years, it seems not to have been disturbed at all. No one has tried to dig out the grave site." In reply, Ryabov wrote: "I am stunned by the confirmation that our friend has discovered the planking. Without exaggerating, it made my flesh crawl."[38]

To be more certain, Avdonin and Kuchurov took soil samples from the suspected area. They knew, from Yurovsky's account, that the grave had been doused with sulfuric acid, and they wanted to test the earth to see if there were any indications of this. The soil drawn from the area surrounding the planking, as Avdonin recalled, was "soft," "black," and "oily," and "with a faintly unpleasant smell." They conducted pH tests, which "confirmed" a "highly acidic environment."[39] With winter fast approaching in the Urals, the men decided to wait until the following year to investigate the suspected grave.

On May 31, 1979, Avdonin and Kuchurov returned to the site and began a full-scale dig. They were joined by five others, including Avdonin's wife, Galina: Ryabov and his wife, Margaret; Gennady Vassiliev, a fellow geologist and friend of Avdonin; and Vladislav Pesotsky, a friend of Ryabov from the Red Army.[40] Before proceeding, as Ryabov later admitted, the group sought and received official permission to conduct "a geological dig."[41] They removed the first layer of topsoil, covered with peat and wild grass, using trowels to scoop away the wet earth. According to Ryabov, there were three layers of railroad ties between the actual grave and the topsoil. The second layer rested directly on top of the first, and beneath this was a muddy mixture of branches, stones, and old brick. Once this had been cleared, they found a third layer of railroad ties some 60 centimeters beneath the surface. Beneath this, they struck water—a narrow underground channel that flooded the site—followed by a layer of wet clay and, finally, the actual grave itself.[42]

None of those involved were trained archaeologists with experience in the exhumation of graves, and their amateurish efforts considerably destroyed the integrity of the original site. At a depth of 80 centimeters they made their first discovery: a blackened segment of bone. After this, they uncovered still more bones, which Ryabov suspected were vertebrae, ribs, and the bones of a hand. As they dug, the site continually flooded with water, which they unsuccessfully attempted to bail out with an old, rusty pail they had found on the road nearby. Finally, Pesotsky reached into the soggy pit and began to feel beneath the water; in a few minutes, he extracted a skull. According to Ryabov, this still held "remains of medium brown hair" and "a rotted brain" whose fragments in places "retained their color and structures."[43] These remains were simply yanked from the pit—breaking connecting bones that tied them to the skeleton not uncovered. Avdonin and Vassiliev found a second skull; when washed, the group saw that the lower jaw held six gold crowns on the remaining teeth. Pesotsky extracted a third skull, along with further bones and pieces of some kind of ceramic pot.[44] On the following day, June 1, they uncovered still more bones, and further fragments of ceramic pots.[45]

"When we held all this," Ryabov later said, "our hands were shaking. It's impossible, it's scary."[46] "We stopped our digging," Avdonin explained, "as we assumed that the remains we had exhumed were enough to determine whether they belonged to the Romanovs."[47]

The group took photographs of their excavation and of the skulls and bones they had exhumed, then covered the pit back over. No attempt was made to excavate the entire grave. At the beginning of September 1979, the group returned to the burial site. Having read Yurovsky's note, they knew that, according to his story, the remains of two of those shot that night should be nearby. They searched the soil with a probe but could find no signs of any fire in the area; frustrated, they widened their efforts to include the old mines and ravines in the encircling forest, hoping to discover the remnants of an old bonfire and any human remains. They probed the earth every two to three feet, over the length of the entire meadow, and into the surrounding forests; in only one place, southeast of the grave at the edge of the forest, did they find an indication of a previous fire, buried just over a foot beneath the topsoil. When they excavated the site, however, they found only undisturbed virgin soil.[48]

The group divided what they had found. Avdonin kept the skull that they all believed belonged to the remains of Nicholas II, while Ryabov took the other two with him back to Moscow. "I intended to examine them to establish the sex and age of the people they came from," Ryabov later said. "I failed to do so because everyone I talked to refused to examine the skulls."[49] In fact, Ryabov went straight to the Ministry of the Interior with his "secret" find, requesting official help. But, as he later explained, "no one would sanction this job through official channels, and it was impossible to get it done through my friends there."[50] Thwarted, he turned to his friends at the KGB. "I reported what had been found to the KGB," he revealed in 1998, "thinking they might help. Instead, they told me to cover over the grave and to keep silent about it. I was given to understand that I would be arrested, and that my future would be tragic."[51]

In July 1980, the men reburied the skulls. Having first taken plaster casts, they constructed a box in which to reinter them. Each skull was placed inside a plastic bag, along with various bone fragments, and sealed within the box. At midnight on July 7, 1980, they took it to the forest and buried it in the grave by the light of a lantern. Before closing the box, they put an icon in it, with an inscription from Matthew 24: "He who endures to the end will be saved."[52]

For nearly a decade, these men carefully guarded the secret of their discovery in Koptyaki Forest. Then, on April 10, 1989, the Soviet journal *Moscow News* printed a startling article. In "The Earth Yields Up Its Secrets," Geli Ryabov revealed that the bodies of the imperial family had been discovered in a mass grave on the outskirts of Sverdlovsk. "Even for me," Ryabov declared, "it was not difficult to identify them, the number of bodies, the character of the wounds, false teeth which had frequently been described in foreign publications, and the remnants of smashed ceramic pots of acid around the bodies." He spoke at length of the great need for secrecy which had cloaked the search: "Ten years ago, when we opened up the grave where the naked bodies were thrown and even later, I just could not publish the results of my investigation." He refused to reveal the location of the burial pit. "I am prepared to show the remains that I found," he said, "to any panel of experts, but only on the condition that they give permission for a decent, Christian burial which, as human beings, they deserve."[53]

This unexpected bombshell found an eager home in newspapers and on television reports around the world, seemingly promising, as it did, an end to the mysteries surrounding the fate of the Romanovs. "It was a sign of the general credulity of reporters," said author Peter Kurth, "that they simply wrote this down, without asking questions, without checking facts, without even wondering, apparently, how it had come about that a 'crime writer' in the Soviet Union, poking around in archives and combing the forest with spades, had dug up the Tsar without being stopped."[54]

Ryabov was interviewed several times, and a Soviet television crew came to his apartment to record a longer version of his story. For the son of an official in the Red Army and a former favorite of the Soviet minister of the interior, Ryabov's apartment provided an intense glimpse into the private world of a man who was quite obviously consumed with the Romanovs. Nearly every inch of space—walls, bookcases, and the tops of tables—was covered with hundreds of framed photographs of the imperial family, oil paintings, postcards, and icons. It was nothing if not a monument to the former dynasty, and specifically to Nicholas II; at the center, a plaster cast of one of the skulls recovered from the Koptyaki grave—Ryabov believed it to be that of Nicholas himself—gazed out across this scene from empty sockets. There was something slightly sinister—"unbalanced," as Russian author Edvard Radzinsky declared—in this excessive display of passion for a family Ryabov never knew.[55]

During the course of his lengthy television interview—which was later translated, reproduced, and distributed by the Russian Orthodox Holy Archangels Center in Washington, D.C., "in memory" of the imperial family—Ryabov gave a lengthy—and highly inaccurate—account of both the search for the remains and precisely what had been discovered. He described the Soviet Union as a country "cursed by God, each of us is indebted [sic] to it. For what has been done in the past. In 1917, in 1920, in 1937. More than 100 million people perished here and each of us must remember that those people died, that they were killed by the Communists, killed by Lenin, killed by butchers."[56]

He described his first visit to Sverdlovsk, adding that it had been named after the "butcher, Bolshevik, friend of Lenin," Yakov Sverdlov. Using a series of photographs and his notebooks as visual aides, he outlined the search and what was taken from the burial site:

> In these photographs you can see how our research progressed. Here we discovered our first find. It was the skull of Nicholas II. Then we found more bones. Here you can see the bones of Nicholas II. Here you can see his jaw, with golden teeth. We also found the skeletons of Alexandra Nikolaievich [sic], and Tsarevna Anastasia. In the head of Alexandra Feodorovna was a bullet hole 9mm in diameter which proved that a large caliber gun was used. In the back of her skull was a hole with greater damage. It was a terrible sight, a terrible sight, but confirmation that we had found what we had been searching for all these years. I can note the following proof: (1) Bullet wounds; (2) the number of skeletal remains—not less than nine; (3) remains of broken jars of sulfuric acid used after the murder of Nicholas's family. There may be some questions as to why the acid didn't completely destroy the remains. Probably, because the acid had filtered deeper into the earth after partially corroding the bodies. The skin was completely destroyed but some particles of hair have been recovered. The bones and skulls weren't destroyed but were colored black and green from the acid. These photographs which have been enlarged were taken at the site. Here you can see the skull of Emperor Nicholas Alexandrovich. The upper jaws don't exist. The simple explanation is that after the family was killed Yurovsky ordered his men to break their facial bones with rifles before the bodies were buried." His litany of pictures was accompanied by an absurd slide show, punctuated with increasingly extravagant and wild claims: "This is the skeleton of Nicholas. . . . Here is either the skull of Tsesarevich Alexei or Tsarevna Anastasia, we still haven't determined the identity. . . . This is the skull of Empress Alexandra Feodorovna, again from an open grave. . . . There was water everywhere so working was difficult. . . . Again the jaw of Nicholas. . . . Another view of the grave. . . . Two skulls next to each other. . . . The skull of Nicholas from a different side . . .

and on Ryabov went, describing each faded photograph as he held it up to the camera.[57]

Ryabov completed his interview with a declaration of his own personal views: "The final end would be the redeeming of that blood which was spilled as a result of the horror which ruled in Russia during the October Revolution, during the Civil War, Stalin's times, and afterwards. We have to reject all that and even cast the dust of it from our feet. There's simply no other way. The redemption of that blood can be accomplished only if the innocent Romanovs, executed without court trial, can be exhumed from that pit and buried with the proper Orthodox ritual. . . . The whole of our nation needs this. Without it, it is simply impossible to go on living."[58]

This hysterical tone was the first of many echoes that would attempt to link the murder of the Romanovs in 1918 to every crime—whether real or imagined—committed in the Soviet Union. More specifically, Ryabov—and after him a host of others—went out of his or her way to inject the element of religion into the story. His somewhat petulant declaration that it was necessary to "reject" and "cast the dust" of seventy years of Soviet history unwittingly struck a chord as well, as the next two, tumultuous years of events in Russia would amply demonstrate. And his mention of Anastasia—when any such identification was clearly presumptuous—would repeatedly surface in this case, as the Russian forensic experts involved in the case made continual efforts and assertions to prove that she had indeed died with her family in 1918.

Ryabov produced no evidence to support his claims other than the faded photographs, and much of what he had declared was clearly—to be generous—hopeful fabrication. He had no dental records with which to compare the teeth in the skulls, no identifying features, no forensic expertise with which to identify the unknown skulls. His references to these skulls and to "the pelvic bone of Nicholas II" were preposterous. Yet Ryabov repeatedly expressed that he was "a trained investigator, a police specialist . . . and I can analyze. I was taught that."[59]

Not everyone was quite so easily taken in by these claims. "In the end," wrote Peter Kurth in 1993, "the absurdities in the story were hard to miss. Ryabov claimed to have identified the skeletons from, among other things, their 'treated' teeth, but since no dental records of the Imperial Family are known to exist, it was a meaningless assertion."[60] "He'd just made too many claims," said Radzinsky. "He couldn't go forward, he couldn't go backward, he just went out."[61]

In none of Ryabov's interviews had he once mentioned the name of Alexander Avdonin, nor those of any of the others involved in the search for, and excavation of, the presumed grave. Instead, his own accounts spoke of "my investigation" and "the remains that I found."[62] Understandably Avdonin was left bitter by the result. "We took a written oath," he says, "that we wouldn't tell anybody until the situation in the country changes, so that we'll be able to tell people that this was done not with sordid motives, but in order to bring justice to Russian history."[63]

Ryabov, in fact, had already begun to make arrangements to publish the news of their discovery several years before 1989, unknown to Avdonin. In 1987, respected German producer Maurice Philip Remy visited Moscow and was approached by Ryabov, who suggested a documentary on the Ekaterinburg murders. He told Remy that "there was exciting news" about the "discovery of their remains."[64]

Shortly before the interview in *Moscow News* was published, Avdonin spoke to Ryabov, and for the first time learned that his former colleague was planning to publish details of the discovery. Avdonin attempted—unsuccessfully—to dissuade him from this move, convinced that the time was not yet right, and fearful that the government itself would seize the remains.[65] When Ryabov allowed the story to be published, Avdonin, as he later said, "considered that he broke his oath of honor to us" to maintain silence until everyone involved agreed that the time was correct to release the news.[66] Ryabov later explained, unconvincingly, that he had included no mention of the other members of the group because at the time Avdonin's wife was a professor in Sverdlovsk, and he did not wish to draw attention to her.[67]

The end result was a complete break between the two men. Boris Yarkov, a journalist in Ekaterinburg, witnessed the effect on Avdonin, calling Ryabov "a less decent person than Avdonin expected. Alexander Nikolaievich was naive. Ryabov broke their agreement. After Avdonin was betrayed, he stopped trusting people who are trying to correct him. He now can't bear it if someone points out a mistake."[68] The two men "no longer speak," not only to each other but also of each other, except when using words like "betrayal" and "treachery."[69]

In the years following Ryabov's announcement, and more specifically after the burial site was exhumed by the government in 1991, any number of suggestions appeared in both the Russian and Western media that the grave had been a carefully contrived plot instituted by the KGB. Rumors that the grave had been opened by the KGB in 1946 were spread by Russian émigrés, who strongly suspected a Communist plot.[70] Nor did the Russian Orthodox Church remain above the fray. In 1990 the Orthodox publication *Tsar-Kolokol* carried an article simply titled "The Forgery," which alleged that Ryabov was a KGB operative who had been under instructions by the Soviet government to uncover the grave. This, the article insisted, was a Cheka forgery, deliberately planted to deceive the White investigators in 1918. As evidence, the article offered as "fact" the allegation made by Deterikhs and repeated by Melgunov that the heads of the victims had been severed and taken to Moscow and hence could not possibly be discovered in the genuine grave. It also contained vehement assertions of Jewish involvement: "The most urgent goal of this forgery," the article declared, "and the artificial sensation surrounding it is to conceal the ritual nature of the murder, and disguise the role of International Jewry in its organization and fulfillment."[71]

There also were various reports—none of them firsthand and none conclusive, though all widely repeated—that unknown individuals were observed engaged in some activity in the area of the grave. One report placed this "tampering," as Ekaterinburg researcher Vladimir Bolshakov later termed it, in April 1979—a month before Avdonin and Ryabov first opened the grave.[72] Lyudmilla Koryakova, a Russian expert who would work on the Romanov case and who lived in Ekaterinburg, later spoke of "several people in the city, who were actually engaged in looking for the bodies."[73] Peter Gritsaenko, another of the Russian forensic experts later involved in the Romanov case, also noted that "others than Avdonin were working on finding the grave."[74] Other, more conspiratorially minded parties suggested that the pit was that of unknown victims, simply strewn with old, genuine Romanov bones culled from other graves in an attempt to provide sufficient evidence for an eventual DNA verdict.

In Russia, government-appointed officials went out of their way to refute these charges. "There is talk, especially abroad," said Boris Soloviev, the man who officially headed the investigation, "that this grave was not the grave of the Tsar's family; that this burial was 'fixed' or arranged by the KGB or the Cheka or one of the other organs of olden days. They say that Ryabov was, and is, an agent of the KGB. The fact is that we now have access to the KGB files, and I have officially checked this allegation against both Avdonin and Ryabov. . . . All of the rumors that this discovery was an action of the KGB or other special organs is ridiculous."[75]

Soloviev's assertion that the KGB had not arranged the grave was true enough. But he also made another claim, one not supported by the facts: "I give you word of honor, knowing those times and those circumstances, that if this grave site had been known to either the KGB or the Party, it would have existed for exactly the amount of time necessary to gather up a crowd of soldiers and get them to that site."[76]

Clearly, Soloviev was not as well briefed as he contended. The location of the grave had been known to officials in the Urals since the morning of the burial, and it remained an open secret for decades. The site was roughly nine miles from the center of Ekaterinburg. In 1918, Pig's Meadow had been a sizable clearing, but by 1978, the vegetation had grown up around the area, ringing it with a fringe of tall pine and birch trees. The old Koptyaki Road, which once led from Verkh-Isetsk to Koptyaki Village, and over which the Fiat bearing the corpses had traveled, cut through the oval glade. The grave itself was along the old roadway, which, by 1978, had all but disappeared in the intervening years, overgrown with wild grass and weeds. A new highway some two hundred yards from the disused road and running parallel to the former tract had long replaced Koptyaki Road, but the old road—and thus the actual burial site itself—were visible from the new roadway, separated only by a grove of birch trees. It was a peculiar spot for their burial, visible, in 1918, to anyone passing between Ekaterinburg and Koptyaki.[77]

Considering the furor raised by the Bolsheviks in Koptyaki Forest between July 17 and 19, 1918—the roadblocks, search parties, and convoys of trucks to and from the mine shaft, as well as members of the Ural Regional Soviet and the Ekaterinburg Cheka openly bragging about destroying the bodies of the imperial family—it is surprising that the grave site was not discovered prior to 1978. Peasants in the area obviously knew what was taking place in Koptyaki Forest, as did the keeper of the Grade Crossing 184. And no one familiar with the area could have failed to notice the railroad ties lying across the roadway; the ties had not been there before July 17.

The burial site was well known, both to Soviet officials and to many people in Ekaterinburg. It is one of the great canards in the Romanov story that it remained an enigmatic, hidden secret until the late 1970s. In 1920, at the request of historian Michael Pokrovsky, Yurovsky wrote the first of his three transcribed sets of memoirs, the so-called Yurovsky note. Clearly intended to be the official account of the Romanov executions, it concisely presented Yurovsky's story of that night, and was deposited in the Kremlin Archives, where it was subsequently available to all Soviet leaders. This was written only after the White Army retreated from the Urals, and Sokolov's proposed theory that all eleven bodies had been burned had become known due to a series of articles published by Robert Wilton's soon-to-be coauthor, George Telberg. At this time, Yurovsky knew that the Whites were not going to uncover the grave, having abandoned the area, and that there was no danger in admitting, in a memoir strictly for internal consumption, that the entire family had been shot. And yet Yurovsky's famous note, in which he gives details of the murder for Soviet officials, was cursory at best; it failed to mention many of the difficulties encountered that night by the execution squad: the thick gun smoke that impeded the shooting; the survival of at least two of the daughters after Yurovsky himself had checked their pulses and declared them dead; the continuous breakdowns of the Fiat; and he gave only the briefest mention of the difficulties presented by the disposal of the bodies. The note was typed, and contained both corrections to the text in Yurovsky's handwriting, and, on the final page, a handwritten paragraph that gave the precise location of the grave outside of Ekaterinburg. This addendum was written not by Yurovsky but by Pokrovsky himself, a fact confirmed after an analysis of the handwriting by the Office of the Public Prosecutor of the Russian Federation in 1997.[78]

Thus, not only was the location of the grave known to Soviet authorities but also, throughout the 1920s and 1930s, many of those concerned with the executions of the Romanovs and the burial of the corpses spoke openly of the site. In 1928, when Vladimir Mayakovsky visited Ekaterinburg, Paramonov, the chairman of the Presidium of the Ural Regional Soviet, showed the poet the grave.[79] Mayakovsky even wrote a poem in which he cryptically described the site:

Past Iset—
the mines and cliffs
Past Iset—
the whistling wind,
at verst Number Nine
the ispolkom driver
stopped, stood,
silent . . .
Here is a cedar,
axed over and over,
notches straight through the bark
By the root of the cedar
a highway
and in it an Emperor—
buried.[80]

The fact that he knew, on arrival in the city, to ask to see the grave itself, alone demonstrated that word of the "secret" grave had widely spread beyond a tightly controlled group of high-ranking officials. And, as Mayakovsky was duly shown the site, there can be no question that authorities in the city knew of it. Avdonin himself, ironically, knew Paramonov well, and discussed both the murder and the poet's visit with him.[81] Presumably, then, Avdonin learned that a grave actually existed from a man who knew precisely where it could be found. Peter Ermakov had himself photographed at the exact spot on several occasions, and these souvenirs were well known in the city. In 1934, when Yurovsky spoke to a Congress of Old Bolsheviks in Sverdlovsk, he detailed rather precisely how and where the bodies had been buried, again leaving little doubt as to where the grave could be found.

Ryabov's absurdly obvious manner during his own research not only provided a clear path to others interested in pursuing the issue, but also convincingly made the case for those seeking some larger conspiracy. His 1976 journey to the Urals, orchestrated by the Soviet minister of the interior, resulted in a meeting with Avdonin, carefully arranged by one of the region's top Communist officials, which commenced the search for the grave, carried out, as both researchers' attested, with the cooperation and permission of Schelekov himself, and encouraged by the KGB. Both the ministry and the KGB supplied Ryabov with privileged access to materials, persons, and maps to aid his quest. When the grave was found, Ryabov promptly reported this to both the minister of the interior and to the KGB. Authorities in the Soviet government, however, had no need to pursue the whereabouts of the burial site in Sverdlovsk for, in the Moscow archives, they had Yurovsky's own 1920 note, with Pokrovsky's handwritten directions on its precise location. Clearly, then, Soloviev's contention that the KGB—and therefore the highest levels of the Soviet government—knew nothing of the grave's location was quite clearly, demonstrably wrong.

Given the extent of Soviet involvement in, and knowledge of, both the actual location of the grave and the search conducted by Avdonin and Ryabov to discover it, it is difficult not to acknowledge that this quest bore all the hallmarks of an official government mission. Ryabov now only rarely speaks of the search for the grave, making it impossible to determine the precise nature of these convoluted encounters, meetings, extended privileges, and courtesies, which reached to the highest levels of the Soviet bureaucracy. If Ryabov knew nothing of what can only be read as official promotion of his eventual search, he certainly acted according to their wishes. Avdonin has made no secret of his belief that he was not only betrayed by Ryabov but also, in some unspoken way, manipulated through the entire experience. Under these circumstances it is quite possible that he was cast in the role of convenient witness, unknowingly launched on a deliberate Soviet adventure whose end result was never in any doubt.

Avdonin attempted, as he later declared, to maintain a watch over the site, to ensure that it was not disturbed, and events conspired to increase his growing suspicion. Shortly after Ryabov reported the discovery to the KGB, Avdonin's friend Michael Kochurov—who had helped excavate the site—was found dead, apparently the victim of an accidental drowning in a remote Siberian river. Within another two years, Nicholas Schelekov—the Soviet minister of the interior who had approved Ryabov's search and assisted him—also was found dead, the victim of a self-inflicted gunshot wound to the head. In early summer 1989, Ryabov published an article on the discovery in the journal *Rodina*, in which he hinted at the location of the pit. "Now," recalls Avdonin, "they knew that place existed. Here in Ekaterinburg we have monarchists and anarchists and adventurers and all these people rushed out into the forest. And I watched the grave for ten years, from 1979 to 1989 when Ryabov made his statement and it's a long period of time, I tell you, it's very difficult to keep a secret so that nobody finds it, it is very, very difficult. But I still went there and looked around. Only in winter I knew I didn't need to worry, nobody would be digging frosted soil in winter. After Ryabov's information I started to notice that people were looking, people from the KGB. They were looking for it in different places but gradually the circle contracted."[82]

The official exhumation of the grave in 1991 revealed a number of unexplained anomalies that strongly suggested the pit had been opened at some unknown time, by parties other than Ryabov and Avdonin. During the 1991 exhumation, strips of earth were discovered along the northeastern walls of the pit, at a spot where neither Avdonin nor Ryabov had conducted their excavations; the color and position indicated that this soil had been deposited some time after the original grave was dug.[83] Beneath the soil, the layers of railroad ties, so carefully described by Ryabov, had completely disintegrated.[84] In place of the arrangement seen by the investigators in 1979, the 1991 exhumation report noted only "pieces of rotted wood" and "fragments of railroad ties."[85]

On further digging, the 1991 exhumation revealed the clear outlines of the 1979 excavations, visible along the southwestern edges of the pit. Along the western edges of the pit, the investigators discovered a power cable, some 15 centimeters in diameter, which crossed through the grave along the southwestern perimeters. This cable ran parallel to the thorax of skeleton 7 and had considerably disturbed the integrity of the remains, overturning and disrupting bones.[86] In 1992 Nikolai Nevolin, the chief forensic medical expert at the Sverdlovsk Provincial Department of Health, declared that the cable had been laid in 1972.[87] In this, however, he was contradicted by his assistant, Peter Gritsaenko, who said: "About a year and a half before we opened the grave, the cable was laid there. I spoke to one of the men who did the cutting in of the line, and he told me that the grave was not known to the local people who worked in the area."[88]

The cable, as Lyudmilla Koryakova, an archaeologist at the laboratory of the History and Archaeology Institute of the Urals Science Center of the USSR Academy of Sciences, and who participated in the 1991 exhumation, declared had actually "turned over" some of the bones in the grave.[89] "The grave was disturbed," she said, "and bones were spoiled to some extent. I was surprised that the bones were lying in such disorder. If a skeleton is lying the way it is without interruption, all the bones are supposed to be in anatomical order. In this case the bones were disordered, and many interrupted."[90]

Neither Avdonin nor Ryabov made any reference to the presence of a cable in the notes or accounts of their 1979 excavation. This is not surprising, as the pit they excavated was filled with muddy water, making it impossible to see the bottom. Yet their excavations extended to a depth of 100 centimeters: the three skulls they extracted—nos. 1, 5, and 6—belonged to remains situated at respective depths of 90 centimeters, 92 centimeters, and 100 centimeters.[91] The cable, which ran in a roughly southwesterly direction, was discovered at a depth of only 80 centimeters, above these remains.[92] This indicates that Nevolin was wrong in stating that the cable was laid in 1972, while Gritsaenko—who said he spoke to one of the men who had done the work—was correct in placing the time at about the beginning of 1990. More disturbing was the fact that the power cable itself was discovered beneath the layer of rotted ties. It could scarcely have ended up below them and in the grave itself unless placed there—evidence that the ties were removed at some point, during which they were damaged and fragmented. It is, of course, possible that this was done by the crew that laid the cable, but if so, they can scarcely have failed to notice the skeletal remains in the trench they dug, particularly as the 1991 exhumation protocol indicates that the cable itself caused significant disruption to the integrity of the bones, and the level of the cable itself coincided with several of the sets of remains.

The most significant indication that the grave was secretly opened between 1980 and 1991, however, was a clue discovered in the pit itself. In 1980, Avdonin and Ryabov had returned the three exhumed skulls, placed in plastic bags contained within a box they buried at the southwestern edge of the site; inside the box, in addition to the bones, the men had placed a metal icon, also wrapped in a protective plastic bag. When the pit was exhumed in 1991, this box—subjected to eleven years of wet soil—split apart, but the skulls and bones within remained intact in their plastic bags. The metal icon, which the men had placed in a plastic bag within the box, however, was found rusted and broken into pieces, contained in "several polyethylene bags"—not intact, in a single bag, as the men had encased it in 1980, but fragmented, in multiple bags.[93] Over the course of eleven years, a metal icon might have rusted and fragmented, but it could not have fragmented into more than its original, single bag.

Ryabov himself found all of this highly suspicious. It was not, he asserted, a question of the ties having simply rotted away, or a simple mistake in recalling how the icon had been placed. Instead, he ascribed these anomalies to "the dialectics of our former Soviet life," a clear signal that he believed the government was directly responsible for the condition in which the items were found in 1991. He went further, saying, with more than a hint of paranoia, that those in charge of the Romanov investigation—"Soloviev, Plaskin, and others"—were "ex-Communists. They are unable to get rid of their inner alter ego. It's simply impossible for them. They still live in their sweet Communist past, and their hand is all over this question. It's all being concealed."[94]

It is probable that the answer can be found in the nature of the searches from 1976 to 1979. The Soviet government organized and propelled Ryabov's search for the Romanov remains, although they themselves quite clearly knew where the grave could be found. At a time of growing Western interest in the fate of the Romanovs, it seems that officials in Moscow decided to end the increasing speculation; rather than reveal that they were aware of the burial site, evidence was fed to Ryabov, a trusted official in the Ministry of the Interior, allowing, with Avdonin as an unknowing witness and partner, to embark on a quest whose outcome was orchestrated by the ruling powers. In this way the Romanov grave could be revealed and the remains produced; at the same time, Yurovsky's note—which conveniently explained the two missing bodies—could be published, providing a final, official end to the troublesome questions arising in the West over the former dynasty. Having encouraged this adventure, the shadowy realms of Soviet bureaucracy and the KGB were then free to conduct their own subsequent, unofficial exhumation, perhaps to verify Yurovsky's claim of two missing bodies and anticipate subsequent questions when the news was finally revealed.

While this hypothesis accords with the available evidence, it does not indicate a larger plot in which the entire grave was some sort of elaborate hoax engineered by the KGB. Clearly, the grave was that of the Romanovs, in exactly the same place it had been in 1918, and with the same number of remains Yurovsky had described. Yet the manner in which the site was found, coupled with the undeniable involvement of Soviet officials, has fed a number of conspiracy theories that the continuing veil of secrecy has only further augmented. The discovery of their grave, like so many aspects of the end of the imperial family, remains clouded with enigmatic questions that shroud the Romanov case.

18

"An Unknown Grave from the Soviet Period"

FROM JULY 11 TO 13, 1991, the grave in Koptyaki Forest was opened, the expedition led by a group of Russian officials, police, archaeologists, forensic experts, and cameramen. Looking on in triumph was Alexander Avdonin. After the appearance of Ryabov's articles, he worried that the grave would be subjected to tampering by the government, and began his watch on the area. After observing men he described as officials from the KGB, he formed Obretenyie [Recovery], a foundation ostensibly conceived "to keep the place itself safe, and maintain a watch over it," though whose real objectives were quite a bit different.[1] At the beginning of 1991, Avdonin asked Edvard Rossel, head of the Sverdlovsk Regional Executive Committee, if the local officials in Sverdlovsk would assist in exhuming the grave. Rossel, in turn, sought permission from Moscow. On July 5, 1991, he had his answer: the Russian government had agreed to the exhumation and would provide the necessary funds to conduct the investigation.[2] The man who had given permission was the same man who, fourteen years earlier, had directed the razing of the Ipatiev House: the newly elected president of the Russian Federation, Boris Yeltsin.

The exhumation was a hasty affair: Rossel ordered officials to round up a team of experts within a day to undertake the work.[3] One of those contacted, Lyudmilla Koryakova, was a professor of archaeology in the USSR Academy of Sciences Division at Ural State University. A dynamic blonde in her thirties, Koryakova was told that she was needed to exhume "an unknown grave from the Soviet period." Her husband, Dr. Igor Koryakov, assistant professor of mathematics sciences and head of the Algebra and Geometry Divisions of Ural State University, also was asked to participate. Officials refused to supply any further information; all she could gather was that everything was "a secret, a big secret."[4] "My husband and I knew, from both newspapers and television, what the grave had to be," she later said. "We discussed this problem, and decided to take part because the others were not trained archaeologists, and had no experience."[5]

The exhumation was supervised by V. A. Volkov, assistant to the Sverdlovsk regional prosecutor, N. N. Zaitsev. With Volkov were eight experts: two Soviet military forensic specialists; two civilian forensic experts; one archaeological expert; a mathematician; and two specialists in infectious diseases.[6] There also were three official witnesses: Avdonin, and two military observers, Nikolai Nachapkin and Nikolai Eryomenko.[7] There were, however, others present. Koryakova recalled more than a dozen mysterious men who "came and went" at intervals throughout the three days of work; they were not members of the exhumation team who, once they arrived in Pig's Meadow, were forbidden to leave.[8]

For an event of such historical importance, the exhumation was carried out in a haphazard manner. Before it began, the participants were warned that they could not refuse or in any way deviate from the orders given.[9] Koryakova would later explain that it had all been arranged "much too quickly," with no proper preparation. "We had only one big digging machine, some military trucks, and several spades," she later complained. Everything was done "too fast." She noted with horror that it was not just the trained archaeologists and forensic specialists who undertook the recovery, but "everyone," trampling through the pit and yanking skeletal remains from connecting bones as they were uncovered.[10]

The remains were removed from the pit as they were uncovered. Although the official exhumation protocol stated that "brushes and knives were used to remove the skeletal remains, and to clean the burial site in accordance with archaeological practices," this assertion of care was not supported by the facts.[11] The exhumation videotape provides a revealing look at not only the grave through the various stages of extrication, but also of the way in which these remains were manhandled. In several instances, Avdonin himself can be observed standing atop bodies in the pit, pulling remains from the mud; in other scenes, skulls are seen being wrenched from the ground. Such incautious behavior, which damaged the integrity of the remains, led Koryakova to make repeated protests. "I wanted to do all the excavation in order," she recalls, "all the stages of an archeological excavation. But people thought that it is not an excavation, it's a sensation. I didn't feel very comfortable. I just wanted to finish the work. We should have had a historian in our group, but we had no one who knew anything about this case. The entire exhumation should have been organized. Under normal conditions, we would have spent a month in research and preparation, and then several weeks in the actual work. In this case, there was no time. The work should have been done by trained anthropologists and archaeologists and other specialists. In this case, it wasn't."[12]

Koryakova's judgment was echoed by the late Dr. William Maples, a respected American forensic anthropologist who himself became involved in the case. "The entire exhumation," he said, "was badly conceived. You had only a few trained specialists there, and apparently when they protested, their objections were ignored. The dig was conducted in a very poor manner. Had we done this work, it would have taken several weeks, not just a few days. They ignored the usual procedures, had no depth control, and let anyone corrupt the site by allowing them to dig as well, whether or not they were trained."[13] Three times Koryakova attempted to leave in disgust, but was forced to return by the military authorities.[14] Despite this, the protocol asserted that "no declarations, complaints, or criticism was received from any of the witnesses or participants concerning the manner in which the exhumation was conducted."[15]

The exhumation began late on the morning of July 11, 1991. It was a chilly day in Koptyaki Forest, overcast and rainy. To protect the site and to shield the workers from curious onlookers, a temporary fence was erected around the meadow, an army tent enclosing the burial site at the center of the overgrown roadway.[16] After several hours of digging, they found the rotted railroad ties, along with redeposited soil, at a depth of 30 centimeters along the southeastern wall of the pit. As the work continued, the group uncovered branches, rotted wood, and stones, but no evidence of human remains.[17] At 8:10 that night, under the powerful illumination of the portable klieg lights within the tent, forensic expert Peter Gritsaenko discovered the first human remains, a left pelvic bone, at a depth of 50 centimeters. Then the wooden box, still intact, which Avdonin and Ryabov had buried in the pit in 1980.[18] As the box was extracted, the wood gave way, and its contents were examined: they noted "several polyethylene bags with icon fragments"; individual bags containing the three previously exhumed skulls; a sacrum; glass ampoules and vials, the first with some remains of human hair inside, the second with fragments of skin; two lumbar vertebrae; a kneecap; two jaw fragments with teeth; a lower jaw; two loose teeth; two vertebrae from a neck; a right rib bone; two metacarpal bones; a right hipbone, with evidence of having been damaged by a sharp blow; and portions of a left shoulder bone. At eleven, the dig was halted for the night.[19]

Although the operation was officially a secret, Koryakova noted that Avdonin was allowed to leave; he immediately sought out a television crew and gave interviews about the exhumation. To her, this was "strange, very strange," especially "since none of the specialists were allowed to leave the site."[20] This odd behavior left an unfavorable impression.[21] "The entire atmosphere," she later said, "was very mysterious, very secret."[22]

The exhumation resumed just after eight the following morning. As the work progressed, Koryakova and others determined that the 1979 dig had done considerable damage to both the integrity of the 1918 pit and to its contents.[23] With the pit widened and deepened, the team discovered multiple remains: a skull fragment, two ribs, fragments of a lower jaw, shoulder bones, and foot bones were found in the southwestern corner of the grave, separated from the remains they had once belonged to "apparently by the laying of the cable."[24] There were a number of ceramic fragments, believed to have come from the vessels containing acid.[25] In the eastern edge of the pit, two more skulls were discovered, lying at depths of 85 to 90 centimeters. Both lay face up, empty eye sockets cloaked in mud; beneath them the team discovered "fragments of carbonized wood." Another skull lay in the southwestern corner, near a number of bones believed to have come from the hands and feet of the victim. As the center of the pit was cleared, two more bodies, dumped one on top of the other, were revealed.[26] With two decades of experience, Koryakova had "never seen so many remains, so badly damaged. It was a terrible picture."[27] The bones, she recalled, were "extremely disordered. If a skeleton is found lying the way it was, without interruption, all the bones are supposed to be in anatomical order." Some of this, she believed, had been caused by the cable and 1979 exhumation; but the majority of the damage "looked very odd."[28]

The grave itself, being shallow, meant that the corpses had been thrown in, one atop another, sometimes jammed sideways or bent to fit the small area. The first body thrown into the grave, found at a depth of 107 to 119 centimeters, was that of the emperor; the remains of Trupp lay on a downward slope, ranging from 100 to 120 centimeters. Kharitonov had been next, discovered at a depth of 99 to 113 centimeters, followed by Botkin, at 90 to 100 centimeters; the three grand duchesses, at 92 to 100 centimeters; Demidova, at 90 centimeters; and the empress, whose remains were discovered near the top of the pit, at a depth of 79 to 96 centimeters.[29] Some of the remains still bore traces of the ropes used to pull them from the Four Brothers after the first burial. The majority of the remains were only skeletal, although a few bones bore traces of fatty tissue and clumps of hair that had somehow survived the passage of time.[30]

In all, nine sets of skeletal remains were discovered, though in no case was a skeleton discovered intact. Later, forensic and DNA analyses were made. Skeleton 1, later identified as that of Anna Demidova, was found along the eastern edge of the pit, its legs pointing south; the skull, extracted in 1979, was found in the wooden box. Of the left leg, portions of foot bones, shinbones, thighbones, and hipbones were found; the right was represented by a single shinbone, thighbones, and hipbones. A fragmented backbone, encased in mud, was discovered next to a number of broken ribs. Clavicles and several shoulder bones were uncovered, but little remained to suggest arms: only a single right forearm bone, with a few fragmented bones from a hand, were unearthed from the bottom of the pit.[31]

Skeleton 2, that of Dr. Eugene Botkin, was discovered face down in the pit, the bones of his left leg along the northern edge of the grave. The lower jaw was found near segments of the spine. The skull was extracted haphazardly, pulled with great pressure, which wrenched it from the cervical vertebrae and crushed it and collapsed it into a number of separate

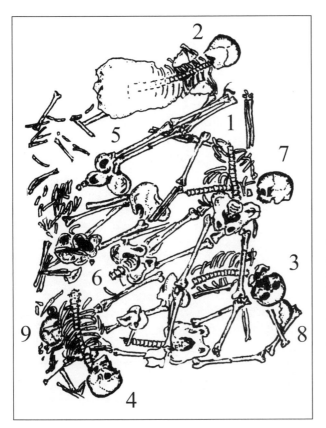

The positions of the skeletons in the grave, as designated by the American forensic experts.
1. Anna S. Demidova
2. Dr. Evgeny S. Botkin
3. Grand Duchess Olga
4. Emperor Nicholas II
5. Grand Duchess Marie
6. Grand Duchess Tatiana
7. Empress Alexandra
8. Ivan M. Kharitonov
9. Alexei I. Trupp

pieces. The sacrum, pelvic region, ribs, lumbar vertebrae, and a few clavicle bones were held together with adipocere, a substance formed when bodies decompose in closed, moist environments. Of the arms and hands, only a few bones were discovered, while the legs and lower extremities were represented only by a right shinbone and a left thighbone.[32]

Skeleton 3, that of Grand Duchess Olga Nikolaievna, lay along the southern edge of the pit, half concealed by the remains of Demidova, who had been thrown atop her, and by the body of her mother. Recovered were two fragments of the lower jaw; left and right clavicles; a number of cervical, thoracic, and lumbar vertebrae; a sacrum and pelvic bones; forearm bones; femurs; a right tibia; and a left tibia and fibula.[33]

The remains of skeleton 4, Nicholas II, lay along the western edge of the pit. While the skull was being extracted, it, like that of Botkin, collapsed while being ripped from the ground.[34] Fragments of cervical and lumbar vertebrae; clavicles; ribs; forearm bones; pelvic bones; femurs; a right tibia and fibula; kneecaps; a left tibia; and some small foot bones were all later identified as belonging to the remains.[35]

Skeleton 5, one of the imperial daughters, was found along the northern edge of the pit, bent double. Avdonin and Ryabov had previously extracted the skull in 1979. In the mud, the investigators found ribs and vertebrae that had become separated during burial; pelvic bones; left and right thighbones, two shinbones; and some foot bones.[36]

The remains of skeleton 6, another grand duchess, were discovered at the center of the pit, missing the skull that Avdonin and Ryabov had taken in 1979. A sacrum and three lumbar vertebrae represented the torso, while the lower extremities included pelvic bones; left and right tibias; a left femur with adipocere; and a right femur.[37]

Skeleton 7, that of Empress Alexandra, also lay in the middle of the pit. When extracted, the skull's jaws were found to have a number of crowns. Right and left shoulder bones were discovered, along with vertebrae, clavicle bones, and humerus bones. The sacrum was recovered, along with pelvic bones displaying signs of adipocere. The lower extremities were represented only by left and right femurs.[38]

Skeleton 8, later identified as that of Kharitonov, was found along the southern edge of the pit. The skull, not extracted by Avdonin and Ryabov, was all but missing, with only a few cranial fragments and a small section of mandible. Very little was left of the skeleton: a carbonized sacrum, which fell apart when pulled from the grave; a few pelvic bone fragments; a partial left femur; a few fragments of the right femur; and a few bones representing a right tibia.[39]

The remains of skeleton 9, that of Alexei Trupp, were discovered at the southern edge of the pit. When extracted, the skull was found—like most of the others—to be heavily damaged. The upper portion of the skeleton was represented by the clavicle bones, a segment of the sternum, and a few rib fragments. From the pelvic region were a sacrum and some pelvic bones. Extremities consisted of a few left and right radius and ulna bones, right and left femurs, and a left tibia and fibula.[40]

Within the pit, the team found forty-five fragments of the pots that had contained sulfuric acid, as well as the corroded firing mechanism from a hand grenade.[41] There were also fourteen bullets, which had remained in the victims when they were thrown in the pit.[42] One, apparently fired from a 7.63 mm Mauser, was misshapen from striking a mass of bone, which deformed its head.[43] Another four bullets, fired from Browning, Colt, and Smith & Wesson pistols, also were deformed. The majority of the bullets—nine in number—had come from Russian Nagant revolvers.[44] Investigators also discovered two separate, loose upper teeth in the grave.[45] A few carbonized fragments of wood were found, along with some bones, also described as "carbonized." Beneath Kharitonov, the soil was black, with more "fragments of charred materials."[46] Soil samples showed that the earth had been drenched with acid, resulting in an unusual blue tinge noted by those exhuming the pit—a reaction between the acid and the metal content, specifically copper—found in the region's earth. This high concentration of acid, however, also meant that, under ordinary conditions, the remains should have been considerably more intact, with soft tissue remnants. Acid sufficient to turn the earth blue would prevent production and spread of bacteria, which ate away at the soft tissue. When poured over the corpses, the acid would have melted away fat, turning the skin black as it dripped from body to body.[47]

The exhumation ended on July 13, 1991. Koryakova and her husband returned to their Sverdlovsk apartment, tired, hungry, and uncertain of their experience. "It was strange," Koryakova recalls. "I never took part in such an expedition. In twenty years I've never been in such atmosphere. There was nothing usual about this work, nothing ordinary in the way it was done. Everything was 'secret,' everything was rushed. It was too strange for me."[48]

Beginning on July 23, 1991, and lasting for two days, the hundreds of bone fragments, skulls, and other relics exhumed from the grave were taken in a series of military packing cases to the Upper Verkh-Isetsk Police Department's shooting range, on the outskirts of Sverdlovsk.[49] Here they were simply dumped on ten sheets of plain brown wrapping paper laid on the cement floor directly beneath the targets, as a few officials attempted to sort them out.[50] Their immediate fate rested in the hands of Nikolai Nevolin, chief of the Sverdlovsk Forensic Bureau, and his deputy, Peter Gritsaenko. A week after the exhumation, they were joined by Dr. Victor Zvyagin, who arrived in Sverdlovsk on July 24 to assist in the investigation.[51]

The hundreds of bone fragments were first cleaned and washed by department employees, a move later criticized as having potentially destroyed evidence. "They told me that when the bones were first washed," remembered Maples, "some of them crumbled into dust or disintegrated while being handled. That should never have been done except by trained professionals. And the state of each and every bone should have been documented in photographs and videotape before being cleaned."[52] Once washed, the bones were air-dried; then Nevolin, Zvyagin, and Gritsaenko began the arduous process of sorting through the piles of remains. In addition to the nine sets of related remains, a tenth pile of bones lay on a paper wrapper—various fragments collected from the grave which, disarticulated, could have belonged to any of the victims.

On August 8, 1991, Moscow authorized a formal investigation, under the direction of Dr. Vladislav Plaskin, the Russian Federation's minister of public health. The Sverdlovsk Regional Forensic Medicine Investigatory Bureau was designated as the local authority, with the Central Urals Scientific Research Laboratory of Forensics asked to supply the necessary experts to help determine identity.[53] Two weeks later, in the midst of the attempted hard-line Communist coup in Moscow, Moscow's experts arrived in Sverdlovsk, including Dr. Vyacheslav Lysy, a criminologist from the University of Krasnoyarsk; Sergei Nikitin, a specialist in facial reconstruction; and Dr. Sergei Abramov, a forensic expert who chaired the Department of New Technology in the Russian Federation's Central Forensic Medicine Division. "All the bones," recalls Abramov, "were numbered with white paint. Depending on which of the nine skeletons a bone was belonging to, every bone was numbered accordingly, from 1 to 9; the tenth group of bones also were numbered."[54] For ten days the group attempted to reconstruct the remains. "We were trying to put many bones together from tiny pieces," Abramov recalls, "especially facial parts." It was, he noted, "impossible to properly work in the basement of the police station."[55]

At the end of September, Abramov and his team returned, to find that the remains had been moved to the Department of Criminal Pathology morgue in Sverdlovsk, hidden in a labyrinth of passages concealed by a steel door bearing this notice: "Families may collect their corpses daily from 9 to 5. Closed on Sundays."[56] On the third floor, behind a gated and locked door, the bones lay on bare, metal autopsy tables ranged around the perimeter of the small, green-walled room. They were not covered or protected from any environmental contamination, nor was the room air conditioned or subjected to climate controls. "The conditions were abysmal," Dr. William Maples later said. "Under those circumstances, you could expect to have all kinds of bacterial contamination."[57] On this second trip, Abramov spent only three days in Sverdlovsk. "We spent most of our time," he recalls, "trying to find computers to use in helping identify them. Unfortunately there were no computers there. Finally, we got a computer on loan and set up the first stages of an imaging system to compare skulls to photographs. But we could only do this for a day before we had to return to Moscow."[58]

Although more than 500 bones had been retrieved, this fell far short of what the investigators should have uncovered. A human skeleton is composed of 206 bones; with nine victims, there should have been 1,854 bones in the pit; instead, fewer than a third of this was found—enough to account for just over two complete sets of remains. It was, Abramov later said, "obvious that not all of the bones had been taken out. Some facial bones were missing. And also hand and feet bones—mainly smaller ones."[59] Abramov suggested that a second exhumation be conducted, apparently in the hope that the first team had been so incompetent it had missed more than 1,000 bones. This second exhumation took place in October 1991, supervised by Dr. Vyacheslav Lysy. One of Lyudmilla Koryakova's colleagues later told her what he had seen. Like the first dig, he said, this had been done "suddenly, secretly," with the team "very badly prepared."[60] Some 20 tons of earth were removed and washed through a sieve; not just from the burial pit, but the entire meadow itself was churned up, until it resembled a plowed field. During this work, they uncovered just under 300 additional bone fragments. Found in the burial pit itself were 13 loose teeth, 11 bullets, 150 small pieces of fatty tissue, and further rope and ceramic fragments.[61]

The investigators now had just over 800 bones and bone fragments with which to work. This still came nowhere near the total amount they should have uncovered; more than half of the skeletal remains were never found. How and why more than half of the remains simply disappeared is an issue that has never been explained. "The substantial lack of remains," Maples commented, "isn't necessarily unusual if you're dealing with one or two victims; with eleven—and nine in that grave—it does become problematic."[62]

Over the next two years, a team of Russian scientists and forensic experts labored over the identification of the remains. Plaskin assembled what he termed "the best Russian forensic scientists" to conduct the case.[63] Working under him was a team including Nikolai Nevolin, director of the Sverdlovsk Regional Bureau of Forensic Medicine; his deputy, Peter Gritsaenko; Dr. Svetlana Gurtovaya, a serological and fiber expert from the Ministry of Health; Dr. Victor Zvyagin, from the

Central Forensic Research Institute in Moscow; and Dr. Vyacheslav Popov, a forensic odontologist from the St. Petersburg Academy of Military Medicine. From the very beginning, a tense, bitter rivalry over the remains plagued the case. Authorities in the newly renamed Ekaterinburg, led by Edvard Rossel, and his deputy, Alexander Blokhin, insisted that the remains formed part of their heritage and could not be removed from the city. Moscow insisted on its own primacy, but lacked the strength to compel the Urals to give in to their demands, a curious and significant echo of the summer of 1918 when Ekaterinburg, in open defiance of Lenin's government, had shot the entire imperial family. Ekaterinburg was convinced that Moscow wanted the bones for their own ends, while Moscow authorities believed—with some justification—that those in the Urals hoped to exploit them by turning Ekaterinburg into, as Edvard Radzinsky once declared, "Tsarland."[64]

The Romanov investigation was, from the very beginning, hampered by a general lack of funds, resources, equipment, and knowledge of the imperial family by those charged with resolving the case. In December 1991, Sergei Abramov told Volkov that he would no longer be able to continue his work in Ekaterinburg unless the regional or federation government stepped in with funding. He eventually worked out a deal with the television production company Rus, under which they would provide the necessary funds in exchange for exclusive rights to film the remains and sell the images. The entire episode, recalls Abramov, was "a travesty. They came, did their filming, then left. And as soon as Rossel and Blokhin learned of this, they demanded that all of the film and photographs be returned. They were furious with me, insisting that I had to leave all of my own materials and files in Ekaterinburg when I was finished."[65]

Given that the Romanovs had been a forbidden subject in the Soviet Union for almost three-quarters of a century, it was not surprising that those officials appointed to the case knew very little about the imperial family or those murdered with them. Throughout the 1990s, information on the Romanovs—books, films, and magazine and newspaper articles—was published and released at an alarming rate in Russia, though much of this was fragmentary at best, and often inaccurate. Thus, Plaskin—the man charged with the official investigation—continually referred to "Dr. Serge Botkin," while Peter Gritsaenko expressed surprise that their efforts to track down Tatiana Botkin Melnik—who, he said in 1993, lived in Yugoslavia (in fact, she had lived in Paris and died several years earlier)—had failed.[66] Dr. Victor Zvyagin, head of the Central Forensic Research Institute in Moscow, later admitted: "When I first began this, I did not even know who Sokolov was and what he had done."[67] Nevertheless, Plaskin was highly critical of amateur historians, experts, and monarchists who attached themselves to the case. He dismissed Avdonin and Ryabov as belonging to the first category, and repeatedly stressed that it was for the experts, for science, to proceed with the investigation. "The question is too important," he declared. "We haven't got a right to make mistakes."[68]

Throughout the fall of 1991 and into 1992, these scientists worked on the remains, conducting varied tests in an attempt to ascertain their identities. Two-millimeter sections were cut from the various tubular bones and examined, then compared to physical analysis of the skulls and pelvic remains. Inevitably there were problems, arising not only through lack of funding but also from the intense rivalry between Ekaterinburg and Moscow, whose respective teams frequently fought each other. Professor V. N. Kryukov, who was charged by Plaskin with determining the injuries to the remains, later complained that Abramov had deliberately impeded his work.[69] Few of the experts cooperated with each other, with the effect that the investigation was hopelessly fragmented into smaller inquiries, each possessing its own materials, and jealously guarding their findings from the others.[70]

By early 1992, the Russian team began to draw its conclusions. They estimated that the skeletons had been in the ground for approximately sixty years; this fit perfectly with the 1918 murders of the imperial family.[71] They represented two groups, one undoubtedly a family, indicated in the skulls of skeletons 3, 5, 6, and 7, which shared a distinctive characteristic, lambdoid sutures.[72]

Skeleton 1, that of Anna Demidova, posed a number of difficulties for the Russian experts. In the few ankle joints that remained, there was evidence of surface extension, "as if the woman had spent many hours crouching or kneeling."[73] A bullet wound was found in the upper left femur, indicating a shot fired through the thigh, from behind the victim.[74]

Although the pelvis was clearly that of a fully mature female, and the sutures on the skull indicated female gender, the forensic and anthropological experts assumed that the body was that of Nicholas II. Abramov himself had given an earlier evaluation of the three skulls exhumed in 1979—those that belonged to skeletons 1, 5, and 6—that proved wildly inaccurate. After reading Ryabov's article in 1989, he contacted the author and studied the plaster casts as well as a number of photographs. In Abramov's report, admittedly based on less than ideal conditions, he declared skull 1 to be that of a male, forty to sixty years of age; skull 5 (one of the grand duchesses) he identified as a male between twelve and sixteen years; and skull 6 (which likewise belonged to one of the grand duchesses) was that of a female between sixteen and twenty years of age. He further stated, after having compared the skulls in question with numerous photographs of the imperial family, that none belonged to any of the Romanovs, but that they were, in fact, a father, son, and daughter.[75]

Abramov was later forced to amend his opinions but, for more than a year, as he recalled, "until we determined that it wasn't a man," the experts "worked according to the theory" that skeleton 1 belonged to Nicholas II. "We didn't talk much about that," he later said, "because we didn't want much ado, since we had two versions. And when we got the idea who really was skeleton 1, then we made results of our research public."[76] The skull was missing many of its facial bones, from the tops of the eye sockets to the mouth, and the upper jaw, but the mandible, or lower jaw, contained a fragmented bridge of six gold teeth, a fact that led the Russians to conclude that it must have belonged to Nicholas II himself.[77]

Skeleton 2, identified as Dr. Eugene Botkin, was missing more than half of its bones: most of the rib cage, clavicle bones, right forearm and hand, lower left forearm and hand, right foot, and lower left leg and foot, were never found. The skull's upper jaw was devoid of teeth, with a "complete atrophy of the maxilla alveolar arches," indicating that they had been lost during life.[78] This strongly suggested that the remains belonged to Botkin, whose upper plate of dentures had been found at the Four Brothers mine in late summer 1918.

The torso, uniquely among the remains discovered in the pit, was still somewhat intact, due to an accumulation of adipocere that preserved a substantial amount of soft tissue. From this, two bullets were recovered: one from the pelvic region, and one from the lower lumbar vertebrae.[79] Two other wounds indicated a shot angled downward, which entered the left parietal area of the forehead, just below the hairline, and exited the right side of the skull after passing through the brain; and a similar, traversing wound through both legs, just below the kneecaps, fired from right to left.[80]

Skeleton 3 was identified as Grand Duchess Olga Nikolaievna. The skull was missing most of its central facial bones, lower right and left facial bones, and lower jaw. The remains were largely incomplete: most of the rib cage, clavicle bones, lower forearm bones, both right and left hands, most of the right leg, and most of the left leg, were never found.[81] There was evidence of a single, fatal bullet wound in the skull, fired from below through the mandible, which traversed the skull at an upward angle through the brain before exiting through the top of the forehead.[82] The prominent forehead suggested that of Grand Duchess Olga, while the remaining teeth contained fully developed roots of the third molars, indicating mature growth. A number of amalgam fillings in the remaining teeth bore testament to both excessive fondness for sweets and a consistent level of dental care.[83]

Skeleton 4, from a Caucasian man of roughly five feet, six inches in height and approximately fifty years of age, was that of Nicholas II.[84] The skull was in terrible condition. The face seemed to have been smashed in by repeated blows, destroying all of the features. Between the left and right edges of the eye sockets, and from the sockets to the base of the nasal cavity, everything was gone. The middle section of the upper jaw held only two remnants of teeth, with six worn stubs, and two missing front teeth, in the lower jaw. The inner cranium, when examined, still contained the emperor's desiccated brain.[85]

The remains were incomplete, missing the majority of the rib cage, the right hand, the lower left forearm and hand, and the feet. The investigation revealed "complete osteal knitting and hyperostosis [extension] of the left sacroiliac joint" and "thorn and crest osteal proliferation along vertebrae edges." To the scientists, this indicated a certain degree of posterior and lumbar pain in life, along with deterioration in mobility. They also found hyperostosis of the femurs, an indication that the person had perhaps spent a significant amount of time in the saddle. A callus observed over the second right rib, which had been broken and knitted during life, also agreed with the known facts—in this case, a riding accident Nicholas had suffered at Livadia.[86] There were signs of three bullet wounds: one to the left chest, which passed through the sternum and exited out the back; and two shots, tracked through the remnants of fractured ribs, fired from the left front and exited out the back.[87]

The jaw and few remaining teeth showed advanced stages of severe periodontal disease. None of the teeth evinced any sign of having been treated or filled, and were riddled with cavities, gray and worn almost to the jawline.[88] The state of the jaw, the clear signs of advanced periodontal disease, and the state of the remaining teeth clearly indicated that such conditions had been present for many years during the emperor's life and gone unchecked.[89]

The right parietal aspect of the cranium, though showing faint signs of etching from acid, did not bear any indication of something that should have been there: scars or marks from the two saber blows Nicholas had received during his 1891 visit to the Japanese town of Otsu. These wounds

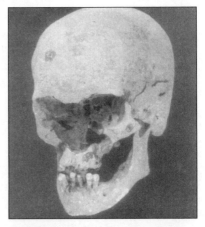

Skull 4, identified as belonging to Emperor Nicholas II, showing the extensive damage done to his face, though he was killed in the first volley of shots.

were described in some detail in a report to Alexander III: "The first or occiptal-parietal, wound is linear in form, measuring nine centimeters, with torn edges, and has penetrated the whole thickness of the skin down to the bone; it is situated in the area of the right parietal bone six centimeters from the upper edge of the ear, extending slightly downward. Furthermore, vessels of the nape and temporal arteries have been cut. At the rear edge of the wound, the parietal bone has lost about a centimeter of periosteum, consistent with a blow from a sharp saber. The second, or front parietal wound, is situated some six centimeters higher than the first and runs almost parallel, being ten centimeters in length; it has penetrated right through the skin down to the bone and occupies the area of the parietal and part of the frontal bone."[90]

During the White investigation into the murders of the Romanovs, Dr. Vladimir Derevenko testified that should the remains be found, he could identify the skull of Nicholas II by both this scar and by a thickening of the bone over the wound, which formed a callus.[91] Neither of these two features—the scar or the thickening of a bone callus—was ever found on the skull attributed to Nicholas II.

Skeleton 5 would prove highly controversial. The skull was among the most fragmented of those found, missing nearly the entire face. From the tops of the eye sockets down, nothing remained, indicating that they had been subjected to repeated blows. In the fragment of the recovered upper jaw were three intact teeth and one broken tooth; like those found in skull 3, they bore numerous amalgam fillings.

A majority of the remains were missing. In addition to the facial bones, this included most of the rib bones, clavicle bones, right hand, lower left forearm and hand, and both feet. A piece of soft tissue, preserved in adipocere, was found on the upper right thigh; within, investigators discovered a single gunshot wound, fired through the upper left thigh, traversing from front to back.[92] Abramov, who had first identified the skull as that of a twelve- to sixteen-year-old male, was forced to revise his opinion after working with the remains.[93]

Skeleton 6 also proved highly contentious. The skull was extremely fragmented, missing most of the face from the edges of the eye sockets across, the bones of the midface, and the nasal cavity; the upper jaw had been broken away, while sections of the lower left jaw were never found. Repeated blows to the face had broken off one tooth in the middle of the upper jaw, while pushing others out of alignment; another tooth was missing from the right front mandible.[94] The skull bore evidence of a single gunshot wound, on the upper left occipital area of the cranium, which passed through the cranial cavity and exited out of the upper right parietal area.[95] The remains themselves were incomplete, missing most of the clavicle bones, a majority of the rib cage, the right hand, the upper left arm and lower left forearms, the knee bones, and the feet.

Skeleton 7 was identified as that of Empress Alexandra. The skull, like others, had been subjected to repeated blows that left most of the central facial bones between the eye sockets and jaw either missing or fragmented. It bore a single bullet wound, which had entered just before the left ear and exited from the same spot on the right side of the head. In the upper jaw were eight complete teeth and the broken fragment of another tooth; in the lower jaw, five teeth were missing—three on the right side of the mandible and two on the left front. The remaining teeth displayed expensive platinum crowns, along with "beautifully wrought" gold fillings.[96] Unlike her husband, the empress had taken meticulous care of her teeth.

A majority of the skeletal remains were missing, including portions of the rib cage; clavicle bones; the lower left and right forearm bones and hands; the lower right leg bones; and both feet. In the remaining lumbar vertebrae, investigators discovered "a pronounced vertical inclination of the superior pectoral vertebrae spinal process." This indicated "a possible lack of vertical dorsiflexion" of the back during life, with a noticeable straight posture, one of the hallmarks of the empress.[97] A few of the ribs bore some evidence that the empress had been stabbed with a bayonet.[98]

Skeleton 8 was assumed to be one of the male retainers—Kharitonov or Trupp—though the Russians could not be certain which. There was almost nothing left. Of the skull, only a few fragments and portions of the jaw were discovered. Missing were most of the clavicle bones; the ribs; the lower right forearm and hand; the lower left forearm and hand; most of the pelvis; most of the right femur and most of the lower right leg, including the foot; and the lower left leg and foot. Due to the fragmented condition, the Russian scientists were unable to determine the sex of the remains.[99] As the body at the bottom of the grave, it had been subjected to greater destruction from acid that dripped from corpse to corpse before collecting against the bedrock floor, forming a natural pool in which the remains had lain for seventy-three years.[100]

Skeleton 9 was later identified as that of Alexei Trupp. The skull was fragmented, its rear missing, as were the clavicles; most of the rib cage; most of the lower right forearm and the hand; most of the left arm and hand; and the majority of the upper and lower leg bones, as well as the feet. From the remaining vertebrae, the Russians determined that Trupp had most likely suffered from lumbar pains and occasional paralysis in his legs.[101] The skull showed evidence of a bullet wound, fired at an upward angle through the right side of the head and exiting just above the left ear. A second bullet, fired through the upper left thigh, struck the outside left hipbone, while a third hit the lower right thigh.[102]

None of the remains exhibited any "evidence of thermal destruction such as carbonization or ash content." The few carbonized bone fragments and pieces of carbonized wood recovered were, experts believed, the result of reaction with the acid, which would have had a similar effect on both bone and wood.[103]

The remains displayed four distinctive categories of damage. The first were indications of ballistic damage.[104] Some of the damage observed, particularly to fragmented ribs and vertebrae, could not definitely be ascertained, owing to the incomplete state of the remains.[105] Four of the skeletons bore gunshot wounds in the femurs and tibias, indicating that they had been shot in the legs when the thick smoke impeded the executions.[106] Five of the remains—nos. 2, 3, 6, 7, and 9—bore gunshot wounds to the head.[107] The second category of damage was stab wounds, which had scarred the bones. These were inflicted by bayonets.[108] The third category of damage was blunt force trauma injury, primarily to the facial areas of the remains. No determination could be made whether they were ante- or postmortem in nature.[109] The final, fourth category of damage was postmortem, the result of the sulfuric acid, which had a corrosive effect on the remains. Those bodies deepest in the grave suffered the worst effects, with the remains attributed to Kharitonov and Trupp showing severe etching and destruction.[110]

Dr. Svetlana Gurtovaya from Moscow was charged with conducting tests on the hair recovered from the grave, as well as standard blood grouping work on the remains. The hair was "very fragile, easily broken, and subject to fracture when touched."[111] Although there were hair samples from the imperial family preserved among their scrapbooks in the Moscow Archives, apparently the hair from the grave was in such bad condition that it could not be compared.[112]

Dr. Vyacheslav Popov from St. Petersburg examined the fifteen loose teeth found in the burial pit. Thirteen were identified as having belonged to the recovered remains, while two were contentious. Popov said that these two belonged to a person fourteen to sixteen years of age, while Abramov—who had no specialized knowledge of forensic odontology—publicly declared that they had come from someone "no more than sixteen." Popov speculated that they were male teeth, most likely from Tsesarevich Alexei.[113]

"They can't," Popov asserted, "fit anybody buried in the grave, because first of all, they belonged to a teenager about fourteen years of age. Alexei was about this old at the time of his death. It's very important to know that these teeth can't fit any of the nine people buried there. I think that is very significant. . . . These two teeth were exposed to something else besides the environment of the grave. They have a particular brownish hue. It might have been caused by fire, or by

etching of acid.[114] If they did indeed belong to Alexei, as Popov speculated, these two teeth should not have been found in the burial pit.
According to Yurovsky, the tsesarevich was burned not at the burial site
but a short distance away. While it was possible that two teeth—
knocked loose when the faces were smashed in—fell out and somehow
became attached to one of the other naked corpses, this precluded their
having been subjected to fire. According to all accounts, the two corpses
were burned, then buried some distance from the others, and thereafter
had no contact with the bodies thrown into the common grave.

By 1992, work on identification of the remains had been under way
for six months. The Russian experts, however, were continually hampered in their quest by a lack of funds, and the continuing conflict over
the bones waged by Moscow and Ekaterinburg. "It became necessary
for us," recalls Peter Gritsaenko, "to have help from foreign experts,
who had access to better equipment and could either confirm or deny
our results."[115]

At this moment, February 14, 1992, U.S. secretary of state James
Baker arrived in Ekaterinburg during a visit to Russia. He and State
Department spokeswoman Margaret Tutwiler had dinner with Rossel
while in Ekaterinburg. During the evening, Tutwiler asked if they could
be taken to the site of the Ipatiev House; instead, Rossel offered to show
them the actual remains. This took place on the following day, with
Gritsaenko and Avdonin present at the morgue.

"I was at the meeting with James Baker when he came to Ekaterinburg," Gritsaenko recalls. "He came to our Bureau, and listened to
everything with great attention. For twenty minutes, Avdonin told him
the story of how the remains had been found, and showed Baker some
pictures of the exhumation."[116] During this talk, Baker himself picked
up one of the bones lying on one of the autopsy tables, examining it.[117]
Aware that only nine sets of remains had been recovered, Tutwiler asked
if the missing daughter was Anastasia. "Anastasia is in this room!" came
the stinging reply.[118]

Before Baker left Ekaterinburg, he promised Rossel that he would
send a team of American forensics experts to assist the Russians in their
identification of the remains. The request had come from Rossel himself, who—well aware of the shortcomings of the Russian experts, their
conflicting opinions, and the general lack of resources—wanted the
question resolved by a more authoritative panel.[119] This decision would
cause immense resentment among the Russian experts from Moscow,
reveal conflicts in the evidence, and ultimately revive the unwelcome
question of the fate of Anastasia.

19

Bones of Contention

O N HIS RETURN TO THE UNITED STATES, Secretary of State James Baker quietly made arrangements to do as Rossel and Nevolin had asked, requesting a forensics team to travel to Russia and assist in the identification of the presumed Romanov remains. At Baker's request, Dr. Richard Froede, a forensic pathologist and former president of the American Academy of Forensic Sciences, began to gather a team of highly qualified experts. This included Dr. Alan Robilliard of the FBI and forensic anthropologist Dr. William Rodriquez. Then, just days before they were to leave for Russia, they learned that authorities in Ekaterinburg had selected another American team, headed by Dr. William Maples.[1]

In the winter of 1992, Maples, one of the world's most respected forensic anthropologists and director of the C. A. Pound Human Identification Laboratory at the University of Florida, was attending the American Academy of Forensic Sciences convention in New Orleans. When he learned of the Russian request for assistance, he asked the head of the Armed Forces Institute of Pathology if an American team had been organized; hearing that one had not, he decided to assemble his own and volunteer their services to the Ekaterinburg authorities.[2]

With Maples were a group of scientists he termed "an exceptional team."[3] This included Dr. Michael Baden, former chief medical examiner for New York City, former chairman of the House of Representatives Select Committee on Assassinations, which reinvestigated the deaths of President John F. Kennedy, Dr. Martin Luther King Jr., and Senator Robert F. Kennedy, and director of the New York State Police

Forensic Services Division; Dr. Lowell J. Levine, a forensic odontologist with the New York State Police Forensic Services Division, who also had worked on identifying the remains of infamous Nazi Dr. Josef Mengele; Dr. Catherine Oakes, a hair and fiber expert from the New York State Police Forensic Services Division; Dr. William Hamilton, a forensic pathologist from the State of Florida's Criminal Forensics Department; his colleague Dr. Alexander Melamud; and William Goza, a historian.[4] Once his team was assembled, Maples contacted authorities in Ekaterinburg. Alexander Blokhin, Edvard Rossel's deputy, extended a formal invitation to Maples and his fellow scientists to assist in identifying the remains, unaware that the State Department had arranged a team drawn from the Armed Forces Institute of Pathology and Walter Reed Army Medical Center. "It was my understanding that Dr. Maples and his team knew of the official U.S. government team and their plans," says Dr. Rodriquez. Forced to cancel their journey to Ekaterinburg, they fell victim, as Rodriquez says, to the jurisdictional fight over who had legal authority in the case.[5]

Authorities in Ekaterinburg, as Rodriquez hinted, kept word of the agreement to themselves. This was a political decision, the latest salvo in the ongoing war between Ekaterinburg and Moscow, in which Maples and his team were unwittingly caught. Although Baker's visit—and his promise to dispatch a team of American forensics experts to assist in the identification—were both known and widely reported in Russian and international media, Abramov and his fellow scientists from Moscow later evinced shock over the entire episode, saying they had known nothing of a foreign group until they arrived in the city. The American team's arrival in Ekaterinburg provoked a good deal of animosity, in both Plaskin's offices in Moscow and among Abramov and his team.

"The legal procedure was violated," Plaskin complained to a Moscow newspaper, but these words concealed a bevy of unexpressed sentiment.[6] To the Russians—and particularly to those in Moscow—the Romanov case was a part of their national heritage, albeit a part that they had strenuously suppressed and rejected for nearly three-quarters of a century. They became intensely possessive of the imperial family. Increasingly, the memory of Nicholas II—and the murder of the Romanovs—evolved into a semimystical cult, permeated with nationalistic pride and nearly subsumed in the quasi-religious aura with which the victims were surrounded. The Romanovs belonged to Russia, and the intrusion of anyone else into the story—even officially invited forensics experts—struck a bitter, extraordinarily sensitive nerve in the collective national pride. "It's humiliating and insufferable," the *Moscow Komsomolets* newspaper declared, "to watch how the best Russian specialists carry out a brilliant study while the government begs for foreign help."[7]

The American team arrived in Ekaterinburg on July 19, two days past the seventy-fourth anniversary of the murders.[8] This came just a week before a scheduled international conference on the murders of the Romanovs, hosted by the Sverdlovsk Regional Administration. To promote the event, they joined forces with a Swiss firm to form Inter-Ural, which attempted to charge foreign attendees a registration fee of $1,000; only after threats of a media boycott did they relent and waive the fee. But when journalists asked to photograph the remains, they were charged upwards of $10,000 to do so.[9]

Although the regional conference was scheduled to formally discuss outstanding issues in the Romanov case and reveal the results obtained, the team from Plaskin's office "deliberately undercut" the conference, Gritsaenko later said, by releasing news of their findings first, "to try to steal attention away from our work. Plaskin, Abramov, and the others were concerned with putting themselves forward as the only Russian experts working on the case, and the ones who had solved this mystery."[10]

A few weeks before the conference opened, the British magazine *Hello* quoted Abramov as saying he was not been able to identify the individual daughters "because they were so close in age to each other."[11] Plaskin affirmed this point, saying, "Not all of the skeletons will be identified."[12] In the official report to be presented at the conference, the Moscow team confirmed their identification of skeleton 1 as Nicholas, no. 2 as Botkin, and no. 7 as the empress, but stated "this is as far as the identification can go."[13]

Then came a startling reversal. While the official report held to the identifications of Nicholas, Alexandra, and Botkin, a new, fourth name was added: Anastasia, who, the Russians asserted, was skeleton 6.[14] These identifications incorporated forensic anthropology but rested primarily on photo comparisons. This first identification of skeleton 6 as Anastasia, as Abramov admitted, was made "very quickly," owing to time constraints. It was a decision from which the Russians would not waver; having made it, Abramov and his team clung to it stubbornly, repeatedly attempting—in the face of a rising tide of critical analysis that challenged this view—to argue and persuade the rest of the world that they had proved Anastasia dead.[15]

Abramov's task of identifying the remains was admittedly complicated, and he frequently complained that the lack of funding prevented him and members of his team from spending the necessary time in Ekaterinburg working with the remains themselves to make proper forensic and anthropological evaluations. Nor did the battles between Moscow and Ekaterinburg do anything but impede the progress of the investigation, with both sides complaining of misconduct and deliberate interference. An almost complete lack of medical records for the imperial family, Botkin, Demidova, Kharitonov, and Trupp made the inquiries more difficult. The Romanovs had been among the most well-cared-for and cosseted families in the world, attended by a contingent of physicians, specialists, dentists, pediatricians, obstetricians, and surgeons, yet all of their files seemingly vanished after the Revolution. No charts or records existed for the imperial teeth, making it impossible to compare those found in the exhumed skulls to known dental histories.

The Russian effort was further hindered by outdated forensic and scientific training and the antiquated technologies of the obsolete Soviet system. "We have nothing," Peter Gritsaenko reluctantly acknowledged, "nothing at all. No money, no training, no facilities, no equipment. It's all far below that of any European nation."[16] Under Gorbachev, the situation changed gradually, and Dr. Lowell Levine, a member of William Maples' team, himself regularly helped train visiting Russian homicide detectives and forensics experts. "They had no modern techniques or methodology," he recalls of his 1992 visit to Ekaterinburg. "They're all quite capable, but they're hampered by the technological and scientific lag the Soviet system imposed on their careers."[17]

When physical identification of the remains proved increasingly difficult, Abramov's team began what Peter Gritsaenko later referred to as "secondary, less specific methods," focusing primarily on analysis of the skulls, utilizing a computer program to compare them to photographs.[18] "We knew that we wouldn't be able to apply the usual methods of forensic medicine during our research in Ekaterinburg," Abramov recalls. "It was not possible to take good pictures in that small room where we were doing research. So we had to find a new method, that of superimposition, on the computers because the authorities in Ekaterinburg prevented us from doing proper scientific and forensic analysis of the remains. On our second trip to Ekaterinburg we spent eight days only, which is why we had to make these identifications without traditional scientific methods."[19]

The use of photo superimposition to help identify skeletal remains was not new. In the 1930s, Sir Bernard Spillsbury, the great British forensic pathologist, successfully utilized the technology to corroborate identity in several cases, superimposing photos over skulls. As a tool of forensic anthropology, it is widely used to assist in identification where a victim was believed known. There was, however, a substantial difference in the methodology and technique as deployed by most forensic pathologists and anthropologists, and those developed and used by Abramov.

Even obtaining photographs to use in the comparisons became an ordeal in the new Russia. The State Archives of the Russian Federation contain dozens of the imperial family's photograph albums, each crammed with hundreds of images, yet it took Plaskin, a government official, nearly a year to gain access. Two photographs proved of particular importance in Abramov's work. Taken by Pierre Gilliard in spring 1917, they showed the five imperial children facing both front and back, after their heads had been shaved owing to illness, allowing the best match to skulls. "Pictures taken several years prior to their death might be useless in superimposition,' Abramov explained. "The skull would grow out of the face in those pictures, especially with the children, that's why it might not coincide. As for the pictures taken in 1917, the skull could not change that much for one year, that's why these pictures are very important."[20]

A traditional method of photo superimposition utilizes only three pieces of equipment: two video cameras and a monitor. One camera is focused on the skull, the other on the photograph to be compared. The skull is manually turned at variant angles to match the photographs, and the two video images are then overlapped on the screen, to compare and contrast points of congruence. Such a method, as Maples later explained, precluded any manipulation.[21] The system developed by Abramov did not follow this method. Because his team had no time or ability to work in Ekaterinburg, they videotaped the skulls, then used these videotaped images in an anthropological computer program designed by the Russians to fit photographs of the victims onto these skulls. Abramov selected cardinal points on each skull, "which don't change in a person's life," then compared these cardinal points with photographs of the Romanovs.[22] This introduced, Maples later complained, distortion into the process. "It was designed to match skulls to photos, from various angles," he said. "This removed the objectivity necessary if you are going to use this method. The computer sought those matches."[23]

Abramov explained his technique in great detail: "We do comparison of skull contours with face contours. We make a model of the skull based on sixteen constant points. Thus we have got a volume model of the skull, which the computer digitizes. We can then project this model on any number of photographs. The model shows the right position of the skull to make it fit in the picture of the face. We just have to make sure that constant points coincide. The results are more exact with this method than with comparing photographs or using models. And we can tell right away whether this face corresponds to this skull or not." Once the image of a skull was formed into a three-dimensional computer model, it was compared with photographs of the imperial family that had been scanned into the software. To increase statistical probability, Abramov explained, they also used a control group of "about seventy skulls."[24]

The program appeared sophisticated, leading author Robert Massie to refer to it as "space age mathematics."[25] But it was tempered with some curious imbalances. Abramov dismissed suggestions that the work should be evaluated by computer and mathematics experts to determine both its reliability and dependence on human interpretation, saying, "I don't agree with that. I think our forensic experts can evaluate this."[26] Rather than submit the program's calculations to an independent evaluation, Abramov said he tested his own measurements with "an abacus, which we use to count the angles and calculations. The thing is, a computer is good at doing complicated calculations, but it can't do simple things like these angles, it's no good at that."[27]

Abramov acknowledged that his computer superimposition method was "subjective, and that many scientists in Russia have called for further study." Nor did he attempt to match every skull to a photograph. "Those worth superimposing," he said, "were selected. Superimposition was not applied to everyone. It was selective. First it was determined who should be superimposed and who can be skipped. So it was done selectively for who we thought we had. We used superimposition to determine for sure who was missing."[28]

"This is unacceptable," Maples later said. "They did not use a regular superimposition method, but forced a computer to seek matches. To make it worse, they failed to employ regular anthropological standards. They should have attempted matches and exclusions with each and every skull, not just a select few. Superimposition can be useful in helping establish identification, but it should never be the primary method."[29] Dr. Lowell Levine concurred: "In the United States, it's used all the time, but not as the principal means of identifying someone. It's always subjective, no matter what the technology, especially if you are actively seeking a match."[30]

"It's still too early to talk about any significant success in this approach," said Dr. Victor Zvyagin, head of the Central Forensic Research Institute in Moscow, "but it has a big future." He believed that superimposition in the Romanov case would not give accurate results "because the nose bones, the middle face, and the edges of the upper jaw and sides are missing" on skulls 5 and 6. "In this case, the reconstruction of the missing parts was needed, and this introduced alteration to the objects."[31]

When Nevolin led Maples, Baden, Levine, and the other members of the American team into the morgue and to the remains, they were met, as Maples recalled, "by a very chilly reception." A few people immediately objected, "and there was a lot of yelling back and forth in Russian, which I didn't understand. They managed to calm them down, but as soon as we began our setup, and they saw our cameras, it began again." Someone explained that "it might be best if we went to lunch while they sorted the problem out, and so we left. I don't know what was said, but by the time we came back, no one in the room said or did anything to prevent a proper examination of the remains."[32]

"Nevolin was a straight arrow with us," remembers Dr. Levine. "He did everything he could to help us out. I can't really say that about most of the others there. In general, the experts from Ekaterinburg were very well-meaning, though because of the language problems, we couldn't speak to them except through interpreters. So there wasn't a lot of discussion."[33]

Abramov arrived a day after the Americans had begun their examinations. According to Levine, he was "dumbfounded when he saw us there with the bones."[34] Although aware that foreign specialists had been asked to help identify the remains, the Moscow team did not expect to find them at the Ekaterinburg morgue. "It was uncomfortable," Maples recalled, "and it was obvious that we were viewed with suspicion."[35]

"That situation was really strange," Abramov said afterward. "Plaskin could get foreign experts involved in the research, but we learned Plaskin hadn't invited the Americans. It was done by Ekaterinburg authorities. And they didn't tell us about that. We were wondering what was going on. Was it an alternative investigation? Is Dr. Maples our competitor or somebody else? And we still don't know. He is doing the same research we do. Who is he doing it for? We were not sure whether it would be appropriate for us to talk about the results of our research at the conference with Americans or not. If they were our competitors and were doing alternative research, we were not supposed to tell them our data."[36]

On the first day, the American team spent their time doing what Maples termed "preliminary identifications, based on the few known facts of the case."[37] It took Maples himself little time to examine the remains and to "assign them tentative identifications. The speed and accuracy of my initial analysis produced a gratifying response: suddenly the Russians were looking at us with unfeigned respect. They had taken months to make their identifications, using numerous experts in various fields, working independently. We had arrived at roughly the same conclusions in a few hours."[38]

Skeleton 1 proved contentious. Abramov had previously identified the skull, without benefit of examination, as that of a male forty to sixty years of age.[39] It was a conclusion shared by Dr. Zvyagin.[40] As work progressed, Abramov had doubts, but in their report of July 27, 1992, the Moscow team asserted: "Skulls 3, 5, 6, according to their anatomic features, anomalies, and features of asymmetry, occupy an intermediate position between no. 1 and no. 7, which makes it possible to conclude that all five persons are members of the same family. Two generations of the parents, no. 1, and no. 7, are observed. Their children are nos. 3, 5, and 6."[41] According to the Russians, the three grand duchesses were the children of nos. 1 and 7—Demidova and the empress.

Such claims, as well as the identification of skeleton 1 as that of the emperor, greatly surprised the American forensic experts.[42] The sex of a skull is easily determined by both its shape and by the sutures on the top of the cranium. In cases where the skull is missing, or too badly fragmented, gender can quickly be resolved by examining the pelvic bones. Female pelvises are of a greater width than those of a male, with a wider subpubic angle. "I don't know how or why they could have missed the obvious cranial sutures," Maples later said, "or the female pelvis, for that matter. When we first looked at the remains, it took us all of a minute to determine that skeleton 1 belonged to a female."[43] Such an obvious misidentification of what was clearly a female skull failed to lend to Abramov's work the mark of scientific finality for which he had hoped.

The Russian and American experts agreed that skeleton 2—a large, mature male who had worn an upper plate of dentures—was that of Dr. Botkin.[44] Skeleton 3 had remained unidentified by the Russians. The skull was that of a mature female; based on the complete roots on the wisdom teeth, Dr. Levine placed her in her midtwenties.[45] Although most of the facial bones were missing, the prominent forehead on the skull suggested that of Grand Duchess Olga Nikolaievna. When Maples went to examine the remains to estimate height, he found that the leg bones—one of the primary indicators used to gauge how tall a person may have been—had been cut into sections by the Russians. He was forced to measure the bones of the arms, a less reliable method, and estimated her height at roughly 64.9 inches. The Americans identified her as Olga, a judgment with which the Russians concurred.[46]

Skeleton 4 posed a number of difficulties. The indication, as Maples later wrote, that Nicholas "must have had a great horror of dentists, and because he was Tsar, no one could force him to visit one," led to strenuous objections from several of the Russian experts.[47] It was, like so many issues in the Romanov case, a matter of national pride. Dr. Vyacheslav Popov suggested that the decay resulted from exposure to acid, though such a hypothesis failed to explain the advanced stages of periodontal disease. "Nicholas II," he added, "was a courageous person as our Emperor, and not afraid of the dentist as has been suggested."[48]

From the pelvis and from the sutures on the skull, the remains were easily identified as those of a mature male. Maples and Baden were concerned with the overall state of the remains. Both men believed, after examining them, that the Russians had attributed numerous bones that did not belong to the skeleton. This became most obvious when they examined skeleton 9, that of Alexei Trupp. In the grave, Nicholas and Trupp had been thrown one atop the other, and over almost three-quarters of a century, as their skeletal structures collapsed, their bones mingled. The forearm bones of skeleton 9, Maples noted, were "very, very delicate, and not particularly well muscled. The leg bones, however, were quite rugged. But these same bones in skeleton 4, even though they are incomplete, are much larger, and more rugged, and that's the reverse of what should be seen. Nicholas was short, while skeleton 9 was a tall individual. We all believe that these bones are on the wrong tables and should be switched. This also raises a very troubling question: How extensive is this commingling, and where does it stop? The shoulder blades, upper limb bones, and clavicles all appear too small for skeleton 9. There's a real problem with these being mixed up."[49]

The Americans found a number of bones suspect. A great many bore initial numbering in white paint, which had been crossed off in favor of new numbering, indicating that they had been moved from table to table. Many of those marked with a "9" had previously been numbered with sequences beginning "4," which had later been changed.[50] They believed that the sternum attributed to skeleton 9, which bore a bayonet thrust penetrating the breastbone and exiting out the rear, was that of Nicholas II. "There's been a number of people working on these remains," Maples said. "And it wouldn't surprise me to see one team coming and moving the bones around in the belief that they had been mixed up. But then the bones keep getting moved back and forth, from table to table—and it's not just bodies 4 and 9 that seem to have confusion in this area."[51] Speaking in 2002, Dr. Levine added, "To this day, I wouldn't bet money that they got all of the right bones in the right places."[52]

Maples discussed this problem with the Russian scientists, who agreed that perhaps some of the remains had been misattributed. This was in July 1992. When Maples returned to Ekaterinburg exactly one year later, however, he found that nothing had been changed and that the remains were still mislabeled. This upset Maples. "I personally feel rather strongly," he said, "that when we have something as different as this case, then somebody has to make some sort of decision about it."[53]

With skeleton 6 identified as Anastasia by Abramov, no. 5 had, of necessity, to be one of the grand duchesses. Once the Russians accepted the American identification of no. 3 as Olga, that left Marie or Tatiana as the only possibilities. The remains belonged to a Caucasian female. With everything from the tops of the eye sockets missing, an accurate photographic comparison was, in their opinion, too risky. Maples and the American team placed her height at roughly 5 feet, 7 inches, while the

Russian estimate ranged from 5 feet, 5 inches to 5 feet, 7 inches.[54] She was, he later wrote, "the youngest of the five women whose skeletons lay before us. We concluded this from the fact that the root tips of her third molars were incomplete. Her sacrum, in the back of her pelvis, was not completely developed. Her limb bones showed that growth had only recently ended. Her back showed evidence of immaturity, but it was nevertheless the back of a woman at least eighteen years old." Based on these and other factors, the scientific team from the United States believed that the remains were those of Grand Duchess Marie Nikolaievna.[55]

The Russian team disagreed with these findings, citing both photo comparisons and anthropological evidence. Among other factors, the final Russian report declared that skeleton 5 displayed "complete osteal knitting of the fifth lumbar vertebrae process."[56] This assertion, however, stood in complete contrast to the report by the American team, who had based their conclusions on age not only on the state of dental maturity but also on the absence of any complete knitting on the vertebrae, indicating that the growth process was only recently completed. To the Russians, however, skeleton 5 became Grand Duchess Tatiana.

Skeleton 6 also proved controversial. Abramov identified the remains as Anastasia; Maples and his team, however, believed that she had been a bit older than twenty, with an estimated height of approximately 5 feet, 7 inches.[57] The Russians estimated the height between 5 feet, 4 inches and 5 feet, 7 inches.[58] "Body 6," Maples wrote, "belonged to a young woman who was nevertheless fully grown. Her dental and skeletal development fell neatly between that of bodies 3 and 5. There was no evidence of recent growth in her limb bones. Her sacrum and pelvic rim were mature, which made her at least eighteen." The collarbone, he noted, "was mature, making her at least twenty years old."[59] The Americans discovered that the Russians had wrongly attributed a number of bones to skeleton 6, including those of the forearm. Their report noted that they were not "identical or symmetrical. The absence of this similarity can be seen under ultraviolet light, in which the bones luminesce at different shades."[60]

The American team placed her between skeleton 3 and skeleton 5 in age. If Anastasia was no. 5, then skeleton no. 6, according to the Americans, was either Tatiana or Marie. If Anastasia was missing, however, skeleton 6 could only be Tatiana. In the end, on the basis of dental analysis and anthropological comparisons of bone development, Maples and his colleagues believed that skeleton 6 was that of Grand Duchess Tatiana Nikolaievna.[61]

Abramov's identification of skeleton 6 as Anastasia had, as he himself admitted, been done "very quickly," based on the superimposition of four photographs he digitized in his computer.[62] The Americans pointed out the danger inherent in such a photographic evaluation, saying that the forensic and anthropological evidence, including the dental development, the maturity of the vertebrae, pelvis, and sacrum, and the estimated height, all contradicted Abramov's identification.[63] One Russian forensics expert, Professor Filipchuk, disagreed with both Abramov and Maples, insisting, contrary to all available evidence, that skeleton 5 was the tallest of the young women whose remains had been recovered. He identified her as Tatiana, while assigning Grand Duchess Marie to skeleton 6.[64]

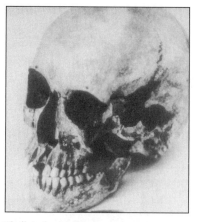

Skull 6, shown after massive reconstruction of the facial structures. When it was exhumed, this skull had nothing below the browbone. The Russian experts believe that this was Anastasia; the American experts think it was Tatiana.

The Russians and Americans both agreed that skeleton 7 was that of the empress.[65] Skeleton 8 was more problematic, owing to its fragmented condition. While the Russians had been unable to determine gender, Maples and his colleagues had little difficulty in identifying it as male by examining the few remaining pelvic bones and hipbones. They believed he was about forty-fifty years of age and of short stature. The right femur demonstrated a pronounced thickening, while the left did not. This indicated that again, the bones had been mixed up with another set of remains.[66] The little that remained, Maples recalled, had been "grievously damaged by acid."[67] Based on estimated height and on the size of the bones, the Russian and American teams believed that skeleton 8 was most likely that of Kharitonov.[68] Skeleton 9 was identified by both the Russian and the American teams as that of Alexei Trupp, though the Americans, having noticed peculiarities, concluded that the Russians had misidentified multiple bone and bone fragments attributed to these remains.[69]

"Two were missing," Dr. Baden said simply. "We found that they were Alexei and Anastasia."[70] There were no remains that could be attributed to the tsesarevich, a determination with which the Russians agreed. It was the question of Anastasia that hung heavily over the two teams, drawing each into polarized, vehemently opposite beliefs.

The Americans determined that Anastasia was missing based on the forensic and anthropological evidence available for study among the remains. Here, there were three primary factors: development of the vertebrae, clavicles, and sacrum; estimated height; and development of the teeth. Of the first, Maples and Baden noted the development of the vertebrae on bodies 3, 5, and 6 as one key piece of evidence. As a person develops, the lumbar, thoracic, and cervical vertebrae change along a definable pattern. In the late teens, cartilage forms over the vertebrae and fuses them together, completing the growth of the spine and setting an individual's height. By examining the state of vertebrae, age can therefore be estimated. This is not an exact science, and can be used only to determine the various stages of the growth process, but it gives an indication that can then be confirmed or denied according to other evidence.

With skeletons 5 and 6, Maples and Baden noted that the fusion of the cervical, thoracic, and lumbar vertebrae was complete, indicating that the two individuals were fully mature. This made sense for the twenty-one-year-old Tatiana and the nineteen-year-old Marie but not for Anastasia, who was seventeen years, one month at the time of her death. "If Anastasia was present," Maples said, "then some vertebra on that table or some other table should show immaturity, marked immaturity. And they don't. None of the bones show immaturity. The collarbone in that body is completely united. It is clearly an adult, and that doesn't happen until around twenty years of age. But Anastasia at seventeen years, one month—to find closed rings in her vertebrae—that's never, ever been seen before. So unless these bones are completely mixed up with another body, Anastasia is clearly missing. And even if, as the Russians believe, Anastasia is there, then on at least one of those nine tables, somewhere, anywhere, you should find a bone, any bone, that shows marked immaturity as you would see in a seventeen-year-old girl. There isn't any bone here that shows marked immaturity. That makes it clear that Anastasia wasn't among the nine buried in that grave."[71]

Estimation of height, while not indicating age, was another factor for the Americans. Photographs taken in the Tobolsk period indicate the respective heights of the four grand duchesses in relation to each other. Of the sisters, Tatiana seems to have been the tallest, though Marie had come close as her final growth cycle was completed. They seem to have been within an inch or two of each other. Olga was somewhat shorter than both, perhaps by as much as two to three inches. None of the sisters, however, was as short as Anastasia, who was several inches shorter than Olga. It was unlikely, Maples and Baden believed, that Anastasia, over the six months that followed, suddenly grew more than five to six inches to fit either of the heights estimated for skeletons 5 or 6.[72]

A third piece of evidence was the work undertaken by forensic odontologist Dr. Lowell Levine. He found that skulls 3, 5, and 6 all bore evidence of advanced development of the third molars, or wisdom teeth. In skull 3, the roots were obviously complete; in skulls 5 and 6, the development of the roots was complete, more so in no. 6 than in no. 5, which led Levine to determine that of the two, no. 5 was in the youngest stages of development. Even so, the stages of growth exhibited in the roots of the teeth discovered in skulls 5 and 6 precluded the possibility that either represented the remains of a seventeen-year-old female.[73]

Skulls 5 and 6 had been missing nearly all of their facial bones, from the tops of their eyes to their jaws. Both had been "manfully" reconstructed, as Maples later said, "with generous dollops of glue, stretched across wide gaps. They had been forced to estimate over and over again, while reassembling these fragments, almost none of which were touching each other."[74] Dr. Levine recalls the "wide stretches of wax" inserted between the bones "to help fill the gaps. The faces were simply missing, and in just too bad of shape to reliably be put back together."[75]

Abramov's photo superimposition technique, Maples declared, "rested on a shaky foundation—that the features of skulls 5 and 6 had been accurately reconstructed. With so many bones missing—and so many hundreds of bones and fragments confused and mixed up in that room—I wouldn't like to give any guess as to how likely it is that they even got the correct bones into those skulls. There was a lot of confusion about the remains. Facial reconstruction isn't new, and I use it, but it has to be done very carefully—it's a very delicate operation. You have to use special glues that don't expand and distort the angles. And here, none of that was done."[76]

The American team worked with the remains throughout the last week of July 1992. On Sunday, July 26, the two-day conference on the fate of the Romanovs, christened with the rather hopeful title of "The Last Page of the History of the Imperial Family," opened in the Ekaterinburg Theater, attended by two hundred people, mainly journalists and officials.[77] The conference was revealing in several respects. Avdonin's talk to the gathering, focusing on his own role in the initial exhumation, also inadvertently focused attention on the Russian lack of knowledge of the Romanovs. Avdonin began his talk by saying that "everyone knows that on March 14 [sic], 1917, Nicholas II was forced to abdicate the Russian throne," and proceeded to launch into a lengthy retelling of the period of exile, imprisonment, and murder that was replete with such errors. He stated that the imperial family was removed from Tsarskoye Selo to Tobolsk in 1918; declared four times that he had first begun to work with Geli Ryabov in the 1960s; that Nicholas, Alexandra, and Marie were first taken to the Ipatiev House "in buses"; and that the truck that carried the bodies into Koptyaki Forest was "a Ford, not a Fiat." He declared that it took Yurovsky and his men "until dusk of July 17" to finish throwing the bodies into the Four Brothers mine; and that Yurovsky decided to burn all the bodies, which Avdonin said was done at the Four Brothers mine itself. He contended that Yurovsky confused the identity of the female body he supposedly burned because "all the women were charred and looked pretty much the same," an assertion completely unsupported by both the eyewitness accounts and forensic examination of the remains themselves. Avdonin also claimed, contrary to what Plaskin's team would announce, that it was Tatiana's body that was burned and therefore missing.[78]

The main focus of the conference, however, was to announce the identification of the remains. The official Russian report—which misidentified skeleton 1 as that of Nicholas—had already been prepared, and Plaskin was thus put in the uncomfortable position of having to publicly disavow his own presentation: "The experts do not always get positive results. In some cases, it is impossible to identify a skeleton. And it is not professional to give false evidence. At the moment, only the following can be said: the skull of Alexandra Feodorovna, and the skull of Dr. Botkin, have been positively identified using the method of superimposition. As to the third finding, the skull of Nicholas II, at this point it is not possible to say for sure that we are now dealing with his skull, because there are other skulls which have similar features. . . . Not all the skeletons will be identified. Their condition is different, they had been buried for a long time, they were subjected to acid."[79]

Abramov, too, had to distance himself from Plaskin's report. He explained how the software had been developed to "help speed up our identifications" using the computer, and declared confidently that "our superimposition is the last, final stage in positive identification." He declared: "For sure, we have the Emperor, the Empress; for sure we have Botkin. Also we have the girls. Now we have to determine who is who." And yet, with skull 1 misidentified in the official report on the basis of superimposition, Abramov confidently declared: "The entire research work done prior to the superimposition makes it possible to trust the validity of the superimposition itself. Superimposition confirms everything that has been discovered earlier."[80]

During the panel discussion, a Russian journalist asked Abramov pointedly: "Why is American intelligence involved in all this? Why did the American FBI and Defense Department pay to have these people come here?"

"I don't know," Abramov replied. "The thing is, when Baker was here, he promised some assistance. He asked whether help was needed. And the Administration said, 'Yes, of course.' So he kept his word. Too bad we don't have enough translators. I would like to speak with them, but I don't speak the language. So we just smile and nod to each other but cannot say a word. And we are dying to know the level of their work, what they think of us. This is important. We don't have any contacts with American scientists, absolutely none. And we don't know what level of expertise their work is at, how they perform examinations, how trained they are."[81]

This rather unsubtle questioning of the qualification of the American team members, Maples later said, made him rather upset. "When we did our work," he explained, "we often disagreed with what the Russians claimed, but I don't think any of us publicly went out and said that we didn't know how qualified they were as scientists. That was unnecessary."[82]

Maples received a rather pointed question as well. "What do you think of the level of Russian forensic medical research? It took about a year for Russians to do the same thing Americans did in three days. What do you think of that?"

"In my opinion," Maples replied diplomatically, "the level of scientific work that have been done on these remains is extremely high. I would be proud to welcome each and every one of the participants into the American Academy of Forensic Sciences. As far as the amount of time, the type of technology and procedures that were used was very time-consuming here in Russia. But remember they had to first bring together the correct bones for each skeleton. They had to reconstruct broken faces and skulls. These things take time. They did so much preliminary work."[83]

Maples' answer skirted the obvious issue. Later, he would answer similar questions more freely but, as he explained, "in that kind of situation, where you're with fellow professionals, in a foreign country, the last thing in the world you do is criticize someone's job performance or question their work. That's why, when Abramov did it to us, it really made me angry."[84]

The American conclusions—and particularly their contention that Anastasia was missing—quickly became the central focus of the conference. The issue of who had been identified and who was missing became even more muddied as the session continued. Dr. Filipchuk, a forensic expert from the Ukraine, believed that no. 5 was a young woman aged about twenty, based on examination of bone lengths, measurements, and vertebrae analysis. He agreed that skeleton 5 was that of Grand Duchess Marie, though he believed that she had been the tallest of the three remains. He placed skeleton 6 between nos. 3 and 5 in age, consistent with the American team.[85] This view was echoed by the work of Dr. Vyacheslav Popov, a forensic dentistry expert from the St. Petersburg Military Medical Academy. Using the development of the teeth, he identified skeleton 5 as that of "a young woman, of about twenty years." According to Popov, skeleton 5 could be either Tatiana or Marie but could not be Anastasia, as the odontology revealed mature development.[86]

The Moscow team went out of their way to do all they could to argue that Anastasia was dead. When asked about the possibility of survivors, Abramov was clearly on uncertain ground. "There are special documents of Sokolov's investigation that testify to the fact that on July 17, eleven people were killed," he declared, as if these accounts in and of themselves provided irrefutable evidence of the death of everyone in the Ipatiev House. It was a peculiar way of addressing the issue, used time and time again throughout the investigation: Sokolov had declared that all eleven were dead; therefore it was a proven fact. Abramov attempted to bolster the case by referring to "a book written by Meyer. It's about the murder of the Emperor's family, published in Austria, and he was convinced no one survived." This was a reference to Hans Johann Meyer, but Abramov got nearly every fact wrong. Meyer never wrote a book, but rather was interviewed, not in an Austrian book, but in the German magazine 7-*Tage*. He claimed to have been in the Ipatiev House and seen the bodies of all of the victims. Apparently Abramov did not know that Meyer had come forth in the 1950s with a handful of forged documents that helped bolster his case and that he attempted to submit as evidence in the Hamburg trial of Anna Anderson. The West German court later branded Meyer a perjurer and declared his documents forgeries.[87]

When questioned directly about the contradiction between his identification of skeleton 6 as Anastasia and the American team's finding that her remains were not present, Abramov replied with a tortured and disingenuous answer: "Our American colleagues," he declared, "said very carefully that the skeleton of Anastasia is missing, but they didn't say that it's missing for certain."[88] This was certainly news to Maples, Baden, Levine, and the other American experts, who were quite categorical that none of the remains exhumed could be attributed to Anastasia. No one contradicted Abramov, or corrected the record, believing, as Maples later said, "it was best to restate our opinions later, and not turn the session into a shouting match."[89]

Another issue raised during the session was that of the two loose teeth found in the grave, which, according to Dr. Popov, did not appear to belong to any of the exhumed remains. Abramov identified them as those of a male between ages fourteen and sixteen. He was adamant that they could not have come from anyone older than sixteen—"no more than sixteen at most" were his exact words.[90] Dr. Lowell Levine, one of the world's foremost forensic odontologists, strongly disagreed with Popov's assertions. He expressed surprise that Popov would claim the ability to identify the gender of their owner, given their deteriorated condition. While Popov stated that they were second molars, Levine believed that they were upper third molars, indicating that they would have come from one of the grand duchesses recovered from the grave.[91] He further disagreed with Popov's assertion that the damage observed on the teeth could have resulted from exposure to fire, believing this had resulted from exposure to acid.[92]

Analysis of the teeth, as both Maples and Levine discovered, was being conducted using an old system developed in the United States in 1932; it apparently was the only technology available to the Russians.[93] The Russians would later undertake a complete reversal of their 1992 position, and agree with Levine that the two teeth were, in fact, from one of the exhumed skulls. They would attempt to use them, however, to again prove that Anastasia was dead, claiming they had belonged to skeleton 6. It was an assertion that failed to convince Levine. "It's too convoluted, and ignores all the evidence," he said.[94]

After two days of this—from Russian insistence that they had Anastasia's remains, Abramov's open questioning of the credentials and level of knowledge of the American experts, to the sometimes obvious hostility of some of the Russians, innuendo that they were paid agents of the FBI, and consistent lack of cooperation—Maples, at least, was tired of "a political situation of which we knew absolutely nothing."[95] After the conference had ended, Maples and Levine spoke freely to reporters, their answers indicating the strain of the past week as well as what had diplomatically been left unsaid in the official sessions. "They suggest that skeleton 1," Maples said, "was a male, and while there may have been some problem dealing with the cranial remains, the pelvis is just clearly female. So I don't understand that. They used a lot of high-tech stuff that probably we wouldn't have used, but not even basic forensic science. They worked very independently from one another. One person worked with hands, and one person worked with blood type, and had no idea what anyone else was doing. So the results came in a little more chopped up than they would have had they been coordinated by a central agency conducting the investigation."[96] Levine added: "There are a lot of loose threads that need to be tightened up. Right now, it's not within reasonable scientific certainty. I think one of the problems in this case, one of the problems in all these types of cases, in the United States and in other countries, is that usually you don't have one unified joint effort by all the best people involved working together to a common goal. You still get very different agendas. And that's where you have problems here. We're a little disappointed, I guess." He added: "As far as a high-profile case, this is getting short shrift in the examination and investigation phase. This isn't even the quality of investigation that the average American citizen would get. And certainly it seems like what's happening here is mixed up with political and religious issues, which we'll leave to the politicians and to the Church."[97]

Maples was highly critical—as Dr. Lyudmilla Koryakova had been before—of the manner in which the two exhumations had been undertaken. "Our plan would have been to dig down 20 or 30 centimeters with sharp-pointed shovels, not the machines they used," Maples said. "We would have come in and used techniques like ground-penetrating radar, perhaps, soil resistance equipment, core tools, taking core samples over a system with a lot more method in planning, a lot more diagrams of exactly what's been done. And we would do everything we could not to disturb the overall soil, so we could continue to take electronic data and that sort of thing."[98]

Near the end of the conference, Abramov took Maples aside and warned him that he should not make any further announcement that Anastasia was missing. He declared that the Russians had "spent a year" working with the remains, while Maples "had spent only three days." Abramov said he did not want Maples to look foolish.[99]

One of the popular misconceptions surrounding the American identifications—and one largely propagated through repetition—was that they had claimed Anastasia to be missing based only on their estimations of heights. In fact, in examining skeletons 5 and 6, they based this determination on four distinct indicators: estimated height of remains; development of the wisdom teeth and roots; pelvic development; and vertebrae development. Thus, even if their height estimations were somehow wrong, the three other factors stood as separate pieces in the evidentiary puzzle to bolster their conclusions.

This overt emphasis on estimated heights was unfortunately propagated by Maples himself, in a casual remark he made to reporters at the 1992 conference. When asked to describe how the American team had come to its conclusions, Maples explained: "All the skeletons appear too tall to be Anastasia, and in the skeletal material we have looked at there is nothing that could represent Alexei."[100] In giving this statement, Maples neglected to address the three other forensic and anthropological factors that had led the Americans to their conclusion; to the public at large, the American determination seemed to rest on a single factor.

The issue became lost in the media frenzy that followed the American announcement. Suddenly, one of the greatest mysteries of the twentieth century was evoked, and for the first time, there appeared to be solid reasons for believing that perhaps the most famous member of the Russian imperial family had somehow escaped the fate of her family. It was a question whose resolution would dominate the case and determine the investigation.

20

"It's All Secret, All Political"

TWO WEEKS AFTER the Ekaterinburg conference, the Russian government formed a special commission designed to investigate the circumstances of the execution of the Romanovs and finalize the identification of the corpses found within the grave.[1] The most pressing concern was that of the two missing sets of remains. Throughout 1992 and continuing to the present day, lengthy and ultimately futile searches would be carried out in Koptyaki Forest, in an effort to provide final resolution to the Romanov case.

The two men responsible for the initial discovery of the remains—Geli Ryabov and Alexander Avdonin—had no doubt but that the two missing victims had indeed died that night and that their remains would ultimately be found. "We have no instances of the Communists ever, anywhere, having mercy on anyone," Ryabov declared. "If people understood that, it would not occur to them that Communists could let a member of the Emperor's family survive. It's simply impossible."[2]

Following the flurry of initial press interviews, Ryabov—and his outrageous and contradictory claims—were largely ignored by the media, which increasingly viewed him as a less than credible source. Avdonin, who helped organize the 1992 conference, pointedly excluded his former partner, a move Peter Gritsaenko ascribed to Avdonin's "tension and anger over the case, and Ryabov's betrayal of their oath."[3] By 1993, however, with the wave of media speculation about the fate of Anastasia rampant, Ryabov once again found himself in the spotlight, sought out for interviews and theories. Time had done nothing to alter his penchant for inaccuracy; instead, his monarchist fervor had dramatically increased, channeled into long-winded condemnations of the former Soviet Union, error-filled pronouncements on the case, and more than a hint of jealousy over Avdonin's role in the entire affair. Speaking in 1993, Ryabov continued to insist that one of the three skulls exhumed in 1979 had been that of Nicholas II, while the other two were "maybe the Heir Alexei, or maybe two of the daughters," an assertion contradicted by both the American and Russian experts. He refused to give way: "I am totally convinced that we exhumed Nicholas II's skull," he declared, adding—seemingly oblivious to the public pronouncements on the issue—"the tests don't refute it." Proudly once again displaying his faded color photographs from the 1979 exhumation, he pointed to the skulls and said, "Here, you see, is the moment when we pulled out the skull of Alexei Nikolaievich." He continually referred to the Romanovs as "our Saints, our martyrs," and criticized those then involved in the case—"Plaskin, Abramov, Nevolin"—as "not decent, very bad people," and "ex-Communists who still live in their sweet Soviet past." When questioned about the proposal to bury the remains in a new church to be built on the site of the Ipatiev House, Ryabov was horrified: "Saints cannot be buried where they were killed!" he exclaimed. "In my opinion, it would be sacrilege." He was full of gushing admiration for Nicholas Sokolov, whom he called "the greatest Russian man ever, a convinced monarchist." He declared that Sokolov's investigation "contained no inconsistencies, no contradictions, everything proves he was right," in apparent oblivion to the wealth of sound criticism leveled at his case. For good measure, Ryabov declared: "I, too, am a convinced monarchist. I am convinced that Russia was a great country, that it became a great country under the scepter of the Russian sovereigns. And that is why I am convinced that once the development of Russia under monarchy was forcibly interrupted, Russia was killed. For seventy-four years Russia was ruled by madmen, mentally ill people, bastards, butchers. I believe that if we still had an Emperor, the United States, God knows, would probably envy Russia, and fear us. Without an Emperor, Russia will never be a wonderful country, never, I am absolutely sure. And no one will respect us. I am totally convinced that everyone was happier under the Emperor, and there can't be any opinion other than this."[4]

As for Avdonin, he, too, fell victim to the prevailing intrigues and monarchist sentiment that engulfed the case. By 1993 he was referring to the executions as "the precise event that ushered in the era of the most cruel terrorist, bloody acts, which were camouflaged by a shroud of diverse, false versions and assertions, legends and speculations." It had, he said, "brought about executioners who specialized in the most cultivated methods of annihilation."[5]

Boris Yarkov, an Ekaterinburg journalist who worked closely with

Avdonin until the two fell out, described him as "a person who does things without thinking, like his association with Ryabov. After he was betrayed, he refused to trust anyone again. And after the scientists and politicians got involved, Avdonin got caught up in that. I think the important thing to know is that this is an entirely political case—everything having to do with those bones has political implications. And Avdonin was swept up into that, and he has become like them—secretive, jealous, insecure. There are constant intrigues over this case, secrets, people interested in keeping things hidden, and people who want to do everything in the open. I think the truth is obvious, but no one here wants to admit to it—it's lost between opinions, somewhere in the middle. Avdonin's over his head, and doesn't know it. When people abandon truth in favor of political principles, that's when problems emerge. And I think Avdonin has fallen into this trap."[6]

Of the two men, only Avdonin remained a part of the ongoing investigation. Like Ryabov, he was convinced that there were no survivors, explaining, "All the people taken to Ipatiev's House were shot. I think maybe Anna Anderson could be Anastasia, but only if Anastasia had not gone into that house. We know everyone who went into that house was killed, including Anastasia." Like Ryabov, he bolstered this assertion by referring to Sokolov: "It really happened," he declared. "We know they all died. They were really shot. And we know because it's been proved by Sokolov." More peculiarly, Avdonin dismissed the possibility of survival on the most unusual grounds: "There are many Anastasias and Alexeis out there, now and in the past. Now, I think, two Alexeis are alive. But if Alexei survived, there should be just one Alexei. But there are two of them, and many more. There were more Anastasias. Anastasia's children live here now, says one. She died in the fifties and was buried in Omsk. She was Anastasia Spiridovna. Anna Anderson was another pretender from [sic] the United States. Who is the real Anastasia? If Anastasia survived, there should be just one pretender, same with Alexei. So more than one means we here in Russia consider them all false."[7]

Avdonin, like Ryabov, believed that the two sets of missing remains could be found in Koptyaki Forest. To this end, he formed his foundation Obretenyie (Recovery), ostensibly to hunt for the two bodies. While this was the stated intent of the organization, Avdonin revealed that the actual motives were somewhat different: "Obretenyie stands for the restoration of moral values in Russia," he declared. "Our special task is establishing the truth of Russian history."[8] Initially, Obretenyie included several others, but all left after falling out with Avdonin. In May 1992 Avdonin offered his friend and fellow geologist Vyacheslav Blinkov the post of deputy in the organization. Blinkov soon learned that aside from himself, the only other person in the organization was

Avdonin, as everyone else refused to work with him. Blinkov got a taste
of this soon enough, and abruptly quit. Avdonin, he says, "was very jealous of everything concerning the Imperial relics and thinks he is the
only one with the right to publish or give out information. When other
reporters appear, with information from different people, he just can't
stand it. When Obretenyie was set up, Avdonin had it written in the
foundation documents that only Obretenyie had the right to publish
material about the family and the finding of the bones."[9]

Blinkov's experiences echoed those of Dr. Lyudmilla Koryakova.
Having been forced, against her objections, to remain at the 1991 exhumation, she was infuriated that Avdonin himself had swept into the pit
and grabbed at the bones, disarticulating them, and given interviews the
first night—while the Russian military stood guard and refused to let
her return to her home for fresh clothes "for security reasons." After the
exhumation, she refused to have anything to do with Avdonin. Her
superiors at Ural State University pressured her to work with
Obretenyie, but she was adamant. That Avdonin wielded such influence, and was allowed to do as he pleased, gave Koryakova enough reason to distance herself.[10]

Koryakova saw intrigue everywhere, and she was not alone. "All difficulties here," Peter Gritsaenko said in 1993, "come from this question.
It's all secret, all political. I think if only scientists and experts were in
charge of the whole thing, and the church and politicians wouldn't
interfere, we could solve many problems. But there are others involved,
too many people, with powerful motives, and they want certain things,
certain outcomes, their own conclusions confirmed."[11]

The attitude was widespread. The Romanovs—their lives, their
deaths, and now their bones—belonged to Russia, and to Russia alone.
Foreigners—and their opinions—were not welcome. In 1993, Avdonin
declared that he was "uniting patriots, real Russians, people interested in
the history of the country and their region. Restoration must happen—
of morals, nationalism, and we hope the Romanovs. Russia needs them
now, to keep out criminals from our lives, bad elements, foreigners who
murdered the sovereign."[12] This was an ominous echo of both the claims
of Jewish ritual murder and the frequent assertions that the murder had
been carried out only by non-Russians. Only foreigners, it was said, had
been responsible for all of Russia's misfortunes. In such a manner did the
murders in 1918 come to be understood and accepted. It had, claimed
one author after another, all come about, not from the Russian people
themselves, but from these nebulous foreigners—the Germans, the
Communists, the Letts, the Jews—anyone and everyone had a hand in
the crime, and everyone was responsible—except, of course, for the
Russians themselves. Thus they came to terms with their past.

The fetid stench of anti-Semitism steadily engulfed the case, as it had under the Whites, under Sokolov, and under those who carried bright the monarchist flame into exile. "Everyone knows," one monarchist group in Russia declared, that the exhumed remains were not those of the Romanovs, "because the Jews ate them."[13] Such talk ran high across Ekaterinburg in the 1990s. Like the site on which the Ipatiev House—torn down in 1977—had once stood, the burial pit became the focus of much attention, a modern shrine. Avdonin erected an Orthodox cross of rough birch branches next to the grave, declaring, "We consider this a Holy Place."[14] The site itself, a gaping, muddy pit filled with water in spring and summer, stood like a painful, open wound, an uncomfortable reminder of the violent past.

When Avdonin, Kochurov, and Ryabov had first examined the area around both Pig's Meadow and the Four Brothers mine, they looked carefully at the few traces of bonfires they discovered. All were of recent origin, while those at the mine itself could not, according to Yurovsky and the others who left accounts, possibly be connected to the two bodies said to have been burned near the actual grave. In the spring of 1993, Professor Veniamin Alekseev, head of the Institute of History and Archaeology in Ekaterinburg, himself led a team into Koptyaki Forest and excavated selected sites in Pig's Meadow. As a trained archaeologist, Alekseev attempted to conduct the dig under strict scientific terms; a team of men used a small bulldozer to remove the top layer of soil at a few selected spots, however, disturbing the ground covering. Although the actual exhumations were conducted carefully, tales soon spread among certain segments in Ekaterinburg that Alekseev, who by this time had joined Avdonin's growing list of enemies, had deliberately

The pile of ashes found by investigators at the Four Brothers.

gone into Koptyaki Forest and simply plowed the entire meadow in his search. In fact, Alekseev had focused on only three selected sites, but he, too, had been unable to find any human remains.[15]

Every summer since 1992, dedicated groups, mostly young men, have filled the clearings and dense forest, examining, digging, searching for a prize that inevitably eluded them. One young man engaged in the search explained: "Honestly, the work is very hard, climate, living conditions, everything is terrible. But this place is sanctified, because this is the burial place of the people who were killed and which were innocent. Each person feels a quivering at this place. All people, who participated in excavations, feel this strange emotional condition. Here you can sob. Many people call this an act of honor and conscience of the whole of Russia. The conscience of Russia is represented by these nine people, and we haven't anybody else. We are trying to expiate the past sins of the Russian people that they committed a long time ago, the sin of murdering the Emperor. The ten of us working here represent the whole of Russia."[16]

Such efforts were often met with skepticism and hostility from unusual quarters. One Orthodox priest, speaking at the grave in 1993, declared: "I can tell you just one thing. No bodies can be possibly found here. You have to look for them in the Kremlin, not in this swamp. These people here spread false information, because they want us to go in a wrong direction, to mock the Imperial Martyrs and the whole of sacred Holy Russia. Satan wants to take people away from the truth of this crime, while the Imperial Martyrs live their sacred lives in Heaven. What is happening here is very sad. God save you all. You have to search for these sufferers in Heaven, not on Earth, because they are Saints."[17]

The Russians hoped to discover the missing remains before a second conference, held in Ekaterinburg from July 14 to 15, 1993. With no bodies, however, the 1993 conference became a mere repetition of the forensic and anthropological evidence of the previous year. Titled "The History of the Romanov Dynasty in Russia," the 1993 conference was organized not by Avdonin, but by his fierce enemy Veniamin Alekseev. There still was much confusion over the remains. At the conference, Dr. Vyacheslav Popov doubted that skeleton 5 would ever be accurately identified, saying it was impossible to determine whether the remains were those of Tatiana or of Marie.

Abramov had continued working with the photo superimposition program, but the new tests simply repeated his first results. To the Russians, Anastasia had been identified as skeleton 6, and neither Abramov nor anyone else from Moscow attempted to refute the development of the teeth, the vertebrae and clavicles, and the pelvic rim, all of which had clearly indicated to the American team a fully mature female of recently completed growth. Instead, Abramov focused solely on criticizing Maples's claim that all of the remains were too tall to be Anastasia. When Maples met with Abramov at his offices in April 1993, Maples again raised the outstanding questions: What of the missing remains? How did the Russians reconcile their identification of skeleton 6 as Anastasia with the clear forensic and anthropological evidence that indicated the remains were those of a young but fully mature woman? Had the issue of the commingled bones from skeletons 4, 6, and 9 been resolved? According to Maples, Abramov "attempted to refute our position by simply referring to different indications of height. He didn't touch on any of the other subjects. When I asked about the mixup in the remains a second time, he merely shrugged his shoulders."[18]

Abramov had grown weary of the issue. As far as he was concerned, he had proved Anastasia was in the grave, and the American announcement that she was missing had led to nothing but unwelcome speculation. Abramov became more vocal in his criticism of the American team. "They didn't use all of the methods available to make their identifications," he declared. But as he continued to speak, it was clear that he meant only his photo superimposition technique: "They didn't use photo superimposition. And so their results can't be final. As for us, we're continuing with our superimposition to determine which girl is missing."[19] As much as the Russians attempted to ignore the question of Anastasia's fate, it refused to die. While they initially blamed the American team for having raised the issue, the country's media were soon awash with similar stories—not just about Anna Anderson, but also about other, Russian claimants. No one, it seemed, was convinced by Abramov's declaration that Anastasia had already been identified.

Maples returned to Ekaterinburg for the 1993 conference, filming segments with the remains to be used in four separate documentaries on the case: Cymru Film's splendidly insightful *The Mystery of the Last Tsar;* a thoughtful British program, *Bones of Contention;* and episodes of the American public television series *Nova* and the NBC television series *Unsolved Mysteries.* The previous year, Moscow had reached an agreement with the British Home Office Laboratories and the Forensic Science Services to test the remains using DNA technology. For this, Dr. Pavel Ivanov had sectioned segments from the femurs of all nine skeletons, which he then delivered to England. Ekaterinburg authorities were suspicious of this, and wanted their own testing done, to either support or refute those commissioned by Moscow. They asked Maples to assist.[20] Teeth, as Maples knew, were a far better source for uncorrupted DNA than the bone sections taken by Ivanov. In the Romanov case, where the bones themselves had become mingled, with no guarantee that they had been correctly identified; laid in the mineral-rich soil of the Urals; been subjected to acid dripping from one bone to another, etching them as it went, and forming a pool in which the lowest remains rested; and been subjected to the yearly flood of water that filled the grave, teeth, Maples explained, "were the best source for uncorrupted DNA."[21] With the permission of the Ekaterinburg authorities, he left the city with a number of teeth, extracted from skulls 1, 3–7, and 9, and sections of femurs from skeletons 2 and 8, to be used in independent DNA testing.[22]

When Moscow learned of this, they moved quickly to end Ekaterinburg's independence. At the beginning of August, the Office of the Public Prosecutor in Moscow ordered that all materials connected to the Romanov case—the actual remains, all investigative matter, testing, photographs, and even videotape of the skeletons—was henceforth under their sole control and authority. To oversee the task, the Russian government appointed Vladimir Soloviev chief investigator for the Office of the Public Prosecutor, who immediately designated it as Criminal Case 18/123666/93, the murders of the imperial family and their four retainers.[23] One of his first tasks was to redirect the investigation, away from the contentious issue of the identification of the remains, and turn it toward a more traditional analysis of the circumstances and nature of the murders themselves. To accomplish this, Soloviev searched for the various weapons believed to have been used in the murders, including a number of guns given by the executioners to museums in the 1920s. Two of Yurovsky's guns—a Colt, model 71905, with a cartridge clip holding seven bullets, and a wooden-stocked Mauser, no. 16177, with a cartridge clip of ten bullets—had gone to the Museum of the October Revolution in Moscow in 1927.[24] Kudrin also had given his Browning revolver no. 389965 to the same institution, while Ermakov handed over his Mauser, no. 16174, to Ekaterinburg's Museum of the Revolution in 1927. These guns were tested by Soloviev, but their age had all but eradicated the usual channeling marks left on their bullets. Nor did the bullets retrieved from the burial pit contain any clear indications; acid had corroded them, making valid comparisons impossible.[25]

Soloviev formed a special government commission chaired by Yuri Yarov, the deputy premier of the Russian Federation, charged with both an evaluation of the evidence and the ultimate burial of the remains. Among others, this group included St. Petersburg mayor Anatoly Sobchak, Vladislav Plaskin, Avdonin, Edvard Rossel, and author Edvard Radzinsky.[26] A second group, the Commission of Forensic Medical Examination of the Skeletal Remains, was given the task of providing final identifications. Headed by Soloviev, it included Plaskin; Abramov; Dr. I. A. Gedygushev, deputy chief of the Bureau of Forensic Medicine in the Ministry of Health; Dr. Svetlana Gurtovaya, head of the Forensic Biological Department in the Ministry of Health; Dr. Pavel Ivanov, head of the Genetic Analysis Laboratory in the Ministry of Health; Dr. V. N. Kryukov, head of the Department of Forensic Medicine at Russian State Medical University; and Professor I. Ye. Kuznetsov, a representative from the Department of Forensic Medicine at the same institute.[27] Excluded from Soloviev's group were Drs. Popov, Filipchuk, Nevolin, and Zvyagin, four scientists who had worked extensively with the remains and who disagreed with the commission's findings.

The commission relied almost exclusively on Abramov's photo superimposition. Their 1993 report, "Conclusions of the Commission of Forensic Medicine on Examination of the Skeletal Remains," concluded that five of the skeletons—nos. 3–7—constituted a family group, and identified them as Olga (no. 3), Nicholas (no. 4), Tatiana (no. 5), Anastasia (no. 6), and Alexandra (no. 7). Demidova was identified as skeleton 1, while Botkin was named as skeleton 2. The remains of Ivan Kharitonov and Alexei Trupp—skeletons 8 and 9, respectively—could only be identified through a process of elimination, on a conditional basis. Lest there be any doubt about how these identifications were to be pursued—or, indeed, how the identifications of skeletons 1–7 had been achieved—the report added: "Identification of I. M. Kharitonov and A. Y. Trupp by additional photographic methods can only be conducted when photographic documents are compared to the bones kept in Ekaterinburg in an additional examination."[28] These identifications became the official Russian verdict. Thus were the remains labeled and, in 1998, eventually buried, though not without a hint of controversy, given the very real doubts that remain to the present day. Skeleton 5, which all American experts believed was Marie, was buried as Tatiana. Skeleton 6, believed by the Americans to be Tatiana, was buried as Anastasia.

The 1993 report confirmed that none of the remains recovered from the burial pit bore any indication of having been subjected to fire. "No evidence of thermal destruction," it declared, "such as carbonization, or ash content, has been detected in any of the remains."[29] The 1993 report failed to address the American team's concerns that various arm and leg bones, as well as the sternum bearing the bayonet wound, had been wrongly attributed to skeletons 4, 6, and 9, a point with which even Abramov had reluctantly agreed.[30]

Although the commission delivered their final report in December 1993, its contents were not released until nearly nine months later. On September 6, 1994, Soloviev granted an interview to the Moscow newspaper *Sevodnya* in which he declared with finality, "The remains of Grand Duchess Anastasia Nikolaievna are indeed present, along with those of her parents, and two of her sisters." Soloviev refused to release the entire report, however, saying that the commission was awaiting completion of the DNA tests in the United Kingdom.[31]

Lacking the technology to conduct their own genetic tests, the Russian Ministry of Health had signed an agreement authorizing the British Home Office to perform DNA analysis on the exhumed remains. The tests would be performed by a team including Dr. Peter Gill, director of Biology Research at the Home Office Forensic Science Services Laboratory; Sir Alec Jeffreys, who had helped develop the genetic fingerprint; Dr. Erika Hagelberg, of Cambridge University; and Dr. Pavel Ivanov, who represented the Russian Ministry of Health. If enough uncontaminated DNA could be extracted from the remains, the scientists hoped to compare it with samples extracted from living relatives of the imperial family.

On September 15, 1992, Ivanov arrived in London, carrying with him sectioned pieces from the femurs and tibias of the nine skeletons. The initial testing took ten months, owing to the age and deterioration of the bones.[32] Gill and Ivanov found the material too degraded to subject it to standard genetic testing; instead, they used the relatively new polymerase chain reaction method, or PCR, a system developed by Nobel Prize winner Dr. Kary B. Mullis.[33] This amplified the available genetic data, producing the quantity of nuclear DNA necessary to conduct accurate tests.

During the initial testing, some suggestion was made that the DNA extracted from skeleton 7, identified as that of Empress Alexandra, should be subjected to chromosomal analysis, to confirm that it carried the defective X chromosomes through which hemophilia is passed. The remains attributed to the grand duchesses also could be tested, establishing if they had been hemophilia carriers. But the nature of the work, coupled with both time and financial restraints, eventually prevented such secondary testing.

Nuclear DNA tests, conducted using an identification known as short tandem repeats, or STRs, established relationships among the nine remains. Repeated base pairs in the analyzed chromosomes, known as hypervariable regions, showed that skeletons 3, 5, and 6 were the children of nos. 4 and 7, Nicholas and Alexandra. Positively identifying skeleton 2 as Dr. Botkin was more problematic. Although Marina Botkin Schweitzer, his granddaughter, donated blood for testing, her nuclear DNA, combining as it did not only the genetic codes of her father, Gleb, but also her late mother, produced only half of the Botkin DNA profile. With no available sample of Botkin's wife's DNA, the scientists were forced to make their identification on exclusion, utilizing the profile drawn from Marina Botkin Schweitzer against one from her half sister to examine the strand of Botkin nuclear DNA. When isolated, this allowed Gill and Ivanov to successfully match the contemporary nuclear DNA pattern to that of skeleton 2.[34]

Identifying the exhumed remains as those of the Romanovs, however, proved difficult. The best hope was the use of mitochondrial DNA, or mtDNA, derived from genetic material in the nucleus of each cell. Mitochondrial DNA, unlike nuclear DNA, is passed only through the matrilineal line, from mothers to their children, but only from their daughters to their own children, following female descent. In an unbroken matrilineal line, a woman could be traced directly through genetic analysis to her own mother, grandmother, great-grandmother, and so forth, across hundreds of years. The remains of the empress and her daughters would therefore contain mtDNA sequences identical to those of the empress's grandmother Queen Victoria.

A blood sample provided by Prince Philip, the duke of Edinburgh and consort of Queen Elizabeth II, helped lessen doubts that lingered over the remains. His mother, Princess Alice of Greece, was the daughter of the empress's eldest sister, Victoria, marchioness of Milford Haven. Both Alexandra and Victoria shared a common mitochondrial DNA sequence inherited from their grandmother Queen Victoria. Prince Philip, separated from the empress by only two generations, was one of Alexandra's closest living relatives, a beneficial position from a scientific standpoint.

Mitochondrial DNA retrieved from the Ekaterinburg remains proved to be highly corrupted, one of the risks involved when extracting sequences from old bones. In the Romanov case, full sequences could not be achieved for the empress and her three daughters; in the string of base pairs forming the mtDNA pattern, entire stretches were missing. To obtain a complete sequence, or mtDNA fingerprint, Gill and Ivanov were forced to look for overlapping, repetitive strands, which were then spliced together to form the missing links in the genetic chain. Although standard practice, this scientific necessity did not provide an unaltered genetic code for the remains, but rather one achieved through manipulation of the available data based on estimation.[35] The sequences derived through this method matched that provided by the duke of Edinburgh, itself considered rare in the early years of genetic research when the testing was conducted: statistical estimation placed the likelihood of finding the same genetic profile at 1 in every 6,000 European Caucasians.[36] This supported the belief that skeletons 7, 3, 5, and 6 shared descent from a common ancestor, in turn suggesting that the remains were those of the empress and three of her daughters.

Finding a donor to provide a genetic profile against which the presumptive remains of Nicholas II could be tested was more complicated. His nearest living relative, and the one person unquestionably sharing direct maternal descent from his mother, Dowager Empress Marie Feodorovna, was his nephew Tikhon Kulikovsky, son of the emperor's sister Grand Duchess Olga Alexandrovna. Kulikovsky, born in 1917, lived in Canada, where he made no secret of his belief that the Ekaterinburg remains were an elaborate hoax engineered by the KGB. He refused to cooperate in tests undertaken by British or Russian scientists, saying he would provide a sample only on condition that analysis was done by a country with no interest in the outcome. Here, Kulikovsky said, England did not qualify, given both the refusal of George V to grant the imperial family asylum in 1917, and also in the belief that the British royal family had personally swindled his mother out of hundreds of thousands of dollars following the sale of certain jewelry to Queen Mary.[37] This forced Gill and Ivanov to go back a generation, to Marie Feodorovna's mother, Queen Louise of Denmark, and her descendants in an unbroken female line. Eventually two candidates were found: the duke of Fife, descended from Queen Louise through her granddaughter Princess Louise; and Madame Xenia Sfiris, a great-great-granddaughter of Marie Feodorovna through Nicholas II's sister Grand Duchess Xenia Alexandrovna.

Gill and Ivanov found distinct similarities between the sequence from skeleton 4 and those derived from the duke of Fife and Xenia Sfiris, but also a deviation in a single position among the bare pairs. This mutation, or heteroplasmy, indicated a serious problem in the identification work.[38] As a genetic condition, heteroplasmy was not unknown in DNA science, indicating that the sample tested had a mutation. In the early 1990s, during the Romanov tests, DNA science itself was so new, and so subject to rapid evolution and development, that no clear, recognized procedures existed for resolving the problem Gill and Ivanov faced. They eventually decided to clone the DNA sample derived from the bones using the PCR process, to see if the heteroplasmy reproduced itself, or if their testing procedure itself had resulted in the anomaly. When cloned, the genetic profile drawn from skeleton 4 indeed contained a single mutated hypervariable region, indicating that the problem originated not with the scientists but with the emperor's own genetic code. This discovery also meant that it was impossible to say conclusively that the remains were those of Nicholas II.

In July 1993 the Forensic Science Services Laboratory announced that the Ekaterinburg remains had been identified as those of Alexandra, three of her daughters, and, tentatively, Nicholas II; the heteroplasmy remained a problem, and would require further testing before any conclusions could accurately be made. Nevertheless, according to the scientists, identity had been established to a 98.5 percent degree of certainty in this case. This figure, their report noted, was "the lowest interpretation of the DNA evidence. A more generous interpretation would increase it to over 99 percent."[39]

This figure, reported around the world as conclusive evidence in the Romanov case, was deceptive. It reflected not the odds that the actual DNA profiling was correct, but the accumulation of forensic, anthropological, and genetic evidence that together strongly suggested that these were indeed the Romanov remains. Professor Brian Sykes, himself a pioneering geneticist, suggested that an estimate of the DNA probabilities alone would have been "significantly lower," particularly given that the tests were conducted in the "early days of research," at a time when genetic databases represented only hundreds of profiles from which these numbers were extrapolated.[40]

The heteroplasmy remained an unresolved issue and, without the blood of Tikhon Kulikovsky, who died in 1993, the Russians were forced to seek alternative solutions. Investigators combed through the State Archives of the Russian Federation, where locks of Nicholas's baby hair were preserved, but these failed to render any useful results. It was then suggested that they approach the Japanese government, which still held a handkerchief used to stem the flow of blood after Nicholas was attacked while visiting Otsu in 1891. After initial reluctance, Japanese authorities finally agreed to allow testing, but then the issue became financial: Who would pay for the tests? The Russian government had no money, and the Forensic Science Services Laboratory in Great Britain had completed the terms of its agreement.

Vladimir Soloviev suggested the alternative: exhumation of Nicholas II's brother Grand Duke George Alexandrovich from his tomb in the Cathedral of the Fortress of St. Peter and St. Paul in St. Petersburg. This proposal resulted in an outcry of horror from the Russian Orthodox Church, which regarded the idea as desecration bordering on sacrilege, and it took Soloviev nearly a year before he finally obtained official permission to proceed. In May 1993 the burial vault was opened, and the rotting, blackened corpse of the grand duke was raised into the nave of the cathedral, watched over by a priest and a string of black-clad nuns who held lighted tapers and chanted solemnly throughout. Lacking the resources to conduct the testing themselves, the Russian government sent samples from the grand duke to the Armed Forces Institute of Pathology in the United States, where they were sequenced and compared against the mtDNA profile derived by Gill and Ivanov from the remains of skeleton 4. Badly corrupted, the mtDNA sequence nevertheless matched that of Nicholas II exactly, containing the heteroplasmy at the same hypervariable region.

In the ten years since these tests were conducted, DNA studies have evolved, new advances in methodology and technique replacing much of what, in 1993, represented the very edge of scientific knowledge. Gill and Ivan used a six-point STR comparison to establish a family relationship among skeletons 3–7. At the time, this was a fairly new standard, yet ten-point testing has shown results based on six-point tests to often produce false matches and exclusions. The Forensic Science Services Laboratory itself switched to the more accurate ten-point STR testing method in 2000, yet within two years, this, too, had become obsolete, replaced first by a sixteen-, then a twenty-point system.[41]

Nor, as genetic databases grow larger and more reflective of a wider cross-section of humanity, do the mtDNA matches in the Romanov case suggest the exclusive identification widely believed in the 1990s. Geneticist Brian Sykes, in a pioneering examination on the spread of mtDNA profiles, has shown that individuals unrelated to one another through hundreds of generations can still share the same genetic fingerprint. Sykes found, in comparing his own mtDNA to that extracted from Nicholas II, that the profiles very nearly matched. This theory that mtDNA profiles are not as unique as first believed has been confirmed as the science itself matures.[42]

Inevitably, such developments led to critical analysis of the DNA work in the Romanov case, the latest in August 2001. A team of Japanese scientists, headed by Dr. Tatsuo Nagai, professor of forensic medicine at Kitasato University's Graduate School of Medical Science, challenged the mtDNA profile that Gill had produced for Nicholas II in 1993. Although they requested access to the remaining Ekaterinburg bone samples, Professor Nagai and his team were refused permission. What they did have, however, was something denied to Gill and Ivanov, and that served, Nagai declared, as their "gold standard": the blood and DNA sequence of Tikhon Kulikovsky. After his death in 1993, Kulikovsky left a will allowing for future testing, and his widow, Olga Nikolaievna, granted Nagai access to a section of tissue preserved in a Toronto hospital archive.[43] The Japanese team also had an mtDNA sequence extracted from the jawbone, hair, and nails of Grand Duke George Alexandrovich, and one from sweat-stained clothing that had belonged to Nicholas II. Having remained unlaundered for more than eighty years, it still contained sweat stains from which a genetic profile could be drawn.

After comparing six hundred patterns in the three individual mtDNA profiles, the researchers determined that all were related. The mtDNA profile extracted from the clothing matched exactly the genetic fingerprint of his brother George Alexandrovich, as did the sample from Kulikovsky's tissue. They then compared these three profiles against that derived by Gill and Ivanov and found five discrepancies between the two sequences. In a science where a single hypervariable region meant identification could not be established without further corroborative tests, these five new anomalies raised serious questions regarding the 1993 profile.

"Analysis of the DNA shows that the remains could not be those of Nicholas II," Nagai declared. The professor's assertion was a direct challenge, not only to the various identifications, but more importantly to the recognized mtDNA sequence produced for Nicholas II in 1993.[44] Word of Nagai's results, presented at the Nineteenth International Conference of Forensic Genetics in Muenster, Germany, caused an immediate stir. Several other scientists followed this with their own tests, including a team of genetics experts led by Professor Bronte, president of the International Association of Forensic Physicians. Bronte's tests apparently confirmed Nagai's results, and he, too, openly suggested that the Ekaterinburg remains were not those of the Romanovs.[45] Such a line of attack, however, seemed futile. Not only was Hessian mtDNA present in four of the bodies, but also that of Dr. Botkin was successfully identified, albeit through exclusion. While questions remain over the exact genetic profile of Nicholas II, the grave itself provided the ultimate evidence. The odds of it being discovered in the correct historical location; bearing the correct mtDNA sequences; and bones answering to the correct forensic and anthropological assessment, yet not containing the Romanovs—would have been too staggering to calculate.

Recently, proposals have been made to rebury Dowager Empress Marie Feodorovna, laid to rest after her death in 1928 in Roskilde Cathedral in Denmark, alongside her husband, Alexander III, in the Cathedral of the Fortress of St. Peter and St. Paul. Such a transfer would present, as critic Professor Lev Zhivotovsky pointed out, an opportunity to confirm the validity of the DNA tests in the Romanov case. Zhivotovsky also has proposed utilizing the comparatively new method of Y-chromosome haplotype analysis, allowing DNA profiles from direct male descendants to be tested if the vault containing Alexander III is opened. This newest DNA method was most recently utilized in testing conducted on descendants of Sally Hemmings, to learn if they shared a sequence with Thomas Jefferson. No one has yet approached any member of the Romanov family about such tests. "I must say," declares Tikhon Kulikovsky's grandnephew Paul Kulikovsky, "that I doubt very much if the Russians would be given permission to do this."[46]

In their 1993 statement, the Forensic Science Services Laboratory referred to their work on the Romanov remains as "pioneering." In this case, it would be difficult to find a more accurate description of tests conducted at the edge of known science, portions of which have become obsolete in ten years. Such "pioneering" work, while important, rarely forms the final verdict, and the initial round of tests seems destined to become only the first step in a complete DNA investigation of the remains.

The DNA tests did little to assuage the growing doubts over the Romanov case, not only about the identification of the remains unearthed in Koptyaki Forest but also about the veracity of those involved in the discovery and testing. In the United States, three members of the Russian Nobility Association formed the Russian Expert Commission Abroad. Headed by Peter Koltypin-Wollovskoy and including Prince Alexei Scherbatow, the group repeatedly dispatched letters to Boris Yeltsin, released press statements, and decried the lack of access by independent experts to the remains and the testing processes under way. These men, all members of the Russian Orthodox Church Outside Russia, rejected the exhumed remains, dismissing them as a KGB hoax; they insisted that the only genuine remains were those collected by Sokolov and taken from Russia when he fled the Bolsheviks. One of their letters asserted that no skull could possibly be identified as that of Nicholas II, since "it is a known fact that the head of the last Emperor was taken to Moscow."[47]

Another unlikely scenario emanated from Vadim Viner, curator of the Komsomol Museum in Ekaterinburg, and chairman of the International Independent Commission to Investigate the Murder of the Romanov Family. Viner claimed to have six pages from the 1918 diary of Stephan Vaganov that related a far different version of events. According to Viner, after the murders, Vaganov—at the point of a gun, no less— forced Yurovsky to hand over the Romanov corpses by showing him an order from Sverdlov. Yurovsky was given a second truck, filled with the corpses of a family named Ardashev, which, conveniently for this story, possessed not only a husband and wife, but also a young son, four young daughters, three male servants, and a maid. These were the corpses, Viner said, that Yurovsky labored over to bury. The Romanovs, according to this version, were secretly buried elsewhere, but not before their bodies apparently were cut up and portions taken to the eventual Koptyaki grave, to confuse anyone who might discover it.[48]

Viner's story rapidly became a mere footnote to the Romanov drama, its convolutions unsupported by any evidence. But it reflected a growing trend that, in the aftermath of Ryabov's 1989 announcement, brought forth a host of varied rescue scenarios, elaborate hoaxes, and stories of numerous survivors. This reached its zenith in the claims of one author, Anatoly Gryannik, who produced a book declaring that the entire imperial family had been rescued from the Ipatiev House and quietly lived in the southern fringes of the Soviet Union. Unhappily for his theory, and highlighting the distinct lack of knowledge of the Romanovs among most Russians in these years, he also claimed that they had been joined by such family members as Grand Duchess Elizabeth Feodorovna, the empress's sister whose body had been recovered from a mine shaft in Alapayevsk, and even Nicholas II's sister Grand Duchess Olga Alexandrovna, who lived quite openly in Canada until her death in 1960.

On September 20, 1995, an official from the office of the Russian general prosecutor announced that the Government commission had completed its work and that the exhumed remains had all been satisfactorily identified. The commission released selected portions of their report, outlining the tests conducted and asserting that they had the remains of Nicholas, Alexandra, Olga, Tatiana, Anastasia, Botkin, Demidova, Kharitonov, and Trupp. Lingering doubts about the veracity of the remains and their contentious identification were abruptly dismissed without explanation.[49]

Intended to be the final Russian word on identification of the remains, the 1993 report failed to address contradictions and questions raised not only by the American experts but also by Russian scientists who had worked extensively with the bones. As such, it proved less than conclusive, and the unwelcome specter of Anastasia continued to hover over the case, leaving the Russians exasperated, increasingly defensive, and insistent on the veracity of their own results. With a sense of frustrated desperation, a number of those involved began to make claims that had never previously formed part of their contentious identification of Anastasia, in an attempt to prove that she had died. In 1997, Soloviev himself gave an interview to *Rossiiskaya gazeta* that focused almost solely on the question of Anastasia. He declared that Russian experts identified skull 6 as that of Anastasia because it bore no gap between the front teeth, something he claimed could be readily observed in photographs of Grand Duchess Marie Nikolaievna, an assertion later echoed by forensic expert Sergei Nikitin.[50]

This convoluted explanation rested not on positive identification of skeleton 6 as Anastasia but rather on the view that skeleton 5 could not possibly be Grand Duchess Marie, a view disputed not only by the Americans but also by many of the Russian experts involved. By assigning one questionable identity to skeleton 5, it propelled an equally doubtful claim to a second, ignoring the anthropological objections to both. The faces of both skulls had been subjected to repeated blows that shattered their facial bones, destroying their structure and breaking teeth. Skull 5 bore only a fragment of the upper jaw, with three intact teeth, and one broken tooth, while that of skeleton 6 had missing teeth in both the upper and lower jaws, the repeated blows to the face having loosened and bent the remaining teeth. These factors made any identification based on presumed—and unproved—gaps highly questionable.

Nor did Nikitin's confirmation add to the story's veracity; he also would claim to know where the two missing remains were, only to be denounced by Avdonin himself as a liar.[51]

In the winter of 1998, the situation became even more complicated when a second forensic team from the United States challenged the Russian identifications. William Maples, suffering from a brain tumor, had retired as director of the C. A. Pound Human Identification Laboratory shortly before his death in February 1998. His colleague Professor Anthony Falsetti not only replaced Maples as director but also inherited the controversial Romanov case. Falsetti had become friendly with Peter Sarandinaki, an American with close ties to the fate of the imperial family. Sarandinaki's great-grandfather General Sergei Rozanov as well as his grandfather Kirill Naryshkin had both been friends of Nicholas Sokolov, and recommended him to Admiral Kolchak to lead the White Army investigation. Sarandinaki considered it a matter of personal honor to locate the two missing bodies, forming an organization called SEARCH (Scientific Expedition to Account for the Romanov Children), and contacting Alexander Avdonin to inquire about future searches of Koptyaki Forest. When Sarandinaki suggested that a new team of experts in forensic anthropology be brought to Ekaterinburg, specialists in locating human remains, Avdonin readily agreed.[52]

Falsetti, who knew details of the case, joined a team from Necro-Search International, an organization that assists law enforcement officials in locating human remains, and widely recognized as the world's leading group of forensic investigators. In the end, Sarandinaki could fund only two individuals: Diane France, director of the Human Identification Laboratory at Colorado State University, and geologist Jim Reed. Just before the trip, France—one of the world's most respected forensic anthropologists—had been appointed chair of the Physical Anthropology Section of the American Academy of Forensic Sciences. The trip was only a preliminary investigation, in anticipation of a return that summer, when a search could be conducted in Koptyaki Forest.[53]

In Ekaterinburg, the team met Avdonin and his wife, Galina, who acted as an interpreter during their visit. On their first day, they were shown the remains, still enclosed under their Plexiglas lids in a locked and guarded room at the Ekaterinburg morgue. Avdonin watched as France and Falsetti moved from skeleton to skeleton; at table 6, which held the bones identified by the Russians as Anastasia, France paused, and began a careful examination of the skull, clavicles, and vertebrae. She thought that the bones and teeth showed marked signs of maturity, inconsistent with a girl of seventeen years of age. The more she looked, the more convinced she became. Pulling Falsetti aside, she whispered,

"I'm not convinced that this is Anastasia." Falsetti nodded, but the two agreed to say nothing of their doubts.[54]

The following day, however, the Americans were forced to take a stand. Avdonin presented them with a contract that specified that, on returning in the summer, they would be looking for "the remains of Alexei and Marie." France and Falsetti objected to this, saying that they could not sign the document given the serious doubts about the Russian identification of skeleton 6 as Anastasia.[55]

On hearing this, Avdonin turned "beet red," screaming, "Marie and Alexei are missing, not Anastasia!" When France asked how he could be so certain, Avdonin replied, "Photographic superimposition!" This convinced France that she and Falsetti—like Maples, Baden, and Levine before them—were correct in doubting that Anastasia had been found. In her work, France utilized photographic superimposition as an aid, but never as the only means for achieving a positive identification, as the Russians had done. Under the best of circumstances, it was only a useful tool; with completely reconstructed faces—and faces still missing entire sections, as were the Romanov skulls—it was an impossibility.[56]

The two Americans suggested that Avdonin make the contract less specific, but the idea that the Russians were being challenged sent him into a frenzy. "Who are you," he yelled, "to question all these other scientists?" Eighty Russian experts, he declared, all agreed that Anastasia was present; as he continued, turning "shades of red and purple" as his fury increased, this soon became "a hundred Russian experts," then "two hundred worldwide scientists." His wife stumbled through this in English, first apologizing for Avdonin's behavior, then herself screaming, "See what you're doing to my poor husband!"[57]

This scene went on for nearly four hours, Avdonin hysterical in his insistence that Anastasia was skeleton 6.[58] Eventually Sarandinaki, who had arranged the entire visit, sided with Falsetti and France. "They were simply trying to get at the truth," he later explained, "but Avdonin couldn't deal with the idea that the Russian scientists might have been wrong. It was a case of protesting just a little too much. So we ended up going home."[59] Not surprisingly, neither Falsetti, France, nor anyone from NecroSearch, was ever asked to return to assist in the quest for the missing remains.[60]

Despite such pointed criticisms, the Russians stuck firmly to their identification of Anastasia. It became their central focus, subsuming all other questions, their determination to prove her death in 1918 rising vehemently in the face of each challenge. Aware of the case of Anna Anderson and the interest in the fate of Anastasia in the West, they had attempted to end such conjectures. Beginning with Ryabov's error-laden interviews in 1989, Russian officials and forensic experts went out of their way to speak of her death, efforts that culminated in Abramov's hasty identification using photographic superimposition. Such a move, coming as it did less than a month before the first Ekaterinburg conference, seemed to confirm this preoccupation. Previously both Abramov and Plaskin had announced that the remains attributed to the three grand duchesses could not be identified; with the specter of Anastasia's possible survival alive in the Western press, efforts suddenly focused on ending the unwelcome speculation, and photographic superimposition became Abramov's coup de grâce in ending it. None of the other as yet unidentified young female remains were singled out for such scrutiny, nor accorded any intensive attempts at identification; nor was it simply a question of pursuing an obvious resemblance with skeleton 6, whose entire face had been missing. Once confronted with the forensic and anthropological data indicating Anastasia had not been found, the Russians simply stopped responding, asserting their increasingly obstinate position again and again while ignoring the contrary evidence raised by others.

This curious and dogmatic insistence seemed to come from three distinct motives. The first, as with the White investigators before, was a need to prove those involved in the murder guilty of the ruthless massacre of women and children. In the new post-Soviet Russia, anti-Bolshevik sentiment reached fevered levels, and the murder of the Romanovs once again became a tool used by those seeking to paint the old regime in the worst possible light. Then, too, while some Russians actively engaged in and even promoted survival stories, they most often did so with native claimants, those who—unlike Anna Anderson—lived and died in Russia, had Russian families, Russian ties; Anderson had been embraced by the West, by émigrés, even by Hollywood motion pictures, creating a true twentieth-century phenomenon of which Russia formed no part. As each new Russian claimant appeared and generated media attention, they were, to some extent, embraced if only because of their nationality. Finally, the issue of Anastasia's identification became a matter of national pride. The country's media, as well as the Russian experts involved, were embarrassed by the state of their scientific abilities. The fact that DNA samples had to be sent to a foreign country for testing was a sore point, as was the continued involvement of American scientists who openly questioned the Russian identifications. Rather than admit that mistakes were made, or even address the outstanding questions posed by Western experts, the Russians clung to their inexplicable position.

Continuing doubts almost certainly led to the latest Russian salvo fired in this ongoing war of forensic and anthropological experts. In 2001, Abramov returned to the subject, in yet another attempt to prove to the world that he was correct and that Anastasia was dead. Titled "Anatomical Appraisal of the Skulls and Teeth Associated with the Family of Tsar Nikolai Romanov," the study, coauthored by Dr. Lev Kolesnikov, professor of anatomy at Moscow State Medical Stomatological University, and his colleague Dr. Gurgen Pashinyan, insisted that "more objective methods were clearly necessary to more accurately identify the remains."[61] These identifications were made "by utilizing, in objective ways, the only antemortem documentation available, i.e., photographic portraits."[62] Thus the entire raison d'être of the new study was a justification for and defense of Abramov's photo superimposition technique, adding a new statistical analysis to prove "with a high likelihood of certainty," based on "very strong evidence," that "Anastasia was killed in 1918."[63]

The authors spent much time criticizing the work by Maples and the American team and by Dr. Zvyagin, claiming that they had based their identifications on "subjective judgments regarding their similarities to photographs."[64] This was inexplicable, particularly in the case of the Americans, who utilized no such comparisons save for two photographs of Nicholas II and Grand Duchess Olga Nikolaievna to study the shape of their foreheads. It was Abramov himself who introduced his own "subjective judgments" with the superimposition technique.

The American team in 1992—as well as France and Falsetti in 1998—failed to identify Anastasia among the remains based on five factors: the issue of height; lack of signs of immaturity in the vertebrae and bones; the age and development of the pelvic rim; age and development of the clavicles; and age and development of the dental roots. Yet the 2001 report noted only the first two, dismissing the question of height and insisting, contrary to the evidence, that the forensic data indicated a young woman not yet fully grown; the remaining three areas were simply ignored.[65]

While asserting that neither the Americans nor Zvyagin "used objective methods of comparison between postmortem remains and antemortem documentation to make their identifications," the study made evident that the "objective methods" referred to were, in fact, only one, photographic superimposition.[66] It attacked the American team and Zvyagin by claiming their identifications suffered "from the fact that the bones in the skeletons were not complete. Therefore, unavoidable errors may have taken place as the skeletons were assembled from a great number of dispersed and injured bones. Additionally, the methods used for determination of gender, age and height were not perfect."[67] This was an absurd statement, ignoring the fact that Abramov himself faced these same problems.

The study was interesting for what it left unsaid. There was no mention of the findings of Dr. Filipchuk or Dr. Nevolin, who agreed with the American position that none of the remains showed the necessary immaturity to represent Anastasia. The misidentified bones, which the Russians never resolved, were only briefly noted, then dismissed as insignificant, nor was there any mention of the erroneous identification of skeleton 1 as a male. Such exclusions of Russian mistakes while focusing criticism on the work of the American team suggested that the study itself was conceived in a rather different light than a simple appraisal of Abramov's superimposition methods.

The study utilized the same software program developed in 1992 to match skulls to specific photographs, using fifty-four points, marked on each skull and photograph, then compared for correlation. Significantly, however, it failed to include a list of what these points were; how many had been matched to each skull; and how many did not match using superimposition. More importantly, the authors admitted that "of fifty-four variables, some, naturally, had to be omitted from particular skulls" owing to extensive facial damage and missing bones, leaving the validity of the testing subject not to rigorous controls applied evenly but rather to variable selectivity.[68] The end results, which claimed Tatiana was skeleton 5 and Anastasia 6 based solely on photographic superimposition, were "essentially consistent" with the 1992 tests.[69]

The authors engaged in a bit of statistical wizardry in an effort to bolster their results. An estimate of the possibility of erroneous identification according to superimposition failed to include tables on how these data were reached; give statistical tables for each skull to show methodology; or demonstrate the reliability of superimposition itself on reconstructed skulls. The estimates given of the "probability of false identification" of the skeletons of "rarer than 2 times in 100 trillion cases" was not a figure reflecting the reliability of superimposition, but rather represented a combined statistical analysis of all relevant data, including the likelihood of finding nine skeletons of those particular ages, races, genders, and relationships, and bearing the damage observed, in Koptyaki Forest. In the end, the statistical analysis did little more than show that this was indeed the Romanov grave.[70]

A smaller portion of the article reviewed the dental evidence, focusing largely on the two "orphan" teeth. In 1992 Dr. Vyacheslav Popov suggested that they came from a male between the ages of fourteen and sixteen years, a view echoed by Abramov, who insisted that they represented someone "no more than sixteen at the most."[71] In 2001, Abramov completely reversed himself, and the two teeth were declared to be third molars, from one of the recovered skulls, as Dr. Lowell Levine had originally asserted.[72] Typically, though, these two teeth were used in an attempt to prove that they had belonged to Anastasia, and thus that she was dead and in the grave itself. While a comparison of the two teeth with those remaining in skull 6 revealed "a similarity in their relative proportions," the authors asserted, "it is probable that the two loose teeth are the third maxillary molars of Anastasia," based on the photographic superimposition that had labeled skeleton 6 as the youngest grand duchess.[73]

The report concluded by saying that Popov, Zvyagin, and Maples were in "broad agreement" with these new results, claiming, "We all agree on the identifications of the Tsar, his wife, his retainers and his daughters Olga and Tatiana."[74] This blatant misrepresentation ignored the fact that Maples, Popov, and Zvyagin had disagreed with the Russian identification of skeleton 5 as that of Tatiana. Thus there was no unanimity of opinion regarding the identification, as the authors suggested.

If Abramov's tests, completed years earlier, had produced such satisfactory results, one wonders why the new study was necessary. Based on his superimposition, the 1993 state commission had declared with finality that Anastasia was present among the remains, and skeleton 6 had been buried as such in 1998. Almost certainly the study was conceived and designed as yet another Russian attempt to justify their identification of Anastasia, a preoccupation highlighted by frequent references to her throughout the text. If there was any lingering doubt, the authors concluded their report with words that, in the context, carry an almost melancholy, embarrassing plea: "The identification of skull 6 and loose teeth as those of Anastasia," they asserted, "has the same strength as the other identifications, and should not be dismissed."[75]

Given the frequency with which such attempts have previously occurred to justify the identification of skeleton 6 as that of Anastasia, the 2001 study is unlikely to be the final Russian word on the subject. Despite determined efforts to convince the world, the Russians cannot escape the widespread doubts that continue to surround their controversial identifications. In the end, Abramov's photographic superimposition changed no one's mind. As Maples had presciently predicted after the 1992 conference, "We're still left with a mystery."[76]

21

The Secret of Koptyaki Forest

A lie is best concealed between two truths.

—RUSSIAN PROVERB

THE WORLD WILL NEVER know what has become of them."
Thus declared Peter Voikov, the Ural regional commissar of
supplies, on the disappearance of the Romanovs.[1] And,
indeed, for the first few years following their murder, the fate of the
Romanovs remained uncertain. The publication of Paul Bykov's book
in 1921 provided the first Soviet admission that they had indeed been
killed, despite the inability of Nicholas Sokolov to prove the case with
actual human remains. Bykov himself explained this conundrum by
asserting: "What remained of the bodies after burning was taken a considerable distance from the pits, and buried in a swamp, in an area
where the volunteers and investigators made no excavations. There the
bodies remained and by now have rotted away."[2]

For seventy-three years the story of the end of the imperial family
rested largely with the orthodox version presented by Sokolov. The discovery of the Koptyaki grave, coupled with publication of materials
related to the execution, ended this monopoly and helped answer many
of the outstanding questions in what were, in the end, unsolved murders. And yet, despite the 1991 exhumation, the string of forensic and
genetic tests conducted on the remains, and the continued Russian
insistence that the escape of Anastasia was nothing more than a Western
legend, one undeniable fact remains: two bodies are missing.

History found its answer in the accounts of the Ural Bolsheviks, who claimed—in a distinct echo of Sokolov's original theory—that two of the bodies had been burned. In all, six men left memoirs detailing this cremation: Yurovsky, who gave three versions, as did Ermakov; two statements said to derive from Peter Voikov; and the memoirs of Michael Kudrin, Isai Rodzinsky, and Gregory Sukhorukov. These eleven accounts seem definitive, yet close examination reveals serious discrepancies that ultimately undermine their assertions.

The decision to burn some of the remains has never been fully explained. Yurovsky explained it away as an attempt to divert attention from a Romanov mass grave, where White investigators would have expected to find all eleven corpses. Given the time frame against which the Bolsheviks were working, however, this seems odd. By the early morning of July 19, the fall of Ekaterinburg was only days away, and none of those gathered in Koptyaki Forest knew how long the Red Army would hold out against the advancing White and Czech forces. Already, counterrevolutionary agents had infiltrated Ekaterinburg, and the boom of artillery could be heard as it drew nearer and nearer. If the Bolsheviks wished to confuse an exhumation, certainly the quickest and least traumatic option would simply have been to bury the bodies separately, or in groups of twos or threes; they had, after all, hundreds of acres of forest, conveniently cordoned off, at their disposal. Yurovsky, in fact, relates that such an idea was strongly considered, but abandoned. Instead, according to his memoirs, he opted for the time-consuming, dangerous, and uncertain course of destroying selected bodies by fire. Had they wished to destroy the bodies, they could easily have utilized the smelter at the Verkh-Isetsk factory. After all, they had, in the end, to bury the charred remains.

Yurovsky's 1920 note was quite clear about the cremation. It took place "around four-thirty" on the morning of July 19, after the truck "got permanently stuck" in Pig's Meadow. While the common grave was dug, the two corpses were burned; as both endeavors were concurrently supervised by Yurovsky himself, logic dictates that they took place close to one another. While they had wanted to burn Alexei and Alexandra, Yurovsky recalled, the men instead burned Alexei and Demidova. When the cremation had ended, the remains were buried beneath the fire, and covered with earth, "to cover completely any trace of digging."[3] In his 1922 memoirs, he repeated many of these claims: the cremation took place in Pig's Meadow; he supervised both the fire and the digging of the mass grave; once it ended, they cleared the coals, dug a grave, and "threw the bones in. We built another fire over this grave to hide all traces. Then we kicked around the ashes to further blur the traces. The traces were covered."[4] In 1934, speaking at a meeting of Ural Bolsheviks, Yurovsky recalled: "While the grave was being readied we burned two corpses: Alexei and, apparently, Demidova, instead of Alexandra Feodorovna, as we had always intended. We dug a pit by the spot where they were burned, piled in the bones, evened it over, lit another big fire, and covered all traces with ashes."[5]

Like Yurovsky, Peter Ermakov also left three versions of these events, in which he flamboyantly claimed, as he wrote in 1932, not that two of the corpses had been burned, but that "all of the bodies" were cremated "to ash"; this, he added for good measure, had been done "personally, by me."[6] He echoed this assertion in an interview the following year, speaking of "a funeral pyre of cut logs" onto which he personally "lifted the corpses" after dousing them with "five tins of gasoline" and "two buckets of sulfuric acid." In time, he claimed, all eleven bodies were "reduced to powder," the ashes "pitched into the air" with a shovel, where the wind "caught them like dust and carried them out across the woods."[7] Fourteen years later, Ermakov repeated these claims, writing that all of the corpses, having been doused with gasoline and sulfuric acid, were "burned to ash" on the night of July 17, 1918.[8]

While Ermakov was certainly a participant in the actual shooting and in the first events in Koptyaki Forest immediately following the murders, his tales reveal a man determined, through outright fabrication, to claim for himself the lead role in what was clearly a historical event. He made no attempt to tailor his stories to those of Yurovsky, but instead seemed bent on repeating what the White Army investigators had erroneously asserted: that no bodies had been found because they had all been burned to ash. With the discovery of the grave in Koptyaki Forest, such claims were easily put to rest.

Peter Voikov left no written statement, and both accounts attributed to him were secondhand, recorded, it is said, in the aftermath of a drunken dinner party in Warsaw during the former Ural regional commissar of supplies' tenure as Soviet ambassador to Poland. The first appeared in a book by an enigmatic Russian émigré, Gregory Bessedowsky, the second apparently discovered many years later when the Soviet Army occupied Warsaw during World War II. Even allowing that the stories—which coincide to a remarkable degree—reflected Voikov's account that night, they did little more than repeat what was commonly believed: that all of the corpses had been burned to ash.[9] Presumably he had no wish, even in his inebriated state, to disclose the truth behind the ultimate disposition of the remains.

In 1963, Michael Kudrin wrote in his memoirs that "the bodies of Nicholas II, Alexei, the Empress, and Dr. Botkin" were doused with gasoline and set on fire at the Four Brothers mine. "The corpses were frozen," he declared, "and they smoked, hissed, and smelled horribly, but they would not burn." Having failed to cremate them, the Bolsheviks "loaded all eleven corpses onto the truck (four of them partially charred)," and drove off, only to become stuck in Pig's Meadow, where they were all buried in a single grave.[10]

This account contains numerous mistakes. Kudrin asserted that the attempted cremation took place at the Four Brothers mine, in contradiction to Yurovsky. Kudrin also claimed that four of the corpses were burned, including those of Nicholas II, the empress, and Dr. Botkin, again in opposition to both Yurovsky and to the forensic evidence of the exhumed remains. Finally, according to Kudrin, all eleven bodies, including the four the Bolsheviks had attempted to destroy, were buried together in the mass grave, an assertion contradicted by Yurovsky and by the forensic evidence.

Kudrin admitted that he was not present during these events, saying that he learned of them from both Yurovsky and Isai Rodzinsky. Clearly, though, Kudrin could not have heard such details from Yurovsky, whose own accounts dispute that of Kudrin. If Kudrin's source was indeed Isai Rodzinsky, it is even more difficult to reconcile Kudrin's account, for Rodzinsky spoke of the alleged cremation in detail. It took place, he said, after the truck broke down in Pig's Meadow, as "night was approaching." He recalled: "I remember we burned Nicholas II. Botkin, too. And Alexei." In total, he declared, "four, five, or perhaps six people" were cremated, including "a few of the women." This, he said, "took a long time, so much so in fact that I had time to go into Ekaterinburg and make a report."[11]

Rodzinsky's account of the attempted cremation—like that of Kudrin—is so starkly at odds with Yurovsky's statements and with the exhumed remains themselves that it cannot be considered as evidence. He misplaced the time of day when the truck broke down in Pig's Meadow; he placed the cremation after the other remains had been buried; he named definitely both Nicholas II and Dr. Botkin as having been burned, in complete contradiction to both Yurovsky and to the forensic evidence; he alleged that four to six bodies were burned, again in direct opposition to Yurovsky and the exhumed remains; he claimed that "a few of the women were burned," again inconsistent with the forensic evidence; and he claimed, in direct opposition to the nine sets of remains recovered from the Koptyaki grave, that these charred bodies—between four and six in number—were buried separately from the rest of the victims.

In fact, according to Yurovsky, Rodzinsky was not even present when the cremation was attempted. Yurovsky recalled, "The boys from the Regional Cheka who had lost track of us—Comrades Isai Rodzinsky, Gorin, and someone else—arrived when we had already finished up everything."[12] This, with the evidence drawn from the Koptyaki grave and forensic examination of the remains, invalidate the accounts of both Rodzinsky and Kudrin.

In 1928, Gregory Sukhorukov left an account of the disposal of the bodies that largely agreed with those of Yurovsky. "We decided," he wrote, "to burn two bodies. For our 'sacrificial altar' we took the heir. The second body was that of Anastasia, the youngest daughter. After the two were burned, we took what remained, dug a pit in the center, shoveled in the unburned remains, built a fire atop the spot, and completed the work."[13]

While this agreed in general with Yurovsky, there is confusion over who was burned. While Yurovsky specified Alexei and Demidova, Sukhorukov spoke definitely of the tsesarevich and Anastasia. What, we are forced to ask, did Sukhorukov see that made him certain of his own identification, when apparently he had never personally laid eyes on the imperial family, while Yurovsky, who had been in constant contact with them since July 4, was unable to be as precise? Is it likely that Yurovsky was mistaken, and Sukhorukov correct?

This confusion over the identities of the two allegedly burned corpses has been explained away by referring to the appearance of the bodies themselves. The late Dr. William Maples speculated:

> Blood would have soaked the disheveled hair of the victims, which would have then dried into a dark hard mass. The bodies had decomposed for three days in daytime temperatures averaging roughly 70 degrees Fahrenheit. Bloating would be pronounced, and bloating makes it very difficult to guess the original weight or girth of a set of remains. . . . The nude and bloated torsos of the females would have taken on a remarkable, balloonish anonymity. Next, flies must be considered. Flies lay their eggs during the first daylight hours in which they can reach a dead body. Those eggs begin to hatch a couple of days later in a sudden burst of activity. There were plenty of flies in that area—I observed them myself, during my visit. These bodies had many wounds. Their faces had been smashed to bloody pulps. They were left in the open near the shaft of the Four Brothers Mine all day long after the executions, then thrown into a mine shaft and hand grenades were flung down on them, further mangling the remains. Flies would have had ample opportunity to lay eggs on the eyes, nostrils and other apertures, along with the open wounds. These eggs and the resulting maggots, deposited in a thick, foamy froth over the mutilated faces, would have further masked the bodies' identities. . . . The bloating, the hard,

blood-soaked hair of the women, the absence of clothing and the encrustation of fly eggs and maggots on their faces, the enveloping darkness—all these factors would have rendered the remains very hard to identify. It would be quite possible to mistake one female for another.[14]

Author Robert Massie cited Maples' conjecture as a convenient resolution to the confusion over which corpses were allegedly burned. This explanation, however, ignores the facts of the case. The corpses were not left "in the open" at the Four Brothers "all day long," but thrown into the cool shaft within five hours of being shot. From the first light of dawn on July 17 until the mass grave was dug, forty-eight hours, not "three days," passed. The faces of the victims had not "been smashed to bloody pulps"; much of the extensive facial and cranial damage to the corpses was inflicted on the morning of July 19, as they were buried. Nor did this account fully analyze the window of opportunity during which changes to the bodies could have occurred, particularly in reference to insect activity. In fact, as amply demonstrated in the work of Professor Neal Haskell, the only full-time forensic entomologist in the world, a precise system regulates insect infestation and damage. This varies according to temperature as well as location. Heat and daylight speed the process, while night and cold prevent it. In the known weather conditions in Ekaterinburg between July 17 and 19, 1918, and the hours of sunrise and sunset for those two days, we find then a window of approximately thirty-two hours, spread over two days, during which insect infestation could have occurred. A forensic entomologist, however, calculates the time necessary for development of blowflies and larvae in accumulated degree-hours measured from the time a fly lays its eggs to the time they hatch and consume the rotting flesh of the victim. The thirty-two hours of daylight between the mornings of July 17 and 19, the known weather conditions, and times of sunrise and sunset, according to Professor Haskell, puts visible and disruptive insect development on the corpses—if any—at the "lowest threshold. There would have been some infestation in the first few hours on the morning of July 17, but once the corpses were in the pit, and covered over with dirt and brush, it would have impeded activity. It's not a long period of time." Had flies laid eggs, they would likely have hatched only after sunrise on the morning of July 19—after the corpses were allegedly burned and buried. Although perhaps minor infestation took place, as Professor Haskell explains, "it wouldn't have been very extensive, and certainly wouldn't have resulted in damage that made the features unrecognizable."[15]

It was possible, given the conditions of the corpses some thirty hours after they had been shot, and in the dim light of Koptyaki Forest, for Yurovsky to have mistaken one middle-aged woman, Demidova, for another, Alexandra, in a heap of bodies, bloated and still covered with dried blood. Far more damaging to Yurovsky's claim was his assertion that it was the body of a middle-aged female that was burned. The two missing corpses were Alexei and Anastasia, not Alexei and Demidova or Alexandra. Even given the unfavorable conditions under which the alleged cremations took place, and Yurovsky's nervous exhaustion, it is difficult to understand how he could possibly have believed the corpse of seventeen-year-old Anastasia to have been that of a middle-aged woman.

Unfortunately for Sukhorukov, if the Russian experts were correct in their identification of skeleton 6, he, too, got his facts wrong in naming Anastasia as having been cremated. But he made other claims, unsupported by the evidence, that undermine his credibility and ultimately cast doubt on his veracity as a witness. He named Ural regional Cheka head Feodor Lukoyanov as the man who, on the evening of July 17, assembled his group and instructed them on their mission. Yet Lukoyanov had not been in Ekaterinburg since late June; instead, he was in Perm, hundreds of miles to the northwest, a fact confirmed by a number of cables dispatched to him there by Beloborodov throughout these weeks; the last was sent on the morning of July 19, within hours of the alleged cremations.[16] Sukhorukov remembered that both Yurovsky and his friend Pavlushin were present when the group rode out to the Four Brothers. Yet Yurovsky was still in Ekaterinburg, as was Pavlushin—the latter in bed with a sprained ankle. Here he remained, as Yurovsky recalled, absent throughout the events that followed. Nor, according to Yurovsky, did he meet any group of men, but rather arrived at the mine to discover them at work early on the morning of July 18.[17] Finally, according to Sukhorukov, when the bodies were exhumed from the mine, all were naked except for Alexei, who "had on a sailor shirt but no trousers."[18] This was in direct contradiction to the other accounts, which stated explicitly that all of the corpses were completely stripped, and their clothing searched and then all burned.[19]

In fact, as Yurovsky wrote in 1922, when he arrived at the Four Brothers mine on the morning of July 18 to supervise the exhumation of the corpses, he found a number of soldiers he did not know, friends of Ermakov, who had begun to retrieve the bodies. "I sent these men to Koptyaki village," he wrote, "to instruct the people there not to leave because a search was under way, and it was possible that they might be caught in an exchange of gunfire. We then began our work when the riders left us."[20] Although Sukhorukov was undoubtedly at the Four Brothers mine on the morning of July 18, and assisted in the initial work, he was almost certainly dismissed, as one of Ermakov's friends, on

Yurovsky's arrival, only to return later that night, after the exhumation was completed.

In recounting an event, some variance is to be expected, especially in statements given at a distance of two to forty-six years after the particular occurrence. Yet here, with the alleged cremations, a number of erroneous statements, from the versions left by Ermakov and Voikov to those of Rodzinsky and Kudrin, muddy the historical waters, contradicting not only each other but also the forensic evidence of the exhumed remains themselves. Such discrepancies are not easily resolved nor lightly excused away; this was, after all, no ordinary event, but the disposal of the remains of Russia's last emperor and his family, as well as four loyal retainers. It is difficult to imagine that it was not burned into the minds of those involved, yet their accounts leave more questions than answers. This is inexplicable given the importance of the issue, where the alleged cremations form the only proffered explanation as to why two bodies would be missing from the grave. In the end, only Yurovsky and, perhaps, Sukhorukov witnessed what took place in Pig's Meadow on the morning of July 19.

Yet even Yurovsky himself left a dramatically different account of that momentous morning, one that completely contradicts not only Sukhorukov but also his own statements. In 1922 he wrote: "I ordered that we begin the burning with Alexei. We laid his body down, and soaked it with gasoline, and quickly set it on fire, just to see if it would work, since no one knew how to go about this. At the same time, we were digging a grave, about three arshins [seven feet] square. It was already morning. It was not possible for us to burn any more of the bodies, for the farmers and workers were beginning to be about, and therefore, we had to bury the remaining bodies in the grave. After they had been dumped into the pit, we covered them with acid, then dirt, and finally laid railroad ties over them. We then drove over it to help flatten it out. On the place where we had tried to burn the body, we dug another grave, and threw the bones in. We built another fire over this grave to hide all traces. Then we kicked around the ashes to further blur the traces. The traces were covered."[21] This was not a simple mistake by Yurovsky: his original manuscript is quite clear in its wording and intent. Nor was he imprecise as to the other corpses: "It was not possible for us to burn any more of the bodies," and all but that of the tsesarevich were dumped into the mass grave.

Yurovsky's 1920 note claimed that Alexei and Demidova were burned; in 1934 he altered this to "probably Demidova." But in 1922 he wrote flatly that only one body—that of Tsesarevich Alexei—had been subjected to attempted cremation, and that the process was abandoned owing to lack of time. If true, the mass grave should have contained ten

bodies, not nine; even given the significant lack of human remains discovered, nothing excuses the lack of a tenth skull, or its teeth, which
should have been within the burial pit.

Both Yurovsky and Sukhorukov state that the cremation was
attempted only after the truck carrying the bodies became irretrievably
stuck in Pig's Meadow. This, Yurovsky wrote in 1920, was "around
four-thirty" on the morning of July 19.[22] In 1922 he placed it "after
four," and completed "around six."[23] Twelve years later he declared
that both the cremation and burial were over between "five or six in the
morning."[24] After this, Yurovsky ordered the barriers along Koptyaki
Road pulled down; this took place at 6:00 A.M. on July 19.[25] These two
events—the breakdown of the Fiat in Pig's Meadow, and the opening of
Koptyaki Road—set the timetable during which the two bodies could
have been burned: no more than ninety minutes.

Within that time frame, it would have been scientifically impossible
for the Bolsheviks to have destroyed any substantial portion of one
body, let alone two. We find a contemporary parallel in the fate of
Adolf Hitler and Eva Braun. On the afternoon of April 25, 1945, as the
Soviets surrounded Berlin and advanced toward the shattered ruins of
Albert Speer's Reichschancellery, the leader of the Third Reich and his
small entourage huddled in the Führerbunker, sunk deep within the
chancellery garden. With the sound of Soviet artillery booming
through the thirty-foot ceilings of reinforced concrete, Hitler asked
Heinze Ligne, his valet and personal bodyguard, to his study.[26] He
declared that he would commit suicide by shooting himself, and that
afterward, Ligne himself must take responsibility for the complete
destruction of his body by fire. "No one," he said, "must see and recognize me after death."[27]

Otto Guensche, Hitler's SS adjutant, ordered some 200 liters of
gasoline to accomplish the grisly task; with Berlin in chaos, only 180
liters could be found.[28] After the suicides of the Führer and his new
wife, Eva Braun, their corpses, wrapped in dark brown army blankets,
were carried up four steep flights of steps and out into the chancellery
garden. Placed in a bomb crater, they were doused with gasoline, then
set ablaze.[29] According to one witness, the "flesh boiled away, but the
bones remained eerily visible through the flames. For more than two
and a half hours, the flames kept burning, and then they died down."[30]
This attempted cremation continued for some three hours.[31] While the
bodies were repeatedly drenched with gasoline, the fire soon died out of
its own volition.[32] Finally, the two corpses—charred, horribly disfigured, but still clearly articulated and recognizable as human beings—
were pulled from the crater and buried in a shallow grave in the
chancellery garden.[33]

When the Soviet Army took the Reichschancellery, they instituted a search of the garden and, with the assistance of Ligne, who had fallen into their hands, located the two burned corpses. They also discovered the charred remains of Minister of Propaganda Josef Goebbels and his wife, Magda, as well as the uncremated remains of their six children, who had been poisoned. The four charred corpses were taken by the Soviets to a secret facility, where thorough forensic examinations were made on May 8, 1945. These examinations are particularly instructive in assessing how little damage such cremations could inflict. While the epidermal layer and some fat had been consumed by the fires, the remains of Hitler and Eva Braun had not been reduced to ash. Musculature remained on the skeletons, along with entire sections of tissue, which the fires had simply seared and sealed, as well as the skeletal structure, skulls, and teeth. Examination of internal organs also was conducted, revealing just how substantial the remains had been. While Hitler's left foot was missing, and his skull shattered, the rest of his body, though disfigured, remained intact. A slightly lesser degree of damage was observed during the autopsy on Eva Braun. The bodies of Josef and Magda Goebbels had not even completely lost their epidermal layer.[34] These remains were photographed, then buried in Magdeburg. In 1970 they were secretly exhumed by Soviet officials, once again examined, then subjected to a second cremation. Even so, substantial bones remained, and these had to be ground into ash before being dumped into a tributary of the Elbe River.[35]

What happened in the Reichschancellery garden is startlingly similar to the scene described in Koptyaki Forest. In both cases, large quantities of gasoline were used to produce an intense fire. In the case of the bodies of Hitler and Eva Braun, some 47.6 gallons of gasoline were brought to the Reichschancellery; in Koptyaki Forest, Sokolov estimated that Yurovsky had roughly 160 gallons of gasoline.[36] The quantity of gasoline, however, matters little. Continual dousing of the remains, as evidenced in the attempted cremations of Hitler and Braun, did nothing to speed the destruction process. At the end of three hours, the remains were largely intact, with only the outer layers of skin and musculature destroyed or charred. In Koptyaki Forest, with no more than ninety minutes at their disposal, would the Bolsheviks have been able to achieve results that evaded the men of Hitler's SS some twenty-seven years later?

When a body is subjected to fire, whether doused with gasoline or some other accelerate, the process is the same. First, the epidermal layer chars, along with the subcutaneous tissues and fat. In effect, this sears the body, creating a kind of protective shell that prevents further destruction beyond the upper layers of musculature and tissue, and external features. Thus the skeletal structure is largely preserved, as is the skull; within the body, the internal organs may be seared or boiled, but they, too, remain largely intact.[37] In an open-air cremation, the efficiency of such a fire is further reduced, with the lack of confined, concentrated heat.

In modern cremations, a body is subjected to a controlled environment in which the temperature is raised to roughly 1,700 degrees Fahrenheit.[38] A cremation, even under these favorable conditions, takes several hours, and leaves a substantial amount of bone and human remains. These are systematically collected and run through a machine, which pulverizes them.[39] Thus, even in the most modern situation, under highly controlled, scientific conditions, it is impossible to completely destroy a human body in the time available to the Bolsheviks. Not only would there have been remains, but very substantial remains, largely intact, articulated skeletons with nearly all of their musculature, and only the outer epidermal layer charred or burned. They would have been rather gruesome, but still clearly recognizable as human bodies.

Russian experts involved in the identification of the exhumed remains were themselves skeptical that the two missing bodies could have been burned as alleged. In 1992, Plaskin declared: "It's very, very doubtful that these two bodies could have been burned to ash in the condition of the open air, on bonfires. There would have been large remains."[40] Abramov agreed, saying: "If they tried to burn the bodies, they would not have been able to burn them completely, even if they poured gasoline on them."[41] By 1998, however, after seven years of failed searches for the two sets of missing remains, Abramov changed his position, asserting in 2001 that the bodies "were burned to ashes."[42] Vladimir Soloviev, in overall charge of the Romanov case, was himself forced to recant the previous official Russian position, saying simply that the missing bodies had been "burned to ash."[43]

Such assertions conveniently explain the two missing skeletons at the expense of historical and scientific fact. In addition to Avdonin, Alekseev, and a handful of others, American Peter Sarandinaki has led several expeditions to Koptyaki Forest, subjecting the area of the Four Brothers mine and that of Pig's Meadow to lengthy searches, all without positive result. In the intervening years, various reports have surfaced from Russia, all claiming to have discovered the missing remains. On January 30, 1998, Edvard Rossel, former governor of Sverdlovsk Province, declared that Avdonin had discovered the burial site, but would only reveal it when the Romanovs were buried in Ekaterinburg. Avdonin added: "It's outside Ekaterinburg, and we'll investigate over the summer of 1998."[44] Just two months later, Avdonin repeated both his claim and his refusal to reveal the precise location.[45] After an extensive search in September 1998, however, Sarandinaki announced that no human remains had been found, and Avdonin was forced to recant. In combing through Koptyaki Forest, the group had discovered several topaz beads, an old Russian Nagant revolver bullet, and animal bones.[46]

Less than a month later, the story that the missing remains had been found resurfaced. Sergei Nikitin, a member of Avdonin's organization and the same man who earlier that year had declared that the Russian experts had "without question" identified Anastasia among the exhumed remains, told the newspaper *Moskovsky Komsomolets* that the two men had "incontrovertible proof that on this very spot the executioners burned the bodies of Grand Duchess Marie and Tsesarevich Alexei." Within a week, however, Avdonin himself denounced Nikitin as a liar, saying his colleague had fabricated the entire episode.[47]

In May 2000, officials in Ekaterinburg announced that they had found two sets of remains while excavating the site of the Ipatiev House, and the Russian press quickly picked up the story, speculating, despite the location, that these were the missing Romanov bodies. A few days later, however, it was revealed that the remains had been discovered in rotted caskets and came from the old eighteenth-century cemetery that had once occupied the site.[48] Almost exactly a year later, and at the same location, two skulls and a femur were discovered, again raising unlikely speculation that these belonged to the missing Romanov children. Within days, this report, too, was dismissed by officials.[49]

Despite the annual excavations, no bodies, no human remains, have been found in Koptyaki Forest. Yurovsky's accounts make clear that these alleged cremations took place in Pig's Meadow, near the mass grave, to allow him to supervise both operations. Yet the entire length of the clearing and its surrounding forests have failed to yield the slightest trace of human remains. Almost certainly, the answer to this conundrum is what is most obvious: the remains of Alexei and Anastasia —despite the continued efforts of the Russians to insist on her presence in the Koptyaki grave—cannot be found because they were never there, never burned. The clumsy, contentious, and scientifically impossible accounts woven by the Bolsheviks attempted to conceal what they could not explain, a masquerade shrouded in deception that evolved to encompass contradictory claims offering not answers but an illusion of shared truth. It is the only conclusion supported by the evidence, leading us inexorably back to the early-morning hours of July 17, 1918, and to the basement of the Ipatiev House, where, in the midst of that terrible carnage and the uncertain hours that followed, circumstance collided with the destinies of the two youngest victims.

Some experts have argued that it was impossible for anyone to have survived the executions. There were too many men present, they declare, too many people confined in too small a room, too many shots fired, and too many bayonets thrust at defenseless victims, for anyone to have lived. "From all my years of experience," the late Dr. William Maples declared, "and from the crime scene itself, I'm certain that Alexei and Anastasia died that night."[50] Such sentiments form the prevailing consensus. How, skeptics ask, could anyone have survived the slaughter in the basement of the Ipatiev House?

And yet, in returning to that night, we know that intended victims left the murder room alive. Two separate volleys failed to finish off the prisoners: bodices and undergarments filled with jewelry deflected bullets, leaving not corpses but a room of screaming, convulsing, struggling victims. Both Olga and Tatiana sustained fatal gunshot wounds that ripped through their brains, but Marie and Anastasia remained alive, suffering repeated bayonet stabs before, according to Yurovsky, being "finished off with head shots."[51] The forensic evidence from the exhumed remains, however, contradicts this: Marie suffered only a single bullet wound, to her thigh. The drunken Ermakov leveled his gun to her head at point-blank range, but his bullet failed to hit her. Anastasia, Yurovsky contended, suffered the same fate. If Ermakov's bullet hit her, it did not prove fatal: after Yurovsky and Kudrin had checked pulses, both Marie and Anastasia sat up screaming.[52–54] Unable to shoot, Strekotin recalled, Ermakov again grabbed his bayonet, attempting to stab them as they struggled, only to fail to penetrate their bodies. He finally resorted to a nearby rifle, using the butt to smash away at their screaming faces until they were once again still.[55]

Were these wounds enough to kill Marie and Anastasia? Marie certainly died that night, though we do not know if this final assault killed her, or if, during the hours that followed, while the bodies were being transported to the Four Brothers mine, she bled to death or died from her injuries. The evidence, as it stands, does not support any such conclusion about the possible deaths of either Grand Duchess Anastasia or Tsesarevich Alexei. It is at least possible that one or more of the intended victims of the execution remained alive as the Fiat wound its way through Ekaterinburg and out along Koptyaki Road toward the Four Brothers mine. How, we must ask ourselves, do we know the precise moment when, or if, on that long drive through the dark summer night, Anastasia and Alexei died? Survival of the executions at the Ipatiev House does not provide evidence of rescue, nor are two missing bodies irrefutable proof of continued life. In the end, however, the complete absence of any trace of their remains means that the deaths of Anastasia and Alexei that night are only a theory of history.

The old Koptyaki Forest today is severed by a modern highway, which slices through the dense growth of trees. Pig's Meadow, overgrown with wild grass and ringed by the white trunks of birch trees and lofty pines, has become a place of pilgrimage, dedicated to the memory of the Romanovs who, for seventy-three years, rested in this muddy ground. Searches continue, but with each passing year, enthusiasm wanes and hope fades. Only the ancient pines towering over the glade remain, circling Pig's Meadow and silently guarding the secrets of Koptyaki Forest.

22

"Drowned in This Mist of Holiness"

And if you had died on the Throne, what a fuss they would
have made, what pompous ceremonies there would have been
in every church, in every country. But today because you are
fallen from power, an exile, they try to ignore you.[1]

F OR SEVEN LONG YEARS, from August 1991 to mid-July 1998
the remains of the Romanovs and their four retainers lay on cold
metal autopsy tables in an isolated, third-floor room, hidden
behind iron grating and locked doors, in the Ekaterinburg morgue.
Over those years, the bones were examined by experts; cut into pieces
for testing; photographed and filmed; and picked up and scrutinized by
both those with legitimate connections and by those who managed to
buy their way in to the supposedly protected and sterile environment.
Skulls were held aloft, empty eye sockets gazed at, and small bones
shuffled from table to table by incautious curiosity-seekers. Some were
religious devotees, who, knowing that hard currency often bought
access, simply bribed officials, often with the simple idea that such an
adventure would bring them into close proximity with their idols, and,
occasionally, in the hope that they might be able to procure for themselves some tangible fragment of their holy royal martyrs. As a result,
actual remains disappeared from time to time; the last such disappearance, in late June 1998, involved several vertebrae and a finger bone,
which, though an extensive search was conducted and those in charge
relentlessly grilled, remain missing. Several of these bones are now held
by private individuals in the United States.[2]

472

One of the first public pronouncements on the issue of what to do with the remains came from Nicholas Romanov, a grandson of Grand Duke Peter Nikolaievich, and president of the Romanov Family Association, an organization created in 1979 with the declared intent to reintroduce the former dynasty back into Russian life through charitable contributions, but whose preoccupation with the nonexistent throne seemed to overwhelm the majority of both their time and their increasingly frequent statements. Commenting in 1992, Romanov told the *Times* of London that he believed the idea of a state funeral for the remains would be an error. He openly questioned the validity of the remains, suggesting that the entire story had more to do with Russia's need to put the entire episode behind them.[3]

In the years that followed, Romanov and members of his association offered frequent comments on the issue of what to do with the remains. On July 10, 1993, the *Times* quoted "descendants of the Romanov family" as saying that the remains "should now be given a proper burial, preferably at Ekaterinburg."[4]

The idea of burial in Ekaterinburg—a city that, for the Romanovs and those killed with them, had no association other than their imprisonment and murders—struck many as abhorrent. Over the five years that followed, various plans and proposals were suggested, calling for burial in Ekaterinburg, in St. Petersburg—as tradition dictated—or even in Moscow. Some curious arguments were spun around the proposal regarding Ekaterinburg. The late Bishop Basil Rodzianko, of the Orthodox Church in America, himself supported the idea of leaving them in the Urals. "The bones should not be separated from the bodies," he declared. "The bodies are there in different form, but they are there in the soil. Therefore, to take the bones away and place them in St. Petersburg means a dismembering of the bodies. To me, this is sacrilege."[5] This was seemingly predicated on the erroneous belief that the Romanovs would be buried in Koptyaki Forest, where, he assumed, hundreds of their bones still lay undiscovered in the soil. No such human remains have ever emerged from the various exhumations, however, leaving the bishop's theory in some question.

At the opposite end of the spectrum, Grand Duchess Maria Vladimirovna, head of the imperial house, supported the idea of burial in St. Petersburg for the Romanovs, though she left open the question of the ultimate fate of the four retainers gunned down with the family. This idea was met with furious resistance by the Romanov Family Association. "It makes sense to leave them in Ekaterinburg," Rostislav Romanov declared. "If you're going to canonize them in martyrdom, why not bury them where they were martyred? If you bury them in St. Petersburg with the other Tsars, you're pretending that nothing ever happened."[6]

These various plans became entangled in a distasteful, increasing swirl of arrogant snobbery that sought to separate the Romanovs in death from Botkin, Demidova, Kharitonov, and Trupp, the faithful retainers who, through their own loyalty, had voluntarily joined their masters in both captivity and, ultimately, death. Marina Botkin Schweitzer, granddaughter of Dr. Botkin, expressed her own displeasure, saying that if the bodies were separated, she wanted to see her grandfather laid to rest in the family plot in St. Petersburg, not in Ekaterinburg. "If they are to be buried together, that's fine," said Richard Schweitzer, Marina's husband. "They died together. There was nothing that tied Marina's grandfather to that place except misery and death."[7]

And yet, to some monarchists, the thought of burying servants with the imperial remains was anathema. One particularly virulent commentator perversely declared that such a move would be tantamount to the ultimate triumph of communism.[8] And yet, such sentiments ignored the realities of the situation. Writer Grant Menzies brilliantly summed up this dilemma and the moral iniquities of the proposed separation:

> The Romanovs were not gunned down with people unknown to them. They went down in a hail of bullets with no less mortality than did Demidova or Botkin. They had all been through experiences, which must have shattered their lives even before the guns were leveled at them. This gave them over to common ground even as it delivered them to a common fate. History abounds with many servants who have literally given their lives as well as their hearts to their employers. Life breaks people down, it removes them from where they were happy, from those they loved, and changes how people see things and their world. Surely one of the few bright spots in the lives of the Imperial Family prior to their murder was that they were together with old faces from their old life, people they could trust. People who are as sure of themselves as real aristocracy, as old royalty, are, do not entertain such parvenu prejudices concerning their servants. The Empress's sister Ella is buried in Jerusalem side by side with the nun who died with her at Alapayevsk, and there were no protests on behalf of monarchists at that. The bodies of Louis XVI and Marie Antoinette were dumped into a common grave with other victims of the Terror. Though bones have been recovered and reinterred at St. Denis, it is by no means certain, it is, in fact, impossible to believe, that they are the authentic relics of the French sovereigns. The tomb at St. Denis is a memorial to the King and Queen and to the victims of the Revolution. Nothing else, and nothing less, is now being suggested in regard to the Romanovs and their retainers. In fact, the family already had been buried with the servants, for seventy-five years. It seems oddly cold now to try to separate

them by class. In death their blood mingled together as it ran across the floor; in death, their bones collapsed into each other and their flesh rotted together.[9]

For several years, the arguments continued without resolution as the Russian government itself struggled to reach a conclusion about the burials. In October 1993, Sergei Filatov, president Yeltsin's chief of staff, declared: "We have to rebury the remnants of the Tsar's family. Today it is becoming a painful question." He suggested that the issue would likely be resolved by the beginning of 1994, when the government hoped to announce definite plans for a funeral service.[10]

As promised, at the beginning of 1994, the Russian government did indeed announce that a date for the funeral had been set: May 18, which was Nicholas II's birthday. By March, however, this proved too optimistic. The Russian Orthodox Church and its patriarch, Alexei II, demanded further proof of identity before they would allow the remains to be buried. The government then changed the date, setting July 3, 1994, as the day on which the funeral would take place. By the end of June, this, too, fell through, and, for the second time, the funeral was canceled.

Throughout the summer of 1994, the government commission charged with the Romanov case met and fought among themselves and with the Russian Orthodox Church, which remained adamant in its decision to deny both recognition and burial to the remains until they were provided with further proof. A third proposed date—March 5, 1995—was announced, but in November 1994 this, too, was canceled.[11] Throughout these struggles, the remains themselves continued to lay in the Ekaterinburg morgue beneath Plexiglas shields, "a haunting reminder of unsettled history," as one news report acutely observed.[12]

Nearly a year passed. In early September 1995, Boris Yeltsin publicly declared that he wished to see the remains properly buried in St. Petersburg. Three weeks later, author Edvard Radzinsky, a member of the government commission, announced that the Russian prosecutor-general, Boris Soloviev, had received final confirmation of identity from forensic and genetic experts. "We all agree," Radzinsky said, "that Russia's last emperor should be laid to rest in the Cathedral of St. Peter and St. Paul, alongside other Tsars from the Romanov Dynasty." The commission, which proposed a date of February 25, 1996, was, however, reticent as to the fate of the other victims, suggesting that the empress and her three daughters might be separated and interred in the Grand Ducal Chapel, adjacent to the main church; there was no mention of the four retainers.[13]

The Russian Orthodox Church, however, still was not satisfied. They objected strenuously to the proposal, announcing that no positive proof had yet been offered to show that these were, indeed, the remains of the Romanovs. They composed a list of ten questions, demanding that they be satisfactorily answered before they would assent to any burial. These were first presented to the state commission on October 6, 1995, and once again on July 17, 1997. Among other items, the list demanded clarification on the issue of whether it was possible to burn two sets of human remains to ash in the time the Bolsheviks had; why Sokolov found the finger, Dr. Botkin's dentures, two pieces of skin, and some forty bone fragments at the Four Brothers mine, when the exhumed remains had come from a common grave some five miles distant; demanded a formal inquiry into the authorship of the 1920 Yurovsky note; asked to whom the loose teeth had belonged; inquired about the circumstances of the murder itself, in an attempt to clarify long-standing accusations among the more conspiratorially minded that it had been "ritual" in nature; and asked why no evidence existed of the Otsu wound on the skull presumed to be that of Nicholas II.[14]

In time, the church did indeed receive partial answers to these queries, but not to their satisfaction. The state commission under Soloviev admitted that the two bodies said to have been burned by Yurovsky would have left substantial remains and not been reduced to ash, although the commission later contradicted this. They admitted that there was no explanation as to the discrepancy in Dr. Derevenko's testimony about the bone callus over the Otsu wound on the emperor's skull and the lack of such a mark on the exhumed skull. Only in addressing the issue of the remains discovered by Sokolov was the commission on firm ground, declaring with some confidence that the finger and skin had come most likely after the bodies were subjected to damage from grenades; they had, however, no explanation for the number of bones discovered at the Four Brothers mine. The church was unimpressed, and asked that the state commission release its final, full report; portions of this were made available, but, significantly, the forensic section, which dealt with the issue of the two missing bodies, remained unseen by those outside the commission itself.

Then, too, certain elements within the church had already begun to consider whether to canonize Nicholas II and his family, a move that would, of necessity, call for a display of their remains for veneration. The question of burial thus became inexorably linked to that of possible canonization, providing a further stumbling block that, in the end, led to the fourth proposed date—February 25, 1996—being canceled.[15]

For nearly two years, these internal Russian struggles continued. At the beginning of November 1997, Edvard Rossel declared on Russian television, that "this burial must take place in the city of both myself, and of our president, Yeltsin."[16] Three weeks later, the government commission once again announced that all forensic testing had been satisfactorily concluded and that no doubts remained as to the identity of the remains. The Russian Orthodox Church, however, still was not convinced, particularly when the commission announced that this last round of conclusive testing had been the photographic superimposition and computer matching work conducted by Sergei Abramov. "Scholars have said that it will take them two months to reach a final answer," the patriarch said in a public statement. "I agree that after the reconciliation of the two versions it will be necessary to conduct a burial and put an end to this horrible period of regicide and the general destruction of our people."[17]

Despite this, Boris Nemtsov, first deputy prime minister, announced that he would present the commission's findings to President Yeltsin, along with their recommendations for the eventual burial. Along with Ekaterinburg and the Cathedral of the St. Peter and St. Paul Fortress in St. Petersburg, a third spot was proposed, the newly rebuilt Cathedral of Christ the Savior in Moscow, an enormous nineteenth-century edifice that had been destroyed on Stalin's orders.[18]

Rossel was quick to act, taking his case to Sverdlovsk District Court. On November 25, 1997, Judge Valery Romashkov issued a ruling that forbade the removal of the remains from Ekaterinburg. The judge cited Article 244 of the Russian Federation's Criminal Code, which made it illegal to desecrate the bodies of the deceased. "In his resolution," noted one report, "he asks agencies to guarantee the proper preservation of the remains and also to protect the rights of citizens in matters of morality." The judge himself declared that, according to his ruling, the remains could be removed "only if a decision has been made regarding their burial."[19]

On January 11, 1998, Nemtsov presided over a press conference during which he declared: "Experts have carried out enormous work, and now we can solemnly announce that the remains belong to the family of Nicholas II. Now no one, even the greatest skeptics, must have no doubts left." Nemtsov added that the government commission would meet again at the end of January, when it would formally present their recommendation to President Yeltsin, and expressed his "very firm" hope that the burial would take place that same year.[20]

With the government commission's announcement and the apparent softening of the church's previously inflexible attitude, officials in St. Petersburg moved quickly. Within two days of Nemtsov's press conference, St. Petersburg governor Vladimir Yakovlev made his own bid for a role in the funeral. In an open letter to Boris Yeltsin, he presented a meticulous proposal calling for an elaborate burial in the former imperial capital. "We suggested," the letter declared, "that the place of burial should be the proper resting place of all Russian Emperors, the Cathedral of the St. Peter and St. Paul Fortress. The remains of not only Nicholas II, but of all of his family members shot with him, as well as their attendants, should be committed to the earth in the Chapel of St. Catherine within the Cathedral."[21]

Yakovlev's plan was suitably dignified, and throughout January was reviewed by Yeltsin and Nemtsov. It was an impressive bid, and one that, though in the end it was considerably scaled back, was to form the actual basis of the eventual funeral rites. Much of the media attention focused not only on the issue of where the remains should be buried but also on the symbolic significance of such an act. "Should the nation honor the last Emperor of all the Russias," asked journalist Maura Reynolds, "or simply inter a discredited despot?" Most Russians involved in the case had little difficulty choosing between the two. "From a historical point of view," said Sergei Mironenko, director of the State Archives of the Russian Federation, "by burying the Emperor and his family, we will be putting a very clear end to this tragedy." Nicholas Romanov, head of the Romanov Family Association, himself conceded this, but added, "Russia has too much history. We need to achieve a certain symbolism, and then move on."[22]

Given these announcements, it did not take long for other parties to interject their own proposals and pleas into the Romanov case. At the end of January 1998, before any firm announcement had been made, the All-Russian Party of the Monarchist Center issued an appeal to Patriarch Alexei II, asking that the church refuse to participate in the burial of the "alleged remains," as they termed them. Referring to Yakovlev's proposal, the group declared that "the Protocol provides that it is you who will perform the funeral over these unknown bones in St. Isaac's Cathedral," adding that the government was exerting pressure on the patriarch "as, without the Church, the splendid funeral that is being planned will assume a questionable and hideous character, deprived of religious significance and grace." The group warned that the identity of the remains had not been established, nor had the church's outstanding questions received official answers. The patriarch's cooperation, they declared, would be tantamount to "a fatal adventure for Your Holiness" and "a Satanic insult, not only against the Holy Memory of the Tsar-Martyr and His August Family, but against the entire Orthodox Faith." They concluded their appeal by urging Alexei II to "resist this impure, dangerous intention. All of us who are not deceived by these false remains and their propaganda expect this of You, and we urge You to hold Yourself and the Holy Church as far away from this political intrigue as possible."[23]

Three weeks later, the Russian government announced its decision.

On February 27, 1998, the government declared that the remains would be buried on July 17, 1998—the eightieth anniversary of the Ekaterinburg murders—in St. Petersburg, in St. Catherine's Chapel, as Vladimir Yakovlev had originally suggested.[24] At the same time, the special Commission for the Burial of the Romanov Remains was established to plan the event. This was headed by Georgi Vilinbakhov, master of ceremonies and chairman of the State Heraldry Division of the office of the president of the Russian Federation. He was joined by Ivan Artishevsky, representing members of the Romanov family in exile, and respected historian Dimitri Likhachev.[25]

This announcement caught the Russian Orthodox Church by surprise. Presented with this fait accompli, they reacted in typical fashion. Having previously declared that they saw no objection to a burial once they received answers to the list of ten questions they had posed to the government commission, they now re-emphasized these points, saying that they did not recognize the Ekaterinburg remains as those of the Romanovs. "The decision on the identification of the relics, as belonging to the family of Emperor Nicholas II, caused serious doubts and even confrontations in the Church and society," they declared in a public statement. "In this connection, the Holy Synod takes the view that these relics should be buried without delay in a temporary, symbolic grave. The final decision on the place of their burial should only be taken when all doubts regarding the Ekaterinburg relics are dispelled."[26]

This announcement only confused the entire issue. The Russian press began to refer to the eventual grave, only half jokingly, as "The Tomb of the Unknown Emperor."[27] While such comments drew chuckles from some, others took the unfolding events far more seriously. Prime Minister Viktor Chernomyrdin openly declared that when the funeral took place, it would be "devoid of pomp or splendor," suggesting the first crack in Vladimir Yakovlev's elaborate proposal.[28]

On March 12, 1998, Sergei Skorogobatov, secretary of the Supreme Monarchist Council, held a press conference in Moscow at which he issued an ominous warning: "There will be no funeral!," he declared. "We will lay down across the railroad tracks to prevent these remains from being removed from Ekaterinburg." A small fringe group, the Public Committee for the Protection of the Holy Remains of the Tsarist Martyrs, was immediately formed in Moscow, with a stated goal of preventing the removal of the remains from Ekaterinburg and thus the funeral itself. "If the remains are authentic," they declared, "then according to the Orthodox Church canons they are Holy Remains, and such remains should not be buried. If the remains are not authentic, their pompous burial is even more inappropriate because it may turn the memory of the Tsar-Martyr into a mass mockery."[29]

Such pressures undoubtedly influenced the church, which, by the middle of April, publicly announced that they were again considering whether to participate in any funeral. On April 10, Patriarch Alexei II chaired a closed-door meeting of the holy synod's twelve bishops, discussing what official stance the Orthodox Church would take. While no official public announcement was forthcoming, the newspaper *Kommersant Daily* reported that the church hierarchy had decided to boycott the planned ceremony.[30]

Within a month, not only the church, but also Yeltsin himself, was pulling away from the intended ceremony. On May 11, an enormous battle erupted among various officials in the president's office, the church and holy synod, the office of the Moscow mayor, Yuri Luzhkov, and Yakovlev's office in St. Petersburg, played out on television and in the pages of national newspapers. Yeltsin's office suggested he might not attend, while Luzhkov suggested that the proposed funeral simply be canceled. This followed the announcement of official government spokesman Viktor Aksyuchits—a deputy aide to Boris Nemtsov—that "in all probability the president and the patriarch will not take part." The patriarch's decision rested on the issue of possible identification and on that of future canonization; if the church, in the future, decided to canonize the Romanovs, Alexei II's attendance at the proposed funeral might cause potential difficulties. Yeltsin himself had strongly allied his office to the church, and, given his tenuous hold on power, dared not go against a more powerful organization. Luzhkov himself openly questioned the veracity of the remains, saying that there was "no complete certainty in identification." There was more than a hint of suspicion in the press, however, that Luzhkov's doubts stemmed more from a desire to cancel the funeral and influence officials to reschedule it to take place in his own city, Moscow, than with any real concerns over the validity of the remains themselves. Luzhkov, commented *Kommersant Daily*, was defending Moscow's interests and "making yet one more curtsy to the Moscow Patriarchy." It pointed out that Luzhkov was the man responsible for the rebuilding of the Cathedral of Christ the Savior, one of the proposed burial sites. Officials in Ekaterinburg, meanwhile, forced into the unwelcome reality of a funeral in St. Petersburg, announced their own grandiose plans for an official ceremony in Voznesensky Cathedral and solemn procession through the city streets. On Rossel's orders, Ekaterinburg officials issued invitations to only Grand Duchess Maria Vladimirovna; her mother, Grand Duchess Leonida Georgievna; and Maria's sixteen-year-old son, Grand Duke George, while pointedly ignoring the members of the Romanov Family Association.[31]

Official confirmation of Yeltsin's decision was a month in coming.

On June 14, Boris Nemtsov finally announced that the president—and Patriarch Alexei II—would not attend the proposed funeral.[32] This came four days after the patriarch released an official statement on the remains and the proposed funeral:

> The seventeenth of July 1998 marks the eightieth anniversary of the murder of the Russian Emperor Nicholas and members of his family. . . . On this day we call upon and bless the Archbishops and Bishops of our Holy Church to conduct requiem services commemorating the murdered Emperor Nicholas II, his wife, Empress Alexandra, and their children, Olga, Tatiana, Marie, Anastasia, Alexei, and their faithful servants and all those martyred and slain in the time of fierce persecution for the faith of Christ, whose names are known to the Lord. Making this appeal, we profoundly regret that the sad anniversary of the murder of the Emperor and his family has been darkened by hard arguments around the remains found near Ekaterinburg. On this day, the seventeenth of July, these remains will be buried at the Cathedral of St. Peter and St. Paul in St. Petersburg. The State Commission identified them as those of the Imperial Family. As is known, the decision of the Commission has provoked a twofold response in our society and the Church. Along with those who trust the Commission's conclusions, there are those who do not accept them. The Church and the secular public have been divided in their judgment, and this division is apparently confrontational and painful. In this situation, the Supreme Church Authority, whose duty it is to take care of the unity of the Church and to promote civic peace and accord, is called by the very logic of the conflict to restrain from supporting a particular point of view. Requiem services for the murdered Emperor, his family and all those martyred in the years of persecution will be conducted on this day in our churches; the same requiem service will be conducted at the Cathedral of St. Peter and St. Paul in the city on the Neva. This divine service will not be an act of recognition or nonrecognition of the scientific conclusions with regard to the "Ekaterinburg remains" but rather a fulfillment of Christian duty, the Church's response to the requests for conducting a service for the repose of the souls during the burial of the remains.

The Statement was endorsed and signed by all of the members of the holy synod.[33]

Although the government itself had known this announcement was coming, they reacted strongly. Nemtsov declared: "It is a matter of conscience and honor to bury the remains of the Tsar and his relatives on July 17 in St. Petersburg, on the eightieth anniversary of the shooting of the Imperial Family. I think one should do this even if Patriarch Alexei II will not take part in the funeral."[34]

Yeltsin's decision to stay away from the funeral was clearly a political move, as Moscow journalist Andrei Zolotov pointed out: "Without the Patriarch's participation, President Boris Yeltsin decided he also could not attend. He needed the Church to give the burial legitimacy, and help him establish his Government as the heir to Imperial Russia. By deciding to distance itself from the funeral, the ruling Holy Synod placed the Church's internal unity above cozy relations with the Kremlin. The Church could not afford to ignore the strong opposition from within its ranks to the findings of the Government Commission." The church itself was suspicious of the government, believing, as Maxim Kozlov, an associate professor at Moscow Theological Seminary, noted, "This is clearly not the motions of the soul, but a political game. By distancing ourselves from the ceremony, we are retaining maximum freedom in the issue of canonization."[35]

The church's decision also rested on the fact that the state commission had refused to provide satisfactory answers to ten questions the holy synod put to them concerning the identification of the remains. "Without these," said Metropolitan Yuvenaly, "we as a Church cannot in good conscience move forward and simply ignore these issues." He spoke at length of the state commission, saying, "These men, we must remember, are all bound to Soviet-style secrecy over this matter. There has never been any openness on their part, only statements that things had been decided." There was more at work, however, in the question of the church. "We are working on the question of possible canonization," Yuvenaly declared, "and we expect this to be resolved in 2000. Any such recognition of the remains before this decision is taken would be premature."[36]

There was another issue as well. Andrei Zolotov, a journalist in St. Petersburg, summed up the church's dilemma thus: "If the Patriarch had succumbed to the government's pressure to endorse the positive identification of the bones, it would force the church—in the year 2000, when the final decision on canonization is expected—to recognize the Ekaterinburg remains as holy relics. This measure would not only be viewed as a sacrilege by many Russian Orthodox believers but would also put a definite end to prospects of reunification with the Church Abroad, which has staunchly opposed the investigation and all dealings with the Kremlin throughout. Even more alarming, opposition from within the Russian Church could be moved to break away and join the Church Abroad."[37]

The Russian Orthodox Church Outside Russia, which had canonized the imperial family in 1981, believed strenuously in the work of Nicholas Sokolov, who asserted that the remains had all been burned and dissolved in acid; they held to the belief that the only genuine remains, therefore, could be those thought to be in Belgium. Using this line of reasoning, they took the position that no remains could possibly be found and, by extension, those exhumed in Ekaterinburg in 1991 were part of some elaborate forgery. In both Europe and the United States, there was much talk of KGB infiltration of the church in Russia, and tales that Alexei II was himself a paid KGB agent. This position was defined by Metropolitan Vitaly of the Russian Orthodox Church Outside Russia, who, on March 23, 1998, declared in a pastoral letter that "when the Bolsheviks led by Lenin came to dominate almost all of the Russian soil," the "voice of Holy Russia left the Russian Land." He charged that the patriarch in Moscow was simply "a government institution, devoid of Divine Grace, and those who make up its ranks are no more than Government officials in cassocks."[38]

For many of the Orthodox faithful, the continuing struggle in Russia itself was of little consequence. In a letter to the editor of *Royalty Monthly*, a magazine published in Great Britain, one reader declared, in reference to allegations that Anastasia was still missing, that "there should be no fear as to the results of these tests for the Orthodox Church has spoken and Anastasia is numbered among the Saints. Faithful Orthodox Christians who are concerned with the spiritual significance of the new Martyrs of Russia and Russia's spiritual renewal are not—and should not be—afraid of the truth, for the Orthodox Church is the epitome of the truth. The truth was revealed in 1981 when the Glorification of the New Martyrs of Russia was proclaimed in New York at the Cathedral of Our Lady of the Sign. To believe otherwise is to doubt the infallibility of the Holy Spirit and His guidance. They are all dead; all having suffered for the True Faith, and are now all Passion Bearers of Christ. This quest for verification of the remains is merely an exercise in futility. The answer has already been decided and no one should think otherwise."[39] Such sentiments clearly reflected the view of Russian émigrés and the church in exile, though they ignored the fact that, under the Soviet government, church officials were no more subject to the state than they had been under the empire since Peter the Great stripped the patriarch and holy synod of their independent voice and power.

Despite the furor over the funeral and its tangential threads, the preparations continued at an increasingly frantic pace. Vladimir Yakovlev's initial elaborate proposal for a state funeral was, as the months passed, greatly scaled back, element after element being dropped as it became apparent that opposition was growing, not only from the office of the president and the patriarch and holy synod in participating, but also from any number of diverse political factions—monarchists, Communists, and moderates—who saw the ceremony as divisive and, in some instances, offensive. The plan for a train journey from Ekaterinburg to Tsarskoye Selo was dropped; there would be no state procession with elaborate catafalques through the city, along roadways lined with a military guard of honor; no service at St. Isaac's Cathedral. Instead, the remains would be flown to the airport just outside of St. Petersburg, and transported in a series of regular hearses to the Fortress of St. Peter and St. Paul, where the service would be held. The only aspect of Yakovlev's original plan that was retained was interment in St. Catherine's Chapel within the fortress cathedral. "I don't think we need too much pomp," Boris Arakcheyev, director of the St. Petersburg History Museum and a member of the burial commission, explained somewhat pathetically.[40]

With the ceremony previously postponed four times, no one knew for certain that it would even take place. As the weeks went by and as preparations continued, the internal Russian struggles over the remains, as well as the political battles and doubts expressed by members of the émigré community, began to have an impact on the very nature of the ceremony itself. On July 10, 1993, following the announcement that the first round of DNA tests had confirmed the presence of five of the Romanovs within the exhumed remains, the *Times* of London commented in an editorial: "The Queen can now make the first visit by a British monarch to Russia since the Revolution for the belated ceremonial funeral of her cousin."[41]

This set the tone for public expectations in the West at least, as, in the minds of many in Europe and America, the proposed funeral quickly assumed the mantle of what was popularly conceived as perhaps the most magnificent and historical royal ceremony the twentieth century had ever witnessed. Nearly 150 members of Europe's royal houses, along with heads of state, were invited to attend the ceremony.[42] In the end, such hopes were to be dashed. There was some irony in the fact that public and media speculation over eventual attendance at the proposed ceremony centered largely on whether Elizabeth II—granddaughter of King George V, who had been solely responsible for denying his cousins British asylum in 1917—herself would go to Russia for the occasion. In autumn 1994 she visited St. Petersburg with the duke of Edinburgh, touring the fortress cathedral and looking at the marble tombs of Russia's sovereigns. Privately, a Buckingham Palace spokesperson confirmed that the queen had expressed the wish to attend the funeral service. "She would see it as the dignified closing of a great cycle of dynastic history," the source confirmed. "She would go to any ceremony as head of state, not in a private capacity—which is reserved for close family and friends. But no formal invitation has been received. The Queen would only act after intense consultation with ministers." This latter comment spoke to the potential political implications of such attendance, particularly given the continuing arguments over the remains and growing schism within the government, the church, and the émigré community.[43]

By 1998, the queen herself had been through one of the most historic—and distinct—funerals in royal history, that of Diana, Princess of Wales, following her tragic death in a Paris car crash on August 31, 1997. The Russian ceremony, however, differed in many important respects, however much the media—particularly in the United Kingdom—speculated on what comparisons might be made between the two events. Aside from the fact that the victims had been dead for eighty years, the Russian government as a body—with the notable exception of Vladimir Yakovlev himself—never tried to invest the ceremony for the Romanovs with the kind of grandeur and solemnity that might reasonably have been expected. The Romanov funeral, rather, was always viewed through the twin filters of historical significance and of national reconciliation, a public recognition of a terrible past crime. In the process, however, those charged with the Romanov case—and even those attached to it—from members of the state commission responsible for identifying the remains, and members of the government, to politicians, the church, and those planning the event—changed the structure of the significance. By the beginning of summer 1998, the intended ceremony was not simply a recognition of the Ekaterinburg murders and proper burial of the remains, but instead had assumed the mantle of a pompous display of the expiation of some imagined collective guilt, over not only this particular murder, but also for every single crime—both real and illusory—committed by the Soviet state between 1918 and 1991. The Russian people, this reasoning went, were all bound together by this crime, and all shared in the ultimate responsibility for not only its commission but also for the unfortunate events that followed. A particular—and peculiar—mind-set developed, which cast the Ekaterinburg murders into an overblown, historically undeserved role, some kind of arbitrary threshold that, when crossed, forever branded the Russian people as guilty.

As ridiculous as this was—tantamount to assigning collective guilt to every German, for example—even those born after the events—for the horrors of Adolf Hitler, it struck a peculiarly Russian chord. It was *sudba* (fate), inexorable, inescapable, a delirious submission that echoed that of Nicholas II himself. "Burying the Tsar is an event that is too political for our people," said Andrei Sokolov, deputy director of the Institute of Russian History. "They still can't look calmly on their Soviet past." The sentiment was echoed—and elaborated on—by Alexander Kravets, secretary to the Communist Party's Ideological

Committee. "The state is trying to exploit its power to reject the Soviet period of our history," he said, aptly summing up what was, indeed, one of the principal motivations of all concerned.[44]

By the end of June, the funeral also had become a political platform of a different kind, exposing the schism within the Romanov family itself. This was no accident, but rather took place by the designs of Dimitri Likhachev, a ninety-one-year-old respected scholar and victim of Stalin's gulags, and a man who exerted a powerful influence over Boris Yeltsin. Likhachev actively promoted the idea of using the funeral as a symbolic expiation of Russia's past crimes, thus sacrificing the religious and historical significance of the event to a forceful desire to make a bold public declaration that the days of Soviet influence had ended. In a letter to Yeltsin at the beginning of July, Likhachev urged the president to attend the funeral, asserting that the murder of the Romanovs "became the symbol of all the mass repression" that followed.[45]

As the leading member of the Commission for the Burial of the Romanov Remains, Likhachev heavily influenced the tenor of the coming ceremony, including the official guest list. And here, Likhachev moved what should have been a rather straightforward matter of inviting all members of the exiled Romanov family into a deliberate political campaign. Likhachev was a friend of Nicholas Romanov, head of the Romanov Family Association and claimant to the nonexistent throne. As such, Likhachev opposed the claim of Grand Duchess Maria Vladimirovna, and proved himself her vehement enemy. Only a year earlier, Likhachev had flooded Yeltsin's office with a barrage of letters and telephone calls urging the president to deny the grand duchess's request that she and her son be allowed to live in Russia. In the summer of 1997 he continued his campaign against the grand duchess, again using his powerful position to cancel what would have been an official ceremony at Ipatiev Monastery in Kostroma to mark Grand Duke George's sixteenth birthday.[46] As plans for the St. Petersburg funeral were under way, Likhachev once again spoke out against Grand Duchess Maria Vladimirovna in a series of open letters to President Yeltsin.[47]

Ivan Artishevsky, Yakovlev's representative on the Commission for the Burial of the Romanov Remains, also was opposed to the grand duchess's claims, and, together with Likhachev, did all he could to ensure that she would be denied her rightful status at the ceremony.[48] These two men used the funeral ceremony as a political platform, to deliver a series of deliberate slights that seemed designed to ensure that she would remain absent when the actual burial took place. Invitations were issued to all members of the far-flung family, but Nicholas Romanov was to be styled as "prince"—something to which he was not entitled with the surname of Romanov—and given precedence as the most senior surviving male. The grand duchess, her mother, and the grand duchess's young son were all identified as "princess" or "prince," downgrading their titles. This was all quite contrary to the actual Pauline Laws that governed the imperial succession and that did not allow for any vacancy on the throne. The Russian Orthodox Church, the Supreme Monarchist Council, the Russian Federation itself, and most European royal houses recognized the grand duchess as the rightful claimant to the throne. These moves, therefore, had the twofold desired effect of ensuring that Maria Vladimirovna would stay away from the ceremony to avoid humiliation, while at the same time actively promoting the claim of Nicholas Romanov to the throne. Likhachev, says Alexander Zakatov, private secretary to the grand duchess, "allowed himself to be used by enemies of the Imperial House, in a dishonorable way, to suit their own ends."[49]

This decision impacted the ceremony in an unsuspected way, with only one major member of a European royal house—Great Britain's Prince Michael of Kent—electing to attend the burial. Neither Queen Elizabeth II nor the duke of Edinburgh; Queen Margrethe of Denmark or Queen Beatrix of the Netherlands; King Harald of Norway or King Carl Gustaf of Sweden; King Juan Carlos of Spain or the exiled King Constantine of the Hellenes—all related to the Romanovs by blood and/or marriage—attended the ceremony. Instead, nearly the entire congregation would be composed of members of the Romanov Family Association and other nonroyal guests. This mass exodus of European monarchs was officially ascribed to the ongoing political struggles over the remains, though privately at least two of the crowned heads admitted that they had no wish to publicly choose sides in the Romanov family by attending the service.[50]

The weeks leading up to July 17 saw a frantic buzz of activity, along with a fair amount of criticism leveled not only at the church and office of the president, but also at the Commission for the Burial of the Romanov Remains, and officials in St. Petersburg charged with organizing the event. As early as April, the *St. Petersburg Times* reported that "hotels and tourist firms have condemned City Hall's lack of forward planning for the July 17 funeral of Tsar Nicholas II." The paper noted, somewhat cynically, that the city administration "has made no concrete plans yet either to promote the event as a reason to visit the city, or to prepare for those who may do so." When asked to comment on the lack of souvenirs that would be available, Sergei Ilchinko, a spokesman for the St. Petersburg Cultural Committee, said in disbelief, "What souvenirs—the Tsar's bones?" But others—particularly those involved in the tourist business—saw the funeral not as religious ceremony, or even some nebulous national expiation of collective guilt, but purely in terms of increased revenue. "The city will explode!" declared Polina Rogozhnikova of the Scandinavia-Petersburg Tour Company. "The city cannot cope with the number of tourists." And Alexander Krasnenkov, director-general of the Astoria Hotel, complained, "It's a big event, and the city could make more efforts to make more money."[51]

Such concerns reflected both the economic realities of the new Russia and the general public indifference most Russians felt toward the Romanovs and the proposed burial. "What funeral?" asked one young man in Ekaterinburg just three days before the ceremony. It was a view echoed by many in the city where the Romanovs had died. "Throughout Ekaterinburg," noted one reporter, "many people cannot quite figure out—or care about—what is going on."[52] It was a sentiment echoed throughout Russia, from Moscow to St. Petersburg itself, reflecting the apathy over the former dynasty and the great national "symbolic repentance."

By the end of the first week of July, preparations had assumed a frenzied pace. The state budget had allocated just $833,000 for the entire ceremony and expenses, although, by the end of the first week of July, none of the workers in St. Petersburg had yet been paid. Plans to repaint the fortress cathedral had to be abandoned at the last minute, as did the laying of a new mosaic tile floor in St. Catherine's Chapel; instead, Irina Bobrova, the cathedral curator, was forced to select ordinary wall-to-wall carpeting in purple. "It's not perfect, but it will do," she declared. Rather than bury the remains in regular-size coffins, special miniature caskets were specially created, lending an oddly surreal quality to the proceedings. When the money allocated by the government failed to appear, the plans for handcarved Italian marble tombstones had to be abandoned, replaced instead with wooden plaques covered with imitation marble plastic sheeting used for kitchen countertops; to these were affixed peel-and-stick gold letters, carefully cut from a book with a knife.[53] As word of these plans leaked out, one Moscow newspaper dubbed the ceremony "the strangest funeral of the twentieth century."[54]

On Wednesday, July 15, the nine caskets from St. Petersburg arrived by airplane in Ekaterinburg and were taken to the city morgue. The coffins, made of golden Caucasian oak, were lined with copper and upholstered in quilted white velvet. Each set of remains was wrapped in a white silk shroud and placed in a separate casket. The coffins bore four ormolu handles, and all, except for one, bore gilded Orthodox crosses affixed to their tops; the only exception was the casket bearing the remains of Alexei Trupp, who, as a Roman Catholic, had a gilded crucifix. The caskets of the Romanovs were trimmed in gold fringe, with tassels of gold bullion at each corner, and were ornamented with ormolu double-headed eagles; those of the retainers were edged with silver thread fringe and tassels. The caskets of Nicholas and Alexandra bore gold and black corner tassels; in addition, Nicholas's casket bore the imperial insignia, and his also had seven gilded coats of arms. The caskets of Nicholas and Alexandra were draped with the old cloth of gold imperial standards, embroidered with black double-headed eagles; atop the emperor's coffin rested an unsheathed sword, crossed over its scabbard.[55]

Once installed in the caskets, the nine sets of remains were taken in hearses to Voznesensky Cathedral, situated just across the avenue from the site of the Ipatiev House, where they lay in state for the night. On Thursday morning, the archbishop of Ekaterinburg conducted a memorial service over the remains, then blessed the caskets as they were carried out to a series of waiting hearses amidst the peal of the cathedral's bell and beneath a blue sky suddenly filled with rain, and driven to the local airport, where they were placed on a plane and flown to St. Petersburg.[56]

The plane arrived at Pulkovo Airport, between St. Petersburg and Tsarskoye Selo, at two on the afternoon of July 16. Vladimir Yakovlev, members of the Commission for the Burial of the Romanov Remains, officials, and members of the exiled Romanov family all stood waiting on the tarmac as the plane eased to a stop. The caskets were taken off the airplane in reverse order of precedence, beginning with the four retainers, then the three grand duchesses, and finally, the remains of the emperor and the empress. As the first seven caskets were carried off the plane, a military band played a funeral march composed by an imperial guard regiment in 1908; at the appearance of the empress's coffin, the band switched to the hymn "How Glorious," which continued as her and her husband's coffins were taken from the plane across a ribbon of crimson carpet and placed in a series of waiting, dark-green vans, which then drove through the suburbs and into St. Petersburg.[57]

The crowds along St. Petersburg's streets, noted one observer, "were distinctly thin."[58] Indeed, the vast majority of those watching the procession were members of the official party itself, including the soldiers and students from the city's military academies sporting black crepe armbands. As the cortege passed the Winter Palace, the flag above the roof was lowered to half staff in salute. Crossing the Neva, the procession turned and drove to the Ioannovsky Bridge, leading to the Fortress of St. Peter and St. Paul. Boughs of cypress, woven with immortelles, and black crepe swags adorned the iron railings of the bridge over which the procession passed. As the vans reached the bridge itself, they were greeted by the solemn tolling of the cathedral's bell, ringing out once each minute throughout the procession.[59]

Inside the cathedral, with its cool sea-foam green marble walls and painted vaults, the caskets were placed on a large, three-tiered, black marble catafalque draped with swags of cloth of gold tied with ribbons of black, white, and gold crepe—representing the colors of the Romanov house standard—and adorned with gold and silver bullion; this stood in front of the carved and gilded wooden iconostasis. The coffins of the four retainers were placed on the lowest level, with the three grand duchesses on the second tier, and Nicholas and Alexandra at the top. Here, amid the flickering candles, they lay in state during the night.

That evening, all main Russian television networks carried both extensive coverage dedicated to the ceremony, and special documentaries, interviews, and analyses on the Romanovs and the reign of Nicholas II. A series of such programs on NTV, the largest privately owned network, "all but canonized Nicholas and endorsed autocracy," as one reporter noted. "His Russia," NTV told its viewers, was a country of "order and prosperity. One young historian argued that Nicholas was a statesman of almost supernatural insight. The guiding logic of the programs seemed to be that if the Bolsheviks hated Nicholas, he must have been a wonderful man."[60]

Such attitudes certainly reflected the more nationalistic elements within Russia. On the eve of the funeral itself, *Pamyat*, an ultraconservative, reactionary political party, issued a statement that summed up much of this sentiment:

> Patriots! Nationalists! Monarchists! July 17 is a tragic day in Russian and world history. On this terrible day will be the funeral of the false remains of Russian Emperor Nicholas II and His Family. Most of us know that the Russian Emperor and His Family were shot in Ekaterinburg, according to a special order of the Zionist-Bolshevik authorities: the Jews Sverdlov, Lenin, Trotsky, and others. On the night of July 17, 1918, in the basement of Ipatiev's House the Bolshevik hangmen, under orders from the Jew Yurovsky, killed the Emperor's Family. After the murders the killers wrote on the wall of the basement a ritual inscription in Hebrew. Then the Jewish-Bolshevik gangsters dissolved the bodies of Nicholas and His Family in sulfuric acid! This is a historically documented fact. When the glorious White Army entered Ekaterinburg, Prosecutor Sokolov opened a criminal investigation into the murders which proved the bodies had all been destroyed by acid and by burning. The killing of the Emperor and His Family was a Jewish ritual murder. We recommend the book by Robert Wilton, which we published under our own press. But this Jewish ritual murder has been kept secret by agents of the Soviet Power, controlled by Zionists, and by the Western powers, also under Jewish control. Only in the last few years have faithful Orthodox Russians been able to learn the truth

behind this Jewish ritual murder. Today's false funeral is undoubtedly a Zionist conspiracy, Jewish propaganda to blame good Russian men for their own murderous deeds. Even today, Zionist forces want to conceal this truth of Jewish ritual murder from the world and distract good Russian Orthodox believers and even world society from the truth. The National Patriotic Front Pamyat has attempted to stop this Zionist propaganda. We are aware that the alleged remains are fake. We have appealed to the Government and to the Patriarch, but the Zionist forces have won. We must not relent in our struggle against World Jewry. Today's Zionist action must be denounced through all means available. All good Russian Orthodox believers must arm ourselves for the fight against these dark Zionists and their crimes. If we do not fight with every weapon at our command, we will be consumed by the hungry Zionists and become slaves of World Jewry! God, Emperor, Nation![61]

The following morning, July 17, 1998—the eightieth anniversary of the murders—dawned bright and hot in St. Petersburg. At noon, an artillery salute shattered the silence of the summer morning, signaling the start of the actual service. It had taken seven years and four cancellations, but the historic moment had finally arrived. It was marked by a last-minute surprise: the appearance of President Boris Yeltsin. Only a week earlier, a spokesman had confirmed that Yeltsin would not attend, in deference to the Russian Orthodox Church. On Thursday, July 16, however, he received a pivotal telephone call from Likhachev, who pleaded with Yeltsin to change his mind; Yeltsin bowed to the pressure, and quickly made arrangement to fly to St. Petersburg early the next day. At eleven-thirty, he appeared, together with his wife, Naina, both dressed in black and she wrapped in a veil, and joined the congregation inside the cathedral.

In the absence of the patriarch and the metropolitan of St. Petersburg, the service was conducted by Archpriest Boris Glebov, assisted by six priests and five deacons.[62] Glebov had received a stern warning from the holy synod that he was not to mention the names of Nicholas, Alexandra, their children, or any of the retainers; instead, they were to be referred to only as "Christian victims of the Revolution." Said Glebov in an interview the day before the service: "The truth is I don't know who I am burying. I am just doing what the Church tells me. It is not up to me to decide whose bones these are. I am just a priest doing my job. Tsar, beggar, general—before God, we are all the same. To me, it's just a normal funeral. Same words, same prayers."[63] This lent the service a slightly surreal quality; not once during the nearly hour-long ceremony were the names of the victims mentioned by the priests; the only other modern royal parallel had been the

The funeral service showing the small coffins of the murdered imperial party.

1986 funeral of the duchess of Windsor, similarly distinguished by a complete lack of mention of the deceased's name.

Throughout the requiem, a robed choir sang deeply, while the priests and deacons, attired in their glittering copes and miters, circled the dais, following by trails of sweet-smelling incense that floated through the ornate cathedral. A crowd of some fifteen hundred people had gathered along the Kronwerks facing the bastions of the fortress; a few held icons and portraits of the emperor, while a small group of Communists protested the ceremony.[64] Inside the cathedral itself, the president and his wife stood silently before the catafalque, holding lighted tapers; beside them, seated, was a triumphant Dimitri Likhachev, and behind him, a sea of several hundred invited guests, including authors Edvard Radzinsky and Robert Massie. The members of the Romanov family stood on the right side of the cathedral, Nicholas Romanov beside Prince Michael of Kent; also present were most of the grandchildren of Nicholas II's sister Grand Duchess Xenia Alexandrovna and her husband, Grand Duke Alexander Mikhailovich, as well as Xenia Sfiris, granddaughter of Rasputin's assassin; Prince Felix Yusupov; and Paul Ilinsky, son of Yusupov's fellow conspirator Grand Duke Dimitri Pavlovich.

At the conclusion of the ceremony, the coffins were, one by one beginning with those of the four retainers, carried by goose-stepping Russian soldiers through the cathedral to St. Catherine's Chapel, where they would be interred. The chapel, a small room originally used during the completion of the cathedral for private worship, had been hastily restored to the designs of Andrei Gunich from the

Lenproektrestavratsiya Institute, with lower walls faced in red marble below the series of arched memorials of wood covered in faux marble bearing the names of the victims. The actual vault was sunk into the floor next to the chapel's single window. The caskets of the four retainers were lowered in first, then covered with beams on which rested the coffins of the three grand duchesses, including one said by the Russians to contain the remains of Grand Duchess Anastasia Nikolaievna. A second level of beams was placed over these, and, on top of this, the men lowered the caskets of first Alexandra, then Nicholas. As the emperor's casket was lowered into the vault, the guns of the fortress began to fire a salute of nineteen rounds, downgraded from the usual twenty-one, to signify that he had died as an abdicated monarch. Before the vault was sealed, the mourners crowded through the chapel, casting handfuls of white sand into the open grave and bowing their heads in respectful silence.[65]

When the vault was sealed, it was covered with a large sarcophagus in imitation of those over the vaults in the main cathedral itself; like the tombstones, this was a temporary measure, constructed of plywood and covered with laminated faux marble sheeting. Plans called for the eventual replacement of this and the tombstones with items carved from Carrara marble; a wrought-iron baldachin was to be erected over the tomb, and a new iconostasis constructed, to separate the front half of the chapel from the vault area.

In the end, the ceremony of July 17, 1998, did little to achieve the goals that had completely subsumed the religious significance of the event. For all of the talk of national repentance and collective guilt, an end to discussion of Soviet history and the endowment of Yeltsin and his government with the mantle of rightful inheritors of the imperial tradition, such sentiments failed to strike a chord in the vast majority of Russians. Yet those who had achieved what had previously eluded them clung desperately to these assertions. In the end, the Romanov funeral became not a religious burial for the last imperial family but a public statement by official powers of a desperate quest for legitimacy. "The new Russia," commented one prescient journalist, "is searching through its pre-Revolutionary epochs to find acceptable connections that might provide historical continuity, reassurance, and peace. Russian history disturbs the Russians and, in their search for an identity, after a century of catastrophes, having to reinvent that identity is embarrassing to them. The demythologization of the Communist past, begun by Gorbachev, is now followed by the increasing mythological consumption of the pre-Revolutionary world and, above all, the figures of Nicholas II and his family. The driving force behind this has remained the same: The salvation of Russian national honor."[66] And a writer for the paper *Nezavisimaya Gazeta* commented: "It is quite obvious that the condemnation of the crime committed eighty years ago in the capital of the Urals has been used by Russian propaganda not for a restoration of historical truth, but for the creation of mass recognition of an idealized image of the Russian autocrat. Nicholas II, who has been transformed into an official icon, could reestablish the historical and legal succession between the Russian empire and the presidential republic of Russia. The present regime could surmount its faulty traditional legitimacy. This quest for the political over the spiritual rightly led the Patriarch to remain away from what, in the end, became nothing more than a hollow, sad ceremony whose meaning had long before been stripped of true grace."[67]

Although the Romanovs had been buried, they continued to haunt Russia. Two years after the remains were interred in St. Petersburg, the Russian Orthodox Church glorified Nicholas II and his family as passion bearers, the lowest level of sainthood. This canonization, the latest chapter in the Romanov drama, also was the most controversial, appeasing many of the Orthodox faithful and members of the Russian émigré community while falling victim to the political expediencies of those most concerned.

In exile, the ineptitude of Nicholas II's reign; his personal anti-Semitic convictions; the thousands of subjects killed during his autocratic rule—all of these were quickly forgotten once the terrible massacre in Ekaterinburg became known. That single event became a far more potent piece of Romanov propaganda than anything the Bolsheviks were ever to do or claim. The deaths of the imperial family in the cellar of the Ipatiev House became, to many of the Orthodox faithful, their earthly apotheosis, an arbitrary line that, once crossed, subsumed in its wake all criticism and sins of the old regime and its principal representatives in the Romanovs. As the years passed, the last imperial family slowly faded from reality and slipped into carefully contrived myth. Émigré memoirs painted largely sympathetic portraits of the Romanovs, emphasizing not the errors of Nicholas II's reign but a cult of personality devoid of historical significance but redolent with lovingly drawn representations of the emperor and his family as preternaturally pious, loyal to each other, devoted only to the welfare of Russia, pure, holy, and, for the children, innocent of any hint of misbehavior, indiscretion, or even reality. This concentration became the primary focus: Nicholas and Alexandra increasingly came to be viewed only in terms of their private lives: the great love story; the quest for an heir; the beautiful daughters; the despair that drove them to Rasputin; their personal struggles in the last years of the dynasty; and their imprisonment and death. The grandeur that was the Russian imperial court, the savage murders, the lingering possibility throughout the twentieth century that Anastasia had somehow survived, and the apparent embodiment of evil in the Soviet regime that replaced the Romanov Dynasty—all contributed to this mystical romanticism that came to embody the story.

In 1981, the Russian Orthodox Church Outside Russia, based in New York, canonized Nicholas II and his family as martyrs. This decision rested on assertions that the Ekaterinburg murders had resulted from the intent to kill Nicholas, as officials claimed, "precisely because he was an Orthodox Tsar," an absurd statement that highlighted the very uncertain canonical grounds on which the decision rested. In reality, the move had largely been a political one, undertaken by the fiercely anti-Communist Russian Orthodox Church Outside Russia in an attempt to portray the Soviet regime as cruel and despotic slayers of helpless women and children. In this, the church echoed the passionate, often exaggerated portrayals by the White Army. The 1981 canonizations were also troubling for the reasoning expressed. The church's position and public statements evoked the specter of a ritual murder, a scenario long promoted by the most virulent and extremist elements in the Russian émigré community that squarely blamed the Jews.

The church in Russia had, by order of Alexei II in 1992, formally established the Holy Synod Commission on the Canonization of Saints in Regard to the Martyrdom of the Imperial Family, presided over by Metropolitan Yuvenaly. In 1996 they released a report that recommended eventual canonization. The commission focused on "the historical, moral, and religious aspects of the reign of the Romanov Dynasty's last Emperor," providing a far more thorough analysis of the circumstances of and conditions on which their decision was predicated than had the Russian Orthodox Church Outside Russia. Yuvenaly began in 1992 with a series of questions, outlining "the need for an objective examination of all circumstances of the lives of the members of the imperial family in the context of the historical events and in their Ecclesiastical interpretation aside from ideological stereotypes which prevailed in our country for the duration of past decades."

This examination became their starting point. They noted honestly that the 1981 canonization "generated a far from positive reaction among the Russian emigration as well as in Russia itself. A number of representatives did not find sufficient grounds for it. And what could be said of the unprecedented historical analogy, from the Orthodox point of view, of the decision of the Synod Abroad to include among those canonized with the Imperial Family, the Martyred Emperor's servant of the Roman Catholic faith Alexei Igorovich Trupp and Court Tutor of the Lutheran faith Catherine Adolfovna Schneider? The Commission could not ignore the conflicting and the contradictory views concerning the canonization of the Imperial Family which were published both in the secular and ecclesiastical media, as well as the correspondence received from representatives of the Hierarchy, the Clergy and Laity of the Russian Orthodox Church."

This was a stinging rebuke of the 1981 decision, but one based on firm canon law and church tradition. Having disposed of the Russian Orthodox Church Outside Russia, the commission report examined at length the principal questions that provided possible impediments to canonization. The first of these concerned the actual abdication of the emperor in 1917, an act that was explored to determine if, in so doing, Nicholas II had violated any sacred oath made on his accession to the throne or at his coronation. No such objections were found, nor contradictions with church teaching.

A second issue concerned "The Ecclesiastical Policy of Emperor Nicholas II." This was an examination of his role in reference to the Russian Orthodox Church during his reign. The commission pointed out the number of new churches and monasteries built between 1894 and 1917, and the canonization of seven new saints in these years—the largest number so glorified in any Romanov reign. These examples, coupled with a thorough study of the Emperor's personal religious beliefs and writings, as well as those of his family, comprised the collected evidence compiled by the commission. There was scant attention paid to the emperor's anti-Semitism, for which a body of his own writings and involvement also existed.

The largest concentration, however, was given to the study of the final days of the Romanovs in captivity, and the "relationship of the prisoners to historical roles of passion bearers in Church history." This focused almost exclusively on two aspects: the suffering of the victims during their period of captivity; and their religious and philosophical lives in these last weeks and days. The evidence collected by the commission, particularly that concerning their time in the Ipatiev House, relied largely on sources that frequently exaggerated tales of abuse of the Romanovs; inflated actual incidents; misinterpreted facts; or simply alleged incidents and circumstances known not to have been true. The church's commission failed to critically examine these tales, leading them to paint an erroneous portrait of life in the Ipatiev House.

Study of these three factors took nearly a year. At the end of their investigation, the commission recommended that further study be made, but on the strength of the work thus completed, adopted a resolution that called for canonization of Nicholas, Alexandra, and their children, but not of the four retainers murdered with them. After some discussion, Yuvenaly returned to the commission and reported that additional factors would have to be weighed against the historical record; any decision, he warned, must—unlike the 1981 canonization undertaken by the Russian Orthodox Church Outside Russia—be based firmly in canon law and "to determine the criteria and methodology most correct on which to base our recommendations."

Given these conclusions, the commission began a second period of intense study, during which they examined at great length Nicholas II's reign from a political point of view, with a special emphasis on "the Orthodox view" of his policies. This was one area where the commission moved carefully, aware that, despite the Romanov revival in Russia in the 1990s, a majority of the population in their country harbored negative views of the last emperor's reign and his personal role in the events leading up to the 1917 Revolution. After intensive study, the commission, as they declared in their report, did not find "sufficient grounds" for the emperor's canonization based on any factor thus far considered: nothing in his personal piety, or in his role as political leader of the Russian nation, made him a suitable candidate for glorification. Patriarch Alexei II himself said openly: "Emperor Nicholas II and his family do not deserve sainthood, because of the way he ruled the country and led the Church before being executed in 1918. His life, his actions, the first Russian Revolution, the Abdication—all of this is regarded by the Church and Society in a very ambivalent way."[68]

Given this, the commission, which had already recommended canonization, turned to the one area that seemed to provide ample opportunity for such an event: the lives of the emperor and his family in captivity. Here, they noted, they found numerous examples of those who, though as Christians they had "led a sinful life following Baptism," were nevertheless accorded canonization "precisely because they atoned for their sins not only by repentance but by special feats, through martyrdom or asceticism." In an attempt to thus find suitable grounds to justify their own earlier resolution, the commission examined the imperial family's "last days, which were burdened with severe suffering and the martyrs' death of its members."

On this determination the commission recommended that Nicholas II and his family be honored as passion bearers. This was a precise designation, and contrasted strongly with the 1981 decision. The commission pointed out that if glorification of the Romanovs was to occur, they could only be considered as passion bearers, not as martyrs, who, of necessity, were required to have suffered and been killed precisely for their Christian faith. This again was a direct rebuke to the very grounds on which the Russian Orthodox Church Outside Russia had asserted their decision. The commission noted carefully that "not every political murder, especially during the time of instability, can be looked upon as a feat of martyrdom. The Church makes an assessment of every political event within the framework of moral judgment. The Bolsheviks, in their systematic and methodical murder of all Romanovs who fell into their hands, were first of all motivated by an ideology and then by politics, since in the people's consciousness the Emperor continued to be God's Anointed and the whole Imperial Family symbolized Russia of the past and Russia to be destroyed." To underline this, Yuvenaly quoted from Patriarch Tikhon's words at a memorial service for the imperial family in Moscow in 1918. Speaking of the emperor, he declared: "Following his Abdication he could have chosen a safe and a comparatively peaceful life abroad, but he did not do this, desiring to suffer along with Russia. He did nothing to improve his situation, submissively resigning himself to fate." This, of course, was certainly the view in 1918, but time had long since rendered such sentiments obsolete, contradicting, as they did, Nicholas II's very real desire to go to England after his abdication. The commission, however, elected not to explore the issue, since willingness to leave Russia did not fit in with the comprehensive portrait they were attempting to piece together.

The last two factors considered by the commission were those of veneration of the imperial family, and whether there was sufficient evidence of miracles attributed to the victims. In connection with the first, the report noted the growing devotion to the Romanovs among many segments of Russian society; to support the second contention, the commission cited published reports of "miraculous events" said to have taken place in connection with veneration of the Romanovs.

As to Botkin, Demidova, Kharitonov, and Trupp, the commission declared that they "do not think it is possible at the present time to make a final judgment if there is a basis for the canonization of this group of laymen whose duty it was to accompany the Imperial Family during the period of their confinement and who suffered violent death. The Commission does not have any evidence of broad prayerful veneration of these laymen as well as of miracles connected with them. Furthermore, there is at present a lack of any substantial evidence about the religious life and personal piety of all these laymen with the exception of some fragmentary witness about the spiritual life of E. S. Botkin." They asserted that "the most appropriate way in which to honor the Christian feats of the Imperial Family's loyal servants who shared in their tragic fate, would be to immortalize this feat" in a book written on the lives of the Romanovs. Finally, the report declared that Botkin, Demidova, Kharitonov, and Trupp, as well as others who were killed—Tatischev, Dolgoruky, Hendrikova, Schneider, Nagorny, and Ivan Sednev—had been "servants doing their moral duty by remaining with the Imperial Family; in fulfilling this duty, they did not commit themselves to the role of martyrs."[69]

The recommendations of, and reasoning used by, the holy synod commission addressed specific concerns yet seemed contradictory to the evidence available. The contention that the Romanovs were, in their last days, subjected to suffering—one of the principal assertions on which the decision to recommend canonization was made—is without merit, resting as it does on often erroneous accounts. The idea that the victims met their deaths without resistance defies explanation; during the executions, there was no opportunity to ponder the decision and, in addition, we know that many of the victims did indeed, as pure logic would dictate, attempt to resist the bayonets and gunfire of their assassins. Nor does the position that this acceptance of death reflected some measure of awareness by the Romanovs, or a decision to remain where they were and face death willingly, follow the available evidence, given that there was no indication of any such awareness by the imperial family, nor were they unwilling to flee, as shown by their answers to the "Officer" letters. When these findings were challenged, the church, in the person of spokesman Father Maxim, declared: "The Imperial Family was an example of purity. They were killed not as simple people but as representatives of Russia's Christian life."[70] This was precisely the same reasoning that the Russian Orthodox Church Outside Russia had used in justifying their 1981 decision, and completely contradicted the report.

The pronouncement regarding Botkin, Demidova, Kharitonov, and Trupp—as well as the other members of the suite and household—was staggering in its implication. While the commission did indeed have a body of letters to support the majority of the imperial family's religious feelings, such was not necessarily the case with all of the victims—for example, the few preserved writings of Tsesarevich Alexei demonstrate, as one might expect of an immature thirteen-year-old boy, little in the way of considered religious thought, while the writings of Anastasia preserved from this period are of no greater religious content than the correspondence of Dr. Botkin. If the church might reasonably excuse Trupp from consideration as a Roman Catholic, there was little reason to do so with Botkin. All four of those killed with the imperial family at the Ipatiev House, in fact, made clear, distinct choices to remain under arrest, and with the Romanovs as prisoners, choices that the Romanovs themselves never faced. If anything, their choices spoke more of "meekness" and submission than did the actions of the Romanovs themselves. Under the commission's own criteria, Botkin was as deserving of canonization as the Romanovs, and certainly more so than all of the imperial children.

Yet on this rather questionable interpretation of circumstances did the holy synod recommend canonization. The announcement was duly noted in the press and received much critical commentary. One reporter wrote: "As a bellwether of Russian popular opinion, the decision is instructive. The Russian Orthodox Church survived for centuries first by serving the autocratic rule of the czars and then subjugating itself under the oppressively atheistic rule of the Soviet Communists. Now, struggling to reinvent itself yet again in the new, free-market Russia, the Church is tapping a popular, nationalist nostalgia for the tradition and order associated with Imperial Russia."[71]

A lengthy and critical analysis of the proposed canonization appeared in an April 1998 issue of *Izvestiia* in which the author wrote:

> The horrible death of the Emperor and the Family cannot but evoke grief and sympathy. But it does not provide a basis to consider the Emperor a saint. The notion of the canonization of Emperor Nicholas II is far-fetched. The purpose of this action is to divert attention of Orthodox Christians from the really sore problems of the contemporary life of the Church in Russia. This issue is useful to the nationalist and monarchist forces in order to deal with their political, but by no means Christian, agenda, in particular for transforming the Russian Orthodox Holy Synod into an ideological institution and for using it as an ideological lever in leading the popular masses. The death of Nicholas II was one of the first in a series of many millions of deaths which were brought on as the results of the two decades of his rule in Russia. In some sense his abdication was a blessing for the Church that he forgot in the moment of his abdication, since it permitted the Provisional Government in a brief period to summon the Local Council which managed to adopt very important measures that fortified the will of the Orthodox people for its heirs and for Orthodoxy, before its descent into the chaos and terror that transformed Russia into a concentration camp and the Orthodox Church into a handmaiden of KGB. . . . The canonization of Emperor Nicholas II, if it follows, will be an offense against the Christian conscience of many believing people.[72]

One difficulty faced by the commission was the small number of questionable "miracles" said to have been achieved through the intercession of the imperial family. Although they received dozens of accounts from ordinary Russians testifying, for example, that Grand Duchess Marie Nikolaievna had appeared during an illness to give tea, or an alcoholic was cured after visiting the site of the Ipatiev House, none of these stories provided the proof needed.[73] In spring 1999, however, the church finally had what it had long sought: an apparent, investigated miracle. An icon of Nicholas II was said to ooze myrrh. In the spring of 1999 the icon was taken across Russia to be venerated by the faithful. The icon in question was only two years old, painted in California in 1997, and on its travels across Russia hundreds of the faithful were said to have witnessed the myrrh streaming from the surface.[74]

Given this icon, the commission rapidly moved forward, announcing that the canonizations would take place in August 2000. This news stirred up a round of vocal protests. Pinchas Goldschmidt, chief rabbi in Moscow, said, "We would rather this not happen. It might give the wrong signal to believers, especially in rural areas that are led by extreme nationalists. People may say that if a person was a saint then he can do nothing wrong, so if he was persecuting Jews then he must have been right to do that." In Ekaterinburg itself, a group of self-appointed guardians of the Ipatiev House site echoed the worst of Goldschmidt's sentiments. One of them, Alexander Vassiliech, declared that no pogroms ever took place in imperial Russia and that "the 1918 crime was all a part of a Jewish ritual murder." Vassiliech and other members of his group fully supported the canonizations, at the same time proudly displaying anti-Semitic banners at the Ipatiev House site, presumably with the approval of Ekaterinburg bishop Vikenty.[75]

Such anti-Semitic, nationalistic worries were prevalent despite the commission's finding that no evidence existed to support the contention that the Ekaterinburg crime had been a Jewish ritual murder. Of far more concern to the Russian press was the increasing attribution of questionable "miracles" to the imperial family in an effort to bolster the decision of the holy synod. "After the Bishops' Council of 1997," one report noted, "a whole 'industry' of miracle working arose around Nicholas II. Icons began weeping; sick people were healed. Of course it could be said that we were faced with a rare if not unique case in the history of the church when a part of the flock was not merely venerating a famous ascetic or martyr as a saint, but was demanding of the hierarchy, in a very clear manner, a canonization. The canonization of Nicholas II is a gigantic gesture to the side of 'archaism,' that is, a profound, mythological, alarmist view of the world."[76]

Yet those who promoted and pursued canonization were a small, but more vocal, minority, filling the Ipatiev House site with icons and portraits of the Romanovs. One visiting American got a taste of this determination when, during a stay in Ekaterinburg, he approached an elderly woman kneeling in the dirt and began to question her about the proposed canonizations. "They are already saints!" she angrily replied. "They head the saints in the Cathedral of Heaven! It's only here in Russia that we've been slow to know this. The Russian Church Abroad canonized them long ago. Abroad, the Mother of God took them up to Heaven." She spoke at length of her own beliefs: "In the Church where I worship, the Mother of God has told St. John the Baptist that they are her Ladies-in-Waiting, her favorite children."[77]

The canonizations took place over the course of two days—Saturday, August 19 and Sunday, August 20, 2000. They were held in the newly rebuilt Cathedral of Christ the Savior in Moscow, once considered as a potential place of interment for the Romanov remains. Patriarch Alexei II and nearly two hundred archbishops, bishops, and priests, all attired in glittering stoles and mantles and copes studded with precious jewels, moved through the vast new building, with its magnificent marble walls and luminous frescoes; a robed choir chanted solemnly from the gallery circling the central dome as the patriarch led the procession of clergy into the enormous church, followed by Grand Duchess Maria Vladimirovna; her mother, Grand Duchess Leonida Georgievna; and the grand duchess's son, Grand Duke George—the only Romanovs who had chosen to attend the ceremony. During the four-hour service on Saturday night, the Romanovs, along with 853 other new martyrs, were celebrated with a liturgy.[78] A new icon commissioned for the canonizations depicted the Romanovs with "the elongated bodies and court robes of Byzantine saints," as Colin Thurbon wrote, "tapering hands held up white crosses. Crowned and haloed, they seemed to gaze out with a sad foreknowledge of their end. Their features echoed one another, as in some inbred clan, and they were all washed in the same amber light. All the vitality of remembered photographs—the moods and stains of real life—was emptied and stilled. Sainthood did not allow for them. Even the emergent individuality of the princesses—the imperious beauty Tatiana, the plump tomboy Anastasia—was drowned in this mist of holiness."[79]

Just before the canonizations, the holy synod, through Metropolitan Yuvenaly, declared, "Since no new data have emerged over the past years, the position of the Church has not changed. Thus, the remains buried in the St. Peter and St. Paul Cathedral in St. Petersburg will not be considered as holy relics of the glorified Imperial Family."[80] The Orthodox Church in Russia, with this announcement, proclaimed its continuing disbelief in the Ekaterinburg remains; officially, to the Russian Orthodox Church in Russia, the physical remains of the Romanovs have never been found.

The canonizations became accomplished facts; Nicholas II and his family were now officially saints in the Russian Orthodox Church. There was, however, a subtle but important distinction between the 2000 decision and the 1981 glorification ceremony. The former had made quite clear that the emperor, his wife, and children were officially passion bearers, not martyrs, in contrast to the 1981 ruling by the Russian Orthodox Church Outside Russia. Their lives, the 2000 decision had declared, were not worthy of sainthood; only their deaths met any requirements for such a designation, and even here, the arguments used to support the elevation to passion bearers were conflicted and rested on exaggerated evidence of their life in the Ipatiev House.

Most Russians regarded the canonizations as they had the burial—with disinterest. A poll taken just days after the event showed that only 29 percent of the country's Orthodox population supported the canonization ceremony.[81] To most, it was viewed as a political decision by the church, designed to achieve three undeclared but nevertheless understood goals. The first was to help facilitate possible reconciliation with the Russian Orthodox Church Outside Russia, which had canonized the imperial family in 1981. The second was to appease the more conservative, vocal elements of the church in Russia and abroad, which had been insistent in their demands that the patriarch recognize the Romanovs as martyred saints. The third factor, left unsaid by church officials, was nonetheless an important point in their decision. This was an attempt to end the spreading veneration of Nicholas II and his family as martyrs, a far different distinction than that of passion bearers. Among the Russian Orthodox Church Outside Russia, Nicholas had already become "tsar-martyr," and this language, incorrectly picked up and spread by those in Russia, had begun to filter through society at large. The designation of "martyr" was one specifically reserved for someone who was killed precisely for their faith, and their refusal, after deliberation, to renounce that faith. In the Orthodox Church, a passion bearer need only be someone who accepted their fate and did not resist death. The appellation of passion bearer to the names of the imperial family largely ignored the fact that none of the victims of Ekaterinburg had been presented with any choice at the time of their deaths, as had the most famous passion bearers in the church, the medieval Princes Boris and Gleb. The church had referred to the period leading up to the Romanovs' death as a *povdig*, a spiritual struggle that mirrored the Passion of Jesus Christ. It was one of their principal arguments in making their decision. Few questioned that the members of the imperial family killed that night all died as Orthodox Christians, but the church's designation and explanations did little to satisfy those who remained highly critical of the entire episode. In the end, the decision, embroiling the memory of the Romanovs once again in controversy, seemed a fitting epilogue to the reign of the last emperor of Russia.

Epilogue

SEVEN WEEKS AFTER THE Ekaterinburg murders, in the midst
of the newly inaugurated Red Terror, the remaining members of
the imperial suite who had been imprisoned in Ekaterinburg and
thus far escaped execution were taken into a forest outside the city of
Perm. The three—Countess Anastasia Hendrikova, lady-in-waiting to
the empress; Mademoiselle Catherine Schneider, the empress's lectrice;
and Alexei Volkov, the empress's kammer diner (valet de chambre)—
had been transferred by train from Ekaterinburg just two days after the
Romanovs were murdered. As Bolshevik soldiers ordered the trio to
march across a glade in the early-morning hours of September 4, shots
suddenly rang out. The sixty-year-old Volkov ran, not daring to look
back, and disappeared into the woods; behind him, the bodies of
Hendrikova and Schneider lay in the tall grass.[1] Their deaths closed the
string of executions by the Ural Bolsheviks directed against the
Romanovs and their retainers. Over eighty-four days, they had ordered
the deaths of twenty-seven people—fourteen Romanovs, and thirteen
members of the former imperial suite and household.

Four months later, on January 27, 1919, Grand Dukes Paul
Alexandrovich, Dimitri Konstantinovich, and Nicholas and George
Mikhailovich were all taken from their cells in the Trubetskoy Bastion
in Petrograd's Fortress of St. Peter and St. Paul and executed. With the
exception of Dimitri Konstantinovich—whose body was retrieved by a
faithful valet and secretly buried in a Petrograd garden—their corpses
were simply dumped into a mass grave in the fortress.[2] These four
grand dukes were the last Romanovs to be executed in Russia.

The vast majority of the surviving members of the suite and household gradually made their way out of Russia when it became obvious, in
1919, that the White Army was on the run. Dr. Eugene Botkin's two
children, Tatiana and Gleb, had remained at Tobolsk after their father's
departure for Ekaterinburg. When the city fell on July 25, Gleb Botkin

rushed to Ekaterinburg, desperately hoping to find his father. When he returned to his sister in Tobolsk, he could only report that no one knew with any certainty what had happened to the imperial family and those imprisoned with them.

Tatiana and Gleb remained in Tobolsk, the latter making frequent journeys back to the Urals to speak with the various investigators. In the fall of 1918, Tatiana married Konstantin Melnik; by 1920, both she and her husband, as well as Gleb himself, had fled Russia. Tatiana settled in Europe, Gleb in America; both became firm supporters of Anna Anderson's claim to be Grand Duchess Anastasia, with Gleb her most dedicated champion. He died in the 1960s, his sister some twenty years later.

Baroness Sophie Buxhoeveden, too, had returned to Tobolsk with the members of the imperial household expelled from Ekaterinburg in June 1918. She was the only member of the former imperial suite to survive captivity. That Buxhoeveden was so intimately involved in the betrayal of the Romanovs is starkly at odds with the lovingly devoted young woman usually described in Romanov literature, who acted as confidante to the grand duchesses. Yet Buxhoeveden's actions in presumably absconding with Soloviev's funds and her subsequent revelations of the imperial family's hidden jewels were not aberrations. While still in Siberia, she borrowed 1,300 rubles from tutor Charles Sydney Gibbes, explaining that she would return the money. At the time, Gibbes himself was in desperate financial circumstances. When he later asked the baroness for the money, she insisted that no such loan had ever been made. In a letter to Gilliard, Gibbes complained: "I knew she was greedy, but I never thought she would go so far!"[3]

Buxhoeveden left Siberia with half a dozen trunks of Romanov possessions. In exile, she lived first in Copenhagen with her father; then at Hemmelmark, the estate of the empress's sister Princess Irene and her husband, Prince Heinrich of Prussia; and finally in Kensington Palace in London, where she acted as an unofficial lady-in-waiting to the empress's eldest sister, Victoria, marchioness of Milford Haven. In 1938 Buxhoeveden applied for British naturalization, which was granted.[4] Buxhoeveden remained with the marchioness until her death, and became a close friend and confidante of her son Earl Mountbatten of Burma. Surviving members of the Romanov family, however, were deeply suspicious of her behavior in Siberia. Buxhoeveden was unique among those attached to the Romanovs, not only by virtue of her seemingly inexplicable escape from death, but also in her relations with the White investigators. Of the surviving members of the suite and household, she alone refused to cooperate with the investigation into the fate of the imperial family. She ignored requests from Sergeyev to be interviewed; when she learned that he had dispatched an official to question her in Tobolsk, she quickly fled to Omsk and asked for passage out of the country.[5] In exile, she ignored repeated requests from Nicholas Sokolov to be questioned about her time in Tobolsk. "It is obvious," Sokolov commented, "that her conscience in regard to that period is not entirely clear."[6]

In the 1920s, when Buxhoeveden first came to London to live with the marchioness of Milford Haven, Grand Duchess Xenia Alexandrovna fired off a number of angry letters to Victoria, warning that the baroness was not to be trusted. Buxhoeveden, she declared, was guilty of treachery in Siberia, and Xenia consistently refused to receive her. When Buxhoeveden died in November 1956, she apparently left hundreds of imperial objects she had taken from Tobolsk to members of the British royal family and certain surviving Romanovs.[7]

The emperor's old valet Terenty Chemodurov was released from the Ekaterinburg Prison hospital ward when the city fell to the Whites in July 1918, and assisted Nametkin and Sergeyev with their investigations. Throughout, Chemodurov repeatedly insisted that the empress and her children had managed to escape, though he refused to reveal precisely how he knew this or where they were. In 1919 he returned to Tobolsk, where he died.[8]

Dr. Vladimir Derevenko spent the first several months after the fall of Ekaterinburg in the city, assisting Nametkin and Sergeyev with their investigations. At the end of the year he took his family to Perm, where he worked under the Bolsheviks as a professor at Perm University's hospital. In 1919, when the Civil War surrounded the city, he moved his family to the Siberian town of Tomsk, where he became head of the district military hospital.[9] Although in White hands, the city fell within eight months, and Derevenko, who always enjoyed an easy relationship with the Bolsheviks, remained behind, much to the consternation of General Deterikhs, who complained bitterly in his book that the former court doctor had "abandoned himself amongst the enemies in Siberia."[10] In the early 1930s, Derevenko was ruthlessly interrogated by the NKVD, successor to the Cheka, in their efforts to locate the missing Romanov jewels. He died in 1936, while in Soviet detention.[11]

When the Soviets began their crackdown on Derevenko, his son, twenty-four-year-old Nicholas Vladimirovich—Alexei's former friend Kolya—left Siberia, making his way across the country to Europe. For a time he worked as an engineer in Prague; just before World War II erupted, he emmigrated to Canada, where he quietly settled into obscurity. Until his death in 1999, he consistently refused to speak about the imperial family or his father's time in Ekaterinburg.[12]

Elizabeth Ersberg, Alexandra's third Kamer-Jungferi, or lady's maid, and Maria Tutelberg, second Kamer-Jungferi, both assisted Sokolov with his investigation into the imperial family's murders. Ersberg temporarily left Russia, living in Europe, where the dowager empress supported her. On the latter's death, Ersberg returned to Russia after signing an official promise never to discuss the Romanovs. She died of starvation in March 1942, during the siege of Leningrad.[13] Tutelberg also immigrated to Europe and eventually settled in South Africa.

Charles Sydney Gibbes, the imperial children's tutor of English, assisted Sokolov during his investigation. Near the end of the White retreat from Siberia, he made his way to Harbin, where he met a fifteen-year-old orphan, George Paveliev, whom he adopted. The two journeyed to England, where, in 1934, Gibbes formally adopted the Orthodox faith. Gibbes was a curious man: a quiet homosexual, in his later life he harbored an obsessive interest in the tsesarevich, and tried, unsuccessfully, to assume the name Father Alexei in his honor; instead, he became Father Nicholas. He settled in Oxford, where he created a small Russian Orthodox chapel decorated with many of the imperial family's icons, and lit by the glass chandelier that had formerly hung in the bedroom of the grand duchesses in the Ipatiev House. He died in 1963.[14]

Gibbes's comrade Pierre Gilliard also worked extensively with Sokolov before he, too, left Siberia, in 1920. He returned to his native Switzerland, where, in 1922, he married Alexandra Tegleva, the former imperial nurse. Gilliard died in 1962, his wife a few years later.

Colonel Eugene Kobylinsky, who had faithfully acted as commander of the special detachment in Tobolsk and sought to protect the Romanovs from the growing Siberian menace, joined the White Army in 1918, eventually serving as quartermaster on Admiral Kolchak's staff in Omsk. Captured by the Bolsheviks, he was freed by the Whites and returned to Tobolsk, where he married Klaudia Bittner, who had come to the town to give music lessons to the imperial children during their captivity. Conspicuous in the small town where he had formerly presided over the Romanovs, Kobylinsky moved his wife and only son, Innokenty, to the Siberian town of Ribinsk in an effort to escape official scrutiny.[15] In 1927 Kobylinsky was arrested, charged with anti-Soviet activities, and executed. His wife and son attempted to disappear, moving to the small town of Orechovo, where she took a job as a factory worker. At the end of the 1920s and into the 1930s, however, Bittner was repeatedly questioned by the NKVD concerning the missing Romanov jewels before being executed in 1935.[16]

Leonid Sednev, the fourteen-year-old kitchen boy spared by Yurovsky just six hours before the Ekaterinburg murders, was put on a train on July 20 by officials from the Ural Regional Soviet and sent to Kaluga District, where he still had relatives. Sednev wrote a brief set of memoirs of his time in the Ipatiev House before his death in 1929, at age twenty-five.[17]

Of the others intimately involved with the final drama of the Romanovs, little is known. Paul Khokryakov, who had guarded the children in Tobolsk during their parents' absence and accompanied them on their perilous voyage aboard the *Rus*, died on August 17, 1918, fighting in the Civil War.[18] Prince George Lvov, former prime minister of the first provisional government, and the man responsible for a number of highly inaccurate stories regarding the life of the Romanovs in the Ipatiev House and their murders, immigrated to France, where he died in 1925.[19] General Michael Deterikhs published his book on the murders of the imperial family in Vladivostok in 1922; shortly thereafter, he, too, left Russia, settling in France, where in 1937 he died. Sokolov's faithful aide Paul Bulygin immigrated to Argentina, where he was apparently shot and killed in the 1930s.[20] Robert Wilton, who produced the first, unreliable, and virulently anti-Semitic account of the Romanov murders, was fired as a correspondent for the *Times* a few years after his book was published. In justification, they explained that Wilton "did not command full confidence."[21] Wilton loudly complained that he had been "flung out on the streets practically penniless . . . after giving the best years of my life to the service of the *Times*."[22] He made his way to Paris, where he spent his last years with Sokolov, Gilliard, and Bulygin before dying in 1925. Nicholas Ipatiev, in whose house the imperial family had lived and died, immigrated to Czechoslovakia, dying in Prague in April 1938.[23]

The enigmatic Konstantin Myachin, whose appearance in Tobolsk under the name Vassili Yakovlev signaled the beginning of the end for the Romanovs, himself barely escaped the vengeance of the Ural Bolsheviks. Through political expediency or personal inclination, he defected to the White Army and joined forces with the Constituent Assembly Party.[24] Yakovlev eventually migrated to Chita, where he claimed to have switched allegiance once again, this time returning to the Bolshevik fold. There seems to have been no real evidence of his Bolshevik involvement, however, for, on his return to Russia in 1928, he was quickly arrested as a traitor, and dispatched to a Soviet labor camp in Kem. Released in 1933, he began a systematic campaign of appeals to Stalin to defend his record, his letters now contradicting his own 1918 statements, and claiming that before he left Moscow, Sverdlov had told him, "The Council of People's Commissars has resolved to move the Romanovs from Tobolsk to the Urals for the present time."[25] Every indication suggests that this was a move designed not only to defend his record but also, more importantly, to save his life. Had Yakovlev admitted that Ekaterinburg had simply outmaneuvered Moscow in

1918, he would undoubtedly have sealed his own fate. As things turned out, within a few years, he was again arrested, and in 1938, shot on Stalin's orders.[26]

As 1919 drew to a close, Bolshevik soldiers pushed the previously strong White and Czech forces back across the Urals and east, toward the dead end of Vladivostok and their inevitable retreat from Siberia. With their flight, members of the Ural Regional Soviet who had fled the previous year gradually returned to Ekaterinburg. They found a city in chaos: the wide avenues were nearly deserted; the only faces to be seen—old men and bent babushkas—bore, according to Yakov Yurovsky, the "unmistakable mark of fear." Typhus had ravaged the city, the hospitals and infirmaries were filled with the dying, morgues piled with infected corpses. There was a singular lack of young men: thousands had been drafted into the anti-Bolshevik forces, while hundreds more lay rotting in shallow graves, victims of mass executions by the White Army. Even the children, with their emaciated faces and sunken eyes, bore "a haunted look."[27]

Nearly all of the city's Jewish citizens—some two thousand in all—had been massacred by soldiers of the White Army in a savage act of venal retribution before they abandoned Ekaterinburg in the summer of 1919.[28] Given the intense anti-Semitism prevalent among the men who formed the White forces, such brutality was common, but rarely was it inflicted on such a scale, and against a city's entire Jewish population. As Richard Pipes notes, to these White soldiers, "the fate of the ex-Tsar was identified with the martyrdom of Christ, and interpreted in the light of the *Protocols*."[29]

After fleeing Ekaterinburg on July 19, 1918, Yurovsky had disappeared from view. For the year that they held power over Siberia, the Whites considered him the most wanted man in all of Russia, and they spent a considerable amount of time and effort attempting to find him. As late as 1922, when General Michael Deterikhs published his work on the Ekaterinburg murders, Yurovsky's fate was still unknown; Deterikhs suggested that he was captured and executed by the Whites.[30]

In fact, Yurovsky had gone to Moscow, where he was joined by his wife and children.[31] He was appointed head of the Moscow Regional Cheka, and served as a member of the Moscow City Cheka for just over a year. Then, in late 1919, he was transferred back to Ekaterinburg, to take up his appointment as chairman of the Ural Regional Cheka.[32]

It was in Ekaterinburg, on March 8, 1920, that British officer Francis McCullagh managed what had eluded Sokolov and every other White investigator: he came face to face with Yakov Yurovsky, and even interviewed him.[33] The interview conducted by McCullagh seems to be the only one Yurovsky ever granted. Although he himself wrote three sets of memoirs, and often spoke publicly—albeit to groups of trusted Bolsheviks—of his role in the Romanov executions, Yurovsky, at least in these early years, avoided publicity. McCullagh's account, therefore, is of intense interest, not only as a personal glimpse of the man who led the execution squad, but also for its revelation of the aura of intrigue that surrounded him in Ekaterinburg.

McCullagh had expected to find Yurovsky a celebrated hero of the Revolution in this, of all cities; instead, he was surprised to hear him spoken of in whispers as "the man who murdered the emperor." No one, it seemed, wanted to associate with Yurovsky. "In restaurants and public places," McCullagh wrote, "men and women" hastened out of his way "with a readiness savoring of panic." Children, passing him in the street, stared wide-eyed. "I was surprised," McCullagh noted, "to find that even the Bolsheviks shun him. They have given him a good house, money, food, everything he asks for; but they avoid him and do not like even to speak about him."[34]

McCullagh discovered this firsthand when he attempted to find a local resident to accompany him on his visit. One man "declined, with a shudder." Another said simply, "No, I would rather not go." And a third declared, "It was a horrible business. I wouldn't like to go near that man." This struck McCullagh as peculiar: "They would accompany me anywhere else I liked," he recalled, "and they went to great pains to show me everything, but the mere mention of Yurovsky's name always caused a shadow to pass across the faces of the most bloodthirsty of them, and they suddenly remembered that they had an engagement elsewhere."[35]

Yurovsky, as he later told McCullagh, hated to be recognized, with the whispers and fears of vengeance that inevitably followed. He even tried to alter his appearance, shaving off his beard and wearing a hat pulled low over his brow. According to McCullagh, he had "a morbid dislike of saying anything" about the murders: "A look of horror crosses his face when any reference is made to it, and he becomes perfectly silent."[36] But as much as he tried to escape his past, Yurovsky was forced to confront it daily. The house the authorities had provided for him stood on Voznesensky Prospekt; from the windows of his drawing room he could look out over the roadway to the Ipatiev House, standing silent guard over his life.[37]

Although McCullagh was careful not to raise the subject of the Romanovs, inevitably echoes of the drama crept into the conversation. During their interview, McCullagh became conscious of Yurovsky's "feelings of remorse and horror" at the murders of the Romanovs.[38] He also had a distinct impression of a "dreadful secret" that "weighed on Yurovsky when I met him."[39]

Within a year, Yurovsky was back in Moscow, where he took up a position in the newly created State Diamond Fund in the Kremlin, charged with cataloging and assessing the confiscated wealth of the Romanovs.[40] In 1927, in anticipation of the tenth anniversary of the October Revolution, members of an Ekaterinburg group made a formal proposal that they should be allowed to write and publish their memoirs of the murders into a book. The request was signed by Yurovsky, Kudrin, Nikulin, and Goloshchokin and forwarded to the Kremlin. But when Goloshchokin approached Stalin with the idea, he was met with an angry response: "Not a word about the Romanovs!"[41]

In 1934 Yurovsky returned to Ekaterinburg—now renamed Sverdlovsk—and to the Ipatiev House, where he attended a reunion of former members of the Ural Regional Soviet. Here, surrounded by the empty rooms where he had once held power over the former imperial family, Yurovsky gave a speech on the events of July 1918—the last time he would ever speak publicly about those events.[42] The following year, Yurovsky's life began to unravel. His daughter Rimma, who had served as a leader in the Komsomol Youth Organization and as secretary of the Komsomol Central Committee, was arrested on suspicion of counter-revolutionary activity and sent to a Soviet labor camp, where she spent the next quarter century imprisoned under Stalin.[43] Her father, increasingly ill from heart trouble and an ulcer, worked only sporadically, first as director of the Red Victory factory near Moscow, then as an assistant at the Polytechnic Museum.[44] In his last days, as his son Alexander recalled, he expressed great regret over his role in the murders. On August 2, 1938, Yakov Yurovsky died in a Kremlin hospital at age sixty. He was buried in Novodievechy Cemetery outside Moscow.[45]

Michael Medvedev, known by his party name of Kudrin, lived quietly over the decades that followed the events of 1918. In December 1963, at the request of his son, Michael Mikhailovich Medvedev, he wrote a lengthy account of the murders that was quietly deposited in the State Archives.[46] Although Kudrin himself was not present when the bodies were exhumed from the mine shaft, nor when the alleged attempt at cremation was made and the corpses finally buried in the mass grave, he wrote fully of these events, leaving a version filled with conflicting claims and erroneous details. Throughout, he was careful to repeatedly delineate, that "all eleven" corpses were always accounted for.[47] As evidence, given Kudrin's absence from these events after the morning of July 17, such statements mean little; yet the constant repetition and insistence on this point stand as distinctly peculiar, an overt declaration of what would only have been obvious. Kudrin died in 1964, having left his Browning pistol no. 389965 to the Museum of the Revolution in Moscow.[48]

That same year, his son, Michael Medvedev, conducted prerecorded interviews for Moscow State Radio with Gregory Nikulin, Yurovsky's former deputy, and Isai Rodzinsky, the member of the Ekaterinburg Cheka who had copied out the forged "Officer" letters received by the Romanovs. Nikulin had fled Ekaterinburg with Yurovsky on July 19, 1918, when both men went to Moscow. For a time, Nikulin worked in the administrative offices of the Moscow Soviet, charged with the supervision of the city's prisons; later he became head of the Moscow Criminal Investigatory Division, chairman of the state insurance offices, and chief of the Moscow water supply stations.[49] Following the evacuation of Ekaterinburg in 1918, Rodzinsky had served as secretary of the Caucasus Regional Executive Committee for a time, then found himself pursued over his participation in the Ekaterinburg murders by Stalin. He was arrested in 1937; his apartment was searched and all of his personal papers and documents related to the Romanovs were seized and, he was later told, "destroyed" by Soviet authorities. Finally released in 1940, Rodzinsky was ominously warned that he "was subject to continued investigation."[50]

It had been Medvedev's idea to bring these two men—-the last survivors from the Ural Regional Soviet and Ekaterinburg Cheka of July 1918—together to record their experiences. Both men had remained friendly with his father, and accepted Medvedev's invitation to finally break their silence about the Romanovs. The interviews, conducted by Medvedev himself, were done separately, but were never broadcast; the transcripts were, however, deposited in the State Television and Radio Archives.[51] A short time later, both Rodzinsky and Nikulin died, the latter being buried near Yurovsky in Novodievechy Cemetery.[52]

Like other Ural Bolsheviks, Peter Ermakov had fled Ekaterinburg on the approach of the White Army. In the eight years that followed the murders of the Romanovs, he served in the Red Army's militia; then, in 1927, Moscow appointed him director of prisons for the Urals and sent him back to Sverdlovsk.[53]

Unlike Yurovsky, Ermakov positively relished his role in the Romanov murders. On December 10, 1927, he proudly handed over his Mauser revolver, no. 16174, to the Museum of the Revolution in Sverdlovsk, along with a short note claiming that with it he had personally killed Nicholas II.[54] He delighted in bringing friends to the museum and pointing out the gun, explaining in graphic detail the events of that night. Thieves attempted to steal the Mauser on five separate occasions, but this relic of the Ekaterinburg crimes was always discovered and returned to the safety of the museum.[55]

Ermakov cut a wide swath through Sverdlovsk. "He was very proud of this whole thing," recalls one elderly woman who knew him. "Now, they call him 'Emperor Killer,' and curse him, but at the time, here he was our number one person. . . . We lived near where he lived. We knew him and his whole family, brothers. He was a very harsh and determined person. Everybody was afraid of him. He could usually be seen riding in the street on horse with lash in his hand. He ended up an alcoholic."[56] Alexander Avdonin, himself destined to play a role in the Romanov case, remembered Ermakov making "appearances in schools, speaking in front of students and workers. He told his audience all about his 'heroic deeds,' though the details sounded more like a crime. He always spoke with great pride in what he had done."[57]

Despite his alcoholism, and the unreliability it brought with it, Ermakov was never censured or relieved of his duties. To the contrary, he was continually rewarded, given promotions, better apartments, and even additional pay. When he retired, he received not a state pension but a personal pension, "a privilege not accorded to many who had served the Regime," as one historian has noted.[58] Ermakov died in 1952. As a reward for his state service, he was buried with full honors near the War Memorial in Moscow, and his name was given to a street in Sverdlovsk.[59]

Peter Voikov, the former Ural Regional commissar of supplies, served as a deputy in the People's Commissariat for Provisions from December 1918 to July 1919. Following this, he held posts in the Central Union of Consumers' Cooperatives and in the Commissariat for Foreign Trade.[60] In 1924 he was named Soviet ambassador to Poland. Three years later, on July 7, 1927, a seventeen-year-old student from Vilna, Boris Koverda, casually strolled up to Voikov at Warsaw Central Station, pulled out a revolver, and shot him six times, fatally. Quickly dubbed "the assassin's assassin" by the press, Koverda, a monarchist, apparently killed Voikov "as an act of private vengeance."[61]

Following the evacuation of Ekaterinburg in July 1918, Alexander Beloborodov fled to Moscow. Here he had expected to join his wife and children, who had been sent away from the Urals, accompanied by Myasnikov; only when Beloborodov arrived in Moscow did he learn of the ferry accident on the Vytchegda River in which his wife and children had drowned.[62] In March 1919 Beloborodov became a member of the Central Committee in Moscow; four years later he was appointed interior commissar and a member of the NKVD, successor to the Cheka. Then, in 1927, he was expelled from the Bolshevik Party as a Trotskyite, and expelled from Moscow. Three years later he was rehabilitated, and allowed to return to the Party.[63]

Russian author Edvard Radzinsky raised the possibility that, in 1935, Beloborodov, using the pseudonym Nicholas Sokolov, came to

Paris to seek treatment for throat cancer. According to the daughter of one official, Beloborodov had remained at the Soviet embassy in Paris; believing that he was dying, he expressed regret over the murders of the Romanovs, saying that it was "a sin on his conscience."[64]

In August 1936 Beloborodov was once again arrested as a Trotskyite and expelled from the Bolshevik Party. This time he was imprisoned on Stalin's orders, first in Moscow's notorious Lubyanka Prison, and finally in a Soviet labor camp. Like so many millions who were to follow him into the gulags, Beloborodov never emerged alive. In February 1938 he was apparently shot on Stalin's orders. Twenty years later, he was finally rehabilitated under Khrushchev and cleared of any crimes.[65]

Beloborodov's compatriot Goloshchokin served as a member of the Central Committee; apparently he also held positions in the Cheka and its successors. In 1924 he was appointed head of the Republic of Kazakhstan, where he served for nine years. Returning to Moscow, he became the chief arbiter of the Sovnarkom in 1933, a post he held for nearly eight years.[66] In summer 1941 Goloshchokin was arrested on Stalin's orders and sent to an NKVD prison camp near Kuibyshev. On October 28 he was executed according to a Kremlin directive. Like Beloborodov, he was later rehabilitated under Khrushchev and cleared of any crimes.[67]

Alexander Avdayev, the first commandant of the House of Special Purpose, seems to have suffered no repercussions over his role in the Romanov drama, perhaps because he was not involved in the actual murders themselves. Apparently he disappeared from Ekaterinburg for a time, leaving the Whites to speculate that he had been sent to the front and killed.[68] In fact, after the evacuation of the city, he seems simply to have hidden himself in a small peasant hut near Koptyaki, where he remained until the Whites fled the area in July 1919. He held a series of menial jobs in the string of factories that ringed the city. Avdayev was later recalled by those who knew him as a warm, loving man who adored children. Sterile himself, in 1924, following the death of his sister Augusta, the wife of Serge Lyukhanov, he adopted his young niece Antonina, and lived quietly in Ekaterinburg, ignored by the Soviet authorities. In 1947 he died of tuberculosis.[69]

Avdayev's sister Augusta was married to Serge Lyukhanov, the man who had driven the Fiat loaded with corpses from the Ipatiev House to Koptyaki Forest in the early morning of July 17, 1918. With the advance of the White and Czech forces on Ekaterinburg in July 1918, Serge Lyukhanov and his wife fled to the town of Osa, near Perm, where he obtained a job in a lumber mill. Sometime in 1920 or 1921 the pair separated, with Augusta taking their four children and returning to Ekaterinburg to be near her brother; apparently this was the result of a discovery by Augusta that her husband had engaged in some activity with which she strongly disagreed.[70]

There has been intense speculation as to precisely what this discovery may have been. In contrast to his wife, who became the inspector of children's homes for the Ural Region, Lyukhanov—although he had joined the Bolshevik Party in 1907—seems to have grown less certain and lost his revolutionary ardor.[71] According to his son Alexei Lyukhanov, before her death Augusta apparently forgave her former husband for his indiscretion.[72] As Lyukhanov did not remarry until 1923, one man who knew him suggested that this indiscretion was not some romantic dalliance but rather an "ideological" break between the pair.[73] Lyukhanov, according to his son, rarely stayed in one place for long after 1926, when he left his job as chief of the Osa electrical station. There followed "jobs in various towns in the Urals," usually as a mechanic, and "many" moves until 1939, when he settled in Perm and took a position as a lathe operator in a hospital. He never applied for the government pension for which he was entitled; according to his son, "he was very taciturn, and spoke rarely." He died in 1954.[74]

Of the 105 men who had served guard duty at the House of Special Purpose, most fled Ekaterinburg just before the city fell to the advancing White and Czech Armies. Most disappeared into obscurity, although it has been possible to trace the subsequent lives of several of these men.

Alexei Churkin, one of the men signed from the Syssert factory in May, joined the Red Army and was killed while fighting in the Caucasus in 1919. Konstantin Dobrynin, another Syssert worker who was described by his friend Alexander Strekotin as "clever and intelligent," joined the Third Red Army in Ekaterinburg after the Whites had fled in 1919; he died barely six months later, while working in the army's Political Section. Feodor Emiliyanov, a third Syssert worker, remained in Ekaterinburg throughout the Civil War, having returned to his job at the factory. Alive in 1934, nothing is known of his subsequent fate.[75]

The two Kabanov brothers, Alexei and Michael, left the city within a few days of the murders of the Romanovs. Before his death in Khabarovsk in the 1960s, Alexei Kabanov wrote his set of memoirs on his time in the Ipatiev House.[76] Seventeen-year-old Ivan Kleshchev, the guard who had openly declared his intention of rescuing one of the grand duchesses and marrying her, had been on duty at the Ipatiev House on the night of the murders. He was so horrified by the executions that he immediately quit the Bolshevik Party and fled to Perm, where he took a job as a guard at a suburban military depot. Apparently he was caught stealing some cloth from the depot, and sentenced to six months at hard labor. Released at the end of 1918, just as the White Army captured the town, apparently he fled once again, never to be seen again.[77]

Ivan Kotegov, a friend of the Strekotin brothers from the Syssert factory, remained in the industrial suburb, continuing his previous job. He was still alive in 1934; after this, all traces of him vanish.[78] Rudolf Lacher, a man who had almost certainly participated in the assassinations and accompanied the Fiat on its drive to Koptyaki Forest, returned to his native Austria, where he lived quietly in the small town of Steinach. In the 1960s, the eighty-year-old former prisoner of war found himself in the public eye when he testified in the trial of Anna Anderson to prove her identity as Anastasia. Lacher offered contradictory accounts, on which Anderson's lawyer quickly seized, suspecting that the witness had, in fact, been a member of the execution squad. When asked about the murders, Lacher said coldly, "What did I care? They weren't my relatives." Before his death in 1974, Lacher declared enigmatically, "I served the Bolsheviks well. I kept my silence."[79]

The two Letemin brothers, Kuzma and Michael, remained in Ekaterinburg after it fell to the Whites. They were discovered when, on passing their house, a group of officers recognized Alexei's spaniel Joy sitting in their front yard. On further investigation, Michael was found to have more than a hundred personal items that had belonged to the Romanovs—all stolen from the Ipatiev House after the murders. He was interrogated and gave his secondhand story of the executions to White investigators. Although only seventeen years old, not involved in the murders, and not even a member of the Bolshevik Party, Michael Letemin was summarily executed by the Whites in an act of pure revenge.[80] Valentin Lyukhanov, son of Serge Lyukhanov, the official driver to the Ipatiev House, fled the town with his father after the murders. In later years he followed his father's curious odyssey as he moved from town to town.[81]

Paul Medvedev fled with the Bolsheviks on the liberation of Ekaterinburg. Apparently he never mentioned his tenure in the Ipatiev House. Then, in Perm, in the late summer of 1918, he fell ill with German measles and while in the 139th Hospital he read a newspaper account of the Romanovs' time in Ekaterinburg.[82] One of the nurses came around and he protested at the tone of the article, saying, "It is not true, Sister, what is written in the newspaper. I am an eyewitness. That the detachment fed them badly and treated them worse is not true. The guards' attitude towards them, that is to say, towards the Emperor's Family, was very good. They were well fed. They always had meat cutlets and vegetables and soup and there was a quart of milk a day."[83]

The nurse to whom Medvedev had confessed, Lydia Guseva, told no one about his identity, and he gave himself up to the Whites on Christmas Eve 1918, when they took Perm.[84] When the Whites tried to interrogate Guseva at the Red Cross Association house where she lived, the directress said she was ill; they insisted, and it turned out Guseva was trying to avoid them, although she knew nothing beyond what Medvedev had told her.[85]

Medvedev himself seems to have been harshly treated while in White hands. His wife, Maria Medvedeva, complained that he seemed "disconnected. He doesn't recognize anyone and has stopped caring about his family."[86] Gradually he revealed his story, and the Whites and Nicholas Sokolov—and thus history—had its only eyewitness account of the executions until the Soviet archives disgorged their previously secret contents. After giving two versions of the murder—one to Sergeyev, one to Alexeiev—Medvedev died under mysterious circumstances, the victim of either typhus, a heart attack, or torture.[87]

Victor Netrebin, one of the men brought in to the Ipatiev House on July 8 and who participated in the executions, remained in the Ekaterinburg area, writing his memoirs before his death. Alexander Orlov, a worker from Syssert and a member of the Bolshevik Party, died in 1932. Nicholas Popov, another worker from the Syssert factory, died in the Civil War, fighting for the Red Army. Eighteen-year-old Philip Proskuryakov was forced into the Red Army and sent off to fight in the Civil War; he died in 1920. Alexander Sadurov, the youngest and, according to Alexander Strekotin, the "most handsome" of the men and "the darling of the whole company," returned to his job at the Syssert factory after his time in the Ipatiev House. The last known mention of Sadurov comes in Strekotin's 1934 memoirs, in which he stated that his friend still lived near the Syssert factory.[88]

Nicholas Sadchikov, another Syssert worker, was so depressed over the murders of the Romanovs that, within six months of the executions, he committed suicide. Benjamin Safonov, another Syssert worker and the only Jewish member of the Ipatiev House guard, returned to work at the factory after the Red Army had recaptured Ekaterinburg in 1919. In 1931 he fell beneath a streetcar on the old Voznesensky Prospekt and lost his hand. Unable to work, he received a disability pension and still lived in Syssert in 1934, when Strekotin wrote his memoirs.[89]

Andrei Starkov, the oldest of the Ipatiev House guards, was forcibly conscripted into the Red Army after Ekaterinburg fell and was sent to the Dutov Front. He was wounded in the Civil War and had to have his foot amputated. He was still alive and friendly with Alexander Strekotin in 1934. Starkov's son was not as fortunate. Seventeen-year-old Ivan Starkov was captured by the Whites when they took Ekaterinburg, forced at gunpoint to dig his own grave, then hacked to pieces by White officers with their sabers.[90]

Andrei Strekotin entered the Red Army after Ekaterinburg fell to the Whites. In August 1918 he was killed in a skirmish with the Whites in Koptyaki Forest, and—ironically—his body was flung into an abandoned mine. Only in 1919, after the Bolsheviks had once again seized control of the city, could his family retrieve his corpse; he was buried in Novotikhvinsky Cemetery in Ekaterinburg. His younger brother Alexander, although not a Bolshevik, was forcibly conscripted into the Red Army to fight in the Civil War. At the end of the conflict, he moved away from Ekaterinburg to Sarapulsk, where he worked as the director of the Rasakonikovsky machine tractor factory. In 1934 he wrote his memoirs of his time in the Ipatiev House and deposited them in the Sverdlovsk Soviet Party Archive. His subsequent fate is not known.[91]

Ivan Talapov left Ekaterinburg after the city fell to the Whites and traveled to Petrograd, where he became involved with the local city administration. In 1920 he was killed while attempting to put down an abortive putsch at Kronstadt. Semyon Turgin, a worker from the Syssert factory and a member of the Bolshevik Party, quietly returned to private life after his term of service at the Ipatiev House, working as a tailor. He was still alive in 1934; after this, nothing is known of him.[92] Anatoly Yakimov, one of the most loquacious of the Ipatiev House guards, was captured by the Whites and provided them with his second-hand testimony of the murders. A month later, he—like Medvedev and Michael Letemin before them—died under White captivity, said to be the victim of pneumonia.[93] Of the remaining members of the Ipatiev House guard, nothing is known; the vast majority vanished into a chaotic Russia engulfed in the Civil War, never to be heard from again.

In the ten years that had passed between the murders in July 1918 and Mayakovsky's visit in 1928, Ekaterinburg had changed considerably. Voznesensky Prospekt was renamed Karl Liebknecht Street, and the city was crossed with the usual assortment of Soviet names—"Prospekt Lenin," "Workers' Square," and "Rosa Luxemburg Prospekt." Statues of Peter the Great and Catherine the Great had been knocked from their pedestals, replaced with a glowering statue of Sverdlov and marble bust of Karl Marx.[94] In the center of the city, which was renamed Sverdlovsk in honor of its most famous native son, Voznesensky Square was renamed first Komsomol Square, and then, in a more sinister nod, The Square of National Revenge.[95]

The Ipatiev House itself remained the ominous central attraction of the city. Following the evacuation of Ekaterinburg and its occupation by the Whites, it was used as a residence by Czech general Rudolf Gaida, who lodged himself in the corner bedroom where once the emperor and empress had slept. Throughout the winter of 1918 and into the summer of 1919, the house was carefully examined. Its contents were inventoried and packed into some fifty crates, and, when the Whites fled the city, these were shipped by train east, to be taken from the country and sent to Grand Duchess Xenia Alexandrovna in England.[96]

By 1920 the Ipatiev House had been turned into the Museum of the People's Vengeance, marked by a red flag flying over its iron roof.[97] In a few rooms, the museum curator lived with his wife and children, as author Valentin Speranski recalled during a visit in 1924: "He felt that living in this house was an enviable thing. So he lives in this house, raises his children there, received invitations there, hosts Soviet feast-days there, and he eats on the same wooden table as the Imperial Family once did. The conscience of the Bolshevik is flexible and conforms to whatever material need he has. And so this man sleeps easily without bad dreams."[98] He explained to Speranski that "it would be truly sad to lose sight of the beauty of this house because of the events which took place here. The truly wonderful thing is that a member of the prole-tariat could live in a house that would not shame the St. Petersburg bourgeoisie."[99]

Speranski found a young woman in the house, an assistant to the curator, who—like him—also resided here. "I never wanted to live in this house," she whispered. "I think that God can curse a house—like this one, where there is no more warmth and light to be found."[100]

The majority of the rooms on the main floor were devoted to the museum itself. "There are posters and diagrams on the wall," wrote Richard Halliburton, who visited in 1934, "announcing the glories of Communism, and showing how many more tractors and ingots of steel were made under Bolshevism than under Tsarism, and how many more airplanes and suits of underwear . . . as if, in this house, anybody cared.

The Ipatiev House in winter 1920. Housing the Museum of the People's Vengeance, the building is decorated with red stars and bunting.

I had to manhandle the guide to get him away from his glories-of-Communism rigmarole long enough to ask him which room was occupied by the Princesses, which by the Tsar and Tsarina—the room where Yurovsky brought the fatal message to 'assemble below' on that fearful July night. I soon found that the guide didn't know exactly, and wasn't interested. . . . This was a temple of the Red Revolutionists—not a memorial to their victims."[101]

In the southeastern corner room, used by Anna Demidova, were the only references to the Romanovs. A few glass cases contained some photographs of the imperial family, along with copies of their letters and some other documents; one letter, written by Rasputin in 1914, predicted disaster should war erupt. But the centerpiece of the room was an immense painting, ten feet long by seven feet high, by the artist Chelyin and titled "The Delivery of the Romanovs to the Ural Soviet." This depicted the handover of the Romanovs by Yakovlev to the Ural Regional Soviet on April 30, 1918.[102]

While the upper floor was given over to the museum, the ground-floor rooms were devoted to the Sverdlovsk Bolshevik Club. A sign, affixed above the side doorway that opened onto the former Voznesensky Lane, marked the entrance to the club; visitors entered the small hallway, passing the closed and locked set of double doors on their right that opened to the murder room.[103]

Valentin Speranski vividly recounted his visit to the murder room:

"The enormous keys resonated, the lock ground as it turned, and the large doors swung slowly open to reveal the terrible room of execution. My face felt the cool dampness of the grave as the air flowed out from the room. What I had heard was confirmed—the uniquely shaped window let in only a small amount of filtered light, and the room was dark with the corners obscure and shadowy. The atmosphere was oppressive and crushing. I forced myself to examine calmly the details of this historical room through the duskiness that obscured my view. Despite these troubles, the first thing I noticed were the slabs removed with care from the parquet floor and the pieces of paper removed from the walls. The room resembled a small cave, not being more than fifty meters square. In the darkness, it appeared to be quite narrow. I thought about how close a fit it would have been for eleven victims and eleven executioners. The smoke from the powder became dense and impenetrable. In this unbreathable atmosphere, the assassins would certainly have lost their heads, and would not have known who they were shooting or if their bullets struck anyone. And later, they could have been striking their bayonets at bodies that were not yet cadavers. All this time, I was looking at the damages and stains on the walls and floor. . . . I was given the opportunity to examine, as closely as possible in the semi-obscurity, the holes in all four walls that were left when the bullets were extracted. One of the holes had traces of blood-soaked duvet-feathers sticking to the inside edge. Perhaps it was here that a bullet penetrated the bloody pillow clutched by Anna Demidova, and lodged itself in the wall.[104]

During World War II, Sverdlovsk served, ironically, as a depository for many of the former Romanov treasures, shipped from Leningrad to avoid capture by the invading German army. At the end of the war, the museum in the Ipatiev House was dismantled, and it served as offices for Ural State University.[105] The city languished as a restricted destination, a region in the Urals strictly off-limits to foreigners. The Ipatiev House remained the city's chief claim to fame, its most notorious landmark, the object of intense curiosity by the few Western visitors allowed into Sverdlovsk. Nor was it only foreigners who flocked to the brooding little villa. "On certain dates, like the date of Nicholas's birthday, and the date of their murder," recalls Alexander Avdonin, "there were always flowers at the Ipatiev House, and people used to go there on these dates."[106]

In 1977, the house was finally torn down. This followed years of revived interest in the Romanovs in the West, and speculation over the fate of the imperial family. Such interest played a decisive role in the order to raze the house. In July 1975, KGB chairman Yuri Andropov submitted a proposal to the Politburo in Moscow that read: "Anti-Soviet circles in the West periodically inspire propaganda campaigns of various kinds about the Romanov Imperial Family and in this connection the former house of the merchant Ipatiev in Sverdlovsk is mentioned. The Ipatiev House still stands in the center of the town. It now accommodates a study center of the Regional Cultural Administration. . . . Foreign specialists have recently begun visiting Sverdlovsk. The number of foreigners may greatly increase in the future and the Ipatiev House could become an object of serious attention. It therefore seems sensible to instruct the Sverdlovsk Regional Party Committee to deal with the question by demolishing the house as part of the planned reconstruction of the city."[107]

In his memoirs, Boris Yeltsin claimed that the Ipatiev House was razed "in the middle of the night, and by next morning, nothing was left of the building."[108] This claim has been picked up by recent authors and repeated. "On the night of July 27, 1977," wrote Robert Massie, "a giant ball wrecker accompanied by bulldozers arrived in front of the house. By morning, the building, reduced to brick and stones, had been carried off to the city dump."[109] This story, however, was untrue, as

The murder room in the Ipatiev House prepared for demolition. The plaster wall between the storeroom and the actual murder room has been removed, as have the doors seen in the foreground.

Yeltsin himself later admitted in a 1990 interview: "We were given three days to tear the house down," he recalled, a fact confirmed by residents of the city and by existing photographs that show the destruction process.[110] A few relics from the house, including the elaborately carved chimney piece from the dining room, were salvaged and carefully hidden away, later to be resurrected in a local museum under Mikhail Gorbachev's glasnost. Where the Ipatiev House had once stood, only a barren patch of sloped ground remained, desolate, pitted with rubble, and as the years passed, lost in a tangle of weeds and creeping vines.

On September 4, 1991—nine weeks after the exhumation of the mass grave in Koptyaki Forest—Sverdlovsk formally reverted to the name of Ekaterinburg. Like so many aspects of recent Russian history, it was both a deliberate rejection of the Soviet past and an embrace of the vanished empire, which increasingly captivated the struggling citizens. The collapse of one totalitarian state left a void, quickly filled with half-understood but eagerly believed tales of a golden prerevolutionary life. Such mystical reflections took on a more overt—and distasteful—form in Ekaterinburg itself. As much of Russia was swept up in a Romanov revival, engulfed in a near-cult that glorified Nicholas II and his family as paragons of every known virtue, people in Ekaterinburg began to flock to the site of the Ipatiev House, taking photographs, leaving flowers, praying. The desolate rubble was replaced with raked gravel, and beds of carefully tended, if perpetually dying, flowers, encircled by the nearby rise of grim, Soviet-era apartment blocks on the old Voznesensky Prospekt.

At the center of the site, monarchists from the Union for the Resurrection of Great Russia laid out a series of flat granite slabs marking off the approximate location of the murder room; at its center rose a tall Orthodox cross, the object of intense veneration. In 1990 the union obtained permission from the City Council to erect a small wooden chapel near the site, guarded day and night by priests and burly, bearded men adorned in prerevolutionary Cossack uniforms. They led rallies in which the glories of the Romanovs were praised while Russia's traditional scapegoats, the Jews, were once again invoked as responsible for the murders, for communism, for all of Russia's misfortunes.[111]

A typical display came on July 17, 1993, the seventy-fifth anniversary of the Ekaterinburg murders. After attending a memorial service for the imperial family, a group of men in Cossack uniforms led a large crowd through the city streets to the glowering statue of Yakov Sverdlov. "This statue," declared one man, "is protected by the Police! This is a disgrace for our sacred Russian land! Brother Cossacks! We are monarchists, descendants of the Emperor's own Cossacks! We believe in Russia, and Orthodox Autocracy, and we call upon the Police to let us tear down this statue of Yankel Sverdlov, Communist Jew, the butcher of the Imperial Family, the butcher of Cossacks, the butcher of the Russian people! Cossacks cannot accept that this blood-sucking Yid is still standing! The enemies of Christ and Russia, Communist Jews, ritually murdered Nicholas II and his family. This statue and all Commie Jews must be destroyed!"

The crowd—carrying icons, pictures of Tsesarevich Alexei, and anti-Semitic newspapers—cheered loudly. As the police attempted to disperse the mob, they were met with angry shouts. "You guys," yelled one woman, "are in the pay of filthy Jews and their parasitic friends!" Eventually the police managed to steer the swelling crowd away from the statue and back into the city streets. As they left, they fervently crossed themselves and sang "God Save the Tsar."[112]

Eventual plans called for construction of the Cathedral of the Savior on Spilled Blood on the site of the Ipatiev House. After holding an open competition, the Ekaterinburg City Council awarded the commission to Konstantin Efremov, a young, curly-haired local architect who produced a grandiose plan with a memorial chapel crowned with seven gilded onion domes, to be constructed on the site of the murder room; it was to sit next to a massive new cathedral bristling with onion domes—the entire complex to be conveniently placed beside a new steel and glass hotel for tourists. "Once this place is built," Efremov declared, "I believe the pilgrims will come."[113]

Work on this complex was delayed for more than five years, due to lack of funds. In summer 2000 ground was finally broken on the new construction site, though little work was done other than clearing the site. In the seven to eight years that had passed, Efremov's huge design was greatly scaled back and placed in the hands of Vladimir Grachev, who produced plans that called for a moderate-size, traditional medieval-style building of whitewashed brick, with side chapels dedicated to Botkin,

Demidova, Kharitonov, and Trupp placed in small apses extending from the main body; each of the four corners would be topped with a small spire and gilded onion dome and, in the center, the entire cathedral would be crowned with a large drum and gilded cupola. The main, or upper church would contain an elaborate carved and gilded iconostasis, featuring icons depicting the imperial family and, authorities hoped, relics from the exhumed remains. Like the Ipatiev House itself, the new cathedral would be built into the side of the sloped hill; the ground floor would contain a lower church, where, perversely, the murder room would be re-created in exact detail, and on the precise spot where it had once stood. This would be separated from the church, not by the original double doors leading into the corridor, but by an iconostasis, for the replica of the murder room was to serve as the sanctuary, complete with an altar.

Construction on the cathedral continued throughout 2001 and it remains a work in progress, rising slowly, gradually, whenever funds are available. It is not, however, the only Ekaterinburg church built in honor of the Romanovs. Eleven miles west of the city, at the site of the Four Brothers mine in Koptyaki Forest, the entire clearing has been transformed. A large wooden church, capped with seventeen copper onion domes, has risen in the midst of the pine and birch trees; just beyond it, surrounded by railings and marked with a large cross and a bronze plaque, are the old shafts themselves. The building, the Church of St. Nicholas, is only one of seven planned chapels, of which five have already been constructed. When they are completed, the complex, christened the Monastery of the Imperial Passion Bearers, will function, as its name suggests, as a working monastery dedicated to the memory of the Romanovs.

The monastery proceeds from the still-unchanged position of the Russian Orthodox Church, which does not recognize the remains exhumed in 1991 as those of the Romanovs, and the similar belief espoused by the Russian Orthodox Church Outside Russia, which contends that the only genuine relics are those discovered by the various White investigators in 1918–1919 and taken from Russia in Sokolov's famous box. According to this view, Sokolov's contention that the bodies of the victims were completely burned, then dissolved in sulfuric acid—despite its scientific impossibility—was correct, and the remains unearthed by Ryabov and Avdonin were part of a KGB plot. Thus, what little remained of the corpses—ash and traces of fat—vanished into the forest surrounding the Four Brothers mine, literally becoming part of the encircling forest. "Those are the Emperor and Empress," explained monastery director Anatoly Kozhayev, pointing to two birch trees near the shaft. He identified five smaller trees as "the Tsesarevich and the four daughters." Apparently the remains of the four faithful retainers failed to sprout any trees. "The landscape itself testifies that this is a holy place," Kozhayev said.[114]

The Monastery of the Imperial Passion Bearers stands just over a mile away from Pig's Meadow, where the mass grave now competes with the new complex for the honor of having been the true resting place for the corpses of the Romanovs. "My foundation," Avdonin declared in 1993, "has plans to build a memorial park in the meadow. A nice lake can be built for families, and the grave must be restored and covered up with railway ties, as in the original. And of course some kind of chapel or worthy monument must be erected."[115]

Avdonin's plans, however, never materialized. Pig's Meadow lay abandoned, silent except for the nearly ceaseless—and ultimately futile—excavations undertaken to locate the two missing corpses. The mass grave itself, an open, muddy pit filled with water in summer and ice in the winter, was marked with an Orthodox cross. In 2001, however, once plans for the Monastery of the Imperial Passion Bearers were announced, authorities in Ekaterinburg moved quickly to provide their own pilgrimage site. A new lane was cut through the forest, to link the new highway with the old Koptyaki Road. At the edge of the clearing, at Grade Crossing 184, they built a set of wooden gates crowned with a sign that announced, "Romanov Memorial." The road beyond, a half-mile stretch that cleaved through the trees and opened into Pig's Meadow, was widened and smoothed, and the grave itself was surrounded by a concrete viewing platform, marked with a black Orthodox cross and a marble plaque declaring it the site of the Romanov grave. In death, as in life, Nicholas II continues to divide Russia.

IN HIS "ESSAYS," Macauley cast a typically critical eye on Charles I, and the swell of popular sentiment that excused the errors of his reign by looking to his private life:

> What, after all, are the virtues ascribed to Charles I? A religious zeal, not more sincere than that of his son, and fully as weak and narrow-minded, and a few of the ordinary household decencies which half the tombstones in England claim for those who lie beneath them. A good father! Ample apologies indeed for fifteen years of persecution, tyranny and falsehood! We charge him with having broken his Coronation Oath, and we are told that he kept his marriage vow! We accuse him of having given up his people to the merciless inflictions of the most hotheaded and hard-hearted of prelates, and the defense is that he took his little son on his knee and kissed him! We censure him for having violated the articles of the Petition of Rights after having, for good and valuable consideration,

promised to observe them, and we are informed that he was accustomed to hear prayers at six o'clock in the morning! It is to such considerations as these, together with his Van Dyck dress, his handsome face, and his peaked beard, that he owes, we truly believe, most of his popularity with the present generation. For ourselves, we own that we do not understand the common phrase, a good man, but a bad king. We can as easily conceive a good man but an unnatural father, or a good man and treacherous friend. We cannot, in estimating the character of an individual, leave out of our consideration his conduct in the most important of all human relations; and if in that relation we find him to have been selfish, cruel, and deceitful, we shall take the liberty to call him a bad man, in spite of all his temperance at table and all his regularity at chapel."[116]

This is an eerie echo of the sentiment that now surrounds Nicholas II and his family. Macauley sought justification for the execution of the sovereign. Had Nicholas II himself alone been killed by the Bolsheviks, and his family spared, the link might be yet stronger. But the murders of the empress and her children transcended the historical model, an uncompromising and unnecessary determination by the Ural Bolsheviks to eradicate a problem whose terrible end provided a window, not onto the systematic, state-sponsored mass murder described by Professor Richard Pipes, but to the infinitely more recognizable and thus, to us today, more poignant slaughter of innocent women and children who have danced through the collective twentieth-century imagination to become secular saints.

In the modern age, religion and romance, mystery and adulation have combined in an attempt to transform Nicholas II and his family into something quite distinct from any other ruling family, or, indeed, any semblance of their actual selves. If not the bloodthirsty tyrants used to invoke the country to discontent and to the eventual Revolution, nor were they paragons of all moral virtues, as they have increasingly come to be viewed at the beginning of the twenty-first century. Hopelessly naive, and clinging desperately to an archaic and inept religious autocracy that swathed him in mysticism and allowed him to plead his conscience as the final arbiter of Russian rule, Nicholas II came to the imperial throne with a self-fulfilling sense of impending doom. Unprepared for the onerous duties of his demanding office and lacking the necessary vision or strength of will to follow in the bold footsteps of his eighteenth-century ancestors, the last emperor of Russia played a game of captive rule, unwilling and unable to break free of the ponderous weight of the rotting dynasty as it collapsed on his shoulders. He surrendered to fate, *sudba*, the inexorable force that, in his passivity, he believed controlled his life. It was his ultimate tragedy—and Russia's misfortune—that he inflicted this personal weakness on an entire empire just as it reached its most crucial turning point.

Nicholas the inept ruler, the weak-willed husband, the brutal and authoritarian dictator who ruthlessly crushed the 1905 Revolution, the virulent anti-Semite, the passive observer of his empire's martyrdom—all of these historical truths have been subsumed by the romantic nostalgia that has increasingly come to view him not as Russia's last sovereign but as a man, a husband, and a father. The history of his reign has fallen victim to the story of his private life, unpleasant incidents and less than admirable characteristics ignored in favor of sentimental words, as Macauley argued in the case of Charles I, and vivid photographs that speak of a time and a place—and a family—that in reality never existed in the terms of which they are most frequently and lovingly evoked.

The entire world was changed as a result of Nicholas II's abdication and the subsequent rise of the Soviet Union. To many, something regarded as so intensely evil must, of necessity, have replaced its moral counterweight. The Ekaterinburg massacre transformed Nicholas II and his family into powerful symbols, evoked to this day by elements as diverse as the remnants of Russia's Communist Party to rabid monarchists and the Orthodox faithful in an eighty-five-year-old propaganda war. As a result, rumor has replaced fact, legend becomes enshrined as truth, and those involved in the final drama of the Romanovs are subsumed in a polarized mythology carefully crafted according to varied agendas.

Nicholas himself is largely responsible for the cult of devotees that surrounds his family. As shortsighted as he could be, in one respect Nicholas was far ahead of his contemporary monarchs: with an uncanny sense of the value of his own family, he eagerly offered them up as paragons of modern morality, waging a propaganda war that continues to this day. The idea of an imperial or royal family as living embodiments of national and moral virtue was, in his reign, relatively new. The only comparable model was in England, where Queen Victoria and Prince Albert had consciously embarked on a careful program to rehabilitate the tarnished image of the British royal family after the less-than-upright reigns of George IV and William IV. Their efforts helped transform the idea of a paternal monarchy into a familial one, where God, family, and country-bourgeois, middle-class values replaced the smart, intellectual amusements and fast manners and diversions of the previous generation. With Nicholas and Alexandra it was much the same; their values were solidly middle-class, if their own personal views were slightly reactionary. Alexandra, at least, was deeply suspicious of amusements, at anything that hinted at wasted time, at frivolity, and—with her prim moral sensibilities—at temptation and sin.

"The flamboyant domesticity of Nicholas I had made the home the model of service to state and nation," writes Richard Wortman. "Nicholas and Alexandra's life in the home, on the contrary, represented a haven from the demands of rule. But unlike his father, for whom the family was also a haven, Nicholas II made his domestic virtues a public sign of his supreme humanity. From the beginning of his reign Nicholas cultivated the image of himself as an ideal family man who doted on his children."[117]

The decision was deliberate and indicates, perhaps more than anything else, that Nicholas II, if neither the idiot described by Bolsheviks nor the decisive man encountered in émigré memoirs, was at the very least cunning. If he had lost control of Russia politically, been forced to grant the hated Duma, and bowed repeatedly to his wife's wishes, there was one area over which he still remained master: the presentation of his family to the nation and the world. Nor was he shy about using his family, especially his beautiful daughters and handsome young son, to evoke patriotism and loyalty to the throne. With his approval their faces smiled from hundreds of official photographs and postcards, creating a new cult of personality never before seen in Russia, and one that lasts to this day.

Two generations have passed since the Ekaterinburg murders. Yet somehow, the events of that night, and its victims, stand at the forefront of public interest. The inadequacies of Alexander III and Marie Feodorovna, which crushed their eldest son's character and crippled his chances of navigating the traumatic twentieth century, have been washed away in lovingly painted portraits of happy family life. Alexandra's determination to preserve the autocracy for her only son has been forgiven by extending sympathy for her all-too-human plight. The marked immaturity and bad behavior of the tsesarevich fall away when compared to his horrible pain and suffering. The sad and thwarted lives of the four grand duchesses, made difficult by their cloistered existence and domineering mother, disappear in the haze of revolver smoke that enveloped their last minutes in the Ipatiev House. The resonance of the ultimate fate of the last Russian imperial family has stripped them of their humanity, shrouded them in mystical mantles, and washed from the faces that now adorn icons any trace of reality. Perversely, in death, the once-despised emperor and his family have become all things to all people, embodying romance, sentiment, nostalgia, national pride, religion, and myth. This is the true fate of the Romanovs.

Ekaterinburg Guards

Members of the Special Detachment Guarding the House of Special Purpose

Alexeiev, Alexander Kronidovich. Signed May 11, from the Syssert factory.

Belogoik, Semyon.

Belomoinov, Semyon Nikolaievich. Signed May 11, from the Syssert factory. Bolshevik Party member.

Brusyanin, Leonid. Signed May 30, from the Zlokazov factory.

Cherepanov. Signed May 11, from the Syssert factory. No party affiliation.

Churkin, Alexei Ivanovich (1897–1919). Signed May 11, from the Syssert factory. Member of the Bolshevik Party. Killed in a Red Army battle in the Caucasus.

Deryabin, Nikita. Signed May 30, from the Zlokazov factory.

Dimitriev, Semyon. Signed May 30, from the Zlokazov factory.

Dobrynin, Konstantin Stepanovich (1896–1920). Signed May 11, from the Syssert factory. Bolshevik Party member. Died January 1920 while engaged in the political section of the Third Army in Ekaterinburg.

Droyadov (or Drozdov, Droydov), Igor Alexeievich. Signed May 11, from the Syssert factory.

Emiliyanov, Feodor Vassilievich (1898–?). Signed May 11, from the Syssert factory. Bolshevik Party member. Still living in Syssert in 1934.

Fomin. Signed May 30, from the Zlokazov factory.

Gonshkevich (or Gonihkevich), Vassili. Signed June 11, from the Zlokazov factory.

Kabanov, Alexei Gregorievich. Signed July 8, from Verkh-Isetsk.

Kabanov, Michael Gregorievich. Signed July 8, from Verkh-Isetsk.

Khokryakov, Philip Polievich.

Khokryakov, Stephan. Signed from the Zlokazov factory.

Kissarev, Gregory Alexandrovich. Signed May 11, from the Syssert factory.

Kleshchev, Ivan Nicholaievich. Signed May 11, from the Syssert factory.

Komendantov. Signed June 11, from the Zlokazov factory.

Koryakin. Signed June 11, from the Zlokazov factory.

Kotchenkov, Prokopy.

Kotegov, Alexander Alexeievich. Signed May 11, from the Syssert factory.

Kotegov, Ivan Pavlovich. Signed May 11, from the Syssert factory. Still living in Syssert in 1934.

Koterlov, Ivan.

Kotlov, Alexander.

Kotlov, Ivan.

Kotov, Michael Pavlovich. Signed May 11, from the Syssert factory. Bolshevik Party member.

Korzukhin, Alexander. Signed from the Zlokazov factory.

Krashennikov. Signed June 11, from the Zlokazov factory.

Kscheshcheyev, Ivan. Signed from the Zlokazov factory.

Labishev (or Laboushev). Signed June 11, from the Zlokazov factory.

Lacher, Rudolf (1893–1974). Signed July 8, from Verkh-Isetsk.

Lepa, Adolf. Signed July 8, from Verkh-Isetsk. Commander of the "Lett" detachment.

Lesnikov, Gregory. Signed from the Zlokazov factory.

Letemin, Kuzma Ivanovich. Signed from the Syssert factory. Brother of Michael Letemin. No party affiliation.

Letemin, Michael Ivanovich. Signed May 11, from the Syssert factory. Brother of Kuzma Letemin. No party affiliation. Joined the Red Army in 1918. Remained in Ekaterinburg after it fell to Whites on July 25, 1918. Executed by Whites after interrogation.

Loginov, Ivan. Signed June 11, from the Zlokazov factory. Brother of Vassili Loginov and friend of Alexander Moshkin.

Loginov, Vassili. Signed June 11, from the Zlokazov factory. Brother of Ivan Loginov and friend of Alexander Moshkin.

Lygovoi, Victor Konstantinovich. Signed May 11, from the Syssert factory.

Lyukhanov, Valentin Sergeievich (1900–?). Signed June 11, from the Zlokazov factory. Son of Sergei Ivanovich Lyukhanov, official driver to the Ipatiev House.

Medvedev, Paul Spiridonovich. Signed May 11, from the Syssert factory. Senior guard commander at the Ipatiev House. Bolshevik Party member, Red Army member.

Mishkevich, Nicholas. Signed June 11, from the Zlokazov factory. Pole.

Mishkevich, Stanislaus. Signed June 11, from the Zlokazov factory. Pole.

Nadasyakov (or Nedoeshikov), Peter.

Netrebin, Victor Nikiforovich (1900–?). Signed July 8, from Verkh-Isetsk.

Nikiforov, Alexei Nikitavich. Signed May 11, from the Syssert factory.

Nodkorstov, Nicholas.

Orlov, Alexander Grigorievich (1899–1932). Signed May 11, from the Syssert factory. Bolshevik Party member.

Osokin, Alexander. Signed from the Zlokazov factory.

Pelegov, Vassili. Signed from the Zlokazov factory.

Permyakov, Ivan. Signed June 11, from the Zlokazov factory. Friend of Alexander Moshkin.

Petrov, Avksenti. Signed from the Zlokazov factory. Friend of Alexander Moshkin.

Petrov, Vassili. Signed June 11, from the Zlokazov factory. Friend of Alexander Moshkin.

Podkoryitov, Nicholas Ivanovich (1899–?). Signed May 11, from the Syssert factory. Bolshevik Party member.

Popov, Nicholas Ivanovich (1894–1919). Signed May 11, from the Syssert factory. Bolshevik Party member. Died while serving in the Red Army.

Prokhorov, Alexander. Signed from the Zlokazov factory.

Proskuryakov, Philip Poliektovich. Signed May 11, from the Syssert factory. No party affiliation. Arrested by Whites August 1918; imprisoned until 1920 in Irkutsk Prison.

Putilov, Nicholas. Signed from the Zlokazov factory.

Romanov, Ivan. Signed from the Zlokazov factory.

Rysakov (or Russakov), Nicholas Mikhailovich. Signed May 11, from the Syssert factory.

Sadchikov, Boris Viktorovich (1897–?). Signed May 11, from the Syssert factory.

Sadchikov, Nicholas Stepanovich (1897–1918). Signed May 11, from the Syssert factory. Committed suicide from depression.

Sadurov, Alexander Feodorovich (1901–?). Signed May 11, from the Syssert factory. No party affiliation. Youngest Ipatiev House guard; called "Kerensky" by fellow guards. From Ekaterinburg, still alive in 1934.

Safonov, Benjamin Yakovlevich. Signed May 11, from the Syssert factory. Bolshevik Party member. Jewish. Injured in 1931 in streetcar accident in Sverdlovsk when hand ripped off; still living in Sverdlovsk in 1934.

Semyonov, Vassili Igorovich. Signed May 11, from the Syssert factory.

Shevelev, Semyon Stepanovich. Signed May 11, from the Syssert factory. Bolshevik Party member.

Shulin, Ivan. Signed June 11, from the Zlokazov factory. Friend of Alexander Moshkin.

Sidorov, Alexei. Signed June 11, from the Zlokazov factory. Friend of Alexander Moshkin.

Skorokhodov, Ivan. Signed June 11, from the Zlokazov factory. Expelled from Ipatiev House on June 28.

Smorodyakov, Alexander. Signed from the Zlokazov factory. Brother of Michael Smorodyakov.

Smorodyakov, Michael. Signed June 11, from the Zlokazov factory. Brother of Alexander Smorodyakov and friend of Alexander Moshkin.

Soames. Signed July 8, from Verkh-Isetsk.

Soloviev, Alexander. Signed June 11, from the Zlokazov factory. Friend of Alexander Moshkin.

Starkov, Andrei Semyonovich. Signed June 11, from the Syssert factory. No party affiliation. Father of Ivan Starkov; oldest member of the guard at the Ipatiev House. Hired to replace Kotegov as cook for the detachment. Shot in the leg and had amputation in the Civil War. Still living in Syssert in 1934.

Starkov, Ivan Andreievich. Signed May 11, from the Syssert factory. Bolshevik Party member. Red Army soldier; previously served on Dutov Front. After the fall of Ekaterinburg he served in the Red Army. Captured 1918 by Whites, made to dig own grave then stabbed to death by White officers with sabers.

Stolov, Igor Alexeievich. Signed May 11, from the Syssert factory.

Strekotin, Alexander Andreievich (1897–?). Signed May 11, from the Syssert factory. No party affiliation in 1918. As of 1934 still alive in Rayon Sarabulsk, working as manager at the Riskolnikov machine tractor station.

Strekotin, Andrei Andreievich (1891–1918). Signed May 11, from the Syssert factory. Bolshevik Party member. Brother of Alexander Strekotin. Captured August 1918 while fighting in the Civil War. Killed by Whites, body thrown into mine shaft, recovered and reburied in 1919.

Talanov, Konstantin.

Talapov, Ivan Semyonovich (1900–1920). Signed May 11, from the Syssert factory. Bolshevik Party member. Died while fighting in Kronstadt putsch, 1920.

Tetkin, Roman Ivanovich. Signed May 11, from the Syssert factory.

Turigin, Semyon Mikhailovich (1899–?). Signed May 11, from the Syssert factory. Bolshevik Party member.

Ukraintsev, Alexander. Signed June 11, from the Zlokazov factory.

Ukraintsev, Konstantin Ivanovich. First assistant to Alexander Avdayev; probably from the Zlokazov factory. Married to the sister-in-law of a local engineer named Kormouchkin.

Ustinov, Alexander. Signed from the Zlokazov factory.

Varakushev, Alexander. Signed from the Zlokazov factory.

Verhas, Andras. Signed July 8, from Verkh-Isetsk.

Vyatkin, Paul Grigorievich. Signed from the Zlokazovv factory or the Syssert factory.

Vyatkin, Stephan Grigorievich. Signed May 11, from the Syssert factory. Brother of Paul Vyatkin. Bolshevik Party member.

Yakimov, Anatoly Alexandrovich. Signed June 11, from the Zlokazov factory. No party affiliation.
Zaitsev, Nicholas Stepanovich (?–1918). Signed May 11, from the Syssert factory. No party affiliation. Killed serving in the Red Army in 1918.

Ermakov's Verkh-Isetsk Contingent

Bolotov, Alexander
Desyatov, Gregory
Grydin, Alexei
Guskin
Kamayev
Kazantsev, Nicholas
Kostoysov, Alexander
Kurilov, Michael
Kurilov, Vassili
Levatnikh, Vassili
Medvedev, Alexander
Oreshkin, Kapiton
Perin, Ilya
Prosvernin, Ivan
Puzanov, Peter
Puzanov, Serge
Shadrin, Michael
Shalin, Igor
Skorynin, Igor
Sorokin, Michael
Tretyakov, Polycarp
Vaganov, Stephan
Vaganov, Victor
Yaroslavtsev, Peter
Zaishutsin, Ivan[1]

Inventory of Romanov Possessions in Ekaterinburg

Nametkin's complete inventory of the Ipatiev House and those objects that had belonged to the Romanovs is reproduced below. His inventory divided the objects he found at the Ipatiev House into several classifications.

In the stoves, he listed:

1 mauve silk Fabergé jewel case, lined in satin
Pieces of black hemming
1 brown leather coin purse
Pieces of a tissue container
Pieces of a tissue with brass rings
Portions of a lady's garter that had been burned
A burned iron buckle
1 lid for a small box
1 bronze handle
Fragments of an icon, burned
1 sheet of writing paper, on which was written "Sednev," "nostalgia," "grief," and "terrible"
Parts of a bronze box
Rib from a wall calendar
A vial of yellow glass
6 glass fragments
1 burned toothbrush
1 bronze charger
3 porcelain fragments
Portions of an artificial flower
1 small glass vial
3 pieces of burned fabric
Burned portion of epaulette braid with monogram "N. II"
1 box with gramophone needles
1 porcelain pin container
Fragments of a nailbrush
Burned pieces of iron
Pieces of burned dominoes

2 locks
Fragments of a metal picture frame
Fragments of porcelain and glass objects
2 metal candlesticks
1 belt buckle
Burned rib from a corset
Burned metal back from a calendar
2 sets of tongs
1 thimble
2 burned hooks
Fragments of nails
A burned mesh strainer
Hairpins
A partially burned wooden lid to a box
1 small porcelain box
Portions of a man's toilette kit
Burned portions of several ladies' handbags
Portions of small metal picture frames
4 metal belt buckles
6 metal box lids
Fragments of a handle
1 key
1 button from a lady's glove
Fragments of a small lamp
Parts of an air mattress
1 box with buttons
2 glass crosses
Knitting needles
Fragments of gold, melted
Fragments of wooden brushes
4 revolver cartridges from a Nagant revolver

Ormolu mounts
1 small black purse
1 lady's handkerchief
Portions of a burned playing card
Burned pieces of fabric
Fragments of thread and gold braid
A burned metal medallion
The cockade from an officer's hat
2 metal plates
4 men's buckles
6 military buttons crested with double-
    headed eagles
3 glass buttons
Fragments of buttons in mother-of-pearl
Parts of a man's shoe
Fragments from ladies' stockings

In the rubbish pit of the Ipatiev House, Nametkin found:

4 wooden icons
1 white blouse
1 cambric handkerchief, white
1 black silk purse
1 black moire ribbon from the Order of
    St. Vladimir
Fragment of pink silk ribbon
1 ribbon from the Order of St. George
Fragments of gold braid
9 glass bottles
Fragments of a brown purse
A glass vial containing cosmetics
1 oval picture frame
Fragments of a metal frame
2 small gold lockets.
Fragment of a *nécessaire*
1 tube of ointment
1 bottle filled with powder
1 lip to a metal soap box
1 metal jar
Fragments of a teacup
Fragments from various medicine and
    scent bottles
4 pewter miniature boats
1 pewter cavalry figure
1 cameo depicting a female in profile
1 5-kopeck coin
6 charred wooden building blocks

1 soup tureen cover
1 metal thimble

In the stoves of the Popov House, across Voznesensky Lane, Nametkin found the following objects:

1 wooden icon of Christ, inscribed on
    the reverse in the empress's hand,
    "Christ is Risen, March 25, 1912,
    Livadia"
3 cartridges of Kodak film
3 metal nameplates, 1 engraved with
    monogram "A. F."
1 cardboard box with ten slides[1]

The following is a list of items that belonged to the imperial family and that were discovered in the possession of former Ipatiev House guard Michael Letemin:

Camera
Box with 16 glass negative plates
Box with 17 glass negative plates
Diary for 1917 inscribed "To My Dear
    Alexei from Yr. Mama, Tsarskoye
    Selo"
An account book
Yellow metal cross with the image of St.
    Alexei on one side and Jesus Christ on
    the other, probably gold
Silver cross with inscription "St.
    Pimeon's"
Icon of St. Alexei of Moscow, in silver
    frame decorated with jewels
Shell rosary
Glass tureen
2 small buckles in jeweled silver frames
Vial with small quantity of perfume
Metal thermometer
2 oil lamps
2 wax candles
1 spirit lamp
2 pair scissors
1 empty vial

2 small buttons with imperial crest
6 black buttons
4 small buttons with diamonds
1 light-colored button
1 pepper cellar
1 ball of white thread
1 black pen set
2 scraps of paper, with needles
1 box with 8 electric lamps
1 small birch bark box with flour
1 small pillow with pins
1 broken mirror
1 clasp penknife, for opening envelopes
1 traveling box, with ormolu mounts on
   corners
1 knapsack, with yellow leather corners
1 broken metal knife
1 pair of white gloves
1 glass soap dish
1 can with fruit drops
11 big white envelopes
3 small envelopes
1 brass bell
1 can with small holes
1 tea glass
2 small envelopes
1 pair of steel tongs
1 red pencil
1 toothbrush
1 hairbrush
1 paintbrush
1 gumbrush
1 man's comb
1 box with wicks
1 silver spirit lamp
1 glass jar
1 tin lid
1 lady's black silk umbrella with ebony
   handle and silver grasp
1 porcelain jar
1 tea glass and two tea saucers
2 small plates
1 faience cover
2 padlocks with four keys
1 empty tin box
1 tin box with rice
1 linen shirtfront with imperial crest
1 man's unbleached linen shirt
1 velvet tablecloth with red tassels

1 unbleached sheet with a mark cleaned
   out
1 cambric sheet with mark and crown
   over numbers "72/95"
1 thin silk violet pillow with a bow in the
   middle
1 feather pillow with 3 cases, upper of
   white cambric with crested "A. F.,"
   second of pink silk
1 white knitted tablecloth
1 thin white knitted tablecloth
1 small lace doily
1 white lace piece
4 white knitted tablecloths
4 small knitted tablecloths
1 crimson knitted tablecloth
1 unstitched white linen pillowcase
1 white linen cover for pillow with lace
1 small lace doily
1 pair men's black lace-up boots
1 pair lady's cream-colored shoes, one
   marked "M"
1 leather belt
2 little caps
1 wooden box with 23 metal toys
1 notebook, within a note with address
   "142 Kuznechnaya Street, Vasse
   Stepanovna Isakovoi"
1 note in form of a will: "After my death
   hand over all the items below to my
   two brothers," altogether 8 lines
9 porcelain plates
Joy, Alexei's purebred male spaniel,
   brown with white spots[2]

Letemin's brother and fellow Ipatiev House guard, Kuzma, also was found in possession of seven toys that had belonged to the tsesarevich, which Kuzma said he had received from his brother.[3]

The following items were discovered by the investigators during a search of the house of Ipatiev House guard Paul Medvedev:

3 pairs of gray gloves
A compass
An unwound bandage
2 cufflinks
1 silver ring with blue enamel face
1 silver ring with black enamel face
1 linen napkin
1 pair of wool socks
1 red Moroccan leather notebook
1 travel case of yellow leather[4]

At the house of Ivan Starkov, the White investigators discovered the following items from the Ipatiev House:

A bottle of scent
A file with wooden handle
2 red wax candles
3 forks
1 thermometer
1 small wooden box
1 small wooden frame holding a water-color of the imperial yacht *Standart*
4 handkerchiefs of white cambric from which the monograms had been cut
1 picture frame covered in mauve leather
2 picture frames of blue Moroccan leather
1 picture frame covered in gold filigree-work
1 pair of tweezers with ebony handle[5]

At the house of Peter Lyluv, treasurer of the Ekaterinburg Soviet, White investigators discovered the following items:

1 pencil encased in mauve enamel, engraved with "A. F." and "1915"
1 picture frame, green glass
1 picture frame, pearl enamel with rose garlands
1 green enamel box with powder
1 picture frame, bronze, crested with laurel wreaths
1 gold wedding band

1 enameled hatpin, with stone missing
8 gold medallions
1 gold locket engraved "February 6, 1875" containing lock of Nicholas II's baby hair
1 small silver crucifix
1 small gold cross
1 atomizer
3 pieces of soap
1 white silk parasol with ivory handle and jasper and gold mounts
1 black silk parasol with silver handle and mounts
4 small combs
4 gold trinkets from a charm bracelet
4 bottles of varied cosmetics
1 gold necklace with 3 crosses
1 small cross, in gold
3 gold medallions with the image of Christ
3 silk bodices
1 silk bodice with mother-of-pearl buttons
1 silk bodice, boned
1 silk bodice, the bones removed
1 piece of white silk moiré
1 length of white madapolam fabric
1 umbrella, white linen
3 silk corsets in blue, cream, and pink
1 small white porcelain Easter egg with "N. II"
1 small black brooch
2 sofa cushions
1 long bolster for a sofa—one side chamois, the other satin
1 small oil lamp
4 birch knitting needles
2 medicine bottles labeled "Court Pharmacy"
14 white linen table napkins with monogram "N" and sewn with the imperial crown
1 dress of light gray, with matching jacket
1 icon of St. John the Baptist
56 rolls of silk thread, in various colors
1 bodice in gray, with striped gray silk cuffs and collars
1 skirt and matching bodice, in gray cambric
1 long jacket, white linen

1 lady's traveling costume in white wool
1 lady's jacket, white wool
1 lady's blouse, white silk
1 man's silk shirt, white
1 lady's pleated skirt, light gray
1 lady's muslin skirt, white
1 lady's blouse, gray silk
3 ladies' underskirts, black silk
3 ladies' underskirts, white cambric
1 lady's bodice, black linen
1 lady's summer costume, cambric, light
    blue
1 lady's fur hat
1 lady's skirt, gray wool
1 lady's skirt, white linen
1 lady's blouse, white linen
1 lady's skirt, pleated
1 lining of a dress coat, white cambric
2 ladies' dresses, dark cambric
1 lady's blouse, linen
1 lady's bodice, mint green silk
1 lady's bodice, pink sink
Parts of a waistband in silk
Edging from a lady's skirt in silk
4 ladies' bodices in muslin
1 lady's bodice, green silk
1 lady's dress in mauve velvet, with
    matching jacket
1 lady's camisole, in silk with mother-of-
    pearl buttons
1 lady's skirt panel, white wool
1 tablecloth, white linen
1 white scarf in gauze
2 silk shawls, multicolored, with
    Oriental designs
3 tulle veils, white
1 black silk scarf
1 lady's belt, white silk
1 silk scarf with Oriental designs
1 piece of yellow silk moiré
1 pair of lady's stockings, black silk
1 pair of lady's stockings, white
2 silk bands, embroidered with blue flo-
    ral designs
1 white silk scarf
Portions of a shirt in mauve silk
Spools of mauve, blue, and gray silk
    ribbon
1 silk blanket lined with fur
1 piece of yellow silk embroidery,
    unfinished

1 pair of lady's house slippers covered in
    lace
1 sofa cushion cover, silk
1 eiderdown
1 bolster embroidered with lace
1 linen pillowcase
1 lady's sweater, brown wool
1 man's shirt
1 man's shirt, brown pinstripes
1 pair man's socks, gray wool
1 man's vest, gray with black pinstripes
1 sewn bedspread embroidered with
    lace[6]

The following is a list of the imperial family's belongings packed by
members of the interior guard at
the Ipatiev House and shipped
from Ekaterinburg to Moscow:

Clothing:

2 silk dresses, gray
1 wool dress, gray
3 wool dresses, blue
4 silk jackets, knitted
1 knitted skirt, red
2 silk blouses, brown
2 dresses, lilac
3 dresses, white
4 cashmere dresses, various colors
3 midlength dresses, blue silk
1 formal evening gown, mauve silk and
    velvet
1 formal evening gown, brown silk sewn
    with pearls
2 ladies' summer traveling suits, white
    cotton
1 lady's cotton jacket, blue
4 ladies' skirts, brown
2 ladies' skirts, blue
2 ladies' skirts, white
4 ladies' blouses, white silk
4 ladies' short jackets, dark blue
2 ladies' skirts, gray crepe
3 pairs ladies' undergarments, white
2 pairs ladies' undergarments, pink
11 pairs ladies' stockings, white

1 lady's night dress, white cambric
2 ladies' night dresses, fine white cambric
3 ladies' camisoles, white and pink cambric
1 man's shirt, white with pearl buttons
1 man's shirt, brown, with bone buttons
3 pairs men's long underwear, white, marked "Jaeger" and "N. II"
2 men's undershirts, white cotton
4 pair assorted men's underwear, white
11 pair men's socks, various colors
2 men's bathrobes, silk brocade and velvet
1 pair of trousers, black
2 pair men's trousers, white canvas
1 Circassian caftan, gray
1 guard's jacket, khaki
1 pair of trousers, khaki
1 Circassian caftan, crimson
1 Circassian caftan, white
1 Circassian caftan, cream
1 Circassian caftan, blue
1 soldier's tunic, beige
1 pair of trousers, khaki
1 silk shirt, crimson
1 Circassian caftan, crimson
1 pair of cloth trousers, khaki
2 pairs of trousers, blue
1 pair of braided trousers, black
1 bathrobe, blue
14 pairs of summer sailors' trousers, white
4 sailors' shirts, white-and-blue-striped
2 summer canvas outfits, white
2 dresses trimmed in sable, crimson

Coats, cloaks, hats, and muffs:

8 sable muffs
2 soldiers' tunics
4 large astrakhan fur jackets
4 sealskin hats
3 astrakhan fur hats
8 ermine muffs
2 beaver caps
4 velvet caps trimmed with lamb's wool
2 sable collars
4 ermine collars
5 sable wraps
2 boas, white

2 lamb's wool mufflers, gray
1 feather boa, gray
2 astrakhan fur muffs
3 sable fur boas
1 astrakhan fur hat
1 rabbitskin fur hat
4 ermine boas
1 man's gray sheepskin hat
3 down muffs, gray
3 velvet muffs, gray
1 felt coat, black
2 military cadets' greatcoats, black
Officer's greatcoat, gray
1 cloth cloak, black
1 flannel sailor's jacket, black
1 guard's jacket, khaki
1 sheepskin papakha, gray
1 Astrakhan papakha, gray
1 lambskin papakha, white with gold braid
1 lambskin papakha, black with red trim
1 Cossack cloak, crimson

Clothing accessories, shoes, gloves, and fans:

2 silver belt buckles studded with pearls
1 gold belt buckle studded with uncut diamonds
1 lady's shoe, crimson silk
2 pairs ladies' shoes, blue silk
3 pairs ladies' shoes, suede
1 lady's shoe, bronze silk
3 pairs ladies' shoes, white silk
4 pairs military boots, black leather
1 child's military boot, black leather
2 pairs ladies' shoes, white cloth
9 pairs ladies' gloves, kid
2 pairs ladies' gloves, doeskin
1 lady's fan, painted
1 lady's fan, broken
2 parasols, white cloth with silver-gilt handles
1 umbrella, black with ivory handle

Vases and housewares:

7 faience vases
4 silver vases
2 small colored-glass vases marked "M. B."

1 large Chinese vase
4 ivory vases with bas-reliefs
2 small crystal vases
1 white sheepskin lap rug
1 knitted blanket
1 blanket, sewn with "Ataman" in Cyrillic
1 cotton blanket, beige
4 embroidered bedspreads, various colors
1 small silver inkpot
1 silver matchbox
1 tape measure in silver case
1 thermometer
1 silver box
1 small oil lantern
1 silver washbasin

Picture frames, decorative objects, and photographic materials:

1 enamel frame containing a portrait of Alexandra
1 enamel frame containing a portrait of Marie Feodorovna
1 enamel frame containing a portrait of the imperial family
1 enamel frame, round
1 enamel frame, round, with gold border
1 round frame in shape of a heart
1 white enamel frame, round
1 enamel frame, round
1 gold frame, round
1 gold frame composed of four linked ovals
1 silver frame with mirror
9 small picture frames, silver
3 large picture frames, silver
2 large picture frames, ormolu
2 small Fabergé picture frames, ormolu with diamonds and pearls
7 wooden picture frames
2 small Karelian birch picture frames
1 oval picture frame, engraved gold
1 ebony picture frame with tortoiseshell mounts
3 connected picture frames, gilt and ivory
3 red Moroccan leather photograph albums

13 blue Moroccan leather photograph albums
2 cloth-covered scrapbooks

Toiletries:

15 vials and bottles with silver lids, 5 with monogram "T. N." and 10 with monogram "A. F."
1 powder case
1 silver button-fastener for gloves
1 toothbrush
1 pestle
1 silver-plated soap dish with monogram "T. N."
1 spirit lamp and hair tongs with monogram "T. N."
2 hairbrushes with monogram "A. F."
1 silver case containing comb
1 silver case for pomade
1 silver and ivory manicure set
2 silver toilet sets, each composed of 17 separate pieces
1 silver toilet box with engraved gilt cover
1 perfume vial
1 fastening hook for shoes

Kitchenwares:

2 porcelain trays, handpainted
11 porcelain dinner plates, with monogram "N. II" and painted with decorative scenes
9 matching porcelain cups and saucers with gilt edges, marked "Tsarskoye Selo"
2 large silver carving knives with imperial crest
9 large porcelain bowls in various colors
3 small porcelain bowls with applied floral motifs in various colors
8 gilt chargers
6 crystal tumblers etched with imperial crest
4 tall crystal tumblers etched with imperial crest
1 blue wineglass with silver mounts
3 etched crystal wineglasses with imperial crest
17 assorted crystal glasses
1 ladle, silver, with broken handle

1 silver funnel
3 silver coffeepots
1 silver spoon
11 silver teapots
15 silver sugar bowls
1 silver pitcher, large
2 silver cream jugs
4 silver milk jugs
13 silver trays
3 large silver ladles
9 silver tea strainers
4 silver sugar tongs
1 small silver teapot with monogram "A. F."
1 small silver sugar basin with monogram "A. F."
1 small silver cream jug with monogram "A. F."
1 silver drinking cup
1 small silver cup
1 silver napkin ring
6 silver dessert spoons
2 silver biscuit dishes
1 silver teaspoon

Desk accessories:

1 silver desk clock engraved with date "1894"
1 small coach clock, silver
1 gold letter opener with enamel handle
1 notebook with gold pencil attached
3 silver inkwells
2 fountain pens in ormolu mounts
1 silver pencil sharpener
1 silver blotter
1 baize blotting pad
Mauve and cream crested writing paper and envelopes
1 small knife, metal
Various pencils and pens, some silver, gold, or mother-of-pearl
2 silver candlesticks with monogram "A. F."

1 silver inkwell with gold filigree lid
1 silver basket for visiting cards
1 silver, three-cornered ashtray, engraved "Sevastopol, cruiser *Mockba*, May 6, 1886"
1 silver ashtray engraved with autographs of the family of Alexander III

Miscellaneous items:

1 ormolu Romanov double-headed eagle monogram
1 gold cross with small icon attached
30 gold chains, mementos, and other items
1 icon, in silver frame
2 silver crosses
1 gold chain with enamel portrait
3 small gold plaques, engraved
1 cross, bronze
1 travel clock, folding, in blue enamel case
1 pocket watch with gold case
1 gold cigar case engraved with arms of the Order of St. Andrew
1 gold cigar case engraved "Livadia, November 14, 1911, Alix"
1 gold cigar case set with ruby and mounted with sapphire lock, engraved "1903"
2 small assorted pieces of silver
1 folding icon in a red enamel case
1 small wooden whistle
2 spirit lamps
1 case filled with needlework
1 box containing diaries and letters of Nicholas II; Alexandra; Tsesarevich Alexei; the four grand duchesses; and correspondence from Rasputin
1 large wooden chest marked with Romanov double-headed eagle and containing personal correspondence of the Romanovs and letters from various relatives[7]

The Romanovs' Jewels

The following is a list of the Romanovs' jewels taken by the imperial family when they left Tsarskoye Selo and later recovered by the Soviets. All were hidden in and around Tobolsk and were dispersed by the Romanovs for safekeeping before they left for Ekaterinburg:

Diamond brooch, 100 carats, valued at 1,200,000 rubles (£3,600,000, or $5,868,000 in 2002 currency)

Diamond crescent with 5 large diamonds of up to 70 carats each, valued at 310,000 rubles (£930,000, or $1,515,900)

2 Diamond hatpins, 36 carats each, valued at 350,000 rubles each (£1,050,000, or $1,711,500)

Diamond pin, 44 carats, valued at 700,000 rubles (£2,100,000, or $3,423,000)

Diamond necklace, pearl and ruby pendants, valued at 50,000 rubles (£150,000, or $244,500)

Emperor's diamond monogram with 8-carat diamond, valued at 22,000 rubles (£66,000, or $107,580)

2 Diamond hairpins, valued at 3,500 rubles each (£21,000, or $34,230)

2 Diamond bow brooches, valued at 3,000 rubles each (£18,000, or $29,340)

Diamond brooch, with pearls, valued at 8,000 rubles (£24,000, or $39,120)

2 hairpins of pearls and diamonds, valued at 10,000 rubles each (£60,000, or $97,800)

Diamond tiara with 8-carat central diamond, other smaller side diamonds, and other smaller diamonds, valued at 25,000 rubles (£75,000, or $122,250)

Diamond tiara with pearls, valued at 25,000 rubles (£75,000, or $122,250)

Diamond tiara, studded with kunzite stones, valued at 2,000 rubles (£6,000, or $9,780)

Diamond tiara, with almandin stones, valued at 5,000 rubles (£15,000, or $24,450)

Diamond tiara, with turquoises, valued at 7,500 rubles (£22,500, or $36,675)

Diamond hairpin, valued at 1,000 rubles (£3,000, or $4,890)

5 diamond medallions, valued at 5,000 rubles each (£15,000, or $24,450)

2 panagias, valued at 2,000 rubles each (£12,000, or $19,560)

2 panagias, valued at 1,000 rubles each (£6,000, or $9,780)

Pendant, with diamonds, valued at 9,500 rubles (£28,500, or $46,455)

Brooch with diamonds, valued at 1,500 rubles (£4,500, or $7,335)

Gold chain with emeralds, valued at 3,000 rubles (£10,500, or $17,115)

Ornament with pearl and diamond pendants, valued at 2,500 rubles (£7,500, or $12,225)

Ornament with pearls and small trinkets, valued at 1,500 rubles (£4,500, or $7,335)

Pendant with medallions, roses, and pearls, valued at 1,500 rubles (£4,500, or $7,335)

Gold chain, with small turquoise and trinkets, valued at 120 rubles (£360, or $587)

Twisted chain with petals of gold and diamonds, valued at 150 rubles (£450, or $734)

Gold chain with emerald drops, pearls, and diamonds, valued at 250 rubles (£750, or $1,223)

Gold chain with amethyst cabochon and pendants, valued at 150 rubles (£450, or $734)

Ornament with small medallions and pendants, valued at 200 rubles (£600, or $978)

Ornament with large pearl, turquoise, and trinkets, valued at 150 rubles (£450, or $734)

Lady's waistband with amethyst and moonstone, valued at 100 rubles (£300, or $489)

Lady's enamel watch with gold chain, valued at 50 rubles (£150, or $245)

Lady's watch with monogram "T. N." valued at 50 rubles (£150, or $245)

Gold necklace with bell trinkets, valued at 50 rubles (£150, or $245)

Gold necklace with pearls, valued at 150 rubles (£450, or $734)

Gold necklace with aquamarines, diamonds, and pearls, valued at 2,500 rubles (£7,500, or $12,225)

Pendant with diamond portrait and small pearl chain, valued at 2,500 rubles (£7,500, or $12,225)

Pendant with a 5-carat diamond, amethyst, and a pearl weave, valued at 6,000 rubles (£18,000, or $29,340)

Brooch with diamond and beryl, valued at 2,000 rubles (£6,000, or $9,780)

Necklace with small diamonds and amethysts, valued at 1,200 rubles (£3,600, or $5,868)

Bracelet with diamonds and amethysts, valued at 800 rubles (£2,400, or $3,912)

Pendant with chain of diamonds and kunzite stones, valued at 600 rubles (£1,800, or $2,934)

Pendant with platinum chain with shorls and chrysoprases, valued at 150 rubles (£450, or $734)

Diamond band, valued at 600 rubles (£1,800, or $2,934)

Pendant with gold chain and four small gold bells, valued at 200 rubles (£600, or $978)

Cross with pearls and emeralds, valued at 100 rubles (£300, or $489)

9 pendants with platinum chains, valued at 100 rubles each (£2,700, or $4,401)

Pendant with handing cross and mounted gems, valued at 700 rubles (£2,100, or $3,423)

Brooch in form of twigs studded with diamonds and aquamarines, valued at 800 rubles (£2,400, or $3,912)

4 hairpins with small diamonds, valued at 250 rubles each (£3,000, or $4,890)

Watch in bracelet with diamonds, valued at 200 rubles (£600, or $978)

Anchor-shaped pin with diamonds, valued at 300 rubles (£900, or $1,467)

Pendant with moonstones, valued at 80 rubles (£240, or $391)

Pendant studded with diamonds and aquamarines, valued at 100 rubles (£300, or $489)

Pendant with small diamond and aquamarine, valued at 120 rubles (£360, or $587)

Pendant, globe with shorls, with diamonds, valued at 130 rubles (£390, or $636)

Aquamarine trinket, valued at 40 rubles (£120, or $196)

3 studs with moonstones, valued at 10 rubles each (£30, or $49)

Small trinket with agate, valued at 20 rubles (£60, or $98)

Small trinket with lily of the valley in moonstone, valued at 15 rubles (£45, or $73)

Small trinket studded with diamonds, valued at 80 rubles (£240, or $391)

Small trinket with diamonds and an amethyst, valued at 60 rubles (£180, or $293)

2 studs with diamonds, valued at 35 rubles each (£2,100, or $3,423)

Platinum trinket, dated 1912, valued at 20 rubles (£60, or $98)

Cross with aquamarine, valued at 40 rubles (£120, or $196)

4 national brooches, valued at 5 rubles each (£60, or $98)

Brooch with swastika, valued at 5 rubles (£15, or $24)

Metal brooch shaped like swastika, valued at 15 rubles (£45, or $73)

Trinket with swastika, valued at 2 rubles (£6, or $9.70)

2 trinkets with monogram "T," valued at 5 rubles each (£30, or $49)

Trinket with monogram "A. F," valued at 5 rubles (£15, or $24)

3 silver pendants with monograms, valued in total at 5 rubles (£15, or $24)

3 pins, valued at 2 rubles each (£18, or $29.34)

Trinket with roses and rubies, valued at 30 rubles (£90, or $147)

2 Red Cross medallions, valued at 2.5 rubles each (£15, or $24.45)

Gold pencil with pearl, valued at 15 rubles (£45, or $73)

Trinket with monogram and sapphire, valued at 10 rubles (£30, or $49)

Gold coin of 7 rubles, 50 kopecks (£22.50, or $37)

Gold cross with alexandrite, valued at 5 rubles (£15, or $24)

2 gold trinkets, valued at 5 rubles each (£30, or $49)

Pendant with emerald bas-relief of woman, with diamonds, valued at 7,000 rubles (£21,000, or $34,230)

Pearl pinhead studded with diamonds, valued at 2,000 rubles (£6,000, or $9,780)

3 pearl pendants, valued at 1,200 rubles each (£3,600, or $5,868)

Brooch of gems and diamonds, valued at 2,500 rubles (£7,500, or $12,225)

Brooch with gem of golden rock crystal with diamonds, valued at 2,000 rubles (£6,000, or $9,780)

Brooch of aquamarine studded with diamonds and roses, valued at 800 rubles (£2,400, or $3,912)

Oval brooch of aquamarines studded with uncut diamonds, valued at 800 rubles (£2,400, or $3,912)

Pendant of amethyst and diamonds, valued at 700 rubles (£2,100, or $3,423)

Aquamarine brooch with diamond rim, valued at 200 rubles (£600, or $978)

Brooch of aquamarine, triangle-shaped with diamonds, valued at 300 rubles (£900, or $1,467)

Brooch with emerald, ellipse-shaped, studded with diamonds, valued at 300 rubles (£900, or $1,467)

Brooch of agate and small diamonds, valued at 100 rubles (£300, or $489)

Brooch of zetrin, studded with diamonds, valued at 120 rubles (£360, or $587)

Brooch of amethyst with diamonds and 2 pearls, valued at 250 rubles (£750, or $1,223)

Brooch with amethyst and studded with diamonds, valued at 200 rubles (£600, or $978)

Brooch of beryl with diamonds, valued at 150 rubles (£450, or $734)

Brooch of amethysts with marquis diamonds, valued at 400 rubles (£1,200, or $1,956)

Brooch with a moonstone in form of a small heart with diamonds, valued at 175 rubles (£525, or $856)

Pendant from small pearls, valued at 700 rubles (£2,100, or $3,423)

Brooch with emeralds and diamonds, valued at 500 rubles (£1,500, or $2,445)

2 amethyst brooches studded with diamonds, valued at 150 rubles each (£900, or $1,467)

Brooch with small ellipse-shaped aquamarine with diamonds, valued at 75 rubles (£225, or $367)

Brooch with square rubies and diamonds, valued at 250 rubles (£750, or $1,223)

Brooch with 3 small crowns with sapphires and garnets, valued at 120 rubles (£360, or $587)

Brooch with 4 moonstones studded with diamonds, valued at 75 rubles (£225, or $367)

Square brooch with an inner small crown with pearls and small diamonds, valued at 60 rubles (£180, or $293)

Brooch with two small clasps with amethyst and studded with diamonds, valued at 45 rubles (£135, or $220)

Brooch in form of cross with almandite gems and studded with diamonds, valued at 85 rubles (£255, or $416)

Brooch with agate, studded with small roses, valued at 40 rubles (£120, or $196)

2 brooches, with sapphires, valued at 15 rubles each (£90, or $147)

Brooch, round, enameled with small pearls and studded with diamonds, valued at 60 rubles (£180, or $293)

Brooch with shorl, valued at 20 rubles (£60, or $98)

Brooch with oblong aquamarine and roses, valued at 120 rubles (£360, or $587)

Brooch with 3 pendants, cornelian, garnet, and amethyst, valued at 60 rubles (£180, or $293)

Brooch with image of flag, valued at 3 rubles (£9, or $15)

Pendant with sapphire, diamonds, and uncut diamonds, valued at 175 rubles (£525, or $856)

Brooch with round aquamarine, valued at 300 rubles (£900, or $1,467)

Blue aquamarine, oval shape, valued at 300 rubles (£900, or $1,467)

Pendant of aquamarine in form of pear and studded with diamonds, valued at 180 rubles (£540, or $880)

Chain bracelet with 3 rubies and diamonds, valued at 2,500 rubles (£7,500, or $12,225)

Platinum bracelet with 3 aquamarines in form of a heart, and 2 kunzite stones, valued at 250 rubles (£750, or $1,223)

Bracelet with small emeralds cabochon, one pearl and studded with diamonds, valued at 50 rubles (£150, or $245)

Bracelet with 4 aquamarines, valued at 35 rubles (£105, or $171)

Bracelet with turquoises and studded with diamonds, valued at 50 rubles (£150, or $245)

Bracelet with agate, valued at 30 rubles (£90, or $147)

Bracelet with amethyst, valued at 55 rubles (£165, or $269)

Bracelet with 2 rubies, valued at 250 rubles (£750, or $1,223)

2 plain gold bracelets, valued at 10 rubles each (£60, or $98)

Bracelet of gold engraved "Alexandra," studded with uncut diamonds, valued at 500 rubles (£1,500, or $2,445)

Chain bracelet with trinket, 1914, valued at 10 rubles (£30, or $49)

2 iron bracelets, no value

Gold locket, valued at 5 rubles (£15, or $24)

2 decorations with emeralds and studded with diamonds, valued at 325 rubles each (£1,950, or $3,178)

Bracelet with diamonds and rubies, valued at 500 rubles (£1,500, or $2,445)

Bracelet with ruby, valued at 500 rubles (£1,500, or $2,445)

Bracelet with aquamarine with small uncut diamonds, valued at 50 rubles (£150, or $245)

Bracelet with 2 sapphires and diamond, valued at 75 rubles (£225, or $367)

Bracelet with agate and small uncut diamonds, valued at 20 rubles (£60, or $98)

Bracelet with diamonds, valued at 150 rubles (£450, or $734)

Waistband of small pearls with 11 big rubies, studded with diamonds and rubies, valued at 75,000 rubles (£225,000, or $366,750)

2 silver panagias with gold chain, valued at 200 rubles each (£1,200, or $1,956)

Silver panagia with gold chain and gems, valued at 300 rubles (£900, or $1,467)

Silver panagia with gems, valued at 100 rubles (£300, or $489)

Mother-of-pearl panagia with silver chain, valued at 50 rubles (£150, or $245)

Silver panagia with pearls, valued at 150 rubles (£450, or $734)

Silver panagia, valued at 25 rubles (£75, or $122)

3 crosses with gems, valued at 150 rubles each (£1,350, or $2,201)

Cross with gems, valued at 80 rubles (£240, or $391)

Cross with gems, valued at 75 rubles (£225, or $367)

Mother-of-pearl cross, valued at 25 rubles (£75, or $122)

Silver cross with gems, valued at 180 rubles (£540, or $880)

Gold chain with cross, valued at 100 rubles (£300, or $489)

5 small silver icons, no value[1]

Acknowledgments

This book began long before its two authors had even met, as we each researched and formulated our own separate accounts of the last days of the captivity and murders of the Romanovs. Thus, when we agreed in spring 2000 to join efforts and produce a joint book, we each brought to the project not only much material, but also those people who had assisted us individually throughout the years.

No book rests on the shoulders of the authors alone, and nowhere has this been truer than in the present work. This was a massive project, and we were fortunate to be able to draw on the talents and support of hundreds of people. Many worked on our behalf in various archives in Russia, Europe, and North America, searching out documents and attempting to verify their contents. Some of those we have interviewed and who have given us assistance have asked that we maintain their privacy, particularly when they spoke candidly or accessed sensitive or restricted archival material on our behalf. We have respected their wishes, but all involved in this work have our heartfelt gratitude.

We would like to thank HIH The Grand Duchess Maria Vladimirovna of Russia for taking time out of her busy schedule to assist us in our inquiries concerning the eventual fate of the human remains in the Sokolov box, and certain questions surrounding the 1998 Romanov funeral. Alexander Zakatov, secretary to Her Imperial Highness, provided helpful answers and offered information previously unavailable.

Those who have contributed to this book, supported its research, answered questions, and provided important materials to help in its completion include: David Adams; Bob Atchison; Thomas Berry; Lisa Davidson; Marlene Eilers; George Fedoroff; Julia Gelardi; Christine Harper; Andrew Hartsook; Dr. Neal Haskell; Gretchen and David Haskin; DeeAnn Hoff; Brien Horan; Ingrid Kane; John Kendrick; Paul Kulikovsky; Dr. Lowell Levine; Ian Lilburn; Thomas Mansfield; the late Dr. William Maples; Grant Menzies; Susanne Meslans; Ilana Miller; Ronald Moe; Greg Rittenhouse; Dr. William Rodriquez; Peter

Sarandinaki; Marilyn Swezey; Dr. Idris Traylor; David Vernall-Downes; and the late Dimitry Volkogonov. Many others, who must go unnamed, supported our efforts financially and emotionally, allowing us to access the materials that form this work. They all have our most grateful thanks.

In Germany, two individuals merit our most appreciative thanks. Professor Eckhart Franz and his staff at the Staatsarchiv in Darmstadt were uncompromisingly helpful in our research, providing us unfettered access to the unique treasures of the Hessian Royal Archives. They were all most encouraging and treated us with the greatest kindness and consideration. Producer Maurice Philip Remy, and his entire staff at MPR Productions in Munich, offered us their complete cooperation in examining MPR's extensive Romanov Archive, freely sharing important information and resources. A special thanks to the ever-helpful Ulrike Nieder-Vahrenholz, who did much to make our stay in Munich and our research at MPR Productions a memorable experience.

The list of those who have, over the years, been instrumental in assisting us in our work, either individually or together, is extensive, reflecting the collaborative nature of such an endeavor. In Russia we would like to thank Sergei Alfresnov; Alla Alimpieva; Ekaterina Ardischeva; Mikhail Balovnik; Pavel Bernstov; Irina Bevlisky; Peter Biflovskya; Ivan Bordunov; Nikolai and Xenia Botsugnev; Olga Burgieff; Igor Davidov; Lev Deminkin; Grigorii Denhovich; Aaron Dinsky; Yelizabeta Divlovsky; Tamara Efremov; Filipp Egremov; Georgi Elston; Ilya Emdachnov; Konstantin Endrokov; Alexander Eristov; Dimitry Faure; Lyudmilla Fenin; Max Fillipov; Alexandra Fillips; Irina Fomenko; Sergei Fratskaya; Artur and Katia Fromelov; Vassili Gendrikoff; Ludwig Grossmann; Evgeni Iakovlev; Pavel Ignatiev; Katrina Ignatsky; Zorin Imin; Mikhail Iroshnikov; Avram Ishchel; Isaac Jacobs; Vladimir Kazalovsky; Terenty Komnin; Olga Kudrin; Julia Kudrina; Mikhail Lashevets; Alexei Lidval; Yakov Litovsky; Ivan Livprodsky; Dimitry Mamen; Konstantin Mamnetsky; Ilya Menshikov; Feliks Menuilin; Stanislav Mersh; Pavel and Tatiana Merzinsky; Svetlana Morozov; Nikolai Murovsky; Gennady Nabokov; Peter Nikolaiev; Serge Nikolsky; Alexander Nomintz; Elizabeta Nurichnin; Elena Nyslander; Alexei Orlov; Feodor Ormetsky; Nikolai Pahlen; Sergei Panin; Artur Persin; Anton Pilovsky; Evgeni Pomgradskaya; Linda Predovsky; Maria Puchelsky; Kirill Ragonoff; Nikita Ridel; Alexander Rodzinsky; Feodor Romanov; Igor Romanovsky; Ioann Rudnikov; Vassili Serin; Lev Sorin; Markus Tan; Peter Tarvolets; Vladimir Tevlov; Grigorii Timmons; Anna Tompkins; Ekaterina Tutaschev; Anne Ullmann; Sergei Uvalensky; Anastasia

Worontsov; Max Wottle; Alois Wrichtmann; Paulina Yurovskaya; Vassili Yurovsky; and Feodor Yuvenaly.

In North America we wish to thank Jason Adams; Betty Aronson; Lee Atweiler; Lucia Bequaert; George Bobrick; Thomas and Mary Botford; Erna Bringe; Lorraine Butterfield; Jill Camps; Vincent Cartwright; Harry Cernan; Luke Connor; Ben Curry; Cyndi Darling; Louise David; Mona and Gerald Dennings; Sam Dettlemore; Greg Dunmassy; Keith Eaton; Brian Ebford; Fred Ernest; Edward Fine; Beth Fry; Michelle Fumkin; Andrei Gaddis; Kathryn George; Nick Gorman; Dan Gretsky; Roger Gringle; Larry Gross; Linda Grundvald; Mike Harris; John Harrison; Marina Hart; Candice Hearst; William Hemple; Bill Hennings; Steve Hervet; Craig Hohman; Elizabeth Hoss; Allison Hume; Francine Imford; Nagori Iskaguchi; Max Jacobs; Irving Jadschmidt; Hans Jergin; Terry and Michael Jorgenson; Greg Julia; Kerry Karnet; Natasha Kennet; Will Kevin; Harvey Kew; Scott Laforce; Brandon Lamont; Ian Lanoge; Gabrielle Lasher; Anne Little; Julia Loman; Peter Longford; Mike Lumis; Justin Maris; Thomas Matt; Shay McNeal; Edgar McNeil; Irina Mishop; Roger Morris; Jay Moss; Christopher Mowlens; Sue Nardin; Claudia Nervin; Felix Norris; Rick Owens; Bill Partridge; Bob Perricault; Hank Pettigrew; Marsha and Ashton Porman; Ron Questen; George Ransome; Linda and Phil Rascul; Viki Sams; William Samuels; John Sandford; Rachel Sattle; Matt Selford; Tim Simmons; John Simon; Corey Sommers; Cynthia Sulden; Ryan Tager; Josh Tanner; Eleanor Tibble; Diana Totesmore; Michael Townsend; Fanny Ulman; Eugene Unwin; Anna Victor; Michel Vusgek; Henry Walters; Burt Washington; Curtis Welborne; Zora and Peter Welcome; Dale Wilmington; Allen Wilson; Nadine Womack; Cathy Wycliff; Shiguro Yukihama; Gleb Yuvenshky; and Mark Zendor.

In Germany we would like to thank Hans Aronsen; Ulrike Atavinsky; Felix Bonhoeffer; Klaus Butlefeld; Richard Carlysle; Nicola Carvin; Marlene Cedrick; Louisa Demmhof; Charlotta Duddlemann; Erich Egmann; Karl Friedrich; Franz Gross; Josef Hochleitner; Maria and Wilhelm Hudle; Ernst Janson; Peter Jergin; Heiner Jerofsky, Direktor von Presse und Offentlichkeitsarbeit for the Darmstadt Police Archives; Gustaf Justmann; Norbert Kliege; Stefan Krebentischler; Markus Krugger; Nikolas Kundelman; Marcel Leggat; Elisabeth Lemmon; Bertita Lumvoert; Friedrich Manson; Birgitte Mattlehof; Julia Michelmann; Tomas Momford; Wilhelm Nardon; Augustus Nirovenko; Karl Orleans; Daniella Otford; Sissy and Michael Pegmand; Siegfried Rathlef; Cosima Richards; Sunny Rinaldi; Franz Romero; Maria and Heinrich Rudenfeld; Jude Sailer; Anton Sandor; Beatta Seamhof; Sylvie Semdon; Maurice Suder; Franc Tagert; Nikita Talipov; Lazlo Tamet; Victor Tarfrod; Alexandra Tiritsii; Katherine

Tomas; Klaus Ullmann; Possa Ulvandon; David Vasnor; Jurgen Vertor; Thor Vierck; Luitpold Viktor; Diedrich Vomritz; Nikolas Wagfield; Felix Wagner; Marta and Kurt Wagner; Tristan Wonanberg; Gretel Wurlack; and the courteous and attentive staffs at the lovely Hotel Prinz Heinrich in Darmstadt, and at the extraordinary Schloss-Hotel Lisl in Hohenschwangau.

In France we would like to thank Catherine Amboise; Jacques and Bridget Balsan; Philippe Berrin; Michel Borman; Nicolas Carriere; Louis Coughlan; Chance Deinfoire; Marcel Dorman; Étienne Elford; David Ensfield; Terry Étienne; Eric Fallows; Jacqueline Formin; Philippe Forquet; Mansfield Grasse; Peter Henri; Yvette Honseur; Ingrid Iffly; Consuelo Jacques; Victor Jenkins; Maria and Charles Jerome; Elisabeth Justine; Hélène Klayman; Violet Kureva; Marcus Lindercoste; Yves Ludendorff; Gaston Mafel-Troyant; Pierre Morris; Stephen Munitz; Claude Orphen; Gills Ostrikov; Rodney Papin; Victoria Perrin; François Phillips; Guy Pomeroy; Nicole Purgunard; Justin Redincourt; Vladislav Rostov; Gerard Rumage; Michel Savage; Julia Serricault; Fredric Sisson; Lucy Somm; Diana Sutre; Charlotte Thierry; Andrea Tomas; and Albert Wyland.

In the United Kingdom we would like to thank Allen Abrams; Danielle Ascher; Frederick Bast; Christine Benagh; Mike Betford; Kate Blanchard; David Bloom; Felix Bortz; Nicholas Buggle; Seth Carson; Aline Castle; Feodor Cawielki; William Clarke; Irina and Paul Daniels; Thomas David; Nick Davidoff; Elizabeth Densmuire; Elliot Depholm; Colin Dern; Mary Derry; Gerald Detmire; Anne Dillard; Victoria Dimoire; Henry Dorrit; Catherine Duschenay; George Egmont; Diana Emmons; Cecilia Eton; Una Fadurov; Susan Famen; Jocelyn Femboch; Richard Firch; Erich Firth; Terrance Flyght; Ivor Foreman; Philip Fotlemen; Mike Grady; Arthur Grassle; Lawrence Grintock; Amanda Grisholm; Diana Guryev; Coryne Hall; Roger Hansen; Sebastian Hanson; Charles Hawson; Dale Headington; Anna Heffler; Harry Henman; Barbara Hervey; Trina Hettle; Robert Hirsch; Ian Hogg; Michael Homes; Orlando Humewood; Peter Isles; Jean Jeffreys; Adrian Johns; Kathryn Johnston; Schlomo Kaneda; David Kennedy; George Kettle; Thomas King; John King; Christopher Koerner; John Kurtiss; William Lawrence; David Lermon; Ella Little; Prince and Princess M. Lobanov-Rostovsky; Rupert Loman; Robin Luwis; Nicholas Mason; Barbara Mersey; Anne and Roger Metz; Stephen Middlefield; Paul Mirsky; Ian Morris; Annette Nason-Waters; Ophelia Nicholls; Kip Noll; Nigel Olson; Colin Organ; Franklin Ormond; Henrietta Ottoline; William Percy; Robin Piguet; Charles Restin; Mike Rimmer; Edward Romanov; Sue Rutledge; Christine Sarband; Penelope Sergeant; Nicola Simms; Beatrice Simons; Madeleine Sommers; Brian Suchenay;

Alexander Tell; Gianni Timpkins; Peter Tomas; Erich Torrence; David Tuttle; Mona and Philip Usher; Lawton Vesty; Katrina Warne; Harry Washington; Richard Wellington; Edward Williams; Katherine Wishburne; Mary Wormington; Marion Wynne; and Charlotte Zeepvat.

Our agent, Frank Weimann, of Literary Group International in New York, took on this project and saw it through its varied perambulations to its present form. At a time when the very subject of the book itself seemed overwhelming, he offered helpful advice that resulted in the present work. Our editor at John Wiley & Sons, Stephen S. Power, has proved extraordinarily understanding of the difficulties and disasters that plague any book of this length, with the inevitable pleas for deadline extensions that naturally follow. And Mike Thompson, editorial assistant at John Wiley & Sons, provided invaluable assistance in the final process.

Penny Wilson would like to extend her gratitude and appreciation to the following members of the History and Language Departments at the University of California at Riverside: Dr. J. Arch Getty; the late Dr. John Phillips; Dr. Sharon Salinger; Dr. Louis A. Pedrotti; Dr. Jules Levin; Dr. Josef Purkhart; and Serena Anderlini. We are sometimes fortunate in encountering teachers whose passion for their work is inspirational; their influence will be felt for a lifetime.

Special thanks to the 1999–2000 Chapter Council members at the Epilson Pi chapter of Kappa Kappa Gamma, who on more than one occasion good-naturedly agreed to participate in trial reenactment of various items on our timeline. Samantha Allswang; Jennifer Beaver; Barbara Cohen; Amy Crawford; Jamie Farr; Shawna Garg; Sara Gewirtz; Shruti Joshi; Yvonne Kim; Cory Malone; Alexandra Patarias; Breana Pearce; and Michelle Shirk were our willing guinea pigs: They have our gratitude and best wishes for bright and successful futures.

The long-suffering friends and subscribers of our *Atlantis Magazine* are thanked for their forbearance and patience with our erratic publishing schedule, knowing the difficulties faced in a project of such magnitude. To those who do not wish to be named, and to those below, we extend out sincere gratitude for your understanding: Kay Adler; Charles Altman; Joseph Ambro; Mark Andersen; Varya Anderson; Joseph Ambro; Ann Arlen; Natalia Ayers; Amy Ballard; William Beall; Lynn Blick; Michael Boardman; Edward Boshears; Estelle Bouthillier; Susan Burkhart; Mary Cassidy; Diana deCourcy-Ireland; Russell Clarke; Betty Cornish; Ellen Davis; Bettye Dolinsky; Lois Eyre; Mary Ann Fogarty; Marie Graham; Helene Higgins; Wayne Hodges; Bernardette Inzani; Bruce Jones; John Kelleher; Petra Kleinpenning; Harold Larsen; Carolina Liljedahl; Eric Carrera Lowe; Dr. Edgar Lucidi; John McClure; Mary D. McLeod; Father Nicholas Monk and the brothers of Holy Trinity Monastery in Brookline, Massachusetts;

Claudia Moreno; Laura Mustard; Michele Nelson; Edward Pattillo; Christopher Pierce; Kassandra Pollock; Jennifer van Proeyen; Heather Redding; Ingrid Roeder; Karen Roth; Harvey and Ija Schmidt; Dorothy Shearn; Jean Snyder; Peter Sparks; Russann Spotti; Yuri Tarala; William von Weiland; David N. Westwood; and Chris Wise-Pappas.

Penny Wilson would like to thank Dr. Robert Clark of Centrum Analytical Laboratories for both his support and kindness in providing a flexible and understanding work environment, and in giving professional opinions in certain environmental areas germane to the subject of this book. Heartfelt thanks also go to the staff of Centrum, some of whose jobs were undoubtedly made more difficult through the frequent absences and unreasonable demands of the resident author: Kurt Baumbauer; Jeff Betty; Cathy Reichel-Clark; Margaret Dutton; Marilu and Kirk Escher; Ryan Frankenberger; Gail Fuson; Ryan Gates; Nehemias Gutierrez; Jerad Hunt; Jennifer Iniguez; Julia Lakes; Stefanie LeDoux; Zalen Liley; Ken Nguyen; Connie Phoong; Trish Reed; Kevin Scott; Pat and Gloria Smith; Joe Sprockett; Larry Stewart; John Tangeman; Rudy Vergara and Brian Stout; Richard Villafania; Andrew Walsh; and Andrew Williamson. Special thanks to Centrum's UPS driver, Steve LaCroix, who carried and delivered several hundred pounds of books over the past three years.

Greg King would like to acknowledge the unswerving support of Half Price Books, a company that has made his continued work possible through its generosity. Particularly he extends his thanks to Tim Brown; Dennis Demercer; Melinda Gardner; Joseph Gramer; Molly Harvey; Jennifer Holland; Nikki Kent; Mathew Kirshner; Beth Kuffel; Jay Larson; Joey Owens; Crystal Perrigoue; Judy Prince; Guy Tennis; Derek Turner; Michelle and Corey Urbach; Craig Windham; and especially to Cynthia Melin, who, as always, has been extraordinarily understanding of the complexities and demands of a writer's life.

The Internet has created a new world of online communities, and Penny Wilson has been fortunate to have been welcomed by the good people at Planetsocks.com. Without their peculiar brand of wit and wisdom, the past three years of solitude would have been much darker and far lonelier. Thanks to: Kimberly Benson; Boy Blunder; Fabio; Gobanana; Julie Hopkins; Neckbone the Conquerer; Cheryl Norman; Jessica; Kaleoaloha; Elizabeth Kennedy; Hope Lives; Lori Muccino; Steve Nelson; Mikhail Nikolai; Mark Pletcher; Qwijybo; Robnoxious; Laurie Singer; Cory "Corndog" Sklar; Rob Tomlin; Trish; Jim Trzaska; and especially to Dogstalker; Wench; Weezie; and AC, who is, after all, everyone else.

With such intensive hours of work and the total concentration demanded by such an undertaking, we have both been buoyed by those who have served as models of determination to us, and by those who have filled our long days and nights with humor, courage, and diversion: Dario Argento; Rupert Everett; Christopher Gorham, Penelope Keith; Felicity Kendall; Nicole Kidman; Christopher Lee; Trey Parker and Matt Stone; Paul Rudd; Duncan Sheik; and Ian Thorpe. They all have our warmest thanks.

The death of former Canadian prime minister Pierre Trudeau during the early stages of this book once again reminded us of his great intellect, and his thoughtful model of "reason before passion," an important example that we have attempted to follow in analyzing the complexities of the Romanov case. To his family, and especially to his sons Justin and Sacha, we extend our heartfelt thanks for having shared so noble a man with the world.

As always, friends have been a constant source of support, and especially understanding of the demands placed on our lives as we struggled to bring this book to fruition. Past and present, they have been sounding boards for ideas, and often were the first to offer encouragement outside of our families. They also were the people who have seen the least of us over the past three years, never complaining of our temporary absences from their lives. We would like to thank Sharlene Aadland; Jacqui Axelson; Daniel Briere; Dan Brite; the late Cheryl Brown; Carrie Carlson; Sally Dick; Liz and Andy Eaton; Laura Enstone; Pablo Fonseca; Jake Gariepy; Ella Gaumer; Sally Hampton; Nils Hanson; Barbara and Paul Harper; Louise Hayes; Kathy Hoefler; Lise Everett Holden; Diane Huntley; Ruxandra Ionescu-Purice; Kimberly Kacker; Christopher Kinsman; Jonathan Kinsman; Rosann Kinsman; Chuck and Eileen Knaus; Angela Manning; Cecelia Manning; Mark Manning; Gigi McDonald; Nancy Mellon; Denis Meslans; Russ and Deb Minugh; Jennifer Mottershaw; Steve O'Donnell; Robin Olson; Lisa Palmer; the late Sister Paraclete, mother superior of the Sisters of Divine Providence, Kingston, Massachusetts; Amy and Adam Perlstein; Jeremy Perlstein; David Perry, now in Bujumbura, Burundi; Philip Proctor; Alan Reed; Anne Shawyer; Mary Silzel; Masaru and Yoko Takayama; Debra Tate; and Ed West. Every partnership begins with an introduction, and ours came from an old mutual friend, Candace Metz-Longinette-Gahring. We would like to extend our deepest appreciation to her for beginning what has proved to be a happy, productive, and enduring relationship.

Penny Wilson would like to thank her extended family, who have given enthusiastic support and encouragement in this endeavor: Ceri, Stephen, Mark, and Bethan Chichester; Marianne Cowan; Brian, Julie, Samantha, and Bethan Holland; Gerald and Ann Holland; Kevin, Cherylle, Ashbie, and Christine Holland; Angela McKenna; Joanne

Menzies; Bill and Anne O'Hanlon; Brian O'Hanlon; Helen O'Hanlon; Mark O'Hanlon; Adrian Osborne; Edmund Osborne; John Osborne; Michael Osborne; and Richard Osborne. Special thanks go to Betty and Jim Heeney of Kilmarnock, Scotland, who spent sleepless nights carefully documenting the quality of light on July nights in a part of Scotland on latitude similar to that in Ekaterinburg.

The patience of close family members was particularly important in this process, for it would have been impossible to properly research and write this work without their understanding over missed family holidays and celebrations, rushed visits, preoccupied phone calls, and just plain absences over long periods of time. They are loved and appreciated more than they know. Penny Wilson thanks Peggy and Darren Cartwright; Beth Kelsey; Jean Landrum; Jamie and Lindsey Phillips; Jon and Jacqui Phillips; Tricia Phillips; Liz Wilson; and Paul Wilson. During the three years it has taken to complete this project, Penny Wilson has become an aunt to two little boys, Eric and Ryan Cartwright. Because of the demands of this work, she has missed many of their early milestones, and hereby promises to make it up to them. Peggy Bennion is immensely appreciated for her lifelong support and kindness. The lives and long memories of Penny's late grandparents, John and Anne O'Hanlon and Gwen and Len Bennion, were original inspirations in her passion for the past. They will always be missed. Penny's sister-in-law, Lynne O'Hanlon, has long been a source of strength, honesty, and common sense; her brother, Peter O'Hanlon, a bottomless well of support and encouragement, is quite simply the best brother in the world.

Special thanks to Penny's parents, Edward and Mary O'Hanlon, who have been enthusiastic and supportive through this long process and have borne the brunt of missed holidays and short tempers. Over the years and in many ways, they have proven just how valuable parents may be.

Penny's husband, Tom, has uncomplainingly worked long overtime hours to support the Wilson household over the past three years. He has also good-naturedly provided computer support and expertise, even when roused from sleep at four o'clock in the morning by a shrieking Valkyrie. This book literally would not have been possible without him; he has Penny's endless love and Greg's eternal gratitude.

Greg King, as always, thanks his parents, Roger and Helena King, for their unfailing support, particularly over the last few, difficult years as this book has taken shape.

Sue Woolmans endured much on our behalf. From helping to facilitate our research in London to providing us with invaluable leads drawn from a number of inaccessible sources, her generous cooperation has allowed us to seek out avenues otherwise closed to us. And her husband, Mike, always patient, deserves special thanks for having understood the demands of the book.

Ellen Vinsant has been generous with her time, reading and critiquing various chapters as her busy family schedule has allowed. In several areas she was the first to read our work, and we appreciate the honesty and kindness of her appraisals. The book would be much the less without her insight.

Dimitry Macedonsky provided formidable information, materials, and advice on much of this book's content. Working with a reliable group of dedicated researchers across Russia, he undertook repeated searches for missing memoirs and confirming dates for incidents discussed herein. His discoveries, and those of his friends in the former Soviet Archives, have enabled this book to bring to the public much new and important material.

Victoria Lewis and Frank Simone of Cymru Films in San Francisco have proved steadfast supporters of our work over the past few years. Through their generosity, we have been able to access a number of important interviews from the first years following the 1991 exhumations, conducted at a time when the participants spoke more freely and revealed more of the truth. The transcripts of their extraordinary film The Mystery of the Last Tsar—itself an invaluable source for any researcher on the subject—provided us with much new and important information.

Barbara Wilson is not only Penny Wilson's mother-in-law but also a research librarian at the Tomas Rivera Library at the University of California, Riverside. With the motivated assistance of Janet Moores and Maria Mendoza at interlibrary loan, she has tracked down, ordered, and coordinated literally hundreds of rare books, manuscripts, dissertations, journals, and other volumes for our use. Her calmness and organization in the face of increasingly frantic and erratic lists of requests have been both admirable and immensely supportive. All three ladies have our deepest gratitude.

Penny Wilson's friend Mark Horan has undertaken a great deal of work in the creation of *www.thefateoftheromanovs.com*, this book's Web site. With unfailing patience and goodwill, Mark has brought his considerable talent and artistry in crafting a superb companion to this book. We thank him for his friendship and for the strength of his vision. Our sincere thanks also to artist Andrew Pinedo for his assistance on the site.

If there were one person we wish we could thank in person for his help and support in researching Russian history, it would be the late

Dmitri Volkogonov. General Volkogonov generously gave advice, assistance, and access to his personal archives, including several rare photographs that appear in this book. It is six years since his death; his kindness and encouragement are still missed.

Janet Ashton has been instrumental in helping to form the finished work. She has sacrificed her own time; run down obscure books; copied old letters; and undertaken any number of tasks to assist us. Her arguments and thoughts have proved invaluable, and helped us both form our arguments and reconsider certain elements within this book. She has not agreed with everything said within, yet has continually been on our side, especially during difficult times when it was not in her best interests to do so. For that, we thank her.

Pepsi Nunes must be singled out for our special thanks. Over the past two years she has been an unfailing source of constant support and encouragement, literally making possible our numerous research trips through her generosity and connections. At times when opposition to the creation of this book seemed overwhelming, Pepsi stood by us, supporting our efforts and assisting in every imaginable way. It would not have been possible without her.

Peter Kurth, running true to form, has been one of the few people unwavering in their support of this project. From the very beginning, he has facilitated interviews and contacts; made available information; and provided thousands of documents from his extensive private archives on the Romanov case. Along the way, he offered criticism and helpful comment, and pointed us in directions we might otherwise not have discovered. His realism and common sense where the Romanovs are concerned proved a remarkable road map, one we have been honored to follow.

Greg King and Penny Wilson
December 2002

Notes

Unless otherwise noted, all archival sources quoted or cited within the text are provided with their complete archival citation references in the following notes. A list of the various archives, as well as abbreviations used, can be found in its own section below. Most newspaper and magazine articles are given full citations within the notes and are not repeated in the bibliography.

The Nicholas Sokolov Archive is divided among multiple locations. Volumes are in the State Archives of the Russian Federation, Moscow; Houghton Library, Harvard University; in a private collection in Europe, made available to the authors for study; and in the Henry Ford Museum Archives in Dearborn, Michigan. None of these sources contains a complete set of the Sokolov dossier and its compendiums. We have therefore utilized a broad approach when dealing with the Sokolov materials, giving the name of the person making the deposition, the date, and the volume and document numbers where the information can be found (which remain consistent in all copies of the dossier viewed by us).

We also have utilized the origial transcript of "The Mystery of the Last Tsar," generously made available to us by producers Victoria Lewis and Frank Simone of Cymru Films, San Francisco, California.

List of abbreviations used in these notes:

AF: Alexandra Feodorovna

APRF: Arkhiv Presidentsii Rossiya Federatsii, Moscow

Cymru: Transcripts from "The Mystery of the Last Tsar," Cymru Films

GARF: State Archives of the Russian Federation, Moscow

MF: Marie Feodorovna

N: Nicholas II

PRO: Public Records Office, Kew, United Kingdom

RTsKhIDNI: Russkia tsentr dokumentatsii Istorii, Moscow

SA: Sokolov Archive

TsDOOSO: Tsentr dokumentatsii obshchestvennykh organizatsii Sverdlovskoi oblasti, Ekaterinburg (formerly Sverdlovsk Party Archives).

Introduction

1. Pares, 399.
2. Cowles, *The Russian Dagger*, 240–249.
3. Pipes, *The Russian Revolution*, 788.
4. Volkogonov, 217–218.
5. Iroshnikov, Protsai, and Shelayev, 43.
6. Wilton and Telberg, 294–295.
7. Ibid., 212.
8. Pierre Gilliard, "Tutor to the Tsarevich," *Atlantic Monthly* 1153 (September 1933): 286.
9. McCullagh, 141.
10. See Pipes, *Russian Revolution*, 762; and Steinberg and Krustalev, 280, for further discussion.
11. Steinberg and Krustalev, 280.
12. At the time he left Russia in 1920, Sokolov apparently made a number of copies of his dossier. In 1990, when Sotheby's auctioned one of the dossiers in London, their catalog asserted that "Sokolov compiled four or five dossiers. One was for his own use, one for Kolchak, and another for Wilton" (Sotheby's catalog, 64). Yet the actual number of complete copies must have been six. One copy was given to General Michael Deterikhs and one to Robert Wilton; a third was given to Henry Ford and eventually ended up in the Henry Ford Archive in Dearborn, Michigan; and portions of a fourth seem to have

been given to Charles Sydney Gibbes, the tutor of English to the imperial children (George Gibbes to King, May 1989). Sokolov had two complete copies of his dossier in exile. Both remained with him in Paris for the first years of his exile. One was a master copy, the other, a working copy, which he took with him when he traveled the Continent to interview further witnesses. In early 1921 Sokolov was staying at the Berlin house of a Colonel Freiberg, conducting further interviews. He had brought with him the seven volumes of his working copy of the dossier. One night, the house was raided by a band of armed Russian agents and German Communists. They stole only Sokolov's dossier. This entire episode seems to have been arranged at the request of the Soviet government, apparently anxious to see what information had been gathered (Bulygin and Kerensky, 274). A later inquiry by the Berlin authorities indicated that the stolen papers had been taken first to Prague, then on to Moscow, where they disappeared (Bulygin and Kerensky, 273–274). When General Deterikhs eventually left Russia, he carried his copy of the dossier into European exile. After his death in 1937, the dossier disappeared. It may have been placed on the market and quietly purchased by the grand ducal family of Liechtenstein, who, until the 1990s, owned a copy of Sokolov's dossier; it also may have been the copy of the dossier that was placed on auction at Sotheby's in London in 1990. Wilton died shortly after Sokolov. In 1937, Wilton's copy of the dossier was sold by his widow in auction at Sotheby's in London. The purchaser was Maggs Brothers of Mayfair, an antiquarian bookstore, which, in turn, sold the dossier a short time later to a private collector. Sometime later, the dossier was sold to a retired chairman of the Cincinnati Bell Telephone Company, Bayard Kilgour, an American with a great interest in Russian history. In 1964 Kilgour's copy—and thus Wilton's copy—was donated to the Houghton Library at Harvard University (Summers and Man-

gold, 60–61). Ford's copy remained in the automotive baron's archives in Michigan. In many ways, the Ford copy of the dossier is the most complete version compiled, with several additional volumes of evidence not included in the collection of bound volumes owned by Deterikhs or Wilton, both of which represented only the evidence as gathered to 1920. The Ford dossier contains, for example, copies of the depositions and testimony collected by Sokolov during his years of exile in Europe—vital pieces of information missing from the Wilton dossier at Harvard University. The copy of the dossier owned by Charles Sydney Gibbes seems to have been only fragmentary at best, consisting of several bound volumes of testimony. The tutor's son, the late George Gibbes, also retained a small wooden chest that contained copies of the original glass negative plates of photographs related to the investigation (George Gibbes to King, May 1989). After Sokolov's death, he left his own personal copy of the dossier to Prince Nicholas Orlov, his benefactor in exile. Orlov's copy of the dossier seems to have disappeared, although its history is perhaps better documented than any other set of the documents. On October 9, 1950, following Orlov's death, the trunks containing the dossier and the glass negatives were auctioned at the Salle Drouot in Paris. They were purchased by M. I. Gurvich, a Russian antiques dealer, who promptly stored them in his attic. There they remained untouched until April 1962, when author Victor Alexandrov, searching for materials on a biography of Catherine the Great, discovered the trunks, still marked "N. Sokolov," in a dusty corner of Gurvich's attic in his house in the Val-de-Grâce district of Paris (Alexandrov, 14–15). Alexandrov had discovered the glass plates and some incidental materials but not Orlov's copy of the dossier itself. An elderly White officer, a certain General Pozdnyshev, hinted that the Germans had stolen Orlov's copy of the dossier after they invaded France in 1940. Its location, said Pozdnyshev, was unknown, although he admitted that another copy of the entire dossier was still in private hands (Summers and Mangold, 60). The issue seems to have been unnecessarily complicated by Bulygin, who, in his book, asserted that Sokolov had brought "only one copy" of the dossier from Siberia (Bulygin and Kerensky, 158). Yet this was untrue, as he himself related in the same book that a second copy had been stolen in Berlin in 1921. In fact, Bulygin had an eleven-volume copy of the complete dossier, including his own handwritten notes, which remains in private hands in Europe and which has been made available for use in this book. The fate of the dossier that belonged to Deterikhs remains uncertain; it was most likely the dossier that belonged to the grand ducal family of Liechtenstein and that was presented to the State Archives of the Russian Federation in the 1990s. Wilton's original copy remains in the Houghton Library at Harvard University, while the copy presented to Henry Ford is in Dearborn, Michigan. Sokolov's working copy, stolen in Berlin in 1921, was sent, via Prague, to Moscow, where it disappeared. The fate of Orlov's copy remains an enigma. If, as Pozdnyshev claimed, it was stolen by Nazi troops during the occupation of Paris, it presumably remained hidden for many years. It is possible that this was the copy that belonged to the Liechtenstein family, and not the Deterikhs copy. One of these two complete copies of the dossier—either the Deterikhs copy or the Sokolov-Orlov copy—was certainly in their private archive in Vaduz Castle before it was presented to the Russian Federation.

13. Wilton, 15–16.
14. Deterikhs, vol. 1, 258.
15. O'Connor, 169.
16. Bulygin and Kerensky, 154.
17. Ibid., 155.
18. Melgunov, 399; Bykov, *Last Days*, 3; Volkogonov, 210.
19. Bykov, *Last Days*, 82.
20. Root, 225–227; Halliburton, 150.
21. See Halliburton, *Seven League Boots*, 150–159. Halliburton returned to Moscow and sent a triumphant letter to his parents: "The Sverdlovsk expedition was a grand and glorious success, beyond my wildest hopes. The man who murdered the Tsar and all his family, the actual assassin who was jailer, executioner, undertaker, cremator, has kept silent for seventeen years. I got him on his sick bed, and heard his story poured out—unguarded, complete and terrifically vivid. I happened, by this good break, to be his confessor. He's never spoken to any other person. I'm still a little weak over the melodramatics of the thing. This interview should ensure the success of our book. It was history he told me" (Halliburton, *Richard Halliburton*, 359–360). Stoneman, still at the Hotel Metropole, listened as Halliburton poured out his excited account of his interview with the "dying" Ermakov. "You're a story-teller posing as a journalist," Stoneman declared candidly. "The next thing you'll tell me is that Ermakov died in your arms!" (Root, 231).
22. Root, 232.
23. Ibid., 227.
24. Summers and Mangold, 181.
25. Medvedev, February 21–22, 1919, in SA, vol. 2, doc. 86.
26. See *Atlantis Magazine: In the Courts of Memory*, at www.atlantis-magazine.com.
27. See King, *The Last Empress*.

Chapter 1: The Ruin of an Empire

1. Bulygin and Kerensky, 34–35.
2. Paleologue, vol. 1, 260.
3. Hall, 54.
4. Mossolov, 6.
5. Surguchev, 26.
6. Lowe, 255.
7. Marie, Queen of Romania, vol. 1, 332, 573.
8. Benckendorff, 113–114.
9. Kobylinsky, April 6–10, 1919, in SA, vol. 3, doc. 29.
10. Gibbes, July 1, 1919, in SA, vol. 5, doc. 31.
11. Mossolov, 11.
12. Alexander Izvolsky, "Souvenirs de mon ministère," *Revue des deux mondes* (July 1, 1919), 105.
13. Witte, 535.

14. Gilliard, 48.
15. *Krasnii Arkhiv* 2 (1922): 43.
16. Report of General Trepov to Nicholas II, August 6, 1905, in *Krasnii Arkhiv* 11–12 (1925): 435.
17. Andrew Rothstein in Bykov, *Last Days*, 5.
18. Trotsky, *Russian Revolution*, vol. 1, 69.
19. *Krasnii Arkhiv* 11–12 (1925): 439.
20. Bing, 206, 210; *Krasnii Arkhiv* 11–12 (1925): 436.
21. Elbogen, 398–399.
22. Florinsky, 17–18.
23. Sacher, 311.
24. Laqueur, *Russia and Germany*, 96; Witte, 589.
25. *Krymskii Vestnik* (September 14, 1917).
26. Elbogen, 396–397; Oldenburg, vol. 3, 188 n; vol. 3, 190 n.
27. Johnson, 365; Sachar, 320.
28. *Krasnii Arkhiv* 2 (1922): 43.
29. Elbogen, 394.
30. Johnson, 365; Elbogen, 395; Sachar, 321.
31. Nicholas II to Marie Feodorovna, October 27, 1905, in Bing, 190–191; and in *Krasnii Arkhiv* (1927), vol. 22, 169.
32. *Krasnii Arkhiv* 5 (1924): 105; Kokovtsov, 166–168.
33. Laqueur, *Russia and Germany*, 99–100.
34. See *Poslednie Novosti*, Paris (May 1, 1921); *La Tribune Juive* (May 14, 1921); Schwartz-Bostunich, *Juedischer Imperialismus*, 359, cited in Laqueur, *Russia and Germany*, 100–101; Cohn, 90–98.
35. V. L. Burtsev, "Protokoly sionskikh mudretsov," in *Dokazannia podlog*, Paris (1938), 105–106, cited in Warth, 158.
36. Laqueur, *Russia and Germany*, 100–101; Cohn, 90–98; Elbogen, 397, 563. Nicholas II's own copy of Nilus's book is now in the Library of Congress in Washington, D.C. See Elbogen, 734 n.
37. V. L. Burtsev, "Protokly sionskikh mudretsov," in *Dokazannia podlog*, Paris (1938), 106, quoted in Laqueur, *Russia and Germany*, 79; Boris Ananich and Rafail Ganelin, "Nikolai II," *Voprosy istorii* 2 (1993): 58–76.
38. Testimony of Klaudia Bittner to Sokolov, in Ross, 422; Nicholas's diary, March 27, 1918, in GARF, f. 601, op. 1, d. 265.
39. Laqueur, *Russia and Germany*, 83; A. Chernovskii, ed., *Soyuz Russkovo Naroda* (Moscow 1929), 411, cited in Laqueur, *Russia and Germany*, 80.
40. Oldenburg, vol. 2, 178; Warth, 102; Laqueur, *Russia and Germany*, 83–84.
41. Tager, 11–12.
42. Laqueur, *Russia and Germany*, 83–84; Frumkin, 43.
43. Shulgin, 102; Oldenburg, vol. 3, 131.
44. Shulgin, 102–103; Oldenburg, vol. 3, 131–132.
45. Shulgin, 103–105; Samuel, 17, 26–27; Cohn, 90–98, 108–125; Pipes, *Russia under the Bolshevik Regime*, 255–257; Tager, 39–40; Rogger, *Jewish Policies*, 40–55.
46. Oldenburg, vol. 3, 130; Shulgin, 105.
47. Oldenburg, vol. 1, 132; Shulgin, 105–107.
48. Shulgin, 107–108; Samuel, 55–59; Cohn, 90–98; Tager, 40–47; Figes, 243–244.
49. Oldenburg, vol. 3, 214 n; Shulgin, 110–112; Figes, 243–244; Samuel, 55–59; Cohn, 108–125; Pipes, *Russia under the Bolshevik Regime*, 255–257.
50. Figes, 244; Samuel, 55–59; Cohn, 121; Tager, 40–47.
51. Miliukov, 285.
52. Oldenburg, vol. 3, 132.
53. Crankshaw, 308.
54. Abrikossow, 227.
55. Cymru transcripts.
56. Peter Botkine, 15.
57. Buxhoeveden, *Life*, 166.
58. Gilliard, 83.
59. Buxhoeveden, *Life*, 150.
60. AF to N, March 13, 1916, in GARF, f. 601, op. 1, d. 1150.
61. Marie of Romania, vol. 1, 574.
62. Gilliard, 76.
63. Olga Nikolaievna to AF, December 4, 1908, in GARF, f. 640, op. 1, d. 116.
64. Tatiana Nikolaievna to AF, January 17, 1909, in GARF, f. 640, op. 1, d. 116.
65. Olga Nikolaievna to Marie Feodorovna, September 9, 1913, in GARF, f. 642, op. 1, d. 2435.
66. Tatiana Nikolaievna to AF, August 7, 1915, in GARF, f. 640, op. 1, d. 118.
67. AF to Marie Nikolaievna, December 6, 1910, in GARF, f. 685, op. 1, d. 67.
68. Botkin, *Romanovs*, 27.
69. Marie of Romania, vol. 1, 574.
70. Botkin, *Romanovs*, 27.
71. AF to Olga Nikolaievna, September 17, 1909, in GARF, f. 673, op. 1, d. 71.

72. Gibbes, July 1, 1919, in SA, vol. 5, doc. 31.
73. Vyrubova, 78.
74. AF to N, April 10, 1916, in GARF, f. 601, op. 1, d. 1150.
75. AF to N, March 13, 1916, in GARF, f. 601, op. 1, d. 1150.
76. Botkin, *Romanovs*, 27.
77. Trewin, 73.
78. Mossolov, 63–64.
79. Dehn, 76.
80. Vyrubova, 79.
81. Gilliard, 75.
82. Gibbes, July 1, 1919, in SA, vol. 5, doc. 31.
83. Kobylinksy, April 6–10, 1919, in SA, vol. 3, doc. 29.
84. Trewin, 73.
85. Bokhanov, ed., *Romanovs*, 127.
86. Gibbes, July 1, 1919, in SA, vol. 5, doc. 31.
87. Buxhoeveden, *Life*, 154.
88. Gilliard, 75.
89. Vorres, 53.
90. Botkin, *Romanovs*, 28.
91. Hough, *Louis and Victoria*, 265.
92. Gibbes, July 1, 1919, in SA, vol. 5, doc. 31.
93. Kobylinksy, April 6–10, 1919, in SA, vol. 3, doc. 29.
94. Dehn, 78; Gilliard, 75; Vyrubova, 78.
95. AF to Marie Nikolaievna, March 7, 1910, in GARF, f. 685, op. 1, d. 67.
96. AF to Marie Nikolaievna, March 11, 1910, in GARF, f. 685, op. 1, d. 67.
97. Wood, 105–106.
98. Botkin, *Romanovs*, 28; Botkin, *Woman*, 18.
99. Tatiana Botkine, 81.
100. Chavchavadze, *Crowns*, 57; testimony of Princess Xenia Georgievna of Russia at Hamburg court trial of Anna Anderson, quoted in Kurth, 202.
101. Gibbes, July 1, 1919, in SA, vol. 5, doc. 31.
102. Ibid.
103. Tatiana Botkine, 81.
104. Pares, 198; Asprey, 57–107.
105. Mossolov, 61.
106. Tatiana Botkine, 81; Vyrubova, 79.
107. Buxhoeveden, *Life*, 155.
108. Ibid.
109. Fletcher, "Royal Mothers and Their Children," *Good Housekeeping* 54 (April 1912): 455–456.
110. Mossolov, 247.
111. Naryshkina-Kuryakina, 196.
112. Gilliard, 72.
113. Ibid., 40.
114. Vyrubova, 82; Radziwill, *Taint*, 232.
115. Eugenie de Greece, 16–17.
116. Gibbes, July 1, 1919, in SA, vol. 5, doc. 31.
117. Ibid.
118. Grand Duke Konstantin Konstantinovich, diary entry of March 30, 1912, in GARF, f. 660, op. 2, d. 53.
119. de Stoeckl, 126.
120. Fromenko, 31.
121. Botkin, *Woman*, 22.
122. Eager, 160–161.
123. Tuchman, 75.
124. Golovine, 45–50.
125. Ibid., 34.
126. Pares, 198; Asprey, 57–107.
127. Paleologue, vol. 1, 107.
128. Pares, 198.
129. AF to N, September 24, 1914, in GARF, f. 601, op. 1, d. 1148.
130. Golovine, 214.
131. Pares, 230.
132. Golovine, 145.
133. Ibid., 98.
134. See King, 224–228, for further details of the 1915 assumption of supreme command and the feud between the empress and the grand duke.
135. Robert Wilton to Wickham Steed, November 16, 1916, in *The History of the Times*, vol. 4, 244.
136. Benckendorff, 47.
137. de Basily, 131–132.
138. *Krasnii Arkhiv* 22 (1927): 137.
139. Kerensky, 110.
140. AF diary, March 8, 1917, in GARF, f. 640, op. 1, d. 333.
141. Alexandrov, 156.
142. Benckendorff, 33.
143. Gilliard, 217.
144. Note from N to General Alexeiev, March 4, 1917, in *Krasnii Arkhiv* 22 (1927): 53–54.
145. N diary, July 31, 1917, in GARF, f. 601, op. 1, d. 265, l. 174.
146. Gilliard, 234–235; Alexei's diary, July 31, 1917, photo caption 16, in Alexandrov;

diary of Elizabeth Naryshkina-Kuryak-ina, chief comptroller of the empress's household, August 1, 1917, in *Poslednie Novosti*, Paris, (May 10, 1936).

147. Volkov, 106–107.
148. Kerensky in Bulygin and Kerensky, 130.
149. Stopford, 188.
150. Kerensky in Bulygin and Kerensky, 129.
151. Stopford, 156; Radziwill, *Taint*, 232–233.
152. Tatiana Botkine, 66.
153. N diary, August 1, 1917, in GARF, f. 601, op. I, d. 265.
154. Buxhoeveden, *Life*, 306.
155. Sir George Buchanan, vol. 2, 74. There is general disagreement concerning various events and times involved in the departure of the imperial family. In his account, Kerensky wrote that he arrived in Tsarskoye Selo that night after 11:00 P.M., following a meeting in Petrograd (Kerensky in Bulygin and Kerensky, 120). But Alexei Volkov gave two differing times in his book: 10:00 P.M. (p. 108) and 11:00 P.M. (p. 106). And Volkov declared that Kerensky "arrived on the train that he had arranged would transport us," which is certainly incorrect (Volkov, 106–107). Nor is there any agreement concerning the timing of the visit of Grand Duke Michael Alexandrovich. In her diary, Alexandra wrote: "11: Kerensky brought Misha to see N. for 10 minutes" (AF diary July 31, 1917). In his account, Volkov gives the time as 10:00 P.M. (see Volkov, 107–108). And Nicholas II, in his diary, gives a third time: "Around 10:30, dear Misha came" (diary of Nicholas II, August 1, 1917, in GARF, f. 601, op. 1, d. 265). Nor is there agreement as to who remained in the Alexander Palace and who waited for the trains in the meadow at the station. According to Volkov: "Except for the Imperial Family, all those who were to travel with them—Suite and Servants—were already assembled in the place designated for them, in the middle of the field between Tsarskoye and Alexandrovsky Station on the Warsaw line (Volkov, 106–107). This is contradicted in the accounts of Count Benckendorff, Elizabeth Naryshkin-Kuryakina, and Pierre Gilliard, who all stated that they were in the palace, along with Tatischev, Dolgoruky, and Botkin (see Benckendorff, 106–112; diary of Naryshkina-Kuryakina, August 1, 1917, in *Poslednie Novosti*, Paris [May 10, 1936]; and Gilliard, 234–235). There is no consensus on the time when the trains arrived from Petrograd. Volkov writes that they came at 6:00 A.M. (Volkov, 107). Elizabeth Naryshkina-Kuryakina agrees with this time (diary of Naryshkina-Kuryakina, August 1, 1917, in *Poslednie Novosti*, Paris, May 10, 1936). Yet Gilliard writes that "about five o'clock" they were told that the trains were ready, while, in his diary, Nicholas II writes that Kerensky told the family at 5:15 A.M. that the trains were waiting (see Gilliard, 235; diary of Nicholas II August 1, 1917, in GARF, f. 601, op. 1, d. 265) when, according to Volkov, Benckendorff, and Naryshkina-Kuryakina, they had not yet arrived. Benckendorff insisted that it was not until 6:00 A.M. that they were told to leave (Benckendorff, 111). And finally there is a wide variety of times given for the actual departure. Benckendorff wrote that it left the station at 7:30 A.M. (Benckendorff, 112). Gilliard insisted in his book (p. 235) that the train left at exactly 5:50 A.M. (ten minutes before, according to Benckendorff, Volkov, and Naryshkina-Kuryakina, the train even arrived), while Nicholas, in his diary, gave the time as exactly 6:10 A.M. (diary of Nicholas II, August 1, 1917, in GARF, f. 601, op. 1, d. 265).
156. Bykov, 40.
157. Kobylinksy, April 6–10, 1919, in SA, vol. 3, doc. 29.
158. Kirill Vladimirovich, 112.
159. Mossolov, 60.
160. Botkin, *Romanovs*, 79.
161. Buxhoeveden, *Life*, vii.
162. Peter Botkine, 5.
163. Botkin, *Romanovs*, 55–56.
164. Peter Botkine, 8.
165. Ibid.
166. Grey, 32.
167. Peter Botkine, 18–19.
168. Ibid., 5.

169. Private information to authors; see also G. Ioffe, "V sushchnosti ya uzhe umer" in *Literaturnaya gazeta* (September 1, 1993), 13; N. Bubnova, "Slovo chesti oplacheno zhizn'yu" in *Oblastnaya gazeta* (June 27, 1995), 3.

170. Peter Botkine, 23–25.

171. Botkin, *Romanovs*, 10.

172. Ibid., 15.

173. Tatiana Botkine, 68.

174. Botkin, *Romanovs*, 79.

175. Ibid., 142.

176. Gilliard, 17.

177. Botkin, *Romanovs*, 79.

178. Ibid., 80.

179. Sokolov, *Enquete*, 34.

180. Vyrubova, 218.

181. Radzinsky, 116; information provided to the authors by Dimitry Macedonsky.

182. Benagh, 224.

183. Sokolov, *Enquete*, 33.

184. Details drawn from Volkov's own memoirs.

185. Speranski, 166.

186. Proskuryakov, April 3, 1919, in SA, vol. 5, doc. 17.

187. Yakimov, May 7–11, 1919, in SA, vol. 5, doc. 18.

188. Proskuryakov, April 3, 1919, in SA, vol. 5, doc. 17.

189. Interview with Dr. William Maples, July 16, 1993, Ekaterinburg, Cymru.

190. Tatiana Botkine, 115.

191. Proskuryakov, April 3, 1919, in SA, vol. 5, doc. 17; Yakimov, May 7–11, 1919, in SA, vol. 5, doc. 18.

192. Grey, 33; Proskuryakov, April 3, 1919, in SA, vol. 5, doc. 17; Yakimov, May 7–11, 1919, in SA, vol. 5, doc. 18.

193. Benckendorff, 128.

194. Sokolov, 88.

195. Benckendorff, 129.

196. Markov, 126.

197. Markov, 128–129.

198. Bulygin and Kerensky, 197.

199. Ibid., 198–199.

200. Markov, 148.

201. Kasvinov, 401; Markov, 149.

202. Bulygin and Kerensky, 198.

203. Kasvinov, 403.

204. Bulygin and Kerensky, 199.

205. Kasvinov, 403.

206. Markov, 152; Kasvinov, 403.

207. Maria Rasputin, manuscript in a private collection in the United States; Bykov, October 17, 1927, in TsDOOSO, f. 41, op. 1, d. 149.

208. AF to Vyrubova, February 4, 1918, in Vyrubova, 322.

209. Markov, 255–256.

210. Markov, 259.

211. See Maria Rasputin, manuscript in a private collection in the United States; Bykov, October 17, 1927, in TsDOOSO, f. 41, op. 1, d. 149; memoirs of Tatiana Teumina in TsDOOSO, f. 221, op. 2, d. 848.

212. Bykov, October 17, 1927, in TsDOOSO, f. 41, op. 1, d. 149; see also memoirs of Tatiana Teumina in TsDOOSO, f. 221, op. 2, d. 848; Markov, 228–262; Kasvinov, 399–406.

213. Benckendorff, 129.

214. Maria Rasputin, manuscript, in a private collection in the United States.

215. Markov, 212.

216. Ibid., 214–215.

217. See Markov, 214–215; Maria Rasputin, manuscript in a private collection in the United States; Kasvinov, 403–405; Interrogation of N. V. Lepilin, November 17, 1918, by Kirsta, certified copy in authors' collection.

218. Kobylinsky, April 6–10, 1919, in SA, vol. 3, doc. 29.

219. See Benckendorff, 130, and Clarke, 138.

220. Buxhoeveden, *Left Behind*, 58–61.

221. Gibbes, July 1, 1919, in SA, vol. 5, doc. 31.

222. Romanov jewel inventory list, in TsDOOSO, in documents collection "The Romanov Valuables," f. 221, op. 1, d. 89.

223. Alexander Kirpichnikov statements, November 11–12, 1933; December 22, 1933; January 31, 1934; and March 8, 1934, in TsDOOSO, in documents collection "The Romanov Valuables," f. 221, op. 1, d. 1, l. 60, 69, 138; op. 2, l. 106, 130–131.

Chapter 2: A Traitor to the Revolution

1. Wilton and Telberg, 277.

2. Nevolin, in GARF, f. 601, op. 2, d. 33; Sakovich, in GARF, f. 601, op. 2, d. 51.

3. Volkogonov, 6.

4. Bunyan and Fisher, 6.

5. Ulyanova-Yelizarova, *Vospomininaniya*, 126–128.

6. Ulyanova-Yelizarova in *Proletarskaya Revolyutsiya* 2–3 (February–March 1927): 284, quoted in Salisbury, 32.

7. Ulyanova-Yelizarova, *Vospomininaniya*, 127.

8. Ulyanova-Yelizarova, "O V. I. Lenine I semie Ulyanovykh," in Volkogonov, 15.

9. Volkogonov, 19.

10. Ibid., 52–59.

11. Payne, *Lenin*, 24–27.

12. Salisbury, 148.

13. Cited in Salisbury, 152.

14. *Sochineny*, vol. 20, 167.

15. Ibid., 21:17; see also A. Latyshev, "Rasstrel tsarskoi sem'i: znal li o nyom Lenin?" in *Vechernii Yekaterinburg* (July 27, 1993); and A. Latyshev, "Lenin v rasstrele ne uchastvoval," *Rodina* 8 (1993): 68–73.

16. Trotsky, *O Lenine*, 91–93.

17. Volkogonov, 175.

18. A. M. Spirin, "Klassy I partii v grazhdanskii voine vi Rossii," cited in Pipes, *Russia under the Bolshevik Regime*, 24.

19. Volkogonov, 173.

20. Ibid., 175.

21. "The Socialist Fatherland in Danger!" in *Pravda* (February, 9–22, 1918).

22. Payne, *Lenin*, 517.

23. Lenin, *Sochineny*, vol. 35, 186.

24. Trotsky, *O Lenine*, 104–105.

25. Steinberg, *In the Workshop of the Revolution*, 134.

26. Ibid., 145.

27. Levytsky, 22.

28. Bunyan, 227.

29. Bromage, 9–11; Levytsky, 22.

30. Volkogonov, 183.

31. Wheeler-Bennett, 269.

32. Ibid., 276.

33. Volkogonov, 185.

34. "Nemetskii imperator i russkii gosudar," *Pravda* (February 10–23, 1918).

35. Alexandrov, 71.

36. Deterikhs, vol. 1, 78.

37. Letter of Grand Duke Andrei to Serge Botkin, December 8, 1927, in Kurth Papers.

38. Ibid.

39. Markov, 228.

40. Ioffe, *Revoliutsiia i sud'ba Romanovki*, 303–353.

41. Bykov, in *Rabochaya revoliutsiya na Urale*, 7; Bykov, *Last Days*, 63.

42. Avdayev, in *Krasnaia Nov* 5 (1928): 187.

43. Memoirs of Tatiana Teumina, in TsDOOSO, f. 221, op. 2, d. 848.

44. Avdayev, in *Krasnaia Nov* 5 (1928): 187.

45. Bulygin and Kerensky, 205; Sokolov, *Enquete*, 70; Melgunov, *Sud'ba Imperatora Nikolaya*, 277–279.

46. Memoirs of Tatiana Teumina, in TsDOOSO, f. 221, op. 2, d. 848.

47. Ibid.; Bykov, *Last Days*, 63; Sokolov, *Enquete*, 70.

48. Special detachment meeting of April 22, 1918, minutes, in GARF, f. 601, op. 2, d. 33, l. 27–28.

49. Memoirs of Tatiana Teumina, in TsDOOSO, f. 221, op. 2, d. 848; Bykov, *Last Days*, 64; Kobylinsky, April 6–10, 1919, in SA, vol. 3, doc. 29; Gilliard, March 5, 1919, in SA, Vol. 2, doc. 55.

50. Ural Regional Soviet to Sverdlov, cable of April 6, 1918, in GARF, f. 1235, op. 34, d. 36, l. 31.

51. Bykov, *Last Days*, 65–66; Melgunov, *Sud'ba Imperatora Nikolaya*, 278; Sokolov, *Enquete*, 71–72.

52. Sokolov, *Enquete*, 71–72; memoirs of Tatiana Teumina, in TsDOOSO, f. 221, op. 2, d. 848.

53. Sokolov, *Enquete*, 71; Bulygin and Kerensky, 206.

54. Didkovsky, Ural Regional Soviet, to VTsIK, Sovnarkom, cable of April 13, 1918, in GARF, f. 130, op. 2, d. 1109.

55. Minutes of session of VTsIK, April 1, 1918, in GARF, f. 1235, op. 3, d. 36.

56. Minutes of session of VTsIK, April 6, 1918, in GARF, f. 1235, op. 34, d. 36.

57. Sverdlov to the Ural Regional Soviet, letter of April 9, 1918, in GARF, f. 601, op. 2, d. 33.

58. Yakovlev's unpublished memoirs, in TsDOOSO, f. 221, op. 2, d. 964.

59. Yakovlev's memoirs, in Party Archive of Bashkirov, f. 1832, op. 2, d. 33; Yakovlev's unpublished memoirs, in TsDOOSO, f. 221, op. 2, d. 964; Radzinsky, 257; Kobylinksy, April 6–10, 1919, in SA, vol. 3, doc. 29.

60. Yakovlev's unpublished memoirs, in TsDOOSO, f. 221, op. 2, d. 964; Ioffe, *Revoliutsiia i sud'ba Romanovki*, 167–175.

61. Alexandrov, 144.

62. Mstislavskii, 87.

63. Yakovlev's unpublished memoirs, in TsDOOSO, f. 221, op. 2, d. 964.

64. Ibid.

65. Kobylinksy, April 6–10, 1919, in SA, vol. 3, doc. 29.

66. Yakovlev's unpublished memoirs, in TsDOOSO, f. 221, op. 2, d. 964; Platonov, *Ubiistvo tsarskoi semi*, 371; Kasvinov, 372; Petrov, Lysenko, and Egorov, 41.

67. Bykov, *Last Days*, 64–65.

68. Ibid., 65.

69. Ibid.

70. Kobylinksy, April 6–10, 1919, in SA, Vol. 3, Doc. 29.

71. Sokolov, *Enquete*, 67.

72. Unpublished memoirs of Serge Galkin, in TsDOOSO, f. 221, op. 2, d. 304.

73. N diary, April 23, 1918, in GARF, f. 601, op. 1, d. 266.

74. Yakovlev's unpublished memoirs, in TsDOOSO, f. 221, op. 2, d. 964.

75. Ibid.

76. Tatiana Botkine, 63.

77. N diary, April 23, 1918, in GARF, f. 601, op. 1, d. 266.

78. Kobylinksy, April 6–10, 1919, in SA, vol. 3, doc. 29; Tegleva, July 5–6, 1919, in SA, vol. 5, doc. 36; Bulygin and Kerensky, 201.

79. Volkov, 117.

80. AF diary, April 23, 1918, in GARF, f. 640, op. 1, d. 326.

81. Gilliard diary, April 23, 1918, in Gilliard, 259–260.

82. Cable of April 23, 1918, in GARF f. 601, op. 2, d. 33.

83. Kobylinsky, in Sokolov, *Enquete*, 73.

84. Kobylinksy, April 6–10, 1919, in SA, vol. 3, doc. 29.

85. Volkov, 118–119.

86. Ibid., 119–120.

87. Kobylinksy, April 6–10, 1919, in SA, vol. 3, doc. 29.

88. Yakovlev's unpublished memoirs, in TsDOOSO, f. 221, op. 2, d. 964.

89. Kobylinksy, April 6–10, 1919, in SA, vol. 3, doc. 29.

90. Yakovlev's unpublished memoirs, in TsDOOSO, f. 221, op. 2, d. 964.

91. Kobylinksy, April 6–10, 1919, in SA, vol. 3, doc. 29.

92. Gilliard, March 5, 1919, in SA, vol. 2, doc. 55.

93. Kobylinksy, April 6–10, 1919, in SA, vol. 3, doc. 29.

94. *Krasnaia Nov* 27 (1928): 17.

95. Avdayev, in *Krasnaia Nov* 5 (1928): 195.

96. Paul Matveyev, unpublished memoirs, in Sverdlovsk Party Archive, TsDOOSO, f. 41, op. 1, d. 149.

97. Smirnoff, 123; Melgunov, *Sud'ba Imperatora Nikolaya II*, 282.

98. Dolgoruky to Chemodurov, in Sokolov, *Enquete*, 108–109.

99. Tatiana Botkine, 106.

100. Botkin, *Romanovs*, 194.

101. Gilliard, *Thirteen Years*, 260.

102. Gilliard, in Sokolov, *Enquete*, 75–76.

103. Tutelberg, in Sokolov, *Enquete*, 77.

104. Gilliard, in Sokolov, *Enquete*, 76.

105. Gilliard, *Thirteen Years*, 261.

106. Buxhoeveden, *Life*, 329.

107. Gilliard, *Thirteen Years*, 261.

108. Gilliard, March 5, 1919, in SA, vol. 2, doc. 55.

109. Volkov, in Sokolov, *Enquete*, 77.

110. Tatiana Botkine, 109.

111. Gilliard, *Thirteen Years*, 262.

112. Trewin, 98.

113. Bykov, *Last Days*, 68.

114. Tatiana Botkine, 110.

115. Tatiana Botkine, 110.

116. Bittner, August 4, 1919, in Ross, 422.

117. Buxhoeveden, *Life*, 331.

118. Volkov, 122.

119. Bury, 170.

120. Gilliard, March 5, 1919, in SA, vol. 2, doc. 55.

121. Bykov, *Last Days*, 66.

122. Tatiana Botkine, 110–111.

123. Kobylinsky, April 6–10, 1919, in SA, vol. 3, doc. 29.

124. Bittner, in Sokolov, *Enquete*, 79.

125. Tatiana Botkine, 111.

126. Letter from Marie Nikolaievna to Zenaide Tolstoy, May 17, 1918, in Speranski, 12.

127. AF diary, April 26, 1918, in GARF, f. 640, op. 1, d. 326.

128. N diary, April 27, 1918, in GARF, f. 601, op. 1, d. 266.

129. AF diary, April 27, 1918, in GARF, f. 640, op. 1, d. 326.

130. Bykov, *Last Days*, 68; Bulygin and Kerensky, 212.
131. Nevolin, in GARF, f. 601, op. 2, d. 33.
132. Sakovich, in GARF, f. 601, op. 2, d. 51.
133. Bykov, *Last Days*, 67.
134. Ibid., 68.
135. Yakovlev to Goloshchokin, April 27, 1918, in GARF, f. 601, op. 2, d. 33; and to Silig, in Tyumen, April 27, 1918, in GARF, f. 601, op. 2, d. 33.
136. Bykov, *Last Days*, 69.
137. AF diary, April 27, 1918, in GARF, f. 640, op. 1, d. 326; N diary, April 27, 1918, in GARF, f. 601, op. 1, d. 266.
138. Bulygin and Kerensky, 212; AF diary, April 27, 1918, in GARF, f. 640, op. 1, d. 326; N diary, April 27, 1918, in GARF, f. 601, op. 1, d. 266; Kobylinksy, April 6–10, 1919, in SA, vol. 3, doc. 29.
139. Kobylinksy, April 6–10, 1919, in SA, vol. 3, doc. 29.
140. Kasvinov, 454–455.
141. Yakovlev's unpublished memoirs, in TsDOOSO, f. 221, op. 2, d. 964.
142. AF diary, April 27, 1918, in GARF, f. 640, op. 1, d. 326; N diary, April 27, 1918, in GARF, f. 601, op. 1, d. 266.
143. N diary, April 27, 1918, in GARF, f. 601, op. 1, d. 266.
144. AF diary, April 27, 1918, in GARF, f. 640, op. 1, d. 326.
145. Yakovlev's unpublished memoirs, in TsDOOSO, f. 221, op. 2, d. 992.
146. Yakovlev to Goloshchokin, Tyumen to Ekaterinburg, April 27, 1918, in GARF, f. 601, op. 2, d. 33.
147. Yakovlev to Sverdlov, Tyumen to Moscow, April 27, 1918, in GARF, f. 601, op. 2, d. 32.
148. Telegraphic conversation between Sverdlov and Yakovlev, Tyumen to Moscow, April 27, 1918, in GARF, f. 601, op. 2, d. 32.
149. Sverdlov to Kosarev, Moscow to Omsk, April 28, 1918, GARF, f. 601, op. 2, d. 33.
150. Avdayev, in *Krasnaia Nov* 5 (1928): 195–196; Bykov, *Last Days*, 69.
151. Sokolov, *Enquete*, 83.
152. N diary, April 28, 1918, in GARF, f. 601, op. 1, d. 266.
153. Ibid.
154. Yakovlev, in *Izvestiia*, no. 96 (May 16, 1918), 2.
155. Avdayev, in *Krasnaia Nov* 5 (1928): 1 Bykov, *Last Days*, 69.
156. Beloborodov to Sverdlov, Ekaterinburg to Moscow, April 29, 1918, in GARF, f. 601, op. 2, d. 27.
157. Bykov, *Last Days*, 72.
158. Sverdlov to Beloborodov, Moscow to Ekaterinburg, April 28 or 29, 1918, in GARF, f. 601, op. 2, d. 7709.
159. Melgunov, *Sud'ba Imperatora Nikolaya II*, 290.
160. Yakovlev's unpublished memoirs, in TsDOOSO, f. 221, op. 2, d. 964.
161. Beloborodov to Kosarev, Ekaterinburg to Omsk, April 29, 1918, in GARF, f. 601, op. 2, d. 32.
162. Yakovlev to Sverdlov, Omsk to Moscow, April 29, 1918, in GARF, f. 130, op. 2, d. 1109.
163. Sokolov, *Enquete*, 109.
164. Yakovlev to Sverdlov and Lenin, Ekaterinburg to Moscow, April 30, 1918, in GARF, f. 601, op. 2, d. 38.
165. Yakovlev declaration of April 30, 1918, in GARF, f. 601, op. 2, d. 32.
166. AF diary, April 29, 1918, in GARF, f. 601, op. 1, d. 266.
167. Paul Matveyev, unpublished memoirs, in Sverdlovsk Party Archive, TsDOOSO, f. 41, op. 1, d. 149.
168. N diary, April 30, 1918, in GARF, f. 601, op. 1, d. 266; AF diary, April 30, 1918, in GARF, f. 640, op. 1, d. 326.
169. Yakovlev's unpublished memoirs, in TsDOOSO, f. 221, op. 2, d. 964.
170. Ibid.
171. Ibid.
172. Ibid.
173. N Diary, April 30, 1918, in GARF, f. 601, op. 1, d. 266; AF diary, April 30, 1918, in GARF, f. 640, op. 1, d. 326.
174. Yakovlev's unpublished memoirs, in TsDOOSO, f. 221, op. 2, d. 964.
175. Avdayev, in *Krasnaia Nov* 5 (1928): 197.
176. AF diary, April 30, 1918, in GARF, f. 640, op. 1, d. 326.
177. Avdayev, in *Krasnaia Nov* 5 (1928): 197.
178. AF diary, April 30, 1918, in GARF, f. 640, op. 1, d. 326.
179. Receipt for Romanovs, April 30, 1918, signed by Beloborodov, in GARF, f. 601, op. 2, d. 1109.
180. Avdayev, in *Krasnaia Nov* 5 (1928): 197.

181. N diary, April 30, 1918, in GARF, f. 601, op. 1, d. 266; AF diary, April 30, 1918, in GARF, f. 640, op. 1, d. 326.
182. AF diary, April 30, 1918, in GARF, f. 640, op. 1, d. 326.
183. Nicholas Ipatiev, unpublished memoirs, in SA, vol. 2, doc. 22; Ipatiev, 217; Bykov, *Last Days*, 72; Order 2778 from Ural Regional Soviet Housing commissar Zhilinsky, in SA, vol. 2, doc. 4.
184. Bykov, *Last Days*, 58; Speranski, 30–31.
185. Bulygin and Kerensky, 232.
186. Arrest order signed by Beloborodov, April 30, 1918, in GARF, f. 601, op. 2, d. 4.
187. Avdayev, in *Krasnaia Nov* 5 (1928): 197–198.
188. Bykov, *Last Days*, 71.
189. Chemodurov testimony, August 15–16, 1918, in SA, vol. 1, doc. 23.
190. Avdayev, in *Krasnaia Nov* 5 (1928): 198.
191. Vyrubova, 341–342.

Chapter 3: The House of Special Purpose

1. Beable, 61.
2. Ackerman, 76; Beable, 32.
3. Wilton and Telberg, 420.
4. Beable, 60.
5. Bobrick, 328.
6. Preston, 89; McCullagh, 114.
7. Pascal, 67.
8. Ackerman, 75.
9. Bury, 40–41.
10. Preston, 46.
11. Ackerman, 75.
12. Smirnoff, 120.
13. Ibid., 120; Solzhenitsyn, vol. 2, 681.
14. Bury, 83.
15. Ibid.
16. Ibid., 85.
17. Victoria, marchioness of Milford Haven, unpublished "Recollections," 303, in Broadlands Archives, Hartley Library, Southampton University, United Kingdom, quoted in Hough, *Louis and Victoria*, 332.
18. Ibid.
19. Sokolov, *Enquete*, 154–155; Grey, 17; Speranski, 29–30.
20. See "The Memoirs of Nicholas Ipatiev" in SA, vol. 2, doc. 22.

21. McCullagh, 124.
22. See AP report, May 31, 2000.
23. Speranski, 29.
24. Ibid., 37.
25. Sokolov, *Enquete*, 155–156; Speranski, 35; McCullagh, 125.
26. McCullagh, 126; Nametkin search, August 2, 3, 6–8, 1918, in SA, vol. 3, doc. 27.
27. Nametkin search, August 2, 3, 6–8, 1918, in SA, vol. 3, doc. 27.
28. Ibid.
29. Ibid.; Sokolov, *Enquete*, 156; Ackerman, 85.
30. Sokolov, *Enquete*, 157.
31. Nametkin search, August 2, 3, 6–8, 1918, in SA, vol. 3, doc. 27; McCullagh, 128; Sokolov, *Enquete*, 157.
32. Nametkin search, August 2, 3, 6–8, 1918, in SA, vol. 3, doc. 27; Trewin, 148.
33. Nametkin search, August 2, 3, 6–8, 1918, in SA, vol. 3, doc. 27; Sokolov, *Enquete*, 156–157; Ackerman, 85.
34. Nametkin search, August 2, 3, 6–8, 1918, in SA, vol. 3, doc. 27; Sergeyev search, August 11–14, 1918, in SA, vol. 3, doc. 54; Sokolov, *Enquete*, 157–158; Ackerman, 85.
35. AF diary, April 30, 1918, in GARF, f. 640, op. 1, d. 326.
36. N diary, April 30, 1918, in GARF, f. 601, op. 1, d. 266.
37. Letter from Marie Nikolaievna to Zenaide Tolstoy, May 17, 1918, quoted in Speranski, 12.
38. Report of inspection of the Ipatiev House by Sokolov, April 15–25, 1919, in SA, vol. 3, doc. 42; Gilliard, March 5–6, 1919, in SA, vol. 2, doc. 55.
39. Alexandrov, 87.
40. Ibid.
41. Deterikhs, vol. 1, 283.
42. Pipes, *Russian Revolution*, 748; Alexandrov, 88; Radzinsky, 235.
43. Alexandrov, 88; Bulygin and Kerensky, 243.
44. Alexandrov, 89; Trotsky, *Stalin*, 137.
45. Radzinsky, 235.
46. Sverdlov, 32.
47. Goloshchokin, "Vospominaniya uchastnikov Velikogo Oktyabrya," in *Istoricheskii arkhiv* 5 (1957): 198, cited in Volkogonov, 218; Lenin, *Biograficheskaya Khronika*, vol. 5, 64.

48. Alexandrov, 88.
49. Wilton, 230.
50. Radzinsky, 395.
51. Alexandrov, 91; Sokolov, *Enquete*, 137; Timms, 390–391.
52. Glafira Stepanovna, in Speranski, 204.
53. Radzinsky, 395.
54. Sokolov, *Enquete*, 137.
55. Ibid., 135–136. Ermakov's Verkh-Isetsk detachment was composed of the two Vaganov brothers, Alexander Medvedev, Peter Puzanov, Igor Skoryanin, Michael Shadrin, Peter Yaroslavtsev, Vassili Kurilov, Michael Kurilov, Nicholas Kazantsev, Michael Sorokin, Ilia Perin, Gregory Desyatov, Ivan Prosvirnin, Igor Shalin, Polikarp Tretyakov, Ivan Zaushitsin, Alexander Rybnikov, Gushkin, and Oreshkin.
56. Radzinsky, 321; Timms, 386.
57. Nikita Tchernikin, in Speranski, 151.
58. Radzinsky, 419.
59. Ibid., 252.
60. Ibid., 292.
61. Radzinsky, 279–280.
62. Ibid., 328.
63. Preston, 97.
64. Gilliard, *Thirteen Years*, 282.
65. Sokolov, *Enquete*, 154; Speranski, 13–16.
66. Speranski, 135.
67. Speranski, 45–46; Yakimov, May 7–11, 1919, in SA, vol. 5, doc. 18.
68. Yakimov, May 7–11, 1919, in SA, vol. 5, doc. 18.
69. Speranski, 47–48.
70. Yakimov, May 7–11, 1919, in SA, vol. 5, doc. 18.
71. Kobylinsky, April 6–10, 1919, in SA, vol. 3, doc. 29.
72. Sister Agnes, mistress of novices at Novotikhvinsky Convent in Ekaterinburg, in Speranski, 135–139.
73. Speranski, 149.
74. Rodzinsky, December 1963, in RTsKhIDNI, f. 588, op. 3, d. 14.
75. Sokolov, *Enquete*, 52.
76. Yakimov, May 7–11, 1919, in SA, vol. 5, doc. 18; Medvedev, February 21–22, 1919, vol. 2, doc. 86; Speranski, 89.
77. Medvedev, February 21–22, 1919, in SA, vol. 2, doc. 86.
78. Speranski, 45.
79. Proskuryakov, April 3, 1919, in SA, vol.

5, doc. 17; Yakimov, May 7–11, 1919, in SA, vol. 5, doc. 18.
80. Pipes, *Russian Revolution*, 629; Grey, 36.
81. Strekotin, 1934, in TsDOOSO, f. 221, op. 2, d. 849; Medvedev, February 21–22, 1919, in SA, vol. 2, doc. 86; Platonov, 445–446.
82. Strekotin, 1934, in TsDOOSO, f. 221, op. 2, d. 849; Deterikhs, vol. 1, 277; Medvedev, February 21–22, 1919, in SA, vol. 2, doc. 86; Platonov, *Ternovyi venets Rossi*, 445–446, 507.
83. Deterikhs, vol. 1, 378.
84. Ibid.
85. Ibid., 379.
86. Ibid.
87. Ibid.
88. Ibid., 379–380.
89. Strekotin, 1934, in TsDOOSO, f. 221, op. 2, d. 849.
90. Ibid.; Deterikhs, vol. 1, 277; May notebook for Ipatiev House pay, in Sotheby's auction catalog, 74–75.
91. Sokolov, *Enquete*, 109; Deterikhs, vol. 1, 105.
92. Strekotin, 1934, in TsDOOSO, f. 221, op. 2, d. 849.
93. Ibid.
94. Medvedev, February 21–22, 1919, in SA, vol. 2, doc. 86; Strekotin, 1934, in TsDOOSO, f. 221, op. 2, d. 849.
95. Ibid.
96. Medvedev, February 21–22, 1919, in SA, vol. 2, doc. 86.
97. Ibid.
98. Strekotin, 1934, in TsDOOSO, f. 221, op. 2, d. 849.
99. Ibid.; May notebook for Ipatiev House pay, in Sotheby's auction catalog, 74–75; Deterikhs, vol. 1, 278–279; Platonov, *Ternovyi venets Rossi*, 445.
100. Proskuryakov, April 3, 1919, in SA, vol. 5, doc. 17.
101. Deterikhs, vol. 1, 417, 1:400; Strekotin, 1934, in TsDOOSO, f. 221, op. 2, d. 849.
102. Strekotin, 1934, in TsDOOSO, f. 221, op. 2, d. 849; Medvedev, February 21–22, 1919, in SA, vol. 2, doc. 86.
103. Strekotin, 1934, in TsDOOSO, f. 221, op. 2, d. 849.
104. Ibid.
105. Yakimov, May 7–11, 1919, in SA, vol. 5, doc. 18.

106. Ibid.
107. Ibid.; Medvedev, February 21–22, 1919, in SA, vol. 2, doc. 86; Platonov, *Ternovyi venets Rossi*, 445–446.
108. Yakimov, May 7–11, 1919, in SA, vol. 5, doc. 18.
109. Ibid.
110. N diary, May 8, 1918, in GARF, f. 601, op. 1, d. 266.
111. Avdayev, in *Krasnaia Nov* 5 (1928): 198.
112. Proskuryakov, April 3, 1919, in SA, vol. 5, doc. 17.
113. Medvedev, February 21–22, 1919, in SA, vol. 2, doc. 86; Proskuryakov, April 3, 1919, in SA, vol. 5, doc. 17.
114. Medvedev, February 21–22, 1919, in SA, vol. 2, doc. 86.
115. Yakimov, May 7–11, 1919, in SA, vol. 5, doc. 18.
116. Pipes, *Russian Revolution*, 629; Grey, 36.
117. Proskuryakov, April 3, 1919, in SA, vol. 5, doc. 17; Medvedev, February 21–22, 1919, in SA, vol. 2, doc. 86.
118. Proskuryakov, April 3, 1919, in SA, vol. 5, doc. 17.
119. Yakimov, May 7–11, 1919, in SA, vol. 5, doc. 18.
120. Medvedev, February 21–22, 1919, in SA, vol. 2, doc. 86; Yakimov, May 7–11, 1919, in SA, vol. 5, doc. 18.
121. Yakimov, May 7–11, 1919, in SA, vol. 5, doc. 18.
122. Ibid.; Proskuryakov, April 3, 1919, in SA, vol. 5, doc. 17; Yakimov, May 7–11, 1919, in SA, vol. 5, doc. 18.
123. Yakimov, May 7–11, 1919, in SA, vol. 5, doc. 18; Medvedev, February 21–22, 1919, in SA, vol. 2, doc. 86; Proskuryakov, April 3, 1919, in SA, vol. 5, doc. 17.
124. Deterikhs, vol. 1, 378.
125. Ian Lilburn to Wilson, July 29, 2000.
126. Yakimov, May 7–11, 1919, in SA, vol. 5, doc. 18.
127. Ibid.; Medvedev, February 21–22, 1919, in SA, vol. 2, doc. 86.
128. Yakimov, May 7–11, 1919, in SA, vol. 5, doc. 18.
129. Ibid.; Medvedev, February 21–22, 1919, in SA, vol. 2, doc. 86; Ipatiev House guard duty book, in GARF, f. 601, op. 2, d. 24. On June 11 the following Zlokazov workers were added to the Special Detachment: three brothers named

Loginov; Stanislaus Mishkevich, whose brother Nicholas had already joined the Special Detachment; Soloviev; Gonikhevich; Koriakin; Krashennikov; Sidorov; Oukrainzev; Komendantov; Laboushev; Valentine Lyukhanov; and Ivan Skorokhodov.
130. Yakimov, May 7–11, 1919, in SA, vol. 5, doc. 18; Medvedev, February 21–22, 1919, in SA, vol. 2, doc. 86.
131. Yakimov, May 7–11, 1919, in SA, vol. 5, doc. 18; Proskuryakov, April 3, 1919, in SA, vol. 5, doc. 17; Medvedev, February 21, 1919, in SA, vol. 2, doc. 86; Yurovsky, unpublished memoirs, 1922, in APRF, f. 3, op. 58, d. 280.
132. Yakimov, May 7–11, 1919, in SA, vol. 5, doc. 18.
133. Ibid.
134. Strekotin, 1934, in TsDOOSO, f. 221, op. 2, d. 849; Yakimov, May 7–11, 1919, in SA, vol. 5, doc. 18; Speranski, 100–101; Proskuryakov, April 3, 1919, in SA, vol. 5, doc. 17; McCullagh, 125.
135. Strekotin, 1934, in TsDOOSO, f. 221, op. 2, d. 849.
136. Proskuryakov, April 3, 1919, in SA, vol. 5, doc. 18.
137. Speranski, 89–90.
138. Medvedev, February 21–22, 1919, in SA, vol. 2, doc. 86.
139. Ibid.; Yakimov, May 7–11, 1919, in SA, vol. 5, doc. 18.

Chapter 4: "It Was Dreadful, What They Did . . ."

1. AF diary, May 1, 1918, in GARF, f. 640, op. 1, d. 326; Marie Nikolaievna to Olga Nikolaievna, with notes by Alexandra and Nicholas, May 1, 1918, in GARF, f. 673, op. 1, d. 78.
2. N diary, May 1, 1918, in GARF, f. 601, op. 1, d. 266.
3. Strekotin, 1934, in TsDOOSO, f. 221, op. 2, d. 849.
4. Marie Nikolaievna to Olga Nikolaievna, with notes by Alexandra and Nicholas, May 1, 1918, in GARF, f. 673, op. 1, d. 78.
5. AF diary, May 1, 1918, in GARF, f. 640, op. 1, d. 326.
6. Marie Nikolaievna to Olga Nikolaievna, May 3, 1918, in GARF, f. 673, op. 1, d. 82.

7. AF diary, May 2, 1918, in GARF, f. 640, op. 1, d. 326.
8. Ibid.
9. Ibid.
10. N diary, May 3, 1918, in GARF, f. 601, op. 1, d. 266.
11. Letter from Alexandra and Marie Nikolaievna to Olga Nikolaievna, May 2, 1918, in GARF, f. 673, op. I, d. 78.
12. AF diary, May 3, 1918, in GARF, f. 640, op. 1, d. 326.
13. Kozlov, 125.
14. N diary, May 4, 1918, in GARF, f. 601, op. 1, d. 266.
15. AF and N diaries, May 4, 1918, in GARF, f. 640, op. 1, d. 326, and f. 601, op. 1, d. 266.
16. AF diary, May 5, 1918, in GARF, f. 640, op. 1, d. 326.
17. N diary, May 4, 1918, in GARF, f. 601, op. 1, d. 266.
18. Avdayev, in *Krasnaia Nov* 5 (1928): 204.
19. N diary, May 7, 1918, in GARF, f. 601, op. 1, d. 266.
20. In GARF, f. 673, op. 1, d. 74.
21. N diary, May 8, 1918, in GARF, f. 601, op. 1, d. 266.
22. N diary, May 8, 1918, in GARF, f. 601, op. 1, d. 266.
23. N diary, May 10, 1918, in GARF, f. 601, op. 1, d. 266; AF diary, May 10, 1918, f. 640, op. 1, d. 326.
24. N diary, May 10, 1918, in GARF, f. 601, op. 1, d. 266.
25. Proskuryakov, April 3, 1919, in SA, vol. 5, doc. 17.
26. Proskuryakov, April 3, 1919, in SA, vol. 5, doc. 17; AF diary, July 4, 1918, in GARF, f. 640, op. 1, d. 326.
27. AF diary, May 10, 1918, in GARF, f. 601, op. 1, d. 266.
28. Ibid.; AF diary, May 10, 1918, in GARF, f. 640, op. 1, d. 326.
29. N diary, May 12, 1918, in GARF, f. 601, op. 1, d. 266.
30. N diary May, 9, 1918, in GARF, f. 601, op. 1, d. 266.
31. AF diary, May 9, 1918, in GARF, f. 640, op. 1, d. 326; N diary, May 10, 1918, in GARF, f. 601, op. 1, d. 266.
32. N diary, May 10, 1918, in GARF, f. 601, op. 1, d. 266.
33. Marie Nikolaievna to Olga Nikolaievna,

May 10, 1918, in GARF, f. 685, op. 1, d. 276.
34. Guard duty book, May 11–13, 1918, in GARF, f. 601, op. 2, d. 24.
35. AF diary, May 14, 1918, in GARF, f. 640, op. 1, d. 326.
36. N diary, May 14, 1918, in GARF, f. 601, op. 1, d. 266.
37. Ibid.
38. AF diary, May 15, 1918, in GARF, f. 640, op. 1, d. 326.
39. AF diary, May 20, 1918, in GARF, f. 640, op. 1, d. 326.
40. Guard duty book, May 15, 1918, in GARF, f. 601, op. 2, d. 24.
41. Guard duty book, May 20–21, 1918, in GARF, f. 601, op. 2, d. 24.
42. N diary, May 1–23, 1918, in GARF, f. 601, op. 1, d. 266; AF diary, May 1–23, 1918, in GARF, f. 640, op. 1, d. 326; guard duty book for Ipatiev House, May 1–23, 1918, in GARF, f. 601, op. 2, d. 24; N diary, May 22, 1918, in GARF, f. 601, op. 1, d. 266.
43. AF diary, May 19, 1918, in GARF, f. 640, op. 1, d. 326.
44. N diary, May 19, 1918, in GARF, f. 601, op. 1, d. 266.
45. Ibid.
46. AF diary, May 21, 1918, in GARF, f. 640, op. 1, d. 326; N diary, May 21, 1918, in GARF, f. 601, op. 1, d. 266.
47. N diary, May 22, 1918, in GARF, f. 601, op. 1, d. 266.
48. Volkov, 122.
49. Gilliard, *Thirteen Years*, 263; see also Gilliard, March 5, 1919, in SA, vol. 2, doc. 55.
50. Gilliard, *Thirteen Years*, 263.
51. Gilliard, diary for May 2, 1918, in Gilliard, *Thirteen Years*, 264.
52. Hendrikova, diary for May 3, 1918, in SA, vol. 4.
53. Gilliard, diary for May 3, 1918, in Gilliard, *Thirteen Years*, 264.
54. Kobylinsky, April 6–10, 1919, in SA, vol. 3, doc. 29.
55. Gilliard, diary for May 4, 1918, in Gilliard, *Thirteen Years*, 264.
56. Letter from Anastasia Nikolaievna to Marie Nikolaievna and her parents in Ekaterinburg, May 7, 1918, in GARF, f. 685, op. I, d. 40.

57. Trewin, 101.

58. Bulygin and Kerensky, 232.

59. Newman and Bressler, 42.

60. Tegleva, in Sokolov, *Enquete*, 105; also letter from Minister of Justice Starynkevich to the Ministry of Foreign Affairs Executive Board, Omsk, February 19, 1919 (original certified Russian copy in authors' possession).

61. Newman and Bressler, 42.

62. Unpublished memoirs of Tatiana Teumina, in TsDOOSO, f. 221, op. 2, d. 848.

63. Sokolov, *Enquete*, 109.

64. Unpublished memoirs of Tatiana Teumina, in TsDOOSO, f. 221, op. 2, d. 848; Volkov, 123; see also Gibbes, July 1, 1919, in SA, vol. 5, doc. 31. The Latvian Regiment consisted of: First Platoon: Zen, Kokorouch, Drerve, Nebrotchnik, Ikovnok or Ikovien, Viksna, Gravit, Strazdan, Tarkch, Pourine, Ivseitchick, Prous, Alenkoutz or Liasikoutz, Brandt or Breidt, Gredzen or Grezden, Lepine, Egel, Guerounas, and Ozoline. Second Platoon: Ploume, Grike, Pranoutchkis or Tranoutchkis, Bilskam, Vilemsen, Tsekoulit, Makon, Yakubovski, Alchkine, Baranof, Rolman, Kraino, Oiaver, Kirchansk, Froul, Bloume, Malne or Melne, Iaounzen or Iaounzem, Timan, Dzirkal or Dzirkam, Korsak or Karsak, Larichef or Laristchef, Sternberg, and Guintar. Third Platoon: Doubould or Douboult, Aounine, Berzine, Sirsnik or Sirsnine, Tabak, Schteller, Tchsalnek, Seia, Reinhold, Boilik or Bailik, Hertz, Zivert, Tarkanine, Dief, Zaline, Ligbard, Poumpour, Heide, Volkof, and Keire. The machine gunners were: Haussman, Litzit, Perlantsek, Tobok, Tsalit or Tsalitsch, Zilbert, Berzine, Orlof, and Goussatchenko.

65. Volkov, 123.

66. Ibid., 124.

67. Benagh, 187.

68. Buxhoeveden, *Life*, 336.

69. Tegleva, July 5–6, 1919, in SA, vol. 5, doc. 36.

70. Alexei diary, May 14, 1918, in Eugenie de Greece, 279.

71. Botkin, *Romanovs*, 207.

72. Affidavit of Gleb Botkin, July 20, 1938, in dossier of Edward H. Fallows, prepared by Dr. Paul Leverkuehn and Dr. Kurt

Vermehren, August 17, 1938, Berlin (original in authors' possession).

73. Botkin, *Romanovs*, 208.

74. Trewin, 100.

75. Gibbes's diary, May 19, 1918, in Trewin, 102.

76. Tegleva, July 5–6, 1919, in SA, vol. 5, doc. 36; also in Bulygin and Kerensky, 203.

77. Receipt, May 22, 1918, Western Siberian Trading Company, for 270 rubles paid by Khokryakov to the porter of *Rus*, in GARF, f. 601, op. 2, d. 49.

78. Gilliard, March 5, 1919, in SA, vol. 2, doc. 55; Buxhoeveden, *Left Behind*, 69.

79. Volkov, 123.

80. Buxhoeveden, *Life*, 363.

81. Bykov, *Last Days*, 74; Kobylinsky, April 6–10, 1919, in SA, vol. 3, doc. 29; Gibbes, July 1, 1919, in SA, vol. 5, doc. 31; Volkov, 126; Buxhoeveden, *Life*, 336.

82. Buxhoeveden, *Left Behind*, 68–69.

83. Ibid., 69.

84. Ibid., 70.

85. Volkov, 126.

86. Buxhoeveden, *Life*, 338.

87. Volkov, 126.

88. Gilliard, March 5, 1919, in SA, vol. 2, doc. 55; Gilliard, *Thirteen Years*, 265; Kobylinsky, April 6–10, 1919, in SA, vol. 3, doc. 29; Tegleva, July 5–6, 1919, in SA, vol. 5, doc. 36; Volkov, 126; George Gibbes to King, May 1989.

89. Tegleva, July 5–6, 1919, in SA, vol. 5, doc. 36.

90. Buxhoeveden, *Left Behind*, 69.

91. Volkov, 126.

92. George Gibbes to King, May 1989.

93. According to Volkov, the weather during the journey was indeed warm until the prisoners reached Ekaterinburg, when, as he wrote, "it became very cold." See Volkov, 127.

94. Trewin, 103.

95. Buxhoeveden, *Left Behind*, 69–70.

96. Bykov, October 17, 1927, in TsDOOSO, f. 41, op. 1, d. 149.

97. Ibid.

98. Bulygin and Kerensky, 214.

99. George Gibbes to King, May 1989.

100. Isai Rodzinsky, May 13, 1964, statement, in RTsKhIDNI, f. 588, op. 3, d. 14.

101. Yakov Yurovsky, unpublished memoirs, 1922, in Archives of the President of the Russian Federation (APRF), f. 3, op. 58, d. 280.

102. Bill of the steamship office of the Western Siberian Trading Company to Khokryakov "for expenses incurred for select passengers" aboard *Rus*, May 22, 1918, in GARF, f. 601, op. 2, d. 49.

103. Buxhoeveden, *Left Behind*, 72.

104. In his book, Volkov errs in naming the date of arrival in Tyumen as May 21. See Volkov, 126.

105. Diary of Maria Rasputin, May 22, 1918, in GARF, f. 601, op. 2, d. 75, l. 20, cited in Steinberg and Krustalev, 365.

106. Gibbes, July 1, 1919, in SA, vol. 5, doc. 31; Volkov, 126.

107. Buxhoeveden, *Life*, 338.

108. Buxhoeveden, *Left Behind*, 70; Volkov, 126; Buxhoeveden, *Life*, 338.

109. Buxhoeveden, *Left Behind*, 70–71.

110. N diary, May 23, 1918, in GARF, f. 601, op. 1, d. 266.

111. Volkov, 127.

112. N diary, May 23, 1918, in GARF, f. 601, op. 1, d. 266.

113. Buxhoeveden, *Left Behind*, 73.

114. Ibid., 75.

115. Ibid.

116. Ibid., 76.

117. Volkov, 128.

118. Buxhoeveden, *Left Behind*, 73.

119. Speranski, 166.

120. Halliburton, *Seven League Boots*, 124.

121. Speranski, 160–161.

122. Volkov, 129; Buxhoeveden, *Left Behind*, 73.

123. Buxhoeveden, *Life*, 339. Nearly every account of the Romanovs in Ekaterinburg mentions the presence of only two dogs, Joy and Jemmy, but Buxhoeveden's account—as well as the memoirs of both the guards at the Ipatiev House and the eventual assassins—allows us for the first time to state that all three dogs, Ortino, Joy, and Jemmy, were in the Ipatiev House until the shooting of the family. Further complicating matters is the issue of Jemmy's ownership. The King Charles spaniel had been given to Tatiana by Anna Vyrubova (see Vyrubova, 53). Jemmy has caused countless errors in books written on the imperial family and especially their murders. Nearly every author on the subject has written of Jemmy as Anastasia's dog; even those in the suite and household, who should have known better, including Gibbes, later mistakenly declared that Jemmy had belonged to Anastasia (Gibbes, July 1, 1919, in SA, vol. 5, doc. 31). The discovery of Jemmy's corpse after the Ekaterinburg murders was, for eighty years, cited as proof that his presumed mistress had died as well. The errors continue to the present day, when scholars such as Orlando Figes and the late W. Bruce Lincoln perpetuate the error. See Figes, 640, and Lincoln, *Red Victory*, 153.

124. Gilliard, *Thirteen Years*, 269.

125. Bulygin and Kerensky, 233; Trewin, 103–104; Bykov, *Last Days*, 74; Gilliard, March 5, 1919, in SA, vol. 2, doc. 55.

126. N diary, May 23, 1918, in GARF, f. 601, op. 1, d. 266.

127. Volkov, 128–129.

128. Gilliard, March 5, 1919, in SA, vol. 2, doc. 55.

129. Volkov, 128–129.

130. Ibid., 129–130.

131. Ibid., 131.

132. Gibbes, July 1, 1919, in SA, vol. 5, doc. 31; Gilliard, March 5, 1919, in SA, vol. 2, doc. 55.

133. Buxhoeveden, *Left Behind*, 74.

134. Ibid.

135. Gilliard, *Thirteen Years*, 270.

136. George Gibbes to King, May 1989.

137. Bykov, October 17, 1927, in TsDOOSO, f. 41, op. 1, d. 149.

138. Ibid.

139. See Derevenko in *Rodina* 4 (1989): 96.

140. Helen of Serbia and of Russia, 21.

141. Botkin, *Romanovs*, 223.

142. Avdayev, in *Krasnaia Nov* 5 (1928): 202.

143. Catherine Tomilova, interrogation of November 4, 1918, in GARF, f. 601, op. 2, d. 51.

144. Deterikhs, vol. 1, 299.

145. Yakimov, May 7–11, 1919, in SA, vol. 5, doc. 18.

146. Volkov, 133.

147. Ibid., 133–134.

148. Ibid., 134.

149. Ibid.
150. Gilliard, *Le Tragique Destin*, 302; this is omitted from Gilliard's English-language version.
151. Preston, 98.
152. Ibid., 99.
153. Volkov, 134.
154. Buxhoeveden, *Left Behind*, 78.
155. Buxhoeveden, *Life*, 339; Gilliard, *Thirteen Years*, 271–272; Gilliard, March 5, 1919, in SA, vol. 2, doc. 55.
156. Buxhoeveden, *Left Behind*, 77–79.
157. Gilliard, *Thirteen Years*, 270–271. British consul Thomas Preston also writes that Buxhoeveden came on several occasions, something that Gilliard does not mention. See Preston, 98.
158. Gilliard, *Thirteen Years*, 270–271.
159. Buxhoeveden, *Life*, 339.
160. Buxhoeveden, *Left Behind*, 80; see also Gilliard, *Thirteen Years*, 272.
161. Trewin, 114.
162. Buxhoeveden, *Left Behind*, 91.
163. Ibid., 91; Trewin, 115.
164. Buxhoeveden, *Left Behind*, 91.
165. George Gibbes to King, May 1989.
166. Buxhoeveden, *Left Behind*, 92.
167. Kobylinsky, April 6–10, 1919, in SA, vol. 3, doc. 29.

Chapter 5: The Seventy-eight Days

1. Wilton and Telberg, 294.
2. Ibid., 295.
3. Ibid., 212.
4. N diary, May 23, 1918, in GARF, f. 601, op. 1, d. 266.
5. Gibbes, July 1, 1919, in SA, vol. 5, doc. 31; Medvedev, February 21–22, 1919, in SA, vol. 2, doc. 86.
6. AF diary, May 23, 1918, in GARF, f. 640, op. 1, d. 326.
7. N diary, May 23, 1918, in GARF, f. 601, op. 1, d. 266.
8. AF diary, May 24, 1918, in GARF, f. 640, op. 1, d. 326.
9. Document given to the Ural Regional Soviet and signed by Nagorny, May 24, 1918, in GARF, f. 601, op. 2, d. 38.
10. AF diary, May 24, 1918, in GARF, f. 640, op. 1, d. 326.
11. Ibid.; N diary, May 24, 1918, in GARF, f. 601, op. 1, d. 266; guard duty book, May 24, 1918, in GARF, f. 601, op. 2, d. 24.

12. Deterikhs, vol. 1, 26; Medvedev, February 21–22, 1919, in SA, vol. 2, doc. 86.
13. Letter from Botkin to the Presidium of the Ural Regional Soviet, May 24, 1918, in GARF, f. 601, op. 2, d. 37.
14. Avdayev, in *Krasnaia Nov* 5 (1928): 200.
15. Avdayev's note, appended to the bottom of the Botkin letter, in GARF, f. 601, op. 2, d. 37.
16. AF diary, May 25, 1918, in GARF, f. 640, op. 1, d. 326.
17. N diary, May 26, 1918, in GARF, f. 601, op. 1, d. 266.
18. N diary, May 27, 1918, in GARF, f. 601, op. 1, d. 266.
19. AF diary, May 27, 1918, in GARF, f. 640, op. 1, d. 326.
20. Ibid.
21. Gilliard, *Thirteen Years*, 265; Kobylinsky, April 6–10, 1919, in SA, vol. 3, doc. 29. In his book, Gilliard correctly states that the service took place. In his original deposition to Sokolov, given on March 5, 1919, he declared, "Khokryakov forbade it, saying that no time should be wasted." Gilliard, March 5, 1919, in SA, vol. 2, doc. 55.
22. Lvov statement in Sokolov, *Enquete*, 130; Gibbes, July 1, 1919, in SA, vol. 5, doc. 31.
23. Letter of Prince George Lvov to President Woodrow Wilson, October 12, 1918, in the Richard Teller Crane Papers, MS Division, Library, Georgetown University, Washington, D.C., cited in McNeal, 167; see also S. Alekseyev, "Yekaterinburgskii uznik ne tolko Nikolai II, no i knyaz GE Lvov," *Kongress sootechestvennikov* 2 (1991).
24. Lasies, 86.
25. Summers and Mangold, 94.
26. N diary, May 27, 1918, in GARF, f. 601, op. 1, d. 266; AF diary, May 17, 1918, in GARF, f. 640, op. 1, d. 326.
27. Buxhoeveden, *Life*, 342.
28. Speranski, 166.
29. Radzinsky, 300.
30. AF diary, May 28, 1918, in GARF, f. 640, op. 1, d. 326.
31. AF diary, May 29, 1918, in GARF, f. 640, op. 1, d. 326.
32. Avdayev, in *Krasnaia Nov* 5 (1928): 202; AF diary, May 30, 1918, in GARF, f. 640,

op. 1, d. 326; N diary, June 3, 1918, in GARF, f. 601, op. 1, d. 266; N diary, June 4, 1918, in GARF, f. 601, op. 1, d. 266; AF diary, June 4, 1918, in GARF, f. 640, op. 1, d. 326; see Derevenko in *Rodina* 4 (1989): 96.

33. Avdayev, in *Krasnaia Nov* 5 (1928): 203; Proskuryakov, April 3, 1919, in SA, vol. 5, doc. 17.

34. Avdayev, in *Krasnaia Nov* 5 (1928): 203.

35. Chemodurov, August 15–16, 1918, in SA, vol. 1, doc. 23.

36. Wilton and Telberg, 296.

37. Buxhoeveden, *Life*, 334–335.

38. Chemodurov, August 15–16, 1918, in SA, vol. 1, doc. 23.

39. Wilton and Telberg, 295.

40. Buxhoeveden, *Life*, 334.

41. AF diary, May 2, 1918, in GARF, f. 640, op. 1, d. 326.

42. Bykov, *Last Days*, 68; Strekotin, 1934, in TsDOOSO, f. 221, op. 2, d. 849; Proskuryakov, April 3, 1919, in SA, vol. 5, doc. 17; Proskuryakov, April 3, 1919, in SA, vol. 5, doc. 17; Avdayev, in *Krasnaia Nov* 5 (1928): 202.

43. Catherine Tomilova, interrogation of November 4, 1918, in GARF, f. 601, op. 2, d. 51; N diary, May 14, 1918, in GARF, f. 601, op. 1, d. 266.

44. AF diary, May 7, 1918, in GARF, f. 640, op. 1, d. 326.

45. Avdayev, in *Krasnaia Nov* 5 (1928): 200; Avdayev, in *Krasnaia Nov* 5 (1928): 202.

46. AF diary, May 17, 1918, in GARF, f. 640, op. 1, d. 326.

47. Strekotin, 1934, in TsDOOSO, f. 221, op. 2, d. 849; see also guard duty book, May 29, 1918, in GARF, f. 601, op. 2, d. 24.

48. Avdayev, in *Krasnaia Nov* 5 (1928): 202.

49. Buxhoeveden, *Left Behind*, 116; Buxhoeveden, *Life*, 334–335.

50. Yakimov, May 7–11, 1919, in SA, vol. 5, doc. 18.

51. Ibid.

52. Chemodurov, August 15–16, 1918, in SA, vol. 1, doc. 23.

53. Lvov, in Sokolov, *Enquete*, 130.

54. Wilton and Telberg, 296.

55. Buxhoeveden, *Life*, 334–335.

56. Yakimov, May 7–11, 1919, in SA, vol. 5, doc. 18.

57. Nametkin search of Ipatiev House, August 7–8, 1918, in SA, vol. 3, doc. 27; Sergeyev, inspection of the Ipatiev House, August 11–14, 1918, in SA, vol. 1, doc. 19; Sokolov, inspection of the Ipatiev House, April 15–25, 1919, in SA, vol. 3, doc. 42; Sokolov, report on inspection of materials removed from Ipatiev House by Sergeyev, May 19, 1919, in SA, vol. 4, doc. 37.

58. Proskuryakov, April 3, 1919, in SA, vol. 5, doc. 17.

59. Ibid.

60. Gilliard, March 5, 1919, in SA, vol. 2, doc. 55.

61. Gilliard. *Thirteen Years*, 282.

62. Yakimov, May 7–11, 1919, in SA, vol. 5, doc. 18.

63. N diary, June 14, 1918, in GARF, f. 601, op. 1, d. 266.

64. Strekotin, 1934, in TsDOOSO, f. 221, op. 2, d. 849.

65. Speranski, 149.

66. Sister Agnes, mistress of novices at Novotikhvinsky Convent in Ekaterinburg, in Speranski, 135–139.

67. Melgunov, *Sud'ba Imperator Nikolaia II*, 376; Wilton and Telberg, 299.

68. N diary, July 4, 1918, in GARF, f. 601, op. 1, d. 266.

69. Gilliard, March 5, 1919, in SA, vol. 2, doc. 55; Wilton and Telberg, 34.

70. Buxhoeveden, *Left Behind*, 116; Buxhoeveden, *Life*, 334–335.

71. Proskuryakov, April 3, 1919, in SA, vol. 5, doc. 17.

72. Strekotin, 1934, in TsDOOSO, f. 221, op. 2, d. 849.

73. N diary, May 27, 1918, in GARF, f. 601, op. 1, d. 266.

74. N diary, June 3, 1918, in GARF, f. 601, op. 1, d. 266.

75. Guard duty book, June 24, 1918, in GARF, f. 601, op. 2, d. 24.

76. Proskuryakov, April 3, 1919, in SA, vol. 5, doc. 17.

77. Wilton and Telberg, 149.

78. Bykov, *Last Days*, 79.

79. Strekotin, 1934, in TsDOOSO, f. 221, op. 2, d. 849.

80. N diary, May 27, 1918, in GARF, f. 601, op. 1, d. 266.

81. Proskuryakov, April 3, 1919, in SA, vol. 5, doc. 17.

82. Avdayev, in *Krasnaia Nov* 5 (1928): 203.
83. Chemodurov, August 15–16, 1918, in SA, vol. 1, doc. 23.
84. Yakimov, May 7–11, 1919, in SA, vol. 5, doc. 18.
85. Wilton and Telberg, 296.
86. Lvov, in Sokolov, *Enquete*, 129.
87. AF diary, May 4, 1918, in GARF, f. 640, op. 1, d. 326.
88. N diary, May 1–23, 1918, in GARF, f. 601, op. 1, d. 266; AF diary, May 1–23, 1918, in GARF, f. 640, op. 1, d. 326; guard duty book for the Ipatiev House, May 1–23, 1918, in GARF, f. 601, op. 2, d. 24.
89. See AF diary, July 11–16, 1918, in GARF, f. 640, op. 1, d. 326; N diary July 11–13, 1918, in GARF, f. 601, op. 1, d. 266; guard duty book for the Ipatiev House, July 11–15, 1918, in GARF, f. 601, op. 2, d. 24.
90. Bykov, *Last Days*, 70.
91. Guard duty book for the Ipatiev House, May 20, 1918, in GARF, f. 601, op. 2, d. 24.
92. Strekotin, 1934, in TsDOOSO, f. 221, op. 2, d. 849.
93. Ibid.
94. Ibid.
95. Ibid.
96. Avdayev, in *Krasnaia Nov* 5 (1928): 202.
97. Picture caption 56, Alexandrov.
98. Trewin, 107.
99. McCullagh, 128.
100. Avdayev, in *Krasnaia Nov* 5 (1928): 202.
101. AF diary, June 21, 1918, in GARF, f. 640, op. 1, d. 326.
102. Wilton and Telberg, 149.
103. AF diary, May 28, 1918, in GARF, f. 640, op. 1, d. 326.
104. Bykov, *Last Days*, 68; Strekotin, 1934, in TsDOOSO, f. 221, op. 2, d. 849; Proskuryakov, April 3, 1919, in SA, vol. 5, doc. 17.
105. Catherine Tomilova, interrogation of November 4, 1918, in GARF, f. 601, op. 2, d. 51.
106. Ibid.
107. Buxhoeveden, *Left Behind*, 117.
108. Chemodurov, August 15–16, 1918, in SA, vol. 1, doc. 23.
109. Wilton and Telberg, 295.
110. Buxhoeveden, *Life*, 334–335.
111. N diary, May 8, 1918, in GARF, f. 601, op. 1, d. 266.
112. Kobylinsky April, 6–10, 1919, in SA, vol. 3, doc. 29.
113. Wilton and Telberg, 129.
114. Bulygin and Kerensky, 232.
115. Wilton and Telberg, 34.
116. Buxhoeveden, *Life*, 334–335.
117. Speranski, 50.
118. Avdayev, in *Krasnaia Nov* 5 (1928): 202.
119. See N diary, May 26, 1918, in GARF, f. 601, op. 1, d. 266.
120. N diary, March 27, 1918, in GARF, f. 601, op. 1, d. 266. For more on this issue see King and Wilson, "Inheritance of Blood: Official Anti-Semitism and the Last of the Romanovs," *Atlantis Magazine* 3, no. 3 (2002): 26–51; also www.atlantis-magazine.com. See AF diary, May 3, 5, 6, 7, and 12, 1918, in GARF, f. 640, op. 1, d. 326.
121. Yakimov, May 7–11, 1919, in SA, vol. 5, doc. 18; Proskuryakov, April 3, 1919, in SA, vol. 5, doc. 17.
122. Lvov, in Sokolov, *Enquete*, 129–130.
123. Wilton and Telberg, 296.
124. Yakimov, May 7–11, 1919, in SA, vol. 5, doc. 18; Proskuryakov, April 3, 1919, in SA, vol. 5, doc. 17.
125. Ibid.
126. N diary, May 8, 1918, in GARF, f. 601, op. 1, d. 266.
127. Yakimov, May 7–11, 1919, in SA, vol. 5, doc. 18.
128. Guard duty book, June 1, 1918, in GARF, f. 601, op. 2, d. 24.
129. Storozhev, interviewed October 8–10, 1918, by Sergeyev, in Sokolov, *Enquete*, 32–35.
130. N diary, June 2, 1918, in GARF, f. 601, op. 1, d. 266.
131. N Diary, June 4, 1918, in GARF, f. 601, op. 1, d. 266; guard duty book, June 3, 1918, in GARF, f. 601, op. 2, d. 24.
132. N diary, June 4, 1918, in GARF, f. 601, op. 1, d. 266; AF diary, June 4, 1918, in GARF, f. 640, op. 1, d. 326.
133. Avdayev, in *Krasnaia Nov* 5 (1928): 202.
134. AF diary, June 4, 1918, in GARF, f. 640, op. 1, d. 326.
135. AF diary, June 5, 1918, in GARF, f. 640, op. 1, d. 326; guard duty book, June 5, 1918, in GARF, f. 601, op. 2, d. 24; N

diary, June 5, 1918, in GARF, f. 601, op. 1, d. 266.

136. AF diary, June 5, 1918, in GARF, f. 640, op. 1, d. 326.

137. Ibid.; guard duty book, June 5, 1918, in GARF, f. 601, op. 2, d. 24.

138. Guard duty book, June 6, 1918, in GARF, f. 601, op. 2, d. 24.

139. AF diary, June 6, 1918, in GARF, f. 640, op. 1, d. 326; N diary, June 6, 1918, in GARF, f. 601, op. 1, d. 266.

140. N diary, June 6, 1918, in GARF, f. 601, op. 1, d. 266.

141. Guard duty book, June 7, 1918, in GARF, f. 601, op. 2, d. 24; AF diary, June 7, 1918, in GARF, f. 640, op. 1, d. 326.

142. Guard duty book, June 8, 1918, in GARF, f. 601, op. 2, d. 24.

143. Salisbury, 589–590.

144. Melgunov, *Sud'ba Imperatora Nikolaya II*, 362.

145. AF diary, June 8, 1918, in GARF, f. 640, op. 1, d. 326.

146. Guard duty book, June 9, 1918, GARF, f. 601, op. 2, d. 24.

147. Strekotin, 1934, in TsDOOSO, f. 221, op. 2, d. 849.

148. *New York Times*, July 12, 1918.

149. Summers and Mangold, 316.

150. Quoted in Summers and Mangold, 316.

151. Olga Petrova, interrogation of November 5, 1918, by Military CID, in GARF, f. 601, op. 2, d. 51.

152. Guard duty book, June 12, 1918, in GARF, f. 601, op. 2, d. 24.

153. N diary, June 10, 1918, in GARF, f. 601, op. 1, d. 266.

154. Strekotin, 1934, in TsDOOSO, f. 221, op. 2, d. 849. Victor Alexandrov, in his book *The End of the Romanovs*, p. 81, asserted that this took place on June 9, an allegation recently repeated by authors Rosemary and Donald Crawford (see Crawfords, 354). We know, however, that the uprising did, indeed, take place on June 12, from the accounts of both Avdayev and Strekotin. See also Avdayev, *Krasnaia Nov* 5 (1928): 202; and Bykov, *Arkhiv Russkoi Revolyutsii*, volume 17, 313, in which Bykov alleges that the date for this uprising was May 1, 1918.

155. Avdayev, *Krasnaia Nov* 5 (1928): 202; see also Rodzinsky, May 13, 1964, in RTsKhIDNI, f. 588, op. 3, d. 14.

Chapter 6: Russia in Chaos

1. Bunyan and Fisher, 233.

2. Joost, 1967, 17–63, cited in Pipes, *Russian Revolution*, 615.

3. Kennan, *Decision to Intervene*, vol. 2, 357.

4. Knightly, 153.

5. Reed, 74; Knightly, 149.

6. U.S. Department of State, Foreign Relations, 1918, Russia, 519–521, cited in Kennan, *Decision to Intervene*, 215.

7. *Biograficheskaya Khronika* 5 (1918): 459.

8. Alexandrov, 71.

9. Zeman, 94.

10. Ibid., 100–105.

11. Fleming, 145; Snow, 12–19.

12. I. M. Bikerman, in "Rossiia I Evrei," in *Sbornik* (Berlin, 1924), 22–23, cited in Pipes, *Russia under the Bolshevik Regime*, 100–101.

13. Pipes, *Russian Revolution*, 792.

14. Alexandrov, 78.

15. Baerlein, 180.

16. Pipes, *Russian Revolution*, 629.

17. Kennan, *Decision to Intervene*, 137; Lehovich, 220.

18. Kennan, *Decision to Intervene*, 137.

19. Luckett, 161.

20. *Biograficheskaia Khronika* 5 (1918): 318–319; Ullman, 152.

21. Luckett, 162.

22. Klante, *Von der Wolga*, 100, cited in Pipes, *Russian Revolution*, 627.

23. Ullman, 154–155.

24. Chamberlain, vol. 2, 4.

25. Gaida, 38.

26. Ioffe, *Revoliutsiia i sud'ba Romanovki*, 231–239; Pipes, *Russian Revolution*, 624–631.

27. Krachtovil, *Cesta Revoluce*, 42, quoted in Luckett, 161.

28. Fleming, 21.

29. Gaida, 40–41.

30. Klante, in Pipes, *Russian Revolution*, 632.

31. Luckett, 163.

32. Bradley, 93; Gaida, 9–22.

33. Gaida, 56–58; Luckett, 163.

34. Gaida, 58–59; Luckett, 163; Fleming, 24.

35. Gaida, 59–60.

36. Ibid., 61.

37. Fleming, 23.

38. Ibid., 24.
39. Ernest Lloyd Harris Papers, MSS, files of the U.S. consul general in Vladivostok from 1918–1920, cited in Kennan, *Decision to Intervene*, 164.
40. Baerlein, 22–25.
41. Luckett, 162; Gaida, 76.
42. Gaida, 48–51.
43. Kennan, *Decision to Intervene*, 163.
44. Ibid., 162.
45. Ibid., 164.
46. Fleming, 24.
47. Ioffe, *Revoliutsiia i sud'ba Romanovki*, 231–239; Pipes, *Russian Revolution*, 624–630.
48. Pipes, *Russia under the Bolshevik Regime*, 24.
49. Pipes, *Russian Revolution*, 630.
50. Chamberlain, vol. 2, 7–8.
51. Pipes, *Russia under the Bolshevik Regime*, 24; Luckett, 164.
52. Kennan, *Decision to Intervene*, 292.
53. Pipes, *Russian Revolution*, 632.
54. Preston, 81.
55. Bunyan and Fisher, 235.
56. Melgunov, *Sud'ba Imperatora Nikolaya II,"* 350–351.
57. Chamberlain, vol. 2, 66; Luckett, 170.
58. Bunyan and Fisher, 235.
59. Lenin, *Sochineny*, vol. 35, 334.
60. "Perepiska Sekretariata TsK . . . (noiabr' 1917g–fevral' 1918g)," 380, cited in Snow, 220.
61. Bunyan and Fisher, 237.
62. Ibid., 238.
63. Rosenberg, 236–238.
64. Lenin, *Sochineny*, vol. 27, 329–330.
65. Ibid., vol. 28, 536.
66. Pipes, *Russian Revolution*, 636.
67. Bunyan, 197–198.
68. Bunyan and Fisher, 237.
69. Pipes, *Russian Revolution*, 558.
70. Ibid.
71. Ibid., 559
72. Ibid.
73. Ibid., 561.
74. Bunyan and Fisher, 236.
75. Pipes, *Russian Revolution*, 561.
76. Ibid., 562.
77. Ibid., 560.
78. Ibid., 564.
79. Bunyan and Fisher, 238; Pipes, *Russian Revolution*, 563; Solzhenitsyn, vol. 1, 30.
80. Pipes, *Russian Revolution*, 568.
81. *Izvestiia*, June 16, 1918.
82. Bunyan and Fisher, 237.
83. Lenin, *Sochineny*, vol. 50, 106.
84. Bunyan and Fisher, 235.
85. Erdmann, 270–271, 279–280.
86. Ibid., 118.
87. Zeman, 167.
88. Ibid., 139.

Chapter 7: The First to Die

1. Abrikossow, 233.
2. Buchanan to Arthur Balfour, September 8, 1917, PRO FO 371/3015.
3. *Biografischeskaya Khronika* 5 (1918): 165–166.
4. Perry and Pleshakov, 201.
5. Pipes, *Russian Revolution*, 746.
6. Bykov, *Last Days*, 83.
7. Ibid., 84.
8. Sokolov, *Enquete*, 298.
9. Bykov, *Last Days*, 84; Alferyev, 395.
10. Bykov, *Last Days*, 84.
11. Crawfords, 351.
12. Melgunov, *Sud'ba Imperatora Nikolaya II*, 350–351, 388–396; Sokolov, *Enquete*, 265–266; Alferyev, 393–394.
13. Crawfords, 350.
14. Vera Lukoyanov, interrogation on July 2, 1919, in Sokolov, *Enquete*, 299–300.
15. Crawfords, 355–356.
16. Volkogonov, 210.
17. Volkov, in Sokolov, *Enquete*, 299; Melgunov, *Sud'ba Imperatora Nikolaya II*, 392–394; Poutianine, 309–310.
18. Crawfords, 352–358; Melgunov, *Sud'ba Imperatora Nikolaya II*, 389.
19. Crawfords, 355; Bykov, *Last Days*, 85.
20. *Perskye Izvestiia*, June 13, 1918, quoted in Melgunov, *Sud'ba Imperatora Nikolaya II*, 388.
21. Bykov, *Last Days*, 73.
22. *New York Times*, July 4, 1918.
23. *New York Times*, July 15, 1918.
24. Pipes, *Russian Revolution*, 748.
25. Bykov, *Last Days*, 81; Sokolov, *Enquete*, 266.
26. See "Sud'ba Mikhaila Romanova: Publikatsiya dokumentov, podgotovka k pechati i presidloviye I. A. Mirikinoi i V. M. Khrustalyova," *Voprosy istorii* 9 (1990): 158–163; V. K. Vinogradov, "Ya chasto dumayu za chto yego kasnili," *Nezavisimaya gazeta* (April 1994): 17–19;

"Rasskaz zaveduiushchei Permskim par-tarkhivom N. Alikinoi o vstrechakh s Markovym i prieme Leninym Markova posle ubiista Mikhaila," *Vecherniaia Perm* (February 3, 1990): 48–51; G. Myasnikov, "Filosofiya ubiistva, ili pochemu i kak ya ubil Mikhaila Romanova," *Minuvsheye Vypusk* 15 (1995): 183–194; I. A. Mirkina and V. M. Krustalev, "Sud'ba Mikhaila Romanova," *Voprosy istorii* 9 (1990): 11–16; A. Markov, "Sud'ba Mikhaila Romanova," *Vecherniaia Perm* 15 (January 15, 1990); and G. Sostavitel, *Samosud. Ubiistvo velikogo knyazya Mikhaila Romanova v Permi v iyune 1918 g: Dokumenty i publikatsii,* 62–134.

27. Bulygin and Kerensky, 244; Massie, 255.

28. Maylunas and Mironenko, 630.

29. Bulygin and Kerensky, 255; Sokolov, *Enquete,* 299–301; Wilton and Telberg, 319.

30. Pipes, *Russian Revolution,* 765.

31. Sokolov, *Enquete,* 302.

32. Bulygin and Kerensky, 255.

33. Platonov, *Ternovyi ventes Rossi,* 391–392.

34. Crawfords, 361–362; "Sud'ba Mikhaila Romanova: Publikatsiya dokumentov, podgotovka k pechati i presidloviye I. A. Mirikinoi i V. M. Khrustalyova" in *Voprosy istorii* 9 (1990): 158–163; V. K. Vinogradov, "Ya chasto dumayu za chto yego kasnili" in *Nezavisimaya gazeta* (April 1994): 17–19; "Rasskaz zaveduiushchei Permskim partarkhivom N. Alikinoi o vstrechakh s Markovym i prieme Leninym Markova posle ubiista Mikhaila" in *Vecherniaia Perm* (February 3, 1990): 48–51; G. Myasnikov, "Filosofiya ubiistva, ili pochemu i kak ya ubil Mikhaila Romanova" in *Minuvsheye Vypusk* 15 (1995): 183–194; I. A. Mirkina and V. M. Krustalev, "Sud'ba Mikhaila Romanova" in *Voprosy istorii* 9 (1990): 11–16; A. Markov, "Sud'ba Mikhaila Romanova" in *Vecherniaia Perm* 15 (January 15, 1990); and G. I. Sostavitel, *Samosud. Ubiistvo velikogo knyazya Mikhaila Romanova v Permi v iyune 1918 g: Dokumenty i publikatsii,* 62–134.

35. Crawfords, 360.

36. Bykov, *Last Days,* 85.

37. See Crawfords, 354.

38. Kudrin, December 1963, in RTsKhIDNI,

f. 588, op. 3, d. 14; Rodzinsky, May 13, 1964, in RTsKhIDNI, f. 588, op. 3, d. 14.

Chapter 8: The June Conspiracies

1. Jagow, 393.

2. Wilhelm II to Christian X, FO document A.S. 1356 (draft), quoted in Summers and Mangold, 278.

3. *Marie Feodorovna,* 48.

4. Bulygin and Kerensky, 202; testimonies of Krivoshein (January 17, 1921, and February 6, 1921), Neigart (January 27 and 29, 1921, and May 29, 1921), and Trepov (February 16, 1921), in Sokolov, *Enquete,* 104–107.

5. Melgunov, *Sud'ba Imperatora Nikolaya II,* 228–231.

6. Cited in Summers and Mangold, 278.

7. Ibid., 279.

8. Jagow, 393; German FO document, Mirbach to Berlin on May 10, 1918, telegram, German Foreign Office Archives A. 19964.

9. Vladimir Burtsev, November 15, 1920, in SA, vol. 6, doc. 73.

10. Mirbach report telegram to Berlin, June 21, 1918, in German Foreign Office Archives, telegram 338, A. 19964.

11. Report of British ambassador in Berne to FO, June 19, 1918, in PRO/FO 370/3328.

12. State secretary von Kuhlmann to von Grunau, June 22, 1918, PRO GFM 6/139, A. 26851.

13. Wilton and Telberg, 232.

14. AF diary, June 13, 1918, in GARF, f. 640, op. 1, d. 326.

15. N diary, June 13, 1918, in GARF, f. 601, op. 1, d. 266; guard duty book, June 13, 1918, in GARF, f. 601, op. 2, d. 24.

16. N diary, June 13, 1918, in GARF, f. 601, op. 1, d. 266.

17. Ibid.; AF diary, June 13, 1918, in GARF, f. 640, op. 1, d. 326.

18. AF diary, June 13, 1918, in GARF, f. 640, op. 1, d. 326.

19. N diary, June 14, 1918, in GARF, f. 601, op. 1, d. 266.

20. Guard duty book, June 14, 1918, in GARF, f. 601, op. 2, d. 24.

21. N diary, June 14, 1918, in GARF, f. 601, op. 1, d. 266.

22. See Bykov, *Arkhiv Russkoi Revolyutsii* 17

(1928): 313; Avdayev, *Krasnaia Nov* 5 (1928): 202.

23. Luckett, 166; Kasvinov, 113.

24. Sotheby's auction catalog, 73.

25. Guard duty book, June 15, 1918, in GARF, f. 601, op. 2, d. 24.

26. AF diary, June 16, 1918, in GARF, f. 640, op. 1, d. 326.

27. Guard duty book, June 16, 1918, in GARF, f. 601, op. 2, d. 24.

28. Sister Agnes, mistress of novices at Novotikhvinsky Convent in Ekaterinburg, in Speranski, 135–139.

29. AF diary, June 17, 1918, in GARF, f. 640, op. 1, d. 326.

30. AF diary, June 18, 1918, in GARF, f. 640, op. 1, d. 326; N diary, June 18, 1918, in GARF, f. 601, op. 1, d. 266.

31. AF diary, June 18, 1918, in GARF, f. 640, op. 1, d. 326.

32. Guard duty book, June 18, 1918, in GARF, f. 601, op. 2, d. 24.

33. Ibid., June 19, 1918.

34. Bykov, *Last Days*, 76.

35. Kudrin, December 1963, in RTsKhIDNI, f. 588, op. 3, d. 14.

36. Bykov, *Last Days*, 77.

37. Salisbury, 594.

38. Bykov, *Last Days*, 77.

39. Helen of Serbia and of Russia, 20; Smirnoff, 102–103; Millar, 203.

40. Paley, 199.

41. Ibid., 200.

42. Helen of Serbia and of Russia, 20.

43. Bykov, *Last Days*, 76–77.

44. Semchevskaya, 34.

45. Bykov, *Last Days*, 78.

46. Alexandrov, 220.

47. Smirnoff, 104.

48. Helen of Serbia and of Russia, 22.

49. Preston, 101.

50. Helen of Serbia and of Russia, 30.

51. Bykov, in *Arkhiv Russkoi Revolyutsii* 17 (1928): 312; Melgunov, *Sud'ba Imperatora Nikolaifa II*, 376; *Krasnii Arkhiv* 26 (1928): 130–135.

52. Cable from Starkov, Moscow, June 22, 1918, to Alapayevsk Soviet, in Sotheby's auction catalog, 98.

53. Rodzinsky, May 13, 1964, in RTsKhIDNI, f. 588, op. 3, d. 14.

54. Ibid.

55. Deterikhs, vol. 1, 377.

56. Semchevskaia, 34.

57. Dimitri Malinovskii, testimony of June 17, 1919, in SA, vol. 5, doc. 8; Alexandrov, 80–81.

58. Avdayev, in *Krasnaia Nov* 5 (1928): 202. Avdayev believed the letter had been written by a Serbian officer, Major Jarko Konstantinovich Michich (Avdayev, in *Krasnaia Nov* 5 [1928]: 201). Michich, however, did not arrive in Ekaterinburg until the evening of July 4, two weeks after the letter was intercepted (Smirnoff, 102–103). At the time the letter was sent, Michich was either in Petrograd or traveling to the Urals. This, and the three "Officer" letters that followed, were first published in the Moscow newspaper *Vechernye Izvestiia* in April 1919; seven months later they appeared for the first time in English, in a series of articles written by journalist Isaac Don Levine for the *Chicago Daily News* in December 1919. Levine, a distinguished reporter and one of the few foreign journalists to befriend high-level Bolsheviks during the Civil War, had been given copies of the letters by the Soviet historian Michael Pokrovsky (Isaac Don Levine in the *Chicago Daily News*, November 6, 1919; see also the reproduction of the articles in the *Chicago Daily News*, December 18, 1919; and Levine, 138–141).

59. Avdayev, in *Krasnaia Nov* 5 (1928): 202.

60. Yurovsky, unpublished memoirs, 1922, in APRF, f. 3, op. 58, d. 280.

61. Kudrin, December 1964, in RTsKhIDNI, f. 588, op. 3, d. 14; Rodzinsky, May 13, 1964, in RTsKhIDNI, f. 588, op. 3, d. 14.

62. In GARF, f. 601, op. 2, d. 27.

63. Avdayev, in *Krasnaia Nov* 5 (1928): 202.

64. In GARF, f. 601, op. 2, d. 27.

65. AF diary, June 21, 1918, in GARF, f. 640, op. 1, d. 326.

66. Ibid.

67. N diary, June 22, 1918, in GARF, f. 601, op. 1, d. 266.

68. Ibid.; AF diary, June 22, 1918, in GARF, f. 640, op. 1, d. 326.

69. N diary, June 22, 1918, in GARF, f. 601, op. 1, d. 266.

70. AF diary, June 22, 1918, in GARF, f. 640, op. 1, d. 326.

71. N diary, June 22, 1918, in GARF, f. 601, op. 1, d. 266.

72. *Nashe Slovo* 48 (June 19, 1918), as reported in *Nash Vek* 97/121 (June 29, 1918), in Pipes, *Russian Revolution*, 765; *Biografischeskaya Khronika* 5: 552.

73. *Nash Vek* 96/120 (June 19, 1918): 2, in Pipes, *Russian Revolution*, 765.

74. de Robien, 267–268.

75. See *New York Times* (June 26, 1918), and Pipes, *Russian Revolution*, 765.

76. *Nash Vek* 100/124 (June 23, 1918): 2, in Pipes, *Russian Revolution*, 765.

77. Jagow, 411.

78. Ibid., 413.

79. Vladimir Bonch-Bruyevich to Beloborodov, June 20, 1918, in Sotheby's auction catalog, 73.

80. Stark, in Moscow, to Beloborodov, sent June 21, 1918, received June 24, 1918, Ekaterinburg, in GARF, f. 601, op. 2, d. 38.

81. *Krasnii Arkhiv* 26 (1927): 135.

82. Melgunov, *Sud'ba Imperatora Nikolaya II*, 377–378; Dimitri Volkogonov to Penny Wilson.

83. Telegraph operators' testimony, report 1497 of Criminal Investigating Division, in SA, vol. 1, doc. 30.

84. Melgunov, *Sud'ba Imperatora Nikolaya II*, 377–378; *Krasnii Arkhiv* 26 (1927): 135.

85. Stark, in Moscow, to Vorobyov in Ekaterinburg, June 24, 1918, in Sotheby's auction catalog, 73.

86. Telegram from Muravyov, in Ogloblin, to Kazan, then Moscow, Berzin, copied to the Sovnarkom VTsIK and Military Press Bureau by Moscow recipient, June 28, 1918, in GARF, f. 130, op. 2, d. 1109; also dated June 27, 1918, 12:05 A.M., military telegram 487, to Moscow from Ekaterinburg headquarters 3190, June 27, 1918, in SA, vol. 2, doc. 66; Deterikhs, vol. 1, 46–48.

87. Pipes, *Russian Revolution*, 765.

88. N diary, June 23, 1918, in GARF, f. 601, op. 1, d. 266; also AF diary, June 23, 1918, in GARF, f. 640, op. 1, d. 326; and guard duty book, June 23, 1918, in GARF, f. 601, op. 2, d. 24.

89. N diary, June 23, 1918, in GARF, f. 601, op. 1, d. 266; AF diary, June 23, 1918, in GARF, f. 640, op. 1, d. 326.

90. AF diary, June 23, 1918, in GARF, f. 640, op. 1, d. 326.

91. Ibid.

92. Ibid.

93. N diary, June, 23, 1918, in GARF, f. 601, op. 1, d. 266.

94. AF diary, June 23, 1918, in GARF, f. 640, op. 1, d. 326.

95. Bykov, *Last Days*, 78.

96. Rodzinsky, May 13, 1964, in RTsKhIDNI, f. 588, op. 3, d. 14.

97. Kudrin, December 1963, in RTsKhIDNI, f. 588, op. 3, d. 14.

98. Rodzinsky, May 13, 1964, in RTsKhIDNI, f. 588, op. 3, d. 14.

99. Avdayev, in *Krasnaia Nov* 5 (1928): 202; Bykov, *Last Days*, 92–94; Radzinsky, 320–322; Ioffe, *Revoliutsiia i sud'ba Romanovki*, 294–296; Pipes, *Russian Revolution*, 767–768; Steinberg and Krustalev, 284. In his book on Nicholas II, Edvard Radzinsky contends that an enormous conspiracy was in place in Ekaterinburg. He begins with Ivan Sidorov; apparently unaware that Sidorov was a former adjutant to the emperor, he refers to this as "an obvious pseudonym" and suggests that Sidorov was a Bolshevik agent. "Through Dr. Derevenko," Radzinsky writes, "Sidorov made contact with the Novotikhvinsky Monastery and, simultaneously, with Commandant Avdayev. Soon after, the suddenly softhearted Commandant allowed food to be brought from the Monastery for the family, and to fatten his own pocket—with the money Dr. Derevenko offered him for the food. Thus the Tsar's family began to connect the Monastery with their good, loyal friends. That was why they believed in the letters. . . . Then the simple-hearted Avdayev suddenly proved surprisingly vigilant: he carefully checked all the food from the Monastery and 'discovered' the correspondence." Radzinsky's imaginative scenario holds that the Romanovs were being spied on even while at Tobolsk. He named Feodor Lukoyanov, chairman of the Ural Regional Cheka, as the man who, under cover of an alias, actually lived in the Governor's House in Tobolsk, where he kept careful track of the Romanovs. Radzinsky offered no evidence to support this allegation, nor did he explain how the head of the Ural

Regional Cheka could have been in Tobolsk for several months, ignoring his duties in the Urals, but this did not stop him from taking the allegations even farther. He alleged that Lukoyanov also regularly read the emperor's diary at the Ipatiev House, including the admissions that the prisoners had sat up for several nights, awaiting a rescue. "I can imagine his triumph," Radzinsky wrote of Lukoyanov: "the family went out for a walk, and he read Nicholas's entry in the diary. Yes, he had calculated it all. He felt like an astronomer who has calculated the presence of a star and sees it through his telescope in the sky." Not content to end with such fanciful dramatics, Radzinsky asserted that Nicholas himself knew of this from the very beginning and deliberately played along, willingly sealing his own death warrant (Radzinsky, 322–324). Radzinsky cited no evidence to support this contention, nor did he help establish his credibility by "imagining" the feelings of his alleged villain. There is no evidence that Avdayev was bribed by Derevenko, and certainly no evidence that the emperor himself somehow willingly condemned himself and his family to certain death.

100. AF diary, June 24, 1918, in GARF, f. 640, op. 1, d. 326.
101. Rodzinsky, May 13, 1964, in RTsKhIDNI, f. 588, op. 3, d. 14; Kudrin, December 1963, in RTsKhIDNI, f. 588, op. 3, d. 14.
102. In GARF, f. 601, op. 2, d. 27.
103. Ibid.
104. N diary, June 25, 1918, in GARF, f. 601, op. 1, d. 266.
105. AF diary, June 25, 1918, in GARF, f. 640, op. 1, d. 326.
106. N diary, June 25, 1918, in GARF, f. 601, op. 1, d. 266.
107. AF diary, June 26, 1918, in GARF, f. 640, op. 1, d. 326.
108. Ibid.
109. Ibid.
110. AF diary, June 27, 1918, in GARF, f. 640, op. 1, d. 326.
111. Ibid.; AF diary, July 4, 1918, in GARF, f. 640, op. 1, d. 326.
112. AF diary, June 27, 1918, in GARF, f. 640, op. 1, d. 326.
113. Kudrin, December 1963, in RTsKhIDNI, f. 588, op. 3, d. 14.
114. N diary, June 26, 1918, in GARF, f. 601, op. 1, d. 266.
115. AF diary, June 28, 1918, in GARF, f. 640, op. 1, d. 326.
116. In GARF, f. 601, op. 2, d. 27.
117. Ibid.
118. AF diary, June 29, 1918, in GARF, f. 640, op. 1, d. 326.

Chapter 9: "A Happy Hour with the Grandest People in the World"

1. Sokolov, *Enquete*, 97.
2. Speranski, 202.
3. Ibid., 102.
4. Yakimov, May 7–11, 1919, in SA, vol. 5, doc. 18.
5. Rodzinsky, December 1963, in RTsKhIDNI, f. 588, op. 3, d. 14.
6. Strekotin, 1934, in TsDOOSO, f. 221, op. 2, d. 849; Halliburton, *Seven League Boots*, 126.
7. Yurovsky, unpublished memoirs, 1922, in APRF, f. 3, op. 58, d. 280.
8. Speranski, 51.
9. Yakimov, May 7–11, 1919, in SA, vol. 5, doc. 18.
10. Speranski, 49–53.
11. Kabanov, unpublished memoirs, in Khabarovsk Regional Party Archives, f. 117, op. 2, d. 27.
12. Avdayev, in *Krasnaia Nov* 5 (1928): 203.
13. Strekotin, 1934, in TsDOOSO, f. 221, op. 2, d. 849; Yakimov, May 7–11, 1919, in SA, vol. 5, doc. 18.
14. Bykov, *Last Days*, 67.
15. Ermakov, in Halliburton, *Seven League Boots*, 126.
16. Victor Vorobiev, in Radzinsky, 291.
17. Rodzinsky, May 13, 1964, in RTsKhIDNI, f. 588, op. 3, d. 14.
18. Speranski, 50.
19. Strekotin, 1934, in TsDOOSO, f. 221, op. 2, d. 849; Yakimov, May 7–11, 1919, in SA, vol. 5, doc. 18.
20. Rodzinsky, May 13, 1964, in RTsKhIDNI, f. 588, op. 3, d. 14.
21. Bykov, *Last Days*, 64.
22. Ermakov, in Halliburton, *Seven League Boots*, 126.

23. Kabanov, unpublished memoirs, in Khabarovsk Regional Party Archives, f. 117, op. 2, d. 27.

24. Vorobiev, in Radzinsky, 291–292.

25. Halliburton, *Seven League Boots*, 128.

26. Rodzinsky, May 13, 1964, in RTsKhIDNI, f. 588, op. 3, d. 14.

27. Speranski, 54.

28. Kabanov, unpublished memoirs, in Khabarovsk Regional Party Archives, f. 117, op. 2, d. 27.

29. N diary, July 4, 1918, in GARF, f. 601, op. 1, d. 266.

30. Speranski, 55.

31. Strekotin, 1934, in TsDOOSO, f. 221, op. 2, d. 849.

32. Yakimov, May 7–11, 1919, in SA, vol. 5, doc. 18.

33. Speranski, 55.

34. Ibid., 50.

35. Strekotin, 1934, in TsDOOSO, f. 221, op. 2, d. 849.

36. Speranski, 55.

37. Yurovsky, unpublished memoirs, 1922, in APRF, f. 3, op. 58, d. 280.

38. Strekotin, 1934, in TsDOOSO, f. 221, op. 2, d. 849.

39. Speranski, 56.

40. Ibid., 161.

41. Bulygin and Kerensky, 231.

42. Speranski, 34.

43. Kudrin, December 1963, in RTsKhIDNI, f. 588, op. 3, d. 14.

44. In GARF, f. 601, op. 2, d. 27.

45. Bulygin and Kerensky, 242.

46. Speranski, 201.

47. Voikov, *Gutek* file, in Alexandrov, 231.

48. Yurovsky, unpublished memoirs, 1922, in APRF, f. 3, op. 58, d. 280.

49. Strekotin, 1934, in TsDOOSO, f. 221, op. 2, d. 849.

50. Vyrubova, 80.

51. Strekotin, 1934, in TsDOOSO, f. 221, op. 2, d. 849.

52. Ibid.

53. Speranski, 55.

54. Avdayev, in *Krasnaia Nov* 5 (1928): 203.

55. Yurovsky, unpublished memoirs, 1922, in APRF, f. 3, op. 58, d. 280.

56. Avdayev, in *Krasnaia Nov* 5 (1928): 203.

57. Yurovsky, unpublished memoirs, 1922, in APRF, f. 3, op. 58, d. 280.

58. Bykov, *Last Days*, 79.

59. Yurovsky, unpublished memoirs, 1922, in APRF, f. 3, op. 58, d. 280.

60. Ermakov, in Halliburton, *Seven League Boots*, 128.

61. Speranski, 160.

62. Strekotin, 1934, in TsDOOSO, f. 221, op. 2, d. 849.

63. Ibid.

64. Speranski, 33.

65. Ibid., 56–57.

66. Ibid., 57.

67. Ibid., 79–80.

68. Deterikhs, vol. 1, 379–380.

69. Ermakov, in Halliburton, *Seven League Boots*, 127.

70. AF diary, June 27, 1918, in GARF, f. 640, op. 1, d. 326.

71. Yakimov, May 7–11, 1919, in SA, vol. 5, doc. 18; Strekotin, 1934, in TsDOOSO, f. 221, op. 2, d. 849; Deterikhs, vol. 1, 276–277.

72. Yakimov, May 7–11, 1919, in SA, vol. 5, doc. 18; Proskuryakov, April 3, 1919, in SA, vol. 5, doc. 17.

73. Ermakov, in Halliburton, *Seven League Boots*, 128.

74. AF diary, June 27, 1918, in GARF, f. 640, op. 1, d. 326.

75. Letter of Alois Hochleitner, March 6, 1926, in Rathlef-Keilmann, 199–200.

76. Rodzinsky, May 13, 1964, in RTsKhIDNI, f. 588, op. 3, d. 14.

77. Netrebin, in TsDOOSO, f. 41, op. 1, d. 149.

78. Yurovsky, unpublished memoirs, 1922, in APRF, f. 3, op. 58, d. 280.

79. Guard duty book, May 17, 1918, in GARF, f. 601, op. 2, d. 24.

80. Strekotin, 1934, in TsDOOSO, f. 221, op. 2, d. 849.

81. Netrebin, in TsDOOSO, f. 41, op. 1, d. 149.

82. Yurovsky, unpublished memoirs, 1922, in APRF, f. 3, op. 58, d. 280.

83. Yakimov, May 7–11, 1919, in SA, vol. 5, doc. 18; Deterikhs, vol. 1, 276–277.

84. Strekotin, 1934, in TsDOOSO, f. 221, op. 2, d. 849.

85. Kennan, *Decision to Intervene*, 448.

86. Kudrin, December 1963, in RTsKhIDNI, f. 588, op. 3, d. 14.

87. Ibid.

88. Bykov, *Last Days*, 80.

89. *Ural'skii rabochii* (June 28, 1918).

90. *Biograficheskaia Khronika* 5: 616.
91. AF diary, June 29, 1918, in GARF, f. 640, op. 1, d. 326.
92. Minutes of Ural Regional Soviet meeting of June 29, 1918, in *Istoria borby uralskogo proletariata* 9 (1923): 173–177, Ekaterinburg. An edited version of these minutes was published in Bykov, *Last Days*, 75–76.
93. AF diary, June 29, 1918, in GARF, f. 640, op. 1, d. 326.
94. Alexandrov, 81–83.
95. Sister Agnes, mistress of novices at Novotikhvinsky Convent in Ekaterinburg, in Speranski, 135–139.
96. Rodzinsky, May 13, 1964, in RTsKhIDNI, f. 588, op. 3, d. 14.
97. Payne, *Lenin*, 461.
98. Speranski, 55.
99. Buxhoeveden, *Life*, 342.
100. Buranov and Krustalev, *Gibel*, 255. Great mystery surrounds the Yurovsky family's ethnic origins. Most authorities have concluded that they were Jewish. This clearly suited the interests of the majority of the Whites and monarchists, who believed that Jews—Russia's traditional scapegoats—were all Bolsheviks; in time, like so many other elements in the Romanov case, this assertion became accepted fact, repeated endlessly from book to book. Thus Robert Wilton spoke of "Yankel Yurovsky, the son of a Jew convict" (Wilton and Telberg, 299). The deliberate alteration by Wilton of Yurovsky's Christian name, from Yakov to the Jewish Yankel, indicates both Wilton's own anti-Semitism and his tendency to fabricate information to suit his own ends. Unfortunately, such assertions continue to cloud the issue. The author Marina Grey, daughter of White general Denikin, not only repeated Wilton's assertion but also added to it, referring in her book to Yurovsky as "Yankel Chaimovich" (Grey, 43). The story seemingly gained instant credibility when, in his book, *Enquete judicare sur l'Assassinat de la Famille Imperiale Russe*, Sokolov reported—based on evidence obtained directly from Yurovsky's elder brother Leonti—that Yurovsky's grandfather had been a Polish rabbi (Sokolov, *Enquete*, 135; testimonies of Leonti Mikhailovich Yurovsky and Anna Yurovskaia in SA, vol. 7, docs. 1 and 2). Yet, on examination, this evidence is far from conclusive. Leonti Mikhailovich Yurovsky and his family were living in Tomsk when, in November 1918, soldiers of the White Army stormed their house. After engaging in what can only be described as punitive destruction—the smashing in of walls, ripping apart of furniture, and burning of clothing and personal effects—Leonti and his wife, Anna, were arrested. Leonti was forcibly removed to Irkutsk, while his wife and their children were kept under house arrest in Tomsk. During the eight months of his imprisonment in Irkutsk, Leonti Yurovsky was subjected to daily interrogations and torture, the Whites threatening to shoot his wife and children unless he gave them the information they wanted. In Tomsk, Anna, too, was subjected to repeated threats and humiliations, and told that her husband would be shot unless she supplied her interrogators with facts they demanded (Yurovsky, unpublished memoirs, 1922, in APRF, f. 3, op. 58, d. 280). Such threats and torture formed common elements in White Army interrogations, and it is not surprising—given that they were dealing with the brother of the man who had killed the Romanovs—that they would have treated him and his wife in such a barbaric manner. The cruelty of the Whites often matched that of their more infamous Red counterparts. Even former prime minister Alexander Kerensky—himself no friend of the Bolsheviks—told a group of foreign journalists in the summer of 1919: "There is no crime the agents of Admiral Kolchak would not commit. . . . Executions and torture have been committed in Siberia, and often the population of whole villages have been flogged, including the teachers and intellectuals" (Archives of NKVD-KGB, Archive 501, t. 3, l. 616, cited in Volkogonov, 202). Yet information obtained under such circumstances must be treated with

great caution. This is particularly true in the case of Leonti and Anna Yurovsky, where daily beatings, torture, and threats were implemented to elicit specific responses. With anti-Semitism rampant among the White Army, it is not surprising that the ethnic origin of the family should have loomed large in their interrogations. Then, too, we know from multiple source material and evidence available that conscious attempts were made by the Whites to indeed link the Jews to the murders in Ekaterinburg. Given these conditions, there are solid reasons for questioning the content of Leonti Yurovsky's testimony. On the identification of his grandfather as a Jewish rabbi, we find very serious doubts. The Yurovsky family itself was Russian Orthodox, not Jewish; Yurovsky himself seethed with a fair amount of anti-Semitism in his youth—something bred into a majority of ethnic Russians and often encouraged by the church itself. Then, too, in the depositions of both Leonti and his wife, we find rather startling descriptions of Yakov Yurovsky himself. Allegedly, his brother and sister-in-law described him as a "despot" and a man who "liked to oppress people" (testimonies of Leonti Mikhailovich Yurovsky and Anna Yurovskaia, in SA, vol. 7, docs. 1 and 2). Among all of the testimonies collected during the investigation, these two statements were the most damning to investigators—and, indeed, to historians who have come after. They stand in contrast to the great majority of opinion about Yurovsky. It is left to his own brother and sister-in-law—in the hands of the Whites—to portray him as a "despot." Yet the brothers enjoyed an excellent, close relationship. After Leonti Yurovsky was freed from the Irkutsk prison in August 1919 by advancing Red soldiers—and had provided this damning testimony to the White investigators—he did not shun his brother; instead, they spent a great deal of time together, during which Leonti described his arrest and imprisonment. Under such circumstances, the testimonies of both Leonti Yurovsky and Anna Yurovskaia were at best tainted; at worst, they were certainly extracted under torture, perhaps even designed to provide exactly the information that the White Army had hoped to elicit. Steinberg and Krustalev note that "as arrested relatives of the Tsar's alleged murderer," both Leonti and his wife, "facing a monarchist court, certainly had reason to ingratiate themselves with their interrogators" (Steinberg and Krustalev, 285). Given the conflicting evidence available about the family's religious practices, the conditions under which these admissions were gathered, the undue emphasis that the Whites placed on the issue of identifying Bolsheviks as Jews, and the continued close relationship between Leonti and Yakov Yurovsky, these seemingly damning pieces of information cannot be considered as historical fact. The issue of Yakov Yurovsky's racial background is of little historical interest. Perhaps he was Jewish, though he was certainly raised in the Russian Orthodox Church. His racial heritage played no part in the role he enacted in the Romanov drama. It mattered only to the White investigators.

101. Yurovsky, 1938, letter, written from Kremlin hospital to his children, quoted in Radzinsky, 244.

102. Yurovsky, unpublished memoirs, 1922, in APRF, f. 3, op. 58, d. 280.

103. Yurovsky, 1938, letter written from Kremlin hospital to his children, quoted in Radzinsky, 303–304.

104. Yurovsky, unpublished memoirs, 1922, in APRF, f. 3, op. 58, d. 280.

105. Ibid.

106. Ibid.

107. Ibid.

108. Ibid.

109. Ibid.

110. Ibid.

111. Buranov and Krustalev, *Gibel*, 255.

112. Outemskii, 513–514.

113. Yurovsky, unpublished memoirs, 1922, in APRF, f. 3, op. 58, d. 280.

114. Outemskii, 513–514.

115. Yurovsky, unpublished memoirs, 1922, in APRF, f. 3, op. 58, d. 280.

116. Ibid.
117. Ibid.
118. Yurovsky, 1938, letter written from Kremlin hospital to his children, quoted in Radzinsky, 244.
119. Yurovsky, unpublished memoirs, 1922, in APRF, f. 3, op. 58, d. 280.
120. Ibid.
121. Ibid.; Ioffe, *Revoliutsiia i sud'ba Romanovki*, 317–319.
122. Yurovsky, unpublished memoirs, 1922, in APRF, f. 3, op. 58, d. 280; Steinberg and Krustalev, 285.
123. Yurovsky, 1938, letter written from Kremlin hospital to his children, quoted in Radzinsky, 244.
124. Speranski, 138.
125. Yurovsky, unpublished memoirs, 1922, in APRF, f. 3, op. 58, d. 280.
126. Radzinsky, 244; Buranov and Krustalev, *Gibel*, 255.
127. Speranski, 152.
128. Yurovsky, unpublished memoirs, 1922, in APRF, f. 3, op. 58, d. 280.
129. In SA, vol. 1, doc. 81; Radzinsky, 244; Buranov and Krustalev, *Gibel*, 255; Alexandrov, 90.
130. Alexandrov, 90.
131. Speranski, 152–153.
132. Alexandrov, 90.
133. Buranov and Krustalev, *Gibel*, 255; Steinberg and Krustalev, 285; Radzinsky, 245.
134. Yurovsky, unpublished memoirs, 1922, in APRF, f. 3, op. 58, d. 280; McCullagh, 126.
135. Speranski, 91.
136. In SA, vol. 1, doc. 81; interrogation of Nicholas Arsenyevich Sakovich, in GARF, f. 601, op. 2, d. 51.
137. Speranski, 139.
138. Ibid., 95–96.
139. Rodzinsky, May 13, 1964, in RTsKhIDNI, f. 588, op. 3, d. 14.
140. Yurovsky, unpublished memoirs, 1922, in APRF, f. 3, op. 58, d. 280.
141. Ibid.
142. Markov, 254.
143. Ibid., 254.
144. Baedecker, 260.
145. Preston, 111.
146. Ibid., 107.
147. Cable 5351, "Boyar," Ekaterinburg, on French consulate form with official stamp, to French embassy, Moscow, July 9, 1918, in Sotheby's auction catalog, 88; Alexandrov, illustration 43, also 216.
148. Smirnoff, 96–104; Helen of Serbia and of Russia, 24.
149. Smirnoff, 104–105; Helen of Serbia and of Russia, 24.
150. Bykov, *Last Days*, 77.
151. See Bykov, *Last Days*, 77; also, cable 4650, Beloborodov to Sverdlov, Ekaterinburg to Moscow, July 9, 1918, in Sotheby's auction catalog, 84.
152. Gaida, 152.
153. Rodzinsky, May 13, 1964, in RTsKhIDNI, f. 588, op. 3, d. 14.
154. Preston, 99.
155. Wilton and Telberg, 367; Buxhoeveden, *Left Behind*, 117.
156. Michael Mikhailovich Medvedev, in Radzinsky, 286–287.
157. Alexandrov, 77.
158. Melgunov, *Sud'ba Imperatora Nikolaya II*, 370.
159. McCullagh, 129.
160. Summers and Mangold, 51.

Chapter 10: The Coming Storm: Enter Yurovsky

1. AF diary, July 1, 1918, in GARF, f. 640, op. 1, d. 326.
2. AF diary, July 2, 1918, in GARF, f. 640, op. 1, d. 326.
3. See AF diary, July 7–10 and 15, 1918, in GARF, f. 640, op. 1, d. 326. According to General Deterikhs, Derevenko visited the Ipatiev House sometime after July 4, when Yakov Yurovsky took over from Avdayev as commandant. Deterikhs wrote that after Yurovsky's appointment, "He invited Dr. Derevenko to the house. After this visit the doctor stopped visiting the Imperial Family altogether. The reason for this was explained by Derevenko himself to interested friends as follows: when he, in response to the invitation referred to, arrived at the house, Yurovsky brought him, as the story has it, to the Tsesarevich, who was prostrate with a sore leg, and asked Derevenko's opinion about the state of His Highness' illness. Derevenko replied that he considered the

condition of the Tsesarevich's leg to be very serious and would not permit him to walk under any circumstances. Then, according to the account, Yurovsky himself took hold of the Tsesarevich's leg, began to feel it crudely and knead it, and asserted that it was perfectly well. According to this story, this crude medical treatment of the suffering Tsesarevich by Yurovsky so upset the doctor that he decided not to go back to the Ipatiev House." Deterikhs had this story second-hand, and he never spoke to Derevenko personally. The diary entries of both Nicholas and Alexandra do not indicate that Alexei had suffered any relapse in his illness; on the contrary, his leg continued to improve after his injuries in April in Tobolsk, and again on the night of May 23 in the Ipatiev House. The very fact that Alexandra does not mention a visit by Derevenko after July 2—and, on the contrary, rather pointedly expressed concern over his continued absence— makes it unlikely that he was in the Ipatiev House again after July 2. See Deterikhs, vol. 1, 299–300, for further discussion.

4. AF diary, July 3, 1918, in GARF, f. 640, op. 1, d. 326.
5. In GARF, f. 740, op. 1, d. 12.
6. N diary, July 4, 1918, in GARF, f. 601, op. 1, d. 266; AF diary, July 4, 1918, in GARF, f. 640, op. 1, d. 326.
7. N diary, July 4, 1918, in GARF, f. 601, op. 1, d. 266.
8. AF diary, July 4, 1918, in GARF, f. 640, op. 1, d. 326.
9. Yurovsky, unpublished memoirs, 1922, in APRF, f. 3, op. 58, d. 280.
10. Ibid.
11. AF diary, July 4, 1918, in GARF, f. 640, op. 1, d. 326.
12. Yurovsky, unpublished memoirs, 1922, in APRF, f. 3, op. 58, d. 280.
13. Ibid.
14. AF diary, July 4, 1918, in GARF, f. 640, op. 1, d. 326.
15. Yurovsky, unpublished memoirs, 1922, in APRF, f. 3, op. 58, d. 280.
16. Rodzinsky, May 13, 1964, in RTsKhIDNI, f. 588, op. 3, d. 14.
17. Yurovsky, unpublished memoirs, 1922, in APRF, f. 3, op. 58, d. 280.

18. Nikulin, May 13, 1964, in RTsKhIDNI, f. 588, op. 3, d. 14.
19. Medvedev, February 21–22, 1919, vol. 2, doc. 86.
20. AF diary, July 4, 1918, in GARF, f. 640, op. 1, d. 326.
21. Lorrain, *La Nuit de L'Oural*, 304; Strekotin, 1934, in TsDOOSO, f. 221, op. 2, d. 849.
22. N diary, July 6, 1918, in GARF, f. 601, op. 1, d. 266.
23. AF diary, July 5, 1918, in GARF, f. 640, op. 1, d. 326; N diary, July 6, 1918, in GARF, f. 601, op. 1, d. 266.
24. Yurovsky, unpublished memoirs, 1922, in APRF, f. 3, op. 58, d. 280.
25. In GARF, f. 601, op. 2, d. 27.
26. AF diary, July 6, 1918, in GARF, f. 640, op. 1, d. 326.
27. N diary, July 6, 1918, in GARF, f. 601, op. 1, d. 266.
28. AF diary, July 6, 1918, in GARF, f. 640, op. 1, d. 326.
29. Ibid.
30. AF diary, July 7, 1918, in GARF, f. 640, op. 1, d. 326.
31. Previously, this change in guard has always been assigned to July 4—the same day on which Yurovsky himself was introduced into the Ipatiev House. However, we know from six disparate sources—the diary of Nicholas II, Yurovsky's unpublished memoirs, and the testimonies of guards Paul Medvedev, Anatoly Yakimov, Philip Proskuryakov, and Victor Netrebin—that this change was made not on July 4, but on July 8. See N diary, July 8, 1918, in GARF, f. 601, op. 1, d. 266; Yurovsky, unpublished memoirs, 1922, in APRF, f. 3, op. 58, d. 280; Medvedev, February 21–22, 1919, vol. 2, doc. 86; Yakimov, May 7–11, 1919, in SA, vol. 4, doc. 18; Proskuryakov, April 3, 1919, in SA, vol. 5, doc. 17; and Netrebin, in TsDOOSO, f. 41, op. 1, d. 149.
32. Yakimov, May 7–11, 1919, in SA, vol. 5, doc. 18.
33. Ibid.
34. Rules for guards at Ipatiev House drawn up by Yurovsky, July 4, 1918, in GARF, f. 601, op. 2, d. 23.
35. N diary, July 8, 1918, in GARF, f. 601, op. 1, d. 266.

36. Yakimov, May 7–11, 1919, in SA, vol. 5, doc. 18.
37. Speranski, 39.
38. Alexandrov, 83; in SA, vol. 3, doc. 9; Yurovsky, unpublished memoirs, 1922, in APRF, f. 3, op. 58, d. 280.
39. Netrebin, in TsDOOSO, f. 41, op. 1, d. 149.
40. Alexandrov, 83.
41. Rudolf Lacher, testimony of January 17–18, 1966, in the case of *Anna Anderson v. Barbara, Duchess of Mecklenburg, Oberlandesgericht-Hamburg*, III, ZPO 139/67.
42. Yakimov, May 7–11, 1919, in SA, vol. 5, doc. 18; Proskuryakov, April 3, 1919, in SA, vol. 5, doc. 17.
43. Netrebin, in TsDOOSO, f. 41, op. 1, d. 149.
44. Proskuryakov, April 3, 1919, in SA, vol. 5, doc. 17.
45. Yakimov, May 7–11, 1919, in SA, vol. 5, doc. 18.
46. Yurovsky, unpublished memoirs, 1922, in APRF, f. 3, op. 58, d. 280.
47. Yakimov, May 7–11, 1919, in SA, vol. 5, doc. 18; Speranski, 100–101; Proskuryakov, April 3, 1919, in SA, vol. 5, doc. 17; McCullagh, 125; guard duty book, July 6, 1918, in GARF, f. 601, op. 2, d. 24.
48. Yurovsky, unpublished memoirs, 1922, in APRF, f. 3, op. 58, d. 280.
49. Ibid.
50. Ibid.
51. Ibid.
52. Ibid.
53. Ibid.
54. Yakimov, May 7–11, 1919, in SA, vol. 5, doc. 18; Yurovsky, unpublished memoirs, 1922, in APRF, f. 3, op. 58, d. 280.
55. Yurovsky, unpublished memoirs, 1922, in APRF, f. 3, op. 58, d. 280.
56. Ibid.
57. Ibid.
58. AF diary, July 11, 1918, in GARF, f. 640, op. 1, d. 326.
59. N diary, July 11, 1918, in GARF, f. 601, op. 1, d. 266.
60. AF diary, July 11, 1918, in GARF, f. 640, op. 1, d. 326; Yurovsky, unpublished memoirs, 1922, in APRF, f. 3, op. 58, d. 280.
61. AF diary, July 12, 1918, in GARF, f. 640, op. 1, d. 326.
62. AF diary, July 13, 1918, in GARF, f. 640, op. 1, d. 326.
63. Ibid.
64. Yurovsky, unpublished memoirs, 1922, in APRF, f. 3, op. 58, d. 280.
65. N diary, July 13, 1918, in GARF, f. 601, op. 1, d. 266.
66. AF diary, July 14, 1918, in GARF, f. 640, op. 1, d. 326.
67. Storozhev, in Sokolov, *Enquete*, 122.
68. Ibid.
69. Storozhev, in Sokolov, *Enquete*, 123.
70. Ibid., 123–124.
71. Ibid., 124–126.
72. AF diary, July 15, 1918, in GARF, f. 640, op. 1, d. 326; Alexandrov, 85–87.
73. Sokolov, *Enquete*, 127.
74. Medvedev, February 21–22, 1919, vol. 2, doc. 86.
75. Starodymova, November 11, 1918, in Sokolov, *Enquete*, 128.
76. Varvara Dryagina, November 11, 1918, in Sokolov, *Enquete*, 129.
77. Eudokia Semyonovna, in Speranski, 117–124.
78. AF diary, July 16, 1918, in GARF, f. 640, op. 1, d. 326.
79. Sokolov, *Enquete*, 138.
80. Proskuryakov, April 3, 1919, in SA, vol. 5, doc. 17.
81. Ibid.
82. Nikulin, May 13, 1964, in RTsKhIDNI, f. 558, op. 3, d. 13.
83. AF diary, July 16, 1918, in GARF, f. 640, op. 1, d. 326.
84. Paul Medvedev, as related to Proskuryakov, April 3, 1919, in SA, vol. 5, doc. 17.
85. Yakimov, May 7–11, 1919, in SA, vol. 5, doc. 18.
86. Letemin, interrogated August 7, 1918, by Kirsta, head of the Criminal Investigating Division, Ekaterinburg Office, in letters and materials of Minister of Justice Starynkevich, February 19, 1919; certified original copies in authors' possession.
87. Proskuryakov, April 3, 1919, in SA, vol. 5, doc. 17.
88. Yurovsky, 1920 note, in GARF, f. 601, op. 2, d. 35; Yurovsky, unpublished memoirs, 1922, in APRF, f. 3, op. 58, d. 280; Kudrin, December 1963, in RTsKhIDNI,

f. 588, op. 3, d. 14; Ermakov, October 29, 1947, in Sverdlovsk Party Archives, TsDOOSO, f. 221, op. 2, d. 774.

89. AF diary, July 16, 1918, in GARF, f. 640, op. 1, d. 326.

90. Yurovsky, unpublished memoirs, 1922, in APRF, f. 3, op. 58, d. 280.

91. There has previously been much confusion as to precisely when Sednev was removed from the Ipatiev House. The contradictory accounts come from those witnesses who should have been the most reliable: Yurovsky himself, and members of the Special Detachment who were on guard duty. In his three detailed sets of recollections of that night, Yurovsky gave three different times for this removal. In his first, 1920 account—the "Yurovsky note"—he wrote: "On 16 July, at about two in the afternoon, I called the young servant Sednev, and told him that his uncle wished to see him" (Yurovsky, 1920 note, in GARF, f. 601, op. 2, d. 35). In his unpublished memoirs, written two years later, he said: "While the prisoners were having dinner, I summoned the young servant Sednev and told him that he should leave the Ipatiev House that night to join his uncle" (Yurovsky, unpublished memoirs, 1922, in APRF, f. 3, op. 58, d. 280). And in his 1934 recollections he declared: "On the morning of the 16th, I sent away the kitchen boy Sednev, under the pretext of a meeting with his uncle who had come to Ekaterinburg" (Yurovsky, February 1, 1934, in TsDOOSO, f. 41, op. 1, d. 151). Clearly, only Yurovsky's 1922 memoirs was accurate in its recall of the event, as it agrees with the diary of the empress. Yet the other accounts vary widely. Anatoly Yakimov testified that he had seen Sednev taken out of the Ipatiev House on the previous day, July 15 (Yakimov, May 7–11, 1919, in SA, vol. 5, doc. 18). And both Paul Medvedev and Gregory Nikulin later declared that the young boy had been removed early in the afternoon (Medvedev, February 21–22, 1919, vol. 2, doc. 86; Nikulin, May 13, 1964, in RTsKhIDNI, f. 558, op. 3, d. 13).

92. Yurovsky, unpublished memoirs, 1922, in APRF, f. 3, op. 58, d. 280.

93. AF diary, July 16, 1918, in GARF, f. 640, op. 1, d. 326.

94. Yakimov, May 7–11, 1919, in SA, vol. 5, doc. 18.

95. Preston, 102.

96. McCullagh, 129.

97. Preston, 102.

98. Ibid.

99. AF diary, July 16, 1918, in GARF, f. 640, op. 1, d. 326.

Chapter 11: Murderous Intentions

1. Kudrin, December 1963, in RTsKhIDNI, f. 588, op. 3, d. 14.

2. Sokolov, *Enquete*, 142.

3. Massie, 12.

4. Pipes, *Russian Revolution*, 770.

5. Radzinsky, 325–326.

6. Figes, 638.

7. *Biograficheskaya Khronika*, 5: 374.

8. Cited in Pipes, *Russian Revolution*, 738.

9. *Sovetskaia Rossiia* 161, issue 9 (July 12, 1987): 412.

10. Trotsky, diary entry for April 9, 1935, in *Diary in Exile*, 80.

11. *Biograficheskaya Khronika*, 5: 242.

12. Steinberg, *Spiridonova*, 195.

13. *Nash Vek* 73 (April 14, 1918).

14. Trotsky, diary entry for April 9, 1935, in *Diary in Exile*, 80.

15. Voikov, in Bessedowsky, 203.

16. Radzinsky, 330.

17. Pipes, *Russian Revolution*, 636.

18. Salisbury, 603.

19. Bunyan, 198–204.

20. Bruce Lockhart, *British Agent*, 298–300; Chamberlain, vol. 2, 53–55; Bunyan and Fisher, 232; Erdmann, 713–714.

21. Bunyan and Fisher, 232.

22. Lockhart, *British Agent*, 298–300; Chamberlain, vol. 2, 53–55; Salisbury, 604; Pipes, *Russian Revolution*, 640; Fisher and Bunyan, 232.

23. Pipes, *Russian Revolution*, 640–641.

24. Ibid.; Lockhart, *British Agent*, 298–300; Chamberlain, vol. 2, 53–55; Salisbury, 604.

25. Trotsky, *O Lenine*, 156–157; German foreign minister von Lersner to Foreign Ministry, July 13, 1918, in PRO/GFM 6/139, A29982; Kennan, *Decision to Intervene*, 446. On July 15 Lenin boldly announced to the Presidium of the

Central Executive Committee that allowing a German battalion into Moscow would mark "the beginning of the occupation by foreign powers"; he added that "there are limits" to how far Russia could be pushed, and promised that Russians, "to a man," would "defend the country with arms" (Sochineny, vol. 50, 113). It was all a charade, calculated on Lenin's presumption that Germany could not afford to embark on a full-scale invasion of Russia and a return to a two-front war.

26. Bunyan and Fisher, 242; Sir Robert Bruce Lockhart, *British Agent*, 298–300; Chamberlain, vol. 2, 53–55; Salisbury, 604; Pipes, *Russian Revolution*, 644.

27. Bunyan and Fisher, 242.

28. Report of Nicholas Sokolov, in British Library, 24.aa.19.

29. Bunyan and Fisher, 242; Salisbury, 605; Payne, *Lenin*, 462.

30. Bonch-Bruyevich, 203; Bunyan and Fisher, 242.

31. Kudrin, December 1963, in RTsKhIDNI, f. 588, op. 3, d. 14.

32. Kokovtsov, *Out of My Past*, 461.

33. Bykov, *Last Days*, 89.

34. Voikov, in Bessedowsky, 204.

35. Ibid.

36. Ibid., 205.

37. Nikulin, May 13, 1964, in RTsKhIDNI, f. 558, op. 3, d. 13.

38. Melgunov, *Sud'ba Imperatora Nikolaya II*, 401.

39. This admission came in Bykov, "The Last Days of the Romanovs," *Rabochaya revolyutsiya na Urale*, 3. Published in 1921 in Ekaterinburg, this book was quickly confiscated by Soviet authorities on orders from Moscow; only a few copies survived. Bykov subsequently removed this statement indicating that the Ural authorities had acted on their own initiative and without Moscow's approval when he wrote his own account of the murders, presumably on orders from the same Soviet government that had seized the first offending work.

40. Rodzinsky, May 13, 1964, in RTsKhIDNI, f. 588, op. 3, d. 14; Yurovsky, unpublished memoirs, 1922, in APRF, f. 3, op. 58, d. 280.

41. Netrebin, in TsDOOSO, f. 41, op. 1, d. 149.

42. Voikov, in Bessedowsky, 203.

43. Sokolov, *Enquete*, 140. Peter Ermakov, who mistakenly placed this event on July 14, identified the third man as his friend Stephan Vaganov (Ermakov, in Halliburton, *Seven League Boots*, 132).

44. Fesenko, in Yurovsky, 140.

45. M. A. Volokitin, June 21, 1919, in Sokolov, *Enquete*, 139.

46. A number of variant accounts all claim numerous meetings of the Ural Regional Soviet between July 12 and 16 held to discuss the fate of the Romanovs. Two of these are said to emanate from Peter Voikov, who placed one meeting on July 13, and yet another on July 15 (Voikov, *Gutek*, in Alexandrov, 238; Voikov, in Bessedowsky, 311). The third, which often has been cited as evidence that Moscow ordered the executions, comes in the form of an alleged resolution adopted by the Ural Regional Soviet on July 14, following "an order from Sverdlov" that the Romanovs be killed: "At the proposal of the Military Revolutionary Committee, the meeting unanimously resolved to liquidate the former Emperor Nicholas Romanov and his family, as well as their servants. It was further agreed to carry out this resolution not later than July 18, 1918, and to appoint Comrade Y. M. Yurovsky from the Extraordinary Commission to fulfill this task" (quoted in Alferyev, 398–399). It was reproduced in the book *Pis'ma tsarskoi sem'i iz zatocheniia* (Letters of the Tsar's Family from Captivity), published by the Russian Orthodox Church Outside Russia's Holy Trinity Monastery in Jordanville, New York. The document—along with others quoted in the book—have been shown to be forgeries, concocted in the 1950s by Johann Meyer, a man who tried to interject himself into the then ongoing trial of Anna Anderson to establish her identity as Anastasia. One of Meyer's friends explained to the West German court how Meyer had fabricated the documents. A historian carefully examined them at the judge's request and declared them to be second-rate forgeries, containing numerous errors. (See Ioffe, *Revoliutsiia in sud'ba Romanovki,*

320–321, and Summers and Mangold, 106–107). Although exposed as forgeries, they continue to be reproduced in numerous works on the Romanovs.

47. In addition to Goloshchokin, those in attendance included Alexander Beloborodov, Peter Voikov, Gregory Safarov, and Vladimir Gorin from the Ural Regional Presidium; and Isai Rodzinsky, Michael Kudrin, and Yakov Yurovsky from the Ekaterinburg Cheka (Kudrin, December 1963, in RTsKhIDNI, f. 588, op. 3, d. 14). In his account, Kudrin places this meeting on the evening of July 16, but clearly, from the content, he is referring to two separate meetings: one on July 12, the other on the evening of July 16. Therefore we have utilized his account in both respects, with this proviso.

48. Kudrin, December 1963, in RTsKhIDNI, f. 588, op. 3, d. 14.

49. Voikov, in Bessedowsky, 205.

50. Bykov, *Last Days*, 75.

51. Bykov, in *Rabochaya revolyutsiya na Urale*, 10.

52. Kudrin, December 1963, in RTsKhIDNI, f. 588, op. 3, d. 14.

53. Bykov, *Last Days*, 89.

54. Y. M. Sverdlov, *Izbranniye Proizvedeniya*, 312, cited in Salisbury, 607.

55. Ibid.

56. Kudrin, December 1963, in RTsKhIDNI, f. 588, op. 3, d. 14.

57. Nikulin, May 13, 1964, in RTsKhIDNI, f. 558, op. 3, d. 13.

58. Yurovsky, unpublished memoirs, 1922, in APRF, f. 3, op. 58, d. 280.

59. Zinoviev to Moscow, Lenin, July 16, 1918, in GARF, f. 130, op. 2, d. 653.

60. Given the lack of evidence, it is important to examine the state of communications between Ekaterinburg and Moscow on July 16. The telegraph system was established in Ekaterinburg in 1861; by 1862 it employed eleven full-time workers. By 1873, and reflecting the growing importance of Ekaterinburg itself, the number of staff had grown to forty-four, responsible for handling some 620 cables each day. At the beginning of World War I, the system included seven long-distance telegraph lines, six local lines, and one city line, which handled some

6,600 cables per day. In 1917 the office added the Whitestone and Morse apparatus as well as a Hughes telegraph line, the latter commonly referred to as the "direct line." All official communications between Petrograd and Moscow were conducted using the Hughes wire. (See www.etel.ru/company/history.htm for further information.)

61. Steinberg and Krustalev, 378; *Biografich-eskaya Khronika*, 5: 640.

62. Radzinsky, 378.

63. Beloborodov to Lenin and Sverdlov, July 17, 1918, in GARF, f. 601, op. 2, d. 27.

64. Steinberg and Krustalev, 294.

65. Radzinsky, 345–346.

66. Akimov, "Vospominaniya," *Konstrukziia gazeta* 96, issue 460 (August 11, 1957): 2.

67. Yurovsky, 1920 note, in GARF, f. 601, op. 2, d. 35.

68. Radzinsky, 342–344.

69. Russian historians Buranov and Krustalev have contended that this cable from Perm ordering the execution was actually a cablegram from Moscow sent in response to the Zinoviev cable and read over the telephone (Buranov and Krustalev, *Gibel*, 189). This, they reason, explains why no record of any such communication has ever been found. But such a hypothesis ignores the difficulties inherent in the time frame given by Yurovsky, who clearly stated that the Perm cable was received before the Zinoviev cable was even dispatched.

70. On July 2, the Sovnarkom in Moscow formally adopted a resolution that called for the nationalization of all former Romanov properties. This was signed on July 13, but not published until July 19, a move viewed by some historians as evidence of Moscow's complicity. (See Pipes, *Russian Revolution*, 771.) Yet a number of issues were discussed during these sessions, and not only Romanov properties were nationalized: large industry and numerous mineral reserves also were seized (*Izvestiia*, July 19, 1918). This nationalization policy was undertaken not in advance of looming Romanov executions, but rather in anticipation of the Congress of Soviets to take place the third week of July. As with other frequently cited incidents, it cannot be read

as proof of Moscow's foreknowledge of the Ekaterinburg murders.

71. Trotsky, *Diary in Exile*, 80–81.
72. Steinberg and Krustalev, 293.
73. Trotsky, *Stalin*, 162.
74. Kennan, *Decision to Intervene*, 449.
75. Cockfield, 242.

Chapter 12: Götterdämmerung

1. McCullagh, 129.
2. Yurovsky, February 1, 1934, in TsDOOSO, f. 41, op. 1, d. 151.
3. Wilton and Telberg, 88.
4. Summers and Mangold, 74; Massie, 4.
5. Sokolov, *Enquete*, 157, 307.
6. Medvedev, February 21–22, 1919, vol. 2, doc. 86.
7. *Taina tsarskikh ostankov*, 92–109; Sokolov, *Enquete*, 222–224. See also Medvedev, February 21–22, 1919, vol. 2, doc. 86; Ermakov, October 29, 1947, in Sverdlovsk Party Archive, f. 221, op. 2, d. 774; Kudrin, December 1963, in RTsKhIDNI, f. 588, op. 3, d. 14; Netrebin, in TsDOOSO, f. 41, op. 1, d. 149; Yurovsky, unpublished memoirs, 1922, in APRF, f. 3, op. 58, d. 280; Kabanov, unpublished memoirs, in Khabarovsk Regional Party Archives, f. 117, op. 2, d. 27. Information on the guns used that night is drawn not only from the varied accounts of participants but also from the White Army investigation of the murder room, and the bullets recovered, as well as forensic evidence recovered from the Koptyaki Forest grave and the exhumed remains. Thirteen bullets were recovered from the murder room in the Ipatiev House, including one from a Colt, seven from Russian Nagant revolvers, and five from other guns, including Brownings and Smith & Wessons. At the Four Brothers mine, investigators found two Nagant bullets and one empty shell casing (Sokolov, 215–222). From the 1991 exhumations in Koptyaki Forest, twenty-five bullets were recovered, including one possible Mauser bullet; nine rounds fired from 7.62 Nagant revolvers; and four bullets from Browning, Colt, and Smith & Wessons (*Taina tsarskikh ostankov*, 104). The Russian Nagant revolvers had been standard issue to the Imperial Army since 1895, when the Belgian brothers Emil

and Leon Nagant joined forces with Russian S. I. Mosin to design a rifle and a revolver to be supplied to troops. Each Nagant used that night carried seven bullets, fired at a velocity of 1,000 feet per second; in the process, propellant gases escaped from the end of the chamber, resulting in immediate thick, acrid clouds of smoke (Miller, 51; Hartink, 14, 19, 38, 54, 82, 106; Ezell, 28, 49, 84, 91–92). Kudrin's .28-caliber (6.43 mm) Browning pistol, made in 1910 by Fabrique Nationale in Belgium, held a clip of seven cartridges, with a velocity of 925 feet per second (Miller, 14). Yurovsky's 1911 model .45-caliber (11.43 mm) American Colt pistol held a clip of seven bullets, with a velocity of 860 feet per second (Miller, 114). Both Yurovsky and Ermakov carried 1896 .32-caliber (7.63 mm) Mauser pistols, each holding a clip of ten cartridges, with a velocity of 1,400 feet per second (Miller, 36). The 1908 Smith & Wesson .42-caliber (10.66 mm) revolver used that night held six bullets, with a velocity of 650 feet per second; a gap at the rear of the chamber allowed the gunpowder to escape, resulting in thick, black smoke (Miller, 132). From the number of bullets recovered from the various locations, a total of at least forty-one shots were fired in the murder room that night. The fourteen guns used that night held a total of 103 possible shots: twenty shots between the two Mausers; fourteen shots between the two Colts; fourteen total shots between the two Brownings; six total shots in the Smith & Wesson; and forty-nine possible shots among the seven Nagant revolvers.

8. Yurovsky, February 1, 1934, in TsDOOSO, f. 41, op. 1, d. 151.
9. Ermakov, October 29, 1947, in Sverdlovsk Party Archive, f. 221, op. 2, d. 774.
10. Kudrin, December 1963, in RTsKhIDNI, f. 588, op. 3, d. 14.
11. Yurovsky, February 1, 1934, in TsDOOSO, f. 41, op. 1, d. 151.
12. Yurovsky, 1920 note, in GARF, f. 601, op. 2, d. 35.
13. Yurovsky, unpublished memoirs, 1922, in APRF, f. 3, op. 58, d. 280; Yurovsky, February 1, 1934, in TsDOOSO, f. 41, op. 1, d. 151.

14. Kudrin, December 1963, in RTsKhIDNI, f. 588, op. 3, d. 14; Nikulin, May 13, 1964, in RTsKhIDNI, f. 558, op. 3, d. 13.
15. Medvedev, February 21–22, 1919, vol. 2, doc. 86.
16. Maria Medvedev, in SA, vol. 2, doc. 21.
17. Yakimov, May 7–11, 1919, in SA, vol. 5, doc. 18.
18. Andrei Strekotin to Yakimov, May 7–11, 1919, in SA, vol. 5, doc. 19; Strekotin, 1934, in TsDOOSO, f. 221, op. 2, d. 849.
19. Alferyev, 399.
20. Summers and Mangold, 211–214; Ioffe, *Revoliutsiia i sud'ba Romanovki*, 320–321; Steinberg and Krustalev, 296; Paganuzzi, "Tschaikowska-Anna Anderson-Manahan," 14–15.
21. The enigmatic Lacher's role in events that night is difficult to determine. In the Anna Anderson trial of 1964–1967, he changed his story several times. When first interviewed, he claimed that he had "seen nothing, heard nothing, and knew nothing," claiming that, for reasons he could not explain, Yurovsky had locked him into his room at midnight (in *Le Figaro*, June 4, 1965). He certainly had a number of objects that had belonged to the Romanovs, including a gold case, an embroidered handkerchief, and one of the emperor's cigarette holders (Kurth, 350). During his closed-session testimony of January 17–18, 1966, in Göttingen, Lacher insisted that although locked in his room during the murders, he had watched through the keyhole of his door as the victims passed, noting that all of the grand duchesses were sobbing as they descended the staircase. Later, he said, after a number of shots, he climbed on his bed and peered out of the window, counting "eleven bloody bundles" as they were loaded onto the waiting Fiat. (See Rudolf Lacher, testimony of January 17–18, 1966, in the case of *Anna Anderson v. Barbara, Duchess of Mecklenburg*, Oberlandesgericht-Hamburg, III, ZPO 139/67.) Lacher's room, directly beneath Yurovsky's office, had one small window, with double panes of glass, sunk deeply into the two-foot-thick stone wall; between it and the courtyard gate, into which Lyukhanov had backed the Fiat, the first palisade was attached to the eastern facade of the Ipatiev House and, beyond this, the main stairs, with high concrete piers on either side, further obscuring the view and eliminating any possibility that Lacher could have seen what he claimed. Anderson's lawyer, quick to discern the impossibility of Lacher's statements, seized on the contradictions, yelling, "Where were you that night?" "I told you," Lacher replied, "I was locked in my room." "Either you're lying when you say you were locked in your room," the lawyer replied, "or you're lying when you say you saw the bodies." The lawyer suspected that Lacher had, in fact, been among the members of the execution squad. (Cited in Kurth, 351.) In fact, this is supported inferentially in the memoirs of Netrebin, who recalled that, of his comrades, only Lepa and Verhas did not participate in the shooting.
22. Netrebin, in TsDOOSO, f. 41, op. 1, d. 149.
23. Yurovsky, unpublished memoirs, 1922, in APRF, f. 3, op. 58, d. 280.
24. Netrebin, in TsDOOSO, f. 41, op. 1, d. 149.
25. Letemin, in SA, vol. 1, doc. 44.
26. Yurovsky, unpublished memoirs, 1922, in APRF, f. 3, op. 58, d. 280.
27. Kudrin, December 1963, in RTsKhIDNI, f. 588, op. 3, d. 14.
28. Yakimov, May 7–11, 1919, in SA, vol. 5, doc. 18.
29. Peter Leonov, in a letter from Minister of Justice Starynkevich to the Ministry of Foreign Affairs Executive Board about preliminary findings on the assassination of the imperial family, Omsk, February 19, 1919; certified copy in authors' possession.
30. Kudrin, December 1963, in RTsKhIDNI, f. 588, op. 3, d. 14.
31. Yurovsky, February 1, 1934, in TsDOOSO, f. 41, op. 1, d. 151.
32. Yurovsky, unpublished memoirs, 1922, in APRF, f. 3, op. 58, d. 280.
33. Ibid.; Yurovsky, February 1, 1934, in TsDOOSO, f. 41, op. 1, d. 151.
34. Ibid.

35. Yurovsky, 1920 note, in GARF, f. 601, op. 2, d. 35.

36. Yurovsky, unpublished memoirs, 1922, in APRF, f. 3, op. 58, d. 280.

37. Ibid.

38. Ermakov, in Halliburton, *Seven League Boots*, 132.

39. Kudrin, December 1963, in RTsKhIDNI, f. 588, op. 3, d. 14.

40. Yurovsky, February 1, 1934, in TsDOOSO, f. 41, op. 1, d. 151.

41. Yurovsky, unpublished memoirs, 1922, in APRF, f. 3, op. 58, d. 280.

42. Netrebin, in TsDOOSO, f. 41, op. 1, d. 149.

43. Yakimov, May 7–11, 1919, in SA, vol. 5, doc. 18.

44. Strekotin, 1934, in TsDOOSO, f. 221, op. 2, d. 849.

45. Ibid.

46. Ibid.

47. Ibid.

48. Netrebin, in TsDOOSO, f. 41, op. 1, d. 149.

49. Yurovsky, unpublished memoirs, 1922, in APRF, f. 3, op. 58, d. 280; Ermakov, in Halliburton, *Seven League Boots*, 134.

50. Yurovsky, 1920 note, in GARF, f. 601, op. 2, d. 35; Yurovsky, unpublished memoirs, 1922, in APRF, f. 3, op. 58, d. 280; Yurovsky, February 1, 1934, in TsDOOSO, f. 41, op. 1, d. 151; Kudrin, December 1963, in RTsKhIDNI, f. 588, op. 3, d. 14.

51. Kabanov, unpublished memoirs, in Khabarovsk Regional Party Archives, f. 117, op. 2, d. 27.

52. Medvedev, February 21–22, 1919, vol. 2, doc. 86.

53. Kudrin, December 1963, in RTsKhIDNI, f. 588, op. 3, d. 14.

54. Ibid.

55. Medvedev, February 21–22, 1919, vol. 2, doc. 86.

56. Yurovsky, February 1, 1934, in TsDOOSO, f. 41, op. 1, d. 151.

57. Kudrin, December 1963, in RTsKhIDNI, f. 588, op. 3, d. 14.

58. Ermakov, in Halliburton, *Seven League Boots*, 135.

59. Netrebin, in TsDOOSO, f. 41, op. 1, d. 149.

60. Yurovsky, 1920 note, in GARF, f. 601, op. 2, d. 35.

61. Kudrin, December 1963, in RTsKhIDNI, f. 588, op. 3, d. 14.

62. Yurovsky, 1920 note, in GARF, f. 601, op. 2, d. 35.

63. Kudrin, December 1963, in RTsKhIDNI, f. 588, op. 3, d. 14.

64. Yurovsky, unpublished memoirs, 1922, in APRF, f. 3, op. 58, d. 280.

65. Positions in the murder room are drawn from Yurovsky, 1920 note, in GARF, f. 601, op. 2, d. 35; Yurovsky, unpublished memoirs, 1922, in APRF, f. 3, op. 58, d. 280; Yurovsky, February 1, 1934, in TsDOOSO, f. 41, op. 1, d. 151; Kudrin, December 1963, in RTsKhIDNI, f. 588, op. 3, d. 14; Nikulin, May 13, 1964, in RTsKhIDNI, f. 558, op. 3, d. 13; Strekotin, 1934, in TsDOOSO, f. 221, op. 2, d. 849; Ermakov, in Halliburton, *Seven League Boots*, 136–137; Ermakov, October 29, 1947, in Sverdlovsk Party Archive, f. 221, op. 2, d. 774; Medvedev, February 21–22, 1919, vol. 2, doc. 86; Kabanov, unpublished memoirs, in Khabarovsk Regional Party Archives, f. 117, op. 2, d. 27; Rodzinsky, May 13, 1964, statement, in RTsKhIDNI, f. 588, op. 3, d. 14; Yakimov, May 7–11, 1919, in SA, vol. 5, doc. 18; and Netrebin, in TsDOOSO, f. 41, op. 1, d. 149.

66. Yurovsky, unpublished memoirs, 1922, in APRF, f. 3, op. 58, d. 280.

67. Ibid.

68. Kudrin, December 1963, in RTsKhIDNI, f. 588, op. 3, d. 14.

69. Kabanov, unpublished memoirs, in Khabarovsk Regional Party Archives, f. 117, op. 2, d. 27.

70. Ermakov, in Halliburton, *Seven League Boots*, 136.

71. Ermakov, October 29, 1947, in Sverdlovsk Party Archive, f. 221, op. 2, d. 774; Kudrin, December 1963, in RTsKhIDNI, f. 588, op. 3, d. 14; Rodzinsky, May 13, 1964, statement, in RTsKhIDNI, f. 588, op. 3, d. 14.

72. Yurovsky, unpublished memoirs, 1922, in APRF, f. 3, op. 58, d. 280; Kudrin, December 1963, in RTsKhIDNI, f. 588, op. 3, d. 14.

73. Yurovsky, unpublished memoirs, 1922, in APRF, f. 3, op. 58, d. 280; Yurovsky, February 1, 1934, in TsDOOSO, f. 41, op. 1, d. 151.

74. Yurovsky, unpublished memoirs, 1922, in APRF, f. 3, op. 58, d. 280.
75. Kudrin, December 1963, in RTsKhIDNI, f. 588, op. 3, d. 14.
76. Kabanov, unpublished memoirs, in Khabarovsk Regional Party Archives, f. 117, op. 2, d. 27.
77. Netrebin, in TsDOOSO, f. 41, op. 1, d. 149.
78. Yurovsky, unpublished memoirs, 1922, in APRF, f. 3, op. 58, d. 280.
79. Kudrin, December 1963, in RTsKhIDNI, f. 588, op. 3, d. 14.
80. Yurovsky, 1920 note, in GARF, f. 601, op. 2, d. 35.
81. Kudrin, December 1963, in RTsKhIDNI, f. 588, op. 3, d. 14.
82. Nikulin, May 13, 1964, in RTsKhIDNI, f. 558, op. 3, d. 13.
83. Strekotin, 1934, in TsDOOSO, f. 221, op. 2, d. 849.
84. Ibid.
85. Yurovsky, 1920 note, in GARF, f. 601, op. 2, d. 35.
86. Strekotin, 1934, in TsDOOSO, f. 221, op. 2, d. 849.
87. Yurovsky, unpublished memoirs, 1922, in APRF, f. 3, op. 58, d. 280.
88. Yurovsky, 1920 note, in GARF, f. 601, op. 2, d. 35; Kudrin, December 1963, in RTsKhIDNI, f. 588, op. 3, d. 14.
89. Strekotin, 1934, in TsDOOSO, f. 221, op. 2, d. 849.
90. *Taina tsarskikh ostankov*, 108.
91. Kabanov, unpublished memoirs, in Khabarovsk Regional Party Archives, f. 117, op. 2, d. 27.
92. Yurovsky, unpublished memoirs, 1922, in APRF, f. 3, op. 58, d. 280.
93. Kudrin, December 1963, in RTsKhIDNI, f. 588, op. 3, d. 14.
94. Yurovsky, unpublished memoirs, 1922, in APRF, f. 3, op. 58, d. 280.
95. Kabanov, unpublished memoirs, in Khabarovsk Regional Party Archives, f. 117, op. 2, d. 27.
96. Yurovsky, February 1, 1934, in TsDOOSO, f. 41, op. 1, d. 151.
97. Yurovsky, unpublished memoirs, 1922, in APRF, f. 3, op. 58, d. 280.
98. Yurovsky, February 1, 1934, in TsDOOSO, f. 41, op. 1, d. 151.
99. Yurovsky, 1920 note, in GARF, f. 601, op. 2, d. 35; Kudrin, December 1963, in RTsKhIDNI, f. 588, op. 3, d. 14; Yurovsky, February 1, 1934, in TsDOOSO, f. 41, op. 1, d. 151.
100. Yurovsky, unpublished memoirs, 1922, in APRF, f. 3, op. 58, d. 280.
101. Yurovsky, February 1, 1934, in TsDOOSO, f. 41, op. 1, d. 151.
102. Netrebin, in TsDOOSO, f. 41, op. 1, d. 149.
103. Yurovsky, unpublished memoirs, 1922, in APRF, f. 3, op. 58, d. 280; *Taina tsarskikh ostankov*, 107.
104. Yurovsky, 1920 note, in GARF, f. 601, op. 2, d. 35; *Taina tsarskikh ostankov*, 107.
105. Strekotin, 1934, in TsDOOSO, f. 221, op. 2, d. 849.
106. Ermakov, in Halliburton, *Seven League Boots*, 140.
107. Strekotin, 1934, in TsDOOSO, f. 221, op. 2, d. 849.
108. Yurovsky, unpublished memoirs, 1922, in APRF, f. 3, op. 58, d. 280; *Taina tsarskikh ostankov*, 108.
109. Kudrin, December 1963, in RTsKhIDNI, f. 588, op. 3, d. 14.
110. Strekotin, 1934, in TsDOOSO, f. 221, op. 2, d. 849.
111. Yurovsky, February 1, 1934, in TsDOOSO, f. 41, op. 1, d. 151.
112. Kudrin, December 1963, in RTsKhIDNI, f. 588, op. 3, d. 14.
113. Yurovsky, unpublished memoirs, 1922, in APRF, f. 3, op. 58, d. 280.
114. Ibid.
115. Kabanov, unpublished memoirs, in Khabarovsk Regional Party Archives, f. 117, op. 2, d. 27.
116. Yurovsky, 1920 note, in GARF, f. 601, op. 2, d. 35; Yurovsky, unpublished memoirs, 1922, in APRF, f. 3, op. 58, d. 280; Kudrin, December 1963, in RTsKhIDNI, f. 588, op. 3, d. 14.
117. Yurovsky, unpublished memoirs, 1922, in APRF, f. 3, op. 58, d. 280; *Taina tsarskikh ostankov*, 109.
118. Yurovsky, February 1, 1934, in TsDOOSO, f. 41, op. 1, d. 151.
119. Netrebin, in TsDOOSO, f. 41, op. 1, d. 149.
120. Yurovsky, 1927 note, in RTsKhIDNI, f. 588, op. 3, d. 11.
121. Kudrin, December 1963, in RTsKhIDNI, f. 588, op. 3, d. 14.

122. Medvedev, February 21–22, 1919, vol. 2, doc. 86.
123. Sokolov, *Enquete*, 217; Yurovsky, unpublished memoirs, 1922, in APRF, f. 3, op. 58, d. 280.
124. Yurovsky, unpublished memoirs, 1922, in APRF, f. 3, op. 58, d. 280.
125. Ibid.
126. Netrebin, in TsDOOSO, f. 41, op. 1, d. 149.
127. Medvedev, February 21–22, 1919, vol. 2, doc. 86.
128. Yurovsky, unpublished memoirs, 1922, in APRF, f. 3, op. 58, d. 280.
129. Yurovsky, February 1, 1934, in TsDOOSO, f. 41, op. 1, d. 151.
130. Yurovsky, unpublished memoirs, 1922, in APRF, f. 3, op. 58, d. 280.
131. Kabanov, unpublished memoirs, in Khabarovsk Regional Party Archives, f. 117, op. 2, d. 27.
132. Yurovsky, unpublished memoirs, 1922, in APRF, f. 3, op. 58, d. 280.
133. Netrebin, in TsDOOSO, f. 41, op. 1, d. 149; *Taina tsarskikh ostankov*, 109–110.
134. Netrebin, in TsDOOSO, f. 41, op. 1, d. 149.
135. Yurovsky, unpublished memoirs, 1922, in APRF, f. 3, op. 58, d. 280; *Taina tsarskikh ostankov*, 110.
136. Kudrin, December 1963, in RTsKhIDNI, f. 588, op. 3, d. 14.
137. Kabanov, unpublished memoirs, in Khabarovsk Regional Party Archives, f. 117, op. 2, d. 27.
138. Yurovsky, unpublished memoirs, 1922, in APRF, f. 3, op. 58, d. 280; *Taina tsarskikh ostankov*, 110.
139. Kabanov, unpublished memoirs, in Khabarovsk Regional Party Archives, f. 117, op. 2, d. 27.
140. Yurovsky, 1920 note, in GARF, f. 601, op. 2, d. 35.
141. Yurovsky, unpublished memoirs, 1922, in APRF, f. 3, op. 58, d. 280.
142. Ibid.
143. Ibid.; Sokolov, *Enquete*, 109.
144. Kudrin, December 1963, in RTsKhIDNI, f. 588, op. 3, d. 14.
145. Kabanov, unpublished memoirs, in Khabarovsk Regional Party Archives, f. 117, op. 2, d. 27.
146. *Taina tsarskikh ostankov*, 110–111.

147. Ibid., 110.
148. Yurovsky, unpublished memoirs, 1922, in APRF, f. 3, op. 58, d. 280.
149. Yurovsky, unpublished memoirs, 1922, in APRF, f. 3, op. 58, d. 280; also Yurovsky, 1920 note, in GARF, f. 601, op. 2, d. 35; Yurovsky, February 1, 1934, in TsDOOSO, f. 41, op. 1, d. 151; Kudrin, December 1963, in RTsKhIDNI, f. 588, op. 3, d. 14.
150. Victor Buivid, August 10, 1918, in letter from Minister of Justice Starynkevich to the minister of foreign affairs, Omsk, February 19, 1919; certified copy in authors' possession.
151. Medvedev, February 21–22, 1919, vol. 2, doc. 86.
152. Yakimov, May 7–11, 1919, in SA, vol. 5, doc. 18.
153. Ermakov, in Halliburton, *Seven League Boots*, 141.
154. Yurovsky, February 1, 1934, in TsDOOSO, f. 41, op. 1, d. 151.
155. Kudrin, December 1963, in RTsKhIDNI, f. 588, op. 3, d. 14.
156. Voikov, in Bessedowsky, 208.
157. Kudrin, December 1963, in RTsKhIDNI, f. 588, op. 3, d. 14.
158. Ibid.
159. Strekotin, 1934, in TsDOOSO, f. 221, op. 2, d. 849.
160. Yurovsky, unpublished memoirs, 1922, in APRF, f. 3, op. 58, d. 280.
161. Yurovsky, February 1, 1934, in TsDOOSO, f. 41, op. 1, d. 151.
162. Kudrin, December 1963, in RTsKhIDNI, f. 588, op. 3, d. 14.
163. Ibid.
164. Yurovsky, unpublished memoirs, 1922, in APRF, f. 3, op. 58, d. 280.
165. Rodzinsky, May 13, 1964, statement, in RTsKhIDNI, f. 588, op. 3, d. 14.
166. Yurovsky, unpublished memoirs, 1922, in APRF, f. 3, op. 58, d. 280; also Yurovsky, 1920 note, in GARF, f. 601, op. 2, d. 35; Yurovsky, February 1, 1934, in TsDOOSO, f. 41, op. 1, d. 151; Nikulin, May 13, 1964, in RTsKhIDNI, f. 558, op. 3, d. 13; Kudrin, December 1963, in RTsKhIDNI, f. 588, op. 3, d. 14.
167. Strekotin, 1934, in TsDOOSO, f. 221, op. 2, d. 849.
168. Voikov, in Bessedowsky, 210.

169. Strekotin, 1934, in TsDOOSO, f. 221, op. 2, d. 849.
170. Voikov, in Bessedowsky, 211.
171. Proskuryakov, April 3, 1919, in SA, vol. 5, doc. 17; Andrei Strekotin to Yakimov, May 7–11, 1919, in SA, vol. 5, doc. 18.
172. See *Le Figaro,* June 4, 1965.
173. Kudrin, December 1963, in RTsKhIDNI, f. 588, op. 3, d. 14.
174. Yurovsky, February 1, 1934, in TsDOOSO, f. 41, op. 1, d. 151.
175. Ibid.
176. Yurovsky, unpublished memoirs, 1922, in APRF, f. 3, op. 58, d. 280.
177. Strekotin, 1934, in TsDOOSO, f. 221, op. 2, d. 849.
178. Kudrin, December 1963, in RTsKhIDNI, f. 588, op. 3, d. 14.
179. Ibid.
180. Ibid.
181. Ibid.
182. Yurovsky, unpublished memoirs, 1922, in APRF, f. 3, op. 58, d. 280.
183. Yurovsky, February 1, 1934, in TsDOOSO, f. 41, op. 1, d. 151.
184. Yurovsky, unpublished memoirs, 1922, in APRF, f. 3, op. 58, d. 280.
185. Tsetsegov, in Sokolov, *Enquete,* 109.

Chapter 13: The Four Brothers

1. Kudrin, December 1963, in RTsKhIDNI, f. 588, op. 3, d. 14; also Yurovsky, unpublished memoirs, 1922, in APRF, f. 3, op. 58, d. 280.
2. Brithodko, in Sokolov, *Enquete,* 187.
3. Yurovsky, unpublished memoirs, 1922, in APRF, f. 3, op. 58, d. 280.
4. Ibid.
5. Ibid.
6. Ibid.
7. Halliburton, *Seven League Boots,* 142.
8. Yurovsky, unpublished memoirs, 1922, in APRF, f. 3, op. 58, d. 280.
9. Yurovsky, February 1, 1934, in TsDOOSO, f. 41, op. 1, d. 151.
10. Yurovsky, unpublished memoirs, 1922, in APRF, f. 3, op. 58, d. 280.
11. Ibid.
12. Ibid.
13. Ibid.
14. Ibid.
15. Ibid.
16. Ibid.
17. Sokolov, *Enquete,* 176.
18. Ibid., 178.
19. Natasha Zukova, in Sokolov, *Enquete,* 178–179.
20. Zukovs, questioned by Sokolov on June 27 and 29, 1919, in Sokolov, *Enquete,* 179.
21. Papin to Sokolov, June 1919, in Sokolov, *Enquete,* 180.
22. Sheremetievsky, in Sokolov, *Enquete,* 180.
23. Yurovsky, unpublished memoirs, 1922, in APRF, f. 3, op. 58, d. 280.
24. Ibid.
25. Yurovsky, February 1, 1934, in TsDOOSO, f. 41, op. 1, d. 151.
26. Yurovsky, unpublished memoirs, 1922, in APRF, f. 3, op. 58, d. 280.
27. Sokolov, *Enquete,* 176–178.
28. Kudrin, December 1963, in RTsKhIDNI, f. 588, op. 3, d. 14; Yurovsky, unpublished memoirs, 1922, in APRF, f. 3, op. 58, d. 280.
29. Yurovsky, February 1, 1934, in TsDOOSO, f. 41, op. 1, d. 151.
30. Yurovsky, unpublished memoirs, 1922, in APRF, f. 3, op. 58, d. 280.
31. Ibid.
32. Not surprisingly, many of those attached to the Ural Regional Soviet and Ekaterinburg Cheka—some of whom had participated in the actual executions only a few hours earlier—later claimed that they, too, had been at the Four Brothers mine that morning, witnesses to what took place. This number includes Peter Voikov, who arrived at the Ipatiev House only after the executions had ended; and Kudrin, who left memoirs that contain assertions based in fact but that fail to prove his presence at the mine itself through the first events of that morning. Kudrin's account is riddled with errors and contradictions: he placed himself in the cab of the Fiat on the drive into Koptyaki Forest; he asserted that Yurovsky arrived only much later at the mine, and in an automobile; he failed to mention the numerous breakdowns suffered by the truck on its journey; he misplaced events in the chronological narrative at the mine itself; and he directly contradicted Yurovsky's own accounts of these events of the morning of July 17 in

Koptyaki Forest. According to Yurovsky's 1922 memoirs, he arrived at the Four Brothers only while the corpses were being unloaded. See Kudrin, December 1963, in RTsKhIDNI, f. 588, op. 3, d. 14.

33. Yurovsky, unpublished memoirs, 1922, in APRF, f. 3, op. 58, d. 280.

34. Kudrin, December 1963, in RTsKhIDNI, f. 588, op. 3, d. 14.

35. Yurovsky, unpublished memoirs, 1922, in APRF, f. 3, op. 58, d. 280; Yurovsky, February 1, 1934, in TsDOOSO, f. 41, op. 1, d. 151.

36. Yurovsky, 1920 note, in GARF, f. 601, op. 2, d. 35; Yurovsky, unpublished memoirs, 1922, in APRF, f. 3, op. 58, d. 280; Yurovsky, February 1, 1934, in TsDOOSO, f. 41, op. 1, d. 151; Ermakov, October 29, 1947, in Sverdlovsk Party Archives, TsDOOSO, f. 221, op. 2, d. 774.

37. Yurovsky, unpublished memoirs, 1922, in APRF, f. 3, op. 58, d. 280.

38. Yurovsky, 1920 note, in GARF, f. 601, op. 2, d. 35; Yurovsky, unpublished memoirs, 1922, in APRF, f. 3, op. 58, d. 280; Yurovsky, February 1, 1934, in TsDOOSO, f. 41, op. 1, d. 151; Kudrin, December 1963, in RTsKhIDNI, f. 588, op. 3, d. 14.

39. Yurovsky, February 1, 1934, in TsDOOSO, f. 41, op. 1, d. 151.

40. Ibid.

41. Yurovsky, unpublished memoirs, 1922, in APRF, f. 3, op. 58, d. 280.

42. Yurovsky, 1920 note, in GARF, f. 601, op. 2, d. 35; Yurovsky, unpublished memoirs, 1922, in APRF, f. 3, op. 58, d. 280.

43. Yurovsky, unpublished memoirs, 1922, in APRF, f. 3, op. 58, d. 280; Yurovsky, February 1, 1934, in TsDOOSO, f. 41, op. 1, d. 151.

44. Yurovsky, February 1, 1934, in TsDOOSO, f. 41, op. 1, d. 151.

45. Yurovsky, 1920 note, in GARF, f. 601, op. 2, d. 35.

46. Yurovsky, unpublished memoirs, 1922, in APRF, f. 3, op. 58, d. 280.

47. Ibid.; Kudrin, December 1963, in RTsKhIDNI, f. 588, op. 3, d. 14.

48. Yurovsky, unpublished memoirs, 1922, in APRF, f. 3, op. 58, d. 280.

49. Ibid.; Kudrin, December 1963, in RTsKhIDNI, f. 588, op. 3, d. 14.

50. Rodzinsky, May 13, 1964, in RTsKhIDNI, f. 588, op. 3, d. 14.

51. Yurovsky, unpublished memoirs, 1922, in APRF, f. 3, op. 58, d. 280.

52. Ibid.

53. Yurovsky, February 1, 1934, in TsDOOSO, f. 41, op. 1, d. 151.

54. Rodzinsky, May 13, 1964, in RTsKhIDNI, f. 588, op. 3, d. 14.

55. Yurovsky, unpublished memoirs, 1922, in APRF, f. 3, op. 58, d. 280; Kudrin, December 1963, in RTsKhIDNI, f. 588, op. 3, d. 14.

56. Yurovsky, unpublished memoirs, 1922, in APRF, f. 3, op. 58, d. 280.

57. Ibid.

58. Ibid.

59. Ibid.

60. Ibid.

61. Sokolov, 189; see order from Voikov for immediate delivery of 5 poods (181 pounds) of sulfuric acid on July 17, 1918, in GARF, f. 1837, op. 1, d. 1530; and order from Voikov for an additional three jugs of Japanese sulfuric acid on July 17, 1918, in GARF, f. 1837, op. 1, d. 19.

62. Yurovsky, unpublished memoirs, 1922, in APRF, f. 3, op. 58, d. 280.

63. Sokolov, *Enquete*, 189.

64. Yurovsky, unpublished memoirs, 1922, in APRF, f. 3, op. 58, d. 280.

65. Ibid.

66. Ibid.

67. Sukhorukov, April 3, 1928, in TsDOOSO, f. 41. op. 1, d. 149.

68. Kudrin, December 1963, in RTsKhIDNI, f. 588, op. 3, d. 14.

69. Rodzinsky, May 13, 1964, in RTsKhIDNI, f. 588, op. 3, d. 14.

70. Yurovsky, unpublished memoirs, 1922, in APRF, f. 3, op. 58, d. 280.

71. Ibid.

72. Yurovsky, unpublished memoirs, 1922, in APRF, f. 3, op. 58, d. 280.

73. Kudrin, December 1963, in RTsKhIDNI, f. 588, op. 3, d. 14.

74. Yurovsky, unpublished memoirs, 1922, in APRF, f. 3, op. 58, d. 280.

75. Ibid.

76. Ibid.

77. Sokolov, *Enquete*, 189.

78. Yurovsky, unpublished memoirs, 1922, in APRF, f. 3, op. 58, d. 280.

79. Ibid.

80. Ibid.

81. Sukhorukov, April 3, 1928, in TsDOOSO, f. 41. op. 1, d. 149.

82. Yurovsky, unpublished memoirs, 1922, in APRF, f. 3, op. 58, d. 280.

83. Ibid.

84. Yurovsky, February 1, 1934, in TsDOOSO, f. 41, op. 1, d. 151.

85. Ibid.

86. Yurovsky, unpublished memoirs, 1922, in APRF, f. 3, op. 58, d. 280.

87. Kudrin, December 1963, in RTsKhIDNI, f. 588, op. 3, d. 14.

88. Rodzinsky, May 13, 1964, in RTsKhIDNI, f. 588, op. 3, d. 14.

89. Yurovsky, 1920 note, in GARF, f. 601, op. 2, d. 35.

90. Yurovsky, unpublished memoirs, 1922, in APRF, f. 3, op. 58, d. 280; Yurovsky, February 1, 1934, in TsDOOSO, f. 41, op. 1, d. 151; Sukhorukov, April 3, 1928, in TsDOOSO, f. 41, op. 1, d. 149.

91. Yurovsky, 1920 note, in GARF, f. 601, op. 2, d. 35.

92. Ibid.; Yurovsky, unpublished memoirs, 1922, in APRF, f. 3, op. 58, d. 280; Yurovsky, February 1, 1934, in TsDOOSO, f. 41, op. 1, d. 151.

93. Yurovsky, February 1, 1934, in TsDOOSO, f. 41, op. 1, d. 151.

94. Yurovsky, unpublished memoirs, 1922, in APRF, f. 3, op. 58, d. 280.

95. Sokolov, *Enquete*, 179.

Chapter 14: Aftermath

1. Proskuryakov, April 3, 1919, in SA, vol. 5, doc. 17.

2. Halliburton, *Seven League Boots*, 144.

3. Sokolov, *Enquete*, 221.

4. Yakimov, May 7–11, 1919, in SA, vol. 5, doc. 18.

5. Grey, 57.

6. Capitolina Agafonovna, testimony of November 4, 1918, in SA, vol. 2, doc. 17.

7. Speranski, 39.

8. Ibid., 202.

9. Strekotin, 1934, in TsDOOSO, f. 221, op. 2, d. 849.

10. Yakimov, May 7–11, 1919, in SA, vol. 5, doc. 18.

11. Ibid.

12. Ibid.

13. Telegram from Ural Regional Soviet to Lenin and Sverdlov, July 17, 1918, in GARF, f. 601, op. 2, d. 27.

14. Sokolov, *Enquete*, 221.

15. Bulygin and Kerensky, 336; Sokolov, 296.

16. Sokolov, *Enquete*, 261.

17. Kudrin, December 1963, in RTsKhIDNI, f. 588, op. 3, d. 14; Nikulin, RTsKhIDNI, f. 558, op. 3, d. 13.

18. Sokolov, *Enquete*, 297.

19. *Biograficheskaya Khronika*, 5: 648–649.

20. In GARF, f. 601, op. 2, d. 27; Robert Bruce Lockhart to FO, July 18, 1918, 339, in PRO/FO 371/3335.

21. Petrov, Lysenko, and Egorov, 84.

22. Deterikhs, vol. 1, 154–155.

23. Ibid., 231.

24. Ibid., 311.

25. Wilton and Telberg, 326.

26. Kudrin, December 1963, in RTsKhIDNI, f. 588, op. 3, d. 14.

27. Sokolov, *Enquete*, 151.

28. Wilton and Telberg, 325–326.

29. McCullagh, 130.

30. Bykov, *Last Days*, 82.

31. Kudrin, December 1963, in RTsKhIDNI, f. 588, op. 3, d. 14.

32. Deterikhs, vol. 1, 408.

33. Rodzinsky, May 13, 1964, in RTsKhIDNI, f. 588, op. 3, d. 14.

34. Bykov, *Last Days*, 89.

35. Sokolov, *Enquete*, 154.

36. Kudrin, December 1963, in RTsKhIDNI, f. 588, op. 3, d. 14.

37. Netrebin, in TsDOOSO, f. 41, op. 1, d. 149.

38. Ibid.

39. Ibid.

40. Kabanov, unpublished memoirs, in Khabarovsk Regional Party Archives, f. 117, op. 2, d. 27.

41. Netrebin, in TsDOOSO, f. 41, op. 1, d. 149.

42. Ibid.

43. Nametkin protocol, August 2, 5, 6, 7, 8, 1918, in SA, vol. 1, doc. 9.

44. Ibid.

Chapter 15: The Investigations

1. Sokolov, *Enquete*, 167.

2. Report of the public prosecutor of the Kazan Court of Assizes, N. Mirobulov,

December 12, 1918, communiqué 28, in GARF, f. 601, op. 2, d. 36, l. 27–29.

3. Bykov, *Last Days*, 87.

4. Deterikhs, vol. 1, 94.

5. Ibid., 97.

6. Ibid.

7. See letter from Minister of Justice Starynkevich to the Ministry of Foreign Affairs Executive Board about preliminary findings on the assassination of the imperial family, Omsk, February 19, 1919, signed Starynkevich, dated February 19, 1919, from Omsk; certified original copy in authors' collection. In "Le Crime d'Ekaterinbourg" by Nicolas de Berg-Poggenpohl, in *Revue des deux mondes* for August 1, 1920, it was explained and verified that this train, which has loomed large in conspiracy theories in the past few decades, in fact carried the imprisoned members of the former imperial suite, including Mademoiselle Schneider, Countess Hendrikova, and Alexei Volkov, along with the luggage packed from the Romanov possessions in the Ipatiev House.

8. Sonin, 35.

9. Ibid., 36.

10. See Nametkin's inventory protocol, August 2, 5, 6, 7, 8, 1918, in SA, vol. 1, doc. 9.

11. Sokolov, *Enquete*, 20.

12. Wilton and Telberg, 335.

13. Bulygin and Kerensky, 247.

14. Deterikhs, vol. 1, 127.

15. Sonin, 38.

16. Deterikhs, vol. 1, 127–128.

17. Ibid., 127.

18. Wilton and Telberg, 134–135.

19. Deterikhs, vol. 1, 146.

20. Report of December 12, 1918, Military Intelligence Division, in U.S. National Archives, Navy and Old Army Branch, Military Archives Division, Washington, D.C., Doc. 184/112.

21. Report of December 5, 1918, French Ministry of War, Général des Affaires de Guerre, Franco-Américaines, cited in Summers and Mangold, 95.

22. See Michael Thornton, "Anastasia: Mystery Remains Unsolved," *London Sunday Express*, May 17, 1992.

23. Lasies, 87.

24. B. A. Gavrilov, testimony of September 17–19, 1919, in GARF, f. 601, op. 2, d. 51.

25. Samson Matikov testimony, in Ross, 128–130.

26. Luckett, 218.

27. Pipes, *Russia under the Bolshevik Regime*, 49.

28. Knox, telegram of January 29, 1919, quoted in Luckett, 245.

29. General Knox to War Office in Russia 1, 1919, in Laqueur, *Russia and Germany*, 93.

30. Milner manuscript, Moscow, March 31, 1918, quoted in Laqueur, *Russia and Germany*, 91.

31. Laqueur, *Russia and Germany*, 91.

32. See, for example, A. A. Alferyev, whose work, published by the Russian Orthodox Church Outside Russia's Holy Trinity Monastery, contended that the executions were ordered by American Jewish financier Jacob Schiff (Alferyev, *Imperator Nikolai II*, 115). For a refutation of these stories see Heifets, 14–27.

33. Deterikhs, vol. 1, 19.

34. Klier and Mingay, 79.

35. Deterikhs, vol. 1, 340.

36. Ibid.; ibid., 346.

37. Sokolov, *Enquete*, 17–18.

38. Peter Sarandinaki to King, August 2002.

39. Memorandum of General Deterikhs, April 10, 1919, in memorandum of Carl-August Wollmann, December 30, 1963, in collection of Ian Lilburn.

40. Deterikhs, vol. 1, 177; Bulygin and Kerensky, 184.

41. Ibid.

42. Deterikhs, vol. 1, 177.

43. Bulygin and Kerensky, 53, 183.

44. Ibid., 183

45. Knightly, 141; Wilton and Telberg, 213.

46. Summers and Mangold, 103.

47. Ibid.

48. Wilton and Telberg, 312.

49. Ibid., 352.

50. Ibid., 410.

51. Ibid., 392.

52. Ibid., 360.

53. Ibid.

54. Ibid., 385.

55. Ibid., 393.

56. Lasies, 83.

57. Sokolov, *Enquete*, 189.
58. Summers and Mangold found this suspect, particularly given that General Deterikhs himself later claimed that Medvedev had died from a heart attack within a few days of being questioned (see *New York Times*, August 1, 1920). Sir Thomas Preston, the former British consul in Ekaterinburg, told Summers and Mangold that Medvedev had been interrogated "under torture," and the authors also discovered that a former White Army staff captain, Nicholas Belotserkovsky, claimed Medvedev had died because "I hit him once too often" (interview with Thomas Preston, 1971, by Summers and Mangold, in Summers and Mangold, 127; Staff Captain Nicholas Belotserkovsky, in Summers and Mangold, 127). Further, Summers and Mangold discovered a letter from a Professor Valery Jordansky, assigned to the Romanov case in 1919 by Nikander Mirolyubov, public prosecutor of the Kazan District Court, in which the former voiced suspicions that the interrogation had taken place under suspicious circumstances, and, more important, that there had been only one interrogation (Summers and Mangold, 126). This not only led them to question the official cause of death and how many times Medvedev had been interrogated, but also whether the prisoner had even been Medvedev. Of the first, it is entirely possible that the Whites tortured Medvedev and that this led to his presumably inadvertent death. In many instances the Whites were just as cruel as their Bolshevik counterparts. Former Ipatiev House guard Michael Letemin, the seventeen-year-old who had not participated in the murders and was not even a member of the Bolshevik Party, was killed by a group of White Army officers in an act of retaliation shortly after giving his testimony. Given the corruption that pervaded the White Army organization in Siberia in 1919, a proposition such as that suggested by Summers and Mangold regarding the nature of Medvedev's death is not beyond reason. Their other conjectures, however, were less tenable. Jordansky, the man who originally stated that Medvedev had been questioned only once, was himself not a part of the official investigation. He had a consultative role, during the transitional period between Sergeyev and Sokolov. Undoubtedly, Jordansky's statement—contrasting as it does with the fact that two separate depositions clearly exist in the Sokolov Archives—was made in error. Nor does the idea that the man interrogated may not have been Medvedev have any evidence. The details of Medvedev's confessions can be verified against known facts, and against the accounts of others involved in the Romanov executions—accounts that were certainly not known to anyone other than the actual assassins in 1919.

59. Sokolov, *Enquete*, 125.
60. Ibid., 126.
61. Ibid., 127.
62. Ibid., 129–132. When Sokolov examined the room, he discovered five bullet holes that Sergeyev had missed. These were in the cornices and arches of the vaulted ceiling. It is possible that Sergeyev missed the five bullet holes located by Sokolov, since they were hidden in the arches of the room. Critics, however, find this suspicious, and cite a number of contradictory accounts left by those who visited the Ipatiev House as proof that the number of bullet holes was being deliberately altered as time went on to prove that the imperial family had been executed. The first recorded visit made to the murder room following the shootings was by the guard Michael Letemin. He recalled: "All that I learned about the murder of the Emperor and his family deeply interested me and I was determined to confirm, in so far as possible, the information I had received. For this purpose, on July 18 I went into the room in which the shooting occurred. I saw that the floor was clean, and I did not find any stains on the walls. On the rear wall, to the left as one enters the room, I saw three small holes of a depth of about one centimeter each; I saw no other evidence whatsoever of firing. In general I did not find traces of blood anywhere" (Michael

Letemin, in SA, vol. 1, doc. 44). This was the day after the alleged murders. The next recorded visit was that of Sir Charles Eliot, the British high commissioner in Siberia. In his report to London, he recalled: "On the wall opposite the door and on the floor were the marks of seventeen bullets or, to be more accurate, marks showing where pieces of the wall and floor had been cut out in order to remove the bullet holes, the officials charged with the investigation having thought fit to take them away for examination elsewhere. They stated that Browning revolver bullets were found and that some of them were stained with blood. Otherwise no traces of blood were visible" (Eliot report to Foreign Office, London, in PRO/FO, 371/3977 at Kew). British officer Francis McCullagh visited the Ipatiev House in 1920. He wrote: "There are sixteen bullet holes in the wall, and sixteen bullets were extracted from them by the Whites after they arrived. Some of those bullets must have gone through the bodies of the victims before entering into the plaster. Several, which had penetrated for a short distance into the floor, must have passed through the corpses as they lay on the ground" (McCullagh, 138). Finally, there are two seemingly contradictory accounts left by Pierre Gilliard. He visited the Ipatiev House in late August 1918 and swore in a deposition: "At the time I left the house I could not believe that the Imperial Family had really perished. There were such a small number of bullet holes in the room which I had inspected, that I thought it impossible for everybody to have been executed" (Gilliard, March 5, 1919, in SA, vol. 2, doc. 55). In his book published in 1921, Gilliard recalled his visit to the Ipatiev House like this: "I went down to the bottom floor, the greater part of which was below the level of the ground. It was with intense emotion that I entered the room in which perhaps—I was still in doubt—they had met their death. Its appearance was sinister beyond expression. The only light filtered through a barred window at the height of a man's head. The walls and floor showed numerous traces of bullets and bayonet scars. The first glance showed that an odious crime had been perpetrated there and that several people had been done to death. I became convinced that the Emperor had perished and, granting that, I could not believe that the Tsarina had survived him" (Gilliard, *Le Tragique Destin*, 274). A closer look at this evidence, however, raises considerable doubt about the critics' assumptions. Sergeyev listed twenty-seven bullet holes in the walls and floor, while Sokolov, examining the room five months later, found thirty-two. While it may seem unlikely that Sergeyev missed these five bullet holes, it cannot be ruled out, particularly as they were in upper cornices of walls. If, as the critics argue, evidence was being planted, it is hardly likely that an additional five bullet holes would help sway anyone's conclusions as to the fate of the imperial family. But the critics go farther, refusing to accept—in light of the testimony of others—that Sergeyev found twenty-seven bullet holes at all. They suggest that this number was altered on the official record at the time when Sergeyev handed over his dossier of evidence to Deterikhs after he was relieved of his position, and changed before the documents came into the possession of Sokolov. Thus, according to this theory, the testimony of others carries more weight than the official record. The problem with this theory is that it ignores the very obvious explanation for the seemingly multiplying number of bullet holes: that they were not multiplying at all. On July 18, Letemin saw only three bullet holes in the murder room—seemingly damning testimony in light of Sergeyev's and Sokolov's conclusions. But Letemin, in the same deposition in which he described his visit to the murder room, also makes quite clear that his visit took place in the evening—when the light was poor—and that he had to look hurriedly, since he feared being caught. Because Sergeyev had to dig out many of the bullets from the plaster walls, it is likely that they were hidden in the poor light in which Letemin viewed the scene. Under these circumstances,

Letemin might well have missed the great number of bullet holes, especially as we do not know how long he spent examining the room. On the surface, the testimony of Sir Charles Eliot, a trained diplomat said to have been fastidious about details, seem to demolish the contention that Sergeyev found twenty-seven bullet holes and Sokolov thirty-two. But Eliot's report contained a number of errors, and here the wording is extremely important. He noted: "On the wall opposite the door and on the floor were the marks of seventeen bullets." And it was on the eastern wall—the wall opposite the door—that Sergeyev did indeed list sixteen bullet holes, and Sokolov seventeen. Summers and Mangold take great pains to emphasize that Eliot was a precise man; assuming this is true, it is likely that, in describing the "seventeen" bullet holes on "the wall opposite the door," Eliot was describing the number of marks on the eastern wall and not the actual number of bullet holes within the room itself. He makes no mention, for instance, of the bullet holes in the doors or cornices, which both Sergeyev and Sokolov listed in their reports. Further, it is not known if Eliot personally counted the number of bullet holes in the room, or if his guide at the Ipatiev House informed him of this figure. Given the other erroneous claims made in Eliot's report, this cannot be considered damning proof that the ballistic evidence in the murder room was being falsified. McCullagh's account, as well, is cited as proof that the evidence was being tampered with. But McCullagh visited the Ipatiev House in February 1920—months after both Sergeyev and Sokolov had cataloged their findings. Again, reading McCullagh's statement at face value, he merely confirms that sixteen bullet holes were found on the eastern wall. As such, his account cannot be used to confirm that evidence was being planted. Gilliard's two differing impressions stem, in all probability, from the benefit of hindsight. When he was sworn and deposed in 1919, the tutor held out hope that the imperial family might still

be alive. But when Gilliard wrote his book two years later, he believed that the entire family had perished, and his memory of his visit to the basement room of the Ipatiev House reflects this belief in his presentation of a different, dramatic impression. In short, not one piece of evidence cited by the critics seriously threatens the credibility of either the Sergeyev or the Sokolov accounts of the number of bullet holes discovered in the murder room.

63. Sokolov, report of November 15, 1920, Paris to Foreign Office, London, in PRO/FO, 371/3977 at Kew.

64. Sokolov, Enquete, 129.

65. Wilton and Telberg, 342.

66. Ibid., 408.

67. Klier and Mingay, 83–84.

68. These assertions found favor among the more rabid monarchist elements, and continue to reappear on Internet sites dedicated to Nicholas II and his family.

69. Sokolov, Enquete, 156.

70. Deterikhs, vol. 1, 44–46.

71. General Deterikhs was clearly suspicious of Derevenko. No doubt Derevenko was aware of both the apparent respect with which he had been treated by the Bolshevik authorities in Ekaterinburg, and puzzled by the question of his continued liberty in the city with the permission of the Ural Regional Soviet. In his book he claimed: "Dr. Derevenko did not offer his testimony. He was questioned by no one, neither by the investigator, Nametkin, nor by the member of the Court, Sergeyev, nor by the public prosecutor— by no one. And when the case passed into the hands of the investigator, N. A. Sokolov, who urgently sought out for questioning all of the people of the court who had been with the Imperial Family, Dr. Derevenko was not in Ekaterinburg: he had gone somewhere into the depths of Siberia and now remains in Tomsk with the Bolsheviks" (Deterikhs, vol. 1, 44–45). This, however, was not quite correct. Derevenko, in fact, remained in Ekaterinburg for at least six weeks after the fall of the city to the Whites, and he certainly assisted the first two investigators on the case, Nametkin and Sergeyev,

by helping to identify objects found at both the Ipatiev House and at the Four Brothers mine as having belonged to the imperial family—a fact certainly known to Deterikhs, who reported as much in his book. And on September 11, 1919, he was questioned by military authorities in Tomsk at some length (Sokolov, *Enquete*, 135). Derevenko apparently remained with the Whites for little over a year. In the fall of 1919, when Nicholas Sokolov was in Chita, Derevenko was brought in and asked to confront two men who had been arrested on suspicion of being Yakov Yurovsky, the last commandant of the Ipatiev House and leader of the execution squad. Apparently Derevenko agreed, and testified that one was indeed Yakov Yurovsky. In fact, these two men were Yurovsky's brothers, whom Derevenko had presumably never met before, whereas he certainly did know Yurovsky: on May 26, Yurovsky had accompanied him on his visit to the Ipatiev House, and the two men certainly spent several hours together (AF diary, May 26, 1918, in GARF, f. 640, op. 1, d. 326; N diary, May 26, 1918, in GARF, f. 601, op. 1, d. 266). Why he willingly misidentified one of them as the commandant and gave false evidence remains a mystery. This episode cannot be easily explained away as a case of confusion or mistaken identity. There were four Yurovsky brothers: Leyba, Leonti, Ilya, and Yakov, who was the youngest. Leonti and Ilya had been arrested, and were the pair confronted by Derevenko. After Derevenko made his positive identification, he was released, and promptly disappeared. When the White officials investigated the identification, they quickly learned that they had been duped, but on seeking Derevenko for clarification, they learned that he had gone over to the Bolsheviks, taking a position at a Soviet military hospital (Bulygin and Kerensky, 260–261; Deterikhs, vol. 1, 45).

72. Deterikhs, vol. 1, 46–49.
73. Sokolov, *Enquete*, 187.
74. Magnitsky testimony, in SA, vol. 1, doc. 77; Deterikhs, vol. 1, 44.

75. Sokolov, *Enquete*, 191.
76. Bulygin and Kerensky, 252; Wilton and Telberg, 349.
77. Deterikhs, vol. 1, 229.
78. Sokolov, *Enquete*, 197.
79. Ibid.
80. Summers and Mangold, 155.
81. Wilton and Telberg, 113.
82. Ibid., 146; Deterikhs, vol. 1, 43.
83. Sokolov, *Enquete*, 199.
84. Ibid.
85. See Gibbes, June 27, 1919, in SA, vol. 4, doc. 14; Gilliard, *Thirteen Years*, 289; Vyrubova, 252.
86. Wilton and Telberg, 116, 334, 345.
87. Sokolov, *Enquete*, 199.
88. Ibid.; Wilton and Telberg, 116.
89. Summers and Mangold, 162.
90. See ibid., 163–165.
91. Summers and Mangold, 164.
92. Sokolov, *Enquete*, 201.
93. Alexandrov, 102.
94. Bulygin and Kerensky, 266.
95. Alexandrov, 102.
96. Information from Peter Sarandinaki to King, August 3, 2002.
97. Bulygin and Kerensky, 266–267.
98. Ibid., 158.
99. Summers and Mangold, 173.
100. Bulygin and Kerensky, 158.
101. Ibid., 273.
102. Summers and Mangold, 173.
103. Orlov, in Sokolov, *Enquete*, 17–18.
104. Memorandum in files, Office of American Naval Intelligence, reg. no. 16406, March 25, 1924, Navy and Old Army Branch, Military Archives Division, U.S. National Archives, quoted in Summers and Mangold, 173.
105. *New York Times*, January 29, 1924.
106. Ibid., February 6, 1924.
107. Summers and Mangold, 175.
108. Sokolov to Mirolyubov, April 22, 1922, in Mirolyubov Papers, Hoover Institution Archives, Stanford University, cited in Summers and Mangold, 176.
109. Bulygin and Kerensky, 159.
110. Orlov, in Sokolov, *Enquete*, 18.

Chapter 16: "Holy Relics of Our Saints"

1. Janin, 304–305.

2. Bulygin and Kerensky, 254.
3. Trewin, 136.
4. In PRO/FO, 371/4047, January–February 1920.
5. *New York Times*, December 18, 19, 20, 1930.
6. Sproul in *New York Times*, March 28, 1925.
7. Sokolov, *Enquete*, 17.
8. In PRO/FO, 371/4047 at Kew.
9. Ibid.
10. *New York Times*, December 18–20, 1930.
11. Trewin, 137.
12. Sokolov, *Enquete*, 17.
13. Gilliard, *Thirteen Years*, 301.
14. Janin, 304.
15. Fleming, 235.
16. Gilliard, *Thirteen Years*, 302; Sotheby's auction catalog, 65; Janin, 304.
17. Information from Peter Sarandinaki to King, August 3, 2002.
18. Janin, in *Petit Journal*, December 1930.
19. Ibid.; Nostitz, 226; Fleming, 237.
20. Buxhoeveden papers, in Mountbatten Family Archives, Broadlands House, quoted in Clarke, 155–156.
21. Lady Violet Kirkpatrik, in *Times* of London, April 14, 1971.
22. Sir Thomas Preston, in *Spectator*, February 1972.
23. Interview with Prince Serge Obolensky, BBC, 1971, cited in Summers and Mangold, 370.
24. Prince Dimitri Alexandrovich, in *Picture Post*, February 11, 1967.
25. Vorres, 171.
26. Janin, in *Petit Journal*, December 1930.
27. Janin, 305.
28. Information from H.I.H. The Grand Duchess Maria Vladimirovna of Russia to King, August 2002.
29. Letter of Grand Duke Kirill Vladimirovich, August 8, 1924, in the private family papers of H.I.H. The Grand Duchess Maria Vladimirovna of Russia, supplied to the authors by the latter, August 2002.
30. Prince G. Sidamon-Eristov, supplement, in Bykov, *Les derniers jours des Romanov* (Paris: Payot, 1931), 175–176.
31. Information from H.I.H. The Grand Duchess Maria Vladimirovna of Russia to the authors, August 2002.
32. Alexandrov, 15–16.
33. Summers and Mangold, 371.
34. Alexandrov, 16.
35. Vorres, 171; see also Trewin, 130.
36. See Clarke, 156; Summers and Mangold, 371.
37. Massie, 126.
38. Clarke, 156.
39. Ibid.
40. Massie, 126.
41. "Head of Russian Church Abroad Says Genuine Remains of Tsar Are in Belgium," Itar-Tass, February 9, 1998; Buranov and Krustalev, *Pravda o Ekaterinburgskoi Tragedii*, 276.
42. Clarke, 156.
43. BBC interviews with Grand Duke Vladimir Kirillovich, 1971 and 1974, quoted in Summers and Mangold, 371.
44. Information from H.I.H. The Grand Duchess Maria Vladimirovna of Russia to the authors, August 2002.
45. Information from Maurice Philip Remy to the authors, July 2000. During our research, Mr. Remy generously shared his copy of this file with us, which included a complete photographic inventory of the box in the wall of St. Ioann in Brussels. In addition, he made available to us letters from officials at the church confirming that the presumed human remains had, in fact, remained in the possession of Grand Duke Kirill Vladimirovich.
46. Information from Romanov family member to Wilson.
47. Speranski, 257–258.
48. Alferyev, *Pis'ma tsarskoi sem'i iz zatocheniia*, 492.
49. Warth, 274.
50. Millar, 241–242; Philaret statement in Joseph Gambardello, "Czar, 30,000 Canonized," UPI, November 2, 1981.
51. Joseph Gambardello, "Czar, 30,000, Canonized," UPI, November 2, 1981; Stuart Vincent, "Mass Sainthood: Russian Rulers to Be Canonized," *Albany (N.Y.) Times Union*, October 21, 1981.

Chapter 17: Unearthing the Past

1. Avdonin, in *Taina tsarskikh ostankov*, 27–28.
2. Avdonin, August 8, 1991, to Sverdlovsk Region public prosecutor Tiukov, quoted in Alekseev, 277–278.

3. Ryabov, in "Revenge of the Romanovs."
4. Ryabov, in "New Findings."
5. Ryabov, September 14, 1991, to Sverdlovsk Region public prosecutor Tiukov, quoted in Alekseev, 279–282.
6. Ryabov, in "New Findings."
7. Ryabov, September 14, 1991, to Sverdlovsk Region public prosecutor Tiukov, quoted in Alekseev, 279–282; *Imperii Novovo Vremeni*, 253–256; *Gosudarstvennaya Legitimnost*, 276–279.
8. Ryabov, in "New Findings"; Ryabov, "Zhelayushchikh ne nashlos," *Za vlast Sovetov* 8–9, 11 (1991); *Imperii Novovo Vremeni*, 278.
9. Ryabov, September 14, 1991, to Sverdlovsk Region public prosecutor Tiukov, quoted in Alekseev, 279–282; *Imperii Novovo Vremeni*, 280.
10. Avdonin, August 8, 1991, to Sverdlovsk Region public prosecutor Tiukov, quoted in Alekseev, 277–278; Ryabov, September 14, 1991, to Sverdlovsk Region public prosecutor Tiukov, quoted in Alekseev, 279–282.
11. *Gosudarstvennaya Legitimnost*, 281.
12. *Imperii Novovo Vremeni*, 285.
13. Ryabov, in "New Findings."
14. Ryabov, September 14, 1991, to Sverdlovsk Region public prosecutor Tiukov, quoted in Alekseev, 279–282.
15. Ryabov, in "New Findings."
16. Ryabov, September 14, 1991, to Sverdlovsk Region public prosecutor Tiukov, quoted in Alekseev, 279–282; *Gosudarstvennaya Legitimnost*, 286.
17. Ryabov, in "New Findings."
18. Ryabov, Cymru; see also Ryabov, "Zhelayushchikh ne nashlos," *Za vlast Sovetov* 8–9, 11 (1991); *Imperii Novovo Vremeni*, 283; Avdonin, Cymru; "Istoriyu ne zakopat," *Na smenu!* 24 (December 1992): 2; Avdonin, "In Search of the Place of Burial of the Remains of the Czar's Family," *Historical Genealogy* 1 (1993): 96–98; Avdonin, "Investigation of the Sources on the Death of the Romanovs and the Search for Their Remains," *Historical Genealogy* 2 (1993): 83–86; Avdonin, "Versiya staroi Koptyakovskoi dorogi. Ob istorii poiskov ostankov imperatorskoi sem'i," *Istochnik* 5 (1994): 60–76; Yakubovskii, *Rasstrel v*

Podvale, 289–293; *Gosudarstvennaya Legitimnost*, 286–288.
19. Avdonin, August 8, 1991, to Sverdlovsk Region public prosecutor Tiukov, quoted in Alekseev, 277–278.
20. Avdonin, Cymru.
21. Gritsaenko, Cymru.
22. Ryabov, in "New Findings."
23. Ryabov, September 14, 1991, to Sverdlovsk Region public prosecutor Tiukov, quoted in Alekseev, 279–282; *Imperii Novovo Vremeni*, 288.
24. Ryabov, in "New Findings."
25. Ibid.
26. Ryabov, Cymru.
27. Ryabov, in "Revenge of the Romanovs"; "Istoriyu ne zakopat," *Na smenu!* 24 (December 1992): 2; Avdonin, "In Search of the Place of Burial of the Remains of the Czar's Family," *Historical Genealogy* 1 (1993): 96–98; Avdonin, "Investigation of the Sources on the Death of the Romanovs and the Search for Their Remains," *Historical Genealogy* 2 (1993): 83–86; Avdonin, "Versiya staroi Koptyakovskoi dorogi. Ob istorii poiskov ostankov imperatorskoi sem'i," *Istochnik* 5 (1994): 60–76; Yakubovskii, *Rasstrel v Podvale*, 289–293.
28. Ryabov, September 14, 1991, to Sverdlovsk Region public prosecutor Tiukov, quoted in Alekseev, 279–282.
29. Ryabov, in "Revenge of the Romanovs."
30. See "Istoriyu ne zakopat," *Na smenu!* 24 (December 1992): 2; Avdonin, "In Search of the Place of Burial of the Remains of the Czar's Family," *Historical Genealogy* 1 (1993): 96–98; Avdonin, "Investigation of the Sources on the Death of the Romanovs and the Search for Their Remains," *Historical Genealogy* 2 (1993): 83–86; Avdonin, "Versiya staroi Koptyakovskoi dorogi. Ob istorii poiskov ostankov imperatorskoi sem'i," *Istochnik* 5 (1994): 60–76; Yakubovskii, *Rasstrel v Podvale*, 289–293.
31. "Istoriyu ne zakopat," *Na smenu!* 24 (December 1992): 2; Avdonin, "Versiya staroi Koptyakovskoi dorogi. Ob istorii poiskov ostankov imperatorskoi sem'i," *Istochnik* 5 (1994): 60–76; Yakubovskii, *Rasstrel v Podvale*, 295; *Gosudarstvennaya Legitimnost*, 287.

32. Avdonin, in *Taina tsarskikh ostankov*, 29–30; *Imperii Novovo Vremeni*, 294.
33. Avdonin, August 8, 1991, to Sverdlovsk Region public prosecutor Tiukov, quoted in Alekseev, 277–278.
34. In *Taina tsarskikh ostankov*, 15–18; *Imperii Novovo Vremeni*, 279; *Gosudarstvennaya Legitimnost*, 292.
35. Avdonin, August 8, 1991, to Sverdlovsk Region public prosecutor Tiukov, quoted in Alekseev, 277–278.
36. Ryabov, September 14, 1991, to Sverdlovsk Region public prosecutor Tiukov, quoted in Alekseev, 279–282.
37. In *Taina tsarskikh ostankov*, 15–18.
38. Ibid.
39. *Gosudarstvennaya Legitimnost*, 293.
40. In *Taina traskikh ostraniv*, 18; *Gosudarstvennaya Legitimnost*, 295–297.
41. Ryabov diary, June 1, 1979, in Alekseev, 284.
42. Ibid.
43. Ibid.
44. Ibid., 285.
45. Ibid., June 2, 1979, 286.
46. Ryabov, Cymru.
47. Avdonin, August 8, 1991, to Sverdlovsk Region public prosecutor Tiukov, quoted in Alekseev, 277–278.
48. Ryabov diary, September 6–10, 1979, in Alekseev, 287.
49. Ryabov, September 14, 1991, to Sverdlovsk Region public prosecutor Tiukov, quoted in Alekseev, 279–282; *Imperii Novovo Vremeni*, 286.
50. Ryabov, Cymru.
51. Ibid.
52. Ryabov diary, July 7, 1980, in Alekseev, 289; Kurth, "The Mystery of the Romanov Bones," *Vanity Fair* (January 1993): 101.
53. *Moscow News*, April 10, 1989.
54. Kurth, "The Mystery of the Romanov Bones," *Vanity Fair* (January 1993): 100.
55. Radzinsky to King, June 1992.
56. Ryabov, in "New Findings."
57. Ibid.
58. Ibid.
59. Ibid.
60. Ibid.
61. Ibid.
62. *Moscow News*, April 10, 1989.
63. Avdonin, Cymru.

64. Remy to authors, July 2000.
65. Massie, 36.
66. Avdonin, Cymru.
67. Massie, 36.
68. Boris Yarkov, Cymru.
69. Massie, 36; Kurth to authors.
70. Zhivotovsky, 572.
71. "Forgery," *Tsar-Kolokol* 2 (1990): 10–28.
72. Vladimir Bolshakov, quoted in an article by Vitaly Kozlikin and Cathy Scott-Clark in *London Sunday Express*, January 24, 1993.
73. Koryakova to Kurth.
74. Gritsaenko, Cymru.
75. Massie, 129.
76. Ibid.
77. In *Taina tsarskikh ostankov*, 57–65; Platonov, *Ternovyi venets Rossi*, 198; information to authors from Peter Kurth.
78. Timms, 381; Ross, "'Zapiska Iurovskogo' ili 'Zapiska Pokrovskogo?,'" *Russkaia mysl'* 4168 (April 10–16, 1997): 16.
79. Avdonin, Cymru; Radzinsky, 417.
80. Leskovsky, "Za chto my ubili Gosudarya imperatora?," *LG-Dos'e* 5 (1993): 3, 13; Bubnova, "Ot Vindzorskogo zamka do Koptyakov," *Oblastnaya gazeta* (April 26, 1995): 3; G. Nazarov, *Vosprositel'nye znaki and mogilami*, 18–31.
81. Avdonin, Cymru; "Istoriyu ne zakopat," *Na smenu!* 24 (December 1992): 2; Avdonin, "In Search of the Place of Burial of the Remains of the Czar's Family," *Historical Genealogy* 1 (1993): 96–98; Avdonin, "Investigation of the Sources on the Death of the Romanovs and the Search for Their Remains," *Historical Genealogy* 2 (1993): 83–86; Avdonin, "Versiya staroi Koptyakovskoi dorogi. Ob istorii poiskov ostankov imperatorskoi sem'i," *Istochnik* 5 (1994): 60–76; Yakubovskii, *Rasstrel v Podvale*, 289–293; *Gosudarstvennaya Legitimnost*, 286–288.
82. Avdonin, Cymru.
83. *Taina tsarskikh ostankov*, 54–57.
84. Ryabov diary, June 1, 1979, in Alekseev, 284.
85. *Taina tsarskikh ostankov*, 58.
86. Ibid., 64.
87. *Taina tsarskikh ostankov*, 57–65; *Imperii Novovo Vremeni*, 298.
88. Gritsaenko, Cymru.
89. Information from Peter Kurth to authors.

90. "Raskopki na lesnoi polyane," *Za vlast Sovetov* 131 (1991); L. Koryakova and I. Koryakov, "Raskopki na lesnoi polyane," *Nauka Urala* (September 14, 1991).
91. *Taina tsarskikh ostankov*, 57–65.
92. Ibid., 63.
93. Ibid., 56.
94. Ryabov, Cymru.

Chapter 18: "An Unknown Grave from the Soviet Period"

1. Avdonin, Cymru.
2. *Taina tsarskikh ostankov*, 70.
3. Ibid., 59.
4. Koryakova to Kurth; "Raskopki na lesnoi polyane," *Za vlast Sovetov* 31 (1993); L. Koryakova and I. Koryakov, "Raskopki na lesnoi polyane," *Nauka Urala* (September 14, 1991).
5. Ibid.
6. The group was composed of V. D. Vorobiev, chief of the Verkh-Isetsk militia and member of the Regional Executive Committee; his deputy, Sergeant V. G. Novikov; Professor Lyudmilla Koryakova, from the Institute of History and Archaeology, Ural State University, Russian Academy of Sciences; her husband, I. O. Koryakov, assistant professor of Mathematics Sciences and head of the Algebra and Geometry Divisions of Ural State University; Peter Gritsaensko, specialist in forensic medicine and deputy head of the Sverdlovsk Regional Forensic Medicine Bureau; V. S. Gromov, senior forensic medicine expert and head of the Physio-Technical Division of the Sverdlovsk Regional Forensic Medicine Bureau; Dr. A. M. Bayevsky, from the Department of General Hygiene at the Sverdlovsk Regional Epidemiological Center; and Dr. N. Y. Fedoseyev, a specialist in infectious diseases from the Sverdlovsk Regional Epidemiological Center (*Taina tsarskikh ostankov*, 60).
7. *Taina tsarskikh ostankov*, 60.
8. "Raskopki na lesnoi polyane," *Za vlast Sovetov* 31 (1991); L. Koryakova and I. Koryakov, "Raskopki na lesnoi polyane," *Nauka Urala*, (September 14, 1991).
9. *Taina tsarskikh ostankov*, 57.
10. Koryakova to Kurth.
11. *Taina tsarskikh ostankov*, 59–61.
12. "Raskopki na lesnoi polyane," *Za vlast Sovetov* 31 (1991); L. Koryakova and I. Koryakov, "Raskopki na lesnoi polyane," *Nauka Urala* (September 14, 1991).
13. Maples to King, January 1994.
14. Abramov to Massie in *Romanovs*, 46.
15. *Gosudarstvennaya Legitimnost*, 295–297.
16. *Taina tsarskikh ostankov*, 59.
17. Ibid., 58–59.
18. Ibid., 55.
19. Ibid., 58.
20. Koryakova to Kurth.
21. Ibid.
22. "Raskopki na lesnoi polyane," *Za vlast Sovetov* 31 (1991); L. Koryakova and I. Koryakov, "Raskopki na lesnoi polyane," *Nauka Urala* (September 14, 1991).
23. *Taina tsarskikh ostankov*, 58.
24. Ibid., 59.
25. Ibid.
26. Ibid., 60.
27. Koryakova to Kurth.
28. "Raskopki na lesnoi polyane," *Za vlast Sovetov* 31 (1991); L. Koryakova and I. Koryakov, "Raskopki na lesnoi polyane," *Nauka Urala* (September 14, 1991).
29. *Taina tsarskikh ostankov*, 62.
30. Ibid., 63.
31. Ibid., 61.
32. Ibid., 62.
33. Ibid., 65.
34. Ibid.
35. Ibid., 62.
36. Ibid., 64.
37. Ibid., 63.
38. Ibid., 64.
39. Ibid., 61–62.
40. Ibid., 62.
41. Ibid., 63.
42. Ibid., 104–108.
43. Ibid., 104.
44. Ibid.
45. Popov, *Gde Vy, Vashe Velichestvo?*, 135–136.
46. *Taina tsarskikh ostankov*, 64.
47. Dr. Bob Clark to Wilson, May 16, 2001.
48. "Raskopki na lesnoi polyane," *Za vlast Sovetov* 31 (1991); L. Koryakova and I. Koryakov, "Raskopki na lesnoi polyane," *Nauka Urala* (September 14, 1991).
49. Kurth, "The Mystery of the Romanov Bones," *Vanity Fair* (January 1993): 120.
50. Abramov, April 23, 1993, Cymru.

51. Gritsaenko, Cymru.
52. Maples to King, January 1994.
53. *Gosudarstvennaya Legitimnost*, 297.
54. Abramov, April 23, 1993, Cymru.
55. Ibid.
56. Kurth, "The Mystery of the Romanov Bones," *Vanity Fair* (January 1993): 124.
57. Maples to King, January 1994.
58. Abramov, April 23, 1993, Cymru.
59. Ibid.
60. Koryakova to Kurth.
61. *Gosudarstvennaya Legitimnost*, 298.
62. Maples to King, January 1994.
63. Information from Kurth to authors.
64. Radzinsky to King, June 1992.
65. Abramov, April 23, 1993, Cymru; see also Massie, 47–48.
66. Gritsaenko, Cymru.
67. Zvyagin, Cymru.
68. Plaskin to Kurth.
69. *Taina tsarskikh ostankov*, 62.
70. Petrov, Lysenko, and Egorov, 94.
71. *Taina tsarskikh ostankov*, 59.
72. Ibid., 62.
73. Maples and Browning, 254.
74. In *Taina tsarskikh ostankov*, 117.
75. Ryabov, September 14, 1991, to Sverdlovsk Region public prosecutor Tiukov, quoted in Alekseev, 279–282.
76. Abramov, Romanov conference, July 27, 1992, Ekaterinburg.
77. Maples and Browning, 253.
78. *Gosudarstvennaya Legitimnost*, 307.
79. Maples and Browning, 254.
80. Ibid., 255.
81. *Taina tsarskikh ostankov*, 116; Popov, *Gde Vy, Vashe Velichestvo?*, 152–153.
82. Maples and Browning, 255.
83. Ibid.
84. Popov, *Gde Vy, Vashe Velichestvo?*, 152–153.
85. Maples and Browning, 260.
86. *Gosudarstvennaya Legitimnost*, 307; Maples and Browning, 259; *Taina tsarskikh ostankov*, 119.
87. Maples and Browning, 259.
88. Ibid., 259.
89. Levine to King, June 2002.
90. In GARF, op. 677, op. 1, d. 701.
91. Letter from Minister of Justice Starynkevich to the minister of foreign affairs, Omsk, February 19, 1919; certified copy in authors' possession.
92. Maples and Browning, 256.
93. *Gosudarstvennaya Legitimnost*, 311–314.
94. Maples and Browning, 257.
95. Ibid., 256.
96. Ibid., 258.
97. *Gosudarstvennaya Legitimnost*, 311–314.
98. Maples and Browning, 258.
99. Romanov conference, Ekaterinburg, July 27, 1992.
100. Levine to King, June 2002.
101. *Gosudarstvennaya Legitimnost*, 316–317.
102. Maples to King, January 1994.
103. *Gosudarstvennaya Legitimnost*, 316–317.
104. *Taina tsarskikh ostankov*, 127–128.
105. *Gosudarstvennaya Legitimnost*, 316–317.
106. *Taina tsarskikh ostankov*, 95–97.
107. Maples and Browning, 254.
108. *Gosudarstvennaya Legitimnost*, 319–320; *Taina tsarskikh ostankov*, 57–65.
109. *Gosudarstvennaya Legitimnost*, 319.
110. Ibid., 322.
111. *Taina tsarskikh ostankov*, 129–132.
112. Levine to King, June 2002.
113. Popov, July 21, 1993, Cymru; Romanov conference, Monday, July 27, 1992, Ekaterinburg.
114. Popov, July 21, 1993, Cymru.
115. Gritsaenko, Cymru.
116. Ibid.
117. Massie, 51.
118. Ibid.
119. "U.S. Help Promised in Czar Mystery," AP (February 16, 1992).

Chapter 19: Bones of Contention

1. Rodriquez to King, August 2002.
2. Maples to King, January 1994.
3. Ibid.
4. Maples and Browning, 251–252.
5. Rodriquez to King, August 2002.
6. Quoted in Kurth, "The Mystery of the Romanov Bones," *Vanity Fair* (January 1993): 123.
7. Ibid., 123; Ye. Shvortsova, "Yekaterinburg zhazhdet arii varyazhskogo gostya," *Rabochaya tribuna* (August 14, 1992).
8. Maples and Browning, 252.
9. Information from Kurth to authors.
10. Gritsaenko, Cymru.
11. In "Scientists Claim Russia's Last Tsar Is Now Identified," *Hello* 12 (July 11, 1992): 53.

12. *Taina tsarskikh ostankov*, 36, for July 26, 1992.
13. Ibid.
14. AP report, June 23, 1992.
15. See Lev L. Kolesnikov, Gurgen A. Pashinyan, and Sergei S. Abramov, "Anatomical Appraisal of the Skulls and Teeth Associated with the Family of Tsar Nicolay Romanov," *The Anatomical Record* 265, no. 1 (2001).
16. Gritsaenko, Cymru.
17. Levine to King, June 2002.
18. Gritsaenko, Cymru.
19. Abramov, April 23, 1993, Cymru.
20. Ibid.
21. See Maples and Austin-Smith for further information.
22. Abramov, April 23, 1993, Cymru.
23. Maples to King, January 1994.
24. Abramov, April 23, 1993, Cymru.
25. Massie, 42.
26. Abramov, April 23, 1993, Cymru.
27. Ibid.
28. Ibid.
29. Maples to King, January 1994.
30. Levine to King, June 2002.
31. Zvyagin, Cymru.
32. Maples to King, January 1994.
33. Levine to King, June 2002.
34. Ibid.
35. Maples to King, January 1994.
36. Abramov, April 23, 1993, Cymru.
37. Maples to King, January 1994.
38. Maples and Browning, 252–253.
39. Ryabov, September 14, 1991, to Sverdlovsk Region public prosecutor Tiukov, quoted in Alekseev, 279–282.
40. Massie, 71.
41. Romanov conference, July 27, 1992, Ekaterinburg.
42. Maples to King, January 1994; Levine to King, June 2002.
43. Maples to King, January 1994.
44. Maples, 254–255.
45. Levine to King, June 2002.
46. Maples and Browning, 255.
47. Ibid., 260.
48. Popov, July 21, 1993, Cymru.
49. Maples, July 16, 1993, Ekaterinburg, Cymru.
50. Ibid.
51. Maples to King, January 1994.
52. Levine to King, June 2002.

53. Maples to King, January 1994.
54. Maples and Browning, 256–257; *Taina tsarskikh ostankov*, 146; Popov, *Gde Vy, Vashe Velichestvo?*, 166.
55. Maples and Browning, 256.
56. *Gosudarstvennaya Legitimnost*, 311–314.
57. Maples and Browning, 256–257; *Taina tsarskikh ostankov*, 122.
58. Popov, *Gde Vy, Vashe Velichestvo?*, 152–153.
59. Maples and Browning, 256.
60. In *Taina tsarskikh ostankov*, 107–112.
61. Maples and Browning, 257.
62. Massie, 45.
63. Maples and Browning, 257; Levine to King, June 2002.
64. Massie, 71.
65. Maples and Browning, 258.
66. Maples, 257–258; *Gosudarstvennaya Legitimnost*, 316–317; *Taina tsarskikh ostankov*, 105–111.
67. Maples and Browning, 257.
68. Ibid., 258.
69. Ibid.
70. Baden, 183.
71. Maples and Browning, July 16, 1993, Ekaterinburg, Cymru.
72. Ibid. Given the furor over these identifications, it is worth taking the time to compare the exact measurements attributed by both the American and Russian teams to each set of skeletal remains. The American team estimated the height of skeleton 1 at approximately 66 inches (in *Taina tsarskhik ostankov*, 143–144). This was 167.64 centimeters. The Russians produced two estimates of height: the first, in 1992, of 161–168 centimeters (63.4–66.1 inches); the second, in 2001, of 164–168 centimeters (64.6–66.1 inches) (Popov, *Gde Vy, Vashe Velichestvo?*, 154–155; Kolesnikov, Pashinyan, and Abramov, "Anatomical Appraisal of the Skulls and Teeth Associated with the Family of Tsar Nicolay Romanov," *Anatomical Record* 265, no. 1 [2001]). The height of skeleton 2 was placed at approximately 69 inches (175.26 centimeters) by the American team (in *Taina tsarskhik ostankov*, 154). The Russians gave two estimates, in 1992 and 2001, both 171–177 centimeters (67.3–69.7 inches) (Popov, *Gde Vy, Vashe Velichestvo?*, 156;

Kolesnikov, Pashinyan, and Abramov, "Anatomical Appraisal of the Skulls and Teeth Associated with the Family of Tsar Nicolay Romanov," *Anatomical Record* 265, no. 1 [2001]). Skeleton 3's height was estimated by the American team at roughly 64.9 inches (164.8 centimeters) (Maples and Browning, 255). The 1992 Russian estimate placed it at 158–165 centimeters (62.2–64.96 inches) (in *Taina tsarskikh ostankov*, 156–159). Their 2001 estimate placed the height at 161–165 centimeters (63.4–65 inches) (Kolesnikov, Pashinyan, and Abramov, "Anatomical Appraisal of the Skulls and Teeth Associated with the Family of Tsar Nicolay Romanov," *Anatomical Record* 265, no. 1 [2001]). The American team placed skeleton 4 at roughly 66 inches (167.64 centimeters) (Maples and Browning, 260). The Russians estimated the height of the remains in 1992 at 165–170 centimeters (65–67 inches) (Popov, *Gde Vy, Vashe Velichestvo?*, 159–160). In 2001 they estimated the height at 165–169 centimeters (65–66 inches) (Kolesnikov, Pashinyan, and Abramov, "Anatomical Appraisal of the Skulls and Teeth Associated with the Family of Tsar Nicolay Romanov," *Anatomical Record* 265, no. 1 [2001]). Skeleton 5 was placed by Maples and the American team at roughly 67.5 inches (171.45 centimeters) (Maples and Browning, 256). In 1992 the Russians estimated her height at 166–171 centimeters (65.4–67.3 inches) (Popov, *Gde Vy, Vashe Velichestvo?*, 162). In 2001 the Russians estimated her height at 166–169 centimeters (65.4–67 inches) (Kolesnikov, Pashinyan, and Abramov, "Anatomical Appraisal of the Skulls and Teeth Associated with the Family of Tsar Nicolay Romanov," *Anatomical Record* 265, no. 1 [2001]). Skeleton 6 was given an estimated height of approximately 65.6 inches (166.62 centimeters) by the Americans (Maples and Browning, 256–257; *Taina tsarskikh ostankov*, 146). In 1992 the Russians estimated the height at 162–171 centimeters (63.7–67.3 inches) (Popov, *Gde Vy, Vashe Velichestvo?*, 166). In 2001 they gave an estimated height of

162–166 centimeters (63.7–65.3 inches) (Kolesnikov, Pashinyan, and Abramov, "Anatomical Appraisal of the Skulls and Teeth Associated with the Family of Tsar Nicolay Romanov," *Anatomical Record* 265, no. 1 [2001]). The American team estimated skeleton 7 at 67.5 inches (171.45 centimeters) (Maples and Browning, 258). The 1992 Russian estimate placed her height at 163–168 centimeters (64.17–66.14 inches) (Popov, *Gde Vy, Vashe Velichestvo?*, 166). In 2001 they gave the same estimate (Kolesnikov, Pashinyan, and Abramov, "Anatomical Appraisal of the Skulls and Teeth Associated with the Family of Tsar Nicolay Romanov," *Anatomical Record* 265, no. 1 [2001]). The American team did not fix an estimated height to skeleton 8, other than saying that he was a man of short stature (Maples and Browning, 257–258; *Gosudarstvennaya Legitimnost*, 319–322; *Taina tsarskikh ostankov*, 113). The Russians did not attempt an estimate of height until 2001, when they suggested he was 163–167 centimeters (64.17–65.8 inches) (Kolesnikov, Pashinyan, and Abramov, "Anatomical Appraisal of the Skulls and Teeth Associated with the Family of Tsar Nicolay Romanov," *Anatomical Record* 265, no. 1 [2001]). Skeleton 9 was estimated at approximately 71 inches (180.34 centimeters) by the American team (Maples and Browning, 258). In 1992 the Russians estimated his height at 172–181 centimeters (67.7–71.3 inches) (Popov, *Gde Vy, Vashe Velichestvo?*, 167). In 2001 they gave an estimate of 173–180 centimeters (68.1–70.9 inches) (Kolesnikov, Pashinyan, and Abramov, "Anatomical Appraisal of the Skulls and Teeth Associated with the Family of Tsar Nicolay Romanov," *Anatomical Record* 265, no. 1 [2001]). The Americans believed Demidova to be roughly 5 feet, 6 inches, while Russian estimates placed her between 5 feet, 3 inches and 5 feet, 5 inches. The Americans placed Botkin at 5 feet, 9 inches, while the Russians placed him between 5 feet, 7 inches and 5 feet, 10 inches— approximately within the range of the American estimate. There was more discrepancy with skeleton 3. The Americans placed Grand Duchess Olga at 5 feet, 5 inches, while the Russians placed her between 5 feet, 2 inches and 5 feet, 5 inches. There was general agreement with skeleton 4: the Americans placed Nicholas II at 5 feet, 6 inches, while the Russians placed him at 5 feet, 6 inches to 5 feet, 7 inches. Skeleton 5—believed by the Americans to be Grand Duchess Marie—was more problematic. The Americans placed her at 5 feet, 7½ inches, while the Russians placed her at 5 feet, 5 inches to 5 feet, 7 inches. Skeleton 6—presumed by the Americans to be Grand Duchess Tatiana and by the Russians to be Grand Duchess Anastasia—was likewise given a wider range in the estimates. She was placed at 5 feet, 6 inches by the Americans, and between 5 feet, 4 inches and 5 feet, 7 inches by the Russians in 1992, and between 5 feet, 4 inches and 5 feet, 5 inches by the Russians in 2001. The Americans placed Empress Alexandra at 5 feet, 7 inches, while the Russians placed her between 5 feet, 4 inches and 5 feet, 6 inches in both 1992 and 2001. The Americans placed Kharitonov at 5 feet, 6 inches, while the Russians placed him between 5 feet, 4 inches and 5 feet, 6 inches in 2001. The Americans placed Trupp at 5 feet, 11 inches, while the Russians placed him at 5 feet, 8 inches to 5 feet, 11 inches in both 1992 and 2001. The biggest discrepancies are with skeletons 1, 2, 3, 5, 6, and 7. Once the issue of Demidova's true gender and identity was resolved, the question of her height faded into the background. The estimates for Botkin show some variations, of 3 inches from the shortest to the tallest. While both the Americans and the Russians agreed that skeleton 3 was that of Grand Duchess Olga, the Russian estimate at the low end of her height at 5 feet, 2 inches was clearly incorrect, as revealed in any number of contemporary photographs. A particularly telling photograph is one taken in winter 1918 in Tobolsk, which shows Olga and Anastasia standing side by side in the snow-covered courtyard of the Governor's House. In this photograph,

Olga stands slightly forward of Anastasia, who appears to be not only between 6 and 12 inches behind her sister, but also standing on a slightly higher bank of snow. While both are wearing hats, the difference in height is obvious, with Anastasia's nose roughly in a straight line with the bottom of Olga's chin. The difference in height between the two sisters can reasonably be extrapolated at roughly 3 to 4 inches. A Russian estimate of Olga's height at 5 feet, 2 inches at the lowest, and 5 feet, 5 inches at the tallest contains the seeds of its own destruction in relation to their identification of skeleton 6 as that of Anastasia. Skeleton 6, according to the Russians in 1992, was between 5 feet, 4 inches and 5 feet, 7 inches, and between 5 feet, 4 inches and 5 feet, 5 inches according to their 2001 estimate. If one accepts the Russian estimation of height in these cases, then one is forced to conclude that in the space of six months—between winter 1918 and July 16, 1918—Anastasia grew at least 2 inches, and more likely 3 inches, in height. Given this, it therefore seems reasonable to conclude that the Russian estimate of 5 feet, 2 inches is off by several inches. With skeleton 5, believed by the Americans to be the youngest of the remains, there was a discrepancy of some 2 inches in the American and Russian estimates of height. Again, contemporary photographs reveal that the Russian estimates are in contrast with the evidence. The Russians identified no. 5 as Tatiana, who was, until the winter of 1918 at least, known to be the tallest of the four daughters. And yet, with a top Russian estimated height of 5 feet, 7 inches, such an identification is problematic. A photograph taken by Pierre Gilliard of the four sisters in the garden at Tsarskoye Selo in July 1917 clearly shows that Tatiana stood a good 4 to 5 inches or more taller than Anastasia, with Marie slightly taller than Olga. And yet, according to the Russian identification of nos. 5 and 6, and their estimates of height, Anastasia was only 1 inch shorter than Tatiana at the low end, and 3 inches shorter at the high end, again indicating that to fit these estimates Anastasia would have had to have began an extreme growth spurt in the last six months of her life.

73. Maples and Browning, 255–257; Levine to King, June 2002.
74. Maples and Browning, 257.
75. Levine to King, June 2002.
76. Maples to King, January 1994; see also Maples and Austin-Smith, 446–455.
77. Information from Kurth to the authors.
78. Avdonin, in *Taina tsarskikh ostankov*, 25–26.
79. Plaskin, Romanov conference, July 26, 1992, Ekaterinburg.
80. Abramov, Romanov conference, July 27, 1992, Ekaterinburg.
81. Ibid.
82. Maples to King, January 1994.
83. Maples, Romanov conference, July 27, 1992, Ekaterinburg.
84. Maples to King, January 1994.
85. In *Taina tsarskikh ostankov*, 137–139.
86. Ibid.
87. Abramov, Romanov conference, July 27, 1992, Ekaterinburg.
88. Ibid.
89. Maples to King, January 1994.
90. Abramov, Romanov conference, July 27, 1922, Ekaterinburg.
91. *Taina tsarskikh ostankov*, 133–135; Levine to King, June 2002.
92. Ibid.
93. Maples, July 26, 1992, Ekaterinburg, Cymru.
94. Levine to King, June 2002.
95. Maples to King, January 1994.
96. Maples, July 27, 1992, Ekaterinburg, Cymru.
97. Levine, July 27, 1992, Ekaterinburg, Cymru.
98. Maples, July 16, 1993, Ekaterinburg, Cymru.
99. Massie, 74.
100. AP wire report, July 29, 1992.

Chapter 20: "It's All Secret, All Political"

1. Petrov, Lysenko, and Egorov, 95.
2. "Czar: Mystery Is Unraveling," AP, February 3, 1993.
3. Gritsaenko, Cymru.
4. Ryabov, 1993, Cymru.
5. Avdonin, 1993 Romanov conference, Ekaterinburg, in *Gosudarstvennaya Legitimnost*, 299.
6. Boris Yarkov, Cymru.
7. Avdonin, Cymru; Avdonin and Zaitsev, "Rossiskii Imperatorskii Dom: Poslednii put/Fond 'Obreteniye,'" Ekaterinburg, 1993; Avdonin, "Istoriyu ne zakopat," *Na smenu!* 24 (December 1992).
8. Avdonin, Cymru.
9. Blinkov to Kurth.
10. Koryakova to Kurth.
11. Gritsaenko, Cymru.
12. Avdonin, Cymru.
13. Kurth, "The Mystery of the Romanov Bones," *Vanity Fair* (January 1993): 117.
14. Avdonin, Romanov conference, July 27, 1992.
15. Information from Sergei Louchenko to authors.
16. In Cymru transcripts.
17. Ibid.
18. Maples to King, January 1994.
19. Abramov, April 23, 1993, Cymru.
20. See Massie, 98–99.
21. Maples to King, January 1994.
22. Massie, 98–99; also Gritsaenko, Cymru.
23. Popov, *Gde Vy, Vashe Velichestvo?*, 220.
24. Radzinsky, 375.
25. Massie, 121.
26. Ibid., 117–118.
27. *Gosudarstvennaya Legitimnost*, 301–319.
28. Ibid.
29. Ibid.
30. Ibid.
31. Soloviev, in *Sevodnya*, Moscow, September 7, 1994.
32. Massie, 89.
33. Ibid.
34. Private information to authors.
35. Sykes, 66–68.
36. Ibid., 71.
37. Paul Kulikovsky to King, August 2002; see also "Monarkhiya-eto sostoyaniye dukhas," *Moskovskiye novosti* 57 (1994): 11.
38. Sykes, 69.
39. News release from FSS, Home Office release, London, July 9, 1993; also Gill et al., "Identification of the Remains of the Romanov Family by DNA Analysis," *Nature Genetics* 6 (February 1994).

40. Sykes, 70.
41. See BBC news online, November 2, 2000.
42. Sykes, 76.
43. Paul Kulikovsky to King, August 2002; see also "Monarkhiya-eto sostoyaniye dukhas," *Moskovskiye novosti* 57 (1994): 11.
44. See "Researchers Cast Doubts on Bones Thought to Be Tsar's," *Asahi Shimbun* (July 18, 2001); Nagai and Okazaki, nineteenth International Conference on Forensic Genetics, Muenster, Germany, August 28, 2001; information from Carsten Hohoff, the Local Congress Arrangement Committee, Muenster, Germany, to authors.
45. In *Istina* (September 22, 2001): 20; see also "Researchers Cast Doubts on Bones Thought to Be Tsar's," *Asahi Shimbun* (July 18, 2001); Nagai and Okazaki, nineteenth International Conference on Forensic Genetics, Muenster, Germany, August 28, 2001; information from Carsten Hohoff, the Local Congress Arrangement Committee, Muenster, Germany, to authors.
46. Paul Kulikovsky to King, August 2002.
47. Letter of RECA, December 25, 1993, to Yeltsin; see also letter of RECA, January 18, 1998.
48. Vadim Viner, September 20, 1993, Cymru; Peter Kurth to authors; Kurth, "The Mystery of the Romanov Bones," *Vanity Fair* (January 1993): 199; "Skol'ko lyudei, stol'ko i versii: Podborka materialov," *Oblastnaya gazeta* (December 1, 1992); Viner, "Vmesto tochki-zapyataya," *Oblastnaya gazeta* (May 25, 1993); Viner, "Yest' takaya versiya," *Vechernii Yekaterinburg* (August 6, 1993).
49. "Russian Officials Reject Doubts on Tsar's Remains," Moscow, Reuters, September 27, 1995; E. Yakubovsky, "Itak, ona zvalas' Mariya?," *Vechernii Yekaterinburg* (September 23, 1994).
50. Andrei Papushin, "Anastasia's Escape Is Simply a Myth," *Rossiiskaia gazeta* (November 6, 1997); Alexander Astafyev, "Beyond the Tsar's Bones," Itar/Tass (August 27, 1998).
51. Kolesnikov, Pashinyan, and Abramov, "Anatomical Appraisal of the Skulls and Teeth Associated with the Family of Tsar Nicolay Romanov," *Anatomical Record* 265, no. 1 (2001).
52. Peter Sarandinaki to King, August 2002.
53. Ibid.
54. Jackson, 350–351.
55. Ibid., 354.
56. Ibid.
57. Ibid.
58. Ibid., 355.
59. Peter Sarandinaki to King, August 2002.
60. Jackson, 356.
61. Kolesnikov, Pashinyan, and Abramov, "Anatomical Appraisal of the Skulls and Teeth Associated with the Family of Tsar Nicolay Romanov," *Anatomical Record* 265, no. 1 (2001): 21.
62. Ibid., 22.
63. Ibid., 21.
64. Ibid., 19.
65. Ibid., 20.
66. Ibid., 20–21.
67. Ibid., 22.
68. Ibid., 25.
69. Ibid., 25–26.
70. Ibid., 29.
71. Popov, Romanov conference, July 27, 1992, Ekaterinburg; Abramov, Romanov conference, July 27, 1992, Ekaterinburg.
72. Levine to King, June 2002.
73. Kolesnikov, Pashinyan, and Abramov, "Anatomical Appraisal of the Skulls and Teeth Associated with the Family of Tsar Nicolay Romanov," *Anatomical Record* 265, no. 1 (2001): 31.
74. Ibid.
75. Ibid., 32.
76. Maples, AP report, July 29, 1992.

Chapter 21: The Secret of Koptyaki Forest

1. Bulygin and Kerensky, 239.
2. Bykov, *Last Days*, 88.
3. Yurovsky, 1920 note, in GARF, f. 601, op. 2, d. 27.
4. Yurovsky, unpublished memoirs, 1922, in APRF, f. 3, op. 58, d. 280.
5. Yurovsky, February 1, 1934, in TsDOOSO, f. 41, op. 1, d. 151.
6. Ermakov, August 3, 1932, in TsDOOSO, f. 41, op. 2, d. 79.
7. Halliburton, *Seven League Boots*, 143.
8. Ermakov, October 29, 1947, in TsDOOSO, f. 221, op. 2, d. 774.

9. Bessedowsky, 210–211; Alexandrov, 233.

10. Kudrin, December 1963, in RTsKhIDNI, f. 588, op. 3, d. 14.

11. Rodzinsky, May 13, 1964, in RTsKhIDNI, f. 588, op. 3, d. 14.

12. Yurovsky, February 1, 1934, in TsDOOSO, f. 41, op. 1, d. 151.

13. Sukhorukov, April 3, 1928, in TsDOOSO, f. 41, op. 1, d. 149.

14. Maples and Browning, 263.

15. Haskell to King, March 2003; Baden, 164.

16. See Steinberg and Krustalev, 291; see also Beloborodov to Lukoyanov, Matveyev, and Syromolotov, cable of July 7, 1918, in Deterikhs, vol. 1, 212; cable 4640, Beloborodov to Lukoyanov, Matveyev, and Syromolotov, July 8, 1918, in Sotheby's auction catalog, 88; Deterikhs, vol. 1, 212; and Beloborodov to Gorbunov, Moscow, cable 4369, July 8, 1918, in Sokolov, Enquete, 150.

17. Yurovsky, unpublished memoirs, 1922, in APRF, f. 3, op. 58, d. 280.

18. Sukhorukov, April 3, 1928, in TsDOOSO, f. 41, op. 1, d. 149.

19. See Kudrin, December 1963, in RTsKhIDNI, f. 588, op. 3, d. 14; Yurovsky, 1920 note, in GARF, f. 601, op. 2, d. 27; Yurovsky, unpublished memoirs, 1922, in APRF, f. 3, op. 58, d. 280; and Yurovsky, February 1, 1934, in TsDOOSO, f. 41, op. 1, d. 151.

20. Yurovsky, unpublished memoirs, 1922, in APRF, f. 3, op. 58, d. 280.

21. Ibid.

22. Yurovsky, 1920 note, in GARF, f. 601, op. 2, d. 27.

23. Yurovsky, unpublished memoirs, 1922, in APRF, f. 3, op. 58, d. 280.

24. Yurovsky, February 1, 1934, in TsDOOSO, f. 41, op. 1, d. 151.

25. Sokolov, Enquete, 216; Deterikhs, vol. 1, 182.

26. Toland, 857–858.

27. Payne, Hitler, 548.

28. Ibid., 566.

29. Toland, 889; Payne, Hitler, 568.

30. Payne, Hitler, 568.

31. Petrova and Watson, xi.

32. Ibid., 40.

33. Toland, 890; Payne, Hitler, 568.

34. See Bezymenski for details of these autopsy reports.

35. Petrova and Watson, 88–89.

36. Sokolov, Enquete, 190.

37. See Maples and Browning, 135–137.

38. Ibid., 137.

39. Ibid., 137–140.

40. Plaskin, Romanov conference, July 27, 1992, Ekaterinburg.

41. Abramov, Romanov conference, July 27, 1992, Ekaterinburg.

42. Kolesnikov, Pashinyan, and Abramov, "Anatomical Appraisal of the Skulls and Teeth Associated with the Family of Tsar Nicolay Romanov," Anatomical Record 265, no. 1 (2001): 23.

43. AP report, January 23, 1998.

44. Reuters wire report, Moscow, February 9, 1998.

45. London Sunday Telegraph, April 19, 1998.

46. Sarandinaki to King, August 3, 2002.

47. London Independent, October 25, 1998.

48. AP report, "Remains Found in Czar Killing Site," May 31, 2000.

49. Interfax report, May 2, 2002; REN-TV report, repeated by the BBC monitoring service, May 25, 2002.

50. Maples to King, January 1994.

51. Yurovsky, unpublished memoirs, 1922, in APRF, f. 3, op. 58, d. 280.

52. Yurovsky, unpublished memoirs, 1922, in APRF, f. 3, op. 58, d. 280; also Yurovsky, 1920 note, in GARF, f. 601, op. 2, d. 27; Yurovsky, February 1, 1934, in TsDOOSO, f. 41, op. 1, d. 151; Kudrin, December 1963, in RTsKhIDNI, f. 588, op. 3, d. 14.

53. Strekotin, 1934, in TsDOOSO, f. 221, op. 2, d. 849.

54. Bessedowsky, 209–210.

55. Strekotin, 1934, in TsDOOSO, f. 221, op. 2, d. 849.

Chapter 22: "Drowned in This Mist of Holiness"

1. Marie, Queen of Romania diary of July 31, 1918, in Marie, Queen of Romania, vol. 2, 368.

2. Private information; Merridale, 322; Seamus Martin, in Irish Times, July 18, 1998.

3. Nicholas Romanov in Times of London, May 13, 1992.

4. Nigel Hawkes, "Scientists Identify Bones of the Tsar," Times of London, July 10, 1993.

5. Massie, 135.

6. Ibid., 136.

7. Ronald J. Hansen, "Story of Romanovs Is Not Yet Laid to Rest," *Charlottesville (Va.) Daily Progress*, November 12, 1995.

8. Private information to authors.

9. Grant Menzies, writing on alt.talk. royalty, February 26, 1997.

10. Sergei Shargorodsky, "Tsar's Family to Get Proper Burial," AP, Moscow, October 20, 1993.

11. Massie, 138.

12. Maura Reynolds, "Russia to Decide How to Bury the Czar," AP, January 23, 1998.

13. "Russian Czar's Burial Debated," AP, September 26, 1995.

14. "Romanov Leader Explains Stand on Funeral: 'We Should Not Live in the Past Anymore,'" *Segodnya*, June 19, 1998.

15. In *London Sunday Telegraph*, January 14, 1996.

16. Rossel on "Itogi," November 1, 1997.

17. "Patriarch Explains Hesitation on Tsar's Burial: On Reburial of the Remains of the Imperial Family," *Izvestiia*, November 21, 1997.

18. In *St. Petersburg Times*, November 24, 1997.

19. Ekaterina Grigorieva, "Imperial Family Must Remain in Ekaterinburg: Judge Forbids Removal of Tsar's Relics; Complete Surprise for All Officials," *Nezavisimaia gazeta*, November 26, 1997.

20. "Nemtsov Says Tests on Tsar's Bones Over," Reuters, January 12, 1998; "Remains Accepted as Tsar's," Agence France-Presse, January 13, 1998.

21. *Nezavisimaia gazeta*, January 13, 1998.

22. Maura Reynolds, "Russia to Decide How to Bury Czar," AP, January 23, 1998.

23. "Monarchists Call on Patriarch to Refrain from Burial," Itar/Tass report, January 26, 1997.

24. UPI report, February 27, 1998.

25. *Last Journey*, 4.

26. Ibid.

27. Fred Weir, *Hindustan Times*, March 2, 1998.

28. Yevgenia Borisova, "Protests to Greet Funeral for Tsar," *St. Petersburg Times*, March 16, 1997.

29. Ibid.

30. Alice Lagnado and Andrei Zolotov, "Patriarch Boycott of Tsar Burial Is Possible," *St. Petersburg Times*, April 13, 1998.

31. Alice Lagnado, "President May Miss Burial of Last Tsar," *St. Petersburg Times*, May 12, 1998.

32. "Yeltsin Not to Attend Czar Burial," Reuters, June 15, 1998.

33. Statement of Alexei II, June 10, 1998, signed by twelve metropolitans, archbishops, and bishops of the holy synod, in Itar/Tass, June 11, 1998.

34. Philippa Fletcher, "Russia to Bury Tsar Remains in Patriarch's Absence," Reuters, June 10, 1998.

35. Andrei Zolotov, "Stance on Tsar Shows Church's Independence," *Moscow Times*, June 18, 1998.

36. Itar/Tass report, July 10, 1998.

37. Andrei Zolotov, "Church Can't Afford to Ignore Opposition," *St. Petersburg Times*, July 10, 1998.

38. Letter of Metropolitan Vitaly, March 23, 1998, released by ROCOR.

39. Letter of Philip Trahan in *Royalty Monthly* 13, no. 5 (December 1994): 96.

40. Konstantin Trifonov, "Russia Plans Modest Burial for Royal Remains," June 10, 1998, Reuters; *Sunday Times* of London, July 12, 1998.

41. *Times* of London, July 10, 1993.

42. Mark Franchetti, in *Sunday Times* of London, July 12, 1998.

43. Christy Campbell and Marcus Warren, "Tsar's Funeral Row Stops Queen's Visit," *Sunday London Telegraph*, January 14, 1996.

44. Betsy McKay, "Bones of Nicholas II Will Get Decent Burial, but Not a Fete," *Wall Street Journal*, July 8, 1998.

45. In *Baltimore Sun*, July 23, 1998.

46. Alice Lagnado, "Monarchy's Heirs Inherit Family Feud," *St. Petersburg Times*, June 30, 1998.

47. See, for example, Itar/Tass, February 12, 1998; also, information to authors from H.I.H. The Grand Duchess Maria Vladimirovna of Russia.

48. Alice Lagnado, "Monarchy's Heirs Inherit Family Feud," *St. Petersburg Times*, June 30, 1998.

49. Information to authors from H.I.H. The Grand Duchess Maria Vladimirovna of Russia.

50. Private information.
51. Alice Lagnado, "City Hall: 'Early' to Prepare for Tsar," *St. Petersburg Times*, April 19, 1998.
52. Vladimir Isachenkov, "Little Enthusiasm for Czar Burial," AP, July 14, 1998.
53. Mark Franchetti, *Sunday Times* of London, July 12, 1998.
54. Betsy McKay, "Bones of Nicholas II Will Get Decent Burial, but Not a Fete," *Wall Street Journal*, July 8, 1998.
55. Vladimir Isachenkov, "Little Enthusiasm for Czar Burial," AP, July 14, 1998; Fogarty, 83.
56. Vladimir Isachenkov, "Little Enthusiasm for Czar Burial," AP, July 14, 1998; Betsy McKay, "Bones of Nicholas II Will Get Decent Burial, but Not a Fete," *Wall Street Journal*, July 8, 1998; Zeepvat, "Funeral," 41.
57. *Last Journey*, 6; Fogarty, 83; Zeepvat, "Funeral," 41.
58. Merridale, 322.
59. *Last Journey*, 6–8; Fogarty, 83; Zeepvat, "Funeral," 41.
60. Paul Quinn-Judge, "Final Rites for the Czar: After 80 Years, the Romanovs Are Laid to Rest with More Russian Politics Than National Repentance," *Time* (July 27, 1998).
61. National-Patriotic Front "Pamyat," statement of July 17, 1998, posted on their Web site at http://www.geocities.com/Colosseum/loge/8461.
62. Fogarty, 83.
63. Mark Franchetti, *Sunday Times* of London, July 12, 1998.
64. Maura Reynolds, "Russia Buries Its Final Czar," AP, July 17, 1998.
65. *Last Journey*, 5.
66. Klaus Helge Donath, "Everyone Wants to Be a Russian Messiah," *Die Weltwoche*, July 16, 1998.
67. Yury Borisov, "Idealnyi Nikolai II," *Nezavisimaia gazeta*, August 5, 1998.
68. Statement of Alexei II in *Orthodox Observer*, September 1997.
69. "Report of the Holy Synod Commission on the Canonization of Saints with Respect to the Martyrdom of the Imperial Family," compiled by Metropolitan Yuvenaly and presented at the October 9–10, 1996, session of the holy synod under the direction of Patriarch Alexei II, Moscow, including the papers "On the Relation of the Church to Passion Bearers," "The Orthodox View on the Governing Activity of Emperor Nicholas II," "Emperor Nicholas II and the Events of January 9, 1905, in St. Petersburg," "On the Ecclesiastical Policy of Emperor Nicholas II," "The Reasons behind the Abdication of Emperor Nicholas II from the Throne and the Orthodox View of This Act," "The Royal Family and Rasputin," "The Last Days of the Royal Family," and "The Life and Suffering of the Righteous Tsar Nicholas Alexandrovich and His Family," as well as "Draft of the Act of the Canonization of the Imperial Family."
70. Uli Schmetzer, "Last Russian Czar Almost Certain to Be Church's New Saint," *Chicago Tribune*, October 16, 1996; "Kanonizatsiya tsarskoi sem'i snova otlozhena," *Izvestiya*, October 10, 1995.
71. Uli Schmetzer, "Last Russian Czar Almost Certain to Be Church's New Saint," *Chicago Tribune*, October 16, 1996.
72. Marina Silonova, "Muscovite Orthodox Believer Opposes Canonization of Last Tsar: 'Emperor Nicholas II Is Unworthy of Canonization,'" *Izvestiya*, April 23, 1998.
73. See Serfes Web page http://www.fr-d-serfes.org for details.
74. "Icon of Nicholas II to Travel over Russia," Itar-Tass, April 2, 1999.
75. Frank Brown, "Tsar's Canonization Might Fan Anti-Semitism: Sainthood's Troublesome Symbolism," Religion News Service from Orthodox Christian News Service, August 6, 2000.
76. Itar/Tass report, August 9, 2000.
77. Thurbon, 10.
78. AP report, August 21, 2000; *Times* of London, August 21, 2000.
79. Thurbon, 10–11.
80. See *Moscow Times*, August 15, 2000.
81. Itar/Tass report, August 23, 2000.

Epilogue

1. Volkov, 126.
2. Information from Romanov family to Penny Wilson.

3. Welch, 82.
4. Application for naturalization, Buxhoeveden, January 1, 1937, to December 31, 1938, Home Office File 405/2265, Ministry of Home Security, Aliens Personal Files.
5. Report of General Kirsta, November 17, 1918, in collection of Ian Lilburn, London.
6. Ian Lilburn to authors, July 2000.
7. Private information to authors, September 2000.
8. Buranov and Krustalev, *Pravda o Ekaterinburgskoi Tragedii*, 462.
9. Ibid., 464.
10. Deterikhs, vol. 1, 286.
11. Paganuzzi, *Pravda*, 46.
12. See ibid.; Alferyev, *Imperator Nikolai II*, 140; Sonin, 311; Yakubovskii, 276; private information.
13. Sonin, 309; information provided to the authors by Dimitry Macedonsky.
14. See Trewin, 141–145, and Welch for further information.
15. Platonov, *Ternovyi venets Rossi*, 506.
16. Sonin, 311; Yakubovskii, 279.
17. Platonov, *Ternovyi venets Rossi*, 514; Sonin, 312; Yakubovskii, 281; and information to the authors from Maurice Philip Remy, July 2000.
18. Steinberg and Krustalev, 385–386; Platonov, *Ternovyi venets Rossi*, 503.
19. Steinberg and Krustalev, 387.
20. Summers and Mangold, 176.
21. In *The History of The Times*, vol. 4, 244.
22. Knightly, 169.
23. See "The Memoirs of Nicholas Ipatiev" in SA, vol. 2, doc. 22; and Ipatiev, *The Memoirs of a Chemist*, for further details.
24. Letters and declarations from Yakovlev, 1931–1937, family archive of Yakovlev, in Alekseev, *Gibel'*, 72–82; Lyoshkin, "Poslednii reis Romanovykh," *Rifey-89* (Chelyabinsk 1989): 72 (October–November 1976), quoted in Radzinsky, 282–284; Ioffe, *Revoliutsiia i sud'ba Romanovki*, 199–207.
25. Letters and declarations from Yakovlev, 1931–1937, family archive of Yakovlev, in Alekseev, *Gibel'*, 72–82; Ioffe, *Revoliutsiia i sud'ba Romanovki*, 199–207.
26. *Posledniye dni Romanovkh*, 44–45; Ioffe, *Revoliutsiia i sud'ba Romanovki*, 199–207.
27. Yurovsky, unpublished memoirs, 1922, in APRF, f. 3, op. 58, d. 280.
28. Bobrick, 406.
29. Pipes, *Russia under the Bolshevik Regime*, 105.
30. Deterikhs, vol. 1, 94.
31. Yurovsky, unpublished memoirs, 1922, in APRF, f. 3, op. 58, d. 280.
32. In *Pravda* 212 (August 3, 1938): 5; see also A. Gubanov, "Krasnye tsareubiitsy," *Russkie vesti* 175 (1997): 4–5; Sonin, 299; Yakubovskii, 282–283.
33. McCullagh, 131.
34. Ibid., 142.
35. Ibid., 145.
36. Ibid., 145–146.
37. Ibid., 142–144.
38. Ibid., 142.
39. Ibid., 136.
40. Sonin, 286.
41. See A. Gubanov, "Krasnye tsareubiitsy," *Russkie vesti* 175 (1997): 4–5.
42. E. Bovkun, "Ubiitsa sidit ne v kazhdom," *Izvestiya*, October 3, 1997.
43. Buranov and Krustalev, *Pravda*, 399; Platonov, *Ternovyi venets Rossi*, 512.
44. Radzinsky, 375.
45. *Pravda* 212 (August 3, 1938): 5; G. Ryabov and G. Ioffe in *Rodina* 5 (1989): 12; Alexandrov, 244.
46. Sonin, 307.
47. Rodzinsky, May 13, 1964, in RTsKhIDNI, f. 588, op. 3, d. 14.
48. Buranov and Krustalev, *Pravda*, 453.
49. Sonin, 308; Platonov, *Ternovyi venets Rossi*, 510.
50. Rodzinsky, May 13, 1964, in RTsKhIDNI, f. 588, op. 3, d. 14.
51. Radzinsky, 321, 429; Lorrain, *La Nuit de L'Oural*, 313; Lorraine, *La Fin*, 299.
52. Platonov, *Ternovyi venets Rossi*, 512.
53. A. Murzin, "O chem rasskazal pered smert'iu tsareubiitsa Petr Ermakov," *Komsomolskaia Pravda* 217 (November 25, 1987): 1–4.
54. Radzinsky, 396.
55. Cymru transcripts.
56. Ibid.
57. Avdonin, Cymru.
58. A. Gubanov, "Krasnye tsareubiitsy," *Russkie vesti* 175 (1997): 4–5; A. Murzin, "O chem rasskazal pered smert'iu tsareubiitsa Petr Ermakov," *Komsomol-*

skaia Pravda 217 (November 25, 1987): 4.; Sonin, 306; Zaitsev, 254.

59. Lorrain, *La Nuit de L'Oural*, 313; Platonov, *Ternovyi venets Rossi*, 507; Steinberg and Krustalev, 393.

60. Platonov, *Ternovyi venets Rossi*, 507.

61. Solzhenitsyn, vol. 1, 41; Steinberg and Krustalev, 392; Alexandrov, 228.

62. Sonin, 274.

63. Steinberg and Krustalev, 380; Platonov, *Ternovyi venets Rossi*, 501.

64. Radzinsky, 427.

65. Steinberg and Krustalev, 380; Platonov, *Ternovyi venets Rossi*, 501; Solzhenitsyn, vol. 1, 333; vol. 2, 680; Alexandrov, 244.

66. Steinberg and Krustalev, 384; Platonov, *Ternovyi venets Rossi*, 504; *Literaturnaya Rossiya* 39 (September 28, 1990): 19; Radzinsky, 428.

67. Ibid.; Sonin, 301.

68. Platonov, *Ternovyi venets Rossi*, 504.

69. Steinberg and Krustalev, 380; Grey, 37; Sonin, 297.

70. Alexei Lyukhanov, in Radzinsky, 419.

71. Radzinsky, 252.

72. Alexei Lyukhanov, in Radzinsky, 419.

73. Radzinsky, 414.

74. Alexei Lyukhanov, in Radzinsky, 419.

75. Strekotin, 1934, in TsDOOSO, f. 221, op. 2, d. 849.

76. Sonin, 314.

77. Deterikhs, vol. 1, 378–380.

78. Strekotin, 1934, in TsDOOSO, f. 221, op. 2, d. 849.

79. Rudolf Lacher, testimony of January 17–18, 1966, *Anna Anderson v. Barbara, Duchess of Mecklenburg, Oberlandesgericht-Hamburg*, III, ZPO, 139/67.

80. Deterikhs, vol. 1, 105; Steinberg and Krustalev, 387; Strekotin, 1934, in TsDOOSO, f. 221, op. 2, d. 849.

81. Radzinsky, 292.

82. O. Bozhov, "O stat'e Zhotesa Medvedeva 'Do i posle tragedii,'" *Ural* 4 (1992): 190–191.

83. Deterikhs, vol. 1, 279.

84. Ibid., 280.

85. Ibid., 280–281.

86. Maria Danilovna Medvedeva, interviewed by Peter Foskin, head of the Syssert Committee of the People's Power, and Acting Syssert Commandant Alexei Orlov, in GARF, f. 601, op. 2, d. 51.

87. O. Bozhov, "O stat'e Zhotesa Medvedeva 'Do i posle tragedii,'" in *Ural* 4 (1992): 191.

88. Strekotin, 1934, in TsDOOSO, f. 221, op. 2, d. 849.

89. Ibid.

90. Ibid.

91. Ibid.

92. Ibid.

93. Steinberg and Krustalev, 387; Strekotin, 1934, in TsDOOSO, f. 221, op. 2, d. 849.

94. McCullagh, 115; Ackerman, 75.

95. McCullagh, 115.

96. Buranov and Krustalev, *Pravda*, 422.

97. McCullagh, 115.

98. Speranski, 31.

99. Ibid., 32.

100. Ibid., 38.

101. Halliburton, *Seven League Boots*, 151.

102. Ibid., 152.

103. McCullagh, 126.

104. Speranski, 42–44.

105. Avdonin, 1993 Ekaterinburg conference.

106. Avdonin, Cymru.

107. Yuri Andropov, "Proposal to Remove the Ipatiev House," memorandum submitted to the Politburo on July 26, 1975, quoted in Volkogonov, 219.

108. Yeltsin, 190.

109. Massie, 24.

110. Yeltsin interview with Alexander Olbiks, in *Sovietskaya Molodezh*, Riga, January 3–4, 1990, in Morrison, 39.

111. In *New York Times*, November 21, 1990; AP report, July 21, 1993.

112. In "Bones of Contention."

113. Efremov, in "Bones of Contention."

114. Maura Reynolds, "A Tale of Two Royal Grave Sites," *Los Angeles Times*, June 18, 2002.

115. Avdonin, in "Bones of Contention."

116. Macauley, 36–37.

117. Wortman, vol. 2, 336.

Appendix 1: Ekaterinburg Guards

1. Guard details are drawn from Deterikhs, vol. 1, 276–277; May notebook for Ipatiev House pay in Sotheby's auction catalog, 74–75; Yakimov, May 7–11, 1919, in SA, vol. 5, doc. 18; Strekotin, 1934, in TsDOOSO, f. 221, op. 2, d. 849;

Medvedev, February 21–22, 1919, in SA, vol. 2, doc. 86; Platonov, *Ternovyi venets Rossi*, 445–446; McCullagh, 167; Radzinsky, 292; Sokolov, *Enquete*, 117–122; Kabanov, unpublished memoirs, in Khabarovsk Regional Party Archives, f. 117, op. 2, d. 27; and Netrebin, in TsDOOSO, f. 41, op. 1, d. 149.

Appendix 2: Inventory of Romanov Possessions in Ekaterinburg

1. Nametkin's Inventory of Ipatiev House, August 2, 5, 6, 7, 8, 1918, in SA, vol. 1, doc. 9; also reproduced in Sokolov, 317–334.
2. Kirsta, Report of the Military-Criminal Investigating Division, in GARF, f. 601, op. 2, d. 51; Nametkin's inventory of the Ipatiev House, August 2, 5, 6, 7, 8, 1918, in SA, vol. 1, doc. 9; also reproduced in Sokolov, *Enquete*, 317–334.

3. Ibid.
4. Nametkin's Inventory of the Ipatiev House, August 2, 5, 6, 7, 8, 1918, in SA, vol. 1, doc. 9; also reproduced in Sokolov, *Enquete*, 317–334.
5. Ibid.
6. Ibid.
7. In GARF, f. 601, op. 2, d. 41, l. 3–3ob; l. 4; l. 5–5ob; l. 6; l. 7–7ob; l. 9; l. 21–21ob.

Appendix 3: The Romanovs' Jewels

1. Romanov jewel inventory list, in TsDOOSO, in documents collection "The Romanov Valuables," f. 221, op. 1, d. 89.

Bibliography

Books and Manuscripts

Abraham, Richard. *Alexander Kerensky: The First Love of the Revolution*. New York: Columbia University Press, 1987.

Abramovitch, Raphael R. *The Soviet Revolution, 1917–1939*. New York: International Universities Press, 1962.

Abrikossow, Dimitri. *Revelations of a Russian Diplomat: The Memoirs of Dimitri Abrikossow*. Edited by George Alexander Lensen. Seattle: University of Washington Press, 1964.

Ackerman, Carl. *Trailing the Bolsheviki*. New York: Charles Scribner's Sons, 1919.

Airlie, Mabell, Countess of. *Thatched with Gold: The Memoirs of Mabell, Countess of Airlie*. Edited and arranged by Jennifer Ellis. London: Hutchinson, 1962.

Albertson, Ralph. *Fighting without a War: An Account of Military Intervention in North Russia*. New York: Harcourt, Brace, & Howe, 1920.

Alekseev, Veniamin A. *Gibel' tsarskoi sem'i: mify i real'nost'. Novye dokumenty o tragedii na Urale*. Ekaterinburg: Central Ural Publishing, 1993.

Alexander Mikhailovich, Grand Duke of Russia. *Once a Grand Duke*. New York: Farrar & Rinehart, 1932.

Alexandrov, Victor. *The End of the Romanovs*. Boston: Little, Brown, 1966.

Alferyev, Ye., ed. *Pis'ma tsarskoi sem'i iz zatocheniia*. Jordanville, N.Y.: Holy Trinity Monastery, 1974.

———. *Imperator Nikolai II kak chelovek silnoi voli*. Jordanville, N.Y.: Holy Trinity Monastery, 1983.

Asprey, Robert. *The German High Command at War*. New York: William Morrow/Avon, 1991.

Aucleres, Dominique. *Anastasia, qui êtes-vous?* Paris: Hachette, 1962.

Baden, Michael. *Dead Reckoning*. New York: Simon & Schuster, 2001.

Baden, Prince Max of. *The Memoirs of Prince Max of Baden*. Translated by W. M. Calder and C. W. H. Sutton. 2 vols. London: Constable, 1928.

Baedecker, Karl. *Russia with Teheran, Port Arthur, and Peking*. New York: Baedeker, 1914.

Baerlein, Henry. *The March of the Seventy Thousand*. London: Leonard Parsons, 1926.

Bariatinsky, Princess Anatole. *My Russian Life*. London: Hutchinson, 1923.

Barkovets, Alia, and Valentina Tenikhina. *Nicholas II: The Imperial Family*. Edited by Olga Akbulatova. Translated by Valery Fateyev. St. Petersburg: Arbis, 1998.

Barton, George. *Celebrated Spies and Famous Mysteries of the Great War*. Boston: Page, 1919.

de Basily, Nicolas. *The Abdication of Emperor Nicholas II of Russia*. Princeton, N.J.: Princeton University Press, 1984.

Baumgart, Winfried. *Deutsche Ostpolitik 1918*. Vienna-Munich: Schampfer, 1966.

Beable, William. *Russian Gazetter & Guide*. London: Russian Outlook, 1919.

Beaumont, A. *Heroic Story of the Czecho-Slovak Legions*. Prague: Czechoslovakian Foreigners' Office, 1919.

Belyakova, Zoya. *The Romanovs: The Way It Was*. St. Petersburg: Ego, 2000.

Benagh, Christine. *An Englishman in the Court of the Tsar*. Ben Lomond, Calif.: Conciliar Press, 2000.

Benckendorff, Count Paul. *Last Days at Tsarskoye Selo*. London: William Heinemann, 1927.

Benvenuti, Francesco. *The Bolsheviks and the Red Army, 1918–1922*. Cambridge: Cambridge University Press, 1988.

Bergamini, John. *The Tragic Dynasty*. New York: G. P. Putnam's Sons, 1969.

Bessedowsky, Gregory. *Im Dienste Der Sowjets*. Leipzig: Grethlein, 1930.

Bezymenski, Lev. *The Death of Adolf Hitler: Unknown Documents from Soviet Archives*. London: Michael Joseph, 1968.

Blair, Dorian, and C. H. Dand. *Russian Hazard: The Adventures of a British Secret Service Agent in Russia*. London: Robert Hale, 1937.

Bobrick, Benson. *East of the Sun: The Epic Conquest and Tragic History of Siberia*. New York: Poseidon, 1992.

Bokhanov, Alexander. *Rossiiskii Imperatorskii Dom: Dnevniki, Pis'ma, Fotografii*. Moscow: Perspektiva, 1992.

_____, ed. *The Romanovs: Love, Power, and Tragedy*. London: Leppi, 1993.

Bonch-Bruyevich, Michael, M.D. *Vsye Vlast Sovetem*. Moscow: Central University, 1964.

Bor'ba za Vlast' Sovetov b Tobol'skoi (Tyumenskoi) Gyberni. Tyumen: Sibirskii Knigii, 1998.

Botkin, Gleb. *The Real Romanovs*. New York: Fleming H. Revell, 1932.

_____. *The Woman Who Rose Again*. New York: Fleming H. Revell, 1937.

Botkine, Peter. *Les Morts sans Tombes*. Paris: Louis Conard, 1921.

Botkine, Tatiana. *Au Temps des Tsars*. Paris: Grasset, 1980.

Bradley, John. *Allied Intervention in Russia 1919–1920*. New York: Basic Books, 1968.

_____. *Civil War in Russia 1917–1920*. London: Batsford, 1975.

Brinkley, George. *The Volunteer Army and Allied Intervention in South Russia, 1917–1921*. Notre Dame, Ind.: University of Notre Dame Press, 1966.

Bromage, Bernard. *Man of Terror: Dzherzhinskii*. London: Peter Owen, 1933.

Browder, Robert P., and Alexander F. Kerensky, eds. *The Russian Provisional Government 1917: Documents*. 3 vols. Palo Alto, Calif.: Stanford University Press, 1961.

Bruce Lockhart, Sir Robert. *Memoirs of a British Agent*. London: G. P. Putnam's Sons, 1932.

_____. *Diaries*. London: Macmillan, 1973.

Bruce Lockhart, Robin. *Ace of Spies*. London: Hodder & Stoughton, 1967.

Buchanan, Meriel. *The Dissolution of an Empire*. London: John Murray, 1932.

_____. *Queen Victoria's Relations*. London: Cassell, 1954.

_____. *Victorian Gallery*. London: Cassell, 1956.

_____. *Ambassador's Daughter*. London: Cassell, 1958.

Buchanan, Sir George. *My Mission to Russia*. 2 vols. Boston: Little, Brown, 1923.

Bulygin, Paul, and Alexander Kerensky. *The Murder of the Romanovs*. London: Hutchinson, 1935.

Bunyan, James, ed. *Intervention, Civil War and Communism in Russia: Documents and Materials*. Philadelphia: J. B. Lippincott, 1936.

Bunyan, James, and H. H. Fisher. *The Bolshevik Revolution 1917–1918*. London: Oxford University Press, 1934.

Buranov, Yuri, and V. Krustalev. *Gibel' imperatorskogo doma 1917–1919gg*. Moscow: Progress, 1992.

_____. *Ubiisty tsaria. Unichtozhenie dinastii*. Moscow: Progress, 1997.

_____. *Pravda o Ekaterinburgskoi Tragedii: Sbornik Statei*. Moscow: Progress, 1998.

Bury, Herbert, Right Reverend, D.D. *Russian Life Today*. London: A. R. Mowbray, 1915.

Buxhoeveden, Baroness Sophie. *Left Behind: Fourteen Months in Siberia during the Revolution, December 1917–February 1919*. London: Longmans, Green, 1919.

_____. *The Life and Tragedy of Alexandra Feodorovna*. London: Longmans, Green, 1928.

_____. *Before the Storm*. London: Macmillan, 1938.

Bykov, Paul. "Posledniye dni poslednego tsarya." In *Rabochaya revolyutsiya na Urale. Episody i fakty*. Ekaterinburg: Ural State, 1921.

_____. *The Last Days of Tsar Nicholas*. New York: International Publishers, 1934.

Byrnes, Robert F. *Pobedonostsev: His Life and Thought*. Bloomington: Indiana University Press, 1968.

Chamberlain, William Henry. *The Russian Revolution*. 2 vols. London: Hutchinson, 1935.

Charques, Richard. *The Twilight of Imperial Russia*. London: Oxford University Press, 1958.

Chavchavadze, David. *Crowns and Trenchcoats*. New York: Atlantic International, 1990.

———. *The Grand Dukes*. New York: Atlantic International, 1990.

Chicherin, G. *Stat'i rechi po voprosam mezhdunarodnoi politiki*. Moscow: Izdat'stvo sotsial'no-ekonomicheskoi literatury, 1961.

Clarke, William. *The Lost Fortune of the Tsars*. New York: St. Martin's Press, 1994.

Cockfield, Jamie. *White Crow: The Life and Times of Grand Duke Nicholas Mikhailovich of Russia, 1859–1919*. Westport, CT: Praeger, 2002.

Cohen, Naomi W. *Jacob Schiff: A Study in American Jewish Leadership*. Hanover, N.H.: University Press of New England, Brandeis University Press, 1999.

Cohn, Norman. *Warrant for Genocide: The Myth of the Jewish World Conspiracy and the Protocols of the Elders of Zion*. New York: Viking, 1967.

Cowles, Virginia. *The Russian Dagger: Cold War in the Days of the Czars*. New York: Harper & Row, 1969.

———. *The Last Tsar*. New York: G. P. Putnam's Sons, 1977.

Crankshaw, Edward. *The Shadow of the Winter Palace: Russia's Drift to Revolution 1825–1917*. New York: Viking, 1976.

Crawford, Rosemary and Donald. *Michael and Natasha: The Life and Love of the Last Tsar of Russia*. London: George Weidenfeld & Nicolson, 1997.

Danilov, Yu. N. *Na puti k krusheniyu. Ocherki iz poslednego perioda russkoi monarkhii*. Moscow: Voyyenizdat, 1992.

Degras, Jane, ed. *Soviet Documents on Foreign Policy*. 3 vols. London: Oxford University Press, 1948.

Dehn, Lili. *The Real Tsaritsa*. London: Thornton Butterworth, 1922.

Delane, John Thadeus, ed. *The History of The Times*. 5 vols. London: The Times, 1935–1952.

Deterikhs, General Michael. *Ubiistvo tsarskoi sem'i i chlenov doma Romanovykh na Urale*. 2 vols. Vladivostok: Vladivostok Military Academy, 1922.

Dorr, Rheta Childe. *Inside the Russian Revolution*. New York: Macmillan, 1918.

Dukes, Sir Paul. *The Story of "ST 25": Adventures and Romance of the Secret Intelligence Service in Red Russia*. London: Cassell, 1938.

Eager, Margaretta. *Six Years at the Russian Court*. London: Hurst & Blackett, 1906.

Elbogen, Ismar. *A Century of Jewish Life*. Translated by Moses Hadas. Philadelphia: Jewish Publication Society of America, 1944.

d'Encausse, Hélène Carrere. *The Russian Syndrome: One Thousand Years of Political Murder*. New York: Holmes & Meier, 1992.

———. *Nicholas II: The Interrupted Transition*. Translated by George Holoch. New York: Holmes & Meier, 2000.

Enel [Michael Vladimirovich Skaryatin]. *Sacrifice*. Brussels, 1923.

Erdmann, K. D. *Kurt Riezler: Tagebucher, Aufsatze, Dokumente*. Göttingen: Hirmer, 1972.

Ernst Ludwig, Grand Duke of Hesse and by Rhine. *Erinnertes: Aufzeichnungen des letzten Grossherzogs Ernst Ludwig von Hessen und bei Rhein*. Darmstadt: Eduard Roether, 1983.

Essad-Bey, Mohammed. *Nicholas II: Prisoner of the Purple*. London: Hutchinson, 1936.

Ezell, Edward. *Handguns of the World*. New York: Barnes & Noble, 1993.

Figes, Orlando. *A People's Tragedy: The Russian Revolution 1891–1924*. London: Random House, 1996.

Fleming, Robert. *The Fate of Admiral Kolchak*. London: Rupert Hart-Davis, 1963.

Florinsky, Michael T. *The End of the Russian Empire*. New York: Collier, 1961.

Fogelsong, David S. *America's Secret War against Bolshevism: U.S. Intervention in the Russian Civil War 1917–1920*. Chapel Hill: University of North Carolina Press, 1995.

Frankel, Jonathan. *Prophecy and Politics: Socialism, Nationalism, and the Russian Jews 1862–1917*. Cambridge: Cambridge University Press, 1981.

Fraser, John Foster. *The Real Siberia: Together with an Account of a Dash through Manchuria*. London: Cassell, 1902.

Freund, G. *Unholy Alliance: Russian-German Relations from the Treaty of Brest-Litovsk to the Treaty of Berlin*. London: Chatto & Windus, 1957.

Fromenko, Irina. "Krymskii Al'bom Nikolaya II." In *Krymskii Al'bom: Istoriko-kraevedcheskii i literaturno-khudozh*, ed. Irina Fromenko. Sevastopol: Taurida, 1998.

Frumkin, Jacob. *Russian Jewry 1860–1917*. New York: Viking, 1966.

Fry, L. *Waters Flowing Eastward: The War against the Kingship of Christ*. London: Hutchinson, 1965.

Fuhrman, Joseph T. *Rasputin: A Life*. New York: Praeger, 1990.

———. *The Complete Wartime Correspondence of Tsar Nicholas II and the Empress Alexandra, April 1914–March 1917*. Westport, Conn.: Greenwood, 1999.

Gaida, Rudolf. *Moje Pameti: Ceskoslovanska Anabase Zpet na Ural proti bolsevikum Admiral Kolcak*. Prague: Vesmir, 1924.

George, Grand Duchess of Russia. *A Romanov Diary*. New York: Atlantic International, 1988.

Gilliard, Pierre. *Le Tragique Destin de Nicolas II et de sa Famille*. Paris: Payot, 1921.

———. *Thirteen Years at the Russian Court*. New York: George H. Doran, 1923.

Golovine, Nicholas. *The Russian Army in 1914*. New York: Viking, 1933.

Gorkii, M., ed., with V. Molotov, K. Voroshilov, S. Kirov, A. Zhdanov, and Josef Stalin. *The History of the Civil War in the USSR*. New York: International Publishers, 1936.

Gorodetsky, Ye., and Yu. Shuranov. *Sverdlov*. Moscow: Moscow State, 1971.

Gosudarstvennaya Legitimnost: Sbornik materialov posvyashchennii dorasslidovanniyu ubiistvo Tsarskoi Sem'i. St. Petersburg: Mezhdu Narodni Foundation, 1994.

Graves, Major General William S. *America's Siberian Adventure 1918–1920*. New York: Jonathan Cape and Harrison Smith, 1931.

Grebelsky, P., and A. Mirvis. *Dom Romanovykh: Biograficheskiye svedeniya o ehlenaskh tsarstvo-vavshego doma, ikh predlakh i rodstvennikakh-2 isdaniye dopolennoye i pereabotannoye*. St. Petersburg: Redaktor, 1992.

Greece, Eugenie de. *Le tsarevich: Enfant Martyr*. Paris: Perrin, 1990.

Grey, Marina. *Enquete sur le massacre des Romanov*. Paris: Librairie Academique, 1987.

Gryannik, Anatoly. *Zaveshchaniye Nikolaya II*. Riga: Kondus, 1993.

Hall, Coryne. *Little Mother of Russia*. London: Shepheard-Walwyn, 1999.

Halliburton, Richard. *Seven League Boots*. London: Unwin, 1936.

———. *Richard Halliburton: The Story of His Life's Adventure*. Garden City, N.Y.: Garden City, 1942.

Hanbury-Williams, Major General Sir John. *The Emperor Nicholas II as I Knew Him*. London: Arthur L. Humphreys, 1922.

Harcave, Sidney. *Years of the Golden Cockerel: The Last Romanov Tsars 1814–1917*. New York: Macmillan, 1968.

Hartink, A. E. *Encyclopedia of Pistols and Revolvers*. Amsterdam: Rebo, 1996.

Heifets, Mikhail. *Tsareubiistvo v 1918 g Versiya prestupleniya i ofitsialnogo sledstviya*. Moscow: Festival, 1992.

Helen, Princess of Serbia and of Russia. "Memoirs." New York: MS Collection, Box 42, Collection H, Bahkmatieff Archive, Rare Book and Manuscript Library, Columbia University, 1952.

Hoffmann, Max. *War Diaries and Other Papers*. London: Martin Secker, 1929.

Hough, Richard. *Louis and Victoria: The First Mountbattens*. London: Hutchinson, 1974.

———. *Mountbatten*. London: Macmillan, 1980.

Ignatiev, Lieutenant General A. A. *A Subaltern in Old Russia*. Translated by Ivor Montagu. London: Hutchinson, 1944.

Ioffe, Genrikh. *Revoliutsiia i sud'ba Romanovki*. Moscow: Republika, 1992.

Ipatieff, Vladimir. *The Memoirs of a Chemist*. Evanston, Ill.: Northwestern University Press, 1959.

Iroshnikov, Mikhail, Liudmila Protsai, and Yuri Shelayev. *The Sunset of the Romanov Dynasty*. Moscow: Terra, 1992.

Jackson, Steve. *No Stone Unturned*. New York: Kensington, 2002.

Jagow, Gottlieb von. *Documents from the Prussian Archives of the Ministry of Foreign Affairs*. Berlin: Monatshefte, 1935.

Janin, General Maurice. *Ma Mission en Siberie*. Paris: Payot, 1933.

Johnson, Paul. *A History of the Jews*. New York: Harper & Row, 1987.

Jones, Steven. *The Language of Genes: Solving the Mysteries of Our Genetic Past, Present, and Future*. New York: Doubleday, Anchor, 1994.

de Jonge, Alex. *The Life and Times of Grigorii Rasputin*. New York: Coward, McCann, & Geoghegan, 1982.

Joost, Wilhelm. *Botschafter bei den roten Zaren*. Vienna: Furst, 1967.

Kasvinov, M. *Dvadstat' tri stupeni vniz*. Moscow: Central State, 1982.

Katkov, George. *Russia 1917: The February Revolution*. London: Longman, Green, 1967.

Kennan, George. *Russia Leaves the War*. Vol. 1 of *Soviet-American Relations 1917–1920*. New York: W. W. Norton, 1958.

———. *The Decision to Intervene*. Vol. 2 of *Soviet-American Relations 1917–1920*. Princeton, N.J.: Princeton University Press, 1958.

King, Greg. *The Last Empress: The Life and Times of Alexandra Feodorovna, Tsarina of Russia*. New York: Carol, 1994.

Kirill, H. I. H., Grand Duke of Russia. *My Life in Russia's Service—Then and Now*. London: Selwyn & Blount, 1939.

Klier, John, and Helen Mingay. *The Quest for Anastasia: Solving the Mystery of the Lost Romanovs*. London: Smith Gryphon, 1995.

Knightly, Phillip. *The First Casualty: From the Crimea to Vietnam: The War Correspondent as Hero, Propagandist, and Myth Maker*. New York: Harcourt Brace Jovanovich, 1975.

Knodt, Manfred. *Ernst Ludwig, Grossherzog von Hesse und Bei Rhine*. Darmstadt: H. L. Schlapp, 1986.

Knox, Alfred. *With the Russian Army*. New York: E. P. Dutton, 1921.

Kokovtsov, Count Vladimir. *Out of My Past: The Memoirs of Count Kokovtsov*. Palo Alto, Calif.: Stanford University Press, 1935.

Kozlov, Vladimir, and Vladimir Krustalev, eds. *The Last Diary of Tsaritsa Alexandra*. New Haven, Conn.: Yale University Press, 1997.

Krupskaya, N. *Vospominaniya o Lenine*. Moscow: Partizdat, 1934.

———. *Izbrannie Pedagogicheskie Proizvedeniya*. Moscow: Izdatelstvo, Akademii Pedagogicheskikh Nauk, 1955.

———. *O Lenine: Sbornik Statei*. Moscow: Partizdat, 1960.

Kudrina, Julia. *Imperatritsa Maria Fedorovna*. Moscow: Mokba Olma, 2001.

Kurth, Peter. *Anastasia: The Riddle of Anna Anderson*. Boston: Little, Brown, 1983.

Lasies, Joseph. *La Tragedie Siberienne: le drame d'Ekaterinbourg*. Paris: L'Édition Française Illustrée, 1920.

The Last Journey: The Funeral of the Romanovs. St. Petersburg: Liki Rossi, 1998.

Leggett, George. *The Cheka: Lenin's Political Police*. Oxford: Clarendon Press, 1981.

Lehovich, Dmitry. *White against Red: The Life of General Anton Denikin*. New York: W. W. Norton, 1973.

Lenin, V. I. *Polnoe Sobranie Sochineny*, 5th ed., 55 vols. Moscow: Institut Markszima-Leninizma, 1958–1965.

———. *Biograficheskaia Khronika, 1870–1924*. 13 vols. Moscow: Institut Markszima-Leninizma, 1970–1985.

Laqueuer, Walter. *Russia and Germany: A Century of Conflict*. London: George Weidenfeld & Nicolson, 1966.

———. *The Fate of the Revolution*. New York: Macmillan, 1967.

Levenda, Peter. *Unholy Alliance*. New York: Avon, 1995.

Levine, Isaac Don. *Eyewitness to History*. New York: Hawthorn, 1973.

Levytsky, Boris. *The Uses of Terror: The Soviet Secret Service 1917–1970*. London: Sidgwick & Jackson, 1971.

Lieven, Dominic. *Nicholas II: Twilight of the Empire*. New York: St. Martin's Press, 1993.

Lincoln, W. Bruce. *Red Victory: A History of the Russian Civil War*. New York: Simon & Schuster, 1989.

———. *Passage through Armageddon*. New York: Simon & Schuster, 1990.

Lorrain, Pierre. *La Nuit de L'Oural: l'assassinait des Romanov*. Paris: Bartillat, 1996.

———. *La Fin Tragique des Romanov*. Paris: Bartillat, 1998.

Lowe, Charles. *Alexander III*. New York: Macmillan, 1895.

Luckett, Richard. *The White Generals: An Account of the White Movement and the Russian Civil War*. London: Longman, 1971.

Ludendorff, E. *My War Memories, 1914–1918*. London: Hutchinson, 1919.

Ludwig, Emil. *Kaiser Wilhelm II*. London: G. P. Putman's Sons, 1926.

Lukomsky, General Alexander. *Memoirs of the Russian Revolution*. London: T. Fisher Unwin, 1922.

Lyubashkova, T. A. *K istorii izdaniya istoricheskikh istochnikov o dome Romanovykh; Aktualnye voprosy teorii, metodologii i istorii publikatsii istoricheskikh dokumentov*. Moscow: Perspekta, 1991.

Macauley, Thomas. *Historical and Critical Essays*. Vol. 1. London: Longman, Brown, & Green, 1843.

Major, H. D. A. *The Life and Letters of William Boyd-Carpenter*. London: John Murray, 1925.

Maples, Dr. William R., and Michael Browning. *Dead Men Do Tell Tales*. New York: Doubleday, 1994.

Marie Feodorovna, Empress of Russia: An Exhibition about the Danish Princess Who Became Empress of Russia. Exhibition catalog. Copenhagen: Christiansborg Palace-Der Kongelige Udstillingsfond, 1997.

Marie Pavlovna, Grand Duchess of Russia. *Education of a Princess*. New York: Viking, 1931.

Marie, Queen of Romania. *The Story of My Life*. New York: Charles Scribner's Sons, 1934.

Markov, Serge. *How We Tried to Save the Tsaritsa*. London: G. P. Putnam's Sons, 1929.

Masaryk, Thomas. *Die Welt-Revolution: Erinnerungen und Betrachtungen 1914–1918*. Berlin: Erich Reiss, 1925.

Massie, Robert. *The Romanovs: The Final Chapter*. New York: Random House, 1995.

Mawdsley, Evan. *The Russian Civil War*. Winchester, Mass.: Allen & Unwin, 1987.

Maylunas, Andrei, and Sergei Mironenko. *A Lifelong Passion: Nicholas and Alexandra: Their Own Story*. London: George Weidenfeld & Nicolson, 1996.

McCullagh, Francis. *A Prisoner of the Reds: The Story of a British Officer Captured in Siberia*. London: John Murray, 1921.

McLees, Nun Nectaria. *A Gathered Radiance: The Life of Alexandra Romanov, Russia's Last Empress*. Chico, Calif.: Valaam Society of America, 1992.

McNeal, Shay. *The Plots to Rescue the Tsar*. London: Random Century, 2001.

Melgunov, Serge Petrovich. *The Red Terror in Russia*. London: J. M. Dent, 1926.

———. *Sud'ba Imperatora Nikolaya II poslye otrecheniya*. Paris: La Renaissance, 1951.

Merridale, Catherine. *Night of Stone: Death and Memory in Twentieth-Century Russia*. New York: Viking, 2000.

Miliukov, Paul. *Political Memoirs*. Translated by Carl Goldberg. Ann Arbor: University of Michigan Press, 1967.

Millar, Lyubov. *Grand Duchess Elizabeth of Russia: New Martyr of the Communist Yoke*. Redding, Calif.: Nikodemos Orthodox Publication Society, 1991.

Miller, David, ed. *The Illustrated Book of Guns*. San Diego, Calif.: Thunder Bay Press, 2000.

Morrison, John. *Boris Yeltsin: From Bolshevik to Democrat*. New York: E. P. Dutton, 1991.

Mossolov, Alexander. *At the Court of the Last Tsar*. London: Metheun, 1935.

Mstislavskii, Sergei. *Five Days which Transformed Russia*. Translated by Elizabeth Zelensky. London: Hutchinson, 1988.

Nadtochii, Yu. *Ubitsy imenem revolyutsii: Dokumentumentalnaya povest' o poslednikh dnyakh zhizni Nikolaya II i yego sem'i*. Tiumen: Uralskii, 1994.

Naryshkina-Kuryakin, Elizabeth. *Under Three Tsars*. New York: E. P. Dutton, 1931.

Nazorov, G. *Vosprositel' nye znaki and mogilami*. Moscow: Tsentrali, 1969.

Newman, Karoline, and Karen Bressler. *A Century of Style: Lingerie*. London: Apple, 1996.

Noel, Gerard. *Princess Alice: Queen Victoria's Forgotten Daughter*. London: Hutchinson, 1974.

Nostitz, Countess Lilie. *Romance and Revolutions*. London: Hutchinson, 1937.

Obninsky, V. *Poslednii samoderzhets: Ocherk zhizni i tsarstvovanita imperatora Rossii Nikolaya II*. Moscow: Republika, 1992.

Occleshaw, Michael. *The Romanov Conspiracies*. London: Chapman's, 1993.

O'Connor, John F. *The Sokolov Investigation of the Alleged Murder of the Russian Imperial Family*. New York: Robert Speller & Sons, 1971.

Oldenburg, S. S. *Last Tsar: Nicholas II, His Reign, His Russia*. Gulf Breeze, Fla.: Academic International, 1977.

Outemskii, N. V. *Travels in the East of Nicholas II, Emperor of Russia, when Tsesarevich, 1890–1891*. 2 vols. London: Constable, 1896–1900.

Paganuzzi, Paul. *Pravda ob ubiistv' Tsarskoi Sem'i*. Jordanville, N.Y.: Holy Trinity Monastery, 1981.

———. *Tschaikowska-Anna Anderson-Manahan: Tsar's Daughter or Imposter?: A Historical Critical Essay*. St. Petersburg, Fla., 1987.

Paleologue, Maurice. *An Ambassador's Memoirs*. 3 vols. New York: Doran, 1925.

Paley, Princess Olga. *Memories of Russia 1916–1919*. London: Herbert Jenkins, 1924.

Pares, Sir Bernard. *The Fall of the Russian Monarchy*. New York: Alfred A. Knopf, 1939.

Pascal, Pierre. *Mon Journal de Russie à la Mission Militaire Française 1916–1918*. Lausanne, Switz.: Éditions L'Age d'Homme, 1975.

Payne, Robert. *The Life and Death of Lenin*. New York: Simon & Schuster, 1964.

———. *The Life and Death of Adolf Hitler*. New York: Praeger, 1973.

Perry, John Curtis, and Constantine Pleshakov. *The Flight of the Romanovs*. New York: Basic Books, 1999.

Petrov, Vadim, Igor Lysenko, and Georgy Egorov. *The Escape of Alexei: Son of Tsar Nicholas II*. New York: Harry N. Abrams, 1998.

Petrova, Ada, and Peter Watson. *The Death of Hitler: The Final Words from Russia's Secret Archives*. London: Richard Cohen Books, 1995.

Pipes, Richard. *The Russian Revolution*. New York: Alfred A. Knopf, 1991.

———. *Russia under the Bolshevik Regime*. New York: Alfred A. Knopf, 1993.

Platonov, O. *Ubiistvo tsarskoi semi*. Moscow: Sovetskaya Rossiya, 1991.

———. *Ternovyi venets Rossi. Zagovor tsareubiits*. Moscow: Rodnik, 1996.

de Ponfilly, Raymond. *Guide des Russes en France*. Paris: Éditions Horay, 1990.

Ponsonby, Sir Frederick. *Recollections of Three Reigns*. New York: E. P. Dutton, 1952.

Pope-Hennessy, James. *Queen Mary*. London: George Allen & Unwin, 1959.

Popov, V. *Gde Vy, Vashe Velichestvo?* St. Petersburg: Perspekta, 1996.

Posledni dni Romanovykh: Dokumenti, Materialni Sledstviya, Dnevniki, Versii. Sverdlovsk: Central-Ural, 1991.

Posledniye dni imperatorskoi vlastic: Po neizdannym dokumentam. Minsk: Sostavitel A. Blok, 1991.

Posledniye dni Romanovykh. Moscow: Kniga, 1991.

Preston, Sir Thomas H. *Before the Curtain*. London: Murray, 1950.

Prishchev, V., and A. Aleksandrov. *Rassledovanie tsareubiistva: sekretnye dokumenty*. Moscow: Progress, 1993.

Radek, Karl. *Vneshniaia politika sovetskoi Rossii*. Moscow: Gosizdat, 1923.

Radzinsky, Edvard. *The Last Tsar: The Life and Death of Nicholas II*. New York: Doubleday, 1992.

Radziwill, Princess Catherine. *The Intimate Life of the Last Tsarina*. London: Cassell, 1929.

———. *Nicholas II: The Last of the Tsars*. London: Cassell, 1931.

———. *The Taint of the Romanovs*. London: Cassell, 1931.

Ransome, Arthur. *Six Weeks in Russia in 1919*. London: George Allen & Unwin, 1919.

Rasputin, Maria, and Patte Barham. *Rasputin: The Man behind the Myth*. Englewood Cliffs, N.J.: Prentice-Hall, 1977.

Rathlef-Keilmann, Harriet von. *Anastasia: The Survivor of Ekaterinburg*. New York: G. P. Putnam's Sons, 1928.

Riezler, Kurt. *Tagebucher-Aufsatze-Dokumente: Eingeleiter und herausgegben von Karl Dietrich Erdmann*. Göttingen: Vandenhoek & Rupprecht, 1972.

de Robien, Louis. *The Diary of a Diplomat in Russia, 1917–1918*. New York: Praeger, 1967.

Rodzianko, Paul. *Tattered Banners: An Autobiography*. London: Seeley Service, 1939.

Rogger, Hans. *Russia in the Age of Modernization and Revolution, 1881–1917*. London: Sidgwick, 1983.

———. *Jewish Policies and Right-Wing Politics in Imperial Russia*. Berkeley: University of California Press, 1986.

Root, Jonathan. *Halliburton: The Magnificent Myth*. Toronto: Longman, 1965.

Ross, Nikolai. ed. *Gibel' tsarskoi sem'i: Materialy sledstviia po delu ob ubiistve Tsarskoi sem'i (avgust 1918–fevral' 1920)*. Frankfurt: Possev, 1987.

Russian, a. *Russian Court Memoirs, 1914–1916*. New York: E. P. Dutton, 1916.

Russkaia Letopis. Vols. 1–4, Paris: Russkii Ochag, 1921–1922.

Sachar, Abram Leon. *A History of the Jews*. New York: Alfred A. Knopf, 1964.

Sadoul, Jacques. *Notes sur la revolution Bolchevique Octobre 1917–Janvier 1919*. Paris: Éditions de la Sirene, 1919.

Salisbury, Harrison. *Black Night, White Snow: Russia's Revolutions 1905–1917*. Garden City, N.Y.: Doubleday, 1977.

Samuel, Maurice. *Blood Accusation: The Strange History of the Beilis Case*. New York: Alfred A. Knopf, 1966.

Sell, Dr. *Alice, Grand Duchess of Hesse, Princess of Great Britain and Ireland*. London: John Murrary, 1884.

Seton-Watson, Hugh. *The Decline of Imperial Russia*. New York: Praeger, 1964.

Shchegolev, P., ed. *Padenie tsarskogo rezhima: Stenografisheskie otchety doprosov I pokazanii, dannisk v 1917 g v. Chrezvychainoi Sledstvennoi Komissii Vremennogo Pravitel'stva*. 7 vols. Moscow: State Publishing, 1924–1927.

Shulgin, Vassili. *The Years*. New York: Hippocrene Books, 1984.

Smirnoff, Serge. *Autour de L'Assassinat des Grands-Ducs: Ekaterinbourg, Alapaievsk, Perm, Petrograd*. Paris: Payot, 1928.

Smith, Lacey Baldwin. *Fools, Martyrs, Traitors: The Story of Martyrdom in the Western World*. New York: Alfred A. Knopf, 1997.

Snow, Russell E. *The Bolsheviks in Siberia 1917–1918*. London: Associated University Presses, 1977.

Sokolov, Nicholas. *Enquete judiciare sur l'Assassinat de la Famille Imperiale Russe*. Paris: Payot, 1924.

———. *Ubiistvo tsarskoi sem'i*. Berlin: Slovo, 1925.

Solzhenitsyn, Alexander. *The Gulag Archipelago, 1918–1956: An Experiment in Literary Investigation*. 3 vols. New York: Harper & Row, 1973.

Sonin, Lev. *Poker Na Kostyakh, ili, Kak Skrivaiyut pravdy o syd'be Nikolaiya II.* Ekaterinburg: Perspekta, 1998.

Sostavitel, G. *Samosud. Ubiistvo velikogo knyazya Mikhaila Romanova v Permi v iyune 1918 g: Dokumenty i publikatsii.* Perm: Ural, 1992.

Sotheby's auction catalog. *The Romanovs: Documents and Photographs Relating to the Russian Imperial House.* London: Thursday, April 5, 1990.

Speranski, Valentin. *La Maison à Destination Speciale.* Paris: J. Ferenczi & Fils, Éditeurs, 1928.

Steinberg, Isaac. *Spiridonova, Revolutionary Terrorist.* London: Hutchinson, 1935.

―――. *In the Workshop of the Revolution.* New York: Rinehart, 1935.

Steinberg, Mark, and Vladimir Krustalev. *The Fall of the Romanovs: Political Dreams and Personal Struggles in a Time of Revolution.* New Haven, Conn.: Yale University Press, 1995.

Stewart, George. *The White Armies of Russia: A Chronicle of Counterrevolution and Allied Intervention.* New York: Russell & Russell, 1970.

de Stoeckl, Baroness Agnes. *My Dear Marquis.* London: John Murray, 1952.

[Stopford, Hon. Bertie]. *The Russian Diary of an Englishman, Petrograd 1915–1917.* London: William Heinemann, 1919.

Strakhovsky, Leonid I. *Intervention at Archangel: The Story of Allied Intervention and Russian Counterrevolution in North Russia, 1918–1920.* New York: Howard Fertig, 1971.

Summers, Anthony, and Tom Mangold. *The File on the Tsar.* New York: Harper & Row, 1976.

Surguchev, I. *Detstvo Imperatora Nikolaia II.* Paris: Payot, 1953.

Sverdlova, Klaudia. *Jacob M. Sverdlov.* Moscow: Progress, 1945.

Sykes, Brian. *The Seven Daughters of Eve.* New York: W. W. Norton, 2001.

Tager, A. B. *The Decay of Tsarism: The Beilis Trial.* Philadelphia: J. B. Lippincott, 1935.

Taina tsarskikh ostankov. Materialy nauchnoi konferentsii 'Posledniaia stanitsa istorii tsarskoi sem'i: itogi izucheniia Ekaterinburgskoi tragedii. Ekaterinburg: Uralskii, 1994.

Taylor, Edmund. *The Fall of the Dynasties: The Collapse of the Old Order 1905–1922.* Garden City, N.Y.: Doubleday, 1963.

Thurbon, Colin. *In Siberia.* New York: HarperCollins, 1999.

Timms, Robert, ed. *Nicholas and Alexandra: The Last Imperial Family of Tsarist Russia.* New York: Harry N. Abrams, 1998.

Toland, John. *Adolf Hitler.* New York: Ballantine Books, 1976.

Trewin, J. C. *The House of Special Purpose.* London: Macmillan, 1975.

Trotsky, Leon. *O Lenine.* Moscow: State Central Publishing, 1927.

―――. *A History of the Russian Revolution.* 3 vols. New York: Simon & Schuster, 1932.

―――. *Stalin.* London: Hollis & Carter, 1947.

―――. *Diary in Exile, 1935.* Cambridge, Mass.: Harvard University Press, 1953.

Trufanov, Sergei. *The Mad Monk of Russia: Life, Memoirs, and Confessions of Sergei Mikhailovich Trufanov (Iliodor).* New York: Century, 1918.

Tuchman, Barbara. *The Guns of August.* New York: Dell, 1963.

Tupper, Harmon. *To the Great Ocean: Siberia and the Trans-Siberian Railway.* Boston: Little, Brown, 1965.

Ubiistvo tsarskoi semi Romanovykh, Sbornik dokumentov, statei, vospominanii. Sverdlovsk: Vest, Ural-Sovety, 1991.

Ullman, Richard H. *Intervention and the War.* Vol. 1 of *Anglo-Soviet Relations 1917–1921.* Princeton, N.J.: Princeton University Press, 1961.

Ulyanova-Yelizarova, Anna. *Vospomininaniya ob Ilyiche.* Moscow: Partinoe Izdatelstvo, 1934.

U.S. Department of State. *Papers Relating to the Foreign Relations of the United States, 1918; Russia, 1918.* 3 vols. Washington, D.C.: U.S. Government Printing Office, 1931–1932.

―――. *Papers Relating to the Foreign Relations of the United States, 1919; Russia, 1919.* Washington, D.C.: U.S. Government Printing Office, 1937.

———. *Papers Relating to the Foreign Relations of the United States; 1920, Russia, 1920*. Washington, D.C.: U.S. Government Printing Office, 1936.

———. *Papers Relating to the Foreign Relations of the United States: The Lansing Papers, 1914–1920*. 2 vols. Washington, D.C.: U.S. Government Printing Office, 1939–1940.

Varneck, Elena, and H. H. Fisher. *The Testimony of Kolchak and Other Siberian Materials*. Palo Alto, Calif.: Stanford University Press, 1935.

Vassili, Count Paul [Princess Catherine Radziwill]. *Behind the Veil at the Russian Court*. London: Cassell, 1913.

Verner, Andrew. *The Crisis of Russian Autocracy: Nicholas II and the 1905 Revolution*. Princeton, N.J.: Princeton University Press, 1990.

Vickers, Hugo. *Alice, Princess Andrew of Greece*. London: Hamish Hamilton, 2000.

Volkogonov, Dmitri. *Lenin*. New York: Free Press, 1994.

Volkov, Alexei. *Souvenirs d'Alexis Volkov, Valet de Chambre de Tsarina Alexandra Feodorovna, 1910–1918*. Paris: Payot, 1928.

Vorres, Ian. *The Last Grand Duchess*. London: Hutchinson, 1964.

Vyrubova, Anna. *Memories of the Russian Court*. New York: Macmillan, 1923.

Walsh, Edmund A. *The Fall of the Russian Empire*. Boston: Little, Brown, 1928.

Ward, Colonel John. *With the "Die-Hards" in Siberia*. New York: George H. Doran, 1920.

Warth, Robert D. *Nicholas II: The Life and Reign of Russia's Last Monarch*. Westport, Conn.: Praeger, 1997.

Waters, General Hely-Hutchinson Wallscourt. *Potsdam and Doorn*. London: John Murray, 1935.

Welch, Frances. *The Romanovs and Mr. Gibbes*. London: Short Books, 2002.

Wheeler-Bennett, John W. *Brest-Litovsk: The Forgotten Peace, March 1917*. London: Macmillan, 1963.

White, John Albert. *The Siberian Intervention*. Princeton, N.J.: Princeton University Press, 1950.

Wilson, Colin. *Clues! A History of Forensic Detection*. New York: Warner Books, 1991.

Wilton, Robert, and George Gustav Telberg. *The Last Days of the Romanovs*. London: Thorton Butterworth, 1920.

Witte, Count Serge. *The Memoirs of Count Witte*. Edited by Sydney Harcave. Armonk, New York: M. E. Sharpe, 1990.

Wonlar-Larsky, Nadine. *The Russia That I Loved*. London: Elsie MacSwinney, 1937.

Wood, Ruth Kedzie. *Honeymooning in Russia*. New York, Dodd, Mead, 1911.

Wortman, Richard. *Scenarios of Power: Myth and Ceremony in Russian Monarchy, from Alexander II to the Abdication of Nicholas II*. Princeton, N.J.: Princeton University Press, 2000.

Yakubovskii, Edvard. *Rasstrel v Podvale*. Ekaterinburg: Bank Kylityrnoi Informatsii, 1998.

Yeltsin, Boris. *Against the Grain*. New York: Summit Books, 1990.

Zaitsev, Georgii. *Romanovi v Ekaterinburge: 78 Dnei*. Moscow: Sokrat, 1998.

Zeman, Z. A. B., ed. *Germany and the Revolution in Russia 1915–1918: Documents from the Archives of the German Foreign Ministry*. London: Oxford University Press, 1958.

Znamenov, Vadim. *Nicholas II: The Imperial Family*. St. Petersburg: Arbis, 1998.

Zuliani, Mariolina Doria de. *Tsarskaya semya: Poslednii akt tragededii*. Moscow: Khudozhestvennaya Literatura, 1991.

Periodicals and Newspapers

"A on umer v svoyei krovati." *Vechernii Yekaterinburg*, January 17, 1996.

Ackerman, Carl. "How the Czar Was Doomed to Death." *Current History Monthly* 9, no. 2, 1919.

Akimov, Alexei. "Vospominaniya." *Konstrukziia gazeta* 96, August 11, 1957.

Alekseev, S., and G. Kaeta. "Ot aresta do rasstrela, 1." *Ural'skii rabochii* 213, September 16, 1990.

_____. "Ot aresta do rasstrela, 2." *Ural'skii rabochii* 219, September 23, 1990.

Alekseyev, D. "Tsar' sam sebe stiral ispodneye i gotovil na primuse." *Golos*, August 16–22, 1993.

Alekseev, S. "Yekaterinburgskii uznik ne tolko Nikolai II, no i knyaz GE Lvov." *Kongress sootechestvennikov* 2, 1991.

Alexandrov, A. "Poslednii put' poslednego tsarya." *Udmurtskaia Pravda*, August 11–12, 1993.

Ananich, Boris, and Rafail Ganelon. "Nikolai II." *Voprosy istorii* 2, 1993.

Anderson, A. "BBC protic Sokolova ili eshchyo odna versiya rasstrela tsarskoi semi." *Na smenu!*, May 21, 1991.

Anisov, L. "Sledstvennoye delo Nikolaya Sokolova." *Literaturnaya Rossiya* 40, October 5, 1990.

Arsen'ev, V., and I. Kots. "Sledovatel' Solov'ev zakryvayet 'delo Romanovykh.'" *Komsomolskaia Pravda*, February 7, 1995.

Avdayev, Alexander. "Nikolai Romanovi v Tobolsk v Ekaterinburge." *Krasnaia Nov* 5, 1928.

Avdonin, Alexander. "Taina tsarskoi mogily." *Uralskii rabochii* 5, November 1991.

_____. "Istoriyu ne zakopat: Beseda s predsedatelem fonda 'Obreteniye.'" *Na smenu!* 24, December 1992.

_____. "In Search of the Place of Burial of the Remains of the Czar's Family." *Historical Genealogy* 1, 1993.

_____. "Investigation of the Sources on the Death of the Romanovs and the Search for Their Remains." *Historical Genealogy* 2, 1993.

_____. "Versiya staroi Koptyakovskoi dorogi. Ob istorii poiskov ostankov imperatorskoi sem'i." *Istochnik* 5, 1994.

Belikov, Yurii. "Pokhozhe, obnaruzheno mesto kazni braa poslednego imperatora." *Komsomolskaia Pravda*, June 13, 1996.

Blazhnova, T. "On k nam vozvrashchaetsya." *Knizhnoe obozreniye* 36, 1993.

Bogoslovskaia, E. Ugolovnoe delo po povodu Nikolaia II zakryto." *Chas pik* 7/641, September 22, 1995.

_____. "Taina tsasaevicha: dlinnaia doroga k istine." *Chas pik* 8/747, February 8, 1997.

Bolotin, A. "A taina ostalas' tainoi." *Uralskii rabochii*, June 18, 1993.

Borovikov, D., and D. Gavrilov. "Rasstrelyany proletarskoi rukoi: eshchyo odin neizvestnyi document ob ubiistve tsarskoi semi." *Ural* 11, 1990.

Bovkun, E. "Ubiitsa sidit ne v kazhdom." *Izvestiia*, October 3, 1997.

Bozhov, N. "O stat'e Zhotesa Medvedeva 'Do i posle tragedii.'" *Ural* 4, 1992.

Bubnova, N. "Ot Vindzorskogo zamka do Koptyakov." *Oblastnaya gazeta*, April 26, 1995.

_____. "Taina Porosenkova loga perestala byt' tainoi." *Oblastnaya gazeta*, May 26, 1995.

_____. "Slovo chesti oplacheno zhizn'yu." *Oblastnaya gazeta*, June 27, 1995.

Buranov, Yu., and V. Krustalev. "Pokhishcheniye pretendenta: Neizvestnyi dnevnik Mikhaila Romanova." *Sovershenno sekretno* 9, 1990.

Bykov, Paul. "Posledniye dni poslednego tsarya." *Arkhiv Russkoi Revolyutsii* 17, 1928.

Chikin, M. "Tsarya nashli, a gde tsarevich?" *Komsomolskaia Pravda*, July 14, 1993.

Chuyev, F. "Sto sorok besed s Molotovym: (Iz dnevnika)." *Rodina* 3, 1991.

Davydova, I. "Pyat tomov o rasstrele tsarskoi semi." *Moskovskiye novosti* 1, 1993.

"Dni pokayaniya v Yekaterinburge." *Russky vestnit* 28–29, 1992.

"Dokumenty v istorii i istoriya v dokumentakh: [Ob obstoyatel'stvakh rassledovaiya uniistva tsarskoi sem'i]." *Oblastnaya gazeta*, December 9, 1992.

Eggert, K. "Taina 'Anastasii' bluzka k razresheniyu." *Izvestiya*, May 20, 1994.

"Eksperty utverzhdayut: ostanki poslednego imperatora naideny." *Uralskii rabochkii*, July 1, 1992.

"Fal'shivaya Anastasiya." *Rossiiskaya gazeta*, October 21, 1994.

Fletcher, Richard. "Royal Mothers and Their Children." *Good Housekeeping* 54, no. 4, April 1912.

Fogarty, Mary Ann. "Attending the Romanov Funeral." *Royalty Digest* 8, no. 3/87, September 1998.

Frolova, I. "Delo o tsarskikh kostiakh. Peterburgskie eksperty schitaiut, chto v nem rano stavit' tochku." *Komsomol'skaya pravda* 225, December 5, 1997.

Ganichev, V., and S. Ganicheva. "Kremlevskaya kukgnya." *Moskva* 11, 1991.

Gavrilov, D. "Mir nikogda ne uznayet, chto my s nimi sdelali." *Ural* 12, 1993.

"Generalnyi prokuror RF V. Stepankov podgotovil dlya glavy pravitelstva Chernomyrdina dokladnuyu zapisku s predlozheniyem o sozdanii gosudarstvennoi komissii po issledovaniyu predpolagaemykh ostankov imperatorskoi semi Nikolaya II." *Na smeni!*, August 4, 1993.

Gill, Peter, et al. "Identification of the Remains of the Romanov Family by DNA Analysis." *Nature Genetics* 6, February 1994.

Gilliard, Pierre. "Tutor to the Tsarevich." *Atlantic Monthly* 1153, September 1933.

Gintsel, L. "Sokrovishcha imperatora: Sud'ba dragotsennostei: ostavlennikh tsarskoi sem'ei v 1918 gody v Tobolskom monastyre." *Oblastnaya gazeta* 104–106, nos. 9, 11, 15, December 1992.

Glinski, B. "Tsarskiye deti i ikh nastavniki. Istoricheskiye ocherki s portretami i illyustratsiyami." *Moskovskii zhurnal* 9, 1992.

Golovnin, V. "Eksponaty zagovoryat?" *Uralskii rabochii*, February 23, 1993.

––––––. "Ranen v Yaponii, ubit na Urale. Analiz-v Anglii." *Rabochya tribuna*, June 19, 1993.

Goriachkin, D. "Togda chekisty eshche boialis' oglaski." *Ekspert* 36, September 22, 1997.

Goza, William. "William R. Maples, Forensic Historian." *Journal of Forensic Sciences* 44, no. 4, 1999.

Gubanov, A. "Krasnye tsareubiitsy." *Russkie vesti* 175/1342, 1997.

Gurnov, A. "Net tsarya v svoyom Otechestve?" *Komsomolskaya Pravda*, July 8, 1993.

"Informatsiya [Rossikiye i amerikanskiye spetsialisty postavili okonchatalnunyu tochku v rassledovanii sub'by Romanovykh]." *Yalskii rabochii*, September 2, 1995.

Ioffe, G. "Dom osobogo naznacheniya: Yurovsky Ya. M. Vospominaniya komendanta Doma osobogo naznacheniya v Yekaterinburge." *Korona i eshalfot*, Moscow, 1991.

––––––. "V sushchnosti ya uzhe umer." *Literaturnaya gazeta*, September 1, 1993.

––––––. "Mezhdu Tobolskom i Yekaterinburgom. Novye dannye o sube tsarskoi semi." *Nauka i zhizn* 10, 1993.

"Istoriyu ne zakopat." *Na smenu!*, December 24, 1992.

Kamenshchik, V. "Kammi yego Velichestva: [O zaderzhanii organami OBKhSS v Sverdlovske v 1942 g. khranitelei tsarskikh dragotsennostei pri poputke prodazhi]." *Uralskii sledopyt* 10, 1992.

"Kanonizatsiya tsarskoi sem'i snova otlozhena." *Izvestiya*, October 10, 1995.

Kashits, V. "Vse li deti Nikolaya rasstrelyany v Yekaterinburge? Eshchyo odna versiya o sudbe tsarskoi semi." *Literaturnaya gazeta* 39, July 31, 1991.

––––––. "Tsarskiye nasledniki sredi nas (Pochti detektivnaya dokumental'naya istoriya trekhletnikh poiskov dokazatel'stv)." *Rossiyane* 10–11, 1994.

Kasvinov, M. K. "Twenty-three Steps Down." *Zvezda* 8–9, 1972; 7–10, 1973.

"Khoronit li tsarya v Yekaterinburge? Zayavleniye Velikoi knyagini Leonidy Georgiyevny dlya Rossiskogo televideniya i pressy." *Vechernii Yekaterinburge*, November 24, 1992.

King, Greg, and Penny Wilson. "Inheritance of Blood: Official Anti-Semitism and the Last of the Romanovs." *Atlantis Magazine: In the Courts of Memory* 3, no. 3, 2002.

Kirsanovna, N. "Poslednii put poslednego tsarya." *Ekho planety* 40, 1992.

Kokovtsov, Count Vladimir. "La Verite sur la Tragedie d'Ekaterinbourg." *Revue des Deux Mondes*, October 1, 1929.

Kolesnikov, Lev, Gurgen Pashinyan, and Sergei Abramov. "Anatomical Appraisal of the

Skulls and Teeth Associated with the Family of Tsar Nicolay Romanov." *Anatomical Record* 265, no. 1, 2001.

Koridorov, Ye. "Prakh osyadet v koshel'kakh?" *Na smenu!*, October 27, 1992.

Koryakova, L., and I. Koryakov. "Raskopki na lesnoi polyane." *Nauka Urala*, September 14, 1991.

———. "Taina lesnoi polyany. Rasskazyvayut uchastniki iyulskikh raskopok." *Verchernii Yekaterinburg*, November 12, 1991.

Krayukhin, Sergei. "Sud'bu ubitykh v Yekaterinburge Romanovykh soznatel'no razdelili ikh priblizhennyye." *Izvestiya*, April 5, 1996.

Kudryashova, T. "Rossiya, Romanovy, Ural." *Uralskii Rabochii*, April 30, 1993.

Kulikovskaga-Romanova, O. "Monarkhiya-eto sostoyaniye dukhas." *Moskovskiye novosti* 57, 1994.

Kurasheva, T. "A taina ostalas tainoi." *Uralskii rabochii*, June 18, 1993.

———. "Zagadka na dolgiye gody." *Uralskii rabochii*, July 14, 1995.

Kurth, Peter. "The Mystery of the Romanov Bones." *Vanity Fair*, January 1993.

Kuzmin, S. "Tsarskaya semya eshcho ne v sbore." *Komsomolskaya Pravda*, July 23, 1993.

Latyshev, A. "Mesto ubiisty vakantno, Novye dokumenty o rasstrele tsarskoi semi." *Rossiiskaya gazeta*, August 29, 1992.

———. "Lenin v rasstrele ne uchastvoval." *Rodina* 8, 1993.

———. "Rasstrel tsarskoi semi: znal li o nyom Lenin?" *Vechernii Yekaterinburg*, July 27, 1993.

Leshovsky, M. "Za cho my ubili Gosudarya imperatora?" *LG-Dos ê* 5, 1993.

Lyoshkin, N. "Poslednii reis Romanovykh." *Rifey-89*, Chelyabinsk, 1989.

Maksimova, Ye. "Naidennyye pod Yekaterinburgom ostanki deistvitel'no yavyalyutsya ostankami chlenov tsarskoi sem'i." *Izvestiya*, April 6, 1994.

Mamysheva, N. "Oshiblas' li istoriya?" *Slovo* 7–8, 1994.

Maples, William, and D. Austin-Smith. "The Reliability of Skull/Photograph Superimposition in Individual Identification." *Journal of Forensic Sciences* 39, no. 2, 1994.

Markov, A. "Sudba Mikhaila Romanova." *Vecherniaia Perm*, January 15, 1990.

Mirkina, I. A., and V. Krustalev. "Sudba Mikhaila Romanova." *Voprosy istorii* 9, Moscow, 1990.

Murzin, A. "O chem rasskazal pered smert'iu tsareubiitsa Petr Ermakov." *Komsomolskaia Pravda* 217, November 25, 1987.

Myasnikov, G. "Filosofiya ubiistva, ili pochemu i kak ya ubil Mikhaila Romanova." *Minuvsheye Vypusk* 15, 1995.

Naymov, S. "Tsareubiitsy: o nekotorykh obstoyatelstavkh gibeli tsarskoi semi." *Molodaya gvardiya* 7, 1990.

Nepein, I. "Komnatnaya devushka Yego Velichestva [Iz zhizni tsarskoi semi v Tobolske v 1917 g. Po stranitsam dnevnika Demidovi]." *Irtysh* 1, 1991.

"Obrashchenie uchastnikov nauchnoi konferentsii—Po tsarskomy delu." *Sovetskaia Rossia* 3/11592, January 9, 1998.

"O predvaritel'nykh itogakh raboty pravitel'stvennoi komissii po izucheniyu voprosov, svyazannykh s issledovaniyem i perezakhoroneniyem ostankov rossiskogo imperatora Nikolaya II i chlenov yego sem'i (informatsiya dlya pressy)." *Vechernii Yekaterinburg*, October 21, 1994.

Orlov, A. "Poslednii imperator Rossii [informatsiya o vystavke v manezhe, Moskva]." *Rossiiskaya gazeta*, May 22, 1993.

"Ostanki tsarskoi semi naideny: Sensatsiya ili falsifikatsiya." *Kongress sootechestvennikov* 2, 1991.

Poutianine, Princess Olga. "Le Grand Duc Michael Alexandrovich." *Revue des Deux Mondes* 18, November 15, 1926.

"Prodazha tsarskikh paltsev-mif. schitaet amerikanskii antripolog Villiam Maples." *Uralskii rabochii*, May 13, 1993.

"Raskopki na lesnoi polyane." *Za vlast Sovetov* 31, 1991.

"Rasskaz zaveduiushchei Permskim partarkhivom N. Alikinoi o vstrechakh s Markovym i prieme Leninym Markova posle ubiista Mikhaila." *Vecherniaia Perm*, February 3, 1990.

"Romanovs Find Closure in DNA." *Nature Genetics* 12, April 1996.

"Romanovy ili net? Ekspertiza prodolzhaetsya." *Vechernii Yekaterinburg*, December 1, 1993.

"Romanovy: Zagadka ostayetsya [Soveshchaniye sudebno meditsinskikh ekspertov v Yekaterinburge]." *Na smenu!*, May 5, 1992.

Ross, Nikolai. "Zapiska Iurovskogo' ili 'Zapiska Pokrovskogo?" *Russkaia mysl'* 4168, April 10–16, 1997.

Ryabov, G. "Zhelayushchikh ne nashlos." *Za vlast Sovetov* 8–9, 11, 1991.

Ryabov, G., and G. Ioffe. "Prinuzhdeny Vas rasstreliat." *Rodina* 4–5, 1989.

Semchevskaya, E. "Velikii Knyazii." *Douglavy Orel* 15, 1921.

Shvortsova, Ye. "Yekaterinburg zhazhdet arii varyazhskogo gostya." *Rabochaya tribuna*, August 14, 1992.

"Skelety-to ne vse." *Na smenu!*, August 4, 1993.

"Skol'ko lyudei, stol'ko i versii: Podborka materialov." *Oblastnaya gazeta*, December 1, 1992.

"Sluchainoye sovpadeniye pochti neveroyatno Zaklyuchebiye voronezhskikh ekspertov po povody predpolagaemykh ostankov tsarskoi semi." *Uralskii rabochii*, February 29, 1992.

Smetanina, S. "Briussel'skaia mogila russkogo tsaria." *Kommersant deili* 21, February 10, 1998.

Sorkin, Yu. "Na stantsii Yekaterinburg-1." *Nauka Urala* 27, July 18–25, 1991.

Stepanov, A. "Vagon absurda. Voina ambitsii iz-za ostankov tsarskoi sem'i pozorit Rossiiu." *Novye Izvestiia* 17, November 27, 1997.

"Sudba Mikhaila Romanova: Publikatsiya dokumentov, podgotovka k pechati i presidloviye I A Mirikinoi i VM Khrustalyova." *Voprosy istorii* 9, 1990.

Ulyanova-Yelizarova, Anna I. "O Lenine." *Proletarskaya Revolyutsiya* 2–3, February–March 1927.

"Universitet v avstraliiskom g. Melbourn raspolagayet unikalnymi dokumentami dopolnyayushchimi uzhe izvestnye fakty ubiistva tsarskoi semi v Yekaterinburge." *Rossiskiye vesti*, September 30, 1993.

Viner, V. "Vmesto tochki-zapyataya." *Oblastnaya gazeta*, May 25, 1993.

———. "Yest' takaya versiya." *Vechernii Yekaterinburg*, August 6, 1993.

Vinogradov, V. "Ya chasto dumayu za chto yego kasnili." *Nezavisimaya gazeta*, April 1994.

Yakovlev, V. V. [Konstantin Miachin]. "Poslednii reis Romanovykh. Vospiminaniia." *Ural* 8, 1988.

Yakubovsky, E. "V pogone za sensatsiyei. V istorii s identifikatsiyei ostankov tochku stavit rano." *Vechernii Yekaterinburg*, June 23, 1992.

———. "Versiya, Versiya . . . Yeshchylo versiya?" *Verchenii Yekaterinburg*, June 1, 1994.

———. "Itak, ona zvalas' Mariya?" *Vechernii Yekaterinburg*, September 23, 1994.

———. "Romanovskoye delo-vzglyad iz za okeana." *Vechernii Yekaterinburg*, October 17, 1995.

Zeepvat, Charlotte. "The Lost Tsar." *Royalty Digest* 8, no. 1/85, July 1998.

———. "The Funeral of the Last Tsar." *Royalty Digest* 8, no. 2/86, August 1998.

Zhivotovsky, Dr. Lev. "Annuals of Human Biology." *Journal of the Society for the Study of Human Biology* 26, no. 6, November–December 1999.

Archival Source

Germany

Hessian Staatsarkhiv, Darmstadt

MPR Productions Archive, Munich

Russia
Arkhiv Presidentsii Rossiya Federatsii, Moscow
Russkia tsentr dokumentatsii Istorii, Moscow
State Archives of the Russian Federation, Moscow
Tsentr dokumentatsii obshchestvennykh organizatsii Sverdlovskoi oblasti, Ekaterinburg

United Kingdom
Public Record Office, Kew

United States
Bahkmatieff Archive, Columbia University, New York
National Archives, Washington, D.C.

Private Collections

The following individuals have generously provided us with use of archival materials, photographs, manuscripts, and other documents that they retain in private collections:
    Patte Barham
    Gretchen Haskin
    Brien Horan
    Peter Kurth
    Victoria Lewis and Frank Simone
    Ian Lilburn
    Dimitry Macedonsky
    Greg Rittenhouse
    Dimitri Volkogonov

Other Media

"Anastasia: Dead or Alive?" Produced by Michael Barnes for Nova, PBS Television, 1995.
"Bones of Contention." Produced and directed by Elliot Halpern and Simcha Jacobovici, Reunion Films Ltd., 1993, UK/Canada.
"The Mystery of the Last Tsar." Produced and directed by Victoria Lewis and Frank Simone, Cymru Films, 1997.
"New Findings" (interview with Geli Ryabov), April 1989. U.S. distribution through the Holy Archangels Center, Washington, D.C.
"Nicholas and Alexandra." Hosted by Prince Michael of Kent. Executive producers for Granada TV, U.K.: Dianne Nelmes, Simon Welfare; produced by Armorer Wason; produced and directed by Michael Beckham. Granada TV, U.K., 1994.
"Revenge of the Romanovs." Produced by Home Vision Entertainment, France, 1998.

Index

Page numbers in *italic type* indicate illustrations

Abramov, Sergei, 7, 407–15, 418,
    421–27, 430–31, 432, 434, 436,
    440–41, 442–43, 454–57, 468, 477
Abrikossow, Dimitri, 43, 202
Ackerman, Carl, 104, 350
Agafonov, Gregory, 347
Agnes, Sister, 21, 118, 119
    on Avdayev, 166, 216–17, 251
    on Yurovsky, 257
Akimov, Alexei, 292–93
Aksyuchits, Viktor, 480
Akulov. *See* Nikulin, Gregory
Alapayevsk executions, 210, 219–21,
    250, 336–37, 355, 451, 474
Alekseev, Veniamin, 439–40, 469
Alexander, king of Serbia, 11
Alexander I, emperor, 11
Alexander II, emperor, 1, 11, 31, 39,
    254
Alexander III, emperor, 2, 32, 34, 39,
    40, 49, 72, 449, 528
Alexander Mikhailovich, grand duke,
    2, 492
Alexandra, queen of Great Britain and
    Ireland, 4, 49, 372, 373
Alexandra Feodorovna, empress, 1, 20,
    32, 98, 100–102, 112, 129–35,
    213, 342
    arrest of, 57
    coronation of, 36–37
    departure for Tobolsk by, 59
    departure from Tobolsk by, 85–87,
        88–90, 102
    early life of, 33–34
    execution of, 303–5
    funeral for, 489–93
    hemophilia and, 51–52

ill health of, 43–44, 46, 51, 237
jewels of, 135–36, 319, 322–23, 372
marriage of, 34, 36
posthumous romanticization of,
    494–95
relationship with daughters of,
    45–51, 53
relationship with son of, 51, 53, 54
religious piety of, 34, 48, 51
remains of, 403, 405, 414, 427, 430,
    443, 451, 459–60, 464
royal relatives of, 4
Special Detachment's attitude
    toward, 234, 236–37
title of, 26
on Yakolev, 84
Yakovlev on, 95
See also imperial family
Alexandrov, Victor, 374
Alexeiev, Michael, 55, 187
Alexei II, patriarch, 475, 477, 478,
    480–81, 483, 494, 495, 497, 502
Alexei Nikolaievich, tsesarevich, 1, 20,
    78, 139, 143, 145, 170–72, 202
    Derevenko's treatment of, 155, 156,
        157, 159, 172, 179, 215, 216, 223,
        228–29, 343, 584–85n. 3
    execution of, 303–5, 309–10
    fate of, 180–81, 415–16, 427, 437,
        459–62, 464, 465, 469–70
    frailty of, 139, 140
    hemophilia of, 51, 52–53, 84, 271
    personal qualities of, 51–54
    reported burning of corpse of, 330
    SEARCH and, 452
    Special Detachment's attitude
        toward, 234, 237–38

Storozhev on, 177–78
succession to throne by, 57
title of, 26
unfound remains of, x
Yakovlev and, 83–84
See also imperial family
Alice, princess of Greece, 445
Alix of Hesse. *See* Alexandra
  Feodorovna
All-Russian Party of the Monarchist
  Center, 478
American forensic team, x, 22, 417–34,
  455
anarchists, 38, 181, 215–16, 249, 261,
  262
"Anastasia: Dead or Alive?" (television
  documentary), 441
Anastasia: The Riddle of Anna Anderson
  (Kurth), ix
Anastasia Nikolaievna, grand duchess,
  1, 45, 47, 59, 66, 138, 377, 378,
  391, 502
  execution of, 303–4, 310–11, 347,
    470
  fate of, ix–x, 22, 416, 419, 425–28,
    431–34, 437, 440–41, 443,
    451–57, 458, 462, 464, 469–70,
    483, 495, 505, 516. *See also*
    Anderson, Anna
  missing remains of, 22, 483
  personal qualities of, 50, 240–41
  rifle incident and, 169
  SEARCH and, 452
  Special Detachment's attitude
    toward, 238–39, 246–47
  See also grand duchesses; imperial
    family
"Anatomical Appraisal of the Skulls
  and Teeth Associated with the
  Family of Tsar Nikolai Romanov"
  (Kolesnikov and Pashinyan),
  455–56
Anderson, Anna, ix, x, 299, 377, 378,
  432, 437, 453, 505, 516, 591n. 21
Andrei Vladimirovich, grand duke, 78
Andropov, Yuri, 384, 521

anti-Semitism, 14, 253, 286–87, 299
  of Alexander III, 39, 40
  blame for imperial family murders
    and, 350, 352–53, 356, 359, 367,
    392, 439, 490–91, 495, 501, 523
  of Ford, 366–67
  of Nicholas II, 39–42, 496, 527
  Revolution of 1905 pograms, 39–40
  of White Army, 18, 24, 186–87, 509
Antonina, sister, 20, 276, 279
Arakcheyev, Boris, 484
Artishevsky, Ivan, 479, 486
Avdayev, Alexander, 5, 15, 20, 79–80,
  82, 83, 94, 101, 116, 117–19, 125,
  126, 149, 251, 264, 514
  as commandant of Ipatiev House,
    130, 154–82, 215–28, 248–49
  treatment of imperial family by,
    164–67, 234, 235, 239–40,
    579–80n. 99
Avdayeva, Augusta, 116, 117, 514, 515
Avdonin, Alexander, 7, 381–84,
  386–88, 392–93, 395–98, 400,
  401, 403, 410, 416, 429–30,
  435–39, 442, 452, 452–53,
  468–69, 513, 521, 525
Avdonin, Galina, 452–53

Baden, Michael, 7, 417, 422, 424,
  427–28, 432
Baker, James, 416, 417, 418, 430
Balfour, Arthur, 352
Bashmakov, A., 374
Basily, Nicholas, 57
Beatrix, queen of the Netherlands, 487
Beilis, Mendel, 42
Beloborodov, Alexander, 5, 79, 81,
  95–96, 99, 101, 112–13, 117, 145,
  209, 219–28, 244, 245, 249, 250,
  264, 279, 513–14
Belogradsky, Anatoly, 343
Benckendorff, Count Paul von, 3, 34,
  60, 66, 68, 213
Berzin, Pashka, 351
Berzin, Reinhold, 5, 224, 225–27, 245,
  286, 290, 293

Bessedowsky, Gregory, 460
Biron, George, 351
Bittner, Klaudia, 6, 60, 63, 507
Black Hundreds, 41
Blank, Maria Alexandrovna, 71
Blinkov, Vyacheslav, 437–38
Blokhin, Alexander, 7, 409, 418
"Bloody Sunday" massacre (1905),
    37–38
Bobrova, Irina, 488
Boki, Gleb, 287
Bolshakov, Vladimir, 392–93
Bolshevik Party
  abortive coup of July 1917, 58
  demonstrations against, 181–82, 284
  divergencies in, 24–25
  Ekaterinburg evacuation by, 341
  elections and, 199
  German peace negotiations by,
      76–77
  German threat to, 284–85, 287, 289
  Gregorian calendar changeover by,
      27
  Ipatiev House guards and, 120, 124,
      234
  leading members of, 5–6
  Lenin's power struggle with, 196–97
  murder of imperial family by, 13–14,
      201
  overthrow of Provisional
      Government by, 66, 71
  Romanov exiles from, 294
  Romanovs as targets of, 201, 203,
      208–10, 218–21, 261
  Yurovsky and, 255, 256
  See also Central Executive
      Committee; Civil War
Bolshevik Revolution (1917). See
    October Revolution
Bonch-Bruyevich, Vladimir, 204, 225,
    226, 227
bones. See skeletal remains
Bones of Contention (television film),
    441
Born to the Revolution (documentary
    film), 382

Botkin, Dimitri, 62
Botkin, Eugene, 3, 20, 60, 61–62, 89,
    91, 92, 101, 130, 155, 215, 216,
    263–64, 272, 280, 376, 380, 498,
    499, 523
  on Alexandra's maladies, 43
  execution of, 290, 301, 303, 305,
      308–9, 312–13
  remains of, 403, 404–5, 411, 420,
      424, 430, 443, 449, 451, 460–61,
      474, 476
Botkin, Gleb, 44, 46, 49, 50, 54, 62,
    63, 86, 137–38, 149, 504–5
Botkin, Peter, 61, 62
Botkin, Serge, 61
Botkin, Tatiana, 50, 62, 86, 87–88,
    137–38, 409, 504–5
Botkin, Yuri, 62
Brasol, Boris, 366
Braun, Eva, 466–67
Brest-Litovsk. See Treaty of Brest-
    Litovsk
Bronte, Professor (genetics expert),
    449
Brotherhood of St. John of Tobolsk,
    67–68
Brussels, Belgium, 22, 375, 376, 377,
    378, 483
Brusyanin, Leonid, 280, 300, 312,
    357
Buchanan, Sir George, 203
Buimirov, Vassili Afanasievich, 105–6,
    131, 134, 177, 227, 274–76
Buivid, Victor, 311–12
Bulygin, Paul, 6, 18, 174, 207, 239,
    349, 355, 361, 365, 366, 368,
    371–72, 508
burial controversy. See funeral of
    imperial family
Burtsev, Vladimir, 213–14
Bury, William, 105–6
Buxhoeveden, Sophie, baroness, 3, 20,
    45, 48, 50, 60–61, 139–44, 251,
    372, 505–6
  betrayal of Romanovs by, 68–69,
      141–43, 148, 265, 505

credibility of Ekaterinburg reports of, 158–59, 160, 161, 163, 167, 1174
release from Ekaterinburg of, 147–48, 151–53
Bykov, Paul, 5, 18–19, 79, 82–83, 90, 94, 117, 168–69, 170, 172, 204–5, 210, 216, 217–18, 219, 228, 236, 237, 241, 246, 249, 288, 339, 381, 458

canonization, 13, 21–22, 378, 476, 482, 494–503
burial controversy and, 476, 480
Carl Gustaf, king of Sweden, 487
Cathedral of Christ the Savior (Moscow), 477, 480, 502
Cathedral of Our Lady of the Sign (New York City), 380, 483
Cathedral of Peter and Paul Fortress (St. Petersburg), 447, 449
imperial family burial in, xi, 21–22, 475, 478, 479, 484, 488–93
Cathedral of the Savior on Spilled Blood (Ekaterinburg), 523–24
Catherine the Great, empress, 11, 30
Ekaterinburg named after, 103
Pale of Settlement created by, 39
Cecilie, crown princess of Germany, 214
Cemetery of St. Geneviève de Bois (Paris), 375, 378
Central Executive Committee (Soviet), 9, 24, 75, 79, 214, 284, 289, 334–35, 337–38, 338
fabricated rescue plot and, 228
Presidum (VTsIK), 83, 93, 97, 195, 197
Yakovlev and, 71, 82
See also Ural Regional Soviet
Chachavadze, prince, 374
Chaplinsky (Kiev prosecutor), 42
Charles I, king of England, 11, 525–26, 527
Cheka, 9, 20, 187, 198, 199, 393, 509
Buxhoeveden questioned by, 148

Ermakov and, 115
state terror and, 76, 188
See also Ekaterinburg Cheka; GPU; KGB; NKVD; Perm Cheka
Chelyabinsk, 191–94
Chelyin (artist), 100, 520
Chemodurov, Terenty, 3, 20, 60, 64, 89, 92, 101, 130, 155, 160, 165, 169, 170, 174, 175, 343, 344, 360, 506
departure from Ipatiev House, 156
Cherepanov, Ivan, 121
Chernomyrdin, Viktor, 479
Chicago Daily News, 19
Chicherin, G. V., 5, 213, 225
Christian IX, king of Denmark, 31
Christian X, king of Denmark, 212
Chukazev, Serge, 117, 250, 324
Church of St. Job the Sufferer (Brussels), 22, 375, 376, 377, 378
Church of St. Nicholas (Four Brothers mine site), 524
Churkin, Alexei, 515
Civil War, 185–200, 212, 214, 236, 262, 289, 334, 390, 506
Bolsheviks and, 58, 66, 71, 181–82, 284, 509
Chelyabinsk occupation and, 191–94
Constitutional Democrats and, 75, 194, 196
Czech Corps and, 179, 180, 194–95, 262
Ekaterinburg and, 10, 78, 195, 248, 258, 261, 280–81, 282, 289, 325, 341, 346, 365, 459, 522
fall of Perm and, 348
Kerensky and, 5, 18, 58, 59, 66, 71, 189, 355
Left SRs and, 285–86
martial law and, 198, 199
Mensheviks and, 75, 196, 197, 199
retreat of White and Czech forces, 509
Soviet government move to Moscow, 77, 203
Tobolsk taken by Whites and, 153

Civil War *(continued)*
  Trans-Siberian Railway and, 78, 190, 195, 262, 289
Clarke, William, 375, 376
Commission for the Burial of the Romanov Remains, 479, 486, 487, 489
Commission of Forensic Medical Examination of the Skeletal Remains, 442–43
Committee for the Examination of the Question of Windows in the House of Special Purpose, 178, 217
Committee for the Investigation and Preservation of the Holy Imperial Relics, 374
Congress of Old Bolsheviks, 395
Constantine, king of the Hellenes, 487
Constituent Assembly, 9, 74–75, 179, 194, 197, 198, 283, 508
Constitutional Democrats, 75, 194, 196
constitutional monarchy, 38
Council of People's Commissars, 9, 75, 204, 283
Council of Workers' Representatives, 198
counterrevolutionary demonstrations, 181–82
Crankshaw, Edward, 43
Crawford, Rosemary and Donald, 207, 209
cremation, 330, 376, 459–68, 469, 511
  process of, 467–68
Czech Corps, 133, 179, 180, 189–95, 200, 205, 212, 227, 248, 258, 261, 280–81, 282, 289, 325, 459, 509
Czechoslovakian National Council, 189, 190

daylight saving time, 27, 178–79, 296
de Freedericksz, Vladimir, 3
Dehn, Julia ("Lili"), 6, 44, 48, 66
Dehn, Karl Akimovich von, 44

"Delivery of the Romanovs to the Ural Soviet, The" (painting), *100*, 520
Demidov, J. P., 28–29
Demidova, Anna, 3, 60, 63–64, 87, 89, 92, 101, 130, 135, 155, 322, 380, 498, 499, 524
  execution of, 290, 303–4, 308–9, 311
  remains of, 403, 404, 410, 420, 443, 451, 459–60, 462, 464, 465, 474
Denikin, Anton, 55, 187, 372
Derevenko, Nicholas, 3, 52–53, 62, 171, 506
Derevenko, Vladimir, 3, 60, 62, 85–86, 139, 143, 148–50, 181, 220, 263, 348, 360, 361–62, 413, 476, 506
  treatment of Alexei by, 155, 156, 157, 159, 172, 179, 215, 216, 223, 228–29, 343, 584–85n. 3
Deryabin, Nikita, 280, 300, 308, 312, 357
Deterikhs, Michael, 6, 17–18, 19, 78, 112–13, 121, 123, 149, *193*, 339, 347–50, 352, 354, 365, 368–69, 370–72, 392, 506, 508, 509
Diana, princess of Wales, 485
Diary in Exile (Trotsky), 293–94
Didkovsky, Boris, 80, 99, 101, 117, 250
Dimitri Alexandrovich, prince, 373
Dimitri Konstantinovich, grand duke, 2, 295, 504
Dimitri Pavlovich, grand duke, 492
DNA testing, 22, 393, 403, 441–42, 444–50, 484
  of Anna Anderson, ix
  for hemophilia, 444
  methods, 444, 444–45, 446, 448
  Y-chromosome haplotype, 449
Dobrynin, Anatoly, 167, 178, 515
Dobrynin, Konstantin, 126, 268, 280, 300, 302, 312
dogs of Romanovs, ix–x, 146, 156, 303, 312, 334, 344, 363–64, 516, 571n.123
Dolgoruky, Vassili, prince, 3, 59, 60, 66, 69, 86, 87, 89, 92, 498
  arrest of, 101, 131

death of, 150–51, 261–62
Domnin, Parfen Alekseivich, 350
Dosifei, Metropolitan, 378
Draga, queen of Serbia, 11
Dryagina, Varvara, 277
Duma, creation of, 38
Dzerzhinsky, Felix, 5, 9, 76, 115, 199,
    221, 285

"Earth Yields Up Its Secrets, The"
    (Ryabov), 388–89
Easter Massacre of 1903, 39
Edelshtein, Isidor, 299
Edinburgh, duke of, 445, 484, 487
Efremov, Konstantin, 523
Eichhorn, Hermann von, 286
Ekaterinburg, 9, 10, 78, 341, 488, 522
    bomb incident report, 180–81
    defense of, 258–59, 261
    description of, 103–6, 259–60,
        509–11, 518
    imperial family transported to, 15,
        78–102, 135–45, 248
    later status of, 517–25
    memorial service in, 480, 489
    occupation of, 341, 346, 459
    as proposed final burial site, 473, 477
    White and Czech forces' advance on,
        195, 248, 258, 280–81, 282, 289,
        325, 459, 518
    White Army victims in, 509
    White rule ended in, 365, 509
    Yurovsky's reputation in, 510
    See also Ipatiev House; Ural Regional
        Soviet
Ekaterinburg II (goods depot), 99–100,
    144–45
Ekaterinburg Cheka, 115–17, 123, 394
    rescue attempt fabrications by,
        228–29, 245, 249, 250, 266–67,
        289–90, 292, 334–35, 339–40, 512
Ekaterinburg executions, ix, x, 10–15,
    57, 201, 282–315, 371
    aftermath of, 332–45
    anniversary memorials, 523
    books about, 17–22, 25

disposal of remains. See remains of
    imperial family
eyewitness accounts of, 19–21
false evidence from, 363–64
funeral on eightieth anniversary of,
    479
investigations of, 346–65
Ipatiev House murder room, 10,
    108, 111, 304, 306, 332, 349, 356,
    357–60, 382, 520–21, 522,
    599–601n. 62
Kudrin's memoir of, 511–12
looting during, 313–14
media and, 419, 434
Michael Alexandrovich's murder and,
    207, 208, 210–11, 212
of Romanov retainers, 473–75, 504
speculated survivors of, 470
squad composition, 298–99
symbolism of, 11–15, 527
weapons for, 297–98, 358, 590n. 7
Western view of, 14–15
Yurovsky's accounts of, 509–11
See also Four Brothers mine; Grade
    Crossing 184; Pig's Meadow
Ekaterinburg guards. See Special
    Detachment
Ekaterinburg Soviet, 249, 536
Electoral Commission, disbanding of,
    74
Elizabeth II, queen of Great Britain,
    484–85, 487
Elizabeth Feodorovna ("Ella"), grand
    duchess, 2, 33, 40, 60, 213, 219,
    336, 451, 474
Emiliyanov, Feodor, 515
Enquete judiciare sur l'Assassinat de la
    Famille Imperiale Russe (Sokolov),
    17
Ermakov, Peter, 5, 19–20, 25, 114–15,
    159, 234–38, 241, 243, 250, 261,
    298–99, 301–3, 305, 308–11,
    313–14, 316–19, 321–31, 395,
    459
    on cremation of imperial family
        remains, 459, 460

Ermakov, Peter *(continued)*
    list of Verkh-Isetsk Special
        Detachment contingent, 532
    on role in Romanov murders,
        512–13
Ernst Ludwig, grand duke of Hesse
    und bei Rhine, 4, 77–78
Ersberg, Elizabeth, 3, 60, 63, 139, 143,
    147, 506–7
Eryomenko, Nikolai, 401
"Essays" (Macauley), 525–26
executions. *See* Alapayevsk executions;
    Ekaterinburg executions; Perm
    executions
exhumations
    in 1978–79, 386–89, 429, 434, 436
    in 1991, 397–98, 400–406, 408, 434,
        458, 468, 483
exile entourage of imperial family, 3–4,
    59–65, 101, 139, 498, 499
    burial controversy, 473–74
    executions of, 473–75, 504
    funeral for, 489, 493
    surviving members, 504–8
exiles, Romanov, 295, 519. *See also*
    Romanov Family Association
Extraordinary Commission for
    Combating Counterrevolution
    and Sabotage, 76, 115

Falsetti, Anthony, 7, 452–53, 455
famine, 186, 196, 198, 289
February Revolution (1917), 5, 18, 24,
    203, 256
Fekete, Emil, 299
Fesenko, Ivan, 288
Fife, duke of, 446
Fifth Congress of Soviets, 198, 199,
    210, 285
Figes, Orlando, 283
Filatov, Sergei, 475
Filipchuk, Professor (forensic expert),
    427, 431, 456
Finland, 195
Fischer, Louis, 198
Fisher, Anzelm, 299

Fleming, Peter, 192
Ford, Henry, 366–67
forensic entomology, 463
forensic pathology
    American team, x, 22, 417–34, 455
    DNA testing, ix, 22, 393, 403,
        441–42, 444–50, 484
    exhumation (1978–79), 386–89, 429,
        434, 436
    exhumation (1991), 397–98,
        400–406, 408, 434, 458, 468
    final confirmation of Romanov
        remains by, 475, 477
    modern investigators, 7–8
    photo superimposition identification,
        326–27, 420–22, 429, 430,
        440–41, 443, 453–57, 477
"Forgery, The" (newspaper article),
    392
Fortress of St. Peter and St. Paul. *See*
    Cathedral of St. Peter and St. Paul
    Fortress
Four Brothers mine, 18, 288, 321–31,
    346, 348–49, 356, 360, 361–62,
    365, 377, 386, 429, 439
    chapel built on site, 524
    description of, 321
    remains found at, 370–71, 476
    report of attempted cremation at,
        461–62, 463, 464, 468–70
France, Diane, 7, 452–53, 455
Francis, David, 184
Freemasonry, 40
French Revolution, 11
Froede, Richard, 417
Frolova-Bagreeva, Catherine
    Mikhailovna, 53–54
funeral of imperial family, xi, 21–22,
    443, 473–94
    controversies surrounding, 473–84
    miniature caskets and, 488–89, 490,
        492, 493
    Orthodox churches and, 475–77,
        482–83
    proposed burial sites, 473, 475,
        477–78

symbolism of, 485–86, 493
tourism and, 487–88

Gaida, Rudolf, 191, 193, 194, 250, 261, 518
Galkin, Serge, 83
Ganina Works, 321
Ganin's Pit, *323*
Gedygushev, I. A., 442
genetic testing. *See* DNA testing
George V, king of Great Britain, 4, 58, 203, 350–51, 370, 372, 373, 446, 484
George, grand duke, 480, 486, 502
George Alexandrovich, grand duke, 2, 31, 447, 448
George Mikhailovich, grand duke, 295, 504
Germany, 371, 376
  Bolshevik peace negotiation with, 76–77. *See also* Treaty of Brest-Litovsk
  as Bolshevik threat, 284–85, 287, 289, 338
  double-game Russian policy of, 185–86
  Hitler-Braun cremation in, 466–67
  imperial family rescue and, 78, 212–14, 284
  imperial family's ties with, 4, 77, 212–13, 214
  Russia at war with, 54–56, 212
  Western Front offensive by, 183–84
  See also Mirbach, Wilhelm von;
Gibbes, Charles Sidney, 3, 20, 35, 47, 48, 50, 60, 63, 64, 87, 138, 139, 144, 360, 371–72, 507
  Buxhoeveden and, 142, 505
  Ekaterinburg departure by, 151–53
  on harassment of grand duchesses aboard *Rus*, 140–41
  Ipatiev House reports by, 157
  on Tsesarevich Alexei, 53
Giers, Nicholas de, 372, 373, 374
Gill, Peter, 7, 444–46

Gilliard, Pierre, 3, 16, 20, 60, 135, 139, 144, 150, 360, 365, 371–72, 421, 507
  on Buxhoeveden, 142
  Ekaterinburg departure by, 151–53
  on grand duchesses, 44, 45, 48–49
  imprisonment and, 58, 63, 84, 85
  Ipatiev House reports by, 157, 164, 167
  on Tsesarevich Alexei, 52
glasnost, 522
Glebov, Boris, archpriest, 491
Goebbels, Josef and Magda, 467
Goldschmidt, Pinchas, 501
Golitsyn, Major General, 341
Goloshchokin, Philip [Isaac], 5, 79, 80, 82, 90, 92–93, 101, 222, 224, 228, 230, 232, 244, 245, 248, 249, 250, 282, 284, 287, 291, 293, 300, 305, 314, 324, 328, 335, 339, 511, 514
  power of, 113–14
Gorbachev, Mikhail, 21, 420, 493, 522
Gorbunov, Paul, 326
Gorshokov, Feodor, 347
Gorvat, Lazlo, 299
Goza, William, 418
GPU, 9, 19
Grachev, Vladimir, 523
Grade Crossing 184, 318–19, 325–26, 327, 330, 361, 385–86, 394
  memorial sign, 525
grand duchesses, x, 1, 44
  departure for Tobolsk by, 59
  diaries of, 20
  funeral for, 489–93
  harassment aboard *Rus* of, 140–41, 247
  Ipatiev House guards and, 238–47, 249
  jewels found on corpses of, 319, 322
  rearing of, 45–51, 53
  See also Anastasia Nikolaievna; Marie Nikolaievna; Olga Nikolaievna; Tatiana Nikolaievna
Graves, William, 188

Great and the Small and the Coming of the Antichrist, The. See *Protocols of the Zionist Elders*

Great Britain
  denial of Romanov asylum by, 4, 58, 203, 370, 484
  DNA testing of imperial family remains and, 445
  imperial family funeral and, 484–85, 487, 492
  imperial family's possessions and, 372–73, 519
  imperial family's remains and, 370, 372–73
  imperial family's ties with, 4, 49, 58, 203, 370, 445, 446, 484
  Romanov exiles in, 295, 519
  World War I and, 179, 180, 184

Great War. See World War I

Gregorian calendar, 27

Grinfeld, Viktor, 299

Gritsaenko, Peter, 8, 384, 393, 397–98, 402, 406–7, 408, 416, 420, 435, 438

Gryannik, Anatoly, 450–51

guards, Ipatiev House. See Special Detachment

Guchkov, Alexander, 57

Guensche, Otto, 466

Gunich, Andrei, 492–93

Gurtovaya, Svetlana, 8, 408, 415, 443

Guseva, Lydia, 516–17

Hagelberg, Erika, 444

Halliburton, Richard, 19–20, 519–20

Hamilton, William, 418

Harald, king of Norway, 487

Harris, Ernest, 369–71

Haskell, Neal, 463

Heinrich, prince of Prussia, 505

Helen Petrovna, princess, 2, 85, 148–49, 219–20, 260–61

Hello (magazine), 419

hemophilia
  DNA testing for, 444

of Tsesarevich Alexei, 51, 52–53, 84, 271

Hendrikova, Anastasia, 4, 51, 59, 60, 135, 139, 142, 143, 144, 146, 147, 372, 498, 504

Hermogen, bishop of Tobolsk Province, 6, 68, 69

heteroplasmy, 446–47

Hindenburg, Paul von, 185

"History of the Romanov Dynasty in Russia, The" (1993 conference), 440–41

Hitler, Adolf, 466–67

Hochleitner, Alois, 244, 245, 246

Holy Synod Commission on the Canonization of Saints in Regard to the Martyrdom of the Imperial Family, 495–502

Holy Trinity Monastery, Orthodox Church Outside Russia, 299

Hotel Amerika, *107*, 112
  death sentence meetings in, 250–51, 279, 289, 291, 298

House of Romanov. See Romanov Dynasty

"House of Special Purpose, The." See Ipatiev House

Igor Konstantinovich, prince, 2, 219, 336

Ilchinko, Sergei, 487

Ilinsky, Paul, 492

Imperial Army, 28–29, 54

imperial family, 1–3
  arrest of, 57
  asylum and, 58, 77, 203, 212–13, 214, 370, 446, 484
  attitudes toward Avdayev, 166–67
  Avdayev's treatment of, 164–67, 516
  bathing and, 273, 344
  canonization of, 13, 21–22, 378, 476, 482, 494–503
  conspiracies against, 66–70
  correspondence by, 171
  court, suite, and household of, 3–4
  Czech Corps and, 193

daily walks by, 169–71

death rumors and, 224, 225, 226

death sentence of, 250

dogs of, ix–x, 146, 156, 303, 312, 344, 363–64, 516, 571n. 123

escape attempts by, 214–15

execution of. *See* Ekaterinburg executions

exile entourage of, 3–4, 59–65, 101, 139, 473–74, 498, 499

exile in Tobolsk of, 58–70, 77–78, 135–39, 203, 429

family life of, 43–45, 527–28

funeral and final burial of, xi, 21–22, 443, 489–93

German rescue plan and, 78

hemophilia and, 51

imprisonment at Tsarskoye Selo, 57–59, 235–36

imprisonment at Ipatiev House. *See* Ipatiev House

inventory of Ekaterinburg possessions, 533–40

jewels taken into exile by, 70, 135–37, 265, 279, 319, 322–23, 333–34, 340, 341, 372, 506, 507, 541–45

laundry routine of, 161

legends about, 14

list of members, 1

posthumous mythologizing of, 14–15, 45

Rasputin and, 10, 48, 51–52, 56, 164, 242, 322, 341, 494

religious services and, 177–78, 273–76

remains of. *See* remains of imperial family

rescue attempts and, 215, 217–32, 245, 258, 450

revisionist views of, 494–95

Revolution of 1905 and, 37–38, 43

royal relatives of, 4, 49, 58, 77, 203, 212–14, 370, 445, 446, 484, 487, 492

Special Detachments' sympathy for, 233–43, 298, 333

spiritual symbolism of, 352–53, 391, 418, 494–95, 526–28

veneration of, 13, 15, 21–22, 378, 476, 482, 494–503, 522, 524

See also individual members

International Independent Commission to Investigate the Murder of the Romanov Family, 450

Internet sites, Nicholas and Alexandra, 15

inventories

at Four Brothers mine, 18, 348–49

of Ipatiev House, 18, 342–45, 349–50, 357, 518–19, 533–34

list of Romanov possessions, 533–40

of Romanov jewels, 511, 541–45

Ioann Konstantinovich, prince, 2, 85, 148, 219, 336

Ioffe, Adolph, 5, 78, 185, 212–13, 214, 225

Ipatiev, Nicholas, 6, 101, 106, 508

Ipatiev House, ix

bombing incident, 176–77, 180

daily routine, 159–78, 223

description of, 106–12, 127–28, *162, 224,* 233, 297, 518

eyewitness memoirs of life at, 20–21

floor plans of, *109, 111*

graffiti, 163–64, 342

guards. *See* Special Detachment

imperial family's remains and, 469

imperial family's arrival at, 101–2, 117

imperial family members' reunion at, 146

inventories of, 18, 342–45, 349–50, 357, 518–19, 533–34

laundry routine, 161

meals at, 160–61, 172–75, 217

monarchist site memorial, 439, 522–23

murder room, 10, *108, 111, 304, 306,* 332, 349, 356, 357–60, 382, 520–21, *522,* 599–601n. 62

Ipatiev House (continued)
  as Museum of the People's
    Vengeance, 519–21
  post-execution cleanup of, 332–45
  razing of, 384, 400, 439, 521–22
  religious services at, 131, 134,
    177–78, 273–76
  Ryabov's tour of, 382–83
  thefts at, 176
  as Ural Regional Soviet reunion site,
    511
  vulnerability of, 233
  windows of, 131, 168–69, 178, 217,
    222–23, 224, 227, 230, 272
  Yurovsky as commandant of, 264–81
Ipatiev Monastery (Kostroma), 107,
  486
Irene, princess of Prussia, 505
Irina Alexandrovna, princess, 56
Irkutsk, 195, 262
Ivanchenko, Vassili, 205
Ivanov, Pavel, 8, 139, 441, 443, 444–47
Ivan the Terrible, tsar, 10, 76
Izvestia, 338, 500

Jackson, Margaret, 34
Janin, General (France), 371–72, 373
Japanese geneticists, 22
Jeffreys, Alec, 444
jewelry, 70, 265, 279, 333–34, 340,
  341, 506, 507
  Buxhoeveden's treachery and,
    141–43, 505
  concealment of, 135–37, 310, 372
  as evidence, 346, 348–49, 360–61,
    364–65
  inventory list of, 541–45
  looting of, 314–16, 319, 322–23,
    326
  State Diamond Fund and, 511
Jews. See anti-Semitism
Jews Have Killed the Emperor, The
  (pamphlet), 353
Johnson, Nicholas, 204, 206–8
Juan Carlos, king of Spain, 487
Julian calendar, 27

Kabanov, Alexei, 20, 237, 238, 250,
  269, 271, 299–300, 303, 305, 307,
  309–11, 334, 515
Kabanov, Michael, 20, 235, 269,
  299–300, 334, 515
Kamkov, Boris, 197
Karakhan, Lev, 213
Kennan, George, 194
Kerensky, Alexander, 5, 18, 189, 355
  imperial family's exile and, 58, 59
  overthrow of, 66, 71
KGB, 9, 385, 388, 392, 393, 395–96,
  399, 400, 450, 483, 500, 521
Kharitonov, Ivan, 4, 49, 60, 65, 139,
  144, 147, 160, 172, 174, 176, 217,
  230, 271, 272, 380, 498, 499, 523
  execution of, 290, 303–4, 308, 309
  remains of, 403, 405, 414, 420, 427,
    443, 451, 474
Khokhryakov, Paul, 5, 79–80, 137,
  140, 143, 145, 216, 508
Khrushchev, Nikita, 514
Khrustaev, V., 374
Kirill Vladimirovich, grand duke, 60,
  295, 374, 376, 377–78
Kirkpatrik, Violet, 372–73
Kirpichnikov, Alexander, 60
Kirsta, Alexander, 347–48, 357
Kleshchev, Ivan, 121–22, 224, 243,
  280, 300, 302, 312, 357, 515
Kleshchev, Nicholas, 121–22
Knightly, Philip, 355
Knox, Alfred, 352, 356
Kobylinsky, Eugene, 6, 34–35, 47, 48,
  49, 135, 174
  on Avdayev, 118
  as imperial family guard, 58, 63, 66,
    69, 80, 82–84, 91, 507
Kobylinsky, Innokenty, 507
Kochurov, Michael, 386, 396, 439
Kokovtsov, Vladimir, 287
Kolchak, Alexander, 6, 17, 193, 352,
  365, 452, 507
Kolesnikov, Lev, 455–56
Kolpashchikov, Ivan, 205, 206
Koltypin-Wollovskoy, Peter, 450

Kommersant Daily (newspaper), 480
Komsomolskaya Pravda (newspaper),
   382
Konovnizin, count, 41
Konstantin Konstantinovich, prince, 2,
   53, 219, 336
Koptyaki Forest, 333, 393–94, 458–71
   Romanov remains and, 316–31,
   473
   See also Four Brothers mine; Grade
   Crossing 184; Pig's Meadow
Koptyaki Road, 317, 318, 330, 331,
   361, 386, 393, 466, 470, 525
Koptyaki Village, 320, 321, 331
Korevo, N., 374
Korlykhanov, Ivan, 382–83
Kornilov, Lavr, 57, 187
Koryakov, Igor, 400–401, 406
Koryakova, Ludmilla, x–xi, 8, 393, 397,
   400–402, 406, 434, 438
Kosarev, Vladimir, 5, 93, 94, 96, 196
Kotegov, Ivan, 125, 516
Kovalevsky, Pierre, 374
Koverda, Boris, 513
Kozhayev, Anatoly, 524
Kozlov, Maxim, 482, 499
Krasnenkov, Alexander, 488
Krasnov, General, 187
Kravets, Alexander, 485–86
Krokhaleva, Marie, 216
Krustalev, Vladimir, 16–17, 292
Krylenko, Nicholas, 284
Kryukov, V. N., 410, 443
Kudrin, Michael, 5, 20, 115, 210, 218,
   228–29, 231, 249, 267, 290,
   298–99, 300, 301–305, 307, 308–14,
   316, 322, 323, 326, 327, 330, 336,
   338, 339, 364, 459, 460–61, 470
   memoir of Romanov murders by,
   511–12
Kuhlmann, Wilhelm von, 214
Kulikovsky, Paul, 449
Kulikovsky, Tikhon, 446, 447, 448
Kurth, Peter, ix–xi, 389, 391
Kutuzov, Alexander, 347, 348, 349
Kuznetsov, I. Ye., 443

Lacher, Rudolf, 269–70, 300, 313, 314,
   316, 516, 591n. 21
Lampson, Miles, 368–70, 372–73
Lasies, Joseph, 356
Last Days of the Romanovs, The
   (Wilton), 17, 356
Last Days of Tsardom, The (*The Last
   Days of Tsar Nicholas*) (Bykov), 19
"Last Page of the History of the
   Imperial Family, The" (1992 con-
   ference), 429–34
Last Tsar, The (Radzinsky), x
Latsis, Martin, 285
Latypov, Mohammed Abdul, 120, 239
Lebedev, V. I., 194
Left SRs, 75, 76, 196, 197–98, 261
   Ekaterinburg Soviet and, 249
   rebellion against Bolsheviks by,
   285–86
Lenin, Vladimir, 5, 9, 24, 98, 113, 114,
   249, 283, 483
   daylight saving time and, 27, 178–79,
   296
   early life of, 71–74
   famine policy of, 196, 198, 289
   imperial family's execution and, 13,
   282–83, 288, 291, 292–95,
   334–38, 504
   on imperial family's safety, 224, 226
   martial law declaration of, 198, 199
   Michael Alexandrovich and, 203,
   204, 205, 209, 210
   Nechayev's influence on, 73, 74
   power struggles and, 74–76, 82, 92,
   186, 195–98, 212, 214, 248, 284,
   289
   proposed trial of Nicholas II and,
   284, 287, 294, 335–36
   state terror policy of, 75–76, 200
   Treaty of Brest-Litovsk and, 185,
   196–97
Leonida Georgievna, grand duchess,
   480, 502
Leonov, Peter, 300, 325
Lepa, Adolf, 250, 269, 300
Lesnikov, Gregory, 280, 300, 312

Letemin, Kuzma, 516, 535
Letemin, Michael Ivanovich, 122, 279,
    300, 355, 357, 364, 516
  list of Romanov items taken by,
    534–35
Letters of the *Tsar's Family from
    Captivity*, 299
Lett squad, 137, 139–41, 268–70,
    298–99, 300, 347
Levine, Lowell, 8, 418, 420, 422–34,
    456
Ligne, Heinze, 466–67
Likhachev, Dimitri, 479, 486–87, 491,
    492
Lisin, Gennady, 381
Livadia (imperial compound), 43
Lloyd George, David, 184
Lobukhin, Vassili, 318, 385–86
Lockhart, Robert Bruce, 337–38, 352
looting, 313–14, 319, 322–23, 326,
    342, 472
Lopukhin, Alexei, 39
Louis XVI, king of France, 11, 474
Louise, princess of Denmark, 446
Louis of Battenberg. *See* Mountbatten,
    Lord
Ludendorff, Erich, 185
Ludwig IV, grand duke of Hesse, 33
Lukoyanov, Feodor, 5, 115, 205, 464
Luzhkov, Yuri, 480
Lvov, George, 6, 20, 58, 351, 508
  credibility of, 158, 163, 170, 176
Lyluv, Peter, 536–37
Lysy, Vyacheslav, 407, 408
Lyukhanov, Alexei, 515
Lyukhanov, Serge, 5, 116–17, 291,
    300–301, 305, 314–19, 321, 329,
    331, 514–15
Lyukhanov, Valentin, 116, 516

Macauley, Thomas, 525–26, 527
Magdelana, Abbess, 105–6, 118
Malinovsky, Dimitri, 221, 348
Mangold, Tom, 180–81, 297, 363,
    367
Manifesto of October 17, 1905, 38

Maples, William, 8, 402, 407, 408,
    417–18, 422–34, 441–42, 452,
    455, 457, 462–63, 470
Margrethe, queen of Denmark, 487
Maria, Sister, 20, 276, 279
Maria Vladimirovna, grand duchess,
    473, 480, 486, 487, 502
Marie, queen of Romania, 33, 45
Marie Antoinette, queen of France, 11,
    474
Marie Feodorovna, dowager empress,
    2, 31, 202, 355, 366, 372, 446,
    449, 528
Marie Nikolaievna, grand duchess, 1,
    45, *47*, 66, 100–101, 112, 129–35,
    239, 499
  departure for Tobolsk by, 59
  departure from Tobolsk by, 88–89
  execution of, 303–4, 308, 310–11,
    470
  personal qualities of, 49–50, 240–41
  remains of, 403, 425–27, 428, 431,
    440, 443
  Skorokhodov incident and, 243–47,
    249
  Special Detachment's attitude
    toward, 238, 242, 246–47
  See also grand duchesses; imperial
    family
Markov, Andrei, 205, 206
Markov, Nicholas (Markov II), 66–68,
    374
Markov, Serge, 6, 66–68, 78, 260
Martov, Julius, 197
martyrs, imperial family canonized as,
    21, 495, 497, 502
Mary, queen of Great Britain, 372, 446
Masaryk, Thomas, 189, 190
Massie, Robert, 207, 283, 297, 375,
    422, 463, 492, 521
Mather, Annie, 69
Matveyev, Paul, 83, 98–99
Maximilian, emperor of Mexico, 11
Mayakovsky, Vladimir, 394–95, 518
"May Laws" of 1882, 39
Maylunas, Andrei, 207

McCullagh, Francis, 509–11
media
  exhumations and, 388–89
  forensic investigations and, 419, 434,
    435–36, 454
  Romanov funeral and, 478, 484, 485,
    488, 490
Medvedev, Michael. *See* Kudrin,
  Michael
Medvedev, Michael Mikhailovich
  (Kudrin's son), 511–12
Medvedev, Paul Spiridonovich, 17,
  120, 122–23, 125, 134, 168, 215,
  266, 267–68, 272, 598–99n. 58
  duties of, 126–27, 276–77, 280, 332,
    334, 516–17
  imperial family execution and,
    297–300, 302–3, 309, 310, 312,
    355, 357
  Romanov possessions and, 535–36
Medvedeva, Maria, 517
Mejantz, Pauline, 139
Melamud, Alexander, 418
Meledin, Anatoly, 131, 134, 177, 227,
  273–74
Melgunov, Serge, 180, 392
Melnik, Konstantin, 505
Melnik, Tatiana Botkin. *See* Botkin,
  Tatiana
Mensheviks, 75, 196, 197, 199
Menzies, Grant, 474–75
Merezhovskii, Dimitri, 30
Meyer, Hans Johann, 299, 432
Michael, first Romanov emperor, 10, 42
Michael, prince of Kent, 487, 492
Michael Alexandrovich, grand duke, 2,
  31, 130–31, 201–12, 295
  arrest and murder of, 201, 204–11,
    212, 215, 289, 294, 335, 336
  personality of, 201–2
  as regent, 57, 201
Michael Mikhailovich, grand duke,
  295
Michich, Jarko Konstantinovich, 260
Military-Criminal Investigating
  Division, 346

Miliukov, Paul, 42
Mirbach, Wilhelm von, 7, 183, 185,
  195, 198, 200, 213, 214, 225
  murder of, 285, 287, 338
Mironenko, Sergei, 207, 478
Mishkevich brothers, 120
mitochondrial DNA testing, 445, 447,
  448, 449
Moltke, Count von, 212
monarchists, 24, 193, 194, 354, 365,
  366, 378, 435, 439
  burial of executed retainers and, 474
  burial of Romanov remains and, 478,
    479
  Ipatiev House site memorial of,
    522–23
  rescue plots of, 213, 214, 218,
    221–32, 245, 282–83
Monastery of the Imperial Passion
  Bearers (Ekaterinburg), 524–25
Moscow
  as proposed Romanov burial site,
    477
  Soviet government moved to, 77,
    203
  Yurovsky in, 509, 511
Moscow News (journal), 388–89, 392
Moscow Regional Cheka, 509
Moscow Soviet, 197
  Michael Alexandrovich's murder and,
    210, 211
  plans for imperial family's execution
    and, 282–88, 291–94, 295
  reports of imperial family's execution
    to, 334–37, 338–39
Moscow State Radio, 512
Moshkin, Alexander Mikhailovich,
  119, 132–33, 157, 160, 175–76,
  251, 264
Moskovsky Komsomolets (newspaper),
  418, 469
Mossolov, Alexander, 48, 51
Mountbatten, Lord, 49, 350–51, 505
Mrachkovsky, Serge, 123, 125
Mullis, Kary B., 444
Muravyev, Michael, 286

Murder of the Romanovs, The (Bulygin), 18

murder room (Ipatiev House), *108,* *111, 304, 306,* 349, 356, 357–60, 382–83, *522,* 599–601n. 62
cleanup of, 332
description of, 520–21

Murmansk, Allied landing in, 200

Museum of the People's Vengeance (Ekaterinburg), 519–21

Myachin, Konstantin. *See* Yakovlev, Vassili

Myasnikov, Gabriel, 205, 206, 209, 210, 250

Mystery of the Last Tsar, The (documentary film), 441

Nachapkin, Nikolai, 401

Nagai, Tatsuo, 448–49

Nage, Imre, 299

Nagorny, Klementy, 4, 20, 52, 60, 64, 139, 143, 145, 155–56, 170, 215, 498
imprisonment and killing of, 157–59, 177

Nametkin, Alexander, 7, 161–62, 163, 348–49, 356, 357, 360, 362, 506
inventory of Ipatiev House by, 342–45, 533–34

Narodnaya Voliya (terrorist group), 72

Naryshkin, Kirill, 365, 452

Naryshkina–Kuryakina, Elizabeth, 51, 372

Nashe Slovo (newspaper), 224

Nash Vek (newspaper), 225

National Tidende (newspaper), 291

Nazier-Vachot, Philippe, 40, 51

Nechayev, Serge, 73, 74

NecroSearch International, 452–53

Nemtsov, Boris, 477–78, 481

Nemtsov, Nicholas, 85

Netrebin, Victor, 20, 244, 245, 246, 248, 269, 288, 299–300, 303–4, 308, 334, 340–41, 517

Nevolin, Alexander, 90–91

Nevolin, Nikolai, 8, 397–98, 406–7, 408, 422–23, 436, 456

New York Times (newspaper), 180, 207, 350, 367, 369–70

Nezavisimaya Gazeta (newspaper), 493–94

Nicholas I, emperor, 254, 528

Nicholas II, emperor, 1
abdication of, 14, 27, 57, 201, 295
anti-Semitism of, 39–42, 496, 527
biography authorized by, 44–45
brother Michael's relationship with, 202–3
canonization of, 13, 21–22, 378
coronation of, 36–37
Czech prisoners of war and, 192–93
death rumors and, 208–9, 291
departure from Tobolsk by, 88–89, 98–99
diary routine of, 20, 180, 231, 236, 247, 273, 341
early years of, 30–33
in Ekaterinburg, 98, 100–102, 129–35
execution of, 10, 11–12, 303–9, 312
family life focus of, 43, 44–45, 54
funeral for, 489–93
hemorrhoids and, 179, 341
Lenin on, 74
marriage of, 34, 36
personal qualities of, 34–35, 43–44, 526–27
plots against, 13–14, 24, 31–32
proposed trial of, 86, 283–84, 287–88, 335–36
Rasputin and, 10, 494
reign of, 35–44
remains of, 403, 405, 411, 412–13, 424–25, 430, 443, 445–46, 450, 451, 460–61, 476
restoration of, 186
revisionist glorification of, 522
Revolution of 1905 and, 37–38
royal relatives of, 4
Russian posthumous idealized image of, 490–91, 494–95

son's hemophilia and, 51
Special Detachment's sympathy for, 234–36
spiritual symbolism of, 352–53, 391, 418, 494–95, 526–28
title of, 26
unpopularity of, 13–14
World War I and, 47, 54, 55–56
Yakovlev and, 82, 83–84, 95
Yurovsky and, 253–54, 271
See also imperial family
Nicholas Konstantinovich, grand duke, 295
Nicholas Mikhailovich, grand duke, 2, 295, 504
Nicholas Nikolaievich, grand duke, 2, 38, 55, 366, 372, 373, 374
Nikiforov, Alexei, 125, 300–301
Nikitin, Sergei, 8, 407, 451–52, 469
Nikolaeva, Alexandrine, 142
Nikulin, Gregory ("Akulov"), 5, 115, 246, 262, 264–66, 272, 279, 290, 299, 302–3, 305, 306, 309, 314, 336, 340, 511, 512
Nilus, Serge, 40–41, 175, 344
Nina Georgievna, princess, 50
NKVD, 9, 506, 507, 514
Northern Ural Siberian Front, 224, 225, 227, 290, 293
Novaya Zhizn (newspaper), 199
Novo-Nikolayevsk, 194
Novoselov, Igor, 205, 206
Novotikhvinsky Monastery and Convent, 20, 118
Novyoe Vremya (newspaper), 42

Oakes, Catherine, 418
Obolensky, Dimitri, 213
Obolensky, Serge, prince, 373
Obretenyie (Recovery) foundation, 400, 437–38
October Revolution (1917), 11–12, 27, 71, 189, 203, 390
State Central Archives of, 385
Officers' Commission investigation, 346, 347, 360

Okhrana (Secret Police), 9, 40, 76, 113, 175, 202, 256
Olga, queen of the Hellenes, 214
Olga Alexandrovna, grand duchess, 2, 31, 49, 131, 366, 373, 375, 446, 451
Olga Nikolaievna, grand duchess, 1, 45, 53, 132, 139–40, 246, *248*
execution of, 303–4, 310, 470
harassment on *Rus* and, 140–41, 247
personal qualities of, 46–47, 48, 139–40, 141, 240, 241, 242
remains of, 403, 405, 411, 424, 425, 428, 443, 451
Special Detachment's attitude toward, 238
See also grand duchesses; imperial family
Omsk, 94, 96, 194
Onassis, Jacqueline Kennedy, x
Oprichniki, 76
Orlov, Alexander, 517
Orlov, Nicholas, prince, 366, 367
Orthodox Church. *See* Russian Orthodox Church; Russian Orthodox Church Outside Russia
OSVAG (anti-Bolshevik propaganda office), 352

Pale of Settlement, 39
Paley, Vladimir, 219, 336
Pamyat (ultraconservative political party), 490–91
Pascal, Pierre, 104
Pashinyan, Gurgen, 455
passion bearers, 21, 497, 502, 503
Paul Alexandrovich, grand duke, 2, 64, 219, 295, 504
Paul I, emperor, 11
Paveliev, George, 507
Payne, Robert, 75
peasant revolt, 196–97
Penza, 194
Perm, 85, 348
Perm Cheka, 204, 205, 209

Perm executions, 204–11, 224, 355, 504

Perry, John Curtis, 203

Peter I (the Great), emperor, 26, 30, 483

Peter III, emperor, 11, 30

Peter Nikolaievich, grand duke, 473

Petit Journal (periodical), 372, 373

Petotsky, Vladislav, 387

Petrograd
    Soviet government move from, 77, 203
    World War I conditions, 56–57
    See also St. Petersburg

Petropavlosk, 194

Petrova, Olga, 181

Philaret, metropolitan, 379

Philip, duke of Edinburgh, 445, 484, 487

photo superimposition remains identification, 326–27, 420–22, 429, 430, 440–41, 443, 453–57, 477

Pichon, M., 351

Pig's Meadow, 329–31, 439, 468–71
    cremation attempt at, 459–61, 466
    mass grave at, 330–31, 393–95, 401–6
    mass grave discovery (1978), 386–89
    as pilgrimage site, 471, 525
    Sokolov's investigation of, 361–62
    unloading of corpses at, 318, 330
    See also exhumations

Pipes, Richard, 12, 16, 188, 194, 198, 204, 207–8, 227, 283, 509, 526

Plaskin, Vladislav, 8, 407, 408–10, 418, 421, 423, 430, 436, 442, 454, 468

Platonov, O., 209

Plehve, Vyacheslav, 39

Pleshakov, Constantine, 203

Pobedonostsev, Konstantin, 32

Podkorytov, Nicholas, 167–68

pogroms, 38–42

Pokrovsky, Michael, 385, 394, 396

polymerase chain reaction (PCR), 444, 446

Popov, Nicholas, 517

Popov, Vyacheslav, 8, 409, 415, 424, 431, 432–33, 440, 456–57

Popov Battalion, 285–86

Popov House, 126, 127, 245, 270, 300, 333

Poradelov, N., 194

Pravda (newspaper), 76, 77, 181, 338

Preobrajenksy Guards Regiment, 32

Presidium. *See* VTsIK

Preston, Thomas, 104–5, 150, 195, 220, 262, 373

Privalova, Catherine, 328

Proskuryakov, Philip, 123, 159, 164, 167, 169, 175–76, 279–80, 313, 332, 355, 357, 517

Protocols of the Elders of Zion, 40–41, 175, 344, 352, 353, 509

Provisional Government, 203, 500
    Bolshevik's overthrow of, 66, 71
    Czech Corps formed by, 189
    imperial family and, 57, 58
    Kerensky and, 58, 59, 189

Public Committee for the Protection of the Holy Remains of the Tsarist Martyrs, 479

Radek, Karl, 213

Radzinsky, Edvard, x, 283, 291, 292, 389, 409, 442, 475, 492, 513–14

Ramez, Feodor, 336

Rasputin, Gregory, 14, 166, 237, 520
    background of, 51–52
    imperial family and, 48, 56, 164, 242, 322, 341, 494
    murder of, 56, 492
    threat by, 10

Rasputin, Maria, 68, 69, 91, 143

Red Army, 188, 262, 286, 289

Red Cross Officers' Organization, 221

Red Terror, 504

Ree, Poul, 181

Reed, Jim, 452

remains of imperial family, 326–27, 340–41, 402–34, 440–58, 472–94, 524
    burial controversy, 473–83

cremation reports, 330, 376, 459–68,
469
DNA testing of, 22, 393, 441–42,
444–50
exhumation (1978–79), 386–89, 429,
434, 436
exhumation (1991), 397–98,
400–406, 408, 434, 458, 468
funeral for (1998), 21–22, 488–94
investigation of, 406–16
Koptyaki Forest and, 316–31, 473
NecroSearch International and,
452–53
new discovery of, 21–22
Pig's Meadow mass grave for,
330–31, 386–89
removal and burial of, 316–31,
458–71
rumored whereabouts of, 370–80
skeletal, x–xi, 403–6, 410–16,
419–34, 440–42, 443–50, 455–57,
464, 472, 608–10n. 72
Sokolov's cases containing, 368–75,
376
thefts of, 472
two missing bodies, 22, 376, 458,
464, 468, 525
See also canonization; forensic
pathology
Remy, Maurice Philip, 377, 391
Rennenkampf, Paul, 54
rescue attempts, 217–32, 240, 245, 450
fabricated, 228–29, 245, 249,
266–67, 289–90, 292, 334–35,
339–40, 512
retainers. *See* exile entourage of imperial family
Revolt of the Evacuated Invalids, 262
Revolutionary Catechism (Nechayev), 73
Revolution of 1905, 37–40, 43, 255
anti-Semitic pogroms, 39–40
Revolution of February 1917. *See*
February Revolution
Revolution of October 1917. *See*
October Revolution
Reynolds, Maura, 478

Riezler, Kurt, 183, 200
Riza-Kuli-Mirza, prince, 347
"Road to Tragedy, The" (Kerensky), 18
Robien, Louis de, 225
Robilliard, Alan, 417
Rodina (journal), 396
Rodionov, Nicholas, 137–40, 145–48
Rodriquez, William, 417, 418
Rodzianko, Basil, 473
Rodzinsky, Isai, 5, 20, 118–19, 142,
210, 221, 222, 228–29, 234, 236,
237, 238, 244, 245, 246, 248, 251,
258, 265, 266–67, 288, 290, 324,
326, 330, 339, 459, 461–62, 512
Rogozhnikova, Polina, 488
Romanov, Nicholas, 473, 478, 486–87,
492
Romanov, Rostislav, 473
Romanova, Anna, 60, 142
Romanov Dynasty
Bolshevik treatment of, 201, 203–4,
209–10, 218–21, 261, 295
burial site of, 475
end of rule by, 29, 57, 201
executions of members, 10–11, 30,
38, 295, 504. *See also* Ekaterinburg
execution
founding of, 10, 42, 107
members of, 1–3
royal relatives of, 4, 33–34, 487, 492
St. Petersburg burial site, 475, 478
succession laws, 51, 57, 201, 487
titles of, 26
See also imperial family; *individual
members*
Romanov Family Association, 473,
478, 480, 486, 487, 489, 492
Romashkov, Valery, 477
Rossel, Edvard, 8, 400, 409, 416, 418,
442, 468, 476, 477, 480
Royalty Monthly (magazine), 483
Rozanov, Sergei, 452
Rus (steamship), 139–43
harassment of grand duchesses
aboard, 140–41, 247

Russian Expert Commission Abroad, 450

Russian National Society, 366

Russian Nobility Association, 375, 450

Russian Orthodox Church, xi, 35, 44, 234, 392, 447, 479–83
  canonization of imperial family by, 13, 15, 16, 21, 476, 480, 494–503, 524
  imperial family burial and, 475–77, 478, 479–80, 481, 491
  Rasputin and, 52
  Romanov throne succession and, 487
  Special Detachment and, 234

Russian Orthodox Church Abroad, 377, 379, 380

Russian Orthodox Church Outside Russia, 21, 299, 363, 375, 376, 450
  canonization of imperial family by, 13, 21–22, 378, 476, 482–83, 497, 501, 503, 524

Russian Orthodox Holy Archangels Center (Washington, D.C.), 389–90

Russiiskaya gazeta (publication), 451

Russo-Japanese War, 37, 61, 113

Ryabov, Geli, 8, 21, 382–93, 400, 410, 429, 435–37, 439, 453

Sacrifice (Skariatin), 359

Sadchikov, Nicholas, 333, 517

Sadurov, Alexander Feodorovich, 123, 517

Safarov, Gregory, 5, 117, 250, 324

Safonov, Benjamin, 126, 168, 169, 268, 517

St. Catherine's Chapel, 478, 479, 484, 488, 492–93

St. Genevieve de Bois cemetery (Paris), 375, 378

St. Petersburg, 484
  as Romanovs' final burial site, 4, 21, 473, 475, 477–78, 479, 487, 489–90, 491
  See also Petrograd

St. Petersburg Military Academy of the General Staff, 218

St. Petersburg Times, 487

Sakovich, Nicholas, 90, 257

Salisbury, Harrison, 180

Samara, capture of, 179, 180, 194

Samokhavlov, Parfen, 101

Samsonov, Alexander, 54

Sarandinaki, Peter, 452, 453, 468–69

Scavenius, Harald, 212

Schelekov, Nicholas, 382, 384, 385, 395, 396

Scherbatow, Alexis, prince, 375, 376, 377, 450

Schneider, Catherine, 4, 59–60, 139, 142, 143, 146, 147, 495, 498, 504

Schweitzer, Marina Botkin, 444, 474

Schweitzer, Richard, 474

SEARCH (Scientific Expedition to Account for the Romanov Children), 452

Secret Police. *See* Okhrana

Sednev, Ivan, 4, 20, 60, 64–65, 89, 92, 101, 130, 134, 155, 215, 498
  imprisonment and killing of, 157–59, 177, 280

Sednev, Leonid, 4, 60, 65, 139, 144, 147, 171, 172, 174, 230, 271, 280, 290, 333, 507–8

Sedov, Nicholas, 67, 68

Semyonov (rogue Cossack), 187–88, 365

Semyonovna, Eudokia, 277

Serge Alexandrovich, grand duke, 3, 11, 33, 38, 40

Serge Mikhailovich, grand duke, 3, 219, 336

Sergeyev, Ivan, 7, 163, 349–53, 356, 357, 360, 505–6

Seven League Boots (Halliburton), 19

Sevodnya (newspaper), 443

Sfiris, Xenia, 446, 492

Shamarin, A. A., 205

Sheremetievsky, Andrei, 346, 360

short tandem repeat (STR) DNA testing, 444–45, 448

Shulgin, Vassili, 57
Siberia. *See* Ekaterinburg; Perm; Tobolsk
Sidamon-Eristov, prince, 374
Sidorov, Alexei, 133, 176, 179, 181, 216, 245–46, 342
Sidorov, Ivan, 221
7-Tage (magazine), 299, 432
Skariatin, Michael, 359
skeletal remains, x–xi, 403–6, 410–16, 419–34, 440–42, 443–50, 455–57, 464, 472, 608–10n. 72
Skorogobatov, Sergei, 479
Skorokhodov, Ivan, 47–48, 243–44, 247–48, 249
Soames, 300, 314, 316
Sobchak, Anatoly, 442
Social Democrats, 181
Socialist Revolutionaries, 75, 77, 194, 199, 261, 262
   Czech support for, 193
   Ekaterinburg Soviet and, 249
   support of peasant revolt by, 196
   See also Civil War; Left SRs
Sokolov, Andrei, 485
Sokolov, Nicholas, x, 7, 17, 18, 19, 21, 24, 119, 159, 174, 206, 207, 208, 233, 283, 297, 320, 331, 337, 349, 376, 381, 386, 394, 409, 432, 437, 450, 452, 458, 467, 476, 482, 506, 513
   Romanov murder investigation by, x, 353–67
   suitcases of Romanov remains and, 368–86
Solodovnikov, Boris, 193–94, 393
Soloviev, Boris, 7, 67–69, 141, 396, 475
Soloviev, Vladimir, 442, 443–44, 447, 451, 468, 476
"Sorrowful Quest, The" (Bulygin), 18
Soviet Press Bureau, 225, 284
Soviet state, 14, 21, 485–86
   demythologization of, 493, 495
   Fifth Congress of Soviets, 198, 199, 210, 285

first admission of Romanovs' execution by, 458
   government move to Moscow, 77, 203
   Museum of the People's Vengeance and, 519–21
   terror policy, 75–76, 114, 200. *See also* Cheka; KGB; NKVD
   See also Bolshevik Party; Central Executive Committee; Red Army; Ural Regional Soviet; VTsIK
Sovnarkom. *See* Council of People's Commissars
Spalaikovich, 151, 260–61
Special Detachment (Ipatiev House guards), 20, 21, 23, 120–28, 137, 162–64, 333
   disbanding of, 341
   duty book of, 20, 216, 245
   later years of, 509–18
   Lett squad, 137, 139–41, 268–70, 298–99, 300, 347
   list of members, 529–32
   Romanov possessions and, 534–36
   sympathy for imperial family of, 233–43, 298, 333
   treatment of imperial family by, 23, 167–69, 516
   vulnerability of Ipatiev House and, 233
   Yurovsky's rules for, 268
   See also individual members
Special Detachment (Tobolsk), 58, 66, 69, 79–81, 137
Speranski, Valentin, 378, 519, 520–21
Spillsbury, Bernard, 420
Spiridonovna, Maria, 198
Spiridovna, Anastasia, 437
spiritual symbolism
   of Ekaterinburg execution, 11, 12–15, 527
   of imperial family, 352–53, 391, 418, 494–95, 526–28
Sproul, Arthur Elliot, 369–70
Stalin, Josef, 5, 190, 294, 390, 477, 509, 511, 514

Starkov, Andrei, 125, 221–22, 268,
    302, 312, 517
Starkov, Ivan, 517, 536
Starodumova, Maria, 276–77
State Central Archives of the October
    Revolution, 385
State Diamond Fund, 511
Steinberg, Isaac, 76, 83, 283, 284, 292
Steinberg, Mark, 16–17
Stepanovna, Glafira, 239
Stolov, Igor, 279–80
Stolypin, Peter, 41
Stoneman, William, 19–20
Storozhev, Ioann, 21, 177–78, 245,
    255, 274–76
Strekotin, Alexander, 121, 122, 124,
    164–71, 180, 181, 234, 236, 238,
    240–42, 246, 299, 302, 307–9,
    313, 470, 515, 517–18
Strekotin, Andrei, 123–24, 164, 299,
    302
Suatin, Gregory, 239
sudba (fate), 16, 36, 485, 526
Sukhorukov, Gregory, 326, 459, 462,
    464–66
Summers, Anthony, 180–81, 297, 363,
    367
Supreme Investigatory Commission,
    284
Supreme Monarchist Council, 479,
    487
Svenska Dagbladt (newspaper), 181
Sverdlov, Yakov, 5, 79, 80–81, 82, 83,
    92, 94, 96–97, 98, 113–14, 196,
    213–14, 248, 249, 284–85,
    286–87, 291, 293, 334–40, 390
    monarchists' attack on statue of, 523
    murder of Michael Romanov and,
    205, 208, 209, 210, 211
Sverdlovsk. *See* Ekaterinburg
Sverdlovsk Bolshevik Club, 520
Sykes, Brian, 8, 448

Talapov, Ivan, 123, 180, 518
Tarasov-Rodionov. *See* Yakovlev,
    Vassili

Tatiana Nikolaievna, grand duchess, 1,
    45, *47*, *248*, 342, 363, 502
    execution of, 303–4, 310, 470
    personal qualities of, 48–49, 87, 145,
    241
    remains of, 28, 403, 425–27, 430,
    431, 440, 443, 451, 456
    Special Detachment's attitude
    toward, 238, 242
    See also grand duchesses; imperial
    family
Tatishchev, Ilya, 4, 59, 66, 85, 87, 139,
    143, 144, 146, 147, 498
    disappearance of, 150
    execution of, 261
Tchelyshev, Vassili, 206
Tchernikin, Nikita, 118
Tegleva, Alexandra, 4, 60, 63, 136,
    138–39, 144, 365, 507
Telberg, George, 17, 394
Teumina, Tatiana, 79
Thomas, Arthur, 262, 281, 296
Thurbon, Colin, 502
Times of London (newspaper), 7, 56,
    114, 154, 184, 207, 355, 473, 484
Tobolsk
    imperial family's exile in, 58–70,
    77–78, 135–39, 203, 235–36, 429
    removal of imperial family from, 15,
    85–87, 88–90, 102
    taken by Whites, 153
Tolstoy, Zenaide, 89, 112
Tomilova, Catherine, 21, 149, 172–74,
    181
Tomsk, 194
Trans-Siberian Railway, 78, 190, 195,
    262, 289
Treaty of Brest-Litovsk (1918), 77, 85,
    152, 183, 184–85, 197, 284, 289
    peasant protest of, 196–97
    round up of Romanov family mem-
    bers following, 203–4, 218–21
Trinkina, Antonina, 216
Trotsky, Leon, 6, 24, 77, 200, 285–86,
    293–94
    Czech Corps and, 191–92

proposed trial of Nicholas II and, 283–84, 287

Trupp, Alexei, 4, 60, 65, 139, 147, 155–56, 380, 495, 498, 499, 524
burial of, 488
execution of, 290, 303–4, 308–9
remains of, 403, 405–6, 414–15, 420, 425, 427, 443, 451, 474

Tsar-Kolokol (publication), 392

Tsarskoye Selo, 37, 43, 429
imperial family's imprisoned at, 57–59, 235–36

Tsar: The Lost World of Nicholas and Alexandra (Kurth), ix

Tsetsegov, Peter, 315

Turgin, Semyon, 518

Turkin, M. P., 210

Tutelberg, Maria, 4, 60, 63, 86–87, 139, 507

Tutwiler, Margaret, 416

Tyumen, 89, 90–91, 92, 139–43, 153

Ufa, 195, 286

Ukraine, 195

Ukrainstsev, Konstantin, 130–31, 132, 133

Ulyanov, Alexander (Lenin's brother), 32, 72

Ulyanov, Ilya (Lenin's father), 72

Union for the Resurrection of Great Russia, 522–23

Union of the Russian People (anti-Semitic organization), 41

Unsolved Mysteries (television documentary), 441

Ural Regional Soviet, 9, 15, 78–81, 233, 353, 394–95
Avdayev removed by, 251
Buxhoeveden questioned by, 148
on cremation of Romanov remains, 459
executions by, 504
imperial family in custody of, 112–28, 520
imperial family's death sentence by, 250

imperial family's execution and, 282, 284, 288–93, 295, 334, 338
imperial family's transport to Ekaterinburg and, 83–97
Michael Alexandrovich assassination and, 210–11
rescue attempt fabrications by, 228–29, 245, 249, 266–67, 289–90, 292, 334–35, 339–40, 512
rescue attempt fears of, 215, 217–32, 240, 261
return to Ekaterinburg by, 509
Romanov jewels and, 265
Yakovlev as traitor to, 96, 119
Yurovsky and, 256, 324, 329, 460, 509, 511

Uralskii Rabochii (newspaper), 236, 249, 339–40, 383

Uritsky, Michael, 74–75, 204, 221

U.S. Senate Committee on Labor and Education hearings (1922), 188

Utkin, Anna, 60

Vaganov, Serge, 299

Vaganov, Stephan, 115, 320, 450

Vaganov, Victor, 115

Vassiliev, Alexander, 7, 67, 501

Vassiliev, Gennady, 387

Vergazi, Andras, 299

Verhas, Andras, 269, 300, 315, 316

Victoria, marchioness of Milford Haven, 445, 505, 506

Victoria, princess of Battenberg, 106

Victoria, princess of Great Britain, 49

Victoria, queen of Great Britain, 33–34, 51, 445

Vilinbakhov, Georgi, 479

Viner, Vadim, 8, 450

Vitaly, metropolitan, 376, 483

Vladimir Kirillovich, grand duke, 376–77, 380

Vladivostok, 184, 195, 200, 509

Voikov, Peter, 6, 20, 116, 117, 171, 222, 228, 239, 250, 266, 284, 287, 288, 312–13, 325, 458–59, 460, 513

Voitinsky, Vladimir, 73
Volkogonov, Dimitri, 12, 77
Volkov, Alexei, 4, 20, 60, 64, 84, 135, 137, 139, 140, 144, 146, 147, 150, 206, 504
  Rus, 141
Volkov, V., 8, 401, 409
Volodarsky, V., 199
Volunteer Army. *See* White Army
Vorobyev, Victor, 20, 226, 236, 237
Vorres, Ian, 375
Voznesensky Cathedral, *107*, 480, 489
Voznesensky Prospekt, *107*, 510
Voznesensky Square, 107, 110, 518
VTsIK (Presidium), 83, 93, 97, 195, 197
Vyrubova, Anna, 7, 44, 47, 66, 67, 102, 171, 363

Warsaw, fall of, 55
Warth, Robert, 379
Western Siberian Regional Soviet, 96
White Army, 17, 21, 24, 185–87, 205, 227, 233, 248, 258, 261, 280–81, 282, 289, 325, 341–42, 346, 459
  anti-Semitism of, 18, 24, 186–87
  atrocities by, 187–88
  Ekaterinburg fall to, 518
  Ekaterinburg victims of, 509
  four generals, *193*
  retreat to Vladivostok by, 509
  Samara taken by, 179, 180
  Tobolsk taken by, 153
White Cross Officers' Organization, 221
White Russians, 13, 16, 185, 214, 352, 365
Wilhelm II, emperor of Germany, 4, 77, 212–13, 214
Wilton, Robert, 7, 56, 114, 207, 214–15, 297, 349, 350, 355–56, 359, 361, 365, 378, 508
  credibility of Ekaterinburg reports of, 15–16, 17, 18, 19, 154–55, 160, 163, 168, 169, 170, 174
World War I, 55, 179, 184

Alexandra and, 44
Bolshevik-German peace negotiation, 76–77. *See also* Treaty of Brest-Litovsk
Botkin family and, 62
conditions in Petrograd, 56–57
German Western Front offensive, 183–84
Murmansk, 200
Nicholas II and, 47, 54, 55–56
Russian involvement in, 13, 28–29, 44, 54–56, 76–77, 185–86, 212, 338, 371, 376
Wortman, Richard, 528
Wulfert, Nathalia Sheremetevskaia, 201–3, 205

Xenia Alexandrovna, grand duchess, 3, 31, 53, 372, 373, 446, 492, 506, 519

Yakimov, Anatoly Alexandrovich, 17, 118, 124–27, 162–65, 169, 170, 175–76, 247, 268, 279, 280, 289, 299, 300, 312, 355, 357, 508–9, 518
  on Alexandra, 237
  sympathy toward imperial family and, 233–34, 235, 333–34
Yakimova, Capitolina, 347
Yakovlev, Vassili, 6, 15, 135, 520
  arrest of, 98
  imperial family's transport to Ekaterinburg and, 71, 81–100, 119, 227
  as traitor to the Revolution, 96
Yakovlev, Vladimir, 477–78, 479, 480, 483–84, 485, 489
Yakovleva, Barbara, 219, 336
Yarkov, Boris, 392, 436–37
Yaroshinsky, Karol, 66
Yaroslavl, 286
Yarov, Yuri, 375, 442
Y-chromosome haplotype, 449
Yeltsin, Boris, 8, 400, 450, 475–78, 480–82, 486, 493

at imperial family's funeral, 491, 492
on Ipatiev House razing, 521, 522
Yeltsin, Naina, 491, 492
Yurovsky, Alexander, 385, 511
Yurovsky, Rimma, 383, 385, 511
Yurovsky, Yakov, 6, 20, 115, 143, 168,
    230, 234, 250, 395, 582–83n. 100
as commandant of Ipatiev House,
    239–48, 251, 264–81, 340
early life of, 251–56
on imperial family, 271–72
imperial family's execution and, 258,
    288, 290–91, 296–315, 382, 470,
    510–11
imperial family's remains and,
    316–19, 321–31, 363, 376, 429,
    459–62, 464–66, 467, 469
later life of, 509–11
Yurovsky note (1920), 19, 293, 384–87,
    388, 394, 396, 399, 459, 465, 476

Yusupov, Felix, prince, 56, 373, 492
Yuvenaly, metropolitan, 482, 495, 496,
    498

Zaitsev, Nicholas, 8, 121, 401
Zakatov, Alexander, 487
Zanotti, Madeleine, 4, 60
Zaslavsky, Semyon, 79–80, 91
Zhivotovsky, Lev, 449
Zhuzhgov, Nicholas, 205, 206
Zinoviev, Gregory, 6, 24, 200, 291,
    292, 335, 336
Zlokazov, Nicholas, 118
Zolotov, Andrei, 482
Zukova, Natasha and Nicholas, 320
Zvyagin, Victor, 8, 407, 408–10, 422,
    423, 455, 457
Zvyorgin, Feodor, 320